in the 20th Century

START OF THE SEVENTIES 1 JAN 1970	START OF THE EIGHTIES* 1 JAN 1980	CATEGORY
3,704,000,000	4,410,000,000*	*World Population*
55,534,000	55,883,100*	*Great Britain & Northern Ireland Population*
Tōkyō-to 11,462,230 (July 1969)	Tōkyō-to 11.5 million	*Largest Conurbation*
141	165*	*Number of Sovereign Countries*
24,790.8 mph *39 897,0 km/h* Cdrs Cernan & Young, Col. Stafford USAF Apollo X. Re-entry after lunar orbit. 26 May 1969	→	*Absolute Human Speed*
248,433 miles *399 814 km*. Cdr. Cernan & Col. Stafford, USAF Apollo X lunar module. Circum lunar flight. 22 May 1969.	248,655 miles *400 187 km*. US Apollo XIII. Capt. Lovell, F. Haise & J. Swigert. Abortive lunar landing mission. 15 April 1970.	*Absolute Human Altitude*
242,000,000 miles *389,450,000 km* Mars 1. USSR. 1 Nov 1962	1,905,000,000 miles *3 067 000 000 km* Pioneer 10 Rocket, launched 2 Mar 1972*	*Greatest Space Penetration by Rocket*
35,760 ft *10 900 m* US Bathyscaphe *Trieste* (Dr. J. Piccard, Lt. D. Walsh USN) Marianas Trench, Pacific. 23 Jan 1960.	→	*Deepest Underwater Descent*
25,340 ft *7723 m* Oil Well. Pecos County West Texas, USA 1958.	31,911 ft *9726 m* Geological Research Kola Peninsula, USSR. July 1979.*	*Deepest Boring*
11,246 ft *3427 m* East Rand Proprietary Mine, Boksburg, South Africa 1959	3582 m *11,752 ft* Western Deep Levels Carletonville, South Africa.	*Deepest Mine*
3842 ft *1171 m* Reseau de la Pierre St. Martin, France. ARSIP Aug 1966	4370 ft *1332 m* Reseau de la Pierre St. Martin, France. ARSIP August 1975*	*Deepest Cave Penetration*
est. 13,000 million light years. Quasar 4C 25.5 E. Olsen. Palomar, California, July 1968.	est. 15,500 million light years. Quasar OQ 172. E. J. Wampler *et al*. Lick Observatory, California. April 1973	*Most Distant Measured Heavenly Body*
104	107	*Number of Elements Discovered*
2063 ft *628 m* KTHI TV Mast, Fargo, Dakota, USA, 1963	2120.6 ft *646,38 m* Warszawa Radio Mast, Plock, Poland. 1974	*Tallest Structure*
1472 ft *449 m* (with completion on 1 May 1951 of TV antenna) Empire State Building, New York City, USA.	1454 ft *443 m* Sears Tower, Chicago, Illinois, 1974.	*Tallest Skyscraper*
200,000,000 ft² *5 600 600 m²* Boeing Assembly Plant, Everett, Washington, USA. Completed 1968	→	*Largest Commercial Building*
935 ft *285 m* Grande Dixence, Switzerland, 1961	1082 ft *330 m* (building). Rogunsky, Tadzhikistan, USSR	*Tallest Dam*
6,096,000 kw Krasnoyarsk. USSR. On Yenisey River. Completed 1968	6,480,000 kw Grande Coulee, Washington State, USA. On Columbia River (Present capacity)	*Most Powerful Power Station*
4260 ft *1298 m* Verrazano-Narrows, Brooklyn – Staten Island, USA. 1964	4626 ft *1410 m* Humber Estuary, England. Decking not completed until 18 July 1980	*Longest Bridge Span*
→	22,2 km *13.79 miles* Oshimizu, Honshū, Japan	*Longest Rail Tunnel*
7.27 miles *11,7 m* Mont Blanc, France – Italy, 1965	8.7 miles *14,0 km* Arlberg, West Austria 1978*	*Longest Road Tunnel*
326,833 dwt *Universe Iran*. 1135 ft *346 m* long, completed 1969	555,031 dwt *Pierre Guillaumat* 1359 ft *414 m* long, completed 9 Nov 1977.*	*Largest Tanker*
613.995 mph *988,13 km/h Spirit of America Sonic I*. Norman Breedlove (US) at Bonneville, Utah, USA. 15 Nov 1965	739.666 mph *1190,377 km/h* (Mach 1.01) *Budweiser Rocket*. Stan Barratt (US) at Edwards A. F. Base, California, USA. 17 Dec 1979	*Fastest Car*
285.213 mph *459,00 km/h Hustler* Lee Taylor (US) Lake Guntersville, Alabama, 30 June 1967.	319.62 mph *514,39 km/h Spirit of Australia*. Ken Warby (Australian) at Blowering Dam Lake, NSW. 8 Oct 1978.	*Fastest Water Speed*
57 megatons. USSR Thermo-nuclear device. Novaya–Zemlya 30 Oct 1961	→	*Largest Explosion (TNT)*
£1,785,714 (equivalent current value £8.1 million) da Vinci's *Ginerva de' Benci* bought by National Gallery, Washington, in 1967.	£2,310,000 (equivalent current value £8.75 million) Velázquéz's *Juan de Pareja* bought by Wildenstein Gallery, New York, in 1970*	*Highest Sale Price for a Painting*
→	→	*...ture*
−126.9°F *−88,3°C* Vostok, Antarctica. 24 Aug 1960	→	*...ture*
→	→	
→	est. 100 st (1400 lb) *635 kg* John B. M... (USA) (b. 1941) (Peak March 1978)	

GUINNESS LICENSED PRODUCTS

Amongst the products licensed by Guinness Superlatives Ltd are the following:

Guinness Mindbender Electronic Cassett Quiz – audio cassette quizzes based on the *Guinness Book of Records* introduced by Norris McWhirter – Ivan Berg Associates (Audio Publishing) Ltd.

Guinness World Record Breakers Collectors Stickers and Album – F.K.S. Publishers Ltd. – A collection for younge readers.

Guinness Book of Records Diary – published by But Is It Art.
Guinness Book of Records Crossword Puzzle – Onsworld Ltd
The Guinness Calendar of World Records – a full-colour engage ment calendar – Hallmark Cards Inc.

The above products are not available from Guinness Superlatives Ltd., but through the reta trade.

VIEWDATA

Guinness Superlatives Ltd. is one of the leading information providers on 'Prestel', the Post Office's viewdata system. Viewdata is a new means of communication, linking the user of an adapted television set through a telephone line to a large store of computer-based information. By keying the Guinness index page number (321) you will be able to gain access to a wide rang of information, including up-to-date records, sports champion and quizzes to test your knowledge.

Prestel is a trade mark of the Post Office

GUINNESS MUSEUMS OF WORLD RECORDS

Several permanent exhibition halls featuring world records have been established in the USA and other parts of the world. The exhibits seek to bring world records from the realm of imagination to visual reality. Those already established are:

Empire State Building, New York City, USA
Myrtle Beach, South Carolina, USA
Gatlinburg, Tennessee, USA

Lake of the Ozarks, Missouri, USA
Fisherman's Wharf, San Francisco, California, USA
Niagara Falls, Ontario, Canada
Gröna Lund, Stockholm, Sweden
Mount Fuji Safari Park, Japan
Linna Mati Amusement Park, Helsinki, Finland
Museums are also being planned in a number of other locations

Acknowledgements

J. W. Arblaster, AIM; Richard Ayling; Howard Bass; Pat Besford; James Bond; British Airways; British Museum (Natura History); British Rail; British Travel; British Waterworks Association; L. J. Boughey; Henry G. Button; Kenneth H. Chandler Central Electricity Generating Board; Central Office of Information; Dr A. J. C. Charig; Sq Ldr D. H. Clarke, DFC, AFC; Clerk o Dail Eireann; The late Peter T. Cunningham (Chairman 1975–8); Albert Dormer; Clive Everton; Fédération Aéronautiqu Internationale; Fédération Internationale de l'Automobile; Fédération Internationale des Hôpitaux; Frank L. Forster, Esq. M. H. Ford; Darryl Francis; Dr Francis C. Fraser; Bill Frindall; John George; Colin W. Graham; General Post Office; A. Herb ert, (New Zealand); Dr Arthur H. Hughes (Chairman, 1954–66); Derek Hurst; Imperial War Museum; Institute of Strategi Studies; Sir Peter Johnson; Erich Kamper; Kline Iron and Steel Company; Mr Michael D. Lampen; John Lees; The Library o Congress, Washington DC; *Lloyd's Register of Shipping*; London Transport Board; The late T. L. Marks, OBE, TD (Chairma 1966–71); K. G. McWhirter, MA, MSc; Dr G. T. Meaden, Editor *Journal of Meteorology*; Meteorological Office; Metropolita Police; Alan Mitchell, BA, BAg. (For); David Mondey; Music Research Bureau; National Aeronautics and Space Administration National Geographic Society; National Maritime Museum; National Physical Laboratory; Doug Nye; Mrs Susann Palmer; Chri stopher Plumridge; E. T. Pugh, Editor *Manned Spacecraft*; A. J. R. Purssell (Chairman 1971–5); *The Racing Pigeon*, Londor John Randall; Jean Reville; Chris Rhys; Tim Rice; Jack Rollin; Royal Astronomical Society; Royal Botanic Gardens; Royal Geo graphic Society; Royal National Life-boat Institution; Rugby Football League; Alan Russell; SAS City Profiles; Wm L. Schult Graham Snowdon; John H. Stephens; Dave Terry; Lance Tingay; UN Statistical Office; Juhani Virola; J. N. P. Watson; Baruc H. Wood; Gerry L. Wood, FZS; World Meteorological Organization; Francis Albert Young; Zoological Society of London, an various sports associations and governing bodies.

Colin C. Smith (Correspondence Editor); Linda Hull (Editor's Secretary); Beverley Waites (Sports Editor's Assistant); Peter J Matthews and Bernadette Bidwell; the late A. Ross McWhirter (Co-editor 1954–75).

Also to Barbara Anderson, Maureen Anderson, Anne Belsham, Sally V. Bennett, Christine Bethlehem, Rosemary Bevan, D Richard Bowen, Signa. Wendy Cirillo, Amanda Clark, Pamela Croome, Mary Crowder, Trudy Doyle, Mlle Béatrice Frei, G Howard Garrard, DSC, Jacqueline Gould, Susan Gullen, Tessa Hegley, E. C. Henniker, David N. Hewlett, Allan Hicks, Angel Hoaen, David F. Hoy (Managing Director), Eileen Jackson, Hilary Leavey, Diana Lloyd, Jane Mayo, G. M. Nutbrown, W. E Nutbrown, Margaret Orr-Deas, Peter B. Page (1954–7), Lucie Phillippo, John Rivers, Suzi M. Ross-Browne, Judith Sleath Anne Symonds, Andrew Thomas (Associate Editor 1964–8), Gillian Turner, Winnie Ulrich, Peter Whatley, Stephen Jame Clarke (1974–76) (Management Accountant).

Front Cover Illustrations: *left to right:* Jack Nicklaus (see Golf); Eric Heiden (see Ice Skating); CN Tower (see p. 121); Paul Kimmelman (see p. 14); the world's longest car owned by Rev Gerald Manning (se p. 138–9); the Pygmy marmoset (see p. 32).

GUINNESS
BOOK OF
RECORDS

EDITION 28

Editor and Compiler NORRIS McWHIRTER

Assistant Editor MOIRA F. STOWE

Sports Editor STAN GREENBERG

GUINNESS SUPERLATIVES LIMITED

2 CECIL COURT, LONDON ROAD, ENFIELD, MIDDLESEX

OVERSEAS AND FOREIGN LANGUAGE EDITIONS

Language		Title	No. of Editions	Latest Publication	Publisher
American	(Casebound)	Guinness Book of World Records	20	1981	Sterling Publishing Co. Inc, New York City, NY, USA
American	(Paperback)	Guinness Book of World Records		1981	Bantam Books Inc, New York City, NY, USA
Arabic		Contracted for publication	–	—	Near East Business Development Company, Beirut, Lebanon and Saudia Arabia
Chinese	(Paperback)	健力士 世界 紀錄 大全	1	1981	Kite International Ltd, Hong Kong
Czech	(Casebound)	Guinnessova Kniha Rekordu	1	1975	Olympia, Prague, Czechoslovakia
Danish	(Casebound)	Guinness Rekordbog	8	1981	Forlaget Komma A/S, Copenhagen, Denmark
Dutch	(Casebound)	Het Groot Guinness Record Boek	6	1981	Uitgeverij Luitingh BV, Laren, Netherlands
Farsi		Contracted for publication	–	—	Amir Kabir Publishing Group, Tehran, Iran
Finnish	(Casebound)	Guinness Suuri Ennätys Kirja	5	1981	Sanoma Osakeyhtio, Helsinki, Finland
French	(Casebound)	Livre Guinness Des Records	8	1981	Edition No 1, Paris, France
German	(Casebound)	Guinness Buch der Rekorde	11	1981	Verlag Ullstein GmbH, Berlin, West Germany
Greek	(Casebound)	Τά Παράξενα καί τά Ρεκόρ τοῦ Κόσμου	1	1980	Imex Rigas Athanasios Ltd, Thessaloniki, Greece
Hebrew	(Casebound)	Guinness Sēfēr Ha'siim	4	1981	Carta, The Israel Map & Publishing Company, Jerusalem, Israel
Icelandic	(Casebound)	Heimsmetabok Guinness	2	1980	Bokautgafan Örn og Örlygur hf, Reykjavik, Iceland
Italian	(Casebound)	Il Guinness Dei Primati	5	1981	Arnoldo Mondadori Editore, Milan, Italy
Indonesian	(Paperback)	Guinness Rekaman Rekor Dunia	1	1980	P. T. Gramedia, Jakarta, Indonesia
Japanese	(Casebound)	Guinness Korega Sekai Ichi	7	1981	Kodansha Ltd, Tokyo, Japan
Norwegian	(Casebound)	Guinness Rekordboken Først og Størst	7	1980	Chr. Schibsteds Forlag, Oslo, Norway
Portuguese	(Casebound)	Guinness O Livro dos Recordes	2	1981	Augusto Sa Da Costa., Lda, Lisbon, Portugal
Serbo-Croat	(Casebound)	Guinnessova Knjiga Rekorda	1	1977	Prosvjeta, Zagreb, Yugoslavia
Slovenian	(Casebound)	Guinnessova Knjiga Rekordov	1	1978	Mladinska Knjiga, Ljubljana, Yugoslavia
Spanish	(Casebound)	Guinness Libro de los Records	6	1981	Exclusivas Graficas Catalanas S.A., Barcelona, Spain
Swedish	(Casebound)	Guinness Rekordbok Först och Störst	11	1981	Bokforlaget Forum AB., Stockholm, Sweden
Turkish	(Paperback)	Guinness Rekorlar Kitabi	1	1981	Karacan Yayinlari, Istanbul, Turkey

UK Editions with a supplement have been published annually for Australia since 1972.

British Library Cataloguing in Publication Data

Guinness book of records.—28th ed (1982).
1. Curiosities and wonders—Periodicals
032'.02   AG240

ISBN 0–85112–232–9

Standard Book Number ISBN: 0 85112 232 9
Standard Book Number ISBN: 0 85112 233 7
(Australian Edition)

Printed and bound in Great Britain by
REDWOOD BURN LIMITED Trowbridge, Wiltshire

OVERSEAS AGENTS

CANADA Adams, Colbourne & Reynolds Ltd, 2344 Spruce Street, Vancouver, BC, V6H 2P4. David Drew Associates, 9 Birchcroft Road, Islington, Ontario, M9A 2L3. Gordon R. Totten, 1533 Birmingham Street, Halifax, Nova Scotia, B3J 2J3.
EASTERN CARIBBEAN Poseidon Publishing Company, PO Box 582, Trinidad, West Indies.
EUROPE D. Richard Bowen, Post Box 30037, S–200 61, Malmö 30, Sweden
REPUBLIC OF IRELAND J. A. McGarry, 5 Second Avenue, Douglas, Isle of Man
LATIN AMERICA Eti Feeny, c/o Wm Collins Sons & Co. Ltd, 14 St. James's Place, London, SW1.
MIDDLE EAST, NORTH AFRICA and KENYA Nigel M. Ealand, Ealand Enterprises, Platanidia, Volos, Greece

OVERSEAS SOLE DISTRIBUTORS

AUSTRALIA Wm Collins Pty Ltd, 55 Clarence Street, Sydney 2000.
CHANNEL ISLANDS LST, 9 Patriotic Street, St Helier, Jersey
HONG KONG, TAIWAN Federal Publications (HK) Ltd, Unit D, 2nd floor, Freder Centre, 68 Sung Wong Toi Road, Tokwawan, Kowloon, Hong Kong.
INDIA UBS Publishers Distributors Ltd, 5 Ansari Road, PO Box 7015, New Delhi, 110002, India
KENYA Textbook Centre, Kijabe Street, PO Box 47540, Nairobi, Kenya.
MALTA Agius & Agius Ltd, 42a South Street, Valetta, Malta
NETHERLANDS Uitgeverij Luitingh BV, Hilversumseweg 16, Laren NH, Holland.
NEW ZEALAND Whitcoulls Ltd, Private Bag, Christchurch, New Zealand
NIGERIA J. L. Morison Son & Jones (Nigeria) Ltd
OMAN Family Bookshop & Co., PO Box 3376 Ruwi, Oman
SOUTH AFRICA Collins Vaal (Pty) Ltd, 1, Hardy Street, City and Suburban, Johannesburg 2001.
SOUTH EAST ASIA (Singapore, Malaysia, Brunei, Indonesia) Times Distributors Sdn. Bhd., Times Centre, 1 New Industrial Road, Singapore 1953.
THAILAND Far East Publications Ltd, 5th floor, Central Building, Silan Road, Bangkok.
UNITED ARAB EMIRATES Alnasr Novelty Stores, PO Box 1949, Riqa, Dubai, UAE

FOREWORD
by the Rt. Hon. the Earl of Iveagh

Now that our *Guinness Book of Records* has reached its 28th edition it has long since moved from the status of an annual to that of a perennial.

When we first brought out this book, twenty-six years ago, we did so in the hope of providing a means for peaceful settling of arguments about record performances in this record-breaking world in which we live. We realise, of course, that much joy lies in the argument, but how exasperating it can be if there is no final means of finding the answer.

About a quarter of the many thousands of records listed have to be changed from one edition to the next. In this edition we are again obliged to revise our own entry that records that the global sales of this book, now being published in 23 languages, have surpassed the 42 000 000 mark.

Whether the discussion concerns the highest that any man has jumped over his own height, the greatest weight lifted by a woman, the nationality of the first woman to climb Everest, or—an old bone of contention—the longest time for anyone to become a Saint, I can but quote the words used in introducing the first edition, 'How much heat these innocent questions can raise: Guinness, in producing this book, hopes that it may assist in resolving many such disputes, and may, we hope, turn heat into light'.

Iveagh

Chairman
Arthur Guinness, Son & Co., Ltd.

October 1981

NOTES ON THE ACCEPTABILITY OF RECORDS

We are *likely* to publish only those records which improve upon previous records or which are newly significant in having become the subject of widespread and preferably international competitiveness.

It should be stressed that unique occurrences and interesting peculiarities are not in themselves necessarily records. Records in our sense essentially have to be both measurable and comparable. Records which are *qualified* in some way, for example, by age, day of the week, county, etc, cannot be accommodated in a reference work so general as *The Guinness Book of Records*.

Claimants should send independent corroboration in the form of local or national newspaper cuttings, radio or TV coverage reports and signed authentication by independent adult witnesses or representatives of organisations of standing in their community. Signed log books should show there has been unremitting surveillance in the case of endurance events. Action photographs (preferably colour transparencies) should also be supplied. Five minutes rest intervals (optional but aggregable) are *permitted* after each completed hour in marathon events except for those very few 'non-stop' categories in which minimal intervals may be taken only for purposes other than for resting.

If an activity is one controlled by a recognised world or national governing body, that body should be consulted and involved in ratifying it.

The publishers do not publish gratuitously dangerous categories such as the lowest height for a handcuffed free-fall parachutist or the thinnest burning rope suspending a man in a strait-jacket from a helicopter.

The publishers do *not* normally supply personnel to invigilate record attempts but reserve the right to do so.

PREFACE

This 28th Edition has been not only completely revised but re-illustrated throughout.

Due to the significant fluctuations in comparative foreign exchange rates, currency conversions have been converted at the rate ruling at the time of the event or record. To indicate this the word '*then*' has been inserted before the relevant conversion.

There has been in recent years a marked increase in efforts to establish records for sheer endurance in many activities. In the very nature of record breaking the duration of such 'marathons' will tend to be pushed to greater and greater extremes and it should be stressed that marathon attempts are not without possible dangers. Organisers of marathon events would be well counselled to seek medical advice before and surveillance during marathons which involve extended periods with little or no sleep. (See above for notes on rest periods).

If there are discrepancies between entries in one edition and another, it may be generally assumed that the *later* entry is the product of the more up to date research. Readers should consult the Stop Press section and the index, where an asterisk indicates that there is an additional entry in the Stop Press.

Finally the editorial office, which is concerned with maintaining and improving the quality of each succeeding edition, is unable to perform also the function of a free general information bureau for quiz competitions and the like, by telephone or by correspondence.

Norris McWhirter

Editor and compiler

October 1981
Guinness Superlatives Limited, 2 Cecil Court, London Road, Enfield, Middlesex EN2 6DJ

Design and Layout by David Roberts   *Artwork by Don Roberts (no kin)*

Additional Artwork by Eddie Botchway, Pat Gibbon, Matthew Hillier, Herbie Barrett and Mike Roffe.
Colour Film supplied by Format Graphics (Bristol) Ltd. and NEWSELE Litho Ltd. (Director Janice Tennant)

CONTENTS

ACKNOWLEDGEMENTS   4

FOREWORD by *The Rt Hon. Earl of Iveagh* 7

PREFACE by *Norris McWhirter*   7

CHAPTER ONE

The Human Being
1. *Dimensions*   9
2. *Origins*   14
3. *Longevity*   15
4. *Reproductivity*   16
5. *Physiology and Anatomy*   20

CHAPTER TWO

The Living World
Animal Kingdom—General   26
1. *Mammals*   28
2. *Birds*   36
3. *Reptiles*   40
4. *Amphibians*   42
5. *Fishes*   43
6. *Starfishes*   44
7. *Arachnids*   44
8. *Crustaceans*   45
9. *Insects*   45
10. *Centipedes*   47
11. *Millipedes*   47
12. *Segmented Worms*   48
13. *Molluscs*   48
14. *Ribbon Worms*   48
15. *Jelly Fishes*   48
16. *Sponges*   49
17. *Extinct Animals*   49

The Plant Kingdom   50
Kingdom Protista   57
Kingdom Fungi   57
Kingdom Procaryota   57
Parks, Zoos, Oceanaria and Aquaria 58

CHAPTER THREE

The Natural World
1. *Weather*   59
2. *Natural Phenomena*   63
3. *Structure and Dimensions*   64

CHAPTER FOUR

The Universe and Space   72
Rocketry and Missiles   77

CHAPTER FIVE

The Scientific World
1. *Elements*   79
2. *Drink*   81
3. *Telescopes*   82
4. *Photography*   83
5. *Gems & Other Precious Materials* 84
6. *Numerology*   85
7. *Physical Extremes*   85

CHAPTER SIX

The Arts and Entertainments
1. *Painting*   88
2. *Sculpture*   91
3. *Language & Literature*   92
4. *Music*   102
5. *Gramophone*   106
6. *Theatre*   108
7. *Cinema*   109
8. *Radio Broadcasting*   111
9. *Television*   112

CHAPTER SEVEN

The World's Structures
1. *Buildings for Working*   114
2. *Buildings for Living*   116
3. *Buildings for Entertainment*   118
4. *Towers and Masts*   121
5. *Bridges*   121
6. *Canals*   123
7. *Dams*   124
8. *Tunnels*   125
9. *Specialised Structures*   126
10. *Borings and Mines*   131

CHAPTER EIGHT

The Mechanical World
1. *Ships*   133
2. *Road Vehicles*   137
3. *Railways*   142
4. *Aircraft*   145
5. *Power Producers*   151
6. *Engineering*   152

CHAPTER NINE

The Business World
1. *Commerce*   156
2. *Manufactured Articles*   162
3. *Agriculture*   169

CHAPTER TEN

Human Achievements
1. *Endurance and Endeavour*   173
2. *Honours, Decorations and Awards* 198

CHAPTER ELEVEN

The Human World
1. *Political and Social*   202
2. *Royalty and Heads of State*   206
3. *Legislatures*   207
4. *Military and Defence*   212
5. *Judicial*   215
6. *Economic*   223
7. *Education*   233
8. *Religions*   235
9. *Accidents and Disasters*   238

CHAPTER TWELVE

Sports, Games and Pastimes   239–339

All Sports
Aerobatics
Angling
Archery
Association Football (see Football)
Athletics (see Track and Field)
Backgammon (see Gambling)
Badminton
Baseball
Basketball
Beagling (see Coursing)
Billiards and Snooker
Board Sailing (see Yachting)
Bobsleigh
Bowling (Tenpin)
Bowls
Boxing
Bridge (see Indoor Pastimes)
Bullfighting
Canoeing
Caving
Chess (see Indoor Pastimes)
Coursing
Cribbage (see Indoor Pastimes)
Cricket
Croquet
Cross-Country Running
Curling
Cycling
Darts (see Indoor Pastimes)
Diving (see Swimming)
Dominoes (see Indoor Pastimes)
Draughts (see Indoor Pastimes)
Equestrian Sports
Fell Running (see Mountaineering)
Fencing
Fives (Eton and Rugby)
Football (Association, Gaelic, Rugby League, Rugby Union)
Fox Hunting
Gaelic Football (see Football)
Gambling (Betting, Bingo, Pools)
Gliding and Hang Gliding
Golf
Greyhound Racing
Gymnastics
Handball (Court and Field)
Harness Racing
Hockey
Horse Racing
Hurling
Ice Hockey
Ice Skating (Figure and Speed)
Ice and Sand Yachting
Indoor Pastimes
Judo (Ju-Jitsu)
Karate
Lacrosse
Lawn Tennis
Lugeing (see Bobsleigh)
Marbles
Modern Pentathlon
Monopoly (see Indoor Pastimes)
Motorcycle Racing
Motor Racing

Mountaineering
Netball
Olympic Games
Orienteering
Parachuting
Pelota Vasca (Jai Alai)
Pigeon Racing
Polo
Pool (see Billiards)
Power Boat Racing
Punting (see Rowing)
Rackets
Real Tennis (see Tennis)
Rodeo
Roller Cycling (see Cycling)
Roller Skating
Rowing
Rugby League (see Football)
Rugby Union (see Football)
Scrabble (see Indoor Pastimes)
Shinty
Shooting
Skiing
Skittles (see Bowling)
Snooker (see Billiards)
Softball
Speedway
Squash Rackets
Surfing
Swimming
Table Football (see Indoor Pastimes)
Table Tennis
Tennis (Real or Royal)
Tiddlywinks (see Indoor Pastimes)
Tobogganing (see Bobsleigh)
Track and Field Athletics
Trampolining
Trotting and Pacing (see Harness Racing)
Tug of War
Volleyball
Walking
Water Polo
Water Skiing
Weightlifting
Whist (see Indoor Pastimes)
Windsurfing (see Board Sailing)
Women's Cricket (see Cricket)
Wrestling
Yachting

STOP PRESS

INDEX

1. THE HUMAN BEING

---

1. DIMENSIONS

TALLEST GIANTS

The height of human giants is a subject on which accurate information is frequently obscured by exaggeration and commercial dishonesty. The only admissible evidence on the true height of giants is that collected in the last 100 years under impartial medical supervision. Some medical papers themselves, however, have published fanciful, as opposed to measured, heights as recently as 1962.

The assertion that Goliath of Gath (*c.* 1060 BC) stood 6 cubits and a span (9 ft 6½ in *290 cm*) suggests a confusion of units or some over-zealous exaggeration by the Hebrew chroniclers. The Jewish historian Flavius Josephus (born AD 37/38, died *c.* AD 100) and some of the manuscripts of the Septuagint (the earliest Greek translation of the Old Testament) attribute to Goliath the quite credible height of 4 Greek cubits and a span (6 ft 10 in *208 cm*).

Extreme mediaeval data, taken from bone measurements, invariably refer to specimens of extinct whale, giant cave bear, mastodon, woolly rhinoceros or other prehistoric non-human remains.

Circus giants and others who are exhibited are normally under contract not to be measured and are, almost traditionally, billed by their promoters at heights up to 18 in *45 cm* in excess of their true heights. There are many notable examples of this, and 23 instances were listed in the *Guinness Book of Records* (14th edition). The acromegalic giant Eddie Carmel (b. Tel Aviv, Israel, 1938), formerly 'The Tallest Man on Earth' of Ringling Bros. and Barnum & Bailey's Circus (1961–8) was allegedly 9 ft 0⅝ in *275 cm* tall (weighing 38 st 3 lb *242 kg*), but photographic evidence suggests that his true height was about 7 ft 6⅝ in *229,6 cm*. He died in New York City on 14 Aug 1972 when his standing height, due to severe kyphoscoliosis, (two dimensional spinal curvature), was *c.* 7 ft *212 cm*.

An extreme case of exaggeration concerned Siah Khān ibn Kashmir Khān (b. 1913) of Bushehr (Bushire), Iran. Prof. D. H. Fuchs showed photographs of him at a meeting of the Society of Physicians in Vienna, Austria, in January 1935, claiming that he was 320 cm *10 ft 6 in* tall. Later, when Siah Khān entered the Imperial Hospital in Teheran for an operation, it was revealed that his actual height was a full metre less at 220 cm *7 ft 2.6 in*.

World

Modern opinion is that the tallest recorded man of whom there is irrefutable evidence was the pre-acromegalic giant Robert Pershing Wadlow, born at 6.30 a.m. on 22 Feb 1918 in Alton, Illinois, USA.

He was born to Mrs Addie Mae Wadlow (1896–1980) weighing 8½ lb *3,85 kg*. His abnormal growth started at the age of 2 following a double hernia operation. His height progressed as follows:

Age in Years	Height		Weight		Age in Years	Height		Weight	
			lb	kg				lb	kg
5	5'4"	163 cm	105	48	15	7'8"	234 cm	355	161
8	6'0"	183 cm	169	77	16	7'10½"	240 cm	374	170
9	6'2½"	189 cm	180	82	17	8'0½"	245 cm	315[1]	143
10	6'5"	196 cm	210	95	18	8'3½"	253 cm	—	—
11	6'7"	200 cm	—	—	19	8'5½"	258 cm	480	218
12	6'10½"	210 cm	—	—	20	8'6¾"	261 cm	—	—
13	7'1¾"	218 cm	255	116	21	8'8¼"	265 cm	491	223
14	7'5"	226 cm	301	137	22.4[2]	8'11"	272 cm	439	199

[1] Following severe influenza and infection of the foot.
[2] Wadlow was still growing during his terminal illness.

Dr C. M. Charles, Associate Professor of Anatomy at Washington University's School of Medicine in St Louis, Missouri and Dr Cyril MacBryde measured Robert Wadlow at 272 cm *8 ft 11.1 in* in St Louis on 27 June 1940. Wadlow died 18 days later, at 1.30 a.m. on 15 July 1940, in Manistee, Michigan as a result of cellulitis (inflammation of cellular tissue) of the right ankle aggravated by a poorly fitted brace, which had been fitted only a week earlier.

9

Robert Wadlow, the world's tallest ever human at 272 cm *8 ft 11.1 in* with some of the workers who built his outsize shoes. The photograph was taken in St. Louis, Missouri, USA in 1940.

He was buried in Oakwood Cemetery, Alton, Illinois in a coffin measuring 10 ft 9 in *328 cm* in length, 32 in *81 cm* wide and 30 in *76 cm* deep. His greatest recorded weight was 35 st 1 lb *222,71 kg*, on his 21st birthday. He weighed 31 st 5 lb *199 kg* at the time of his death. His shoes were size 37AA (18½ in *47 cm* long) and his hands measured 12¾ in *32,5 cm* from the wrist to the tip of the middle finger (*cf.* the depth of this page at 11¼ in *28,6 cm*).

His arm span was 9 ft 5¾ in *288 cm* and his peak daily consumption attained 8000 calories. At the age of 9 he was able to carry his father, Harold F Wadlow (d. Sept 1967) later Mayor of Alton, who stood 5 ft 11 in *182 cm* and weighed 170 lb *72 kg*, up the stairs of the family home.

The only other men for whom heights of 8 ft *244 cm* or more have been reliably reported are the ten listed below. In seven cases, gigantism was followed by acromegaly, a disorder which causes an enlargement of the nose, lips, tongue, lower jaw, hands and feet, due to renewed activity by an already swollen pituitary gland, which is located at the base of the brain.

John F. Carroll (1932–69) of Buffalo, New York State, USA [1] 8 ft 7¾ in *263,5 cm*.

John William Rogan (1871–1905), a Negro of Gallatin, Tennessee, USA [2] 8 ft 6 in *259,1 cm*.

Muhammad Alam Channa (b. 1954–*fl.* 1981) of Sehwan Sharif, Pakistan [3] 8 ft 3 in *251,4 cm*.

Don Koehler (1925–81) of Denton, Montana, USA [4] 8 ft 2 in *248,9 cm*, latterly lived in Chicago.

Bernard Coyne (1897–1921) of Anthon, Iowa USA [5] 8 ft 2 in *248,9 cm*

Väinö Myllyrinne (1909–63) of Helsinki, Finland [6] 8 ft 1.2 in *247 cm*.

Patrick Cotter O'Brien (1760–1806) of Kinsale, County Cork, Ireland [7] 8 ft 1 in *246 cm*.

'Constantine' (1872–1902) of Reutlingen, West Germany [8] 8 ft 0.8 in *245,8 cm*.

Sulaimān 'Ali Nashnush (b.1943–*fl.* 1981) of Tripoli, Libya [9] 8 ft 0.4 in *245 cm*.

Gabriel Estevao Monjane (b.1944–*fl.* 1981) of Monjacaze, Mozambique [10] *c.* 8 ft 0 in *243,8 cm*.

(1) *Severe kypho-scoliosis (two dimensional spinal curvature). The figure represents his height with assumed normal spinal curvature, calculated from a standing height of 8 ft 0 in 244 cm, measured on 14 Oct 1959. His standing height was 7 ft 8¼ in 234 cm shortly before his death.*
(2) *Measured in a sitting position. Unable to stand owing to ankylosis (stiffening of the joints through the formation of adhesions) of the knees and hips.*
(3) *Started growing abnormally at the age of 10. Has been credited with heights up to 8 ft 6 in 259 cm.*
(4) *Spinal curvature reduced his standing height to c. 7 ft 10 in 238,4 cm. He had a twin sister who is 5 ft 9 in 175 cm tall. His father was 6 ft 2 in 187 cm and his mother 5 ft 10 in 177 cm.*
(5) *Eunuchoidal giant (Daddy long-legs syndrome). Rejected by Army in 1918 when 7 ft 9 in 236 cm.*
(6) *Stood 7 ft 3½ in 222 cm at the age of 21 years. Experienced a second phase of growth in his late thirties and may have stood 8 ft 3 in 251 cm at one time.*
(7) *Revised height based on skeletal remeasurement in 1975.*
(8) *Eunuchoidal. Height estimated, as both legs were amputated after they turned gangrenous. He claimed a height of 8 ft 6 in 259 cm.*
(9) *Operation in Rome to correct abnormal growth was successful in 1960.*
(10) *Eunuchoidal. Measured 7 ft 5 in 226 cm at the age of 16 and 7 ft 10 in 238,7 cm in Dec 1965. Has not been anthropometrically assessed since joining a Portuguese circus (billed height 265 cm 8 ft 8⅓ in).*

A table of the tallest giants of all-time in the 31 countries with men taller than 7 ft 4 in *223,5 cm* was listed in the 15th edition of the *Guinness Book of Records* (1968) at page 9.

The tallest known living human is Muhammad Alam Channa (b. 1956), who works as an attendant at the shrine of Lal Shahbaz Qalandar in Pakistan. He began growing abnormally from the age of 12 and reached a height of 7 ft *231 cm* by the age of 20. He is now 8 ft 3 in *251 cm* and weighs more than 180 kg *28 st 5 lb*.

England
The tallest Englishman ever recorded was William Bradley (1787–1820), born in Market Weighton, Humberside. He stood 7 ft 9 in *236 cm*. John Middleton (1578–1623), the famous Childe of Hale, from near Liverpool, was credited with a height of 9 ft 3 in *282 cm* but a life-size impression of his right hand (length 11½ in *29,2 cm*, *cf.* Wadlow's 12¾ in *32,4 cm*) painted on a panel in Brasenose College, Oxford indicates his true stature was nearer 7 ft 8 in *233,3 cm*. James Toller (1795–1819) of St Neots, Cambridgeshire was alleged to be 8 ft 6 in *259 cm* but was actually 7 ft 6 in *229 cm*. Albert Brough (1871–1919), a publican of Nottingham, reached a height of 7 ft 7½ in *232 cm*. Frederick Kempster (1889–1918) of Bayswater, London, was reported to have measured 8 ft 4½ in *255 cm* at the time of his death, but photographic evidence suggests that his height was 7 ft 8½ in *235 cm*. He measured 234 cm *7 ft 8.1 in* in 1913. Henry Daglish, who stood 7 ft 7 in *231 cm*. died in Upper Stratton, Wiltshire, on 16 March 1951, aged 25. The much-publicised Edward (Ted) Evans (1924–58) of Englefield Green, Surrey, was reputed to be 9 ft 3 in *282 cm* but actually stood 7 ft 8½ in *235 cm*. The tallest fully mobile man now living in Great Britain is Christopher Paul Greener (b. New Brighton, Merseyside, 21 Nov 1943) of Hayes,

Kent, who measures 7 ft 6¼ in *229 cm.* (weight 26 st *165 kg*). Terence Keenan (b. 1942) of Rock Ferry, Merseyside measured 7 ft 6 in *229 cm* in 1968, but is confined to a wheelchair owing to a leg condition. His abnormal growth began at the age of 17 when he was only 5 ft 4 in *163 cm* tall.

Scotland

The tallest Scotsman, and the tallest recorded 'true' (non-pathological) giant, was Angus Macaskill (1825–63), born on the island of Berneray, in the Sound of Harris, in the Western Isles. He stood 7 ft 9 in *236 cm* and died in St Anns', on Cape Breton Island, Nova Scotia, Canada. Lambert Quételet (1796–1874), a Belgian anthropometrist, considered that a Scotsman named MacQuail, known as 'the Scotch Giant', stood 8 ft 3 in *251 cm*. He served in the famous regiment of giants of Frederick William I (1688–1740), King of Prussia. His skeleton, now in the Staatliche Museum zu Berlin, East Germany, measures 220 cm *7 ft 2.6 in*. Sam McDonald (1762–1802) of Lairg in Sutherland, was reputed to be 8 ft *244 cm* tall but actually stood 6 ft 10 in *208 cm*. The tallest Scotsman now living is George Gracie (b. 1938) of Forth, Strathclyde. He stands 7 ft 3 in *221 cm* and weighs 28 st *178 kg*. His brother Hugh (b. 1941) is 7 ft 0½ in *215 cm*.

Wales

The tallest Welshman on record was William Evans (1599–1634) of Monmouthshire, who was porter to King James I. He stood 7 ft 6 in *228,2 cm*.

Ireland

The tallest Irishman was Patrick Cotter O'Brien (1760–1806), born in Kinsale, County Cork. He died at Hotwells, Bristol (See Table p. 10). The tallest Irishman now living is believed to be Jim Cully (b. 1926) of Tipperary, a former boxer and wrestler. He stands 7 ft 2 in *218 cm*.

Twins

The tallest twins (identical) ever recorded were the Knipe brothers (b. 1761–*fl.* 1780) of Magherafelt, near Londonderry, Northern Ireland, who both measured 7 ft 2 in *218,4 cm*. The world's tallest living twins (also identical) are Dan and Doug Busch of Flagstaff, Arizona, USA who both measure 6 ft 11 in *210,8 cm*. Britain's tallest twins are the 6 ft 8 in *2,03 m* tall David and John Moore (b. 29 Mar 1963) of Erith, Kent.

TALLEST GIANTESSES
World *All-time*

Giantesses are rarer than giants but their heights are still spectacular. The tallest woman in medical history was the acromegalic giantess Jane ('Ginny') Bunford, born on 26 July 1895 at Bartley Green, Northfield, West Midlands, England. Her abnormal growth started at the age of 11 following a head injury, and on her 13th birthday she measured 6 ft 6 in *198 cm*. Shortly before her death on 1 April 1922 she stood 7 ft 7 in *231 cm* tall, but she had severe kyphoscoliosis and would have measured about 7 ft 11 in *241 cm* with assumed normal spinal curvature. Her skeleton, now preserved in the Anatomical Museum in the Medical School at Birmingham University, has a mounted height of 7 ft 4 in *223,5 cm*. Anna Hanen Swan (1846–88) of Nova Scotia, Canada, was billed at 8 ft 1 in *246 cm* but actually measured 7 ft 5½ in *227 cm*. In London on 17 June 1871 she married Martin van Buren Bates (1845–1919) of Whitesburg, Letcher County, Kentucky, USA, who stood 7 ft 2½ in *220 cm* making them the tallest married couple on record.

Living

The tallest living woman is Zeng Jinlian (pronounced San Chung Lin) (b. 26 June 1964) of Yujiang village in the Bright Moon Commune, Hunan Province, central China. In November 1980 she was reported to be 240 cm *7 ft 10½ in* and to weigh 147 kg *23 st 2 lb*. She began to grow rapidly at the age of 4 months and stood 156 cm *5 ft 1½ in* before her 4th birthday and 217 cm *7 ft 1½ in* when she was 13. Her hands measure 25,5 cm *10 in* and her feet 35,5 cm *14 in* in length. She is acromegalic and suffers from both scoliosis and diabetes. Her parents are 163 cm *5 ft 4½ in* and 156 cm *5 ft 1½ in* while her brother was 158 cm *5 ft 2½ in* aged 18.

SHORTEST DWARFS

The strictures which apply to giants apply equally to dwarfs, except that exaggeration gives way to understatement. In the

The world's tallest living woman, Zeng Jinlian of Yujiang village in central China, who was 240 cm *7 ft 10½ in* tall in Nov 1980 and has become the first 8 foot *2,44 m* giantess. (*China Features*)

same way as 9 ft *274 cm* may be regarded as the limit towards which the tallest giants tend, so 23 in *58 cm* must be regarded as the limit towards which the shortest mature dwarfs tend (*cf.* the average length of new-born babies is 18–20 in *46–50 cm*). In the case of child dwarfs their *ages* are often enhanced by their agents or managers.

There are many forms of human dwarfism. Ateleiotic dwarfs, known as midgets, have essentially normal proportions but suffer from growth hormone deficiency. Such dwarfs tended to be even shorter at a time when human stature was generally shorter due to lower nutritional standards.

World *All-time*

The shortest mature human of whom there is independent evidence was Pauline Musters ('Princess Pauline'), a Dutch midget. She was born at Ossendrecht, on 26 Feb 1876 and measured 30 cm *12 in* at birth. At the age of 9 she was 55 cm *21.65 in* tall and weighed only 1,5 kg *3 lb 5 oz*. She died, at the age of 19, of pneumonia, with meningitis, her heart weakened from alcoholic excesses, on 1 Mar 1895 in New York City, NY, USA. Although she was billed at 48 cm *19 in*, she had earlier been medically measured to be 59 cm *23.2 in* tall. A *post mortem* examination showed her to be exactly 61 cm *24 in* (there was some elongation after death). Her mature weight varied from 3,4–4 kg *7½–9 lb* and her 'vital statistics' were 47–48–43 cm *18½–19–17 in*, which suggests she was overweight.

A height of 19 in *48 cm* was attributed to Paul Del Rio (b. Madrid, Spain, 1920) by *Life Magazine* in 1938. The fact he created no 'fuss' in Hollywood and weighed as much as 12 lb *5,4 kg* indicates that he was taller.

In 1979 a height of 50 cm *19.68 in* and a weight of 4 lb 6 oz *1,98 kg* were reported for a nine-year-old Greek girl named Stamatoula being cared for at the Lyrion Convent, Athens. The child, believed to be the survivor of twins, is suffering from Seckel's 'bird-face' syndrome and growth has allegedly ceased, but in a similar case from Corsica the girl eventually reached a height of 34 in *86,3 cm* and a weight of 26 lb *11,8 kg*.

Male All-time

The shortest recorded adult male dwarf was Calvin Phillips, born on 14 Jan 1791 in Bridgewater, Massachusetts, USA. He weighed 2 lb *907 g* at birth and stopped growing at the age of 5. When he was 19 he measured 26½ in *67 cm* tall and weighed 12 lb *5,4 kg* with his clothes on. He died two years later, in April 1812, from progeria, a rare disorder characterised by dwarfism and premature senility.

The most famous midget in history was Charles Sherwood Stratton, *alias* 'General Tom Thumb', born on 4 Jan 1838. When he got into the clutches of the circus proprietor Mr. Barnum his birth date was changed to 4 Jan 1832 so that when billed at 30½ in *77 cm* at the age of 18 he was in fact 12. He died in his birthplace of Bridgeport, Connecticut, USA of apoplexy on 15 July 1883 aged 45 (not 51) and was 3 ft 4 in *102 cm*.

Another celebrated midget was Józef ('Count') Boruwalaski (b. November 1739) of Poland. He measured only 8 in *20 cm* long at

At 37 in *94 cm* tall Michael Henbury-Ballam is Britain's shortest adult. He is standing beside his twin brother Malcolm. (*Bitterne Photographs*)

birth, growing to 14 in *36 cm* at the age of 1 year. He stood 17 in *43 cm* at 6 years, 21 in *53 cm* at 10, 25 in *64 cm* at 15, 35 in *89 cm* at 25 and 39 in *99 cm* at 30. He died near Durham, England, on 5 Sept 1837, aged 97.

William E. Jackson, *alias* 'Major Mite', born on 2 Oct 1864 in Dunedin, New Zealand, measured 9 in *23 cm* long and weighed 12 oz *340 g* at birth. In November 1880 he stood 21 in *53 cm* and weighed 9 lb *4 kg*. He died in New York City, NY, USA, on 9 Dec 1900, when he measured 27 in *70 cm*.

Living

The world's shortest living adult human is Nruturam (b. 28 May 1929) a rachitic dwarf of Naydwar, India, who measures 28 in *71 cm*. The circus acrobatic dancer Süleyman Eris (b. 24 Jan 1955 in Turkey) was medically measured on 3 Mar 1977 to be 76,5 cm *30.1 in* and weighed 11,4 kg *25 lb 2 oz*. He and his brother (83,5 cm *32.8 in*) and sister (96,5 cm *38 in*) are primordial dwarfs.

United Kingdom

The shortest mature human ever recorded in Britain was Miss Joyce Carpenter (b. 21 Dec 1929), a rachitic dwarf of Charford, Hereford and Worcester, who stood 29 in *74 cm* tall and weighed 30 lb *13,60 kg*. She died on 7 Aug 1973 aged 43. Hopkins Hopkins (1737–54) of Llantrisant, Mid Glamorgan was 31 in *79 cm*. Hopkins, who died from progeria weighed 19 lb *8,62 kg* at the age of 7 and 13 lb *6 kg* at the time of his death. There are an estimated 2000 people of severely restricted growth, i.e. under 4 ft 8 in *142 cm*, living in Britain today.

The shortest adult living in Britain is Michael Henbury-Ballam (b. 26 Nov 1958) of Bassett, Southampton, who is 37 in *94 cm* tall and weighs 4 st 11 lb *30,38 kg*. A 5 lb 14 oz *2,66 kg* baby, he stopped growing at the age of 13 years. His twin brother Malcolm is 5 ft 9 in *175 cm* tall and weighs 11 st 7 lb *73 kg*.

Oldest

There are only two centenarian dwarfs on record. The first was Miss Anne Clowes of Matlock, Derbyshire, who died on 5 Aug 1784 aged 103 years. She was 3 ft 9 in *114 cm* tall and weighed 48 lb *21,7 kg*. On 6 Apr 1981 Hungarian-born Miss Susanna Bokoyni ('Princess Susanna') of Newton, New Jersey, USA celebrated her 102nd birthday. She is 3 ft 4 in *101 cm* tall and weighs 37 lb *16,78 kg*.

Most variable stature

Adam Rainer, born in Graz, Austria, in 1899, measured 118 cm *3 ft 10.45 in* at the age of 21. But then he suddenly started growing upwards at a rapid rate, and by 1931 he had reached 218 cm *7 ft 1¾ in*. He became so weak as a result that he was bed-ridden for the rest of his life. He died on 4 March 1950 aged 51 and was the only person in medical history to have been both a giant and a dwarf.

TRIBES

Tallest

The tallest major tribe in the world is the Tutsi (also Watussi), Nilotic herdsmen of Rwanda and Burundi, Central Africa whose young adult males average 180 cm *5 ft 10¾ in*. The Tehuelches of Patagonia, long regarded as of gigantic stature (*i.e.* 7–8 ft *213–244 cm*), have in fact an average height (males) of 5 ft 10 in *178 cm*. The Montenegrins of Yugoslavia, with a male average of 5 ft 10 in *178 cm* (in the town of Trebinje the average height is 6 ft *183 cm*), compares with the men of Sutherland, at 5 ft 9½ in *176,5 cm*. In 1912 the average height of the men living in Balmaclellan, in the Kircudbright district of Dumfries and Galloway was reported to be 5 ft 10.4 in *179 cm*.

Shortest

The smallest pygmies are the Mbuti, with an average height of 4 ft 6 in *137 cm* for men and 4 ft 5 in *135 cm* for women, with some groups averaging only 4 ft 4 in *132 cm* for men and 4 ft 1 in *124 cm* for women. They live in the forests near the river Ituri in Zaïre, Africa.

WEIGHT

Heaviest men *World*

The heaviest human in medical history has been Jon Brower Minnoch (b. 29 Sept 1941) of Bainbridge Island, Washington

USA, who was carried on planking by a rescue team into the University Hospital, Seattle in March 1978. Dr. Robert Schwartz, the endocrinological consultant, estimated by extrapolating his intake and elmination rates that he was 'probably more' than 1400 lb *635 kg* (100 st). To roll him over in his hospital bed it took 18 attendants. After nearly 2 years on a 1200 calorie per day diet he was down to 450 lb *205 kg*. This former taxi-cab driver stands 6 ft 1 in *1,85 m* tall. He was 400 lb *180 kg* in 1963, 700 lb *315 kg* in 1966 and about 975 lb *440 kg* in late 1976 but is still aiming for a stable 210 lb *95 kg*.

The only other men for whom weights of more than 60 st (840 lb) *381 kg* have been reliably reported are the nine listed below:

	st	lb	kg
Michael Walker *né* Francis Lang (b. 1934) USA (6 ft 2 in *188 cm*)[1]	84	11	538
Robert Earl Hughes (1926–58) USA (6 ft 0½ in *184 cm*)	76	5	485
Mills Darden (1798–1857) USA (7 ft 6 in *229 cm*)	72	12	463
John Hanson Craig (1856–94) USA (6 ft 5 in *195 cm*)[2]	64	11	411
Arthur Knorr (1914–60) USA (6 ft 1 in *185 cm*)[3]	64	4	408
Toubi (b. 1946) Cameroon	61	3½	389
T. J. Albert (b. 1957) St. Albans, W. Virginia, USA[4]	61	2	388
T. A. Valenzuela (1895–1937) Mexico (5 ft 11 in *180 cm*)	60	10	386
Joseph Schorr (1934–80) USA (6 ft 4 in *193 cm*)	60	6	384

[1] *Reduced to 369 lb 167 kg by Feb. 1980. Peak weight was estimated in 1971.*
[2] *Won $1000 in a 'Bonny Baby' contest in New York City in 1858.*
[3] *Gained 300 lb 136 kg in the last 6 months of his life.*
[4] *A French press report attributed a weight of 470 kg 1036 lb to him in 1979.*

Great Britain

The heaviest recorded man in Great Britain was William Campbell, who was born in Glasgow in 1856 and died on 16 June 1878, when a publican at High Bridge, Newcastle upon Tyne, Tyne and Wear. He was 6 ft 3 in *191 cm* tall and weighed 53 st 8 lb *340 kg* with an 85-in *216 cm* waist and a 96-in *244 cm* chest. His coffin weighed 1500 lb *680 kg*. He was 'a man of considerable intelligence and humour'. The only other British man with a recorded weight of more than 50 st *317,5 kg* was the celebrated Daniel Lambert (1770–1809) of Leicester. He stood 5 ft 11 in *180 cm* tall, weighed 52 st 11 lb *335 kg* shortly before his death and had a girth of more than 92 in *234 cm*.

The highest weight attained by any man living in Britain today was that of Eric Keeling (b. 1933) of Islington, Greater London who scaled 47 st *299 kg* in mid-1971. An 11 lb *5 kg* baby he weighed 18 st *114,5 kg* at the age of 13. By November 1973 he had reduced by dieting (600 calories per day) to 33 st *210 kg*. He is 6 ft 5 in *195,5 cm* tall.

George Macaree (b. 24 Dec 1923) of Newham, Greater London, who attained a peak weight of 41 st *253 kg* in April 1980, was taken ill shortly afterwards and is now on a special 1000 calories per day diet. By March 1981 he had reduced to 30 st 10 lb *195 kg*, and he hopes eventually to stabilise at 20 st *127 kg*.

Britain's heaviest man is now Jack Taylor (b. 1950) of Bradford, Yorkshire, who tipped the scales at 39 st 7 lb *251 kg* in January 1981.

Ireland

The heaviest Irishman is reputed to have been Roger Byrne, who was buried in Rosenallis, County Laoighis (Leix), on 14 Mar 1804. He died in his 54th year and his coffin and its contents weighed 52 st *330 kg*. Another Irish heavyweight was Lovelace Love (1731–66), born in Brook Hill, County Mayo. He weighed 'upward of 40 st *254 kg*' at the time of his death.

Heaviest women *World*
The heaviest woman ever recorded was the late Mrs Percy Pearl Washington, 46 who died in a hospital in Milwaukee, on 9 Oct

1972. The hospital scales registered only up to 800 lb (57 st 2 lb) *362,8 kg* but she was believed to weigh about 880 lb (62 st 12 lb) *399,1 kg*. The previous feminine weight record had been set 84 years earlier at 850 lb (60 st 10 lb) *386 kg* although a wholly unsubstantiated report exists of a woman Mrs Ida Maitland (1898–1932) of Springfield, Mississippi, USA, who reputedly weighed 65 st 1 lb (911 lb) *413,2 kg*.

A more reliable and better documented case was that of Mrs Flora Mae Jackson (*née* King), a 5 ft 9 in *175 cm* Negress born in 1930 at Shuqualak, Mississippi, USA. She weighed 10 lb *4,5 kg* at birth, 19 st 1 lb (267 lb) *121 kg* at the age of 11, 44 st 5 lb (621 lb) *282 kg* at 25 and 60 st (840 lb) *381 kg* shortly before her death in Meridian, Mississippi, on 9 Dec 1965. She was known in show business as 'Baby Flo'.

Great Britain and Ireland
The heaviest woman ever recorded in Great Britain was Mrs Muriel Hopkins (b. 1931) of Tipton, West Midlands who weighed 43 st 11 lb *278 kg* (height 5 ft 11 in *180 cm*) in 1978. Shortly before her death on 22 Apr 1979 she reportedly scaled 52 st *330 kg*, but this was only an estimate and her actual weight was believed to have been about 47½ st *301 kg*. Her coffin measured 6 ft 3 in *190 cm* in length, 4 ft 6 in *137 cm* wide and 3 ft *91 cm* deep. The heaviest weight of a woman living in Britain today was that of Miss Jean Renwick (b. 1939) of Brixton, London, who weighed 40 st 2 lb *254 kg* (height 5 ft 3½ in *161 cm*) in January 1972. Since dieting her lowest weight has been 22 st 2 lb *141 kg*.

Heaviest twins
The heaviest twins in the world were Billy Leon (1946–79) and Benny Loyd (b. 7 Dec 1946) McCrary *alias* McGuire of Hendersonville, North Carolina, USA, who in November 1978 were weighed 743 lb *337 kg* (Billy) and 723 lb *328 kg* (Benny) and had 84 in *213 cm* waists. As professional tag wrestling performers they were *billed* at weights up to 770 lb *349 kg*. After one 6 week strict slimming course in a hospital, they emerged weighing 5 lb *2,26 kg* more. Billy died at Niagara Falls, Ontario, Canada on 13 July 1979 after a mini-motorcycle accident.

Lightest World
The lightest adult human on record was Lucia Zarate (b. San Carlos, Mexico 2 Jan 1863, d. October 1889), an emaciated Mexican ateleiotic dwarf of 26½ in *67 cm*, who weighed 2,125 kg *4.7 lb* at the age of 17. She 'fattened up' to 13 lb *5,9 kg* by her 20th birthday. At birth she weighed 2½ lb *1,1 kg*. The lightest adult ever recorded in the United Kingdom was Hopkins Hopkins (Shortest dwarfs, see p. 12).

The thinnest recorded adults of normal height are those suffering from Simmonds' Disease (Hypophyseal cachexia). Losses up to 65 per cent of the original body-weight have been recorded in females, with a 'low' of 3 st 3 lb *20 kg* in the case of Emma Shaller (b. St Louis, Missouri 8 July 1868, d. 4 Oct 1890), who stood 5 ft 2 in *157 cm*. Edward C. Hagner (1892–1962), *alias* Eddie Masher (USA) is alleged to have weighed only 3 st 8 lb *22 kg* at a height of 5 ft 7 in *170 cm*. He was also known as 'the Skeleton Dude'. In August 1825 the biceps measurement of Claude-Ambroise Seurat (b. 10 Apr 1797, d. 6 Apr 1826) of Troyes, France was 4 in *10 cm* and the distance between his back and his chest was less than 3 in *8 cm*. According to one report he stood 5 ft 7½ in *171 cm* and weighed 5 st 8 lb *35 kg*, but in another account was described as 5 ft 4 in *163 cm* and only 2 st 8 lb *16 kg*. It was recorded that the American exhibitionist Rosa Lee Plemons (b. 1873) weighed 27 lb *12 kg* at the age of 18. In March 1978 the death was reported of an anorexic 47-year-old woman in Hounslow, Middx, who scaled only 4 st 3 lb *26,7 kg* (height 5 ft 2 in *157 cm*).

In February 1981 a weight of 3 st 12 lb *24,5 kg* was recorded for a 31-year-old woman suffering from what is known as the 'total allergy syndrome' (aversion to anything that has a synthetic base).

Lightest Great Britain
Robert Thorn (b. 1842) of March, Cambridgeshire weighed 49 lb *22 kg* at the age of 32. He was 4 ft 6 in *137 cm* tall and had a 27 in *68 cm* chest (expanded) and 4½ in *11 cm* biceps.

Slimming

The greatest recorded slimming feat was that of William J. Cobb (b. 1926), *alias* 'Happy Humphrey', a professional wrestler of Macon, Georgia, USA. It was reported in July 1965 that he had reduced from 57 st 4 lb *364 kg* to 16 st 8 lb *105 kg*, a loss of 40 st 10 lb *259 kg* in 3 years. His waist measurement declined from 101 to 44 in *257 to 112 cm*. In October 1973 it was reported that 'Happy' was back to his normal weight of 46½ st or 650 lb *295 kg*. By February 1980 Michael Walker (see table p. 13) had reduced to 369 lb *167 kg*; if the peak weight quoted for him was authentic, this indicates a weight loss of 58 st 6 lb *371 kg* in the period 1971–80.

The US circus fat lady Mrs Celesta Geyer (b. 1901), *alias* Dolly Dimples, reduced from 553 lb *251 kg* to 152 lb *69 kg* in 1950–51, a loss of 401 lb *182 kg* in 14 months. Her vital statistics diminished *pari passu* from 79–84–84 in *200–213–213 cm* to a *svelte* 34–28–36 in *86–71–91 cm*. Her book 'How I lost 400 lbs' was not a best-seller because of the difficulty of would-be readers identifying themselves with the dress-making problems of losing more than 28 st *178 kg* when 4 ft 11 in *150 cm* tall. In December 1967 she was reportedly down to 7 st 12 lb *50 kg*. The speed record for slimming was established by Paul M. Kimelman, 21, of Pittsburgh, Pennsylvania, USA, who from 25 Dec 1966 to August 1967 went on a crash diet of 300–600 calories per day to reduce from 487 lb (34 st 11 lb) *215,9 kg* to 130 lb (9 st 4 lb) *59 kg*—a total loss of 357 lb (25 st 7 lb) *156,9 kg*. He has now stabilised at 175 lb (12 st 7 lb) *79 kg*. On 4–8 Feb 1951 Mrs Gertrude Levandowski (b. 1893) of Burnips, Michigan, USA successfully underwent a series of operations to reduce her weight from 44 st *280 kg* to 22 st *140 kg*.

Claude Halls (b. 1937) of Sible Hedingham, Essex reduced from 33 st 6¾ lb *212,6 kg* to 12 st 10 lb *80,7 kg*—a loss of 20 st 10¾ lb *131,8 kg*—in the 14 months January 1974 to March 1975. In the first 7 days with Weight Watchers he lost 5 st 7 lb *35 kg*.

The feminine Weight Watchers champion in Britain was Mrs Dolly Wager (b. 1933) of Charlton, London, who, between September 1971 and 22 May 1973 reduced from 31 st 7 lb *197 kg* to 11 st *69,8 kg* so losing 20 st 7 lb *130 kg*.

Weight gaining

A probable record for gaining weight was set by Arthur Knorr (b. 17 May 1914), who died on 7 July 1960, aged 46, in Reseda, California, USA. He gained 21 st 6 lb *136 kg* in the last 6 months of his life and weighed 64 st 4 lb *408 kg* when he died. Miss Doris James of San Francisco, California, USA is alleged to have gained 23 st 3 lb *147 kg* in the 12 months before her death in August 1965, aged 38, at a weight of 48 st 3 lb *306 kg*. She was only 5 ft 2 in *157 cm* tall.

Greatest differential

The greatest weight differential recorded for a married couple is 65 st 12 lb *419 kg* in the case of Mills Darden (72 st 12 lb *463 kg*—see p. 13) and his wife Mary (7 st *44,5 kg*). Despite her diminutiveness, however, Mrs Darden bore her husband 3 (perhaps 5) children before her death in 1837.

2. ORIGINS

EARLIEST MAN

SCALE OF TIME
If the age of the Earth-Moon system (latest estimate at least 4700 million years) is likened to a single year, Handy Man appeared on the scene at about 8.35 p.m. on 31 December, Britain's earliest known inhabitants arrived at about 11.27 p.m., the Christian era began about 13 seconds before midnight and the life span of a 115-year-old person (pp. 16 & 17) would be about three-quarters of a second. Present calculations indicate that the Sun's increased heat, as it becomes a 'red giant', will make life insupportable on Earth in about 10,000 million years. Meanwhile there may well be colder epicycles. The period of 1000 million years is sometimes referred to as an aeon.

Man (*Homo sapiens*) is a species in the sub-family Homininae of the family Hominidae of the super-family Hominoidea of the sub-order Simiae (or Anthropoidea) of the order Primates of the infra-class Eutheria of the sub-class Theria of the class Mammalia of the sub-phylum Vertebrata (Craniata) of the phylum Chordata of the sub-kingdom Metazoa of the animal kingdom.

Earliest *Primate*

The earliest known primates appeared in the Palaeocene period of about 80,000,000 years ago. The sub-order of higher primates, called Simiae (or Anthropoidea) evolved from the catarrhine or old-world sect more than 40,000,000 years later in the

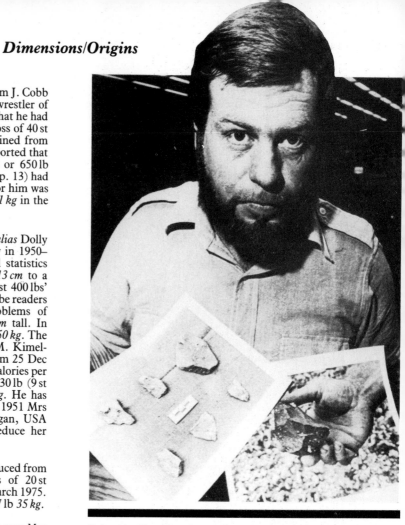

Photographs of the earliest evidence of toolmaking collected from the Gona River site in the Afar region of NE Ethiopia. The stone tools are believed to be 2.6 million years old, a half a million years older than any previously found and were discovered by Dr. Jack Harris of the University of Pittsburgh in 1977. (*Topham/AP*)

Lower Oligocene period. During the Middle and Upper Oligocene the super-family Hominoidea emerged. This contains three accepted families, *viz* Hominidae (bipedal, ground-dwelling man or near man), Pongidae (brachiating forest apes) and Oreopithecidae. The earliest known hominoid (man-like) fossil found is the *Oligopithecus savagei* found in El Faiyum, Egypt and dated to *c*. 33 million years ago.

Earliest *Hominid (Near Man)*

The characteristics of the Hominidae, such as a large brain, very fully distinguish them from any of the other Hominoidea. Evidence published in August 1969 indicated that *Ramapithecus*, discovered by G. Edward Lewis at Siwalik Hills, northern India in 1932 can be dated from 8 to 13 million years ago.

Earliest *Genus* Homo (*True Man*)

The greatest age attributed to fossils of the genus *Homo* is for the remains of 8 adults and 3 children discovered in the summer of 1975 at Laetolil, Tanzania by Dr Mary Leakey and dated by the University of California, Berkeley to between 3,350,000 and 3,750,000 BC. An arm bone fragment from Kanapoi has been tentatively regarded as from *Homo* and has been dated *c*. 4 million years ago.

The most complete of the earliest skeletons of *Homo* is that of 'Lucy' (40 per cent complete) found by Dr Donald C. Johanson and named *Australopithecus afarensis* found in the Afar region of Ethiopia in November 1974 dating 3–4 million years BC.

Seven proto-human footprints dating from 1.5 million years ago were reported from Lake Turkana, Kenya in Nov. 1979. Though they were 10½ in *26,6 cm* long the *Homo erectus* concerned was estimated to be 5 ft 2 in *158 cm* tall.

Earliest *Homo sapiens*

The earliest recorded remains of the species *Homo sapiens*, variously dated from 300,000 to 450,000 years ago in the Middle Pleistocene, were discovered on 24 Aug 1965 by Dr László

Vértes in a limestone quarry at Vértesszöllös, about 30 miles west of Budapest, Hungary. The remains, designated *Homo sapiens palaeo-hungaricus*, comprised an almost complete occipital bone, part of a skull with an estimated cranial capacity of nearly 1400 cm³ *85 in³*.

Earliest man in the Americas dates from at least 50,000 BC and 'more probably 100,000 BC' according to the late Dr Leakey after the examination of some hearth stones found in the Mojave Desert, California and announced in October 1970. The earliest human relic is a skull found in the area of Los Angeles, California dated in December 1970 to be from 22,000 BC.

Great Britain

The earliest evidence for the presence of humans in Great Britain dates from the time of the Cromerian interglacial (400,000–500,000 BC). Five worked flint artefacts of this period were found in deposits of this interglacial in a quarry near Westbury-sub-Mendip, Somerset, and described in 1975 by Michael J. Bishop. The oldest human remains ever found in Britain are pieces of a brain case from a specimen of *Homo sapiens fossilis*, believed to be a woman, recovered in June 1935 and March 1936 by Dr Alvan T. Marston from the Boyn Hill terrace in the Barnfield Pit, near Swanscombe, northern Kent. This find is attributed to Acheulian man, type *III* or *IV*, dating from the Hoxnian interglacial period.

3. LONGEVITY

No single subject is more obscured by vanity, deceit, falsehood and deliberate fraud than the extremes of human longevity. Extreme claims are generally made on behalf of the very aged rather than *by* them.

Many hundreds of claims throughout history have been made for persons living well into their second century and some, insulting to the intelligence, for people living even into their third. Centenarians surviving beyond their 110th year are in fact of the extremest rarity and the present absolute proven limit of human longevity does not yet admit of anyone living to celebrate any birthday after their 115th.

It is highly significant that in Sweden, where alone proper and thorough official investigations follow the death of every allegedly very aged citizen, none has been found to have surpassed 110 years. The most reliably pedigreed large group of people in the world, the British peerage, has, after ten centuries, produced only two centenarian peers, but only one reached his 101st birthday. However, this is possibly not unconnected with the extreme draughtiness of many of their residences and the amount of lead in their game.

Scientific research into extreme old age reveals that the correlation between the claimed density of centenarians in a country and its regional illiteracy is 0.83 ± 0.03. In late life, very old people often tend to advance their ages at the rate of about 17 years per decade. This was nicely corroborated by a cross analysis of the 1901 and 1911 censuses of England and Wales. Early claims must necessarily be without the elementary corroboration of birth dates. England was among the earliest of all countries to introduce compulsory local registers (September 1538) and official birth registration (1 July 1837) which was made fully compulsory only in 1874. Even in the United States, 45 per cent of births occurring between 1890 and 1920 were unregistered.

Several celebrated super-centenarians are believed to have been double lives (father and son, relations with the same names or successive bearers of a title). The most famous example is Christian Jakobsen Drackenberg allegedly born in Stavanger, Norway on 18 Nov 1626 and died in Aarhus, Denmark aged seemingly 145 years 326 days on 9 Oct 1772. A number of instances have been commercially sponsored, while a fourth category of recent claims are those made for political ends, such as the 100 citizens of the Russian Soviet Federative Socialist Republic (population about 132,000,000 at mid-1967) claimed in

Paul Kimelman of Pittsburgh, Pennsylvania who lost 357 lb *156,9 kg* in 8 months while on a crash diet of 300–600 calories per day.

March 1960 to be between 120 and 156. From data on documented centenarians, actuaries have shown that only one 115-year life can be expected in 2100 million lives (*cf.* world population was estimated to be 4470 million at mid-1980).

The height of credulity was reached on 5 May 1933, when a news agency solemnly filed a story from China with a Peking date-line that Li Chung-yun, the 'oldest man on Earth', born in 1680, had just died aged 256 years (*sic*). Recently the most extreme case of longevity claimed in the USSR has been 168 years for Shirali 'Baba' Mislimov of Barzavu, Azerbaijan, who died on 2 Sept 1973 and was reputedly born on 26 Mar 1805. No interview of this man has ever been permitted to any Western journalist or scientist. He was said to have celebrated the 100th birthday of his third wife Hartun, in 1966, and that of one of his grandchildren in August 1973. It was reported in 1954 that in the Abkhasian Republic of Georgia, USSR, where aged citizens are invested with an almost saint-like status, 2.58 per cent of the population was aged over 90—25 times the proportion in the USA.

Official Soviet insistence in 1961 on the unrivalled longevity of the country's citizenry is curious in view of the fact that the 592 persons in their unique 'over 120' category must have spent at least the first 78 years of their prolonged lives under Tsarism. It has recently been suggested that the extreme ages claimed by some men in Georgia, USSR, are the result of attempts to avoid military service when they were younger, by assuming the identities of older men.

Dr Zhores A. Medvedev, the expelled Soviet gerontologist, in Washington DC, on 30 Apr 1974 referring to USSR claims stated 'The whole phenomenon looks like a falsification' adding 'He [Stalin] liked the idea that [other] Georgians lived to be a 100

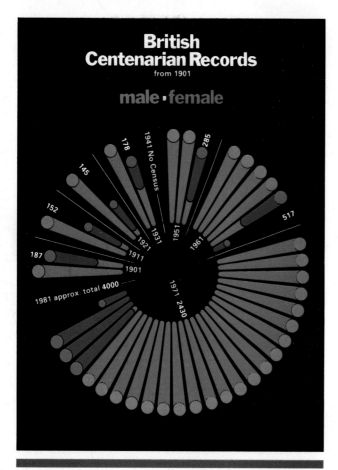

British Centenarian Records
from 1901

male · female

178
1941 No Census
285
145
152
517
1951
1931
1961
1921
1911
187
1901
1981 approx total 4000
1971 2430

A chart showing how Britain's centenarian population has increased over 21 fold this century. (*Source: Office of Population Censuses and Surveys*)

or more.' 'Local officials tried hard to find more and more cases for Stalin.' He points out (a) the *average* life-span in the regions claiming the highest incidence of centenarians is lower than the USSR average and (b) the number of centenarians claimed in the Caucasus has declined rapidly from 8000 in 1950 to 4500 in 1970. Dr I. M. Spector, of the Institute of Traumatology, Kazan, USSR quoted the maximum life-span of man in April 1974 as '110–115 years', though Dr Medvedev, in December 1977, put the proven limit in the USSR as low as 108 years.

After 4 years the Andean valley of Vilcabamba in Ecuador ceased, from February 1978, to be the source of highly publicised and uncritical reports about very aged humans. These, it was said, lived up to 25 years beyond the so far acceptable limit of about 115 years. The discovery by Mazess and Forman was published in March 1978 that inhabitants had pointed to baptismal entries of their fathers, and even their grandfathers, as their own, reduced the age of the valley's oldest man from 140 to 96. The lucrative income from tourism is expected to decline *pari passu*.

Charlie Smith of Bartow, Florida, USA obtained a Social Security card in 1955 when claiming to be born on 4 July 1842 in Liberia. The US Department of Health, Education and Welfare stated that they were 'unable to disclose the type of evidence used' to determine Mr Smith's age because such disclosure 'would infringe on the confidentiality of the individual's record'. He celebrated what he reckoned to be his 137th birthday on 4 July 1979. However a reference to the county records at Arcadia, Florida (Book 2, page 392) reveals a marriage contracted aged 35 on 8 Jan 1910 and hence an exaggeration of at least 33 years. He died on 7 Oct 1979. According to census research by A. Ross Eckler he was most probably two months short of his 100th birthday.

The 1900 US Federal Census for Crawfish Springs Militia District of Walker County, Georgia, records an age of 77 for a

Mark Thrash. If the Mark Thrash (reputedly born in Georgia in December 1822) who died near Chattanooga, Tennessee on 17 Dec 1943 was he, and the age attributed was accurate, then he would have survived for 121 years.

Oldest authentic centenarian *World*
The greatest *authenticated* age to which any human has ever lived is a unique 116th birthday in the case of Shigechiyo Izumi of Asan on Tokunoshima Island, 820 miles *1320 km* SW of Tokyo, Japan. He was born where he lives on 29 June 1865 and recorded as a 6-year-old in Japan's first census of 1871. He watches television and says the best way to a long life is 'not to worry' and to leave things to 'God, the Sun, and Buddha'. He was visited by the Editor on 3 Apr 1980.

Oldest authentic centenarian *Great Britain*
The United Kingdom has an estimated population of some 4000 centenarians of whom only 22 per cent were male (see also table left). Miss Alice Stevenson (1861–1973) (see Table, p. 17) is the only UK citizen with birth and death certificates more than 112 years apart. In April 1706 a John Bailes was buried at All Saints Church, Northampton, having apparently been baptised on 20 Aug 1592. If the same person, he would have been 113 years 8 months. The oldest centenarian living in Britain is Miss Janetta Jane Thomas of Cowbridge, South Glamorgan, Wales (born Llantrisant, Glamorgan 2 Dec 1869) who reached 111 years 119 days on 1 Apr 1981.

Oldest Triplets
The longest-lived triplets on record were Faith, Hope and Charity Caughlin born at Marlboro, Massachusetts, USA on 27 Mar 1868. The first to die was Mrs (Ellen) Hope Daniels aged 93 on 2 Mar 1962.

Oldest twins *World*
The chances of identical twins both reaching 100 are said to be one in 700 million. The oldest recorded twins were Eli and John Phipps (b. 14 Feb 1803, Affinghton, Virginia). Eli died at Hennessey, Oklahoma, USA on 23 Feb 1911 aged 108 years 9 days on which day John was still living in Shenandoah, Iowa. On 16 June 1980, identical twin sisters, Naemi Bomanson and Elin Hagmark of Mariehamn, Finland, celebrated their 100th birthday.

Great Britain
The oldest twins on record in Great Britain have been the Bean twins Robert, of Birkenhead, Merseyside and Mary (now Mrs Simpson) of Etton, Cambridgeshire who celebrated their 100th birthday on 19 Oct 1973. Robert died before the end of 1973.

Last 18th-century link
The last known Briton with 18th-century paternity was Miss Alice J. Grigg of Belvedere, Kent (d. 28 Apr 1970) whose father William was born on 26 Oct 1799.

Most reigns
The greatest number of reigns during which any English subject could have lived is ten. A person born on the day (11 April) that Henry VI was deposed in 1471 had to live to only the comparatively modest age of 87 years 7 months and 6 days to see the accession of Elizabeth I on 17 Nov 1558. Such a person could have been Thomas Carn of London, reputedly born in 1471 and died 28 Jan 1578 in his 107th year.

Oldest Mummy
Mummification (from the Persian word *mãm*, wax) dates from 2700 BC or the 2nd dynasty of the Egyptian pharaohs. The practice began to decline from *c* 1000 BC.

4. REPRODUCTIVITY

MOTHERHOOD
Most children *World*
The greatest officially recorded number of children produced by a mother is 69 by the first of the two wives of Feodor Vassilyev

AUTHENTICATED NATIONAL LONGEVITY RECORDS

	Years	Days		Born		Died	
Japan	116	—	Shigechiyo Izumi	29 June	1865	*fl.* 29 June	1981
United States[1]	113	273	Fannie Thomas	24 Apr	1867	22 Jan	1981
Canada[2]	113	124	Pierre Joubert	15 July	1701	16 Nov	1814
Spain	112	228	Josefa Salas Mateo	14 July	1860	27 Feb	1973
France	112	66	Augustine Teissier (Sister Julia)	2 Jan	1869	9 Mar	1981
United Kingdom[3]	112	39	Alice Stevenson	10 July	1861	18 Aug	1973
Morocco	>112		El Hadj Mohammed el Mokri (Grand Vizier)		1844	16 Sept	1957
Poland	112	+	Roswlia Mielzcarak (Mrs)		1868	7 Jan	1981
Ireland	111	327	The Hon. Katherine Plunket	22 Nov	1820	14 Oct	1932
Australia	111	235	Jane Piercy (Mrs)	2 Sept	1869	3 May	1981
South Africa[4]	111	151	Johanna Booyson	17 Jan	1857	16 June	1968
Czechoslovakia	111	+	Marie Bernatkova	22 Oct	1857	*fl.* Oct	1968
Channel Islands	110	321	Margaret Ann Neve (*née* Harvey)	18 May	1792	4 April	1903
Northern Ireland	110	234	Elizabeth Watkins (Mrs)	10 Mar	1863	31 Oct	1973
Yugoslavia	110	150+	Demitrius Philipovitch	9 Mar	1818	*fl.* Aug	1928
Netherlands[5]	110	141	Gerada Hurenkamp-Bosgoed	5 Jan	1870	25 May	1980
Greece	110	+	Lambrini Tsiatoura (Mrs)		1870	19 Feb	1981
USSR[6]	110	+	Khasako Dzugayev	7 Aug	1860	*fl.* Aug	1970
Norway	109	208	Marie Olsen (Mrs)	1 May	1850	24 Nov	1959
Tasmania (State of)	109	179	Mary Ann Crow (Mrs)	2 Feb	1836	31 July	1945
Sweden	109	94	Anna Mathilda Johansson	21 Nov	1865	23 Feb	1975
Italy	109	179	Rosalia Spoto	25 Aug	1847	20 Feb	1957
Scotland	109	14	Rachel MacArthur (Mrs)	26 Nov	1827	10 Dec.	1936
Belgium	108	327	Mathilda Vertommen-Hellemans	12 Aug	1868	4 July	1977
Germany[7]	108	128	Luise Schwarz	27 Sept	1849	2 Feb	1958
Portugal[8]	108	+	Maria Luisa Jorge	7 June	1859	*fl.* July	1967
Finland	107	221	Amalia Wallenius (Mrs)	6 Aug	1867	24 Mar.	1975
Austria	106	231	Anna Migschitz	3 Feb	1850	1 Nov	1956
Malaysia	106	+	Hassan Bin Yusoff	14 Aug	1865	*fl.* Jan	1972
Isle of Man	105	221	John Kneen	12 Nov	1852	9 June	1958

1 *Ex-slave Mrs Martha Graham died at Fayetteville, North Carolina on 25 June 1959 reputedly aged 117 or 118. Census researches by Eckler show that she was seemingly born in Dec 1844 and hence aged 114 years 6 months. Mrs Rena Glover Brailsford died in Summerton, South Carolina, USA on 6 Dec 1977 reputedly aged 118 years. Mrs Rosario Reina Vasquez who died in California on 2 Sept 1980 was reputedly born in Sonora, Mexico on 3 June 1866, which would make her 114 years 93 days.*

2 *Mrs Ellen Carroll died in North River, Newfoundland, Canada on 8 Dec 1943, reputedly aged 115 years 49 days.*

3 *London-born Miss Isabella Shepheard was allegedly 115 years old when she died at St Asaph, Clwyd, North Wales, on 20 Nov 1948, but her actual age was believed to have been 109 years 90 days. Charles Alfred Nunez Arnold died in Liverpool on 15 Nov 1941 reputedly aged 112 years 66 days based on a baptismal claim (London, 10 Sept 1829). Mrs Elizabeth Cornish (née Veale) who was buried at Stratton, Cornwall on 10 Mar 1691/2 was reputedly baptized on 16 Oct 1578, 113 years 4 months earlier.*

4 *Mrs Susan Johanna Deporter of Port Elizabeth, South Africa, was reputedly 114 years old when she died on 4 Aug 1954. Mrs Sarah Lawrence, Cape Town, South Africa was reputedly 112 on 3 June 1968.*

5 *Thomas Peters was recorded to have been born on 6 Apr 1745 in Leeuwarden and died aged 111 years 354 days on 26 Mar 1857 in Arnhem.*

6 *There are allegedly 21,700 centenarians in USSR (cf. 7000 in USA). Of these 21,000 are ascribed to the Georgian SSR i.e. one in every 232. In July 1962 it was reported that 128, mostly male, were in the one village of Medini.*

7 *Friedrich Sadowski of Heidelberg reputedly celebrated his 111th birthday on 31 Oct 1936. Franz Joseph Eder d. Spitzburg 3 May 1911, allegedly aged 116.*

8 *Senhora Jesuina da Conceicao of Lisbon was reputedly 113 years old when she died on 10 June 1965.*

Note: *fl* is the abbreviation for *floruit*, latin for he (or she) was living at the relevant date.

(b. 1707–*fl.* 1782), a peasant from Shuya, 150 miles *241 km* east of Moscow, who, in 27 confinements, gave birth to 16 pairs of twins, 7 sets of triplets and 4 sets of quadruplets. The case was reported by the Monastery of Nikolskiy on 27 Feb 1782 to Moscow. At least 67 survived infancy. Empress Ekaterina II (The Great) (1762–96) was reputed to have evinced interest. The children, of whom almost all survived to their majority, were born in the period *c.* 1725–65.

Currently the world's most prolific mother is reported to be Leontina Albina (*née* Espinosa) (b. 1925) of San Antonio, Chile, who was reported pregnant in November 1980 having already produced 44 children. Her husband Gerardo Secundo Albina (b. 1921) has no written records of the 24 children born before 1955. The first birth in this 'two bus family' was a triplet birth in 1939; many of the others were of twins and at least 6 babies died in infancy.

Great Britain

The British record is seemingly held by Elizabeth, wife of John Mott married in 1676 of Monks Kirby, Warwickshire, who produced 42 live-born children. She died in 1720, 44 years later. According to an inscription on a gravestone in Conway Church cemetery, Gwynedd, North Wales, Nicholas Hookes (d. 27 Mar 1637) was the 41st child of his mother Alice Hookes, but further details are lacking. It has not been possible to corroborate or refute this report. The highest recent reported figure is 25 children, including 3 sets of twins, born to Mrs Ada Watson (b. Cambridge, 23 June 1886) of Roehampton, who died on 5 Feb 1974.

Great Britain's champion mothers of today are believed to be Mrs Margaret McNaught (b. 1923), of Balsall Heath, Birmingham (12 boys and 10 girls, all single births) and Mrs Mabel Constable (b. 1920), of Long Itchington, Warwickshire who also has had 22 children including a set of triplets and two sets of twins.

Oldest mother *World*

Medical literature contains extreme but unauthenticated cases of septuagenarian mothers, such as Mrs Ellen Ellis, aged 72, of Four Crosses, Clwyd, who allegedly produced a still-born 13th child on 15 May 1776 in her 46th year of marriage. Many cases are cover-ups for illegitimate grandchildren. The oldest recorded mother of whom there is certain evidence is Mrs Ruth Alice Kistler (*née* Taylor), formerly Mrs Shepard, of Portland, Oregon, USA. She was born at Wakefield, Massachusetts, on 11 June 1899 and gave birth to a daughter, Suzan, at Glendale, near Los Angeles, California, on 18 Oct 1956, when her age was 57 years 129 days. The incidence of quinquagenarian births varies widely with the highest purported rate being in Albania (with nearly 5500 per million) compared with 2 per million in England & Wales.

Great Britain

The oldest British mother reliably recorded is Mrs Winifred Wilson (*née* Stanley) of Eccles, Greater Manchester. She was born in Wolverhampton on 11 Nov 1881 or 1882 and had her tenth child, a daughter Shirley, on 14 Nov 1936, when aged 54 or 55 years and 3 days. She died aged 91 or 92 in January 1974. At Southampton, on 10 Feb 1916, Mrs Elizabeth Pearce gave birth to a son when aged 54 years 40 days.

Ireland

The oldest Irish mother recorded was Mrs Mary Higgins of Cork, County Cork (b. 7 Jan 1876) who gave birth to a daughter, Patricia, on 17 Mar 1931 when aged 55 years 69 days.

Descendants

In polygamous countries, the number of a person's descendants can become incalculable. The last Sharifian Emperor of Morocco, Moulay Ismail (1672–1727), known as 'The Bloodthirsty', was reputed to have fathered a total of 548 sons and 340 daughters.

Heidi Henriksen and both her brothers Olav and Lief-Martin celebrate their birthdays together only every fourth year. They were all born on Leap Days (see p. 20).

Capt Wilson Kettle (b. 1860) of Grand Bay, Port aux Basques, Newfoundland, Canada, died on 25 Jan 1963, aged 102, leaving 11 children by two wives, 65 grandchildren, 201 great-grandchildren and 305 great-great-grandchildren, a total of 582 living descendants. Mrs Johanna Booyson (see page 17), of Belfast, Transvaal, was estimated to have 600 living descendants in South Africa in January 1968.

Mrs Sarah Crawshaw (d. 25 Dec 1844) left 397 descendants according to her gravestone in Stones Church, Ripponden, Halifax, West Yorkshire.

Multiple great-grandparents

Theoretically a great-great-great-great-grandparent is a possibility, though in practice countries in which young mothers are common, generally have a low expectation of life. At least twenty-two cases of great-great-great-grandparents have been reported in the last 28 years. Of these cases the youngest person to learn that their great-granddaughter had become a grandmother was Mrs Ann V. Weirick (1888–1978) of Paxtonville, Pennsylvania, USA, who received news of her great-great-great-grandson Matthew Stork (b. 9 Sept 1976) when aged only 88. She died on 6 Jan 1978. Britain's youngest 3 greats grandmother is Mrs Violet Lewis (b. June 1885) of Southampton.

Most living ascendants

Jesse Jones Werkmeister (b. 27 Oct 1979) of Tilden Nebraska, USA, had a full set of grandparents and great-grandparents and four great-great-grandparents, making 18 direct ascendants.

MULTIPLE BIRTHS
Lightest twins

The lightest recorded birthweight for a pair of surviving twins has been 2 lb 3 oz *992 g* in the case of Mary 16 oz *453 g* and Margaret 19 oz *538 g* born to Mrs Florence Stimson, Queens Road, Old Fletton, Peterborough, England, delivered by Dr Macaulay on 16 Aug 1931. Margaret is now Mrs M. J. Hurst.

'Siamese' twins

Conjoined twins derived the name 'Siamese' from the celebrated Chang and Eng Bunker (known in Thailand as Chan and In) born at Maklong, on 11 May 1811. They were joined by a cartila-

ginous band at the chest and married in April 1843 the Misses Sarah and Adelaide Yates and fathered ten and twelve children respectively. They died within three hours of each other on 1 Jan 1874, aged 62. The only known British example to reach maturity were Daisy and Violet Hilton born in Brighton Sussex on 5 Feb 1908, who were joined at the hip. They died in Charlotte, North Carolina, USA, on 5 Jan 1969, aged 60. The earliest successful separation of Siamese twins was performed on Prisma and Napit Atkinson (b. May 1953 in Thailand) by D Dragstedt at the University of Chicago on 29 Mar 1955.

The rarest form of conjoined twins is Dicephales tetrabrachius dipus (two heads, four arms and two legs) of which only three examples are known today. They are the pair Masha and Dasha born in the USSR on 4 Jan 1950, an unnamed pair separated in a 10-hour operation in Washington, DC, USA on 23 June 1977 and Fonda Michelle and Shannon Elaine Beaver of Forest City North Carolina, USA born on 9 Feb 1980. The only known British example were the 'Scottish brothers', who were born near Glasgow in 1490. They were brought to the Court of King James IV of Scotland the following year, and lived under the king's patronage for the rest of his reign. They died in 1518 aged 28 years, one brother succumbing five days before the other, who 'moaned piteously as he crept about the castle gardens, carrying with him the dead body of the brother from whom only death could separate him and to whom death would again join him.'

Fastest triplet birth

The fastest recorded natural birth of triplets has been 2 minutes in the case of Mrs James E. Duck of Memphis, Tennessee (Bradley, Christopher and Carmon) on 21 Mar 1977.

Quindecaplets

It was announced by Dr Gennaro Montanino of Rome that he had removed the foetuses of 10 girls and 5 boys from the womb of a 35-year-old housewife on 22 July 1971. A fertility drug was responsible for this unique and unsurpassed instance of quindecaplets.

Longest pregnancy

Claims up to 413 days have been widely reported but accurate data are bedevilled by the increasing use of oral contraceptives

Ruth Alice Kistler who was 57 years 129 days when she gave birth to her daughter Suzan at Glendale, near Los Angeles on 18 Oct 1956 (see p. 17).

pills which is a cause of amenorrhoea. Some women on becoming pregnant erroneously add some preceding periodless months to their pregnancy. In the pre-pill era English law has accepted pregnancies with extremes of 174 days (*Clark* v. *Clark*, 1939) and 349 days (*Hadlum* v. *Hadlum*, 1949).

Most proximate births and shortest pregnancies
Mrs Gloria Kuehn of Lemay, Missouri, USA gave birth to a daughter, Amy Elizabeth, on 9 June 1978 and a son, Gregory Charles, on 19 Jan 1979, 224 days later.

BABIES
Heaviest *World*
The heaviest normal new-born child reported in modern times was a boy weighing 11 kg *24 lb 4 oz*, born on 3 June 1961 to Mrs Saadat Cor of Cegham, Southern Turkey. It was revealed in January 1978 however that, although relayed by a major news agency, no reliance can be placed on this report. Mrs. Anna Bates *née* Swan, the 7 ft 5½ in *227 cm* Canadian giantess (see page 11) gave birth to a boy weighing 23 lb 12 oz *10,77 kg* (length 30 in *76 cm*) at her home in Seville, Ohio, USA on 19 Jan 1879, but the baby died less than 24 hours later. Her first child, an 18 lb *8,16 kg* girl (length 24 in *61 cm*) was still-born when she was delivered in 1872. In May 1939 a deformed baby weighing 29 lb 4 oz *13,26 kg* was born in a hospital at Effingham, Illinois, USA, but died two hours later from respiratory problems.

Heaviest *United Kingdom*
The greatest recorded live birth weight in the United Kingdom is 21 lb *9,53 kg* for a child born on Christmas Day, 1852. It was reported in a letter to the *British Medical Journal* (1 Feb 1879) from a doctor in Torpoint, Cornwall. The only other reported birth weight in excess of 20 lb *9,07 kg* is 20 lb 2 oz *9,13 kg* for a boy born to a 33-year-old schoolmistress in Crewe, Cheshire, on 12 Nov 1884 with a 14½ in *36,8 cm* chest. A baby of 33 lb *14,97 kg* was reportedly born to a Mrs Lambert of Wandsworth Road, London *c.* 1930 but its measurements indicate a weight of about 17 lb *7,7 kg*.

Most bouncing baby
The most bouncing baby on record was probably James Weir (1819–1821) who, according to his headstone in Cambushnethan, Old Parish Cemetery, Wishaw, Strathclyde, Scotland was

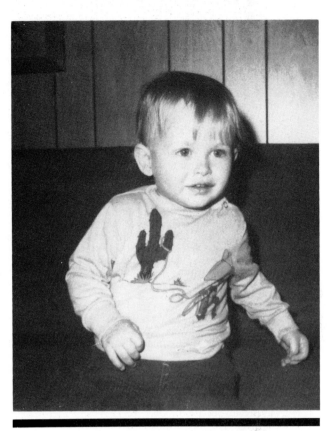

Jesse Jones Werkmeister, who had 18 direct ascendants living when he was born on 27 Oct 1979. These included 4 great-great-grandparents (see p. 18).

8 st or 112 lb *50,8 kg* at 13 months, 3 ft 4 in *1,01 m* in height and 39 in *99 cm* in girth.

Therese Parentean, who died in Rouyn, Quebec, Canada on 11 May 1936 aged 9 years, weighed 24 st 4 lb *154 kg*. (*cf.* 27 st

MULTIPLE BIRTHS

	World	United Kingdom
Highest number reported at single birth	10 (decaplets) (2 male, 8 female) Bacacay, Brazil, 22 Apr 1946 (also report from Spain, 1924 and China, 12 May 1936)	
Highest number medically recorded	9 (nonuplets) (5 male, 4 female) to Mrs Geraldine Broderick at Royal Hospital, Sydney, Australia on 13 June 1971. 2 males stillborn. Richard (12 oz *340 g*) survived 6 days 9 (all also died) to patient at University of Pennsylvania, Philadelphia 29 May 1972 9 (all died) reported from Bagerhat, Bangladesh, *c.* 11 May 1977 to 30-year-old mother	6 (sextuplets) (2 male, 4 female) to Mrs Sheila Ann Thorns (*née* Manning) at New Birmingham Maternity Hospital on 2 Oct 1968. Three survive 6 (1 male, 5 female) to Mrs Rosemary Letts (*née* Egerton) at University College Hospital, Greater London, on 15 Dec 1969. One boy and 4 girls survive
Highest number surviving[1]	6 out of 6 (3 males, 3 females) to Mrs Susan Jane Rosenkowitz (*née* Scoones) (b. Colombo, Sri Lanka, 28 Oct 1947) at Mowbray, Cape Town, South Africa on 11 Jan 1974. In order of birth they were: David, Nicolette, Jason, Emma, Grant and Elizabeth. They totalled 24 lb 1 oz *10,915 kg* 6 out of 6 (4 males, 2 females) to Mrs Rosanna Giannini (b. 1952) at Careggi Hospital, Florence, Italy on 11 Jan. 1980. They are Francesco, Fabrizio, Giorgio, Roberto, Letizia and Linda	5 out of 6 (as above) and also 5 out of 5 (5 females) to Mrs Irene Mary Hanson (*née* Brown) at Queen Charlotte's Hospital London on 13 Nov 1969 and 5 out of 5 (1 male, 4 females) to Mrs James Bostock of Armadale, Lothian, Scotland (no use of fertility drugs) on 14 Apr 1972
	Heaviest	**Most Sets**
Quintuplets *World*	25 lb *11,35 kg* Mrs Lui Saulien, Chekiang, China, 7 June 1953 25 lb *11,35 kg* Mrs Kamalammal, Pondicherry, India, 30 Dec 1956	No recorded case of more than a single set
Quadruplets *World*	10,35 kg *22 lb 13 oz* Mrs Ayako Takeda, Tsuchihashi Maternity Hospital, Kagoshima, Japan, 4 Oct 1978 (4 girls)	4 Mde Feodor Vassilyev, Shuya, Russia (d. *ante* 1770)
Triplets *World* *UK*	26 lb 6 oz *11,96 kg* (unconfirmed) Iranian case (2 male, 1 female) 18 Mar 1968 24 lb 0 oz *10,886 kg* Mrs Mary McDermott, of Bearpark, Co Durham, 18 Nov 1914	15 Maddalena Granata (1839–*fl.* 1886)
Twins *World*	27 lb 12 oz *12,590 kg* (surviving Mrs J. P. Haskin, Fort Smith, Arkansas, USA, 20 Feb 1924) The 35 lb 8 oz *16,1 kg* reported in *The Lancet* from Derbyshire, England, on 6 Dec 1884 for the Warren Case (2 males liveborn) is believed to be a misprint for 25 lb 8 oz *11,6 kg*	16 Mde Vassilyev (see above). *Note also* Mrs Barbara Zulu of Barbeton, South Africa bore 3 sets of girls and 3 mixed sets in 7 years (1967–73) 15 Mrs Mary Jonas of Chester (d. 4 Dec 1899)—all sets were boy and girl

[1] The South African press were unable to verify the birth of 5 babies to Mrs Charmaine Craig (*née* Peterson) in Cape Town on 16 Oct 1980 and a sixth on 8 Nov. The reported names were Frank, Salome, John, Andrew, William and belatedly Deborah.

171 kg for Robert Earl Hughes at the age of ten [see weight table p. 13 and Chest measurements right]).

Lightest
The lowest birth weight for a surviving infant, of which there is definite evidence, is 10 oz *283 g* in the case of Marion Chapman, born on 5 June 1938 in South Shields, Tyne and Wear. She was 12¼ in *31 cm* long. By her first birthday her weight had increased to 13 lb 14 oz *6,29kg*. She was born unattended and was nursed by Dr D. A. Shearer, who fed her hourly through a fountain-pen filler. Her weight on her 21st birthday was 7 st 8 lb *48,08kg*. The smallest viable baby reported from the United States has been Jacqueline Benson born at Palatine, Illinois, on 20 Feb 1936, weighing 12 oz *340 g*.

A weight of 8 oz *227 g* was reported on 20 Mar 1938 for a baby born prematurely to Mrs John Womack, after she had been knocked down by a lorry in East St Louis, Illinois, USA. The baby was taken alive to St Mary's Hospital, but further information is lacking. On 23 Feb 1952 it was reported that a 6 oz *170 g* baby only 6½ in *17 cm* long lived for 12 hours in a hospital in Indianapolis, Indiana, USA. A twin was still-born.

Coincident birthdates
The only verified example of a family producing five single children with coincident birthdays is that of Catherine (1952); Carol (1953); Charles (1956); Claudia (1961) and Cecilia (1966), born to Ralph and Carolyn Cummins of Clintwood, Virginia, USA, all on 20 February. The random odds against five single siblings sharing a birthdate are one in 17,797,577,730—almost 4 times the world's population.

The three children of the Henriksen family of Andenes, Norway, Heidi (b. 1960); Olav (b. 1964) and Lief-Martin (b. 1968) all celebrate their birthday infrequently, because these all fall on Leap Day – February 29.

Most southerly birth
Emilio Marcos Palma born 7 Jan 1978 at the Sargento Cabral Base, Antarctica is the only infant who can claim to be the first born on any continent.

Test tube baby *Earliest*
Louise Brown (5 lb 12 oz *2,6 kg*) was delivered by Caesarian section from Lesley Brown, 31, in Oldham General Hospital, Lancashire, at 11.47 p.m. on 25 July 1978. She was externally conceived on 10 Nov 1977.

---

5. PHYSIOLOGY AND ANATOMY

Hydrogen (63 per cent) and oxygen (25.5 per cent) constitute the commonest of the 24 elements in the human body. In 1972 four more trace elements were added—fluorine, silicon, tin and vanadium. The 'essentiality' of nickel has not yet been finally pronounced upon.

BONES
Longest
Excluding a variable number of sesamoids, there are 206 bones in the human body. The thigh bone or *femur* is the longest. It constitutes usually 27½ per cent of a person's stature, and may be expected to be 19¾ in *50 cm* long in a 6 ft *183 cm*-tall man. The longest recorded bone was the femur of the German giant Constantine, who died in Mons, Belgium, on 30 Mar 1902, aged 30 (see p. 10). It measured 76 cm *29,9 in*. The femur of Robert Wadlow, the tallest man ever recorded, measured an estimated 29½ in *75 cm*.

Smallest
The *stapes* or stirrup bone, one of the three auditory ossicles in the middle ear, is the smallest human bone, measuring from 2,6 to 3,4 mm *0.10 to 0.17 in* in length and weighing from 2,0 to 4,3 mg *0.03 to 0.065 g*.

MUSCLES
Largest
Muscles normally account for 40 per cent of the body weight and the bulkiest of the 639 muscles in the human body is the *gluteus maximus* or buttock muscle, which extends the thigh.

Smallest
The smallest muscle is the *stapedius*, which controls the *stapes* (see above), an auditory ossicle in the middle ear, and which is less than 1/20th of an inch *0,127 cm* long.

Smallest waists
Queen Catherine de Medici (1519–89) decreed a waist measurement of 13 in *33 cm* for ladies of the French Court. This was at a time when females were more diminutive. The smallest recorded waist among women of normal stature in the 20th century is a reputed 13 in *33 cm* in the case of the French actress Mlle Polaire (1881–1939) and Mrs Ethel Granger (b. 12 Apr 1905) of Peterborough who reduced from a natural 22 in *56 cm* over the period 1929–39.

Largest chest measurements
The largest chest measurements are among endomorphs (those with a tendency towards globularity). In the extreme case of Hughes (see pp. 13 & 19–20) this was reportedly 124 in *315 cm*, but in the light of his known height and weight a figure of 104 in *264 cm* would be more supportable. George Macaree (formerly Britain's heaviest man) has a chest measurement of 75 in *190 cm* at a bodyweight of 30 st 10 lb *195 kg*. Among muscular subjects (mesomorphs) of normal height *expanded* chest measurements above 56 in *142 cm* are extremely rare. Louis Cyr (1865–1912), the famous French-Canadian strongman, had a chest measurement of 59 in *150 cm* at his best weight of 300 lb *136 kg*. Arnold Schwarzennegger (b. 1948) of Graz, Austria, the 6 ft 1 in *185 cm* former Mr Universe and 'the most perfectly developed man in the history of the world', had a chest measurement of 57 in *145 cm* at a bodyweight of 235 lb *107 kg* at his peak. He also boasted a 22 in *56 cm* upper arm. Lou Ferrigno, the 6 ft 5 in *195 cm* American actor who plays the *Incredible Hulk* in the television series of that name, has a 59 in *150 cm* chest and a 22½ in *57 cm* upper arm at a body weight of 252 lb *114 kg*.

Longest necks
The maximum measured extension of the neck by the successive fitting of copper coils, as practised by the Padaung or Karen people of Burma, is 15¾ in *40 cm*.

BRAIN AND BRAIN POWER
Largest
The brain has 10×10^{10} nerve cells or neurons interconnected by dendrites or filaments and 10×10^{11} glia. Some of the brain's chemical reactions require only one millionth of a second. A comparison between computer performance and brain power, published by *Business Week* attributes a storage capacity of 1.25 $\times 10^{14}$ characters to the human brain—equivalent to that of 50 million floppy discs. After the age of 18 the brain loses some 10^3 cells per day. The brain of an average adult male (*i.e.* 30–59 years) weighs 1410 g *3 lb 1.73 oz*, falling to 1030 g *2 lb 4.31 oz*. The heaviest brain ever recorded has been that of a 50-year-old white male weighing 4 lb 8.29 oz *2049 g* reported by Dr Thomas F. Hegert, Chief Medical Examiner for District 9, State of Florida on 23 Oct 1975. The brain of Oliver Cromwell (1599–1658) reputedly weighed 2222 g *4 lb 14.8 oz*, but the size of his head in portraits does not support this extreme figure. The brain of Lord Byron, who died in Greece in 1824 aged 36, reportedly weighed 6 Neapolitan pounds (1924 g or *4 lb 3.86 oz,*) but this also included a certain amount of blood. In January 1891 the *Edinburgh Medical Journal* reported the case of a 75-year-old man in the Royal Edinburgh Asylum whose brain weighed 1829 g *4 lb 0.5 oz*.

Smallest
The non-atrophied brain of the writer Anatole France (1844–1924) weighed only 1017 g *35.8 oz* without the membrane. Brains in extreme cases of microcephaly may weigh as little as 300 g *10.6 oz* (*cf.* 20 oz *567 g* for the adult male gorilla, and 16–20 oz *454–567 g* for other anthropoid apes).

Human brains are getting heavier. Examination of post-mortem records shows that the average male brain weight has increased from 1372 g, *48.4 oz* in 1860 to 1424 g *50.2 oz* today. Women's brains have also put on weight, from 1242 g *43.8 oz* to 1265 g *44.6 oz* and in recent years have been growing almost as fast as men's! (*Source—Curious Facts by John May*)

ghest IQ
On the Stanford Binet or Terman index for Intelligence Quotients, (ceiling 200) 150 represents 'genius' level. Only 100 persons in a million have IQs above 160. Comparison close to the ceilings are impracticable as are comparabilities between one scale and another. Those closest to the ceiling are Dr Bruce R. Whiting, PhD (Boston) (b. 1947) of the International Society for Philosophical Enquiry; Kevin Langdon of Berkeley, California; Chris Harding (606 Society) of Rockhampton, Queensland, Australia; Robert Bryzman of Baltimore, Maryland and Ms Leta Speyer of New York, reported to have returned 196 on the Stanford Binet scale.

The highest IQ published for a national population is 106.6 for the Japanese (*cf*. 100 for the UK).

uman computer
The fastest extraction of a 13th root from a 100 digit number is in 1 min 28.8 sec by Willem Klein (b. 1914, Netherlands) on 7 Apr 1981 at the National Laboratory for High Energy Physics (KEK), Tsukuba, Japan. Mrs Shakuntala Devi of India demonstrated the multiplication of two 13-digit numbers 7,686,369,774,870 × 2,465,099,745,779 picked at random by the Computer Department of Imperial College, London on 18 June 1980, in 28 sec. Her correct answer was 18,947,668,177,995,426,462,773,730.

uman memory
Mehmed Ali Halici of Ankara, Turkey on 14 Oct 1967 recited 6666 verses of the Koran from memory in 6 hours. The recitation was followed by six Koran scholars. Rare instances of eidetic memory—the ability to re-project and hence 'visually' recall material—are known to science.

he greatest number of places of π
The greatest number of places to which Pi (ratio of circle's circumference to diameter) has been memorised and recited is 20,013 by Creighton Carvello on 27 June 1980 in 9 hr 10 min at the Saltscar Comprehensive School, Redcar, Cleveland, England. Note: It is only the *approximation* of π at $^{22}/_{7}$ which recurs after its sixth decimal place and can, of course, be recited *ad nauseam*. The true value is a string of random numbers fiendishly difficult to memorise. The average ability for memorizing random numbers is 7.

HANDS AND HAIR
ouch sensitivity
The extreme sensitivity of the fingers is such that a vibration with a movement of 0.02 of a micron can be detected.

ost fingers
In 1938 the extreme case of a baby girl with 14 fingers and 12 toes was reported from St George's Hospital, Hyde Park, Greater London.

ongest finger nails
The longest finger nail ever reported is one of 26½ in *67,3 cm* grown by Romesh Sharma of Delhi after 13 years, measured on 7 Apr 1980. On 22 Mar 1981 Shridhar Chillal, (b. 1937) of Poona, India achieved a measured aggregate of 108½ in *275,6 cm* for the 5 nails on his left hand (thumb 27½ in *69,8 cm*) uncut since 1952.

ongest hair
Swami Pandarasannadhi, the head of the Tirudaduturai monastery, Tanjore district, Madras, India was reported in 1949 to have hair 26 ft *7,93 m* in length. From photographs it appears that he was affected with the disease Plica caudiformis. The length of hair of Miss Skuldfrid Sjorgren (b. Stockholm) was reported from Toronto, Canada in 1927 to have attained twice her height at 10 ft 6 in *3,20 m*.

ongest beard
The longest beard preserved was that of Hans N. Langseth (b. 1846 near Eidsroll, Norway) which measured 17½ ft *5,33 m* at the time of his burial at Kensett, Iowa in 1927 after 15 years residence in the United States. The beard was presented to the Smithsonian Institution, Washington, DC in 1967. Richard Latter (b. Pembury, Kent, 1831) of Tunbridge Wells, Kent, who died in 1914 aged 83, reputedly had a beard 16 ft *4,87 m* long but contemporary independent corroboration is lacking

and photographic evidence indicates this figure was exaggerated. The beard of the bearded lady Janice Deveree (b. Bracken Co., Kentucky, USA, 1842) was measured at 14 in *36 cm* in 1884.

Longest moustache
The longest moustache on record was that of Masuriya Din (b. 1908), a Brahmin of the Partabgarh district in Uttar Pradesh, India. It grew to an extended span of 8 ft 6 in *2,59 m* between 1949 and 1962. Karna Ram Bheel (b. 1928) was granted permission by a New Delhi prison governor in February 1979 to keep his 7 ft 10 in *238 cm* moustache grown since 1949 during his life sentence. The longest moustache in Great Britain is that of Mr John Roy (b. 14 Jan 1910), of Weeley, near Clacton, Essex. It attained a peak span of 68½ in *174 cm* between 1939 and when measured on the BBC-TV 'Nationwide' programme on 2 Apr 1976.

DENTITION
Earliest
The first deciduous or milk teeth normally appear in infants at 5–8 months, these being the mandibular and maxillary first incisors. There are many records of children born with teeth, the most distinguished example being Prince Louis Dieudonné, later Louis XIV of France, who was born with two teeth on 5 Sept 1638. Molars usually appear at 24 months, but in Pindborg's case published in Denmark in 1970 a 6-week premature baby was documented with 8 natal teeth of which 4 were in the molar region.

Most
Cases of the growth in late life of a third set of teeth have been recorded several times. A reference to an extreme case in France of a fourth dentition, known as Lison's case, was published in 1896. A triple row of teeth was noted in 1680 by Albertus Hellwigius.

Most dedicated dentist
Brother Giovanni Battista Orsenigo of the Ospedale Fatebenefratelli, Rome, Italy, a religious dentist, conserved all the teeth he extracted in three enormous cases during the time he exercised his profession from 1868 to 1904. In 1903 the number was counted and found to be 2,000,744 teeth.

OPTICS
Smallest visible object
The resolving power of the human eye is 0.0003 of a radian or an arc of one minute (1/60th of a degree), which corresponds to 100 microns at 10 in. A micron is a thousandth of a millimetre, hence 100 microns is 0.003937, or less than four thousandths, of an inch. The human eye can, however, detect a bright light source shining through an aperture only 3 to 4 microns across. In October 1972 the University of Stuttgart, W. Germany reported that their student Frl Veronica Seider (b. 1953) possessed a visual acuity 20 times better than average. She could identify people at a distance of more than a mile *1,6 km*. The Russians are reputedly working on a new type of lens implant which will give the wearer super-human sight.

Colour sensitivity
The unaided human eye, under the best possible viewing conditions, comparing large areas of colour, in good illumination, using both eyes, can distinguish 10,000,000 different colour surfaces. The most accurate photo-electric spectrophotometers possess a precision probably only 40 per cent as good as this. About 7.5 per cent of men and 0.1 per cent of women are colour blind. The most extreme form, monochromatic vision, is very rare. The highest recorded rate of red-green colour blindness is in Czechoslovakia and the lowest rate among Fijians and Brazilian Indians.

VOICE
Highest and lowest
The highest and lowest recorded notes attained by the human voice before this century were a staccato E in *alt altissimo* (e^{iv}) by the American Ellen Beach Yaw (1869–1947) in Carnegie Hall, New York City on 19 Jan 1896, and an A$_1$ (55 cycles per sec) by Kasper Foster (1617–73). Madeleine Marie Robin (1918–60) the French operatic coloratura could produce and sustain the B above high C in the Lucia mad scene in *Lucia di Lammermoor*.

Since 1950 singers have achieved high and low notes far beyond the hitherto accepted extremes. However, notes at the bass and treble extremities of the register tend to lack harmonics and are of little musical value. Frl Marita Gunther, trained by Alfred Wolfsohn, has covered the range of the piano from the lowest note, A_{11}, to c^v. Of this range of 7¼ octaves, six octaves are considered to be of musical value. Mr Roy Hart, also trained by Wolfsohn, has reached notes below the range of the piano. Barry Girard of Canton, Ohio in May 1975 reached the e (4340 Hz) above the piano's top note. The highest note put into song is G^{iv} first occurring in *Popoli di Tessaglia* by Mozart. The lowest note put into song is a D_{11} by the singer Tom King, of King's Langley, Hertfordshire. Stefan Zucker sang A in *alt altissimo* for 3.8 sec in the tenor role of Salvini in the world première of Bellini's *Adelson e Salvini* in New York City, USA on 12 Sept 1972.

Greatest range
The normal intelligible outdoor range of the male human voice in still air is 200 yd *180 m*. The *silbo*, the whistled language of the Spanish-speaking Canary Island of La Gomera, is intelligible across the valleys, under ideal conditions, at five miles *8 km*. There is a recorded case, under freak acoustic conditions, of the human voice being detectable at a distance of 10½ miles *17 km* across still water at night. It was said that Mills Darden (see table page 13) could be heard 6 miles *9 km* away when he shouted at the top of his voice.

The world record for shouting is 118 decibels by Joanne Brown, 15, of Dronfield Woodhouse, Sheffield, N. Yorkshire on 24 June 1981 at Leeds Castle, Kent. Stan Lemkuil achieved 117 decibels on 25 Oct 1979 at the intersection of 2nd and K St., Old Sacramento, California, USA. Peter Van de Vooren twice achieved 112 decibels while whistling, on Radio 2SM Sydney, Australia on 9 Feb 1980.

Lowest detectable sound
The intensity of noise or sound is measured in terms of pressure. The pressure of the quietest sound that can be detected by a person of normal hearing at the most sensitive frequency of *c.* 2750 Hz is 2×10^{-5} pascal. One tenth of the logarithm to this standard provides a unit termed a decibel (dBA). Prolonged noise above 150 decibels will cause immediate permanent deafness while 200 decibels could be fatal. A noise of 30 decibels is negligible.

Highest detectable pitch
The upper limit of hearing by the human ear has long been regarded as 20,000 Hz (cycles per sec), although children with asthma can often detect a sound of 30,000 cycles per sec. It was announced in February 1964 that experiments in the USSR had conclusively proved that oscillations as high as 200,000 cycles per sec can be heard if the oscillator is pressed against the skull.

Fastest talker
Few people are able to speak *articulately* at a sustained speed above 300 words per min. The fastest broadcaster has been regarded as Gerry Wilmot (b. Victoria BC, Canada 6 Oct 1914) the ice hockey commentator in the post-World War II period. Raymond Glendenning (1907–74), the BBC horseracing commentator, once spoke 176 words in 30 sec while commentating on a greyhound race. In public life the highest speed recorded is a 327 words per min burst in a speech made in December 1961 by John Fitzgerald Kennedy (1917–63), then President of the United States. Tapes of attempts to recite Hamlet's 262-word Soliloquy in under 24 sec (655 w.p.m.) have proved unintelligible. Patricia Keeling-Andrich delivered 403 words from W. S. Gilbert's 'The Nightmare' in a test in 60 sec at Chabot College, Hayward, California on 16 Mar 1978.

BLOOD
Blood groups
The preponderance of one blood group varies greatly from one locality to another. On a world basis Group O is the most common (46 per cent), but in some areas, for example Norway, Group A predominates.

The full description of the commonest sub-group in Britain is O MsNs, P+, Rr, Lu(a−), K−, Le(a−b+), Fy(a+b+), Jk(a+b+), which occurs in one in every 270 people.

The rarest blood group on the ABO system, one of 14 systems, AB, which occurs in less than 3 per cent of persons in the Briti Isles. The rarest type in the world is a type of Bombay blo (sub-type A-h) found so far only in a Czechoslovak nurse in 19 and in a brother (Rh positive) and sister (Rh negative) nam Jalbert in Massachusetts, USA reported in February 1968. T American male has started a blood bank for himself.

Richest natural resources
Joe Thomas of Detroit, Michigan, USA was reported in Augu 1970 to have the highest known count of Anti-Lewis B, the ra blood antibody. A US biological supply firm pays him $1500 p quart *1,13 l*. The Internal Revenue regard this income as a ta able liquid asset.

Champion blood donor
Ed 'Spike' Howard (1877–1946), the professional strongman Philadelphia, USA donated a lifetime total of 1056 US pints *499,66 l*. The present-day normal limit on donations is 5 pin per annum. A 50-year-old haemophiliac Warren C. Jyri required 2400 donor units *1080 l* of blood when undergoi open heart surgery at the Michael Reese Hospital, Chicag USA in December 1970.

Largest vein
The largest vein in the human body is the *inferior vena cav* which returns most of the blood from the body below the level the heart.

Most alcoholic subject
It is recorded that a hard drinker named Vanhorn (1750–1811 born in London, averaged more than four bottles of ruby po per day for the 23 years from 1788 to his death aged 61 in 181 The total of his 'empties' was put at 35,688.

The youngest recorded death from alcoholic poisoning was th of a 4-year-old boy, Joseph Sweet, in Wolverhampton, Englan in 1827 reported in the Stafford Assizes case *R. v. Martin*.

The United Kingdom's legal limit for motorists is 80 mg of alc hol per 100 ml of blood. The hitherto recorded highest figure medical literature of 656 mg per 100 ml was submerged whe the late Samuel Riley (b. 1922) of Sefton Park, Merseyside, wa found by a disbelieving pathologist to have a level of 1220 mg o 28 Mar 1979. He had expired in his flat and had been an inspe tor at the plant of a well-known motor manufacturer.

BODY TEMPERATURE
Highest body temperature
In Kalow's case (*Lancet*, 31 Oct 1970) a woman following hal thane anaesthesia ran a temperature of 112°F *44,4°C*. She re covered after a procainamide infusion. Marathon runners in he weather attain 105.8°F *41°C*.

A temperature of 115°F *46,1°C* was recorded in the case Christopher Legge in the Hospital for Tropical Disease: London, on 9 Feb 1934. A subsequent examination of the the mometer disclosed a flaw in the bulb, but it is regarded as certa that the patient sustained a temperature of more than 110° *43,3°C*.

Lowest body temperature
There are two recorded cases of patients surviving body tem peratures as low as 60.8°F *16,0°C*. Dorothy Mae Stevens (1929–74) was found in an alley in Chicago, Illinois on 1 Fe 1951 and Vickie Mary Davis aged 2 years 1 month in an un heated house in Marshalltown, Iowa on 21 Jan 1956, both wit this temperature.

ILLNESS AND DISEASE
Commonest disease
The commonest non-contagious disease in the world is dent caries or tooth decay. In Great Britain 13 per cent of people hav lost all their teeth before they are 21 years old. During their life time few completely escape its effects. Infestation with pinwor (*Enterobius vermicularis*) approaches 100 per cent in some area of the world.

Physiology and Anatomy

The commonest contagious disease in the world is coryza (acute nasopharyngitis) or the common cold. Only 1,725,000 working days were reportedly lost as a result of this illness in Great Britain between mid 1979 and mid 1980, since absences of less than three days are not reported. The greatest reported loss of working time in Britain is from bronchitis, which accounted for 25,868,000, or 7.2 per cent, of the total of 358,638,000 working days lost in the same period.

The most resistant recorded case to being infected at the Medical Research Council Common Cold Unit, Salisbury, Wiltshire is J. Brophy, who has had one mild reaction in 24 visits.

Rarest disease
Medical literature periodically records hitherto undescribed diseases. A disease as yet undescribed but predicted by a Norwegian doctor is podocytoma of the kidney—a tumour of the epithelial cells lining the glomerulus of the kidney. The last case of endemic Smallpox was recorded in Ali Maow Maalin in Merka, Somalia on 26 Oct 1977.

Kuru, or laughing sickness, afflicts only the Fore tribe of eastern New Guinea and is 100 per cent fatal. This was formally attributed to the cannibalistic practice of eating human brains. The rarest fatal diseases in England and Wales have been those from which the last deaths (all males) were all recorded more than 40 years ago—yellow fever (1930), cholera nostras (1928) and bubonic plague (1926).

Most and least infectious disease
The most infectious of all diseases is the pneumonic form of plague, which also has a mortality rate of about 99.99 per cent. Leprosy transmitted by *Mycobacterium leprae* is the least infectious and most bacilliferous of communicable diseases.

Highest mortality
Rabies in humans has been regarded as uniformly fatal when associated with the hydrophobia symptom. A 25-year-old woman Candida de Sousa Barbosa of Rio de Janeiro, Brazil, was believed to be the first ever survivor of the disease in November 1968, though some sources give priority to Matthew Winkler, 6, who, on 10 Oct 1970, was bitten by a rabid bat.

Leading cause of death
The leading cause of death in industrialised countries is arteriosclerosis (thickening of the arterial wall) which underlies much coronary and cerebrovascular disease.

Most notorious carrier
The most publicized of all typhoid carriers has been Mary Mallon, known as Typhoid Mary, of New York City, NY, USA. She was the source of nine outbreaks, notably that of 1903. She was placed under permanent detention from 1915 until her death in 1938. A still anonymous dairy farmer from Camden, N.Y. was the source of 409 cases (40 fatal) in Aug. 1909.

Parkinson's disease
The most protracted case of Parkinson's disease (named after Dr James Parkinson's essay of 1817) for which the earliest treatments were not published until 1946, is 56 years in the case of Frederick G. Humphries of Croydon, Greater London whose symptoms became detectable in 1923.

Dr. Bruce Whiting who has the distinction of having the highest IQ in the 200 member International Society for Philosophical Enquiry with an IQ of 190 (see p. 21).

MEDICAL EXTREMES
Heart stoppage
The longest recorded heart stoppage is a minimum of 3 hr 32 min in the case of Miss Jean Jawbone, 20, who was revived by a team of 26, using peritoneal dialysis, in Winnipeg Medical Centre, Manitoba, Canada on 19 Jan 1977. In February 1974 Vegard Slettmoen, 5, fell through the ice on the river Nitselv, Norway. He was found 40 min later 2,5 m *8 ft* down but was revived in Akerhaus Central Hospital without brain-damage.

The longest recorded interval in a *post mortem* birth was one of at least 80 min in Magnolia, Mississippi, USA. Dr. Robert E. Drake found Fanella Anderson, aged 25, dead in her home at 11.40 p.m. on 15 Oct 1966 and he delivered her of a son weighing 6 lb 4 oz *2,83 kg* by Caesarean operation in the Beacham Memorial Hospital on 16 Oct 1966.

Pulse rates
A normal adult pulse rate is 70–72 beats per min at rest for males and 78–82 for females. Rates increase to 200 or more during violent exercise and drop to as low as 12 in the extreme case of Dorothy Mae Stevens (see Lowest body temperature, p. 22), and Jean Hilliard (b. 1962) of Fosston, Minnesota, USA on 20 Dec 1980.

Longest coma
The longest recorded coma was that undergone by Elaine Esposito (b. 3 Dec 1934) of Tarpon Springs, Florida, USA. She never stirred since an appendicectomy on 6 Aug 1941, when she was 6, in Chicago, Illinois, USA. and she died on 25 Nov 1978 aged 43 years 357 days, having been in a coma for 37 years 111 days. Paul Balay (b. 1936) of Lons le Saunier, Dijon, France has been in a coma since 11 Dec 1955 following a car accident.

Longest dream
Dreaming sleep is characterised by rapid eye movements known as REM. The longest recorded period of REM is one of 2 hr 23 min on 15 Feb 1967 at the department of Psychology, University of Illinois, Chicago on Bill Carskadon, who had had his previous sleep interrupted.

Largest stone
The largest stone or vesical calculus reported in medical literature was one of 13 lb 14 oz *6294 g* removed from an 80-year-old

The heaviest quadruplets in the world, who weighed a total of 10,35 kg *22 lb 13 oz* when born to Mrs Ayako Takeda in Kagoshima, Japan on 4 Oct 1978 (see p. 19).

woman by Dr Humphrey Arthure at Charing Cross Hospital, London, on 29 Dec 1952.

Longest in iron lung

The longest recorded survival by an 'iron lung' patient is that of Mrs Laurel Nisbet (b. 17 Nov 1912) of La Crescenta, California, USA. She has been in an iron lung continuously since 25 June 1948. The longest survival in an 'iron lung' in Britain has been 30 years by Denis Atkin in Lodge Moor Hospital, Sheffield, South Yorkshire. Miss Kathy Crowhurst of West Hendon Hospital, London has been dependent upon a respirator since July 1957. Paul Bates of Horsham, West Sussex was harnessed to a mechanical positive pressure respirator on 13 Aug 1954. He has received an estimated 198,494,498 respirations into his lungs *via* his trachea up to 1 May 1981.

Fastest nerve impulses

The results of experiments published in 1966 have shown that the fastest messages transmitted by the human nervous system travel as fast as 180 mph *288 km/h*. With advancing age impulses are carried 15 per cent more slowly.

Hiccoughing

The longest recorded attack of hiccoughs or singultus is that afflicting Charles Osborne (b. 1894) of Anthon, Iowa, USA, from 1922 to date. He contracted it when slaughtering a hog. His first wife left him and he is unable to keep in his false teeth. The infirmary at Newcastle upon Tyne is recorded to have admitted a young man from Long Witton, Northumberland on 25 Mar 1769 suffering from hiccoughs which were reportedly audible at a range of more than a mile.

Sneezing

The most chronic sneezing fit ever recorded is that of Patricia Reay, aged 12, of Sutton Coldfield, West Midlands. She started sneezing on 15 Oct 1979 after catching a cold. The sneezing stopped after treatment, at Le Chalet St. George, a clinic at Font Romeu in the French Pyrénées, on 25 Apr 1980 after 194 days. The highest speed at which expelled particles have been measured to travel is 103.6 mph *167 km/h*.

Snoring *Loudest*

Research at the Ear, Nose and Throat Department of St Mary's Hospital, London, published in November 1968, shows that a rasping snore can attain a loudness of 69 decibels (*cf.* 70–90 for a pneumatic drill).

Yawning

In Lee's case, reported in 1888, a 15-year-old female patient yawned continuously for a period of 5 weeks.

Sleeplessness

Researches indicate that on the Circadian cycle for the majority peak efficiency is attained between 8 and 9 p.m. and the low point comes at 4 a.m. The longest recorded period for which a person has voluntarily gone without sleep is 449 hr (18 days 17 hr) by Mrs Maureen Weston of Peterborough, Cambridgeshire in a rocking chair marathon on 14 Apr–2 May 1977. Though she tended to hallucinate toward the end of this surely ill-advised test, she surprisingly suffered no lasting ill-effects. W. Ananda Upali of Veyangoda, Sri Lanka voluntarily went without sleep for 353 hr 10 min (14 days 17 hr 10 min) from 20 Aug to 4 Sept 1979.

Motionlessness

The longest that anyone has voluntarily remained motionless is 7 hr 2 min by Wolfgang Kreuzer on T.V. Channel 7 in Brisbane, Australia on 4 Apr 1980. The longest recorded case of involuntarily being made to stand to attention was when Staff Sgt Samuel B. Moody USAF, was so punished in Narumi prison camp, Nagoya, Japan for 53 hr in Spring of 1945. He survived to write *Reprieve from Hell*.

Swallowing

The worst reported case of compulsive swallowing was an insane female Mrs H. aged 42, who complained of a 'slight abdominal pain'. She proved to have 2533 objects, including 947 bent pins, in her stomach. These were removed by Drs Chalk and Foucar in June 1927 at the Ontario Hospital, Canada. The heaviest object extracted from a human stomach has been a 5 lb 3 oz *2,530 kg* ball of hair in Swain's case from a 20-year-old female in

the South Devon and East Cornwall Hospital, England on 30 Mar 1895.

Sword

'Count Desmond' (b. 1941 of Birmingham, NY, USA) swallowed thirteen 23 in *58,4 cm* long blades to below his xiphisternum and injured himself in the process. *This category has now been retired and no further claims will be entertained.*

Fasting

Most humans experience considerable discomfort after an abstinence from food for even 12 hr but this often passes off after 24–48 hr. Records claimed without unremitting medical surveillance are of little value. The longest period for which anyone has gone without solid food is 382 days by Angus Barbieri (b. 1940) of Tayport, Fife, who lived on tea, coffee, water, soda water and vitamins in Maryfield Hospital, Dundee, Angus, from June 1965 to July 1966. His weight declined from 33 st 10 lb *214,1 kg* to 12 st 10 lb *8,74 kg*. Sister Therese Neumann survived 35 years on the 'bread' of the Holy Eucharist wafer at Mass each morning at Konnersreuth, Germany.

Hunger strike

The longest recorded hunger strike was one of 94 days by John and Peter Crowley, Thomas Donovan, Michael Burke, Michael O'Reilly, Christopher Upton, John Power, Joseph Kenny and Seán Hennessy in Cork Prison, Ireland, from 11 Aug to 12 Nov 1920. These nine survivors from 12 prisoners owed their lives to expert medical attention and an appeal by Arthur Griffith. The longest recorded hunger strike in a British gaol is 385 days from 28 June 1972 to 18 July 1973 by Denis Galer Goodwin in Wakefield Prison, West Yorkshire protesting his innocence of a rape charge. He was fed by tube orally.

The longest recorded case of survival without food *and* water is 18 days by Andreas Mihavecz, 18, of Bregenz, Austria who was put into a holding cell on 1 Apr 1979 in a local government building in Höchst, Austria but was totally forgotten by the police. On 18 Apr 1979 he was discovered close to death having had neither food nor water. He had been a passenger in a crashed car.

Most voracious fire eaters

Jon Zealando (NZ) blew a flame from his mouth to a distance of 24½ ft *7,45 m* at the Henderson Square Shopping Centre, Auckland on 19 Oct 1979. On 25 Aug 1979 at the 'Six Bells' Stoke Poges, Bucks, Jean Chapman extinguished 4593 torches of flame successively in her mouth in 2 hrs.

Human salamanders

The highest dry-air temperature endured by naked men in the US Air Force experiments in 1960 was 400° F *204,4° C* and for heavily clothed men 500° F *260° C*. Steaks require only 325° F *162,8° C*. Temperatures of 140° C *284° F* have been found quite bearable in *Sauna* baths.

The highest temperature recorded by pyrometer for the coals in any fire walk was 1494° F *812° C* for a walk by 'Komar' (Vernon E. Craig) of Wooster, Ohio at the International Festival of Yoga and Esoteric Sciences, Maidenhead, England on 14 Aug 1976.

Underwater

The world record for voluntarily staying underwater is 13 min 42.5 sec by Robert Foster, aged 32, an electronics technician of Richmond, California, who stayed under 10 ft *3,05 m* of water in the swimming pool of the Bermuda Palms Motel at San Rafael, California, USA, on 15 Mar 1959. He hyperventilated with oxygen for 30 min before his descent.

g forces

The acceleration g, due to gravity, is 32 ft 1.05 in per sec per sec *978,02 cm/sec²* at sea-level at the Equator. A *sustained* acceleration of 25 g was withstood in a dry capsule during astronautic research by Dr Carter Collins of California, USA. The highest g value endured on a water-braked rocket sled is 82.6 g for 0.04 of a sec by Eli L. Beeding Jr. at Holloman Air Force Base, New Mexico, USA, on 16 May 1958. He was put in hospital for 3 days. A man who fell off a 185 ft *56,39 m* cliff (before 1963) has survived a *momentary* g of 209 in decelerating from 68 mph *109 km/h* to stationary in 0.015 of a sec.

The racing driver David Purley GM survived a deceleration from 108 mph *173 km/h* to zero in 26 in *66 cm* in a crash at Silverstone on 13 July 1977 which involved a force of 179.8 g. He suffered 29 fractures, 3 dislocations and 6 heart stoppages.

The land divers of Penecost Island, New Hebrides dive from platforms 70 ft *21,3 m* high with liana vines attached to their ankles. The jerk can transmit a momentary g force in excess of 100.

Electric shock *Highest voltage*
Excluding lightning bolts, the highest reported voltage electric shock survived was one of 230,000 volts by Brian Latasa, 17, on the tower of an ultra-high-voltage power line in Griffith Park, Los Angeles on 9 Nov 1967. Highly insulated individuals have touched 1,200,000 volt cables in bare-hand live cable work without harm.

Isolation
The longest recorded period for which any volunteer has been able to withstand total deprivation of all sensory stimulation (sight, hearing and touch) is 92 hr, recorded in 1962 at Lancaster Moor Hospital, Lancashire.

The farthest that any human has been isolated from all other humans has been the lone pilots of lunar command modules when antipodal to their Apollo missions, two lunar explorers 2200 miles *3540 km* distant.

Pill-taking
The highest recorded total of pills swallowed by a patient is 359,061 between 9 June 1967 and 1 Jan 1981 by C. H. A. Kilner (b. 1926) of Malawi, following a successful pancreatectomy.

Most injections
The diabetic Mrs Evelyn Ruth Winder of Invercargill, New Zealand gave an estimated 54,190 insulin injections to herself over 50 years to May 1981.

Most tattoos
The seeming ultimate in being tatooed is represented by Wilfred Hardy of Huthwaite, Nottinghamshire, England. Not content with a perilous approach to within 4% totality, he has been tatooed on the inside of his cheek, his tongue, gums and eyebrows. Britain's most decorated woman is Mrs Rusty Skuse *née* Field (b. 1944) of Aldershot, Hampshire, who after 12 years under the needle of Mr Skuse, came within 15 per cent of totality. He stated he always had designs on her.

OPERATIONS
Longest
The most protracted reported operation, for surgical as opposed to medical control purposes, has been one of 47 hr performed on James Boydston, 26 on 15–17 June 1979 at the Veterans Administration medical center, Des Moines, Iowa, USA.

Most major
On 20 Aug 1975 Mr Charles Hill (b. 1914) of Sydney, New South Wales, Australia underwent his 87th major operation. Most of the surgery has been abdominal.

Oldest subject
The greatest recorded age at which a person has been subjected to an operation is 111 years 105 days in the case of James Henry Brett, Jr (b. 25 July 1849, d. 10 Feb 1961) of Houston, Texas, USA. He underwent a hip operation on 7 Nov 1960. The oldest age established in Britain was the case of Miss Mary Wright (b. 28 Feb 1862) who died during a thigh operation at Boston, Lincolnshire on 22 Apr 1971 aged 109 years 53 days.

Earliest heart transplant
The first human heart transplant operation was performed on Louis Washkansky, aged 55, at the Groote Schuur Hospital Cape Town, South Africa, between 1.00 a.m. and 6 a.m., on 3 Dec 1967, by a team of 30 headed by Prof. Christiaan Neethling Barnard (b. Beaufort West, South Africa, 8 Oct 1922). The donor was Miss Denise Ann Darvall, aged 25. Washkansky died on 21 Dec 1967. The longest surviving heart transplantee has been Emmanuel Vitria, of Marseilles, France who received a heart transplant on 28 Nov 1968 and entered the twelfth year of his new life in 1979. Britain's longest-surviving heart transplant patient is Mr Keith Castle (b. 1927) of Battersea, London who received his new heart on 18 Aug 1979 at Papworth Hospital, Cambridge.

Earliest kidney transplant
R. H. Lawler (b. 1895) (USA) performed the first homo transplantation of the kidney in the human in 1950. The longest survival, as between identical twins, has been 20 years.

Earliest appendicectomy
The earliest recorded successful appendix operation was performed in 1736 by Claudius Amyand (1680–1740). He was Serjeant Surgeon to King George II (reigned 1727–60).

Earliest anaesthesia
The earliest recorded operation under general anaesthesia was for the removal of a cyst from the neck of James Venable by Dr Crawford Williamson Long (1815–78), using diethyl ether ($C_2H_5)_2O$, in Jefferson, Georgia, USA, on 30 Mar 1842. The earliest amputation under an anaesthetic in Great Britain was by Dr William Scott and Dr James McLauchlan at the Dumfries and Galloway Infirmary, Scotland on 19 Dec 1846.

Most durable cancer patient
The most extreme recorded case of survival from diagnosed cancer is that of Mrs Winona Mildred Melick (*née* Douglass) (b. 22 Oct. 1876) of Long Beach, California. She had four cancer operations in 1918, 1933, 1966 and 1968 but celebrated her 104th birthday in 1980.

Laryngectomy
On 24 July 1924 John I. Poole of Plymouth, Devon after diagnosis of carcinoma, then aged 33 underwent total laryngectomy in Edinburgh. He died on 19 June 1979 after surviving nearly 55 years as a 'neck-breather'.

Fastest amputation
The shortest time recorded for a leg amputation in the pre-anaesthetic era was 13–15 sec by Napoleon's chief surgeon Dominique Larrey. There could have been no ligation.

Surgical instruments
The largest surgical instruments are robot retractors used in abdominal surgery introduced by Abbey Surgical Instruments of Chingford, Essex in 1968 and weighing 11 lb *5 kg*. Some bronchoscopic forceps measure 60 cm *23½ in* in length. The smallest are Elliot's eye trephine, which has a blade 0.078 in *0.20 cm* in diameter and 'straight' stapes picks with a needle-type tip or blade of 0,3 mm *0.013 in* long.

PSYCHIC FORCES
Extra-sensory perception
The two most extreme published examples of ESP in scientific literature have been those of the Reiss case of a 26 year old female at Hunter College, New York State, USA in 1936 and of Pavel Stepánek (Czechoslovakia) in 1967–68. The importance which might be attached to their cases has been diminished by subsequent developments. The Reiss subject refused to undergo any further tests under stricter conditions. When Stepánek was retested at Edinburgh University with plastic cards he 'failed to display any clairvoyant ability'. Much smaller departures from the laws of probability have however been displayed in less extreme cases carried out under strict conditions.

Most durable ghosts
Ghosts are not immortal and, according to the *Gazetteer of British Ghosts*, seem to deteriorate after 400 years. The most outstanding exception to their normal 'half-life' would be the ghosts of Roman soldiers thrice reported still marching through the cellars of the Treasurer's House, York Minster after nearly 19 centuries. The book's author, Peter Underwood, states that Britain has more reported ghosts per square mile than any other country with Borley Rectory near Long Melford, Suffolk the site of unrivalled activity between 1863 and its destruction by fire in 1939. Andrew M. Green, author of *Ghost Hunting, A Practical Guide* claims to possess the only known letter from a *poltergeist*.

2.
THE ANIMAL & PLANT KINGDOMS

ANIMAL KINGDOM
GENERAL RECORDS

Note—Guinness Superlatives Ltd has published a specialist volume entitled *The Guinness Book of Animal Facts and Feats* (2nd Edition) by Gerald L. Wood (price £6.50). This work treats the dimensions and performances of the Classes of the Animal Kingdom in greater detail, giving also the sources and authorities for much of the material in this chapter.

Largest and heaviest
The largest and heaviest animal in the world is the Blue or Sulphur-bottom whale (*Balaenoptera musculus*), also called Sibbald's rorqual. The largest specimen ever recorded was a female landed at the Cia Argentina de Pesca, South Georgia some time in the period 1904–20 which measured 107 Norwegian fot 33,58 m *110 ft 2½ in* in length. Another female measuring 27,6 m *90 ft 6 in* caught in the Southern Ocean by the Soviet *Slava* whaling fleet on 20 Mar 1947, weighed 190 tonnes *18.tons*.

Tallest
The tallest living animal is the giraffe (*Giraffa camelopardalis*) which is now found only in the dry savannah and semi-desert areas of Africa south of the Sahara. The tallest ever recorded was a Masai bull (*G. camelopardalis tippelskirchi*) named 'George' received at Chester Zoo, England on 8 Jan 1959 from Kenya. His head *almost* touched the roof of the 20 ft *6,09 m* high Giraffe House when he was 9 years old. George died on 22 July 1969. Less credible heights of up to 23 ft *7 m* (between pegs) have been claimed for bulls shot in the field.

Longest
The longest animal ever recorded is the ribbon worm *Lineus longissimus* also known as the 'Boot-lace worm', which is found in the shallow coastal waters of the North Sea. In 1864 a specimen measuring more than 180 ft *54 m* was washed ashore at St Andrews, Fifeshire, Scotland after a storm.

Rarest
The best claimants to the title of the world's rarest land animals are those species which are known only from a single (type) specimen. One of these is Fontoynont's hedgehog-tenrec *Dasogale fontoynonti*, which is known only from a specimen collected

The Three-toed sloth (or Ai) of tropical America, the slowest moving land mammal, whose average ground speed is so slow that he would require 31 days non-stop to cover a mile (see p. 29). (*Günter Ziesler*)

in eastern Madagascar (Malagasy Republic) and now preserved in the Museum d'Histoire Naturelle, Paris.

Commonest
It has been estimated that man shares the earth with about 3,000,000,000,000,000,000,000,000,000,000,000 (3000 quintillion or 3×10^{33}) other living things. The number of nematode sea-worms has been estimated at 4×10^{25}.

Fastest
The fastest-moving animal is the Peregrine falcon (*Falco peregrinus*), which has recently been timed electronically at 350 km/h *217 mph* in Germany while making a stoop at a 45-degree angle of descent. In a vertical fall of 5000 ft *1524 m*, it has been calculated a stooping Peregrine in display could probably reach 230–240 mph *370–386 km/h*, but it usually strikes its prey at about half this velocity. The fastest bird in level flight is the White-throated spinetail swift (*Hirundapus caudacutus*) of Asia. In 1942 air speeds up to 171 km/h *106.25 mph* were recorded for this species in the USSR (cf. 60 mph *96 km/h* for the Peregrine). This bird has a blood temperature of 112.5 °F *44,7 °C*.

Longest lived
Few non-bacterial creatures live longer than humans. It would appear that tortoises are the longest lived such animals. The greatest authentic age recorded for a tortoise is 152-plus years for a male Marion's tortoise (*Testudo sumeirii*) brought from the Seychelles to Mauritius in 1766 by the Chevalier de Fresne, who presented it to the Port Louis army garrison. This specimen (it went blind in 1908) was accidentally killed in 1918. When the famous Royal Tongan tortoise 'Tu'malilia' (believed to be a specimen of *Testudo radiata*) died on 19 May 1966 it was reputed to be over 200 years old, having been presented to the then King of Tonga by Captain James Cook (1728–79) on 22 Oct 1773, but this record may well have been compiled from two (or more) overlapping residents.

The bacteria *Thermoactinomyces vulgaris* have been found alive in cores of mud taken from the bottom of Windermere, Cumbria, England which have been dated to 1500 years before the present.

Heaviest brain
The Sperm whale (*Physeter catodon*) has the heaviest brain of any living animal. The brain of a 49 ft *14,93 m* bull processed in the Japanese factory ship *Nissin Maru No. 1* in the Antarctic on 11 Dec 1949 weighed 9,2 kg *20.24 lb* compared with 6,9 kg *15.38 lb* for a 90 ft *27 m* Blue whale. The heaviest brain recorded for an elephant was an exceptional 16.5 lb *7,5 kg* in the case of a 1.94 ton *1957 kg* Asiatic cow. The brain of the adult bull African elephant is normally 9¼–12 lb *4,2–5,4 kg*.

Largest eye
The giant squid (*Architeuthis* sp.) has the largest eye of any living animal. The ocular diameter may exceed 38 cm *15 in* (cf. 30 cm *11.81 in* for a 33⅓ long-playing record).

Largest egg
The largest egg of any living animal is that of the Whale shark (*Rhiniodon typus*). One egg case measuring 12 in by 5.5 in by 3.5 in *30 × 14 × 9 cm* was picked up by the shrimp trawler *Doris* on 29 June 1953 at a depth of 31 fathoms (186 ft *56,6 m*) in the Gulf of Mexico 130 miles *209 km* south of Port Isabel, Texas, USA. The egg contained a perfect embryo of a Whale shark 13.78 in *35 cm* long.

Longest gestation
The viviparous Alpine black salamander (*Salamandra atra*) has a gestation period of up to 38 months at altitudes above 1400 m *4600 ft* in the Swiss Alps, but this drops to 24–26 months at lower altitudes.

Fastest and slowest growth
The fastest growth in the Animal Kingdom is that of the Blue whale calf (see p. 26). A barely visible ovum weighing a fraction of a milligramme (*0.000035 oz*) grows to a weight of *c.* 26 tons *26 tonnes* in 22¾ months, made up of 10¾ months gestation and the first 12 months of life. This is equivalent to an increase of 30,000 million-fold. The slowest growth in the Animal Kingdom is that of the deep-sea clam *Tindaria callistiformis* of the North Atlantic, which takes an estimated 100 years to reach a length of 8 mm *0.31 in*.

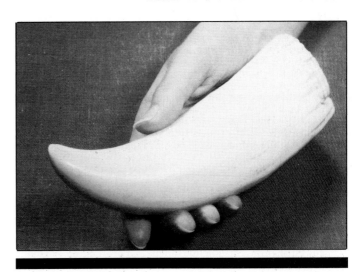

A small part of the dental armament of an adult bull sperm whale, the worlds largest toothed mammal. Mandibular teeth can exceed 160 mm *6¼ in* in height. (*Ronald A Chapman*)

Greatest size difference between sexes
The largest female deep-sea angler fish of the species *Ceratias holboelki* on record weighed half a million times as much as the smallest known parasitic male. It has been suggested that this fish would make an appropriate emblem for the Women's Lib. Movement.

Highest g force
The highest force encountered in nature is the 400 g *averaged* by the Click beetle *Athous haemorrhoidalis* (a common British species) when 'jack-knifing' into the air to escape predators. One example measuring 12 mm *0,47 in* in length and weighing 40 mg *0.00014 oz* which jumped to a height of 30 cm *11¾ in* was calculated to have 'endured' a peak brain deceleration of 2300 g at the end of the movement.

Blood temperatures
The highest mammalian blood temperature is that of the Domestic goat (*Capra hircus*) with an average of 103.8°F *39,9°C*, and a normal range of 101.7°–105.3°F *38,7°–40,7°C*. The lowest mammalian blood temperature is that of the Spiny anteater (*Tachyglossus aculeatus*), a monotreme found in Australia and New Guinea, with a normal range of 72°–87°F *22,2°–24,4°C*. The blood temperature of the Golden hamster (*Mesocricetus auratus*) sometimes falls as low as 38.3°F *3,5°C* during hibernation, and an extreme figure of 29.6°F *1,3°C* has been reported for a Myotis bat (family Vespertilionidae) during a deep sleep.

Most prodigious eater
The most phenomenal eating machine in nature is the larva of the Polyphemus moth (*Antheraea polyphemus*) of North America which, in the first 48 hours of its life, consumes an amount equal to 86,000 times its own birthweight. In human terms, this would be equivalent to a 7 lb *3,17 kg* baby taking in 269 tons *273 tonnes* of nourishment!

Most valuable furs
The highest-priced animal pelts are those of the Sea otter (*Enhydra lutris*), also known as the Kamchatka beaver, which fetched up to $2700 (then £675) before their 55-year-long protection started in 1912. The protection ended in 1967, and at the first legal auction of Sea otter pelts at Seattle, Washington, USA on 31 Jan 1968, Neiman-Marcus, the famous Dallas department store, paid $9200 (then £3832) for four pelts from Alaska. In May 1970 a Kojah (a mink-sable cross) coat costing $125,000 (*then £52,083*) was sold by Neiman-Marcus to Welsh actor Richard Burton for his then wife, Elizabeth Taylor.

Heaviest ambergris
The heaviest piece of ambergris (a fatty deposit in the intestine of the Sperm whale) on record was a 1003 lb *455 kg* lump recovered from a Sperm whale (*Physeter catodon*) taken in Australian waters on 3 Dec 1912 by a Norwegian whaling fleet. It was later sold in London for £23,000.

Most valuable
The most valuable animals in cash terms are thoroughbred race-horses. It was announced in March 1980 that *Spectacular Bid* (see Chap. XII Horseracing) would be syndicated for $22 million (*£10 million*). The most valuable zoo exhibit is the Giant panda (*Ailuropoda melanoleuca*) for which $250,000 (*£104,160*) was offered by the San Diego Zoological Gardens for a fertile pair in 1971. The most valuable marine exhibit is the Killer whale (*Orcinus orca*) 'Orky' at Marineland, Palos Verdes, Los Angeles. He has grown to 14,000 lb *6350 kg* since 1964 and is valued at not less than $250,000 (*£115,000*).

1. MAMMALS

Largest and heaviest *World*
For details of the Blue whale (*Balaenoptera musculus*) see page 26. Further information: the tongue and heart of the 190 tonne *187 ton* female taken by the *Slava* whaling fleet in the Southern Ocean on 20 Mar 1947 weighed 4.22 tons *4,29 tonnes* and 1540 lb *698,5 kg* respectively.

Largest and heaviest *British waters*
The largest Blue whale ever recorded in British waters was probably an 88 ft *26,8 m* specimen killed near the Bunaveneader station in Harris in the Western Isles, Scotland in 1904. In Sept 1750 a Blue whale allegedly measuring 101 ft *30,75 m* in length ran aground in the River Humber estuary. Another specimen stranded on the west coast of Lewis, Western Isles, Scotland in *c.* 1870 was credited with a length of 105 ft *32 m* but the carcase was cut up by the local people before the length could be verified. In both cases the length was probably exaggerated or taken along the curve of the body instead of in a straight line from the tip of the snout to the notch in the flukes. Four Blue whales have been stranded on British coasts since 1913, at least two of them after being harpooned by whalers. The last occurrence (*c.* 60 ft *18 m*) was at Wick, Highland, Scotland on 15 Oct 1923.

Blue whales inhabit the colder seas and migrate to warmer waters in the winter for breeding. Observations made in the Antarctic in 1947–8 showed that a Blue whale can maintain a speed of 20 knots (23 mph *37 km/h*) for 10 min when frightened. It has been calculated that a 90 ft *27 m* Blue whale travelling at 20 knots *37 km/h* would develop 520 hp *527 cv*. Newborn calves measure 6,5–8,6 m *21 ft 3½ in–28 ft 6 in* in length and weigh up to 3000 kg *2.95 tons*.

It has been estimated that there were between 21,000 and 23,000 Blue whales living throughout the oceans in 1980. The species has been protected *de jure* since 1967, although non-member countries of the International Whaling Commission, *e.g.* Panama and Taiwan, are not bound by this agreement.

Deepest dive
The greatest *recorded* depth to which a whale has dived is 620 fathoms (3720 ft *1134 m*) by a 47 ft *14,32 m* bull Sperm whale (*Physeter catodon*) found with its jaw entangled with a submarine cable running between Santa Elena, Ecuador and Chorillos, Peru, on 14 Oct 1955. At this depth the whale withstood a pressure of 1680 lb/in² *118 kg.f/cm²* of body surface. On 25 Aug 1969 another bull Sperm whale was killed 100 miles *160 km* south of Durban after it had surfaced from a dive lasting 1 hr 52 min, and inside its stomach were found two small sharks which had been swallowed about an hour earlier. These were later identified as *Scymnodon* sp., a species found only on the sea floor. At this point from land the depth of water is in excess of 1646 fathoms (10,476 ft *3193 m*) for a radius of 30–40 miles *48–64 km*, which now suggests that the Sperm whale sometimes may descend to a depth of over 10,000 ft *3000 m* when seeking food.

Largest on land *World*
The largest living land animal is the African bush elephant (*Loxodonta africana africana*). The average adult bull stands 10 ft 6 in *3,2 m* at the shoulder and weighs 5.6 tons *5,7 tonnes*. The largest specimen ever recorded, and the largest land animal of modern times, was a bull shot 25 miles *40 km* north-northeast of Mucusso, southern Angola on 7 Nov 1974. Lying on its side this elephant measured 13 ft 8 in *4,16 m* in a projected line from the

highest point of the shoulder to the base of the forefoot, indicating that its standing height must have been about 13 *3,96 m*. Other measurements included an over-all length of 35 *10,67 m* (tip of extended trunk to tip of extended tail) and a fore foot circumference of 5 ft 11 in *1,80 m*. The weight was computed to be 26,998 lb (12.05 tons, *12,24 tonnes*) (see also Shootin Chapter 12).

Largest on land *Britain*
The largest wild mammal in the British Isles is the Red de (*Cervus elaphus*). A full-grown stag stands 3 ft 8 in *1,11 m* at t shoulder and weighs 230–250 lb *104–113 kg*. The heaviest ev recorded was probably a stag killed at Glenfiddich, Banff, Sco land in 1831, which weighed 525 lb *238 kg*. The heaviest pa Red deer on record was a stag weighing 476 lb *215 kg* (height shoulder 4 ft 6 in *1,37 m*) killed at Woburn, Bedfordshire 1836. The wild pony (*Equus caballus*) may weigh up to 700 *320 kg* but now lives under semi-feral conditions.

Tallest
The tallest mammal is the giraffe (*Giraffa camelopardalis*). F details see p. 26.

Smallest *Land*
The smallest recorded land mammal is the rare Kitti's ho nosed bat (*Craseonycteris thonglongyai*) or Bumblebee bat, whi is restricted to two caves near the forestry station at Ban Sai Yo on the Kwae Noi River, Kanchanaburi, Thailand. Mature spec mens (both sexes) have a wing span of *c.* 160 mm *6.29 in* a weigh 1,75–2 g *0.062–0.071 oz*. The smallest mammal found the British Isles is the European pygmy shrew (*Sorex minutu* Mature specimens have a head and body length of 43–64 m *1.69–2.5 in*, a tail length of 31–46 mm *1.22–1.81 in* and wei between 2,4 and 6,1 g *0.084 and 0.213 oz*.

Smallest *Marine*
The smallest totally marine mammal in terms of weight is pro ably Commerson's dolphin (*Cephalorhynchus commersoni*) al known as Le Jacobite, which is found in the waters off t southern tip of South America. In one series of six adult spec mens the weights ranged from 23 kg *50.7 lb* to 35 kg *77.1* The Sea otter (*Enhydra lutris*) is of comparable size (55–81.4 *25–38,5 kg*), but this species sometimes comes ashore durin storms.

Rarest
A number of mammals are known only from a single (typ specimen, including Fontoynont's hedgehog-tenrec, (*Dasoga fontoynonti*) (see pp. 26–7). Among sub-species, the Javan tig (*Panthera tigris sondaica*) was reduced to 4 specimens by Janua 1980, all of them in the Meru Betiri reserve in eastern Java. 1979 scientists uncovered the first evidence that the Bali leopa (*Panthera pardus balica*) and the Bali tiger (*Panthera tigris balic* still existed on the island. The Arabian oryx (*Oryx leucoryx*) ha not been reported in the wild since 3 were killed and 4 capture in South Oman in 1972. In April 1980 five animals from the he at San Diego Zoo were sent to Oman for future release in th open desert.

The total British population of the now fully-protected Commo otter (*Lutra lutra*) is now less than 300, compared to 14,0 before the Second World War. No otters have been killed England since 1975, but 3 were killed in Wales in 1976.

Fastest *World*
The fastest of all land animals over a short distance (*i.e.* up 600 yd *549 m*) is the Cheetah or Hunting leopard (*Acinony jubatus*) of the open plains of East Africa, Iran, Turkmenia an Afghanistan, with a probable maximum speed of 60–63 mph 9 *101 km/h* over suitably level ground. Speeds of 71, 84 and eve 90 mph, *114, 135 and 145 km/h* have been claimed for th animal, but these figures must be considered exaggerated. Tes in London in 1937 showed that on an oval greyhound track ove 345 yd *316 m* a female cheetah's average speed over three ru was 43.4 mph *69,8 km/h* (cf. 43.26 mph *69,6 km/h* for the faste racehorse), but this specimen was not running flat out and ha great difficulty negotiating bends. The fastest land animal over sustained distance (*i.e.* 1000 yd *914 m* or more) is the Pronghor antelope (*Antilocapra americana*) of the western United State

Specimens have been observed to travel at 35 mph for 4 miles *56 km/h for 6 km*, at 42 mph for 1 mile *67 km/h for 1,6 km* and 55 mph for half a mile *88,5 km/h for 0,8 km*. On 14 Aug 1936 at Spanish Lake, in Lake County, Oregon a hard-pressed buck was timed by a car speedometer at 61 mph *98 km/h* over 200 yd *183 m*.

Fastest *Britain*
The fastest British land mammal over a sustained distance is the Roe deer (*Capreolus capreolus*), which can cruise at 25–30 mph *40–48 km/h* for more than 20 miles *32 km*, with occasional bursts of up to 40 mph *64 km/h*. On 19 Oct 1970 a frightened runaway Red deer (*Cervus elaphus*) registered a speed of 42 mph *67,5 km/ h* on a police radar trap as it charged through a street in Stalybridge, Greater Manchester.

Slowest
The slowest moving land mammal is the Ai or Three-toed sloth (*Bradypus tridactylus*) of tropical America. The average ground speed is 6–8 ft *1,83–2,44 m* a minute (0.068–0.098 mph *0,109– 0,158 km/h*), but in the trees it can 'accelerate' to 15 ft *4,57 m* a minute (0.17 mph *0,272 km/h*) (*cf.* these figures with the 0.03 mph *0,05 km/h* of the common garden snail and the 0.17 mph *0,27 km/h* of the giant tortoise).

Longest lived
No other mammal can match the extreme proven 115 years attained by Man (*Homo sapiens*) (see pp. 16 and 17). It is probable that the closest approach is among Blue and Fin whales (*Balaenoptera musculus* and *B. physalus*). Studies of the annual growth layers or laminations found in the wax-like plug deposited in the outer ear indicate a maximum life-span of 90–100 years.

The longest-living land mammal, excluding Man, is the Asiatic elephant (*Elephas maximus*). The greatest age that has been verified with certainty is 70 years in the case of a bull timber elephant 'Kyaw Thee' (Tusker 1342), who died in the Taunggyi Forest division, southern Shan States, Burma in 1965. The famous circus cow elephant 'Modoc' was reportedly 78 years old when she died in Santa Clara, California, USA on 17 July 1975, but this claim has never been fully authenticated.

Highest living
The highest living wild mammal in the world is probably the Yak (*Bos grunniens*), of Tibet and the Szechwanese Alps, China, which occasionally climbs to an altitude of 20,000 ft *6100 m* when foraging. The Bharal (*Pseudois nayaur*) and the Pika or Mouse hare (*Ochotona thibetana*) may also reach this height in the Himalayas. In 1890 the tracks of an elephant were found at 15,000 ft *4750 m* on Kilimanjaro, Tanzania.

Largest herds
The largest herds on record were those of the Springbok (*Antidorcas marsupialis*) during migration across the plains of the western parts of southern Africa in the 19th century. In 1849 John (later Sir John) Fraser observed a *trekbokken* that took three days to pass through the settlement of Beaufort West, Cape Province. Another herd seen moving near Nels Poortje, Cape Province in 1888 was estimated to contain 100,000,000 head, although 10,000,000 is probably a more realistic figure. A herd estimated to be 15 miles *24 km* wide and more than 100 miles *160 km* long was reported from Karree Kloof, Orange River, South Africa in July 1896.

The largest concentration of wild mammals found living anywhere in the world today is that of the Mexican free-tailed Bat *Tadarida mexicana* in Bracken Cave, San Antonio, Texas, USA, where up to twenty million animals assemble after migration from Mexico.

Longest and shortest gestation periods
The longest of all mammalian gestation periods is that of the Asiatic elephant (*Elephas maximus*), with an average of 609 days or just over 20 months and a maximum of 760 days—more than two and a half times that of a human. The gestation period of the American opossum (*Didelphis marsupialis*), also called the Virginian opossum, is normally 12–13 days but may be as short as 8 days.

'George' (far right) the tallest ever Giraffe from Chester Zoo whose peak height was just under 20 ft *6,09 m* (see p. 26). (*Kenneth W Green, ARPS*)

The gestation periods of the rare Water opossum or Yapok (*Chironectes minimus*) of Central and northern South America (average 12–13 days) and the Eastern native cat (*Dasyurus viverrinus*) of Australia (average 12 days) may also be as short as 8 days.

Largest litter
The greatest recorded number of young born to a *wild* mammal at a single birth is 32 (not all of which survived) in the case of the Common tenrec (*Centetes ecaudatus*) found in Madagascar and the Comoro Islands. The average litter is 12–16. In March 1961 a litter of 32 was also reported for a House mouse (*Mus musculus*) at the Roswell Park Memorial Institute in Buffalo, NY, USA (average litter 13–21) (see also Chapter 9 Agriculture, prolificacy records—pigs).

Youngest breeder
The Streaked tenrec (*Hemicentetes semispinosus*) of Madagascar is weaned after only 5 days, and females are capable of breeding 3–4 weeks after birth.

CARNIVORES
Largest Land *World*
The largest living terrestrial carnivore is the Kodiak bear (*Ursus arctos middendorffi*), which is found on Kodiak Island and the adjacent Afognak and Shuyak islands in the Gulf of Alaska, USA. The average adult male has a nose to tail length of 8 ft *2,4 m* (tail about 4 in *10 cm*), stands 52 in *132 cm* at the shoulder and weighs between 1050 and 1175 lb *476–533 kg*. In 1894 a weight of 1656 lb *751 kg* was recorded for a male shot at English Bay, Kodiak Island, whose *stretched* skin measured 13 ft 6 in *4,11 m* from the tip of the nose to the root of the tail. This weight was exceeded by a 'cage-fat' male in the Cheyenne Mountain Zoological Park, Colorado Springs, Colorado, USA which scaled 1670 lb *757 kg* at the time of its death on 22 Sept 1955.

Weights in excess of 1600 lb *725 kg* have also been reported for the Polar bear (*Ursus maritimus*), but the average adult male weighs 850–900 lb *386–408 kg* and measures 7¾ ft *2,4 m* nose to tail. In 1960 a Polar bear allegedly weighing 2210 lb *1002 kg* before skinning was shot at the polar entrance to Kotzebue Sound, north-west Alaska. The mounted specimen has a standing height of 11 ft 1¼ in *3,38 m*.

Largest Land *Britain*
The largest land carnivore found in Britain is the Badger (*Meles meles*). The average adult boar (sows are slightly smaller) measures 3 ft *90 cm* in length—including a 4 in *10 cm* tail—and weighs 27 lb *12,3 kg* in the early spring and 32 lb *14,5 kg* at the end of the summer when it is in 'grease'. In December 1952 a boar weighing exactly 60 lb *27,2 kg* was killed near Rotherham, South Yorkshire.

Largest Marine
The largest toothed mammal ever recorded is the Sperm whale (*Physeter catodon*), also called the cachalot. The average adult bull measures 47 ft *14,3 m* in length and weighs about 33 tons *33,5 tonnes*. The largest accurately measured specimen on record was a 67 ft 11 in *20,7 m* bull captured off the Kurile Islands, north-west Pacific, by a USSR whaling fleet in the summer of 1950. Twelve cachalots have been stranded on British coasts since 1913. The largest, a bull measuring 61 ft 5 in *19 m*, was washed ashore at Birchington, Kent on 18 Oct 1914. Another bull estimated at 65 ft *19,8 m* but badly decomposed was stranded at Ferryloughan, Co. Galway, Ireland on 2 Jan 1952.

Smallest
The smallest living member of the Order Carnivora is the Least weasel (*Mustela rixosa*), also called the Dwarf weasel, which is circumpolar in distribution. Four races are recognised, the smallest of which is *M. r. pygmaea* of Siberia. Mature specimens have an overall length of 177–207 mm *6.96–8.14 in* and weigh between 35 and 70 g *1¼–2½ oz*.

Largest feline
The largest member of the cat family (Felidae) is the long-furred Siberian tiger (*Panthera tigris altaica*), also called the Amur or Manchurian tiger. Adult males average 10 ft 4 in *3,15 m* in length (nose to tip of extended tail), stand 39–42 in *99–107 cm* at the shoulder and weigh about 585 lb *265 kg*. In 1950 a male weighing 384 kg *846.5 lb* was shot in the Sikhote Alin Mts, Maritime Territory, USSR. In November 1967 David H. Hasinger of Philadelphia, USA shot an outsized Indian tiger (*Panthera tigris tigris*) in northern Uttar Pradesh which measured 10 ft 7 in *3,22 m* between pegs (11 ft 1 in *3,37 m* over the curves) and weighed 857 lb *388,7 kg* (*cf.* 9 ft 3 in *2,82 m* and 420 lb *190 kg* for average adult male). It is now on display in the US Museum of Natural History, Smithsonian Institution, Washington, DC.

The average adult African lion (*Pantheria leo*) measures 9 ft *2,7 m* overall, stands 36–38 in *91–97 cm* at the shoulder and weighs 400–410 lb *181–185 kg*. The heaviest wild specimen on record was one weighing 690 lb *313 kg* shot by Mr Lennox Anderson just outside Hectorspruit in the eastern Transvaal, South Africa in 1936. In July 1970 a weight of 826 lb *375 kg* was reported for a black-maned lion named 'Simba' (b. Dublin Zoo, 1959) at Colchester Zoo, Essex. He died on 16 Jan 1973 at Knaresborough Zoo, North Yorkshire, where his stuffed body is currently on display.

Smallest feline
The smallest member of the cat family is the Rusty-spotted cat (*Felis rubiginosa*) of southern India and Sri Lanka. The average adult male has an overall length of 25–28 in *64–71 cm* (tail 9–10 in *23–25 cm*) and weighs about 3 lb *1,35 kg*.

PINNIPEDS (Seals, Sea-lions and Walruses)
Largest *World*
The largest of the 32 known species of pinniped is the Southern elephant seal (*Mirounga leonina*), which inhabits the sub-Antarctic islands. Adult bulls average 16½ ft *5 m* in length (tip of inflated snout to the extremities of the outstretched tail flippers), 12 ft *3,7 m* in maximum bodily girth and weigh about 5000 lb (2.18 tons *2 268 kg*). The largest accurately measured specimen on record was a bull killed in Possession Bay, South Georgia on 28 Feb 1913 which measured 21 ft 4 in *6,5 m* after flensing (original length about 22½ ft *6,85 m*) and probably weighed at least 4 tons/*tonnes*. There are old records of bulls

measuring 25–30 ft *7,62–9,14 m* and even 35 ft *10,66 m* b these figures must be considered exaggerated.

Largest *British*
The largest pinniped among British fauna is the Grey seal (*Ha choerus grypus*), also called the Atlantic seal. In 1772 an e tremely bulky bull measuring 9 ft *2,74 m* in length, 7 ft 6 *2,28 m* in maximum bodily girth and weighing 658 lb *298 kg* w killed in the Farne Islands.

Smallest
The smallest pinnipeds are the Baikal seal (*Pusa sibirica*) of Lal Baykal, USSR and the Ringed seal (*Pusa hispida*) of the Arcti Adult specimens measure up to 5 ft 6 in *1,67 m* and weigh up 280 lb *127 kg*.

Most abundant
The most abundant species of pinniped is the Crabeater se (*Lobodon carcinophagus*) of Antarctica. In 1978 the total popu lation was believed to be nearly 15,000,000.

Rarest
The Caribbean or West Indian monk seal (*Monachus tropicali* has not been recorded since 1962 when a single specimen w sighted on the beach of Isla Mujeres off the Yucatan Peninsul Mexico, and the species is now believed to be on the verge extinction.

Fastest and deepest
The highest swimming speed recorded for a pinniped is 25 mp *40 km/h* for a Californian sea lion (*Zalophus californianus*). Th deepest dive recorded for a pinniped is 600 m *1968 ft* for a bu Weddell seal (*Leptonychotes weddelli*) in McMurdo Soun Antarctica in March 1966. At this depth the seal withstood pressure of 875 lb/in² *6033 kPa* of body area. The exceptionall large eyes of the Southern elephant seal (*Mirounga leonina*) point to a deep-diving ability, and unconfirmed measuremen down to 2000 ft *609 m* have been claimed.

Longest lived
A female Grey seal (*Halichoerus grypus*) shot at Shunni Wick the Shetland Islands on 23 Apr 1969 was believed to be 'at lea 46 years old' based on a count of dental annuli.

BATS
Largest *World*
The only flying mammals are bats (order Chiroptera), of whic there are about 1000 living species. That with the greatest win span is the Bismarck flying fox (*Pteropus neohibernicus*) of th Bismarck Archipelago and New Guinea. One specimen pr served in the American Museum of Natural History has a win spread of 165 cm *5 ft 5 in* but some unmeasured bats probabl reach 183 cm *6 ft*.

Largest *Britain*
The largest bat found in Britain is the very rare Large mouse eared bat (*Myotis myotis*). Mature specimens have a wing spa of 355–450 mm *13.97–17.71 in* and weigh up to 45 g *1.58 o* (females).

Smallest *World*
For details of Kitti's hog-nosed bat see p. 28.

Smallest *Britain*
The smallest native British bat is the Pipistrelle (*Pipistrellus pip strellus*). Mature specimens have a wing span of 190–250 mr *7.48–9.84 in* and weigh between 3 and 8 g *0.1–0.28 oz*.

Rarest *World*
At least three species of bat are known only from the type speci men. They are: the Small-toothed fruit bat (*Neopteryx frost* from Tamalanti, West Celebes (1938/39); *Paracoelops megalot* from Vinh, Vietnam (1945); and *Latidens salimalii* from th High Wavy Mountains, southern India (1948).

Rarest *Britain*
The rarest native British bat is Bechstein's bat (*Myotis bech steini*), which is confined to Southern England. There have bee

The female Asiatic elephant 'Modoc' regarded by some as the oldest ever land mammal when she died at the reputed age of 78 years (see p. 29). *(Ralph Helfer)*

about thirty records to date (including 16 from Dorset). In January 1965 fifteen specimens of the Grey long-eared bat (*Plecotus austriacus*) were discovered in the roof of the Nature Conservancy's Research Station at Furzebrook, Dorset. Up to then this species, which is found all over Europe, had only been recorded once in Britain (Hampshire, 1875). In November 1976 another specimen was found in Sussex.

Fastest
Because of the great practical difficulties few data on bat speeds have been published. The greatest velocity attributed to a bat is 32 mph *51 km/h* in the case of a Mexican free-tailed bat (*Tadarida mexicana*), but this may have been wind-assisted. In one American experiment using an artificial mine tunnel and 17 different kinds of bat, only four of them managed to exceed 13 mph *20,8 km/h* in level flight.

Longest lived
The greatest age reliably reported for a bat is 31 years 5 months for an Indian flying fox (*Pteropus giganteus*) which died at London Zoo on 11 Jan 1979.

Highest detectable pitch
Because of their ultrasonic echolocation bats have the most acute hearing of any terrestrial animal. Vampire bats (*Desmodontidae*) and fruit bats (*Pteropodidae*) can hear frequencies as high as 150 kHz (*cf.* 20 kHz for the adult human limit but 153 kHz for the Bottle-nosed dolphin (*Tursiopis truncatus*)).

PRIMATES
Largest
The largest living primate is the Eastern lowland gorilla (*Gorilla gorilla graueri*) which inhabits the lowlands of the eastern part of Zaïre (formerly Democratic Republic of the Congo) and southwestern Uganda. The average adult male stands 5 ft 9 in *1,75 m* tall (including crest), measures 58–60 in *147–152 cm* round the chest and weighs about 360 lb *163 kg*. The greatest height (top of crest to heel) recorded for a gorilla is 6 ft 2 in *1,88 m* for a male

of the Mountain race (*Gorilla g. beringei*) shot in the eastern Congo in *c.* 1921.

The heaviest gorilla ever kept in captivity was a male of the mountain race named 'N'gagi', who died in San Diego Zoo, California, USA on 12 January 1944 aged 18 years. He scaled 683 lb *310 kg* at his heaviest in 1943, and weighed 636 lb *288 kg* at the time of his death. He was 5 ft 7¾ in *1,72 m* tall and boasted a record chest measurement of 78 in *198 cm*. The heaviest gorilla living in captivity today is a Western lowland (*Gorilla g. gorilla*) male called 'Zaak', who was received at Kobe Oji Zoo, Japan in December 1962. He tipped the scales at 628 lb *285 kg* in June 1976, but has not been weighed since.

Smallest
The smallest known primate is the rare Pen-tailed shrew (*Ptilocercus lowii*) of Malaysia, Sumatra and Borneo. Adult specimens have a total length of 230–330 mm *9–13 in* (head and body 100–140 mm *3.93–5.51 in*, tail 130–190 mm *5.1–7.5 in*) and weigh

David Hasinger with the 857 lb *388,7 kg* tiger he shot in northern India in November 1967 (see p. 30).

35–50 g *1.23–1.76 oz.* The Pygmy marmoset (*Cebuella pygmae*) of the Upper Amazon Basin and the Lesser mouse-lemur (*Microcebus murinus*) of Madagascar are also of comparable length but heavier, adults weighing 50–75 g *1.76–2.64 oz* and 45–80 g *1.58–2.82 oz* respectively.

Rarest
The rarest primate is the Hairy-eared dwarf lemur (*Allocebus trichotis*) of Madagascar which, until fairly recently, was known only from the type specimen and two skins. In 1966, however, a live example was found on the east coast near Mananara.

Longest lived
The greatest irrefutable age reported for a non-human primate is *c*. 59 years in the case of a male Orang-utan (*Pongo pygmaeus*) named 'Guas', who died in Philadelphia Zoological Garden, Pennsylvania, USA on 9 Feb 1977. When he was received on 1 May 1931 he was at least 13 years of age. The world's oldest living primate is a male Chimpanzee (*Pan troglodytes*) named 'Jimmy' at Seneca Zoo, Rochester, N.Y., USA, who was still alive in December 1980 aged 50 years 6 months.

Strength
In 1924 'Boma', a 165 lb *74,80 kg* male chimpanzee at Bronx Zoo, New York, NY, USA recorded a right-handed pull (feet braced) of 847 lb *384 kg* on a dynamometer (*cf.* 210 lb *95 kg* for a man of the same weight). On another occasion an adult female chimpanzee named 'Suzette' (estimated weight 135 lb *61 kg*) at the same zoo registered a right-handed pull of 1260 lb *572 kg* while in a rage. A record from the USA of a 100 lb *45 kg* chimpanzee achieving a two-handed dead lift of 600 lb *272 kg* with ease suggests that a male gorilla could with training raise 1800 lb *816 kg!*

MONKEYS
Largest
The only species of monkey reliably credited with weights of more than 100 lb *45 kg* is the Mandrill (*Mandrillus sphinx*) of equatorial West Africa. The greatest reliable weight recorded is 119 lb *54 kg* for a male but an unconfirmed weight of 130 lb *59 kg* has been reported. (Adult females are about half the size of males).

Smallest
The smallest known monkey is the Pygmy marmoset (*Cebuella pygmaea*) of the Upper Amazon Basin (see Primate Smallest).

Oldest
The greatest reliable age recorded for a monkey is 46 years 11 months for a White-throated capuchin (*Cebus capucinus*) which died in Evansville Zoo, Indiana, USA on 12 Apr 1976.

RODENTS
Largest
The world's largest rodent is the Capybara (*Hydrochoerus hydrochaeris*), also called the Carpincho or Water hog, which is found in tropical South America. Mature specimens have a head and body length of 3¼–4½ ft *0,99–1,4 m* and weigh up to 174 lb *79 kg*. Britain's largest rodent is now the Coypu (*Myocastor coypus*), also known as the Nutria, which was introduced from Argentina by East Anglian fur-breeders in 1929. Three years later, the first escapes were recorded and by 1960 at least 200,000 coypus were living in East Anglia. About 80 per cent were killed by the winter of 1963 and a government campaign of extermination has reduced the population to *c.* 8000 animals. Adult males measure 30–36 in *76–91 cm* in length (including short tail) and weigh up to 28 lb *13 kg* in the wild state (40 lb *18 kg* in captivity).

Smallest
The smallest known rodent is the Northern Pygmy mouse (*Baiomys taylori*) of central Mexico and southern Arizona and Texas, USA, which measures up to 109 mm *4.3 in* in total length and weighs 7–8 g *0.24–0.28 oz.* Britain's smallest rodent is the Old World harvest mouse (*Micromys minutus*), which measures up to 135 mm *5.3 in* in total length and weighs 7–10 g *0.24–0.35 oz.*

Rarest
The rarest rodent in the world is believed to be the James Island rice rat (*Oryzomys swarthi*), also called Swarth's rice rat. Four

specimens were collected on this island in the Galapagos group in 1906, and it was not heard of again until January 1966 when recent skull was found.

Longest lived
The greatest reliable age reported for a rodent is 27 years months for a Sumatran crested porcupine (*Hystrix brachyura* which died in National Zoological Park, Washington DC, USA on 12 Jan 1965.

Fastest breeder
The female Meadow vole (*Microtus agrestis*) found in Britain, ca reproduce from the age of 25 days and have up to 17 litters of 6–young in a year.

INSECTIVORES
Largest
The largest insectivore is the Moon rat (*Echinosorex gymnurus*) also known as Raffles' gymnure, which is found in Burma Thailand, Malaysia, Sumatra and Borneo. Mature specimen have a head and body length of 265–445 mm *10.43–17.52 in*, tail measuring 200–210 mm *7.87–8.26 in* and weigh up to 1400 *3.08 lb.* Although the much larger Anteaters (family Tachy glossidae and Myrmecophagidae) feed on termites and othe soft-bodied insects they are not insectivores, but belong to th orders Monotremata and Edentata, which means 'withou teeth'.

Smallest
The smallest insectivore is Savi's white-toothed pygmy shrev (*Suncus etruscus*), also called the Etruscan shrew, which is found along the coast of the northern Mediterranean and southward to Cape Province, South Africa. Mature specimens have a hea and body length of 36–52 mm *1.32–2.04 in*, a tail length of 24 29 mm *0.94–1.14 in* and weigh between 1,5 and 2,5 g *0.052 an 0.09 oz.*

Longest lived
The greatest reliable age recorded for an insectivore is 14+ year for a Lesser hedgehog-tenrec (*Echinops telfairi*), which was bor in Amsterdam Zoo, Netherlands in 1966 and was later sent t Jersey Zoo. It was still alive on 24 Dec 1980.

ANTELOPES
Largest
The largest of all antelopes is the rare Giant eland (*Tragelaphu derbianus*), of West and Central Africa, which may surpas 2000 lb *907 kg*. The Common eland (*T. oryx*) of East and Sout Africa has the same shoulder height of up to 5 ft 10 in *1,78 m* bu is not quite so massive, although there is one record of a 5 ft 5 i *1,65 m* bull shot in Nyasaland (now Malawi) in *c.* 1937 whic weighed 2078 lb *943 kg*.

Smallest
The smallest known antelope is the Royal antelope (*Neotragu pygmaeus*) of West Africa. Mature specimens measure 10–12 i *25–31 cm* at the shoulder and weigh only 7–8 lb *3–3,6 kg* whic is the size of a large Brown hare (*Lepus europaeus*). Salt's dik-di (*Madoqua saltina*) of NE Ethiopia and Somalia weighs only 5- 6 lb *2,2–2,7 kg* when adult, but this species stands about 14 i *35,5 cm* at the withers.

Rarest
The rarest antelope is the Arabian oryx (*Oryx leucoryx*) (se Mammals Rarest).

Oldest
The greatest reliable age recorded for an antelope is 25 years months for an Addax (*Addax nasomaculatus*) which died i Brookfield Zoo, Chicago, Illinois, USA on 15 Oct 1960.

DEER
Largest
The largest deer is the Alaskan moose (*Alces alces gigas*). A bul standing 7 ft 8 in *2,3 m* at the withers and weighing an estimate 1800 lb *816 kg* was shot on the Yukon River in the Yukon Terri tory, Canada in September 1897. Unconfirmed measurement up to 8½ ft *2,59 m* at the withers and estimated weights up to

Mammals

2600 lb *1180 kg* have been claimed. The record antler span is 78½ in *199 cm*.

Smallest

The smallest true deer (family Cervidae) is the Northern pudu (*Pudu mephistophiles*) of Ecuador and Columbia. Mature specimens measure 13–14 in *33–35 cm* at the shoulder and weigh 16–18 lb *7,2–8,1 kg*. The smallest ruminant is the Lesser Malay chevrotain (*Tragulus javanicus*) of SE Asia, Sumatra and Borneo. Adult specimens measure 8–10 in *20–25 cm* at the shoulder and weigh 6–7 lb *2,7–3,2 kg*.

Rarest

The rarest deer in the world is Fea's muntjac (*Muntiacus feae*), which until recently, was known only from two specimens collected on the borders of S Burma and W Thailand. In December 1977 a female was received at Bangkok Zoo.

Oldest

The greatest reliable age recorded for a deer is 26 years 8 months for a Red deer (*Cervus elaphus scoticus*) which died in Milwaukee Zoo, Wisconsin, USA on 28 June 1954.

MARSUPIALS

Largest

The largest of all marsupials is the Red kangaroo (*Macropus rufus*) of southern and eastern Australia. Adult males or 'boomers' stand up to 7 feet *2,13 m* tall, weigh up to 175 lb *79 kg* and measure up to 8 ft 11 in *2,71 m* in a straight line from the nose to the tip of the extended tail.

Smallest

The smallest known marsupial is the very rare Ingram's planigale (*Planigale ingrami*), a flat-skulled mouse found only in the Kimberley district of Western Australia. Adult males have a head and body length of 44 mm *1.7 in*, a tail length of 50 mm *2 in* and weigh about 4 g *0.141 oz*.

Rarest

The rarest marsupial is probably the Thylacine (*Thylacinus cynocephalus*), also known as the 'Tasmanian tiger', the largest of the carnivorous marsupials, which reportedly became extinct some time in the mid-1930s (the last captive specimen died in Hobart Zoo, Tasmania in 1934). In 1961, however, a young male was accidentally killed by fishermen at Sandy Cape, western Tasmania, and in December 1966 the traces of a thylacine lair were found at White River, near Mawbanna. In July 1977 a positive sighting was made of another specimen near Derby on the northwestern side of the island.

Longest lived

The greatest reliable age recorded for a marsupial is 26 years 0 months 22 days for a Common Wombat (*Vombatus ursinus*) which died in London Zoo on 20 Apr 1906.

Highest and longest jumps

The greatest measured height cleared by a hunted kangaroo is 10 ft 6 in *3,20 m* over a pile of timber. During the course of a chase in January 1951 a female Red kangaroo (*Macropus rufus*) made a series of bounds which included one of 42 ft *12,80 m*. There is also an unconfirmed report of a Great grey kangaroo (*M. canguru*) jumping nearly 13,5 m *44 ft 8½ in* on the flat.

TUSKS

Longest

The longest recorded elephant tusks (excluding prehistoric examples) are a pair from Zaïre preserved in the National Collection of Heads and Horns kept by the New York Zoological Society in Bronx Park, New York City, NY, USA. The right tusk measures 11 ft 5½ in *3,49 m* along the outside curve and the left 11 ft *3,35 m*. Their combined weight is 293 lb *133 kg*. A single tusk of 11 ft 6 in *3,5 m* has been reported, but further details are lacking.

Heaviest

The heaviest recorded tusks are a pair in the British Museum (Natural History) which were collected from an aged bull shot by an Arab with a muzzle-loading gun at the foot of Mt. Kilimanjaro, Kenya in 1897. They weigh 240 lb *109 kg* (length 10 ft

Although there was a positive sighting in 1977 of the Thylacine or 'Tasmanian tiger' it still ranks as the rarest carnivorous marsupial. The last captive specimen died in 1934.

2½ in *3,11 m*) and 225 lb *102 kg* (length 10 ft 5½ in *3,18 m*) respectively, giving a combined weight of 465 lb *211 kg*.

The greatest weight ever recorded for an elephant tusk is 117 kg *258 lb* for a specimen collected in Benin, West Africa and exhibited at the Paris Exposition in 1900.

HORNS
Longest

The longest recorded animal horn was one measuring 81¼ in *206 cm* on the outside curve, with a circumference of 18¼ in *46 cm*, found on a specimen of domestic Ankole cattle (*Bos taurus*) near Lake Ngami, Botswana. The largest head (horns measured from tip to tip across the forehead) is one of 13 ft 11 in *4,24 m* for a specimen of wild buffalo (*Bubalus bubalus*) shot in India in 1955. The maximum recorded for a Texas Longhorn steer is 9 ft 9 in *2,97 m* from tip to tip.

Longest *Rhinoceros*

The longest recorded anterior horn for a rhinoceros is one of 62¼ in *158 cm* found on a female southern race White rhinoceros (*Ceratotheriam simum simum*) shot in South Africa in *c*. 1848. The interior horn measured 22¼ in *57 cm*. There is also an unconfirmed record of an anterior horn measuring 81 in *206 cm*.

HORSES AND PONIES
The world's horse population is estimated to be 75,000,000.

Largest

The heaviest horse ever recorded was a 19.2-hand (6 ft 6 in *1,98 m*) pure-bred Belgian stallion named 'Brooklyn Supreme' (foaled 12 Apr 1928) owned by Ralph Fogleman of Callender, Iowa, USA which weighed 3200 lb 1.42 tons *1,44 tonnes* shortly before his death on 6 Sept 1948 aged 20.

In April 1973 the Belgian mare 'Wilma du Bos' (foaled 15 July 1966), owned by Mrs Virgie Arden of Reno, Nevada, USA was reported to weigh slightly in excess of 3200 lb *1451 kg* when in foal and being shipped from Antwerp. The normal weight of this 18.2-hand *1,88 m* mare is about 2400 lb *1088 kg*. The British weight record is held by the 17.2-hand (5 ft 10 in *1,78 m*) Shire stallion 'Honest Tom 5123' (foaled in 1884), owned by James Forshaw of Littleport, Cambridgeshire, which scaled 2912 lb *1325 kg* in 1891. This poundage may have been exceeded by another huge Shire stallion named 'Great Britain 978', bred by Henry Bultitaft of Ely, Cambridgeshire in 1876, but no weight details are available. In 1888 this horse was sold to Phineas T. Barnum, the American showman, for exhibition purposes.

The heaviest horse living in Britain today is the champion Percheron stallion 'Pinchbeck Union Crest' (foaled 27 Jan 1964), owned by Mr. George Sneath of Pinchbeck, Spalding, Lincs., which weighs 23½ cwt *1194 kg*.

Tallest

The tallest horse documented was the Percheron-Shire cross 'Firpon' (foaled 1959), owned by Julio Falabella which stood

21.1 hands (7 ft 1 in *2,16 m*) and weighed 2976 lb *1350 kg*. He died on the Recco de Roca Ranch near Buenos Aires, Argentina on 14 Mar 1972. A height of 21.1 hands was also claimed for the Clydesdale gelding 'Big Jim' (foaled 1950) bred by Lyall M. Anderson of West Broomley, Montrose, Scotland. He died in St Louis, Missouri in 1957. A claim for 21.2 hands (7 ft 2 in *2,18 m*) was made in 1908 for a horse named 'Morocco' weighing 2835 lb *1286 kg* in Allentown, Pennsylvania, USA. The tallest horse living in Britain today is the Shire stallion 'Ryton Regent' (foaled 1971), owned by Mr. Robert Brickell of Witney, Oxfordshire, which stands 19.1½ hands (6 ft 5½ in *1,97 m*) and weighs over 20 cwt (2240 lb *1016 kg*).

Smallest

The smallest breed of horse (*sic*) is the Falabella of Argentina which was developed over a period of 45 years by crossing and recrossing a small group of undersized English Thoroughbreds with Shetland ponies. Adult specimens stand 15–30 in *38–74 cm* at the shoulder and weigh 40–80 lb *18–36 kg*. Foals of 3 hands (12 in *30,4 cm*) have been twice recorded by Norman J. Mitchell of Glenorie, NSW, Australia in the cases of 'Tung Dynasty' (8 Feb 1978) and 'Quicksilver' (1975).

Oldest

The greatest reliable age recorded for a horse is 62 years in the case of 'Old Billy' (foaled 1760), believed to be a cross between a Cleveland and Eastern blood, who was bred by Mr Edward Robinson of Wild Grave Farm in Woolston, Lancashire. In 1762 or 1763 he was sold to the Mersey and Irwell Navigation Company and remained with them in a working capacity (*i.e.* marshalling and towing barges) until 1819 when he was retired to a farm at Latchford, near Warrington, where he died on 27 Nov 1822. The skull of this horse is preserved in the Manchester Museum, and his stuffed head is now on display in the Bedford Museum. The greatest reliable age recorded for a pony is 54 years for a stallion owned by a farmer in Central France which was still alive in 1919. The greatest age recorded for a thoroughbred racehorse is 42 years in the case of the bay gelding 'Tango Duke' (foaled 1935), owned by Mrs Carmen J. Koper of Barongarook, Victoria, Australia. The horse died on 25 Jan 1978.

Strongest *draught*

The greatest load ever hauled by a pair of draught-horses was 48 short tons *43,5 tonnes* (= 50 pine logs or 36,055 board-feet of timber) on a special sledge litter *pulled across snow* for a distance of 275 yd *251 m* at the Nester Estate, Ewen, Ontanagon County, Michigan, USA on 26 Feb 1893. The two horses, both Clydesdales, had a combined weight of 3500 lb *1587 kg*. On 4 Sept 1924

'Heidan Dark Blue' Britain's heaviest ever dog whose peak weight was 20 st 7 lb *130 kg* in March 1981. (*Nicol Plummer*)

'Max of Pangoula' trained by Chief Prison Officer Alec Mann, setting the canine high jump record with 11 ft 5⅛ in *3,48 m* (see p. 35)

a pair of Shire geldings owned by Liverpool Corporation registered a much more impressive *maximum* pull equivalent to a starting load of 50 tons *51 tonnes* on a dynamometer at the British Empire Exhibition at Wembley, London.

DOGS *UK dog population 5,542,000 (1981 estimate) compared with 41,000,000 for the USA).*

Largest

The heaviest breed of domestic dog (*Canis familiaris*) is the St Bernard. The heaviest recorded example is 'Benedictine Schwarzwald Hof', owned by Thomas C. and Ann E. Irwin of Grand Rapids, Michigan, USA. He was whelped on 17 Dec 1970 and weighed 21 st 11 lb *138,34 kg* in May 1978, (height at shoulder 39 in *99 cm*). The heaviest dog ever recorded in Britain is 'Heidan Dark Blue' (whelped 23 Apr 1978) also called 'Jason', a St Bernard owned by Nicol Plummer of Skeffington, Leics. On 16 Mar 1981 he scaled 20 st 7 lb *130 kg*. He measures 34 in *86,3 cm* at the shoulder and boasts a 52 in *132 cm* chest.

Tallest

The tallest breeds of dog are the Great Dane and the Irish wolfhound, both of which can exceed 39 in *99 cm* at the shoulder. In the case of the Great Dane the extreme recorded example is 'Shamgret Danzas' (whelped in 1975), owned by Mrs G. Comley of Milton Keynes, Bucks. He stands 40½ in *102,9 cm* and weighs 16 st *101,6 kg*. The Irish Wolfhound 'Broadbridge Michael' (whelped in 1920), owned by Mrs Mary Beynon of Sutton-at-Hone, Kent, stood 39½ in *100,3 cm* at the age of 2 years.

Smallest

The world's smallest breeds of dog are the Yorkshire terrier, the Chihuahua and the Toy poodle, *miniature* versions of which have been known to weigh less than 16 oz *453 g* when adult. In April 1971 a weight of 10 oz *283 g* was reliably reported for a fully-grown Yorkshire terrier called 'Sylvia' (shoulder height 3½ in *89 mm*) owned by Mrs Connie Hutchins of Walthamstow, Greater London.

Oldest

Authentic records of dogs living over 20 years are extremely rare, but even 34 years has been accepted by one authority. The greatest reliable age recorded for a dog is 29 years 5 months for a Queensland 'heeler' named 'Bluey', owned by Mr Les Hall of Rochester, Victoria, Australia. The dog was obtained as a puppy in 1910 and worked among cattle and sheep for nearly 20 years. He was put to sleep on 14 Nov 1939. The British record is 27 years 313 days for a Welsh collie named 'Taffy' owned by Mrs Evelyn Brown of Forge Farm, West Bromwich, W. Midlands. He was whelped on 2 Apr 1952 and was put to sleep on 9 Feb 1980.

Strength and endurance
The greatest load ever shifted by a dog was 6400½ lb *2905 kg* of railroad steel pulled by a 176 lb *80 kg* St Bernard named 'Ryettes Brandy Bear' at Bothell, Washington, USA on 21 July 1978. The 4-year-old dog, owned by Douglas Alexander of Monroe, Washington, pulled the weight on a four-wheeled carrier across a cement surface for a distance of 15 ft *4,57 m* in less than 90 sec. The strongest dog in the world in terms of most proportionate weight hauled is 'Barbara-Allen's Dark Hans', a 97 lb *44 kg* Newfoundland, who pulled 5045½ lb *2289 kg* (= 52 lb *23,5 kg* per lb *0,45 kg* body weight) across a cement surface at Bothell on 20 July 1979. The dog, owned by Miss Terri Dickinson of Kenmore, Washington, was only 12 months old when he made the attempt. The record time for the annual 1100 mile *1770 km* dog sled race from Anchorage to Nome, Alaska is 14 days 7 hr 11 min by a dog owned by Mr Joe May in the 1980 race.

Rarest
The world's rarest breed of dog is the Tahltan bear dog, which was formerly used by the Tahltan Indians of western Canada for hunting big game. Only five known examples of this hound still survive, and four of these are spayed bitches, which means the Tahltan has now passed the point of no return unless a breeding pair can be found. The solitary dog, 'Iskut' (whelped 14 Mar 1967), is owned by Mrs. Winnie Acheson of Atlin, British Columbia, where three of the bitches also live.

Guide dog
The longest period of *active service* reported for a guide dog is 13 years 2 months in the case of a Labrador-retriever bitch named 'Polly' (whelped 10 Oct 1956), owned by Miss Rose Resnick of San Rafael, California, USA. The dog was put to sleep on 15 Dec 1971.

Largest litter
The largest recorded litter of puppies is one of 23 thrown on 19 June 1944 by 'Lena', a foxhound bitch owned by Commander W. N. Ely of Ambler, Pennsylvania, USA. On 6–7 Feb 1975 'Careless Ann', a St Bernard bitch, owned by Robert and Alice Rodden of Lebanon, Missouri, USA also produced a litter of 23, 14 of which survived. The British record is held by 'Settrina Baroness Medina', a Red Setter bitch owned by Mgr M. J. Buckley, Director of the Wood Hall Centre, Wetherby, West Yorkshire. The bitch gave birth to 22 puppies, 15 of which survived, on 10 Jan 1974. All 17 puppies born in February 1977 to 'Trudi', an Irish setter owned by Mr Alan Jenkins of Wolverhampton, survived.

Most prolific
The greatest sire of all time was the champion greyhound 'Low Pressure', nicknamed 'Timmy', whelped in September 1957 and owned by Mrs Bruna Amhurst of Regent's Park, London. From December 1961 until his death on 27 Nov 1969 he fathered 2414 registered puppies, with at least 600 others unregistered.

Most valuable
In June 1972 Mrs Judith Thurlow of Great Ashfield, Suffolk turned down an offer of £14,000 for her racing greyhound 'Super Rory' (b. October 1970). Show dogs have also fetched extremely high prices, and in July 1976 Mrs Eiselle Banks of Rayleigh, Essex turned down an American offer of £10,000 for her international champion Lowchen 'Cluneen Adam Adamant' (b. 13 Aug 1969). On 27 June 1972 Mr August Belmont of Easton, Maryland, USA paid $22,000 (*then £8,500*) for his labrador retriever puppy 'Wanapum Lucky Yo Yo'; bred by Eddie Dewitt of Redmond, Washington, USA. This is the highest price *actually paid* for a dog.

An eyeball to eyeball confrontation between a Falabella of Argentina, the most miniature of all horses and a cockerel (see p. 34). (*Lynne Kirkman*)

'Top dog'
The greatest altitude attained by a mammal is 1050 miles *1690 km* by the Samoyed husky bitch fired as a passenger in Sputnik II on 3 Nov 1957. The dog was variously named 'Kudryavka' (feminine form of 'Curly') 'Limonchik' (diminutive of lemon), 'Malyshka', 'Zhuchka' or by the Russian breed name for husky, 'Laika'.

Highest and longest jump
The canine 'high jump' record for a leap and a scramble is held by a German shepherd dog named 'Max of Pangoula', who scaled an 11 ft 5⅛ in *3,48 m* smooth wooden wall, at Chikurubi prison's dog training school near Salisbury, Zimbabwe on 18 Mar 1980. The longest recorded canine long jump was one of 30 ft *9,14 m* by a greyhound named 'Bang' made in jumping a gate in coursing a hare at Brecon Lodge, Gloucestershire in 1849.

Ratting
The greatest ratter of all time was Mr James Searle's bull terrier bitch 'Jenny Lind', who killed 500 rats in 1 hr 30 min at 'The Beehive', Old Crosshall Street, Liverpool on 12 July 1853. Another bull terrier named 'Jacko' owned by Mr Jemmy Shaw, was credited with killing 1000 rats in 1 hr 40 min, but the feat was performed over a period of ten weeks in batches of 100 at a time. The last 100 were accounted for in 5 min 28 sec in London on 1 May 1862.

Tracking
The greatest tracking feat on record was performed by a Dobermann Pinscher named 'Sauer', trained by Detective-Sergeant Herbert Kruger. In 1925 he tracked a stock-thief 100 miles *160 km* across the Great Karroo, South Africa by scent alone. In 1923 a collie dog named 'Bobbie', lost by his owners while they were on holiday in Wolcott, Indiana, USA, turned up at the family home in Silverton, Oregon 6 months later, after covering a distance of some 2000 miles *3200 km*. The dog, later identified by householders who had looked after him along the route, had apparently travelled back through the states of Illinois, Iowa, Nebraska and Colorado, before crossing the Rocky Mountains in the depths of winter and then continuing through Wyoming and Idaho.

Top show dog
The record number of 'Best in Show' awards won by any dog in all breed shows is 127 compiled by the Pekinese International

Champion Chik T'Sun of Caversham, owned by Mr and Mrs Charles C. Venable of Marietta, Georgia, in North America from January 1957 to February 1960.

Top trainer

The most successful dog trainer in the world—and the fastest—is Mrs Barbara Woodhouse of Rickmansworth, Hertfordshire, who has trained 17,094 dogs to obey the basic commands during the period 1951 to 25 Mar 1981. Her record for a single day is 80 dogs (Denver, Colorado, USA June 1973).

Police Dogs

The world's top police dog is 'Trep' of Dade County Crime Force, Florida, USA with $63 million (*then £36 million*) worth of narcotics sniffed out. Demonstrating at a school with 10 hidden packets, Trep once found 11. 'Sergeant Blitz', a drug-sniffing police dog in Savannah, Georgia, USA was the subject of a $10,000 (*£5,250*) 'contract' in January 1977.

Greatest dog funeral

The greatest dog funeral on record was for the mongrel dog 'Lazaras' belonging to the eccentric Emperor Norton I of the United States, Protector of Mexico, held in San Francisco, California in 1862 which was attended by an estimated 10,000 people.

CATS (*UK cat population 4,897,000 (1981 estimate) compared with 23,000,000 for the USA*)

Heaviest

The heaviest domestic cat (*Felis catus*) on record was a long-haired part Persian named 'Tiger' owned by Mrs Phyllis Dacey of Billericay, Essex. During the two-year period ending September 1979 he scaled a constant 42–43 lb *19,05–19,50 kg* (neck 12½ in *31,75 cm*, waist 33 in *83,8 cm*, length 37 in *94 cm*), but after receiving treatment for a hormone imbalance he started to lose weight rapidly. When he was put to sleep on 27 Aug 1980 he was, as a result of kidney trouble, down to 18 lb *8,16 kg*.

Smallest

Because of the reproduction problems involved, there is no recognised smallest breed of cat. Adult weights of under 3 lb *1,36 kg*, however, have been reliably reported in some cases of feline dwarfism (average weight 9–11 lb *4,08–4,98 kg*).

Oldest

Cats are generally longer-lived than dogs. Information on this subject is often obscured by two or more cats bearing the same nickname in succession. The oldest cat ever recorded was probably the tabby 'Puss', owned by Mrs T. Holway of Clayhidon, Devon who celebrated his 36th birthday on 28 Nov 1939 and died the next day. A more recent and better-documented case was that of the female tabby 'Ma', owned by Mrs Alice St George Moore of Drewsteignton, Devon. This cat was put to sleep on 5 Nov 1957 aged 34.

Largest pet litters

ANIMAL	NUMBER	BREED	OWNER
Cat	15	Burmese/Siamese	Mrs Valerie Gane, Church Westcote, Kingham, Oxfordshire.
Dog	23	Foxhound	Cdr W. N. Ely, Ambler, Pennsylvania, USA.
	23	St Bernard	R. and A. Rodden, Lebanon, Missouri, USA.
Rabbit	24	New Zealand White	Joseph Filek, Sydney, Cape Breton, Nova Scotia, Canada.
Guinea Pig	12	—	Laboratory Specimen.
Hamster	18	Golden Hamster	Laboratory Specimen.
	26*	Golden Hamster	L. and S. Miller, Baton Rouge, Louisiana, USA
Mouse	32	House Mouse	Laboratory Specimen (USA).
Gerbil	11	—	Steve Austin, Addington, Surrey
	11	—	Heather James, High Wycombe, Bucks.

* 18 killed by mother

Largest kindle

The largest litter ever recorded was one of 19 kittens (4 stillborn) delivered by Caesarean section to 'Tarawood Antigone', a 4-year-old brown Burmese, on 7 Aug 1970. Her owner, Mrs Valerie Gane of Church Westcote, Kingham, Oxfordshire, said the result was a mis-mating with a half-Siamese. Of the 15 survivors, 14 were males and one female.

The largest live litter (all of which survived) was one of 14 kittens born in December 1974 to a Persian cat named 'Bluebell', owned by Mrs Elenore Dawson of Wellington, Cape Province, South Africa.

Most prolific

A cat named 'Dusty', aged 17, living in Bonham, Texas, USA, gave birth to her 420th kitten on 12 June 1952. A 21-year-old cat 'Tippy' living in Kingston-upon-Hull, Humberside gave birth to her 343rd kitten in June 1933.

Richest and most valuable

Dr William Grier of San Diego, California, USA died in June 1963 leaving his entire estate of $415,000 (*then £148,000*) to his two 15-year-old cats 'Hellcat' and 'Brownie'. When the cats died in 1965 the money went to the George Washington University in Washington, DC. In 1967 Miss Elspeth Sellar of Grafham, Surrey turned down an offer of 2000 guineas (£2100) from an American breeder for her champion copper-eyed white Persian tom 'Coylum Marcus' (b. 28 Mar 1965) who died on 14 Apr 1978.

Best climber

On 28 Feb 1980 a female cat climbed 70 ft *21,3 m* up the sheer pebble-dash outside wall of a five-storey block of flats in Bradford, Yorkshire and took refuge in a roof space. It had been frightened by a dog.

Mousing Champion

The greatest mouser on record was a tabby named 'Mickey', owned by Shepherd & Sons Ltd of Burscough, Lancashire who killed more than 22,000 mice during 23 years with the firm. He died in November 1968.

RABBITS

Largest

The largest breed of domestic rabbit (*Oryctolagus cuniculus*) is the British giant. Adult specimens average 18–20 lb *8,16–9,07 kg* but unconfirmed weights up to 30 lb *13,6 kg* have been reported for bucks. In April 1980 a five month old female French lop weighing 12 kg *26.45 lb* was exhibited at the Reus Fair, NE Spain.

The heaviest recorded wild rabbit (av. weight 3½ lb *1,58 kg*) is one of 6 lb 12 oz *3,06 kg* shot by Mr Monty Forest in the Swinford Estate, Burford, Oxfordshire in February 1976.

Smallest

The smallest breeds of domestic rabbit are the Netherlands dwarf and the Polish, both of which have a maximum British standard weight of 2¼ lb *1,02 kg* at maturity.

Most prolific

The most prolific domestic breeds are the New Zealand white and the Californian. Does produce 5–6 litters a year, each containing 8–12 young (*cf.* five litters and three to seven young for the wild rabbit).

HARES

Largest

In November 1956 a Brown hare (*Lepus europaeus*) weighing 15 lb 1 oz *6,83 kg* was shot near Welford, Northamptonshire. The average adult weight is 8 lb *3,62 kg*.

2. BIRDS (Aves)

Largest *Ratite*

The largest living bird is the North African ostrich (*Struthio camelus camelus*), which is found in reduced numbers south of

GOLDFISH

41 YEARS
'Fred'
Died: Sussex 1980

CAT

34 YEARS
Tabby 'Ma'
Died: Devon 1957

DOG

29 YEARS 5 MONTHS
Queensland 'Heeler' 'Bluey'
Died: Australia 1939

BUDGERIGAR

29 YEARS 2 MONTHS
'Charlie'
Died: London 1977

RABBIT

18 YEARS*
European
Died: 1977

GUINEA PIG

14 YEARS 10½ MONTHS
'Snowball'
Died: Nottinghamshire 1979

GERBIL

7 YEARS 9½ MONTHS
'Squirt'
Died: USA 1977

MOUSE

5 YEARS 11 MONTHS
'Hercules'
Died: Surrey 1976

RAT

5 YEARS 8 MONTHS
Died: USA 1924

Pet longevity

The greatest recorded ages for commonly kept pets

* 18 Years also reported for a doe still living in 1947.

Note: A report of 10 years 2 months for a hamster has been published but details are lacking.

The contrast between largest and smallest living birds. The Bee hummingbird (*Calypte helenae*), shown actual size compared to the eye of an ostrich. The ostrich is 97,000 times more massive.

the Atlas Mountains from Upper Senegal and Niger across to the Sudan and central Ethiopia. Male examples of this flightless or ratite sub-species have been recorded up to 9 ft *2,74 m* in height and 345 lb *156,5 kg* in weight.

Largest *Carinate*
The heaviest flying bird or carinate is the Kori bustard or Paauw (*Otis kori*) of East and South Africa. Weights up to 40 lb *18 kg* have been reliably reported for cock birds shot in South Africa. The Mute swan (*Cygnus olor*), which is resident in Britain, can also reach 40 lb *18 kg* on occasion, and there is a record from Poland of a cob weighing 22,5 kg *49.5 lb* which could not fly. The heaviest bird of prey is the Andean condor (*Vultur gryphus*), adult males averaging 20–25 lb *9,09–11,3 kg*. An unconfirmed weight of 31 lb *14,1 kg* has been claimed for a California condor (*Gymnogyps californianus*) (average weight 20 lb *9 kg*) now preserved in the California Academy of Sciences, Los Angeles.

Largest wing span
The Wandering albatross (*Diomedea exulans*) of the southern oceans has the largest wing span of any living bird, adult males averaging 10 ft 4 in *3,15 m* with wings tightly stretched. The largest recorded specimen was a male measuring 11 ft 11 in *3,63 m* caught by members of the Antarctic research ship USNS *Eltanin* in the Tasman Sea on 18 Sept 1965. The only other bird reliably credited with a wingspread in excess of 11 ft *3,35 m* is the vulture-like Marabou stork (*Leptoptilus crumeniferus*) of Africa. In the 1930s an extreme measurement of 13 ft 4 in *4,06 m* was reported for a male shot in Central Africa, but this species rarely exceeds 9 ft *2,43 m*.

Smallest *World*
The smallest bird in the world is the Bee hummingbird (*Calypte helenae*) of Cuba and the Isle of Pines. Adult males (females are slightly larger) measure 57 mm *2.24 in* in total length, half of

which is taken up by the bill and tail. It weighs 1.6 g *0.056 oz*, which means it is lighter than a Privet hawk-moth (2.4 g *0.084 oz*). The smallest bird of prey is the 35 g *1.23 oz* White-fronted falconet (*Microhierax latifrons*) of NW Borneo which is sparrow-sized.

The smallest sea bird is the Least storm petrel (*Halocyptena microsoma*), which breeds on many of the small islands in the Gulf of California, NW Mexico. Adult specimens average 140 mm *5½ in* in total length.

Smallest *Great Britain*
The smallest regularly-breeding British bird is the Goldcrest (*Regulus regulus*), also known as the Golden crested wren or Kinglet. Adult specimens measure 90 mm *3.5 in* total length and weigh between—3,8 and 4,5 g *0.108* and *0.127 oz*.

Most abundant *Wild*
The most abundant species of wild bird is the Red-billed quelea (*Quelea quelea*) of the drier parts of Africa south of the Sahara with a population estimated at 10,000,000,000 of which a tenth are destroyed each year by pest control units. The most abundant sea bird is probably Wilson's storm-petrel (*Oceanites oceanicus*) of the Antarctic. No population estimates have been published, but the number must run into hundreds of millions. Britain's most abundant sea-bird is the Common guillemot (*Uria aalge*) with an estimated 577,000 breeding pairs in 1969–70.

Most abundant *Domestic*
The most abundant species of domesticated bird is the Chicken, the domesticated form of the wild Red jungle fowl (*Gallus gallus*) of south-east Asia. In 1974 there were believed to be about 4,000,000,000 in the world, or about one chicken for every member of the human race. The fowl stock in Britain was estimated at 130,000,000 in 1972, producing 270,000,000 chicks annually.

Most abundant *Great Britain*
The commonest wild breeding land bird in Great Britain is the wren (*Troglodytes troglodytes*) with an estimated 10 million pairs nesting after a series of mild winters. The Blackbird (*Turdus merula*), Starling (*Sturnus vulgaris*), House Sparrow (*Passer domesticus*) and the Chaffinch (*Fringilla coelebs*) all have a nesting population of about 7 million pairs. It was estimated in 1967 that 250,000 pigeon fanciers owned an average of 40 racing pigeons per loft, making a population of *c.* 10 million in Great Britain.

Rarest *World*
Because of the practical difficulties involved in assessing bird populations in the wild, it is virtually impossible to establish the identity of the world's rarest living bird. The strongest contender, however, must be the Kauai Ooaa (*Moho braccatus*) of Kauai, Hawaiian Islands, of which only a single pair survived in 1979. The total population of the Chatham Island robin-flycatcher (*Petroica traversi*) is now down to 7, and only 8 Japanese crested ibis (*Nipponia nippon*) remain in a government nature reserve on Sado Island off the NW coast of Honshu.

Rarest *Great Britain*
According to the British Ornithologists' Union there are more than 40 species of birds which have been recorded only once in the British Isles—most of them since the end of the Second World War in 1945. That which has not recurred for the longest period is the Black-capped petrel (*Pterodroma hasitata*), of the West Indies. A specimen was caught alive on a heath at Southacre, near Swaffham, Norfolk in March or April 1850. On 28–29 May 1979 an Aleutian tern (*Sterna aleutica*) was sighted on the Farne Islands, Northumberland. This bird breeds on the coasts of Alaska and eastern Siberia, and until then had never been recorded outside the N. Pacific. The most tenuously established British bird is the Snowy owl (*Nyctea scandiaca*). During the period 1969–75 one pair bred regularly on Fetlar, Shetland Isles but no males have been sighted since then.

Fastest flying
The fastest flying bird in level flight is the White-throated spine-tailed swift (*Hirundapus caudacutus*). For details see p. 27.

The bird which presents the hunter with the greatest difficulty is the Red-breasted merganser (*Mergus serrator*). On 29 May 1960 a specimen flushed from the Kukpuk River, Cape Thompson, northern Alaska, USA by a light aircraft recorded an air speed of 80 mph *128 km/h* in level flight for nearly 13 sec before turning aside.

Fastest and slowest wing beat

The fastest recorded wing beat of any bird is that of the Horned sungem *Heliactin cornuta* of tropical South America with a rate of 90 beats a second. Large vultures (family Vulturidae) sometimes exhibit a flapping rate as low as one beat per sec, and condors can cruise 60 miles *96 km* without beating their wings.

Longest lived

The greatest irrefutable age reported for any bird is 72+ years in the case of a male Andean condor (*Vultur gryphus*) named 'Kuzya', which died in Moskovskii Zoologicheskii Park, Moscow, USSR in 1964. This bird had been received as an adult in 1892. The British record is 68+ years in the case of a female European eagle-owl (*Bubo bubo*) which was still alive in 1899. Other records which are regarded as *probably* reliable include 73 years (1818–91) for a Greater sulphur-crested cockatoo (*Cacatua galerita*); 72 years (1797–1869) for an African grey parrot (*Psittacus erithacus*); 70 years (1770–1840) for a Mute swan (*Cygnus olor*) and 69 years for a raven (*Corvus corax*). In 1972 a Southern ostrich (*Sturthio camelus australis*) aged 62 years and 3 months was killed in the Ostrich Abattoir at Oudtshoorn, Cape Province, South Africa. 'Jimmy', a red and green Amazon parrot owned by Mrs Bella Ludford of Liverpool, England was allegedly hatched in captivity on 3 Dec 1870 and lived 104 years in his original brass cage dying on 5 Jan 1975.

Eggs *Largest*

The largest egg produced by any living bird is that of the ostrich (*Struthio camelus*). The average example measures 6–8 in *15–20 cm* in length, 4–6 in *10–15 cm* in diameter and weighs 3.63–3.88 lb *1,65–1,78 kg* (equal to the volume of two dozen hen's eggs). It requires about 40 min for boiling. The shell though 1/16 in *1,5 mm* thick can support the weight of a 20 st *127 kg* man. The largest egg laid by any bird on the British list is that of the Mute swan (*Cygnus olor*), which measures 4.3–4.9 in *109–124 mm* in length and between 2.8 and 3.1 in *71–78,5 mm* in diameter. The weight is 12–13 oz *340–368 g*.

Eggs *Smallest*

The smallest egg laid by any bird is that of the Vervain hummingbird (*Mellisuga minima*) of Jamaica. Two specimens measuring less than 10 mm *0.39 in* in length weighed 0,365 g *0.0128 oz* and 0,375 g *0.0132 oz* respectively (cf 0,5 g *0.176 oz* for the Bee hummingbird). The smallest egg laid by a bird on the British list is that of the Goldcrest (*Regulus regulus*), which measures 12,2–14,5 mm *0.48–0.57 in* in length and between 9,4 and 9,9 mm *0.37* and *0.39 in* in diameter with a weight of 0,6 g *0.021 oz*. Eggs emitted from the oviduct before maturity, known as 'sports', are not reckoned to be of significance in discussion of relative sizes.

Incubation *Longest and shortest*

The longest normal incubation period is that of the Wandering albatross (*Diomedea exulans*), with a normal range of 75–82 days. There is a case of an egg of the Mallee fowl (*Leipoa ocellata*) of Australia taking 90 days to hatch against its normal incubation of 62 days. The shortest incubation period is the 10 days of the Great spotted woodpecker (*Dendrocopus major*) and the Black-billed cuckoo (*Coccyzus erythropthalmus*). The idlest of cock birds include hummingbirds (family Trochilidae), Eider duck (*Somateria mollissima*) and Golden pheasant (*Chrysolophus pictus*) among whom the hen bird does 100 per cent of the incubation, whereas the female Common kiwi (*Apteryx australis*) leaves this entirely to the male for 75–80 days.

Longest flights

The greatest distance covered by a ringed bird during migration is 12,000 miles *19 300 km* by an Arctic tern (*Sterna paradisaea*), which was banded as a nestling on 5 July 1955 in the Kandalaksha Sanctuary on the White Sea coast and was captured alive by a fisherman 8 miles *13 km* south of Fremantle, Western Australia on 16 May 1956.

Highest flying

The highest acceptable altitude recorded for a bird is 27,000 ft *8230 m* for 30 Whooper swans (*Cygnus olor*) flying in from Iceland. They were spotted by an airline pilot over the Outer Hebrides on 9 Dec 1967, and the height was also confirmed by air traffic control in Northern Ireland after the swans had been picked up on radar.

Most airborne

The most aerial of all birds is the Sooty tern (*Sterna fuscata*) which, after leaving the nesting grounds, remains continuously aloft for 3 or 4 years before returning to the breeding grounds. The most aerial land bird is the Common swift (*Apus apus*) which remains 'airborne' for 2–3 years until it is mature enough to breed.

Fastest swimmer

The fastest swimming bird is the Gentoo penguin (*Pygoscelis papua*). In January 1913 a small group were timed at 10 m/sec *22.3 mph* under water near the Bay of Isles, South Georgia. This is a respectable flying speed for some birds. The deepest diving bird is the Emperor penguin (*Aptenodytes forsteri*) of the Antarctic which can reach a depth of 265 m *870 ft* and remain submerged for up to 18 min.

Most acute vision

Birds of prey (Falconiformes) have the keenest eyesight in the avian world, and their visual acuity is at least 8–10 times stronger than that of human vision. The Golden eagle (*Aquila chrysaetos*) can detect an 18 in *46 cm* long hare at a range of 2150 yd *1966 m* (possibly even 2 miles *3,2 km*) in good light and against a contrasting background, and a Peregrine falcon (*Falco peregrinus*) a pigeon at a range of over 3500 ft *1066 m*.

Highest g force

Recent American scientific experiments have revealed that the beak of the Red-headed woodpecker (*Melanerpes erythrocephalus*) hits the bark of a tree with an impact velocity of 1300 mph *2092 km/h*. This means that when the head snaps back the brain is subject to a deceleration of about 1000 g.

Feathers *Longest*

The longest feathers grown by any bird are those of the cock Long-tailed fowl or Onagadori (a strain of *Gallus gallus*) which have been bred in south-western Japan since the mid 17th century. In 1973 a tail covert measuring 10,6 m *34 ft 9½ in* was reported by Masashi Kubota of Kochi, Shikoku. The tail feathers of the flying Reeve's pheasant (*Syrmaticus reevesi*) of north and west China can exceed 8 ft *2,43 m*.

Feathers *Most*

In a series of 'feather counts' on various species of bird a Whistling swan (*Cygnus columbianus*) was found to have 25,216 feathers, 20,177 of which were on the head and neck. The ruby-throated hummingbird (*Archilochus colubris*) has only 940, although hummingbirds have more feathers per area of body surface than any other living bird.

Earliest and latest cuckoo

It is unlikely that the Cuckoo (*Cuculus canorus*) has ever been *heard and seen* in Britain earlier than 2 Mar, on which date one was observed under acceptable conditions by Mr William A. Haynes of Trinder Road, Wantage, Oxfordshire in 1972. The two latest dates are 16 Dec 1912 at Anstey's Cove, Torquay, Devon and 26 Dec 1897 or 1898 in Cheshire.

Champion bird-spotter

The world's leading bird-spotter is George Stuart Keith (b. 1932) (GB) of Ramsey, New Jersey, who is resident ornithologist in the American Museum of Natural History, New York. Since 1947 he has logged 5450 of the 8733 known species (rounded up to the nearest 50).

Nests, *Largest*

The largest bird's nest on record is one 9½ ft *2,9 m* wide and 20 ft *6 m* deep built by a pair of Bald eagles (*Haliaeetus leucocephalus*) and possibly their successors near St Petersburg, Florida, USA reported in 1963 and estimated to weigh more than 2 tons/*tonnes*. The Golden eagle (*Aquila chrysaetos*) also constructs huge nests, and one 15 ft *4,57 m* deep was reported from

The male African grey parrot, 'Prudle' which was the world's most talkative bird, owned by Lyn Logue of London.

Scotland in 1954. It had been in use for 45 years. The incubation mounds built by the Mallee fowl (*Leipoa ocellata*) of Australia are much larger, having been measured up to 15 ft *4,57 m* in height and 35 ft *10,6 m* across, and it has been calculated that the nest site may involve the mounding of 300 yd³ *289 m³* of matter weighing 300 tonnes *295 tons*.

DOMESTICATED BIRDS

Chicken *Heaviest*

The heaviest breed of chicken is one called the White Sully developed by Mr Grant Sullens of West Point, California, USA over a period of 7 years. One monstrous rooster named 'Weirdo' reportedly weighed 22 lb *10 kg* in January 1973, and was so ferocious that he had already killed two cats and crippled a dog which came too close. The heaviest British breed is the Dorking, with roosters weighing up to 14 lb *6,36 kg*.

Chicken flying *for distance*

The record distance flown by a chicken is 310 ft 6 in *94,64 m* by *Shorisha* (means champion) owned by Morimitzu Meura at Hammatzu, Japan on 8 Mar 1981. Hens are better fliers than cocks.

Turkey *Heaviest*

The greatest dressed weight recorded for a turkey (*Meleagris gallopavo*) is 78 lb 11¼ oz *35,69 kg* for a stag reared by Leacroft Turkeys Ltd of Barnwell, Northants. It won the annual 'heaviest turkey' competition held in London on 8 Dec 1980. Turkeys were introduced into Britain *via* Spain from Mexico in 1549.

Most expensive

The highest price reached at auction (auctioneer Bernard Cribbins) for a turkey was the £2200 paid by Peter Lane, managing director of W. Fenn, Covent Garden poulterers for the 78 lb 11¼ oz *35,69 kg* stag (see above) at The Savoy Hotel, London on 8 Dec 1980.

Longest lived

The longest lived domesticated bird (excluding the ostrich) is the domestic goose (*Anser anser domesticus*) which normally lives about 25 years. On 16 Dec 1976 a gander named 'George' owned by Mrs Florence Hull of Thornton, Lancashire, died aged 49 years 8 months. He was hatched out in April 1927. The longest lived small cagebird is the canary (*Serinus canaria*). The oldest example on record was a 34-year-old cock bird named 'Joey' owned by Mrs K. Ross of Hull. The bird was purchased in Calabar, Nigeria in 1941 and died on 8 Apr 1975. The oldest budgerigar (*Melopsittacus undulatus*) on record was a hen bird named 'Charlie' owned by Miss J. Dinsey of Stonebridge, London, which lived for 29 years 2 months. She died on 20 June 1977.

Most talkative

The world's most talkative bird is a male African grey parrot (*Psittacus erythacus*) named 'Prudle', owned by Mrs Lyn Logue of Golders Green, London, which won the 'Best talking parrot-like bird' title at the National Cage and Aviary Bird Show held in London each December for 12 consecutive years (1965–76). Prudle, who has a vocabulary of nearly 1000 words, was taken from a nest in a tree about to be felled at Jinja, Uganda in 1958. He retired undefeated in 1977.

3. REPTILES *(Reptilia)*

(Crocodiles, snakes, turtles, tortoises and lizards.)

Largest and heaviest

The largest reptile in the world is the Estuarine or Salt-water crocodile (*Crocodylus porosus*) of south-east Asia, northern Australia, New Guinea, the Malay archipelago and the Solomon Islands. Adult males average 14–16 ft *4,2–4,8 m* in length and scale about 900–1150 lb *408–520 kg*. In 1823 a notorious man-eater allegedly 27 ft *8,23 m* in length and weighing an estimated 2 tons/*tonnes* was shot at Jala Jala on Luzon Island in the Philippines after terrorising the neighbourhood for many years, but the dimensions of the skull (preserved in the Museum of Comparative Zoology at Harvard University, Cambridge, Massachusetts, USA) suggest this crocodile must have measured about 20 ft *6,09 m*. The holder of the 'official' record is a 20 ft 4 in *6,20 m* male which drowned after getting entangled in a fisherman's net at Obo on the Fly River, Papua New Guinea in 1979. In July 1957 an unconfirmed length of 28 ft 4 in *8,63 m* was reported for an Estuarine crocodile shot by Mrs Kris Pawlowski on MacArthur Bank in the Norman River, north-western Queensland, Australia.

Smallest

The smallest known species of reptile is believed to be *Sphaerodactylus parthenopion*, a tiny gecko found only on the island of Virgin Gorda, one of the British Virgin Islands, in the West Indies. It is known only from 15 specimens, including some gravid females found between 10 and 16 Aug 1964. The three largest females measured 18 mm *0.71 in* from snout to vent, with a tail of approximately the same length. It is possible that another gecko, *Sphaerodactylus elasmorhynchus*, may be even smaller. The only known specimen was an apparently mature female with a snout–vent length of 17 mm *0.67 in* and a tail the same measurement found on 15 March 1966 among the roots of a tree in the western part of the Massif de la Hotte in Haiti. A species of dwarf chameleon, *Evoluticauda tuberculata* found in Madagascar, and known only from a single specimen, has a snout–vent length of 18 mm *0.71 in* and a tail length of 14 mm *0.55 in*. Chameleons, however, are more bulky than geckos, and it is not yet known if this specimen was fully grown.

The smallest reptile found in Britain is the Viviparous or Common lizard (*Lacerta vivipara*). Adult specimens have an overall length of 108–178 mm *4.25–7 in*.

Fastest

The highest speed measured for any reptile on land is 18 mph *29 km/h* for a Six-lined racerunner (*Cnemidophorus sexlineatus*) pursued by a car near McCormick, South Carolina, USA in 1941. The highest speed claimed for any reptile in water is 22 mph *35 km/h* by a frightened Pacific leatherback turtle (see below).

Lizards *Largest*

The largest of all lizards is the Komodo monitor or Ora (*Varanus komodoensis*), a dragonlike reptile found on the Indonesian islands of Komodo, Rintja, Padar and Flores. Adult males average 8 ft *2,43 m* in length and weigh 175–200 lb *79–91 kg*. Lengths up to 23 ft *7 m* (*sic*) have been quoted for this species, but the largest specimen to be accurately measured was a male presented to an American zoologist in 1928 by the Sultan of Bima which taped 3,05 m *10 ft 0.8 in*. In 1937 this animal was put on display in St Louis Zoological Gardens, Missouri, USA for a short period. It then measured 10 ft 2 in *3,10 m* in length and weighed 365 lb *166 kg*. The longest lizard in the world is the

The Estuarine or Salt-water crocodile, the largest reptile in the world. The diet of this particular one did not exclude outboard motors (see p. 40). *(Keystone Press)*

slender Salvadori dragon (*Varanus salvadori*) of New Guinea which has been reliably measured up to 15 ft 7 in *4.75 m* long.

Lizards *Oldest*
The greatest age recorded for a lizard is more than 54 years for a male Slow worm (*Anguis fragilis*) kept in the Zoological Museum in Copenhagen, Denmark from 1892 until 1946.

Chelonians *Largest*
The largest living chelonian is the Pacific leatherback turtle (*Dermochelys coriacea schlegelii*). The average adult measures 6–7 ft *1,83–2,13 m* in overall length (length of carapace 4–5 ft *122–152 cm*) and weighs up to 1000 lb *453 kg*. The greatest weight reliably recorded is 1908 lb *865 kg* for a male captured off Monterey, California, USA on 29 Aug 1961 measuring 8 ft 4 in *2,54 m* overall. The largest chelonian found in British waters is the Atlantic leatherback turtle (*Dermochelys coriacea coriacea*). A male which drowned off Crail, Fifeshire, Scotland measured 6 ft 4 in *1,93 m* in total length and weighed 772 lb *350 kg*.

The largest living tortoise is *Geochelone (Testudo) gigantea* of the Indian Ocean islands of Aldabra, Mauritius, and the Seychelles (introduced 1874). Adult males in the wild sometimes exceed 450 lb *200 kg* in weight but much heavier captive specimens have been recorded. One male preserved in the Rothschild Museum at Tring, Herts., weighed 593 lb *269 kg* when alive.

Chelonians *Longest lived*
Tortoises are the longest lived of all vertebrates. (See page 26.) Other reliable records over 100 years include a Common box tortoise (*Testudo carolina*) of 138 years and a European pond-tortoise (*Emys orbicularis*) of 120+ years. The greatest proven age of a continuously observed tortoise is 116+ years for a Mediterranean spur-thighed tortoise (*Testudo graeca*) which died in Paignton Zoo, Devon in 1957.

Chelonians *Slowest moving*
In a recent 'speed' test carried out in the Seychelles a male giant tortoise (*Geochelone gigantea*) could only cover 5 yd *4,57 m* in 43.5 sec (0.23 mph *0,37 km/h*) despite the enticement of a female tortoise. The National Tortoise Championship record is 18 ft *5,48 m* up a 1 : 12 gradient in 43.7 sec by 'Charlie' at Tickhill, South Yorkshire on 2 July 1977.

SNAKES
Longest *World*
The longest of all snakes (average adult length) is the Reticulated python (*Python reticulatus*) of south-east Asia, Indonesia and the Philippines which regularly exceeds 20 ft *6 m*. In 1912 a specimen measuring exactly 10 m *32 ft 9½ in* was shot near a mining camp on the north coast of Celebes in the Malay Archipelago. Lengths of 37½ ft *11,43 m*, 42 ft *12,8 m* and even 45 ft *13,7 m* have been claimed for the Anaconda (*Eunectes murinus*) of tropical South America, but these extreme measurements were probably based on *stretched* skins. The greatest authenticated length recorded for an anaconda is 27 ft 9 in *8,45 m* for a female killed in Brazil in *c.* 1960.

Longest *In captivity*
The longest (and heaviest) snake ever held in captivity was a female reticulated python (*Python reticulatus*) named 'Colossus' who died in Highland Park Zoo, Pennsylvania, USA on 15 Apr 1963. She measured 28 ft 6 in *8,68 m* in length, and scaled 320 lb *145 kg* at her heaviest. Another female reticulated python named 'Cassius' owned by Mr. Adrian Nyoka of Knaresborough Zoo, North Yorkshire measured about 25 ft 6 in *7,77 m* at the time of her death on 3 Apr 1980. She yielded a 29 ft *8,84 m* skin.

Longest *British*
The longest snake found in Britain is the Grass snake (*Natrix natrix*), which is found throughout southern England, parts of Wales and in Dumfries and Galloway, Scotland. Adult males average 660 mm *26 in* in length and adult females 760 mm *29.92 in*. The longest accurately measured specimen was probably a female killed in South Wales in 1887 which measured 1775 mm *5 ft 10 in*.

Shortest
The shortest known snake is the Thread snake *Leptotyphlops bilineata*, which is found on the islands of Martinique, Barbados and St Lucia in the West Indies. It has a maximum recorded length of 11,9 cm *4.7 in*. The shortest venomous snake is the Striped dwarf garter snake (*Elaps dorsalis*) of South Africa, adults average 6 in *152 mm* in length.

Heaviest
The heaviest snake is the Anaconda (*Eunectes murinus*) which is nearly twice as heavy as a Reticulated python (*Python reticulatus*) of the same length. The specimen shot in Brazil in *c.* 1960 (see Snakes longest world, above) was not weighed, but as it had a maximum bodily girth of 44 in *111 cm* it must have scaled nearly 500 lb *227 kg*. The heaviest venomous snake is the Eastern

41

diamond-back rattlesnake (*Crotalus adamanteus*) of the south-eastern United States. One specimen measuring 7 ft 9 in *2,36 m* in length weighed 34 lb *15 kg*. Less reliable lengths up to 8 ft 9 in *2,66 m* and weights up to 40 lb *18 kg* have been reported. In February 1973 a posthumous weight of 28 lb *12,75 kg* was reported for a 14 ft 5 in *4,39 m* long King cobra (*Ophiophagus hannah*) at New York Zoological Park (Bronx Zoo).

Venomous *Longest and Shortest*

The longest venomous snake in the world is the King cobra (*Ophiophagus hannah*), also called the Hamadryad, of south-east Asia and the Philippines. A specimen collected near Port Dickson in the state of Negri Sembilan, Malaya in April 1937 grew to 18 ft 9 in *5,71 m* in London Zoo. It was destroyed at the outbreak of war in 1939.

Oldest

The greatest irrefutable age recorded for a snake is 40 years 3 months and 14 days for a male Common boa (*Boa constrictor constrictor*) named 'Popeye' at Philadelphia Zoological Garden, Pennsylvania, USA, who was euthanased on 15 Apr 1977 because of medical problems associated with advanced age. He was purchased from a London dealer in December 1936.

Fastest moving

The fastest moving land snake is probably the slender Black mamba (*Dendroaspis polylepis*). On 23 Apr 1906 an angry Black mamba was timed at a speed of 7 mph *11 km/h* over a measured distance of 47 yd *43 m* near Mbuyuni on the Serengeti Plains, Tanzania. Stories that Black mambas can overtake galloping horses (maximum speed 43.26 mph *69,62 km/h*) are wild exaggerations, though a speed of 15 mph *24 km/h* may be possible for short bursts over level ground. The British grass snake (*Natrix natrix*) has a maximum speed of 4.2 mph *6,8 km/h*.

Most venomous

The world's most venomous snake is the sea snake *Hydrophis belcheri* which has a venom one hundred times as toxic as that of the Australian taipan (*Oxyuranus scutellatus*). The snake abounds round Ashmore Reef in the Timor Sea, off the coast of North West Australia. The most venomous land snake is the Small scaled or Fierce snake (*Parademansia microlepidotus*) of south-western Queensland and north-eastern South Australia which has a venom nine times as toxic as that of the Tiger snake (*Notechis scutatus*) of South Australia and Tasmania. One specimen yielded 110 mg *0,00385 oz* after milking, a quantity sufficient to kill at least 125,000 mice. Until 1976 this 2 m 6 ft 6¾ in long snake was regarded as a western form of the taipan, but its venom differs significantly from the latter. It is estimated that between 30,000 and 40,000 people (excluding Chinese and Russians) die from snakebite each year, 75 per cent of them in densely populated India. Burma has the highest mortality rate with 15.4 deaths per 100,000 population per annum.

Most venomous *Britain*

The only venomous snake in Britain is the adder (*Vipera berus*). Since 1890 ten people have died after being bitten by this snake, including six children. The most recently recorded death was on 1 July 1975 when a 5-year-old was bitten at Callander, Central, Scotland and died 44 hr later. The longest recorded specimen was a female measuring 43½ in *110,5 cm* which was killed by Graham Perkins of Paradise Farm, Pontrilas, Hereford and Worcester in August 1977.

Longest fangs

The longest fangs of any snake are those of the Gaboon viper (*Bitis gabonica*) of tropical Africa. In a 6 ft *1,83 m* long specimen they measured 50 mm *1.96 in*. On 12 Feb 1963 a Gaboon viper bit itself to death in the Philadelphia Zoological Gardens, Philadelphia, Pennsylvania, USA. Keepers found the dead snake with its fangs deeply embedded in its own back.

4. AMPHIBIANS *(Amphibia)*

Largest *World*

The largest species of amphibian is the Chinese giant salamander (*Andrias davidianus*), which lives in the cold mountain streams and marshy areas of north-eastern, central and southern China. The average adult measures 3 ft 9 in *1,14 m* in total length and weighs 55–66 lb *25–30 kg*. One huge individual collected in Kweichow (Guizhou) Province in southern China in *c.*1923 measured 5 ft *1,52 m* in total length and weighed nearly 100 lb *45 kg*. The much rarer Japanese giant salamander (*Andrias japonicus*) is slightly smaller, but one captive specimen weighed 40 kg *88 lb* when alive and 45 kg *100 lb* after death, the body having absorbed water from the aquarium.

Largest *Britain*

The heaviest British amphibian is the Common toad (*Bufo bufo*) of which a female has been weighed at 114 g *4 oz*.

The longest is the Warty or Great crested newt (*Triturus cristatus*). One female specimen collected at Hampton, Greater London measured 162 mm *6.37 in* in total length.

Smallest *World*

The smallest species of amphibian is believed to be the arrow-poison frog *Sminthillus limbatus*, found only in Cuba. Adult specimens have a snout–vent length of 8,5–12,4 mm *0.44–0.48 in*.

Smallest *Britain*

The smallest amphibian found in Britain is the Palmate newt (*Triturus helveticus*). Adult specimens measure 7,5–9,2 cm *2.95–3.62 in* in total length and weigh up to 2,39 g *0.083 oz*. The Natterjack or Running toad (*Bufo calamita*) has a maximum snout–vent length of only 8 cm *3.14 in*. but it is a bulkier animal.

Longest lived

The greatest authentic age recorded for an amphibian is about 55 years for a male Japanese giant salamander (*Megalobatrachus japonicus*) which died in the aquarium at Amsterdam Zoological Gardens on 3 June 1881. It was brought to Holland in 1829, at which time it was estimated to be three years old.

Highest and lowest

The greatest altitude at which an amphibian has been found is 8000 m *26,246 ft* for a Common toad (*Bufo vulgaris*) collected in the Himalayas. This species has also been found at a depth of 340 m *1115 ft* in a coal mine.

Most poisonous

The most active known poison is the batrachotoxin derived from the skin secretions of the Two-toned arrow-poison frog or Kokoi (*Phyllobates bicolor*), found in north-western Colombia, South America. Only about 1/100,000th of a gramme *0.0000004 oz* is sufficient to kill a man.

Newt *Largest world*

The largest newt in the world is the Pleurodele or Ribbed newt (*Pleurodeles waltl*), which is found in Morocco and on the Iberian Peninsula. Specimens measuring up to 40 cm *15.74 in* in total length and weighing over 1 lb *450 g* have been reliably reported.

Newt *Smallest world*

The smallest newt in the world is believed to be the Striped newt (*Notophthalmus perstriatus*) of the south-eastern United States. Adult specimens average 51 mm *2.01 in* in total length.

Frog *Largest World*

The largest known frog is the rare Goliath frog (*Rana goliath*) of Cameroun and Equatorial Guinea. A female weighing 3306 g *7 lb 4.5 oz* was caught in the River Mbia, Equatorial Guinea on 23 Aug 1960. It had a snout–vent length of 34 cm *13.38 in* and measured 81,5 cm *32.08 in* overall with legs extended. In December 1960 another giant frog known locally as 'agak' or 'carn-pnag' and said to measure 12–15 in *30–38 cm* snout to vent and weigh over 6 lb *2,7 kg* was reportedly discovered in central New Guinea, but further information is lacking. In 1969 a new species of giant frog was discovered in Sumatra.

Frog *Largest Britain*

The largest frog found in Britain is the *introduced* Marsh frog (*Rana r. ridibunda*). Adult males have been measured up to 96 mm *3.77 in* snout to vent, and adult females up to 133 mm *5.25 in*, the weight ranging from 60 to 95 g *1.7–3 oz*.

Longest jump

The record for three consecutive leaps is 10,3 m *33 ft 5½ in* by a female South African sharp-nosed frog (*Rana oxyrhyncha*) named 'Santjie' at a frog Derby held at Lurula Natal Spa, Paulpietersburg, Natal on 21 May 1977. At the annual Calaveras County Jumping Frog Jubilee at Angels Camp, California, USA in 1975 another specimen 'Ex Lax' made a *single* leap of 17 ft 6¾ in *5,35 m* for its owner Bill Moniz.

Tree frog *Largest*

The largest species of tree frog is *Hyla vasta*, found only on the island of Hispaniola (Haiti and the Dominican Republic) in the West Indies. The average snout–vent length is about 9 cm *3.54 in* but a female collected from the San Juan River, Dominican Republic, in March 1928 measured 14,3 cm *5.63 in*.

Tree frog *Smallest*

The smallest tree frog in the world is the Least tree frog (*Hyla ocularis*), found in the south-eastern United States. It has a maximum snout–vent length of 15,8 mm *0.62 in*.

Toad *Largest World*

The most massive toad in the world is probably the Marine toad (*Bufo marinus*) of tropical South America. An enormous female collected on 24 Nov 1965 at Miraflores Vaupes, Colombia and later exhibited in the Reptile House at Bronx Zoo, New York City, USA had a snout–vent length of 23,8 cm *9.37 in* and weighed 1302 g *2 lb 11¼ oz* at the time of its death in 1967.

Toad *Largest Britain*

The largest toad and heaviest amphibian found in Britain is the Common toad (*Bufo bufo*). Females of up to 102 mm *3.94 in* in length and 114 g *3.2 oz* have been recorded.

Toad *Smallest World*

The smallest toad in the world is the sub-species *Bufo taitanus beiranus*, first discovered in *c.* 1906 near Beira, Mozambique, East Africa. Adult specimens have a maximum recorded snout–vent length of 24 mm *0.94 in*.

Salamander *Smallest*

The smallest species of salamander is the Pygmy salamander (*Desmognathus wrighti*), which is found only in Tennessee, North Carolina and Virginia, USA. Adult specimens measure 37–50,8 mm *1.45–2.0 in* in total length.

---

5. FISHES *(Pisces, Bradyodonti, Selachii, Marsipoli)*

Largest marine *World*

The largest fish in the world is the rare plankton-feeding Whale shark (*Rhiniodon typus*), which is found in the warmer areas of the Atlantic, Pacific and Indian Oceans. It is not, however, the largest marine animal, since it is smaller than the larger species of whales (mammals). In 1919 a Whale shark measuring 10 *wa* (= 60 ft 9 in, *18,5 m*) in length and weighing an estimated 42.4 tons *43 tonnes* was trapped in a bamboo stake-trap at Koh Chik, in the Gulf of Siam. The largest carnivorous fish (excluding plankton eaters) is the comparatively rare Great white shark (*Carcharodon charcharias*), also called the 'Maneater', which ranges from the tropics to temperate zone waters. In June 1930 a specimen measuring 37 ft *11,27 m* in length was reportedly trapped in a herring weir at White Head Island, New Brunswick, Canada but may have been a wrongly identified Basking shark (see below). In June 1978 a great white shark measuring 29 ft 6 in *9 m* in length was killed after a fierce battle by fishermen at San Miguel in the Azores. It weighed more than 10,000 lb *4536 kg*.

The longest of the bony or 'true' fishes (Pisces) is the Russian sturgeon (*Acipenser huso*), also called the Beluga, which is found in the temperate areas of the Adriatic, Black and Caspian Seas but enters large rivers like the Volga and the Danube for spawning. Lengths up to 8 m *26 ft 3 in* have been reliably reported, and a gravid female taken in the estuary of the Volga in 1827 weighed 1474,2 kg *1.44 tons*. The heaviest bony fish in the world is the Ocean sunfish (*Mola mola*), which is found in all tropical, sub-tropical and temperate waters. On 18 Sept 1908 a huge specimen was accidentally struck by the SS *Fiona* off Bird Island about 40 miles *65 km* from Sydney, New South Wales, Australia and towed to Port Jackson. It measured 14 ft *4,26 m* between the anal and dorsal fins and weighed 2.24 tons *2,28 tonnes*.

Britain

The largest fish ever recorded in the waters of the British Isles was a 36 ft 6 in *11,12 m* Basking shark (*Cetorhinus maximus*) washed ashore at Brighton, East Sussex in 1806. It weighed an estimated 8 tons/*tonnes*. The largest bony fish found in British waters is the Ocean sunfish (*Mola mola*). A specimen weighing 800 lb *363 kg* stranded near Montrose, Scotland on 14 Dec 1960 was sent to the Marine Research Institute in Aberdeen.

Largest freshwater *World*

The largest fish which spends its whole life in fresh or brackish water is the rare Pa beuk or Pla buk (*Pangasianodon gigas*), a giant catfish, which is found in the deep waters of the Mekong River of Laos and Thailand. Adult males average 8 ft *2,43 m* in length and weigh about 360 lb *163 kg*. This size was exceeded by the European catfish or Wels (*Silurus glanis*) in earlier times (in the 19th century lengths up to 15 ft *4,57 m* and weights up to 720 lb *336,3 kg* were reported for Russian specimens), but today anything over 6 ft *1,83 m* and 200 lb *91 kg* is considered large. The Arapaima (*Arapaima glanis*), also called the Pirarucu, found in the Amazon and other South American rivers and often claimed to be the largest freshwater fish, averages 6½ ft *2 m* and 150 lb *68 kg*. The largest 'authentically recorded' measured 8 ft 1½ in *2,48 m* in length and weighed 325 lb *147 kg*. It was caught in the Rio Negro, Brazil in 1836. In September 1978, a Nile perch (*Lates niloticus*) weighing 416 lb *188,6 kg* was netted in the eastern part of Lake Victoria, Kenya.

Largest freshwater *Britain*

The largest fish ever caught in a British river was a Common sturgeon (*Acipenser sturio*) weighing 507½ lb *230 kg* and measuring 9 ft *2,74 m*, which was accidentally netted in the Severn at Lydney, Gloucestershire on 1 June 1937. Larger specimens have been taken at sea—notably one weighing 700 lb *317 kg* and 10 ft 5 in *3,18 m* long netted by the trawler *Ben Urie* off Orkney and landed at Aberdeen on 18 Oct 1956.

Smallest Marine

The smallest recorded marine fishes are the Marshall Islands goby (*Eviota zonura*) measuring 12–16 mm *0.47–0.63 in* and *Schindleria praematurus* from Samoa, measuring 12–19 mm *0.47–0.74 in*, both in the Pacific Ocean. Mature specimens of the latter fish, which was not described until 1940, have been known to weigh only 2 mg, equivalent to 17,750 to the oz—the lightest of all vertebrates and the smallest catch possible for any fisherman. The smallest British marine fish is the goby *Lebetus orca*, which grows to a length of 39 mm *1.53 in*. It has been recorded off south-west Cornwall and in the Irish Sea. The smallest known shark is the Long-faced dwarf shark (*Squaliolus laticaudus*) of the western Pacific. Adult specimens measure about 110 mm *4.33 in* in length.

Smallest Freshwater

The shortest known fish, and the shortest of all vertebrates, is the Dwarf pygmy goby (*Pandaka pygmaea*), a colourless and nearly transparent fish found in the streams and lakes of Luzon in the Philippines. Adult males measure only 7,5–9,9 mm *0.28–0.38 in* in length and weigh 4–5 mg *0.00014–0.00017 oz*.

Fastest

The cosmopolitan sailfish (*Istiophorus platypterus*) is generally considered to be the fastest species of fish, although the practical difficulties of measurement make data extremely difficult to secure. A figure of 68.1 mph *109,7 km/h* (100 yd *91 m* in 3 sec) has been cited for one off Florida, USA. The swordfish (*Xiphias gladius*) has also been credited with very high speeds, but the evidence is based mainly on bills that have been found deeply embedded in ships' timbers. A speed of 50 knots (57.6 mph *92,7 km/h*) has been calculated from a penetration of 22 in *56 cm* by a bill into a piece of timber, but 30–35 knots (35–40 mph *56–64 km/h*) is the most conceded by some experts. Speeds in excess of 35 knots (40 mph *64 km/h*) have also been attributed to the

Marlin (*Tetrapturus* sp.), the Wahoo (*Acanthocybium solandri*), the Great blue shark (*Prionace glauca*) and the Bonefish (*Albula vulpes*), and the Bluefin tuna (*Tunnus thynnus*) has been scientifically clocked at 43.4 mph *69,8 km/h* in a 20 sec dash. The Four-winged flying fish (*Cypselurus heterururs*) may also exceed 40 mph *64 km/h* during its rapid rush to the surface before take-off (the average speed in the air is about 35 mph *56 km/h*). Record flights of 90 sec, 36 ft *11 m* in altitude and 1110 m *3640 ft* in length have been recorded in the tropical Altantic.

Longest lived
Aquaria are of too recent origin to be able to establish with certainty which species of fish can be regarded as being the longest lived. Early indications are, however, that it is the Lake sturgeon (*Acipenser fulvescens*) of North America. In one study of the growth rings (annuli) of 966 specimens caught in the Lake Winnebago region, Wisconsin, USA between 1951 and 1954 the oldest sturgeon was found to be a male (length 2,01 m *6 ft 7 in*) which gave a reading of 82 years and was still growing. In July 1974 a growth ring count of 228 years (*sic*) was reported for a female Koi fish, a form of fancy carp, named 'Hanako' living in a pond in Higashi Shirakawa, Gifu Prefecture, Japan, but the greatest authoritatively accepted age for this species is 'more than 50 years'.

In 1948 the death was reported of an 88-year-old female European eel (*Anguilla anguilla*) named 'Putte' in the aquarium at Halsingborg Museum, southern Sweden. She was allegedly born in the Sargasso Sea, North Atlantic in 1860, and was caught in a river as a three-year-old elver.

Oldest goldfish
Goldfish (*Carassius auratus*) have been reported to live for over 40 years in China. The British record is held by a specimen named 'Fred' owned by Mr A. R. Wilson of Worthing, Sussex, which died on 1 Aug 1980, aged 41 years.

Shortest lived
The shortest-lived fishes are probably certain species of the sub-order Cyprinodontei (killifish) found in Africa and South America which normally live about eight months in the wild state.

Most Abundant
The most abundant species of fish in the world is probably the 3 in *76 mm* long deep-sea bristlemouth *Cyclothone elongata* which has a worldwide distribution.

Deepest
The greatest depth from which a fish has been recovered is 8300 m *27,230 ft* in the Puerto Rico Trench (27,488 ft *8366 m*) in the Atlantic by Dr Gilbert L. Voss of the US research vessel *John Elliott* who took a 6½ in *16,5 cm* long *Bassogigas profundissimus* in April 1970. It was only the fifth such brotulid ever caught. Dr Jacques Picard and Lieutenant Don Walsh, US Navy, reported they saw a sole-like fish about 1 ft *33 cm* long (tentatively identified as *Chascanopsetta lugubris*) from the bathyscaphe *Trieste* at a depth of 35,802 ft *10 912 m* in the Challenger Deep (Marianas Trench) in the western Pacific on 24 Jan 1960. This sighting, however, has been questioned by some authorities, who still regard the brotulids of the genus *Bassogigas* as the deepest-living vertebrates.

Most and least eggs
The Ocean sunfish (*Mola mola*) produces up to 300,000,000 eggs, each of them measuring about 0.05 in *1,3 mm* in diameter. The egg yield of the tooth carp *Jordanella floridae* of Florida, USA is only *c.* 20 over a period of several days.

Most Valuable
Benchana, a Japanese ranchu or lion-head goldfish, winner of the Japanese, British and North American triple crown was valued in July 1980 at $10,000 (*then £4250*).

Most venomous
The most venomous fish in the world are the Stonefish (family Synanceidae) of the tropical waters of the Indo-Pacific. Direct contact with the spines of their fins, which contain a strong neurotoxic poison, often proves fatal.

Most electric
The most powerful electric fish is the Electric eel (*Electrophorus electricus*), which is found in the rivers of Brazil, Colombia, Venezuela and Peru. An average sized specimen can discharge 400 volts at 1 ampere, but measurements up to 650 volts have been recorded.

River Thames
The first salmon caught in the Thames since June 1833 was taken at West Thurrock Power Station, Essex in November 1974 and weighed 8 lb 4½ oz *3,757 kg*.

6. STARFISHES *(Asteroidea)*

Largest
The largest of the 1600 known species of starfish in terms of total arm span is the very fragile brisingid *Midgardia xandaros*. A specimen collected by the Texas A & M University research vessel *Alaminos* in the southern part of the Gulf of Mexico in the late summer of 1968, measured 1380 mm *54.33 in* tip to tip, but the diameter of its disc was only 26 mm *1.02 in*. Its dry weight was 70 g *2.46 oz*. The heaviest species of starfish is the five-armed *Thromidia catalai* of the Western Pacific. One specimen collected off Ilot Amedee, New Caledonia on 14 Sept 1969 and later deposited in Noumea Aquarium weighed an estimated 6 kg *13.2 lb* (total arm span 630 mm *24.8 in*). The largest starfish found in British waters is the Spiny starfish (*Marthasterias glacialis*). In January 1979 Jonathon MacNeil of the Isle of Barra, Western Isles, Scotland found a specimen on the beach which originally measured 30 in *76,2 cm* from arm tip to arm tip.

Smallest
The smallest known starfish is *Marginaster capreenis*, found deep in the Mediterranean, which is not known to exceed 20 mm *0.78 in* in diameter. The smallest starfish found in British waters is the Cushion starfish (*Asterina gibbosa*) which measures up to *c.* 60 mm *2.36 in* in diameter but is usually *c.* 25 mm *1 in* across.

Deepest
The greatest depth from which a starfish has been recovered is 7584 m *24,881 ft* for a specimen of *Porcellanaster ivanovi* collected by the USSR research ship *Vityaz* in the Marianas Trench, in the West Pacific *c.* 1962.

7. ARACHNIDS *(Arachnida)*

SPIDERS (order Araneae)
Largest *World*
The world's largest known spider is the bird-eating spider *Theraphosa blondi* of northern South America. A male specimen with a leg span of 10 in *25 cm* when fully extended and a body length of 3½ in *8,9 cm* was collected at Montagne la Gabrielle, French Guiana in April 1925. It weighed nearly 2 oz *56 g*. The heaviest spider ever recorded was a female 'tarantula' of the long-haired species *Lasiodora klugi* collected at Manaos, Brazil in 1945. It measured 9½ in *241 mm* across the legs and weighed almost 3 oz *85 g*.

Largest *Britain*
Of the 617 known British species of spider covering an estimated population of over 500,000,000,000,000, the Cardinal spider (*Tegenaria parietina*) has the greatest leg span. In 1974 one spanning 5.3 in *13,4 cm* was trapped in a house in Wokingham, Berkshire but later escaped. This spider is found only in southern England. The well-known 'Daddy Longlegs' spider (*Pholcus phalangioides*) rarely exceeds 3 in *75 mm* in leg span, but one outsized specimen collected in England measured 6 in *15,2 cm* across. The heaviest spider found in Britain is the orb weaver (*Araneus quadratus*) (formerly called *Araneus reaumuri*). A female, not of extreme size, collected in October 1943 weighed 1174 g *0.041 oz* and measured 15 mm *0.58 in* in body length.

Smallest *World*
The smallest known spider is *Patu marplesi* (family Symphytognathidae) of Western Samoa. The type specimen (male) found in

moss at *c*. 2000 ft *610 m* altitude near Malolelei, Upolu in January 1956 measure 0,43 mm *0.016 in* overall—or half the size of this full stop . The smallest spider found in Britain is the money spider *Glyphesis cottonae*, which is confined to a swamp near Beaulieu Road Station, New Forest, Hampshire and Thursley Common, Surrey. Adult specimens of both sexes have a body length of 1 mm *0.039 in*.

Rarest
The most elusive of all spiders are the rare trapdoor spiders of the genus *Liphistius*, which are found in south-east Asia. The most elusive spiders in Britain are the four species which are known only from the type specimen. These are the jumping spiders *Salticus mutabilis* (1 male Bloxworth, Dorset, 1860) and *Heliophanus melinus* (1 female Bloxworth, 1870); the crab spider *Philodromus buxi* (1 female Bloxworth pre-1879); and the cobweb spider *Robertus insignis* (1 male Norwich, 1906).

Fastest
The highest speed recorded for a spider on a level surface is 1.73 ft/sec *53 cm/sec* (1.17 mph *1,88 km/h*) in the case of a specimen of *Tegenaria atrica*. This is 33 times her body length per sec compared with the human record of 5½ times.

Longest lived
The longest lived of all spiders are the primitive *Mygalomorphae* (tarantulas and allied species). One mature female tarantula collected at Mazatlan, Mexico in 1935 and estimated to be 12 years old at the time, was kept in a laboratory for 16 years, making a total of 28 years. The longest-lived British spider is probably the purse web spider (*Atypus affinis*). One specimen was kept in a greenhouse for nine years.

Largest webs
The largest webs are the aerial ones spun by the tropical orb weavers of the genus *Nephila*, which have been measured up to 18 ft 9¾ in *573 cm* in circumference. The smallest webs are spun by spiders like *Glyphesis cottonae*, etc. which are about the size of a postage stamp.

Most venomous
The most venomous spiders in the world are the Brazilian wandering spiders of the genus Phoneutria, and particularly *P. fera*, which has the most active neurotoxic venom of any living spider. These large and highly aggressive creatures frequently enter human dwellings and hide in clothing or shoes. When disturbed they bite furiously several times, and hundreds of accidents involving these species are reported annually. Fortunately an effective antivenin is available, and when deaths do occur they are usually children under the age of seven.

8. CRUSTACEANS *(Crustacea)*

(Crabs, lobsters, shrimps, prawns, crayfish, barnacles, water fleas, fish lice, woodlice, sandhoppers, krill, etc.)

Largest *World*
The largest of all crustaceans (although not the heaviest) is the sanschouo or giant spider crab (*Macrocheira kaempferi*), also called the stilt crab, which is found in deep waters off the southeastern coast of Japan. Mature specimens usually have a 12–14 in *30–35 cm* wide body and a claw-span of 8–9 ft *2,43–2,74 m* but unconfirmed measurements up to 19 ft *5,79 m* have been reported. A specimen with a claw span of 12 ft 1½ in *3,69 m* weighed 41 lb *18,6 kg*.

The largest species of lobster, and the heaviest of all crustaceans, is the American or North Atlantic lobster (*Homarus americanus*). On 11 Feb 1977 a specimen weighing 44 lb 6 oz *20,14 kg* and measuring 3 ft 6 in *1,06 m* from the end of the tail-fan to the tip of the largest claw was caught off Nova Scotia, Canada and later sold to a New York restaurant owner.

Largest *Britain*
The largest crustacean found in British waters is the Common or European lobster (*Homarus vulgarus*), which averages 2–3 lb *900–1360 g*. In June 1931 an outsized specimen weighing

Scaphistostreptus seychellarum, the Giant Seychelles millipede which can measure nearly 1 ft *30,4 cm* overall (see p. 47). (*J. Watson/WWF*)

20½ lb *5,80 kg* and measuring 4 ft 1½ in *1,26 m* in total length, was caught in a caisson during the construction of No. 3 jetty at Fowey, Cornwall. Its crushing claw weighed 2 lb 10 oz *1188 g* after the meat had been removed. The largest crab found in British waters is the Edible or Great crab (*Cancer pagurus*). In 1895 a crab measuring 11 in *279 mm* across the shell and weighing 14 lb *6,35 kg* was caught off the coast of Cornwall.

Smallest
The smallest known crustaceans are water fleas of the genus *Alonella*, which may measure less than 0,25 mm *0.0098 in* in length. They are found in British waters. The smallest known lobster is the Cape lobster (*Homarus capensis*) of South Africa which measures 10–12 cm *3.9–4.7 in* in total length. The smallest crabs in the world are the aptly named pea crabs (family Pinnotheridae). Some species have a shell diameter of only 0.25 in *6,3 mm*, including *Pinnotheres pisum* which is found in British waters.

Longest lived
The longest lived of all crustaceans is the American lobster (*Homarus americanus*). Very large specimens may be as much as 50 years old.

Vertical distribution
The greatest depth from which a crustacean has been recovered is 9790 m *32,119 ft* for an isopod, *Macrostylis galatheae*, collected by the Galathea Deep Sea Expedition in the Philippine Trench in 1951. The marine crab *Ethusina abyssicola* has been taken at a depth of 4815 m *15,800 ft*. Amphiopods and isopods have also been collected in the Ecuadorean Andes at a height of 13,300 ft *4053 m*.

9. INSECTS *(Insecta)*

Heaviest *World*
The heaviest insects in the world are the Goliath beetles (family *Scarabaeidae*) of equatorial Africa. The largest members of the group are *Goliathus regius* and *Goliathus goliathus* (= *giganteus*) and in one series of fully-grown males the weight ranged from 70 to 100 g *2.5–3.5 oz*.

Heaviest *Britain*
The heaviest insect found in Britain is the Stag beetle (*Lucanus cervus*) which is widely distributed over southern England. The largest specimen on record was a male collected at Sheerness, Kent, in 1871 and now preserved in the British Museum (Natural History), London, which measures 87.4 mm *3.04 in* in length (body plus mandibles) and probably weighed over 6000 mg *0.21 oz* when alive.

BUTTERFLIES AND MOTHS (order Lepidoptera)
Largest *World*
The largest known butterfly is the Queen Alexandra birdwing

(*Ornithoptera alexandrae*) of New Guinea. Females may have a wing span exceeding 280 mm *11.02 in* and weigh over 5 g *0.176 oz*. The largest moth in the world (although not the heaviest) is the Hercules moth (*Cosdinoscera hercules*) of tropical Australia and New Guinea. A wing area of up to 40.8 in² *263,2 cm²* and a wing span of 280 mm *11 in* have been recorded. In 1948 an unconfirmed measurement of 360 mm *14.17 in* was reported for a female captured near the post office at the coastal town of Innisfail, Queensland, Australia. The rare Owlet moth (*Thysania agrippina*) of Brazil has been measured up to 300 mm *11.81 in* wing span, and the Philippine atlas moth (*Attacus crameri caesar*) up to 280 mm *11.02 in*, but both these species are lighter than *C. hercules*.

Largest *Britain*
The largest (but not the heaviest) of the 21,000 species of insect found in Britain is the very rare Death's head hawkmoth (*Acherontia atropos*). One female found dead in a garden at Tiverton, Devon, in 1931 had a wing span of 5.75 in *145 mm* and weighed nearly 3 g *0.10 oz*. The largest butterfly found in Britain is the Monarch butterfly (*Danaus plexippus*), also called the Milkweed or Black-veined brown butterfly, a rare vagrant which breeds in the southern United States and Central America. It has a wing span of up to 5 in *127 mm* and weighs about 1 g *0.04 oz*. The largest *native* butterfly is the Swallowtail (*Papilio machaon brittanicus*), females of which have a wing span up to 100 mm *3.93 in*. This species is now confined to the Norfolk Broads and Wicken Fen, Cambridgeshire.

Smallest *World and Britain*
The smallest of the 140,000 known species of Lepidoptera are the moths *Johanssonia acetosea* (*Stainton*) found in Britain, and *Stigmella ridiculosa* from the Canary Islands, which have a wing span of *c.* 2 mm *0.08 in* with a similar body length. The world's smallest known butterfly is the Dwarf blue (*Brephidium barberae*) of South Africa. It has a wing span of 14 mm *0.55 in*. The smallest butterfly found in Britain is the Small blue (*Cupido minimus*), which has a wing span of 19–25 mm *0.75–1.0 in*.

Rarest
The rarest British butterfly is now probably the Large tortoise-shell (*Nymphalis polycholoris*) of Essex and the Kent/Sussex border. The Large blue (*Maculinea arion*) was officially declared extinct in 1979. Since its demise this butterfly has reportedly been seen in various parts of Britain, but most of these sightings were male examples of the widely-distributed Common blue (*Polyommatus icarus*).

Most acute sense of smell
The most acute sense of smell exhibited in nature is that of the male Emperor moth (*Eudia pavonia*) which, according to German experiments in 1961, can detect the sex attractant of the virgin female at the almost unbelievable range of 11 km *6.8 miles* upwind. This scent has been identified as one of the higher alcohols ($C_{16}H_{29}OH$), of which the female carries less than 0,0001 mg.

Longest
The longest insect in the world is the giant stick-insect *Pharnacia serratipes* of Indonesia, females of which have been measured up to 330 mm *13 in* in body length. The longest known beetles (excluding antennae) are the Hercules beetles (*Dynastes hercules* and *D. neptunus*) of Central and South America, which have been measured up to 190 mm *7.48 in* and 180 mm *7.08 in* respectively. More than half the length however, is taken up by the prothoracic horn.

Smallest *World*
The smallest insects recorded so far are the 'Hairy-winged' beetles of the family *Ptiliidae* (= *Trichopterygidae*) and the 'battle-dore-wing fairy flies' (parasitic wasps) of the family *Myrmaridae*. They measure only 0,2 mm *0.008 in* in length, and the fairy flies have a wing span of only 1 mm *0.04 in*. This makes them smaller than some of the protozoa (single-celled animals). The male bloodsucking banded louse *Enderleinellus zonatus*, ungorged, and the parasitic wasp (*Caraphractus cinctus*) may each weigh as little as 0,005 mg, or *5,670,000 to an oz*. The eggs of the latter each weigh 0,0002 mg, *or 141,750,000 to an oz*.

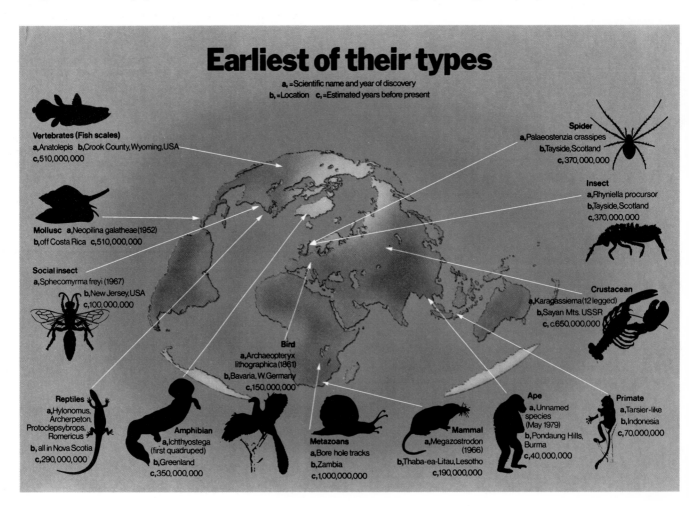

Earliest of their types

a, = Scientific name and year of discovery
b, = Location   c, = Estimated years before present

Vertebrates (Fish scales)
a, Anatolepis b, Crook County, Wyoming, USA
c, 510,000,000

Mollusc a, Neopilina galatheae (1952)
b, off Costa Rica c, 510,000,000

Social insect
a, Sphecomyrma freyi (1967)
b, New Jersey, USA
c, 100,000,000

Reptiles
a, Hylonomus, Archerpeton, Protoclepsybrops, Romericus
b, all in Nova Scotia
c, 290,000,000

Amphibian
a, Ichthyostega (first quadruped)
b, Greenland
c, 350,000,000

Bird
a, Archaeopteryx lithographica (1861)
b, Bavaria, W. Germany
c, 150,000,000

Metazoans
a, Bore hole tracks
b, Zambia
c, 1,000,000,000

Mammal
a, Megazostrodon (1966)
b, Thaba-ea-Litau, Lesotho
c, 190,000,000

Ape
a, Unnamed species (May 1979)
b, Pondaung Hills, Burma
c, 40,000,000

Spider
a, Palaeostenzia crassipes
b, Tayside, Scotland
c, 370,000,000

Insect
a, Rhyniella procursor
b, Tayside, Scotland
c, 370,000,000

Crustacean
a, Karagassiema (12 legged)
b, Sayan Mts. USSR
c, c.650,000,000

Primate
a, Tarsier-like
b, Indonesia
c, 70,000,000

Commonest

The most numerous of all insects are the Springtails (Order Collembola), which have a very wide geographical range. It has been calculated that the top 9 in *288 mm* of soil in one acre of grassland contains 230,000,000 springtails or more than 5000 per square foot *465/m².*

Fastest flying

Experiments have proved that the widely publicised claim by an American entomologist in 1926 that the Deer bot-fly (*Cephenemyia pratti*) could attain a speed of 818 mph *1316 km/h (sic)* was wildly exaggerated. If true it would have generated a supersonic 'pop'! Acceptable modern experiments have now established that the highest maintainable airspeed of any insect, including the Deer bot-fly, is 24 mph *39 km/h*, rising to a maximum of 36 mph *58 km/h* for short bursts. A relay of bees (maximum speed 11 mph *18 km/h*) would use only a gallon of nectar in cruising 4,000,000 miles *6,5 million km* at an average speed of 7 mph *11 km/h.*

Longest lived

The longest-lived insects are the Splendour beetles (*Buprestidae*), some of which remain in the larva stage for more than 30 years. Queen termites (*Isoptera*), previously thought to live 50 years or more, are now known to have a maximum life-span of about 15 years.

Loudest

The loudest of all insects is the male cicada (family Cicadidae). At 7400 pulses/min its tymbal organs produce a noise (officially described by the United States Department of Agriculture as 'Tsh-ee-EEEE-e-ou') detectable more than a quarter of a mile *400 m* distant. The only British species is the very rare Mountain cicada (*Cicadetta montana*), which is confined to the New Forest area in Hampshire.

Southernmost

The farthest south at which any insect has been found is 77° S (900 miles *1450 km* from the South Pole) in the case of a springtail (order Collembola).

Largest locust swarm

The greatest swarm of Desert locusts (*Schistocera gregaria*) ever recorded was one covering an estimated 2000 miles² *5180 km²* observed crossing the Red Sea in 1889. Such a swarm must have contained about 250,000,000,000 insects weighing about 500,000 tons *508 000 tonnes.*

Fastest wing beat

The fastest wing beat of any insect under natural conditions is 62,760 a min by a tiny midge of the genus *Forcipomyia*. In experiments with truncated wings at a temperature of 37° C *98.6° F* the rate increased to 133,080 beats/min. The muscular contraction–expansion cycle in 0.00045 or 1/2218th of a sec, further represents the fastest muscle movement ever measured.

Slowest wing beat

The slowest wing beat of any insect is 300 a min by the swallowtail butterfly (*Papilio machaon*). Most butterflies beat their wings at a rate of 460–636 a min.

Hive record

The greatest reported amount of wild honey ever extracted from a single hive is 404 lb *183,2 kg* recorded by Ormond R. Aebi of Santa Cruz, California on 29 Aug 1974.

Bush-cricket *Largest*

The bush-cricket with the largest wing span is the New Guinean grasshopper *Siliquofera grandis* with female examples measuring more than 10 in *254 mm*. *Pseudophyllanax imperialis*, found on the island of New Caledonia in the south-western Pacific, has antennae measuring up to 8 in *203 mm*. The largest bush-cricket found in Britain is *Tettigonia viridissima*, which normally has a body length of 1¼ in *31,8 mm*. In August 1953 a female measuring 77 mm *3.03 in* in body length (including ovipositor) was caught in a sand pit at Grays, Essex and later presented to the London Zoological Gardens. The largest of the 14 true grasshoppers found in Britain is *Mecostethus grossus*, females of which measure up to 39 mm *1.53 in* in body length.

Dragonflies *Largest*

The largest dragonfly in the world is *Megaloprepes caeruleata* of Central and South America, which has been measured up to 191 mm *7.52 in* across the wings and 120 mm *4.72 in* in body length. The largest dragonfly found in Britain is *Anax imperator*, which has a wing span measurement of up to 106 mm *4.17 in*. The smallest British dragonfly is *Lestes dryas*, which has a wing span of 20–25 mm *0.78–0.98 in.*

Flea *Largest*

The largest known flea is *Hystrichopsylla schefferi schefferi*, which was described from a single specimen taken from the nest of a Mountain beaver (*Aplodontia rufa*) at Puyallup, Washington, USA in 1913. Females measure up to 8 mm *0.31 in* in length which is the diameter of a pencil. The largest flea (61 species) found in Britain is the Mole and Vole flea (*H. talpae*), females of which have been measured up to 6 mm *0.23 in.*

Flea *Longest jump*

The champion jumper among fleas is the common flea (*Pulex irritans*). In one American experiment carried out in 1910 a specimen allowed to leap at will performed a long jump of 13 in *330 mm* and a high jump of 7¾ in *197 mm*. In jumping 130 times its own height a flea subjects itself to a force of 200 g. Siphonapterologists recognise 1830 varieties.

10. CENTIPEDES *(Chilopoda)*

Longest

The longest known species of centipede is a large variant of the widely distributed *Scolopendra morsitans*, found on the Andaman Islands, Bay of Bengal. Specimens have been measured up to 13 in *330 mm* in length and 1½ in *38 mm* in breadth. The longest centipede found in Britain is *Haplophilus subterraneus*, which measures up to 70 mm *2.75 in* in length and 1,4 mm *0.05 in* across the body, but on 1 Nov 1973 Mr Ian Howgate claims to have seen a thin amber-coloured specimen in St Albans, Herts, measuring at least 4½ in *114 mm.*

Shortest

The shortest recorded centipede is an unidentified species which measures only 5 mm *0.19 in*. The shortest centipede found in Britain is *Lithobius dubosequi*, which measures up to 9,5 mm *0.374 in* in length and 1,1 mm *0.043 in* across the body.

Most legs

The centipede with the greatest number of legs is *Himantarum gabrielis* of southern Europe which has 171–177 pairs when adult.

Fastest

The fastest centipede is probably *Scutigera coleoptrata* of southern Europe which can travel at a rate of 50 cm *19.68 in* a sec or 1.1 mph *1,8 km/h.*

11. MILLIPEDES *(Diplopoda)*

Longest

The longest known species of millipede are *Graphidostreptus gigas* of Africa and *Scaphistostreptus seychellarum* of the Seychelles in the Indian Ocean, both of which have been measured up to 280 mm *11.02 in* in length and 20 mm *0.78 in* in diameter. The longest millipede found in Britain is *Cylindroiulus londinensis* which measures up to 50 mm *1.96 in.*

Shortest

The shortest millipede in the world is the British species *Polyxenus lagurus*, which measures 2,1–4,0 mm *0.082–0.15 in* in length.

Most legs

The greatest number of legs reported for a millipede is 355 pairs (710 legs) for an unidentified South African species.

12. SEGMENTED WORMS
(Annelida or Annulata)

Longest
The longest known species of giant earthworm is *Microchaetus rappi* (= *M. microchaetus*) of South Africa. An average-sized specimen measures 136 cm *4 ft 6 in* in length (65 cm *25½ in* when contracted), but much larger examples have been reliably reported. In *c.* 1937 a giant earthworm measuring 22 ft *6,70 m* in length when naturally extended and 20 mm *0.78 in* diameter was collected in the Transvaal, and in November 1967 another specimen measuring 11 ft *3,35 m* in length and 21 ft *6,40 m* when naturally extended was found reaching over the national road (width 6 m *19 ft 8½ in*) near Debe Nek, eastern Cape Province. The longest segmented worm found in Britain is the King rag worm (*Nereis virens*). On 19 Oct 1975 a specimen of 38 in *965 mm* was collected by Mr James Sawyer in Hauxley Bay, Northumberland.

Shortest
The shortest known segmented worm is *Chaetogaster annandalei*, which measures less than 0,5 mm *0.019 in* in length.

13. MOLLUSCS *(Mollusca)*

(Squids, octopuses, shellfish, snails, etc.)

Largest
In November 1896 the remains of an unknown marine animal weighing an estimated 6–7 tons/*tonnes* were found on a beach near St Augustine, Florida, USA. Tissue samples were later sent to the US National Museum in Washington, DC, and in 1970 they were *positively* identified as belonging to a giant form of octopus. It is estimated that this creature had a tentacular span of 200 ft *60,9 m*. The largest octopus found in British waters is the Common octopus (*Octopus vulgaris*), which has been measured up to 7 ft *2,13 m* in radial spread and may weigh more than 10 lb *4,5 kg*.

Largest squid
The largest squid ever recorded was one measuring 55 ft *16,75 m* in total length (head and body 20 ft *6,09 m*, tentacles 35 ft *10,66 m*) captured on 2 Nov 1878 after it had run aground in Thimble Tickle Bay, Newfoundland, Canada. It weighed an estimated 2 tons/*tonnes*. In October 1887 a giant squid (*Architeuthis longimanus*) measuring 57 ft *17,37 m* in total length was washed up in Lyall Bay, New Zealand, but 49 ft *14,93 m* of this was tentacle. The largest squid ever recorded in British waters was one found at the head of Whalefirth Voe, Shetland on 2 Oct 1959 which measured 24 ft *7,31 m* in total length.

Most ancient mollusc
The longest existing living creature is *Neopilina galatheae*, a deep-sea worm-snail which had been believed extinct for about 320,000,000 years. In 1952, however, specimens were found at a depth of 11,400 ft *3 470 m* off Costa Rica by the Danish research vessel *Galathea*. Fossils found in New York State, USA, Newfoundland, Canada, and Sweden show that this mollusc was also living about 500,000,000 years ago.

Longest lived mollusc
The longest lived mollusc is the Quahog (*Venus mercenaria*) a thick-shelled clam found in the North Atlantic. Recent research in America involving the study of microscopic rings laid down annually on the tooth holding the shells together indicates that this species sometimes lives for 150 years.

SHELLS
Largest
The largest of all existing bivalve shells is the marine Giant clam *Tridacna gigas*, which is found on the Indo-Pacific coral reefs. A specimen measuring 43 in *109,2 cm* by 29 in *73,6 cm* and weighing 579½ lb *262,9 kg* (over a quarter of a ton) was collected from the Great Barrier Reef in 1917, and is now preserved in the American Museum of Natural History, New York City, NY,

USA. Another lighter specimen was measured to be 137 cm *53.9 in* overall. The largest bivalve shell found in British waters is the Fan mussel (*Pinna fragilis*). One specimen found at Tor Bay, Devon measured 37 cm *14.56 in* in length and 20 cm *7.87 in* in breadth at the hind end.

Smallest
The smallest bivalve shell found in British waters is the coin-shell *Neolepton sykesi*, which has an average length of 1,2 mm *0.047 in*. This species is only known from a few examples collected off Guernsey, Channel Islands and West Ireland. The smallest British shell is the univalve *Ammonicera rota*, which measures 0,5 mm *0.02 in* in diameter.

Rarest
A second example of the lost species *Tibia serrata* (Perry) first found in 1811 was reported in August 1977 from Bandar Abbas, Iran by Sg Franco Perantoni (Italy). It is grey-cream and golden-yellow and 130 mm *5.1 in* in length. A sum of $10,000 (*then £5,000*) was refused by Phillip Clover of Glen Ellen, California for a *Conus servus* in 1978.

GASTROPODS
Largest
The largest known gastropod is the Trumpet or Baler conch (*Syrinx aruanus*) of Australia. One outsized specimen collected at Bunbury, Western Australia in 1974 and now owned by Morton Hahn of Randolph, New Jersey, USA weighed 35 lb *15,9 kg* when live. Its shell measures 28.1 in *71,3 cm* in length and has a maximum girth of 38 in *96,5 cm*.

The largest known land gastropod is the African giant snail (*Achatina* sp.). An outsized specimen 'Gee Geronimo' found by Christopher Hudson (1955–79) of Hove, E. Sussex, measured 15½ in *39,3 cm* from snout to tail, (shell length 10¾ in *27,3 cm*) in December 1978 and weighed exactly 2 lb *900 g*. The snail was collected in Sierra Leone in June 1976 where shell lengths up to 14 in *35,5 cm* have been reliably reported.

The largest land snail found in Britain is the Roman or Edible snail (*Helix pomatia*), which measures up to 4 in *10 cm* in overall length and weighs up to 3 oz *85 g*. The smallest British land snail is *Punctum pygmaeum*, which has a shell measuring 0.023–0.035 in *0,6–0,9 mm* by 0.047–0.059 in *1,2–1,5 mm*.

Speed
The fastest-moving species of land snail is probably the common garden snail (*Helix aspersa*). According to tests carried out in the United States of America absolute top speed for *Helix aspersa* is 0.0313 mph *0,05 km/h* (or 55 yd *50,3 m* per hr) while some species are at full stretch at 0.00036 mph *0,0005 km/h* (or 23 in *58 cm* per hr). The snail-racing equivalent of a 4-minute mile is 24 inches in 3 minutes or the 7920 minute or 5½-day mile. This was recorded by Colly in 1970.

14. RIBBON WORMS *(Nemertina or Rhynchopods)*

Longest
The longest of the 550 recorded species of ribbon worms, also called nemertines (or nemerteans), is the 'Boot-lace worm' (*Lineus longissimus*), which is found in the shallow waters of the North Sea. A specimen washed ashore at St Andrews, Fife, Scotland in 1864 after a severe storm measured more than 180 ft *55 m* in length, making it easily the longest recorded worm of any variety.

15. JELLYFISHES
(Scyphozoa or Scyphomedusia)

Largest and smallest
The largest jellyfish is the Arctic giant jellyfish (*Cyanea arctica*) of the north-western Atlantic. One specimen washed up in Massachusetts Bay had a bell diameter of 7 ft 6 in *2,28 m* and

tentacles stretching 120 ft *36,5 m*. The largest cnidarian found in British waters is the rare 'Lion's mane' jellyfish (*Cyanea capillata*), also known as the Common sea blubber. One specimen measured at St Andrew's Marine Laboratory, Fife, Scotland had a bell diameter of 91 cm *35.8 in* and tentacles stretching over 13,7 m *45 ft*. Some true jellyfishes have a bell diameter of less than 20 mm *0.78 in*.

Most venomous

The most venomous cnidarian is the Australian sea wasp (*Chironex fleckeri*) which carries a cardio-toxic venom similar in strength to that found in the Asiatic cobra. These box jellyfish have caused the deaths of 66 people off the coast of Queensland, Australia since 1880. Victims die within 1–3 min if medical aid is not available. A most effective defence is women's panty hose, outsize versions of which are now worn by Queensland lifesavers at surf carnivals.

16. SPONGES *(Parazoa, Porifera or Spongida)*

Largest

The largest known sponge is the barrel-shaped Loggerhead sponge (*Spheciospongia vesparium*) of the West Indies and the waters off Florida, USA. Single individuals measure up to 3 ft 6 in *105 cm* in height and 3 ft *91 cm* in diameter. Neptune's cup or goblet (*Poterion patera*) of Indonesia grows to 4 ft *120 cm* in height, but it is a less bulky animal. In 1909 a Wool sponge (*Hippospongia canaliculata*) measuring 6 ft *183 cm* in circumference was collected off the Bahama Islands. When first taken from the water it weighed between 80 and 90 lb *36 and 41 kg* but after it had been dried and relieved of all excrescences it scaled 12 lb *5,44 kg* (this sponge is now preserved in the US National Museum, Washington, DC, USA).

Smallest

The smallest known sponge is the widely distributed *Leucosolenia blanca*, which measures 3 mm *0.11 in* in height when fully grown.

Deepest

Sponges have been recovered from depths of up to 18,500 ft *5637 m*.

17. EXTINCT ANIMALS

Longest *World*

The longest dinosaur so far recorded is Diplodocus ('double-beam'), an attenuated titanosaurid which ranged over Western North America about 150 million years ago. A composite reconstruction in the Carnegie Museum of the Natural Sciences in Pittsburgh, Pennsylvania measures 87 ft 6 in *26,6 m* in total length—head and neck 22 ft *6,7 m*; body 15 ft *4,5 m*; tail 50 ft 6 in *15,4 m*—and has a mounted height of 11 ft 9 in *3,5 m* at the pelvis (the highest point on the body).

Longest *Britain*

In 1975 an amateur fossil-hunter working on the cliff-face near Brightstone, Isle of Wight, uncovered an unusual 228 mm *9 in* long bone which was later identified as the heamal arch (a bone running beneath the vertebrae of the tail) of a Diplodocus-type sauropod.

Heaviest *World*

The heaviest land vertebrates of all time were the massive brachiosaurids ('arm lizards') of the Late Jurassic (135–165 million years ago) of East Africa, the Sahara, Portugal and the south-western USA. A complete skeleton excavated by a German expedition at the famous Tendaguru site, southern Tanganyika (Tanzania) between 1909 and 1911 and now mounted in the Humboldt Museum für Naturkunde, East Berlin measures 74 ft 6 in *22,7 m* in total length (height at shoulder 21 ft *6,4 m*) and has a raised head height of 39 ft *11,8 m. Brachiosaurus brancai*, as it was named, weighed a computed 78,26 tonnes *77 tons* in life.

In the summer of 1972 the remains of another enormous brachiosaurid new to science, were discovered in the Dry Mesa Quarry on the Uncompahgre Plateau, western Colorado, USA. From the evidence of the bones already collected, including 8 ft *2,43 m* long matching shoulder blades, 'Supersaurus', as it has been nicknamed, is about 22 per cent larger than Brachiosaurus: this presupposes an overall length of *c*. 90 ft *27,4 m*, a shoulder height of 26 ft *7,9 m* and a raised head height of nearly 50 ft *15,2 m* if it is built on the same anatomical lines. The weight of such an animal, based on the cube of the fossil dimensions, would be *c*. 140 tonnes *138 tons*. In 1979 another shoulder blade measuring 8 ft 10 in *2,69 m* in length was discovered in the same quarry.

Heaviest *Britain*

Britain's heaviest land vertebrate was the sauropod Cetiosauriscus ('whale lizard'), which roamed across southern England about 150 million years ago. It measured up to 50 ft *15,2 m* in total length and weighed over 15 tonnes/*tons*.

Largest land predator

The largest of the flesh-eating dinosaurs (infraorder *carnosauria*) was probably the 6¾ tons/*tonnes Tyrannosaurus rex* ('king tyrant lizard') which stalked over what are now the states of Montana and Wyoming in the USA about 75,000,000 years ago. No complete skeleton of this dinosaur has ever been discovered, but a composite individual has bipedal height of 18 ft *5,5 m*, and measures 47 ft *14,3 m* in overall length. *Tarbosaurus bataar*, its Mongolian counterpart, was also about the same size (total length 14 m *46 ft*), but although it had a longer skull than Tyrannosaurus its head was less massive and it may have lost out in terms of overall bulk. In 1934 the skeleton of a huge *Antrodemus* (= Allosaurus) with a much heavier body in proportion to its height than the tyrannosaurids was excavated near Kenton, Oklahoma, USA. This carnosaur had a bipedal height of 16 ft *4,87 m* and measured 42 ft *12,8 m* in overall length.

Most brainless

Stegosaurus ('plated reptile'), which measured up to 30 ft *9 m* in total length had a walnut-sized brain weighing only 2½ oz *70 g*, which represented 0.004 of 1 per cent of its computed body weight of 1¾ ton/*tonne* (*cf.* 0.074 of 1 per cent for an elephant and 1.88 per cent for a human). It roamed widely across the Northern Hemisphere about 150,000,000 years ago.

Largest dinosaur eggs

The largest known dinosaur eggs are those of *Hypselosaurus priscus*, a 30 ft *9,14 m* long sauropod which lived about 80,000,000 years ago. Some specimens found in the valley of the Durance near Aix-en-Provence southern France in October 1961 would have had, uncrushed, a length of 12 in *300 mm* and a diameter of 10 in *255 mm*.

Largest flying creature

The largest flying creature is the pterosaur *Quetzalcoatlus northropi* which glided over what is now the state of Texas, USA about 65 million years ago. Partial remains discovered in Big Bend National Park, West Texas in 1971 indicate that this reptile must have had a wing span of 11–12 m *36–39 ft* and weighed about 190 lb *86 kg*.

Largest marine reptile

The largest marine reptile ever recorded was *Stretosaurus macromerus*, a short-necked pliosaur from the Kimmeridge Clay of Stretham, Cambridgeshire and Oxfordshire. A mandible found at Cumnor, Oxfordshire and now in the University Museum, Oxford has a restored length of over 3 m *9 ft 10 in* and must have belonged to a reptile measuring at least 46 ft *14 m* in total length. *Kronosaurus queenslandicus*, another pliosaur, was also of comparable size, and a complete skeleton in the Museum of Comparative Zoology at Harvard University, Cambridge, Massachusetts, USA measures 42 ft *12,8 m* in total length.

Largest crocodile

The largest known crocodile was *Deinosuchus riograndensis*, which lived in the lakes and swamps of what is now the state of Texas, USA about 75,000,000 years ago. Fragmentary remains discovered in Big Bend National Park, West Texas, indicate it must have measured at least 16 m *52 ft 6 in* in total length. The huge gavial *Rhamphosuchus*, which lived in what is now northern

India about 2,000,000 years ago, was even longer reaching 60 ft *18,3 m*, but it was not so heavily built.

Largest chelonians
The largest prehistoric chelonian was *Stupendemys geographicus*, a pelomedusid turtle which lived about 5,000,000 years ago. Fossil remains discovered by a Harvard University paleontological expedition in Northern Venezuela in 1972 indicate that this turtle had a carapace (shell) measuring 218–230 cm *7 ft 2 in–7 ft 6½ in* in mid-line length and probably measured at least 12 ft *3,65 m* in overall length. It had a computed weight of 4500 lb *2041 kg* in life.

Largest tortoise
The largest prehistoric tortoise was probably *Geochelone* (= *Colossochelys*) *atlas*, which lived in what is now northern India, Burma, Java, the Celebes and Timor about 2 million years ago. In 1923 the fossil remains of a specimen with a carapace 5 ft 11 in *180 cm* long (7 ft 4 in *223 cm* over the curve) and 2 ft 11 in *89 cm* high were discovered near Chandigarh in the Siwalik Hills. This animal had a total length of 8 ft *2,44 m* and is computed to have weighed 2100 lb *852 kg* when it was alive. Recently the fossil remains of other giant tortoises (*Geochelone*) have been found in Florida and Texas, USA.

Longest snake
The longest prehistoric snake was the python-like *Gigantophis garstini*, which inhabited what is now Egypt about 55,000,000 years ago. Parts of a spinal column and a small piece of jaw discovered at Fayum in the Western Desert indicate a length of *c.* 37 ft *11 m*. Another fossil giant snake, *Madtsoia bai* from Patagonia, S. America, measured *c.* 10 m *33 ft* in length, comparable with the longest constrictors living today.

Largest amphibian
The largest amphibian ever recorded was the gharial-like *Prionosuchus plummeri* which lived 230,000,000 years ago. In 1972 the fragmented remains of a specimen measuring an estimated 9 m *30 ft* in life, were discovered in North Brazil.

Largest fish
No prehistoric fish larger than living species has yet been discovered. The claim that the Great shark (*Carcharodon megalodon*), which abounded in Miocene seas some 15,000,000 years ago, measured 80 ft *24 m* in length, based on ratios from fossil teeth has now been shown to be in error. The modern estimate is that this shark did not exceed 43 ft *13,1 m*.

Largest insect
The largest prehistoric insect was the dragonfly *Meganeura monyi*, which lived about 280,000,000 years ago. Fossil remains (*i.e.* impressions of wings) discovered at Commentry, central France, indicate that it had a wing expanse of up to 70 cm *27.5 in*.

Britain's largest dragonfly was *Typus* sp. (family *Meganeuridae*), which is only known from a wing impression found on a lump of coal in Bolsover colliery, Derbyshire in July 1978. It had an estimated wing span of 50–60 cm *19.68–23.62 in* and lived about 300,000,000 years ago, making it the oldest flying creature so far recorded.

Most southerly
The most southerly creature yet found is a freshwater salamander-like amphibian *Labyrinthodont*, represented by a 2½ in *63,5 mm* piece of jawbone found near Beardmore Glacier Antarctica, 325 miles *532 km* from the South Pole, dating from the early Jurassic of 200,000,000 years ago. This discovery was made in December 1967.

Largest bird
The largest prehistoric bird was the flightless *Dromornis stirtoni*, a huge emu-like creature which lived in central Australia 11,000,000 years ago. Fossil leg bones found near Alice Springs in 1974 indicate that the bird must have stood *c.* 10 ft *3 m* in height and weighed *c.* 1100 lb *500 kg*. The giant moa *Dinornis maximus* of New Zealand was even taller, attaining a maximum height of 12 ft *3,6 m* but it only weighed about 500 lb *227 kg*.

The largest prehistoric bird actually to fly was a yet unnamed giant teratorn which lived in Argentina about 6 million years ago. Fossil remains discovered at a site 100 miles *160 km* west of Buenos Aires in 1979 indicate that this gigantic vulture had a wing span of *c.* 24 ft *7,3 m* and weighed an estimated 160–170 lb *72,5–77 kg*.

Largest mammals
The largest land mammal ever recorded was *Baluchitherium* (= *Indricotherium*), a long-necked hornless rhinoceros which roamed across western Asia and Europe (Yugoslavia) about 3 million years ago. A restoration in the American Museum of Natural History, New York measures 17 ft 9 in *5,41 m* to the top of the shoulder hump and 37 ft *11,27 m* in total length, and this particular specimen must have weighed about 30 tonnes/*ton* in the flesh. The bones of this gigantic browser were first discovered in the Bugti Hills in east Baluchistan, Pakistan in 1907-08.

The largest marine mammal was the serpentine *Basilosauru* (*Zeuglodon*), which swam in the seas over what are now the American states of Arkansas and Alabama 50 million years ago. It measured up to 70 ft *21,3 m* in length.

Largest mammoth
The largest prehistoric elephant was the Steppe mammoth *Mammuthus (Parelephas) trogontherii*, which roamed over what is now central Europe a million years ago. A fragmentary skeleton found in Mosbach, West Germany indicates a shoulder height of 4,5 m *14 ft 9 in*.

Tusks *Longest*
The longest tusks of any prehistoric animal were those of the straight-tusked elephant *Palaeoloxodon antiquus germanicus*, which lived in northern Germany about 300,000 years ago. The average length in adult bulls was 5 m *16 ft 5 in*. A single tusk of a woolly mammoth (*Mammuthus primigenius*) preserved in the Franzens Museum at Brno, Czechoslovakia measures 5,02 m *16 ft 5½ in* along the outside curve. In *c.* August 1933, a single tusk of an Imperial mammoth (*Mammuthus imperator*) measuring 16+ ft *4,87+ m* (anterior end missing) was unearthed near Post, Gorza County, Texas, USA. In 1934 this tusk was presented to the American Museum of Natural History in New York City, NY, USA.

Tusks *Heaviest*
The heaviest single fossil tusk on record is one weighing 150 kg *330 lb* with a maximum circumference of 35 in *89 cm* now preserved in the Museo Civico di Storia Naturale, Milan, Italy. The specimen (in two pieces) measures 11 ft 9 in *3,58 m* in length. The heaviest recorded fossil tusks are a pair belonging to a 13 ft 4 in *4,06 m* tall Columbian mammoth (*Mammuthus columbi*) in the State Museum, Lincoln, Nebraska, USA which have a combined weight of 498 lb *226 kg* and measure 13 ft 9 in *4,21 m* and 13 ft 7 in *4,14 m* respectively. They were found near Campbell, Nebraska in April 1915.

Antlers *Greatest Span*
The prehistoric Giant deer (*Megaceros giganteus*), which lived in northern Europe and northern Asia as recently as 50,000 BC, had the longest horns of any known animal. One specimen recovered from an Irish bog had greatly palmated antlers measuring 14 ft *4,3m* across.

PLANT KINGDOM *(Plantea)*

PLANTS
Oldest Living Thing
'King Clone', the oldest known clone of the creosote plant (*Larrea tridentata*) found in south west California, was estimated in February 1980 by Prof. Frank C. Vasek to be 11,700 years old.

Rarest
Plants thought to be extinct are rediscovered each year and there are thus many plants of which specimens are known in but a single locality. The small pink blossoms of *Presidio manzanita*

survive in a single specimen reported in June 1978 at an undisclosed site in California. The only known location of the adder's-tongue spearwort (*Ranunculus ophioglossifolius*) in the British Isles is the Badgeworth Nature Reserve, Gloucestershire. Only two of the 5 flowers from Britain's last known colony of ghost orchids (*Epipogium aphyllum*) survived in 1980 in the north west home counties. *Pennantia baylisiana*, a tree found in 1945 on Three Kings Island, off New Zealand, only exists as a female and cannot fruit.

Northernmost
The yellow poppy (*Papaver radicatum*) and the Arctic willow (*Salix arctica*) survive, the latter in an extremely stunted form, on the northernmost land (83° N).

Southernmost
Lichens resembling *Rhinodina frigida* have been found in Moraine Canyon in 86° 09′ S 157° 30′ W in 1971 and in the Horlick Mountain area, Antarctica in 86° 09′ S 131° 14′ W in 1965. The southernmost recorded flowering plant is the carnation (*Colobanthus crassifolius*), which was found in latitude 67° 15′ S on Jenny Island, Margaret Bay, Graham Land (Palmer Peninsula), Antarctica.

Highest
The greatest certain altitude at which any flowering plant has been found is 20,130 ft *6135 m* in the Himalaya for *Stellaria decumbens*. A claim for 23,000 ft *7000 m* in the Himalaya for *Christolea crassifolia* remains inconclusive. A non-flowering plant of *Androsace microphylla* was recorded by A. Zimmermann at 6350 m *20,833 ft* on the 1952 Swiss Everest expedition.

Roots
The greatest reported depth to which roots have penetrated is a calculated 400 ft *120 m* in the case of a wild fig tree at Echo Caves, near Ohrigstad, East Transvaal, South Africa. An elm tree root of at least 360 ft *110 m* was reported from Auchencraig, Largs, Strathclyde *c*. 1950.

A single winter rye plant (*Secale cereale*) has been shown to produce 387 miles *622,8 km* of roots in 1.83 ft³ *0,051 m³* of earth.

Worst weeds
The most intransigent weed is the mat-forming water weed *Salvinia auriculata*, found in Africa. It was detected on the filling of Kariba Lake in May 1959 and within 11 months had choked an area of 77 miles² *199 km²* rising by 1963 to 387 miles² *1002 km²*. The world's worst land weeds are regarded as purple nut sedge, Bermuda grass, barnyard grass, jungle-rice, goose grass, Johnson grass, Guinea grass, cogon grass and lantana. The most damaging and widespread cereal weeds in Britain are the wild oats *Avena fatua* and *A. ludoviciana*. Their seeds can withstand temperatures of 240° F *115,6° C* for 15 min and remain viable.

A blob of *Wolffia punctata*, the flowering aquatic duckweed which has fronds only 1/35 of an inch *0,7 mm* in length. A needle point provides the scale (see p. 52). (*Wayne P. Armstrong*)

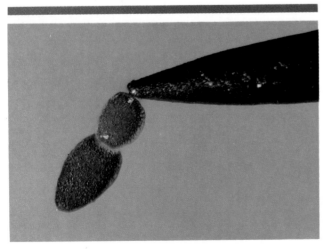

The most expensive orchid *Odontoglossum crispum* which was sold for 1150 guineas (now equivalent to £36,000) to Baron Schröder on 22 Mar 1906 (see p. 54). (*David Sanders*)

Most spreading plant
The greatest area covered by a single clonal growth is that of the wild box huckleberry (*Gaylussacia brachyera*), a mat-forming evergreen shrub first reported in 1796. A colony covering 8 acres, *3,2 hectares* was discovered in 1845 near New Bloomfield, Pennsylvania. Another colony, covering about 100 acres, was 'discovered' on 18 July 1920 near the Juniata River, Pennsylvania. It has been estimated that this colony began 13,000 years ago.

Largest Philodendron
A Philodendron, 300 ft *91,5 m* in length, now grows in La Carreta Restaurant in San Jacinto, California, USA.

Largest aspidistra
The aspidistra (*Aspidistra elatior*) was introduced to Britain as a parlour palm from Japan and China in 1822. The biggest aspidistra in Britain is one 50 in *127 cm* tall with more than 500 leaves spanning 5 ft *1,52 m* grown by Gertie James in Staveley, Chesterfield.

Earliest flower
The oldest fossil of a flowering plant with palm-like imprints was found in Colorado, USA, in 1953 and dated about 65,000,000 years old.

Largest cactus
The largest of all cacti is the saguaro (*Cereus giganteus* or *Carnegiea gigantea*), found in Arizona, south-eastern California, USA and Sonora, Mexico. The green fluted column is surmounted by candelabra-like branches rising to a height of 16,00 m *52 ft 6 in* in the case of a specimen measured on the boundary of the Saguaro National Monument, Arizona. They have waxy white blooms which are followed by edible crimson fruit. An armless cactus 78 ft *24 m* in height was measured in April 1978 by Hube Yates in Cave Creek, Arizona.

Tallest hedge *World*
The world's tallest hedge is the Meikleour beech hedge in Perthshire, Scotland. It was planted in 1746 and has now attained a

Never slow to scent an opportunity, Interflora constructed this largest ever wreath in Western Australia in May 1979 with an external circumference of 42,53 m *139 ft 6 in.* (Western Australian Newspapers Ltd)

trimmed height of 85 ft *26 m*. It is 600 yd *550 m* long. Some of its trees now exceed 100 ft *30,5 m*.

Tallest hedge *Yew*
The tallest yew hedge in the world is in Earl Bathurst's Park, Cirencester, Gloucestershire. It was planted in 1720, runs for 170 yd *155 m*, reaches 36 ft *11 m*, is 15 ft *4,5 m* thick at its base and takes 20 man-days to trim.

Tallest hedge *Box*
The tallest box hedge is 35 ft *10,7 m* in height at Birr Castle, Offaly, Ireland dating from the 18th century.

Mosses
The smallest of mosses is the pygmy moss (*Ephemerum*) and the longest is the brook moss (*Fontinalis*), which forms streamers up to 3 ft *91 cm* long in flowing water.

Longest seaweed
Claims made that seaweed off Tierra del Fuego, South America, grows to 600 ft *182,5 m* and even to 1000 ft *305 m* in length have gained currency. More recent and more reliable records indicate that the longest species of seaweed is the Pacific giant kelp (*Macrocystis pyrifera*), which does not exceed 196 ft *60 m* in length. It can grow 45 cm *18 in* in a day. The longest of the 700 species of British seaweed is the brown seaweed *Chorda filum* which grows up to a length of 20 ft *6,10 m*. The Japanese *Sargassum muticum* introduced *c*. 1970 can grow to 30 ft *9,0 m*.

Largest vines
The largest recorded grape vine was one planted in 1842 at Carpinteria, California, USA. By 1900 it was yielding more than 9 tons/*tonnes* of grapes in some years, and averaging 7 tons/*tonnes* per year. It died in 1920. Britain's largest vine (1898–1964) was at Kippen, Stirling with a girth, measured in 1956, of 5 ft *1,52 m*. England's largest vine is the Great Vine, planted in 1768 at Hampton Court, Greater London. Its girth is 85 in *215,9 cm* with branches up to 114 ft *34,7 m* long and an average yield of 703 lb *318,8 kg*. A yield of 46 kg *101.4 lb* was recorded at The White Lodge, Linton, Kent from an outdoor vine in 1979 with a yield of 77 bottles.

Most northerly and southerly vineyards
A vineyard at Sabile, Latvia, USSR is just north of Lat. 57° N. The most northerly commercial vineyard in Britain is that at Renishaw Hall, Derbyshire with 2,600 vines. It lies in Lat. 53° 18′ N. The most southerly vineyard is operated by Montana Wines Ltd at South Blenheim, South Island, New Zealand in Lat. 41° 12′ S.

BLOOMS AND FLOWERS
Largest bloom *World*
The mottled orange-brown and white parasitic stinking corpse lily (*Rafflesia arnoldii*) has the largest of all blooms. These attach themselves to the cissus vines of the jungle in south-east Asi and measure up to 3 ft *91 cm* across and ¾ inch *1,9 cm* thick, and attain a weight of 15 lb *7 kg*. The spathe and spadix of the les massive green and purple flower of *Amorphophallus titanum* o Sumatra may attain a length of more than 1,5 m *5 ft*.

The largest known inflorescence is that of *Puya raimondii*, a rar Bolivian plant with an erect panicle (diameter 8 ft *2,4 m*) whic emerges to a height of 35 ft *10,7 m*. Each of these bears up t 8000 white blooms (see also Slowest-flowering plant, below) The flower-spike of an agave was in 1974 measured to be 52 f *15,8 m* long in Berkeley, California.

The world's largest blossoming plant is the giant Chines wisteria at Sierra Madre, California, USA. It was planted in 189 and now has branches 500 ft *152 m* long. It covers nearly an acre weighs 225 tons *228 tonnes* and has an estimated 1,500,00 blossoms during its blossoming period of five weeks, when up t 30,000 people pay admission to visit it. In November 1974 Passion plant, fed by a hormone by Dennis and Patti Carlson was reported to have grown to a length of 600 ft *182 m* at Blaine Minnesota, USA.

Largest bloom *Great Britain*
The largest bloom of any indigenous British flowering plant i that of the wild white water lily (*Nymphaea alba*), which meas ures 6 in *15 cm* across. Other species bear much larger inflore scences.

Smallest flower
The floating flowering aquatic duckweed *Wolffia punctata* has fronds only ⅓₅ of an inch *0,7 mm* in length. The 'flower' of a single stamen (male) or single pistil (female) is only ⅟₈₀ × ⅟₁₆₀th of an inch *0,3 × 0,15 mm*. The smallest land plant regularly flowering in Britain is the chaffweed (*Cetunculus minimus*), a single seed of which weighs 0.00003 of a gramme.

Smallest plant
The smallest plant is a uni-cellular alga and is listed under Protista smallest (see p. 57)

Rarest flower
The Burpee Co $20,000 prize offered in 1924 for the first all-white marigold was won in 1945 by Alice Vonk of Sully, Iowa, USA.

Fastest growth
The case of a *Liliacea hesperogucca whipplei* growing 12 ft *3,65 m* in 14 days was reported from Treco Abbey, Isles of Scilly in July 1978.

Slowest flowering plant
The slowest flowering of all plants is the rare *Puyu raimondii*, the largest of all herbs, discovered in Bolivia in 1870. The panicle emerges after about 150 years of the plant's life. It then dies. (See also above under Largest blooms.) Some agaves, erroneously called Century plants, first flower after 40 years.

Largest wreath
The largest wreath constructed was the wreath built by the Interflora Australian Unit Ltd, District 4 at Mt Lawley, W. Australia in May 1979. It measured 13,37 m *43.8 ft* in diameter.

Longest daisy chain
The longest daisy chain is one of 4082 ft *1244 m* at Coediog, Llanelidan, Clwyd, Wales made in 7 hours on 11 June 1978.

Orchid *Largest*
The largest of all orchids is *Grammatophyllum speciosum*, native to Malaysia. Specimens have been recorded up to 25 ft *7,62 m* in height. The largest orchid flower is that of *Phragmipedium caudatum*, found in tropical areas of America. Its petals are up to 18 in *46 cm* long, giving it a maximum outstretched diameter of 3 ft *91 cm*. The flower is, however, much less bulky than that of the stinking corpse lily.

Orchid *Tallest*
The tallest free-standing orchid is *Grammatophyllum speciosum* (see above). *Galeola foliata* may attain 49 ft *15 m* on decaying rainforest trees in Queensland, Australia.

RECORD DIMENSIONS AND WEIGHTS FOR FRUIT, VEGETABLES AND FLOWERS GROWN IN THE UNITED KINGDOM

Many data subsequent to 1958 come from the annual *Garden News* and Phostrogen Ltd. Giant Vegetable and Fruit Contest and the Super Sunflower Contest.

Apple	3 lb 1 oz	1,357 kg	V. Loveridge	Ross-on-Wye, Hereford and Worcester	1965
Artichoke	8 lb	3,625 kg	A. R. Lawson	Tollerton, North Yorkshire	1964
Beetroot	29 lb	13,154 kg	F. A. Pulley	Maidstone, Kent	1964
Broad Bean	23⅜ in	59,3 cm	T. Currie	Jedburgh, Borders	1963
Broccoli	28 lb 14¾ oz	13,100 kg	J. T. Cooke	Funtington, West Sussex	1964
Brussels Sprout[1]	16 lb 1 oz	7,285 kg	E. E. Jenkins	Shipston-on-Stour, Warwickshire	1974
Cabbage[2]	114 lb 3 oz	51,8 kg	P. G. Barton	Cleckheaton, W. Yorkshire	1977
Carrot[3]	7 lb 11½ oz	3,501 kg	A. Howcroft	Huddersfield, W. Yorkshire	1979
Cauliflower	52 lb 11½ oz	23,900 kg	J. T. Cooke	Funtington, W. Sussex	1966
Celery	35 lb	15,875 kg	C. Bowcock	Willaston, Merseyside	1973
Cucumber[4]	11 lb 8 oz (indoor)	5,216 kg	R. Butcher	Stockbridge, Hants.	1978
	8 lb 4 oz (outdoor)	3,740 kg	C. Bowcock	Willaston, Merseyside	1973
Dahlia[5]	9 ft tall	2,74 m	J. Crennan	Abbey Wood, London SE	1975
Dwarf Bean	17½ in	43,4 cm	C. Bowcock	Willaston, Merseyside	1973
Gladiolus*	7 ft 10½ in	2,40 m	W. Wilson	Dunfermline, Fife	1977
Gooseberry	2.06 oz	58,5 g	A. Dingle	Macclesfield, Cheshire	1978
Gourd	196 lb	88,900 kg	J. Leathes	Herringfleet Hall, Suffolk	1846
Grapefruit*	3 lb 8 oz	1,585 kg	A. J. Frost	Willington, Bedfordshire	1977
Hollyhock	24 ft 3 in	7,39 m	W. P. Walshe	Eastbourne, E. Sussex	1961
Kale	12 ft tall	3,65 m	B. T. Newton	Mullion, Cornwall	1950
Leek	9 lb 5½ oz	4,235 kg	C. Bowcock	Willaston, Merseyside	1973
Leek, Pot	100.38 in³	1,644 cm³	R. S. Bell	Ashington, Northumberland	1977
Lemon[6]	3 lb 9 oz	1,628 kg	T. Buckeridge	Isfield, E. Sussex	1978
Lettuce	25 lb	11,335 kg	C. Bowcock	Willaston, Merseyside	1974
Lupin*	6 ft 0½ in	1,84 m	J. Lawlor	New Malden, Surrey	1971
Mangold	54½ lb	24,720 kg	P. F. Scott	Sutton, Humberside	1971
Marrow[7]	69 lb	31,29 kg	D. Payne	Forthampton	1980
Mushroom[8]	54 in circum.	1,37 m	—	Hasketon, Suffolk	1957
Onion	6 lb 7⅛ oz	2,923 kg	B. Rodger	Crail, Fife	1980
Parsnip[9]	10 lb 8½ oz	4,776 kg	C. Moore	Peacehaven, W. Sussex	1980
Pea Pod	10⅛ in	25,7 cm	T. Currie	Jedburgh, Borders	1964
Pear[10]	2 lb 10½ oz	1,200 kg	Mrs. K. Loines	Hythe, Hampshire	1973
Petunia*	8 ft 4 in	2,53 m	G. A. Warner	Dunfermline, Fife	1978
Potato[11]	7 lb 1 oz	3,200 kg	J. H. East	Spalding, Lincolnshire	1963
Pumpkin[12]	229 lb	103,87 kg	R. Butcher	Stockbridge, Hants	1979
Radish[13]	17 lb	7,711 kg	K. Ayliffe	Brecon, Powys	1976
Red Cabbage	42 lb	19,05 kg	R. Straw	Stavely, Derbyshire	1925
Rhubarb	5 lb 11 oz	2,579 kg	A. C. Setterfield	Englefield, Berkshire	1978
Runner Bean	39 in long	99 cm	Mrs. E. Huxley	Churton, Cheshire	1976
Savoy	38 lb 8 oz	17,450 kg	W. H. Neil	Retford, Nottinghamshire	1966
Shallot*	2 lb 12 oz (47 bulbs)	1,245 kg	M. Silverstoff	Falmouth, Cornwall	1977
Strawberry	7¼ oz	205 kg	E. Oxley	Walton-on-the-Naze, Essex	1972
Sugar Beet[14]	28 lb	12,7 kg	W. Featherby	Everingham, Humberside	1977
Sunflower	23 ft 6½ in tall	7,17 m	F. Kelland	Exeter, Devon	1976
Swede	48 lb 12 oz	22,11 kg	A. Foster	Alnwick, Northumberland	1980
Tomato[15]	4 lb 4 oz	1,925 kg	C. Roberts	Eastbourne, East Sussex	1974
Tomato Plant[16]	38 ft 2 in (length)	11,63 m	Chosen Hill School	Gloucester, Glos.	1980
Tomato Truss	20 lb 4 oz	9,175 kg	C. Bowcock	Willaston, Merseyside	1973
Turnip[17]	35 lb 4 oz	15,975 kg	C. W. Butler	Nafferton, Humberside	1972

[1] A Brussels Sprout plant measuring 11 ft 8 in 3,55 m was grown by Ralph G. Sadler of Watchbury Farm, Barford, Warwickshire on 6 July 1978.

[2] The Swalwell, County Durham Red Cabbage of 1865 grown by William Collingwood (d. 8 Oct 1867) reputedly weighed 123 lb 55,7 kg and was 259 in 6,57 m in circumference.

[3] A specimen of 11 lb 4,79 kg was grown by Bob McEwan of Beeac, Victoria, Australia in September 1967.

[4] A 13 lb 5,89 kg example was grown by George J. Kucera of Mexia, Texas, USA in July 1978. A Vietnamese variety 6 ft 1,83 m long was reported by L. Szabo of Debrécen, Hungary in September 1976.

[5] A 10 ft 6½ in 3,21 m dahlia was grown by Michael Power of Waterford, Ireland in 1981.

[6] A 6 lb 4 oz 2,83 kg lemon with a 28¾ in 73 cm girth was reported by Mrs D. Knutzen of Whittier, California USA in January 1977.

[7] A 96 lb 43,525 kg marrow has been reported from Suffolk. A 63½ lb 28,000 kg specimen grown by J. C. Lewis of Blackwood, Gwent, won a contest in 1937.

[8] Same size reported by J. Coombes at Mark, Somerset on 28 July 1965. In September 1968 one weighing 18 lb 10 oz 8,425 kg was reported from Whidbey I. Washington, USA. A mushroom with an estimated circumference of 75 in 190 cm was reported by the Lualaba river, Zaire in 1920.

[9] One 60 in 152 cm long was reported by M. Zaninovich of Waneroo W. Australia.

[10] A specimen weighing 1,405 kg 3.09 lb was harvested on 10 May 1979 at Messrs K. & R. Yeomans, Arding, Armidale, NSW, Australia.

[11] One weighing 18 lb 4 oz 8,275 kg reported dug up by Thomas Siddal in his garden in Chester on 17 Feb 1795. A yield of 515 lb 233,5 kg from a 2½ lb parent seed by Bowcock planted in April 1977. Six tubers weighing 54 lb 8 oz 24,72 kg by Alan Nunn of Rhodes, Greater Manchester were reported on 18 Sept 1949.

[12] A squash (Cucurbita moschata) of 513 lb 232,69 kg was grown by Harold Fulp, Jr., at Ninevah, Indiana, USA in 1977. A pumpkin (C. maxima) of 240 lb 108,8 kg was reported by Merl Sims of Binger, Oklahoma USA in Sept 1980.

[13] A radish of 25 lb 11,34 kg was grown by Glen Tucker of Stanbury, South Australia in August 1974 and by Herbert Breslow of Ruskin, Florida, USA in 1977.

[14] One weighing 45½ lb 20,63 kg was grown by Robert Meyer of Brawley, California in 1974.

[15] Grace's Gardens reported a 6 lb 8 oz 2,94 kg tomato grown by Clarence Daily of Monona, Wisconsin in 1977.

[16] A 21 ft 3½ in 6,48 m plant was grown at Wyckoff, NJ, USA in July 1976 by David Vibert.

[17] A 73 lb 33,1 kg turnip was reported in December 1768.

* Not in official contest.

The heaviest orange is one weighing 3 lb 11 oz 1,77 kg grown by Bill Calendine of Tucson, Arizona, USA in 1977.

Orchid *Smallest*

The smallest orchid is *Bulbophyllum minutissimum*, found in Australia. Claims have also been made for *Notylia norae* found in Venezuela. The smallest orchid flowers are borne by *Stelis graminea*, being less than 1 mm *0.04 in* long.

Orchid *Highest priced*

The highest price ever paid for an orchid is 1150 guinea (£1,207.50), paid by Baron Schröder to Sanders of St Albans for an *Odontoglossum crispum* (variety *pittianum*) at an auction by Protheroe & Morris of Bow Lane, London, on 22 Mar 1906. A Cymbidium orchid called Rosanna Pinkie was sold in the United States for $4500 (then £1600) in 1952.

Largest rhododendron

The largest species of rhododendron is the scarlet *Rhododendron arboreum*, examples of which reach a height of 60 ft *18,25 m* a Mangalbaré, Nepal. The cross-section of the trunk of a *Rhododendron giganteum*, reputedly 90 ft *27,43 m* high from Yunnan China is preserved at Inverewe Garden, Highland. The largest in the United Kingdom is one 25 ft *7,60 m* tall and 272 ft *82,90 m* in circumference at Government House, Hillsborough Co. Down. A specimen 35 ft *10,65 m* high and 3 ft 3 in in circumference has been measured at Tregothan, Truro, Cornwall.

Largest rose tree

A 'Lady Banks' rose tree at Tombstone, Arizona, USA, has a trunk 40 in *101 cm* thick, stands 9 ft *2,74 m* high and covers an area of 5,380 ft² *499 m²* supported by 68 posts and several thousand feet of piping. This enables 150 people to be seated under the arbour. The cutting came from Scotland in 1884.

FRUITS AND VEGETABLES

Most and least nutritive

An analysis of the 38 commonly eaten raw (as opposed to dried) fruits shows that the one with the highest calorific value is avocado (*Persea americana*), with 741 calories per edible pound or *163 cals per 100 gr*. That with the lowest value is cucumber with 73 calories per pound *16 cals per 100 gr*. Avocados probably originated in Central and South America and contain also vitamins A, C, and E and 2.2 per cent protein.

Melon

A watermelon weighing 200 lb *90,7 kg* was reported by Grace's Garden in April 1980. The growers were Ivan and Lloyd Bright of Hope, Arkansas, USA.

left: 'General Sherman', the 289 ft *85 m* tall Californian Big Tree, the most massive living thing on earth. It weighs over 2000 tonnes (see p. 55). *(GAF Corporation)*
below: The remotest tree, at a Saharan oasis in the Ténéré Desert, Niger Republic (see p. 56). *(Monsieur J. Gateaud: Service Geographique)*

Pineapple *Largest*
A pineapple weighing 17 lb *7,71 kg* was picked by H. Retief in Malindi, Kenya in December 1978.

Potato
A record display of 252 varieties of potato (*Solanum tuberosum*) was mounted at the Royal Horticultural Show in Westminster, London by Donald MacLean on 9–10 Oct, 1979.

FERNS
Largest
The largest of all the more than 6000 species of fern is the tree fern (*Alsophila excelsa*) of Norfolk Island, in the South Pacific, which attains a height of up to 60 ft *18,28 m*.

Smallest
The world's smallest ferns are *Hecistopteris pumila*, found in Central America, and *Azolla caroliniana*, which is native to the United States.

GRASSES
Commonest and fastest growing
The world's commonest grass is *Cynodon dactylon* or Bermuda grass. The 'Callie' hybrid, selected in 1966, grows as much as 6 in *15,2 cm* a day and stolons reach 18 ft *5,5 m* in length. The tallest of the 160 grasses found in Great Britain is the common reed (*Phragmites communis*), which reaches a height of 9 ft 9 in *2,97 m*.

Shortest
The shortest grass native to Great Britain is the very rare sand bent (*Mibora minima*) from Anglesey, Gwynedd which has a maximum growing height of under 6 in *15 cm*.

LEAVES
Largest *World*
The largest leaves of any plant belong to the raffia palm (*Raphia raffia*) of the Mascarene Islands, in the Indian Ocean and the Amazonian bamboo palm (*R. toedigera*) of South America, whose leaf blades may measure up to 65 ft *19,81 m* in length with petioles up to 13 ft *3,96 m*.

The largest undivided leaf is that of *Alocasia macrorrhiza*, found in Sabah, East Malaysia. One found in 1966 was 9 ft 11 in *3,02 m* long and 6 ft 3½ in *1,92 m* wide, with a unilateral area of 34.2 ft² *3,17 m²*.

Largest *Great Britain*
The largest leaves to be found in outdoor plants in Great Britain are those of *Gunnera manicata* from Brazil with leaves 6–10 ft *1,82–3,04 m* across on prickly stems 5–8 ft *1,52–2,43 m* long.

Fourteen-leafed clover
A fourteen-leafed white clover (*Trifolium repens*) was found by Randy Farland near Sioux Falls, South Dakota, USA on 16 June 1975.

SEEDS
Largest
The largest seed in the world is that of the double coconut or Coco de Mer (*Lodoicea seychellarum*), the single-seeded fruit of which may weigh 40 lb *18 kg*. This grows only in the Seychelles, in the Indian Ocean.

Smallest
The smallest seeds are those of *Epiphytic* orchids, at 35,000,000 to the oz (*cf.* grass pollens at up to 6,000,000,000 grains/oz). A single plant of the American ragweed can generate 8,000,000,000 pollen grains in five hours.

Most viable
The most protracted claim for the viability of seeds is that made for the Arctic lupin (*Lupinus arcticus*) found in frozen silt at Miller Creek in the Yukon, Canada in July 1954 by Harold Schmidt. The seeds were germinated in 1966 and were dated by the radiocarbon method of associated material to at least 8000 BC and more probably to 13,000 BC.

Most conquering conker
The highest recorded battle honours for an untreated conker (fruit of the Common horse-chestnut or *Aesculus hippocastanum*) is a 'five thousander plus', which won the BBC Conker Conquest in 1954. A professor of botany has however opined that this heroic specimen might well have been a 'ringer', probably an ivory or tagua nut (*Phytelephas macrocarpa*).

TREES AND WOOD
Most massive tree
The most massive living thing on Earth is the biggest known California big tree (*Sequoiadendron giganteum*) named the 'General Sherman', standing 280 ft *85 m* tall, in the Sequoia National Park, California, USA. It has a true girth of 79.8 ft *24,32 m* (1980) (at 5 ft *1,52 m* above the ground). The 'General Sherman' has been estimated to contain the equivalent of 600,120 board feet of timber, sufficient to make 5,000,000,000 matches. The foliage is blue-green, and the red-brown tan bark may be up to 24 in *61 cm* thick in parts. In 1968 the official published figure for its estimated weight was '2145 tons' (1915 long tons *2030 tonnes*). The largest known petrified tree is one of this species with a 295 ft *89,9 m* trunk near Coaldale, Nevada, USA.

The seed of a 'big tree' weighs only 1/6000th of an oz *4,7 mg*. Its growth at maturity may therefore represent an increase in weight of over 250,000 million-fold.

Greatest girth *World*
The Santa Maria del Tule Tree, in the state of Oaxaca, in Mexico is a Montezuma cypress (*Taxodium mucronatum*) with a girth of 112–113 ft *34,1–34,4 m* (1949) at a height of 5 ft *1,52 m* above the ground. A figure of 167 ft *51 m* in circumference was reported for the pollarded European chestnut (*Castanea sativa*) known as the 'Tree of the 100 Horse' (Castagno di Cento Cavalli) on Mount Etna, Sicily, Italy in 1972.

Greatest girth *Britain*
The tree of greatest girth in Britain is a sweet ('Spanish') chestnut (*Castanea sativa*) in the grounds of Canford School, Nr. Wimbourne, Dorset, with a bole 43 ft 9 in *13,33 m* in circumference. The largest-girthed living British oak is one at Bowthorpe Farm near Bourne, south Lincolnshire, measured in September 1973 to be 39 ft 1 in *11,91 m*. The largest 'maiden' (i.e. not pollarded) oak is the Majesty Oak at Fredville Park, near Nonington, Kent, with a girth of (1973) 38 ft 1 in *11,60 m*.

Fastest growing
Discounting bamboo, which is not botanically classified as a tree, but as a woody grass, the fastest rate of growth recorded is 35 ft 3 in *10,74 m* in 13 months by an *Albizzia falcata* planted on 17 June 1974 in Sabah, Malaysia. The youngest recorded age for a tree to reach 100 ft *30,48 m* is 5¾ years for a Camarere (*Eucalyptus deglupta*) in Baku Forest Reserve near Madang, Papua New Guinea.

Slowest growing
The speed of growth of trees depends largely upon conditions, although some species, such as box and yew, are always slow-growing. The extreme is represented by a specimen of Sitka spruce which required 98 years to grow to 11 in *28 cm* tall with a diameter of less than 1 in *2,5 cm* on the Arctic tree-line. The growing of miniature trees or *bonsai* is an oriental cult mentioned as early as *c.* 1320.

Tallest *World*
The world's tallest known species of tree is the coast redwood (*Sequoia sempervirens*), now found growing indigenously only near the coast of California from just across the Oregon border south to Monterey. The tallest measured example is 'Tallest Tree' in Redwood Creek Grove, Humboldt County, California discovered by Dr Paul A. Zahl in 1963 to be 367.8 ft *112,10 m* with a dead top and re-estimated at 366.2 ft *111,60 m* in 1970. It has a girth of 43 ft 11 in *13,38 m*. 'Tallest Tree' is dying back slowly. Several trees with healthy growing tips are 360+ ft *110+ m* in groves by Bull Creek near Weott, California. The tallest non-sequoia is a Douglas fir at Quinault Lake Park trail, Washington, USA of *c.* 310 ft *94,5 m*.

The tallest broadleaf tree in the world is a *Eucalyptus regnans* (mountain ash) growing in the Styx Valley, Tasmania, and measured at 99 m *325 ft*.

Tallest *All-time*

The identity of the tallest tree of all-time has never been satisfactorily resolved. Although there have been claims as high as 525 ft *160 m* (subsequently reduced in May 1889 on re-measurement to 220 ft *67 m*), the now accepted view is that maximum height recorded by a qualified surveyor was the 375 ft *114,3 m* Cornthwaite Tree (*Eucalyptus regnans*, formerly *E. amygdalina*) in Thorpdale, Gippsland, Victoria in 1880. Claims for a Douglas fir (*Pseudotsuga taxifolia*) of 417 ft *127,10 m* with a 77 ft *23,47 m* circumference felled by George Carey in 1895 in British Columbia have been obscured, though not necessarily invalidated by a falsified photograph. The tallest specimen now known is *c.* 310 ft *94,5 m* (see above). A coast redwood of 367 ft 8 in *112,06 m* felled in 1873 near Guerneville, California, USA, was thus almost precisely the same height as 'Tallest Tree' as originally measured.

Tallest *Great Britain*

The tallest trees in Great Britain are a Grand fir (*Abies grandis*) at Strone, Cairndow, Strathclyde, and Douglas firs at The Hermitage, Perth and at Moniac Glen, Inverness. All are a few feet over 190 ft *58 m* (1980). The tallest in England is a Douglas fir (*Pseudotsuga taxifolia*) measured at 172 ft *52,42 m* in 1974 at Dunster, Somerset. The tallest measured in Northern Ireland is a Giant Sequoia (*Sequoiadendron giganteum*), measured in 1976 to be 158 ft *48 m* tall at Caledon Castle, County Tyrone.

Tallest *Ireland*

The tallest tree in Ireland is a Sitka spruce (*Picea sitchensis*) 166 ft *50,59 m* tall at Curraghmore, Waterford, measured in March 1974.

Tallest Christmas Tree

The world's tallest cut Christmas tree was a 221 ft *67,36 m* tall

Douglas fir (*Pseudotsuga taxifolia*) erected at Northgate Shopping Center, Seattle, Washington in December 1950. The tallest Christmas tree erected in Britain was the 85 ft 3¼ in *25,98 m* long spruce from Norway erected for the Canterbury Cathedral appeal on the South Bank, London on 20 Nov 1975.

Oldest tree *World*

The oldest recorded tree was a bristlecone pine (*Pinus longaeva*), designated WPN–114, which grew at 10,750 ft *3275 m* above sea-level on the north-east face of the Wheeler Ridge on the Sierra Nevada, California, USA. During studies in 1963 and 1964 it was found to be about 4900 years old but was cut down with a chain saw. The oldest known *living* tree is the bristlecone pine named *Methuselah* at 10,000 ft *3050 m* in the California side of the White Mountains confirmed as 4600 years old. In March 1974 it was reported that this tree had produced 48 live seedlings. Dendrochronologists estimate the *potential* life-span of bristlecone pine at nearly 5500 years, but that of a 'Big Tree' at perhaps 6000 years. No single cell lives more than 30 years. A report in March 1976 stated that some enormous specimens of Japanese cedar (*Cryptomeria japonica*) had been dated by carbon 14 to 5200 BC. The great ages attributed to the Canary Island dragon tree (*Dracaena draco*) are discounted by botanists.

Oldest tree *Great Britain*

Of all British trees that with the longest life is the yew (*Taxus baccata*), for which a maximum age well in excess of 1000 years is usually conceded. The oldest known is the Fortingall Yew near Aberfeldy, Tayside, part of which still grows. In 1777 this tree was over 50 ft *15,24 m* in girth and it cannot be much less than 1500 years old today. The 1500 years attributed by the Royal Archeological Society to the Eastham yew in Wirral is not accepted by present day expert opinion.

Earliest species

The earliest species of tree still surviving is the maiden-hair tree (*Ginkgo biloba*) of Chekiang, China, which first appeared about 160,000,000 years ago, during the Jurassic era. It was 're-discovered' by Kaempfer (Netherlands) in 1690 and reached England *c.* 1754. It has been grown in Japan since *c.* 1100 where it was known as *ginkyō* ('silver apricot') and is now known as *icho*.

Most leaves

Little work has been done on the laborious task of establishing which species has most leaves. A large oak has perhaps 250,000 but a Cypress may have some 45–50 million leaf scales.

Remotest

The tree remotest from any other tree is believed to be one at an oasis in the Ténéré Desert, Niger Republic. In February 1960 it survived being rammed by a lorry driven by a Frenchman. There were no other trees within 50 km *31 miles*. The tree was transplanted and it is now in the Museum at Niamey, Niger.

Most expensive

The highest price ever paid for a tree is $51,000 (then £18,214) for a single Starkspur Golden Delicious apple tree from near Yakima, Washington, USA, bought by a nursery in Missouri in 1959.

Largest forest *World*

The largest afforested areas in the world are the vast coniferous forests of the northern USSR, lying mainly between latitude 55° N, and the Arctic Circle. The total wooded area amounts to 2,700,000,000 acres *1100 million ha* (25 per cent of the world's forests), of which 38 per cent is Siberian larch. The USSR is 34 per cent afforested.

Largest forest *Great Britain*

The largest forest in England is Kielder Forest (72,336 acres *29 273 ha*), in Northumberland. The largest forest in Wales is the Coed Morgannwg (Forest of Glamorgan) (42,555 acres *17 221 ha*). Scotland's most extensive forest is the Glen Trool Forest (51,376 acres *20 791 ha*) in Kirkcudbrightshire. The United Kingdom is 7 per cent afforested.

Wood *Heaviest*

The heaviest of all woods is black ironwood (*Olea laurifolia*), also called South African ironwood, with a specific gravity of up to

---

TALLEST TREES IN UNITED KINGDOM
By species

		ft	m
Alder (Italian)	Westonbirt, Gloucester	98	30
Alder (Common)	Old Roar Ghyll, St. Leonards, East Sussex	86	26
Ash	Cockington Ct. Devon	121	37
Beech	Whitfield Ho, Hereford & Worcs.	135	41
Beech (Copper)	Chart Park Golf Course, Dorking, Surrey	121	37
Birch (Silver)	Woburn Sands, Bedfordshire	97	29
Cedar (Blue Atlas)	Brockhampton Pk, Hereford & Worcs.	125	38
Cedar (of Lebanon)	Petworth House, West Sussex	132	40
Chestnut (Horse)	Petworth House, West Sussex	125	38
Chestnut (Sweet)	Godinton Park, Kent	118	35
Cypress (Lawson)	Endsleigh, Devon	133	40
Cypress (Leyland)	Bicton, Devon	111	34
Cypress (Monterey)	Montacute House, Somerset	121	37
Douglas Fir	Moniac Glen, Inverness	190+	58+
Elm (Wych)[1]	Rossie Priory, nr Dundee	128	39
Eucalyptus (Blue Gum)	Glengariff, Co. Cork	140	42
Grand Fir	Strone, Cairndow, Strathclyde	190+	58+
Ginkgo	Linton Park (Maidstone), Kent	93	28
Hemlock (Western)	Benmore, Strathclyde	152	46
Holly	Staverton Thicks, Suffolk	74	22
Hornbeam	Wrest Park, Bedfordshire	105	32
Larch (European)	Glenlee, Dumfries & Galloway	150	46
Larch (Japanese)	Blair Castle, Tayside	121	36
Lime	Duncombe Park, North Yorks.	150	45
Metasequoia	Savill Garden, Berks.	72	22
Monkey Puzzle	Lochnaw, Dumfries & Galloway	95	29
Oak (Common)	Petworth House, West Sussex	121	37
Oak (Sessile)	Whitfield Ho., Hereford & Worcs.	140	42
Oak (Red)	Cowdray Park, West Sussex	115	35
Pear	Borde Hill, West Sussex	64	19
Pine (Corsican)	Stanage Park, Powys	144	43
Plane	Bryanston, Dorset	145	44
Poplar (Black Italian)	Fairlawne, Kent	150	46
Poplar (Lombardy)	Marble Hill, Twickenham, G. London	118	35
Redwood (Coast)	Roche's Arboretum, Sussex	140	43
Silver Fir	Benmore, Strathclyde	158	48
Spruce (Sitka)	Murthly, Tayside	174	53
Sycamore	Drumlanrig Castle, Dumfries & Gal.	112	34
Tulip-tree	Taplow House, Buckinghamshire	120	36
Walnut	Bayhurst, Newport Pagnell, Northants.	80	24
Walnut (Black)	Battersea Park, London	105	32
Wellingtonia	Endsleigh, Devon	165	50
Willow (Weeping)	Trinity College, Cambridge	76	23
Wingnut (Caucasian)	Abbotsbury, Dorset	115	35
Yew	Close Walks, Midhurst, W. Sussex	95	29

[1] It was estimated in 1980 that more than 17 million of the 23 million elms in southern England had since 1968 been killed by the fungus that causes Dutch elm disease Ceratocystis ulmi.

1.49, and weighing up to 93 lb/ft³ *1490 kg/m³*. The heaviest British wood is boxwood (*Buxus sempervirens*) with an extreme of 64 lb/ft³ *1025 kg/m³*.

Wood *Lightest*
The lightest wood is *Aeschynomene hispida*, found in Cuba, which has a specific gravity of 0.044 and a weight of only 2¾ lb/ft³ *44 kg/m³*. The wood of the balsa tree (*Ochroma pyramidale*) is of very variable density—between 2½ and 24 lb/ft³ *40 and 384 kg/m³*. The density of cork is 15 lb/ft³ *240 kg/m³*.

Bamboo *Tallest*
The tallest recorded bamboo was a Thorny bamboo culm (*Bambusa arundinacea*) felled at Pattazhi, Travancore, Southern India, in November 1904 measuring 121½ ft *37,03 m*.

Bamboo *Fastest growing*
Some species of the 45 genera of bamboo have attained growth rates of up to 36 in *91 cm* per day (0.00002 mph *0,00003 km/h*), on their way to reaching a height of 100 ft *30 m* in less than three months.

KINGDOM PROTISTA

PROTISTA
Protista were first discovered in 1676 by Anton van Leeuwenhoek of Delft (1632–1723), a Dutch microscopist. Among Protista are characteristics common to both plants and animals. The more plant-like are termed Protophyta (protophytes), including unicellular algae, and the more animal-like are placed in the phylum Protozoa (protozoans), including amoeba and flagellates.

Largest
The largest protozoans which are known to have existed were the now extinct Nummulites, which each had a diameter of 0.95 in *24,1 mm*. The largest existing protozoan is *Pelomyxa palustris*, which may attain a length of up to 0.6 in *15,2 mm*.

Smallest
The smallest of all protophytes is the marine microflagellate alga *Micromonas pusilla*, with a diameter of less than 2 microns or micrometres (2 × 10⁻⁶m) or *0.00008 in*.

Fastest moving
The protozoan *Monas stigmatica* has been measured to move a distance equivalent to 40 times its own length in a second. No human can cover even seven times his own length in a second.

Fastest reproduction
The protozoan *Glaucoma*, which reproduces by binary fission, divides as frequently as every three hours. Thus in the course of a day it could become a 'six greats grandparent' and the progenitor of 510 descendants.

KINGDOM FUNGI

Largest
Matthew Fogarty of Ayton, Berwickshire found a puff ball (*Lycoperdon gigantea*) 64 in *162,5 cm* in circumference and 16¼ in *41,2 cm* high on 9 Mar 1980. A specimen also of 64 in *162,5 cm* in circumference was recorded in New York State, USA in 1877. A 72 lb *32,6 kg* example of the edible mushroom (*Polyporus frondosus*) was reported by Joseph Opple near Solon, Ohio in September 1976.

The largest officially recorded tree fungus was a specimen of *Oxyporus (Fomes) nobilissimus*, measuring 56 in *142 cm* by 37 in *94 cm* and weighing at least 300 lb *136 kg* found by J. Hisey in Washington State, USA, in 1946. The largest recorded in the United Kingdom is an ash fungus (*Fomes fraxineus*) measuring 50 in by 15 in *127 cm* by *38 cm* wide, found by the forester A. D. C. LeSueur on a tree at Waddesdon, Buckinghamshire, in 1954.

Most poisonous toadstool
The yellowish-olive death cap (*Amanita phalloides*) is regarded as the world's most poisonous fungus. It is found in England. From six to fifteen hours after tasting, the effects are vomiting, delirium, collapse and death. Among its victims was Cardinal Giulio de' Medici, Pope Clement VII (b. 1478) on 25 Sept 1534.

The Registrar General's Report states that between 1920 and 1950 there were 39 fatalities from fungus poisoning in the United Kingdom. As the poisonous types are mostly *Amanita* varieties, it is reasonable to assume that the deaths were predominantly due to *Amanita phalloides*. The most recent fatality was probably in 1960.

Aeroflora
Fungi were once classified in the subkingdom Protophyta of the Kingdom Protista. The highest total fungal spore count was 161,037 per m³ near Cardiff on 21 July 1971. A plant tree pollen count of 2160 per m³ was recorded near London on 9 May 1971. The lowest counts of airborne allergens are nil. The highest recorded grass pollen count in Britain was one of 2824 per m³ recorded at Aberystwyth on 29 June 1961.

KINGDOM PROCARYOTA

Earliest life form
Traces of yeast-like cells, *Isuasphaera isua* Pflug from cherty layers of quartzite from SW Greenland dated to 3800 million years ago were announced on 9 Aug 1979, but in January 1981 were rejected as 'fluid inclusions'.

In June 1980 Prof J. William Schopf announced the discovery of 5 microbial life forms in rock dated to 3500 million years old in the 'North Pole' region of northern Western Australia.

The earliest life-form reported from Britain is *Kakabekia barghoorniana*, a microorganism similar in form to an orange slice, found near Harlech, Gwynedd, Wales in 1964 and dated to 2000 million years ago.

BACTERIA
Anton van Leeuwenhoek (1632–1723) was the first to observe bacteria in 1675. The largest of the bacteria is the sulphur bacterium *Beggiatoa mirabilis*, which is from 16 to 45 microns in width and which may form filaments several millimetres long.

Smallest free-living entity
The smallest of all free-living organisms are pleuro-pneumonia-like organisms (PPLO) of the *Mycoplasma*. One of these, *Mycoplasma laidlawii*, first discovered in sewage in 1936, has a diameter during its early existence of only 100 millimicrons, or 0.000004 in. Examples of the strain known as H.39 have a maximum diameter of 300 millimicrons and weigh an estimated 1.0 × 10⁻¹⁶gramme. Thus a 174 ton *177 tonnes* Blue whale would weigh 1.77 × 10²⁴ or 1.7 quadrillion times as much.

Highest
In April 1967 the US National Aeronautics and Space Administration reported that bacteria had been recently discovered at an altitude of 135,000 ft (25.56 miles) *41 100 m*.

Longest lived
The oldest deposits from which living bacteria are claimed to have been extracted are salt layers near Irkutsk, USSR, dating from about 600,000,000 years ago. The discovery was not accepted internationally. The US Dry Valley Drilling Project in Antarctica claimed resuscitated rod-shaped bacteria from caves up to a million years old.

Toughest
The bacterium *Micrococcus radiodurans* can withstand atomic radiation of 6.5 million röntgens or 10,000 times that fatal to the average man.

57

London Zoo's Giraffe House opened 10 years after the zoo was founded in 1826. The building has necessarily retained muc of its original shape.

VIRUSES

Largest

Viruses were discovered by Dmitriy Ivanovsky (1864–1920) in 1892. The largest true viruses are the brick-shaped pox viruses (*e.g.* smallpox, vaccina, orf, etc.) measuring *c.* 250×300 nm (1 nanometer = 1×10^{-9}m).

Smallest

Of more than 1000 identified viruses, the smallest is the sheep scrapie virus with a diameter of 14 nanometers or 14 millionths of a millimetre. Some 40 times smaller still is the nanovariant WSI RNA with a length of 91 nucleotides published by Dr Walter Schaffner of the University of Zürich in 1977.

PARKS, ZOOS, OCEANARIA AND AQUARIA

PARKS

Largest *World*

The world's largest park is the Wood Buffalo National Park in Alberta, Canada (established 1922), which has an area of 11,172,000 acres (17,560 miles² *45 480 km²*).

Largest *Britain*

The largest National Park in Great Britain is the Lake District National Park which has an area of 866 miles² *2240 km²*. The largest private park in the United Kingdom is Woburn Park (3000 acres *1200 ha*), near Woburn Abbey, the seat of the Dukes of Bedford. The largest common in the United Kingdom is Llansantffraed Cwmdauddwr (28,819 acres *11 662 ha*) in Powys, Wales.

ZOOS

Largest game reserve

It has been estimated that throughout the world there are some 500 zoos with an estimated annual attendance of 330,000,000. The largest zoological reserve in the world has been the Etosha Reserve, Namibia established in 1907 with an area which grew to 38,427 miles² *99 525 km²*.

Oldest

The earliest known collection of animals was that set up by

Shulgi, a 3rd dynasty ruler of Ur in 2094–2047 BC at Puzurish i south-east Iraq. The oldest known zoo is that at Schönbrunn Vienna, Austria, built in 1752 by the Holy Roman Empero Franz I for his wife Maria Theresa. The oldest existing privatel owned zoo in the world is that of the Zoological Society o London, founded in 1826. Its collection, housed partly i Regent's Park, London (36 acres *14,5 ha*) and partly at Whip snade Park, Bedfordshire (541 acres *219 ha*) (opened 23 Ma 1931), is the most comprehensive in the United Kingdom. Th stocktaking on 1 Jan 1981 accounted for a total of 10,968 spec mens. These comprised 2154 mammals, 2037 birds, 587 reptile and amphibians, an estimated total of 1971 fish and an estimate total of 4219 invertebrates. Locusts, ants and bees are exclude from these figures. The record annual attendances are 3,031,57 in 1950 for Regent's Park and 756,758 in 1961 for Whipsnade

OCEANARIA

Earliest and largest

The world's first oceanarium is Marineland of Florida, opene in 1938 at a site 18 miles *29 km* south of St Augustine, Florida USA. Up to 5,800,000 gal *26,3 million litres* of sea-water ar pumped daily through two major tanks, one rectangular (100 f *30,48 m* long by 40 ft *12,19 m* wide by 18 ft *5,48 m* deep) con taining 375,000 gal *1,7 million litres* and one circular (233 ft *71 n* in circumference and 12 ft *3,65 m* deep) containing 330,000 ga *1,5 million litres*. The tanks are seascaped, including coral reef and even a shipwreck. The salt water tank at Hanna-Barbera' Marineland, located at Palos Verdes, California, USA is 251½ f *76,65 m* in circumference and 22 ft *6,7 m* deep, with a capacit of 530,000 gal *2,4 million litres*. The total capacity of this whol oceanarium is 2,080,000 gal *9,4 million litres*. Their killer whal 'Orky' at 14,000 lb *6350 kg* is the largest in captivity.

AQUARIA

Largest aquarium

The world's largest aquarium, as opposed to fish farm, is th John G. Shedd Aquarium at 12th Street and Lake Shore Drive Chicago, Illinois, USA, completed in November 1929 at a cost o $3,250,000 (then £668,725). The total capacity of its displa tanks is 375,000 gal *1,7 million litres* with reservoir tanks holdin 1,665,000 gal *7,5 million litres*. Exhibited are 5500 specimen from 350 species. Most of these specimens are collected by th Aquarium collecting boat based in Miami, Florida, and ar shipped by air to Chicago. The record attendances are 78,658 i a day on 21 May 1931, and 4,689,730 visitors in the single year o 1931.

3.
THE
NATURAL WORLD

THE EARTH

The Earth is not a true sphere, but flattened at the poles and hence an ellipsoid. The polar diameter of the Earth (7899.809 miles *12 713,510 km*) is 26.576 miles *42,770 km* less than the equatorial diameter (7926.385 miles *12 756,280 km*). The Earth also has a slight ellipticity of the equator since its long axis (about longitude 37° W) is 174 yd *159 m* greater than the short axis. The greatest departures from the reference ellipsoid are a protuberance of 244 ft *74 m* in the area of Papua/New Guinea and a depression of 354 ft *108 m* south of Sri Lanka, in the Indian Ocean.

The greatest circumference of the Earth, at the equator, is 24,901.47 miles *40 075,03 km*, compared with 24,859.75 miles *40 007,89 km* at the meridian. The area of the surface is estimated to be 196,937,600 miles^2 *510 066 100 km^2*. The period of axial rotation, *i.e.* the true sidereal day, is 23 hr 56 min 4.0996 sec, mean time.

The mass of the Earth is 5,880,000,000,000,000,000,000 tons *5974 × 10^{21} tonnes* and its density is 5.515 times that of water. The volume is an estimated 259,875,620,000 miles^3 *1 083 208 840 000 km^3*. The Earth picks up cosmic dust but estimates vary widely with 30,000 tons/*tonnes* a year being the upper limit. Modern theory is that the Earth has an outer shell or lithosphere about 25 miles *40 km* thick, then an outer and inner rock layer or mantle extending 1800 miles *2900 km* deep, beneath which there is an iron-nickel core at an estimated temperature of 3700° C *6700° F*, and at a pressure of 22,000 tons/*tonnes* per in^2 or 330 GPa. If the iron-nickel core theory is correct, iron must be by far the most abundant element in the Earth.

1. WEATHER

Guinness Superlatives Ltd. published in 1977 a more specialist volume entitled the *Guinness Book of Weather Facts and Feats* by Ingrid Holford (Price £6.50).

The meteorological records given below necessarily relate largely to the last 140–160 years, since data before that time are both sparse and often unreliable. Reliable registering thermometers were introduced as recently as *c.* 1820. The longest continuous observations have been maintained at the Radcliffe Observatory, Oxford since 1815.

Palaeo-entomological evidence is that there was a southern European climate in England *c.* 90,000 BC, while in *c.* 6000 BC the mean summer temperature reached 67° F *19,4° C*, or 6 deg F *3,3 deg C* higher than the present. The earliest authentic recording of British weather relates to the period 26 Aug–17 Sept 55 BC. The earliest reliably known hot summer was in AD 664 during our driest-ever century and the earliest known severe winter was that of AD 763–4. In 1683–4 there was frost in London from November to April. Frosts were recorded during August in the period 1668–89.

Most equable temperature
The location with the most equable recorded temperature over a short period is Garapan, on Saipan, in the Mariana Islands, Pacific Ocean. During the nine years from 1927 to 1935, inclusive, the lowest temperature recorded was 19,6° C *67.3° F* on 30 Jan 1934 and the highest was 31,4° C *88.5° F* on 9 Sept 1931, giving an extreme range of 11,8 deg C *21.2 deg F*. Between 1911 and 1966 the Brazilian off-shore island of Fernando de Noronha had a minimum temperature of 18,6° C *65.5° F* on 17 Nov 1913 and a maximum of 32,0° C *89.6° F* on 2 Mar 1965, an extreme range of 13,4 deg C *24.1 deg F*.

Greatest temperature ranges
The great recorded temperature ranges in the world are around the Siberian 'cold pole' in the eastern USSR. Temperatures in Verkhoyansk (67° 33' N, 133° 23' E) have ranged 192 deg F *106,7 deg C* from −94° F *−70° C* (unofficial) to 98° F *36,7° C*.

The greatest temperature variation recorded in a day is 100 deg F *55,5 deg C* (a fall from 44° F *6,7° C* to −56° F *−48,8° C*) at Browning, Montana, USA, on 23–24 Jan 1916. The most freakish rise was 49 deg F *27,2 deg C* in 2 min at Spearfish, South Dakota, from −4° F *−20° C* at 7.30 a.m. to 45° F *7,2° C* at 7.32 a.m. on 22 Jan 1943. The British record is 29 deg C

The dense equatorial rain forest of Mt Wai-'ale-'ale Kauai, Hawaii, the wettest place on earth (see p. 61). (*Alex Hansen*)

52.2 deg F (−7°C 19.4°F to 22°C 71.6°F) at Tummel Bridge, Tayside on 9 May 1978.

Longest freeze

The longest recorded unremitting freeze (maximum temperature 32°F 0°C and below) in the British Isles was one of 34 days at Moor House, Cumbria, from 23 Dec 1962 to 25 Jan 1963. This was almost certainly exceeded at the neighbouring Great Dun Fell, where the screen temperature never rose above freezing during the whole of January 1963. Less rigorous early data includes a frost from 5 Dec 1607 to 14 Feb 1608 and a 91-day frost on Dartmoor, Devon in 1854–5. No temperature lower than 34°F 1°C has ever been recorded on Bishop Rock, Isles of Scilly.

Upper atmosphere

The lowest temperature ever recorded in the atmosphere is −143°C −225.4°F at an altitude of about 50–60 miles *80,5–96,5 km*, during noctilucent cloud research above Kronogård, Sweden, from 27 July to 7 Aug 1963. A jet stream moving at 408 mph *656 km/h* at 154,200 ft *47 000 m* (29.2 miles *46 km*) was recorded by Skua rocket above South Uist, Outer Hebrides, Scotland on 13 Dec 1967.

Most recent White Christmas and Frost Fair

London has experienced seven 'White' Christmas Days since 1900. These have been 1906, 1917 (slight), 1923 (slight), 1927, 1938, 1956 (slight) and 1970. These were more frequent in the

A plaque commemorating the world's highest surface wind speed, recorded at Mt Washington, New Hampshire, USA (see p. 61) (*Alec Girsman*)

19th century and even more so before the change of the calenda which, by removing 3–13 Sept brought forward all dates subsequent to 2 Sept 1752 by 11 days. The last of the nine recorde Frost Fairs held on the Thames since 1564/65 was from Decen ber 1813 to 26 Jan 1814.

Progressive extremes

The world's extremes of temperature have been noted progress ively thus:

PROGRESSIVE RECORDINGS OF EXTREME HIGH TEMPERATURES WORLD WIDE

127.4° F	53,0° C	Ouargla, Algeria	27 Aug	1884
130° F	54,4° C	Amos, California, USA	17 Aug	1885
130° F	54,4° C	Mammoth Tank, California, USA	17 Aug	1885
134° F	56,7° C	Death Valley, California, USA	10 July	1913
136.4° F	58,0° C	Al'Aziziyah (el-Azizia), Libya*	13 Sept	1922

* *Obtained by the US National Geographical Society but not officially recognised by the Libyan Ministry of Communications.*

A reading of 140° F 60° C at Delta, Mexico, in August 1953 is not now accepted because of over-exposure to roof radiation. The official Mexican record of 136.4° F 58,0° C at San Luis, Sonora on 11 Aug 1933 is not internationally accepted.

A freak heat flash reported from Coimbra, Portugal, in September 1933 said to have caused the temperature to rise to 70° C 158° F for 120 sec is apocryphal.

PROGRESSIVE RECORDINGS OF EXTREME LOW TEMPERATURES WORLD WIDE

−73° F	−58,3° C	Floeberg Bay, Ellesmere I., Canada		1852
−90.4° F	−68° C	Verkhoyansk, Siberia, USSR	3 Jan	1885
−90.4° F	−68° C	Verkhoyansk, Siberia, USSR	5 & 7 Feb	1892
−90.4° F	−68° C	Oymyakon, Siberia, USSR	6 Feb	1933
−100.4° F	−73,5° C	South Pole, Antarctica	11 May	1957
−102.1° F	−74,5° C	South Pole, Antarctica	17 Sept	1957
−109.1° F	−78,34° C	Sovietskaya, Antarctica	2 May	1958
−113.3° F	−80,7° C	Vostok, Antarctica	15 June	1958
−114.1° F	−81,2° C	Sovietskaya, Antarctica	19 June	1958
−117.4° F	−83,0° C	Sovietskaya, Antarctica	25 June	1958
−122.4° F	−85,7° C	Vostok, Antarctica	7–8 Aug	1958
−124.1° F	−86,7° C	Sovietskaya, Antarctica	9 Aug	1958
−125.3° F	−87,4° C	Vostok, Antarctica	25 Aug	1958
−126.9° F	−88,3° C	Vostok, Antarctica	24 Aug	1960

Footnotes to table

(a) *The 100.5° F 38,6° C reported from Tonbridge, Kent was a non-standard exposure and is est mated to be equivalent to 97–98° F 36–36,7° C*

(b) *Vostok is 11,220 ft 3419 m above sea-level. The coldest permanently inhabited place is th Siberian village of Oymyakon (63° 16' N., 143° 15' E.), in the USSR where the temperatur reached −96° F −71,1° C in 1964.*

(c) *The −23° F −30,5° C at Blackadder, Borders, on 4 Dec 1879, and the −20° F −28,9° C Grantown-on-Spey on 24 Feb 1955, were not standard exposures. The −11° F −23,9° reported from Buxton, Derbyshire on 11 Feb 1895 was not standard. The lowest offici temperature in England is −6° F −21,1° C at Bodiam, West Sussex on 20 Jan 1940, Ambleside, Cumbria on 21 Jan 1940 and at Houghall, Durham on 5 Jan 1941 and 4 Marc 1947.*

(d) *This is equal to 7,435 tons 7554 tonnes of rain per acre. Elevation 1200 m 3937 ft.*

(e) *The record for Ireland is 145.4 in 3921 mm near Derriana Lough, County Kerry in 1948.*

(f) *The record for a single snow storm is 189 in 4800 mm at Mt. Shasta, Ski Bowl, California, an for 24 hr, 76 in 1930 mm at Silver Lake, Colorado, USA on 14–15 April 1921. The greates depth of snow on the ground was 25 ft 5 in 7,74 m at Paradise on 17 Apr 1972. London's ea liest recorded snow was on 25 Sept 1885, and the latest on 27 May 1821. Less reliable report suggest snow on 12 Sept 1658 (Old Style) and on 12 June 1791.*

(g) *St Petersburg, Florida, USA, recorded 768 consecutive sunny days from 9 Feb 1967 to 1 March 1969.*

(h) *The south-eastern end of the village of Lochranza, Isle of Arran, Strathclyde is in shadow c mountains from 18 Nov to 8 Feb each winter.*

(j) *The USS Repose, a hospital ship, recorded 25.55 in 856 mb in the eye of a typhoon in 2 35' N 128° 20' E off Okinawa on 16 Sept 1945.*

(k) *The highest speed yet measured in a tornado is 280 mph 450 km/h at Wichita Falls, Texas USA on 2 Apr 1958.*

(l) *The figure of 177.2 mph 285,2 km/h at RAF Saxa Vord, Unst, in the Shetlands, Scotland, on 1 Feb 1962, was not recorded with standard equipment. There were gales of great severity o 15 Jan 1362 and 26 Nov 1703.*

(m) *Between Lat. 35° N. and 35° S. there are some 3200 thunderstorms each 12 night-time hours some of which can be heard at a range of 18 miles 29 km.*

(n) *In Death Valley, California, USA, maximum temperatures of over 120° F 48,9° C were record ed on 43 consecutive days—6 July to 17 Aug 1917. At Marble Bar, Western Australia (max mum 121° F 49,4° C) 160 consecutive days with maximum temperatures of over 100° 37,8° C were recorded—31 Oct 1923 to 7 Apr 1924 at Wyndham, Western Australia, the tem perature reached 90° F 32,2° C or more on 333 days in 1946.*

(o) *The lowest rainfall recorded in a single year was 9.29 in 23,6 cm at one station in Margate Kent in 1921.*

(p) *The longest drought in Scotland was one of 38 days at Port William, Dumfries & Galloway on Apr to 10 May 1938.*

(q) *Much heavier hailstones are sometimes reported. These are usually not single but coalesce stones. An ice block of 1–2 kg 35–70 oz. was reputed at Withington, Manchester on 2 Ap 1973. The Canton Evening News reported on 14 Apr 1981 5 killed and 225 recently injured by hailstorm with stones weighing up to 30 lb 13,6 kg (sic)*

(r) *Lower visibilities occur at higher altitudes. Ben Nevis is reputedly in cloud 300 days per year*

Weather Records

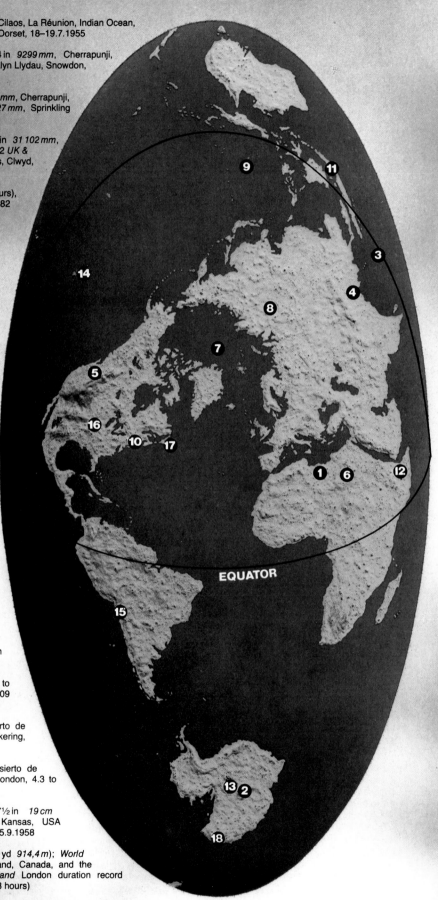

1. HIGHEST SHADE TEMPERATURE: *World* 136.4°F *58° C* Al'Aziziyah, Libya, 13.9.1922 *UK & Ireland* 98°F *<37°C* Raunds, Northants; Epsom, Surrey and Canterbury, Kent 9.8.1911(a)

2. LOWEST SCREEN TEMPERATURE: *World* −126.9°F *−88,3°C* Vostok, Antarctica, 24.8.1960(b). *UK & Ireland* −17°F *−27,2°C*, Braemar, Grampian, Scotland, 11.2.1895(c)

3. GREATEST RAINFALL (24 hours): *World* 73.62 in *1870 mm*, Cilaos, La Réunion, Indian Ocean, 15–16.3.1952(d) *UK & Ireland* 11.00 in *279 mm*, Martinstown, Dorset, 18–19.7.1955

4. GREATEST RAINFALL (Calendar Month): *World* 366.14 in *9299 mm*, Cherrapunji, Meghalaya, India, July 1861 *UK & Ireland* 56.54 in *1436 mm*, Llyn Llydau, Snowdon, Gwynedd, October 1909

GREATEST RAINFALL (12 months): *World* 1041.78 in *26 461 mm*, Cherrapunji, Meghalaya, 1.8.1860–31.7.1861 *UK & Ireland* 257.0 in *6527 mm*, Sprinkling Tarn, Cumbria, in 1954(e)

5. GREATEST SNOWFALL (f) (12 months): *World* 1224.5 in *31 102 mm*, Paradise, Mt Rainier, Washington, USA 19.2.1971 to 18.2.1972 *UK & Ireland* 60 in *1524 mm*, Upper Teesdale and Denbighshire Hills, Clwyd, Wales, 1947

6. MAXIMUM SUNSHINE:(g) *World* >97 per cent (over 4300 hours), eastern Sahara, annual average *UK & Ireland* 78,3 per cent (382 hours) Pendennis Castle, Falmouth, Cornwall, June 1925

7. MINIMUM SUNSHINE: *World* Nil at North Pole—for winter stretches of 186 days *UK & Ireland* Nil in a month at Westminster, London, in December 1890(h)

8. BAROMETRIC PRESSURE (Highest): *World* 1,083.8 mb. *(32.00 in)*, Agata, Siberia, USSR (alt. 862 ft *262 m*), 31.12. 1968. *UK & Ireland* 1054.7 mb. *(31.15 in)*, Aberdeen, 31.1.1902

9. BAROMETRIC PRESSURE (Lowest):(j) *World* 870 mb (*25.69 in*), 300 miles *482 km* west of Guam, Pacific Ocean, 12.10.1979 *UK & Ireland* 925.5 mb (*27.33 in*), Ochtertyre, near Crieff, Tayside, 26.1.1884

10. HIGHEST SURFACE WIND-SPEED:(k) *World* 231 mph *371 km/h*, Mt. Washington (6288 ft *1916 m*), New Hampshire, USA 12.4.1934 *UK & Ireland* 144 mph *231 km/h* (125 knots), Coire Cas ski lift (3525 ft *1074 m*), Cairn Gorm, Highland, 6.3.1967(l)

11. THUNDER-DAYS (Year):(m) *World* 322 days, Bogor (formerly Buitenzorg), Java, Indonesia (average, 1916–19) *UK & Ireland* 38 days, Stonyhurst, Lancashire, 1912 and Huddersfield, West Yorkshire, 1967

12. HOTTEST PLACE (Annual mean):(n) *World* Dallol, Ethiopia, 94°F *34,4°C* (1960–66) *UK & Ireland* Penzance, Cornwall, and Isles of Scilly, both 52.7°F *11,5°C*, average 1931–60

13. COLDEST PLACE (Extrapolated annual mean): *World* Polus Nedostupnosti, Pole of Cold (78°S., 96°E.), Antarctica, −72°F *−57,8°C* Coldest measured: −70°F *−56,6°C* Plateau Station, Antartica *UK & Ireland* Dalwhinnie, Highland 43°F *6,1°C* (alt. 1151 ft *351 m*)

14. WETTEST PLACE (Annual mean): *World* Mt. Wai-'ale-'ale (5148 ft *1569 m*), Kauai, Hawaii, 451 in *11 455 mm* (average1920–72). In 1948 621 in *15 773 mm* *UK & Ireland* Styhead Tarn (1600 ft *487 m*), Cumbria, 172.9 in *4391 mm*

14. MOST RAINY DAYS (Year): *World* Mt. Wai-'ale-'ale up to 350 per annum *UK & Ireland* Ballynahinch, Galway, 309 days in 1923

15. DRIEST PLACE (Annual mean): *World* Nil—in the Desierto de Atacama, near Calama, Chile *UK & Ireland* Great Wakering, Essex, 19.2 in *487 mm* (1916–50)(o)

15. LONGEST DROUGHT: *World* c. 400 years to 1971, Desierto de Atacama, Chile *UK & Ireland* 73 days, Mile End, Greater London, 4.3 to 15.5 1893(p)

16. HEAVIEST HAILSTONES:(q) *World* 1.67 lb *750 g* (7½ in *19 cm* diameter, 17½ in *44,45 cm* circumference), Coffeyville, Kansas, USA 3.9.1970 *UK and Ireland* 5 oz *141 g*, Horsham, West Sussex, 5.9.1958

17. LONGEST SEA LEVEL FOGS (Visibility less than 1000 yd *914,4 m*); *World* Fogs persist for weeks on the Grand Banks, Newfoundland, Canada, and the average is more than 120 days per year(r) *UK & Ireland* London duration record was 26.11 to 1.12.1948 and 5.12 to 9.12.1952 (both 4 days 18 hours)

18. WINDIEST PLACE: *World* The Commonwealth Bay, George V Coast, Antarctica, where gales reach 200 mph *320 km/h* *UK & Ireland* Tiree, Strathclyde (89 ft *27 m*); annual average 17.4 mph *28 km/h*. Fair Isle (1974–78) returned 20.6 mph *33,1 km/h*

The air crew of the US Air Weather Service aircraft back from recording the lowest ever barometric pressure of 870 millibars *25.69 in* in the eye of a 165 kts *305 km/h* Super Typhoon 'Tip' near Gua in the North Pacific (see p. 61). (*USAF*)

Thickest Ice

The greatest recorded thickness of ice on the Earth's surface is 2.97 miles (15,670 ft) *4776 m* measured by radio echo soundings from a U.S. Antarctic Research aircraft at 69° 9′ S 135° 2′ E in Wilkes Land.

Most intense rainfall

Difficulties attend rainfall readings for very short periods but the figure of 1.50 in *38,1 mm* in 1 min at Barst, Guadaloupe on 26 Nov 1970, is regarded as the most intense recorded in modern times. The cloudburst of 'near 2 ft *609 mm* in less than a quarter of half an hour' at Oxford on the afternoon of 31 May (Old Style) 1682 is regarded as unacademically recorded. The most intense rainfall in Britain recorded to modern standards has been 2.0 in *51 mm* in 12 min at Wisbech, Cambridgeshire on 28 June 1970.

Falsest St. Swithin's Days

The legend that the weather on St. Swithin's Day, celebrated on 15 July (Old and New Style) since AD 912, determines the rainfall for the next 40 days is one which has long persisted. There was a brilliant 13½ hr sunshine in London on 15 July 1924, but 30 of the next 40 days were wet. On 15 July 1913 there was a 15-hr downpour, yet it rained on only 9 of the subsequent 40 days in London.

Best and worst British summers

According to Prof. Gordon Manley's survey over the period 1728–1978 the best (*i.e.* driest and hottest) British summer was that of 1976 and the worst (*i.e.* wettest and coldest) that of 1879. Temperatures of >32° C (89.8° F) were recorded on 13 consecutive days (25 June–7 July 1976) within Great Britain including 7 such consecutive days in Cheltenham (1–7 July), where 35,9° C *96.6° F* was reached on 3 July.

Humidity and discomfort

Human comfort or discomfort depends not merely on temperature but on the combination of temperature, humidity, radiation and wind-speed. The United States Weather Bureau uses a Temperature-Humidity Index, which equals two-fifths of the sum of the dry and wet bulb thermometer readings plus 15. A THI of 98.2 has been twice recorded in Death Valley, California—on 27 July 1966 (119° F and 31 per cent) and on 12 Aug 1970 (117° F and 37 per cent). A person driving at 45 mph *72 km/h* in a car without a windscreen in a temperature of −45° F *−42,7° C* would, by the chill factor, experience the equivalent of −125° F *−87,2° C*, *i.e.* within 2 deg F *1,1 deg C* the world record.

Largest mirage

The largest mirage on record was that sighted in the Arctic 83° N 103° W by Donald B. MacMillan in 1913. This type mirage known as the Fata Morgana appeared as the same 'Hill valleys, snow-capped peaks extending through at least 1 degrees of the horizon' that Peary had misidentified as Crock Land 6 years earlier. On 17 July 1939 a mirage of Snaefel Jokull (4715 ft *1437 m*) on Iceland was seen from the sea at distance of 335–350 miles *539–563 km*.

Longest Lasting Rainbow

A rainbow lasting over 3 hours was reported from the coast border of Gwynedd and Clwyd, North Wales on 14 Aug 1979.

Lightning

The visible length of lightning strokes varies greatly. In mou tainous regions, when clouds are very low, the flash may be le than 300 ft *91 m* long. In flat country with very high clouds, cloud-to-earth flash may measure 4 miles *6 km* though in th most extreme cases such flashes have been measured at 20 mile *32 km*. The intensely bright central core of the lightning chann is extremely narrow. Some authorities suggest that its diamet is as little as half an inch *1,27 cm*. This core is surrounded by 'corona envelope' (glow discharge) which may measure 10–20 *3–6 m* in diameter.

The speed of a lightning discharge varies from 100 to 1000 mile sec *160–1600 km/sec* for the downward leader track, and reache up to 87,000 miles/sec *140 000 km/sec* (nearly half the speed light) for the powerful return stroke. In Britain there is a average of 6 strikes/mile² per annum or *3,7 per km²* and a average of 4200 per annum over Greater London alone. Ever few million strokes there is a giant discharge, in which the clou to-earth and the return lightning strokes flash from and to th top of the thunder clouds. In these 'positive giants' energy of u to 3000 million joules (3 × 10¹⁶ ergs) is sometimes recorde The temperature reaches about 30,000° C, which is more tha five times greater than that of the surface of the Sun. A theor that lightning was triggered by cosmic rays was published 1977.

Highest waterspout

The highest waterspout of which there is a reliable record w one observed on 16 May 1898 off Eden, New South Wales, Australia. A theodolite reading from the shore gave its height as 5014 ft *1528 m*. It was about 10 ft *3 m* in diameter. The Spithead waterspout off Ryde, Isle of Wight of 21 Aug 1878 was measured by sextant to be 'about a mile' or *1600 m* in height. A waterspout moved around Torbay, Devon on 17 Sept 1969 which, according to press estimates, was 1000 ft *300 m* in height.

Cloud extremes
The highest standard cloud form is cirrus, averaging 27,000 ft *8250 m* and above, but the rare nacreous or mother-of-pearl formation sometimes reaches nearly 80,000 ft *24 000 m* (see also Noctilucent clouds, Chapter 4). The lowest is stratus, below 3500 ft *1066 m*. The cloud form with the greatest vertical range is cumulo-nimbus, which has been observed to reach a height of nearly 68,000 ft *20 000 m* in the tropics.

Tornadoes
Britain's strongest tornado was at Southsea, Portsmouth on 14 Dec 1810 (Force 8 on the Meaden-TORRO scale). On 19 Oct 1870 fifteen were reported in one day. The Newmarket tornado (Force 6) of 3 Jan 1978 caused property damage estimated at up to £1,000,000.

2. NATURAL PHENOMENA

EARTHQUAKES
(Note: Seismologists record all dates with the year *first*, based not on local time but on Greenwich Mean Time).

Greatest *World*
It is estimated that each year there are some 500,000 detectable seismic or micro-seismic disturbances of which 100,000 can be felt and 1000 cause damage.

An inherent limitation in the widely used Gutenberg–Richter scale (published in 1954) precludes its usefulness when extended to the relative strengths of the strongest earthquakes ever recorded. Its use of surface-wave magnitudes, based on amplitudes of waves of a period of 20 sec, results in the 'damping' of any increase in amplitude where fault ruptures break over a length much above 60 km *37 miles*. These however provenly may reach a length of 800 to 1000 km *500–620 miles*. This 'overload' or 'saturation effect' has resulted in the adoption since 1977 of the Kanamori scale for comparing the most massive earthquakes. Magnitudes are there defined in terms of energy release using the concept of the seismic moment, devised by K-Aki in 1966. Thus the most massive instrumentally recorded earthquake has been the cataclysmic Lebu shock south of Concepción, Chile on 1960 May 22 estimated at 10^{26} ergs. While this uniquely rates a magnitude of 9.5 on the Kanamori scale, it ranks in only equal 4th place (with the 1922 Chilean earthquake) at Magnitude 8.3 on the Gutenberg–Richter scale. For the removal of doubt the progressive records on the two scales are thus.

PROGRESSIVE LIST OF THE WORLD'S STRONGEST INSTRUMENTALLY RECORDED EARTHQUAKES			
Kanamori Scale Magnitudes M_s	**Gutenberg– Richter Scale Magnitude M_w**	Where $M_s = \frac{2}{3}(\log_{10}E - 11.8)$ and $M_w = \frac{2}{3}[\log_{10}(2E \times 10^4) - 10.7]$ Where E = energy released in dyne/cm	
8.8	8.6	Colombia coast	1906 Jan 31
(8.6)	8.6	Assam, India	1950 Aug 15
9.0	(8¼)	Kamchatka, USSR	1952 Nov 4
9.1	(8.3)	Andreanol, Aleutian Is., USA	1957 Mar 9
9.5	(8.3)	Lebu, Chile	1960 May 22

Worst death roll *World*
The greatest loss of life occurred in the earthquake (*ti chen*) in the Shensi, Shansi and Honan provinces of China, of 1556 Feb 2, (new style) (Jan 23 os) when an estimated 830,000 people were killed. The highest death roll in modern times has been in the Tangshan 'quake (Mag. 8.2) in Eastern China on 1976 July 27 (local time was 3 a.m. July 28). A first figure published on 4 Jan

1977 revealed 655,237 killed, later adjusted to 750,000. On 22 Nov 1979 the New China News Agency unaccountably reduced the death toll to 242,000. The greatest material damage was in the 'quake on the Kwanto plain, Japan, of 1923 Sept 1 (Mag. 8.2, epicentre in Lat. 35° 15′ N, Long. 139° 30′ E). In Sagami Bay the sea-bottom in one area sank 400 m *1310 ft*. The official total of persons killed and missing in the *Shinsai* or great 'quake and the resultant fires was 142,807. In Tōkyō and Yokohama 575,000 dwellings were destroyed. The cost of the damage was estimated at £1000 million (now more than £4000 million).

Worst death roll *Great Britain and Ireland*
The East Anglian or Colchester earthquake of 1884 Apr 22 (9.18 a.m.) (epicentres Lat. 51° 48′ N, Long. 0° 53′ E, and Lat. 51° 51′ N, Long. 0° 55′ E) caused damage estimated at £10,000 to 1200 buildings, and according to *The Great English Earthquake* by Peter Haining, the death of at least 3 and possibly 5 people. Langenhoe Church was wrecked. Windows and doors were rattled over an area of 53,000 miles² *137 250 km²* and the shock was felt in Exeter and Ostend, Belgium. It has been estimated to have been of magnitude 6 on the Richter scale. The most marked since 1884 and the worst since instruments have been in use (*i.e.* since 1927) occurred in the Midlands at 3.43 p.m. on 1957 Feb 11, showing a strength of between five and six on the Davison scale. The strongest Scottish tremor occurred at Inverness at 10.45 p.m. on 1816 Aug 13, and was felt over an area of 50,000 miles² *130 000 km²*. The strongest Welsh tremor occurred in Swansea at 9.45 a.m. on 1906 June 27 (epicentre Lat. 51° 38′ N, Long. 4° W). It was felt over an area of 37,800 miles² *97 900 km²*. No earthquake with its epicentre in Ireland has ever been instrumentally measured, though the effects of remoter shocks have been felt. However, there was a shock in 1734 August which damaged 100 dwellings and five churches.

VOLCANOES
The total number of known active volcanoes in the world is 455 with an estimated 80 more that are submarine. The greatest active concentration is in Indonesia, where 77 of its 167 volcanoes have erupted within historic times. The name volcano derives from the now dormant Vulcano Island (from the God of fire Vulcanus) in the Aeolian group in the Mediterranean.

Greatest eruption
The total volume of matter discharged in the eruption of Tambora, a volcano on the island of Sumbawa, in Indonesia, 5–7 Apr 1815, has been estimated at 36.4 miles³ *151,7 km³*. The energy of this eruption which lowered the height of the island from 13,450 ft *4100 m* to 9350 ft *2850 m* was 8.4×10^{26} ergs. The volcano lost about 4100 ft *1250 m* in height and a crater seven miles *11 km* in diameter was formed. This compares with a probable 15 miles³ *62,5 km³* ejected by Santoríni and 4.3 miles³ *18 km³* ejected by Krakatoa (see Greatest explosion). The internal pressure causing the Tambora eruption has been estimated at 46,500,000 lb/in² or more than 20,750 tons/in² *3 270 000 kg/cm²*.

The ejecta in the Taupo eruption in New Zealand *c.* AD 186 has been estimated at 30,000 million tonnes/*tons* of pumice moving at one time at 400 mph *700 km/h*. It flattened 16 000 km² *6180 miles²* (over 26 times the devastated area of Mt. St. Helens). Less than 20 per cent of the 14×10^9 tonnes of pumice ejected in this most violent of all documented volcanic events fell within 200 km *125 miles* of the vent.

Longest lava flow
The longest lava flow in historic times, known as *pahoehoe* (twisted cord-like solidifications), is that from the eruption of Laki in 1783 in south-east Iceland which flowed 65–70 km *40.5–43.5 miles*. The largest known pre-historic flow is the Roza basalt flow in North America *c.* 15 million years ago, which had an unsurpassed length (480 km *300 miles*), area (40 000 km² *15,400 miles²*) and volume (1250 km³ *300 miles³*).

Greatest explosion
The greatest explosion (possibly since Santoríni in the Aegean Sea *c.* 1470 BC) occurred at *c.* 10 a.m. (local time), or 3.00 a.m. GMT, on 27 Aug 1883, with an eruption of Krakatoa, an island (then 18 miles² *47 km²*) in the Sunda Strait, between Sumatra

and Java, in Indonesia. A total of 163 villages were wiped out, and 36,380 people killed by the wave it caused. Rocks were thrown 34 miles *55 km* high and dust fell 3313 miles *5330 km* away 10 days later. The explosion was recorded four hours later on the island of Rodrigues, 2968 miles *4776 km* away, as 'the roar of heavy guns' and was heard over 1/13th part of the surface of the globe. This explosion has been estimated to have had about 26 times the power of the greatest H-bomb test detonation but was still only a fifth part of the Santoríní cataclysm.

Highest *Extinct*
The highest extinct volcano in the world is Cerro Aconcagua (stone centinel) (22,834 ft *6960 m*) on the Argentine side of the Andes. It was first climbed on 14 Jan 1897 by Mathias Zurbriggen and was the highest summit climbed anywhere until 12 June 1907.

Highest *Dormant*
The highest dormant volcano is Volcán Llullaillaco (22,057 ft *6723 m*), on the frontier between Chile and Argentina.

Highest *Active*
The highest volcano regarded as active is Volcán Antofalla (6450 m *21,162 ft*), in Argentina, though a more definite claim is made for Volcán Guayatiri or Guallatiri (19,882 ft *6060 m*), in Chile, which erupted in 1959.

Northernmost and southernmost
The northernmost volcano is Beeren Berg (7470 ft *2276 m*) on the island of Jan Mayen (71° 05′ N) in the Greenland Sea. It erupted on 20 Sept 1970 and the island's 39 inhabitants (all male) had to be evacuated. It was possibly discovered by Henry Hudson in 1607 or 1608, but definitely visited by Jan Jacobsz May (Netherlands) in 1614. It was annexed by Norway on 8 May 1929. The Ostenso seamount (5825 ft *1775 m*) 346 miles *556 km* from the North Pole in Lat. 85° 10′ N, Long. 133° W was volcanic. The most southerly known active volcano is Mount Erebus (12,450 ft *3795 m*) on Ross Island (77° 35′ S), in Antarctica. It was discovered on 28 Jan 1841 by the expedition of Captain (later Rear-Admiral Sir) James Clark Ross, RN (1800–62), and first climbed at 10 a.m. on 10 Mar 1908 by a British party of five, led by Professor (later Lieut.-Col. Sir) Tannatt William Edgeworth David (1858–1934).

Largest crater
The world's largest *caldera* or volcano crater is that of Mount Aso (5223 ft *1590 m*) in Kyūshū, Japan, which measures 17 miles *27 km* north to south, 10 miles *16 km* east to west and 71 miles *114 km* in circumference.

GEYSERS
Tallest World
The Waimangu (Maori, *black water*) geyser, in New Zealand, erupted to a height in excess of 1500 ft *457 m* in 1904, but has not been active since it erupted violently at 6.20 a.m. on 1 Apr 1917 and killed 4 people. Currently the world's tallest active geyser is the US National Parks' Service Steamboat Geyser, which from 1962 to 1969 erupted with intervals ranging from 5 days to 10 months to a height of 250–380 ft *76–115 m*. The greatest measured water discharge has been 825,000 gal *37 850 hl* by the Giant Geyser, also in Yellowstone National Park, Wyoming, which has been dormant since 1955. The *Geysir* ('gusher') near Mount Hekla in south-central Iceland, from which all others have been named, spurts, on occasions, to 180 ft *55 m*, while the adjacent Strokkur, reactivated by drilling in 1963, spurts at 10–15-min intervals.

3. STRUCTURE AND DIMENSIONS

OCEANS
Largest
The area of the Earth covered by sea is estimated to be 139,670,000 miles² *361 740 000 km²* or 70.92 per cent of the total surface. The mean depth of the hydrosphere was once estimated to be 12,450 ft *3795 m*, but recent surveys suggest a lower estimate, of 11,660 ft *3554 m*. The total weight of the water is estimated to be 1.3×10^{18} tons, or 0.022 per cent of the Earth total weight. The volume of the oceans is estimated to be 308,400,000 miles³ *1 285 600 000 km³* compared with on 8,400,000 miles³ *35 000 000 km³* of fresh water.

The largest ocean in the world is the Pacific. Excluding adjacent seas, it represents 45.8 per cent of the world's oceans and about 63,800,000 miles² *165 250 000 km²* in area. The shorte navigable trans-Pacific distance from Guayaquil, Ecuador Bangkok, Thailand is 10,905 miles *17 550 km*.

Deepest *World*
The deepest part of the ocean was first pin-pointed in 1951 HM Survey Ship *Challenger* in the Marianas Trench in the Pacific Ocean. The depth was measured by sounding and by echo sounder and published as 5960 fathoms (35,760 ft *10 900 m* Subsequent visits to this same Challenger Deep have resulted deeper but less reliable claims by echo-sounder only, culminating in one of 6033 fathoms (36,198 ft *11 033 m*) or 6.85 miles the USSR's research ship *Vityaz* in March 1959. On 23 Jan 196 the US Navy bathyscaphe *Trieste* descended to the bottom the but the depth calibrations (made for fresh rather than salt water yielded a figure 60 ft *18 m* deeper than the 1951 survey. A met object, say a pound ball of steel, dropped into water above th trench would take nearly 63 min to fall to the sea-bed 6.85 mil *11,03 km* below. The average depth of the Pacific Ocean 14,000 ft *4267 m*.

Deepest *British waters*
The deepest point in the territorial waters of the United Kin dom is an area 6 cables (*1100 m*) off the island of Raasay, High land, in the Inner Sound at Lat. 57° 30′ 33″ N, Long. 5° 57′ 2 W. A depth of 1038 ft (173 fathoms, *316 m*) was found December 1959 by HMS *Yarnton* (Lt-Cdr A. C. F. David, RN

Largest sea
The largest of the world's seas is the South China Sea, with area of 1,148,500 miles² *2 974 600 km²*. The Malayan Sea, com prising the waters between the Indian Ocean and the South Pacific, south of the Chinese mainland covering 3,144,000 mile *8 142 900 km²* is not now an entity accepted by the Internation Hydrographic Bureau.

Largest gulf
The largest gulf in the world is the Gulf of Mexico, with an are of 580,000 miles² *1 500 000 km²* and a shoreline of 3100 mil *4990 km* from Cape Sable, Florida, USA, to Cabo Catoch Mexico.

Largest bay
The largest bay in the world measured by shore-line length Hudson Bay, northern Canada, with a shoreline of 7623 mil *12 268 km* and with an area of 317,500 miles² *822 300 km²*. Th area of the Bay of Bengal is however 839,000 mile *2 172 000 km²*. Great Britain's largest bay is Cardigan Bay whic has a 140 mile *225 km* long shoreline and measures 72 mil *116 km* across from the Lleyn Peninsula, Gwynedd to St David Head, Dyfed in Wales.

Longest fjords and sea lochs *World*
The world's longest fjord is the Nordvest Fjord arm of th Scoresby Sund in eastern Greenland, which extends inland 19 miles *313 km* from the sea. The longest of Norwegian fjords the Sogne Fjord, which extends 183 km *113.7 miles* inland fro Sygnefest to the head of the Lusterfjord arm at Skjolden. averages barely 4,75 km *3 miles* in width and has a deepest poir of 1245 m *4085 ft*. If measured from Huglo along the Bøml fjord to the head of the Sørfjord arm at Odda, Hardangerfjorde can also be said to extend 183 km *113.7 miles*. The longe: Danish fjord is Limfjorden (100 miles *160 km* long).

Longest fjords and sea lochs *Great Britain*
Scotland's longest sea loch is Loch Fyne, which extends 42 mil *67,5 km* inland into Strathclyde (formerly Argyllshire).

Highest seamount
The highest known submarine mountain, or seamount, is discovered in 1953 near the Tonga Trench, between Samoa an New Zealand. It rises 28,500 ft *8690 m* from the sea bed, with i summit 1200 ft *365 m* below the surface.

Remotest spot from land

The world's most distant point from land is a spot in the South Pacific, approximately 48° 30′ S, 125° 30′ W, which is about 1660 miles *2670 km* from the nearest points of land, namely Pitcairn Island, Ducie Island and Cape Dart, Antarctica. Centred on this spot, therefore, is a circle of water with an area of about 8,657,000 miles² *22 421 500 km²*—about 7000 miles² *18 000 km²* larger than the USSR, the world's largest country (see Chapter 10).

Most southerly

The most southerly part of the oceans is 85° 34′ S, 154° W, at the snout of the Robert Scott Glacier, 305 miles *490 km* from the South Pole.

Longest voyage

The longest possible great circle sea voyage is one of 19,860 miles *31 960 km* from a point 150 miles *240 km* west of Karachi, Pakistan to a point 200 miles *320 km* north of Uka' Kamchatka *via* the Mozambique Channel, Drake Passage and Bering Sea.

Sea temperature

The temperature of the water at the surface of the sea varies from −2° C *28.5° F* in the White Sea to 35,6° C *96° F* in the shallow areas of the Persian Gulf in summer. Ice-focused solar rays have been known to heat lake water to nearly 80° F *26,8° C*. The normal Red Sea temperature is 22° C *71.6° F*. The highest temperature recorded in the ocean is 662° F *350° C*, measured by the research submersible *Alvin* at Lat. 21° N on the East Pacific Rise in November 1979, emanating from a sea-floor geothermal spring at a depth of 2600 m *8530 ft*.

STRAITS

Longest

The longest straits in the world are the Tatarskiy Proliv or Tartar Straits between Sakhalin Island and the USSR mainland running from the Sea of Japan to Sakhalinsky Zaliv. This distance is 800 km *497 miles*—thus marginally longer than the Malacca Straits.

Broadest

The broadest named straits in the world are the Davis Straits between Greenland and Baffin Island with a minimum width of 210 miles *338 km*. The Drake Passage between the Diego Ramirez Islands, Chile and the South Shetland Islands is 710 miles *1140 km* across.

Narrowest

The narrowest navigable straits are those between the Aegean island of Euboea and the mainland of Greece. The gap is only 45 yd *40 m* wide at Khalkis. The Seil Sound, Strathclyde, Scotland, narrows to a point only 20 ft *6 m* wide where the Clachan bridge joins the island of Seil to the mainland and is thus said by the islanders to span the Atlantic.

WAVES

Highest

The highest officially recorded sea wave was measured by Lt Frederic Margraff USN from the USS *Ramapo* proceeding from Manila, Philippines, to San Diego, California, USA, on the night of 6–7 Feb 1933, during a 68-knot (78.3 mph *126 km/h*) hurricane. The wave was computed to be 112 ft *34 m* from trough to crest. The highest instrumentally measured wave was one 86 ft *26,2 m* high, recorded by the British ship *Weather Reporter*, in the North Atlantic on 30 Dec 1972 in Lat. 59° N, Long. 19° W. It has been calculated on the statistics of the Stationary Random Theory that one wave in more than 300,000 may exceed the average by a factor of 4.

On 9 July 1958 a landslip caused a wave to wash 1740 ft *530 m* high along the fjord-like Lituya Bay, Alaska, USA.

Highest seismic wave

The highest estimated height of a *tsunami* (often wrongly called a tidal wave) was one of 85 m *278 ft*, which appeared off Ishigaki Island, Ryukyu Chain on 24 Apr 1971. It tossed a 750 ton block of coral more than 2,5 km *1.3 miles. Tsunami* (a Japanese word meaning *nami*, a wave; *tsu*, overflowing) have been observed to travel at 490 mph *790 km/h*. Between 479 BC and 1977 there were at least 500 instances of *tsunami* of which 270 were destructive.

CURRENTS

Greatest

The greatest current in the oceans of the world is the Antarctic Circumpolar Current or West Wind Drift Current which was measured in 1969 in the Drake Passage between South America and Antarctica to be flowing at a rate of 9500 million ft³ *270 000 000 m³* per sec—nearly treble that of the Gulf Stream. Its width ranges from 185 to 1240 miles *300–2000 km* and has a proven surface flow rate of ⁴⁄₁₀ of a knot *0,75 km/h*.

Strongest

The world's strongest currents are the Nakwakto Rapids, Slingsby Channel, British Columbia, Canada (Lat. 51° 05′ N, Long. 127° 30′ W) where the flow rate may reach 16.0 knots *29,6 km/h*. The fastest current in British territorial waters is 10.7 knots *19,8 km/h* in the Pentland Firth between the Orkney Islands and Caithness, formerly Scotland's northern-most mainland county.

GREATEST TIDES

Extreme tides are due to lunar and solar gravitational forces affected by their perigee, perihelion and conjunctions. Barometric and wind effects can superimpose an added 'surge' element. Coastal and sea-floor configurations can accentuate these forces.

World

The greatest tides in the world occur in the Bay of Fundy, which divides the peninsula of Nova Scotia, Canada, from the United States' north-easternmost state of Maine and the Canadian province of New Brunswick. Burncoat Head in the Minas Basin, Nova Scotia, has the greatest mean spring range with 47.5 ft *14,50 m* and an extreme range of 53.5 ft *16,30 m*.

Great Britain

The place with the greatest mean spring range in Great Britain is Beachley, on the Severn, with a range of 40.7 ft *12,40 m*, compared with the British Isles' average of 15 ft *4,57 m*. Prior to 1933 tides as high as 28.9 ft *8,80 m* above and 22.3 ft *6,80 m* below datum (total range 51.2 ft *15,60 m*) were recorded at Avonmouth though an extreme range of 52.2 ft *15,90 m* for Beachley was officially accepted. In 1883 a freak tide of greater range was reported from Chepstow, Gwent.

Ireland

The greatest mean spring tidal range in Ireland is 17.3 ft *5,27 m* at Mellon, Limerick, on the River Shannon.

ICEBERGS

Largest

The largest iceberg on record was an Antarctic tabular 'berg of over 12,000 miles² *31 000 km²* (208 miles *335 km* long and 60 miles *97 km* wide and thus larger than Belgium) sighted 150 miles *240 km* west of Scott Island, in the South Pacific Ocean, by the USS *Glacier* on 12 Nov 1956. The 200 ft *61 m* thick Arctic ice island T.1 (140 miles² *360 km²*) (discovered in 1946) was tracked for 17 years. The tallest iceberg measured was one of 550 ft *167 m* reported off western Greenland by the US icebreaker *East Wind* in 1958.

Most southerly Arctic

The most southerly Arctic iceberg was sighted in the Atlantic by a USN weather patrol in Lat. 28° 44′ N, Long. 48° 42′ W in April 1935. The southernmost iceberg reported in British home waters was one sighted 60 miles *96 km* from Smith's Knoll, on the Dogger Bank, in the North Sea.

Most northerly Antarctic

The most northerly Antarctic iceberg was a remnant sighted in the Atlantic by the ship *Dochra* in Lat. 26° 30′ S, Long. 25° 40′ W, on 30 Apr 1894.

LAND

There is satisfactory evidence that at one time the Earth's land surface comprised a single primeval continent of 80 million miles² *2 × 10⁸km²*, now termed Pangaea, and that this split about 190 million years ago, during the Jurassic period, into two super-continents, termed Laurasia (Eurasia, Greenland and Northern America) and Gondwanaland (Africa, Arabia, India, South America, Oceania and Antarctica) and named after Gondwana, India, which itself split 120 million years ago. The South

Pole was apparently in the area of the Sahara as recently as the Ordovician period of *c.* 450 million years ago.

ROCKS

The age of the Earth is generally considered to be within the range of 4600 ± 100 million years, by analogy with directly measured ages of meteorites and of the moon. However, no rocks of this great age have yet been found on the Earth since geological processes have presumably destroyed the earliest record.

Oldest *World*

The greatest reported age for any scientifically dated rock is 3800 ± 100 million years for granite gneiss rock found near Granite Falls in the Minnesota river valley, USA as measured by the lead-isotope and rubidium-uranium methods by the US Geological Survey and announced on 26 Jan 1975. These metamorphic samples compare with the Amîtsoq gneiss from Godthaab, Greenland unreservedly accepted to be between 3700 and 3750 million years.

Oldest *Great Britain*

The original volcanic products from which were formed the gneiss and granulite rocks of the Scourian complex in the north west Highlands and the Western Isles may be possibly older than 3000 million years. They were crystallized 2800 million years ago.

Largest

The largest isolated monolith in the world is the 1237 ft *377 m* high Mount Augustus (3627 ft *1105 m* above sea-level), discovered on 3 June 1858, 200 miles *320 km* east of Carnarvon, Western Australia. It is an upfaulted monoclinal gritty conglomerate 5 miles *8 km* long and 2 miles *3 km* across and thus twice the size of the celebrated monolithic arkose Ayer's Rock (1100 ft *335 m*), 250 miles *400 km* south-west of Alice Springs, in Northern Territory, Australia.

CONTINENTS

Largest

Only 29.08 per cent, or an estimated 57,270,000 miles *148 328 000 km²* of the Earth's surface is land, with a mean height of 2480 ft *756 m* above sea-level. The Eurasian land mass is the largest, with an area (including islands) of 20,733,000 miles² *53 698 000 km²*. The Afro-Eurasian land mass, separated artificially only by the Suez Canal covers an area of 32,233,000 miles² *83 483 000 km²* or 56.2% of the Earth's landmass.

Smallest

The smallest is the Australian mainland, with an area of 2,941,526 miles² *7 618 493 km²*, which, together with Tasmania, New Zealand, New Guinea and the Pacific Islands, is described sometimes as Oceania.

Land remotest from the sea *World*

There is an as yet unpinpointed spot in the Dzoosotoyn Elisen (desert), northern Xinjiang Uygur Zizhiqu (Sin Kiang) China's most north westerly province, that is more than 1500 miles *2400 km* from the open sea in any direction. The nearest large city to this point is Ürümqi (Ürümchi) to its south.

Land remotest from the sea *Great Britain*

The point furthest from the sea in Great Britain is a point near Meriden, West Midlands, England, which is 72½ miles *117 km* equidistant from the Severn Bridge, the Dee and Mersey estuaries and the Welland estuary in the Wash. The equivalent point in Scotland is in the Forest of Atholl, north-west Tayside, 40½ miles *65 km* equidistant from the head of Loch Leven Inverness Firth and the Firth of Tay.

Peninsula

The world's largest peninsula is Arabia, with an area of about 1,250,000 miles² *3 250 000 km²*.

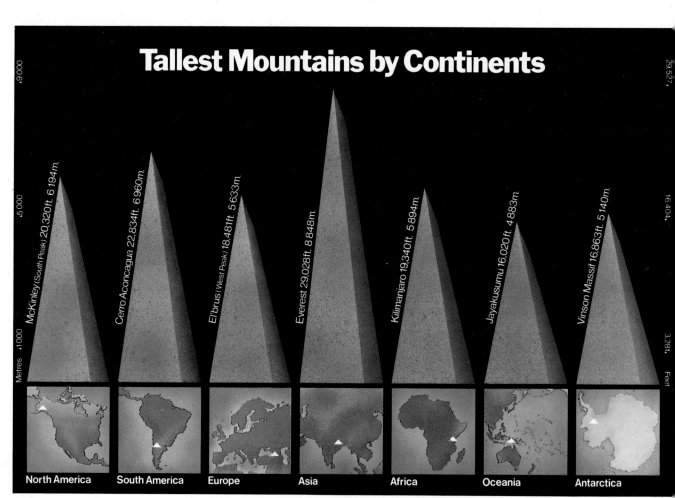

Tallest Mountains by Continents

McKinley (South Peak) 20,320ft. 6 194 m — North America
Cerro Aconcagua 22,834ft. 6 960 m — South America
Elbrus (West Peak) 18,481ft. 5 633 m — Europe
Everest 29,028ft. 8 848 m — Asia
Kilimanjaro 19,340ft. 5 894 m — Africa
Jayakusumu 16,020ft. 4 883 m — Oceania
Vinson Massif 16,863ft. 5 140 m — Antarctica

ISLANDS

Largest *World*

Discounting Australia, which is usually regarded as a continental land mass, the largest island in the world is Greenland (part of the Kingdom of Denmark), with an area of about 840,000 miles² *2 175 000 km²*. There is evidence that Greenland is in fact several islands overlaid by an ice cap without which it would have an area of 650,000 miles² *1 680 000 km²*.

Largest *Great Britain*

The mainland of Great Britain (Scotland, England and Wales) is the eighth largest in the world, with an area of 84,186 miles² *218 041 km²*. It stretches 603½ miles *971 km* from Dunnet Head in the north to Lizard Point in the south and 287½ miles *463 km* across from Porthaflod, Dyfed to Lowestoft, Suffolk. The island of Ireland (32,594 miles² *84 418 km²*) is the 20th largest in the world.

Freshwater

The largest island surrounded by fresh water is the Ilha de Marajó (13,500 miles² *35 000 km²*), in the mouth of the River Amazon, Brazil. The world's largest inland island (*i.e.* land surrounded by rivers) is Ilha do Bananal, Brazil (7000 miles² *18 130 km²*). The largest island in a lake is Manitoulin Island (1068 miles² *2766 km²*) in the Canadian (Ontario) section of Lake Huron. The largest lake island in Great Britain is Inchmurrin in Loch Lomond, Strathclyde/Central, Scotland with an area of 284 acres *115 ha*.

Remotest *World uninhabited*

The remotest island in the world is Bouvet Øya (formerly Liverpool Island), discovered in the South Atlantic by J. B. C. Bouvet de Lozier on 1 Jan 1739, and first landed on by Capt. George Norris on 16 Dec 1825. Its position is 54° 26′ S, 3° 24′ E. This uninhabited Norwegian dependency is about 1050 miles *1700 km* from the nearest land—the uninhabited Queen Maud Land coast of eastern Antarctica.

Remotest *World inhabited*

The remotest inhabited island in the world is Tristan da Cunha, discovered in the South Atlantic by Tristao da Cunha, a Portuguese admiral, in March 1506. It has an area of 38 miles² *98 km²* (habitable area 12 miles² *31 km²*) and was annexed by the United Kingdom on 14 Aug 1816. After evacuation in 1961 (due to volcanic activity), 198 islanders returned in November 1963. The nearest inhabited land is the island of St Helena, 1320 miles *2120 km* to the north-east. The nearest continent, Africa is 1700 miles *2735 km* away.

Remotest *Great Britain*

The remotest of the British islets is Rockall 191 miles *307 km* west of St Kilda, Western Isles. This 70 ft *21 m* high rock measuring 83 ft *25 m* across was not formally annexed until 18 Sept 1955. The remotest British island which has ever been inhabited is North Rona which is 44 miles *70,8 km* from the next nearest land at Cape Wrath and the Butt of Lewis. It was evacuated *c.* 1844. Muckle Flugga, off Unst, in the Shetlands, is the northernmost inhabited with a population of 3 (1971) and is in a latitude north of southern Greenland. Just to the north of it is the rock of Out Stack.

Highest Rock Pinnacle

The world's highest rock pinnacle is Ball's Pyramid near Lord Howe Island, Pacific which is 1843 ft *561 m* high, but has a base axis of only 200 m *220 yd*. It was first scaled in 1965.

Northernmost land

On 26 July 1978 Uffe Petersen of the Danish Geodetic Institute observed the islet of OOdaq Ø 30 m *100 ft* across, 1,36 km *1487 yd* north of Kaffeklubben Ø off Pearyland, Greenland in Lat. 83° 40′ 32.5″ N, Long. 30° 40′ 10.1″ W. The island is 706,4 km *438.9 miles* from the North Pole.

Southernmost land

The South Pole, unlike the North Pole, is on land. The Amundsen-Scott South Polar station was built there at an altitude of 9370 ft *2855 m* in 1957. It is drifting bodily with the ice cap 27–30 ft *8–9 m* per annum in the direction 43° W and was replaced by a new structure in 1975.

The Tongan landing party salute as their national flag is raised over Lateiki Island. This rose from the ocean and was sighted by pilots in June 1979. (*John Topham Picture Library*)

Greatest archipelago

The world's greatest archipelago is the 3500 mile *5600 km* long crescent of more than 13,000 islands which forms Indonesia.

Newest

The world's newest island, Lateiki Island, which appeared after a volcanic eruption, was annexed by Tonga in June 1979.

Largest atoll

The largest atoll in the world is Kwajalein in the Marshall Islands, in the central Pacific Ocean. Its slender 176 mile *283 km* long coral reef encloses a lagoon of 1100 miles² *2850 km²*. The atoll with the largest land area is Christmas Atoll, in the Line Islands, in the central Pacific Ocean. It has an area of 184 miles² *477 km²*. Its two principal settlements, London and Paris, are 4 miles *6 km* apart.

Longest reef

The longest reef is the Great Barrier Reef off Queensland, northeastern Australia, which is 1260 statute miles *2027 km* in length. Between 1959 and 1971 a large section between Cooktown and Townsville was destroyed by the proliferation of the Crown of Thorns starfish (*Acanthaster planci*).

DEPRESSIONS

Deepest *World*

The deepest depression so far discovered is beneath the Hollick-Kenyon Plateau in Marie Byrd Land, Antarctica, where, at a point 5900 ft *1800 m* above sea-level, the ice depth is 14,000 ft *4267 m*, hence indicating a bed rock depression 8100 ft *2468 m* below sea-level. The greatest submarine depression is a large area of the floor of the north-west Pacific which has an average depth of 15,000 ft *4570 m*. The deepest exposed depression on land is the shore surrounding the Dead Sea, 1291 ft *393 m* below sea-level. The deepest point on the bed of this lake is 2600 ft *792 m* below the Mediterranean. The deepest part of the bed of Lake Baykal in Siberia, USSR, is 4872 ft *1484 m* below sea-level.

Deepest *Great Britain*

The lowest lying area in Great Britain is in the Holme Fen area of the Great Ouse, in Cambridgeshire, at 9 ft *2,75 m* below sea-level. The deepest depression in England is the bed of part of Windermere, 94 ft *28,65 m* below sea-level, and in Scotland the bed of Loch Morar, Highland 987 ft *300,8 m* below sea-level.

Largest

The largest exposed depression in the world is the Caspian Sea basin in the Azerbaydzhani, Russian, Kazakh and Turkmen Republics of the USSR and northern Iran (Persia). It is more than 200,000 miles² *518 000 km²* of which 143,550 miles² *371 800 km²* is lake area. The preponderant land area of the depression is the Prikaspiyskaya Nizmennost', lying around the northern third of the lake and stretching inland for a distance of up to 280 miles *450 km.*

CAVES
Longest
The most extensive cave system in the world is that under the Mammoth Cave National Park, Kentucky, USA first discovered in 1799. On 9 Sept 1972 an exploration group led by Dr John P. Wilcox completed a connection, pioneered by Mrs Patricia Crowther on 30 Aug between the Flint Ridge Cave system and the Mammoth Cave system, so making a combined system with a total mapped passageway length of 345 km *213.3 miles.* The longest cave system in Great Britain is the Easegill system which reached 46,3 km *28.8 miles* with the connection of Easegill Caverns, Cumbria with Pippikin Pot, Lancashire on 16 Dec 1978.

Largest cavern
The world's largest cave chamber is the Sarawak Chamber, Lobang Nasip Bagus, in the Gunung Mulu National Park, Sarawak discovered and surveyed by the 1980 British–Malaysian Mulu Expedition. Its length is 700 m *2300 ft*; and its average width is 300 m *980 ft* and it is nowhere less than 70 m *230 ft* high. Wembley Stadium would fit into one end.

Longest stalactite
The longest known stalactite in the world is a wall-supported column extending 195 ft *59 m* from roof to floor in the Cueva de Nerja, near Málaga, Spain. Probably the longest free-hanging stalactite is one of 38 ft *11,60 m* in the Poll an Ionain cave in County Clare, Ireland. The tallest cave column is the 106 ft *32,3 m* tall Bicenntenial Column in Ogle Cave in Carlsbad Cavern National Park, New Mexico USA.

Tallest stalagmite
The tallest known stalagmite in the world is La Grande Stalagmite in the Aven Armand cave, Lozère, France, which has attained a height of 98 ft *29 m* from the cave floor. It was found in September 1897.

DEEPEST CAVES BY COUNTRIES
These depths are subject to continuous revisions.

Depth			
Ft	m		
4600	*1402*	Reseau du Foillis	France
4200	*1280*	Snezhnaya, Caucasus	USSR
4002	*1220*	Sistema Huautla	Mexico
3887	*1185*	Sima de Ukerdi	Spain
3645	*1111*	Schneeloch	Austria
3117	*950*	Antro di Corchia	Italy
2713	*827*	Hölloch, Muotathal, Schwyz	Switzerland
2569	*783*	Jaskini Snieznej Tatras	Poland
2464	*751*	Ghar Parau, Zagros Mountains	Iran
2296	*700*	Kef Toghobeit	Morocco
2247	*685*	Poloska Jama	Yugoslavia
1010	*308*	Ogof Ffynnod Ddu	Wales
702	*214*	Giant's Hole, Oxlow Caverns, Derbyshire	England
587	*179*	Reyfad Pot	N Ireland
459	*140*	Carrowmore Cavern	Rep. of Ireland

MOUNTAINS
The *Guinness Book of Mountains and Mountaineering Facts and Feats* by Edward Pyatt (£8.95) was published in May 1980.

Highest *World*
An eastern Himalayan peak of 29,028 ft *8848 m* above sea-level on the Tibet–Nepal border (in an area first designated Chu-mu-lang-ma on a map of 1717) was discovered to be the world's highest mountain in 1852 by the Survey Department of the Government of India, from theodolite readings taken in 1849 and 1850. In 1860 its height was computed to be 29,002 ft *8840 m.* On 25 July 1973 the Chinese announced a height of 8848,1 m or *29,029 ft 3 in.* In practice the altitude can only be justified as 29,028 ft ± 25 feet or a mean *8848 m.* The 5½ mile *8,85 km* high peak was named Mount Everest after Sir George Everest, CB. (1790–1866), formerly Surveyor-General of India.

Other names for Everest are: Sagarmatha (Nepalese); Qomolongma (Chinese) and Mi-ti Gu-ti Cha-pu Long-na (Tibeten). After a total loss of 11 lives since the first reconnaissance in 1921 Everest was finally conquered at 11.30 a.m. on 29 May 1953 (For details of ascents, see under Mountaineering in Chapter 12.) The mountain whose summit is farthest from the Earth's centre is the Andean peak of Chimborazo (20,561 ft *6267 m*), 98 miles *158 km* south of the equator in Ecuador, South America. Its summit is 7057 ft *2150 m* further from the Earth's centre than the summit of Mt Everest. The highest mountain on the equator is Volcán Cayambe (19,285 ft *5878 m*), Ecuador, in Long. 77° 58′ W.

Highest *Insular*
The highest insular mountain in the world is the unsurveyed Ngga Pulu formerly Mount Sukarno, formerly Carstensz Pyramide in Irian Jaya, Indonesia, once Netherlands New Guinea. According to cross-checked altimeter estimates, it is 16,500 ft *5030 m* high.

Steepest Slope
Mount Rakaposhi rises 6 vertical kilometres *19,685 ft* from the Hanza Valley in 10 horizontal kilometres *32,808 ft* with an overall gradient of 31°.

Highest *UK and Ireland*
A list of the highest points in the 72 geographical divisions of the United Kingdom and the 26 counties of the Republic of Ireland was given on page 63 of the 23rd (1977) Edition.

The highest mountain in the United Kingdom is Ben Nevis (4406 ft *1343 m* excluding the 12 ft *3,65 m* cairn), 4¼ miles *6,85 km* south-east of Fort William, Highland, Scotland. It was climbed before 1720 but though acclaimed the highest in 1790 was not confirmed to be higher than Ben Macdhui (4300 ft *1310 m*) until 1847. In 1834 Ben Macdhui and Ben Nevis (Gaelic, *Beinn Nibheis*) (first reference, 1778) were respectively quoted as 4570 ft *1393 m* and 4370 ft *1332 m.* The highest mountain in England is Scafell Pike (3210 ft *978 m*) in Cumbria, in Wales is Snowdon (*Yr Wyddfa*) (3560 ft *1085 m*) in Gwynedd and in the island of Ireland is Carrauntual (3414 ft *1041 m*) in County Kerry.

There is some evidence that, before being ground down by the ice-cap, mountains in the Loch Bà area of the Isle of Mull, Strathclyde were 15,000 ft *4575 m* above sea-level.

Highest *Peaks over 3000 ft*
There are 577 peaks and tops over 3000 ft *915 m* in the whole British Isles and 165 peaks and 136 tops in Scotland higher than England's highest point, Scafell Pike. The highest mountain of the mainland is Sgùrr Alasdair (3309 ft *1008 m*) on Skye named after Alexander (Gaelic, *Alasdair*) Nicolson, who made the first ascent in 1873.

Highest unclimbed
The highest unclimbed mountain is now only the 31st highest—Zemu Gap Peak (25,526 ft *7780 m*) in the Sikkim Himalaya.

Largest
The world's tallest mountain measured from its submarine base (3280 fathoms *6000 m*) in the Hawaiian Trough to peak is Mauna Kea (Mountain White) on the island of Hawaii, with a combined height of 33,476 ft *10 023 m* of which 13,796 ft *4205 m* are above sea-level. Another mountain whose dimensions, but not height, exceed those of Mount Everest is the volcanic Hawaiian peak of Mauna Loa (Mountain Long) at 13,680 ft *4170 m.* The axes of its elliptical base, 16,322 ft *4975 m* below sea-level, have been estimated at 74 miles *119 m* and 53 miles *85 km.* It should be noted that Cerro Aconcagua (22,834 ft *6960 m*) is more than 38,800 ft *11 826 m* above the 16,000 ft *4875 m* deep Pacific abyssal plain or 42,834 ft *13 055 m* above the Peru-Chile Trench which is 180 miles *290 km* distant in the South Pacific.

Greatest ranges
The world's greatest land mountain range is the Himalaya–Karakoram, which contains 96 of the world's 109 peaks of over 24,000 ft *7315 m.* The greatest of all mountain ranges is

however, the submarine Indian/East Pacific Oceans Cordillera extending 19,200 miles *30 720 km* from the Gulf of Aden to the Gulf of California by way of the seabed between Australia and Antarctica with an average height of 8000 ft *2430 km* above the base ocean depth.

Longest lines of sight

Vatnajökull (6952 ft *2118 m*), Iceland has been sighted from the Faroe Islands 340 miles *550 km* distant. In Alaska Mt McKinley (20,320 ft *6193 m*) has been sighted from Mt Sanford (16,237 ft *4949 m*) from a distance of 230 miles *370 km*. McKinley, so named in 1896, was called Denali (Great One) in the Athabascan language.

Greatest plateau

The most extensive high plateau in the world is the Tibetan Plateau in Central Asia. The average altitude is 16,000 ft *4875 m* and the area is 77,000 miles² *200 000 km²*.

Sheerest wall

The 3200 ft *975 m* wide northwest face of Half Dome, Yosemite, California, USA is 2200 ft *670 m* high but nowhere departs more than 7 degrees from the vertical. It was first climbed (Class VI) in 5 days in July 1957 by Royal Robbins, Jerry Gallwas and Mike Sherrick.

Highest halites

Along the northern shores of the Gulf of Mexico for 725 miles *1160 km* there exists 330 subterranean 'mountains' of salt, some of which rise more than 60,000 ft *18 300 m* from bed rock and appear as the low salt domes first discovered in 1862.

Lowest hill

The official map of Seria, Brunei shows a hillock named Bukit Thompson on the Padang Golf Course at 15 ft *4,5 m*.

LAKES AND INLAND SEAS

Largest *World*

The largest inland sea or lake in the world is the Kaspiskoye More (Caspian Sea) in the southern USSR and Iran (Persia). It is 760 miles *1225 km* long and its total area is 143,550 miles² *371 800 km²*. Of the total area some 55,280 miles² *143 200 km²* (38.6 per cent) is in Iran, where it is named the Darya-ye-Khazar. Its maximum depth is 1025 m *3360 ft* and its surface is 28,5 m *93 ft* below sea-level. Its estimated volume is 21,500 miles³ *89 600 km³* of saline water. Its surface has varied between 32 m *105 ft* (11th century) and 22 m *72 ft* (early 19th century) below sea level. The USSR Government plan to reverse the flow of the upper Pechora River from flowing north to the Barents Sea by blasting a 70 mile *112 km* long canal with nuclear explosives into the south-flowing Kolva river so that *via* the Kama and Volga rivers the Caspian will be replenished.

Lake in a lake

The largest lake in a lake is Manitou Lake (41.09 miles² *106,42 km²*) on the world's largest lake island Manitoulin Island (1068 miles² *2766 km²*) in the Canadian part of Lake Huron. It contains itself a number of islands.

Underground lake

Reputedly the world's largest underground lake is the Lost Sea 300 ft *91 m* subterranean in the Craighead Caverns, Sweetwater, Tennessee, USA measuring 4½ acres *1,8 ha* and discovered in 1905.

Freshwater Lake *World*

The freshwater lake with the greatest surface area is Lake Superior, one of the Great Lakes of North America. The total area is 31,800 miles² *82 350 km²*, of which 20,700 miles² *53 600 km²* are in Minnesota, Wisconsin and Michigan, USA and 11,100 miles² *27 750 km²* in Ontario, Canada. It is 600 ft *182 m* above sea-level. The freshwater lake with the greatest volume is Baykal (see pp. 67 and 70) with an estimated volume of 5520 miles³ *23 000 km³*.

Freshwater lake *United Kingdom*

The largest lake in the United Kingdom is Lough Neagh (48 ft *14,60 m* above sea-level) in Northern Ireland. It is 18 miles *28,9 km* long and 11 miles *17,7 km* wide and has an area of 147.39 miles² *381,73 km²*. Its extreme depth is 102 ft *31 m*.

Freshwater lake *Great Britain*

The largest lake in Great Britain, and the largest inland loch in Scotland is Loch Lomond (23 ft *7,0 m* above sea-level), which is 22.64 miles *36,44 km* long and has a surface area of 27.45 miles² *70,04 km²*. It is situated in the Strathclyde and Central regions and its greatest depth is 623 ft *190 m*. The lake with the greatest volume is however Loch Ness with 263,162,000,000 ft³ *7 451 920 000 m³*. The longest lake is Loch Ness which measures 24.23 miles *38,99 km*. The three arms of the Y-shaped Loch Awe aggregate, however, 25.47 miles *40,99 km*. The largest lake in England is Windermere, in the county of Cumbria. It is 10½ miles *17 km* long and has a surface area of 5.69 miles² *14,74 km²*. Its greatest depth is 219 ft *66,75 m* in the northern half. The largest *natural* lake in Wales is Llyn Tegid, with an area of 1.69 miles² *4,38 km²*, although it should be noted that the largest lake

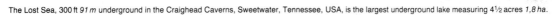

The Lost Sea, 300 ft *91 m* underground in the Craighead Caverns, Sweetwater, Tennessee, USA, is the largest underground lake measuring 4½ acres *1,8 ha*.

in Wales is that formed by the reservoir at Lake Vyrnwy, where the total surface area is 1120 acres *453,25 ha*.

Freshwater lake *Republic of Ireland*
The largest lough in the Republic of Ireland is Lough Corrib in the counties of Mayo and Galway. It measures 27 miles *43,5 km* in length and is 7 miles *11,25 km* across at its widest point with a total surface area of 41,616 acres (65.0 miles² *168 km²*).

Largest Lagoon
The largest lagoon in the world is Lagoa dos Patos in southern-most Brazil. It is 158 miles *254 km* long and extends over 4110 miles² *10 645 km²*.

Deepest *World*
The deepest lake in the world is Ozero (Lake) Baykal in central Siberia, USSR. It is 385 miles *620 km* long and between 20 and 46 miles *32–74 km* wide. In 1957 the lake's Olkhon Crevice was measured to be 1940 m *6365 ft* deep and hence 1485 m *4872 ft* below sea-level (see pp. 67 and 69).

Deepest *Great Britain*
The deepest lake in Great Britain is the 10.30 mile *16,57 km* long Loch Morar, in Highland. Its surface is 30 ft *9 m* above sea-level and its extreme depth 1017 ft *310 m*. England's deepest lake is Wast Water (258 ft *78 m*), in Cumbria. The lake with the greatest mean depth is Loch Ness with c. 450 ft *137 m*.

Highest *World*
The highest steam-navigated lake in the world is Lago Titicaca (maximum depth 1214 ft *370 m*), with an area of about 3200 miles² *8285 km²* (1850 miles² *4790 km²* in Peru, 1350 miles² *3495 km²* in Bolivia), in South America. It is 130 miles *209 km* long and is situated at 12,506 ft *3811 m* above sea-level. There is an unnamed glacial lake near Everest at 19,300 ft *5880 m*. Tibet's largest lake Nam Tso of 722 miles² *1956 km²* is at 15,060 ft *4578 m*.

Highest *United Kingdom*
The highest lake in the United Kingdom is the 1.9 acre *0,76 ha* Lochan Buidhe at 3600 ft *1097 m* above sea-level in the Cairngorm Mountains, Scotland. England's highest is Broad Crag Tarn (2746 ft *837 m* above sea-level) on Scafell Pike, Cumbria and the highest named freshwater in Wales is The Frogs Pool, a tarn near the summit of Carnedd Llywelyn, Gwynedd at c. 2725 ft *830 m*.

Desert *Largest*
Nearly an eighth of the world's land surface is arid with a rainfall of less than 25 cm *9.8 in* per annum. The Sahara Desert in N. Africa is the largest in the world. At its greatest length it is 3200 miles *5150 km* from east to west. From north to south it is between 800 and 1400 miles *1275 and 2250 km*. The area covered by the desert is about 3,250,000 miles² *8 400 000 km²*. The land level varies from 436 ft *132 m* below sea-level in the Qattâra Depression, Egypt, to the mountain Emi Koussi (11,204 ft *3415 m*) in Chad. The diurnal temperature range in the western Sahara may be more than 80° F or *45° C*.

Sand dunes
The world's highest measured sand dunes are those in the Saharan sand sea of Isaouane-n-Tifernine of east central Algeria in Lat. 26° 42′ N, Long. 6° 43′ E. They have a wave-length of near 3 miles *5 km* and attain a height of 1410 ft *430 m*.

Gorge *Largest*
The largest land gorge in the world is the Grand Canyon on the Colorado River in north-central Arizona, USA. It extends from Marble Gorge to the Grand Wash Cliffs, over a distance of 217 miles *349 km*. It varies in width from 4 to 13 miles *6–20 km* and is up to 7000 ft *2133 m* deep. The submarine Labrador Basin canyon is c. 2150 miles *3440 km* long.

Gorge *Deepest*
The deepest canyon in low relief territory is Hell's Canyon, dividing Oregon and Idaho, USA. It plunges 7900 ft *2 400 m* from the Devil Mountain down to the Snake River. A stretch of the Kali River in central Nepal flows 18,000 ft *5485 m* below its flanking summits of the Dhaulagiri and Annapurna groups. The deepest submarine canyon yet discovered is one 25 miles *40 km*

south of Esperance, Western Australia, which is 6000 ft *1800 m* deep and 20 miles *32 km* wide.

Sea cliffs *Highest*
The highest sea cliffs yet pinpointed anywhere in the world are those on the north coast of east Moloka'i, Hawaii near Umileh Point, which descend 3300 ft *1005 m* to the sea at an average gradient of >55°. The highest cliffs in North West Europe are those on the north coast of Achill Island, in County Mayo, Ireland which are 2192 ft *668 m* sheer above the sea at Croaghan. The highest cliffs in the United Kingdom are the 1300 ft *396 m* Cona chair cliffs on St Kilda, Western Isles (1379 ft *425 m*). The highest sheer sea cliffs on the mainland of Great Britain are at Clo Mor, 3 miles *4,8 km* south-east of Cape Wrath, Highland Scotland which drop 921 ft *280,7 m*. England's highest cliffs are Holdstone Hill which descends 1131 ft *344 m* in a ½ mile *800 m* and Great Hangman Hill, near Coombe Martin, also in North Devon, which descends from 1029 ft *313 m* to the sea in less than ¼ mile *400 m*, the last 700 ft *213 m* of which is sheer.

Natural arch *Longest*
The longest natural arch in the world is the Landscape Arch in the Arches National Park, 25 miles *40 km* north of Moab, Utah, USA. This natural sandstone arch spans 291 ft *88 m* and is set about 100 ft *30 m* above the canyon floor. In one place erosion has narrowed its section to 6 ft *1,82 m*. Larger, however, is the Rainbow Bridge, Utah discovered on 14 Aug 1909 with a span of 278 ft *84,7 m* but more than 22 ft *6,7 m* wide.

Natural bridge *Highest*
The highest natural arch is the sandstone arch 25 miles *40 km* WNW of K'ashih, Sinkiang, China, estimated in 1947 to be nearly 1000 ft *312 m* tall with a span of about 150 ft *45 m*.

Longest glaciers
It is estimated that 6,020,000 miles² *15 600 000 km²*, or about 10.4 per cent of the Earth's land surface, is permanently glaciated. The world's longest known glacier is the Lambert Glacier, discovered by an Australian aircraft crew in Australian Antarctic Territory in 1956–7. It is up to 40 miles *64 km* wide and, with its upper section, known as the Mellor Glacier, it measures at least 250 miles *402 km* in length. With the Fisher Glacier limb, the Lambert forms a continuous ice passage about 320 miles *514 km* long. The longest Himalayan glacier is the Siachen (47 miles *75,6 km*) in the Karakoram range, though the Hispar and Biafo combine to form an ice passage 76 miles *122 km* long. The fastest moving major glacier is the Quarayaq in Greenland which flows 20–24 m *65–80 ft* per day.

Greatest avalanches
The greatest natural avalanches, though rarely observed, occur in the Himalaya but no estimates of their volume had been published. It was estimated that 3,500,000 m³ *120 000 000 ft³* of snow fell in an avalanche in the Italian Alps in 1885. The 250 mph *400 km/h* avalanche triggered by the Mount St. Helens eruption in Washington, USA on 18 May 1979 was estimated to measure 2800 million m³ *96,000 million ft³* (see also Disasters, end of Chapter 10).

WATERFALLS
Highest
The highest waterfall (as opposed to vaporized 'Bridal Veil') in the world is the Salto Angel in Venezuela, on a branch of the River Carrao, an upper tributary of the Caroni with a total drop of 3212 ft *979 m*—the longest single drop is 2648 ft *807 m*. It was re-discovered by a United States pilot named James (Jimmy) Angel (died 8 Dec 1956), who crashed nearby on 9 Oct 1937. The falls, known by the Indians as Cherun-Meru, were first reported by Ernesto Sanchez La Cruz in 1910.

Highest *United Kingdom*
The tallest waterfall in the United Kingdom is Eas a'Chùal Aluinn, from Glas Bheinn (2541 ft *774 m*), Highland, Scotland, with a drop of 658 ft *200 m*. England's highest fall above ground is Caldron (or Cauldron) Snout, on the Tees, with a fall of 200 ft *60 m* in 450 ft *135 m* of cataracts, but no sheer leap. It is on the border of Durham and Cumbria. The cascade in the Gaping Gill Cave descends 365 ft *111 m*. The highest Welsh waterfall is the Pistyll-y-Llyn on the Powys-Dyfed border which exceeds 300 ft *90 m* in descent.

Highest *Ireland*

The highest falls in Ireland are the Powerscourt Falls (350 ft *106 m*), on the River Dargle, County Wicklow.

Greatest

On the basis of the average annual flow, the greatest waterfall in the world is the Guairá (374 ft *114 m* high), known also as the Salto dos Sete Quedas, on the Alto Paraná River between Brazil and Paraguay. Although attaining an average height of only 110 ft *33,5 m*, its estimated annual average flow over the lip (5300 yd *4850 m* wide) is 470,000 cusec *13 300 m³/sec*. The amount of water this represents can be imagined by supposing that it was pouring into the dome of St Paul's Cathedral—it would fill it completely in three-fifths of a second. It has a peak flow of 1,750,000 cusec *50 000 m³/sec*. The seven cataracts of the Boyoma (formerly Stanley) Falls in the Congo (Kinshasa) have an average annual flow of 600,000 cusec *17 000 m³/sec*.

It has been calculated that, when some 5,500,000 years ago the Mediterranean basins began to be filled from the Atlantic through the Straits of Gibraltar, a waterfall 26 times greater than the Guairá and perhaps 800 m *2625 ft* high was formed.

Widest

The widest waterfalls in the world are the Khône Falls (50–70 ft *15–21 m* high) in Laos, with a width of 6.7 miles *10,8 km* and a flood flow of 1,500,000 cusec *42 500 m³/sec*.

RIVERS

Longest *World*

The two longest rivers in the world are the Amazon (*Amazonas*), flowing into the South Atlantic, and the Nile (*Bahr-el-Nil*) flowing into the Mediterranean. Which is the longer is more a matter of definition than simple measurement.

The true source of the Amazon was discovered in 1953 to be a stream named Huarco, rising near the summit of Cerro Huagra (17,188 ft *5238 m*) in Peru. This stream progressively becomes the Toro then the Santiago then the Apurimac, which in turn is known as the Ene and then the Tambo before its confluence with the Amazon prime tributary the Ucayali. The length of the Amazon from this source to the South Atlantic *via* the Canal do Norte was measured in 1969 to be 4007 miles *6448 km* (usually quoted to the rounded off figure of 4000 miles *6437 km*).

If, however, a vessel navigating down the river turns to the south of Ilha de Marajó through the straits of Breves and Boiuci into the Pará, the total length of the water-course becomes 4195 miles 6750 km. The Pará is not however a tributary of the Amazon, being hydrologically part of the basin of the Tocantins.

The length of the Nile watercourse, as surveyed by M. Devroey (Belgium) before the loss of a few miles of meanders due to the formation of Lake Nasser, behind the Aswan High Dam, was 4145 miles *6670 km*. This course is the hydrologically acceptable one from the source in Burundi of the Luvironza branch of the Kagera feeder of the Victoria Nyanza *via* the White Nile (*Bahr-el-Jebel*) to the delta.

Longest *Great Britain*

The longest river in Great Britain is the Severn, which empties into the Bristol Channel and is 220 miles *354 km* long. Its basin extends over 4409 miles² *11 419 km²*. It rises in north-western Powys and flows through Shropshire, Hereford and Worcester, Gloucestershire and Avon and has a record 17 tributaries. The longest river *wholly* in England is the Thames, which is 215 miles, *346 km* long to the Nore. Its remotest source is at Seven Springs, Gloucestershire, whence the River Churn joins the other head waters. The source of the Thames proper is Trewsbury Mead, Coates, Cirencester, Gloucestershire. The basin measures 3841 miles² *9948 km²*. The Yorkshire Ouse's 11 tributaries aggregate 629 miles *1012 km*.

The longest river wholly in Wales is the Towy, with a length of 64 miles *102 km*. It rises in Dyfed and flows out into Carmarthen Bay. The longest river in Scotland is the Tay, with Dundee, Tayside, on the shore of the estuary. It is 117 miles *188 km* long from the source of its remotest head-stream, the River Tummel, Tayside and has the greatest volume of any river in Great Britain, with a flow of up to 49,000 cusecs *1387 m³* per sec. Of Scottish rivers the Tweed and the Clyde have most tributaries with 11 each.

Longest *Ireland*

The longest river in Ireland is the Shannon, which is longer than any river in Great Britain. It rises 258 ft *78,6 m* above sea-level, in County Cavan, and flows through a series of loughs to Limerick. It is 240 miles *386 km* long, including the 56 mile *90 km* long estuary to Loop Head. The basin area is 6060 miles² *15 695 km²*.

Shortest river

The world's shortest named river is the D River, Lincoln City, Oregon, USA which connects Devil's Lake to the Pacific Ocean and is 440 ft *134 m* long at low tide.

Largest basin and longest tributary

The largest river basin in the world is that drained by the Amazon (4007 miles *6448 km*). It covers about 2,720,000 miles² *7 045 000 km²*. It has about 15,000 tributaries and subtributaries, of which four are more than 1000 miles *1609 km* long. These include the Madeira, the longest of all tributaries, with a length of 2100 miles *3380 km*, which is surpassed by only 14 rivers in the whole world.

Longest sub-tributary

The longest sub-tributary is the Pilcomayo (1000 miles *1609 km* long) in South America. It is a tributary of the Paraguay (1500 miles *2415 km* long), which is itself a tributary of the Paraná (2500 miles *4025 km*).

Longest estuary

The world's longest estuary is that of the often frozen Ob', in the northern USSR, at 550 miles *885 km*. It is up to 50 miles *80 km* wide.

Largest delta

The world's largest delta is that created by the Ganga (Ganges) and Brahmaputra in Bangla Desh (formerly East Pakistan) and West Bengal, India. It covers an area of 30,000 miles² *75 000 km²*.

Greatest flow

The greatest flow of any river in the world is that of the Amazon, which discharges an average of 4,200,000 cusec *120 000 m³/sec* into the Atlantic Ocean, rising to more than 7,000,000 cusec *200 000 m³/sec* in full flood. The lowest 900 miles *1450 km* of the Amazon average 300 ft *90 m* in depth.

Submarine river

In 1952 a submarine river 250 miles *400 km* wide, known as the Cromwell current, was discovered flowing eastward 300 ft *90 m* below the surface of the Pacific for 3500 miles *5625 km* along the equator. Its volume is 1000 times that of the Mississippi.

Subterranean river

In August 1958 a crypto-river was tracked by radio isotopes flowing under the Nile with 6 times its mean annual flow or 500,000 million m³ *20 million million ft³*.

Largest swamp

The world's largest tract of swamp is in the basin of the Pripet or Pripyat River—a tributary of the Dnieper in the USSR. These swamps cover an estimated area of 18,125 miles² *46 950 km²*.

RIVER BORES
World

The bore on the Ch'ient'ang'kian (Hang-chou-fe) in eastern China is the most remarkable in the world. At Spring tides the wave attains a height of up to 25 ft *7,5 m* and a speed of 13 knots *24 km/h*. It is heard advancing at a range of 14 miles *22 km*. The bore on the Hooghly branch of the Ganges travels for 70 miles *110 km* at more than 15 knots *27 km/h*. The annual downstream flood wave on the Mekong sometimes reaches a height of 46 ft *14 m*. The greatest volume of any tidal bore is that of the Canal do Norte (10 miles *16 km* wide) in the mouth of the Amazon.

Great Britain

The most notable river bore in the United Kingdom is that on the Severn, which attained a measured height of 9¼ ft *2,8 m* on 15 Oct 1966 downstream of Stone-bench, and a speed of 13 mph *20 km/h*. It travels as far up as Severn Stoke in Hereford and Worcester.

71

4. THE UNIVERSE & SPACE

The Guinness Book of Astronomy Facts and Feats by Patrick Moore was published in May 19
price £6.95.

LIGHT-YEAR—that distance travelled by light (speed 186,282.397 miles/sec *299 792,4*
km s⁻¹ or 670,616,629.4 mph *1 079 258 848,8 km h⁻¹ in vacuo*) in one tropical ye
(365.24219878 mean solar days at January 0,12 hours Ephemeris time in AD 1900) and
5,878,499,814,000 miles *9 460 528 405 000 km*. The unit was first used in March 1888.

MAGNITUDE—a measure of stellar brightness such that the light of a star of any magnitud
bears a ratio of 2.511886 to that of a star of the next magnitude. Thus a fifth magnitude star
2.511886 times as bright, while one of the first magnitude is exactly 100 (or 2.511886⁵) times
bright, as a sixth magnitude star. In the case of such exceptionally bright bodies as Sirius, Venu
the Moon (magnitude – 12.71) or the Sun (magnitude – 26.78), the magnitude is expressed as
minus quantity.

PROPER MOTION—that component of a star's motion in space which, at right angles to th
line of sight, constitutes an apparent change of position of the star in the celestial sphere.

The universe is the entirety of space, matter and anti-matter. A
appreciation of its magnitude is best grasped by working out
ward from the Earth, through the Solar System and our ow
Milky Way Galaxy, to the remotest extra-galactic nebulae an
quasars.

METEOROIDS
Meteor shower
Meteoroids are of cometary or asteroidal origin. A meteor is th
light phenomenon caused by the entry of a meteoroid into th
Earth's atmosphere. The greatest meteor 'shower' on recor
occurred on the night of 16–17 Nov 1966, when the Leoni
meteors (which recur every 33¼ years) were visible betwee
western North America and eastern USSR. It was calculate
that meteors passed over Arizona, USA, at a rate of 2300 per mi
for a period of 20 min from 5 a.m. on 17 Nov 1966.

METEORITES
Oldest
It was reported in August 1978 that dust grains in the Murchiso
meteorite which fell in Australia in September 1969 pre-date th
formation of the Solar System.

Largest *World*
When a meteoroid penetrates to the Earth's surface, the rem
nant is described as a meteorite. This occurs about 150 times pe
year over the whole land surface of the Earth. Although th
chances of being struck are deemed negligible, the most anxiou
time of day for meteorophobes is 3 p.m. The largest know
meteorite is one found in 1920 at Hoba West, near Grootfontei
in south-west Africa. This is a block 9 ft *2,75 m* long by 8 f
2,43 m broad, estimated to be 132,000 lb (59 tons/*tonnes*). Th
largest meteorite exhibited by any museum is the 'Tent' meteo
rite, weighing 68,085 lb (30.39 tons *30 882 kg*) found in 189
near Cape York, on the west coast of Greenland, by the ex
pedition of Commander (later Rear-Admiral) Robert Edwi
Peary (1856–1920). It was known to the Eskimos as the Abni
ghito and is now exhibited in the Hayden Planetarium in Ne
York City, NY, USA. The largest piece of stony meteorite re
covered is a piece of 1770 kg *3902 lb* part of a shower whic
struck Jilin (formerly Kirin), China on 8 Mar 1976. The oldes
dated meteorites are from the Allende fall in Chihuahua, Mexic
on 8 Feb 1969 dating back to 4,610 million years.

There was a mysterious explosion of 12½ megatons in Lat. 60
55′ N, Long. 101° 57′ E, in the basin of the Podkamennay
Tunguska river, 40 miles north of Vanavar, in Siberia, USSR, a
00 hrs 17 min 11 sec UT on 30 June 1908. The cause was vari
ously attributed to a meteorite (1927), a comet (1930), a nuclea
explosion (1961) and to anti-matter (1965). This devastated an
area of about 1500 miles² *3885 km²* and the shock was felt as fa
as 1000 km (more than *600 miles*) away. The theory is now
favoured that this was the terminal flare of stony debris from a
comet, possibly Encké's comet, at altitude of only 6 km *or les
than 20,000 ft*. A similar event may have occurred over the Isle o
Axeholm, Lincolnshire a few thousand years before.

Largest *United Kingdom and Ireland*
The heaviest of the 22 meteorites known to have fallen on the
British Isles since 1623 was one weighing at least 102 lb *46,25 k*
(largest piece 17 lb 6 oz *7,88 kg*), which fell at 4.12 p.m. on 2
Dec 1965 at Barwell, Leicestershire. Scotland's largest recorde
meteorite fell in Strathmore, Tayside on 3 Dec 1917. It weighe
22¼ lb *10,09 kg* and was the largest of four stones totalling 29 l
6 oz *13,324 kg*. The largest recorded meteorite to fall in Irelan
was the Limerick Stone of 65 lb *29,5 kg*, part of a shower weigh
ing more than 106 lb *48 kg* which fell near Adare County

Limerick, on 10 Sept 1813. The larger of the two recorded meteorites to land in Wales was one weighing 28 oz *794 g* of which a piece weighing 25½ oz *723 g* went through the roof of the Prince Llewellyn Hotel in Beddgelert, Gwynedd, shortly before 3.15 a.m. on 21 Sept 1949.

Largest craters
It has been estimated that some 2,000 asteroid–Earth collisions have occurred in the last 600 million years. A total of 96 collision sites or astroblemes have been recognized. A crater 150 miles *241 km* in diameter and ½ mile *805 m* deep has been postulated in Wilkes Land, Antarctica since 1962. It would be caused by a 13,000 million ton meteorite striking at 44,000 mph *70 811 km/ h*. USSR scientists reported in December 1970 an astrobleme with a 60 mile *95 km* diameter and a maximum depth of 1300 ft *400 m* in the basin of the River Popigai. There is a possible crater-like formation or astrobleme 275 miles *442,5 km* in diameter on the eastern shore of the Hudson Bay, Canada, where the Nastapoka Islands are just off the coast.

The largest proven crater is the Coon Butte or Barringer crater, discovered in 1891 near Canyon Diablo, Winslow, northern Arizona, USA. It is 4150 ft *1265 m* in diameter and now about 575 ft *175 m* deep, with a parapet rising 130–155 ft *40–48 m* above the surrounding plain. It has been estimated that an iron-nickel mass with a diameter of 200–260 ft *61–79 m* and weighing about 2,000,000 tons/*tonnes* gouged this crater in *c.* 25,000 BC.

Evidence was published in 1963 discounting a meteoric origin for the crypto-volcanic Vredefort Ring (diameter 26 miles *41,8 km*), to the south-west of Johannesburg, South Africa, but this has now been re-asserted. The New Quebec (formerly the Chubb) 'Crater', first sighted on 20 June 1943 in northern Ungava, Canada, is 1325 ft *404 m* deep and measures 6.8 miles *10,9 km* round its rim.

Fireball *Brightest*
The brightest fireball ever photographically recorded was by Dr Zdenek Ceplecha over Sumava, Czechoslovakia on 4 Dec 1974 with a momentary magnitude of −22 or 10,000 times brighter than a full Moon.

Tektites
The largest tektite of which details have been published has been of 3,2 kg *7.04 lb* found in 1932 at Muong Nong, Saravane Province, Laos and now in the Paris Museum.

AURORAE
Most frequent
Polar lights, known since 1560 as Aurora Borealis or Northern Lights in the northern hemisphere and since 1773 as Aurora Australis in the southern hemisphere, are caused by electrical solar discharges in the upper atmosphere and occur most frequently in high latitudes. Aurorae are visible at some time on *every* clear dark night in the polar areas within 20 degrees of the magnetic poles. The extreme height of aurorae has been measured at 1000 km *620 miles*, while the lowest may descend to 45 miles *72,5 km*. Reliable figures exist only from 1952, since when the record high and low number of nights of auroral displays in Shetland (geomagnetic Lat. 63°) has been 203 (1957) and 58 (1965). The most recent great display in north-west Europe was that of 4–5 Sept 1958.

Lowest latitudes
Extreme cases of displays in very low latitudes are Cuzco, Peru (2 Aug 1744); Honolulu, Hawaii (1 Sept 1859) and questionably Singapore (25 Sept 1909).

Noctilucent clouds
Regular observations in Western Europe date only from 1964, since when the record high and low number of nights on which these phenomena (at heights of *c.* 52 miles *85 km*) have been observed have been 41 (1974) and 15 (1970).

THE MOON
The Earth's closest neighbour in space and only natural satellite is the Moon, at a mean distance of 238,855 statute miles *384 400 km* centre to centre or 233,812 miles *376 284 km* surface to surface. Its closest approach (perigee) and most extreme distance away (apogee) measured surface to surface are 216,420

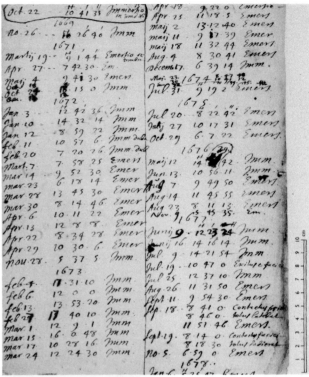

above: A photoprint on Rømer's working log showing 'Emersion' (Emer) and 'Immersion' (Imm) times of Jupiter's moon Io (discovered by Galileo in 1610) between Oct 22 1668 and Jan 1678. The key observation was that on Nov 9 1676. (*Courtesy: Kongelige Bibliotek, Copenhagen*) *left:* Ole Christensen Rømer (1644–1710), the great Danish astronomer, who in 1676 established the first estimate of the finite speed of light. Rømer was working in Paris and predicted that the next 'immersion' of Jupiter's then innermost known satellite Io on 9 Nov 1676 (5 hr 45 min 35 sec) would be 10 minutes later than that logically expected for a moon orbiting its parent planet at a fixed speed. This discrepancy would be due to the fact that the light from it had to cross to the furthest side of the Earth's orbit. He published his brilliant result in *Journal des Sçavans* in Paris on Monday 7 Dec 1676.

and 247,667 miles *348 294 and 398 581 km* respectively or 221,463 and 252,710 miles *356 410 and 406 697 km* measured centre to centre. It has a diameter of 2159.3 miles *3475,0 km* and has a mass of 7.23×10^{19} tons $7,35 \times 10^{19}$ *tonnes* with a mean density of 3.34. The average orbital speed is 2287 mph *3680 km/h*.

The first direct hit on the Moon was achieved at 2 min 24 sec after midnight (Moscow time) on 14 Sept 1959, by the Soviet space probe *Lunik II* near the *Mare Serenitatis*. The first photographic images of the hidden side were collected by the USSR's *Lunik III* from 6.30 a.m. on 7 Oct 1959, from a range of up to 43,750 miles *70 400 km* and transmitted to the Earth from a distance of 470 000 km *292,000 miles*. The first 'soft' landing was made by the USSR's *Luna IX*, in the area of the Ocean of Storms on 3 Feb 1966.

'Blue moon'
Owing to sulphur particles in the upper atmosphere from a forest fire covering 250,000 acres *100 000 ha* between Mile 103 and Mile 119 on the Alaska Highway in northern British Columbia, Canada, the Moon took on a bluish colour, as seen from Great Britain, on the night of 26 Sept 1950. The Moon also appeared green after the Krakatoa eruption of 27 Aug 1883 (see pp. 63–4) and in Stockholm for 3 min on 17 Jan 1884.

Crater *Largest*
Only 59 per cent of the Moon's surface is directly visible from the Earth because it is in 'captured rotation', *i.e.* the period of rotation is equal to the period of orbit. The largest wholly visible crater is the walled plain Bailly, towards the Moon's South Pole, which is 183 miles *295 km* across, with walls rising to 14,000 ft

Saturn V the mightiest rocket of which details have been published. It is seen here lifting a payload of the 73.6 ton/*tonne* Skylab I in 1973 (see pp. 77–8). (*NASA*)

distance from the Sun varies. The orbital speed varies between 65,520 mph *105 450 km/h* (minimum) and 67,750 mph *109 030 km/h*. The average distance of the Sun is 1.000 000 23 astronomical units or 92,955,829 miles *149 597 906 km*.

The closest approach (perihelion) is 91,402,000 miles *147 097 000 km* and the farthest departure (aphelion) is 94,510,000 miles *152 099 000 km*. The Solar System is revolving around the centre of the Milky Way once in each 225,000,000 years, at a speed of 481,000 mph *774 000 km/h* and has a velocity of 42,500 mph *68 400 km/h* relative to stars in our immediate region such as Vega, towards which it is moving.

Temperature and dimensions

The Sun has an internal temperature of about 16 000 000 K, core pressure of 500,000,000 tons/in² *7,7 PPa* and uses up 4,000,000 tons/*tonnes* of hydrogen per sec, thus providing luminosity of 3×10^{27} candlepower, with an intensity of 1,500,000 candles/in² *1 530 000 candelas*. The Sun has the stellar classification of a 'yellow dwarf' and, although its density is only 1.407 times that of water, its mass is 332,946 times as much as that of the Earth. It has a mean diameter of 865,270 miles *1 392 520 km*. The Sun with a mass of 1.958×10^{27} tons *$1,989 \times 10^{27}$ tonnes* represents more than 99 per cent of the total mass of the Solar System.

Sun-spots *Largest*

To be visible to the *protected* naked eye, a Sun-spot must cover about one two-thousandth part of the Sun's disc and thus have an area of about 500,000,000 miles² *1300 million km²*. The largest recorded Sun-spot occurred in the Sun's southern hemisphere on 8 Apr 1947. Its area was about 7000 million miles² *18 000 million km²* with an extreme longitude of 187,000 miles *300 000 km* and an extreme latitude of 90,000 miles *145 000 km*. Sun-spots appear darker because they are more than 1500 deg C cooler than the rest of the Sun's surface temperature of 5525°C. The largest observed solar prominence was one protruding 365,000 miles *588 000 km*, photographed on 19 Dec 1973 during the 3rd and final manned Skylab mission.

Most frequent

In October 1957 a smoothed Sun-spot count showed 263, the highest recorded index since records started in 1755 (*cf.* previous record of 239 in May 1778). In 1943 one Sun-spot lasted for 200 days from June to December.

ECLIPSES
Earliest recorded

The earliest extrapolated eclipses that have been identified are 1361 BC (lunar) and October 2136 BC (solar). For the Middle East only, lunar eclipses have been extrapolated to 3450 BC and solar ones to 4200 BC. No centre of the path of totality for a solar eclipse crossed London for the 575 years from 20 Mar 1140 to 3 May 1715. On 14 June 2151 at 18.25 GMT the eclipse will be 98 per cent total in central London but total in Sheffield and Norfolk. The most recent occasion when a line of totality of a solar eclipse crossed Great Britain was on 29 June 1927 for 24.5 sec at 6.23 a.m. at West Hartlepool, Cleveland and the next instance will clip the coast at St Just, Cornwall at 10.10 a.m. on Wednesday 11 Aug 1999. On 30 June 1954 a total eclipse was witnessed in Unst, Shetland Islands but the centre of the path of totality was to the north of territorial waters.

Longest duration

The maximum *possible* duration of an eclipse of the Sun is 7 min 31 sec. The longest actually *measured* was on 20 June 1955 (7 min 8 sec), seen from the Philippines. One of 7 min 29 sec should occur in mid-Atlantic on 16 July 2186, which will then be the longest for 1469 years. The longest possible in the British Isles is 5½ min. That of 15 June 885 lasted nearly 5 min, as will that of 20 July 2381 in the Border area. Durations can be extended by observers being airborne as on 30 June 1973 when an eclipse was 'extended' to 72 min aboard *Concorde*. An annular eclipse may last for 12 min 24 sec. The longest totality of any lunar eclipse is 104 min. This has occurred many times.

Most and least frequent

The highest number of eclipses possible in a year is seven, as in 1935, when there were five solar and two lunar eclipses; or four solar and three lunar eclipses, as will occur in 1982. The lowest

4250 m. The Orientale Basin, partly on the averted side, measures more than 600 miles *965 km* in diameter.

Crater *Deepest*

The deepest crater is the Newton crater, with a floor estimated to be between 23,000 and 29,000 ft *7000–8850 m* below its rim and 14,000 ft *2250 m* below the level of the plain outside. The brightest directly visible spot on the Moon is *Aristarchus*.

Highest mountains

In the absence of a sea level, lunar altitudes are measured relative to an adopted reference sphere of radius 1738,000 km or *1079.943 miles*. Thus the greatest elevation attained on this basis by any of the 12 US astronauts has been 7830 m *25,688 ft* on the Descartes Highlands by Capt. John Walter Young USN and Major Charles M. Duke Jr on 27 Apr 1972.

Temperature extremes

When the Sun is overhead the temperature on the lunar equator reaches 243°F *117,2°C* (31 deg F *17,2 deg C* above the boiling point of water). By sunset the temperature is 58°F *14,4°C* but after nightfall it sinks to −261°F *−162,7°C*.

Moon samples

The age attributed to the oldest of the moon material brought back to Earth by the *Apollo* programme crews has been soil dated to 4720 million years.

THE SUN
Distance extremes

The Earth's 66,620 mph *107 220 km/h* orbit of 584,017,800 miles *939 885 500 km* around the Sun is elliptical, hence our

74

possible number in a year is two, both of which must be solar, as in 1944 and 1969.

COMETS

Earliest recorded
The earliest records of comets date from the 7th century BC. The speeds of the estimated 2,000,000 comets vary from 700 mph *1125 km/h* in outer space to 1,250,000 mph *2 000 000 km/h* when near the Sun. The successive appearances of Halley's Comet have been traced back to 467 BC. It was first depicted in the Nuremburg Chronicle of AD 684. The first prediction of its return by Edmund Halley (1656–1742) proved true on Christmas Day 1758, 16 years after his death. Its next perihelion should be at 9.9 (*viz.* at 9.30 p.m. on the 9th) February 1986, 75.81 years after the last, which was on 19 Apr 1910. The 33rd sighting may occur as early as December 1984.

Closest approach
On 1 July 1770, Lexell's Comet, travelling at a speed of 23.9 miles/sec *38,5 km/sec* (relative to the Sun), came within 745,000 miles *1 200 000 km* of the Earth. However, the Earth is believed to have passed through the tail of Halley's Comet, most recently on 19 May 1910.

Largest
Comets are so tenuous that it has been estimated that even the head of one rarely contains solid matter much more than *c*. 1 km *0.6 miles* in diameter. Tails, as in the case of the brightest of all, the Great Comet of 1843, may trail for 205,000,000 miles *330 million km*. The head of Holmes Comet of 1892 once measured 1,500,000 miles *2 400 000 km* in diameter. Comet Bennett which appeared in January 1970 was found to be enveloped in a hydrogen cloud measuring some 8,000,000 miles *12 750 000 km* in length.

Shortest period
Of all the recorded periodic comets (these are members of the Solar System), the one which most frequently returns is Encke's Comet, first identified in 1786. Its period of 1206 days (3.3 years) is the shortest established. Not one of its 51 returns (including 1977) has been missed by astronomers. Now increasingly faint, it is expected to 'die' by February 1994. The most frequently observed comets are Schwassmann-Wachmann I, Kopff and Oterma which can be observed every year between Mars and Jupiter.

Longest period
At the other extreme is Delavan's Comet of 1914, whose path was not accurately determined. It is not expected to return for perhaps 24 million years.

PLANETS

Largest
Planets (including the Earth) are bodies within the Solar System and which revolve round the Sun in definite orbits. Jupiter, with an equatorial diameter of 88,780 miles *142 880 km* and a polar diameter of 82,980 miles *133 540 km* is the largest of the nine major planets, with a mass 317.83 times, and a volume 1318 times that of the Earth. It also has the shortest period of rotation resulting in a Jovian day of only 9 hr 50 min 30.003 sec in the equatorial zone.

Smallest and coldest
The smallest and coldest planet is Pluto, (with its partner Charon, announced on 22 June 1978) which have an estimated surface temperature of −360° F *−220° C* (100 deg F *53 deg C* above absolute zero). Their mean distance from the Sun is 3,674,488,000 miles *5 913 514 000 km* and their period of revolution is 248.54 years. The diameter is *c*. 3000 km *1880 miles* and the mass is about 1/500th of that of the Earth. Pluto was first recorded by Clyde William Tombaugh (b. 4 Feb 1906) at Lowell Observatory, Flagstaff, Arizona, USA, on 18 Feb 1930 from photographs taken on 23 and 29 Jan and announced on 13 Mar. Because of its orbital eccentricity Pluto moved closer to the Sun than Neptune between 23 Jan 1979 and 15 Mar 1999.

Fastest
Mercury, which orbits the Sun at an average distance of 35,983,100 miles *57 909 200 km*, has a period of revolution of 87.9686 days, so giving the highest average speed in orbit of 107,030 mph *172 248 km/h*.

Hottest
For Venus a surface temperature of 462° C *864° F* has been estimated from measurements made from the USSR *Venera 7* and US Pioneer Cytherean surface probes.

Nearest
The fellow planet closest to the Earth is Venus, which is, at times, about 25,700,000 miles *41 360 000 km* inside the Earth's orbit, compared with Mars's closest approach of 34,600,000 miles *55 680 000 km* outside the Earth's orbit. Mars, known since 1965 to be cratered, has temperatures ranging from 85° F *29,4° C* to −190° F *−123° C*.

Surface features
By far the highest and most spectacular is Olympus Mons (formerly Nix Olympica) in the Tharsis region with a diameter of 500–600 km *310–370 miles* and a height of 26 ± 3 km *75,450–95,150 ft* above the surrounding plain.

Brightest and faintest
Viewed from the Earth, by far the brightest of the five planets visible to the naked eye (Uranus at magnitude 5.5 is only marginally visible) is Venus, with a maximum magnitude of −4.4. The faintest is Pluto, with a magnitude of 15.0.

Densest and least dense
Earth is the densest planet with an average figure of 5.515 times that of water, whilst Saturn has an average density only about one-eighth of this value or 0.705 times that of water.

Conjunctions
The most dramatic recorded conjunction (coming together) of the other seven principal members of the Solar System (Sun, Moon, Mercury, Venus, Mars, Jupiter and Saturn) occurred on 5 Feb 1962, when 16° covered all seven during an eclipse in the Pacific area. It is possible that the seven-fold conjunction of September 1186 spanned only 12°. The next notable conjunction will take place on 5 May 2000.

SATELLITES

Most
Of the nine major planets, all but Venus and Mercury have satellites. The planet with the most is Jupiter, with four large and ten small moons. Jupiter and Saturn have 16 satellites each, whilst the Earth and Pluto are the only planets with a single satellite. The distance from their parent planets varies from the 5827 miles *9378 km* of *Phobos* from the centre of Mars to the 14,730,000 miles *23 705 000 km* of Jupiter's outer satellite *Sinope* (Jupiter IX). The Solar System has a total of 43 satellites.

Largest and smallest
The largest satellite is *Titan* (Saturn VI), with a diameter of about 3300 miles *5400 km* and a possible atmospheric thickness of 90 miles *150 km*. The heaviest satellite known is *Ganymede* (Jupiter III), which is 2.02 times heavier than our own Moon. The smallest satellite is *Leda* (Jupiter XIII) with a diameter of less than 9 miles *15 km*.

Largest asteroids
In the belt which lies between Mars and Jupiter, there are some 45,000 (only 2319 numbered to January 1981) minor planets or asteroids which are, for the most part, too small to yield to diameter measurement. The largest and first discovered (by G. Piazzi at Palermo, Sicily on 1 Jan 1801) of these is *Ceres*, with a diameter of 637 miles *1025 km*. The only one visible to the naked eye is asteroid 4 *Vesta* (diameter 345 miles *555 km* discovered on 29 Mar 1807 by Dr Heinrich Wilhelm Olbers (1758–1840), a German amateur astronomer. The closest measured approach to the Earth by an asteroid was 485,000 miles *780 000 km* in the case of *Hermes* on 30 Oct 1937 (asteroid now lost). The most distant detected is 2060 *Chiron*, found between Saturn and Uranus on 18–19 Oct 1977, by Charles T. Kowal from the Hale Observatory, California, USA.

STARS

Largest and most massive
The most massive star is the faint-blue R 136a in the Tarantula Nebula (or 30 Doradus), an appendage of the Lesser Magellanic Cloud, announced on 19 Jan 1981 and believed to be of 3500 Solar masses and 150,000 light years distant. Betelgeux (top left

star of Orion) has a diameter of >400 million km *250 million miles* and in 1978 was found to be surrounded by a tenuous 'shell' of potassium 1,6 million million km or 11 000 astronomical units. The light from Betelgeux left it in AD 1460.

Smallest
The least massive stars known are the two components of the binary star *Wolf 424*, a faint star in Virgo. Each of the two stars has only 0.06 solar masses.

Brightest
Sirius A (*Alpha Canis Majoris*), also known as the Dog Star, is apparently the brightest star of the 5776 stars visible in the heavens, with an apparent magnitude of -1.46. It is in the constellation *Canis Major* and is visible in the winter months of the northern hemisphere, being due south at midnight on the last day of the year. The Sirius system is 8.64 light-years distant and has a luminosity 26 times as much as that of the Sun. It has a diameter of 1,450,000 miles *2,33 million km* and a mass of 4.20×10^{27} tons *$4,26 \times 10^{27}$ tonnes*. The faint white dwarf companion Sirius B has a diameter of only 6000 miles *10 000 km* but is 350,000 times heavier than the Earth.

Farthest
The Solar System, with its Sun, nine principal planets, 43 satellites, asteroids and comets, was estimated in 1921 to be about 32,000 light-years from the centre of the lens-shaped Milky Way galaxy (diameter 100,000 light-years) of about 100,000 million stars. The most distant star in our galaxy was therefore estimated to be 80,000 light-years distant. A recalibration, published in 1980, however indicates the Galaxy has a diameter of c. 70,000 light years with the most distant star hence less than 60,000 light years away.

Nearest
Excepting the special case of our own Sun (*q.v.* above) the nearest star is the very faint *Proxima Centauri*, which is 4.22 light-years (24,800,000,000,000 miles *$4,00 \times 10^{13}$ km*) away. The nearest star visible to the naked eye is the southern hemisphere star *Alpha Centauri*, or *Rigel Kentaurus* (4.35 light-years), with a magnitude of -0.29. By AD 11,800 the nearest star will be Barnard's Star (see below under Stellar Planets) at a distance of 3.75 light years.

Most and least luminous
If all stars could be viewed at the same distance, the most luminous would be the apparently faint variable *S. Doradûs*, in the Greater Magellanic Cloud (*Nebecula Major*), which can be nearly 1 million times brighter than the Sun, and has an absolute magnitude of -8.9. The variable η *Carinae* in c. 1840 was perhaps 4 million times more luminous than the sun. The faintest star detected visually is a very red star, known as LP 425–140, 23.5 light years distant with about one millionth of the Sun's brightness.

Brightest super-nova
Super-novae, or temporary 'stars' which flare and then fade, occur perhaps five times in 1000 years in our galaxy. The brightest 'star' ever seen by historic man is believed to be the super-nova SN 1006 in April 1006 near *Lupus* β which flared for 2 years and attained a magnitude of -9 to -10. It is now believed to be the radio source G.327.6 + 14.5 nearly 3000 light-years distant.

Constellations
The largest of the 89 constellations is *Hydra* (the Sea Serpent), which covers 1,302.844 deg^2 or 6.3 per cent of the hemisphere and contains at least 68 stars visible to the naked eye (to 5.5 mag.). The constellation *Centaurus* (Centaur), ranking ninth in area embraces however at least 94 such stars. The smallest constellation is *Crux Australis* (Southern Cross) with an area of 68.477 deg^2 compared with the 41,252.96 deg^2 of the whole sky.

Stellar planets
Planetary companions, with a mass of less than 7 per cent of their parent star, have been reported for 61 *Cygni* (1942), *Lalande* 21185 (1960) *Krüger 60, Ci 2354, BD + 20° 2465* and one of the two components of *70 Ophiuchi*. A planet of 6 times the mass of Jupiter, 750 million miles *1200 million km* from *Epsilon Eridani* (see below) was reported by Peter van de Kamp

in January 1973. In August 1975 van de Kamp reported that Barnard's Star (Munich 15040) possibly had two planets equivalent in mass to Jupiter and Saturn.

Listening operations ('Project Ozma') on *Tau Ceti* and *Epsilon Eridani* were maintained from 4 Apr 1960 to March 1961, using an 85-ft *25,90 m* radio telescope at Deer Creek Valley, Green Bank, West Virginia, USA. The apparatus was probably insufficiently sensitive for any signal from a distance of 10.7 light-years to be received. Monitoring has been conducted from Gorkiy, USSR since 1969.

Longest name
The longest name for any star is *Shurnarkabtishashutu*, the Arabic for 'under the southern horn of the bull'.

Black Holes
The first tentative identification of a Black Hole was announced in December 1972 in the binary-star X-ray source Cygnus X-1. This is a small dark companion of some 10 solar masses from which the escape velocity tends to c (the velocity of light). The critical size has been estimated to be as low as a diameter of 3.67 miles *5,90 km*. In early 1978 supermassive Black Holes were suggested with a mass of 100 million suns—2×10^{35} tonnes.

THE UNIVERSE
Outside the Milky Way galaxy, which is part of the so-called Local Group of galaxies moving toward the centre of the Virgo supercluster 30 million light-years distant, at a speed of *c* 400 km/sec *875,000 mph*, there exist 10,000 million other galaxies. These range in size up to the largest known object in the Universe, the radio galaxy 3C-345, announced from Effelsberg, near Bonn, W. Germany in March 1980, which is 78 million light-years or 72×10^{19} km across. It is estimated to be 5,000 million light-years distant.

Farthest visible object
The remotest heavenly body visible with the naked eye is the Great Galaxy in *Andromeda* (Mag. 3.47), known as Messier 31. This is a rotating nebula in spiral form, and its distance from the Earth is about 2,200,000 light-years, or about 13,000,000,000,000,000,000 miles *21×10^{18} km* and is moving towards us. It is just possible however that, under ideal seeing conditions, Messier 33, the Spiral in Triangulum (Mag. 5.79), can be glimpsed by the naked eye of keen-sighted people at a distance of 2,300,000 light-years.

Quasars
In November 1962 the existence of quasi-stellar radio sources ('quasars' or QSO's) was established with 3C-273, still the brightest known. No satisfactory model has yet been constructed to account for the immensely high luminosity of bodies apparently so distant and of such small diameter. In April 1975 it was announced that 3C-279 had a measured luminosity of 2.75×10^{14} that of the sun. The first double quasar (0957 + 56) among the 1500 known, was announced in May 1980.

Pulsars
The earliest observation of a pulsating radio source or 'pulsar' CP 1919 by Dr Jocelyn Bell Burnell was announced from the Mullard Radio Astronomy Observatory, Cambridgeshire, England, on 29 Feb 1968. The 100th was announced from Jodrell Bank, Cheshire in June 1973. The fastest so far discovered is NP 0532 in the Crab Nebula with a pulse period of 33 milli-sec. The now accepted model is that they are rotating neutron stars with an inner core density of 4.7×10^{15} g/cm^3 *74,400 million tons/in^3*.

Remotest object
The interpretation of very large red shifts exhibited by quasars

The faint star-like image arrowed, QSO 0Q172 is the most distant object known. (*National Geographic–Palomar Observatory Sky Survey*)

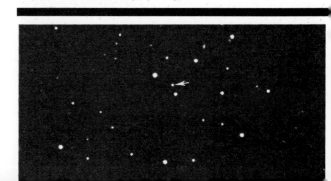

PROGRESSIVE RECORDS OF THE MOST DISTANT MEASURED HEAVENLY BODIES

The possible existence of galaxies external to our own Milky Way system was mooted in 1789 by Sir William Herschel (1738–1822). These extra-galactic nebulae were first termed 'island universes'. Sir John Herschel (1792–1871) opined as early as 1835 that some were 48,000 light-years distant. The first direct measurement of any body outside our Solar System was in 1838.

Estimated Distance in Light Years[1]	Object	Method	Astronomer	Observatory	Date
nearly 11 (now 11.08)	61 Cygni	Parallax	F. Bessel	Königsberg, Germany	1838
>20 (now 26)	Vega	Parallax	F. G. W. Struve	Dorpat (now Tartu), Estonia	1840
c. 200	Limit	Parallax			by 1900
750,000 (now 2.2 m)[2]	Galaxy M31	Cepheid variable	E. P. Hubble	Mt. Wilson, Cal., USA	1923
900,000 (now 2.2 m)[2]	Galaxy M31	Cepheid variable	E. P. Hubble	Mt. Wilson, Cal., USA	1924

Millions of Light Years*	% of c		Red shift[3]			
250	2.5	Ursa Major Galaxy		E. P. Hubble	Mt. Wilson, Cal., USA	by 1934[4]
>350	3.6			M. L. Humason	Palomar, Cal., USA	by 1952
	>10			M. L. Humason	Palomar, Cal., USA	1954
3000	31	Cluster 1448			Palomar, Cal., USA	1956
c. 4500	46	3C 295 in Boötes			Palomar, Cal., USA	June 1960
5300	54.5	QSO 3C 147			Palomar, Cal., USA	April 1964[5]
8700	80	QSO 3C 9		M. Schmidt	Palomar, Cal., USA	May 1965
c. 10,000	81			Margaret Burbidge *et al.*	Palomar, Cal., USA	Dec 1965
	82.2	QSO 1116 + 12		M. Schmidt	Palomar, Cal., USA	Jan 1966
13,000	82.4	QSO PKS 0237–23		J. G. Bolton	Parkes, NSW, Australia	March 1967
	83.8	QSO 4C 25.5		E. Olsen	Palomar, Cal., USA	July 1968
	87.5	QSO 4C 05.34			Kitt Peak, Arizona, USA	May 1970
15,000	92	QSO OH 471		R. F. Carswell *et al.*	Steward Observatory, Arizona, USA	March 1973
15,500[6]	95.5	QSO OQ 172	3.53	Margaret Burbidge *et al.*	Lick Observatory, Cal., USA	April 1973

Note: c is the notation for the speed of light. (see page 72)   [1] Term first utilised in March 1888.   [2] Re-estimate by W. Baade in September 1952.   [3] Discovered by V. M. Slipher from Flagstaff, Arizona, USA 1920.   [4] In this year Hubble opined that the observable horizon would be 3000 m light-years.   [5] Then said that QS0 3C2 and 286 might be more distant—latter claimed by Dr Shklovsky (USSR) to be receding at 55 per cent of c in December 1963.   [6] This distance was attributed at a time when the 'expansion age' estimates for the Universe tended towards 20,000 million years. Recent reassessments have all tended to resile from this figure with 14,500 million years (Schramm, 1978) down to even more recent estimates closer to the 8,000 million years first mooted in 1952. The 7 year reign of OQ172 will almost certainly end with the launch of the Space Telescope in 1983 with a new more distant champion with a higher value of c but a lower figure for estimated distance.

PROGRESSIVE ROCKET ALTITUDE RECORDS

Height in miles	Height in km	Rocket	Place	Launch Date	
0.71	1,14	A 3 in 7,62 cm rocket	near London, England	April	1750
1.24	2	Reinhold Tiling[1] (Germany) solid fuel rocket	Osnabruck, Germany	April	1931
3.1	5	GIRD-X liquid fuel (USSR)	USSR	25 Nov	1933
8.1	13	USSR 'Stratosphere' rocket	USSR		1935
52.46	84,42	A.4 rocket (Germany)	Peenemünde, Germany	3 Oct	1942
c. 85	c. 136	A.4 rocket (Germany)	Heidelager, Poland	early	1944
118	190	A.4 rocket (Germany)	Heidelager, Poland	mid	1944
244	392,6	V-2/W.A.C. Corporal (2-stage) Bumper No. 5 (USA)	White Sands, NM, USA	24 Feb	1949
318	512	GFR (B-5-B) (USSR)	? Tyura Tam, USSR		1950-52
682	1097	Jupiter C (USA)	Cape Canaveral, Florida, USA	20 Sept	1956
>800	>1300	ICBM test flight (USSR)	Tyura Tam/Baikonur, USSR	Aug	1957
>2700	>4345	Farside No. 5 (4-stage) (USA)	Eniwetok Atoll	20 Oct	1957
70,700	113770	Pioneer I-B Lunar Probe (USA)	Cape Canaveral, Florida, USA	11 Oct	1958
215,300,000*	346 480 000	Luna 1 or Mechta (USSR)	Tyura Tam, USSR	2 Jan	1959
242,000,000*	389 450 000	Mars 1 (USSR)	USSR	1 Nov	1962
2,845,000,000[2]	4 580 000 000	Pioneer 10 (USA) (see page 78)	Kennedy Space Center, Cape Canaveral, Florida, USA	2 Mar	1972

* Apogee in solar orbit.   [1] There is some evidence that Tiling may shortly after have reached 9500 m (5.90 miles) with a solid fuel rocket at Wangerooge, East Friesian Islands, W. Germany.   [2] This will be the distance attained in March 1983 when Pioneer 10 crosses the orbit of Neptune. A distance of 4435 million miles 7135 million km will be reached by mid 1989 when crossing the orbit of Pluto and leaving the Solar System's effective gravitational field for deep space.

remains controversial. The record value of Z = 3.53 for Quasar OQ 172 (see Table above) has been interpreted in August 1978 as between 13,500 and 15,500 million light years. On some assessments published in 1979 and 1980 such a recession speed would be consistent with distances of no more than 10,000 light-years. This latter distance was, however, in March 1981 ascribed to the most distant known galaxy 3C 427, which has a red shift of 1.175. The 3° background radiation or primordial hiss discovered in 1965 by Arno Penzias and Robert Wilson of Bell Laboratories appears to be moving at a velocity of 99.9998 per cent c.

Age of the Universe

Estimates of the age of the Universe are dependant upon the value ascribed to Hubble's ratio. Values ranging between 40 and 110 km/s/Mpc yield estimates between 8,000 and 25,000 million years. The most comprehensive survey, published in Aug 1978, gave a value of 14½ ± 1 aeon (an aeon being 1,000 million years) consistent with a value of 60 km/s/Mpc and is known as the Schramm model.

ROCKETRY AND MISSILES

Earliest uses

War rockets, propelled by a charcoal-saltpetre-sulphur gunpowder, were described by Tseng Kung Liang of China in 1042. These early rockets became known in Europe by 1258. The pioneer of military rocketry in Britain was Col. Sir William

Congreve, Bt., MP (1772–1828), Comptroller of the Royal Laboratory, Woolwich, Greater London and Inspector of Military Machines, whose 'six-pound *2,72 kg* rocket' was developed to a range of 2000 yd *1825 m* by 1805 and first used by the Royal Navy against Boulogne, France on 8 Oct 1806.

The first launching of a liquid-fuelled rocket (patented 14 July 1914) was by Dr Robert Hutchings Goddard (1882–1945) of the United States, at Auburn, Massachusetts, USA, on 16 Mar 1926, when his rocket reached an altitude of 41 ft *12,5 m* and travelled a distance of 184 ft *56 m*. The USSR's earliest rocket was the semi-liquid fuelled GIRD-IX tested on 17 Aug 1933.

Longest ranges

On 16 Mar 1962, Nikita Khrushchyov, then Prime Minister of the USSR, claimed in Moscow that the USSR possessed a 'global rocket' with a range of 30 000 km (*about 19,000 miles*) i.e. more than the Earth's semi-circumference and therefore capable of hitting any target from either direction.

Most powerful *World*

It has been suggested that the USSR lunar booster which blew up at Tyura Tam in the summer (? July) of 1969 had a thrust of 10–14 million lb *4,5–6,35 million kg*. There is some evidence of a launch of a USSR 'G' class lunar booster, larger than the US *Saturn V*, on 11 May 1973.

The most powerful rocket that has been publicised is the *Saturn V*, used for the Project Apollo and Skylab programmes on which development began in January 1962, at the John F. Kennedy Space Center, Merritt Island, Florida, USA. The rocket is 363 ft 8 in *110,85 m* tall, with a payload of 74 783 kg *73.60 tons* in the case of *Skylab I*, and gulps 13.4 tons *13,6 tonnes* of propellant per sec for 2½ min (2010 tons *2042 tonnes*). Stage I (S-IC) is 138 ft *42,06 m* tall and is powered by five Rocketdyne F-1 engines, using liquid oxygen (LOX) and kerosene, each delivering 1,514,000 lb *686 680 kg* thrust. Stage II (S-II) is powered by five LOX and liquid hydrogen Rocketdyne J-2 engines with a total thrust of 1,141,453 lb *517 759 kg* while Stage III (designated S-IVB) is powered by a single 228,290 lb *103 550 kg* thrust J-2 engine. The whole assembly generates 175,600,000 hp and weighs up to 7,600,000 lb (3393 tons *3447 tonnes*) fully loaded in the case of *Apollo 17*. It was first launched on 9 Nov 1967, from Cape Canaveral (then Kennedy), Florida.

Highest Pay Load
Skylab I, (launched on 14 May 1973) fell to Earth on its 34,981 st orbit over the Western Australian coast at 16.32 GMT on 11 July 1979 thus leaving *Salyut 6* as the heaviest object in space. Large pieces of *Skylab I* were found 12 km *7.45 miles* south of Rawlinna and sold to a Hong Kong syndicate. The piece which most worried keraunothnetophobes was a 5175 lb *2347 kg* airlock shroud.

Highest velocity
The first space vehicle to achieve the Third Cosmic velocity sufficient to break out of the Solar System was *Pioneer 10* (see page 77). The Atlas SLV-3C launcher with a modified Centaur D second stage and a Thiokol Te-364-4 third stage left the Earth at an unprecedented 32,114 mph *51 682 km/h* on 2 Mar 1972. The highest recorded velocity of any space vehicle has been 240,000 km/h *149,125 mph* in the case of the US-German solar probe *Helios B* launched on 15 Jan 1976. By March 1983 *Pioneer 10* will cross the orbit of Neptune 2845 miles *4580 million km* distant.

Ion rockets
Speeds of up to 100,000 mph *160 000 km/h* are envisaged for rockets powered by an ion discharge. An ion thruster has been maintained for 9715 hours (404 days 19 hrs) at the Lewis Research Center in Cleveland, Ohio, USA. Ion rockets were first used in flight by NASA's SERT I rocket launched on 20 July 1964.

SPACE FLIGHT
The physical laws controlling the flight of artificial satellites were first propounded by Sir Isaac Newton (1642–1727) in his *Philosophiae Naturalis Principia Mathematica* ('Mathematical Principles of Natural Philosophy'), begun in March 1686 and first published in the summer of 1687. The first artificial satellite was successfully put into orbit at an altitude of 142/588 miles *228,5/946 km* and a velocity of more than 17,750 mph *28 565 km/h* from Tyura Tam, a site located 170 miles *275 km* east of the Aral Sea on the night of 4 Oct. 1957. This spherical satellite *Sputnik* ('Fellow Traveller') *1*, officially designated 'Satellite 1957 Alpha 2', weighed 83,6 kg *184.3 lb*, with a diameter of 58 cm *22.8 in*, and its lifetime is believed to have been 92 days, ending on 4 Jan 1958. It was designed under the direction of Dr Sergey Pavlovich Korolyov (1907–66).

Earliest successful manned satellite
The first successful manned space flight began at 9.07 a.m. (Moscow time), or 6.08 a.m. GMT, on 12 Apr 1961. Cosmonaut Flight Major (later Colonel) Yuriy Alekseyevich Gagarin (born 9 Mar 1934) completed a single orbit of the Earth in 89.34 min in the 4.65 ton *4,72 tonnes* space vehicle *Vostok* ('East') 1. The take-off was from Tyura Tam in Kazakhstan, and the landing was 108 min later near the village of Smelovka, near Engels, in the Saratov region of the USSR. The maximum speed was 17,560 mph *28 260 km/h* and the maximum altitude 327 km *203.2 miles* in a flight of 40 868,6 km *25,394.5 miles*. Major Gagarin, invested a Hero of the Soviet Union and awarded the Order of Lenin and the Gold Star Medal, was killed in a jet plane crash near Moscow on 27 Mar 1968.

First woman in space
The first and only woman to orbit the Earth was Junior Lieutenant (now Lt-Col) Valentina Vladimirovna Tereshkova, now Nikolayev (b. 6 Mar 1937), who was launched in *Vostok 6* from Tyura Tam, USSR, at 9.30 a.m. GMT on 16 June 1963, and landed at 8.16 a.m. on 19 June, after a flight of 2 days 22 hr 42 min, during which she completed over 48 orbits (1,225,000 miles *1 971 000 km*) and passed momentarily within 3 miles *4,8 km* of *Vostok 5*. She was formerly a textile worker. Her mission was variously reported to be punctuated with pleas to be brought back due to giddiness and of being extended because of her excellent performance.

First in flight fatality
Col. Vladimir Mikhailovich Komarov (b. 16 Mar 1927) was launched in *Soyuz* ('Union') *1* at 00.35 a.m. GMT on 23 Apr 1967. The spacecraft was in orbit for about 25½ hr but he impacted on the final descent due to parachute failure and was the first man indisputably known to have died during space flight.

First 'walk' in space
The earliest undoubted instance of an astronaut floating free outside a space vehicle was by Astronaut, the late Edward H. White II (killed 27 Jan 1967) for 21 min over Hawaii to the US Atlantic coast on 3 June 1965 from *Gemini IV*. Evidence for the earlier claim of Lt-Col Aleksey A. Leonov from *Voshkod 2* on 18 Mar 1965 is not unreservedly accepted.

Longest manned space flight
The longest time spent in space is 185 days, by Valeriy Ryumin, and Leonid Popov on board the Salyut-Soyuz research station *Salyut 6*. They were launched on 8 Apr 1980 in *Soyuz 35* and landed 180 km *112 miles* SE of Dzhezkhzgan on 11 Oct 1980.

Astronaut *Oldest and youngest*
The oldest of the 104 people in space has been Donald Kent 'Deke' Slayton (b. Sparta, Wisconsin, USA 1 Mar 1924) who was aged 51 years 146 days when launched on the Apollo-Soyuz mission on 24 July 1975. The youngest has been Major (later Col) Gherman Stepanovich Titov (b. 11 Sept 1935), who was aged 25 years 329 days when launched in *Vostok 2* on 6 Aug 1961.

Duration record on the Moon
The crew of *Apollo 17* collected a record 253 lb *114,8 kg* of rock and soil during their 22 hr 5 min 'extra-vehicular acitivity'. They were Capt Eugene A. Cernan, USN. (b. Chicago, 14 Mar 1934) and Dr Harrison H. (Jack) Schmitt (b. Santa Rosa, New Mexico, 3 July 1935) who became the 12th man on the moon. The crew were on the lunar surface for 74 hr 59½ min during this longest of lunar missions which took 12 days 13 hr 51 min on 7–19 Dec 1972.

First extra-terrestrial vehicle
The first wheeled vehicle landed on the Moon was *Lunokhod 1* which began its Earth-controlled travels on 17 Nov 1970. It moved a total of 10,54 km *.54 miles* on gradients up to 30° in the Mare Imbrium and did not become non-functioning until 4 Oct 1971. The lunar speed and distance record was set by the *Apollo 16* Rover with 11.2 mph *18 km/h* downhill and 22.4 miles *33,8 km*.

Closest approach to the Sun
The research spacecraft *Helios B* approached within 27 million miles *43,4 million km* of the Sun, carrying both US and West German instrumentation on 16 Apr 1976.

Largest space object
The heaviest object orbited is the Apollo 15 (spacecraft plus third stage) which, prior to trans-lunar injection in parking orbit weighed 140 512 kg *138.29 tons*. The 442 lb *200 kg* US RAE (radio astronomy explorer) B or Explorer 49 launched on 10 June 1973 has, however, antennae, 1500 ft *415 m* from tip to tip.

Most expensive project
The total cost of the US manned space programme up to and including the lunar mission of *Apollo 17* has been estimated to be $25,541,400,000 (then £9,823,150,000). The first 15 years of the USSR space programme from 1958 to September 1973 has been estimated to have cost $45,000 million. The cost of the NASA Shuttle programme was $9.9 billion (*£4350 million*) to the launch of *Columbia* on 12 Apr 1981.

5. THE SCIENTIFIC WORLD

1. ELEMENTS

All known matter in, on and beyond the Earth is made up of chemical elements. The total of naturally-occurring elements so far detected is 94, comprising, at ordinary temperatures, two liquids, 11 gases and 81 solids. The so-called 'fourth state' of matter is plasma, when negatively charged electrons and positively-charged ions are in flux.

Lightest and heaviest sub-nuclear particles

By August 1980 the existence of 24 'stable particles, 42 meson resonance multiplets and 54 baryon resonance multiplets' was accepted, representing the possible eventual discovery of 224 particles and an equal number of anti-particles. The heaviest 'stable' particle fully accepted is the charmed lambda baryon, symbol Λ^+_c, of mass 2273 ± 6 MeV and lifetime 7×10^{-13} sec, first identified in March 1975 at the Brookhaven National Laboratory, New Upton, Long Island, NY, USA. The heaviest particle known is the upsilon triple prime meson, symbol Y''', of mass 10550 MeV, which consists of a bottom or beauty quark and its anti-quark, and which was first identified in April 1980 by two groups using the Cornell electron storage ring facilities at Cornell University, Ithaca, New York, USA. Sub-atomic concepts require that the masses of the graviton, photon, and neutrino should all be zero. Based on the sensitivities of various cosmological theories, upper limits for the masses of these particles are $7,6 \times 10^{-67}$ g for the graviton; $3,0 \times 10^{-53}$ g for the photon and $1,4 \times 10^{-32}$ g for the neutrino (cf. $9,10953 \times 10^{-28}$ g for the mass of an electron.) The neutrino, so named by Enrico Fermi (1901–54) was postulated in 1931 by Wolfgang Pauli and discovered by Frederick Reines in 1956.

Newest particles

In July–August 1980 two groups using the SPEAR electron storage ring facilities at the Stanford Linear Accelerator Center, Stanford University, Stanford, California, USA, announced the discovery of the charmed eta meson, symbol η_c, of mass 2980 MeV, which is the lowest ground-state of the combination of a charmed quark and its anti-quark.

Bitrex, the bitterest known substance, of which one cup will render 1000 gal *4546 l* of even alcohol unpalatable (see p. 80). (*Menzies and Young*)

THE 107 ELEMENTS

There are 94 known naturally-occurring elements comprising, at ordinary temperatures, two liquids, 11 gases, 72 metals and 9 other solids. To date the discovery of a further 13 transuranic elements (Elements 95 to 107) has been claimed of which 9 are undisputed.

Category	Name	Symbol	Discovery of Element	Record
Commonest (lithosphere)	Oxygen	O	1771 Scheele (Germany-Sweden)	46.60% by weight
Commonest (atmosphere)	Nitrogen	N	1772 Rutherford (GB)	78.09% by volume
Commonest (extra-terrestrial)	Hydrogen	H	1776 Cavendish (GB)	90% of all matter
Rarest (of the 94)	Astatine	At	1940 Corson (US) et al,	1/100th oz *0,35 g* in Earth's crust
Lightest	Hydrogen	H	1776 Cavendish (GB)	0.005612 lb/ft3 *0,00008989 g/cm3*
Lightest (Metal)	Lithium	Li	1817 Arfwedson (Sweden)	33.30 lb/ft3 *0.5334 g/cm3*
Densest[1]	Osmium	Os	1804 Tennant (GB)	1410 lb/ft3 *22,59 g/cm3*
Heaviest (Gas)	Radon	Rn	1900 Dorn (Germany)	*0.6274 lb/ft3* 0.01005 g/cm3 at 0°C
Newest[2]	Unnilseptium	Uns	1976 Oganesyan et al. (USSR)	highest atomic number (element 107)
Purest	Helium	^{4}He	1868 Lockyer (GB) and Jannsen (France)	2 parts in 10^{15} (1978)
Hardest	Carbon	C	— prehistoric	Diamond allotrope, Knoop value 8400
Most Expensive	Californium	Cf	1950 Seaborg (US) et al.	Sold in 1970 for $10 per μg
Most Stable[3]	Tellurium	^{128}Te	1782 von Reichenstein (Austro. Hung)	Half-life of 1.5×10^{24} years
Least Stable	Lithium (isotope 5)	Li 5	1817 Arfwedson (Sweden)	Lifetime of 4.4×10^{-22} sec.
Most Isotopes	Caesium	Cs	1860 Bunsen & Kirchoff (Germ.)	35
	Xenon	Xe	1898 Ramsay and Travers (GB)	35
Least Isotopes	Hydrogen	H	1776 Cavendish (GB)	3 (confirmed)
Most Ductile	Gold	Au	*ante* 3000 BC	1 oz drawn to 43 miles *1 g/2,4 km*
Highest Tensile Strength	Boron	B	1808 Gay-Lussac and Thenard (France)	3.9×10^6 lb f/in2 *26,8 GPa*
Lowest Melting/Boiling Point[4]	Helium	^{4}He	1895 Ramsay (GB)	−272,375°C under pressure 24.985 atm
				(2532 MPa) and −268,928°C
Highest Melting/Boiling Point	Tungsten	W	1783 J. J. & F. d'Elhuyar (Spain)	3422°C and 5730°C
Largest Expansion (negative)	Plutonium	Pu	1940 Seaborg (US) et al.	-5.8×10^{-5} cm/cm/deg C between 450–480°C
				(Delta prime allotrope (disc. 1953)
Lowest Expansion (positive)	Carbon (diamond)	C	— prehistoric	1.0×10^{-6} cm/cm/deg C (at 20°C)
Highest Expansion (metal)	Caesium	Cs	1860 Bunsen & Kirchoff (Germ.)	9.7×10^{-5} cm/cm/deg C (at 20°C)
Highest Expansion (gas)	Nitrogen	N	1916 Beta allotrope	108×10^{-3} cm/cm/deg C (c. −210°C)
Highest Expansion (solid)	Neon	Ne	1898 Ramsay and Travers (GB)	1.94×10^{-3} cm/cm/degC at 248.59°C
Most Toxic	Radium	^{224}R	1898 The Curies and Bemont (France)	naturally occuring isotope 17,000 × more toxic than plutonium 239

[1] *Work published by Robert H Crabtree (Yale University, USA) in 1978 that while the specific gravity of Osmium is 22.59 ± 0.02 that of Iridium is 22.57 ± 0.01 i.e. the difference is smaller than the experimental error involved.*

[2] *Provisional IUPAC name. Evidence alleging the existence of Elements 116, 124 and 126 published on 17 June 1976 subsequently was declared to have been misconceived. Unnilhexium (Unh) or element 106 was identified by Ghiorso (USA) et al. on 9 Sept 1974.*

[3] *Double beta decay estimate. Alpha particle record is Samarium 148 at 8×10^{15} years and Beta particle record is Cadmium 113 at 9×10^{15} years.*

[4] *Monatomic hydrogen H is expected to be a non-liquifiable superfluid gas.*

CHEMICAL COMPOUNDS

It has been estimated that there are 4,040,000 described chemical compounds of which 63,000 are (1978) in common use.

Most Refractory	Tantulum Carbide TaC$_{0.88}$	Melts at 4010° ± 75 deg C
Most Refractory (plastics)	Modified polymides	900°F *482°C* for short periods
Lowest Expansion	Invar metal (Ni-Fe alloy with C and Mn)	1.3×10^{-7} cm/cm/deg C at 20°C
Highest Tensile Strength	Sapphire whisker Al$_2$O$_3$	6×10^6 lb/in2 *42,7 GPa*
Highest Tensile Strength (plastics)	Polyvinyl alcoholic fibres	1.4×10^5 lbf/in2 *1,03 GPa*
Most Magnetic	Cobalt-copper-samarium Co$_3$Cu$_2$Sm	10,500 oersted coercive force
Least Magnetic alloy	Copper nickel alloy CuNi	963 parts Cu to 37 parts Ni
Most Pungent	Vanillaldehyde	Detectable at 2×10^{-8} mg/litre
Sweetest[1]	Talin from arils of katemfe (Thaumatococcus daniellii) discovered in W. Africa	6150 × as sweet as 1% sucrose
Bitterest	Bitrex or Benzyl diethyl ammonium benzoate	200 × as bitter as quinine sulphate
Most Acidic[2]	Perchloric acid (HClO$_4$)	pH value of normal solution tends to 0.
Most Alkaline	Caustic soda (NaOH) and potash (KOH) and tetramethylammonium hydroxide (N(CH$_3$)$_4$OH)	pH value of normal solution is 14.
Highest Specific Impulse	Hydrogen with liquid fluorine	447 lb f/sec/lb *4382 N/sec/kg*
Most Poisonous	Thiopentone (a barbiturate)	Intracardiac injection will kill in 1 to 2 sec
Highest Ductility in tension (max. superplasticity)	Pb38 Sn62	49½ times pre-stressed length by Ahmed and Langdon, Univ. of S. California, 1977

[1] *Found in 1839, reported in 1852 but the protein thaumatin not isolated until 1972.*

[2] *The most powerful acid, assessed on its power as a hydrogen-ion donor, is a solution of antimony pentafluoride in fluorosulphonic acid—SbF$_5$ + FSO$_3$H. Concentrated hydrochloric acid HCL, in aqueous solution has a pH value tending to −1.*

Most and Least stable

In 1974 the proton was measured to be stable against decay for a lifetime in excess of 2×10^{30} years. Theoretical predictions under the 'grand unified theory' suggest the lifetime of a proton may be less than 1×10^{34} years! The least stable or shortest lived nuclear particles discovered are the four baryon resonances N (2600), N (3030), Δ (2850) and Δ (3230), all 1.6×10^{-24} sec.

Substance smelliest

The most evil smelling substance, of the 17,000 smells so far classified, must be a matter of opinion but ethyl mercaptan (C$_2$H$_5$SH) and butyl seleno-mercaptan (C$_4$H$_9$SeH), are powerful claimants, each with a smell reminiscent of a combination of rotting cabbage, garlic, onions and sewer gas.

Most expensive perfume

The retail prices of the most expensive perfumes tend to be fixed at public relations rather than economic levels. The most expensive flagrent ingredient in perfume is pure French middle note jasmine essence at £2900 per kg or £82.20p per oz. The key ingredient is muscone, a macrocyclic ketone, from natural musk oil which in 1980 sold for £15,000 per kg or £425 per oz. The most expensive perfume in the world is *De Berens No 1* retailing at £66.66 per ⅓ oz *9,44 g.*

Most potent poison

The rickettsial disease, Q-fever can be instituted by a *single* organism but is only fatal in 1 in 1000 cases. About 10 organisms of *Francisella tularenesis* (formerly *Pasteurella tularenesis*) can institute tularaemia variously called alkali disease, Francis disease or deerfly fever, and this is fatal in upwards of 10 cases in 1000.

Most powerful nerve gas

In the early 1950s substances known as V-agents, notably VX, 300 times more toxic than phosgene (COCl$_2$) used in World War I, were developed at the Chemical Defence Experimental Establishment, Porton Down, Wiltshire. V-agents are lethal if 0,4 mg is inhaled by an adult. Patents were applied for in 1962 and published in February 1974.

Most powerful drugs

The most powerful commonly available drug is d-Lysergic Acid Diethylamide tartrate (LSD-25, $C_{20}H_{25}N_3O$) first produced in 1938 for common cold research and as a hallucinogen by Dr Albert Hoffman (Swiss) on 16–19 Apr 1943. The most potent analgesic drug is the morphine-like R33799 confirmed in 1978 to have almost 12,000 times the potency of morphine.

Most prescribed drug

The benzodiazepine group tranquillising drug Valium discovered by Hoffmann-La Roche is the world's most widely used drug. More than 40 million prescriptions are issued annually in the US alone.

Most absorbent substance

The US Department of Agriculture Research Service announced on 18 Aug 1974 that 'H-span' or Super Slurper composed of one half starch derivative and one fourth each of acrylamide and acrylic acid can when treated with iron retain water 1300 times its own weight.

Finest powder

Particulate matter of 25–40 Å or 2,5 to $4,0 \times 10^{-7}$ cm *1.0 to 1.5×10^{-7} in* was reportedly produced by an electron beam evaporation process at the Atomic Energy Establishment, Harwell in October 1972. The paper was published by Dr P. RamaKrishnan.

2. DRINK

The strength of spirituous liquor is gauged by degrees proof. In the United Kingdom proof spirit is that mixture of ethyl alcohol (C_2H_5OH) and water which at 51° F *10,55°C* weighs in air 12/13ths of an equal measure of distilled water. Such spirit in fact contains 49.28 per cent alcohol by weight, so that pure or absolute alcohol is 75.35° over proof (OP). In the USA proof is double the actual percentage of alcohol by volume at 60°F *15,6°C*. A 'hangover' is due to toxic congenerics such as amyl alcohol ($C_5H_{11}OH$).

Most alcoholic

Absolute (or 100 per cent) alcohol is 75.35 degrees over proof (UK) or 200 per cent proof spirit (US). During independence (1918–40) the Estonian Liquor Monopoly marketed 98 per cent potato alcohol (196 proof US). In 31 US states *Everclear* 190 proof 95 per cent alcohol, is marketed by the American Distilling Co 'primarily as a base for home-made cordials'. Royal Navy rum, introduced in 1692, was 40° OP (79.8 per cent) before 1948, but was reduced to 4.5° UP (under proof) or 46.3 per cent alcohol by weight, before its abolition on 31 July 1970.

Oldest wine

The oldest datable wine has been an amphora salvaged and drank by Capt. Jacques Cousteau from the wreck of a Greek trader sunk in the Mediterranean *c* 230 BC. Wine jars recovered from the Pompeii eruption of AD 79 were found labelled VESUVINUM—the oldest known trade mark. A bottle of 1748 Rudesheimer Rosewein was auctioned at Christie's, London for £260 on 6 Dec 1979.

Beer *Strongest world*

The world's strongest and most expensive beer is Samichlaus Bier brewed by Brauerai Hürlimann of Zürich, Switzerland, which retails for Sw Fr 10 for a 33,3 cl bottle (equiv. to £4 per pint). It is 13.94 per cent alcohol by volume at 20°C with an original gravity of 1107.6°.

Beer *Strongest Great Britain*

The strongest regularly brewed beer in Britain is Thomas Hardy's brewed by Eldridge Pope & Co at their Dorchester Brewery, Dorset. It has an alcoholic content of 12.48 per cent by volume at 60°F and an original gravity of 1125.8°.

Beer *Weakest*

The weakest liquid ever marketed as beer was a sweet Ersatz beer which was brewed in Germany by Sunner, Colne-Kalk, in 1918. It had an original gravity of 1000.96° and a strength 1/30th that of the weakest beer now obtainable in the United Kingdom.

Some of the 3100 unduplicated whiskies, in an array of containers owned by Signor Edward Giaccone (see p. 82).

Most expensive wine

The highest price paid for any bottle (meaning a container as opposed to a measure) of wine is $31,000 (*then £13,140*) for a bottle of 1822 Château Lafite, bought by John Grisanti at an auction in San Fransisco, USA on 28 May 1980.

Greatest wine auction

The largest single sale of wine was conducted by Christie's of King Street, St James's, London on 10–11 July 1974 at Quaglino's Ballroom, London when 2325 lots comprising 432,000 bottles realised £962,190. The largest ever wine-tasting was held at Nederburg, South Africa for 1737 people with 15 openers, 93 pourers and 2012 bottles on 4 Mar 1978.

Most expensive liqueurs

The most expensive liqueur in France is *Eau de vie de poire avec poire* at 150 F (*now £15.00*) at Fauchon in Paris.

Most expensive spirits

The most expensive bottle of spirits at auction is £780 for a magnum of *Grande Armée Fine Champagne Cognac, 1811* at Christie's Geneva on 13 Nov 1978. *Cognac Delamain* (1875) retails for 3300 F (*now £340*) a bottle at Fauchon. In Britain *Hennessy Private Reserve Grande Champagne* retails for £120 (including VAT) for a standard bottle.

Largest bottles

The largest bottle normally used in the wine and spirit trade is the Jeroboam (equal to 4 bottles of champagne or, rarely, of brandy and from 5 to 6½ bottles of claret according to whether blown or moulded) and the Double Magnum (equal, since *c.* 1934 to 4 bottles of claret or, more rarely, red Burgundy). A complete set of Champagne bottles would consist of a ¼ bottle, through the ½ bottle, bottle, magnum, Jeroboam, Rehoboam, Methuselah, Salmanazar and Balthazar, to the Nebuchadnezzar, which has a capacity of 16 litres *28.14 pt*, and is equivalent to 20 bottles. In May 1958 a 5 ft *152 cm* tall sherry bottle with a capacity of 20½ Imperial gal *93,19 litres* was blown in Stoke-on-Trent, Staffordshire. This bottle, with the capacity of 131 normal bottles, was named an 'Adelaide'.

Smallest bottles

The smallest and meanest bottles of liquor now sold are White Horse bottles of Scotch whisky containing 1,3 millilitres or *22 minims* at 33 p a bottle or £2.16 per 'case' of 12.

Champagne cork flight

The longest distance for a champagne cork to fly from an

untreated and unheated bottle 4 ft *1,22 m* from level ground is 103 ft 8 in *31,59 m* by Ronald Rose at Idlewild Park, Reno, Nevada, USA on 4 July 1979.

Largest collections

The largest reported collection of unduplicated miniature bottles is one of 11,673 as at 17 May 1981 owned by David Maund of Eastleigh, Hants.

The largest recorded collection of distilled spirits or liquors in any public house is 774 unduplicated labels sold at Jake O'Shaugnessey's Bar, 100 Mercer Street, Seattle, Washington, USA as audited in 1980.

The world's greatest collection of whisky bottles is one of 3100 unduplicated labels assembled by Sgn Edward Giaccone at his Whiskyteca, Salo, Lake Garda, Italy.

3. TELESCOPES

Earliest

Although there is evidence that early Arabian scientists understood something of the magnifying power of lenses, their first use to form a telescope has been attributed to Roger Bacon (*c.* 1214–92) in England. The prototype of modern refracting telescopes was that completed by Johannes Lippershey for the Netherlands government on 2 Oct 1608.

below: The world's largest solar telescope at Kitt Peak National Observatory near Tucson, Arizona which measures 480 ft *146,3 m* overall (see p. 83) *(Alex Hansen)*

bottom: The US National Science Foundation VLA (Very Large Array) radio telescopic installation which has 27 mobile railed antennae. *(Alex Hansen)*

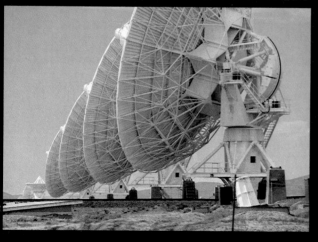

Largest *Reflector World*

The largest telescope in the world is the alt-azimuth mounted 6 m *236.2 in* telescope sited on Mount Semirodriki, near Zelenchukskaya in the Caucasus Mountains, USSR, at an altitude of 6830 ft *2080 m*. Work on the mirror, weighing 70 tons/*tonnes* was not completed until the summer of 1974. Regular observations were begun on 7 Feb 1976 after 16 years work. The weight of the 42 m *138 ft* high assembly is 840 tonnes *827 tons*. Being the most powerful of all telescopes its range, which includes the location of objects down to the 25th magnitude, represents the limits of the observable Universe. Its light-gathering power would enable it to detect the light from a candle at a distance of 15,000 miles *24 000 km*.

A design for a 500 ton 10 metre *393.7 inch* reflector comprising 36 independently controlled fitting hexagonal mirrors was adopted in Oct 1980. If sited on Mauna Kea, Hawaii it would be expected to cost $50 million and be completed by 1989. The design of a 25 m *984 in* composite hexagonal reflector was announced by the USSR in August 1979.

Note: The attachment of an electronic charge-coupled device (CCD) increases the 'light-grasp' of a telescope by a factor up to 100 fold. Thus a 200 in *508 cm* telescope becomes the equivalent of a 2000 in *5080 cm* telescope.

Largest *Reflector Great Britain*

The largest British reflector is the Isaac Newton 98.2 in *249,4 cm* reflector formerly installed at the Royal Greenwich Observatory, Herstmonceux Castle, East Sussex. It was built in Newcastle upon Tyne, Tyne and Wear, weighs 92 tons *93,5 tonnes*, cost £641,000 and was inaugurated on 1 Dec 1967. It has been dismantled and is being re-erected on the 2423m *7949 ft* high Roque de los Muchachos, La Palma, Canary Islands by agreement of the Spanish government made on 26 May 1979. It is hoped that a 4,2 m *167.3 in* reflector will also be sited at this new Northern Hemisphere Observatory.

Largest *Refractor*

The largest refracting (*i.e.* magnification by lenses) telescope in the world is the 62 ft *18,90 m* long 40 in *101,6 cm* telescope completed in 1897 at the Yerkes Observatory, Williams Bay, Wisconsin, and belonging to the University of Chicago, Illinois, USA. In 1900 a 125 cm *49.2 in* refractor 54,85 m *180 ft* in length was built for the Paris Exposition but its optical performance was too poor to justify attempts to use it. The largest in the British Isles is the 28 in *71,1 cm* at the Royal Greenwich Observatory (then in London) completed in 1894.

Radio *Largest steerable dish*

Radio waves of extra-terrestrial origin were first detected by Karl Jansky of Bell Telephone Laboratories, Holmdel, New Jersey, USA using a 100 ft *30,48 m* long shortwave rotatable antenna in 1932. The world's largest trainable dish-type radio telescope is the 100 m *328 ft* diameter, 3000 ton *3048 tonnes* assembly at the Max Planck Institute for Radio Astronomy of Bonn in the Effelsberger Valley, W. Germany; it became operative in May 1971. The cost of the installation begun in November 1967 was 36,920,000 DM (*then £6,150,000*).

Radio *Largest Dish*

The world's largest dish radio telescope is the partially-steerable ionospheric assembly built over a natural bowl at Arecibo, Puerto Rico, completed in November 1963 at a cost of about $9,000,000 (*then £3.75 million*). The dish has a diameter of 1000 ft *304,80 m* and covers 18½ acres *7,28 ha*. Its sensitivity was raised by a factor of 1000 and its range to the edge of the observable Universe at some 15,000 million light-years by the fitting of new aluminium plates at a cost of $8.8 million. Rededication was on 16 Nov 1974. The RATAN-600 radio telescope completed in the Northern Caucasus, USSR in 1976 has 895 metal mirror panels mounted in a circle 576 m *1890 ft* across.

Radio *Largest World*

The world's largest radio telescopic installation is the US National Science Foundation VLA (Very Large Array). It is Y-shaped with each arm 13 miles *20,9 km* long with 27 mobile antennae (each of 25 m *82 ft* diameter) on rails. It is 50 miles

80 km west of Socorro in the Plains of San Augustin, New Mexico, and was dedicated on 10 Oct 1980 at a cost of $78 million (*now £41 million*).

A computer-linked very long base-line array of 25 m *82 ft* radio telescopes stretched over 4200 km *2600 miles* on Latitude 49.3° N has been planned by the Canadian Astronomical Society.

Radio *Largest Great Britain*
The British Science Research Council 5 km radio telescope at Lord's Bridge, Cambridgeshire to be operated by the Mullard Radio Astronomy Observatory of Cambridge University will utilise eight mobile 42 ft *12,80 m* rail-borne computer-controlled dish aerials, which will be equivalent to a single steerable dish 5 km *3 miles 188 yd* in diameter. The project cost more than £2,100,000 and was completed in 1973.

Solar
The world's largest solar telescope is the 480 ft *146,30 m* long McMath telescope at Kitt Peak National Observatory near Tucson, Arizona, USA. It has a focal length of 300 ft *91,44 m* and an 80 in *2,03 m* heliostat mirror. It was completed in 1962 and produces an image measuring 33 in *83,8 cm* in diameter.

Observatory *Highest*
The highest altitude observatory in the world is the University of Denver's High Altitude Observatory at an altitude of 14,100 ft *4297 m*, opened in 1973. The principal instrument is a 24 in *60,48 cm* Ealing Beck reflecting telescope.

Observatory *Oldest*
The oldest astronomical observatory building extant in the world is the Chomsong-dae built in AD 632 in Kyongju, South Korea.

Planetaria *World*
The ancestor of the planetarium is the rotatable Gottorp Globe, built by Andreas Busch in Denmark between 1654 and 1664 to the orders of Olearius, court mathematician to Duke Frederick III of Holstein. It is 34.6 ft *10,54 m* in circumference, weighs nearly 3½ tons/*tonnes* and is now preserved in Leningrad, USSR. The stars were painted on the inside. The earliest optical installation was not until 1923 in the Deutsches Museum, Munich, by Zeiss of Jena, Germany. The world's largest planetarium, is in Moscow, USSR, and has a diameter of 82½ ft *25,15 m*.

Planetaria *Great Britain*
The United Kingdom's first planetarium was opened at Madame Tussaud's, Marylebone Road, London, on 19 Mar 1958. Accurate images of 8900 stars (some below naked eye magnitude) are able to be projected on the 70 ft *21,33 m* high copper dome.

4. PHOTOGRAPHY

CAMERAS
Earliest
The earliest photograph was taken in the summer of 1826 by Joseph Nicéphore Niepce (1765–1833), a French physician and scientist. It showed the courtyard of his country house at Gras, near St Loup-de-Varennes. It probably took eight hours to expose and was taken on a bitumen-coated polished pewter plate measuring 7¾ in by 6½ in *20 × 16,5 cm*. The earliest photograph taken in England was one of a diamond-paned window in Laycock (or Lacock) Abbey, Wiltshire, taken in August 1835 by William Henry Fox Talbot, MP (1800–77), the inventor of the negative–positive process. The negative of this was donated to the Science Museum, London in 1937 by his granddaughter Matilda. The world's earliest aerial photograph was taken in 1858 by Gaspard Félix Tournachon (1820–1910), *alias* Nadar, from a balloon near Villacoublay, on the outskirts of Paris, France.

Largest
The largest camera ever built is the 27 ton/*tonne* Rolls Royce camera built for Product Support (Graphics) Ltd, of Derby,

The worlds most expensive photograph at auction, a portrait of Alexander Dumas père photographed by Gaspard Felix Tournachon in 1857, was sold for $16,000 (*then £7,100*) in New York City on 2 Nov 1979.

England completed in 1959. It measures 8 ft 10 in *2,69 m* high, 8 ft 3 in *2,51 m* wide and 35 ft *10,66 m* in length. The lens is a 63″ f 15 Cooke Apochromatic. Its value after improvements in 1971 was in excess of £100,000.

Smallest
Apart from cameras built for intra-cardiac surgery and espionage, the smallest camera that has been marketed is the circular Japanese 'Petal' camera with a diameter of 1.14 in *2,9 cm* and a thickness of 0.65 in *1,65 cm*. It has a focal length of 12 mm *0.47 in*. The BBC TV programme *Record Breakers* showed prints from this camera on 3 Dec 1974.

Fastest
In 1972 Prof. Basof of the USSR Academy of Sciences published a paper describing an experimental camera with a time resolution of 5×10^{-13} sec or ½ picosec. The fastest production camera in the world is the Imacon 675 manufactured by John Hadland (PI) Ltd of Bovingdon, Hertfordshire which is capable of taking pictures at a *rate* of 600 million per sec. Uses include laser, ballistic, detonic, plasma and corona research.

Most expensive
The most expensive complete range of camera equipment in the world is that of Nikon of Tokyo, Japan, who marketed in 1981 a range of 8 cameras with 70 lenses and 424 accessories. Fox Talbot of London quoted £61,484.49 plus £9222.67 VAT for the whole range. The highest auction price for an antique camera is £21,000 for a J. B. Dancer stereo camera, patented in 1856 and sold at Christie's, South Kensington on 12 Oct 1977.

5. GEMS AND OTHER PRECIOUS MATERIALS

PRECIOUS STONE RECORDS

Note: The carat was standardised at 205mg in 1877. The metric carat of 200mg was introduced in 1914.

Largest	Largest Cut Stone	Other records
Diamond (pure crystallised carbon) 3106 metric carats (over 1¼ lb)—*The Cullinan*, found by Capt M. F. Wells 25 Jan 1905 in the Premier Mine, Pretoria, South Africa.	530.2 metric carats or 74 facets. Cleaved from *The Cullinan* in 1908, by Jak Asscher of Amsterdam and polished by Henri Koe known as *The Star of Africa* or Cullinan I and now in the Royal Sceptre.	Diamond is the *hardest* known naturally-occurring substance, being 90 times as hard as the next hardest mineral, corundum (Al_2O_3). The peak hardness value on the Knoop scale is 8400 compared with an average diamond of 7000. The rarest colour for diamond is blood red. The largest example is a flawless 5.05 ct stone from South Africa now in a private collection in the U.S. It was revealed on 12 Mar 1981 that the Emir of Abu Dhabi paid $20 million for the 170.49 carat 'Star of Peace' which is internally flawless. It was formally owned by Mrs Elinor Loder (US). It was found in Central Africa in 1974 with an uncut weight of more than 500 carats. The diamond per carat record price of $113,000 was set by the 41.3 ct 'Polar Star' bought in Geneva for $4.6 million (*then £1.95 million*) on 21 Nov 1980.
Emerald (green beryl) [$Be_3Al_2(SiO_3)_6$]	2226 gram (11 130 ct) crystal from Stretensk, Ural Mts, USSR, in 1834. Now in the Mineralogical Museum, Moscow.	$520,000 (then £305,000) paid for an 18.35 ct ring sold at Sotheby Parke Bernet, New York, in Apr. 1977. The Swiss customs at Geneva confirmed on 16 Apr 1972 the existence of an hexagonal emerald of about 20,000 carats, thus possibly worth more than $100 million (*then £38.75 million*).
Sapphire (corundum any colour but red) (Al_2O_3) 2302 carat stone found at Anakie, Queensland, Australia, in *c*. 1935, now a 1318 carat head of President Abraham Lincoln (1809–65).	1444 carat black star stone carved from 2097 carats in 1953–5 into a bust of General Dwight David Eisenhower (1890–1969).	Note: both the sapphire busts are in the custody of the Kazanjian Foundation of Los Angeles, California, USA. Auction record for a single stone was set by a step-cut sapphire of 66.03 carats at £579,300 from the Rockefeller collection at Sotheby's Zurich on 8 May 1980.
Ruby (red corundum) (Al_2O_3) 3421 carat broken stone reported found in July 1961 (largest piece 750 carats).	1184 carat natural gem stone of Burmese origin. The largest star ruby is the 138.72 carat Rosser Reeves stone at the Smithsonian Institution.	Since 1955 rubies have been the world's most precious gem attaining a price of up to £4000 per carat by 1969. A world record carat price of $100,639 (*then £46,600*) was set at Christie's sale in Geneva in November 1979 for a 4.12 carat caspian-shaped ruby. The ability to make corundum prisms for laser technology up to over 12 in 30 cm in length seems to have little bearing on the market for natural gems.

RECORDS FOR OTHER PRECIOUS MATERIALS

Largest	Where Found	Notes On Present Location, etc.
Pearl (Molluscan consecretion) 14 lb 1 oz *6,37 kg* 9½ in *24 cm* long by 5½ in *14 cm* in diameter—*Pearl of Laotze*	At Palawan, Philippines, 7 May 1934 in shell of giant clam.	The property since 1936 of Wilburn Dowell Cobb until his death, it was valued at $4,080,000 in July 1971. On 15 May 1980 it was bought at auction in San Francisco by Peter Hoffman, a jeweller, for $200,000 (*then £85,000*).
Opal (SiO_2nH_2O) 220 troy oz (yellow-orange).	Andamooka, South Australia.	The Andamooka specimen (34,215 carats), which was unearthed by a bulldozer, is in two filling pieces making a block $11 \times 10 \times 5$ in *28 × 25 × 12,5 cm*. It is owned by the Palgrave Corp. since September 1969, is displayed in Sydney and is valued in excess of $A1,000,000 (£500,000).
Rock Crystal (quartz) SiO_2 Ball: 106¾ lb *40,48 kg* 12⅞ in *32,7 cm* diameter, the *Warner* sphere	Burma, (originally a 1000 lb *450 kg* piece).	US National Museum, in Washington, DC.
Topaz $Al_2SiO_4(F,OH)_2$ 'Brazilian Princess' 21,327 carat 221 facets.	Light blue: from Brazil.	Exhibited by Smithsonian Institution, November 1978. Valued at $1,066,350 or $50 per carat. Cut from a 79 lb *35,8 kg* crystal. World's largest facetted stone.
Amber (Coniferous fossil resin) 33 lb 10 oz *15,25 kg*.	Reputedly from Burma acquired in 1860.	Bought by John Charles Bowing (d. 1893) for £300 in Canton, China. Natural History Museum, London, since 1940.
Turquoise monolith ($CuAl_6(PO_4)_4(OH)_8.4H_2O$) 218 lb *98,8 kg*.	Riverside County, California, 17 Jan 1975.	Found by Chester Jastromb and Kenneth Casper. Original weight was probably *c*. 250 lb *113,4 kg*.
Nephrite jade $Ca_2(Mg, Fe)_5(Si_4O_{11})_2(OH)_2$ Boulder of 143 tons/*tonnes* and 21,300 ft³ *603 m³*	In China. Reported 17 Sept. 1978.	Jadeite can be almost any colour excepting red or blue.
Marble (Metamorphosed $CaCO_3$) 90 tons/*tonnes* (single slab)	Quarried at Yule, Colorado, USA.	A piece of over 45 tons/*tonnes* was dressed from this slab for the coping stone of the Tomb of the Unknown Soldier in Arlington National Cemetery, Virginia, USA.
Nuggets—Gold (Au) 7560 oz. (472½ lb *214,32 kg*) (reef gold) *Holtermann Nugget*	Beyers & Holtermann Star of Hope Gold Mining Co., Hill End, NSW, Australia, 19 Oct 1872.	The purest large nugget was the *Welcome Stranger*, found at Moliagul, Victoria, Australia, which yielded 2248 troy oz *69,92 kg* of pure gold from 2280¼ oz *70,92 kg*.
Silver (Ag) 2750 lb troy	Sonora, Mexico.	Appropriated by the Spanish Government before 1821.

Other Gems Records:

Largest Crystal of Gem Quality:
A 520,000 carat (2 cwt 5 lb *103,8 kg*) aquamarine, [$Be_3Al_2(SiO_3)_6$] found near Marambaia, Brazil in 1910. Yielded over 200,000 carats of gem quality cut stones.

Rarest Gem Mineral:
Painite ($CaZrB(Al_9O_{18})$) discovered by A C D Pain near Ohngaing, Mogok, Burma in 1951. Deep red crystals of 1.31 and 2.12 gm are in the British Museum (Natural History), London and a third of 0.34 gm at the Gemological Institute of America.

Densest Gem Mineral:
Stibiotantalite [$(SbO)_2(Ta,Nb)_2O_6$] a rare brownish-yellow mineral found in San Diego County, California, has a density of 7.46. The alloy platiniridium has a density of more than 22.0.

Smallest Brilliant Cut Diamond:
A 57 facet diamond of 0.0012 of a carat (0.24 milligrams) by A. Van Moppes & Zoon (Diamant) BV of Amsterdam certified on 26 Jan 1949.

6. NUMEROLOGY

In dealing with large numbers, scientists use the notation of 10 raised to various powers to eliminate a profusion of noughts. For example, 19,160,000,000,000 miles would be written 1.916×10^{13} miles. Similarly, a very small number, for example 0,0000154324 of a gramme, would be written $1,5432 \times 10^{-5}$. Of the prefixes used before numbers the smallest is 'atto-' from the Danish atten for 18, indicating a trillionth part (10^{-18}) of the unit, and the highest is 'exa' (Greek, hexa, six), symbol E, indicating six groups of 3 zeros 10^{18} or a trillion (UK) or a quintillion (US) fold.

Highest numbers

The highest lexicographically accepted named number in the system of successive powers of ten is the centillion, which is 10 raised to the power 600, or one followed by 600 noughts in the British system or 10^{303} in the US system. The highest named number outside the decimal notation is the Buddhist *asankhyeya*, which is equal to 10^{140} or 100 tertio-vigintillions (British system) or 100 quinto-quadragintillions (US system).

The number 10^{100} (10,000 sexdecillion [UK] or 10 duotrigintillion [US]) is designated a Googol. The term was devised by Dr Edward Kasner (US) (d. 1955). Ten raised to the power of a Googol is described as a Googolplex. Some conception of the magnitude of such numbers can be gained when it is said that the number of atoms in some models of the observable Universe does not exceed 10^{85}.

The highest number ever used in a mathematical proof is a bounding value published in 1977 and known as Graham's number. It concerns bichromatic hypercubes and is inexpressible without the special 'arrow' notation, devised by Knuth in 1976, extended to 64 layers.

Longest Roman Numeral

The date requiring most Roman letters is AD 1888 with 13, viz MDCCCLXXXVIII. It was used on the entrance to the former High Court of New South Wales, now the Darlinghurst Courthouse completed in that year in Taylor Square, Sydney Australia. This drew the comment that the building would become equally famous for the length of its sentences.

Prime numbers

A prime number is any positive integer (excluding 1) having no integral factors other than itself and unity, *e.g.* 2, 3, 5, 7 or 11. The lowest prime number is thus 2. The highest known prime number is $2^{44497}-1$ discovered on 8 Apr 1979, after a two month long run on a Cray One computer, at the University of California's Lawrence Livermore Laboratory, by Harry Nelson, 47 and David Slowinski, 25. The number contains 13,395 digits.

Perfect numbers

A number is said to be perfect if it is equal to the sum of its divisors other than itself, *e.g.* $1 + 2 + 4 + 7 + 14 = 28$. The lowest perfect number is 6 $(1 + 2 + 3)$. The highest known and the 26th so far discovered, is $(2^{44497}-1) \times 2^{44496}$. It is a consequence of the highest known prime (see above).

Most innumerate

The most innumerate people are the Nambiquara of the north west Matto Grosso of Brazil who lack any system of numbers. They do however have a verb which means 'they are two alike'.

Most accurate and most inaccurate version of 'pi'

The greatest number of decimal places to which pi (π) has been calculated is 1,000,000 by the French mathematicians Jean Guilloud and Mlle Martine Bouyer achieved on 24 May 1973 on a CDC 7600 computer but not verified until 3 Sept 1973. The published value to a million places, in what has been described as the world's most boring 400 page book, was 3.141592653589793 ... (omitting the next 999,975 places) ... 5779458151. In 1897 the General Assembly of Indiana enacted in House Bill No. 246 that pi was *de jure* 4.

Earliest measures

The earliest known measure of weight is the *beqa* of the Amratian period of Egyptian civilisation c. 3,800 BC found at Naqada, United Arab Republic. The weights are cylindrical with rounded ends from 188.7 to 211.2 g *6.65–7.45 oz*. The unit of length used by the megalithic tomb-builders in Britain c. 3500 BC

appears to have been 2.72 ± 0.003 ft *82,90 cm $\pm$ 0.09 cm*. This was deduced by Prof. Alexander Thom.

Time measure *Longest*

The longest measure of time is the *kalpa* in Hindu chronology. It is equivalent to 4320 million years. In astronomy a cosmic year is the period of rotation of the sun around the centre of the Milky Way galaxy, *i.e.* about 225 million years. In the Late Cretaceous Period of c. 85 million years ago the Earth rotated faster so resulting in 370.3 days per year while in Cambrian times some 600 million years ago there is evidence that the year contained 425 days.

Time measure *Shortest*

Owing to variations in the length of a day, which is estimated to be increasing irregularly at the average rate of about a millisecond per century due to the Moon's tidal drag, the second has been redefined. Instead of being 1/86,400th part of a mean solar day, it has, since 1960, been reckoned as 1/31,556,925,9747th part of the solar (or tropical) year at AD 1900, January 0. 12hr, Ephemeris time. In 1958 the second of Ephemeris time was computed to be equivalent to $9,192,631,770 \pm 20$ cycles of the radiation corresponding to the transition of a caesium 133 atom when unperturbed by exterior fields. The greatest diurnal change recorded has been 10 milliseconds on 8 Aug 1972 due to the most violent solar storm recorded in 370 years of observations. The shortest blip of light is one of 0.2 of a pico-second (0,2×10^{-12} sec) produced by the Center of Laser Studies, University of Southern California in August 1978. In that time light travels 0,06 mm or *0.0023 in*.

Smallest linear unit

The shortest unit of length is the atto-metre which is 1.0×10^{-16} cm.

Longest slide rule

The world's longest slide rule is one 323 ft 9.5 in *98,69 m* in length completed on 11 Nov 1979 by Greg Maggs and Robert Kolstad at the University of Illinois College of Law Building in Champaign, Illinois, USA.

7. PHYSICAL EXTREMES
(Terrestrial)

Temperature *Highest*

The highest man-made temperatures yet attained are those produced in the centre of a thermonuclear fusion bomb, which are of the order of 300,000,000 – 400,000,000° C. Of controllable temperatures, the highest effective laboratory figure reported is 67 million degrees at the University of Rochester's Laser Energetics Laboratory, on 22 May 1979. Prior to 1963 a figure of 3000 million° C was reportedly achieved in the USSR with Ogra injection-mirror equipment.

Temperature *Lowest*

The lowest temperature reached is 5×10^{-8} Kelvins above absolute zero atttained in a two stage nuclear demagnetization cryostat at the Helsinki University of Technology, Otaniema, Finland by the team of Prof. Olli V. Lounasmaa (b. 1920) and announced in March 1979. Absolute or thermodynamic temperatures are defined in terms of ratios rather than as differences reckoned from the unattainable absolute zero, which on the Kelvin scale is $-273,15°$ C or $-459.67°$ F. Thus the lowest temperature ever attained is 1 in 5.5×10^9 of the melting point of ice (0° C or 273.15 K or 32° F).

The lowest equilibrium temperature ever attained is 0.0003 K by nuclear refrigeration in a 1,4 kg *3 lb* copper specimen by Prof. Lounasmaa (see above) and his team at the Helsinki University of Technology, Otaniemi, Finland, on 17 Apr 1974.

Highest pressures

The highest sustained laboratory pressures yet reported are of 1.72 mega bars (11,000 tons force/in² *160 GPa*) achieved in the giant hydraulic diamond-faced press at the Carnegie Institution's Geophysical Laboratory, Washington DC reported in

85

June 1978. This laboratory announced solid hydrogen achieved at 57 kilobars pressure on 2 Mar 1979. If created, metallic hydrogen is expected to be silvery white but soft with a density of 1.1 g/cm³. The pressure required for the transition is estimated by H. K. Mao and P. M. Bell to be 1 Megabar at 25°C. Using dynamic methods and impact speeds of up to 18,000 mph *29 000 km/h*, momentary pressures of 75,000,000 atmospheres (490,000 tons/in² *7000 GPa*) were reported from the United States in 1958.

Highest vacuum

The highest (or 'hardest') vacuums obtained in scientific research are of the order of 10^{-14} torr at the IBM Thomas J. Watson Research Center, Yorktown Heights, New York, USA in October 1976 in a cryogenic system with temperatures down to $-269°C$ *$-452°F$*. This is equivalent to depopulating (baseball-sized) molecules from 1 metre apart to 80 km apart or from 1 yard to 50 miles.

Fastest centrifuge

Ultra-centrifuges were invented by Theodor Svedberg (b. 30 Aug 1884) (Sweden) in 1923. The highest man-made rotary speed ever achieved and the fastest speed of any earth-bound object is 4500 mph *7250 km/h* by a swirling tapered 6 in *15,2 cm* carbon fibre rod in a vacuum at Birmingham University, England reported on 24 Jan 1975.

Most powerful microscope

The world's most powerful microscope was announced by Dr Lawrence Bartell and Charles Ritz of the University of Michigan in July 1974 with an image magnification of 260 million fold. It uses an optical laser to decode holograms produced with 40 KeV radiation and has produced photographs of electron clouds of atoms of neon and argon.

Highest note

The highest note yet attained is one of 60 000 megahertz (60 GHz) (60,000 million vibrations/sec), generated by a 'laser' beam striking a sapphire crystal at the Massachusetts Institute of Technology in Cambridge, Massachusetts, USA, in September 1964.

Hottest Flame

The hottest flame that can be produced is from carbon subnitride (C_4N_2) which at one atmosphere pressure is calculated to reach 5261 K.

Loudest noise

The loudest noise created in a laboratory is 210 decibels or 400,000 acoustic watts reported by NASA from a 48 ft *14,63 m* steel and concrete horn at Huntsville, Alabama, USA in October 1965. Holes can be bored in solid material by this means.

Quietest place

The 'dead room', measuring 35 ft by 28 ft *10,67 × 8,50 m* in the Bell Telephone System laboratory at Murray Hill, New Jersey, USA, is the most anechoic room in the world, eliminating 99.98 per cent of reflected sound.

Finest balance

The most accurate balance in the world is the Sartorius Model 4108 manufactured in Göttingen, W. Germany, which can weigh objects of up to 0,5 g to an accuracy of 0,01 µg or 0,00000001 g which is equivalent to little more than one sixtieth of the weight of the ink on this full stop .

Lowest viscosity

The California Institute of Technology, USA announced on 1 Dec 1957 that there was no measurable viscosity, *i.e.* perfect flow, in liquid helium II, which exists only at temperatures close to absolute zero ($-273,15°C$ or $-459.67°F$).

Lowest friction

The lowest coefficient of static and dynamic friction of any solid is 0.02, in the case of polytetrafluoroethylene ($[C_2F_4]_n$), called PTFE—equivalent to wet ice on wet ice. It was first manufactured in quantity by E. I. du Pont de Nemours & Co Inc in 1943, and is marketed from the USA as Teflon. In the United Kingdom it is marketed by ICI as Fluon.

In the centrifuge at the University of Virginia a 30 lb *13,60 kg* rotor magnetically supported has been spun at 1000 rev/sec in a vacuum of 10^{-6} mm of mercury pressure. It loses only one revolution per second per day, thus spinning for years.

Most powerful electric current

The most powerful electric current generated is that from the Zeus capacitor at the Los Alamos Scientific Laboratory, New Mexico, USA. If fired simultaneously the 4032 capacitors would produce for a few microseconds twice as much current as that generated elsewhere on Earth.

Most powerful particle accelerator

The 2 kilometre *6562 ft* diameter proton synchrotron at the Fermi National Accelerator Laboratory east of Batavia, Illinois, USA is the highest energy 'atom-smasher' in the world. On 14 May 1976 an energy of 500 billion (5×10^{11}) electron volts was attained. Work on doubling the energy to nearly 1 Tera electron volts or 1000 GeV was begun in July 1979. This involves 1000 super-conducting magnets maintained at a temperature of $-452°F$ *$-268,8°C$* by means of the world's largest 4500 litre *990 gal* per hour helium liquefying plant which began operating on 18 Apr 1980.

The £32 million CERN intersecting storage rings (ISR) project near Geneva, Switzerland started on 27 Jan 1971, using two 28 GeV proton beams, and is designed to yield the equivalent of 1700 GeV or 1.7 TeV (1.7 million million electron volts) in its centre of mass experiments.

The ultimate aim of CERN is to collide beams of protons and antiprotons in their Super Proton Synchroton (SPS) at 540 GeV, equivalent to striking a fixed target with protons at 150 TeV or 150 000 GeV.

Largest bubble chamber

The largest bubble chamber in the world is the $7 million installation completed in October 1973 at Weston, Illinois. It is 15 ft *4,57 m* in diameter and contains 7259 gal *33 000 litres* of liquid hydrogen at a temperature of $-247°C$ with a super-conductivity magnet of 30,000 gauss.

Heaviest magnet

The heaviest magnet in the world is one measuring 60 m *196 ft* in diameter, with a weight of 36,000 tons/*tonnes* for the 10 GeV synchrophasotron in the Joint Institute for Nuclear Research at Dubna, near Moscow, USSR. Intermagnetics General Corporation announced in 1975 plans for a 180 kG vanadium-gallium magnet.

Magnetic fields *Strongest and weakest*

The strongest magnetic field strength achieved has been one of 301 kilogauss *30,1 teslas* at the Francis Bitter National Magnet Laboratory at Massachusetts Institute of Technology, by Mathias J. Leupold and Robert J. Weggel, announced in July 1977. The outer magnet is of super-conducting niobium-titanium.

The weakest magnetic field measured is one of 8×10^{-11} gauss in the heavily shielded room at the Francis Bitter National Magnet Laboratory, Cambridge, Massachusetts, USA. It is used for research by Dr David Cohen into the very weak magnetic field generated in the heart and brain.

Finest cut

Biological specimens embedded in epoxy resin can be sectioned by a glass knife microtome under ideal conditions to a thickness of 1/875,000th of an inch *$2,9 \times 10^{-5}$ mm* or 29 µm.

Sharpest objects

The University of California Medical Center, San Francisco announced in July 1974 the ultimate in sharpness—glass electrodes more than 200 times slimmer than a diamond phonograph stylus. These can be used for exploring the cells in the eye. The points are 0.05 µm.

Most powerful laser beams

The first illumination of another celestial body was achieved on 9 May 1962, when a beam of light was successfully reflected from the Moon by the use of a maser (microwave amplification by stimulated emission of radiation) or laser (light amplification by stimulated emission of radiation) attached to a 48 in *121,9 cm* telescope at Massachusetts Institute of Technology, Cambridge, Massachusetts, USA. The spot was estimated to be 4 miles *6,4 km* in diameter on the Moon. The device was propounded in 1958 by Dr Charles Hard Townes (born 1915) of the USA. A maser light flash is focused into liquid nitrogen-cooled ruby crystal. Its chromium atoms are excited into a high energy state in which they emit a red light which is allowed to escape only in the direction desired. Such a flash for 1/5000th of a second can bore a hole through a diamond by vaporization at 10,000°C, produced by 2×10^{23} photons.

The 'Shiva' laser was reported at the Lawrence Livermore Laboratory, California to be concentrating 2.6×10^{13} watts into a pinhead-sized target for 9.5×10^{-11} in a test on 18 May 1978.

Brightest light

The brightest steady artificial light sources are 'laser' beams with an intensity exceeding the Sun's 1,500,000 candles/in² *232 500 candelas/cm²* by a factor well in excess of 1000. In May 1969 the USSR Academy of Sciences announced blast waves travelling through a luminous plasma of inert gases heated to 90,000 K. The flare-up for up to 3 micro-seconds shone at 50,000 times the brightness of the Sun *viz.* 75,000 million candles/in² *11 625 million candelas/cm²*. Of continuously burning sources, the most powerful is a 200 kW high-pressure xenon arc lamp of 600,000 candle-power, reported from the USSR in 1965.

The synchrotron radiation from a 4×0.5 in *100 × 2,5 mm* slit in the SPEAR high energy physics plant at the end of the 2 mile *3,2 km* long Stanford Linear Accelerator, California, USA has been described as the world's most powerful light beam.

The most powerful searchlight ever developed was one produced during the 1939–45 war by the General Electric Company Ltd at the Hirst Research Centre in Wembley, Greater London. It had a consumption of 600 kW and gave an arc luminance of 300,000 candles/in² *46 500 candelas/cm²* and a maximum beam intensity of 2,700,000,000 candles from its parabolic mirror (diameter 10 ft *3,04 m*).

Most durable light

The average bulb lasts for 750–1,000 hr. There is some evidence that a carbon filament bulb burning in the Fire Department, Livermore, south Alameda County, California has been burning since 1901.

Highest Measured Frequency

The highest frequency ever directly measured is a visible yellow light at $5.20206528 \times 10^{14}$ hertz (*c.* 520 terahertz or million million cycles per second) in February 1979 by the US National Bureau of Standards Boulder Laboratories and the National Research Council Laboratory in Ottawa, Canada.

Longest echo

The longest recorded echo in any building in Great Britain is one of 15 sec following the closing of the door of the Chapel of the Mausoleum, Hamilton, Strathclyde built in 1840–55.

Largest wind tunnel *World*

The world's largest wind tunnel is a low-speed tunnel with a 40×80 ft *12,19 × 24,38 m* test section built in 1944 at the Ames Research Center, Moffett Field, California, USA. The tunnel encloses 800 tons/*tonnes* of air and cost approximately $7,000,000 (*then* £1,735,000). The maximum volume of air that can be moved is 60,000,000 ft³ *1 700 000 m³* per min. On 30 July 1974 NASA announced an intention to increase it in size to 80×120 ft *24,38 × 36,57 m* for 345 mph speeds with a 135,000 hp *136 900 cv* system. The most powerful is the 216,000 hp *219 000 cv* installation at the Arnold Engineering Test Center at Tullahoma, Tennessee, USA opened in September 1956. The highest Mach number attained with air is Mach 27 at the works of the Boeing Company in Seattle, Washington State, USA. For periods of micro-seconds, shock Mach numbers of the order of 30 (22,830 mph *36 735 km/h*) have been attained in impulse tubes at Cornell University, Ithaca, New York State, USA.

Crystals of the rarest gem mineral, Painite, discovered in 1951 by A. C. D. Pain (GB) near Ohngaing, Mogok, Burma (see p. 84). (*British Museum: Natural History*)

Largest wind tunnel *Great Britain*

The most powerful wind tunnel in the United Kingdom is the intermittent compressed air type installation at the BAC plant at Warton, Lancashire which can be run at Mach 4, which is equivalent to 3044 mph *4898 km/h* at sea level.

Smallest hole

Inco Nickel Co. were reported in August 1977 to have produced a hole with a diameter of a ten millionth of an inch *0,000004 mm* or one thousand times smaller than a human hair.

A hole of 40 Å was shown visually using a JEM 100C electron microscope and Quantel Electronics devices at the Dept. of Metallurgy, Oxford on 28 Oct. 1979. To find such a hole is equivalent to finding a pinhead in a haystack with sides of 1.2 miles *1,93 km*.

Most Accurate Physical Device

The accuracy of the caesium beam frequency standard approaches 8 parts in 10^{14} compared to 2 parts in 10^{13} for the methane-stabilised helium-neon laser and 6 parts in 10^{13} for the hydrogen maser.

Harry Nelson (left) and David Slowinski, discoverers of the highest known prime number (see p. 85).

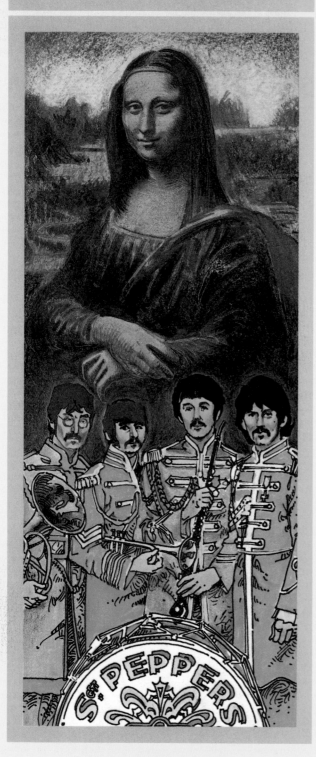

6. THE ARTS & ENTERTAINMENTS

1. PAINTING

Guinness Superlatives has published a more specialist book *Guinness Book of Art Facts and Feats* (£6.95) by John FitzMaurice Mills.

Earliest *World*
Evidence of Palaeolithic art was first found in 1834 at Chaffaud Vienne, France by Brouillet when he recognised an engraving of two deer on a piece of flat bone from the cave, dating to *c* 20,000 BC. The number of stratigraphically dated cave art is limited. The oldest known dated examples come from La Ferrassie, near Les Eyzies in the Perigord, France, in layers dated to *c* 25,000 BC. Blocks of stone were found with engraved animals and female symbols; some of the blocks also had symbols painted in red ochre. Pieces of ochre with ground facets have been found at Lake Mungo, NSW in a context *ante* 30,000 BC but there is no evidence whether these were used for body-painting or art.

Britain
The first cave wall art ever detected in Britain was a cervid head spotted by Dr. Tom Rogers (Canada) in Cave 5615 in the cliffs above Symonds Yat East on the English side of the River Wye in Hereford and Worcester in June 1980. It is of the Upper Palaeolithic dated to *c* 13,000 BC.

Largest World *All time*
Panorama of the Mississippi, completed by John Banvard (1815–91) in 1846, showing the river for 1200 miles *1930 km* in a strip probably 5000 ft *1525 m* long and 12 ft *3,65 m* wide, was the largest painting in the world, with an area of more than 1.3 acres *0,52 ha*. The painting is believed to have been destroyed when the rolls of canvas, stored in a barn at Cold Spring Harbor, Long Island, New York State, USA, caught fire shortly before Banvard's death on 16 May 1891.

Existing
The largest known painting now in existence is *The Battle of Gettysburg*, completed in 1883, after 2½ years of work, by Paul Philippoteaux (France) and 16 assistants. The painting is 410 ft *125 m* long, 70 ft *21,3 m* high and weighs 5.36 tons *5,45 tonnes*. It depicts the climax of the Battle of Gettysburg, in southern Pennsylvania, USA, on 3 July 1863. In 1964 the painting was bought by Joe King of Winston-Salem, North Carolina, USA after being stored by E. W. McConnell in a Chicago warehouse since 1933.

'Old Master'
The largest 'Old Master' is *Il Paradiso*, painted between 1587 and 1590 by Jacopo Robusti, *alias* Tintoretto (1518–94), and his son Domenico (1565–1637) on Wall 'E' of the Sala del Maggior Consiglio in the Palazzo Ducale (Doge's Palace) in Venice, Italy. The work is 22 m *72 ft 2 in* long and 7 m *22 ft 11½ in* high and contains more than 100 human figures.

Largest *Great Britain*
The largest painting in Great Britain is the giant oval *Triumph of Peace and Liberty* by Sir James Thornhill (1676–1734), on the ceiling of the Painted Hall in the Royal Naval College, Greenwich. It measures 106 ft *32,3 m* by 51 ft *15,4 m* and took 20 years (1707–1727) to complete.

A painting 6050 ft² *562 m²* in area and weighing more than a ton was painted for the 4th European Youth Games under the direction of David A. Judge and to the design of Norman G. Warner in Colchester, Essex between 29 Oct 1975 and 24 May 1976 by 365 people.

World's largest Poster
The largest recorded poster is a greeting measuring 53 ft 3 in × 166 ft *16,23 × 50,6 m* delivered to Spalding College Center, Louisville, Kentucky, USA, on its 60th anniversary on 3 Oct 1980 bearing a 'Happy Birthday' inscription and the college's Pelican mascot.

Most valuable
The 'Mona Lisa' (*La Gioconda*) by Leonardo da Vinci (1452–1519) in the Louvre, Paris, was assessed for insurance purposes at the highest ever figure of $100,000,000 (*then £35.7 million*) for

its move for exhibition in Washington, DC, and New York City, NY, USA, from 14 Dec 1962 to 12 Mar 1963. However, insurance was not concluded because the cost of the closest security precautions was less than that of the premiums. It was painted in *c.* 1503–7 and measures 77 × 53 cm *30.5 × 20.9 in.* It is believed to portray Mona (short for Madonna) Lisa Gherardini, the wife of Francesco del Giocondo of Florence, who disliked it and refused to pay for it. Francis I, King of France, bought the painting for his bathroom in 1517 for 4000 gold florins or 492 oz *15,30 kg* of gold worth some £235,000 (mid-1981).

HIGHEST PRICE
Auction price *World*
The highest price ever bid in a public auction for any painting is $6,400,000 (*then £2,689,076*) for *Juliet and Her Nurse* painted by Joseph Mallord William Turner (1775–1851) of London when in Venice, Italy in 1836 and sold on 30 May 1980 at Sotheby Parke Bernet's, New York City, to an undisclosed collector possibly a 'woman in white' from Argentina. The painting had been sold by the Whitney Museum in New York and is 3 ft × 4 ft *91 × 122 cm.*

Private Treaty
It was announced on 12 Nov 1980 that the National Gallery, London had acquired Albrecht Altdorfer's *Christ Taking Leave of His Mother*, valued by Christie's at 'about £6 million', from the trustees of the Wernher collection at Luton Hoo, Bedfordshire.

By A Woman Artist
The highest price ever paid for a painting by a female artist is $150,000 (*then £62,500*), at Parke Bernet, New York on 3 Mar 1971, for *Summertime* by Mary Cassatt (b. Pennsylvania, USA, 1844–d. 1926). She worked mainly from Paris.

Miniature portrait
The highest price ever paid for a portrait miniature is the £75,000 given by an anonymous buyer at a sale held by Sotheby's, London on 24 Mar 1980 for a miniature of Jane Broughton, aged 21, painted on vellum by Nicholas Hilliard (1547–1619) in 1574. The painted surface measures 1.65 in *42 mm* in diameter.

Modern painting
The record for a 20th century painting was set at $3 million (*then £1,310,000*) at Sotheby Parke, Bernet, New York City on 12 May 1980 by Picasso's 1923 portrait of an acrobat *Saltimbanque* bought by Tokyo's Bridgestone Museum. The 19th century record is $5,200,000 (*then £2,270,700*) for Van Gogh's *Le Jardin du Poète, Arles* sold by Christie's in New York City on 13 May 1980.

Living artist *World*
The highest price paid for paintings in the lifetime of the artist is $1,950,000 (*then £812,500*) paid for the two canvases *Two Brothers* (1905) and *Seated Harlequin* (1922) by Pablo Diego José Francisco de Paula Juan Nepomuceno Crispín Crispiano de la Santisima Trinidad Ruiz y Picasso (1881–1973) of Spain. This was paid by the Basle City Government to the Staechelin Foundation to enable the Basle Museum of Arts to retain the painting after an offer of $2,560,000 (£1,066,666) had been received from the United States in December 1967. The highest price at auction for a work by a now living artist is £360,000 at Christie's, London on 30 Mar 1981 for Salvador Dali's *Le Sommeil.*

Joseph Turner's 1836 painting *Juliet and Her Nurse* which realised $6,400,000 (*then £2,689,076*) at auction on 30 May 1980 for the highest price ever bid at a public auction. (*Courtesy: Sotheby's*)

Nicholas Hilliard's painting of Jane Broughton in 1574, the highest priced portrait miniature which was sold for £75,000 on 24 Mar 1980 (see p. 89). (*Sotheby's*)

British and Irish

The highest price for any painting by a living United Kingdom born artist is $160,000 (*then £89,890*) for the painting *Reclining Man with Sculpture* by Francis Bacon (b. Dublin, Ireland, 1909, then part of the United Kingdom) sold on 27 May 1976 at Sotheby Parke Bernet, New York City, USA.

Drawing

The highest price ever attached to any drawing is £804,361 for the cartoon *The Virgin and Child with St John the Baptist and St Anne*, measuring 54½ in × 39¼ in *137 × 100 cm*, drawn in Milan, probably in 1499–1500, by Leonardo da Vinci (1452–1519) of Italy, retained by the National Gallery in 1962. Three United States bids of over $4,000,000 (*then £1,428,570*) were reputed to have been made for the cartoon.

MOST PROLIFIC
Painter

Picasso was the most prolific of all painters in a career which lasted 78 years. It has been estimated that Picasso produced about 13,500 paintings or designs, 100,000 prints or engravings, 34,000 book illustrations and 300 sculptures or ceramics. His life-time *oeuvre* has been valued at £500 million.

Morris Katz (b. 1932) of Greenwich Village, New York City was reported at around noon on 29 June 1979 to have 'knocked off' his 82,000th saleable painting. Described as the 'King of Schlock Art', he sells his paintings 'cheap and often'.

Portraitist

John A. Wismont Jr. (b. New York City, 20 Sept 1941), formerly of Disneyland, Anaheim, California, painted 45,423

water colour paintings in his career (up to 1978) including 9853 in 1976.

Most repetitious painter

Antonio Bin of Paris has painted the *Mona Lisa* on some 300 occasions. These sell for up to £1000 apiece.

Oldest and youngest RA

The oldest ever Royal Academician has been (Thomas) Sidney Cooper C.V.O., who died on 8 Feb 1902 aged 98 yr 136 days, having exhibited 266 paintings over the record span of 69 consecutive years (1833–1902). The youngest ever RA has been Mary Moser (1744–1819) (later Mrs Hugh Lloyd), who was elected on the foundation of the Royal Academy in 1768 when aged 24.

Youngest exhibitor

The youngest ever exhibitor at the Royal Academy of Arts Annual Summer Exhibition has been Lewis Melville 'Gino' Lyons (b. 30 Apr 1962). His *Trees and Monkeys* was painted on 4 June 1965, submitted on 17 Mar 1967 and exhibited to the public on 29 Apr 1967.

Largest gallery

The world's largest art gallery is the Winter Palace and the neighbouring Hermitage in Leningrad, USSR. One has to walk 15 miles *24 km* to visit each of the 322 galleries, which house nearly 3,000,000 works of art and objects of archaeological interest. The world's largest modern art museum is the Georges Pompidou National Centre for Art and Culture opened in Paris in 1977 with 17 700 m² *183,000 ft²* of floor space.

Finest brush

The finest standard brush sold is the 000 in Series 7 by Winsor and Newton known as a 'triple goose'. It is made of 150–200 Kolinsky sable hairs weighing 15 mg *0.000529 oz*.

MURALS
Earliest

The earliest known murals on man-made walls are those at Çatal Hüyük in southern Anatolia, Turkey, dating from *c.* 5850 BC.

Largest

The largest logo and mural painting in the world is the American Revolution Bicentennial symbol, on the curved roof of the Arizona Veterans Memorial Coliseum, Phoenix, Arizona. It occupies 110,000 ft² *10 219 m²* or more than 2½ acres *1,0 ha*. It was painted over in 1977. After being outlined by aid of a computer, it took 45 man days, under the supervision of its designer John M. Glitsos, to apply the necessary 870 gallons *3955 l* of patriotic (red, white and blue) paint on 18–26 Aug 1973.

A ground mural measuring 1400 ft *426,7 m* long by 100 ft *30,4 m* wide named Yellow Brick Road—Leisure Time, painted on a disused runway near the Tamiami Stadium, South Dade, Florida USA was completed on 18 Mar 1976. A wall mural measuring 260 metres long and 2 metres tall *853 ft × 6½ ft*,

HIGHEST-PRICE PAINTINGS–Progressive records

Price	Equivalent 1981 Value	Painter, title, sold by and sold to	Date
£6500	£195,000	Antonio Correggio's *The Magdalen Reading* (in fact spurious) to Elector Friedrich Augustus II of Saxony.	1746
£8500	£235,000	Raphael's *The Sistine Madonna* to Elector Friedrich Augustus II of Saxony.	1759
£16,000	£265,000	Van Eycks' *Adoration of the Lamb*, 6 outer panels of Ghent altarpiece by Edward Solby to the Government of Prussia.	1821
£24,600*	£600,000	Murillo's *The Immaculate Conception* by estate of Marshall Soult to the Louvre (against Czar Nicholas I) in Paris.	1852
£70,000	£2,640,000	Raphael's *Ansidei Madonna* by the 8th Duke of Marlborough to the National Gallery.	1885
£100,000	£3,825,000	Raphael's *The Colonna Altarpiece* by Seldemeyer to J. Pierpoint Morgan.	1901
£102,880	£3,000,000	Van Dyck's *Elena Grimaldi-Cattaneo* (portrait) by Knoedler to Peter Widener (1834–1915).	1906
£102,880	£2,250,000	Rembrandt's *The Mill* by 6th Marquess of Lansdowne to Peter Widener.	1911
£116,500	£2,850,000	Raphael's smaller *Panshanger Madonna* by Joseph (later Baron) Duveen (1869–1939) to Peter Widener.	1913
£310,400	£7,535,000	Leonardo da Vinci's *Benois Madonna* to Czar Nicholas II in Paris.	1914
£821,429*	£4,900,000	Rembrandt's *Aristotle Contemplating the Bust of Homer* by estate of Mr and Mrs Alfred W. Erickson to New York Metropolitan Museum of Art.	1961
£1,785,714	£7,950,000	Leonardo da Vinci's *Ginerva de' Benci* (portrait) by Prince Franz Josef II of Liechtenstein to National Gallery of Art, Washington DC, USA.	1967
£2,310,000*	£8,535,000	Velázquez's *Portrait of Juan de Pareja* by the Earl of Radnor to the Wildenstein Gallery, New York.	1970
£2,729,000	£3,070,000	Turner's *Juliet and Her Nurse* by Trustees of Whitney Museum, New York to undisclosed bidder.	1980

*Indicates price at auction, otherwise prices were by private treaty.

comprising 108 panels from drafts by children was painted from June to December 1980 around St. David's Square, Swansea, West Glamorgan in Wales.

Largest mosaic

The world's largest mosaic is on the walls of the central library of the Universidad Nacional Autónomao de México, Mexico City. There are four walls, the two largest measuring 12,949 ft² *1203 m²* each representing the pre-Hispanic past. The largest Roman mosaic in Britain is the Woodchester Pavement, Gloucestershire of *c.* AD 325, excavated in 1793, now recovered with protective earth until its 8th showing due in 1983. It measures 48 ft 10 in *14,88 m* square comprising 1½ million tesserae.

Largest cartoon

The largest cartoon ever exhibited was one covering five storeys (50 × 150 ft *15 × 45 m*) of a University of Arizona building drawn by Dr Peter A. Kesling for Mom 'n Dad's Day 1954.

MUSEUMS

Oldest

The oldest museum in the world is the Ashmolean Museum in Oxford built in 1679.

Largest

The largest museum in the world is the American Museum of Natural History on 77th to 81st Streets and Central Park West, New York City, NY, USA. Founded in 1874, it comprises 19 interconnected buildings with 23 acres *9 ha* of floor space. The largest museum in the United Kingdom is the British Museum (founded in 1753), which was opened to the public in 1759. The main building in Bloomsbury, London, was built in 1823 and has a total floor area of 17.57 acres *7,11 ha*.

2. SCULPTURE

Earliest *World*

The earliest known examples of sculpture are the so-called Venus figurines from Aurignacian sites, dating to *c.* 25,000–22,000 BC, *e.g.* the famous Venus of Willendorf from Austria and the Venus of Brassempouy (Landes, France). A piece of ox rib found in 1973 at Pech de l'Azé, Dordogne, France in an early Middle Paleolithic layer of the Riss glaciation *c.* 105,000 BC has several engraved lines on one side, thought to be possibly intentional. The earliest authenticated and dated art are engravings of vulvae and animals from La Ferrassie, Périgord, France dated to *c.* 25,000 BC from the early Aurignacian period.

Great Britain

The earliest British art object is an engraving of a horse's head on a piece of rib-bone from Robin Hood Cave, Creswell Crag, Derbyshire. It dates from the Upper Paleolithic period (*c.* 15,000 to 10,000 BC). The earliest Scottish rock carving from Lagalochan, Strathclyde dates from *c.* 3000 BC.

Most expensive *World and Ancient*

The highest price ever paid for a sculpture is $3,900,000 (*then £2,400,000*) paid by private treaty in London in early 1977 by J. Paul Getty's Museum in California for the 4th century BC bronze statue of a youth attributed to the school of Lysippus. It was found by fishermen on the seabed off Faro, Italy in 1963. The £23 million Museum, with 38 galleries, opened in Malibu in January 1974, is the world's most heavily endowed with £700 million.

Living sculptor

The highest price paid for the work of a living sculptor is the $310,000 (*then £130,000*) given at Sotheby's Parke-Bernet Galleries, New York on 22 Oct 1980 for the signed bronze *Double Standing figure* by Henry Moore, OM, CH, (b. Castleford, West Yorkshire, 30 July 1898). It was executed in an edition of two in 1950 and is 88 in *2,23 m* tall.

Largest

The world's largest sculptures are the mounted figures of Jefferson Davis (1808–89), Gen Robert Edward Lee (1807–70) and Gen Thomas Jonathan ('Stonewall') Jackson (1824–63), covering 1.33 acres *0,5 ha* on the face of Stone Mountain, near Atlanta, Georgia. They are 90 ft *27,4 m* high. Roy Faulkner was on the mountain face for 8 years 174 days with a thermo-jet torch working with the sculptor Walker Kirtland Hancock and other helpers from 12 Sept 1963 to 3 Mar 1972. When completed the world's largest sculpture will be that of the Indian chief Tashunca-Uitco (*c.* 1849–77), known as Crazy Horse, of the Oglala tribe of the Dakota or Nadowessioux (Sioux) group. The sculpture was begun on 3 June 1948 near Mount Rushmore, South Dakota, USA. A projected 561 ft *170 m* high and 641 ft *195 m* long, it has required blasting 5,800,000 tons *5 890 000 tonnes* of stone and is the life work of one man, Korczak Ziolkowski.

Ground figures

In the Nazca Desert, south of Lima, Peru there are straight lines (one more than 7 miles *11,2 km* long), geometric shapes and shapes of plants and animals drawn on the ground sometime between 100 BC and AD 700 for an uncertain but probably religious or even astronomical purpose by a still unknown civilization. They were first detected from the air in *c.* 1928.

Hill figures

In August 1968 a 330 ft *100 m* tall figure was found on a hill above Tarapacá, Chile.

The largest human hill carving in Britain is the 'Long Man' of Wilmington, East Sussex, 226 ft *68 m* in length. The oldest of all White Horses in Britain is the Uffington White Horse in Oxfordshire, dating from the late Iron Age (*c.* 150 BC) and measuring 374 ft *114 m* from nose to tail and 120 ft *36 m* from ear to heel.

Most massive mobile

The most massive mobile is *White Cascade* weighing 8 tons/*tonnes* and measuring 100 ft *30,48 m* from top to bottom installed on 24–25 May 1976 at the Federal Reserve Bank of Philadelphia, Pennsylvania, USA. It was designed by Alexander Calder (b. 1898), whose first mobiles were exhibited in Paris in 1932.

White Cascade, the most massive mobile, weighing 8 tons and designed by Alexander Calder. (*Edward J. Bonner*)

3. LANGUAGE & LITERATURE

Earliest
Anthropologists have evidence that the truncated pharynx of Neanderthal man precluded his speaking anything akin to a modern language any more than an ape or a modern baby. Cro-Magnon man of 40,000 BC had however developed an efficient vocal tract. Clay tablets of the neolithic Danubian culture discovered in December 1966 at Tartaria, Moros River, Romania have been dated to the fifth or fourth millennium BC. The tablets bear symbols of bows and arrows, gates and combs. Writing tablets bearing an early form of the Elamite language dating from 3500 BC were found in south-eastern Iran in 1970. Tokens or tallies from Tepe Asiab and Ganji-I-Dareh Tepe in Iran have however been dated to 8500 BC.

Oldest
The written language with the longest continuous history is Egyptian from the earliest hieroglyphic inscriptions on the palette of Narmer dated to *c.* 3100 BC to Coptic used in Churches at the present day more than 5000 years later. Hieroglyphs were used only until AD 394 and thus may be overtaken by Chinese characters as the most durable script in the 21st century.

Oldest words in English
Some as yet unpublished research indicates some words of a pre-Indo-European substrate survive in English—apple (apal), bad (bad), gold (gol) and tin (tin).

Commonest language
Today's world total of languages and dialects still spoken is about 5000 of which some 845 come from India. The language spoken by more people than any other is Northern Chinese, or Mandarin, by an estimated 68 per cent of the population, hence 660 million people in 1980. The so-called national language (*Guóyǔ*) is a standardised form of Northern Chinese (*Běifanghuà*) as spoken in the Peking area. This was alphabetised into *zhùyīn fúhào* of 37 letters in 1918. In 1958 the *pinyin* system, which is a phonetic pronunciation guide, was introduced. The next most commonly spoken language and the most widespread is English, by an estimated 395,000,000 in mid-1980. English is spoken by 10 per cent or more of the population in 37 sovereign countries.

In Great Britain and Ireland there are six indigenous tongues: English, Cornish, Scots Gaelic, Welsh, Irish Gaelic, and Romany (Gipsy). Of these English is, of course, predominant. Mr Edward (Ned) Maddrell (1877–1974) of Glen Chass, Port St Mary, Isle of Man, died as the last islander whose professed tongue was Manx. Cornish, now happily saved, came within an ace of extinction but a dictionary was published in 1887, four years before the death of the then last fluent speaker John Davey. In the Channel Islands, apart from Jersey and Guernsey *normand*, there survive words of Sarkese or *Sèrtchais* in which the Parable of the Sower, as recited by some fishermen, was noted and published by Prince Louis Lucien Bonaparte (1813–91) in 1862.

Rarest language
There are believed to be 20 or more languages including 6 Indian languages in North America in which no-one can converse because there is only one speaker left. Eyak is still spoken in south-east Alaska by two aged sisters if they meet.

Most complex
The following extremes of complexity have been noted: Chippewa, the North American Indian language of Minnesota, USA, has the most verb forms with up to 6000; Tillamook, the North American Indian language of Oregon, USA, has the most prefixes with 30; Tabassaran, a language in Daghestan, USSR, uses the most noun cases with 35, while Eskimaux use 63 forms of the present tense and simple nouns have as many as 252 inflections. In Chinese the 40 volume *Chung-wén Tà Tz'u-tiĕn* dictionary lists 49,905 characters. The fourth tone of 'i' has 84 meanings, varying as widely as 'dress', 'hiccough' and 'licentious'. The written language provides 92 different characters of 'i⁴'. The

most complex written character in Chinese is that representing *xiè* consisting of 64 strokes meaning 'talkative'. The most complex in current use is *yù* with 32 strokes meaning to urge or implore.

Most and least irregular verbs
Esperanto was first published by Dr Ludwig Zamenhof (1859–1917) of Warsaw in 1887 without irregular verbs and is now estimated (by text book sales) to have a million speakers. The even earlier interlanguage Volapuk, invented by Johann Martin Schleyer (1831–1912), also has absolutely regular configuration. Swahili has a strict 6-class pattern of verbs and no verbs which are irregular to this pattern. According to *The Morphology and Syntax of Present-day English* by Prof. Olu Tomori, English has 283 irregular verbs of which all but perhaps 30 verbs repeated with prefixes are admissible.

Rarest and commonest sounds
The rarest speech sound is probably the sound written ř in Czech which occurs in very few languages and is the last sound mastered by Czech children. In the southern Bushman language !xo there is a click articulated with both lips, which is written ʘ. The *l* sound in the Arabic word *Allah*, in some contexts, is pronounced uniquely in that language. The commonest sound is the vowel *a* (as in the English father); no language is known to be without it.

Literature, smallest
Of written languages, that with the smallest literature is Tyrrhenian, also known as Lemnian, once spoken on the island of Lemnon and believed to be related to Etruscan. The only surviving fragment is a 10-line inscription from the sixth century BC.

Vocabulary
The English language contains about 490,000 words plus another 300,000 technical terms, the most in any language, but it is doubtful if any individual uses more than 60,000. Those in Great Britain who have undergone a full 16 years of education use perhaps 5000 words in speech and up to 10,000 words in written communications. The membership of the International Society for Philosophical Enquiry (no admission for IQ's below 148) have an average vocabulary of 36,250 words.

Greatest linguist
If the yardstick of ability to speak with fluency and reasonable accuracy is adhered to, it is doubtful whether any human could maintain fluency in more than 20–25 languages concurrently or achieve fluency in more than 40 in a lifetime.

The most multi-lingual living person in the world is George Henri Schmidt (b. Strasbourg, France, 28 Dec 1914), the Chief of the UN Terminology Section in 1965–71. The 1975 edition of *Who's Who in the United Nations*, listed 'only' 19 languages because he was then unable to find time to 'revive' his former fluency in 12 others. Britain's greatest linguist is George Campbell (b. 1913), who retired from the BBC Overseas Service where he worked, with 39 languages.

Historically the greatest linguists have been proclaimed as Cardinal Mezzofanti (1774–1849) (fluent in 26 or 27), Professor Rask (1787–1832), Sir John Bowering (1792–1872) and Dr Harold Williams of New Zealand (1876–1928), who was fluent in 28 languages.

ALPHABET
Earliest
The development of the use of an alphabet in place of pictograms occurred in the Sinaitic world between 1700 and 1500 BC. This western Semitic language developed the consonantal system based on phonetic and syllabic principles. The oldest letter is 'O', unchanged in shape since its adoption in the Phoenician alphabet *c.* 1300 BC. The newest letters in the English alphabet are 'j' and 'v' which are of post-Shakespearean use *c.* 1630. There are 65 alphabets now in use.

Longest and shortest
The language with most letters is Cambodian with 72 (including useless ones) and Rotokas in central Bougainville Island has least

with 11 (just a, b, e, g, i, k, o, p, ř, t and u). Amharic has 231 formations from 33 basic syllabic forms, each of which has seven modifications, so this Ethiopian language cannot be described as alphabetic.

Most and least consonants and vowels

The language with most consonantal sounds is the Caucasian language Ubyx, with 80, and that with least is Rotokas, with only 6 consonants. The language with the most vowels is Sedang, a central Vietnamese language with 55 distinguishable vowel sounds and those with the least is the Caucasian language Abkhazian with two such. The English record for consecutive vowels is 6 in the musical term *euouae*. The Estonian word jääääre, meaning the edge of the ice, has the same 4 consecutively. Voiauai, a language in Pará State, Brazil consists solely of 7 vowels. The English word 'latchstring' has 6 consecutive consonants, but the German word *Angstschweiss* has 8.

Largest letter

The largest permanent letters in the world are the giant 600 ft *183 m* letters spelling READYMIX on the ground in the Nullarbor near East Balladonia, Western Australia. This was constructed in December 1971.

WORDS

Longest words *World*

The longest word ever to appear in literature occurs in *The Ecclesiazusae*, a comedy by Aristophanes (448–380 BC). In the Greek it is 170 letters long but transliterates into 182 letters in English, thus: lopadotemachoselachogaleokranioleipsanodrim-hypotrimmatosilphioparaomelitokatakechymenokichlepikossy-phophophattoperisteralektryonoptekephalliokigklopeleiolagoi-osiraiobaphetraganopterygon. The term describes a fricassee of

17 sweet and sour ingredients including mullet, brains, honey, vinegar, pickles, marrow and ouzo (a Greek drink laced with anisette).

English

The longest word in the Oxford English Dictionary is floccipau-cinihilipilification (alternatively spelt in hyphenated form with 'n' in seventh place), with 29 letters, meaning 'the action of estimating as worthless', first used in 1741, and later by Sir Walter Scott (1771–1832). Webster's Third International Dictionary lists among its 450,000 entries: pneumon-oultramicroscopicsilicovolcanoconiosises (47 letters) the plural of a lung disease contracted by some miners.

The nonce word used by Dr Edward Strother (1675–1737) to describe the spa waters at Bristol was aequeosalino-calcalinoceraceoaluminosocupreovitriolic of 52 letters.

The longest regularly formed English word is praetertranssub-stantiationalistically (37 letters), used by Mark McShane in his novel *Untimely Ripped*, published in 1963. The medical term hepaticocholangiocholecystenterostomies (39 letters) refers to the surgical creations of new communications between gallbladders and hepatic ducts and between intestines and gallbladders. The longest words in common use are disproportionableness and incomprehensibilities (21 letters). Interdenominationalism (22 letters) is found in Webster's Dictionary and hence perhaps interdenominationalistically (28 letters) is permissible.

Longest palindromes

The longest known palindromic word is *saippuakivikauppias* (19 letters), the Finnish word for a dealer in lye (*i.e.* caustic soda). The longest in the English language is *redivider* (9 letters). The

A sign depicting the longest place name on any map, in North Island, New Zealand (see p. 94).

WORLDS LONGEST WORDS

Japanese	Chi-n-chi-ku-ri-n (12 letters) —a very short person (slang)
French	Anticonstitutionnellement (25 letters) —anticonstitutionally. Anthropoclimatologiquement (26 letters) —anthropoclimatologically
Croatian	Prijestolonasljednikovica (25 letters) —wife of an heir apparent.
Italian	Precipitevolissimevolmente (26 letters) —as fast as possible.
Portuguese	inconstitucionalissimamente (27 letters) —the highest degree of unconstitutionality.
Russian	ryentgyenoelyektrokardiografichyeskogo (33 Cyrillic letters, transliterating as 38) —of the radioelectrocardiographic.
Hungarian	Megszentsegtelenithetetlensegeskedeseitekert (44 letters) —for your unprofaneable actions.
Turkish‡	Cekoslovakyalılastıramadıklarımızdanmıymıssınız (47 letters) —'are you not of that group of persons that we were said to be unable to Czechoslovakianise?'
Dutch‡	Kindercarnavalsoptochtvoorbereidingswerkzaanheden (49 letters) —preparation activities for a children's carnival procession
Mohawk*	tkanuhstasrihsranuhwe'tsraaksahsrakaratattsrayeri' (50 letters) —the praising of the evil of the liking of the finding of the house is right.
Icelandic‡	Haestarréttarmálaflutningsmannsskrifstofustúlkuútidyralykillinn
German†‡	Donaudampfschiffahrtselec tricitaetenhaupt betriebswerkbauunterbeamtengesellschaft (81 letters) —The club for subordinate officials of the head office management of the Danube steamboat electrical services (Name of a pre-war club in Vienna).
Swedish‡	Spårvagnsaktiebolags skensmutsskjutarefack föreningspersonal beklädnadsmagasins förrådsförvaltaren (94 letters) —Manager of the depot for the supply of uniforms to the personnel of the track cleaners' union of the tramway company.

* Lengthy concatenations are a feature of Mohawk. Above is an example.
† The longest dictionary word in every day usage is Kraftfahrzeugreparaturwerkstätten (33 letters or 34 if the ä is written as ae) meaning motor vehicle repair shops (or service garages).
‡ Not found in standard dictionaries.

nine-letter word, *Malayalam*, is a proper noun given to the language of the Malayali people in Kerala, southern India while *Kanakanak* near Dillingham, Alaska is a 9 lettered palindromic place-name. The nine letter word ROTAVATOR is a registered trade mark belonging to Howard Machinery Ltd. The contrived chemical term *detartrated* has 11 letters. Some baptismal fonts in Greece and Turkey bear the circular 25 letter inscription ΝΙΨΟΝ ΑΝΟΜΗΜΑΤΑ ΜΗ ΜΟΝΑΝ ΟΨΙΝ meaning 'wash (my) sins not only (my) face'. This appears at St Mary's Church, Nottingham, St Paul's, Woldingham, Surrey and other churches. The longest palindromic composition devised is one of 22,500 words completed by Edward Benbow of Bewdley, Hereford & Worcs. in February 1980. It begins 'Egad, I have done more, Jeff....' and hence predictably ends '.... Jerome, nod! Eva hid age'.

Longest chemical name

The longest scientific name is that of protein resulting from a fusion of the repressor of ß-galactosidase and ß-galactosidase published in October 1978. It consists of 4059 letters in its abbreviated code form and more than 8000 letters in its full form. The first nine letters are 'Methionyl....'.

Longest anagrams

The longest non-scientific English words which can form anagrams are the 18-letter transpositions 'conservationalists' and 'conversationalists'. The longest scientific transposals are cholecystoduodenostomy/duodenocholecystostomy and hydropneumopericardium/pneumohydropericardium each of 22 letters.

In his research into anagrams A. J. Capper has found only one 4 letter word with 13 and one 5 letter word with 28 anagrams—these are 'aber' and 'aster'.

Longest abbreviation

The longest known abbreviation is S.K.O.M.K.H.P.K.J.C. D.P.W.B., the initials of the Syarikat Kerjasama Orang-orang Melayu Kerajaan Hilir Perak Kerana Jimat Cermat Dan Pinjam-meminjam Wang Berhad. This is the Malay name for the Lower Perak Malay Government Servant's Co-operative Thrift and Loan Society Limited, in Teluk Anson, Perak, West Malaysia (formerly Malaya). The abbreviation for this abbreviation is Skomk. The 55-letter full name of Los Angeles (El Pueblo de Nuestra Señora la Reina de los Angeles de Porciuncula) is abbreviated to LA or 3.63 per cent of its length.

Longest Acronym

The longest acronym is NIIOMTPLABOPARMBETZHELB-ETRABSBOMONIMONKONOTDTEKHSTROMONT with 56 letters (54 in cyrillic) in the *Concise Dictionary of Soviet Terminology* meaning: The laboratory for shuttering, reinforcement, concrete and ferro-concrete operations for composite-monolithic and monolithic constructions of the Department of the Technology of Building—assembly operations the Scientific Research Institute of the Organisation for building mechanisation and technical aid of the Academy of Building and Architecture of the USSR.

Commonest words and letters

In written English the most frequently used words are in order: the, of, and, to, a, in, that, is, I, it, for *and* as. The most used in conversation is I. The commonest letter is 'e' and the commonest initial letter is 'T'.

Most meanings

The most over-worked word in English is the word *set* which has 58 noun uses, 126 verbal uses and 10 as a participial adjective.

Most homophones

The most homophonous sounds in English are *air* and *sol* which, according to the researches of Dora Newhouse of Los Angeles, both have 38 homophones. The homonym with most variant spellings is *Air* with Aire, are, Ayer, Ayr, Ayre, Ear, e'er, ere, eyre and heir.

Most accents

Accents were introduced in French in the reign of Louis XIII (1601–43). The word with most accents is *hétérogénéité*, meaning

heterogeneity. An atoll in the Pacific Ocean 320 miles *516k* E.S.E. of Tahiti is named Héréhérétué.

Shortest holoalphabetic sentence

The contrived headline describing the reaction of despicabl vandals from the valley thwarted by finding a block of quart with carvings (already) upon it as 'Quartz glyph job vex'd cw finks' represents the closest approach to the ultimate in containing all 26 letters in 26 letters and one apostrophe to eliminate th second 'e'. This was devised by Jeff Grant of Hastings, New Zealand. The five words 'fyrd jackbox plegms qvint wuz' all appea in major dictionaries but can hardly be moulded into a cursiv sentence however contrived.

Longest sentence

A sentence of 1300 words appears in 'Absalom Absalom' by Wi liam Faulkner and one of 3153 words in *History of the Church* God composed by Sylvester Hassell of Wilson, North Carolina USA, c. 1884 with 86 semi-colons and 390 commas. The longe sentence recorded to have got past the editor of a major new paper is one of 1286 words in the *New York Times* by Herbe Stein in the issue of 13 Feb 1981. The Report of the President Columbia University 1942–3 contained a sentence of 428 words. The first 40,000 words of *The Gates of Paradise* b George Andrzeyevski (Panther) appear to lack any punctuation Some authors such as James Joyce (1882–1941) appear to esche punctuation altogether.

PLACE-NAMES

Earliest

The earliest recorded British place-name is Belerion, the Pe with peninsula of Cornwall, referred to as such by Pytheas Massilia in c. 308 BC. The name Salakee on St Mary's, Isles Scilly is however arguably of a pre Indo-European substra meaning *tin island*. There are reasons to contend that Leicest (Roman, Ligora Castrum) contains an element reflecting i founding by the Western Mediterranean navigators, the Lig rians, as early as c. 1200 BC. The earliest distinctive name f what is now Great Britain was Albion by Himilco c. 500 BC. Th oldest name among England's 46 counties is Kent, first me tioned in its Roman form of Cantium (from the Celtic *cant* meaning a rim, *i.e.* a coastal district) from the same circumnav gation by Pytheas. The earliest mention of England is the for *Angelcymn*, which appeared in the Anglo-Saxon Chronicle in A 880.

Longest *World*

The official name for Bangkok, the capital city of Thailand, Krungtep Mahanakhon. The full name is however: Krungth Mahanakhon Bovorn Ratanakosin Mahintharayutthaya Mah dilokpop Noparatratchathani Burirom Udomratchanive mahasathan Amornpiman Avatarnsathit Sakkathattiya snukarmprasit (167 letters) which in its most scholarly trans teration emerges with 175 letters. The longest place-name now use in the world is Taumatawhakatangihangakoauauotamat (turipukakapikimaungahoronuku)pokaiwhenuakitanatahu, th unofficial 85-letter version of the name of a hill (1002 ft *305* above sea-level) in the Southern Hawke's Bay district of Nor Island, New Zealand. This Maori name means 'the hill where was played the flute of Tamatea, circumnavigator of lands, f his lady love'. The official version has 57 letters (1 to 36 and 65 85). Ijouaououene, Morocco has 8 consecutive vowels.

Great Britain

The longest place-name in the United Kingdom is the concoct 58-letter name Llanfairpwllgwyngyllgogerychwyrndrobw llantysiliogogogoch, which is translated: 'St Mary's Church in dell of white hazel trees, near the rapid whirlpool, by the r cave of the Church of St Tysilio'. This is the name used for t reopened (April 1973) village railway station in Anglesey, Gw nedd, Wales, but the *official* name consists of only the first letters of what the Welsh would regard as a 51 letter word sin 'll' and 'ch' may be regarded as one. The longest genuine Wel place-name listed in the Ordnance Survey Gazetteer is Low Llanfihangel-y-Creuddyn (26 letters), a village ne Aberystwyth, Dyfed, Wales.

England

The longest single-word (unhyphenated) place-name

England is Blakehopeburnhaugh, a hamlet between Burness and Rochester in Northumberland, of 18 letters. The nearby Cottonshopeburnfoot (19 letters) is locally rendered as one word though not by the Ordnance Survey. The hyphenated Sutton-under-Whitestonecliffe, North Yorkshire has 27 letters on the Ordnance Survey but with the insertion of 'the' and the dropping of the final 'e' 29 letters in the Post Office List. The longest multiple name is North Leverton with Habblesthorpe (30 letters), Nottinghamshire, while the longest parish name is Saint Mary le More and All Hallows with Saint Leonard and Saint Peter, Wallingford (68 letters) in Oxfordshire formed on 5 Apr 1971.

Scotland
The longest single-word place-name in Scotland is Coignafeuinternich in Inverness-shire. Kirkcudbrightshire (also 18 letters) became merged into Dumfries and Galloway on 16 May 1975. A 12-acre *5 ha* loch 9 miles *14 km* west of Stornoway on Lewes, Western Isles is named Loch Airidh Mhic Fhionnlaidh Dhuibh (31 letters).

Ireland
The longest place-name in Ireland is Muckanaghederdauhaulia (22 letters), 4 miles *6 km* from Costello in Camus Bay, County Galway. The name means 'soft place between two seas'.

Shortest
The shortest place names in the world are the French village of Y (population 143), so named since 1241, the Danish village Å on the island Fyn, the Norwegian village of Å (pronounced 'Aw'), the Swedish place Å in Vikholandet, U in the Caroline Islands, Pacific Ocean; and the Japanese town of Sosei which is alternatively called Aioi or O. There was once a 6 in West Virginia, USA. The shortest place-names in Great Britain are the two-lettered villages of Ae (population 199 in 1961) Dumfries and Galloway; Oa on the island of Islay, Strathclyde and Bu on Wyre, Orkney Islands. In the Shetland Islands there are skerries called Ve and two stacks called Aa. The island of Iona was originally I. The River E flows into the southern end of Loch Mhór, Inverness-shire, and O Brook flows on Dartmoor, Devon. The shortest place-name in Ireland is Ta (or Lady's Island) Lough, a sea-inlet on the coast of County Wexford. Tievelough, in County Donegal, is also called Ea.

Most spellings
The spelling of the Dutch town of Leeuwarden has been recorded in 225 versions since AD 1046. The Leicestershire village of Shepshed is recorded in 49 spellings since the Scepesvesde of the Doomsday Book in 1086.

PERSONAL NAMES

Earliest
The earliest personal name which has survived is seemingly that of a predynastic King of Upper Egypt *ante* 3050 BC, who is indicated by the hieroglyphic sign for a scorpion. It has been suggested that the name should be read as Sekhen. The earliest known name of any resident of Britain is Divitiacus, King of the Suessiones, the Gaulish ruler of the Kent area *c.* 75 BC under the name Prydhain. Scotland, unlike England, was never conquered by the Roman occupiers (AD 43–410). Calgācus (b. *c.* AD 40), who led this last resistance was the earliest native of Scotland whose name has been recorded.

Longest pedigree
The only non-Royal English pedigree that can with certainty show a clear pre-Conquest descent is that of the Arden family. Shakespeare's mother was a Mary Arden. It is claimed on behalf of the Clan Mackay that their clan can be traced to Loarn, the Irish invader of south west Pictland, now Strathclyde, *c.* AD 501.

Longest single name
The longest Christian or given name on record is Napuamohala-onaona-a-me-ka- wehiwehi-o-na- kuahiwi-a-me-na-awawa- ke-hoomaka-ke- hoaala-ke-ea-o- na-aina-nani-akea-o- hawaii-i- ka-wanaao (102 letters) in the case of Miss Dawne N. Lee so named in Honolulu, Hawaii, USA in February 1967. The name means 'The abundant, beautiful blossoms of the mountains and valleys begin to fill the air with their fragrance throughout the length and breadth of Hawaii'.

Longest surname *World*
The longest name used by anyone is Adolph Blaine Charles David Earl Frederick Gerald Hubert Irvin John Kenneth Lloyd Martin Nero Oliver Paul Quincy Randolph Sherman Thomas Uncas Victor William Xerxes Yancy Zeus Wolfeschlegelstein-hausenbergerdorff, Senior, who was born at Bergedorf, near Hamburg, Germany, on 29 Feb 1904. On printed forms he uses only his eighth and second Christian names and the first 35 letters of his surname. The full version of the name of 590 letters appeared in the 12th edition of *The Guinness Book of Records*. He now lives in Philadelphia, Pensylvania, USA, and has shortened his surname to Mr Wolfe+585, Senior.

United Kingdom
The longest surname in the United Kingdom was the six-barrelled one borne by the late Major L.S.D.O.F. (Leone Sextus Denys Oswolf Fraudati filius) Tollemache-Tollemache de Orellana Plantagenet Tollemache Tollemache, who was born in 1884 and died of pneumonia in France on 20 Feb 1917. Of non-repetitious surnames, the last example of a five-barrelled one was that of the Lady Caroline Jemima Temple-Nugent-Chandos-Brydges-Grenville (1858–1946). The longest single English surname is Featherstonehaugh, correctly pronounced on occasions (but improbably on the correct occasion) Feather-stonehaw or Festonhaw or Fessonhay or Freestonhugh or Feerstonhaw or Fanshaw.

Scotland
In Scotland the surname nin (feminine of mac) Achinmacdholi-cachinskerray (29 letters) was recorded in an 18th century parish register.

Most Christian names
The great-great-grandson of Carlos III of Spain, Don Alfonso de Borbón y Borbón (1866–1934) had 89 Christian names of which several were lengthened by hyphenation.

Shortest
The single-letter surname O, of which more than 12 examples appear in telephone directories for Brussels, Belgium, besides being the commonest single-letter name is the one obviously causing most distress to those concerned with the prevention of cruelty to computers. There are two one-lettered Burmese names E (calm), pronounced aye and U (egg), pronounced Oo. U *before* the name means 'uncle'. There exist among the 47,000,000 names on the Dept. of Health & Social Security index 6 examples of a one-lettered surname. Their identity has not been disclosed, but they are 'A', 'B', 'J', 'N', 'O' and 'X'. Two-letter British surnames include By and On have recently been joined by Oy, Za and others. The Christian name 'A' has been used for 5 generations in the Lincoln Taber family of Fingringhoe, Essex.

Commonest family name *World*
The commonest family name in the world is the Chinese name Chang which is borne, according to estimates, by between 9.7 and 12.1 per cent of the Chinese population, so indicating even on the lower estimate that there are at least some 75,000,000 Changs—more than the entire population of all but 7 of the 164 other sovereign countries of the world.

English
The commonest surname in the English-speaking world is Smith. The most recent published count showed 659,050 nationally insured Smiths in Great Britain, of whom 10,102 were plain John Smith and another 19,502 were John (plus one or more given names) Smith. Including uninsured persons there were over 800,000 Smiths in England and Wales alone, of whom 81,493 were called A. Smith. There were an estimated 2,382,509 Smiths in the USA in 1973.

'Macs'
There are, however, estimated to be 1,600,000 persons in Britain with M', Mc or Mac (Gaelic 'son of') as part of their surnames. The commonest of these is Macdonald which accounts for about 55,000 of the Scottish population.

Commonest Christian name
From the latest available full year (1979) birth registrations for

England and Wales at St Catherine's House (formerly Somerset House), the most favoured first forename choice of parents from the classless 1.3% sample of 8800 families bearing the commonest surname of Smith are boys David and Andrew equal with a lead over Mark/Marc followed by Matthew and Paul and girls Emma well ahead of Claire, Kelly and Nicola. This survey was carried out by C. V. Appleton. From 1196 to at least 1925 William and John were first and second but by 1979 John had sunk to 24th and William considerably lower.

Most versions

Mr Edward A. Nedelcov of Regina, Saskatchewan, Canada has collected 617 versions of the spelling of his family name. Mzilikazi of Zululand (b. *c.* 1795) had his name chronicled in 325 spellings, according to researches by Dr R. Kent Rasmussen.

Most contrived name

In the United States the determination to derive commercial or other benefit from being the last listing in the local telephone book has resulted in self-given names, starting with up to 9 z's—the extreme example being Zachary Zzzzzzzzzzra in the San Francisco book. Last in the book for Madison, Wisconsin is however the 31-year-old Hero Zzyzzx (pronounced Ziz-icks) whose name, he claims, is 'for real'. The alpha and omega of Britain's 82 directories are Mrs Maude E. Aab of Hull, Humberside and Mr Z. Z. Zzitz of London N16.

TEXTS AND BOOKS

Oldest

The oldest known written text is the pictographic expression of Sumerian speech (see Earliest Language, p. 92). The Sumerian papyri, written in Aramaic, found 8½ miles *13,7 km* north of Jericho are dated 375–335 BC.

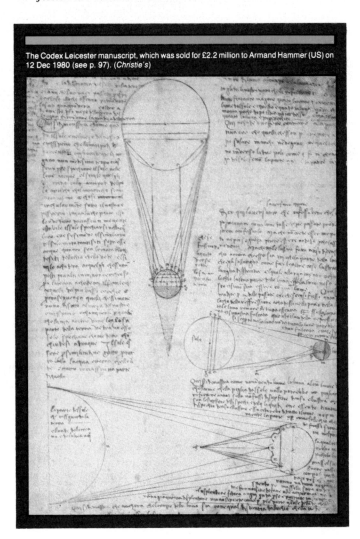

The Codex Leicester manuscript, which was sold for £2.2 million to Armand Hammer (US) on 12 Dec 1980 (see p. 97). (*Christie's*)

Oldest printed

The oldest surviving printed work is a Korean scroll or *sutra* from wooden printing blocks found in the foundations of the Pulguk Sa pagoda, Kyongju, Korea, on 14 Oct 1966. It has been dated no later than AD 704. It was claimed in November 197? that a 28-page book of Tang dynasty poems at Yonsei University, Korea was printed from metal type *c.* 1160.

Oldest mechanically printed

It is widely accepted that the earliest mechanically printed full length book was the 42-line Gutenberg Bible, printed at Mainz, Germany, in *c.* 1454 by Johann Henne zum Gensfleisch zur Laden, called 'zu Gutenberg' (*c.* 1398–*c.* 1468). Work on water marks published in 1967 indicates a copy of a surviving printed 'Donatus' Latin grammar was made from paper in *c.* 1450. The earliest exactly dated printed work is the Psalter completed on 14 Aug 1457 by Johann Fust (*c.* 1400–66) and Peter Schöffer (1425–1502), who had been Gutenberg's chief assistant. The earliest printing by William Caxton (*c.* 1422–1491) though undated would appear to be *The Recuyel of the Historyes of Troye* in late 1473 to spring 1474.

Largest *Book*

The largest book in the world is the *Super Book* measuring 9 ft × 10 ft 2⅛ in *2,74 × 3,07 m* weighing 557 lb *252,6 kg* consisting of 300 pages published in Denver, Colorado, USA in 1976.

Publication

The largest publication in the world is the 1112 volume set of *British Parliamentary Papers* published by the Irish University Press in 1968–72. A complete set weighs 3¼ tons *3,3 tonnes* costs £32,804 and would take 6 years to read at 10 hours per day. The production involved the death of 34,000 Indian goats, and the use of £15,000 worth of gold ingots. The total print is 50? sets.

Dictionary

Deutches Wörterbuch started by Jacob and Wilhelm Grimm in 1854 was completed in 34,519 pages and 33 volumes in 1971. Today's price is DM4,920.30 (*now £1045*). The largest English language dictionary is the 12-volume Royal quarto *The Oxford English Dictionary* of 15,487 pages published between 1884 and 1928 with a first supplement of 963 pages in 1933 with a further 4-volume supplement, edited by R. W. Burchfield, O-sez (due late 1981) and Se-Z and the Bibliography (due 1985) have yet to appear. The work contains 414,825 words, 1,827,306 illustrative quotations and reputedly 227,779,589 letters and figures, 63.8 times more than the Bible. The greatest outside contributor has been Marganita Laski with 175,000 quotations since 1958.

The New Grove Dictionary of Music and Musicians (Editor Stanley Sadie) published in 20 volumes by Macmillan's in February 1981 contains over 22 million words and 4,500 illustrations and is the largest specialist dictionary yet published.

Smallest book

The smallest marketed bound printed book with cursive material is one of 20 pages measuring 1,4 × 1,4 mm ¹/₁₈ × ¹/₁₈ *in*, comprising the children's story 'Ari' (the ant) made by Asao Hoshio in Tokyo, Japan and published in 200 copies in June 1980.

Longest novel

The longest important novel ever published is *Les hommes de bonne volonté* by Louis Henri Jean Farigoule (b. 26 Aug 1885) alias Jules Romains, of France, in 27 volumes in 1932–46. The English version *Men of Good Will* was published in 14 volumes in 1933–46 as a 'novel-cycle'. The 4959 page edition published by Peter Davies Ltd has an estimated 2,070,000 words excluding a 100 page index. The novel *Tokuga-Wa Ieyasu* by Sohachi Yamaoka has been serialised in Japanese daily newspapers since 1951. Now completed it will require nearly 40 volumes in book form.

Encyclopaedias *Earliest*

The earliest known encyclopaedia was compiled by Speusippus (*post* 408–*c.* 338 BC) a nephew of Plato, in Athens *c.* 370 BC. The earliest encyclopaedia compiled by a Briton was *Liber exerptionum* by the Scottish monk Richard (d. 1173) at St Victor's Abbey, Paris *c.* 1140.

Largest

The largest encyclopaedia ever compiled was the *Great Standard Encyclopaedia* of Yung-lo ta tien of 22,937 manuscript chapters (370 still survive), written by 2000 Chinese scholars in 1403–8.

Most comprehensive

The most comprehensive academic encyclopaedia is the *Encyclopaedia Britannica*, first published in Edinburgh, Scotland, in December 1768–1771. A group of booksellers in the United States acquired reprint rights in 1898 and completed ownership in 1899. In 1943 the *Britannica* was given to the University of Chicago, Illinois, USA. The current 30-volume 15th edition contains 33,141 pages and 43,000,000 words from 4277 contributors. It is now edited in Chicago and in London.

Longest index

The Ninth Collective Index of *Chemical Abstracts* completed on 23 Aug 1978 contains 20.55 million entries in 95,882 pages and 57 volumes, and weighs 251 lb *113,8 kg*.

Maps *Oldest*

The oldest known map of any kind is a clay tablet depicting the river Euphrates flowing through northern Mesopotamia, Iraq, dated *c.* 3800 BC. The earliest surviving product of English mapmaking is the Anglo Saxon *mappa mundi*, known as the Cottonian manuscript from the late 10th century. The earliest printed map in the world dates from Isodore of Sevellés *Etymologiarium* of 1472. The earliest printed map of Britain was Ptolemy's outline printed in Bologna, Italy in 1477.

Most expensive *Printed Book*

The highest price ever paid for a printed book is $2,400,000 (*then £1,265,000*) for one of the only 21 complete known copies of the Gutenberg Bible, printed in Mainz, W. Germany in *c.* 1454. It was bought from the Carl and Lily Pforzheimer Foundation by Texas University in a sale arranged by Quaritch of London in New York on 9 June 1978.

Broadsheet

The highest price ever paid for a broadsheet has been $404,000 (*then £168,333*) for one of the 16 known copies of *The Declaration of Independence*, printed in Philadelphia in 1776 by Samuel T. Freeman & Co, and sold to a Texan in May 1969.

Manuscripts

The highest value ever paid for a complete manuscript is £2.2 million by Armand Hammer paid at Christie's, London on 12 Dec 1980 for Leonardo da Vinci's 36-page Codex Leicester manuscript compiled in *c* 1507. It was sold by the trustees of the Holkham estate.

Atlas

The highest price paid for an atlas is £340,000 for a 16th century Mercator atlas of Europe, sold at Sotheby's, London, on 13 Mar 1979.

BIBLE

Oldest

Biblical texts in Hebrew are known to have become standardised as early as AD 70. The oldest leather and papyrus Dead Sea Scrolls date from *c.* 250 BC. The oldest known bible is the *Codex Vaticanus* written in Greek *ante* AD 350 and preserved in the Vatican Museum, Rome. The earliest Bible printed in English was one edited by Miles Coverdale, Bishop of Exeter (*c.* 1488–1569), while living in Antwerp, and printed in 1535. William Tyndale's New Testament in English had, however, been printed in Cologne and in Worms, Germany in 1525.

Longest and shortest books

The longest book in the Authorized version of the Bible is the Book of Psalms, while the longest book incuding prose is the Book of the Prophet Isaiah, with 66 chapters. The shortest is the Third Epistle of John, with 294 words in 14 verses. The Second Epistle of John has only 13 verses but 298 words.

Longest and shortest psalm and verse

Of the 150 Psalms, the longest is the 119th, with 176 verses, and the shortest is the 117th, with two verses. The shortest verse in the Authorised Version (King James) of the Bible is verse 35 of

above: Members of The London Bible Society who are represented in 150 countries and who distribute annually over 550,000 copies of the world's most printed book, the Bible. (see p. 99) (*British and Foreign Bible Society, London*)
below: The print of *The Truth that leads to Eternal Life* published by the Watchtower Bible and Tract Society reached 100 million by April 1981 (see p. 100).

Chapter XI of the Gospel according to St. John, consisting of the two words 'Jesus wept'. The longest is verse 9 of Chapter VIII of the Book of Esther, which extends to a 90-word description of the Persian empire.

Total letters and words, longest name

The total number of letters in the Bible is 3,566,480. The total number of words depends on the method of counting hyphenated words, but is usually given as between 773,692 and 773,746. The word 'and' according to Colin McKay Wilson of the Salvation Army appears 46,227 times. The longest personal name in the Bible is Maher-shalal-hash-baz, the symbolic name of the second son of Isaiah (Isaiah, Chapter VIII, verses 1 and 3). The caption of Psalm 22, however, contains a Hebrew title sometimes rendered Al-'Ayyeleth Hash-Shahar (20 letters).

LETTERS

Longest

The longest personal letter based on a word count is one of 1,113,747 words written in 8 months ending May 1976, by Miss Jacqueline Jones of Lindale, Texas, to her sister, Mrs Jean Stewart, of Springfield, Maine, USA.

To an editor *Longest*

The Upper Dauphin Sentinel of Pennsylvania, USA published a letter of 23,513 words over 8 issues from August to November 1979, written by John Sultzbaugh of Lykens, Pennsylvania.

Most

The only person known to have had over 40 letters published in *The Times* is Mr Hockley Clarke of Surbiton, Surrey in the period 1930–70. Britain's, and seemingly the world's, most indefatigable writer of letters to the editors of newspapers is Raymond L. Cantwell, of Oxford. His total claims are currently under audit.

Shortest

The shortest correspondence on record was that between Victor Marie Hugo (1802–85) and his publisher Hurst and Blackett in 1862. The author was on holiday and anxious to know how his new novel *Les Misérables* was selling. He wrote '?'. The reply was '!'.

In the middle of the 11 month strike of the London *Times*, the Editor received a letter dated 9 July 1979 'Dear Sir, I remain yours faithfully T. P. O'Brien'.

Most personal mail

The highest confirmed mail received by any private citizen in a year is 900,000 letters by the baseball star Hank Aaron reported by the US Postal Department in June 1974. About a third were letters of hate engendered by his bettering of Babe Ruth's career record for 'home runs'. (See Chap. 12.)

Longest diary

The diary of Edward Robb Ellis (b. 1911) of New York City begun in 1927 is estimated after 54 years to run to 15 million words. The diary of T. C. Baskerville of Charlton-cum-Hardy, Manchester maintained since 1939 comprises an estimated 3,606,000 words.

The head office in Tokyo of the *Yomiuri Shimbun*, the newspaper with the worlds highest circulation and advertising rates (see pp. 101 & 102).

Pen pals most durable

The longest sustained correspondence on record is one of 7 years between Mrs E. Darlington of Marple, Cheshire and Mr Gertrude Walker of Hawthorn, South Australia which starte on 5 Jan 1906.

Birthday card—most parsimonious

Mrs Amelia Finch (b. 18 Apr 1912) of Lakehurst, New Jersey USA and Mr Paul E. Warburgh (b. 1 Feb 1902) of Huntington New York have been exchanging the same card since 1 Fe 1927.

Christmas cards

The greatest number of personal Christmas cards sent out is believed to be 62,824 by Mr Werner Erhard of San Francisco, California in December 1975.

AUTOGRAPHS AND SIGNATURES
Earliest

The earliest surviving signatures known are of Oliba, the Spanish Catalan bishop of Vic (*c.* 971–1046) and Oliba I o Cerdanya-Besalú (d. 990). A signum exists for the French Kin Pepin the Short (715–768) and also for William I (the Conqueror) *c* 1070. The earliest English sovereign whose handwriting is known to have survived is Edward III (1327–77). The earliest full signature extant is that of Richard II (dated 26 Jul 1386). The Magna Carta does not bear even the mark of Kin John (reigned 1199–1216), but carries only his seal.

Most expensive

The highest price ever paid on the open market for a single autograph letter signed is $100,000 (*then £45,500*), paid on 18 Oc 1979 at a Charles Hamilton auction in New York City for a brie receipt signed by the Gloucestershire-born Button Gwinnet (1732–77), one of the 56 signatories of the United States' Declaration of Independence of 1776.

The highest price paid for a signed autograph letter of a living person is $6250 (*then £2430*) at the Hamilton Galleries on 1 De 1977 for a letter from ex-President Richard M. Nixon to a briga dier general dated 14 Dec 1971.

Most valuable

Only one example of the signature of Christopher Marlowe (1564–93) is known. It is in the Kent County Archives on a Wil of 1583. It is estimated that a seventh Shakespearean signature would realise at least £1 million at auction.

AUTHORS
Most prolific

The most prolific writer for whom a word count has been published was Charles Hamilton, *alias* Frank Richards (1875-1961), the Englishman who created Billy Bunter. At his height in 1908 he wrote the whole of the boys' comics *Gem* (founded 1907) and *Magnet* (1908–40) and most of two others, totalling 80,000 words a week. His lifetime output has been put a 100,000,000 words. He enjoyed the advantages of the use of electric light rather than candlelight and of being unmarried. The champion of the goose quill era was Jósef Ignacy Kraszewsk (1812–87) of Poland who produced more than 600 volumes o novels and historical works.

Most novels

The greatest number of novels published by any author is 904 by Kathleen Lindsay (Mrs Mary Faulkner) (1903–73) of Somerse West, Cape Province, South Africa. She wrote under six pe names, two of them masculine. The most prolific living novelis is Lauran Paine of California, who has had 834 published unde 71 pen names. After receiving a probable record 743 rejectior slips the British novelist John Creasey MBE (1908–73), under hi own name and 13 *noms de plume* had 564 books totalling mor than 40,000,000 words published from 1932 to his death on June 1973. The British authoress with the greatest total of fulllength titles is Miss Ursula Harvey Bloom (b. Chelmsford, Essex 1892) (Mrs A. C. G. Robinson, formerly Mrs Denham-Cookes), who reached 500 by December 1975, starting in 1924 with *The Great Beginning* and including the best sellers *The Ring Tree* (novel) and *The Rose of Norfolk* (non-fiction). Enid Mary Blyton (1898–1968) (Mrs Darrell Waters) completed 600 titles of children's stories, many of them brief, with 59 in the single year 1955. She was translated into a record 128 languages.

Most text books
Britain's most successful writer of text books is the ex-schoolmaster Ronald Ridout (b. 23 July 1916) who between 1948 and April 1981 had 435 titles published with sales of 74,750,000. His *The First English Workbook* has sold 4,702,000.

The annual aggregate sales of all titles by Louis Alexander of Haslemere, Surrey, reached 4,573,000 in the year 1977.

Highest paid
In 1958 a Mrs Deborah Schneider of Minneapolis, Minnesota, USA, wrote 25 words to complete a sentence in a competition for the best blurb for Plymouth cars. She won from about 1,400,000 entrants the prize of $500 (*then £178*) every month for life. On normal life expectations she would have collected $12,000 (*£4,285*) per word. No known anthology includes Mrs Schneider's deathless prose.

Greatest Advance
The greatest advance paid for any book is $3,208,875 (*then £1.45 million*) by Bantam Books Inc. for *Princess Daisy* by Judith Krantz in an auction in New York City, USA on 5 Sept 1979. Corgi Books paid the highest rights price ever paid in Britain of $450,000 (*then £205,000*).

Top selling
It was announced on 13 Mar 1953 that 672,058,000 copies of the works of Generalissimo Stalin (born Yózef Vissarionovich Dzhugashvili,) (1879–1953), had been sold or distributed in 101 languages.

The all-time estimate of book sales by Erle Stanley Gardner (1889–1970) (US) to 1 Jan 1981 were 313,169,827 copies in 37 languages. The top selling authoress has been Dame Agatha Christie (*née* Miller) (later Lady Mallowan) (1890–1976) whose 87 crime novels sold an estimated 300,000,000 in 103 languages. *Sleeping Murder* was published posthumously in 1977. Currently the top-selling authoress is Barbara Cartland (Mrs McCorquodale) with global sales exceeding 100,000,000 for 248 novels in 17 languages. In both 1977 and 1980 she published 24 titles bringing her overall total of titles to 298.

Highest selling titles
It is believed that 1879 edition of *The McGaffey Reader*, compiled by Henry Vail and published for school distribution in the United States by Van Antwerp Bragg and Co sold 60 million copies in the pre-copyright era.

For details of the *Guinness Book of Records* see p. 100.

Most rejections
The greatest recorded number of publisher's rejections for a manuscript is 137 for *One Man versus the Establishment* by William E. E. Owens of Street, Somerset on a revised form of government.

Oldest authoress
The oldest authoress in the world was Mrs Alice Pollock (*née* Wykeham-Martin (1868–1971), of Haslemere, Surrey, whose book *Portrait of My Victorian Youth* (Johnson Publications) was published in March 1971 when she was aged 102 years 8 months.

Youngest
The youngest recorded commercially published author is Dorothy Straight (b. 25 May 1958) of Washington DC, who wrote *How the World Began* in 1962 aged 4 which was published in August 1964 by Pantheon Books, New York.

Longest literary gestation
The standard German dictionary *Deutsches Wörterbuch*, begun by the brothers Grimm in 1854, was finished in 1971. *Acta Sanctorum* begun by Jean Bolland in 1643, arranged according to saints' days, reached the month of November in 1925 and an introduction for December was published in 1940.

Poet Laureate *Youngest and oldest*
The youngest Poet Laureate was Laurence Eusden (1688–1730), who received the bays on 24 Dec 1718 at the age of 30 years and 3 months. The greatest age at which a poet has succeeded is 73 in the case of William Wordsworth (1770–1850) on 6 Apr 1843. The longest lived Laureate was John Masefield, OM, who died on 12 May 1967, aged 88 years 345 days. The longest which any poet has worn the laurel is 41 years 322 days, in the case of Alfred (later the 1st Lord) Tennyson (1809–92), who was appointed on 19 Nov 1850 and died in office on 6 Oct 1892.

Longest poem
The lengthiest poem ever published has been the Kirghiz folk epic *Manas*, which appeared in printed form in 1958 but which has never been translated into English. It runs to 'more than 500,000 lines'. Short translated passages appear in *The Elek Book of Oriental Verse*.

The longest poem ever written in the English language is one on the life of King Alfred by John Fitchett (1766–1838) of Liverpool which ran to 129,807 lines and took 40 years to write. His editor Robert Riscoe added the concluding 2585 lines.

Roger Brien's (b. Montreal, 1910) *Prométhée—dialogues des vivants et des morts* runs to 262,008 lines. Brien has written another 440,000 lines of French poetry in over 90 published works.

Most Successful
The most translated poem is believed to be *If* by Joseph Rudyard Kipling (1865–1936), first published in 1910. It was put into 27 languages and according to Kipling 'anthologized to weariness'.

HIGHEST PRINTINGS
World
The world's most widely distributed book is the Bible, portions of which have been translated into 1710 languages. This compares with 222 languages by Lenin. It has been estimated that between 1815 and 1975 some 2,500,000,000 copies were printed of which 1,500,000,000 were handled by Bible Societies. The total distribution of complete Bibles by the United Bible Societies (covering 150 countries) in the year 1980 was 9,653,508.

It has been reported that 800,000,000 copies of the red-covered booklet *Quotations from the Works of Mao Tse-tung* were sold or

Edward Robb Ellis of New York whose diary is estimated to run to 15 million words (see p. 98).
(above: Jeff Meyerowitz, right: Ed Rasmussen)

distributed between June 1966, when possession became virtually mandatory in China, and September 1971 when their promoter Marshal Lin Piao was killed.

Non fiction

The total disposal through non-commercial channels by Jehovah's Witnesses of the 192 page hard bound book *The Truth That Leads to Eternal Life* published by the Watchtower Bible and Tract Society of Brooklyn, New York, on 8 May 1968, reached 100 million in 115 languages by 1 Apr 1981.

BEST SELLERS

The world's all-time best *selling* copyright book is the *Guinness Book of Records* first published from 107 Fleet Street, London EC4 in September 1955 by the Guinness Brewery to settle arguments in Britain's 81,400 pubs and edited by Norris Dewar McWhirter (b. 12 Aug 1925) and his twin brother Alan Ross McWhirter (k. 27 Nov 1975). Its cumulative sale in 23 languages to mid-1981 is estimated at over 42 million copies increasing by some 60,000 per week.

Best Seller Lists

The *Sunday Times* best seller list (which excludes books published annually) was first published on 14 Apr 1974. *The Country Diary of an Edwardian Lady* (publisher Michael Joseph) held No 1 position for 59 consecutive weeks up to the paper's 10 month closure which started on 30 Nov 1978.

Fiction

The novel with the highest sales has been *Valley of the Dolls* (first published March 1966) by Jacqueline Susann (Mrs Irving Mansfield) (1921–74) with a world-wide total of 23,686,000 to 1 May 1981. In the first 6 months Bantam sold 6.8 million. In the United Kingdom the highest print order has been 3,000,000 by Penguin Books Ltd. for their paperback edition of *Lady Chatterley's Lover*, by D. H. (David Herbert) Lawrence (1885–1930). The total sales to Jan 1981 were 4,316,759. Alistair Stuart MacLean (b. Scotland, April 1922) between 1955 and 1980 wrote 24 books of which the sales of 18 have exceeded a million copies and 13 have been filmed. *The Cruel Sea* by Nicholas Monsarrat (1910–79) published in 1951 by Cassell, reached sales of 1,200,000 in its *original* edition.

Fastest Publisher

The fastest time in which a book has been published is 46½ hours from receipt of manuscript to finished copies, in the case of *Miracle on Ice* by the staff of *The New York Times* on 27–28–29 Feb 1980. The 96 page story of the US Olympic gold medal ice hockey team was published by Bantam Books Inc.

Slowest seller

The accolade for the world's slowest selling book (known in US publishing as slooow-sellers) probably belongs to David Wilkins's Translation of the New Testament from Coptic into Latin published by Oxford University Press in 1716 in 500 copies. Selling an average of one each 139 days, it was in print for 191 years.

Shortest Review

The Calgary Herald book critic Brian Brennan, after years of frustration as a would-be record-breaker, finally submitted a 3 letter review on our 1980 US edition used on the TV serial *Soap*. It was published on 1 Dec 1979 and merely said 'Wow!'.

PUBLISHERS AND PRINTERS

Publishing

In terms of new titles per annum Britain's most prolific publisher in 1980 was Robert Hale Ltd (founded 1936) with 713 in 1980. The UK published a record 48,158 book titles in 1980 of which a record 10,776 were reprints.

Largest Printer *World*

The largest printers in the world are R. R. Donnelley & Sons Co. of Chicago, Illinois, USA. The company, founded in 1864, has plants in 15 main centres, turning out $957,000,000 (*£435 million*) worth of work per year. More than 60,000 tons of inks and 1,000,000 tons of paper and board are consumed every year.

The largest printer under one roof is the United States Government Printing Office (founded 1860) in Washington, DC, USA. The Superintendent of Documents Division dispatches items worth nearly $48 million (*£20 million*) every year. The inventory is maintained at 25,000 titles in print.

Print order

The initial print order for the 51st Automobile Association Members' Handbook (1980–1) was 4,800,000 copies. The total print since 1908 has been 77,200,000. It is currently printed b web offset by Petty & Sons of Leeds.

LIBRARIES

Largest *World*

The largest library in the world is the United States Library of Congress (founded on 24 Apr 1800), on Capitol Hill, Washington, DC. By 1980 it contained 76,945,360 items, including 19,155,165 volumes and pamphlets. The buildings contain 64. acres *26,14 ha* of floor space and contain 532 miles *856 km* of shelving. The James Madison Memorial Extension was dedicated in April 1980 and has 34.5 acres *14 ha* of floor space.

The largest non-statutory library in the world is the New York Public Library (founded 1895) on Fifth Avenue with a floor space of 525,276 ft² *48 800 m²* and 78.8 miles *126,8 km* of shelving. Its collection including 83 branch libraries embrace 10,018,241 volumes, 11,539,193 manuscripts and 342,06 maps.

Great Britain

The largest library in the United Kingdom is the British Library, dispersed among 18 buildings in London and a 60 acr *24,3 ha* site at Boston Spa, West Yorkshire, with a total staff of over 2000. The British Library Reference Division comprise the former library departments of the British Museum. It contains over 10 million books, and takes in more than 90,000 *different* journals. Under the Copyright Act a copy of every UK publication must be deposited with the British Library an much is acquired from overseas by purchase or exchange. Stock increases involve over 4.5 miles *7.2 km* of additional shelving annually. The British Library's Newspaper Library at Colindale, North London, opened in 1932, has 650,000 volumes and parcels and 95,000 reels of microfilm comprising 45,000 different titles on 20 miles *32 km* of shelving. The British Library Lending Division in West Yorkshire (shelf capacity 96 mile *154,5 km*) runs the largest library inter-lending operation in the world; it handles annually nearly 3 million requests from other libraries (UK and overseas) for items they do not hold in stock. The largest public library in the United Kingdom is the extended Mitchell Library, North Street, Glasgow with a floor area of 510,000 ft² *47 380 m²* or 11.7 acres *4,7 ha* and an ultimate capacity for 4,000,000 volumes. The oldest public library in Scotland is in Kirkwall, Orkney, founded in 1683.

Overdue books

The most overdue book taken out by a known borrower was one reported on 7 Dec 1968, checked out in 1823 from the University of Cincinnati Medical Library on Febrile Diseases (London, 1805 by Dr J. Currie). This was returned by the borrower' great-grandson Richard Dodd. The fine calculated to be $226 (*then £1102 10s*) was waived.

PERIODICALS

Oldest *World*

The oldest continuing periodical in the world is *Philosophica Transactions of the Royal Society*, published in London, which first appeared on 6 Mar 1665.

Great Britain

The Botanical Magazine has been in continuous publication since 1787, as several 'parts' a year forming a series of continuously numbered volumes. Britain's oldest weekly periodical is *Lancet* first published in 1823. The *Scots Magazine* began publication in 1739 and ran till 1826, and with three breaks has been produced continuously since 1924.

Largest circulation *World*

The largest circulation of any weekly periodical is that of *TV Guide* (USA) which in 1974 became the first magazine in history to sell a billion (1000 million) copies in a year. The weekly average for July–December 1980 was 17,981,657. In its 40 basic international editions *The Reader's Digest* (established February

1922) circulates 30,695,000 copies monthly in 16 languages, including a United States edition of more than 17,750,000 copies and a United Kingdom edition (established 1939) of 1,596,837 copies (av. January–December 1980).

Parade, the syndicated Sunday newspaper colour supplement, is distributed with 130 newspapers every Sunday. The current circulation is 21,967,421 (March 1981).

Great Britain
The highest circulation of any periodical in Great Britain is that of the *Radio Times* (instituted on 28 Sept 1923). The average weekly sale for July–December 1980 was 3,373,030 copies with a readership of 9,499,000. The highest sale of any issue was 9,778,062 copies for the Christmas issue of 1955. *TV Times* averaged sales of 3,113,608 in the period July–Dec 1980 with an estimated readership of 9,319,000 (July–December 1980).

Annual
Old Moore's Almanack has been published annually since 1697, when it first appeared as a broadsheet, by Dr Francis Moore (1657–1715) of Southwark, London to advertise his 'physiks'. The annual sale certified by its publishers W. Foulsham & Co. Ltd of Slough England is 1 million copies and its aggregate sale is estimated to be in excess of 108 million.

NEWSPAPERS

Oldest World
The oldest existing newspaper in the world is the Swedish official journal *Post och Inrikes Tidningar*, founded in 1645. It is published by the Royal Swedish Academy of Letters. The oldest existing commercial newspaper is the *Haarlems Dagblad/Oprechte Haarlemsche Courant*, published in Haarlem, in the Netherlands. The *Courant* was first issued as the *Weeckelycke Courante van Europa* on 8 Jan 1656 and a copy of issue No. 1 survives.

United Kingdom
The oldest continuously produced newspaper in the United Kingdom is *Berrow's Worcester Journal* (originally the *Worcester Post Man*), published in Worcester. It was traditionally founded in 1690 and has appeared weekly since June 1709. The *Belfast News Letter* has been published since 16 Feb 1737/38 and the *Public Ledger* daily since 12 Jan 1760. The oldest newspaper in the United Kingdom is *Lloyd's List*, the shipping intelligence bulletin of Lloyd's London, established as a weekly *c.* 1729 and as a bi-weekly on 2 Jan 1740/1. The *London Gazette* (originally the *Oxford Gazette*) was first published on 16 Nov 1665. The oldest Sunday newspaper in the United Kingdom is *The Observer*, first issued on 4 Dec 1791.

Largest and smallest
The most massive single issue of a newspaper was the 7½ lb *3,40 kg New York Times* of Sunday 17 Oct 1965. It comprised 15 sections with a total of 946 pages, including about 1,200,000 lines of advertising. The largest page size ever used has been 51 in × 35 in *130 cm × 89 cm* for *The Constellation*, printed in 1859 by George Roberts as part of the Fourth of July celebrations in New York City, NY, USA. The *Worcestershire Chronicle* was the largest British newspaper. A surviving issue of 16 Feb 1859 measures 32¼ in × 22½ in *82 cm × 57 cm*. The smallest recorded page size has been 3 × 3¾ in *7,6 × 9,5 cm* of the *Daily Banner* (25 cents per month) of Roseberg, Oregon, USA, issues of which, dated 1 and 2 Feb 1876, survive. The *Answers to Correspondents* published by Messrs Carr & Co, Paternoster Square, London in 1888 was 3½ × 4½ in *9 × 11 cm*.

Most expensive
Britain's most expensive paper is *The Sunday Times* at 35p or 7s in the money prior to 15 Feb 1971, or 40 per cent higher than the price of the original 1955 fully bound edition of this publication.

Most
The United States had 1769 English-language daily newspapers at 1 Oct 1979 with a combined net paid circulation of 62,088,960 copies per day. The peak year for US newspapers was 1910, when there were 2202. The leading newspaper readers in the world are the people of Sweden, where 564 newspapers were sold for each 1000 compared with the UK figure of 438.

Longest editorship
The longest editorship of any national newspaper has been more than 59 years by C. P. Scott (1846–1932) of the (then *Manchester*) *Guardian*, who was appointed aged 25 in 1872 and died on 1 Jan 1932. John Watson was editor of the South Australian newspaper *The Border Watch* from 1863 to December 1925—a span of 62 years. Robert Edwards was 4 times appointed editor of a national paper—*Daily Express* (1961); *Daily Express* (1963); *Sunday People* (1966) and *Sunday Mirror* (1972). Dr Thomas Riddle DD (b. 18 Apr 1886) was still editor-in-chief of *The Christian Herald* in April 1981 aged 95 years.

Most durable feature
The longest lasting feature in the British national press from one pen is *Your Stars* by Edward Lyndoe. It has run since 1 Oct 1933 in *The Sunday People*. Frank Lowe has contributed a weekly natural history column to the *Bolton Evening News* every week since 4 Feb 1926.

Most syndicated cartoonist
Ranan R. Lurie (b. 26 May 1932) is the most widely syndicated political cartoonist in the world. His work is published in 45 countries.

Longest lived strip
The most durable newspaper comic strip has been the Katzenjammer Kids (Hans and Fritz) created by Rudolph Dirks and first published in the *New York Journal* on 12 Dec 1897 and perpetuated by his son John. The earliest strip was The Yellow Kid, which first appeared in the New York *Journal* on 18 Oct 1896. The most widely syndicated is *Blondie* (originated in 1930) appearing in 1800 newspapers in 59 countries and in 19 languages.

Most misprints
The record for misprints in *The Times* was set on 22 Aug 1978 when on page 19 there were 97 in 5½ single column inches. The passage concerned 'Pop' (Pope) Paul VI.

Most durable advertiser
The Jos Neel Co, a clothing store in Macon, Georgia, USA (founded 1880) has run an 'ad' in the *Macon Telegraph* every day in the upper left corner of page 2 since 22 Feb 1889 or 30,338 times to mid-1981.

CIRCULATION

Earliest 1,000,000
The first newspaper to achieve a circulation of 1,000,000 was *Le Petit Journal*, published in Paris, France, which reached this figure in 1886, when selling at 5 centimes. The *Daily Mail* first reached a million in May 1900.

Highest World
The highest circulation for any newspaper in the world is that for the *Yomiuri Shimbun* (founded 1874) of Japan which attained a figure of 13,741,921 copies on 1 April 1981. This is achieved by totalling the figures for editions published in various centres with a morning figure of 8,785,477 and an evening figure of 4,956,444.

Great Britain
The highest circulation of any single newspaper in Britain is that of the Sunday newspaper *The News of the World*, printed in Bouverie Street, London. Single issues have attained a sale of 9,000,000 copies with an estimated readership of more than 19,000,000. The paper first appeared on 1 Oct 1843, and surpassed the million mark in 1905. The latest sales figure is 4,197,652 copies per issue (average for 1 July to 31 December 1980), with an estimated readership of 11,369,000.

The highest net sale of any daily newspaper in the United Kingdom is that of *The Sun*, founded in London in 1964. The latest sales figure is 3,741,373 (July–December 1980), with an estimated readership of 11,327,000.

Most read
The newspaper which achieves the closest to a saturation circulation is *The Sunday Post*, established in Glasgow in 1914. In 1980 its estimated readership in Scotland of 2,903,000 represented 72 per cent of the entire population aged 15 and over.

101

CROSSWORDS

First

The earliest crossword was one with 32 clues invented by Arthur Wynne (b. Liverpool, England, d. 1945) and published in the *New York World* on 21 Dec 1913. The first crossword published in a British newspaper was one furnished by C. W. Shepherd in the *Sunday Express* of 2 Nov 1924. However a 25 letter acrostic of Roman provenance was discovered on a wall in Cirencester, England in 1868.

Largest

The world's largest published crossword is one compiled by Stephen Robinson of Coventry, England published by Onsworld Ltd of Stamford, Lincolnshire on 22 Oct. 1979. It contains 6257 clues across and 6051 down and covers 18.5 ft² *1,72 m²*. The largest crosswords regularly published are 'Mammoth' crosswords based on grids of 73 × 73 (5329) squares with up to 828 clues by First Features Ltd of Hastings, East Sussex since 1 May 1970.

Longest

A crossword compiled by Roger F. Squires and published in 1979 by Onsworld Ltd with over 1000 clues, measures 8 ft 0 in *2,43 m* in length.

Fastest and slowest solution

The fastest recorded time for completing *The Times* crossword under test conditions is 3 min 45.0 sec by Roy Dean, 43 of Bromley, Greater London in the BBC 'Today' radio studio on 19 Dec 1970. Dr John Sykes won the Cutty Sark/*Times* championship 4 times (1972–5). The only woman to reach a final has been Mrs Morar Ryton. In May 1966 *The Times* of London received an announcement from a Fijian woman that she had just succeeded in completing their crossword No. 673 in the issue of 4 Apr 1932.

Most durable compilers

Adrian Bell (b. 4 Oct 1901) of Barsham, Suffolk contributed a record 4327 crosswords to *The Times* from 2 Jan 1930 to 1 Mar 1975. R. J. Baddock of Plymouth (b. 30 Oct 1894) has been a regular contributor to national newspapers since 13 Aug 1926. Mrs Phyllis Harvey, 85, of Brighton from December 1924 to December 1979 completed 55 years of contributions to the *Evening News* Junior Cross Word (now Quick Crossword). The most prolific compiler is Roger F. Squires, who compiles 38 published puzzles single-handedly each week. His total output to August 1981 is estimated at over 18,000.

ADVERTISING RATES

The highest ever price for a single page has been $178,060 (*£80,940*) for a four-colour back cover in *Parade* (circulation 21 million per week) in May 1981 (see also page 107). The current record is $173,060 (*£78,600*) for a four colour page in *Parade* (in May 1981). The advertising revenue from the October 1978 US edition of *Readers Digest* was a peak $10,393,200 (*then £5,196,000*).

The highest expenditure ever incurred on a single advertisement in a periodical is $3,200,000 (*£1,600,000*) by Gulf and Western Industries on 5 Feb 1979 for insertions in *Time* Magazine (US and selected overseas editions). The British record is some £100,000 for a 20-page colour supplement by Woolworths in *The Radio Times* of 16 Nov 1972. The colour rate for a single page in *The Radio Times* reached £15,900 on 1 Jan 1981 and £19,400 for an outside back page in Oct/Dec 1981. The world's highest newspaper advertising rate is 31,695,000 Yen (*£65,350*) for a full page in the morning edition and 25,095,000 Yen (*£51,750*) for the evening edition of the *Yomiuri Shimbun* of Tokyo (April 1981). The highest rate in Britain is a full page in *The News of the World* at £29,736 (May 1981).

---

4. MUSIC

The Guinness Book of Music (2nd edition), by Robert and Celia Dearling with Brian Rust was published in Spring 1981 and contains more detailed treatment of musical facts and superlatives.

Origins

The world's oldest surviving musical notation dates from *c.* 1800 BC. A heptonic scale deciphered from a clay tablet by D Duchesne-Guillemin in 1966–7 was found at a site in Nippu Sumer, now Iraq. An Assyrian love song also *c.* 1800 BC to a Ugaritic god from a tablet of notation and lyric was reconstructed for an 11 string lyre at the University of California, Berkele on 6 Mar 1974. Musical history is, however, able to be trace back to the 3rd millennium BC, when the yellow bell (*huan chung*) had a recognised standard musical tone in Chinese templ music. Whistles and flutes made from perforated phalang bones have been found at Upper Palaeolithic sites of the Aurig nacian period (*c.* 25,000–22,000 BC) *e.g.* at Istallósкö, Hungar and in Molodova, USSR.

INSTRUMENTS

Piano Earliest

The earliest pianoforte in existence is one built in Florence Italy, in 1720 by Bartolommeo Cristofori (1655–1731) of Padua and now preserved in the Metropolitan Museum of Art, Ne York City.

Piano Grandest

The grandest grand piano built was one of 1¼ tons/*tonnes* 11 8 in *3,55 m* in length made by Chas. H. Challen & Son Ltd o London in 1935. The longest bass string measured 9 ft 11 i *3,02 m* and the tensile stress on the 6½ cwt *330 kg* frame was 3 tons/*tonnes*.

Piano *Most Expensive*

The highest price ever paid for a piano is $390,000 (*the £177,273*) at Sotheby Parke Bernet, New York City on 26 Ma 1980 for a Steinway grand of *c.* 1888 sold by the Martin Bec Theatre and bought by a non-pianist.

Organ largest *World*

The largest and loudest musical instrument ever constructed i the now only partially functional Auditorium Organ in Atlanti City, New Jersey, USA. Completed in 1930, this heroic instru ment has two consoles (one with seven manuals and anothe movable one with five), 1477 stop controls and 33,112 pipe ranging in tone from ³/₁₆ of an inch *4,7 mm* to the 64 ft *19 m* tone It is powered with blower motors of 365 horsepower *370 cv*, cos $500,000 (*then £102,880*) and has the volume of 25 brass band with a range of seven octaves. The grand organ at Wanamaker Store, Philadelphia, installed in 1911, was enlarged until b 1930 it had 6 manuals and 30,067 pipes including a 64 ft *19 m* tone Gravissima. The world's largest church organ is that i Passau Cathedral, Germany. It was completed in 1928 by D. F Steinmeyer & Co. It was built with 16,000 pipes and fiv manuals. The world's most versatile electric organ is the manual Kawai T.50 built in Japan in 1977 to mark the com pany's golden jubilee.

Great Britain

The largest organ in Great Britain is that completed in Liverpoo Anglican Cathedral on 18 Oct 1926, with two five-manual con soles of which only one is now in use, and 9704 speaking pipe (originally 10,936) ranging from tones of ¾ in to 32 ft *1,9 cm t 9,75 m*.

Organists *Most Durable*

The longest recorded reign as an organist has been 81 years i the case of Charles Bridgeman (1779–1873) of All Saints Paris Church, Hertford, England, who was appointed in 1792 an who was still playing in 1873. The year in which he reached hi crescendo was not recorded.

Loudest organ stop

The loudest organ stop in the world is the Ophicleide stop of th Grand Great in the Solo Organ in the Atlantic City Auditoriu (see above). It is operated by a pressure of 100 in *254 cm* of wate (3½ lb/in² *24 kPa*) and has a pure trumpet note of ear-splitting volume, more than six times the volume of the loudest loco motive whistles.

Brass instrument *Largest*

The largest recorded brass instrument is a tuba standing 7½ f *2,28 m* tall, with 39 ft *11,8 m* of tubing and a bell 3 ft 4 in *1 m* across. This contrabass tuba was constructed for a world tour b the band of John Philip Sousa (1854–1932), the United State composer, in *c.* 1896–8, and is still in use. This instrument is now owned by a circus promoter in South Africa.

Horns *Longest Alphorn*
The longest alphorn is one of 13,4 m *43 ft 11½ in* built from a spruce log by Herr Stocker in Switzerland in 1976. It weighs 32 kg *70½ lb* and was seen on the BBC TV *Record Breakers* Show transmitted on 27 Dec 1980.

Longest blow
The longest recorded blast on a hunting horn is 55.5 sec by Martin Dee of Blockley, Gloucestershire on a 9 in *22,8 cm* Cotswold horn on 19 Mar 1980.

Stringed instrument *Largest*
The largest movable stringed instrument ever constructed was a pantaleon with 270 strings stretched over 50 ft² *4,6 m²* used by George Noel in 1767. The greatest number of musicians required to operate a single instrument was the six required to play the gigantic orchestrion, known as the Apollonican, built in 1816 and played until 1840.

Guitar *Largest and Most Expensive*
The largest and presumably also the loudest playable guitar in the world is one 10 ft 1 in *3,07 m* tall built for Sparkling Ragtime Productions of San Francisco, USA in December 1980. The most expensive standard sized guitar is the German chittara battente by Jacob Stadler, dated 1624, which was sold for £10,500 at Christies, London on 12 June 1974.

Double bass *Largest*
The largest double bass ever constructed was one 14 ft *4,26 m* tall, built in 1924 in Ironia, New Jersey, USA by Arthur K. Ferris, allegedly on orders from the Archangel Gabriel. It weighed 11.6 cwt. *590 kg* with a sound box 8 ft *2,43 m* across, and had leathern strings totalling 104 ft *31,7 m*. Its low notes could be felt rather than heard.

'Cello *Most valuable*
The highest ever auction price for a violoncello is £145,000 at Sotheby's, London on 8 Nov 1978 for a Stradivari made in Cremona, Italy in 1710.

Violin *Most valuable*
The highest ever price paid at auction for a violin is $290,000 (*then £145,000*) for the 'Huberman' *ex* Kreisler Stradivari dated 1733 at Sotheby's, London on 3 May 1979. Some 700 of the 1116 violins by Stradivarius (1644–1737) have survived. His inlaid 'Hellier' violin was sold by private treaty in the U.S. in March 1979 for a reputed $400,000 (*then £200,000*).

Violinist *Underwater*
The only violinist to surmount the problems of playing the violin underwater has been Mark Gottlieb. Submerged in Evergreen State College swimming bath in Olympia, Washington, USA in March 1975 he gave a submarine rendition of Handel's Water Music. He is still working on the problem of bow speed and *détaché*.

Most durable fiddler
Otto E. Funk, 62, walked 4165 miles *6702 km* from New York City to San Francisco, California playing his Hopf violin every step of the way westward. He arrived on 16 June 1929 after 183 days on the road. Rolland S. Tapley retired as a violinist from the Boston Symphony Orchestra after playing for a reputedly unrivalled 58 years from February 1920 to 27 Aug 1978.

Drum *Largest*
The largest drum in the world is the Disneyland Big Bass Drum with a diameter of 10 ft 6 in *3,2 m* and a weight of 450 lb *204 kg*. It was built in 1961 by Remo Inc. of North Hollywood, California, USA and is mounted on wheels and towed by a tractor.

Highest and lowest notes
The extremes of orchestral instruments (excluding the organ) range between a handbell tuned to g^v (6272 cycles/sec) and the sub-contrabass clarinet, which can reach C_{11} or 16.4 cycles/sec. The highest note on a standard pianoforte is c^v (4186 cycles/sec), which is also the violinist's limit. In 1873 a sub double bassoon

able to reach B_{111} # or 14.6 cycles/sec was constructed but no surviving specimen is known. The extremes for the organ are g^{vi} (the sixth G above middle C) (12,544 cycles/sec) and C_{111} (8.12 cycles/sec) obtainable from ¾ in *1,9 cm* and 64 ft *19 m* pipes respectively.

Easiest and most difficult instruments
The American Music Conference announced in September 1977 that the easiest instrument is the ukulele, and the most difficult are the French horn and the oboe, which latter has been described as 'the ill woodwind that no-one blows good'.

ORCHESTRAS
Largest *Orchestra*
The most massive orchestra ever assembled was one of 20,100 at the Ullevaal Stadium, Oslo, of Norges Musikkorps Forbund bands from all Norway on 28 June 1964. On 17 June 1872, Johann Strauss the younger (1825–99) conducted an orchestra of 987 pieces supported by a choir of 20,000, at the World Peace Jubilee in Boston, Massachussetts, USA. The number of first violinists was 400.

Marching band
The largest marching band on record was one of 1976 musicians and 54 drill majors, flag bearers and directors who marched 2 miles *3,2 km* down Pennsylvania Avenue in President Nixon's Inaugural Parade on 20 Jan 1973. The longest recorded musical march is one of 61 km *37.9 miles* from Lillehammer to Hamar, Norway in 15 hours when, on 10 May 1980, 26 of 35 members of the Trondheim Brass Band survived the playing of 135 marches.

Most successful bands
Most British Open Brass band Championship titles (inst. 1853) have been won by the Black Dyke Mills Band which has won 22 times from 1862 to 1974 including three consecutive wins in 1972–4. The most successful pipe band is the Shotts & Dykehead Caledonian Pipe Band with their 10th world title in August 1980.

Greatest attendance *Classical*
The greatest attendance at any classical concert has been 400,000 for the Boston Pops Orchestra, conducted by Arthur Fiedler (1895–1979) at the Hatch Memorial Shell, Boston, Massachusetts, USA on 4 July 1976. At the 1978 concert the 83-year-old conductor was presented with a testimonial bearing a record 500,000 signatures.

Pop Festival
The greatest claimed attendance at a Pop Festival has been 600,000 for the 'Summer Jam' at Watkins Glen, New York, USA, on Sunday 29 July 1973 of whom about 150,000 actually paid. There were 12 'sound towers'. The attendance at the third Pop Festival at East Afton Farm, Freshwater, Isle of Wight, England on 30 Aug 1970 was claimed by its promoters, Fiery Creations, to be 400,000.

Single Performer
The largest live audience ever attracted by a solo performer is an estimated 175,000 in the Maracaña Stadium, Rio de Janiero, Brazil to hear Frank Sinatra (b. 1915) on 26 Jan 1980.

COMPOSERS
Most prolific
The most prolific composer of all time was probably Georg Philipp Telemann (1681–1767) of Germany. He composed 12 complete sets of services (one cantata every Sunday) for a year, 78 services for special occasions, 40 operas, 600 to 700 orchestral suites, 44 Passions, plus concertos and chamber music. The most prolific symphonist was Johann Melchior Molter (c. 1695–1765) of Germany who wrote 165. Joseph Haydn (1732–1809) of Austria wrote 104 numbered symphonies some of which are regularly played today.

Most rapid
Among composers of the classical period the most prolific was Wolfgang Amadeus Mozart (1756–91) of Austria, who wrote *c.* 1000 operas, operettas, symphonies, violin sonatas, divertimenti, serenades, motets, concertos for piano and many other instruments, string quartets, other chamber music, masses and litanies, of which only 70 were published before he died aged 35.

Havergal Brian, composer of the Gothic Symphony which recently required 1 hr 45½ min to broadcast.

His opera *The Clemency of Titus* (1791) was written in 18 days and three symphonic masterpieces, *Symphony No. 39 in E flat major*, *Symphony in G minor* and the *Jupiter Symphony in C*, were reputedly written in the space of 42 days in 1788. His overture *Don Giovanni* was written in full score at one sitting in Prague in 1787 and finished on the day of its opening performance.

Longest symphony

The longest of all single classical symphonies is the orchestral symphony No. 3 in D minor by Gustav Mahler (1860–1911) of Austria. This work, composed in 1896, requires a contralto, a women's and boys' choir in addition to a full orchestra. A full performance requires 1 hr 40 min, of which the first movement alone takes between 30 and 36 min. The Symphony No. 2 (the Gothic, or No. 1), composed in 1919–22 by Havergal Brian (1876–1972) was played by over 800 performers (4 brass bands) in the Victoria Hall, Hanley, Staffordshire on 21 May 1978 (conductor Trevor Stokes). A recent broadcast required 1 hr 45½ min. Brian wrote an even vaster work based on Shelley's 'Prometheus Unbound' lasting 4 hr 11 min but the full score has been missing since 1961.

The symphony *Victory at Sea* written by Richard Rodgers and arranged by Robert Russell Bennett for NBC TV in 1952 lasted for 13 hr.

Longest piano composition

The longest continuous non-repetitious piece for piano ever specifically composed for the piano has been 'The Well-Tuned Piano' by La Monte Young first presented by the Dia Art Foundation at the Concert Hall, Harrison St. New York City on 28 Feb 1980. The piece lasted 4 hr 12 min 10 secs.

Longest silence

The most protracted silence in a modern sheet music is one entitled *4 minutes 33 seconds* in a totally silent *opus* by John Cage (USA). Commenting on this trend among young composers, Igor Fyodorovich Stravinsky (1882–1971) said that he looked forward to their subsequent compositions being 'works of major length'. The longest subsequently submitted, though not marketed, by a serious composer has been a modest 12¾ minutes 'composed' on 30 June 1979.

HIGHEST PAID MUSICIANS
Pianist

Wladziu Valentino Liberace (b. West Allis, Wisconsin, USA, 16 May 1917) earns more than $2 million each 26 week season with a peak of $138,000 (*then £49,285*) for a single night's performance at Madison Square Gardens, New York City, USA in 1954.

The highest paid classical concert pianist was Ignace Jan Paderewski (1860–1941), Prime Minister of Poland (1919–20), who accumulated a fortune estimated at $5,000,000, of which $500,000 (*then £110,000*) was earned in a single season in 1922–23. The *nouveau riche* wife of a US industrialist once required him to play behind a curtain.

Singer *Most Successful*

Of great fortunes earned by singers, the highest on record are those of Enrico Caruso (1873–1921), the Italian tenor, whose estate was about $9,000,000 (*then £1,875,000*) and the Italian-Spanish coloratura soprano Amelita Galli-Curci (1889–1963), who received about $3,000,000 (£750,000). In 1850, up to $653 was paid for a single seat at the concerts given in the United States by Johanna ('Jenny') Maria Lind, later Mrs Otto Goldschmidt (1820–87), the 'Swedish Nightingale'. She had a range from g to e^{III} of which the middle register is still regarded as unrivalled. The tenor Count John Francis McCormack (1884–1945) of Ireland gave up to 10 concerts to capacity audiences in a single season in New York City.

Worst

While no agreement exists as to the identity of history's greatest singer, there is unanimity on the worst. The excursions of the soprano Florence Foster Jenkins (1868–1944) into lieder and even high coloratura culminated on 25 Oct 1944 in her sell-out concert at the Carnegie Hall, New York, USA. The diva's (already high) high F was said to have been made higher in 1943 by a crash in a taxi. It is one of the tragedies of musicology that Madame Jenkins' *Clavelitos*, accompanied by Cosme McMoon, was never recorded for posterity. Her latter day rival is Mrs Hazel Saunders of Clent, Hereford & Worcester.

Violinist

The Austrian-born Fritz Kreisler (1875–1962) is reputed to have received more than £1,000,000 in his career.

Greatest Span

Sergei Vassilievitch Rachmaninov (1873–1953) had a span of 12 white notes and could play a left hand chord of C, E♭, G, C, G.

OPERA
Longest

The longest of commonly performed operas is *Die Meistersinger von Nürnberg* by Wilhelm Richard Wagner (1813–83) of Germany. A normal uncut performance of this opera as performed by the Sadler's Wells company between 24 Aug and 19 Sept 1968 entailed 5 hr 15 min of music. *The Heretics* by Gabriel von Wayditch, a Hungarian-American, is orchestrated for 110 pieces and lasts 8½ hr.

Shortest

The shortest opera published was *The Deliverance of Theseus* by Darius Milhaud (b. September 1892) first performed in 1928 which lasts for 7 min 27 sec.

Aria

The longest single aria, in the sense of an operatic solo, is Brünnhilde's immolation scene in Wagner's *Gotterdammerung*. A well-known recording of this has been precisely timed at 14 min 46 sec.

Opera houses *Largest*

The largest opera house in the world is the Metropolitan Opera House, Lincoln Center, New York City, NY, USA, completed in September 1966 at a cost of $45,700,000 (*then £16,320,000*). It has a capacity of 3800 seats in an auditorium 451 ft *137 m* deep. The stage is 234 ft *71 m* wide and 146 ft *44,5 m* deep. The tallest opera house is one housed in a 42-storey building on Wacker Drive in Chicago, Illinois, USA.

Most tiers

The Teatro della Scala (La Scala) in Milan, Italy, shares with the Bolshoi Theatre in Moscow, USSR, the distinction of having the greatest number of tiers. Each has six, with the topmost being nicknamed the *Galiorka* by Russians.

Opera singers *Youngest and Oldest*

The youngest opera singer in the world has been Jeanette Gloria La Bianca, born in Buffalo, New York on 12 May 1934, who sang Rosina in *The Barber of Seville* at the Teatro dell'Opera, Rome, on 8 May 1950 aged 15 years 361 days, having appeared as Gilda in *Rigoletto* at Velletri 45 days earlier. Ginetta La Bianca was taught by Lucia Carlino and managed by Angelo Carlino. The tenor Giovanni Martinelli sang Emperor Altoum in *Turandot* in Seattle, Washington, USA on 4 Feb 1967 when aged 81.

Longest encore

The longest operatic encore, listed in the *Concise Oxford Dictionary of Opera*, was of the entire opera Cimarosa's' *Il Matrimonio Segreto* at its première in 1792. This was at the request of the Austro-Hungarian Emperor Leopold II (1790–92).

SONG

Oldest

The oldest known song is the *shaduf* chant, which has been sung since time immemorial by irrigation workers on the man-powered pivoted-rod bucket raisers of the Nile water mills (or *saqiyas*) in Egypt. The oldest known harmonized music performed today is the English song *Sumer is icumen in* which dates from *c*. 1240.

National anthems

The oldest national anthem is the *Kimigayo* of Japan, in which the words date from the 9th century. The anthem of Greece constitutes the first four verses of the Solomos poem, which has 158 stanzas. The shortest anthems are those of Japan, Jordan and San Marino, each with only four lines. Of the 23 wordless national anthems the oldest is that of Spain dating from 1770.

Longest rendering

'God Save the King' was played non-stop 16 or 17 times by a German military band on the platform of Rathenau Railway Station, Brandenburg, on the morning of 9 Feb 1909. The reason was that King Edward VII was struggling inside the train with the uniform of a German Field-Marshal before he could emerge.

Top songs of all time

The most frequently sung songs in English are *Happy Birthday to You* (based on the original *Good morning to all*), by Mildred and Patty S. Hill of New York (published in 1935 and in copyright until 2010); *For He's a Jolly Good Fellow* (originally the French *Malbrouk*), known at least as early as 1781, and *Auld Lang Syne* (originally the Strathspey *I fee'd a Lad at Michaelmass*), some words of which were written by Robert Burns (1759–96). *Happy Birthday* was sung in space by the Apollo IX astronauts on 8 Mar 1969.

Top selling sheet music

Sales of three non-copyright pieces are known to have exceeded 20,000,000 namely *The Old Folks at Home* by Stephen Foster (1855), *Listen to the Mocking Bird* (1855) and *The Blue Danube* (1867). Of copyright material the two topsellers are *Let Me Call You Sweetheart* (1910, by Whitson and Friedman) and *Till We Meet Again* (1918, by Egan and Whiting) each with some 6,000,000 by 1967. Other huge sellers have been *St Louis Blues*, *Stardust* and *Tea for Two*.

Most successful songwriter

In terms of sales of single records, the most successful of all song writers has been Paul McCartney (see also Gramophone, pp. 107–8) formerly of the Beatles and now of Wings. Between 1962 and 1 Jan 1978 he wrote jointly or solo 43 songs which sold a million or more.

Eurovision Contest

In the 25 contests since 1956 France has won 4 outright (1958–60–62–77) and shared 1 (1969). Luxembourg also won outright 4 times (1961–65–72–73).The UK won in 1967 (Sandie Shaw, *Puppet On A String*), 1976 (Brotherhood of Man, *Save Your Kisses For Me*), shared in 1969 (Lulu, *Boom, Bang-a-Bang*) and won in 1981 (Bucks Fizz, *Making your mind up*).

HYMNS

Earliest

There are more than 950,000 Christian hymns in existence. The earliest exactly datable hymn is the *Heyr Rimna Smiour* (*Hear, the maker of heaven*) from 1208 by the Icelandic bard and chieftain Kolbeinn Tumason (1173–1208). The music and parts of the text of a hymn in the *Oxyrhynchus Papyri* from the 2nd century are the earliest known hymnody.

Longest and shortest

The longest hymn is *Hora novissima tempora pessima sunt; vigilemus* by Bernard of Cluny (12th century), which runs to 2966 lines. In English the longest is *The Sands of Time are sinking* by

Mrs Anne Ross Cousin, *née* Cundell (1824–1906), which is in full 152 lines, though only 32 lines in the Methodist Hymn Book. The shortest hymn is the single verse in Long Metre *Be Present at our Table Lord*, anon., but attributed to 'J. Leland'.

Most prolific hymnists

Mrs Frances (Fanny) Jane Van Alstyne *née* Crosby (1820–1915) (USA) wrote 8500 hymns although she had been blinded at the age of 6 weeks. She is reputed to have knocked off one hymn in 15 min. Charles Wesley (1707–88) wrote about 6000 hymns. In the seventh (1950) edition of *Hymns Ancient and Modern* the works of John Mason Neale (1818–66) appear 56 times.

BELLS

Oldest *World*

The oldest bell in the world is the tintinnabulum found in the Babylonian Palace of Nimrod in 1849 by Mr (later Sir) Austen Henry Layard (1817–94) dating from *c*. 1100 BC. The oldest known tower bell is one in Pisa, Italy dated MCXVII (1107).

Great Britain

The fragile hand bell known as the Black or Iron Bell of St. Patrick is dated *c*. AD 450. The oldest tower bell in Great Britain is one of 1 cwt *50 kg* at St Botolph, Handham, Sussex still in use but dated *ante* 1100. The oldest inscribed bell is the Gargate bell at Caversfield church, Oxfordshire and is dated *c*. 1200–1210. The oldest *dated* bell in England is one hanging in Lissett church, near Bridlington, Humberside discovered in October 1972 to bear the date MCCLIIII (1254).

Heaviest *World*

The heaviest bell in the world is the Tsar Kolokol, cast on 25 Nov 1735 in Moscow, USSR. It weighs 193 tons *196 tonnes*, measures 5,9 m *19 ft 4¼ in* diameter and 5,87 m *19 ft 3 in* high, and its greatest thickness is 24 in *60 cm*. The bell is cracked, and a fragment, weighing about 11 tons/*tonnes* was broken from it. The bell has stood, unrung, on a platform in the Kremlin, in Moscow, since 1836.

The heaviest bell in use is the Mingun bell, weighing 55,555 viss or *90,52 tons* with a diameter of 16 ft 8½ in *5,09 m* at the lip, in Mandalay, Burma, which is struck by a teak boom from the outside. It was cast at Mingun late in the reign of King Bodawpaya (1782–1819). The heaviest swinging bell in the world is the Petersglocke in the South-West tower of Cologne Cathedral, Germany, cast in 1923 with a diameter of 3,40 m *11 ft 1¾ in* weighing 25,4 tonnes *25.0 tons*.

Great Britain

The heaviest bell hung in Great Britain is 'Great Paul' in the south-west tower of St Paul's Cathedral, London, cast in 1881. It weighs 16 tons 14 cwt 2 qrs 19 lb net *17002 kg* and has a diameter of 9 ft 6½ in *2,90 m* and sounds note E-flat. 'Big Ben', the hour bell in the clock tower of the House of Commons, was cast in 1858 and weighs 13 tons 10 cwt 3 qrs 15 lb *13 761 kg*. It is the most broadcast bell in the world and is note E.

Ringing Peals

A ringing peal is defined as a diatonic 'ring' of five or more bells hung for full-circle change ringing. Of 5,500 rings so hung only 70 are outside the United Kingdom and Ireland. The heaviest ring in the world is that of 13 bells cast in 1938–39 for the Anglican Cathedral, Liverpool. The total bell weight is 16½ tons *16,76 tonnes* of which Emmanuel, the tenor bell note A, weighs 82 cwt 11 lb *4170,8 kg*.

Carillon *Largest*

The largest carillon (minimum of 23 bells) in the world is the Laura Spelman Rockefeller Memorial carillon in Riverside Church, New York City, USA with 74 bells weighing 102 tons. The bourdon, giving the note lower C, weighs 40,926 lb *18 563 kg*. This 18.27 ton bell, cast in England, with a diameter of 10 ft 2 in *3,09 cm* is the largest *tuned* bell in the world.

Heaviest

The heaviest carillon in Great Britain is in St Nicholas Church, Aberdeen, Scotland. It consists of 48 bells, the total weight of which is 25 tons 8 cwt 2 qrs 13 lb *25 838 kg*. The bourdon bell weighs 4 tons 9 cwt 3 qrs 26 lb *4 571 kg* and is the note G-sharp.

Bell ringing

Eight bells have been rung to their full 'extent' (40,320 unrepeated changes of Plain Bob Major) only once without relays. This took place in a bell foundry at Loughborough, Leicestershire, beginning at 6.52 a.m. on 27 July 1963 and ending at 12.50 a.m. on 28 July, after 17 hr 58 min. The peal was composed by Kenneth Lewis of Altrincham, Greater Manchester, and the eight ringers were conducted by Robert B. Smith, aged 25, of Marple, Greater Manchester. Theoretically it would take 37 years 355 days to ring 12 bells (maximus) to their full extent of 479,001,600 changes. The greatest number of peals (minimum of 5040 changes, all in tower bells) rung in a year is 209 by Mark William Marshall of Ashford, Kent in 1973. The late George E. Fearn rang 2666 peals from 1928 to May 1974. Matthew Lakin (1801–1899) was a regular bell-ringer at Tetney Church near Grimsby for 84 years.

The longest running musical show in Britain *The Black and White Minstrel Show* which began on 25 May 1962 and finally closed on 8 Dec 1973 (see pp. 108–9). (*BBC TV*)

Currently the world's most successful pop group ABBA (left to right: Anni-Frid Lyngstad, Benny Andersson, Agnetha Faltskog and Bjorn Ulvaeus). Their world-wide earnings are reputedly a statistically significant part of Sweden's annual gross national product (see p. 107). (*Rex Features*)

5. GRAMOPHONE

Origins

The gramophone (phonograph) was first *conceived* by Charles Cros (1842–88) a French poet and scientist, who described his idea in sealed papers deposited in the French Academy of Sciences on 30 Apr 1877. However the realisation of a practical device was first *achieved* by Thomas Alva Edison (1847–1931) of the USA. The first successful machine was constructed by his mechanic, John Kruesi on 4–6 Dec 1877, demonstrated on 7 Dec and patented on 19 Feb 1878. Pre-recorded tapes were first marketed by Recording Associates in New York City, USA in 1950.

Earliest

The first practical hand cranked, wax coated cylinder phonograph was manufactured in the United States by Chichester Bell and Charles Sumner Tainter in 1886. The forerunner of the modern disc gramophone was patented in 1887 by Emile Berliner (1851–1929), a German immigrant to the USA. Although a toy machine based on his principle was produced in Germany in 1889, the gramophone was not a serious commercial competitor to the cylinder phonograph until 1896.

Most record players

The country with the greatest number of record players is the United States, with a total in excess of 75,000,000. A total of more than half a billion dollars (*now £225 million*) is spent annually on 500,000 juke boxes in the United States. In the US retail sales of discs and tapes reached $4100 million (*then £1440 million*) in 1978 which included sales of 273 million stereo LPs and 190 million singles and 127.8 million stereo tapes. In Sweden disc and tape sales were a record $17.92 (£9.95) per head in 1976.

Smallest record

The smallest functional gramophone record is one 1⅜ in *3,5 cm* in diameter of 'God Save the King' of which 250 were made by HMV Record Co in 1924.

Oldest records
The BBC record library contains over 750,000 records, including 5250 with no known matrix. An Edison solid wax cylinder, recorded in Edison's laboratory and dated 26 June 1888 is the oldest record in the library.

Earliest jazz records
The earliest jazz record made was *Indiana* and *The Dark Town Strutters Ball*, recorded for the Columbia label in New York City, NY, USA, on or about 30 Jan 1917, by the Original Dixieland Jazz Band, led by Dominick (Nick) James La Rocca (1889–1961). This was released on 31 May 1917. The first jazz record to be released was the ODJB's *Livery Stable Blues* (recorded 24 Feb), backed by *The Dixie Jass Band One-Step* (recorded 26 Feb), released by Victor on 7 Mar 1917.

Most successful solo recording artist
On 9 June 1960 the Hollywood Chamber of Commerce presented Harry Lillis (*alias* Bing) Crosby, Jr (1904–77) with a platinum disc to commemorate the alleged sale of 200,000,000 records from the 2600 singles and 125 albums he had recorded. On 15 Sept 1970 he received a second platinum disc when Decca claimed a sale of 300,650,000 discs. Crosby's first commercial recording was *I've Got the Girl* recorded on 18 Oct 1926 (master number W142785 [Take 3] issued on the Columbia label) and his first million-seller was *Sweet Leilani* in 1937. No independently audited figures of his global life-time sales from his royalty reports have ever been published and experts regard figures so high as this before the industry became highly developed, as exaggerated.

Similarly no independently audited figures have been published for Elvis Aron Presley (1935–77). In view of Presley's worldwide tally of over 170 major hits on singles and over 80 top-selling albums from 1956 continuing after his death, it may be assumed that it was he who succeeded Crosby as the top-selling solo artist of all-time.

Most successful group
The singers with the greatest sales of any group have been the Beatles. This group from Liverpool, Merseyside, comprised George Harrison, MBE (b. 25 Feb 1943), John Ono (formerly John Winston) Lennon, MBE (b. 9 Oct 1940–k. 16 Dec 1980), James Paul McCartney, MBE (b. 18 June 1942) and Richard Starkey, MBE *alias* Ringo Starr (b. 7 July 1940). The all-time Beatles sales by the end of 1980 have been estimated at over 100 million singles and over 100 million albums.

All 4 ex-Beatles have sold several million further records as solo artists. Since the break-up of the Beatles in 1970, it is estimated that the most successful group in the world in terms of record sales is the Swedish foursome ABBA (Agnetha Faltskog, Anni-Frid Lyngstad, Bjorn Ulvaeus and Benny Andersson).

Golden discs *Earliest*
The earliest recorded piece eventually to aggregate a total sale of a million copies were performances by Enrico Caruso (b. Naples, Italy, 1873, and d. 2 Aug 1921) of the aria *Vesti la giubba* (*On with the Motley*) from the opera *I Pagliacci* by Ruggiero Leoncavallo (1858–1919), the earliest version of which was recorded with piano on 12 Nov 1902. The first single recording to surpass the million mark was Alma Gluck's *Carry me back to old Virginny* on the Red Seal Victor label on the 12-inch *30,48 cm* single faced (later backed) record 74420. The first actual golden disc was one sprayed by RCA Victor for presentation to the US trombonist and band-leader Alton 'Glenn' Miller (1904–44) for his *Chattanooga Choo Choo* on 10 Feb 1942.

Most
The only *audited* measure of million-selling singles and 500,000 selling albums within the United States, is certification by the Recording Industry Association of America introduced 14 Mar 1958. Out of the 2841 RIAA gold record awards made to 20 May 1981, the most have gone to The Beatles with 42 (plus one with Billy Preston) as a group. McCartney has 21 more awards outside the group and with Wings. The most awards to an individual is 38 to Elvis Presley (1935–77) spanning 1958 to 20 May 1981. Globally however Presley's total of million-selling singles has been authoritatively put at 'approaching 80'.

Most recorded song
Two songs have each been recorded over 1000 times—*Yesterday* written by Paul McCartney and John Lennon (see above) with 1186 versions between 1965 and 1 Jan 1973 and *Tie A Yellow Ribbon Round the old Oak Tree* written by Irwin Levine and L. Russell Brown with more than 1000 from 1973 to 1 Jan 1979.

Most recordings
Miss Lata Mangeshker (b. 1928) between 1948 and 1974 has reportedly recorded not less than 25,000 solo, duet and chorus backed songs in 20 Indian languages. She frequently had 5 sessions in a day and has 'backed' 1800 films to 1974. Mohammed Rafi (d. 1 May 1980) claimed to have recorded 28,000 songs in 11 Indian languages between 1944 and April 1980.

Biggest sellers *Singles*
The greatest seller of any gramophone record to date is *White Christmas* by Irving Berlin (b. Israel Bailin, at Tyumen, Russia, 11 May 1888) with 25,000,000 for the Crosby single (recorded 29 May 1942) and more than 100,000,000 in other versions. The highest claim for any 'pop' record is an unaudited 25,000,000 for *Rock Around the Clock*, copyrighted in 1953 by James E. Myers under the name Jimmy DeKnight and the late Max C. Friedmann and recorded on 12 Apr 1954 by Bill Haley (1927–1981) and the Comets. The top-selling British record of all-time is *I Want to Hold Your Hand* by the Beatles, released in 1963, with world sales of over 13,000,000. The first single to sell over 2,000,000 copies in Great Britain was *Mull of Kintyre*, released in November 1977, by Wings, a group which includes Paul McCartney (see Beatles above), Linda McCartney (b. New York 24 Sept 1942) and Denny Laine (b. Jersey 29 Oct 1944). It was written by McCartney and Laine.

Albums
The best selling album of all time is the double album (4 sides) of the soundtrack of the film *Saturday Night Fever* with 25 million copies globally. The most popular of the songs were written by the Bee Gees comprising the Manx-born Gibb brothers Barry Alan (b. 1 Sept 1946) and the twins Robin and Maurice (b. 22 Dec 1949).

The best selling album by British performers is considered to be *Dark Side of the Moon* recorded by The Pink Floyd (Dave Gilmour, Nick Mason, Roger Waters and Rick Wright) in June 1972–January 1973 in London, with sales of at least 13 million by the end of 1980.

The charts—*US Singles*
Singles record charts were first published by *Billboard* on 20 July 1940 when the No. 1 was *I'll Never Smile Again* by Tommy Dorsey (b. 19 Nov 1905, d. 26 Nov 1956). Three discs have stayed top for a record 13 consecutive weeks—*Frenesi* by Artie Shaw from December 1940; *I've Heard that Song Before* by Harry James from February 1943 and *Goodnight Irene* by Gordon Jenkins and the Weavers from August 1950. *I go crazy* by Paul Davis stayed on the chart for 40 consecutive weeks from August 1977. The Beatles have had most No. 1 records (20) and Elvis Presley has had most hit singles on Billboard's Hot 100— 97 from 1956 to May 1981.

US Albums
Billboard first published an album chart on 15 Mar 1945 when the No. 1 was *King Cole Trio* featuring Nat 'King' Cole (b. 17 Mar 1919, d. 15 Feb 1965). *South Pacific* was No. 1 for 69 weeks (non-consecutive) from May 1949. *Johnny's Greatest Hits* by Johnny Mathis stayed in the chart for 490 weeks (over 9 years) from April 1958. The Beatles had most No. 1's (15) and Presley most hit albums (81 from 1956 to May 1981).

UK Singles
Singles record charts were first published in Britain on 14 Nov 1952 by *New Musical Express*. *I Believe* by Frankie Laine (b. 30 Mar 1913) held No. 1 position for 18 weeks (non-consecutive) from April 1953, with *Rose Marie* by Slim Whitman (b. 20 Jan 1924) the consecutive record holder with 11 weeks from July 1955. The longest stay has been the 122 weeks of *My Way* by Francis Albert Sinatra (b. 12 Dec 1917) in 9 separate runs from 2 Apr 1969 into 1972. The record for an uninterrupted stay is 56 weeks for Engelbert Humperdinck's *Release Me* from 26 Jan

107

1967. The Beatles and Presley hold the record for most No. 1 hits with 17 each, with Presley having an overall record of 98 hits in the UK singles chart from 1956 to 1 Jan 1981. The leading British chart maker is Cliff Richard (b. Harry Webb, 14 Oct 1940) with 72 (plus 1 with Olivia Newton-John) from 1958 to 1 Jan 1981.

The Guinness Book of British Hit Singles (3rd edition) *by Jo and Tim Rice with Paul Gambaccini and Mike Read (£4.99 paperback) lists every one of the 7000 plus records by approximately 2000 acts in the British Top 50 from 14 Nov 1952 to 1 Jan 1981.* The Guinness Book of Hits of the 70's *by the same authors is priced £4.95 paperback and £6.50 hardback.*

Fastest selling LPs

The fastest selling record of all time is *John Fitzgerald Kennedy—A Memorial Album* (Premium Albums), recorded on 22 Nov 1963, the day of Mr Kennedy's assassination, which sold 4,000,000 copies at 99 cents (*then 35p*) in six days (7–12 Dec 1963), thus ironically beating the previous speed record set by the satirical LP *The First Family* in 1962–3. The fastest selling British record is the Beatles' double album *The Beatles* (Apple) with 'nearly 2 million' in its first week in November 1968.

Advance sales

The greatest advance sale was 2,100,000 for *Can't Buy Me Love* by the Beatles, released in the United States on 16 Mar 1964. The Beatles also equalled their British record of 1,000,000 advance sales, set by *I Want to Hold Your Hand* (Parlophone transferred to Apple, Aug 1968) on 29 Nov 1963, with this same record on 20 Mar 1964. The UK record for advance sales of an LP is 750,000 for the Parlophone album *Beatles for Sale* released on 4 Dec 1964.

Loudest *Pop Group*

The amplification at The Who concert at Charlton Athletic Football Ground, London on 31 May 1976 provided by a Tasco PA System had a total power of 76,000 watts from eighty 800 W Crown DC 300 A Amplifiers and twenty 600 W Phase Linear 200's. The readings at 50 m *164 ft* from the front of the sound system were 120 db. *Exposure to such noise levels causes PSH—Permanent Shift of Hearing or partial deafness.*

6. THEATRE

Origins

Theatre in Europe has its origins in Greek drama performed in honour of a god, usually Dionysus. The earliest amphitheatres date from the 5th century BC and the largest of all known is one at Megalopolis in central Greece, where the auditorium reached a height of 75 ft *23 m* and had a capacity of 17,000. The first stone-built theatre in Rome erected in 55 BC could accommodate 40,000 spectators.

Oldest *World*

The oldest indoor theatre in the world is the Teatro Olimpico in Vicenza, Italy. Designed in the Roman style by Andrea di Pietro, *alias* Palladio (1508–80), it was begun three months before his death and finished in 1582 by his pupil Vicenzo Scamozzi (1552–1616). It is preserved today in its original form.

Great Britain

The earliest London theatre was James Burbage's 'The Theatre', built in 1576 near Finsbury Fields, London. The oldest theatre still in use in Great Britain is The Royal, Bristol. The foundation stone was laid on 30 Nov 1764, and the theatre was opened on 30 May 1766 with a 'Concert of Music and a Specimen of Rhetorick'. The City Varieties Music Hall, Leeds was a singing room in 1762 and so claims to outdate the Theatre Royal. Actors were legally rogues and vagabonds until the passing of the Vagrancy Act in 1824. The oldest amateur dramatic society is the Amateur Dramatic Club (ADC) in Cambridge founded in the Hoop Hotel, Jesus Lane by F. C. Burnand in May 1855.

Largest *World*

The world's largest building used for theatre is the National People's Congress Building (*Ren min da hui tang*) on the west side of Tian an men Square, Peking, China. It was completed in 1959 and covers an area of 12.9 acres *5,2 ha*. The theatre seats 10,000 and is occasionally used as such as in 1964 for the play 'The East is Red'. The highest capacity purpose-built theatre is the Perth Entertainment Centre, Western Australia completed at a cost of $A 8.3 million (*then £4.2 million*) in November 1976 with 8003 seats. The stage area is 12,000 ft² *1148 m²*.

Great Britain

The highest capacity theatre is the Odeon, Hammersmith, Greater London, with 3485 seats in 1975. The largest theatre stage in Great Britain is the Opera House in Blackpool, Lancashire. It was re-built in July 1939 and has seats for 2975 people. Behind the 45 ft *14 m* wide proscenium arch the stage is 110 ft *33 m* high, 60 ft *18 m* deep and 100 ft *30 m* wide, and there is dressing room accommodation for 200 artistes.

Britain's largest open air theatre is at Scarborough, North Yorkshire opened in 1932 with a seating capacity of 7000 plus standing room for 9000 and a 182 ft *55 m* long stage.

Smallest

The smallest regularly operated professional theatres in Great Britain are the Mull Little Theatre, near Dervaig, Isle of Mull, Scotland and the Community Theatre, Luton, Bedfordshire each with a maximum capacity of 36 seats.

Largest amphitheatre

The largest amphitheatre ever built is the Flavian amphitheatre or Colosseum of Rome, Italy, completed in AD 80. Covering 5 acres *2 ha* and with a capacity of 87,000, it has a maximum length of 612 ft *187 m* and maximum width of 515 ft *175 m*.

Longest Stage

The largest stage in the world is the Ziegfeld Room Reno, Nevada with 176 ft *53,6 m* passerelle, three main lifts each capable of raising 1200 show girls (64¼ tons *65,3 tonnes*), two 62½ ft *19,1 m* circumference turntables and 800 spotlights.

Longest runs

The longest continuous run of any show in the world is *The Mousetrap* by Dame Agatha Mary Clarissa Christie, DBE (*née* Miller, later Lady Mallowan) (1890–1976). This thriller opened on 25 Nov 1952, at the Ambassadors Theatre (capacity 453) and moved after 8862 performances 'down the road' to St Martin's Theatre on 25 Mar 1974. The Silver Jubilee performance on 25 Nov 1977 was the 10,390th and the 11,500th was on 22 July 1980. The Vicksburg Theatre Guild of Vicksburg, Mississippi, USA have been playing the melodrama *Gold in the Hills*, by J. Frank Davis every season since 1936.

Revue

The greatest number of performances of any theatrical presentation is 39,046 (to 30 Sept 1980) in the case of *The Golden Horseshoe Revue*—a show staged at Disneyland Park, Anaheim, California, USA. The show was first put on 16 July 1955 and has been seen by 15 million people. The three main performers Fulton Burley, Walley Boag and Betty Taylor play as many as five houses a day in a routine lasting 45 min. In Britain, the Brighton Corporation's variety show *Tuesday Night at the Dome* reached its 1485th performance in 35 years to 1 May 1981.

Broadway

The long-run record for any Broadway show was set on 8 Dec 1979 with the 3243rd performance of *Grease* at the Royale Theater where it had opened on 27 Nov 1972. It had first opened at the Eden Theater on 14 Feb 1972. The book, music and lyrics were written by Jim Jacobs (b. Chicago, 1942) and Warren Casey (b. Yonkers, NY, 1935). Profits of $4 million have accrued to the producers Kenneth Waissman and his wife Maxine Fox from the gross $70 million in the US alone. The off-Broadway musical show *The Fantasticks* by Tom Jones and Harvey Schmidt achieved its 8736th performance as it entered its 22nd year at the Sullivan Street Playhouse, Greenwich Village, New York City on 3 May 1981. It has been played in a record 4000 productions in 56 countries.

Musical shows

The longest-running musical show ever performed in Britain

was *The Black and White Minstrel Show* later *Magic of the Minstrels*. The aggregate but discontinuous number of performances was 6464 with a total attendance of 7,794,552. The show opened at the Victoria Palace, London on 25 May 1962 and closed on 4 Nov 1972. It re-opened for a season in June 1973 at the New Victoria and finally closed on 8 Dec 1973.

Jesus Christ Superstar, which opened at Palace Theatre, London on 8 Aug 1972, passed *Oliver* with its 2620th performance on 3 Oct 1978. It closed on 23 Aug 1980 after 3357 performances.

Shortest runs *World*
The shortest run on record was that of *The Intimate Revue* at the Duchess Theatre, London, on 11 Mar 1930. Anything which could go wrong did. With scene changes taking up to 20 min apiece, the management scrapped seven scenes to get the finale on before midnight. The run was described as 'half a performance'. In a number of Broadway productions the opening and closing nights have coincided.

Broadway
The opening and closing nights of many Broadway shows have coincided. Spectacular failures are known as 'turkeys' of which there were 11 in 1978–79. The biggest loss incurred was an estimated $2,000,000 on *Frankenstein* which opened and closed on Broadway on 4 Jan 1981.

Lowest attendance
The first recorded one-man show in which the one man comprised the audience occurred at the Oldman Grange Arts Centre, Lancashire on 23 Oct 1980 when Mr Ronald Bradbury made theatrical history by sitting through *Oh Mistress Mine* in solitary state.

Youngest Broadway producer
Margo Feiden (Margo Eden) (b. New York, 2 Dec 1944) produced the musical *Peter Pan*, which opened on 3 Apr 1961 when she was 16 years 5 months old. She wrote *Out Brief Candle*, which opened on 18 Aug 1962. She is now a leading art dealer.

One-man shows
The longest run of one-man shows is 849 by Victor Borge (b. Copenhagen, 3 Jan 1909) in his *Comedy in Music* from 2 Oct 1953 to 21 Jan 1956 at the Golden Theater, Broadway, New York City. The world aggregate record for one-man shows is 1700 performances of *Brief Lives* by Roy Dotrice (b. Guernsey, 5 May 1923) including 400 straight at the Mayfair Theatre, London ending on 20 July 1974. He was on stage for more than 2½ hr per performance of this 17th century monologue and required 3 hr for make up and 1 hr for removal of make-up so aggregating 40 weeks in the chair.

Most durable leading actress
Dame Anna Neagle, DBE (b. 20 Oct 1904) played the lead role in *Charlie Girl* at the Adelphi Theatre, London for 2062 of 2202 performances between 15 Dec 1965 and 27 Mar 1971. She played the role a further 327 times in 327 performances in Australasia.

Frances Etheridge has played in *Gold in the Hills* (see Longest Runs) for 45 years since 1936.

Most roles
The greatest recorded number of theatrical, film and television roles is 1804 from 1951 to April 1981 by Jan Leighton (US).

Longest play
The longest recorded theatrical production has been *The Warp* by Neil Oram directed by Ken Campbell, a 10 part play cycle played at the Institute of Contemporary Art, The Mall, London, on 18–20 Jan 1979. Russell Denton was on stage for all but 5 min of the 18 hr 5 min. The three intermissions totalled 3 hr 10 min.

Shakespeare
The first all-amateur company to have staged all 37 of Shakespeare's plays was The Southsea Shakespeare Actors, Hampshire, England (founded 1947), when in October 1966 they presented *Cymbeline*. The amateur director throughout was Mr K. Edmonds Gateley, MBE. Ten members of the English Speaking Theatre Amsterdam completed a dramatic reading of all the 37 plays, 154 sonnets and five narrative poems in 30 hr exactly on 26–27 Apr 1980. (*This category has now been retired*). The longest is *Hamlet* with 4042 lines and 29,551 words. Of Shakespeare's 1277 speaking parts the longest is Hamlet with 11,610 words.

Longest chorus line
The 63 'Atomic Girls' of the Shochiku Revue danced in line in the Kokusai Theatre, Tokyo in the revue's 49th season in 1980 in a 4½ minute routine.

Cabaret
The highest paid entertainer is Wayne Newton (b. 1942) who is paid up to $250,000 (*now £113,650*) per performance in Las Vegas hotels by the Summa Corporation.

Ice shows
Holiday on Ice Production Inc, founded by Morris Chalfen in 1945, stages the world's most costly live entertainment with up to seven productions playing simultaneously in several of 75 countries drawing 20,000,000 spectators paying $40 million (*£22.2 million*) in a year. The total skating and other staff exceeds 900. The most prolific producer of Ice Shows is Gerald Palmer with 137 since 1945 including 34 consecutive shows at Empire Pool, Wembley, London with attendances up to 850,000. Hazel Wendy Jolly (b. 1933) has appeared in the Wembley Winter Pantomime for 27 years.

Most ardent theatregoers
It has been estimated by the press that H. Howard Hughes (b. 1904) of Fort Worth, Texas, had seen 4160 shows in the period 1956–76. Britain's leading 'first nighter' Edward Sutro MC (1900–78) saw 3000 first night productions in 1916–56 and possibly more than 5000 in his 60 years of theatre-going. The highest precisely recorded number of theatre attendances in Britain is 3409 shows in 27 years from 28 Mar 1953 to 28 Mar 1981 by John Iles of Salisbury, Wiltshire. He estimates he has travelled 141,527 miles *227 765 km* and seen 159,145 performers in 9014 hours (over 53½ weeks) inside theatres.

The world's largest arts festival is the annual Edinburgh Festival Fringe (instituted in 1959). In 1980, 380 groups gave 6411 performances of 624 shows. Gerald Berkowitz, an associate professor of English at Northern Illinois University, USA attended 145 separate performances at the Edinburgh International Festival in the 25 days (15 Aug–8 Sept 1979) including a peak 17 on 20–21 August.

Fashion shows
The most prolific producer and most durable commentator of fashion shows is Adalene Ross of San Francisco, California with totals over 4674 in both categories to mid-1981.

Professional wrestling
The professional wrestler who has received most for a single bout has been Kanii Antonio Inoki of Japan on 26 Jun 1976. He received $2 million for the drawn wrestler v boxer bout against Muhammad Ali in the Budokan Arena, Tokyo. Lou Thesz has won 7 of the world's many 'world' titles. 'Fabulous' Moolah has won major US women's alliance titles every year since 1956. The heaviest ever wrestler has been William J. Cobb of Macon, Georgia, USA (b. 1926), who was billed in 1962 as the 802 lb *363 kg* (57 st 4 lb) 'Happy' Humphrey. Ed 'Strangler' Lewis (1890–1966) *né* Robert H. Friedrich, fought 6200 bouts in 44 years losing only 33 matches. He won world titles in 1921, 1922, 1928 and 1931–32.

7. CINEMA

Guinness Superlatives has published a more specialist book *Guinness Book of Film Facts and Feats* by Patrick Robertson, priced £8.95.

FILMS
Origins
The greatest impetus in the development of cinematography came from the inventiveness of Etienne Jules Marey (1830–1903) of France in the 1870s.

Earliest silent showings

Louis Aimé Augustine Le Prince (1842–?1890) achieved dim moving outlines on a whitewashed wall at the Institute for the Deaf, Washington Heights, New York, USA as early as 1885. The earliest surviving film is his Traffic scenes on Leeds Bridge, Yorkshire shot in late October 1888. The earliest public demonstration of a celluloid cinematograph film on a screen was given at 44 Rue de Rennes, Paris on 22 Mar 1895 by Auguste Marie Louis Nicolas Lumière (1862–1954) and Louis Jean Lumière (1864–1948). The film was entitled *La Sortie des Ouvriers de l'Usine Lumière* taken probably in August or September 1894 outside the factory gates at Lyons. The earliest demonstration of film projection in Britain was given by Bert Acres (b. USA 23 July 1854, d. Walthamstow, Essex 27 Dec 1918) at the Royal Photographic Society, 12 Hanover Square, London on 14 Jan 1896. The earliest show before a paying public was at the Polytechnic, Regent St., London on 20 Feb 1896.

Earliest 'Talkie'

The earliest sound-on-film motion picture was achieved by Eugene Augustin Lauste (b. Paris 17 Jan 1857) who patented his process on 11 Aug 1906 and produced a workable system using a string galvanometer in 1910 in London. Dr Lee de Forest (1873–1961) was responsible for the screening of the first sound picture before a paying audience at the Rialto Theater, New York City on 15 Apr 1923. The first all-talking feature was Warner Bros' *Lights of New York*, shown at The Strand, New York City, on 6 July 1928.

Most expensive film

The costliest film ever completed has been *Star Trek* which received its world première in Washington D.C. on 6 Dec. 1979. Paramount Studios stated that the cost of this space epic directed by Robert Wise and produced by Gene Roddenberry, was $46 million (*then £21 million*).

Least expensive film

Cecil Hepworth's highly successful release of 1905 *Rescued by Rover* cost £7 13s 9d (*then £37.40*).

Most expensive film rights

The highest price ever paid for film rights is $9,500,000 (*then £4,950,000*) announced on 20 Jan 1978 by Columbia for *Annie*, the Broadway Musical by Charles Strouse starring Andrea McCardle, Dorothy Loudon and Reid Shelton.

Longest film

The longest film ever released was **** by Andy Warhol (b. Andrew Warhola, Cleveland, Ohio, 1931) which lasted 24 hr. It proved not surprisingly, except reportedly to its creator, a commercial failure and was withdrawn and re-released in a 90 minute form as *The Loves of Ondine*. *Noli me tangere* directed by Jacques Rivette (b. Rouen, 1 Mar 1928) lasted 12 hr 40 min but was only shown once at Le Havre on 9–10 Sept 1971 and then re-edited as the 4½ hr *Out One: Spectre*.

The Kommunales Kino, Hannover, West Germany on 30–31 Aug 1980 projected *Der längste Film der Welt* comprising episodes by 336 amateurs for 32 hr 35 min 10 sec non-stop.

Highest box office gross

The film which has had the highest world gross earnings is *Star Wars*, written and directed by George Lucas, and produced by Gary Kurtz which from 25 May 1977 to December 1979 grossed $267 million (*then £133.5 million*).

Largest loss

It was reported on 20 Nov 1980 that United Artists had withdrawn *Heaven Gate* because its total cost including distribution and studio overheads had reached $57,000,000.

Highest earnings *By an actor*

The highest rate of pay in cinema history is being contested between Marlon Brando (b. 3 Apr 1924) for his brief part in *Superman* and Steve McQueen (1930–80) for his role in *Tai Pan*. Both received in excess of $2,500,000 (*then £1,250,000*) but the final amount will depend on box office percentages. In July 1980 it was reported that Burt Reynolds (b. 2 Nov 1936) received $238,095 per day from 20th Century-Fox for his part in *Cannonball Run*.

By a Stuntman

Dar Robinson was paid $100,000 (*then £45,500*) for the 1100 ft *335 m* leap from the CN Tower, Toronto in Nov 1979 for *High Point*. His parachute opened at only 300 ft *91 m* above the ground.

Largest studios

The largest complex of film studios in the world are those at Universal City, L.A., California. The Back Lot contains 561 buildings and there are 34 sound stages.

Oscars *Most*

Walter (Walt) Elias Disney (1901–66) won more 'Oscars'—the awards of the United States Academy of Motion Picture Arts and Sciences, instituted on 16 May 1929 for 1927–8—than any other person. The physical count comprises 20 statuettes, and nine other plaques and certificates including posthumous awards. The only person to win three Oscars in a starring rôle has been Miss Katharine Hepburn, formerly Mrs Ludlow Ogden Smith (b. Hartford, Conn., 9 Nov 1909) in *Morning Glory* (1932–3), *Guess Who's Coming to Dinner* (1967) and *The Lion in Winter* (1968). She was 11 times nominated. Only 4 actors have won two Oscars in starring rôles—Frederic March (1897–1975) in 1932 and 1946, Spencer Tracy in 1937 and 1938, Gary Cooper in 1941 and 1952, and Marlon Brando in 1954 and 1972. Oscars are named after Mr Oscar Pierce of Texas, USA. The films with most awards have been *Ben Hur* (1959) with 11, followed by *Gone With the Wind* (1939) with 10 and *West Side Story* (1961) with 10. The film with the highest number of nominations was *All About Eve* (1950) with 14. It won six. The youngest ever winner was Shirley Temple aged 6 in 1934 and the oldest George Burns, 80 for *The Sunshine Boys* in 1976.

Versatility showbusiness awards

Rita Moreno (b. 11 Dec 1931 Rosa Dolores Alverio in Puerto Rico, now Mrs Leonard Gordon) is the only female entertainer to be awarded an Oscar for *West Side Story* (1962); a Grammy for *Electric Company Album* (1972); a regular Tony for *The Ritz* (1975) and an Emmy for *The Muppet Show* (1977) and *The Rockford Files* (1978). Barbra Streisand (b. 24 Apr 1942 in Brooklyn, NY) received Oscar, Grammy and Emmy awards in addition to a special 'Star of the Decade' Tony award.

CINEMAS

Earliest

The earliest structure designed and exclusively used for exhibiting projected films is believed to be one erected at the Atlanta Show, Georgia USA in October 1895 to exhibit C. F. Jenkins' phantoscope. The earliest cinema constructed in Great Britain was built without permission at Olympia, London, to house the 'Theatregraph' promoted by Robert William Paul (1869–1943). This was completed by 16 Apr 1896.

Largest *World*

The largest cinema in the world is the Radio City Music Hall, New York City, opened on 27 Dec 1932 with 5945 (now 5882) seats. The Roxy, opened in New York City on 11 March 1927 had 6214 (later 5869) seats but was closed on 29 Mar 1960. Cineplex, opened at the Toronto Eaton Centre, Canada on 19 Apr 1979 has 18 separate theatres with an aggregate capacity of 1700.

Great Britain

Great Britain's largest cinema is the Odeon Theatre, Hammersmith, Greater London, with 3485 seats. The Playhouse, Glasgow had 4235 seats.

Drive-In

The world's largest drive-in cinema is Loew's Open Air at Lynn, Mass., USA with a capacity of 5000 cars.

Most cinemas

San Marino has more cinemas per total population than any other country in the world, with 1 cinema for every 1512 inhabitants. Saudi Arabia (population 7.8 million) has no cinemas.

Highest cinema going

The people of the Philippines (population 46.3 million) go to the cinema more often than those of any other country in the world with an average of 19.06 attendances per person per annum (1979–80). The Soviet Union claims to have most cinemas in the world, with 163,400 in 1974, but this includes buildings merely equipped with even 16 mm projectors. The USA has 16,965 actual cinemas (1979). The number of cinemas in the UK reached a peak 4714 in 1944 declining to 1582 by 27 Apr 1981. The average weekly admissions has declined from 33,420,000 in 1944 to 1,940,000 in 1980.

Biggest screen
The permanently installed cinema screen with the largest area is one of 70 ft *21,33 m* tall by 96 ft *29,26 m* wide installed in the Pictorium Theater, Marriott's Great America Entertainment Center, Santa Clara, California on 16 May 1978. It was made by Harkness Screens Ltd at Boreham Wood, Herts. A temporary screen 297 ft × 33 ft *90,5 × 10 m* was used at the 1937 Paris Exposition.

8. RADIO BROADCASTING

Origins
The earliest description of a radio transmission system was written by Dr Mahlon Loomis (USA) (b. Fulton County, NY, 21 July 1826) on 21 July 1864 and demonstrated between two kites more than 14 miles *22 km* apart at Bear's Den, Loudoun County, Virginia in October 1866. He received US patent No. 129,971 entitled Improvement in Telegraphing on 20 July 1872. He died in 1886.

Earliest patent
The first patent for a system of communication by means of electro-magnetic waves, numbered No. 12039, was granted on 2 June 1896 to the Italian-Irish Marchese Guglielmo Marconi, GCVO (Hon) (1874–1937). A public demonstration of wireless transmission of speech was, however, given in the town square of Murray, Kentucky, USA in 1892 by Nathan B. Stubblefield. He died destitute on 28 March 1928. The first permanent wireless installation was at The Needles on the Isle of Wight, by Marconi's Wireless Telegraph Co., Ltd., in November 1896.

Earliest broadcast *World*
The world's first advertised broadcast was made on 24 Dec 1906 by the Canadian born Prof Reginald Aubrey Fessenden (1868–1932) from the 420 ft *128 m* mast of the National Electric Signalling Company at Brant Rock, Massachusetts, USA. The transmission included Handel's *Largo*. Fessenden had achieved the broadcast of speech as early as November 1900 but this was highly distorted.

Great Britain
The first experimental broadcasting transmitter in Great Britain was set up at the Marconi Works in Chelmsford, Essex, in December 1919, and broadcast a news service in February 1920. The earliest regular broadcast was made from the Marconi transmitter '2 MT' at Writtle, Essex, on 14 Feb 1922.

Transatlantic transmissions
The earliest transatlantic wireless signals (the letter S in Morse Code) were received by Marconi, George Stephen Kemp and Percy Paget from a 10 kW station at Poldhu, Cornwall, at Signal Hill, St John's, Newfoundland, Canada, at 12.30 p.m. on 12 Dec 1901. Human speech was first heard across the Atlantic in November 1915 when a transmission from the US Navy station at Arlington, Virginia was received by US radio-telephone engineers on the Eiffel Tower.

Earliest radio-microphones
The radio-microphone, which was in essence also the first 'bug', was devised by Reg Moores (GB) in 1947 and first used on 76 MHz in the ice show *Aladdin* at Brighton Sports Stadium, East Sussex in September 1949.

Longest BBC national broadcast
The longest BBC national broadcast was the reporting of the Coronation of Queen Elizabeth II on 2 June 1953. It began at 10.15 a.m. and finished at 5.30 p.m., after 7 hr 15 min.

Longest continuous broadcast *World*
The longest continuous broadcast (excluding disc-jockeying)

Frederic March (1897–1975), one of only 4 actors to have won 2 oscars in starring rôles, shown here with Janet Gaynor (b. 10 June 1906 Philadelphia, USA) (see p. 110). (*Cinema Bookshop*)

has been one of 336 hr by Bill Tinsley of WATN Radio, Watertown, New York, USA on 17–31 Mar 1979.

Great Britain Local and Hospital radio
The longest local radio transmission has been 48 hrs 30 min by BBC Radio London broadcaster David Carter on 6–8 May 1979. Brian Sheard completed 208 hr 15 min of broadcasting on Manchester Hospital Radio on 15–23 Feb 1980.

Brain of Britain Quiz
The youngest person to become 'Brain of Britain' on BBC radio was Anthony Carr, 16, of Anglesey in 1956. The oldest contestant has been the author and translator Hugh Merrick in his 80th year in August 1977.

Most Durable Broadcaster
Sven Jerring (1898–1979) retired from the Swedish Broadcasting Corporation in 1978 aged 82 having broadcast "Children's Mailbox" 1785 times from 1925 to 1972.

Most durable programmes *BBC*
The longest running BBC radio series is *The Week's Good Cause* beginning on 24 Jan 1926. The longest running record programme is *Desert Island Discs* which began on 29 Jan 1942 and on which programme only one guest, Arthur Askey CBE, has been stranded a fourth time (on the 1572nd show on 20 Dec 1980). The *Desert Island* programme has been presented since its inception by Roy Plomley, OBE who devised the idea. The longest running solo radio feature is *Letter from America* by (Alfred) Alistair Cooke, Hon KBE (b. Salford 20 Nov 1908), first broadcast on 24 Mar 1946. The longest running radio serial is *The Archers* which was created by Godfrey Baseley and was first broadcast on 29 May 1950. Up to May 1981 the signature tune *Barwick Green* had been played over 32,000 times. The only one of 363 roles which has been played without interruption from the start has been that of Philip Archer by Norman Painting OBE (b. Leamington Spa, 23 Apr 1924).

Earliest antipodal reception
Frank Henry Alfred Walker (b. 11 Nov 1904) on the night of 12 Nov 1924 received on his home-made 2 valve receiver on 75 metres, signals from Marconi's yacht *Electra* (call sign ICCM) in Australian waters at Crown Farm, Cuttimore Lane, Walton-on-Thames, Surrey, England.

Most stations
The country with the greatest number of radio broadcasting sta-

tions is the United States, where there were 8608 authorised broadcast stations in 1978 of which 4547 were AM (Amplitude modulation) and 4061 FM (Frequency modulation).

Highest listenership

The peak recorded listenership on BBC Radio was 30,000,000 adults on 6 June 1950 for the boxing fight between Lee Savold (US) and Bruce Woodcock (GB).

Highest response

The highest recorded response from a radio show occurred on 27 Nov 1974 when on a 5 hr talk show on WCAU, Philadelphia, USA, Howard Sheldon, the astrologist registered a call count of 388,299 calls on the 'Bill Corsair Show'.

9. TELEVISION

Invention

The invention of television, the instantaneous viewing of distant objects by electrical transmissions, was not an act but a process of successive and inter-dependent discoveries. The first commercial cathode ray tube was introduced in 1897 by Karl Ferdinand Braun (1850–1918), but was not linked to 'electric vision' until 1907 by Boris Rosing of Russia in St Petersburg (now Leningrad). A. A. Campbell Swinton FRS (1863–1930) published the fundamentals of television transmission on 18 June 1908 in a brief letter to *Nature* entitled 'Distant Electric Vision'. The earliest public demonstration of television was given on 27 Jan 1926 by John Logie Baird (1888–1946) of Scotland, using a development of the mechanical scanning system suggested by Paul Nipkov in 1884. He had achieved the transmission of a Maltese Cross over 10 ft *3,05 m* at 8, Queen's Arcade, Hastings, East Sussex in February 1924 and the first facial image (of William Taynton, 15) at Frith Street on 30 Oct 1925. Taynton had to be bribed with 2s 6d. A patent application for the Iconoscope had been filed on 29 Dec 1923 by Dr Vladimir Kosma Zworykin (born in Russia on 30 July 1889, became a US citizen in 1924), though not issued until 20 Dec 1938. The patent filed by Philo Taylor Farnsworth (US) on 7 Jan 1927 was however granted on 26 Aug 1930. Farnsworth succeeded with a low definition image at 202 Green Street, Los Angeles in November 1927. The first experimental transmission in Britain was on 30 Sept 1929. Public transmissions on 30 lines were made from 22 Aug 1932 until 11 Sept 1935.

Earliest service

The world's first high definition (*i.e.* 405 lines) television broadcasting service was opened from Alexandra Palace, Haringey, Greater London, on 2 Nov 1936, when there were about 100 sets in the United Kingdom. The Chief Engineer was Mr Douglas Birkinshaw. A television station in Berlin, Germany, made a low definition (180 line) transmission from 22 Mar 1935. The transmitter burnt out in Aug 1935.

Transatlantic transmission

The earliest transatlantic transmission by satellite was achieved at 1 a.m. on 11 July 1962, *via* the active satellite *Telstar 1* from Andover, Maine, USA, to Pleumeur Bodou, France. The picture was of Mr Frederick R. Kappell, chairman of the American Telephone and Telegraph Company, which owned the satellite. The first 'live' broadcast was made on 23 July 1962 and the first woman to appear was the *haute couturière*, Ginette Spanier, directrice of Balmain, the next day. On 9 Feb 1928 the image of J. L. Baird (see above) and of a Mrs Howe was transmitted from Station 2 KZ at Coulsdon, Surrey, England to Station 2 CVJ, Hartsdale, NY, USA.

Longest telecast

The longest pre-scheduled telecast on record was a continuous transmission for 163 hr 18 min by GTV 9 of Melbourne, Australia covering the Apollo XI moon mission on 19–26 July 1969. The longest continuous TV transmission under a single director was the Avro Television Production *Open het Dorp* transmitted in the Netherlands on 26–27 Nov 1962 for 23 hr 20 min under the direction of Theo Ordeman.

Video-tape recording

Alexander M. Poniatoff first demonstrated video-tape recording known as Ampex (his initials plus 'ex' for excellence) in 1956.

Most durable shows *World*

The world's most durable TV show is NBC's *Meet the Press* first transmitted on 6 Nov 1947 and weekly since 12 Sept 1948, originated by Lawrence E. Spivak, who appeared weekly as either moderator or panel member until 1975. On 11 Dec 1980 Mike Douglas presented the 4754th version of his show started in 1960.

Great Britain

The longest running TV programme on BBC is *Panorama* which was first transmitted, introduced by Patrick Murphy, on 11 Nov 1953. *Andy Pandy* was first transmitted on 11 July 1950 but consisted of repeats of a cycle of 26 shows until 1970. The seasonal programme *Come Dancing* was first transmitted on 29 Sept 1950. *The News* started on 21 Mar 1938 in sound only. The regular daily TV News began on 5 July 1954. The puppet show *Sooty*, devised by Harry Corbett (b. Bradford, 1918) has been transmitted every year since 1952 and is now presented by his son, Matthew.

Most sets

In 1977 the total estimated number of television transmitters in use or under construction was 20,000 serving 384,000,000 sets (90 for each 1000 of the world population). In the United States where 98 per cent of the population was reached by 1976, the number of homes with colour sets was 63,329,000 by September 1979. The number of licences current in the United Kingdom was 18,667,211 on 31 Mar 1981 of which 13,779,548 (73.81 per cent) were for colour sets. Black and white licences became less commonplace than colour in 1976.

TV Watching

In July 1978 it was estimated that the *average* American child by his or her 18th birthday has watched 710 solid days (17,040 hours) of TV, seen more than 350,600 commercials and more than 15,000 TV murders. There are 571 TV sets per 1000 people in the USA compared with 348 in Sweden and 330 in Britain.

Most television free

Iceland has a TV free day on Thursdays to reduce disruption of family life. Otherwise transmissions are normally limited to between 8 and 11 p.m. Upper Volta had by 1974 only one set per 1000 of the population.

Greatest audience

The greatest estimated number of viewers worldwide for a televised event is 1000 million for the live and recorded transmissions of the XXth and XXIst Olympic Games in Munich, W Germany and Montreal, Canada in 1972 and 1976. The estimate for the papal visit to Ireland by Pope John Paul II on 29 Sept 1979 was also 1000 million. The crowd in Phoenix Park, Dublin for Mass was however at 1.3 million even greater than Radio Telefis Eireann's national audience.

The programme which attracted the highest ever viewership was the episode of *Dallas* transmitted by CBS on 21 Nov 1980 to 53.3 per cent of all households in the United States. It was estimated that some 83 million people watched in these 41.4 million homes which took a 76 per cent share of all viewing at 10 pm, E.S.T.

Largest production

The BBC production of the 37 plays of Shakespeare in 1978–84 will cost a minimum of £6,800,000. The new series was conceived by its producer Cedric Messina.

Largest contracts *World*

The highest rate for any TV contract ever signed was one for $7 million (*then £3,100,000*) for 7 hours of transmission by Marie Osmond by NBC announced on 9 Mar 1981. The figure includes talent and production costs.

Currently television's highest-paid performer is Johnny Carson, the host of *The Tonight Show*. His current NBC contract reportedly calls for annual payment of $5,000,000 (*now £2,275,000*) for his one hour evening show aired four times weekly. The highest-paid current affairs or news performer is Barbara Walters of ABC *The Evening News* programme, who signed a 5-year $1 million (*then £525,000*) a year contract on or about 21 Apr 1976.

Alan Alda, star of the *M*A*S*H* series receives a record

above: Jerry Lewis (US) host of the Labor Day Telethon on 4 Sept 1979 which raised over $30 million dollars in pledges for the Muscular Dystrophy Association. (*MDA*)

left: Barbara Walters (US) of *The Evening News* ABC-TV programme is the world's highest paid current affairs newscaster (see p. 112).

$225,000 (*£102,000*) per episode thereby totalling $5.4 million (*£2,448,000*) for 24 episodes in a year.

Great Britain
The largest contract in British television was one of a reported £9,000,000, inclusive of production expenses, signed by Tom Jones (b. Thomas Jones Woodward, 7 June 1940) of Treforest, Mid Glamorgan, Wales in June 1968 with ABC-TV of the United States and ATV in London for 17 one-hour shows per annum from January 1969 to January 1974.

Highest paid TV actor
Peter Falk (b. 16 Sept 1927), the disarmingly persistent detective *Columbo*, was paid from $300,000 to $350,000 for a single episode of his series of six so totalling $1,950,000 (*then £1,147,000*) in 1976. In 1980 Carroll O'Conner, star of *Archie Bunker's Place* was contracted for $200,000 (*then £90,900*) for each of the season's 24 episodes.

Largest TV prizes *World*
On 24 July 1975 WABC-TV, New York City transmitted the first televised Grand Tier draw of the State Lottery in which the winner took the grand prize of $1,000,000 (*now £454,545*). This was however taxable. Mary Buchanan, 15, won a prize of $25,000 for 40 years (viz. $1,000,000) on WKRQ, Cincinnati on 21 Nov 1980.

Most successful appeals
The Jerry Lewis Labor Day Telethon on 4 Sept 1979 raised $30,075,227 (*then £13,670,550*) in pledges for the Muscular Dystrophy Association. The East African Emergency Appeal broadcast on BBC TV by Sue Lawley on 19 June 1980, reached £5,591,643 in donations (excluding government grant), banked when it closed on 3 Apr 1981 for the five distributing charities.

Biggest sale
The greatest number of episodes of any TV programme ever sold has been 1144 episodes of 'Coronation Street' by Granada Television to CBKST Saskatoon, Saskatchewan, Canada, on 31 May 1971. This constituted 20 days 15 hr 44 min continuous viewing.

Most prolific scriptwriter
The most prolific television writer in the world is the Rt Hon Lord Willis known as Ted Willis (b. 13 Jan 1918), who in the period 1949–80 has created 24 series, including the first seven years and 2,250,000 words of *Dixon of Dock Green* which ran from 1955 to 1976, 25 stage plays and 23 feature films. He had 21 plays produced. His total output since 1942 can be estimated at 16,500,000 words.

Highest TV advertising rates
The highest TV advertising rate has been $550,000 per min (*then £3820 per sec*) for NBC network prime time during the transmission of *Super Bowl* on 24 Jan 1981. In Great Britain the peak time weekday 60 sec spot rate (6.30–10.35 p.m.) for Thames Television is £22,678+VAT for a booking within 4 weeks of transmission (April 1981).

Most takes
The highest number of 'takes' for a TV commercial is 28 in 1973 by Pat Coombs, the comedienne, who has supported Dick Emery on BBC TV. Her explanation was 'Everytime we came to the punch line I just could not remember the name of the product'.

Commercials records
In 1977 James Coburn of Beverly Hills, California was reputed to have been paid $500,000 (*then £250,000*) for uttering two words on a series of Schlitz beer commercials. The words 'Schlitz Light' were thus at a quarter of a million dollars per syllable. Brooke Shields (b. 31 May 1965) was reportedly paid $250,000 (*then £125,000*) for one minute of film by a Japanese TV commercial film maker in 1979. Faye Dunaway was reported in May 1979 to have been paid $900,000 (*then £450,000*) for uttering 6 words for a Japanese department store TV commercial. Britain's most durable TV Commercial has been the Brooke Bond chimpanzee commercial first transmitted on 21 Nov 1971 and 1687 more times to October 1979.

Smallest set
The world's first 2 inch screen TV set to be marketed is the 20 oz *567 g* Sinclair Microvision with overall dimensions of $7 \times 2 \times 3\frac{1}{2}$ in *17,7 × 5,08 × 8,9 mm* and a screen measuring 2 in *5,08 cm* diagonally, manufactured by Sinclair Radionics Ltd of St Ives, Cambridgeshire.

7. THE WORLD'S STRUCTURES

EARLIEST STRUCTURES

World

The earliest known human structure is a rough circle of loosely piled lava blocks found in 1960 on the lowest cultural level at the Lower Paleolithic site at Olduvai Gorge in Tanzania. The structure was associated with artifacts and bones and may represent a work-floor, dating to *c.* 1,750,000 BC. The earliest evidence of *buildings* yet discovered is that of 21 huts with hearths or pebble-lined pits and delimited by stake holes found in October 1965 at the Terra Amata site in Nice, France thought to belong to the Acheulian culture of 120,000 years ago. Excavation carried out between 28 June and 5 July 1966 revealed one hut with palisaded walls with axes of 49 ft *15 m* and 20 ft *6 m*. The oldest free standing structures in the world are now believed to be the megalithic temples at Mgarr and Skorba in Malta and Ggantija in Gozo dating from *c.* 3250 BC. The remains of a stone tower 20 ft *6,1 m* high originally built into the walls of Jericho has been excavated and is dated to 5000 BC.

Great Britain

A rudimentary platform of birch branches, stones and wads of clay thrown down on the edge of a swamp at Star Carr, south of Scarborough, North Yorkshire, may possibly represent the earliest man-made 'dwelling' yet found in Britain (Mesolithic, 7607 BC ± 210). A dwelling area in a depression associated with hearths at Broom Hill, Braishfield, Hants have been dated to 6365 BC ± 150. Remains of the earliest dated stone shelter and cooking pit were discovered in 1967 at Culver Well, Isle of Portland, Dorset (Mesolithic, 5200 BC ± 135). On the Isle of Jura, Strathclyde, Scotland a hearth consisting of three linked stone circles has been dated to the Mesolithic period 6013 ± 200 BC.

Ireland

The earliest known structures in Ireland date from the Mesolithic period *c.* 6850–6500 BC. A series of pits associated with postholes have been excavated at a living site at Mount Sandel, Co. Derry.

1. BUILDINGS FOR WORKING

LARGEST BUILDINGS

Commercial *World*

The greatest ground area covered by any building in the world is that by the Ford Parts Redistribution Center, Pennsylvania Avenue, Brownstown Township, Michigan, USA. It encloses a floor area of 3,100,000 ft² or 71.16 acres *28,8 ha*. It was opened on 20 May 1971 and employs 1400 people. The fire control system comprises 70 miles *112 km* of pipelines with 37,000 sprinklers. The building with the largest cubic capacity in the world is the Boeing Company's main assembly plant at Everett, Washington State, USA completed in 1968 with a capacity of 200 million ft³ *5,6 million m³*.

Great Britain

The largest building in Britain is the Ford Parts Center at Daventry, Northamptonshire, which measures 1,978 × 780 ft *602 × 237 m* and 1.6 million ft² or 36.7 acres *14,86 ha*. It was opened on 6 Sept 1972 at a cost of nearly £8 million. It employs 1600 people and is fitted with 14,000 fluorescent lights.

Scientific

The most capacious scientific building in the world is the Vehicle Assembly Building (VAB) at Complex 39, the selected site for the final assembly and launching of the Apollo moon spacecraft on the Saturn V rocket, at the John F. Kennedy Space Center (KSC) on Merritt Island, Cape Canaveral, Florida, USA. It is a steel-framed building measuring 716 ft *218 m* in length, 518 ft *158 m* in width and 525 ft *160 m* high. The building contains four bays, each with its own door 460 ft *140 m* high. Construction began in April 1963 by the Ursum Consortium. Its floor area is 343,500 ft² (7.87 acres *3,18 ha*) and its capacity is 129,482,000 ft³ *3 666 500 m³*. The building was 'topped out' on 14 Apr 1965 at a cost of $108,700,000 (*then £38.8 million*).

Administrative

The largest ground area covered by any office building is that of the Pentagon, in Arlington, Virginia, USA. Built to house the US Defense Department's offices it was completed on 15 Jan

1943 and cost an estimated $83,000,000 (*then £20,595,000*). Each of the outermost sides of the Pentagon is 921 ft *281 m* long and the perimeter of the building is about 1500 yd *1370 m*. The five storeys of the building enclose a floor area of 6,500,000 ft² *604 000 m²* (149.2 acres *60,3 ha*). During the day 29,000 people work in the building. The telephone system of the building has over 44,000 telephones connected by 160,000 miles *257 500 km* of cable and its 220 staff handle 280,000 calls a day. Two restaurants, six cafeterias and ten snack bars and a staff of 675 form the catering department of the building. The corridors measure 17 miles *27 km* in length and there are 7748 windows to be cleaned.

Office
The largest office buildings with the largest rentable space in the world are The World Trade Center in New York City, USA with a total of 4,370,000 ft² *406 000 m²* (100.32 acres *40,6 ha*) in each of the twin towers of which the taller Tower B is 1362 ft 3¼ in *415,22 m*.

Single office *Great Britain*
The largest single office in the United Kingdom is that of West Midlands Gas at Solihull, West Midlands, built by Spooners (Hull) Ltd in 1962. It now measures 753 ft by 160 ft *230 by 49 m* (2.77 acres *1,12 ha*) in one open plan room accommodating 2170 clerical and managerial workers.

TALLEST BUILDINGS
World
The tallest office building in the world is the Sears Tower, the national headquarters of Sears, Roebuck & Co. in Wacker Drive, Chicago, Illinois with 110 storeys rising to 1454 ft *443 m* and begun in August 1970. Its gross area is 4,400,000 ft² (101.0 acres *40,8 ha*). It was 'topped out' on 4 May 1973. It surpassed the World Trade Center in New York City in height at 2.35 p.m. on 6 Mar 1973 with the first steel column reaching to the 104th storey. The addition of two TV antennae brought the total height to 1559 ft *475,18 m*. The building's population is 16,700 served by 103 elevators and 18 escalators. It has 16,000 windows.

Asia
Asia's tallest building, where many buildings must be made resistant to earthquakes, is the 60 storey 'Sunshine 60' in Ikebukuro, Tōkyō, Japan completed in 1978 to a height of 240 m *787.4 ft*. (See also Passenger lifts, fastest).

Great Britain
The tallest office block in Britain and the tallest cantilevered building in the world is the £72 million National Westminster tower block in Bishopsgate, City of London completed in 1979. It has 49 storeys and 3 basement levels, serviced by 21 lifts, and is 600 ft 4 in *183 m* tall. The gross floor area is 636,373 ft² *59,121 m²* (14.6 acres *5,9 ha*). The view from the top extends over 8 counties.

Merseyside County Council unveiled highly tentative plans for a £500 million 139 storey 1825 ft *556,2 m* tall office block on 9 Nov 1979.

HABITATIONS
Greatest altitude
The highest inhabited buildings in the world are those in the Indian–Tibet border fort of Bāsisi at *c.* 19,700 ft *5988 m*. In April 1961, however, a 3-room dwelling was discovered at 21,650 ft *6600 m* on Cerro Llullaillaco (22,058 ft *6723 m*), on the Argentine–Chile border, believed to date from the late pre-Columbian period *c.* 1480. An unnamed settlement on the T'eli-mo trail in southern Tibet is at an apparent altitude of 19,800 ft *6019 m*.

Northernmost
The most northerly habitation in the world is the Danish Scientific station set up in 1952 in Pearyland, northern Greenland, over 900 miles *1450 km* north of the Arctic Circle. Eskimo hearths dated to before 1000 BC were discovered in Pearyland in 1969. The USSR and the United States have maintained research stations on ice floes in the Arctic. The USSR's 'North Pole 15', which drifted 1250 miles *2000 km*, passed within 1¼ miles *2,8 km* of the North Pole in December 1967.

The most northerly continuously inhabited place is the Canadian Department of National Defence outpost at Alert on Ellesmere Island, Northwest Territories in Lat. 82° 30′ N, Long. 62° W, set up in 1950.

Southernmost
The most southerly permanent human habitation is the United States' Scott–Amundsen South Polar Station (see page 67) completed in 1957 and replaced in 1975.

EMBASSIES AND CIVIC BUILDINGS
Largest
The largest embassy in the world is the USSR embassy on Bei Xiao Jie, Peking, China, in the north-eastern corner of the Northern walled city. The whole 45 acre *18,2 ha* area of the old Orthodox Church mission (established 1728), now known as the *Bei guan*, was handed over to the USSR in 1949. The largest in Great Britain is the United States of America Embassy in Grosvenor Square, London. The Chancery Building, completed in 1960, alone has 600 rooms for a staff of 700 on seven floors with a usable floor area of 255,000 ft² (5.85 acres *2,37 ha*).

Great Britain
The oldest municipal building in Britain is the Exeter Guildhall first referred to in a deed of 1160. The Tudor front was added in 1593.

EXHIBITION CENTRES
Largest *Great Britain*
Britain's largest exhibition centre is the National Exhibition Centre, Birmingham opened in February 1976. Five halls which inter-connect cover 87 180 m² *938,397 ft²* or 21.54 acres with a volume of 1 168 466 m³ or *41.26 million ft³*.

INDUSTRIAL STRUCTURES
Tallest chimneys *World*
The world's tallest chimney is the $5.5 million International Nickel Company's stack 1245 ft 8 in *379,6 m* tall at Copper Cliff, Sudbury, Ontario, Canada, completed in 1970. It was built by Canadian Kellogg Ltd., in 60 days and the diameter tapers from 116.4 ft *35,4 m* at the base to 51.8 ft *15,8 m* at the top. It weighs 38,390 tons *39 006 tonnes* and became operational in 1971. The world's most massive chimney is one of 1148 ft *350 m* at Puentes, Spain, built by M. W. Kellogg Co. It contains 20,600 yd³ *15 750 m³* of concrete and 2.9 million lb *1315 tonnes* of steel and has an internal volume of 6.7 million ft³ *189 720 m³*. Europe's tallest chimney serves the Zasavje thermo-power plant in Trboulje, Yugoslavia completed to 350 metres *1181 ft* on 1 June 1976.

Great Britain
The tallest chimney in Great Britain is one of 850 ft *259 m* at Drax Power Station, North Yorkshire, begun in 1966 and topped out on 16 May 1969. It has an untapered diameter of 87 ft 9 in *26 m* and has the greatest capacity of any chimney. The architects were Clifford Tee & Gale of London. The oldest known industrial chimney in Britain is the Stone Edge Chimney, near Chesterfield, Derbyshire built to a height of 55 ft *16,76 m ante* 1771.

Cooling towers
The largest cooling tower in the world is that adjacent to the nuclear power plant at Uentrop, W. Germany which is 590 ft *179,8 m* tall. It was completed in 1976. The largest in the United Kingdom of the Ferrybridge and Didcot type measure 375 ft *114 m* tall and 300 ft *91 m* across the base.

HANGARS
Largest *World*
The world's largest hangar is the Goodyear Airship hangar at Akron, Ohio, USA which measures 1175 ft *358 m* long, 325 ft *99 m* wide and 200 ft *61 m* high. It covers 364,000 ft² (8.35 acres *3,38 ha*) and has a capacity of 55,000,000 ft³ *1,6 million m³*. The world's largest single fixed-wing aircraft hangar is the Lockheed-Georgia engineering test centre at Marietta, Georgia measuring 630 ft by 480 ft *192 by 146 m* (6.94 acres *2,8 ha*) completed in 1967. The maintenance hangar at Frankfurt/Main Airport, W. Germany has a slightly lesser area but a frontage of 902 ft *275 m*. The cable supported roof has a span of 130 m *426.5 ft*. Delta Air Lines' jet base on a 140 acre *56,6 ha* site at

Hartsfield International Airport, Atlanta, Georgia, has 36 acres *14,5 ha* under roof.

Great Britain
The largest hangar building in the United Kingdom is the Britannia Assembly Hall at the former Bristol Aeroplane Company's works at Filton, Avon, now part of the British Aircraft Corporation. The overall width of the Hall is 1054 ft *321 m* and the overall depth of the centre bay is 420 ft *128 m*. It encloses a floor area of 7½ acres *3,0 ha*. The cubic capacity of the Hall is 33,000,000 ft³ *934 000 m³*. The building was begun in April 1946 and completed by September 1949.

GARAGES
Largest *World*
The world's largest parking garage is at O'Hare Airport, Chicago with 6 levels and a capacity for 9250 cars. It is operated by Allright Auto Parks Inc, the world's largest parking company.

Great Britain
Great Britain's highest capacity underground car park is that under the Victoria Centre, Nottingham with a capacity of 1650 cars, opened in June 1972.

Private
The largest private garage ever built was one for 100 cars at the Long Island, New York mansion of William Kissam Vanderbilt (1849–1920).

Parking lot
The largest parking area in Great Britain is that for 15,000 cars and 200 coaches at the National Exhibition Centre, Birmingham (see p. 115). The parking lots at Disneyland, Anaheim, California cover 107.3 acres *43,4 ha* and have parking for 11,500 vehicles.

Filling station
The largest filling station of the 36,000 in the United Kingdom is the Esso service area on the M4 at Leigh Delamere, Wiltshire, opened on 3 Jan 1972. It has 48 petrol and diesel pumps and extends over 43 acres *17,4 ha*. It cost £650,000, has a staff of 280 and can service two million vehicles a year.

GLASSHOUSE
Largest *Great Britain*
The largest glasshouse in the United Kingdom is one covering 7.34 acres *2,97 ha* owned by Van Heyningen Bros. at Holland Nurseries, Littlehampton, West Sussex.

GRAIN ELEVATOR
Largest
The world's largest single-unit grain elevator is that operated by the C-G-F-Grain Company at Wichita, Kansas, USA. Consisting of a triple row of storage tanks, 123 on each side of the central loading tower or 'head house', the unit is 2,717 ft *828 m* long and 100 ft *30 m* wide. Each tank is 120 ft *37 m* high, with an inside diameter of 30 ft *9 m* giving a total storage capacity of 20,000,000 bushels *7,3 million hl* of wheat. The largest collection of elevators in the world are the 23 at City of Thunder Bay, Ontario, Canada, on Lake Superior with a total capacity of 103.9 million bushels *37,4 million hl*.

SEWAGE WORKS
Largest *World*
The largest single full treatment sewage works in the world is the West-Southwest Treatment Plant, opened in 1940 on a site of 501 acres *203 ha* in Chicago, Illinois, USA. It serves an area containing 2,940,000 people. It treated an average of 835,000,000 US gal *3160 million litres* of wastes per day in 1973. The capacity of its sedimentation and aeration tanks is 1 280 000 m³ *1.6 million yd³*.

Great Britain
The largest full treatment works in Britain and probably in Europe is the GLC Beckton Works which serves a 2,966,000 population and handles a daily flow of 207 million gal *941 million litres* in a tank capacity of 757,000 ft³ *21 400 m³*.

WOODEN BUILDING
Largest
The world's largest buildings in timber are the two US Navy air-

ship hangers built in 1942–3 at Tillamook, Oregon. Now used by the Louisiana-Pacific Corporation as a saw mill they measure 1000 ft long, 170 ft high at the crown and 296 ft wide at the base *(304,8 m × 51,81 m × 90,22 m)* and are worth $6 million *(now £2.7 million)*.

AIR-SUPPORTED BUILDING
Largest
The world's largest air-supported roof is the roof of the 80,600 capacity octagonal Pontiac Silverdome Stadium, Michigan, USA measuring 522 ft *159 m* in width and 722 ft *220 m* in length. The air pressure is 5 lb/in² *34,4 kPa* supporting the 10 acre *4 ha* translucent 'Fiberglas' roofing. The structural engineers were Geiger-Berger Associates of New York City. The largest standard size air hall is one 860 ft *262 m* long, 140 ft *42,6 m* wide and 65 ft *19,8 m* high, at Lima, Ohio, USA, made by Irvin Industries of Stamford, Connecticut, USA.

2. BUILDINGS FOR LIVING

WOODEN BUILDINGS
Oldest
The oldest extant wooden buildings in the world are those comprising the Pagoda, Chumanar gate and the Temple of Horyu (Horyu-ji), at Nara, Japan, dating from *c.* AD 670 and completed in 715. The nearby Daibutsuden, built in 1704–11, once measured 285.4 ft long, 167.3 ft wide and 153.3 ft tall *87 × 51 × 46,75 m*. The present dimensions are 188 × 165.3 × 159.4 ft *57,3 × 50,4 × 48,6 m*.

CASTLES
Earliest *World*
Fortifications existed in all the great early civilisations, including that of ancient Egypt from 3000 BC. Fortified castles in the more accepted sense only existed much later. The oldest in the world is that at Gomdan, in the Yemen, which originally had 20 storeys and dates from before AD 100.

Great Britain
The oldest stone castle extant in Great Britain is Richmond Castle, Yorkshire, built in *c.* 1075. Iron Age relics from the first century BC or AD have been found in the lower levels of the Dover Castle site.

Ireland
The oldest Irish castle is Ferrycarrig near Wexford dating from *c.* 1180. The oldest castle in Northern Ireland is Carrickfergus Castle, County Antrim, Northern Ireland, which dates from before 1210.

Largest *World, UK and Ireland*
The largest inhabited castle in the world is the Royal residence of Windsor Castle at New Windsor, Berkshire. It is primarily of 12th century construction and is in the form of a waisted parallelogram 1890 ft by 540 ft *576 by 164 m*. The total area of Dover Castle however covers 34 acres *13,75 ha* with a width of 1100 ft *335,2 m* and a curtain wall of 1800 ft *550 m* or if underground works are taken in, 2300 ft *700 m*. The overall dimensions of Carisbrooke Castle (450 ft by 360 ft *110 by 137 m*), Isle of Wight, if its earthworks are included, are 1350 ft by 825 ft *411 m by 251 m*. The largest castle in Scotland is Edinburgh Castle with a major axis of 1320 ft *402 m* and measuring 3360 ft *1025 m* along its perimeter wall including the Esplanade. The most capacious of all Irish castles is Carrickfergus (see above) but that with the most extensive fortifications is Trim Castle, County Meath, built in *c.* 1205 with a curtain wall 1455 ft *443 m* long.

Forts *Largest*
The largest ancient castle in the world is Hradčany Castle, Prague, Czechoslovakia originating in the 9th century. It is a very oblong irregular polygon with an axis of 570 m *1870 ft* and an average traverse diameter of 128 m *420 ft* with a surface area of 7,28 hectares *18 acres*. Fort George, Ardersier, Highland built in 1748–69 measures 2100 ft *640 m* in length and has an average width of 620 ft *189 m*. The total site covers 42½ acres *17,2 ha*.

Thickest walls
The walls of Babylon north of Al Hillah, Iraq, built in 600 BC,

were up to 85 ft *26 m* in thickness. The walls of the Great Tower or Donjon of Flint Castle, built in 1277–80 are 23 ft *7,01 m* thick. The largest Norman keep in Britain is that of Colchester Castle measuring 152½ ft *46 m* by 111½ ft *34 m*.

PALACES
Largest *World*
The largest palace in the world is the Imperial Palace (*Gu gong*) in the centre of Peking (*Bei jing*, the northern capital), China, which covers a rectangle 1050 yd by 820 yd *960 by 750 m*, an area of 177.9 acres *72 ha*. The outline survives from the construction of the third Ming Emperor, Yung lo of 1402–24, but due to constant re-arrangements most of the intra-mural buildings are 18th century. These consist of 5 halls and 17 palaces of which the last occupied by the last Empress was the Palace of Accumulated Elegance (*Chu xia gong*) until 1924.

Residential
The largest residential palace in the world is the Vatican Palace, in the Vatican City, an enclave in Rome, Italy. Covering an area of 13½ acres *5,5 ha* it has 1400 rooms, chapels and halls, of which the oldest date from the 15th century.

Great Britain
The largest palace in the United Kingdom in Royal use is Buckingham Palace, London, so named after its site, bought in 1703 by John Sheffield, the 1st Duke of Buckingham and Normandy (1648–1721). Buckingham House was reconstructed in the Palladian style between 1835 and 1836, following the design of John Nash (1752–1835). The 610 ft *186 m* long East Front was built in 1846 and refaced in 1912. The Palace, which stands in 39 acres *15,8 ha* of garden, has 600 rooms including a ballroom 111 ft *34 m* long.

The largest ever Royal palace has been Hampton Court Palace, Greater London, acquired by Henry VIII from Cardinal Wolsey in 1525 and greatly enlarged by the King and later by William III, Anne and George I, whose son George II was its last resident monarch. It covers 4 acres *1,6 ha* of a 669 acre *270,7 ha* site.

Largest moat
The world's largest moats are those which surround the Imperial Palace in Peking (see above). From plans drawn by French sources it appears to measure 54 yd *49 m* wide and have a total length of 3600 yd *3290 m*. The city's moats total in all 23½ miles *38 km*.

FLATS
Largest
The largest blocks of private flats in Britain are the Barbican Estate, London, EC2 with 2011 flats on a 40 acre *16 ha* site with covered parking space for 2000 cars. The architects were Chamberlain, Powell and Bon.

Tallest *World*
The tallest block of flats in the world are Lake Point Towers of 70 storeys, and 645 ft *197 m* in Chicago, Illinois, USA.

Great Britain
The tallest residential block in Great Britain is the Shakespeare Tower in the Barbican in the City of London, which has 116 flats on 44 storeys and rises to a height of 419 ft 2½ in *127,77 m* above the street. The first of the three Barbican towers was 'topped out' in May 1971.

HOTELS
Largest *World*
The hotel with most rooms in the world is the 12 storey Hotel Rossiya in Moscow, USSR, with 3200 rooms providing accommodation for 6,000 guests, opened in 1967. It would thus require more than 8½ years to spend one night in each room. In addition there is a 21 storey 'Presidential' tower in the central courtyard. The hotel employs about 3000 people, and has 93 lifts. The ballroom is reputed to be the world's largest. Muscovites are not permitted as residents while foreigners are charged 16 times more than the very low rate charged to USSR officials.

The largest commercial hotel building in the world is The Waldorf Astoria, on Park Avenue, New York City, NY, USA. It occupies a complete block of 81,337 ft² (1.87 acres *0,75 ha*) and reaches a maximum height of 625 ft 7 in *191 m*. The Waldorf Astoria has 47 storeys and 1852 guests rooms and maintains the largest hotel radio receiving system in the world. The Waldorf can accommodate 10,000 people at one time and has a staff of 1700. The restaurants have catered for parties up to 6000 at a time. The coffee-maker's daily output reaches 1000 US gal *3785 litres*. The electricity bill is $2,000,000 each year. The hotel has housed 6 Heads of States simultaneously. It was opened on 1 Oct 1931.

Great Britain
The greatest sleeping capacity of any hotel in Great Britain is 1859 in the London Penta Hotel, Cromwell Road, London SW7 with a staff of 419. It was opened in 1973. The Regent Palace Hotel, Piccadilly Circus, London, opened 20 May 1915, has however 225 more rooms totalling 1140. The largest hotel is the Grosvenor House Hotel, Park Lane, London, which was opened in 1929. It is of 8 storeys covering 2½ acres *1 ha* and caters for more than 100,000 visitors per year in 470 rooms. The Great Room is the largest hotel room measuring 181 ft by 131 ft *55 by 40 m* with a height of 23 ft *7 m*. Banquets for 1500 are frequently handled.

Tallest
The tallest hotel in the world, measured from the street level of its main entrance to the top, is the 723 ft *220,3 m* tall 70 storey Peachtree Center Plaza, Atlanta, Georgia, USA. The $50 million 1100 room hotel is operated by Western International Hotels and owned by Portman Properties. Their Detroit Plaza measuring from the rear entrance level is however 748 ft *227,9 m* tall. Britain's tallest hotel is the 27 storey 380 ft *132,24 m* tall London Penta Hotel (see above).

The ground was broken in June 1980 for the building of the £100 million Raffles City project in Singapore. The central tower of 71 storeys will be 230 metres *754 ft 7 ins* tall.

Largest Lobby
The world's largest hotel lobby is that of The Grand Hotel, Taipei, Taiwan completed on 10 Oct 1973. It measures 47 × 35 m *154 × 114 ft* and is 9,6 m *31½ ft* high.

Most expensive
The world's costliest hotel accommodation is The Celestial Suite on the ninth floor of the Astro Village Hotel, Houston, Texas which is rented for $3000 (*now* £1330) a day. This compares with the official New York City Presidential Suite in The Waldorf Astoria at $1900 (*now* £860) a day.

The most expensive hotel suite in Britain is the Royal Suite on the 8th floor of the Hotel Inter-Continental, London W1, with 3 bedrooms at £460 (incl. VAT).

Spas
The largest spa in the world measured by number of available hotel rooms is Vichy, Allier, France, with 14,000 rooms. Spas are named after the watering place in the Liège province of Belgium where hydropathy was developed from 1626. The highest French spa is Baréges, Hautes-Pyrénées, at 4068 ft *1240 m* above sea level.

HOUSING
Largest estate
The largest housing estate in the United Kingdom is the 1670-acre *675 ha* Becontree Estate, on a site of 3000 acres *1214 ha* in Barking and Redbridge, Greater London, built between 1921 and 1929. The total number of homes is 26,822, with an estimated population of nearly 90,000.

New towns
Of the 23 new towns being built in Great Britain that with the largest eventual planned population is Milton Keynes, Buckinghamshire, with a projected 250,000 for 1992.

Largest house *World*
The largest private house in the world is the 250-room Biltmore House in Asheville, North Carolina, USA. It is owned by

George and William Cecil, grandsons of George Washington Vanderbilt II (1862–1914). The house was built between 1890 and 1895 in an estate of 119,000 acres *48 160 ha*, at a cost of $4,100,000 (now *£1,708,333*) and now valued at $55,000,000 with 12,000 acres *4856 ha*. The most expensive private house ever built is The Hearst Ranch at San Simeon, California, USA. It was built in 1922–39 for William Randolph Hearst (1863–1951), at a total cost of more than $30,000,000 (*then £6,120,000*). It has more than 100 rooms, a 104 ft *32 m* long heated swimming pool, an 83 ft *25 m* long assembly hall and a garage for 25 limousines. The house required 60 servants to maintain it.

Great Britain

The largest house in Great Britain was Wentworth Woodhouse, near Rotherham, South Yorkshire, formerly the seat of the Earls Fitzwilliam and now a teachers' training college. The main part of the house, built over 300 years ago, has more than 240 rooms with over 1000 windows, and its principle façade is 600 ft *183 m* long. The Royal residence, Sandringham House, Norfolk, has been reported to have had 365 rooms before the demolition of 73 surplus rooms in 1975. The largest house in Ireland is Castletown in County Kildare, owned by the Hon. Desmond Guinness and is the headquarters of the Irish Georgian Society. Scotland's largest house is Hopetoun House, West Lothian, built between 1696 and 1756 with a west façade 675 ft *206 m* long.

Smallest

The smallest house in Britain is the 19th century fisherman's cottage on Conway Quay, Gwynedd. It has a 72 in *182 cm* frontage, is 122 in *309 cm* high and has two tiny rooms and a staircase. The house with the narrowest known frontage is the 58 inches *1,47 m* of 21, Manor Road, Kingston, Portsmouth. It was built over a footpath.

Ex Jutland naval veteran Alexander Wortley (1900–80) lived his last 20 years in a green painted box in the garden of David Moreau in Langley Park, Buckinghamshire. It measured 5 × 4 × 3 feet with an extension for his feet—small enough to keep women out. He paid no rent, rates or taxes and did not believe in insurance, pensions or governments.

Most expensive *Houses*

The highest asking price for any private house is $16.5 million (*then £7.1 million*) in July 1980 for the late Conrad Hilton's (1888–1979) Casa Encantada built in 1938 in an 8½ acre *3,43 ha* estate in Bel-Air, Los Angeles, California, USA. It has 64 rooms and 26 bathrooms and 23,000 ft² *2136 m²* of living space. The Hilton attorney reportedly discouraged viewing by anyone less than a demi centi-millionaire. The most expensive house in Britain is the 14 bedroom Tudor mansion Sutton Place, Guildford, Surrey with 160 acres of garden and 4 tenanted farms sold in 1980 by Lintott Residential to Mr Stanley Seager for £7,750,000.

Penthouse

The world's most expensive penthouse is the four storey Galleria International penthouse on 57th Street between Park and Lexington Avenue, Manhattan, New York City with 4 main bedrooms, a 22 ft swimming pool, a library, a sauna and several solariums. It was on the market in March 1976 for £1,750,000.

Oldest

The oldest house in Britain is Eastry Court near Sandwich, Kent dating from AD 603. Some of the original timbers and stone infill still survives behind its present Georgian façade.

Stately home most visited

The most visited stately home, for which precise figures are published in the United Kingdom, is Beaulieu, Hampshire, owned by Lord Montagu of Beaulieu with 565,000 visitors (1980). The figures for Woburn Abbey, Bedfordshire, owned by the Duke of Bedford, have not been published since 1963 but the annual attendance including that of the Woburn Wild Animal Kingdom exceeds 1,000,000.

Barracks

The oldest purpose built barracks in the world are believed to be Collins Barracks, formerly the Royal Barracks, Dublin, Ireland, completed in 1704 and still in use.

3. BUILDINGS FOR ENTERTAINMENT

STADIUM
Largest *World*

The world's largest stadium is the Strahov Stadium in Praha (Prague), Czechoslovakia. It was completed in 1934 and can accommodate 240,000 spectators for mass displays of up to 40,000 Sokol gymnasts.

Football

The largest football stadium in the world is the Maracaña Municipal Stadium in Rio de Janeiro, Brazil, where the football ground has a normal capacity of 205,000, of whom 155,000 may be seated. A crowd of 199,854 was accommodated for the World Cup final between Brazil and Uruguay on 16 July 1950. A dry moat, 7 ft *2,13 m* wide and more than 5 ft *1,5 m* deep, protects players from spectators and *vice versa*. Britain's most capacious football stadium is Hampden Park, Glasgow opened on 31 Oct 1903 and once surveyed to accommodate 184,000 compared with an attendance of 149,547 on 17 Apr 1937 and the present licensed limit of 135,000.

Covered

The Azteca Stadium, Mexico City, Mexico, opened in 1968, has a capacity of 107,000 of whom nearly all are under cover. The largest covered stadium in Britain is the Empire Stadium Wembley, Brent, Greater London, opened in April 1923. It was the scene of the 1948 Olympic Games and the final of the 1966 World Cup. In 1962–3 the capacity under cover was increased to 100,000 of whom 45,000 may be seated. The original cost was £1,250,000.

Largest roof

The transparent acryl glass 'tent' roof over the Munich Olympic Stadium, W. Germany measures 914,940 ft² (21.0 acres *8,5 ha*) in area resting on a steel net supported by masts. The roof of longest span in the world is the 680 ft *207,2 m* diameter of the Louisiana Superdome (see below). The major axis of the elliptical Texas Stadium completed in 1971 at Irving, Texas is however 240 m *787 ft 4 in*.

Indoor

The world's largest indoor stadium is the 13 acre *5,26 ha* $173 million (*then £75 million*) 273 ft *83,2 m* tall Superdome in New Orleans, Louisiana completed in May 1975. Its maximum seating capacity for conventions is 97,365 or 76,791 for football. Box suites rent for $35,000 excluding the price of admission. A gondola with six 312 in *7,92 m* TV screens produces instant replay.

Ballroom

The dance floor used for championships at Earl's Court Exhibition Hall, Kensington, London extends 256 ft *78 m* in length.

Amusement resort

The world's largest amusement resort is Disney World in 27,443 acres *11 105 ha* of Orange and Osceola counties, 20 miles *32 km* south of west of Orlando in central Florida. It was opened on 1 Oct 1971. This $400 million investment attracted 10,700,000 visitors in its first year. The most attended resort in the world is Disneyland, Anaheim, California (opened 1955) where Gert Schelvis, 26, of Santa Barbara, Calif, became the 200 millionth visitor on 8 Jan 1981 at 11.10 am. The greatest attendance in a day has been 84,000 each spending on average some £15 indicating a gross of over £1¼ million (*then £570,000*).

Holiday camps

The largest holiday camp in Britain is that at Filey, North Yorkshire owned by Butlins Ltd. It extends over 500 acres *200 ha* and can house 10,600 residents.

Largest pleasure beach

The largest pleasure beach in the world is Virginia Beach, Virginia, USA. It has 28 miles *45 km* of beach front on the Atlantic and 10 miles *16 km* of estuary frontage. The area embraces 255 miles² *660 km²* and 134 hotels and motels.

Pleasure pier *Earliest longest and most*

The world's earliest pleasure pier was built at Great Yarmouth,

The most capacious hotel lobby in the world is that of the Grand Hotel, Taipei, Taiwan which has a floor area of 1645 m2 or more than four tenths of an acre (see p. 117).

Norfolk in 1808 but washed away in 1953. The Old Pier at Weymouth, Dorset dates back to 1812. The longest pleasure pier in the world is Southend Pier at Southend-on-Sea in Essex. It is 1.34 miles *2,15 km* in length. It was first opened in August 1889 with final extensions made in 1929. In 1949–50 the pier had 5,750,000 visitors. The pier railway was closed in October 1978.

The resort with most piers is Atlantic City, New Jersey, USA with 6 pre-war and 5 currently. In Britain only Blackpool has 3—North, Central and South.

Earliest fair

The earliest major international fair was the Great Exhibition of 1851 in the Crystal Palace, Hyde Park, City of Westminster, Greater London which in 141 days attracted 6,039,195 admissions.

Largest fair

The largest ever International Fair site was that for the St Louis, Missouri, Louisiana Purchase Exposition which covered 1271.76 acres *514,66 ha*. It also staged the 1904 Olympic Games and drew an attendance of 19,694,855.

Record fair attendance

The record attendance for any fair was 64,218,770 for Expo 70 held on an 815 acre *330 ha* site at Osaka, Japan from March to 13 Sept 1970. It made a profit of 19,439,402,017 yen (*then £22.6 million*).

Big wheel

The original Ferris Wheel, named after its constructor, George W. Ferris (1859–96), was erected in 1893 at the Midway, Chicago, Illinois, at a cost of $385,000 (*then £79,218*). It was 250 ft *76 m* in diameter, 790 ft *240 m* in circumference, weighed 1070 tons *1087 tonnes* and carried 36 cars each seating 60 people, making a total of 2160 passengers. The structure was removed in 1904 to St Louis, Missouri, and was eventually sold as scrap for $1800 (*then £370*). In 1897 a Ferris Wheel with a diameter of 300 ft *91 m* was erected for the Earl's Court Exhibition, London. It had ten 1st-class and 30 2nd-class cars. The largest wheel now operating is at Kobe Portopialand, Kobe, Japan, with a height of 63,5 m *208 ft 4 in*. It was constructed by Hankyu Railway Corporation of Osaka, Japan and completed in March 1981.

Hradčany Castle, Prague, the worlds largest ancient castle, dating from the 9th century (see p. 116). (*Stan Greenberg*)

The world's largest big wheel is that of Kobe's Portopialand Amusement Park, Japan with a height of 63,5 m *208 ft 4 in* opened in March 1981.

Fastest switchback

The maximum speeds claimed for switchbacks, scenic railways or roller coasters have in the past been exaggerated for commercial reasons. The fastest and also the longest roller coaster in the world is *The Beast* at Kings Island near Cincinnati, Ohio, USA. Scientific tests at the base of its 141 ft *42,98 m* high drop returned a speed of 64.77 mph *104,23 km/h* on 5 Apr 1980. The run of 7400 ft or 1.40 miles *2,25 km* incorporates 800 ft *243,8 m* of tunnels and a 540 degree banked helix. The wooded site covers 35 acres *14,1 ha*. The tallest is the Tojoko Land Loop Coaster in Hyogo, Japan opened on 4 Aug 1979. It is 193 ft 5 in *59,96 m* tall.

Longest slide

The longest slide in the world is at Bad Tölz, West Germany. This has a length of 1226 m *0.76 mile* and a vertical drop of 220 m *721 ft*.

Restaurant *Highest*

The highest restaurant in the world is at the Chacaltaya ski resort, Bolivia at 5340 m *17,519 ft*. The highest in Great Britain is the Ptarmigan Observation Restaurant at 3650 ft *1112 m* above sea-level on Cairngorm (4084 ft *1244 m*) near Aviemore, Highland, Scotland.

Night club *Oldest*

The earliest night club (*boite de nuit*) was 'Le Bal des Anglais' at 6 Rue des Anglais, Paris, 5e France. It was founded in 1843 but closed *c.* 1960.

Largest

The largest night club in the world is Gilley's Club (formerly Shelly's) built in 1955 and extended in 1971 on Spencer Highway, Houston, Texas, USA. with a seating capacity of more than 3000 and a total capacity of 5500. In the more classical sense the largest night club in the world is 'The Mikado' in the Akasaka district of Tōkyō, Japan, with a seating capacity of 2000. It is 'manned' by 1250 hostesses. A binocular is essential to an appreciation of the floor show.

Lowest

The lowest night club is the 'Minus 206' in Tiberias, Israel o the shores of the Sea of Galilee. It is 206 m *676 ft* below sea-leve An alternative candidate is 'Outer Limits', opposite the Co Palace, San Francisco, California which was raided for the 151 time on 1 Aug 1971. It has been called 'The Most Busted Join and 'The Slowest to Get the Message'.

PUBLIC HOUSES
Oldest

There are various claimants to the title of the United Kingdom oldest inn. A foremost claimant is 'The Fighting Cocks', S Albans, Hertfordshire (an 11th century structure on an 8th cer tury site). The timber frame of The Royalist Hotel, Digbet Street, Stow-on-the-Wold, Gloucestershire has been dated 1000 years before the present. It was the inn 'The Eagle and th Child' in the 13th century and known to exist in AD 947. A origin as early as AD 560 has been claimed for 'Ye Olde Ferr Boat Inn' at Holywell, Cambridgeshire. There is some evidenc that it antedates the local church, built in 980, but the earlies documents are not dated earlier than 1100. There is evidenc that the 'Bingley Arms', Bardsey, near Leeds, West Yorkshire restored and extended in 1738, existed as the 'Priest's Inn according to Bardsey Church records dated 905.

The oldest pub in Ireland is 'The Brazen Head', Bridge Stree Dublin licensed in 1666 and re-built in 1668. The fact that th former den of iniquity does not sell Draught Guinness is ev dence of its antiquity.

Largest *World*

The largest beer-selling establishment in the world is th Mathäser, Bayerstrasse 5, München (Munich), West German where the daily sale reaches 84,470 pts *48 000 litres*. It was estab lished in 1829, was demolished in World War II and re-built b 1955 and now seats 5500 people. The through-put at the Dub beer halls in the Bantu township of Soweto, Johannesburg South Africa may, however, be higher on some Saturdays whe the average consumption of 6000 gal (48,000 pts *27 280 litres*) far exceeded.

Great Britain

The largest public house in Great Britain is 'The Swan' at Yard ley, West Midlands. It has eight bars with a total drinking are of 13,852 ft² *1287 m²* with 58 taps and 2 miles *3,2 km* of piping The sale of beer is equivalent to 31,000 bottles per week. Th pub can hold well over 1000 customers and 320 for banqueting The permanent staff totals 60 with seven resident. 'The Swan' owned by Allied Breweries and administered by Ansel Limited.

Smallest

The smallest pub in Great Britain is the 17th century 'The Nut shell', Bury St Edmunds, Suffolk with maximum dimensions o 15 ft 10 in by 7 ft 6 in *4,82 × 2,28 m*.

Longest bars *World*

The longest permanent bar with beer pumps is that built in 193 at the Working Men's Club, Mildura, Victoria, Australia. It ha a counter 298 ft *90,8 m* in length, served by 27 pumps. Tempor ary bars have been erected of greater length. The Falstaff Brew ing Corp. put up a temporary bar 336 ft 5 in *102 m* in length o Wharf St, St Louis, Missouri, USA, on 22 June 1970. The Bar a Erickson's on Burnside Street, Portland, Oregon, in its heyda (1883–1920) possessed a bar which ran continuously around an across the main saloon measuring 684 ft *208,48 m*. The chie bouncer Edward 'Spider' Johnson had a chief assistant name 'Jumbo' Reilly who weighed 23 stone and was said to resembl 'an ill natured orang-utan'. Beer was 5 cents for 16 fluid ounces

United Kingdom and Ireland

The longest bars in the United Kingdom with beer pumps ar the Theatre Bar, The Gaiety Bar and the Princes Bar, at Butlin Holiday Camp, Filey, North Yorkshire, each measuring 80 f *24,38 m* in length and each having 40 dispensers (beer an lager). The longest bar in a pub is of 71 ft 11 in *21,92 m* with 2 dispensers in 'The Mount Pleasant Inn', Repton, Derbyshire The Grand Stand Bar at Galway Racecourse, Ireland complete in 1955, measures 210 ft *64 m*.

longest tenure

There are no collated records on licensees but the 'Glan-y-Afon Inn', Milwr near Holywell, North Wales had a 418 year long (1559–1977) run within a family which ended with the retirement of Mrs Mary Evans.

longest name

The pub with the longest name is the 39 letter 'The Thirteenth Mounted Cheshire Rifleman Inn', at Stalybridge, Greater Manchester, but 'The Green Man and Black's Head Royal Hotel' at Ashbourne, Derbyshire has more words.

shortest name

The public house in the United Kingdom with the shortest name is the 'X' (formerly Merry Harrier's) at Westcott, Cullompton, Devon.

commonest name

The commonest pub name in Britain is 'Red Lion' of which there are probably just more than 1000. John A. Blackwell of Ferndown, Dorset has recorded over 4600 different pub names.

highest

The highest public house in the United Kingdom is the 'Tan Hill Inn' in North Yorkshire. It is 1732 ft *528 m* above sea-level, on the moorland road between Reeth, North Yorkshire and Brough, Cumbria. The highest pub open the year round is the 'Cat and Fiddle' in Cheshire, near Buxton, Derbyshire at 1690 ft *515 m*. The White Lady Restaurant, 2550 ft *777 m* up on Cairngorm (4084 ft *1244 m*) near Aviemore, Highland, Scotland is the highest licensed restaurant.

most visits

Stanley House of Totterdown, Bristol has visited 3289 differently named pubs in Britain by way of public transport only to 1 May 1981. Jimmy Young GM BEM, of Better Pubs Ltd claims to have visited over 23,000 different pubs.

4. TOWERS AND MASTS

TALLEST STRUCTURES

World

The tallest structure in the world is the guyed Warszawa Radio mast at Konstantynow near Gabin and Płock 60 miles *96 km* north-west of the capital of Poland. It is 646,38 m *2120 ft 8 in* tall or more than four tenths of a mile. The mast was completed on 18 July 1974 and put into operation on 22 July 1974. It was designed by Jan Polak and weighs 550 tons/*tonnes*. The mast is so high that anyone falling off the top would reach their terminal velocity and hence cease to be accelerating before hitting the ground. Work was begun in July 1970 on this tubular steel construction, with its 15 steel guy ropes. It recaptured for Europe a record held in the USA since the Chrysler Building surpassed the Eiffel Tower in 1929.

Great Britain

The tallest structure in the United Kingdom is the Independent Broadcasting Authority's mast at Belmont, north of Horncastle, Lincolnshire completed in 1965 to a height of 1265 ft *385 m* with 7 ft *2,13 m* added by meteorological equipment installed in September 1967. It serves Yorkshire TV and weighs 210 tons.

TALLEST TOWERS

World

The tallest self-supporting tower (as opposed to a guyed mast) in the world is the $44 million CN Tower in Metro Centre, Toronto, Canada, which rises to 1822 ft 1 in *555,33 m*. Excavation began on 12 Feb 1973 for the 130,000 ton structure of reinforced, post-tensioned concrete topped out on 2 Apr 1975. The 416-seat restaurant revolves in the Sky Pod at 1140 ft *347,5 m* from which the visibility extends to hills 74½ miles *120 km* distant. Lightning strikes the top about 200 times (30 storms) per annum.

The tallest tower built before the era of television masts is the Eiffel Tower, in Paris, France, designed by Alexandre Gustav

Eiffel (1832–1923) for the Paris exhibition and completed on 31 Mar 1889. It was 300,51 m *985 ft 11 in* tall, now extended by a TV antenna to 320,75 m *1052 ft 4 in* and weighs 7340 tonnes *7224 tons*. The maximum sway in high winds is 12,7 cm *5 in*. The whole iron edifice which has 1792 steps, took 2 years, 2 months and 2 days to build and cost 7,799,401 francs 31 centimes.

Great Britain

The tallest self-supported tower in Great Britain is the 1080 ft *329,18 m* tall Independent Broadcasting Authority transmitter at Emley Moor, West Yorkshire, completed in September 1971. The structure, which cost £900,000, has an enclosed room at the 865 ft *263,65 m* level and weighs with its foundations more than 15,000 tons/*tonnes*. The tallest tower of the pre-television era was the New Brighton Tower of 562 ft *171,29 m* built on Merseyside in 1897–1900 and dismantled in 1919–21.

5. BRIDGES

Oldest *World*

Arch construction was understood by the Sumerians as early as 3200 BC and a reference exists to a Nile bridge in 2650 BC. The oldest surviving datable bridge in the world is the slab stone single arch bridge over the River Meles in Smyrna (now Izmir), Turkey, which dates from *c.* 850 BC.

Great Britain

The clapper bridges of Dartmoor and Exmoor (*e.g.* the Tarr Steps over the River Barle, Exmoor, Somerset) are thought to be of prehistoric types although none of the existing examples can be certainly dated. They are made of large slabs of stone placed over boulders. The Romans built stone bridges in England and remains of these have been found at Corbridge (Roman, Corstopitum), Northumberland dating to the 2nd century AD; Chester, Northumberland and Willowford, Cumbria. Remains of a very early wooden bridge have been found at Ardwinkle, Northamptonshire.

LONGEST
Cable suspension *World*

The world's longest bridge span is the main span of the Humber Estuary Bridge, England at 4626 ft *1410 m*. Work began on 27 July 1972, after a decision announced on 22 Jan 1966. The towers are 162,5 m *533 ft 1⅝ in* tall from datum and are 1⅜ in *36 mm* out of parallel, to allow for the curvature of the Earth. Including the Hessle and the Barton side spans, the bridge stretches 2220 m or 1.37 miles. On 22 Mar 1980 an accident occurred with the slinging of the decking. The bridge was structurally completed on 18 July 1980 at a cost of £88 million and was opened by HM the Queen on 17 July 1981. Tolls, ranging between £1 for cars and £7.50 for heavy vehicles, operative from 4 May 1981, are the highest in Britain.

The Mackinac Straits Bridge between Mackinaw City and St Ignace, Michigan, USA, is the longest suspension bridge in the

The CN Tower in Toronto, Canada the tallest self-supporting tower in the world with a height of 1822 ft 1 in *555,33 m* topped out on 2 Apr 1975. For the stair climbing record see page 192.

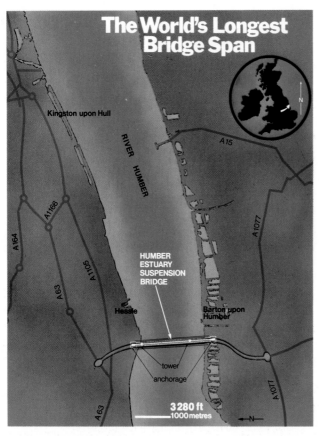

The World's Longest Bridge Span

Kingston upon Hull

RIVER HUMBER

A15

A1166

A164

A1077

A1105

A63

HUMBER ESTUARY SUSPENSION BRIDGE

Hessle

Barton upon Humber

tower

anchorage

A63

A1077

3280 ft
1000 metres

N

suspended length with side spans totalling 11,680 ft *3560 m*. Work began in October 1978 and the eventual cost is expected exceed 1000 billion (10^{12}) yen.

Plans for a Messina Bridge linking Sicily with the Italian main land are dependent upon EEC budgets. One preliminary stu calls for towers 1000 ft *304,8 m* tall and a span of 3000 m *9842* or 1.86 miles. The total cost, it has been estimated, would how ever, exceed £2,000 million.

Cantilever *World*

The Quebec Bridge (Pont de Québec) over the St Lawren River in Canada has the longest cantilever truss span of any the world—1800 ft *549 m* between the piers and 3239 ft *987* overall. It carries a railway track and 2 carriageways. Begun 1899, it was finally opened to traffic on 3 Dec 1917 at a cost of lives, and $Can.22,500,000 (*then £4,623,000*).

Great Britain

The longest cantilever bridge in Great Britain is the For Bridge. Its two main spans are 1710 ft *521 m* long. It carries double railway track over the Firth of Forth 156 ft *47,5 m* abo the water level. Work commenced in November 1882 and t first test trains crossed on 22 Jan 1890 after an expenditure of million. It was officially opened on 4 Mar 1890. Of the 45 workers who built it, 57 were killed in various accidents.

Steel arch *World*

The longest steel arch bridge in the world is the New Riv Gorge bridge, near Fayetteville, West Virginia, USA, co pleted in 1977 with a span of 1700 ft *518,2 m*.

Great Britain

The longest steel arch bridge in Great Britain is the Runcor Widnes bridge, Cheshire opened on 21 July 1961. It has a sp of 1082 ft *329,8 m*.

Floating bridge

The longest floating bridge in the world is the Second La Washington Bridge, Seattle, Washington State, USA. Its to length is 12,596 ft *3839 m* and its floating section measur 7518 ft *2291 m* (1.42 miles *2,29 km*). It was built at a total cost $15,000,000 (*then £5,357,000*) and completed in August 1963

Covered bridge

The longest covered bridge in the world is that at Hartland, Ne

world measured between anchorages (1.58 miles *2543 m*) and has an overall length, including viaducts of the bridge proper measured between abutment bearings, of 3.63 miles *5853,79 m*. It was opened in November 1957 (dedicated 28 June 1958) at a cost of $100 million (*then £35,700,000*) and has a main span of 3800 ft *1158 m*.

The double-deck road-rail Akashi-Kaikyo bridge linking Honshū and Shikoku, Japan is planned to be completed in 1988. The main span will be 5840 ft *1780 m* in length with an overall

A PROGRESSIVE RECORD OF THE WORLD'S TALLEST STRUCTURES

Height in ft	m	Structure	Location	Material	Building or Completion Dates
204	62	Djoser step pyramid (earliest Pyramid)	Saqqâra, Egypt	Tura limestone casing	c. 2650 BC
294	89	Pyramid of Meidum	Meidum, Egypt	Tura limestone casing	c. 2600 BC
c. 336	102	Snefru Bent pyramid	Dahshûr, Egypt	Tura limestone casing	c. 2600 BC
342	104	Snefru North Stone pyramid	Dahshûr, Egypt	Tura limestone casing	c. 2600 BC
480.9[1]	146,5	Great Pyramid of Cheops (Khufu)	El Gizeh, Egypt	Tura limestone casing	c. 2580 BC
525[2]	160	Lincoln Cathedral, Central Tower	Lincoln, England	lead sheathed wood	c. 1307–1548
489[3]	149	St Paul's Cathedral spire	City of London, England	lead sheathed wood	1315–1561
465	141	Minster of Notre Dame	Strasbourg, France	Vosges sandstone	1420–1439
502[4]	153	St Pierre de Beauvais spire	Beauvais, France	lead sheathed wood	–1568
475	144	St Nicholas Church	Hamburg, Germany	stone and iron	1846–1847
485	147	Rouen Cathedral spire	Rouen, France	cast iron	1823–1876
513	156	Köln Cathedral spires	Cologne, W. Germany	stone	–1880
555[5]	169	Washington Monument	Washington, DC, USA	stone	1848–1884
985.9[6]	300,5	Eiffel Tower	Paris, France	iron	1887–1889
1046	318	Chrysler Building	New York City, USA	steel and concrete	1929–1930
1250[7]	381	Empire State Building	New York City, USA	steel and concrete	1929–1930
1572	479	KWTV Television Mast	Oklahoma City, USA	steel	Nov 1954
1610[8]	490	KSWS Television Mast	Roswell, New Mexico, USA	steel	Dec 1956
1619	493	WGAN Television Mast	Portland, Maine, USA	steel	Sept 1959
1676	510	KFVS Television Mast	Cape Girardeau, Missouri, USA	steel	June 1960
1749	533	WTVM & WRBL Television Mast	Columbus, Georgia, USA	steel	May 1962
1749	533	WBIR-TV Mast	Knoxville, Tennessee, USA	steel	Sept 1963
2063	628	KTHI-TV Mast	Fargo, North Dakota, USA	steel	Nov 1963
2120.6	646,38	Warszawa Radio Mast	Płock, Poland	galvanised steel	22 July 1974

[1] *Original height. With loss of pyramidion (topmost stone) height now 449 ft 6 in 137 m*
[2] *Fell in a storm.*
[3] *Struck by lightning and destroyed 4 June 1561.*
[4] *Fell April 1573, shortly after completion.*
[5] *Sinking at a rate of 0.0047 ft per annum or 5 in 12,7 cm since 1884.*
[6] *Original height. With addition of TV antenna in 1957, now 1052 ft 320,75 m.*
[7] *Original height. With addition of TV tower on 1 May 1951 now 1427 ft 449 m. Exterior is clad in limestone from the Empire Quarry, Indiana.*
[8] *Fell in gale in 1960.*

Brunswick, Canada measuring 1282 ft *390,8 m* overall, completed in 1899.

Railway bridge

The longest railway bridge in the world is the Huey P. Long Bridge, Metairie, Louisiana, USA with a railway section 22,996 ft *7009 m* (4.35 miles *7 km*) long. It was completed on 16 Dec 1935 with a longest span of 790 ft *241 m*. The Yangtse River Bridge, completed in 1968 in Nanking, China is the world's longest combined highway and railway bridge. The rail deck is 6772 m *4.20 miles* and the road deck is 4589 m *2.85 miles*.

Great Britain

The longest railway bridge in Britain is the second Tay Bridge (11,653 ft *3552 m*), Tayside, Scotland opened on 20 June 1887. Of the 85 spans, 74 (length 10,289 ft *3136 m*) are over the waterway. The 878 brick arches of the London Bridge to Deptford Creek viaduct built in 1836 extend for 3¾ miles *6,0 km*.

Longest bridging

The world's longest bridging is the Second Lake Pontchartrain Causeway, completed on 23 Mar 1969, joining Lewisburg and Metairie, Louisiana, USA. It has a length of 126,055 ft *38 422 m* (23.87 miles). It cost $29,900,000 (*then £12.45 million*) and is 228 ft *69 m* longer than the adjoining First Causeway completed in 1956. The longest railway viaduct in the world is the rock-filled Great Salt Lake Railroad Trestle, carrying the Southern Pacific Railroad 11.85 miles *19 km* across the Great Salt Lake, Utah, USA. It was opened as a pile and trestle bridge on 8 Mar 1904, but converted to rock fill in 1955–60.

The longest stone arch bridging in the world is the 3810 ft *1161 m* long Rockville Bridge north of Harrisburg, Pennsylvania, USA, with 48 spans containing 196,000 tons/*tonnes* of stone and completed in 1901.

Widest bridge

The world's widest long-span bridge is the 1650 ft *502,9 m* span Sydney Harbour Bridge, Australia (160 ft *48 m* wide). It carries two electric overhead railway tracks, 8 lanes of roadway and a cycle and footway. It was officially opened on 19 Mar 1932. The Crawford Street Bridge in Providence, Rhode Island, USA, has a width of 1147 ft *350 m*. The River Roch is bridged for a distance of 1460 ft *445 m* where the culvert passes through the centre of Rochdale, Greater Manchester and this is sometimes claimed to be a breadth.

HIGHEST
World

The highest bridge in the world is the bridge over the Royal Gorge of the Arkansas River in Colorado, USA. It is 1053 ft *321 m* above the water level. It is a suspension bridge with a main span of 880 ft *268 m* and was constructed in 6 months, ending on 6 Dec 1929. The highest railway bridge in the world is the single track span at Fades, outside Clermont-Ferrand, France. It was built in 1901–9 with a span of 472 ft *144 m* and is 435 ft *132,5 m* above the River Sioule.

Great Britain

The highest railway bridge in Great Britain is the Ballochmyle viaduct over the River Ayr, Strathclyde built 169 ft *51,5 m* over the river bed in 1846–8 with the then world's longest masonry arch span of 181 ft *55,16 m*.

AQUEDUCTS
World longest *Ancient*

The greatest of ancient aqueducts was the Aqueduct of Carthage in Tunisia, which ran 87.6 miles *141 km* from the springs of Zaghouan to Djebel Djougar. It was built by the Romans during the reign of Publius Aelius Hadrianus (AD 117–38). By 1895, 344 arches still survived. Its original capacity has been calculated at 7,000,000 gal *31,8 million litres* per day. The triple-tiered aqueduct Pont du Gard, built in AD 19 near Nîmes, France, is 160 ft *48 m* high. The tallest of the 14 arches of Aguas Livres Aqueduct, built in Lisbon, Portugal, in 1784 is 213 ft 3 in *65 m*.

World longest *Modern*

The world's longest aqueduct, in the modern sense of a water conduit, as opposed to an irrigation canal, is the California State Water Project aqueduct, completed in 1974, to a length of 826 miles *1329 km* of which 385 miles *619 km* is canalised.

Great Britain *longest*

The longest bridged aqueduct in Britain is the Pont Cysylltau in Clwyd on the Frankton to Llantisilio branch of the Shropshire Union Canal. It is 1007 ft *307 m* long, has 19 arches up to 121 ft *36 m* high above low water on the Dee. It was designed by Thomas Telford (1757–1834) of Scotland, and was opened for use in 1805.

6. CANALS

Earliest *World*

Relics of the oldest canals in the world, dated by archaeologists *c.* 4000 BC, were discovered near Mandali, Iraq early in 1968.

Earliest *Great Britain*

The earliest canals in Britain were first cut by the Romans. In the Midlands the 11 mile *17 km* long Fossdyke Canal between Lincoln and the River Trent at Torksey was built in about AD 65 and was scoured in 1122. Part of it is still in use today. Though the Exeter canal was cut as early as 1564–6, the first wholly artificial major navigation canal in the United Kingdom was the 18½ mile *29,7 km* long canal with 14 locks from Whitecoat Point to Newry, Northern Ireland opened on 28 Mar 1742. In Great Britain the Sankey Navigation Canal in Lancashire, 8 miles *12,8 km* in length, with 10 locks, was opened in November 1757.

Longest *World*

The longest canalised system in the world is the Volga–Baltic Canal opened in April 1965. It runs 1850 miles *2300 km* from Astrakhan up the Volga, *via* Kuybyshev, Gor'kiy and Lake Ladoga, to Leningrad, USSR. The longest canal of the ancient world has been the Grand Canal of China from Peking to Hangchou. It was begun in 540 BC and not completed until 1327 by which time it extended (including canalised river sections) for 1107 miles *1781 km*. The estimated work force *c.* AD 600 reached 5,000,000 on the Pien section. Having been allowed by 1950 to silt up to the point that it was, in no place, more than 6 ft *1,8 m* deep, it is now, however, plied by ships of up to 2000 tons/ *tonnes*.

The Beloye More (White Sea) Baltic Canal from Belomorsk to Povenets, in the USSR, is 141 miles *227 km* long with 19 locks. It was completed with the use of forced labour in 1933 and cannot accommodate ships of more than 16 ft *5 m* in draught.

The world's longest big ship canal is the Suez Canal linking the Red and Mediterranean Seas, opened on 16 Nov 1869 but inoperative from June 1967 to June 1975. The canal was planned by the French diplomatist Count Ferdinand de Lesseps (1805–94) and work began on 25 Apr 1859. It is 100.6 miles *161,9 km* in length from Port Said lighthouse to Suez Roads and 197 ft *60 m* wide. The construction work force was 8213 men and 368 camels. The largest vessel to transit has been SS *British Progress* a VLCC (Very Large Crude Carrier) of 228 589 tonnes dwt (length 329,66 m *1081.5 ft*; beam 48,68 m *159.7 ft* at a maximum draft of 25,60 m *84 ft*). This was southbound in ballast on 5 July 1976.

PROGRESSIVE LIST OF HIGHEST STRUCTURES IN GREAT BRITAIN			
Feet	**Metres**		
404	*123*	Salisbury Cathedral Spire	c. 1305–
525	*160*	Lincoln Cathedral	1307–1548
489	*149*	St Paul's Cathedral, London	1315–1561
518.7	*158,1*	Blackpool Tower, Lancashire	1894–
562	*171,29*	New Brighton Tower, Merseyside	1900–1919
820	*250*	GPO Radio Masts, Rugby	1925–
1000*	*304,8*	ITA Mast, Mendlesham, Suffolk	July 1959
1265	*385*	IBA Mast, Emley Moor, Yorkshire	1965–1969†
1265	*385*	IBA Mast, Belmont	1965–
1272	*387,1*	IBA Mast, Belmont	Sept. 1967

*ITA masts of the same height followed at Lichfield, Staffordshire; Black Hill, Strathclyde; Caldbeck, Cumbria; and Durris, Grampian.
†Severely damaged by icing and replaced.

123

Busiest

The busiest big ship canal is the Panama, first transitted on 15 Aug 1914. In 1974 there were a record 14,304 ocean-going transits. The largest liner to transit is *Queen Elizabeth 2* (66,851 gross tons) on 25 Jan 1980 for a toll of $89,154.62. *(then £38,760)* The ships with the greatest beam to transit have been the *Acadia Forest* and the *Atlantic Forest* of 106.9 ft *32,58 m*. The lowest toll was 36 US cents by the swimmer Richard Halliburton in 1928. The fastest transit has been 2 hr 41 min by the US Navy hydrofoil *Pegasus* on 20 June 1979.

Longest *Great Britain*

Inland Waterways in Great Britain, normally defined as nontidal (except for a few tidal 'links' on the Thames, Trent and Yorkshire Ouse) rivers and canals, consist of 2394 miles *3852 km* with 110 miles *177 km* being restored. Of this total 2125 miles *3420 km* are inter-linked.

The longest possible journey on the system would be one of 415¾ miles *669 km* and 157 locks from Bedford, on the Great Ouse to near Ripon, North Yorkshire.

Largest seaway

The world's longest artificial seaway is the St Lawrence Seaway (189 miles *304 km* long) along the New York State–Ontario border from Montreal to Lake Ontario, which enables 80 per cent of all ocean-going ships, and bulk carriers with a capacity of 26,000 tons *26 400 tonnes* to sail 2342 miles *3769 km* from the North Atlantic, up the St Lawrence estuary and across the Great Lakes to Duluth, Minnesota, USA, on Lake Superior (602 ft *183 m* above sea level). The project cost $470,000,000 *(then £168 million)* and was opened on 25 Apr 1959.

Irrigation canal

The longest irrigation canal in the world is the Karakumskiy Kanal, stretching 528 miles *850 km* from Haun-Khan to Ashkhabad, Turkmenistan, USSR. In September 1971 the 'navigable' length reached 280 miles *450 km*. The length of the £370 million project will reach 930 miles *1300 km*.

LOCKS

Largest *World*

The world's largest single lock is that connecting the Schelde with the Kanaaldok system at Zandvliet, west of Antwerp, Belgium. It is 500 m *1640 ft* long and 57 m *187 ft* wide and is an entrance to an impounded sheet of water 18 km *11.2 miles* long.

Largest *Great Britain*

The largest lock in the United Kingdom is the West Dock, Bristol which measures 1200 × 140 ft *366 × 42,7 m* and has a depth of 58 ft *17,7 m*.

Deepest *World*

The world's deepest lock is the John Day dam lock on the Columbia river, Oregon and Washington, USA completed in 1963. It can raise or lower barges 113 ft *34,4 m* and is served by a 982 ton *998 tonne* gate.

Deepest *Great Britain*

The deepest lock in Britain is the rebuilt Lock 8/9 at Bath on the Kennet and Avon Canal which will lower boats 19½ ft *5,94 m*.

Longest flight

The world's highest lock elevator overcomes a head of 68,58 m *225 ft* at Ronquières on the Charleroi-Brussels Canal, Belgium. The two 236 wheeled caissons each able to carry 1350 tons take 22 min to cover the 1432 m *4698 ft* long ramp.

The longest flight of locks in the United Kingdom is on the Worcester and Birmingham Canal at Tardebigge, Hereford and Worcester, where in a 2½ mile *4 km* stretch there are the Tardebigge (30) and Stoke (6) flights which together drop the canal 259 ft *78,9 m*. The highest rise of any boat-carrying plane in Britain was the 225 ft *68,6 m* of the 935 ft *285 m* long Hobbacott Down plane on the Bude Canal, Cornwall.

Largest cut

The Gaillard Cut (known as 'the Ditch') on the Panama Canal is 270 ft *82 m* deep between Gold Hill and Contractor's Hill with a bottom width of 500 ft *152 m*. In one day in 1911 as many as 333 dirt trains each carrying 357 tons *363 tonnes* left this site. The total amount of earth excavated for the whole Panama Canal as of 1 Oct 1979 was 666,194,450 yd³ *509 338 960 m³* which total will be raised by the further widening of the Gaillard Cut.

7. DAMS

Earliest

The earliest known dams were those uncovered by the British School of Archaeology in Jerusalem in 1974 at Jawa in Jordan. These stone-faced earth dams are dated to *c.* 3200 BC.

Most massive

Measured by volume, the largest dam in the world is the 98 ft *29,8 m* high New Cornelia Tailings earth-fill dam, Arizona, USA with a volume of 274,026,000 yd³ *209 506 000 m³* completed in 1973 to a length of 6.74 miles *10,85 km*. The Guri dam across the Caroni River, Venezuela will eventually have a volume of 277,846,000 m³ *363,394,000 yd³*.

Largest concrete

The world's largest concrete dam, and the largest concrete structure in the world, is the Grand Coulee Dam on the Columbia River, Washington State, USA. Work on the dam was begun in 1933, it began working on 22 Mar 1941 and was completed in 1942 at a cost of $56 million. It has a crest length of 4173 ft *1272 m* and is 550 ft *167 m* high. It contains 10,585,000 yd³ *8 092 000 m³* of concrete and weighs about 19,285,000 tons *19 595 000 tonnes*. The hydro-electric power plant (now being extended) will have a capacity of 9,780,000 kW.

Highest

The highest dam in the world is the Grande Dixence in Switzerland, completed in September 1961 at a cost of 1600 million Swiss francs *(then £151,000,000)*. It is 935 ft *285 m* from base to rim, 2296 ft *700 m* long and the total volume of concrete in the dam is 7,792,000 yd³ *5 957 000 m³*. The Rogunsky earth-fill dam will have a final height of 1066 ft *325 m* across the Vakhsh river, Tadzhikistan, USSR with a crest length of only 2165 ft *660 m*.

Longest

The longest river dam in the world is the 62 ft *19 m* high Kiev dam on the river Dnepr, USSR which was completed in 1964 to a length of 33.6 miles *54,1 km*. The Yacyreta–Apipe dam across the Paraná on the Paraguay–Argentina borders will extend for 69,6 km *43.24 miles*. In the early 17th century an impounding dam of moderate height was built in Lake Hungtze, Kiangsu China, to a reputed length of 100 km *62 miles*.

The longest sea dam in the world is the Afsluitdijk stretching 20.195 miles *32,5 km* across the mouth of the Zuider Zee in two sections of 1.553 miles *2,499 km* (mainland of North Holland to the Isle of Wieringen) and 18.641 miles *30 km* from Wieringen to Friesland. It has a sea-level width of 293 ft *89 m* and a height of 24 ft 7 in *7,5 m*.

Strongest

The world's strongest structure will be the 242 m *793 ft* high Sayano-Shusenskaya dam on the River Yenisey, USSR which is under construction and designed to bear a load of 18 000 000 tonnes/*tons* from a fully-filled reservoir of 31,300 million m³ *41,000 million yd³* capacity.

United Kingdom

The most massive (5,630,000 yd³ *4 304 000 m³*), and longest (2050 ft *625 m* crest length) high dam in the United Kingdom is the 240 ft *73 m* high Scammonden Dam, West Yorkshire, begun in November 1966 and completed in the summer of 1970. This rock-fill dam carries the M62 on its crest and was built by Sir Alfred McAlpine's. The cost of the project together with the 6½ miles *10 km* motorway was £8,400,000. There are longer low dams or barrages of the valley cut-off type, notably the Hanningfield Dam, Essex, built from July 1952 to August 1956 to a length of 6850 ft *2088 m* and a height of 64.5 ft *19,7 m*. The rock-fill Llyn Brianne Dam, Dyfed is Britain's highest dam reaching 298½ ft *91 m* in Nov 1971 and becoming operational on 20 July 1972.

Largest reservoir *World*

The most voluminous man-made reservoir is at Bratsk (River Angara) USSR, with a volume of 137,214,000 acre-ft *169,25 km³*. The dam was completed in 1964.

The world's largest artificial lake measured by surface area is Lake Volta, Ghana, formed by the Akosombo dam completed in 1965. By 1969 the lake had filled to an area of 3275 miles² *8482 km²* with a shoreline 4500 miles *7250 km* in length.

The completion in 1954 of the Owen Falls Dam near Jinja, Uganda, across the northern exit of the White Nile from the Victoria Nyanza marginally raised the level of that *natural* lake by adding 166,000,000 acre-ft *204,75 km³*, and technically turned it into a reservoir with a surface area of 17,169,920 acres *6,9 million ha* (26,828 miles² *69 484 km²*).

Largest reservoir *Great Britain*

The largest wholly artificial reservoir in Great Britain is the Queen Mary Reservoir, built from August 1914 to June 1925, at Littleton, near Staines, Surrey, with an available storage capacity of 8130 million gal *369,6 million hl* and a water area of 707 acres *286 ha*. The length of the perimeter embankment is 20,766 ft *6329 m* (3.93 miles *6,32 km*). Of the valley cut-off type reservoirs the most capacious is Kielder Water in the North Tyne valley, Northumberland, which will fill to 44,000 million gallons *2000 million hl* after 18 months by mid-1982. It will overtake Empingham Reservoir (Rutland Water) Leicestershire, which has a capacity of 27,300 million gal *1240 million hl* and has the largest surface area of any reservoir covering 3114 acres *1260 ha*. The deepest reservoir in Europe is Loch Morar, Highland, Scotland, with a maximum depth of 1017 ft *310 m* (see also page 70).

Largest polder

The largest of the five great polders in the old Zuider Zee, Netherlands, will be the 149,000 acre *60 300 ha* (232.8 miles² *602,9 km²*) Markerwaard. Work on the 66 mile *106 km* long surrounding dyke was begun in 1957. The water area remaining after the erection of the 1927–32 dam (20 miles *32 km* in length) is called IJssel Meer, which will have a final area of 487.5 miles² *1262,6 km²*

Largest levees

The most massive levees ever built are the Mississippi levees begun in 1717 but vastly augmented by the US Federal Government after the disastrous floods of 1927. These extend for 1732 miles *2787 km* along the main river from Cape Girardeau, Missouri, to the Gulf of Mexico and comprise more than 1000 million yd³ *765 million m³* of earthworks. Levees on the tributaries comprise an additional 2000 miles *3200 km*. The Pine Bluff, Arkansas to Venice, Louisiana segment of 650 miles *1046 km* is continuous.

8. TUNNELS

LONGEST

Water supply *World*

The world's longest tunnel of any kind is the New York City West Delaware water supply tunnel, begun in 1937 and completed in 1944. It has a diameter of 13 ft 6 in *4,1 m* and runs for 105 miles *168,9 km* from the Rondout Reservoir into the Hillview Reservoir, on the border of Yonkers and New York City, NY, USA.

Water supply *Great Britain*

The longest water supply tunnel in the United Kingdom is the Thames water tunnel from Hampton-on-Thames to Walthamstow, Greater London, completed in 1960 with a circumference of 26 ft 8 in *8,1 m* and a length of 18.8 miles *30,3 km*.

Railway *World*

The world's longest main-line rail tunnel is the 22,2 km (*13 miles 1397 yd*) long Oshimizu Tunnel (Daishimizu) on the Tōkyō–Niigata Joetsu line in central Honshū under the Tanigawa mountain which was holed through on 25 Jan 1979. The cost of the whole project will by March 1981 reach £3150 million. Fatalities in 7 years have been 13.

Railway *Great Britain*

Great Britain's longest main-line railway tunnel is the Severn Tunnel (4 miles 628 yd *6 km*), linking Avon and Gwent completed with 76,400,000 bricks between 1873 and 1886.

Sub-aqueous

The 33.49 mile *53,9 km* long Seikan Rail Tunnel will be 240 m *787 ft* beneath sea level and 100 m *328 ft* below the sea bed of the Tsugaru Strait between Tappi Saki, Honshū, and Fukushima, Hokkaidō, Japan. Once due to be completed by March 1979 at a cost of Yen 200,000 million, major flooding on 6 May 1976 has put back completion beyond 1982. Tests started on the sub-aqueous section (14.5 miles *23,3 km*) in 1963 and construction in June 1972. Currently the world's longest sub-aqueous rail tunnel is the Shin Kanmon Tunnel, completed in May 1974 which runs 11.61 miles *18,7 km* from Honshū to Kyūshū, Japan.

Subway

The world's longest continuous vehicular tunnel is the Moscow Metro underground railway line from Belyaevo to Medvedkovo. It is *c.* 30,7 km *19.07 miles* long and was completed in 1978/9.

Road *World*

The longest road tunnel is the 10.14 mile *16,32 km* long two-lane St Gotthard Road Tunnel from Göschenen, Switzerland, to Airolo, Italy, opened to traffic on 5 Sept 1980. Nineteen lives were lost during the construction which cost Sw Fr 686 million (*then £173.6 million*) since autumn 1969.

Great Britain

The longest road tunnel in the United Kingdom is the Mersey Tunnel, joining Liverpool and Birkenhead, Merseyside. It is 2.13 miles *3,43 km* long, or 2.87 miles *4,62 km* including branch tunnels. Work was begun in December 1925 and it was opened by HM King George V on 18 July 1934. The total cost was £7¾ million. The 36 ft *11 m* wide 4-lane roadway carries nearly 7½ million vehicles a year. The first tube of the second Mersey Tunnel was opened on 24 June 1971.

Largest

The largest diameter road tunnel in the world is that blasted through Yerba Buena Island, San Francisco, California, USA. It is 76 ft *23 m* wide, 58 ft *17 m* high and 540 ft *165 m* long. More than 35,000,000 vehicles pass through on its two decks every year.

Hydro-electric, irrigation or sewerage *World*

The longest irrigation tunnel in the world is the 51.5 mile *82,9 km* long Orange-Fish Rivers Tunnel, South Africa, begun in 1967 at an estimated cost of £60 million. The boring was completed in April 1973. The lining to a minimum thickness of 9 inches *23 cm* will give a completed diameter of 17 ft 6 in *5,33 m*. The Majes project in Peru involves 98 km *60.9 miles* of tunnels for hydroelectric and water supply purposes. The dam is at 4200 m *13,780 ft* altitude. The Chicago TARP (Tunnels and Reservoir Plan) in Illinois, USA involves 120 miles *193 km* of sewerage tunnelling.

Great Britain

The longest in Great Britain is that at Ben Nevis, Highland, which has a mean diameter of 15 ft 2 in *4,6 m* and a length of 15 miles *24 km*. It was begun in June 1926 and was holed through into Loch Treig on 3 Jan 1930 for hydroelectric use. The greatest diameter water tunnel is the 23 ft *7,01 m* tunnel at Clunie, Tayside.

Bridge-Tunnel

The world's longest bridge-tunnel system is the Chesapeake Bay Bridge-Tunnel, extending 17.65 miles *28,40 km* from Eastern Shore, Virginia Peninsula to Virginia Beach, Virginia, USA. It cost $200,000,000 (*then £71,4 million*) and was completed after 42 months and opened to traffic on 15 Apr 1964. The longest bridged section is Trestle C (4.56 miles *7,34 km* long) and the longest tunnel is the Thimble Shoal Channel Tunnel (1.09 miles *1,75 km*).

Canal tunnels *World*

The world's longest canal tunnel is that on the Rove canal between the port of Marseilles, France and the river Rhône, built in 1912–27. It is 4.53 miles *7,29 km* long, 72 ft *22 m* wide and 50 ft *15 m* high, involving 2¼ million yd³ *1,7 million m³* of excavation.

Great Britain

The longest canal tunnel in Great Britain is the Standedge (more properly Stanedge) Tunnel in West Yorkshire on the Huddersfield Narrow Canal built from 1794 to 4 Apr 1811. It measures 3 miles 418 yd *5,21 km* in length and was closed on 21 Dec 1944. The longest *continuous* tunnel of the 43 is the fully restored 3172 yd *3122 m* long Dudley Canal Tunnel which had been abandoned in 1962. The now closed Huddersfield Narrow Canal is the highest in the United Kingdom, reaching a height of 638 ft *194 m* above sea-level.

Tunnelling records

The world's 7 day record for rapid tunnelling was set in the Back River project in Charleston, South Carolina, USA when 1660 ft *506 m* was achieved in 7 consecutive 16 hour periods on 11–17 July 1977 using an M-102 mole by Lovat of Rexdale, Ontario, Canada on a 8½ ft *2,59 m* diameter heading.

The NCB record of 251,4 m *824.8 ft* for a 3,80 m *12½ ft* wide, 2 m *6½ ft* high roadway by a team of 35 pitmen in 5 days was set at West Cannock No 5 Colliery on 30 Mar–3 Apr 1981.

9. SPECIALISED STRUCTURES

Advertising sign Highest *World*

The highest advertising signs in the world are the four Bank of Montreal logos atop the 72 storey 935 ft *285 m* tall First Canadian Place, Toronto. Each sign, built by Claude Neon Industries Ltd, measures 20 × 22 ft *6,09 × 6,70 m* and was lifted by helicopter.

Advertising sign Highest *Great Britain*

The highest advertising sign in Great Britain was the revolving name board of the contractors 'Peter Lind' on the Post Office Tower, London. The illuminated letters were 12 ft *3,7 m* tall and 563 to 575 ft *171 to 175 m* above the street.

Advertising sign Largest

The greatest advertising sign ever erected was the electric Citroën sign on the Eiffel Tower, Paris. It was switched on on 4 July 1925, and could be seen 24 miles *38 km* away. It was in six colours with 250,000 lamps and 56 miles *90 km* of electric cables. The letter 'N' which terminated the name 'Citroën' between the second and third levels measured 68 ft 5 in *20,8 m* in height. The whole apparatus was taken down after 11 years in 1936. For the largest ground sign see Chapter 6, page 93—Largest letter.

The world's largest neon sign was that owned by the Atlantic Coast Line Railroad Company at Port Tampa, Florida, USA. It measured 387 ft 6 in *118 m* long and 76 ft *23 m* high, weighed 175 tons *178 tonnes* and contained about 4200 ft *1280 m* of red neon tubing. It was demolished on 19 Feb 1970. Broadway's largest billboard in New York City is 11,426 ft² *1062 m²* in area—equivalent to 107 ft *32,6 m* square. Britain's largest illuminated sign is the word PLAYHOUSE extending 90 ft *27 m* across the frontage of the new theatre in Leeds, West Yorkshire opened in 1970.

Radio CFMI spelt out its call sign in 400 ft *122 m* letters on Grouse Mountain, Vancouver, BC, Canada on 14 Feb 1980 with 450 flares visible from more than 42 miles *67,5 km* distant.

The world's most massive working sign is reputed to be that outside the Circus Circus Hotel, Reno, Nevada named Topsy, the Clown. It is 127 ft *38,7 m* tall and weighs over 40 tons *40,8 tonnes* with 1.4 miles *2,25 km* of neon tubing. His smile measures 14 ft *4,26 m* across.

Barn Largest

The largest barn in Britain is one at Manor Farm, Cholsey, near Wallingford, Oxfordshire. It is 303 ft *92 m* in length and 54 ft *16 m* in breadth (16,362 ft² *1520 m²*). The Ipsden Barn, Oxford-

shire, is 385½ ft *117 m* long but 30 ft *9 m* wide (11,565 ft² *1074 m²*). The longest tithe barn in Britain is one measuring 268 ft *81 m* long at Wyke Farm, near Sherborne, Dorset.

Bonfire Largest

The largest recorded bonfire constructed in Britain was the Coronation bonfire using 800 tons *812 tonnes* of timber, 1000 gal *4546 litres* each of petroleum and tar. It was octagonal in shape and built to a height of 120 ft *36,67 m* with a base circumference of 155 ft *47,2 m* tapering to 20 ft *6,1 m* at the summit, on Arrowthwhaite Brows at Whitehaven, Cumbria in 1902.

Breakwater Longest *World*

The world's longest breakwater is that which protects the Port of Galveston, Texas, USA. The granite South Breakwater i 6.74 miles *10,85 km* in length.

Breakwater Longest *Great Britain*

The longest breakwater in Great Britain is the North Breakwater at Holyhead, Anglesey, Gwynedd which is 9860 ft (1.86 mile *3005 m*) in length and was completed in 1873.

Buildings demolished by Explosives Largest

The largest building demolished by explosives has been the 21 storey Traymore Hotel, Atlantic City, New Jersey, USA, on 20 May 1972 by Controlled Demolition Inc of Towson, Maryland. This 600 room hotel had a cubic capacity of 6,495,500 ft³ *181 340 m³*. The tallest chimney ever demolished by explosive was the American Smelting and Refining Co Chimney at Crockett, California on 14 June 1973. It stood 605 ft 5 in *184,5 m* and was brought down by the same company.

The greatest recorded smokestack demolition was when 18 were felled at the London Brick Co Coronation Works at Kempston Hardwick, Bedfordshire on 30 Nov 1980 when Mrs Wyn Witherall fired the 100 lb *45,3 kg* of explosives laid by T.W Robinson & Co.

Cemetery Largest

The world's largest cemetery is that in Leningrad, USSR, which contains over 500,000 of the 1,300,000 victims of the German army's siege of 1941–2. The largest cemetery in the United Kingdom is Brookwood Cemetery, Brookwood, Surrey. It is owned by the London Necropolis Co. and is 500 acres *200 ha* in extent with more than 225,000 interments.

Column Tallest

The tallest columns (as opposed to obelisks) in the world are the 36 fluted pillars 90 ft *27,43 m* tall, of Vermont marble in the colonnade of the Education Building, Albany, New York. Their base diameter is 6½ ft *1,98 m*. The tallest load-bearing stone columns in the world are those measuring 69 ft *21 m* in the Hall of Columns of the Temple of Amun at Karnak, opposite Thebes on the Nile, the ancient capital of Upper Egypt. They were built in the 19th dynasty in the reign of Rameses II in *c.* 1270 BC.

Crematorium Earliest

The oldest crematorium in Britain is one built in 1879 at Woking, Surrey. The first cremation took place there on 20 Mar 1885, the practice having been found legal after the cremation of Iesu Grist Price on Caerlan fields on 13 Jan 1884. The total number of people cremated in Britain since, has been 9,023,61 (to 31 Dec 1980), and the percentage (now 64.48%) is the highest in the world for any country in which cremation is voluntary.

Crematorium Largest

The largest crematorium in the world is at the Nikolo Arkhangelskoye Cemetery, East Moscow, with 7 twin cremators of British design, completed in March 1972. It has several Hall of Farewell for atheists. Britain's largest is the City of London Crematorium, E.12, which extends over 165 acres *66,77 ha* and performed a record 5395 cremations in 1979. The all-time total of 247,892 at Golders Green Crematorium (since 1902) remains unsurpassed.

Dock Gate

The world's largest dock gate is that at Nigg Bay, Cromarty Firth, Highlands, Scotland, first operated in March 1974. It measures 408 ft *124 m* long, 50 ft *15,2 m* high with a 4 ft *1,21 m* thick base, is made of reinforced concrete and weigh

above: Broadway's largest billboard, the 11,426 ft² *1062 m²* board in Times Square, New York City (see p. 126) (*John Rivers*) *below:* Empingham Reservoir in Leicestershire which still has the largest surface area of any reservoir in Britain covering 3114 acres *1260 ha* (see p. 125). (*Alexandra Studio*)

16,000 tons *16 257 tonnes* together with its sill, quoins and roundheads. The builders were Brown and Root-Wimpey Highland Fabricators.

Dome Largest *World*
The world's largest dome is the Louisiana Superdome, New Orleans, USA. It has a diameter of 680 ft *207,26 m* (See page 118 for further details.) The largest dome of ancient architecture is that of the Pantheon, built in Rome in AD 112, with a diameter of 142½ ft *43 m*.

Dome Largest *Great Britain*
The largest dome in Britain is that of the Bell Sports Centre, Perth, Scotland, with a diameter of 222 ft *67 m* designed by D. B. Cockburn and constructed in Baltic whitewood by Muirhead & Sons Ltd of Grangemouth, Central, Scotland.

Door Largest *World*
The largest doors in the world are the four in the Vehicle Assembly Building near Cape Kennedy, Florida, with a height of 460 ft *140 m* (see page 114). The world's thickest door is the 43.3 ton *44 tonnes* neutron shield made by Ray Proof Inc for the RTNS-II source at Lawrence Livermore Laboratory, California which is 8 ft *2,43 m* thick.

Door Largest *Great Britain*
The largest doors in Great Britain are those to the Britannia Assembly Hall, at Filton airfield, Avon. The doors are 1035 ft *315 m* in length and 67 ft *20 m* high, divided into three bays each 345 ft *105 m* across. The largest simple hinged door in Britain is that of Ye Old Bull's Head, Beaumaris, Anglesey, Gwynedd, which is 11 ft *3,35 m* wide and 13 ft *3,96 m* high.

Door Oldest
The oldest doors in Britain are those of Hadstock Church, Essex, which date from *c.* 1040 AD and exhibit evidence of Danish workmanship.

Dry dock Largest *World*
The largest dry dock in the world is that at Koyagi, Nagasaki, Japan completed in 1972. It measures 990 m *3248 ft* long; 100 m *328 ft* in width and has a maximum shipbuilding capacity of 1,000,000 tons deadweight.

The largest shipbuilding dry dock in the UK is the Belfast Harbour Commission and Harland and Wolff building dock at Belfast, Northern Ireland. It was excavated by Wimpey's to a length of 1825 ft *556 m* and a width of 305 ft *93 m* and could accommodate tankers of 1,000,000 tons deadweight. Work was begun on 26 Jan 1968 and completed on 30 Nov 1969 and involved the excavation of 400,000 yd³ *306 000 m³*. (See also Largest crane p. 152.) The dry dock under construction at Port Rashid, Dubai, Persian Gulf, opened in March 1979 measures 1722 by 328 ft *525 × 100 m*.

Earthworks Largest *World*
The largest earthworks in the world carried out prior to the mechanical era were the Linear Earth Boundaries of the Benin Empire in the Bendel state of Nigeria. These were first reported in 1900 and partially surveyed in 1967. In April 1973 it was estimated by Mr Patrick Darling that the total length of the earthworks was probably between 4000 and 8000 miles *6400–12 800 km* with the total amount of earth moved estimated at from 500 to 600 million yd³ *380–460 million m³*.

Earthworks Largest *Great Britain*
The greatest prehistoric earthwork in Britain is Wansdyke, originally Woden's Dyke, which ran 86 miles *138 km* from Portishead, Avon to Inkpen Beacon and Ludgershall, south of Hungerford, Berkshire. It is believed to have been built by the pre-Roman Wessex culture. The most extensive single site earthwork is the Dorset Curses near Gussage St. Michael, dating from *c.* 1900 BC. The workings are 6 miles *9,7 km* in length, involving an estimated 250,000 yd³ *191 000 m³* of excavations. The largest of the Celtic hill-forts is that known as Mew Dun, or Maiden Castle, 2 miles *3 km* SW of Dorchester, Dorset. It covers 115 acres *46,5 ha* and was abandoned shortly after AD 43.

Fence Largest
The longest fence in the world is the dingo-proof fence enclosing the main sheep areas of Queensland, Australia. The wire fence is

6 ft *1,8 m* high, 1 ft *30 cm* underground and stretches for 3437 miles *5531 km*.

Flagstaff Tallest *World*
The tallest flagstaff ever erected was that outside the Oregon Building at the 1915 Panama-Pacific International Exposition in San Francisco, California, USA. Trimmed from a Douglas fir, it stood 299 ft 7 in *91 m* in height and weighed 45 tons *47 tonnes*. The tallest unsupported flag pole in the world is a 170 ft *51,8 m* tall (plus 10 ft *3,048 m* below ground) metal pole weighing 28,000 lb *12 700 kg* erected in 1943 at the US Merchant Marine Academy in King's Point, New York, USA. The pole, built by Kearney-National Inc., tapers from 24 in to 5½ in *61 cm to 14 cm* at the jack.

Flagstaff Tallest *Great Britain*
The tallest flagstaff in Great Britain is a 225 ft *68 m* tall Douglas fir staff at Kew, Richmond upon Thames, Greater London. Cut in Canada, it was shipped across the Atlantic and towed up the River Thames on 7 May 1958, to replace the old 214 ft *65 m* tall staff of 1919.

Fountain Tallest *World*
The world's tallest fountain is the Fountain at Fountain Hills, Arizona built at a cost of $1,500,000 for McCulloch Properties Inc. At full pressure of 375 lb/in² *26,3 kg/cm²* and at a rate of 5828 Imp. gal/min *26 500 litres/min* the 560 ft *170 m* tall column of water weighs more than 8 tons/*tonnes*. The nozzle speed achieved by the three 600 hp pumps is 46.7 mph *75 km/h*.

Fountain Tallest *Great Britain*
The tallest fountain in Great Britain is the Emperor Fountain at Chatsworth, Bakewell, Derbyshire. When first tested on 1 Jun 1844, it attained the then unprecedented height of 260 ft *79 m*. Since the war it has not been played to more than 250 ft *76 m* and rarely beyond 180 ft *55 m*.

Garbage dump Biggest
Reclamation Plant No. 1, Fresh Kills, Staten Island, opened in March 1974, is the world's largest sanitary landfill. In its first months 450,000 tons of refuse from New York City was dumped on the site by 700 barges.

Gasholder Largest *World*
The world's largest gasholder is that at Fontaine l'Eveque, Belgium, where disused mines have been adapted to store up to 500 million m³ *17,650 million ft³* of gas at ordinary pressure. Probably the largest conventional gasholder is that at Wien Simmering, Vienna, Austria, completed in 1968, with a height of 274 ft 8 in *84 m* and a capacity of 10.59 million ft³ *300 000 m³*.

Gasholder Largest *Great Britain*
The largest gasholder ever constructed in Great Britain is the East Greenwich Gas Works No. 2 Holder built in 1891 with an original capacity for 12,200,000 ft³ *346 000 m³*. As constructed its capacity is 8.9 million ft³ *252 000 m³* with a water tank 303 ft *92 m* in diameter and a full inflated height of 148 ft *45 m*. The No. 1 holder (capacity 8.6 million ft³ *243 500 m³*) has a height of 200 ft *61 m*. The River Tees Northern Gas Board's 1186 ft *361 m* deep underground storage in use since January 1959 has a capacity of 330,000 ft³ *9300 m³*.

Globe Largest revolving
The world's largest revolving globe is the 21½ ton/*tonnes* 27 ft 11 in *8,50 m* diameter sphere in Babson College Wellesley, Massachusetts, USA completed at a cost of $200,000 (then £71,425) in 1956.

Henges
There are in Britain some 80 henges built *c.* 2500 BC of which the largest was Durrington Walls, Wiltshire with an average diameter of 1550 ft *472 m*. It has been obliterated by road building.

Jetty Longest
The longest deep water jetty in the world is the Quai Hermann du Pasquier at Le Havre, France, with a length of 5000 ft *1524 m*. Part of an enclosed basin, it has a constant depth of water of 32 ft *9,8 m* on both sides.

Kitchen *Largest*
The largest kitchen ever set up has been the Indian Government

field kitchen set up in April 1973 at Ahmadnagar, Maharashtra in the famine area which daily provided 1.2 million subsistence meals.

Lighthouse *Earliest*
see Seven Wonders of the World *page 130*.

Lighthouse Brightest *World*
The lighthouse with the most powerful light in the world is Créac'h d'Ouessant lighthouse, established in 1638 and last altered in 1939 on l'Ile d'Ouessant, Finisterre, Brittany, France. It is 163 ft *50 m* tall and, in times of fog, has a luminous intensity of up to 500 million candelas.

The lights with the greatest visible range are those 1092 ft *332 m* above the ground on the Empire State Building, New York City, NY, USA. Each of the four-arc mercury bulbs has a rated candlepower of 450,000,000, visible 80 miles *130 km* away on the ground and 300 miles *490 km* away from aircraft. They were switched on on 31 Mar 1956.

Lighthouse Brightest *Great Britain*
The lighthouse in Great Britain with the most powerful light is the shorelight Orfordness, Suffolk. It has an intensity of 7,500,000 candelas. The Irish light with the greatest intensity is Aranmore on Rinrawros Point, County Donegal.

Lighthouse Remotest *Great Britain*
The most remote Trinity House lighthouse is The Smalls, about 16 sea miles (18.4 statute miles *29,6 km*) off the Dyfed coast. The most remote Scottish lighthouse is Sule Skerry, 35 miles *56 km* off shore and 45 miles *72 km* northwest of Dunnet Head, Highland. The most remote Irish light is Blackrock, 9 miles *14 km* off the Mayo coast.

Lighthouse Tallest
The world's tallest lighthouse is the steel tower 348 ft *106 m* tall near Yamashita Park in Yokohama, Japan. It has a power of 600,000 candles and a visibility range of 20 miles *32 km*.

Marquee Largest *World*
The largest tent ever erected was one covering an area of 188,368 ft² *17 500 m²* (4.32 acres *1,7 ha*) put up by the firm of Deuter from Augsburg, W. Germany, for the 1958 'Welcome Expo' in Brussels, Belgium.

Marquee Largest *Great Britain*
The largest marquee in Britain is one made by Piggot Brothers in 1951 and used by the Royal Horticultural Society at their annual show (first held in 1913) in the grounds of the Royal Hospital, Kensington and Chelsea, Greater London. The marquee is 310 ft *94 m* long by 480 ft *146 m* wide and consists of 18¾ miles *30 km* of 36 in *91 cm* wide canvas covering a ground area of 148,800 ft² *13 820 m²*. A tent 435 ft *132,5 m* long was erected in one lift by thirty-five men of the Military Corrective Training Centre, Colchester on 23 July 1980.

Maypole
The tallest reported Maypole erected in England was one of Sitka spruce 105 ft 7 in *32,12 m* tall put up in Pelynt, Cornwall on 1 May 1974.

Maze Largest
The world's largest maze is that at Longleat, nr Warminster, Wilts, with 1.61 miles *2,59 km* of paths flanked by 16,180 yew trees. It was opened on 6 June 1978.

Monument Prehistoric *Largest*
Britain's largest megalithic prehistoric monuments are the 28½ acre *11,5 ha* earthworks and stone circles of Avebury, Wiltshire, rediscovered in 1646. The earliest calibrated date in the area of this neolithic site is *c.* 4200 BC. The whole work is 1200 ft *365 m* in diameter with a 40 ft *12 m* ditch around the perimeter and required an estimated 15 million man-hours of work. The largest trilithons exist at Stonehenge, to the south of Salisbury Plain, Wiltshire, with single sarsen blocks weighing over 45 tons/tonnes and requiring over 550 men to drag them up a 9° gradient. The earliest stage of the construction of the ditch has been dated to 2180 ± 105 BC. Whether Stonehenge was a lunar calendar, a temple or an eclipse-predictor remains debatable.

Monument Tallest
The world's tallest monument is the stainless steel Gateway to the West Arch in St Louis, Missouri, USA, completed on 28 Oct 1965 to commemorate the westward expansion after the Louisiana Purchase of 1803. It is a sweeping arch spanning 630 ft *192 m* and rising to the same height of 630 ft *192 m* and costing $29,000,000 (*then £10.35 million*). It was designed in 1947 by Eero Saarinen (d. 1961).

The tallest monumental column in the world is that commemorating the battle of San Jacinto (21 Apr 1836), on the bank of the San Jacinto river near Houston, Texas, USA. General Sam Houston (1793–1863) and his force of 743 Texan troops killed 630 Mexicans (out of a total force of 1600) and captured 700 others, for the loss of nine men killed and 30 wounded. Constructed in 1936–9, at a cost of $1,500,000 (*then £372,000*), the tapering column is 570 ft *173 m* tall, 47 ft *14 m* square at the base, and 30 ft *9 m* square at the observation tower, which is surmounted by a star weighing 196.4 tons *199,6 tonnes*. It is built of concrete, faced with buff limestone, and weighs 31,384 tons *31 888 tonnes*.

Monument, Youngest ancient
The newest scheduled ancient monuments are a hexagonal pill box and 48 concrete tank traps south of Christchurch, Dorset built in World War II and protected since 1973.

Mound Largest *World*
The gravel mound built as a memorial to the Seleucid King Antiochus I (reigned 69–34 BC) on the summit of Nemud Dagi (8205 ft *2494 m*) south east of Malatya, Eastern Turkey measures 197 ft *59,8 m* tall and covers 7.5 acres *3 ha*.

Mound Largest *United Kingdom*
The largest artificial mound in Europe is Silbury Hill, 6 miles *9,7 km* west of Marlborough, Wiltshire, which involved the moving of an estimated 670,000 tons *681 000 tonnes* of chalk to make a cone 130 ft *39 m* high with a base of 5½ acres *2 ha*. Prof. Richard Atkinson in charge of the 1968 excavations showed that it is based on an innermost central mound, similar to contemporary round barrows, and is now dated to 2745 ± 185 BC. The largest long barrow in England is that inside the hill-fort at Maiden Castle (see Earthworks largest GB). It originally had a length of 1800 ft *548 m* and had several enigmatic features such as a ritual pit with pottery, limpet shells, and animal bones. The longest long barrow containing a megalithic chamber is that at West Kennet (*c.* 2200 BC), near Silbury, measuring 385 ft *117 m* in length.

Naturist resorts
The oldest resort is Der Freilichtpark, Klingberg, W. Germany established in 1903. The largest in the world is the Beau Valley Country Club, Warmbaths, South Africa extending over 4 million m² *988 acres* with up to 20,000 visitors a year. However, 100,000 people visit the smaller centre Helio-Marin at Cap d'Agde, southern France, which covers 90 ha *222 acres*. The term 'nudist camp' is deplored by naturists.

Obelisk (Monolithic) Largest
The largest standing obelisk in the world is the Egyptian obelisk brought from Egypt to the Hippodrome of Constantinople in Istanbul, Turkey in AD 390. It stands 58 m *190.2 ft* tall. The largest obelisk in the United Kingdom is Cleopatra's Needle on the Embankment, London, which is 68 ft 5½ in *20 m* tall and weighs 186.36 tons *189,35 tonnes*. It was towed up the Thames from Egypt on 21 Jan 1878 and positioned on 13 Sept.

Obelisk (Monolithic) Oldest
The longest an obelisk has remained *in situ* is that still at Heliopolis, near Cairo, Egypt, erected by Senusret I *c.* 1750 BC.

Pier Longest *World*
The world's longest pier is the Damman Pier, Saudi Arabia, on the Persian Gulf. A rock-filled causeway 4.84 miles *7,79 km* long joins the steel trestle pier 1.80 miles *2,90 km* long, which joins the Main Pier (744 ft *226 m* long), giving an overall length of 6.79 miles *10,93 km*. The work was begun in July 1948 and completed on 15 Mar 1950.

Pier Longest *Great Britain*

The longest pier in Great Britain is the Bee Ness Jetty, completed in 1930, which stretches 8200 ft *2500 m* along the west bank of the River Medway, 5 to 6 miles *8 to 9,6 km* below Rochester, at Kingsnorth, Kent.

Pyramid Largest

The largest pyramid, and the largest monument ever constructed, is the Quetzalcóatl at Cholula de Rivadabia, 63 miles *101 km* south-east of Mexico City, Mexico, It is 177 ft *54 m* tall and its base covers an area of nearly 45 acres *18,2 ha*. Its total volume has been estimated at 4,300,000 yd³ *3 300 000 m³* compared with 3,360,000 yd³ *2,5 million m³* for the Pyramid of Cheops (*see* Seven Wonders of the World). The pyramid-building era here was between the 2nd and 6th centuries AD.

Pyramid Oldest

The oldest known pyramid is the Djoser step pyramid at Saqqâra, Egypt constructed to a height of 204 ft *62 m* originally with a Tura limestone casing in *c.* 2650 BC. The largest known single block comes from the Third Pyramid (the pyramid of Mycerinus) and weighs 290 tonnes *285 tons*. The oldest New World pyramid is that on the island of La Venta in south-eastern Mexico built by the Olmec people *c.* 800 BC. It stands 100 ft *30 m* tall with a base diameter of 420 ft *128 m*.

Scaffolding

The greatest scaffolding structure ever erected was one comprising 750,000 ft (142 miles *228,5 km*) of tubing up to 486 ft *148 m* in height used in the reconstruction of Guy's Hospital, London in 1971.

Seven Wonders of the World

The Seven Wonders of the World were first designated by Antipater of Sidon in the 2nd century BC. They included the Pyramids of Giza, built by three Fourth Dynasty Egyptian Pharaohs, Khwfw (Khufu or Cheops), Kha-f-Ra (Khafre, Khefren or Chepren) and Menkaure (Mycerinus) near El Giza (El Gizeh), south-west of El Qâhira (Cairo) in Egypt. The Great Pyramid ('Horizon of Khufu') was finished *c.* 2580 BC. Its original height was 480 ft 11 in *146,5 m* (now, since the loss of its topmost stones and the pyramidion, reduced to 449 ft 6 in *137 m*) with a base line of 756 ft *230 m* and thus covering slightly more than 13 acres *5 ha*. It has been estimated that a permanent work force of 4000 required 30 years to manoeuvre into position the 2,300,000 limestone blocks averaging 2½ tons/*tonnes* each, totalling about 5,750,000 tons *5 840 000 tonnes* and a volume of 90,700,000 ft³ *2 568 000 m³*. A costing exercise published in December 1974, indicated that it would require 405 men 6 years at a cost of $1.13 billion (*then £500 million*).

Of the other six wonders only fragments remain of the Temple of Artemis (Diana) of the Ephesians, built in *c.* 350 BC. at Ephesus, Turkey (destroyed by the Goths in AD 262), and of the Tomb of King Mausolus of Caria, built at Halicarnassus, now Bodrum, Turkey, in *c.* 325 BC. No trace remains of the Hanging Gardens of Semiramis, at Babylon, Iraq (*c.* 600 BC); the 40 ft *12 m* tall marble, gold and ivory statue of Zeus (Jupiter), by Phidias (5th century BC) at Olympia, Greece (lost in a fire at Istanbul); the 117 ft *35 m* tall statue by Chares of Lindus of the figure of the god Helios (Apollo) called the Colossus of Rhodes (sculptured 292–280 BC, destroyed by an earthquake in 224 BC); or the 400 ft *122 m* tall world's earliest lighthouse, built by Sostratus of Cnidus *c.* 270 BC as a pyramidically shaped tower of white marble, (destroyed by earthquake in AD 1375), on the island of Pharos (Greek, *pharos* = lighthouse), off the coast of El Iskandariya (Alexandria), Egypt.

Stairs Longest *World*

The world's longest stairway is the service staircase for the Niesenbahn funicular which rises to 2365 m *7759 ft* near Spiez, Switzerland. It has 11,674 steps and a bannister. The stone cut T'ai Chan temple stairs of 6600 steps in the Shantung Mountains, China ascend 4700 feet in 5 miles *1428 m* in *8 km*.

Stairs Longest *Great Britain*

The longest stairs in Britain are those from the transformer gallery to the surface 1065 ft *324 m* in the Cruachan Power Station, Argyll, Scotland. They have 1420 steps and the Work Study Dept. allows 27 min 41.4 sec for the ascent.

Statue Longest

Near Bamiyan, Afghanistan there are the remains of the recumbent Sakya Buddha, built of plastered rubble, which was 'about 1000 ft *305 m*' long and is believed to date from the 3rd or 4th century AD.

Statue Tallest

The tallest full-figure statue in the world is that of 'Motherland' an enormous pre-stressed concrete female figure on Mamaye Hill, outside Volgograd, USSR, designed in 1967 by Yevgeny Vuchetich, to commemorate victory in the Battle of Stalingrad (1942–3). The statue from its base to the tip of the sword clenched in her right hand measures 270 ft *82,30 m*. *The India Rope Trick* statue by Calle Örnemark near Jönköping, Sweden measures 103 m *337 ft* from the feet of the *fakir* to the top of the rope 25 cm *9.8 in* in diameter. Its total weight is 144 tonnes *141.6 tons*.

The US sculptor Felix de Welton has announced a plan to replicate the Colossus of Rhodes to a height of 308 ft *93,87 m*.

Tomb Largest

The largest tomb in the world is that of Emperor Nintoku (died *c.* AD 428) south of Osaka, Japan. It measures 1594 ft *485 m* long by 1000 ft *305 m* wide by 150 ft *45 m* high.

Totem pole Tallest

A totem pole 173 ft *52,73 m* tall was raised on 6 June 1973 at Alert Bay, British Columbia, Canada. It tells the story of the Kwakiutl and took 36 man-weeks to carve.

Vats Largest

The largest vat in the world is named 'Strongbow', used by H. P. Bulmer Ltd., the cider makers of Hereford, England. It measures 64½ ft *19,65 m* in height and 75½ ft *23,0 m* in diameter with a capacity of 1,630,000 gallons *74 099 hectolitres*.

The largest wooden wine cask in the world is the Heidelberg Tun completed in 1751 in the cellar of the Friedrichsbau Heidelberg, West Germany. Its capacity is 1855 hectolitres *40,790 gal*.

Wall Longest *World*

The Great Wall of China, completed during the reign of Chhin Shih Huang-ti (246–210 BC), has a main line length of 2150 miles *3460 km* with a further 1780 miles *2860 km* of branches and spurs, with a height of from 15 to 39 ft *4,5 to 12 m* and up to 32 ft *9,8 m* thick. It runs from Shanhaikuan, on the Gulf of Pohai, to Yümên-kuan and Yang-kuan and was kept in repair up to the 16th century. Some 32 miles *51,5 km* of the Wall have been destroyed since 1966. Part of the wall was blown up to make way for a dam in July 1979.

Wall Longest *Great Britain*

The longest of the Roman Walls built in Britain was the 15–20 ft *4,5–6 m* tall Hadrian's Wall, built in the period AD 122–126. It ran across the Tyne-Solway isthmus for 73½ miles *118 km* from Bowness-on-Solway, Cumbria, to Wallsend-on-Tyne, Tyne and Wear, and was abandoned in AD 383.

Water Flumes

The first of the world's now nearly 250 water flumes was built in Newport Beach, California in 1971.

Waterwheel Largest *World*

The largest waterwheel in the world is the Mohammadieh Nori wheel at Hama, Syria with a diameter of 131 ft *40 m* dating from Roman times. The Lady Isabella wheel at Laxey, Isle of Man is the largest in the British Isles and was built for draining a lead mine and completed on 27 Sept 1854, and disused since 1929. It has a circumference of 228 ft *69 m*, a diameter of 72½ ft *22 m* and an axle weighing 9 tons/*tonnes*. The largest waterwheel in England is claimed to be the pitch-back indoor wheel of 45 ft *13,70 m* diameter which provided power from 1862 to 1932 for the mill of James Wilson & Son Ltd. of Lothersdale, near Keighley, West Yorkshire.

Window Largest

The largest sheet of glass ever manufactured was one of 50 m² *538.2 ft²*, or 20 m *65 ft 7 in* by 2,5 m *8 ft 2½ in*, exhibited by the Saint Gobian Company in France at the *Journées Internationale de Miroiterie* in March 1958. The largest single windows in the world are those in the Palace of Industry and Technology at Rondpoint de la Défense, Paris, with an extreme width of 218 m *715.2 ft* and a maximum height of 50 m *164 ft.*

Wine cellar

The largest wine cellars in the world are at Paarl, those of the Ko-operative Wijnbouwers Vereeniging, known as KWV, near Cape Town, in the centre of the wine-growing district of South Africa. They cover an area of 25 acres *10 ha* and have a capacity of 30 million gal *136 million litres.* The Cienega Winery of the Almaden Vineyards in Hollister, California, USA covers 4 acres *1,6 ha* and can house 37,300 oak barrels containing 1.83 million gallons of red wine.

Ziqqurat Largest

The largest surviving ziqqurat (from the verb *zaqaru*, to build high) or stage-tower is the Ziqqurat of Ur (now Muqqayr, Iraq) with a base 200 ft by 150 ft *60 by 45 m* built to at least three storeys of which the first and part of the second now survive to a height of 60 ft *18 m.* It has been variously dated between *c.* 2050 BC and *c.* 2800 BC.

10. BORINGS & MINES

Deepest *World*

Man's deepest penetration into the Earth's crust is a geological exploratory drilling in the Kola peninsula USSR which was announced in November 1980 to have reached 10 500 m *34,450 ft.* Progress was averaging 11 m *36 ft* per day but slowing towards the target of 15,000 m *49,210 ft.*

Deepest *Ocean Drilling*

The deepest recorded drilling into the sea bed by the *Glomar Challenger* of the US Deep Sea Drilling Project is one of 5709 ft *1740 m* off N.W. Spain in 1976. The deepest site is now 7034 m *23,077 ft* below the surface on the western wall of the Marianas Trench (see p. 64) in May 1978.

Oil fields

The largest oil field in the world is the Ghawar field, Saudi Arabia developed by ARAMCO which measures 150 miles by 22 miles *240 km by 35 km.* The Groningen gas field in the Netherlands, exploited since 1965, has reserves of 100×10^{12} ft³. This may be matched by the Dome find of 1972 off Qatar. The area of the designated parts of the UK Continental shelf as at 1 Apr 1975 was 223,550 miles² *579 000 km²* with total recoverable reserves of 3200 million tonnes of oil and 51,000,000 million ft³ *1 443 000 million m³* of gas. Gas was first discovered in the West Sole Field in October 1965 and oil in the Forties Field (Block 22/17) at 11,000 ft *3352 m* from the drilling barge *Sea Quest* on 18 Sept 1970, though a small gasfield was detected near Whitby, N. Yorkshire in 1937.

The most productive oil field is expected to be Brent (found in July 1971) where the B platform was installed in August 1976. Production in 1979 reached 350,000 barrels a day and should peak to 850,000 bbd in 1983. The whole UK production in 1979 was 76,415,581 tonnes or 19,558 million Imperial gal. The deepest drilling in British waters is 2400 ft *731 m* in Block 206, west of Shetland by Shell using the drill ship *Petrel* in April 1980.

The deepest oil exploration is the Blue H-28 in 4876 ft *1486 m* of water 200 miles *320 km* northeast of St John's, Newfoundland, Canada by *Discoverer Seven Seas* spudded in on 28 Apr 1979 and owned by Texaco Shell.

Oil platforms *Largest*

The deepest fixed leg oil platform in the world sits in 1025 ft *312 m* of water 100 miles *160 km* south-east of New Orleans, Louisiana, USA. The overall height of the structure in this $275 million enterprise is 1265 ft *385,5 m.* Experiments have been proceeding with FTL's (Floating tension leg) structures for production platforms at even greater depths.

The world's most massive oil platform is the Central Ninian production and storage platform built at Loch Kishorn, Highland, Scotland, and operated by Chevron Petroleum (UK) Ltd. When towed out to the North Sea site on 5 May 1978 it was the heaviest object ever moved—600,000 tonnes/tons ballasted weight. She was towed by 8 tugs with a combined strength of 92,000 ihp. The height of the concrete structure is 509 ft *155 m* and the overall height 782 ft *238 m.* The tallest fixed leg platform in the North Sea is one 750 ft *228,6 m* in height built by Redpath Dorman Long for Shell-Esso at Methil, Fife and moved to the Brent Field in April 1976.

The production platform in the deepest water is BNOC's Thistle A platform in 530 ft *161,5 m* of water.

Gusher Greatest

The most prolific wildcat recorded is the 1160 ft *353 m* deep Lucas No. 1, at Spindletop, about 3 miles *4,8 km* south of Beaumont, Texas, USA, on 10 Jan 1901. The gusher was heard more than a mile *1,6 km* away and yielded 800,000 barrels during the 9 days it was uncapped. The surrounding ground subsequently yielded 142,000,000 barrels.

Oil Spills Greatest

The slick from the Mexican marine blow-out beneath the drilling rig *Ixtoc I* in the Gulf of Campeche, Gulf of Mexico, on 3 June 1979 reached 400 miles *640 km* by 5 Aug 1979. It eventually was capped on 24 Mar 1980 after a loss of 3,000,000 barrels (535,000 tons).

The worst oil spill in history was of 236,000 tons/*tonnes* of oil from the super-tankers *Atlantic Empress* and *Aegean Captain* when they collided off Tobago on 19 July 1979. The worst oil spill in British waters was from the 118,285 dwt *Torrey Canyon*

Discoverer Seven Seas from which the deepest oil exploration was carried out, to a depth of 4876 ft *1486* m on 28 Apr 1979.

MINES

Earliest (World)	c. 41,000 BC	Haematite (iron ore)	Hhohho district, Swaziland
Earliest (GB)	3390 BC ± 150	Flint	Church Hill, Findon, W. Sussex
Deepest (World)	11,752 ft *3582 m*	Gold, Western Deep Levels (temp 131° F 55° C)	Carletonville, South Africa
Deepest (GB, all-time)	4132 ft *1259 m*	Coal, Arley Seam, Parsonage Colliery (Feb 1949)	Leigh, Greater Manchester
(GB, current)	3690 ft *1127 m*	Coal, Bickershaw Colliery	Bickershaw, Greater Manchester
(Cornwall)	3600 ft *1097 m*	Tin, Williams Shaft, Dolcoath (1910)	Near Cambourne, Cornwall
Copper (largest, open cast)	521,000 tonnes (24 hours)	Copper, Palabora (ore and waste 9 Aug 1980)	Northeast Transvaal, South Africa
Copper (largest underground)	356 miles *573 km* tunnels	San Manuel Mine, Magma Copper Co	Arizona, USA
Lead (largest)	>10 per cent of world output	Viburnum Trend	Southeast Missouri, USA
Goldmining (area)	>51 per cent of world output	38 mines of the Witwatersrand Discovery in 1886	South Africa
Gold Mine (largest, world)	12,100 acres *4900 ha*	East Rand Proprietary Mines Ltd	Boksburg, Transvaal, South Africa
Gold Mine (largest, GB)	120,000 fine oz (1854–1914)	Clogan St Davids (disc. 1836)	Powys, Wales
Gold Mine (richest)	49.4 million fine oz	Crown Mines (all-time yield)	Transvaal, South Africa
Iron Mine (largest)	20,300 million tonnes rich ore	Lebedinsky (45–65% ore)	Kursk region, USSR
Platinum (largest)	1,000,000 oz *28 tonnes* per annum	Rustenberg Group, Impala plant	Springs, South Africa
Tungsten Mine (largest)	2000 tonnes per day	Union Carbide Mount Morgan mine	Near Bishop, California, USA
Uranium (largest)	4687.5 long tons *4762,6 tonnes*	Rio Tinto Zinc open cast pit	Namibia, South West Africa
Spoil Dump (largest, world)	275 million yd³ *210 million m³*	New Cornelia Tailings	Ten Mile Wash, Arizona, USA
Spoil Dump (largest, GB)	114 acre *46 ha* 130 ft *40 m* high	Cutacre Clough Colliery tip	Lancashire
Quarry (largest, world)	2.81 miles² *7,21 km²*. 2540 ft *774 m* deep. 3700 million short tons *3355 million tonnes*	Bingham Canyon Copper Mine	Nr. Salt Lake City, Utah, USA
Quarry (largest, GB)	500 ft *150 m deep*, 1.6 mile *2,6 km* circumference	Old Delabole Slate Quarry (since c. 1570)	Cornwall
Open Cast Coal Mine	820 ft *250 m* deep 4 × 3 km *2.5 × 2 mile* area	Fortuna-Garsdorf lignite	Nr. Bergheim, W. Germany

The world's largest bonfire constructed on Arrowhaite Brows, Whitehaven, Cumbria in 1902 to celebrate the coronation of King Edward VII. It was built to a height of 120 ft *36,67 m* (see p. 126). (*Cumbria County Library: Daniel Hay Library*)

which struck the Pollard Rock off Land's End on 18 Mar 196 resulting in a loss of 106,000 tons of oil.

Flare Greatest
The greatest gas fire was that which burnt at Gassi Touil in the Algerian Sahara from noon on 13 Nov 1961 to 9.30 a.m. on 2 Apr 1962. The pillar of flame rose 450 ft *137 m* and the smoke 600 ft *182 m*. It was eventually extinguished by Paul Nea ('Red') Adair, aged 47, of Austin, Texas, USA, using 550 lb *245 kg* of dynamite. His fee was understood to be abou $1,000,000 (*then £357,000*).

Water well Deepest *World*
The world's deepest water bore is the Stensvad Water Well 11 W1 of 7320 ft *2231 m* drilled by the Great Northern Drilling Co Inc. in Rosebud County, Montana, USA in October–Novembe 1961. The Thermal Power Co. geothermal steam well begun in Sonoma County, California in 1955 is now down to 9029 f *2752 m*.

Water well Deepest *Great Britain*
The deepest well in Great Britain is a water table well 2842 f *866 m* deep in the Staffordshire coal measures at Smestow. The deepest artesian well in Britain is that at the White Heathe Laundry, Stonebridge Park, Brent, Greater London, bored in 1911 to a depth of 2225 ft *678 m*. The deepest private well i probably that of Friningham Farm, Thurnham, Kent sunk t 415 ft *126,5 m* and deepened by bore to 818 ft *249,3 m* in 1940.

Water well *Greatest Flow*
The highest recorded flow rate of any artesian well is 20,000 U gal (16,650 Imp. gal) per min *757 hectolitres/min* certified in 197 for a well 20 miles *32 km* north-west of Orlando, Florida by th Wekiva river.

8.
THE MECHANICAL WORLD

1. SHIPS

EARLIEST BOATS

Evidence for sea faring between the Greek mainland and Melos to trade obsidian *c.* 7250 BC was published in 1971. Oars found in bogs at Magle Mose, Sjaelland, Denmark and Star Carr, North Yorkshire, England, have been dated to the eighth millennium BC.

The oldest surviving boat is the 142 ft *43,4 m* long 40 ton Nile boat buried near the Great Pyramid of Khufu, Egypt *c.* 2515 BC and now re-assembled.

The oldest shipwreck ever found is one of a Cycladic trading vessel located off the islet of Dhókós, near the Greek island of Hydra reported in May 1975 and dated to 2450 BC ± 250.

Earliest power

Propulsion by steam engine was first achieved when in 1783 the Marquis Jouffroy d'Abbans ascended a reach of the river Saône near Lyon, France, in the 180 ton *182 tonnes* paddle steamer *Pyroscaphe*.

The tug *Charlotte Dundas* was the first successful power-driven vessel. She was a paddle-wheel steamer built in Scotland in 1801–2 by William Symington (1763–1831), using a double-acting condensing engine constructed by James Watt (1736–1819). The earliest regular steam run was by the paddle-wheeler *Clermont*, built by Robert Fulton (1765–1815), a US engineer, using a Boulton and Watt engine. She maintained a service from New York to Albany (150 miles *240 km* in 32 hr) from 17 Aug 1807.

Oldest vessels

The oldest mechanically propelled boat in the world of certain date is the 48 ton Bristol steam driven dredger or drag-boat *Bertha* of 50 ft *15,42 m*, designed by I. K. Brunel in 1844 and afloat in the custody of the Exeter Maritime Museum, Devon, England. Mr G. H. Pattinson's 40 ft *12,20 m* steam launch *Dolly*, which was raised after 67 years from Ullswater, Cumbria, in 1962 and now on Lake Windermere, also probably dates from the 1840s. The world's oldest active steam ship is the *Skibladner*, which has plied Lake Mjøsa, Norway since 1856. She has had two major refits and was built in Motala, Sweden. The oldest motor vessel afloat in British waters is the *Proven* on the run from the Clyde to the Inner Hebrides. She was built in Norway in 1866. The oldest vessel on *Lloyd's Yacht Register* is the twin screw steam yacht *Esperence* built on the Clyde in 1869 and salvaged from Windermere in 1941.

The world's largest RoRo (Roll on, Roll off) barge of the *El Rey* class which is 580 ft *176,78 m* in length and can accommodate 376 truck trailers (see p. 135). (Aero-pic Jacksonville)

133

The world's largest tanker *Seawise Giant* which was converted from the *Oppama* and has an overall length well in excess of a quarter of a mile (see p. 135).

Earliest turbine

The first turbine ship was the *Turbinia*, built in 1894 at Wallsend-on-Tyne, Tyne and Wear, to the design of the Hon. Sir Charles Algernon Parsons, OM, KCB (1854–1931). The *Turbinia* was 100 ft *30,48 m* long and of 44½ tons *45,2 tonnes* displacement with machinery consisting of three steam turbines totalling about 2000 shaft horsepower. At her first public demonstration in 1897 she reached a speed of 34.5 knots (39.7 mph *63,9 km/h*).

PASSENGER LINERS

Largest active

The world's largest and the world's longest ever liner is the *Norway* of 70,202.19 grt and 315,66 m *1035 ft 7½ in* in overall length. She was built as the *France* in 1961 and renamed after purchase in June 1979 by Knut Kloster of Norway. Her second maiden voyage was from Southampton on 7 May 1980. Britain's largest liner is RMS *Queen Elizabeth 2* of 66,851 gross tons and with an overall length of 963 ft *293 m* completed for the Cunar

above: Herald of Free Enterprise the car ferry which completed the fastest crossing of the English Channel in 52 min 53 sec on 10 July 1980 (see p. 137).
left: Sea-Land Commerce crossed the Pacific Ocean in 6 days 1 hr 27 min at an average speed of 33.27 knots (see p. 137).

Line Ltd. in 1969. She set a 'turn round' record of 8 hr 3 min at New York on 17 May 1972. In her 1982 World cruise the price of the Queen Mary and the Queen Elizabeth suites was £113,640 (*$225,000*).

Largest ever

The RMS *Queen Elizabeth* (finally 82,998 but formerly 83,673 gross tons), of the Cunard fleet, was the largest passenger vessel ever built and had the largest displacement of any liner in the world. She had an overall length of 1031 ft *314 m* and was 118 ft 7 in *36 m* in breadth and was powered by steam turbines which developed 168,000 hp. Her last passenger voyage ended on 15 Nov 1968. In 1970 she was removed to Hong Kong to serve as a floating marine university and renamed *Seawise University*. On 9 Jan 1972 she was fired by 3 simultaneous outbreaks. Most of the gutted hull had been cut up and removed by December 1977.

WARSHIPS
Battleships *Largest World*
The largest battleship in the world is now the USS *New Jersey* with a full load displacement of 59,000 tons *59 900 tonnes* and an overall length of 888 ft *270 m*. She was the last fire support ship on active service in the world and was de-commissioned on 17 Dec 1969.

Largest all-time
The Japanese battleships *Yamato* (completed on 16 Dec 1941 and sunk south-west of Kyūshū, Japan, by US planes on 7 Apr 1945) and *Musashi* (sunk in the Philippine Sea by 11 bombs and 16 torpedoes on 24 Oct 1944) were the largest battleships ever commissioned, each with a full load displacement of 72,809 tons *73 977 tonnes*. With an overall length of 863 ft *263 m*, a beam of 127 ft *38,7 m* and a full load draught of 35½ ft *10,8 m* they mounted nine 460 mm *18.1 in* guns and three triple turrets. Each gun weighed 162 tons *164,6 tonnes* and was 75 ft *22,8 m* in length firing a 3200 lb *1451 kg* projectile.

Largest Great Britain
Britain's largest ever and last battleship was HMS *Vanguard* with a full load displacement of 51,420 tons *52 245 tonnes*, overall length 814 ft *248,1 m*, beam 108½ ft *33,07 m*, with a maximum draught of 36 ft *10,9 m*. She mounted eight 15 in *38 cm* and sixteen 5.25 in *13,33 cm* guns. A shaft horsepower of 130,000 gave her a sea speed of 29½ knots (34 mph *54 km/h*). The *Vanguard* was laid down in John Brown & Co. Ltd's yard at Clydebank, Strathclyde, on 20 Oct 1941, launched on 30 Nov 1944 and completed on 25 Apr 1946. She was sold in August 1960 for scrap, having cost a total of £14,000,000.

Guns
The largest guns ever mounted in any of HM ships were the 18 in *45 cm* pieces in the light battle cruiser (later aircraft carrier) HMS *Furious* in 1917. In 1918 they were transferred to the monitors HMS *Lord Clive* and *General Wolfe*. The thickest armour ever carried was in HMS *Inflexible* (completed 1881), measuring 24 in *60 cm* backed by teak up to a maximum thickness of 42 in *106,6 cm*.

Fastest destroyer
The highest speed attained by a destroyer was 45.25 knots (51.84 mph *83,42 km/h*) by the 2830 ton/*tonne* French destroyer *Le Terrible* in 1935. She was built in Blainville and powered by four Yarrow small tube boilers and two Rateau geared turbines giving 100,000 shaft horse-power. She was removed from the active list at the end of 1957.

AIRCRAFT CARRIERS
Largest *World*
The warships with the largest full load displacement in the world are the US Navy aircraft carriers USS *Nimitz* and *Dwight D. Eisenhower* at 91,400 tons. They are 1092 ft *332 m* in length overall and have a speed well in excess of 30 knots *56 km/h* from their nuclear-powered 280,000 shp reactors. They have to be re-fuelled after about 900,000 miles *1450 000 km* steaming. Their complement is 6100 and the total cost of the *Eisenhower*, commissioned on 18 Oct 1977, exceeded $2 billion (*then £1052 million*) excluding the 90-plus aircraft carried. USS *Enterprise* is, however, 1102 ft *335,8 m* long and thus still the longest warship ever built.

SUBMARINES
Largest
The world's largest submarine is the first of the USSR Typhoon class code named Oscar. Its completion at the secret covered shipyard at Severodvinsk in the White Sea was announced by NATO on 23 Sept 1980. It is believed to have a dived displacement of 30,000 tons and measure 180 m *590 ft* overall. The largest submarines ever built for the Royal Navy are the four atomic-powered nuclear missile R class boats with a surface displacement of 7500 tons *7620 tonnes* and 8400 tons *8534 tonnes* submerged, a length of 425 ft *129,5 m*, a beam of 33 ft *10 m* and a draught of 30 ft *9,1 m*.

Fastest
The Russian Alfa-Class nuclear-powered submarines have a reported maximum speed of 42 knots *77,8 km/h* down to a depth of 3000 ft *914,4 m*.

Deepest
The two USN vessels able to descend 12,000 ft *3650 m* are the 3-man *Trieste II* (DSV I) of 303 tons recommissioned in November 1973 and the DSV 2 (deep submergence vessel) USS *Alvin*. The *Trieste II* was reconstructed from the record-breaking bathyscaphe *Trieste* but without the Krupp-built sphere, which enabled it to descend to 35,820 ft *10 917 m*. (see Chapter 11 Greatest ocean descent).

TANKERS
Largest
The world's largest tanker and ship of any kind is the 564,763 tons deadweight *Seawise Giant* completed for C. Y. Tung in January 1981. She is 458,54 m *1504 ft* long with a beam of 68,8 m *225 ft 8 in*, has a draught of 29,8 m *94 ft 5 in*. She was converted by Nippon Kokan by adding a 81 m *265 ft 8 in* midship section to the 16.47 knot 422,018 dwt tanker *Oppama*.

CARGO VESSELS
Largest
The largest vessel in the world capable of carrying dry cargo is the Liberian ore/oil carrier *World Gala* of 133,748 grt *282,450 dwt* with a length of 1109 ft *338 m* and a beam of 179 ft *54 m* owned by Liberian Trident Transports Inc. completed in 1973. The largest British ore/oil carrier is the Orient Steam Navigation Co's *Lauderdale*, built in Japan in 1972, of 143,959 grt *260,424 dwt* and a length of 1101 ft *335,6 m*.

Largest whale factory
The largest whale factory ship is the USSR's *Sovietskaya Ukraina* (32,034 gross tons), with a summer deadweight of 46,000 tons *46 738 tonnes* completed in October 1959. She is 217,8 m *714 ft 6 in* in length and 25,8 m *84 ft 7 in* in the beam.

Largest barge
The world's largest RoRo (Roll-on, Roll-off) barge is the *El Rey* and *La Princessa* of 16,700 tons and 580 ft *176,78 m* in length. They are operated by Crowley Maritime Corp of San Francisco between Florida and Puerto Rico with tri-level loading of up to 376 truck-trailers.

Most powerful tugs
The world's largest and most powerful tugs are the *Wolraad Waltemade* and her sister ship *John Ross* of 2822 grt rated at 19,200 shaft horse-power and with a bollard pull of 172.7 tons (90% of full power). They have an overall length of 94,623 m *310 ft 5 in* and a beam of 49 ft 10 in *15,2 m*. They were built to handle the largest tankers and were completed in April 1976 (Leith, Scotland) and in October 1976 (Durban, South Africa).

Largest car ferry
The world's largest car and passenger ferry is the 30.5 knot 24,600 grt GTS *Finnjet* which entered service across the Baltic between Helsinki and Travemünde, West Germany on 13 May 1977. She can carry 350 cars and 1532 passengers.

Largest hydrofoil
The world's largest naval hydrofoil is the 212 ft *65 m* long *Plainview* (310 tons *314 tonnes* full load), launched by the Lockheed Shipbuilding and Construction Co. at Seattle, Washington, USA on 28 June 1965. She has a service speed of 50 knots

(57 mph *92 km/h*). Three 165 ton Supramar PTS 150 Mk III hydrofoils carrying 250 passengers at 40 knots *74 km/h* ply the Malmö-Copenhagen crossing. They were built by Westermoen Hydrofoil Ltd. of Mandal, Norway. A 500 ton wing ground effect vehicle capable of carrying 900 tons has been reported in the USSR.

Most powerful icebreaker
The world's most powerful icebreaker is the 25,000 ton USSR atomic powered *Arktika*, able to smash through ice up to nearly 4 m *13 ft* thick. On 9 Aug 1977 she sailed from Murmansk and reached the North Pole at 2 a.m. GMT on 17 Aug.

The largest *converted* icebreaker has been the 1007 ft *306,9 m* long SS *Manhattan* (43,000 shp), which was converted by the Humble Oil Co. into a 150,000 ton *152 407 tonnes* icebreaker with an armoured prow 69 ft 2 in long. She made a double voyage through the North-West Passage in arctic Canada from 24 Aug to 12 Nov 1969. The North-West Passage was first navigated by Roald Amundsen (Norway) in the sealing sloop *Gjöa* on 11 July 1906.

Yacht most expensive
King Khalid's Saudi Arabian 212 ft *64,6 m* Royal yacht was upstaged as the most expensive in 1979 by a five-deck 282 footer *85,95 m* built by the Benetti Shipyard, Viareggio, Italy for a reputed hull price of $24 million (*then £10.9 million*) to the order of Adnan Khashoggi. It has a helicopter and 5 speed boats.

Largest dredger
The world's most powerful dredger is the 468.4 ft *142,7 m* long *Prins der Nederlanden* of 10,586 grt. She can dredge 20,000 tonnes/*tons* of sand from a depth of 35 m *115 ft via* two suction tubes in less than an hour.

Wooden ship
The heaviest wooden ship ever built was the *Richelieu*, 333 ft 8 in *101,70 m* long and of 8534 tons launched in Toulon, France on 3 Dec 1873. HM Battleship *Lord Warden*, completed in 1869, displaced 7940 tons *8 060 tonnes*. The longest modern wooden ship ever built was the New York built *Rochambeau* (1867–72) formerly *Dunderberg*. She measured 377 ft 4 in *115 m* overall. It should be noted that the biblical length of Noah's Ark was 300 cubits or, at 18 in *45,7 cm* to a cubit, 450 ft *137 m* (but see Junks below).

Largest human powered
The largest human powered ship was the giant Tessarakonteres 3-banked catamaran galley with 4000 rowers built for Ptolemy IV *c.* 210 BC in Alexandria, Egypt. It measured 128 m *420 ft* with up to 8 men to an oar of 38 cubits (*17,5 m 57 ft*) in length.

The world's longest canoe is the 117 ft *35,7 m* long 20 ton Kauri wood Maori war canoe Nga Toki Matawhaorua built by adzes at Kerikeri Inlet, New Zealand in 1940 for a crew of 70 or more.

SAILING SHIPS
Largest
The largest sailing vessel ever built was the *France II* (5806 gross tons), launched at Bordeaux in 1911. The *France II* was a steel-hulled, five-masted barque (square-rigged on four masts and fore and aft rigged on the aftermost mast). Her hull measured 418 ft *127,4 m* overall. Although principally designed as a sailing vessel with a stump topgallant rig, she was also fitted with two steam engines. She was wrecked in 1922. The only seven-masted sailing schooner ever built was the 375.6 ft *114,4 m* long *Thomas W. Lawson* (5218 gross tons) built at Quincy, Massachusetts, USA in 1902 and lost in the English Channel on 15 Dec 1907.

The largest sailing vessel under the Red Ensign is the three-masted topgallant schooner *Captain Scott* of 144 ft *43,8 m* overall and displacing 380 tons/*tonnes* completed in September 1971 and based in Loch Eil, Highland, Scotland.

The world's only surviving First Rate Ship-of-the-Line is the Royal Navy's 104-gun battleship HMS *Victory* laid down at Chatham, Kent on 23 July 1759 constructed from the wood of some 2200 oak trees. She bore the body of Admiral Nelson from Gibraltar to Portsmouth arriving 44 days after serving as his victorious flagship at the Battle of Trafalgar on 21 Oct 1805. In 1922 she was moved to No. 2 dock, Portsmouth—site of the world's oldest graving dock. The total length of her cordage (both standing and running rigging) is 100,962 ft (19.12 miles *30,77 km.*)

Largest junks
The largest junk on record was the sea-going *Cheng Ho*, flagship of Admiral Cheng Ho's 62 treasure ships, of *c.* 1420, with a displacement of 3100 tons *3150 tonnes* and a length variously estimated up to 538 ft *164 m* and believed to have had 9 masts.

A river junk 361 ft *110 m* long, with treadmill-operated paddle-wheels, was recorded in AD 1161. In *c.* AD 280 a floating fortress 600 ft *182,8 m* square, built by Wang Chün on the Yangtze, took part in the Chin-Wu river war. Present-day junks do not, even in the case of the Chiangsu traders, exceed 170 ft *51,8 m* in length.

Longest day's run under sail
The longest day's run claimed by any sailing ship was one of 465 nautical miles (535.45 statute miles *861,72 km*) by the clipper *Champion of the Seas* (2722 registered tons) of the Liverpool Black Ball Line running before a north-westerly gale in the south Indian Ocean under the command of Capt. Alex. Newlands. The elapsed time between the fixes was 23 hr 17 min giving an average of 19.97 knots *37,00 km/h*.

Largest sails
Sails are known to have been used for marine propulsion since 3500 BC. The largest spars ever carried were those in HM Battleship *Temeraire*, completed at Chatham, Kent, on 31 Aug 1877. The fore and main yards measured 115 ft *35 m* in length. The mainsail contained 5100 ft *1555 m* of canvas, weighing 2 tons *2,03 tonnes* and the total sail area was 25,000 ft² *2322 m²*.

Largest wreck
The largest ship ever wrecked has been the 312,186 dwt VLCC (Very Large Crude Carrier) *Energy Determination* which blew up and broke in two in the Straits of Hormuz on 12 Dec 1979. Her full value was $58 million (*then £26.3 million*).

Largest collision
The closest approach to an irrestible force striking an immovable object occurred on 16 Dec 1977, 22 miles *35 km* off the coast of Southern Africa when the tanker *Venoil* (330,954 dwt) struck her sister ship *Venpet* (330,869 dwt).

OCEAN CROSSINGS
Atlantic *Earliest*
The earliest crossing of the Atlantic by a power vessel, as opposed to an auxiliary engined sailing ship, was a 22-day voyage begun in April 1827, from Rotterdam, Netherlands, to the West Indies by the *Curaçao*. She was a 127 ft *38,7 m* wooden paddle boat of 438 tons, built as the *Calpe* in Dover in 1826 and purchased by the Dutch Government for the West Indian mail service. The earliest Atlantic crossing entirely under steam (with intervals for desalting the boilers) was by HMS *Rhadamanthus* from Plymouth to Barbados in 1832. The earliest crossing of the Atlantic under continuous steam power was by the condenser-fitted packet ship *Sirius* (703 tons *714 tonnes*) from Queenstown (now Cóbh), Ireland, to Sandy Hook, New Jersey, USA, in 18 days 10 hr on 4–22 Apr 1838.

Atlantic *Fastest World*
The fastest Atlantic crossing was made by the *United States* (then 51,988, now 38,216 gross tons), former flagship of the United States Lines. On her maiden voyage between 3 and 7 July 1952 from New York City, NY, USA, to Le Havre, France, and Southampton, England, she averaged 35.59 knots, or 40.98 mph *65,95 km/h* for 3 days 10 hr 40 min (6.36 p.m. GMT, 3 July to 5.16 a.m., 7 July) on a route of 2949 nautical miles *5465 km* from the Ambrose Light Vessel to the Bishop Rock Light, Isles of Scilly, Cornwall. During this run, on 6–7 July 1952, she steamed the greatest distance ever covered by any ship in a day's run (24 hr)—868 nautical miles *1609 km*, hence averaging 36.17 knots (41.65 mph *67,02 km/h*). The maximum speed attained from her 240,000 shp engines was 38.32 knots (44.12 mph *71,01 km/h*) on trials on 9–10 June 1952.

Pacific *Fastest*
The fastest crossing of the Pacific Ocean from Yokohama to

Long Beach, California (4840 nautical miles *8960 km*) was 6 days 1 hr 27 min (30 June–6 July 1973) by the container ship *Sea-Land Commerce* (50,315 tons) at an average of 33.27 knots (38.31 mph *61,65 km/h*).

Channel Crossing *Fastest*
The fastest crossing of the English Channel by a commercial ferry is 52 min 53 sec from Dover to Calais by Townsend Thorensen's *Herald of Free Enterprise* in a Force 7–8 Gale on 10 July 1980.

Southernmost
The farthest south ever reached by a ship was achieved on 15 Feb 1912 when the *Fram* reached Lat. 78° 41′ S. off the Antarctic coast.

Deepest anchorage
The deepest anchorage ever achieved is one of 24,600 ft *7498 m* in the mid-Atlantic Romanche Trench by Capt. Jacques-Yves Cousteau's research vessel *Calypso*, with a 5½ mile *8,9 km* long nylon cable, on 29 July 1956.

Greatest roll
The ultimate in rolling was recorded in heavy seas in the 1978 Trans-Tasman single handed race when the yacht of WRM (Bill) Belcher was rolled 360° by each of two successive waves before being dumped on Middleton Reef by a third.

Crossing the Line Ceremony Largest
The largest recorded ceremony on any warship for initiating those who have crossed the equator for the first time occurred aboard the *USS Nimitz* in the South Atlantic in mid-January 1980 when 4421 Nimitz polywogs became shellbacks.

2. ROAD VEHICLES

Guinness Superlatives has now published automotive records in greater detail in the more specialist publication Car Facts and Feats *(3rd edition price £6.95).*

COACHING
Before the widespread use of tarred road surfaces from 1845 coaching was slow and hazardous. The zenith was reached on 13 July 1888 when J. Selby, Esq., drove the 'Old Times' coach 108 miles *173 km* from London to Brighton and back with 8 teams and 14 changes in 7 hr 50 min to average 13.79 mph *22,19 km/h*. Four-horse carriages could maintain a speed of 21⅓ mph *34 km/ h* for nearly an hour. The *Border Union* stage coach, built *c.* 1825, ran 4 in hand from Edinburgh to London (393 miles *632 km*). When it ceased in 1842, due to competition from railways, the allowed schedule was 42 hr 23 min to average better than 9¼ mph *14,9 km/h*.

MOTOR CARS
Most cars
In 1979 it was estimated that in the United States 143,092,000 drivers drove 159,400,000 vehicles 1,525,000 million miles *2 454 000 million km* or 204.9 miles *329,8 km* per week per driver.

Earliest automobiles *Model*
The earliest automobile of which there is record is a two-foot-long steam-powered model constructed by Ferdinand Verbiest (d. 1687) a Belgian Jesuit priest, and described in his *Astronomia Europaea*. His model of 1668 was possibly inspired either by Giovanni Branca's description of a steam turbine, published in

his *La Macchina* in 1629, or by writings on 'fire carts' or *Nan Huai-Jen* during the Chu dynasty (*c.* 800 BC) in the library of the Emperor Khang-hi of China, to whom he was an astronomer during the period *c.* 1665–80.

Earliest automobiles *Passenger-carrying*
The earliest mechanically propelled passenger vehicle was the first of two military steam tractors, completed at the Paris Arsenal in 1769 by Nicolas-Joseph Cugnot (1725–1804). This reached 2¼ mph *3,6 km/h*. Cugnot's second, larger tractor, completed in May 1771, today survives in the *Conservatoire nationale des arts et métiers* in Paris. Britain's first steam carriage carried eight passengers on 24 Dec 1801 in Camborne, Cornwall and was built by Richard Trevithick (1771–1833).

Earliest automobiles *Internal combustion*
The first true internal-combustion engined vehicle was that built by the Londoner Samuel Brown (Patent 5350, 25 Apr 1826) whose 4 hp *4,05 cv* two cylinder atmospheric gas 88 litre engined carriage climbed Shooters Hill, Blackheath, Kent in May 1826. The first successful petrol-driven car, the Motorwagen, built by Karl-Friedrich Benz (1844–1929) of Karlsruhe, ran at Mannheim, Germany, in late 1885. It was a 5 cwt *250 kg* 3-wheeler reaching 8–10 mph *13–16 km/h*. Its single cylinder 4-stroke chain-drive engine (bore 91.4 mm, stroke 160 mm) delivered 0.85 hp *0,86 cv* at 200 rpm. It was patented on 29 Jan 1886. Its first 1 km road test was reported in the local newspaper, the *Neue Badische Landeszeitung*, of 4 June 1886, under the heading 'Miscellaneous'. Two were built in 1885 of which one has been preserved in 'running order' at the Deutsches Museum, Munich.

Earliest automobile *British*
In Britain Edward Butler (1863–1940) built a 1042 cc twin-cylinder 2-stroke petrol-engined tricycle at Erith, Kent in 1888 but the earliest successful British built car with an internal combustion engine was the Bremer car built at Walthamstow, Greater London, by the engineer Frederick William Bremer (1872–1941) which first took the road in December 1894 though the body was not completed until the following month. The car has a single cylinder horizontal, water cooled 600 cc engine with a two-speed chain drive and tiller steering. The maximum speed is about 15 mph and the car in 1964 completed the London-to-Brighton run. It is now housed in the Vestry House Museum, London E17. Henry Hewetson drove an imported Benz Velo in the south-eastern suburbs of London in November 1894.

Registrations *Earliest and Most Expensive*
The world's first plates were probably introduced by the Parisian police in France in 1893. Registration plates were introduced in Britain in 1903. The original A1 plate was secured by the 2nd Earl Russell (1865–1931) for his 12 hp *12,1 cv* Napier. This plate, willed in September 1950 to Mr Trevor T. Laker of Leicester, was sold in August 1959 for £2500 in aid of charity. It was reported in April 1973 that a 'cherished' number plate changed hands for £14,000 in a private deal. On 9 Dec 1978 Sir Run Run Shaw CBE bid HK$330,000 (then £34,800) for a 'Good Fortune' number plate at a Hong Kong Government charity auction.

FASTEST CARS
Diesel engined
The prototype 230 hp 3 litre Mercedes C 111/3 attained 327,3 km/h *203.3 mph* in tests on the Nardo Circuit, Southern Italy on 5–15 Oct 1978.

FASTEST CARS

CATEGORY	MPH	KM/H	CAR	DRIVER	PLACE	DATE
Rocket Engined *(unofficial)*	739.666	1190,377	Budweiser Rocket	Stan Barrett (US)	Edwards Air Base, California, USA	17 Dec 1979
Rocket Engined *(official)*	622.287	1001,473	Blue Flame	Gary Gabelich (US)	Bonneville, Utah, USA	23 Oct 1970
Jet Engined	613.995	988,129	Spirit of America	Norman Breedlove (US)	Bonneville, Utah, USA	15 Nov 1965
Wheel Driven	429.311	690,909	Bluebird	Donald Campbell (UK)	Lake Eyre, Australia	17 July 1964
Piston Engined	418.504	673,516	Goldenrod	Robert Summers (US)	Bonneville, Utah, USA	12 Nov 1965
Racing Car	257.0	413,6	Porsche 917/30 Can-Am	Mark Donohue (US)	Toulon, France	Aug 1973

Rocket Powered Ice Sled

The highest speed recorded is 247.93 mph *399,00 km/h* by *Oxygen* driven by Sammy Miller (b. 15 Apr 1945) on Lake George, NY, USA on 15 Feb 1981.

Road cars

Various detuned track cars have been licensed for road use but are not purchasable production models. Manufacturers of very fast and very expensive models are understandably reluctant to allow maximum speed tests to be carried out. The fastest manufacturer's *claim* (as opposed to independently road-tested) for a production road car, is 315 km/h *195.7 mph* for the Lamborghini Countach P400. The 5.3 litre V8 Aston Martin Lagonda *Bulldog* announced on 15 Apr 1980 has a claimed top speed of 190 mph *305 km/h* and a 0–60 mph *0–96,5 km/h* acceleration of "just over 5 secs".

The highest road-tested acceleration reported is 0–60 mph *0–96,5 km/h* in 4.2 sec and 0–100 mph *0–160,9 km/h* in 9.8 sec by the 7 litre A. C. Cobra 1965, in November 1967 by Roger Bell (*Motor*) and John Bolster (*Autosport*).

LARGEST CARS

World

Of cars produced for private road use, the largest has been the Bugatti 'Royale' type 41, known in Britain as the 'Golden Bugatti', of which only six (not seven) were made at Molsheim, France by the Italian Ettore Bugatti, and some survive. First built in 1927, this machine has an 8-cylinder engine of 12.7 litres capacity, and measures over 22 ft *6,7 m* in length. The bonnet is over 7 ft *2 m* long. Of custom built cars the longest is the stretched 1962 Chevrolet Station Wagon owned by the Rev. Gerald R. Manning of Middletown, Virginia. The finished result is 32 ft 4 in *9,85 m* overall and weighs 4500 lb *2040 kg*. (For cars not intended for private use, see Largest engines.)

Largest engines *All-time and current records*

The world's most powerful piston engine car is 'Quad Al.' It was designed and built in 1964 by Jim Lytle and was first shown in May 1965 at the Los Angeles Sports Arena. The car featured four Allison V12 aircraft engines with a total of 6840 in³ *112,087 cc* displacement and 12,000 hp. The car has 4-wheel drive, 8 wheels and tyres, and dual 6-disc clutch assemblies. The wheelbase is 160 in *406,4 cm*, and weighs 5860 lb *2658 kg*. It has 96 spark plugs and 96 exhaust pipes.

The largest car ever used was the 'White Triplex', sponsored by J. H. White of Philadelphia, Pennsylvania, USA. Completed early in 1928, after two year's work, the car weighed about 4 tons *4,06 tonnes* and was powered by three Liberty V12 aircraft engines with a total capacity of 81,188 cc, developing 1500 bhp at 2,000 rpm. It was used to break the world speed record but crashed at Daytona, Florida on 13 Mar 1929.

Currently the most powerful car on the road is the 6-wheeled Jameson-Merlin, powered by a 27,000 cc 1760 hp Rolls Royce V12 Merlin aero-engine, governed down to a maximum speed of 185 mph *298 km/h*. It has a range of 300 miles *480 km* with tanks of 60 gal *272 litres* capacity. The vehicle weighs 2.65 tons *2,69 tonnes* overall.

Largest engines *Production car*

The highest engine capacity of a production car was 13½ litres *824 in³*, in the case of the US Pierce-Arrow 6–66 Raceabout of 1912–18, the US Peerless 6–60 of 1912–14 and the Fageol of 1918. The largest currently available is the V8 engine of 500.1 in³ *8194 cc*, developing 235 bhp net, used in the 1972 Cadillac Fleetwood Eldorado.

Petrol consumption

The world record for fuel economy on a closed circuit course (one of 14.076 miles *22,00 km*) was set by Ben Visser (US) in a highly modified 1.5 litre *90.8 in³* 1959 Opel CarAvan station wagon in the annual Shell Research Laboratory contest at Wood River, Illinois, driven by Ben and Carolyn Visser on 2 Oct 1973 with 451.90 ton miles per US gal and 376.59 miles *606,0 km* on one US gal, i.e. *3,78 litres*. These figures are equivalent to 542.70 ton miles and 452.26 miles *727,84 km* on an imperial gallon i.e. *4,54 litres*. The tyre pressure was 200 lb/in² and the maximum speed was 12 mph *19,3 km/h*.

In October 1979 at the International Fuel Saving Competition for cars and special vehicles in Switzerland a 20 cc diesel engined 3-wheeler driven by Franz Maier of Stuttgart covered 1284.13 km on 1 litre of fuel—equivalent to 3627.26 miles to the Imperial gallon. Douglas Malewicki drove 451.3 miles *726,2 km* from Los Angeles to San Francisco, California at the US Speed limit of 55 mph *88,5 km/h* on 20 Nov 1980 using only 2.871 US gallons of fuel for an mpg of 157.19 (US), 188.78 (Imperial) or *66,83 km* per litre in his 3 wheeled *California Commuter* road car.

Most durable car

The highest recorded mileage for a car is 1,184,880 authenticated miles *1 906 879 km* by August 1978 for a 1957 Mercedes 180 D owned by Robert O'Reilly of Olympia, Washington State, USA.

Taxis

The largest taxi fleet was that of New York City, which amounted to 29,000 cabs in October 1929, compared with the present figure of 12,500 plus an equal number of 'gypsies'. London's most durable 'cabby' was F. Fuller, who drove from 26 Oct 1908 until he handed in his badge on 16 Sept 1966—57 years later. On 1 May 1981 there were 12,386 cabs and 17,479 drivers in London. In 1923 the London taxi drivers established their one day outing for children. On 5 Aug 1980 157 taxis took 500 children free to Southend, Essex.

MOST EXPENSIVE CARS

Special

The most expensive car to build has been the US Presidential 1969 Lincoln Continental Executive delivered to the US Secret Service on 14 Oct 1968. It has an overall length of 21 ft 6.3 in *6,56 m* with a 13 ft 4 in *4,06 m* wheel-base and with the addition of 2 tons *2,03 tonnes* of armour plate, weighs 5.35 tons *5,43 tonnes* (12,000 lb *5443 kg*). The estimated research, development and manufacture cost was $500,000 (*then £208,000*) but it is rented at $5000 (*now £2300*) per annum. Even if all four tyres were shot out it can travel at 50 mph *80 km/h* on inner rubber-edged steel discs.

Carriage House Motor Cars Ltd of New York City in March 1978 completed 4 years work on converting a 1973 Rolls Royce including lengthening it by 30 in *76,2 cm*. The price tag was $500,000 (*then £263,157*).

Standard

The most expensive British standard car is the Rolls-Royce 8 cylinder 6750 cc Camargue, quoted in *Motor* (May 1981) at £79,160 (incl. tax). More expensive are custom built models. Jack Barclay Ltd of Berkeley Square, London W1 quote £170,000 for an armour-plated Rolls-Royce Phantom VI without tax.

Used

The greatest price paid for any used car has been $421,040 (*then £210,520*), for a 1936 Mercedes-Benz Roadster from the M. L. Cohn collection, by a telephone bidder in Monaco, at Christie's sale on 25 Feb 1979 at the Los Angeles Convention Center. The greatest collection of vintage cars is the William F. Harrah Collection of 1700, estimated to be worth more than $4 million (*£2.3 million*), at Reno, Nevada, USA. Mr Harrah was still looking for a Chalmer's Detroit 1909 Tourabout, an Owen car of 1910–12 and a Nevada Truck of 1915 at the time of his death in 1978.

Most inexpensive

The cheapest car of all-time was the 1922 Red Bug Buckboard, built by Briggs and Stratton Co of Milwaukee, Wisconsin, listed at $150–$125. It had a 62 in *1,57 m* wheel base and weighed 245 lb *111 kg*. The early models of the King Midget cars were sold in kit form for self-assembly for as little as $100 (*then £24 16s*) as late as 1948. By mid-1981 the cheapest quoted new car price in Britain was £1,990 for a Fiat 126 700 cc 2 door car. In France the 49 cc Ligier *Voiturette*, for those without licenses and content with a top speed of 28 mph *45 km/h*, the price is 16,500 Francs (*now £1460*).

Longest production

The longest any car has been in production is 42 years (1938 to date), including wartime interruptions, in the case of the Volkswagen 'Beetle' series, originally designed by Ferdinand

The longest custom-built car, the 1962 'stretched' Chevrolet owned by the Rev. Gerald R. Manning of Middletown, Virginia, which is 32 ft 4 in *9,85 m* in overall length (see Cover and p. 138). (*Rev. Gerald R. Manning*)

Porsche. It ceased production in W. Germany on 19 Jan 1978 with 19,200,000 cars produced since May 1938. Residual production continues in South America. Britain's all-time champion is the 'Flat Twin' engined Jowett (1910–52). Britain's champion seller has been the Mini which originally sold for £496 19s 2d in August 1959. Sales reached 4,988,691 by 1 May 1981.

Round the world driving
The fastest circumnavigation embracing more than an equator's length of driving (24,901.47 road miles *40 075,0 km*) is one in 74 days 1 hr 11 min by Garry Sowerby (driver) and Ken Langley (navigator) of Canada from 6 Sept to 19 Nov 1980 in a Volvo 245 westwards from Toronto, Canada through 4 continents and 23 countries. The distance covered was 42 745,8 km *26,561.0 miles*.

The first recorded round the world drive by lorry was by Daniele Pellegrini and Cesare Gerolimetto of Italy, in a 122 hp Iveco 75 PC 6 cylinder 4 wheel drive Fiat diesel, from Vicenza on 17 Aug 1976 arriving back 2 years 245 days later on 19 Apr 1979. The route took 184 000 km *114,300 miles* including 240 km *1500 miles* off-road.

Round Britain driving
The best recorded time for driving the 3675 miles *5914 km* Round Britain course on an Official Certified Trial under the surveillance of a motoring organisation and with Tachograph readings, is 84 hr 5 min to average 43.31 mph *69,70 km/h* in a Land Rover driven by Ray Sanderson, John Marshall and Simon Le Marchal on 14–18 Apr 1981. This charity trial by Malmesbury & Tetbury Round Table was non-stop by virtue of helicopter refuelling.

Mountain driving
Cars have been driven up Ben Nevis, Highland, Scotland (4406 ft *1343 m*) on 4 occasions. The record times are 7 hr 23 min (ascent) and 1 hr 55 min (descent) by George F. Simpson in an Austin 7 on 6 Oct 1928. Henry Alexander accomplished the feat twice in May 1911 (Model T Ford) and on 13 Sept 1928 (Model A Ford).

Driving in reverse
Charles Creighton (1908–70) and James Hargis of Maplewood, Missouri, USA, drove their Ford Model A 1929 roadster in reverse from New York City 3340 miles *5375 km* to Los Angeles, California on 26 July–13 Aug 1930 without once stopping the engine. They arrived back in New York in reverse on 5 Sept so completing 7180 miles *11 555 km* in 42 days. The highest average speed attained in any non-stop reverse drive exceeding 500 miles was achieved by Gerald Hoagland who drove a 1969 Chevrolet Impala 501 miles *806,2 km* in 17 hr 38 min at Che-

mung Speed Drome, New York, USA on 9–10 July 1976 to average 28.41 mph *45,72 km/h.*

Two Wheel Driving
The longest recorded distance for driving on 2 wheels by a professional stunt man is 5.6 miles *9,01 km* in a Chevrolet Chevelte by Joie Chitwood, Jr on the Indianapolis Speedway, USA on 13 May 1978.

Oldest driver
Roy M. Rawlins (b. 10 July 1870) of Stockton, California, USA, was warned for driving at 95 mph *152 km/h* in a 55 mph *88,5 km/h* zone in June 1974. On 25 Aug 1974 he was awarded a California State licence valid till 1978 by Mr John Burrafato, but Mr Rawlins died on 9 July 1975, one day short of his 105th birthday. Mrs Maude Tull of Inglewood, California, who took to driving aged 91 after her husband died, was issued a renewal on 5 Feb 1976 when aged 104. Britain's only recorded centenarian driver was Herbert Warren (1874–1975) of Whatlington, Norfolk, who drove a 1954 Standard 10. The oldest age at which anyone has passed the Department of Transport driving test has been 88 years 5 months by Mrs Harriet Emma Jack (*née* Morse) (b. 9 Dec 1887) on 18 May 1976 in Bognor Regis, West Sussex. The highest year number ever displayed on a Veteran Motorist's badge was '75' by Walter Herbert Weake, who started his accident free career in 1894 and drove daily until his death in 1969, aged 91.

Youngest driver
Instances of drivers have been recorded in HM Armed Forces much under 17 years. Mrs P. L. M. Williams (b. 3 Feb 1926), now of Risca, Gwent, as Private Patterson in the ATS drove a 5 ton truck in 1941 aged 15. Gordon John Graham of Clydebank, Strathclyde passed his advanced driving test aged 17 years 18 days on 20 Nov 1973.

Driving tests
The record for persistence in taking the Ministry of Transport's Learners' Test is held by Mrs Miriam Hargrave, (b. 3 Apr 1908) of Wakefield, West Yorkshire, who failed her 39th driving test in eight years on 29 Apr 1970 after 'crashing' a set of red lights. She triumphed at her 40th attempt after 212 lessons on 3 Aug 1970. The examiner was alleged not to have known about her previous 39 tests. In 1978 she was reported to dislike right-hand turns. The world's easiest tests have been those in Egypt in which the ability to drive 6 m *19.64 ft* forward and the same in reverse has been deemed sufficient. In 1979 it was reported that accurate reversing had been added between two rubber traffic cones. 'High cone attrition' soon led to the substitution of white lines. Mrs Fannie Turner (b. 1903) of Little Rock, Arkansas,

A 'left-hand down a bit situation' for Dr. Daniele Pellegrini (left) and Cesare Gerolimetto as they drove round the world in their Fiat lorry from 17 Aug 1976 to 19 Apr 1979. They passed through 49 countries (see p. 139). (*Dr Daniele Pellegrini*)

USA passed her *written* test for drivers on her 104th attempt in October 1978.

Buses *Earliest*
The first municipal motor omnibus service in the world was inaugurated on 12 Apr 1903 between Eastbourne railway station and Meads, East Sussex, England. A steam-powered bus named *Royal Patent* ran between Gloucester and Cheltenham for 4 months in 1831.

Longest
The longest buses in the world are the 10.72 ton *10 870 kg*, 76 ft *23,16 m* long articulated buses, with 121 passenger seats and room also for 66 'strap-hangers' built by the Wayne Corporation of Richmond, Indiana, USA for use in the Middle East.

Longest route
The longest regularly scheduled bus route is the Greyhound 'Supercruiser' Miami, Florida, to San Francisco, California, route over 3240 miles *5214 km* in 81 hr 50 min (average speed of travel 39.59 mph *63,71 km/h*). The total Greyhound fleet numbers 5500 buses.

Caravans *Longest journey*
The longest continuous motor caravan journey is one of 143,716

miles *231 288 km* by Harry B. Coleman and Peggy Larson in a Volkswagen Camper from 20 Aug 1976 to 20 Apr 1978 through 113 countries. Saburo Ouchi (b. 7 Feb 1942) of Tokyo, Japan, drove 270 000 km *167,770 miles* in 91 countries from 2 Dec 1969 to 10 Feb 1978.

Largest
The largest caravans built in Britain are 18 m *59 ft 0½ in* in length and 3,5 m *11 ft 5¾ in* wide built by Coventry Steel Caravans Ltd of Newport Pagnell, Buckinghamshire.

Fastest
The world speed record for a caravan is 124.91 mph *201,02 km/h* by an Alpha 14 towed by a Le Mans Aston Martin V8 saloon driven by Robin Hamilton at RAF Elvington, North Yorkshire on 14 Oct 1980.

Vehicles *Most massive*
The most massive vehicle ever constructed is the Marion eight caterpillar crawler used for conveying *Saturn V* rockets to their launching pads at the John F. Kennedy Space Center, Florida (see Chapter 4, Most powerful rocket). It measures 131 ft 4 in *40 m* by 114 ft *34,7 m* and the two built cost $12,300,000 (*then* *£5,125,000*). The loaded train weight is 8036 tons *8165 tonnes*. Its windscreen wipers with 42 in *106 cm* blades are the world's largest.

The most massive automotive land vehicle is 'Big Muskie' the 10,700 ton *10 890 tonnes* mechanical shovel built by Bucyrus Erie for the Musk mine. It is 487 ft *148,43 m* long; 151 ft *46,02 m* wide and 222 ft *67,66 m* high with a grab capacity of 325 tons.

The longest vehicle ever built is the Arctic Snow Train owned by the world famous wire-walker Steve McPeak (US). This 54 wheeled 572 ft *174,3 m* long vehicle was built by R G Le Tourneau Inc of Longview, Texas for the US Army. Its gross train weight is 400 tons with a top speed of 20 mph *32 km/h* and it was driven by a crew of 6 when used as an 'Overland Train' for the military. McPeak repaired it and every punctured wheel lone-handed in often sub-zero temperatures in Alaska. It generates 4,680 shp and has a capacity of 6 522 Imperial gallons *29 648 litres*.

Wrecker *Most powerful*
The world's most powerful wrecker is the Vance Corporation 25 ton *25,4 tonne* 30 ft *9,14 m* long Monster No. 2 stationed at Hammond, Indiana, USA. It can lift in excess of 160 tons *163 tonnes* on its short boom.

Earth mover *Largest*
The world's largest earth mover is the Balderson 'Double Dude' plow (plough) harnessed to a Caterpillar SXS D9H 820 flywheel horsepower tractor. It can cast 14,185 yd³ *10 845 m³* per hour.

Dumper truck *Largest*
The world's largest dump truck is the Terex Titan 33–19 manufactured by the Terex Division of General Motors Corporation. It has a loaded weight of 539.9 tons *548,6 tonnes* and a capacity of 312½ tons *317,5 tonnes*. When tipping its height is 56 ft *17,06 m*. The 16 cylinder engine delivers 3300 hp. The fuel tank holds 1300 Imperial gallons *5904,6 litres*. It went into service in November 1974.

Tractor *Largest*
The world's largest tractor is the $325,000 (*then £162,500*) 58 ton Northern Manufacturing Co 8-wheeled 16V-747. It is 14 ft *4,26 m* tall and 20 ft 7 in *6,27 m* wide with a 707.7 gal *3217 l* tank. It was launched in October 1978.

Fire engine *Most powerful*
The world's most powerful fire appliance is the 860 hp 8-wheel Oshkosh firetruck used for aircraft fires. It can discharge 41,600 gal *190 000 l* of foam through two turrets in just 150 sec. It weighs 59.0 tons *60 tonnes*.

Ambulance Largest
The world's largest ambulances are the 18 m *59 ft 0½ in* long articulated Alligator Jumbulance Mark VI's operated by The

Road Vehicles

Across Trust to convey the sick and handicapped on holidays and pilgrimages to the Continent. They are built by Van Hool of Belgium with Fiat engines and cost £152,000 and convey 44 patients plus staff.

Load heaviest *World*
The greatest weight moved on wheels anywhere in the world is 2744 tonnes *2700 tons* by Snellen-Vermeer and Sarens de Coster NV over 100 m *109 yd* in Rotterdam, Netherlands on 4 Oct 1980. The object moved aboard the Heerema barge H-102 was a buoy 82 m *270 ft* long and 50,3 m *165 ft* in circumference. The train weight of the 1024 wheeled assembly was 3320 tonnes *3267.5 tons*.

The world's record road load is one of a 741 ton *753 tonne* nuclear reactor vessel 6 miles *9,6 km* from Seneca to Marseilles, Illinois on a 384-wheeled Schearele trailer by the Reliance Truck Co on 12 Feb 1977.

Great Britain
The heaviest road load moved in the United Kingdom has been a 395 ton *401,4 tonnes* 121 ft 7¾ in *37,08 m* long reheater pressure vessel from the GEC factory in Larne to Belfast docks, Northern Ireland on 17–18 Dec 1977. The gross weight of the 172 ft 6¾ in *52,6 m* long rig of two pulling and one pushing tractor with the bogies was 625 tons *635,2 tonnes*. The longest load moved on British roads has been a 192 ft *58,5 m* 143 ton Belgian-made main wash column to ICI Wilton on 29 July 1976.

Tyres Largest
The world's largest tyres are manufactured in Topeka, Kansas by the Goodyear Co for giant dumper trucks. They measure 11 ft 6 in *3,50 m* in diameter, weigh 12,500 lb *5670 kg* and cost more than $50,000 (*£23,000*). A tyre 17 ft *5,18 m* in diameter is believed to be the limitation of what is practical.

Skid marks Longest
The longest recorded skid marks on a public road have been those 950 ft *290 m* long left by a Jaguar car involved in an accident on the M1 near Luton, Bedfordshire, on 30 June 1960. Evidence given in the High Court case *Hurlock* v. *Inglis and others* indicated a speed 'in excess of 100 mph *160 km/h*' before the application of the brakes. The skid marks made by the jet-powered *Spirit of America*, driven by Norman Craig Breedlove, after the car went out of control at Bonneville Salt Flats, Utah, USA, on 15 Oct 1964, were nearly 6 miles *9,6 km* long. (see Jet-engined record, p. 137).

Amphibious vehicle circumnavigation
The only circumnavigation by an amphibious vehicle was achieved by Ben Carlin (Australia) (d. 7 Mar 1981) in an amphibious jeep 'Half-Safe'. He completed the last leg of the Atlantic crossing (the English Channel) on 24 Aug 1951. He arrived back in Montreal, Canada on 8 May 1958 having completed a circumnavigation of 39,000 miles *62 765 km* over land and 9600 miles *15 450 km* by sea and river. He was accompanied on the trans Atlantic stage by his ex-wife Elinore (US) and on the long trans Pacific stage (Tokyo to Anchorage) by Broye Lafayette De Mente (b. Missouri, 1928).

Snowmobiles
Tony Lenzini of Sylvania, Ohio, USA drove his Ski-Doo Citation 4500, 5627 miles *9055 km* from Haughton Lake, Michigan to Anchorage, Alaska in 62 days from 7 Jan to 6 Mar 1980.

Rubber-Powered Vehicle
The greatest distance achieved by an elastic-powered car is 482,25 m *527.4 yd* by 'Olive-Goo' designed by a team from Japan on 24 Mar 1980. On 27 Mar 1981 she covered 100 m in 19.34 secs.

Petrol station
The largest gallonage sold through a single pump is 7813.77 gal *35 521,4 litres* in 24 hr on 25 June 1977 at Mornington Motors Ltd, Dunedin, New Zealand.

Tow Longest
The longest tow on record was one of 4759 miles *7 658 km* from Halifax, Nova Scotia to Canada's Pacific Coast, when Frank J. Elliott and George A. Scott of Amherst persuaded 168 passing

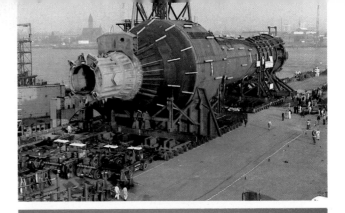

The greatest load (3267½ tons) ever moved on wheels. The 1024 wheeled transporter, here seen moving its load of a giant buoy, along the quay in Rotterdam, Netherlands on 4 Oct 1980.

motorists in 89 days to tow their Model T Ford (in fact engineless) to win a $1000 bet on 15 Oct 1927.

Lawn mowers
The widest gang mower in the world is the 5 ton 60 ft *18,28 m* wide 27 unit Big Green Machine used by the sod farmer Jay Edgar Frick of Monroe, Ohio. It mows an acre in 60 sec. On 28 Mar–1 Apr 1959 a Ransome *Matador* motor mower was driven for 99 hr non-stop over 375 miles *603 km* Edinburgh to London. The greatest distance covered in the annual 12 hour Lawn Mower Race (under the rules of the BLMRA, the British Lawn Mower Racing Association) is 276 miles *84,12 km* by Tony Hazelwood, Derek Bell, Tony Smith and Ray Kilminster at Wisborough Green, W. Sussex on 21–22 June 1980.

MOTORCYCLES

Guinness Superlatives Ltd have published more specialist volumes entitled The Guinness Book of Motor-Cycling Facts and Feats by LJK Setright (£6.95) and The Guinness Guide to Motorcycling by Peter Carrick (£10.95).

Earliest (see also Chapter 12)
The earliest internal combustion-engined motorised bicycle was a wooden-framed machine built at Bad Cannstatt in Oct–Nov 1885 by Gottlieb Daimler (1834–1900) of Germany and first ridden by Wilhelm Maybach (1846–1929). It had a top speed of 12 mph *19 km/h* and developed one-half of one horsepower from its single-cylinder 264 cc four-stroke engine at 700 rpm. Known as the 'Einspur', it was lost in a fire in 1903. The first motorcycles of entirely British production were the 1046 cc Holden flat-four and the 2¾ hp Clyde single both produced in 1898. The earliest factory which made motorcycles in quantity was opened in 1894 by Heinrich and Wilhelm Hildebrand and Alois Wolfmüller at Munich, West Germany. In its first two years this factory produced over 1000 machines, each having a water-cooled 1488 cc twin-cylinder four-stroke engine developing about 2.5 bhp at 600 rpm—the highest capacity motor cycle engine ever put into production.

Fastest road machine
The highest speed returned in an independent road test for a catalogued road machine is 154.2 mph *248,1 km/h* for a Dunstall Suzuki GS 1000 CS.

Fastest racing machine
There is no satisfactory answer to the identity of the fastest track machine other than to say that the current Kawasaki, Suzuki and Yamaha machines have all been geared to attain speeds marginally in excess of 300 km/h *186.4 mph* under race conditions.

Duration record
The longest time a solo motorcycle has been kept in nonstop motion is 500 hr by Owen Fitzgerald, Richard Kennett and Don Mitchell who covered 8432 miles *13 570 km* in Western Australia on 10–31 July 1977.

Most on One Machine
On 20 Apr at Santa Pod Raceway, Podington, Bedfordshire, England, the Magnificent Seven Stunt Team were augmented to 22 riders and covered 440 yd *402,3 m* on an adapted Kawasaki Z 900.

Most expensive
The most expensive road motorcycle available in Britain is the twin rotary Wankel engined 2000 cc Van Veen OCR 1000 made in the Netherlands and priced at £6500. In June 1980 a 1912

The 101 ft 9 in *31,01 m* tall unicycle ridden by Steve McPeak in Las Vegas, Nevada in October 1980. (*Franklin Berger*)

Longest

The longest true tandem bicycle ever built (i.e. without a third stabilizing wheel) is one of 20,40 m *66 ft 11 in* for 35 riders built by the Pedaalstompers Westmalle of Belgium. Their closest approach to covering their own length so far has been 19,2 m *63 ft* on 12 Apr 1980. The machine weighs 1100 kg *2425 lb*.

Smallest

The world's smallest wheeled rideable bicycle is one with 2⅛ in *5,4 cm* wheels weighing 2 lb *900 g* built and ridden by Charli Charles at Circus Circus Hotel, Las Vegas, Nevada, USA.

Largest

A classic Ordinary bicycle with wheels of 64 in *162,5 cm* diameter front and 20 in *50,8 cm* back was built *c.* 1886 by the Pope Manufacturing Co of Massachusetts, USA. It is now owned by Paul Niquette of Connecticut.

Fastest

The world speed records for human powered vehicles are 58.64 mph *94,37 km/h* (single rider) by Dave Grylls at the Ontario Speedway, California on 27 Oct 1980; and 62.92 mph *101,25 km/h* (multiple riders) by Dave Grylls and Leigh Barczewski at the Ontario Speedway on 4 May 1980.

Unicycle records

The tallest unicycle ever mastered is one 101 ft 9 in *31,01 m* tall ridden by Steve McPeak (with a safety wire or mechanic suspended to an overhead crane) for a distance of 376 ft *114,6 m* in Las Vegas in October 1980. The freestyle riding of even taller unicycles (that is without any safety harness) must inevitably lead to serious injury or fatality. Robert Neil 'Bob' McGuinness (b. 1951) unicycled the 6400 km *3976 miles* across Canada from Halifax to Vancouver in 79 days on 6 June–24 Aug 1978. Johnnie Severin of Atwater, California, USA set a record for 100 miles *160,9 km* in 9 hr 20 min 53 sec on 10 Jan 1981. The sprint record from a standing start over 100 metres is 14.89 sec by Floyd Grandall of Pontiac, Michigan, USA, in Tokyo, Japan on 24 Mar 1980.

Place to place

Brian Davis, 33 of Tillicoultry, Clackmannan, Scotland rode 901 miles *1450 km* from Land's End to John O'Groats on 16 May to 4 June 1980 in 19 days 1 hr 45 min.

Penny-farthing record

The record for riding from Land's End to John o'Groats on Ordinary bicycles, more commonly known in the 1870s as Penny-farthings, is 10 days 7 hr 12 min by James Richard Moir, 37 of St Leonards-on-Sea, East Sussex on 5–15 June 1977.

Henderson Model A was auctioned in the US for $18,000 (*then £7825*).

Round Britain

Michael T. Parry of Great Missenden, Buckinghamshire riding a BMW visited all the 62 mainland counties of Great Britain in 38 hours on 16–19 Aug 1980.

BICYCLES
Earliest

The first design for a machine propelled by cranks and pedals, with connecting rods has been attributed to Leonardo da Vinci (1452–1519), or one of his pupils, dated *c.* 1493. The earliest such design actually built was in 1839–40 by Kirkpatrick Macmillan (1810–78) of Dumfries, Scotland. It is now in the Science Museum, Kensington and Chelsea, Greater London.

3. RAILWAYS

The famous Japanese Shinkansen superexpress crossing the Fujigawa River with Mt. Fujiyama in the background. These trains pioneered rail travel at average speeds above 100 mph *160 km/h* (*Nippon Steel Corporation*).

Guinness Superlatives publish railway records in much greater detail in the more specialist publication *Guinness Book of Rail Facts and Feats* 3rd edition (price £6.95).

A progressive table of railway speed records since 1829 was published in the 23rd edition on page 141.

TRAINS

Earliest
Railed trucks were used for mining as early as 1550 at Leberthal, Alsace, and at the Broseley colliery, Shropshire in October 1605, but the first self-propelled locomotive ever to run on rails was that built by Richard Trevithick (1771–1833) for the 3 ft gauge plateway at Coalbrookdale, Shropshire in 1803. The earliest established railway to have a steam-powered locomotive was the Middleton Colliery Railway, set up by an Act of 9 June 1758 running between Middleton Colliery and Leeds Bridge, Yorkshire. This line went over to the use of steam locomotives built by Matthew Murray (1765–1826), in 1812. The Stockton and Darlington Railway, Cleveland, which ran from Shildon through Darlington to Stockton, opened on 27 Sept 1825. The 7 ton/tonne *Locomotion* could pull 48 tons *48,7 tonnes* at a speed of 15 mph *24 km/h*. It was designed and driven by George Stephenson (1781–1848). The first regular steam passenger run was inaugurated over a one mile section (between Bogshole Farm and South Street) on the 6¼ mile *10,05 km* track between Canterbury and Whitstable, Kent, on 3 May 1830 hauled by the engine *Invicta*. The first electric railway was Werner von Siemen's 600 yd *548 m* long Berlin electric track opened for the Berlin Trades' Exhibition on 31 May 1879.

Fastest
The world rail speed record was set up by the US Federal Railroad Administration LIMRV (Linear Induction Motor Research Vehicle) built by the Garrett Corporation on the 6.2 mile *9,97 km* long Pueblo test track, Colorado, USA when a speed of 254.76 mph *410 km/h* was attained on 14 Aug 1974. The highest speed recorded on any national rail system is 236 mph *380 km/h* by the French SNCF high speed train T6V-PSE on trial near Tonnerre on 26 Feb 1981. The TGV (Trés Grand Vitesse) is scheduled to make the Paris–Lyon run of 510 km *317 miles* in exactly two hours (stops included) in 1983.

Steam
The highest speed ever ratified for a steam locomotive was 126 mph *202 km/h* over 440 yd *402 m* by the LNER 4–6–2 No. 4468 *Mallard* (later numbered 60022), which hauled seven coaches weighing 240 tons *243 tonnes* gross, down Stoke Bank, near Essendine, between Grantham, Lincolnshire, and Peterborough, Cambridgeshire, on 3 July 1938. Driver Joseph Duddington was at the controls with Fireman Thomas Bray. The engine suffered severe damage. On 12 June 1905 a speed of 127.06 mph *204,48 km/h* was claimed for the 'Pennsylvania Special' near Ada, Ohio, USA but has never been accepted by leading experts.

Regular run World
The fastest point-to-point schedule in the world is that of the King's Cross-Berwick section of British Rail's Eastern Region HST Service introduced on 14 May 1979 at 106.25 mph *180 km/h*. Speeds of 300 km/h *186.4 mph* are planned for the SNCF Paris-Lyon electrified line by 1982.

Great Britain
British Rail inaugurated their HST (High Speed Train) daily services between London–Bristol and South Wales on 4 Oct 1976. On 10 Apr 1979 one covered the 94 miles *151,2 km* between Paddington, London, and Chippenham, Wiltshire, in 50 min 31 sec for a start-to-stop average of 111.64 mph *179,67 km/h*. The peak speed is 125 mph *201 km/h*. The electric British Rail APT-P (Advanced Passenger Train-Prototype) attained 160 mph *257,5 km/h*, between Glasgow and Carlisle on 20 Dec 1979.

Longest Non-stop
The re-inaugurated Flying Scotsman between London (King's Cross) and Edinburgh is scheduled at 4 hr 43 min. The longest run on British Rail without any advertised stop is the Night Motorail Service from Olympia, Kensington and Chelsea, Greater London to Inverness inaugurated on 21 May 1973. The distance is 565 miles *909 km* and the time taken is 11 hr 15 min.

Most powerful World
The world's most powerful steam locomotive, measured by tractive effort, was No. 700, a triple articulated or triplex 2–8–8–4, the Baldwin Locomotive Co 6-cylinder engine built in 1916 for the Virginian Railroad. It had a tractive force of 166,300 lb *75 432 kg* working compound and 199,560 lb *90 518 kg* working simple.

Probably the heaviest train ever hauled by a single engine was one of 15,300 tons *15 545 tonnes* made up of 250 freight cars stretching 1.6 miles *2,5 km* by the *Matt H. Shay* (No. 5014), a 2–8–8–8–2 engine which ran on the Erie Railroad from May 1914 until 1929.

Longest freight train
The longest and heaviest freight train on record was one about 4 miles *6 km* in length consisting of 500 coal cars with three 3600 hp diesels pulling and three more pushing on the Iaeger, West Virginia, to Portsmouth, Ohio, stretch of 157 miles *252 km* on the Norfolk and Western Railway on 15 Nov 1967. The total weight was nearly 42,000 tons *42 674 tonnes*.

Greatest load
The heaviest single pieces of freight ever conveyed by rail are limited by the capacity of the rolling stock. The only rail carrier with a capacity of 850 tonnes is a 36 axle 86,3 m *283 ft 1½ in* long 'Schnabel' built for a US railway by Krupp, W. Germany, in 1978.

The heaviest load carried by British Rail was a 122 ft *37,1 m* long boiler drum, weighing 275 tons *279 tonnes* which was carried from Immingham Dock to Killinghome, Humberside, in September 1968. They also move their own rails in lengths of 300 feet *91,44 m*.

The heaviest load ever moved on rails is the 10,700 ton Church of the Virgin Mary built in 1548 in the village of Most, Czechoslovakia, in October–November 1975 because it was in the way of coal deposits. It was moved 800 yd *730 m* at 0.0013 mph *0,002 km/h* over 4 weeks at a cost of £9 million.

TRACKS
Longest line
The world's longest run is one of 9438 km *5864½ miles* on the Trans Siberian line from Moscow to Nakhodka, USSR, in the Soviet Far East. There are 97 stops in the journey which takes 8 days 4 hr 25 min. The Baykal-Amur Magistral (BAM) northern line, begun with forced labour in 1938, is expected to be open in 1983 and will cut 500 km *310 miles* off the route round the southern end of Lake Baykal. A total of 10,000 million ft³ *283 million m³* of earth has to be moved and 3700 bridges built in this £8000 million project, which was begun in 1938.

Longest straight
The longest straight in the world is on the Commonwealth Railways Trans Australian line over the Nullarbor Plain from Mile 496 between Nurina and Loongana, Western Australia, to Mile 793 between Ooldea and Watson, South Australia, 297 miles *478 km* dead straight although not level. The longest straight on British Rail is the 18 miles *29 km* between Barlby and Staddlethorpe Junctions on the Selby, North Yorkshire, to Kingston-upon-Hull, Humberside, line.

Widest and Narrowest
The widest gauge in standard use is 5 ft 6 in *1,676 m*. This width is used in Spain, India, Pakistan, Bangladesh, Sri Lanka, Argentina and Chile. In 1885 there was a lumber railway in Oregon, USA, with a gauge of 8 ft *2,4 m*. The narrowest gauge in use on public railways is 1 ft 3 in *0,381 m* on the Ravenglass & Eskdale Railway, Cumbria (7 miles *11,2 km*) and the Romney, Hythe & Dymchurch line in Kent (14 miles *22,53 km*). 'Le Chemin de fer interet locale' between Muir de Bretagne and Caurel, Cote du Nord, France has a gauge of 31 cm *12.2 in* and runs for 5 km *3.1 miles*.

Highest World
The highest standard gauge (4 ft 8½ in *1,43 m*) track in the world is on the Peruvian State Railways at La Cima, on the Morococha Branch at 15,806 ft *4817 m* above sea-level. The highest point on the main line is 15,688 ft *4781 m* in the Galera tunnel.

Great Britain

The highest point of the British Rail system is at the pass of Drumochter on the former Perth–Inverness border, where the track reaches an altitude of 1484 ft *452 m* above sea-level. The highest railway in Britain is the Snowdon Mountain Railway, which rises from Llanberis, Gwynedd, to 3493 ft *1064 m* above sea-level, just below the summit of Snowdon (*Yr Wyddfa*). It has a gauge of 2 ft 7½ in *800 mm*.

Lowest

The lowest point on British Rail is in the Severn Tunnel—144 ft *43,8 m* below sea-level.

Steepest gradient *World*

The world's steepest standard gauge gradient by adhesion is 1:11 between Chedde and Servoz on the metre gauge SNCF Chamonix line, France.

Great Britain

The steepest sustained adhesion-worked gradient on main line in the United Kingdom is the two-mile Lickey incline of 1:37.7 in Hereford and Worcester. From the tunnel bottom to James Street, Liverpool, on the former Mersey Railway, there is a stretch of 1:27; and between Folkestone Junction and Harbour a mile *1,6 km* of 1:30.

Shallowest gradient

The shallowest gradient posted on the British Rail system is one indicated as 1 in 14,400 between Pirbright Junction and Farnborough, Hampshire. This could be described alternatively as England's most obtuse summit.

Busiest rail system

The world's most crowded rail system is the Japanese National Railways, which by 1980 carried 18,584,000 passengers daily. Professional pushers are employed on the Tōkyō Service to squeeze in passengers before the doors can be closed. Among articles lost in 1980 were 543,883 umbrellas, 346,423 clothing items, 194,712 spectacles and hats and also 3 persons' ashes and 29 Buddhist memorial tablets.

Calling All Stations

Alan M. Whitton (b. 1944) of Chorlton, Manchester visited every open British Rail station (2362) in a continuous tour for charity of 16,592¾ miles *26 703 km* in 27,136 minutes on 13 July–28 Aug 1980.

Most Countries in One Day

Burkhard Wendel with Detlef and Andrea Esser travelled by rail in a record 9 countries (Italy, Austria, Liechtenstein, Switzerland, France, Luxembourg, Belgium, West Germany and the Netherlands) on 15 June 1980 in 23 hr 24 min.

David Adams, 24 and Steven Vincent, 22 visited 21 countries in Europe in 6 days 22 hr 10 min on 9–16 Jan 1981 using public transport only.

Handpumped Railcars

The fastest time set in the now annual races at Port Moody, British Columbia, Canada over 300 m *985 ft* by a 5 man team (1 pusher, 4 pumpers) is 34.08 sec on 22 June 1980.

Longest Journey

The longest train journey in the world is the 9 day 2 hour 'odyssey' from Lisbon, Portugal to Khabarovsk in Eastern USSR *via* Omsk.

The longest journey on the British Rail system is from Penzance, Cornwall to Wick, Caithness, Scotland, a round trip of 1860 miles *2993 km*. On 6–9 Feb 1981 Duncan Edmonston and Hugh Mowat made this round trip in 82 hr 4 min.

STATIONS
Largest *World*

The world's largest railway station is Grand Central Terminal, Park Avenue and 43rd Street, New York City, NY, USA, built 1903–13. It covers 48 acres *19 ha* on two levels with 41 tracks on the upper level and 26 on the lower. On average more than 550 trains and 180,000 people per day use it, with a peak of 252,288 on 3 July 1947.

Great Britain

The largest railway station in extent on the British Rail system is the 17-platform Clapham Junction, London, covering 27¾ acres *11,22 ha* with a total face of 11,185 ft *3409 m*. The station with the largest number of platforms is Waterloo, London (24½ acres *9,9 ha*), with 21 main line and two Waterloo and City Line platforms, with a total face of 15,352 ft *4679 m*. Victoria Station (21¾ acres *8,80 ha*) with 17 platforms has, however, a total face length of 18,412 ft *5611 m*. The oldest station in Britain is Liverpool Road Station, Manchester, first used on 15 Sept 1830.

Busiest

The busiest railway junction in Great Britain is Clapham Junction, Wandsworth, Greater London, on the Southern Region of British Rail, with an average of 2400 trains passing through each 24 hr (May 1980).

Highest

The highest station in the world is Condor, Bolivia at 15,705 ft *4786 m* on the metre gauge Rio Mulato to Potosi line. The highest passenger station on British Rail is Corrour, Highland, at an altitude of 1347 ft *410,5 m* above sea-level.

Waiting rooms

The world's largest waiting rooms are those in Peking Station, Chang'an Boulevard, Peking, China, opened in September 1959, with a capacity of 14,000.

Longest platform

The longest railway platform in the world is the Khargpur platform, West Bengal, India, which measures 2733 ft *833 m* in length. The State Street Center subway platform staging on 'The Loop' in Chicago, Illinois, USA, measures 3500 ft *1066 m* in length.

The longest platform in the British Rail system is the 1977 ft 4 in *602,69 m* long platform at Gloucester. The figure of 1981 ft *603,8 m* previously published for Colchester, Essex has proved to be exaggerated by 61 ft *18,59 m*.

UNDERGROUND RAILWAYS
Most extensive

The earliest (first section opened 10 Jan 1863) and one of the most extensive underground or rapid transit railway systems of the 67 in the world is that of the London Transport Executive, with 255 miles *410,3 km* of route, of which 77 miles *124 km* is bored tunnel and 21 miles *33,8 km* is 'cut and cover'. This whole system is operated by a staff of 12,100 serving 279 stations. The 500 trains comprising 4228 cars carried 594,000,000 passengers in 1979. The greatest depth is 221 ft *67,3 m* near Hampstead on the Northern Line. The longest journey without a change is Epping to West Ruislip—34.1 miles *54,8 km*. The record for touring the 278 stations is 18 hr 3 min by John and Stephen Trafford on 20 May 1980.

The subway with most stations in the world is the New York City Transport Authority (first section opened on 27 Oct 1904) with a total of 231.73 route miles *372,93 km* and 1,096,006,529 passengers in 1979. The 462 stations are closer set than London's. The record for travelling the whole system was 21 hr 8½ min by Mayer Wiesen and Charles Emerson on 8 Oct 1973.

Busiest

The world's busiest metro system is that in Greater Moscow with some 6½ million passengers per day. It has 114 stations and 184 km *114 miles* of track. The record transit is 8 hr 18 min 21 sec by Eric Rudkin of Derbyshire on 20 May 1980.

MODEL RAILWAYS

The non-stop duration record for a model train (loco plus 6 coaches, is 864 hr 30 min from 1 June–7 July 1978, covering 678 miles *1091 km*, organised by Roy Catton at 'Pastimes' Toy Store, Mexborough, S. Yorkshire. The longest recorded run by a model *steam* locomotive is 144 miles *231,7 km* in 27 hr 18 mins by the 7¼ inch *18,4 cm* gauge 'Winifred' built in 1974 by Wilf Grove at Thames Ditton, Surrey on 8–9 Sept 1979. 'Winifred' works on 80 lb/in² *5,6 kg/cm²* pressure and is coal-fired with a 2⅛ in *54 mm* bore cylinder and a 3⅛ in *79 mm* stroke. The longest train ever operated was one of 750 cars, plus one caboose, pulled by 10 Lionel engines on a 'O' gauge track, by Stewart E. Roberts at the Rickenbacker Air Force Base in Columbus, Ohio, USA on 26 July 1980 when it traversed its own length (approx 685 ft *208,7 m*).

TRAMS
Longest tram journey
The longest tramway journey now possible is from Krefeld St Tönis to Witten Annen Nord, W. Germany. With luck at the 8 inter-connections the 105,5 km *65.5 mile* trip can be achieved in 5½ hr. By late 1977 there were still some 315 tramway systems surviving of which the longest is that of Leningrad, USSR with 2500 cars on 53 routes.

Oldest
The oldest trams in revenue service in the world are Motor cars 1 and 2 of the Manx Electric Railway dating from 1893.

MONORAIL
Highest speed
The highest speed ever attained on rails is 3090 mph *4972 km/h* (Mach 4.1) by an unmanned rocket-powered sled on the 6.62 mile *10,65 km* long captive track at the US Air Force Missile Development Center at Holloman, New Mexico, USA, on 19 Feb 1959. The highest speed reached carrying a chimpanzee is 1295 mph *2084 km/h*.

The highest speed attained by a tracked hovercraft is 411 km/h *255.3 mph* by the jet-powered *L'Aérotrain* 02, invented by Jean Bertin. An experimental magnetically levitated Japanese National Railway train on a test track near Miyazaki reached 517 km/h *321 mph* on 21 Dec 1979.

4. AIRCRAFT

Guinness Superlatives has published aircraft records in much greater detail in the specialist publication *Guinness Book of Air Facts and Feats* (3rd edition) (price £6.50).

Note—The use of the Mach scale for aircraft speeds was introduced by Prof. Ackeret of Zürich, Switzerland. The Mach number is the ratio of the velocity of a moving body to the local velocity of sound. This ratio was first employed by Dr Ernst Mach (1838–1916) of Vienna, Austria in 1887. Thus Mach 1.0 equals 760.98 mph *1224,67 km/h* at sea-level at 15° C, and is assumed, for convenience, to fall to a constant 659.78 mph *1 061,81 km/h* in the stratosphere, *i.e.* above 11,000 m *36,089 ft*.

EARLIEST FLIGHTS
World
The first controlled and sustained power-driven flight occurred near the Kill Devil Hill, Kitty Hawk, North Carolina, USA, at 10.35 a.m. on 17 Dec 1903, when Orville Wright (1871–1948) flew the 12 hp chain-driven *Flyer I* for a distance of 120 ft *36,5 m* at an airspeed of 30 mph *48 km/h*, a ground speed of 6.8 mph *10,9 km/h* and an altitude of 8–12 ft *2,4–3,6 m* for about 12 sec watched by his brother Wilbur (1867–1912), three life-savers and two others. Both brothers, from Dayton, Ohio, were bachelors because, as Orville put it, they had not the means to 'support a wife as well as an aeroplane'. The *Flyer* is now in the National Air and Space Museum at the Smithsonian Institution, Washington DC.

The first hop by a man-carrying aeroplane entirely under its own power was made when Clément Ader (1841–1925) of France flew in his *Eole* for about 50 m *164 ft* at Armainvilliers, France, on 9 Oct 1890. Richard William Pearce (1877–1953) flew (in uncontrolled flight) for at least 50 yd *45 m* along the Main Waitohi Road, South Canterbury, New Zealand in a self-built petrol-engined monoplane on a date which on best evidence was 31 Mar 1903. The earliest 'rational design' for a flying machine, according to the Royal Aeronautical Society, was that published by Emanuel Swedenborg (1688–1772) in Sweden in 1717.

Great Britain
The first officially recognised flight in the British Isles was made by the US citizen Samuel Franklin Cody (1861–1913) who flew 1390 ft *423 m* in his own biplane at Farnborough, Hampshire, on 16 Oct 1908. Horatio Frederick Phillips (1845–1924) almost certainly covered 500 ft *152 m* in his Phillips II *Venetian blind* aeroplane at Streatham, in 1907. The first resident British citizen to fly in a powered 'plane was Griffith Brewer (1867–1948), as a passenger of Wilbur Wright, on 8 Oct 1908 at Auvours, France.

Cross-Channel
The earliest cross-Channel flight by an aeroplane was made on

Sunday, 25 July 1909 when Louis Blériot (1872–1936) of France flew his *Blériot XI* monoplane, powered by a 23 hp Anzani engine, 26 miles *41,8 km* from Les Baraques, France, to Northfall Meadow near Dover Castle, England, in 36½ min, after taking off at 4.41 a.m.

Jet-engined *World*
Proposals for jet propulsion date back to Captain Marconnet (1909) of France, and Henri Coanda (1886–1972) of Romania, and to the turbojet proposals of Maxime Guillaume in 1921. The earliest tested run was that of the British Power Jets Ltd's experimental WU (Whittle Unit) on 12 Apr 1937, invented by Flying Officer (now Air Commodore Sir) Frank Whittle (b. Coventry, 1 June 1907), who had applied for a patent on jet propulsion in 1930. The first flight by an aeroplane powered by a turbojet engine was made by the Heinkel He 178, piloted by Flug Kapitan Erich Warsitz, at Marienehe, Germany, on 27 Aug 1939. It was powered by a Heinkel He S3b engine (834 lb *378 kg*) as installed with long tailpipe) designed by Dr Hans 'Pabst' von Ohain and first tested in August 1937.

Great Britain
The first British jet flight occurred when Fl Lt P. E. G. 'Jerry' Sayer, OBE (k. 1942) flew the Gloster-Whittle E.28/39 (wing span 29 ft *8,84 m*, length 25 ft 3 in *7,70 m*) fitted with an 860 lb *390 kg* st Whittle W-1 engine for 17 min at Cranwell, Lincolnshire, on 15 May 1941. The maximum speed was *c.* 350 mph *560 km/h*.

Supersonic flight
The first supersonic flight was achieved on 14 Oct 1947 by Capt. (later Brig.-Gen) Charles ('Chuck') Elwood Y.eager, USAF retd (b. 13 Feb 1923), over Edwards Air Force Base, Muroc, California, USA, in a Bell XS-1 rocket plane ('Glamorous Glennis'), with Mach 1.015 (670 mph *1078 km/h*) at an altitude of 42,000 ft *12 800 m*.

The first British aeroplane, and the first turbojet-powered aeroplane in the world, to achieve supersonic speed was a de Havilland D. H. 108 tailless research aircraft which, piloted by John Derry, recorded a Mach number between 1.0 and 1.1 in a dive on 6 Sept 1948.

Trans-Atlantic
The first crossing of the North Atlantic by air was made by Lt-Cdr (later Rear Admiral) Albert Cushion Read (1887–1967) and his crew (Stone, Hinton, Rodd, Rhoads and Breese) in the 84 knot *155 km/h* US Navy/Curtiss flying-boat NC-4 from Trepassey Harbour, Newfoundland, *via* the Azores, to Lisbon, Portugal, on 16–27 May 1919. The whole flight of 4717 miles *7591 km* originating from Rockaway Air Station, Long Island, NY on 8 May, required 53 hr 58 min, terminating at Plymouth, England, on 31 May.

The Newfoundland–Azores flight of 1200 miles *1930 km* took 15 hr 18 min at 81.7 knots *151,4 km/h*.

Non-stop
The first non-stop trans-Atlantic flight was achieved from 4.13 p.m. GMT on 14 June 1919, from Lester's Field, St John's, Newfoundland, 1960 miles *3154 km* to Derrygimla bog near Clifden, County Galway, Ireland, at 8.40 a.m. GMT, 15 June, when the pilot, Capt John William Alcock, DSC (1892–

The B50 Superfortress *Lucky Lady II* touches down at Carswell Airforce base, Fort Worth, Texas, after its record-breaking first non-stop round the world flight (see p. 146). (*Topham/AP*)

1919), and the navigator Lt Arthur Whitten Brown (1886–1948) flew across in a Vickers *Vimy*, powered by two 360 hp Rolls-Royce *Eagle VIII* engines. Both men were created civil KBE's on 21 June 1919 when Alcock was aged 26 years 227 days, and shared a *Daily Mail* prize of £10,000.

Solo

The 79th man to achieve a trans-Atlantic flight but the first to do so solo was Capt (later Brig) Charles Augustus Lindbergh (Hon AFC) (1902–74) who took off in his 220 hp Ryan monoplane 'Spirit of St. Louis' at 12.52 p.m. GMT on 20 May 1927 from Roosevelt Field, Long Island, NY, USA. He landed at 10.21 p.m. GMT on 21 May 1927 at Le Bourget airfield, Paris, France. His flight of 3610 miles *5810 km* lasted 33 hr 29½ min and he won a prize of $25,000 (*then £5300*).

Most Flights

John M. Winston, a senior British Airways Flight Engineer, flew 1277 trans-Atlantic flights from 10 May 1947 to 14 Dec 1978—a total of 20,100 hr.

Trans-Pacific

The first non-stop Pacific flight was by Major Clyde Pangborn and Hugh Herndon in the Bellanca cabin 'plane *Miss Veedol* from Sabishiro Beach, Japan 4558 miles *7335 km* to Wenatchee, Washington, USA in 41 hr 13 min on 3–5 Oct 1931. (For earliest crossing see 1924 flight below).

Circumnavigational flights

Strict circumnavigation requires passing through two antipodal points thus with a minimum distance of 24,859.75 miles *40 007,89 km*. The FAI permits flights which exceed the length of the Tropic of Cancer or Capricorn *viz* 22,858.754 miles *36 787,599 km*.

The earliest such flight of 26,345 miles *42 398 km* was by two US Army Douglas DWC amphibians in 57 'hops'. The *Chicago* was piloted by Lt Lowell H. Smith and Lt Leslie P. Arnold and the *New Orleans* was piloted by Lt Erik H. Nelson and Lt John Harding between 6 Apr and 28 Sept 1924 beginning and ending at Seattle, Washington, USA.

The earliest solo claim was by Wiley Hardemann Post (1898–1935) (US) in the Lockheed Vega 'Winnie Mae' starting and finishing at Floyd Bennett Field, New York City on 15–22 July 1933 in 10 'hops'. The distance of 15,596 miles *25 099 km* with a flying time of 115 hr 36 min was however at too high a latitude to qualify.

The first non-stop round-the-world flight was made by the USAF's Boeing B-50 Superfortress *Lucky Lady II* piloted by Capt James Gallagher from Carswell AFB, Texas in 94 hr 1 min. The aircraft was refuelled 4 times on its 23,452 mile *37 742 km* flight.

The fastest flight has been the non-stop eastabout flight of 45 hr 19 min by three flight-refuelled USAF B-52's led by Maj-Gen Archie J. Old Jr. They covered 24,325 miles *39 147 km* on 16–18 Jan 1957 finishing at March Air Force Base, Riverside, California, having averaged 525 mph *845 km/h* with four in-flight refuellings by KC-97 aerial tankers.

The first circum-polar flight was solo by Capt Elgen M. Long, 44, in a Piper Navajo on 5 Nov–3 Dec 1971. He covered 38,896 miles *62 597 km* in 215 flying hours. The cabin temperature sank to −40°C −40°F over Antarctica.

Circumnavigation *Smallest aircraft*

The smallest aircraft to complete a circumnavigation is the 20 ft 11 in *6,38 m* single-engined 180 hp Thorp T-18 built in his garage by its pilot Donald P. Taylor of Sage, California. His 26,190 mile *42 148 km* flight in 37 stages took 176 flying hours ending at Oshkosh, Wisconsin on 30 Sept 1976.

Largest wing span

The aircraft with the largest wing span ever constructed is the $40 million Hughes H.4 *Hercules* flying-boat, which was raised 70 ft *21,3 m* into the air in a test run of 1000 yd *914 m*, piloted by Howard Hughes (1905–76), off Long Beach Harbor, California, USA, on 2 Nov 1947. The eight-engined 190 ton *193 tonnes* air-

craft had a wing span of 319 ft 11 in *97,51 m* and a length of 218 ft 8 in *66,64 m* and never flew again. She was towed out of her hanger on 30 Oct 1980.

Heaviest

The highest recorded gross take off weight of any aircraft has been 379.9 tons *386,0 tonnes* in the case of a Boeing 747-200B 'Jumbo' jet during certification tests of its Pratt & Whitney JT9D-7Q engines on 23 May 1979.

Lightest

The lightest mechanically powered aeroplane to have flown by early 1981 was the solar-powered *Solar Challenger* designed by a team led by Dr Paul MacCready. *Solar Challenger* had an empty weight of 130 lb *59 kg* and a take-off weight of 275.5 lb *125 kg*, which included its 99 lb *45 kg* pilot, Janice Brown and her parachute. It was flown initially under battery-power to gain essential handling experience, but made its first flight entirely under solar power on 20 Nov 1980. On 5 Dec 1980 *Solar Challenger* was airborne for 1 hr 32 min and attained a height of 4000 ft *1220 m*. On the following day it was flown for 18 miles *29 km* over part of a direct route between Tucson and Phoenix, Arizona, the flight being terminated after 2 hr by a heavy rainstorm.

Smallest

The smallest aeroplane ever flown is the Stits *Skybaby* biplane, designed and built by Ray Stits at Riverside, California, USA, and first flown by Robert H. Starr on 26 May 1952. It was 9 ft 10 in *3 m* long, with a wing span of 7 ft 2 in *2,18 m*, and weighed 452 lb *205 kg* empty. It was powered by an 85 hp Continental C85 engine, giving a top speed of 185 mph *297 km/h*.

Bombers *Heaviest*

The world's heaviest bomber is the eight-jet swept-wing Boeing B-52H *Stratofortress*, which has a maximum take-off weight of 488,000 lb (217.86 tons *221,35 tonnes*). It has a wing span of 185 ft *56,38 m* and is 157 ft 6¾ in *48,02 m* in length, with a speed of over 650 mph *1046 km/h*. The B-52 can carry twelve SRAM thermonuclear short range attack missiles or twenty-four 750 lb *340 kg* bombs under its wings and eight more SRAMs or eighty-four 500 lb *226 kg* bombs in the fuselage. The ten-engined Convair B-36J, weighing 183 tons *185 tonnes*, had a greater wing span, at 230 ft *70,10 m* but it is no longer in service. It had a top speed of 435 mph *700 km/h*.

Fastest

The world's fastest operational bombers are the French Dassault *Mirage IV*, which can fly at Mach 2.2 (1450 mph *2333 km/h*) at 36,000 ft *11 000 m*; the American General Dynamics FB-111A, with a maximum speed of Mach 2.5; and the Soviet swing-wing Tupolev Tu-26 known to NATO as 'Backfire', which has an estimated over-target speed of Mach 2.0 but which may be as fast as Mach 2.5 and a combat radius of up to 3570 miles *5745 km*.

Airliner Largest *World*

The highest capacity jet airliner is the Boeing 747 'Jumbo Jet', first flown on 9 Feb 1969 (see Heaviest aircraft) and has a capacity of from 385 to more than 500 passengers with a maximum speed of 602 mph *969 km/h*. Its wing span is 195.7 ft *59,64 m* and its length 231.8 ft *70,7 m*. It entered service on 22 Jan 1970.

Great Britain

The largest ever British aircraft was the experimental Bristol Type 167 *Brabazon*, which had a maximum take-off weight of 129.4 tons *131,4 tonnes*, a wing span of 230 ft *70,10 m* and a length of 177 ft *53,94 m*. This eight-engined aircraft first flew on 4 Sept 1949. The *Concorde* (see below) has a maximum take-off weight of 408,000 lb *185 065 kg* (182.14 tons).

Airliner Fastest

The supersonic BAC/Aerospatiale *Concorde*, first flown on 2 Mar 1969, with a capacity of 128 passengers, cruises at up to Mach 2.2 (1450 mph *2333 km/h*). It flew at Mach 1.05 on 10 Oct 1969, exceeded Mach 2 for the first time on 4 Nov 1970 and became the first supersonic airliner used on passenger services on 21 Jan 1976 when Air France and British Airways opened services simultaneously between, respectively, Paris–Rio de Janeiro and London–Bahrain. Services between London and

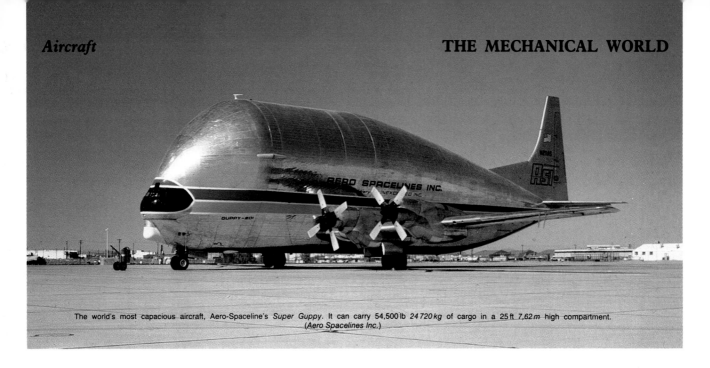

The world's most capacious aircraft, Aero-Spaceline's *Super Guppy*. It can carry 54,500 lb *24 720 kg* of cargo in a 25 ft *7,62 m* high compartment.
(*Aero Spacelines Inc.*)

New York and Paris and New York began on 22 Nov 1977. The New York-London record is 2 hr 59 min 14 sec (average 1166.031 mph *1876,54 km/h*) set on 20 Jan 80.

Most capacious
The capacity of the commercial adaptation of the USAF Lockheed C-5A Galaxy known as the Lockheed 500–3 is 51,707 ft³ *1463 m³* The wing-span is 222.7 ft *67,8 m* and the length 245.9 ft *74,9 m*.

Largest propeller
The largest aircraft propeller ever used was the 22 ft 7½ in *6,9 m* diameter Garuda propeller, fitted to the Linke-Hofmann R II built in Wroclaw, Poland, which flew in 1919. It was driven by four 260 hp Mercedes engines and turned at only 545 rpm.

Scheduled flights *Longest*
The longest distance scheduled non-stop flight is the weekly Pan-Am Sydney-San Francisco non-stop 13 hr 25 min Flight 816, in a Boeing 747 SP, opened in December 1976, over 7475 statue miles *12 030 km*. The longest delivery flight by a commercial jet is 8936 nautical miles or 10,290 statute miles *16 560 km* from Seattle, Washington, USA to Cape Town, South Africa by the South African Airway's Boeing 747 SP (Special performance) 'Matroosberg' with 178 400 kg *175.5 tons* of pre-cooled fuel in 17 hr 22½ min on 23–29 Mar 1976.

Shortest
The shortest scheduled flight in the world is that by Loganair between the Orkney Islands of Westray and Papa Westray which has been flown with Britten-Norman Islander twin-engined 10-seat transports since September 1967. Though scheduled for 2 min, in favourable wind conditions it has been accomplished in 58 sec by Capt Andrew D. Alsop.

Gary W. Rovetto of Island Air on 21 Mar 1980 flew on the scheduled flight from Center Island to Decatur Island, Washington, USA in 41 sec.

London–Edinburgh
The FAI ratified flight record between the capitals of Scotland and England is 26 min 25 sec by Sqn Ldr R. Peart AFC, DSM, on 9 Sept 1977 averaging 750.89 mph *1208,45 km/h* for the 330.6 mile *532 km* flight.

London–New York
The record for central London to downtown New York City is 4 hr 23 min 30.5 sec by Sir Gordon White on 16 Nov 1980.

HIGHEST SPEED
Official record
The official air speed record is 2193.167 mph *3529,56 km/h* by Capt Eldon W. Joersz and Maj George T. Morgan, Jr, in a Lockheed SR-71A near Beale Air Force Base, California, USA over a 15/25 km course on 28 July 1976.

Air-launched record
The fastest fixed-wing aircraft in the world was the US North American Aviation X-15A-2, which flew for the first time (after modification from X-15A) on 28 June 1964 powered by a liquid oxygen and ammonia rocket propulsion system. Ablative materials on the airframe once enabled a temperature of 3000° F to be withstood. The landing speed was 210 knots (242 mph *389,1 km/h*) momentarily. The highest speed attained was 4534 mph *7297 km/h* (Mach 6.72) when piloted by Maj William J. Knight, USAF (b. 1930), on 3 Oct 1967. An earlier version piloted by Joseph A. Walker (1920–66), reached 354,200 ft *107 960 m* (67.08 miles) also over Edwards Air Force Base, California, USA, on 22 Aug 1963. The programme was suspended after the final flight of 24 Oct 1968.

The US NASA Rockwell International Space Shuttle Orbiter *Columbia* was launched from the Kennedy Space Center, Cape Canaveral, Florida commanded by Cdr John W. Young USN and piloted by Robert L. Crippen on 12 Apr 1981 after the expenditure of $9900 million since 1972. *Columbia* broke all records for speed by a fixed wing craft with 16,600 mph *26 715 km/h* at main engine cut-off. After re-entry from 400,000 ft *122 km*, experiencing temperatures of 2160° C *3920° F*, she became the heaviest ever glider at 97 tonnes/*tons* with the highest ever landing speed of 216 mph *347 km/h* on Rogers Dry Lake, California on 14 Apr 1981 after a flight of 54 hr 20 min 32 sec.

Fastest jet
The world's fastest jet aircraft is the USAF Lockheed SR-71 reconnaissance aircraft (see Official record) which was first flown on 22 Dec 1964 and is reportedly capable of attaining an altitude ceiling of close to 100,000 ft *30 480 m*. The SR-71 has a wing span of 55.6 ft *16,94 m* and a length of 107.4 ft *32,73 m* and weighs 170,000 lb (75.9 tons *77,1 tonnes*) at take-off. Its reported range is 2982 miles *4800 km* at Mach 3 at 78,750 ft *24 000 m*. At least 30 are believed to have been built. The fastest combat aircraft in the world is the USSR Mikoyan MiG-25 fighter (code name 'Foxbat'). The reconnaissance 'Foxbat-B' has been tracked by radar at about Mach 3.2 (2110 mph *3395 km/h*). When armed with four large underwing air-to-air missiles known to NATO as 'Acrid', the fighter 'Foxbat-A' is limited to Mach 2.8 (1845 mph *2969 km/h*). The single-seat 'Foxbat-A' spans 45 ft 9 in *13,95 m*, is 73 ft 2 in *22,3 m* long and has a maximum take-off weight of 79,800 lb *36 200 kg*.

Fastest biplane
The fastest recorded biplane was the Italian Fiat C.R.42B, with a 1010 hp Daimler-Benz DB601A engine, which attained 323 mph *520 km/h* in 1941. Only one was built.

Fastest piston-engined aircraft
The fastest speed at which a piston-engined aeroplane has ever been measured was for a cut-down privately owned Hawker *Sea Fury* which attained 520 mph *836 km/h* in level flight over Texas, USA, in August 1966 piloted by Mike Carroll (k. 1969) of Los Angeles. The official record for a piston-engined aircraft is

499.048 mph *803,138 km/h* over Mud Lake, Tonopah, Nevada by Steve Hinton (US) in a modified North American P51D *Mustang* powered by a 3800 hp Rolls-Royce Griffon, over a 3 km *1.86 miles* course at restricted altitude on 14 Aug 1979.

Fastest propeller-driven aircraft
The Soviet Tu-114 turboprop transport is the world's fastest propeller-driven aeroplane. It achieved a recorded speed 545.076 mph *877,212 km/h* carrying heavy payloads over measured circuits. It is developed from the Tupolev Tu-95 bomber, known in the West as the 'Bear', and has four 14,795 hp engines. The turboprop-powered Republic XF-84H prototype US Navy fighter which flew on 22 July 1955 had a top *design* speed of 670 mph *1078 km/h* but was abandoned.

Fastest trans-Atlantic flight
The trans-Atlantic flight record is 1 hr 54 min 56.4 sec by Maj James V. Sullivan, 37, and Maj Noel F. Widdifield, 33 flying a Lockheed SR-71A eastwards on 1 Sept 1974. The average speed, slowed by refuelling by a KC-135 tanker aircraft, for the New York–London stage of 3461.53 miles *5570,80 km* was 1806.963 mph *2908,026 km/h*. The solo record (Gander to Gatwick) is 8 hr 47 min 32 sec by Capt John J. A. Smith in a Rockwell 685 on 12 Mar 1978.

Altitude *Official record*
The official world altitude record by an aircraft taking off from the ground under its own power is 123,524 ft (23.39 miles *37 650 m*) by Aleksandr Fedotov (USSR) in a Mikoyan E.266M, (MiG-25) aircraft, powered by two 30,865 lb *14 000 kg* thrust turbojet engines, on 31 Aug 1977.

The greatest recorded height by any pilot without a pressure cabin or even a pressure suit has been 49,500 ft *15 085 m* by Sq Ldr G. W. H. Reynolds, DFC in a Spitfire Mark VC over Libya in 1942.

Duration
The flight duration record is 64 days, 22 hr 19 min and 5 sec, set up by Robert Timm and John Cook in a Cessna 172 'Hacienda'. They took off from McCarran Airfield, Las Vegas, Nevada, USA, just before 3.53 p.m. local time on 4 Dec 1958, and landed at the same airfield just before 2.12 p.m. on 7 Feb 1959. They covered a distance equivalent to six times round the world with continued refuellings, without landing.

The record for duration without refuelling is 84 hr 32 min, set by Walter E. Lees and Frederic A. Brossy in a Bellanca monoplane with a 225 hp Packard Diesel engine, at Jacksonville, Florida, on 25–28 May 1931.

AIRPORTS
Largest *World*
The world's largest airport is the £2,800 million King Abdul-Aziz International Airport near Jeddah, Saudi Arabia covering an area of 40 miles² *103 km³*. The Hajj Terminal is now the world's largest roofed structure covering 1,5 km² *370 acres*. The present 6 runways and 5 terminal buildings of the Dallas/Fort Worth Airport, Texas, USA are planned to be extended to 9 runways and 13 terminals with 260 gates with an ultimate capacity for 150 million passengers. The world's largest airport terminal is Hartsfield Atlanta International Airport opened on 21 Sept 1980 with floor space covering 50.50 acres *20,43 ha*. It has 138 gates handling currently 42 million passengers a year but has a capacity for 75 million.

Great Britain
Seventy-three airline companies from 68 countries operate scheduled services into Heathrow Airport—London (2819 acres *1140 ha*), and during 1980 there was a total of 273,133 air transport movements handled by a staff of 55,000 employed by the various companies and the British Airports Authority. The total number of passengers, both incoming and outgoing, was 27,770,643. The most flights yet handled by Heathrow in a day was 986 on 19 July 1974 and the largest number of passengers yet handled in a day was 112,880 on 31 Aug 1980. Aircraft fly to more than 90 countries.

Busiest
The world's busiest airport is the Chicago International Airport, O'Hare Field, Illinois, USA with a total of 722,777 movements

and 43,653,167 passengers in the year 1980. This represents a take-off or landing every 43.6 sec round the clock. Heathrow Airport—London handles more *international* traffic than any other.

The busiest landing area ever has been Bien Hoa Air Base, south Vietnam, which handled more than 1,000,000 take-offs and landings in 1970. The world's largest 'helipad' was An Khe, south Vietnam.

Highest and lowest
The highest airport in the world is La Sa (Lhasa) Airport, Tibet at 14,315 ft *4363 m*.

The highest landing ever made by a fixed-wing 'plane is 19,947 ft *6080 m* on Dhaulagiri, Himalaya by a Pilatus Porter, named 'Yeti', supplying the 1960 Swiss Expedition. The lowest landing field is El Lisan on the east shore of the Dead Sea, 1180 ft *360 m* below sea-level, but during World War II BOAC Short C-class flying-boats operated from the surface of the Dead Sea 1292 ft *394 m* below sea level. The lowest international airport is Schiphol, Amsterdam, at 13 ft *3,9 m* below sea-level. Rotterdam's airport is fractionally lower at 15 ft *4,5 m*.

Farthest and Nearest to city centres
The airport farthest from the city centre it allegedly serves is Viracopos, Brazil which is 60 miles *96 km* from São Paulo. The Gibraltar airport is 880 yd *800 m* from the centre.

Longest runway *World*
The longest runway in the world is one of 7 miles *11 km* in length (of which 15,000 ft *4572 m* is concreted) at Edwards Air Force Base on the bed of Rogers Dry Lake at Muroc, California, USA. The whole test centre airfield extends over 65 miles² *168 km²*. In an emergency an auxiliary 12 mile *19 km* strip is available along the bed of the Dry Lake. The world's longest civil airport runway is one of 16,076 ft (3.04 miles *4,89 km*) at Pierre van Ryneveld Airport Upington, South Africa constructed in five months from August 1975 to January 1976.

Great Britain
The longest runway available normally to civil aircraft in the United Kingdom is No. 1 at Heathrow Airport—London, measuring 12,800 ft (2.42 miles *3,90 km*).

HELICOPTERS
Fastest
Bell Helicopters claimed in June 1980 that their Model 301 (US Army XV-15) tilt-rotor research aircraft attained a true air speed of 346.6 mph *557,8 km/h* in level flight. It is powered by two turbo shaft engines. The official world speed record for a pure helicopter is 368,4 km/h *228.9 mph* set by Gourguen Karapetyan in a Mil A-10 on a 15/25 km course near Moscow, USSR on 21 Sept 1978.

Largest
The world's largest helicopter is the Soviet Mil *Mi-12* ('Homer'), also known as the V-12, which set up an international record by lifting a payload of 88,636 lb (39.5 tons *40,2 tonnes*) to a height of 7398 ft *2255 m* on 6 Aug 1969. It is powered by four 6500 hp turboshaft engines and has a span of 219 ft 10 in *67 m* over its rotor tips with a length of 121 ft 4½ in *37,00 m* and weighs 103.3 tons *105 tonnes*.

Smallest
The Aerospace General Co one-man rocket assisted minicopter weighs about 160 lb *72,5 kg* and can cruise 250 miles *400 km* at 85 mph *137 km/h*.

Highest
The altitude record for helicopters is 40,820 ft *12 442 m* by an Aérospatiale SA315B *Lama*, over France on 21 June 1972. The highest recorded landing has been at 23,000 ft *7000 m* below the South-East face of Everest in a rescue sortie in May 1971. The World Trade Center helipad is 1385 ft *422 m* above street level in New York City on the South Tower.

AUTOGYROS
Earliest
The autogyro or gyroplane, a rotorcraft with an unpowered rotor turned by the airflow in flight, preceded the practical heli-

copter with engine-driven rotor. Juan de la Cierva (Spain), made the first successful autogyro flight with his model C.4 (commercially named an *Autogiro*) at Getafe, Spain, on 9 Jan 1923. On 6 Dec 1955, Dr Igor B. Bensen (USA) flew his very simple open-seat Gyro-Copter and then made the design available in kit form to amateur constructor/pilots.

Speed altitude and distance records
Wing Cdr Kenneth H. Wallis (GB) holds the straight-line distance record of 543.27 miles *874,32 km* set in his WA-116F autogyro on 28 Sept 1975 non-stop from Lydd, Kent to Wick, Highland. Wg Cdr Wallis flew his WA-116, with 72 hp McCulloch engine, to a record altitude of 15,220 ft *4639 m* on 11 May 1968, and to a record speed of 111.2 mph *179 km/h* over a 3 km straight course on 12 May 1969.

FLYING-BOAT
Fastest
The fastest flying-boat ever built has been the Martin XP6M-1 *Seamaster*, the US Navy 4 jet engined minelayer flown in 1955–9 with a top speed of 646 mph *1040 km/h*. In September 1946 the Martin JRM-2 *Mars* flying-boat set a payload record of 68,327 lb *30 992 kg*.

The official flying-boat speed record is 566.69 mph *912 km/h*, set up by Nikolai Andrievsky and crew of two in a Soviet Beriev M-10, powered by two AL-7 turbojets, over a 15/25 km course on 7 Aug 1961. The M-10 holds all 12 records listed for jet-powered flying-boats, including an altitude of 49,088 ft *14 962 m* set by Georgiy Buryanov and crew over the Sea of Azov on 9 Sept 1961.

AIRSHIPS
Earliest
The earliest flight in an airship was by Henri Giffard from Paris in his coal-gas 88,300 ft³ *2 500 m³* 144 ft *43,8 m* long airship on 24 Sept 1852. The earliest British airship was a 20,000 ft³ *566 m³* 75 ft *22,8 m* long craft built by Stanley Spencer whose maiden flight was from Crystal Palace, Bromley, Greater London on 22 Sept 1902. The latest airship to be built in Britain is the 181,200 ft³ *5131 m³* 164 ft *50 m* long Aerospace Development AD-500, assembled at RAF Cardington, Bedfordshire. Its maiden flight was on 3 Feb 1979.

Largest *Rigid*
The largest rigid airship ever built was the 210.5 ton *213,9 tonne* German *Graf Zeppelin II* (LZ 130), with a length of 245 m *803.8 ft* and a capacity of 7,062,100 ft³ *199 981 m³*. She made her maiden flight on 14 Sept 1938 and in May and August 1939 made radar spying missions in British air space. She was dismantled in April 1940. Her sister ship *Hindenburg* was 5.6 ft *1,70 m* longer.

British
The largest British airship was the R101 built by the Royal Airship Works, Cardington, Bedfordshire, which first flew on 14 Oct 1929. She was 777 ft *236,8 m* in length and had a capacity of 5,508,800 ft³ *155 995 m³*. She crashed near Beauvais, France, killing 48 aboard on 5 Oct 1930.

Non-Rigid
The largest non-rigid airship ever constructed was the US Navy ZPG 3-W which had a capacity of 1,516,300 ft³ *42 937 m³*, was 403.4 ft *122,9 m* long and 85.1 ft *25,93 m* in diameter, with a crew of 21. She first flew on 21 July 1958, but crashed into the sea in June 1960.

Greatest passenger load
The most people ever carried in an airship was 207 in the US Navy *Akron* in 1931. The trans-Atlantic record is 117 by the German *Hindenburg* in 1937.

Distance record
The FAI accredited distance record for airships is 3967.1 miles *6384,5 km*, set up by the German *Graf Zeppelin*, captained by Dr Hugo Eckener, between 29 Oct and 1 Nov 1928.

Duration record
The longest recorded flight by a non-rigid airship (without refuelling) is 264 hr 12 min by a US Navy Goodyear-built ZPG-

Julian Nott (GB), who, on 31 Oct 1980 attained a new world record altitude for Hot-Air Ballooning when he reached 57,000 ft *17 400 m* in his *Innovation* (see p. 150). (*Jo Whiffen*)

2 class ship (Cdr J. R. Hunt USN) from South Weymouth NAS, Massachusetts, USA on 4-15 Mar 1957 landing back at Key West, Florida having flown 9448 miles *15,205 km*.

BALLOONING
Earliest
The earliest recorded ascent was by a model hot air balloon invented by Father Bartolomeu de Gusmão (*né* Lourenço) (b. Santos, Brazil, 1685), which was flown indoors at the Casa da India, Terreiro do Paço, Portugal on 8 Aug 1709. The claim made on a Soviet postage stamp issued in 1956, that a Russian named Kryakatin had flown in a balloon from Ryazam in 1731, stems from the renowned 19th century forger of manuscripts, A I Sulukadsev, and may be disregarded.

Distance record (*Great-circle distance between take-off and first landing point*)
The record distance travelled by a balloon is 3107.61 miles *5001,22 km* in 137 hr 5 min 50 sec by the American Yost HB-72 helium-filled balloon *Double Eagle II* on 12–17 Aug 1978 from Sprague Farm, Presque Isle, Maine, USA to Coquerel Farm, Miserey, France. The crew on this first North Atlantic crossing was Ben L. Abruzzo, 48, Maxie L. Anderson, 44 and Larry M. Newman, 31 from Albuquerque, New Mexico, USA.

Highest *Unmanned*
The highest altitude attained by an unmanned balloon was

The solar powered aeroplane *Solar Challenger* the lightest ever mechanically powered plane. Its debut under solar power was on 20 Nov 1980 (see p. 146). *(Don Monroe)*

170,000 ft *51 815 m* by a Winzen balloon of 47.8 million ft³ *1,35 million m³* launched at Chico, California in October 1972.

Manned

The greatest altitude reached in a manned balloon is the unofficial 123,800 ft (23.45 miles *37 735 m*) by Nicholas Piantanida (1933–66) of Bricktown, New Jersey, USA, from Sioux Falls, South Dakota, USA, on 1 Feb 1966. He landed in a cornfield in Iowa but did not survive. The official record is 113,740 ft *34 668 m* by Cdr Malcolm D. Ross, USNR and the late Lt-Cdr Victor A. Prother, USN in an ascent from the deck of USS *Antietam* on 4 May 1961, over the Gulf of Mexico.

Largest

The largest balloon built is one with an inflatable volume of 70 million ft³ *2 million m³* by Winzen Research Inc, Minnesota, USA.

Ballooning (*Hot-Air*)

The world's distance record for hot-air ballooning is 419.1 miles *674,53 km* by J. G. (Geoff) Green (GB) set on 30 Sept 1980 in the Cameron balloon A-140 *Sultan* from Northam to Zanthus, Western Australia.

On 31 Oct 1980 Julian Nott (GB) attained an altitude of 57,000 ft *17 400 m* taking off from Denver, Colorado, USA, in the ICI balloon *Innovation*. The largest hot-air balloon ever built is the UK Cameron A-500 500,000 ft³ *14 158 m³ Gerard A. Heineken* (now named *Crest Warrior*) first flown on 18 Aug 1974. The FAI endurance and distance record for a gas and hot-air balloon is 96 hr 24 min and 2074.817 miles *3339,086 km* by *Zanussi* crewed by Donald Allan Cameron (GB) and Major Christopher Davey which failed by only 103 miles *166 km* to achieve the first balloon crossing of the Atlantic on 30 July 1978.

The record altitude in an open basket is 38,789 ft *11 822 m* by Kingswood Sprott Jr, in a Raven S-60A balloon over Lakeland, Florida, USA on 27 Sept 1975.

HOVERCRAFT (skirted air cushion vehicles)

Earliest

The ACV (air-cushion vehicle) was first made a practical proposition by Sir Christopher Sydney Cockerell, CBE, FRS (b. 4 June 1910), a British engineer who had the idea in 1954, published his Ripplecraft Report 1/55 on 25 Oct 1955 and patented it on 12 Dec 1955. The earliest patent relating to an air-cushion craft was applied for in 1877 by John I. Thornycroft (1843–1928) of Chiswick, London and the Finn Toivo Kaario developed the idea in 1935. The first flight by a hovercraft was made by the 4 ton/*tonnes* Saunders-Roe SR-N1 at Cowes on 30 May 1959. With a 1500 lb *680 kg* thrust Viper turbojet engine, this craft reached 68 knots *126 km/h* in June 1961. The first hovercraft public service was run across the Dee Estuary by the 60 knot *111 km/h* 24-

passenger Vickers-Armstrong's VA-3 between July and September 1962.

Largest

The world's largest civil hovercraft is the 305 ton British-built SRN 4 Mk III with a capacity of 416 passengers and 60 cars. It is 186 ft *56,69 m* in length, is powered by 4 Bristol Siddeley Marine Proteus engines giving a maximum speed in excess of the permitted operating speed of 65 knots.

Fastest warship

The world's fastest warship is the 78 ft *23,7 m* long 100 ton/*tonne* US Navy test vehicle SES-100B. She attained 91.9 knots *103.9 mph* on 25 Jan 1980 on the Chesapeake Bay Test Range, Maryland, USA. A contract for a 3000 ton Large Surface Effect Ship (LSES) was placed by the US Department of Defense with Bell Aerospace in September 1977 for delivery in mid-1981.

Longest flight

The longest hovercraft journey was one of 5000 miles *8047 km* through eight West African countries between 15 Oct 1969 and 3 Jan 1970 by the British Trans-African Hovercraft Expedition.

Highest

The greatest altitude at which a hovercraft is operating is on Lago Titicaca, Peru, where since 1975 an HM2 Hoverferry is hovering 12,506 ft *3811 m* above sea level.

PERSONAL AVIATION RECORDS

Oldest and Youngest Passengers

Airborne births are reported every year. The oldest person to fly has been Mr Izumi (see page 16) when he was 108 in 1973 from Tokunashima to Osaka, Japan and return. The oldest Briton to fly was probably Mrs Julia Caroline Black (b. 24 Feb 1874 d. 12 May 1980) on a British Caledonian flight from Abbotsinch to Gatwick on 17 Nov 1978 when aged 104 years 8 months.

Oldest and youngest pilots

The youngest age at which anyone has ever qualified as a military pilot is 15 yr 5 months in the case of Sgt Thomas Dobney (b. 6 May 1926) of the RAF. He had overstated his age (14 yr) on entry. Miss Betty Bennett took off, flew and landed solo at the

The world's mightiest wind generator, the 3000 kilowatt 191 ft *58,2 m* tall Southern California Edison Co machine at San Gorgonio Pass. Note: the girl in orange (see p. 152).

age of 10 on 4 Jan 1952 in Cuba. Clark O. Pelaez (b. 4 May 1957) flew a Piper Tri-Pacer solo at Cebu City, Philippines on 24 Apr 1968 aged 10 yr 11 months. The world's oldest pilot is Ed McCarty (b. 18 Sept 1885) of Kimberly, Idaho, USA, who in 1979 was flying his rebuilt 30-year-old Ercoupe aged 94. Glenn E. Messer of Birmingham, Alabama has been flying 'steady' since 13 May 1911. Albert E. Savoy (b. 22 Feb 1895) was issued with his first PPL aged 82 yr 8 months on 8 Nov 1977.

Most flying hours
Max Conrad (1903–79) (USA) between 1928 and mid-1974 totalled 52,929 hr 40 min logged flight—more than 6 years airborne. He completed 150 trans-Atlantic crossings in light aircraft.

Most take-offs and landings from airports
Al Yates and Bob Phoenix of Texas, USA made 193 take-offs and daylight landings at unduplicated airfields in 14 hr 57 min in a Piper Seminole, on 15 June 1979.

Human-powered flight
The world distance record for human powered flight was set on 12 June 1979 by Dr Paul MacCready's man powered aircraft *Gossamer Albatross*, piloted and pedalled by Bryan Allen. The *Albatross* took off from Folkestone at 05.51 hrs and landed 22.26 miles *35,82 km* distant at Cap Gris Nez, France at 08.40 hrs. The duration was 2 hr 49 min, and this achievement won the £100,000 prize offered by Henry Kremer for the first man-powered crossing of the English Channel.

The 70 lb *31,75 kg Gossamer Condor* (96 ft *29,26 m* wing-span) designed by Dr Paul MacCready flew the figure-of-8 course between pylons 880 yd *804,6 m* apart powered by the 9¾ stone *61,2 kg* Bryan Allen at Shafter Airport, California on 23 Aug 1977 to win the £50,000 Kremer prize. The flight lasted 7 min 27.5 sec.

MODEL AIRCRAFT
Altitude, speed and duration
The World record for altitude is 26,929 ft *8208 m* by Maynard L. Hill (USA) on 6 Sept 1970 using a radio-controlled model. The free flight speed record is 213.70 mph *343,92 km/h* by V. Goukoune and V. Myakinin (both USSR) with a radio-controlled model at Klementyeva, USSR, on 21 Sept 1971. The record duration flight is one of 32 hr 7 min 40 sec by Eduard Svoboda (Czechoslovakia), flying a radio controlled glider on 23–24 Aug 1980.

Cross-channel
The first cross-channel model helicopter flight was achieved by an 11 lb *5,00 kg* model Bell 212 radio controlled by Dieter Zeigler for 32 miles *52 km* between Ashfrod, Kent and Ambleteuse, France on 17 July 1974.

Smallest
The smallest model aircraft to fly is one weighing 0.004 oz *0,1 g* powered by attaching a horsefly and designed by Don Emmick of Seattle, Washington in June 1979. One flew for 5 minutes.

Paper aircraft
The flight duration record for a paper aircraft is 15.0 sec by William Harlan Pryor in the Municipal Auditorium, Nashville, Tennessee, USA on 26 Mar 1975. The indoor record with a 12 ft *3,65 m* ceiling is 1 min 33 sec set in the Fuji TV studios, Tokyo, Japan on 21 Sept 1980. A paper plane was reported and witnessed to have flown 1¼ miles *2,0 km* by 'Chick' C. O. Reinhart from a 10th storey office window at 60 Beaver Street, New York City across the East River to Brooklyn in August 1933. It was helped by a thermal from a coffee-roasting plant.

Indoor
An indoor distance of 140 ft 2 in *42,72 m* was recorded by Tony Felch in the Mary E. Sawyer Auditorium in La Crosse, Wisconsin, USA on 9 Aug 1979.

5. POWER PRODUCERS

Steam engines
The oldest steam engine in working order is the 1812 Boulton & Watt 26 hp 42 in bore beam engine on the Kennet & Avon Canal at Great Bedwyn, Wiltshire. It was restored by the Crofton Society in 1971.

The largest single cylinder steam engine ever built was that designed by Matthew Loam of Cornwall and made by the Hayle Foundry Co in 1849 for installation for land draining at Haarlem, Netherlands. The cylinder was 12 ft *3,65 m* in diameter such that each stroke also of 12 ft lifted 13,440 gallons *61 096 l* or 60 tons of water.

The most efficient steam engine recorded was Taylor's engine built by Michael Loam for the United Mines, Gwennap, Cornwall in 1840. It registered only 1.7 lb of coal per horsepower per hour.

Earliest atomic pile
The world's first atomic pile was built in a disused squash court at Stagg Field, University of Chicago, Illinois, USA. It went 'critical' at 3.25 pm on 2 Dec 1942.

Power plant Largest *World*
The world's largest power station is the USSR's hydroelectric station at Krasnoyarsk on the river Yenisey, Siberia, USSR with a power of 6096 MW. Its third generator turned in March 1968 and the twelfth became operative in December 1970. The turbine hall, completed in June 1968, is 1378 ft *420 m* long. The reservoir backed up by the dam was reported in November 1972 to be 240 miles *386 km* in length.

The largest planned power plant is the Itaipu on the river Paranã on the Brazil-Paraguay border with an ultimate 12,600,000 kW from 18 turbines.

Great Britain
The power station with the greatest installed capacity in Great Britain is Longannet, Fife, Scotland which attained 2400 MW by December 1972. At Drax, North Yorkshire, 6 × 660 MW sets yielding 3960 MW are expected to be in commission by 1984. A 3300 MW oil-fired installation on the Isle of Grain, Kent, is due to be commissioned in 1980.

The largest hydroelectric plant in the United Kingdom is the North of Scotland Hydroelectricity Board's Power Station at Loch Sloy, Central. The installed capacity of this station is 130 MW. The Ben Cruachan Pumped Storage Scheme was opened on 15 Oct 1965 at Loch Awe, Strathclyde, Scotland. It has a capacity of 400 MW and cost £24,000,000. The 1880 MW underground pumped storage scheme at Dinorwic, Gwynedd will be the largest built in Europe with a head of 1739 ft *530 m* and a capacity of 13,770 ft³/sec *390 m³/sec*. Completion is due in 1981.

Nuclear power station *Largest*
The world's largest atomic power station is the Ontario Hydro's Pickering station which in 1973 attained full output of 2160 MW.

Nuclear reactor *Largest*
The largest single nuclear reactor in the world is the 1098 MW Browns Ferry Unit 1 General Electric boiling water type reactor located on the Wheeler Reservoir, near Decatar, Alabama which became operative in 1973. The Grand Gulf Nuclear Station at Port Gibson, Mississippi will have a capacity of 1290 MW in 1980.

Solar power plant
The largest solar furnace in the world is the 5 megawatt Solar Thermal Test Facility at the Sandia Laboratories, Albuquerque, New Mexico, USA completed in December 1977. Sunlight from 222 heliostats is concentrated on a target 114 ft *34,7 m* up in the power tower. Work on the $140 million, 1818 mirror, Solar One near Daggett, Southern California, USA began in January 1980 for completion in early 1982. The 22 acres *8,9 ha* of mirror should yield 10 megawatts.

Tidal power station
The world's first major tidal power station is the *Usine marèmotrice de la Rance*, officially opened on 26 Nov 1966 at the Rance estuary in the Golfe de St Malo, Brittany, France. It was built in

five years at a cost of 420,000,000 francs (£34,685,000), and has a net annual output of 544,000,000 kWh. The 880 yd *804 m* barrage contains 24 turbo alternators. This harnessing of the tides has imperceptibly slowed the Earth's rate of revolution. The $1000 million (£540 million) Passamaquoddy project for the Bay of Fundy in Maine, USA, and New Brunswick, Canada, remains a project.

Boiler Largest
The largest boilers ever designed are those ordered in the United States from The Babcock & Wilcox Company (USA) with a capacity of 1330 MW so involving the evaporation of 9,330,000 lb *4 232 000 kg* of steam per hour. The largest boilers now being installed in the United Kingdom are the three 660 MW units for the Drax Power Station (see p.151) designed and constructed by Babcock & Wilcox Ltd.

Generator Largest
Generators in the 2,000,000 kW (or 2000 MW) range are now in the planning stages both in the UK and the USA. The largest under construction is one of 1300 MW by the Brown Boveri Co of Switzerland for the Tennessee Valley Authority.

Turbines Largest
The largest hydraulic turbines are those rated at 815,000 kw (equivalent to 1.1 million hp), 32 ft *9,7 m* in diameter with a 401 ton *407 tonnes* runner and a 312½ ton *317,5 tonnes* shaft installed by Allis-Chalmers at the Grand Coulee 'Third Powerplant', Washington, USA.

Pump
The world's largest reversible pump-turbine is that made by Allis-Chalmers for the Bath County project, Virginia, USA. It has a maximum rating of 457 Mw as a turbine and maximum operating head of 393 m *1289 ft*. The impeller/runner diameter is 6349 mm *20 ft 9 in* with a synchronous speed of 257.1 rpm.

Longest Lasting Battery
The zinc foil and sulfur dry pile batteries made by Watlin and Hill of London in 1840 have powered ceaseless tintinnabulation inside a bell jar at the Clarendon Laboratory, Oxford since 1840. The first 'perpetual motion' patent filed under the World Patent Cooperation Treaty was No 80/00866 by Edmund and Robert Kraus of California, USA.

Gas works Largest
The flow of natural gas from the North Sea is diminishing the manufacture of gas by the carbonisation of coal and the reforming process using petroleum derivatives. Britain's largest ever gasworks 300 acres *120 ha* were at Beckton, Newham. Currently the most productive gasworks are at the oil re-forming plant at Greenwich, Greater London, with an output of 420.5 million ft³ *11 907 298 m³* per day.

Biggest black-out
The greatest power failure in history struck seven north-eastern US States and Ontario, Canada, on 9–10 Nov 1965. About 30,000,000 people in 80,000 miles² *207 200 km²* were plunged into darkness. Only two were killed. In New York City the power failed at 5.27 pm and was not fully restored for 13½ hr. The total consequential losses in the 52 min New York City power failure of 13 July 1977 including looting was put at $1 billion (*then £580 million*).

Windmill Earliest
The earliest recorded windmills are those used for grinding corn in Iran (Persia) in the 7th century AD.

The earliest date attributed to a windmill in England is 1185 for one at Weedley, near Hull, Humberside. The oldest Dutch mill is the towermill at Zeddam, Gelderland built in c. 1450. The oldest working mill in England is the post-mill at Outwood, Surrey, built in 1665, though the Ivinghoe Mill in Pitstone Green Farm, Buckinghamshire, dating from 1627, has been restored. The postmill in North Ronaldsay, Orkney Islands operated until 1905.

Windmill Largest
The world's most powerful wind generator is the 3000 kw 191 ft *58,2 m* tall Southern California Edison Co machine in San Gorgonio Pass completed in February 1981. It generates 3000 KW

in 40 mph *64 km/h* winds. A 2500 KW wind turbine was under construction in 1980. A £5.6 million 3000 KW aerogenerator with 60 m *196 ft 10 in* blades on Burgar Hill, Evie, Orkney is planned for completion in 1982/83.

Windmill *Largest conventional*
The largest Dutch windmill is the Dijkpolder in Maasland built in 1718. The sails measure 95¾ ft *29 m* from tip to tip. The tallest windmill in the Netherlands is De Walvisch in Schiedam built to a height of 108 ft *33 m* in 1794. The tallest windmill still standing in Britain is the 9 storey Sutton mill, Norfolk built in 1853 which before being struck by lightning in 1941 had sails 73 ft *22,2 m* in diameter with 216 shutters.

Water Mills
There has been a water-powered corn-mill at Priston Mill near Bath, Avon since pre-Norman times. The earliest record is dated AD 931.

6. ENGINEERING

Blast furnace Largest
The world's largest blast furnace is one with an inner volume of 5070 m³ *179,040 ft³* and a 14,8 m *48 ft 6½ in* diameter hearth at the Oita Works, Kyūshū, Japan completed in October 1976 with an annual capacity of 4,380,000 tons *4 451 500 tonnes*.

Cat cracker Largest
The world's largest catalyst cracker is the Exxon Co's Bayway Refinery plant at Linden, New Jersey, USA with a fresh feed rate of 5,040,000 US gal *19 077 000 litres* per day.

Conveyor belt Longest
The world's longest single flight conveyor belt is one of 18 miles *29 km* under construction in Western Australia by Cable Belt Ltd of Camberley, Surrey whose 9 mile *14,5 km* record installation of 1970 in Kentucky, USA will then be doubled. The longest installation in Great Britain is also by Cable Belt and of 5½ miles *8,9 km* underground at Longannet Power Station, Fife, Scotland. The world's longest multi-flight conveyor is one of 100 km *62 miles* between the phosphate mine near Bucraa and the port of El Aaiun, Morocco, built by Krupps and completed in 1972. It has 11 flights of between 9 and 11 km *5.6–6.8 miles* and was driven at 4,5 m/sec *10.06 mph* but has been closed down due to Polisario Front guerrilla activity.

Crane Most Powerful *World*
The world's most powerful crane is the 53,000 ton 584 ft *178 m* long converted tanker *Odin* owned by Heerema Engineering Service of The Hague, Netherlands. On 26 May 1976 she made a test lift on 3000 tonnes *3048 tons* at a radius maximum of 105 ft *32 m* in the Calard Canal, Europoort.

Gantry crane Most powerful
The 92.3 ft *28,14 m* wide Rahco (R. A. Hanson Disc. Ltd) gantry crane at the Grand Coulee Dam Third Powerplant was tested to lift a load of 2232 long tons *2268 tonnes* in 1975. It lowered a 3,944,000 lb *1789 tonne* generator rotor with an accuracy of 1/32 in *0,8 mm*.

Crane Tallest mobile
The tallest mobile crane in the world is the 810 tonnes Rosenkranz K10001 with a lifting capacity of 1000 tonnes *984 tons*, a combined boom and jib height of 202 m *663 ft*. It is carried on 10 trucks each limited to 75 ft 8 in *23,06 m* and an axle weight of 118 tonnes *116 tons*. It can lift 30 tonnes *29.5 tons* to a height of 160 m *525 ft*.

Dragline Largest *World*
The Ural Engineering Works at Ordzhonikidze, USSR, completed in March 1962, has a dragline known as the ES-25(100) with a boom of 100 m *328 ft* and a bucket with a capacity of 31.5 yd³ *24 m³*. The world's largest walking dragline is the Bucyrus-Erie 4250W with an all-up weight of 12,000 tons *12 192 tonnes* and a bucket capacity of 220 yd³ *168 m³* on a 310 ft *94,4 m* boom. This machine, the world's largest mobile land

machine, is now operating on the Central Ohio Coal Company's Muskingum site in Ohio, USA.

Great Britain

The largest dragline excavator in Britain is 'Big Geordie', the Bucyrus-Erie 1550W 6250 gross hp, weighing 3000 tons *3048 tonnes* with a forward mast 160 ft *48,7 m* high. On open-cast coal workings at Butterwell, Northumberland in September 1975, it proved able to strip 100 tons *101 tonnes* of overburden in 65 sec with its 65 yd³ *49,7 m³* bucket on a 265 ft *80,7 m* boom. It is owned by Derek Crouch (Contractors) Ltd of Peterborough, Cambridgeshire.

Escalator Longest

The term was registered in the US on 28 May 1900 but the earliest 'Inclined Escalator' was installed by Jesse W. Reno on the pier at Coney Island, New York in 1896. The first installation in Britain was at Harrods, Knightsbridge, London in November 1898. The escalators on the Leningrad Underground, USSR at Lenin Square have 729 steps and vertical rise of 59,68 m *195 ft 9½ in.* The longest escalators in Britain are the four in the Tyne Tunnel, Tyne and Wear installed in 1951. They measure 192 ft 8 in *58,7 m* between combs with a vertical lift of 85 ft *25,9 m* and a step speed of up to 1.7 mph *2,7 km/h.*

The world's longest 'moving sidewalks' are those installed in 1970 in the Neue Messe Centre, Dusseldorf, W. Germany which measure 225 m *738 ft* between comb plates. The longest in Great Britain is the 375 ft *114,3 m* long Dunlop Starglide at London Airport Terminal 3 installed in March-May 1970.

Excavator Largest

The world's largest excavator is the 13,000 tonne bucket wheel excavator being assembled at the open cast lignite-mine of Hambach, W. Germany with a rating of 200 000 m³ *260,000 yd³* per 20 hr working day. It is 210 m *690 ft* in length and 82 m *269 ft* tall. The wheel is 67,88 m *222 ft* in circumference with 5 m³ *6.5 yd³* buckets.

Forging Largest

The largest forging on record is one of a 450,600 lb *204,4 tonnes* 55 ft *16,76 m* long generator shaft for Japan, forged by the Bethlehem Steel Corp, Pennsylvania in October 1973.

Lathe Largest

The world's largest lathe is the 72 ft *21,9 m* long 385 ton *391 tonnes* giant lathe built by the Dortmunder Rheinstahl firm of Wagner in 1962. The face plate is 15 ft *4,57 m* in diameter and can exert a torque of 289,000 ft/lb *39 955 m/kgf* when handling objects weighing up to 200 tons *203 tonnes.*

Greatest lift

The heaviest lifting operation in engineering history was the 41,000 short ton (36,607 long tons *37 194 tonnes*) roof of the Velodrome in Montreal, Canada in 1975. It was raised by jacks some 4 in *10 cm* to strike its centering.

Oldest machinery *World*

The earliest machinery still in use is the *dâlu*—a water-raising instrument known to have been in use in the Sumerian civilization which originated *c.* 3500 BC in Lower Iraq even earlier than the *Saqiyas* on the Nile.

Great Britain

The oldest piece of machinery (excluding clocks) operating in the United Kingdom is the snuff mill driven by a water wheel at Messrs Wilson & Co's Sharrow Mill in Sheffield, South Yorkshire. It is known to have been operating in 1797 and more probably since 1730.

Nut Largest

The largest nuts ever made weigh 47 cwt *2,39 tonnes* each and have an outside diameter of 50½ in *128,2 cm* and a 31½ in *80 cm* thread. Known as Moorthrust, they are manufactured by Doncaster Moorside Ltd. of Oldham, Greater Manchester for securing propellers.

Oil tank Largest

The largest oil tanks ever constructed are the five Aramco 1½ million barrel storage tanks at Ju'aymah, Saudi Arabia. The tanks are 72 ft *21,94 m* tall with a diameter of 386 ft *117,6 m* and were completed in March 1980.

Passenger lift Fastest *World*

The fastest domestic passenger lifts in the world are the express lifts to the 60th floor of the 240 m *787.4 ft* tall 'Sunshine 60' building, Ikebukuro, Tōkyō, Japan completed 5 Apr 1978. They were built by Mitsubishi Corp and operate at a speed of 2000 ft/min *609,6 m/min* or 22.72 mph *36,56 km/h.* Much higher speeds are achieved in the winding cages of mine shafts. A hoisting shaft 6800 ft *2072 m* deep, owned by Western Deep Levels Ltd in South Africa, winds at speeds of up to 40.9 mph *65,8 km/h* (3595 ft *1095 m* per min). Otitis-media (popping of the ears) presents problems much above even 10 mph *16 km/h.*

Great Britain

The longest lift in the United Kingdom is one 930 ft long inside the B.B.C. T.V. tower at Bilsdale, West Moor, North Yorkshire, built by J. L. Eve Construction Co Ltd. It runs at 130 ft *39,6 m/min.* The longest fast lifts are the two 15-passenger cars in the Post Office Tower, Maple Street, London W1 which travel 540 ft *164 m* up at up to 1,000 ft/min *304 m/min.*

Michael Bracey established an involuntary duration record when trapped in a lift for 59 hr 55 min in Newcastle on Tyne, England on 29 Feb 1980.

Pipeline Longest *Oil*

The longest crude oil pipeline in the world is the Interprovincial Pipe Line Company's installation from Edmonton, Alberta, Canada to Buffalo, New York State, USA, a distance of 1775 miles *2856 km.* Along the length of the pipe 13 pumping stations maintain a flow of 6,900,000 gal *31 367 145 litres* of oil per day.

The eventual length of the Trans-Siberian Pipeline will be 2319 miles *3732 km,* running from Tuimazy through Omsk and Novosibirsk to Irkutsk. The first 30 mile *48 km* section was opened in July 1957.

Submarine pipelines

The longest submarine pipeline is the Ekofisk—Emden line stretching 260 miles *418 km* under the North Sea and completed in July 1975. The deepest North Sea pipeline is that from the Cormorant Field to Firths Voe, Shetland at 530 ft *162 m.*

Natural gas

The longest natural gas pipeline in the world is the Trans-Canada Pipeline which by 1974 had 5654 miles *9099 km* of pipe up to 42 in *106,6 cm* in diameter.

Pipeline Most expensive

The world's most expensive pipeline is the Alaska pipeline running 798 miles *1284 km* from Prudhoe Bay to Valdez. By completion of the first phase in 1977 it had cost at least $6000 million (£3250 million). The pipe is 48 in *1,21 m* in diameter and will eventually carry up to 2 million barrels of crude oil per day.

Press Largest

The world's two most powerful production machines are forging presses in the USA. The Loewy closed-die forging press, in a plant leased from the US Air Force by the Wyman-Gordon Company at North Grafton, Massachusetts, USA weighs 9469 tons *9620 tonnes* and stands 114 ft 2 in *34,79 m* high, of which 66 ft *20,1 m* is sunk below the operating floor. It has a rated capacity of 44,600 tons *45 315 tonnes,* and went into operation in October 1955. The other similar press is at the plant of the Aluminium Company of America at Cleveland, Ohio. There has been a report of a press in the USSR with a capacity of 75 000 tonnes *73,800 tons* at Novo Kramatorsk. The Bêché and Grohs counter-blow forging hammer, manufactured in W. Germany are rated at 60,000 tonnes. The most powerful press in Great Britain is the closed-die forging and extruding press installed in 1967 at the Cameron Iron Works, Livingston, Lothian. The press is 92 ft *28 m* tall (27 ft *8,2 m* below ground) and exerts a force of 30,000 tons *30 481 tonnes.*

Printer Fastest

The world's fastest printer is the Radiation Inc electro-sensitive system at the Lawrence Radiation Laboratory, Livermore, California. High speed recording of up to 30,000 lines each containing 120 alphanumeric characters per minute is attained by controlling electronic pulses through chemically impregnated recording paper which is rapidly moving under closely spaced fixed styli. It can thus print the wordage of the whole Bible (773,692 words) in 65 sec—3333 times as fast as the world's fastest typist.

Radar installation *Largest*

The largest of the three installations in the US Ballistic Missile Early Warning System (BMEWS) is that near Thule, in Greenland, 931 miles *1498 km* from the North Pole, completed in 1960 at a cost of $500,000,000 (*then £178.5 million*). Its sister stations are one at Cape Clear, Alaska, USA, completed in 1961, and a $115,000,000 (*then £41.07 million*) installation at Fylingdales Moor, North Yorkshire, completed in June 1963. The largest scientific radar installation is the 21 acre *84 000 m²* ground array at Jicamarca, Peru.

Ropeway or telepherique Highest *World*

The highest and longest aerial ropeway in the world is the Teleférico Mérida (Mérida téléphérique) in Venezuela, from Mérida City (5379 ft *1639,5 m*) to the summit of Pico Espejo (15,629 ft *4763,7 m*), a rise of 10,250 ft *3124 m*. The ropeway is in four sections, involving 3 car changes in the 8 mile ascent in 1 hr. The fourth span is 10,070 ft *3069 m* in length. The two cars work on the pendulum system—the carrier rope is locked and the cars are hauled by means of three pull ropes powered by a 230 hp *233 cv* motor. They have a maximum capacity of 45 persons and travel at 32 ft *9,7 m* per sec (21.8 mph *35,08 km/h*). The longest single span ropeway is the 13,500 ft *4114 m* long span from the Coachella Valley to Mt San Jacinto (10,821 ft *3298 m*), California, USA, inaugurated on 12 Sept 1963.

Great Britain
Britain's longest cabin lift is that at Llandudno, Gwynedd, opened in June 1969. It has 42 cabins with a capacity of 1000 people per hour and is 5320 ft *1621 m* in length.

Transformer Largest

The world's largest single phase transformers are rated at 1,500,000 kV of which eight are in service with the American Electric Power Service Corporation. Of these five stepdown from 765 to 345 kV. Britain's largest transformers are those rated at 1,000,000 kVa 400/275 kV built by Hackbridge & Hewittic Co Ltd, Walton-on-Thames, Surrey first commissioned for the CEGB in October 1968.

Transmission lines *Longest*

The longest span between pylons of any power line in the world is that across the Sogne Fjord, Norway, between Rabnaberg and Fatlaberg. Erected in 1955 by the Whitecross Co Ltd of Warrington, Cheshire, England as part of the high-tension power cable from Refsdal power station at Vik, it has a span of 16,040 ft *4888 m* and a weight of 12 tons/*tonnes*. In 1967 two further high tensile steel/aluminium lines 16,006 ft *4878 m* long, and weighing 33 tons *33,5 tonnes*, manufactured by Whitecross and BICC were erected here. The longest in Britain are the 5310 ft *1618 m* lines built by J. L. Eve Co across the Severn with main towers each 488 ft *148 m* high.

Highest
The world's highest are those across the Straits of Messina, with towers of 675 ft *205 m* (Sicily side) and 735 ft *224 m* (Calabria) and 11,900 ft *3627 m* apart. The highest lines in Britain are those made by BICC at West Thurrock, Essex, which cross the Thames estuary suspended from 630 ft *192 m* tall towers at a minimum height of 250 ft *76 m*, with a 130 ton *132 tonnes* breaking load. They are 4500 ft *1371 m* in length.

Highest voltages
The highest voltages now carried are 1,330,000 volts 1224 miles *1970 km* on the DC Pacific Inter-tie in the United States. The Ekibastuz DC transmission lines in Kazakhstan, USSR are planned to be 2400 km *1490 miles* long with 1,500,000 volt capacity.

Tubing smallest

The smallest tubing in the world is made by Accles and Pollock, Ltd of Warley, West Midlands. It is of pure nickel with an outer

and inner diameter of 0.0005 in and 0.00013 in and wa announced on 9 Sept 1963. The average human hair measure from 0.002 to 0.003 of an inch *0,05–0,075 mm* diameter. The tubing, which is stainless, can be used for the artificial insemi nation of bees and for the medical process of 'feeding' nerves and weighs only 5 oz *141 gr* per 100 miles *160 km*.

Valve Largest

The world's largest valve is the 32 ft *9,75 m* diameter, 170 ton *tonne* butterfly valve designed by Boving & Co Ltd of Londo for use at the Arnold Airforce Base engine test facility in Ten nessee, USA.

Wire rope Longest and Strongest

The longest wire rope in the world is the stage winder at No shaft Vaal Reefs Gold Mine, South Africa, which measure 15 300 m *9.50 miles* installed in July 1979. They were spun a the Haggie Rand Ltd Ropery at Jupiter, Johannesburg. Each o the two ropes weigh 116 tons/*tonnes*. The thickest ever made are spliced crane strops from wire ropes 28,2 cm *11¼ in* thick mad of 2392 individual wires in March 1979 by British Ropes Ltd o Doncaster at Willington Quay, Tyneside, designed to lift load of up to 3000 tons/*tonnes*.

TIME PIECES
Clock *Oldest*

The earliest mechanical clock, that is one with an escapement was completed in China in AD 725 by I Hsing and Liang Ling tsan.

The oldest surviving working clock in the world is the faceles clock dating from 1386, or possibly earlier, at Salisbury Cathedral, Wiltshire, which was restored in 1956 having struck the hours for 498 years and ticked more than 500 million times Earlier dates, ranging back to *c.* 1335, have been attributed t the weight-driven clock in Wells Cathedral, Somerset, but only the iron frame is original. A model of Giovanni de Dondi's hept agonal astronomical clock of 1348–64 was completed in 1962.

Clock Largest *World*

The world's most massive clock is the Astronomical Clock in the Cathedral of St Pierre, Beauvais, France, constructed betwee 1865 and 1868. It contains 90,000 parts and measures 40 f *12,1 m* high, 20 ft *6,09 m* wide and 9 ft *2,7 m* deep. The Su Sung clock, built in China at K'aifeng in 1088–92, had a 20 to *20,3 tonnes* bronze armillary sphere for 1½ tons, *1,52 tonnes* o water. It was removed to Peking in 1126 and was last known t be working in its 40 ft *12,1 m* high tower in 1136.

Public
The largest four-faced clock in the world is that on the building of the Allen-Bradley Company of Milwaukee, Wisconsin, USA Each face has a diameter of 40 ft 3½ in *12,28 m* with a minute hand 20 ft *6,09 m* in overall length. The tallest four-faced clock in the world is that of the Williamsburgh Savings Bank i Brooklyn, New York City, NY, USA. It is 430 ft *131 m* abov street level.

Great Britain
The largest clock in the United Kingdom is that on the Roya Liver Building (built 1908–11) with dials 25 ft *7,62 m* in diam eter and the 4 minute hands each 14 ft *4,26 m* long. The mechan ism and dials weigh 22 tons and are 220 ft *67 m* above stree level.

Longest stoppage 'Big Ben'

The longest stoppage of the clock in the House of Common clock tower, London since the first tick on 31 May 1859 has been 13 days from noon 4 Apr to noon 17 Apr 1977. In 1945 a host o starlings slowed the minute hand by 5 min.

Clock Most accurate

The most accurate and complicated clockwork in the world i the Olsen clock, installed in the Copenhagen Town Hall, Den mark. The clock, which has more than 14,000 units, took 1 years to make and the mechanism of the clock functions i 570,000 different ways. The celestial pole motion of the clock will take 25,753 years to complete a full circle and is the slowes moving designed mechanism in the world. The clock is accurate

to 0.5 sec in 300 years—50 times more accurate than the previous record.

Clock Most expensive
The highest auction price for any English-made clock is £110,000 for a Thomas Tompion (1639–1713) bracket clock at Christie's in London on 2 June 1980.

Watch Oldest
The oldest watch (portable clockwork time-keeper) is one made of iron by Peter Henlein in Nürnberg (Nüremberg), Bavaria, Germany, in *c*. 1504 and now in the Memorial Hall, Philadelphia, Pennsylvania, USA. The earliest wrist watches were those of Jacquet-Droz and Leschot of Geneva, Switzerland, dating from 1790.

Watch Smallest
The smallest watches in the world are produced by Jaeger Le Coultre of Switzerland. Equipped with a 15-jewelled movement they measure just over ½ in. *1,2 cm* long and ³⁄₁₆ in, *0,476 cm* in width. The movement, with its case, weighs under 0.25 oz *7 g*.

Watch Thinnest
The world's thinnest wrist watch is the Concord Delirium IV. It measures 0,98 mm *0.0385 in* thick and retailed for $16,000 £6800 (including 18 carat gold strap) in June 1980.

Watch Most expensive
Excluding watches with jewelled cases, the most expensive standard men's pocket watch is the Swiss *Grande Complication* by Audemars-Piguet which retailed for £40,000 in May 1981. The *Kallista* watch with 130 carats of precious stones by Vacheron et Constantin of Geneva was valued in Apr 1981 at $5 million (*then* £2,272,000). The record price for an antique watch is $166,300 (*then* £75,600) paid to Capt. Peter Belin USN by L. C. Mannheimer of Zurich at Sotheby Parke Bernet, New York on 29 Nov 1979 for a gold studded case watch of *c*. 1810 by William Anthony of London.

Time measurer Most accurate *World*
The most accurate time-keeping devices are the twin atomic hydrogen masers installed in 1964 in the US Naval Research Laboratory, Washington, DC. They are based on the frequency of the hydrogen atom's transition period of 1,420,450,751,694 cycles/sec. This enables an accuracy to within 1 sec in 1,700,000 years.

COMPUTERS
The first electronic digital computer, called ENIAC, was completed by J. Presper Eckert Jr and John W. Mauchly at the Moore School of Electrical Engineering, University of Pennsylvania, USA in 1946. Computers were then advanced by the invention of the point-contact transistor by John Bardeen and Walter Brattain announced in July 1948, and the junction transistor by R. L. Wallace, Morgan Sparks and Dr William Shockley in early 1951. The Microcomputer was invented in 1969–73 by M. E. Hoff Jr of Intel Corporation with the production of the microprocessor silicon chip '4004'.

The computer planned to be the world's biggest by a factor of 40 is the $50 million NASF (Numerical Aerodynamic Simulation Facility) at NASA's Ames Research Center, Palo Alto, California. The tenders from CDC and Burroughs called for a capacity of 12.8 gigaflops (12,800 million complex calculations per second).

Most powerful and Fastest *World*
The world's most powerful and fastest computer is the CRAY-1, designed by Seymour R. Cray of Cray Research, Inc, Minneapolis, Minnesota. The clock period is 12.5 nanoseconds and memory ranges up to 1,048,576 64-bit words, resulting in a capacity of 8,388,608 bytes of main memory. (N.B. a 'byte' is a unit of storage compressing 8 'bits' collectively equivalent to one alphabetic symbol or two numericals.) It attains speeds of 200 million floating point operations per second. With 32 CRAY DD-19 disk storage units, it has a storage capacity of 7.7568×10^{10} bits. The cost of a mid-range system was quoted in mid-1979 as about $8.8 million (*then* £4 million). The most powerful British computer is the International Computer's Distribution Array Processor – the ICL DAP.

Control Data Corporation announced the CYBER Model 205-444 system from Arden Hill, Minnesota, USA on 2 June 1980 which has a memory of 4 million 64-Bit words and cost $16.5 million (*£7 million*) at delivery in January 1981.

9. THE BUSINESS WORLD

1. COMMERCE

The $(US) has in this chapter been converted at a fixed mean rate of $2.20 to the £ Sterling and at the relevant rates at other dates.

The *Guinness Book of the Business World* by Henry Button and Andrew Lampert (£6.50) contains a more detailed treatment of records and facts in the world of commerce and industry.

Oldest industry

Agriculture is often described as 'the oldest industry in the world', whereas in fact there is no evidence that it was practised before *c.* 11,000 BC. The oldest known industry is flint knapping, involving the production of chopping tools and hand axes, dating from about 1,750,000 years ago. Salt panning could be of comparable antiquity.

Oldest company *World*

The oldest company in the world is the Faversham Oyster Fishery Co, referred to in the Faversham Oyster Fishing Act 1930, as existing 'from time immemorial', *i.e.* in English law from before 1189.

Great Britain

The Royal Mint has origins going back to AD 287. The Oxford University Press celebrated the 500th anniversary of its origins in 1478 in 1978. The Whitechapel Bell Foundry of Whitechapel Road, London, E1, has been in business since 1570. The retail business in Britain with the oldest history is the Cambridge bookshop, which, though under various ownership, has traded from the site of 1 Trinity Street since 1581 and since 1907 under its present title Bowes & Bowes. R. Durtnell & Sons, builders, of Brasted, Kent, has been run by the same family since 1591. The first bill of adventure signed by the English East India Co, was dated 21 Mar 1601.

Greatest assets *World*

The business with the greatest amount in physical assets is the Bell System, which comprises the American Telephone and Telegraph Company, with headquarters at 195 Broadway, New York City, NY, USA, and its subsidiaries. The Bell System's total assets on the consolidated balance sheet at 28 Feb 1981 were valued at $126,424,000,000 (*then £57,465 million*). The plant involved included 142.1 million telephones. The number of employees is 1,045,000. A total of 20,109 shareholders attended the Annual Meeting in April 1961, thereby setting a world record.

The first company to have assets in excess of $1 billion was the United States Steel Corporation with $1400 million (*then £287.73 million*) at the time of its creation by merger in 1900.

Great Britain

The biggest British industrial company is Imperial Chemical Industries Ltd with assets employed of £4698 million as at 31 Dec 1980. Its staff and payroll averaged 143,000 during the year. The company, which has more than 300 UK and overseas subsidiaries, was formed on 7 Dec 1926 by the merger of four concerns—British Dyestuffs Corporation Ltd; Brunner, Mond & Co Ltd; Nobel Industries Ltd and United Alkali Co Ltd. The first chairman was Sir Alfred Moritz Mond (1868–1930), later the 1st Lord Melchett.

The net assets of The 'Shell' Transport and Trading Company, Ltd., at 31 Dec 1980 were £4,834,000,000, comprising mainly its 40 per cent share in the net assets of the Royal Dutch/Shell Group of Companies which stood at £12,039 million. Group companies employ 161,000. 'Shell' Transport was formed in 1897 by Marcus Samuel (1853–1927), later the 1st Viscount Bearsted.

Greatest profit and loss

The greatest net profit ever made by any corporation in 12 months is $6050 million (*£2750 million*) by American Telephone and Telegraph Co from 1 Dec 1979 to 30 Nov 1980.

The greatest loss ever recorded by private enterprise in a year was $1710 million (*£777.2 million*) by the car making Chrysler Corporation in 1980. The record loss was £545,000,000 by the nationalized British Steel Corporation in 1979–80. The record cost to the taxpayer in a year was £567,600,000 or £1079 per minute in 1975 by British Rail.

Greatest sales

The first company to surpass the $1 billion (US) mark in annual sales was the United States Steel Corporation in 1917. Now there are some 450 corporations with sales exceeding £1000 million including 285 from the United States. The list is headed by the Exxon Corporation of New York with $79,106,471,000 (*£35,957,488,000*) in 1979.

The top gross profits in the United Kingdom in *The Times 1,000 1979–80* was British Petroleum with £2,695 million. The biggest loss maker in *The Times 1,000 1979–80* was Govan Shipbuilders with £13,261,000.

Biggest work force

The greatest payroll of any single civilian organisation in the world is that of the USSR National Railway system with a total work force of 2,031,200 in 1976.

Largest take-over

The largest corporate cash take-over in commercial history has been the bid of $3650 million (*£1660 million*) by Shell Oil for the stock of Belridge Oil.

Largest merger

The largest merger ever mooted in British business was that of the Hill Samuel Group (£768 million assets) and Slater, Walker Securities (£469 million) in April 1973 with combined assets of £1237 million. This plan was called off on 19 June 1973.

Biggest write off

The largest reduction of assets in the history of private enterprise was the $800 million *£347 million* write off of Tristar aircraft development costs announced on 23 Nov 1974.

Greatest Bankruptcy

William G. Stern (b. Hungary, 1936), a US citizen since 1957, who set up Wilstar Group Holding Co in the London property market in 1971 was declared bankrupt for £104,390,248 in February 1979.

Companies

The number of companies on the register in Great Britain at 31 Dec 1980 was 828,496 of which 10,325 were public and the balance private companies.

Most directorships

The record for directorships was set in 1961 by Hugh T. Nicholson, formerly senior partner of Harmood Banner & Co, London who, as a liquidating chartered accountant, became director of all 451 companies of the Jasper group in 1961 and had 7 other directorships.

Advertising agency

The largest advertising agency in 1980, as listed in *Advertizing Age*, is Dentsu Incorporated of Japan with estimated billings of $2720 million (*£1236 million*). *Advertising Age* ranks J. Walter Thompson No 1 in Britain with 1980 billings of $323,039,440 (*£146,836,000*).

Biggest advertiser

The world's biggest advertiser is Sears Roebuck and Co, with $545,000,000 (*£248 million*) in 1980 excluding its catalogue.

Aircraft manufacturer

The world's largest aircraft manufacturer is the Boeing Company of Seattle, Washington, USA. The corporation's sales totalled $9,426,000,000 (*£4284 million*) in 1980 and it had 106,000 employees and assets valued at $5,931,000,000 (*then £2696 million*) at 1 Jan 1981. Cessna Aircraft Company of Wichita, Kansas, USA, in the year 1980, had total sales of $1,000,061,000 (*then £454.6 million*). The company has produced more than 167,500 aircraft since Clyde Cessna's first was built in 1911.

Airline *Largest*

The largest airline in the world is the USSR State airline 'Aeroflot', so named since 1932. This was instituted on 9 Feb 1923, with the title of Civil Air Fleet of the Council of Ministers of the USSR, abbreviated to 'Dobrolet'. It operates 1300 aircraft over about 560,000 miles *900 000 km* of routes, employs 400,000 people and carries 100 million passengers to over 105 countries. The commercial airline carrying the greatest number of passengers (April 1980) was Eastern Airlines of Miami, Florida, USA (formed 1938) with 39,052,000 passengers. The company had 40,000 employees and a fleet of 275 jet planes. In March 1981 British Airways were operating a fleet of 201 aircraft (including 36 helicopters). Staff employed on airline activities totalled 52,314 and 17.7 million passengers were carried in 1980 on 361,875 miles *582,381 km* of unduplicated routes.

Oldest

The oldest existing national airline is Koninklijke-Luchtvaart-Maatschappij NV (KLM) of the Netherlands, which opened its first scheduled service (Amsterdam–London) on 17 May 1920, having been established on 7 Oct 1919. One of the original constituents of BOAC, Handley-Page Transport Ltd, was founded in May 1919 and merged into Imperial Airways in 1924. Delag (Deutsche Luftschiffahrt AG) was founded at Frankfurt am Main on 16 Nov 1909 and started a scheduled airship service in June 1910. Chalk's International Airline has been flying amphibians between Miami, Florida and the Bahamas since July 1919. Albert 'Pappy' Chalk flew from 1911 to 1975.

Aluminium producer

The world's largest producer of primary aluminium is the Aluminum Company of America (Alcoa of Pittsburgh, USA) with its affiliated companies. The company had an output of 1,886,000 short tons *1,710,938 tonnes* in 1979. The Aluminum Company of Canada Ltd owns the largest aluminium smelter in the western world, at Arivda, Quebec, with a capacity of 475,000 short tons *431 000 tonnes* per annum. Alcan's total sales for the year 1980 were $5215 million (*then £2370 million*).

Art auctioneering

The largest and oldest firm of art auctioneers in the world is the Sotheby Parke Bernet Group of London and New York, founded in 1744. The turnover in 1979–80 was $553,229,950 (*£251,468,000*). The highest total for any house sale auction was theirs on 18–27 May 1977 at the 6th Earl of Rosebery's home at Mentmore, Buckinghamshire which reached £6,389,933 or *$10.9 million*. HM Government had turned down an offer of £2 million. The total realized at the Robert von Hirsch art sale at Sotheby's, London on 20–27 June 1978 was £18,468,348 (then $36 million).

Bank

The International Bank for Reconstruction and Development (founded 27 Dec 1945), the 'World Bank', a United Nations specialised agency, at 1818 H Street NW, Washington, DC, USA, has an authorized share capital of $43,000 million (*£19,545 million*). There were 139 members with a subscribed capital of $39,000 million (*£17,727 million*) at 30 June 1980. The International Monetary Fund in Washington, DC, USA has 141 members with total quotas of SDR 59,605.5 million (*$72,122.6 million or £32,783 million*) at 31 March 1981.

The private commercial bank with the greatest deposits is the Bank of America National Trust and Savings Association, of San Francisco, California, USA, with $88,426,156,000 (*£40,193,707,000*) at 31 Dec 1980. Its total assets were $111,617,291,000 (*£50,735,130,000*). Barclays Bank (with Barclays Bank International and other subsidiary companies) had some 5000 branches and offices in more than 75 countries (3000 in the United Kingdom) in December 1980. Deposits totalled 31,980 million and assets £37,097 million. The largest bank in the United Kingdom is the National Westminster with total assets of £34,569,000,000 and 3224 branches as at 31 Dec 1980. The bank with most branches is The State Bank of India with 7974 on 1 Jan 1981 with assets of £7,998,435,660.

Bank building

The world's tallest bank building is the Bank of Montreal's First Bank Tower, Toronto, Canada which has 72 stories and stands 935 ft *284,98 m*. The largest bank vault in the world, measuring

350 × 100 × 8 ft *106,7 × 30,4 × 2,4 m* and weighing 879 tons *893 tonnes* is in the Chase Manhattan Building, New York City, completed in May 1961. Its six doors weigh up to 40 tons *40,6 tonnes* apiece but each can be closed by the pressure of a forefinger.

Banquet Greatest *Outdoors*
The greatest banquet ever staged was that by President Loubet, President of France, in the gardens of the Tuileries, Paris, on 22 Sept 1900. He invited the mayors of France and their deputies ending up with 22,295 guests. With the Gallic *penchant* for round numbers, the event has always been referred to as 'le banquet des 100,000 maires'. It was estimated that some 30,000 attended a military feast at Radewitz, Poland on 25 June 1730 thrown by King August II (1709–33).

Indoors
The greatest number of people served indoors at a single sitting was 18,000 municipal leaders at the Palais de l'Industrie, Paris on 18 Aug 1889.

Most expensive
The menu for the main 5½ hr banquet at the Imperial Iranian 2500th Anniversary gathering at Persepolis in October 1971 was probably the most expensive ever compiled. It comprised quail eggs stuffed with Iranian caviar, a mousse of crayfish tails in Nantua sauce, stuffed rack of roast lamb, with a main course of roast peacock stuffed with *foie gras*, fig rings and raspberry sweet champagne sherbet, with wines including *Château Lafite-Rothschild* 1945 at £40 per bottle from the cellars of Maxime, Paris.

Barbers
The largest barbering establishment in the world was Norris of Houston, 3303 Audley, Houston, Texas, USA which employed 60 barbers.

Bicycle factory
The 64-acre *25,9 ha* plant of TI Raleigh Industries Ltd at Nottingham is the largest cycle factory in the world producing complete bicycles and components. The company employs 6,500 and has the capacity to make more than 2,000,000 bicycles.

Book shop
The book shop with most titles and the longest shelving (30 miles *48 km*) in the world is W. & G. Foyle Ltd, City of Westminster, Greater London. First established in 1904 in a small shop in Islington, the company is now at 119–125 Charing Cross Road. The area on one site is 75,825 ft² *7 044 m²*. The most capacious bookstore in the world measured by square footage is Barnes & Noble Bookstore of Fifth Ave at 18th Street, New York City, USA with 154,250 ft² *14 330 m²* and with 12.87 miles *20,71 km* of shelving.

The world's largest second-hand booksellers are Richard Booth (Bookseller) Ltd, of Hay-on-Wye, Powys, Wales with 8.65 miles *13,92 km* of shelving and a running stock of 900,000 to 1,100,000 in 30,091 ft² *2 795 m²* of selling space.

Brewer *Oldest*
The oldest brewery in the world is the Weihenstephan Brewery, Freising, near Munich, W. Germany, founded in AD 1040.

Largest World
The largest single brewer in the world is Anheuser-Busch, Inc in St Louis, Missouri, USA. In 1980 the company sold 50,200,000 US barrels, equivalent to 10,370 million Imp. pints, the greatest annual volume ever produced by a brewing company. The company's St Louis plant covers 100 acres *40,5 ha* and after completion of current modernization projects will have an annual capacity in excess of 12,000,000 US barrels *2478 million Imp. pints*. The largest brewery on a single site is Adolph Coors Co of Golden, Colorado, USA where 13.8 million barrels *3860 million Imperial pints* were sold in 1980.

Europe
The largest brewery in Europe is the Guinness Brewery at St James's Gate, Dublin, Ireland, which extends over 56.15 acres *22,72 ha*. The business was founded in 1759.

Great Britain
The largest brewing company in the United Kingdom based on its 8136 public houses, 985 off-licences and 82 hotels, is Bass Ltd. The company has net assets of £990,600,000, controls 13 breweries and has 63,056 employees (including bar-staff). Their sales figure for the year ending 30 Sept 1980 was £1,262,800,000.

Greatest exports
The largest exporter of beer, ale and stout in the world is Arthur Guinness, Son & Co Ltd, of Dublin, Ireland. Exports of Guinness from the Republic of Ireland in the 52 weeks ending 14 Mar 1981 were 867,676 bulk barrels (bulk barrel = 36 Imperial gallons), which is equivalent to 1,373,026 half pint glasses (*1,300,396 30-centilitre glasses*) per day.

Brickworks
The largest brickworks in the world is the London Brick Company plant at Stewartby, Bedfordshire. The works, established

Foreign Desk

The bustling newsroom of *The Financial Times* which keeps minute by minute tabs on the world's stock markets (see p. 161).

in 1898, now cover 221 acres *90 ha* and has a production capacity of 13,000,000 bricks and brick equivalent each week.

Building contractors
The largest construction company in the United Kingdom is George Wimpey Ltd (founded 1880), of London, who undertake building, civil, mechanical, electrical and chemical engineering work. With 40,000 employees worldwide the turnover of work was £1,216,000,000 in over 30 countries in 1980.

Building societies
The biggest building society in the world is the Halifax Building Society of Halifax, West Yorkshire. It was established in 1853 and has total assets exceeding £10,000,000,000. It has 10,453 employees and over 2000 offices.

Chemist shop chain
The largest chain of chemist shops in the world is Boots The Chemists, which has 1104 retail branches. The firm was founded by Jesse Boot (b. Nottingham, 1850), later the 1st Baron Trent, who died in 1931.

Chocolate factory
The world's largest chocolate factory is that built by Hershey Foods Corp in Hershey, Pennsylvania, USA in 1903–5. It now has 2,000,000 ft² *185,800 m²* of floor space.

Computer company
The world's largest computer firm is International Business Machines (IBM) Corporation of New York which has been resisting since 1969 the Justice Department's largest anti-trust suit. In 1980 assets were $26,703,000,000 (*£12,137 million*) and sales were $26,213,000,000 (*£11,915 million*). In Oct 1979 it made the largest public borrowing in corporate history with $1 billion.

Department stores *World*
F. W. Woolworth, who celebrated their centenary year in 1979, now operate a total of 6537 stores world wide. Frank W. Woolworth opened his first Five and Ten Cent Store in Utica, New York State on 22 Feb 1879. The 1980/81 earnings are $161 million (*£73,181,818*).

Great Britain
The largest department store in the United Kingdom is Harrods Ltd of Knightsbridge, Royal Borough of Kensington and Chelsea, Greater London named after Henry Charles Harrod, who opened a grocery in Knightsbridge Village in 1849. It has a total selling floor space of 16 acres *6,4 ha*, employs 4000 people and had a total of 15,261,673 transactions in 1980.

Highest sales per unit area
The department store with the fastest-moving stock in the world is the Marks & Spencer premier branch, known as 'Marble Arch' at 458 Oxford Street, City of Westminster, Greater London. The figure of £800 worth of goods per square foot of selling space per year is believed to be an understatement. The selling area is 90,400 ft² *8398 m²*. The company has 254 branches in the UK and operates on over 6 million ft² *558 000 m²* of selling space and now has stores on the Continent and Canada.

Distillery
The world's largest distilling company is The Seagram Company Ltd, of Canada. Its sales in the year ending 31 July 1980 totalled US $2,534,952,000 (*£1152 million*) of which $2,047,425,000 (*£930 million*) were from sales by Joseph E. Seagram & Sons, Inc in the United States. The group employs about 15,500 people, including about 11,000 in the United States.

The largest of all Scotch whisky distilleries is Carsebridge at Alloa, Central Region, Scotland, owned by Scottish Grain Distillers Limited. This distillery is capable of producing more than 40,000,000 litres *8,796,000 gal* of alcohol per annum. The largest establishment for blending and bottling Scotch whisky is owned by John Walker & Sons Limited at Kilmarnock, Strathclyde, where over 3 million bottles are filled each week. 'Johnnie Walker' is the world's largest-selling brand of Scotch whisky. The largest malt Scotch whisky distillery is the Tomatin Distillery, Highland, established at 1028 ft *313 m* above sea level in 1897, with an annual capacity of 5.0 million proof gallons. The world's largest-selling brand of gin is Gordon's.

Fisheries
The world's highest recorded catch of fish was 65 700 000 tonnes in 1973. Peru had the largest ever national haul with 12 160 000 tonnes in 1970 comprising mostly anchoveta. The United Kingdom's highest figure was 1 206 000 tonnes in 1948.

Largest net
The largest net yet manufactured is one that can fish 6.8 million m³ *8.8 million yd³* per hour announced from W. Germany in March 1974.

Grocery stores
The largest grocery chain in the world is Safeway Stores, Incorporated of Oakland, California, USA with sales in 1980 of $15,102,673,000 (*£6864 million*) and total current assets valued at $1,268,231,000 (*£576 million*) as at 3 Jan 1981. The company has 2425 stores totalling 62,069,000 ft² *5 766 210 m²*. The total payroll is 150,012.

Hotelier
The top revenue-earning hotel business is Holiday Inns Inc, with a 1980 revenue of $1500 million (*£680 million*), from 1750 inns (300,000 rooms) at 31 Dec 1980 in 59 countries. The business was founded by Charles Kemmons Wilson with his first inn in Summer Avenue, Memphis, Tennessee in 1952.

Insurance
It was estimated in 1978 that the total premiums paid in the United States first surpassed $100 billion (*then £52,600 million*) or $1,400 *£736* per household. The company with the highest volume of insurance in force in the world is the Prudential Insurance Company of America of Newark, New Jersey with $406,572 million (*£184,805 million*) at 31 Dec 1980, which is nearly twice the UK National Debt figure. The admitted assets are $59,778 million (*£27,171 million*).

Great Britain
The largest life assurance company in the United Kingdom is the Prudential Corporation Ltd. At 1 Jan 1981 the tangible assets were £9,969,700,000 and the total amount assured was £45,207,200,000.

Life policies Largest
The largest life assurance policy ever written in Britain was one of £10,000,000 (*then $25,000,000*) for James Derrick Slater (b. 13 Mar 1929), when he was Chairman of Slater, Walker Securities, the City of London Investment bankers. The existence of the policy was made known on 3 June 1971.

Highest pay-out
The highest pay-out on a single life has been some $18 million (*then £7.5 million*) to Mrs Linda Mullendore, wife of an Oklahoma rancher, reported on 14 Nov 1970. Her murdered husband had paid $300,000 in premiums in 1969.

Marine
The largest ever marine insurance loss was the 153,480 grt VLCC (Very Large Crude Carrier), *Energy Determination*. This vessel which was insured at Lloyds and valued at £26.8 million, exploded in the strait of Hormuz on 12 Dec 1979. The 83,000 grt LNG (Liquid Natural Gas) Carrier *Aquarius* built in 1977 by General Dynamics Corporation, Massachusetts, USA is currently insured for $175 million *£103 million*. This vessel is owned by Wilmington Trust Company, Delaware, USA, and chartered to the Burmah Oil Co., Ltd.

The largest sum claimed for consequential losses is $1700 million against owning, operating and building corporations, and Claude Phillips resulting from the 66 million gallon oil spill from M. T. *Amoco Cadiz* on the Brittany Coast on 16 Mar 1978.

A claim for $300 million (*then £127.6 million*) was provisionally agreed by Lloyd's on 31 July 1980 in connection with alleged structural defects in three liquified natural gas carriers being built for El Paso Natural Gas at Avondale Shipyards, New Orleans, Louisiana, USA.

Land *Owner*

The world's largest landowner is the United States Government, with a holding of 775,249,000 acres (1,210,000 miles[2] *3 133 000 km²*) which is more than the area of the world's 8th largest country Argentina and 12.8 times larger than the United Kingdom. The world's largest *private* landowner is reputed to be International Paper Co with 9 million acres *3,64-million ha*. The United Kingdom's greatest ever private landowner was the 3rd Duke of Sutherland, George Granville Sutherland-Leveson-Gower, KG (1828–92), who owned 1,358,000 acres *549 560 ha* in 1883. Currently the largest landholder in Great Britain is the Forestry Commission (instituted 1919) with 3,032,000 acres *1 227 000 ha*. Currently the landowner with the largest known acreage is the 9th Duke of Buccleuch (b. 1923) with 336,000 acres *136,035 ha*. The longest tenure is that by St Paul's Cathedral of land at Tillingham, Essex, given by King Ethelbert before AD 616.

Value Highest

The world's most expensive land is in central Tōkyō, Japan. It is estimated that one square meter of the Tamagama Takashimaya Shopping Centre is worth 12 million yen (*£23,600*) (*£2167 per ft²*). The real estate value per square metre of the two topmost French vineyards, Grande and Petite Cognac vineyards in Bordeaux, has not been recently estimated. The freehold price for a grave site with excellent *Fung Shui* in Hong Kong may cost HK$200,000 for 4 ft × 10 ft or *£19,400 per ft²*. The China Square Inch Land Ltd at a charity auction on 2 Dec 1977 sold 1 cm² *0.155 in²* of land at Sha Tau Kok for HK$2000 (the equivalent of US$17,405,833,737 per acre). The purchasers were Stephen and Tony Nicholson. The most expensive land in Britain is that in the City of London. The freehold price on small prime sites reached £1950/ft² (*£21,230/m²*) in mid 1973.

Greatest auction

The greatest auction was that at Anchorage, Alaska on 11 Sept 1969 for 179 tracts comprising 450,858 acres *182 455 ha* of the oil-bearing North Slope, Alaska. An all-time record bid of $72,277,133 for a 2560 acre *1036 ha* lease was made by the Amerada Hess Corporation—Getty Oil consortium. This £30,115,472 bid indicated a price of $28,233 (*then £11,763*) per acre.

Highest rent

The highest recorded rentals in the world are for prime site shop premises in Hong Kong at US$200 per ft² per *month* or *£120 per ft²* p.a.

Lowest rent

The rent for a 3 room apartment in the Fuggerei in Augsburg, West Germany, since it was built by Jacob Fugger in 1519, has been 1 Rhine guilder, now 1.72 DMk or 31½p. Fugger was the 'millionaire' philanthropist who pioneered social welfare.

Mineral water

The world's largest mineral water firm is Source Perrier, near Nîmes, France with an annual production of more than 2,100,000,000 bottles, of which 1,200,000,000 now come from Perrier and Contrexeville. The French drink about 50 litres *88 pt* of mineral water per person per year.

Motor car manufacturer *Largest World*

In 1980 Japan with 11,043,000 vehicles overtook the USA as the world's No 1 motor manufacturer. The largest manufacturing company in the world is General Motors Corporation of Detroit, Michigan, USA. During 1980 worldwide sales totalled $57,729,000,000 (*£26,240 million*). Its assets at 31 Dec 1980 were valued at $34,581,000,000 (*£15,719 million*). Its total 1980 payroll was $17,799,000,000 (*£8090 million*) to an average of 746,000 employees. Dividends paid in 1979 were $1,533,200,000 (*£696,909,000*).

Great Britain

The largest British manufacturer was BL Ltd with 587,000 vehicles produced and a sales turnover of £2877 million of which £1246 million was overseas sales in 180 markets in 1980. Direct exports of £880 million make BL Britain's largest net earner of foreign currency.

Largest plant

The largest single automobile plant in the world is the Volkswagenwerk, Wolfsburg, West Germany, with 57,000 employees and a capacity for about 4000 vehicles daily. The surface area of the factory buildings is 363 acres *147 ha* and that of the whole plant 4895 acres *1980 ha* with 43.5 miles *70 km* of rail sidings.

Salesmanship

The all-time record for automobile salesmanship in units sold individually in 1425 in 1973 by Joe Girard of Detroit, USA, author of *How to Sell Anything to Anybody*, winner of the No. Car Salesman title each year in 1966–77. His lifetime total of one-at-a-time 'belly to belly' selling was 13,001 sales, all retail. He retired on 1 Jan 1978 to teach others his art and has now had published *How to Sell Yourself*.

Oil company

The world's largest oil company is the Exxon Corporation (formerly Standard Oil Company [New Jersey]), with 177,000 employees and assets valued at $56,576,558,000 (*£25,716 million*) on 1 Jan 1981.

Oil refineries *Largest*

The world'd largest refinery has been the Amerada Hess refinery in St Croix, Virgin Islands with an annual capacity of 34 million tonnes *33.46 million tons*. The largest oil refinery in the United Kingdom is the Esso Refinery at Fawley, Hampshire. Opened in 1921 and much expanded in 1951, it has a capacity of *15.6 million tonnes*/tons per year. The total investment together with the associated chemical plant, on the 1300 acre *526 ha* site is £217 million. The area occupied by the Shell Stanlow Refinery at Ellesmere Port, Cheshire, founded in 1922, and now with a capacity of 18 million tonnes per year in 2000 acres *810 ha*.

Paper mills

The world's largest paper mill is that established in 1936 by the Union Camp Corporation at Savannah, Georgia, USA, with an all-time record output in 1980 of 1,038,656 short tons *942 246 tonnes*. The largest paper mill in the United Kingdom is the Bowaters Kemsley Mill near Sittingbourne, Kent with a complex covering an area of 260 acres *105 ha* and a capacity in excess of 371,000 tons/*tonnes* a year.

Pharmaceuticals

Hoechst of West Germany is the worlds largest pharmaceutical company and is one of the worlds largest 3 chemical companies with a turnover of DM29,915 million (*£6650 million*) in 1980. Britain's largest drug *and* food turnover in 1979–80 was by Glaxo with £618,135,000.

Photographic store

The photographic store with the largest selling area is Jessop of Leicester Ltd's Photo Centre, Hinckley Road, Leicester opened in June 1979 with an area of 20,000 ft² *1858 m²*.

Pop-corn plant

The largest pop-corn plant in the world is The House of Clark Ltd (instituted 1933) of Dagenham, Essex, which in 1979–80 produced 65,000,000 packets of pop-corn.

Public relations

The world's largest public relations firm is Hill and Knowlton Inc of 633 Third Avenue, New York City, NY, USA and fifteen other US cities. The firm employs a full-time staff of more than 1000 and also maintains offices in 22 overseas cities.

The world's pioneer public relations publication is *Public Relations News*, founded by Mrs Denny Griswold in 1944 and which now circulates in 86 countries.

Publishing

The publishing company generating most net revenue is Time Inc of New York City with $2881.8 million (*£1309.9 million*) in 1980. Britain's largest publisher is the International Publishing Corporation Ltd, a subsidiary of Reed International Ltd, with publishing turnover of £400 million as at March 1981. The largest educational book publishing concern in the world is the Book Division of McGraw-Hill Inc of New York with sales of $355,340,000 (*£161.5 million*) in 1980 with 1470 new titles.

Restaurateurs

The largest restaurant chain in the world is that operated by

McDonald's Corporation of Oakbrook, Illinois, USA, founded on 15 April 1955 in Des Plaines, Chicago by Ray A. Kroc BH (Bachelor of Hamburgerology). By 1 Jan 1981 the number of McDonald's restaurants licensed and owned in 26 countries and 3 US territories reached 6263, with an aggregate throughput of 35 billion 100 per cent beef hamburgers under the motto 'Q.S.C. & V.'—for quality, (fast) service, cleanliness and value. Sales systemwide in 1980 were $6226 million (*£2830 million*). The largest hotel, catering and leisure group in the United Kingdom is Trusthouse Forte who employ up to 52,000 full and part-time staff in the UK, 16,000 overseas, and who had a turnover of £772,000,000 in 1979–80. They have 801 hotels world-wide.

Fish and chip restaurant
The world's largest fish and chip shop is Harry Ramsden's, White Cross, Guiseley, West Yorkshire with 180 staff serving 1,600,000 customers per annum, who consumed 290 tons of fish and 450 tons of potatoes.

Retailer
The largest retailing firm in the world is Sears, Roebuck and Co (founded by Richard Warren Sears in North Redwood railway station, Minnesota in 1886) of Chicago, Illinois, USA. World-wide revenues were $25,195,000,000 (*£11,452 million*) in the year ending 31 Jan 1981 when its merchandise group had 854 retail stores and 2778 catalogue, retail and telephone sales offices and independent catalogue merchants in the USA and total assets valued at $28,053,800,000 (*£12,750 million*).

Ship-building
In 1980 there were 13,101,104 tons gross of ships, excluding sailing ships, barges and vessels of less than 100 tons, completed throughout the world. The figures for the USSR and People's Republic of China are incomplete. Japan completed 6,094,142 tons gross (46.52 per cent of the world total). The United Kingdom ranked sixth with 427,122 tons gross. The world's leading shipbuilding firm in 1980 was the Mitsubishi Heavy Industries Co of Japan, which completed 31 vessels of 629,114 gross tons. Physically the largest ship yard in the United Kingdom is Harland and Wolff Ltd of Queen's Island, Belfast, which covers some 300 acres *120 ha*.

Shipping line
The largest shipping owners and operators in the world are the Royal Dutch/Shell Group of Companies (see page 156), whose fleets of owned/managed and chartered ships at 31 Dec 1980 comprised 199 oil tankers (totalling 24 million dwt), 12 gas carriers (totalling 784 000 m³ *1,026,000 yd³* capacity) and 12 dry bulk carriers (1.1 million dwt).

The largest individual ship owner in the world is C. Y. Tung of Hong Kong.

Shopping centre
The world's first shopping centre was Roland Park Shopping Center, Baltimore, Maryland built in 1896. The world's largest shopping centre is the Lakewood Center, California with a gross building area of 2,451,438 ft² *227 745 m²* on a 168 acre *67,9 ha* site with parking for 12,500 cars. The world's largest wholesale merchandise mart is the Dallas Market Center, located on Stemmons Freeway, Dallas, Texas, USA with more than 7 million ft² *650 300 m²* in 6 buildings. The complex covers 135 acres *54 ha* with some 3000 permanent showrooms displaying merchandise of more than 22,000 manufacturers. The center attracts 600,000 buyers each year to its 30 annual markets and trade shows. Britain's largest shopping centre is that at Central Milton Keynes, Buckinghamshire opened at a cost of £40 million in August 1979. The 650 m *2132 ft* long building contains 1,002,275 ft² *93 114 m²* of rentable retail space in 130 shop units.

Soft drinks
The world's most profitable soft drink is Coca-Cola with over 240,000,000 drinks sold per day by the end of 1980 in more than 135 countries. Coke was launched as a tonic by Dr John S. Pemberton of Atlanta, Georgia in 1886. The Coca-Cola Company was formed in 1892 and the famous bottle was patented in 1915.

Steel company *World*
The world's largest producer of steel has been Nippon Steel of Tōkyō, Japan which produced 32.93 million tons *33,45 million-tonnes* of steel and steel products in 1980. The Fukuyama

Works of Nippon Kokan has a capacity of more than 16 000 000 tonnes/*tons* per annum. Its work force is 76,000.

Great Britain
Britain's largest steelworks are those at Scunthorpe, Humberside, which have a capacity of 2.7 million tonnes/*tons* and employ 11,956 people on a 2500 acre *1000 ha* site.

STOCK EXCHANGES
The oldest Stock Exchange of the 138 listed throughout the world is that of Amsterdam, in the Netherlands, founded in 1602.

Most markings
The highest number of markings received in one day on the London Stock Exchange was 32,665 on 14 Oct 1959 following the 1959 General Election. The record for a year is 4,396,175 'marks' in the year ending 31 Mar 1960. There were 7353 securities (*cf*. 9749 peak in June 1973) listed at 31 Dec 1980. Their total nominal value was £138,021 million (gilt-edged £81,676 million) and their market value was £360,745 million (gilt-edged £70,653 million).

The highest figure of *The Financial Times* Industrial Ordinary share index (1 July 1935 = 100) was 558.6 on 4 May 1979. The lowest figure was 49.4 on 26 June 1940. The greatest rise in a day has been 23.7 points to 315.5 on 1 July 1975 in anticipation of anti-inflationary measures, and the greatest fall in a day was 24.0 to 313.8 on 1 Mar 1974 on the realization of a fourth post-war Labour Government.

Highest par value
The highest denomination of any share quoted in the world is a single share in F. Hoffmann-La Roche of Basel worth Sw. Fr 101 000 (*£21,992*) on 23 Apr 1976. The record for the London Stock Exchange is £100 for preference shares in Baring Brothers & Co Ltd, the bankers.

U.S. records
The highest index figure on the Dow Jones average (instituted 8 Oct 1896) of selected industrial stocks at the close of a day's trading was 1051.70 on 11 Jan 1973, when the average of the daily 'highs' of the 30 component stocks was 1067.20. The old record trading volume in a day on the New York Stock Exchange of 16,410,030 shares on 29 Oct 1929, the 'Black Tuesday' of the famous 'crash' was unsurpassed until April 1968. The record day's trading was 92,881,420 shares on 7 Jan 1981. The Dow Jones industrial average, which reached 381.71 on 3 Sept 1929, plunged 30.57 points on 29 Oct 1929, on its way to the Depression's lowest point of 41.22 on 8 July 1932. The largest decline in a day, 38.33 points, occurred on 28 Oct 1929. The total lost in security values from 1 Sept 1929 to 30 June 1932 was $74,000 million (*then £23,000 million*). The greatest paper loss in a year was $209,957 million (*then £87,500 million*) in 1974. The record daily increase of 28.40 on 30 Oct 1929 was most recently bettered on 1 Nov 1978 with 35.34 points to 827.79. The largest transaction on record 'share-wise' was on 14 Mar 1972 for 5,245,000 shares of American Motors at $7.25 each. The largest stock trade in the history of the New York Exchange was a 1,874,300 share block of Cutler-Hammer stock at $55 in a $103,086,500 (*£54½ million*) transaction on 12 June 1978. The highest price paid for a seat on the NY Stock Exchange was $515,000 (*then £214,580*) in 1969. The lowest 20th century price was $17,000 in 1942. The value of stocks listed on the New York Stock Exchange passed $1 trillion in 1981—$1,189,186 million on 31 Jan 1981.

Largest and smallest equity
The greatest aggregate market value of any corporation at year end was $46.8 billion (*then £19,500 million*) at a closing price of $402 multiplied by the 116,400,000 shares of IBM extant on 31 Dec 1972.

Britain's smallest public company is Dura Mill Ltd of Whitworth, Lancashire producers of very high quality yarn with a capitalization of £24,000 in 60 p shares.

Greatest personal loss
The highest recorded personal paper losses on stock values have

The Ingenio de San Cristobal sugar mill in Veracruz, Mexico which set a record for sugar output in one year. (*Mary Saint Albans*)

been those of Ray A. Kroc, Chairman of McDonald's Corporation with $64,901,718 (*then £27 million*) on 8 July 1974 and Edwin H. Land, President of Polaroid Corporation with $59,397,355 on 28–29 May 1974, when Polaroid stock closed $12.12 down at 43¼ on the day.

Largest new issue
The American Telegraph & Telephone Company offered $1375 million's worth of shares in a rights offer on 27,500,000 shares of convertible preferred stock on the New York market on 2 June 1971. The largest offering on the London Stock Exchange by a United Kingdom company was the £186 million rights offer of Consolidated Gold Fields Ltd on 17 Nov 1980.

Largest investment house
The largest investment company in the USA, and once the world's largest partnership with 124 partners, before becoming a corporation in 1959, is Merrill, Lynch, Pierce, Fenner & Smith Inc (founded 6 Jan 1914) of New York City, USA. Its parent, Merrill, Lynch and Co, has assets of $13.2 billion, 31,704 employees, 706 offices and 2.5 million separate accounts. The firm is referred to in the United States stock exchange circles as 'We' or 'We, the people' or 'The Thundering Herd'.

Largest store
The world's largest store is R. H. Macy & Co Inc at Broadway and 34th Street, New York City, NY, USA. It covers 50.5 acres *20,3 ha* and employs 12,000 who handle 400,000 items. The sales of the company and its subsidiaries in 1980 were $2,373,531,000 (*£1079 million*). Mr Rowland Hussey Macy's sales on his first day at his fancy goods store on 6th Avenue, on 27 Oct 1858, were recorded as $11.06 (*then £2.20*).

Sugar Mill
The highest recorded output for any sugar mill was set in 1966–67 by Ingenio de San Cristobal y Anexas, S.A., Veracruz, Mexico with 247,900 tonnes refined from 2,886,074 tonnes of cane ground.

Largest supermarket
The largest supermarket in the United Kingdom is Carrefour in Bristol. Currently it has a selling area of 90,000 ft² *8360 m²* and parking space for 1700 cars. The turnover exceeds £1 million per week. Self-service single level stores with a gross area of more than 50,000 ft² *5000 m²* are commonly referred to as hypermarkets.

Tobacco company
Subsidiary and affiliates of B.A.T. Industries (founded in London in 1902 as British-American Tobacco Co.) comprise the world's largest tobacco concern. They operate 118 tobacco factories in 54 countries: consolidated turnover in 1980 was £4331 million and total assets were £1716 million at 31 Dec 1980. The Group's sales in 1980 topped 560,000 million cigarettes.

The world's largest cigarette plant is the $300 million Philip Morris plant at Richmond, Virginia, USA opened in October 1974. Employing 5500 people the facility produces more than 500 million cigarettes a day.

Toy manufacturer
The world's largest single manufacturer of toys is Mattel Inc of Hawthorne, Los Angeles, USA founded in 1945. Its total sales for the year ending 31 Jan 1980 were $915,690,000 (*£416.2 million*) for 4 divisions of which Mattel Toys is the largest.

Toy shop
The world's biggest toy shop is Hamleys of Regent Street Ltd founded in 1760 in Holborn and removed to Regent Street London, W1 in 1901. It has selling space of 30,000 ft² *2787 m* on 11 floors with over 300 employees during the Christmas season. It was taken over by Debenhams on 12 May 1976.

Vintners
The oldest champagne firm is Ruinart Père et Fils founded in 1729. The oldest cognac firm is Augier Frères & Co, established in 1643.

2. MANUFACTURED ARTICLES

Guinness Superlatives Ltd has published specialist volumes entitled English Pottery and Porcelain (price £7.95), Antique Firearms (price £7.95) and the Guinness Book of Antiques by John FitzMaurice Mills (price £7.95).

Antique *Largest*
The largest antique ever sold has been London Bridge in March 1968. The sale was made by Mr Ivan F. Luckin of the Court of Common Council of the Corporation of London to the McCulloch Oil Corporation of Los Angeles, California, USA for $2,460,000 (*then £1,029,000*). The 10,000 tons/*tonnes* of façade stonework were re-assembled at a cost of £3 million, at Lake Havasu City, Arizona and 're-dedicated' on 10 Oct 1971.

Armour *Most Expensive*
The highest auction price paid for a suit of armour is £25,000 paid in 1924 for the Pembroke suit of armour, made at Greenwich in the 16th century, for the 2nd Earl of Pembroke.

Heaviest
The armour of William Somerset, 3rd Earl of Worcester made at the Royal Workshop, Greenwich *c.* 1570 weighed 81 lb 9 oz *37,0 kg*. If his five bullet-proof exchange elements were substituted the total weight reaches 133 lb 13 oz *60,7 kg*.

Art Nouveau
The highest auction price for any piece of art noveau is $360,000 (*then £163,600*) for a spider-web leaded glass mosaic and bronze table lamp by L. C. Tiffany at Christie's, New York on 8 Apr 1980.

Beds *Largest*
In Bruges, Belgium, Philip, Duke of Burgundy had a bed 12½ ft wide and 19 ft long *3,81 × 5,79 m* erected for the perfunctory *coucher officiel* ceremony with Princess Isabella of Portugal in 1430. The largest bed in Great Britain is the Great Bed of Ware, dating from *c.* 1580, from the Crown Inn, Ware, Hertfordshire, now preserved in the Victoria and Albert Museum, London. It is 10 ft 8½ in wide, 11 ft 1 in long and 8 ft 9 in tall *3,26 × 3,37 × 2,66 m*. The largest bed currently marketed in the United Kingdom is a Super Size Diplomat bed, 9 ft wide by 9 ft long, *2,74 m²* from The London Bedding Centre, Sloane Street, SW1 which would cost more than £4000.

Heaviest
The heaviest bed is a water bed 9 ft 7 in × 9 ft 10 in *2,92 × 2,99 m* owned by Milan Vacek of Canyon Country, California since 1977. The thermostatically heated water alone weighs 4205 lb *1907 kg*.

Beer cans
Beer cans date from a test marketing by Krueger Beer of Newark, New Jersey at Richmond, Virginia in 1935. The largest collection is claimed by John F. Ahrens of Mount Laurel, New Jersey with 13,000 *different* cans. A Rosalie Pilsner can sold for $6000 (*then £2700*) in the US in April 1981.

Beer mats

The world's largest collection of beer mats is owned by Leo Pisker of Vienna, who had collected nearly 84,000 different mats from 147 countries by April 1981. The largest collection of purely British mats is 23,404 by Charles M. Schofield of Glasgow by April 1981.

Blanket

The largest blanket ever made measured 68 × 100 ft *20,7 × 30,48 m* weighing 600 lb *272 kg*. It was knitted in 20,160 6-in *15,24 cm* squares in 10 months (October 1977–July 1978) by *Woman's Weekly* readers for Action Research for The Crippled Child. It was shown on BBC TV *Record Breakers* in October 1978.

Candle

A candle 80 ft *24,38 m* high and 8½ ft *2,59 m* in diameter was exhibited at the 1897 Stockholm Exhibition by the firm of Lindahls. The overall height was 127 ft *38,70 m*.

Carpets and rugs *Earliest*

The earliest carpet known is a woollen pile-knotted carpet, red on white ground excavated at Pazyryk, USSR in 1947, dated to the 5th century BC and now preserved in Leningrad.

Largest

Of ancient carpets the largest on record was the gold-enriched silk carpet of Hashim (dated AD 743) of the Abbasid caliphate in Baghdad, Iraq. It is reputed to have measured 180 by 300 ft *54,86 × 91,44 m*.

The world's largest carpet now consists of 88,000 ft[2] (over two acres *or 0,81 ha*) of maroon carpeting in the Coliseum exhibition hall, Columbus Circle, New York City, NY, USA. This was first used for the International Automobile Show on 28 Apr 1956.

Most expensive

The most magnificent carpet ever made was the Spring carpet of Khusraw made for the audience hall of the Sassanian palace at Ctesiphon, Iraq. It was about 7000 ft[2] *650 m[2]* of silk, gold thread and encrusted with emeralds. It was cut up as booty by military looters in AD 635 and from the known realization value of the pieces must have had an original value of some £100,000,000. In 1946 the Metropolitan Museum, New York, privately paid $1 million (*then £248,138*) for the 26.5 × 13.6 ft *807 × 414 cm* Anhalt Medallion carpet made in Tabriz or Kashan, Persia c. 1590. The highest price ever paid at auction for a carpet is £121,000 for a Mamluk carpet 12 ft 5 in × 7 ft 3 in *378 × 220 cm* presumed woven in Cairo c. 1500, at Sotheby's Bond Street Salerooms, London on 29 Mar 1978.

Most finely woven

The most finely woven carpet known is one with more than 2490 knots per in[2] *38,6 per cm[2]* from a fragment of an Imperial Mughal prayer carpet of the 17th century now in the Altman collections in the Metropolitan Museum of Art, New York City, NY, USA.

Ceramics

The auction record for any ceramic object is £420,000 for the 16¼ in *41,2 cm* Ming blue and white bottle dated 1403–24 acquired by Mrs Helen Glatz, a London dealer, at Sotheby Parke Bernet, London on 2 Apr 1974. The Greek urn painted by Ueuphromios and thrown by Euxitheos in c. 530 BC was bought by private treaty by the Metropolitan Museum of Art, New York for $1.3 million (*then £541,666*) in August 1972.

Chair *Largest*

The world's largest chair is the 9 m *29 ft 6¼ in* tall 4,2 m *13 ft 9¼ in* wide chair outside the Edsbyverken furniture factory in Edsbyn, Sweden since 1944.

Most expensive

The highest price ever paid for a single chair is $85,000 (*then £35,000*) for the John Brown Chippendale mahogany corner chair attributed to John Goddard of Newport, Rhode Island, USA and made in c. 1760. This piece was included in the collection of Mr Lansdell K. Christie dispersed by Sotheby Parke Bernet, New York on 21 Oct 1972.

The World's largest functional Christmas cracker, 56 ft 7 in *17,24 m* in length (see below).

Chandelier *Largest*

The world's largest chandelier was built in Murano, Italy in 1953 for the Casino Knokke, Belgium. It measures 8 m *26 ft 3 in* in circumference and 7 m *23 ft* in height and weighs 37 tons/ *tonnes* with 1896 electric lights.

Christmas cracker

The largest functional cracker ever constructed was one 56 ft 7 in *17,24 m* in length and 9½ ft *2,9 m* in diameter built for British Rail Hull Paragon Station and pulled on 21 Nov 1980.

Cigars *Largest*

The largest smokeable cigar in existence is one 2,78 m *9 ft 1½ in* long, 32,4 cm *12¾ in* in circumference and weighing 27,3 kg *60 lb 3 oz*. It was made by J. P. Schmidt Jnr, Fredericia, Denmark and exhibited in May 1979.

The largest marketed cigar in the world is the 27,8 cm *10.94 in* long Sabah Queen from North Borneo. The Partagas factory in Havana, Cuba, manufactures special gift cigars 50 cm *19.7 in* long, which retail in Europe for £8. Russos' Restaurant, Union Street, San Francisco has the largest known collection of cigar bands with 5000; some dating from 1860.

Most expensive

The most expensive standard cigar in the world is the Montecristo 'A', which retails in Britain at £5.82.

Most voracious smokers

Jim Purol and Mike Papa each smoked 135 cigarettes simultaneously for 5 min on 5 Oct 1978 at Rameys Lounge, Detroit, Michigan, USA. Paul Mears (University of Winnipeg, Manitoba, Canada) won a contest by smoking 35 full-size cigars simultaneously in 1975.

Cigarettes *Consumption*

The heaviest smokers in the world are the people of the United States, where 665,000 million cigarettes (an average of 3900 per adult) were consumed at a cost of some $15,000 million (*£7,900 million*) in 1977. The people of China however were estimated to consume 725,000 million in 1977. The peak consumption in the United Kingdom was 3230 cigarettes per adult in 1973. The peak volume was 243,100,000 lb *110,2 million kg* in 1961, compared with 218,000,000 lb *98,9 million kg* in 1978 when 125,200 million cigarettes were sold.

In the United Kingdom 59 per cent of adult men and 42 per cent of adult women smoke.

Tar/Nicotine content

Of the 132 brands most recently analysed for the Dept of Health and Social Security, the ones with highest tar/nicotine content are *Pall Mall King Size* with 27/2.2 mg and *Capstan Full Strength* with 26/2.7 mg per cigarette. *Silk Cut Ultra Mild, Embassy Ultra Mild* and *John Player King Size Ultra Mild* with < 4/0.3 are at the lower risk end of the league table.

Most popular

The world's most popular cigarette is 'Marlboro', a filter cigarette made by Phillip Morris, which sold 222,800 million units in 1980. The largest selling British cigarette in 1979 was *Benson and Hedges King Size*. The Wills brand 'The Three Castles' was introduced in 1878.

Longest and shortest

The longest cigarettes ever marketed were 'Head Plays', each 11 in *27,9 cm* long and sold in packets of 5 in the United States in about 1930, to save tax. The shortest were 'Lilliput' cigarettes, each 1¼ in *31,7 mm* long, and ⅛ in *3 mm* in diameter, made in Great Britain in 1956.

Largest collection

The world's largest collection of cigarettes is that of Robert E. Kaufman, MD, of 950 Park Avenue, New York City 28, NY, USA. In April 1980 he had 7495 different cigarettes with 43 kinds of tips made in 170 countries. The oldest brand represented is 'Lone Jack', made in the USA in *c.* 1885. Both the longest and shortest (see above) are represented.

Cigarette cards

The earliest known tobacco card is 'Vanity Fair' dated 1876 issued by Wm S. Kimball & Co., Rochester, New York. The earliest British example appeared *c.* 1883 in the form of a calendar issued by Allen & Ginter, of Richmond, Virginia, trading from Holborn Viaduct, City of London. The largest known collection is that of Mr Edward Wharton-Tigar, MBE (b. 1913) of London with a collection of more than 1,000,000 cigarette and trade cards in about 45,000 sets. The highest price paid for a card was $3500 in the U.S. in 1975 for one of the 6 known baseball series cards of Honus Wagner who was a non-smoker.

Cigarette lighter *Most expensive*

The most expensive cigarette pocket lighter in the world is the 18 carat gold and platinum Dunhill lighter, featuring the Union Jack comprising 73 precious stones (diamonds, rubies and sapphires) and selling for $20,000 (*£10,000*) at Dunhill's in New York in 1979. The 18 carat lighthouse table lighter, made by Alfred Dunhill Ltd of St James's, City of Westminster, Greater London, set on an island of amethyst retails for a record £32,500.

Cigarette packets

The earliest surviving cigarette packet is the Finnish 'Petit Canon' packet for 25, made by Tollander & Klärich in 1860 from the Ventegodt Collection. The rarest is the Latvian 700-year anniversary (1201–1901) Riga packet, believed to be unique, from the same collection. The largest private collection is claimed by Roger W. Christiansen of Wisconsin, USA with over 60,000 unduplicated packages.

Credit card collection

The largest collection of valid credit cards at 1 May 1981 is one of 1098 (all different) by Walter Cavanagh (b. 1943) of Santa Clara, California, USA. The cost of acquisition to 'Mr. Plastic Fantastick' was nil, and he keeps them in the world's longest wallet—250 ft *76,2 m* long weighing 34 lb *15,42 kg* worth more than $1.25 million in credit.

Curtain

The largest curtain ever built has been the bright orange-red 4 ton *4064 kg* 185 ft *56 m* high curtain suspended 1350 ft *411 m* across the Rifle Gap, Grand Hogback, Colorado, USA by the Bulgarian-born sculptor Christo, 46 (*né* Javacheff) on 10 Aug 1971. It blew apart in a 50 mph *80 km/h* gust 27 hr later. The total cost involved in displaying this work of art was $750,000 (*then £312,500*).

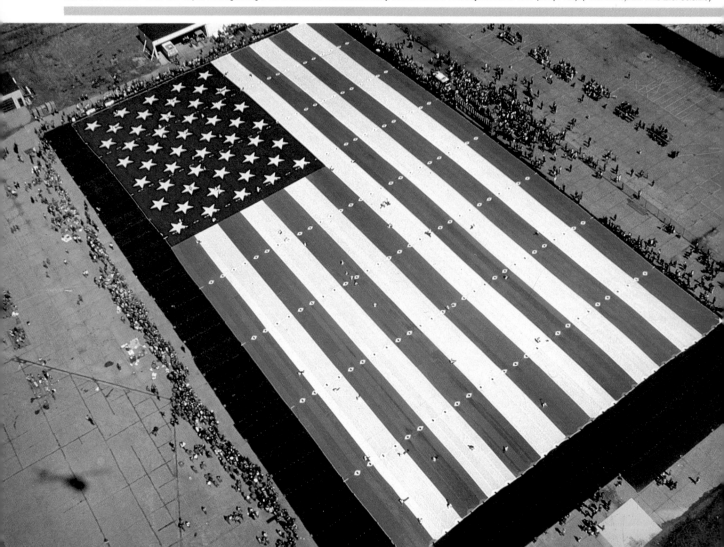

The 86,310 ft² *8018 m²* 'Stars and Stripes' the largest flag in the world which was ceremoniously unfurled in New York City on 2 June 1981 (see p. 165). (*Peter B. Kaplan: Time Life: Colorific*)

The world's largest functional curtain is one 550 ft long × 65 ft high *167,6 × 19,8 m* in the Brabazon Hanger at British Aerospace Filton, Bristol used to enclose aircraft in the paint spraying bay. It is electrically drawn.

Dolls

The highest price paid at auction for dolls is £16,000 for a pair of William and Mary painted wooden dolls in original clothes, 22 in *55,8 cm* high at Sotheby's, London on 19 Apr 1974. After an export licence was refused they were purchased, following a public subscription, by the Victoria and Albert Museum, London. A rag doll 27 ft *8,2 m* in height was made at Macy's, New York City, USA on 26 Aug 1979.

Dress *Most expensive*

The dress with the highest price tag ever exhibited by a Paris fashion house was one in the Schiaparelli spring/summer collection on 23 Jan 1977. 'The Birth of Venus' designed by Serge Lepage with 512 diamonds was priced at Fr. 7,500,000 (*£880,000*).

Emperor Jean-Bédel Bokassa's coronation robe with a 39 ft *11,8 m* long train was encrusted with 785,000 pearls and 1,220,000 crystal beads by Guiselin of Paris for £77,125 for use at Bangui, Central African Empire in December 1977.

Fabrics *Earliest and Most expensive*

The oldest surviving fabric discovered from Level VI A at Çatal Hüyük, Turkey has been radio-carbon dated to 5900 BC.

The most expensive fabric obtainable is an evening-wear fabric 37½ in *95 cm* wide, hand embroidered, sequinned and pearl-beaded in a series of designs on pure silk grounds. One design has as many as 25,000 sequins and pearls per sq metre *29,900 per sq yard* and is designed by Alan Hershman of Duke St, London; it cost £290 per metre in April 1980.

Finest cloth

The most expensive cloth, the brown-grey throat hair of Indian goats, is Shatoosh (or Shatusa), finer, and more expensive than Vicuña. It is sold by Neiman-Marcus of Dallas, Texas, USA, at $1000 (£526) per yard but supplies have now dried up.

Firework

The largest firework ever produced was *Fat Man II* by the New York Pyrotechnic Products Inc fired near Titusville, Florida on 22 Oct 1977. The 720 lb *326,5 kg* shell was 40½ in *102,8 cm* in diameter. The largest firework produced in Britain is one fired on 8 June 1946 from Brock's 25 in *635 mm*, 22 cwt *1117 kg* mortar. The shell weighs 200 lb *90,7 kg* and is 6½ ft *1,98 m* in circumference and was first used in Lisbon in 1886.

Flags *Oldest*

The oldest known flag is one dating to *c*. 500 BC found in the excavation of the princesses graves in Hunan, Changsha, China. The Friesian flag still flown in the Netherlands dates from the 9th century AD.

Largest

The largest flag in the world, the 'Stars and Stripes', was displayed at Evansville, Indiana on 22 Mar 1980 measuring 411 ft *125 m* by 210 ft *64 m* with a weight of 7 tons/*tonnes* in readiness for its hoisting on the Verrazano Narrows Bridge, New York, USA on 4 July 1981. It is the brainchild of advertising man Len Silverfine. The largest Union Flag (or Union Jack) was one 240 × 108 ft *73,15 × 32,91 m* displayed at the Royal Tournament, Earl's Court, London in July 1976. It weighed more than a ton and was made by Form 4Y at Bradley Rowe School, Exeter, Devon. The largest flag *flown* from a public building in Britain is a Union Flag measuring 40 ft *12,19 m* by 20 ft *6,09 m* first flown from the Civic Offices, Newcastle-under-Lyme, Staffordshire on 21 Apr 1977. The study of flags is known as vexillology.

Float

The longest float used in any street carnival is the 200 ft *60 m* long dragon *Sun Loon* used in Bendigo, Victoria, Australia. It has 65,000 mirror scales. Six men are needed to carry its head alone. The largest float is the 150 ft *45,7 m* long, 22 ft *6,7 m* wide 'Agree' Float bearing 51 All-American Homecoming 'Queens'

used at the Orange Bowl parade, Miami, Florida on 29 Dec 1977.

Furniture *Most expensive*

The highest price ever paid for a single piece of furniture is 7,600,000 francs (*then £844,440*) by the J. Paul Getty Museum in Malibu, California, for a 10 ft *3,048 m* high marquetry and ormulu Louis XV corner cabinet made by Dubois, at Sotheby, Parke Bernet, Monte Carlo on 25 June 1979. At Mentmore, Buckinghamshire on 18 May 1977 a bureau *en pente* of *c*. 1735 by Bernard van Risen Burgh was bought in at £280,000.

Oldest British

The oldest surviving piece of British furniture is a three-footed tub with metal bands found at Glastonbury, Somerset, and dating from between 300 and 150 BC.

Largest Piece

The largest item of furniture in the world is the Long Sofa—a wooden bench for old seafarers—measuring 72 m *236 ft* in length at Oskarshamn, Sweden.

Glass

The most priceless example of the art of glass-making is usually regarded as the glass Portland Vase which dates from late in the 1st century BC or 1st century AD. It was made in Italy, and was in the possession of the Barberini family in Rome from at least 1642. It was eventually bought by the Duchess of Portland in 1792 but smashed while in the British Museum in 1847. The auction record is £520,000 for a Roman glass cage-cup of *c*. AD 300 measuring 7 in *17,78 cm* in diameter and 4 in *10,16 cm* in height, sold at Sotheby's, London, on 4 June 1979 to Robin Symes.

Gold plate

The world's highest auction price for a single piece of gold plate is £66,000 (*then $122,000*) for an English George III salver, known as 'The Rutland Salver', made by Paul Storr of London, 1801. The salver, which is 12 in *30.5 cm* in diameter, is engraved with the arms of Manners, Duke of Rutland and of the 16 towns and cities, the gold Freedom boxes of which were melted down to make the salver. It was sold by Sotheby Parke Bernet, London, on May 4 1978.

The gold coffin of the 14th century BC Pharaoh Tutankhamun discovered by Howard Carter on 16 Feb 1923 in Luxor, western Thebes, Egypt weighed 110,4 kg *243 lb*. The exhibition at the British Museum attracted 1,656,151 people (of whom 45.7 per cent bought catalogues) from 30 Mar to 30 Dec 1972, resulting in a profit of £657,731.22.

Guns

The highest price ever paid for a single gun is £125,000 given by the London dealers F. Partridge for a French flintlock fowling piece made for Louis XIII, King of France in *c*. 1615 and attributed to Pierre le Bourgeoys of Lisieux, France (d. 1627). This piece was included in the collection of the late William Goodwin Renwick of the United States sold by Sotheby's, London on 21 Nov 1972 (see also Pistols). It is now in the Metropolitan Museum, New York, USA.

Hat *Most expensive*

The highest price ever paid for a hat is 165,570 francs (*then £14,032*) (incl. tax), by Moët et Chandon at an auction by Maîtres Liery, Rheims et Laurin on 23 Apr 1970 for one last worn by Emperor Napoleon I (1769–1821) on 1 Jan 1815.

Icon *Most expensive*

The record auction price for an icon is $150,000 (*then £67,500*) paid at Christie's, New York on 17 Apr 1980 for the *Last Judgement* (from the George R. Hann collection, Pittsburgh, USA) made in Novgorod in the 16th century.

Jade

The highest price ever paid for an item in jade is 1,250,000 Swiss Francs (*then £156,250*) for a necklace set with 31 graduated beads of Imperial green jade. This was sold by Christie's at the Hotel Richmond, Geneva, Switzerland, on 9 May 1973. The highest price paid for jade objects is HK$1.4 million (*£175,000*) for a pair of 19th-century green jadeite table screens 17¼ in *43,8 cm* in height sold by Sotheby's in Hong Kong on 2 Nov 1976.

Jewels

The highest auction price for any jewels (or any work of art) is £2,825,000 (or £3.1 million with the buyer's premium) for two pear-shaped diamond drop earings of 58.6 and 61 carats at Sotheby's, Geneva on 14 Nov 1980. Neither the buyer nor seller was disclosed.

Jig-saw *Earliest and largest*

The earliest jig-saws were made as 'dissected maps' by John Spilsbury (1739–69) in Russell Court off Drury Lane, London *c.* 1762. The largest jig-saw ever made is one 50 ft 9¾ in × 50 ft 5¾ in *15,48 × 15,38 m* with 10,201 pieces by Richard & Roger Meade unveiled at Earl Wilkes High School, North Carolina, USA on 26 July 1980. Gimbels of New York City sold in 1933 a Ringling Barnum Circus Puzzle 8½ × 13 ft *2,59 × 3,96 m* weighing 597 lb *270 kg* with 50,000 pieces made by Eureka Jig Saw Puzzle Co. of Philadelphia.

Matchbox labels

The oldest match label is that of John Walker, Stockton-on-Tees, Cleveland, England in 1827. Collectors of labels are phillumenists, of bookmatch covers philliberumenists and of matchboxes cumyxaphists. Several labels are only uniquely known such as the Byron Match from Roche & Co., Marseilles and the Canadian Allumettes Frontenac from the Eddy Match Co. both in the Frank J. Mrazik Collection in Quebec, Canada. The world's foremost phillumenist is Teiichi Yoshizawa (b. 1904) of Chiba, Japan, who since 1924 has amassed 559,744 examples from over 100 countries.

Medal or Decoration

The highest price paid at auction for a single medal or decoration is $51,000 (*then £27,568*) for the gold *Comitia Americana* awarded to Brigadier-General 'Mad' Anthony Wayne (1745–1796) of the American Army for his capture of Stony Point, New York on July 15, 1779. The medal was sold by a direct descendant of the general, Anthony Wayne Ridgeway, at Sotheby Parke Bernet, New York, on June 15 1978.

The highest price paid at auction for a group of British orders or decorations is £26,000 at Christie's London on 18 Apr 1979 for the Peninsular gold cross group awarded to Lt. Col. William Stewart (1724–1827).

Nylon Sheerest

The lowest denier nylon yarn ever produced is the 6-denier used for stockings exhibited at the Nylon Fair in London in February 1956. The sheerest stockings normally available are 9-denier. An indication of the thinness is that a hair from the average human head is about 50 denier.

Paperweight

The highest price ever paid for a glass paperweight is £48,000 at Christie's, London on 10 July 1979 for a St Louis 19th century paperweight.

Pencil Longest

The longest pencil was made by the world's oldest pencil factory, the Cumberland Pencil Factory, England to a length of 7 ft *2,13 m*, and a weight of 15¼ lb *6,9 kg* and a lead 1 in *25,4 mm* thick.

Penknife

The penknife with the greatest number of blades is the Year Knife made by the cutlers, Joseph Rodgers & Sons Ltd, of Sheffield, England, whose trade mark was granted in 1682. The knife was built in 1822 with 1822 blades but had to halt at 1973 because there was no further space. It was acquired by Britain's largest hand tool manufacturers, Stanley Works (Great Britain) Ltd of Sheffield, South Yorkshire in 1970.

Pens *Most expensive*

The most expensive writing pens are the 18 carat pair of pens (one fibre-tipped and one ballpoint) capped by diamonds of 3.88 carats sold by Alfred Dunhill (see Cigarette lighter, above) for £9943 the pair (incl. VAT).

Pipe *Most expensive*

A meerschaum pipe with a bowl fashioned in the shape of 'flying horseman' has been marketed in San Fransisco, California for $10,000 (*now £4545*) since August 1978.

Pistols *Most expensive*

The highest price paid for a pair of pistols at auction is the £78,000 given by the London dealer Howard Ricketts Sotheby Parke Bernet, London on 17 Dec 1974 for a pair English Royal flintlock holster pistols made *c.* 1690–1700 Pierre Monlong. They were sent for sale by Anne, Duchess Westminster.

The highest price paid at auction for a pistol is £110,000 Christie's London on 8 July 1980 for a Sadeler wheel-lock ho ster pistol from Munich dated *c.* 1600.

Playing cards

The rarest pack of playing cards is the 17th century 'Lives of th Saints' published by the Bowles family and estimated to b worth £2000. A 7 of diamonds signed by Edward Gibbon in 178 as an IOU for £320 has been sold for £500.

Porcelain and pottery English

The highest price ever paid for a single piece of English po celain is £32,000 for a Chelsea Boar's Head (of the red anch period) sold at Sotheby's on 13 Nov 1973. The pottery record £28,000 for a group of two late 17th century lovers from th Lipski collection sold at Sotheby's on 10 Mar 1981.

European

The highest price paid at auction for a single piece of Europea porcelain is £115,600 (*then $213,675*) for a 38½ in *97.8 cm* hig Meissen white porcelain figure of a Macaw modelled by Johan Joachim Kandler. This piece, from the Robert von Hirsch co lection, was sold at Sotheby's in London on June 27, 1978.

Post cards

Deltiology is claimed to be the third largest collecting hobb next only to stamps and coins. Austria issued the first cards i 1869 followed by Britain in 1872. Values tend to be obscured b the philatelic element.

Pot lid

The highest price paid for a pot lid is £2700 by Richard Cash more for a top to a container of bear's grease, manufactured b Clayton and Co. of London, at Sotheby's, London on 6 Nc 1980.

Ropes largest and longest

The largest rope ever made was a coir fibre launching rope with circumference of 47 in *119 cm* made in 1858 for the British line *Great Eastern* by John and Edwin Wright of Birmingham. It co sisted of four strands, each of 3780 yarns. The longest fibre rop ever made without a splice was one of 10,000 fathoms or 11.3 miles *18 288 m* of 6½ in *16,5 cm* circumference manila by Fro Brothers (now British Ropes Ltd) in London in 1874.

Shoes

James Smith, founder of James Southall & Co of Norwich England introduced sized shoes in 1792. The firm began makin 'Start-rite' children's shoes in 1923.

The most expensive standard shoes obtainable are mink-line golf shoes with 18 carat gold embellishments and ruby-tippe spikes made by Stylo Matchmakers International Ltd of Noi thampton, England which retail for £4,510, or $9920 per pair i the USA.

Largest

Excluding cases of elephantiasis, the largest shoes ever sold are pair size 42 built for the giant Harley Davidson of Avon Parl Florida, USA. The normal limit is size 14. The 1887 Jubile Boot made for the Newark trades procession, Nottinghamshir weighed 81¾ lb *31,7 kg*, is 4 ft 3½ in *131 cm* long and is Siz 141. It is owned by Clarks Shoe Museum, Street, Somerset.

Silver

The highest price ever paid for silver is £612,500 for the pair c Duke of Kingston tureens made in 1735 by Meissonnier an sold by Christie's, Geneva on 8 Nov 1977.

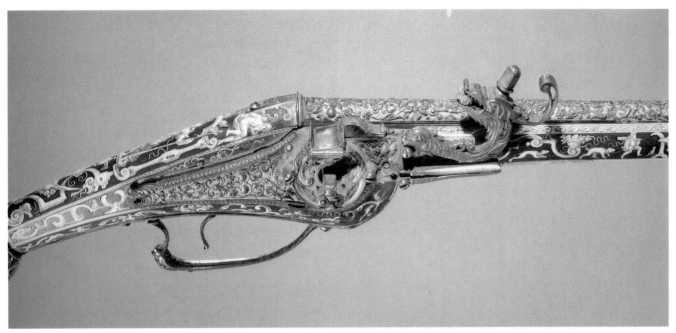

The Sadeler wheel-lock holster pistol dated *c.* 1600 which fetched £10,000 at auction in London on 8 July 1980 (see p. 166). (*Christie's*)

Snuff *Most expensive*

The most expensive snuff obtainable in Britain is 'Café Royale' sold by G. Smith and Sons (est. 1869) of 74, Charing Cross Road, City of Westminster, Greater London. It sells at £1.65 per oz. as at 1 Mar 1981.

Box

The highest price ever paid for a snuff box is Sw. Fr. 480,000 (*then £125,650*) in a sale at Christie's, Geneva on 14 May 1980 for a presentation gold table snuff box presented by Empress Elisabeth to Count Estorazy in 1761.

Sofa *Longest*

The longest standard sofa manufactured for market is the King Talmage Sofa, 12 ft 2 in *3,7 m* in length made by the Talmageville Furniture Manufacturers, California, USA.

Spoons *Most expensive*

The highest price ever paid for a set of 12 spoons is £70,000 paid by Mrs How in a sale at Christie's, London on 26 June 1974. They are Elizabethan silver-gilt spoons, made by Christopher Wace in 1592, known as the 'Tichborne Celebrities'.

Stuffed bird

The highest price ever paid for a stuffed bird is £9000. This was given on 4 Mar 1971 at Messrs Sotheby & Co., London, by the Iceland Natural History Museum for a specimen of the Great Auk (*Alca impennis*) in summer plumage, which was taken in Iceland *c.* 1821; this particular specimen stood 22½ in *57 cm* high. The Great Auk was a flightless North Atlantic seabird, which was finally exterminated on Eldey, Iceland in 1844, becoming extinct through hunting. The last British sightings were at Co. Waterford in 1834 and St Kilda, Western Isles *c.* 1840.

Sword

The highest price paid for a sword is the $145,000 (*then £85,800*) paid for the gold sword of honour presented by the Continental Congress of 1779 to General Marie Jean Joseph Lafayette at Sotheby Parke Bernet, New York City, USA on 20 Nov 1976.

Teiichi Yoshizawa of Chiba, Japan has collected 559,744 unduplicated matchbox labels since 1924 (see p. 166).

One of the 34 panels of The Overlord Embroidery, the largest embroidery ever made which involved 100 man years of work. (*Whitbread & Co. Ltd*)

Table *Longest*

A buffet table 2,606 ft *794,30 m* long was set up by a hotelier in Marienheide, W. Germany to feed 20,000 people attending a charitable fund-raising outdoor event in 1979.

Table cloth

The world's largest table cloth is one 219 yd *200 m* long by 2 yd *1,8 m* wide double damask made by John S. Brown & Sons Ltd of Belfast and shipped to a royal palace in the Middle East. There was also an order for matching napkins for 450 places.

Tapestry *Earliest*

The earliest known examples of tapestry woven linen are three pieces from the tomb of Thutmose IV, the Egyptian Pharaoh and dated to 1483–1411 BC.

Largest

The largest single piece of tapestry ever woven is 'Christ in His Majesty', measuring 72 ft by 39 ft *21,94 × 11,88 m* designed by Graham Vivian Sutherland OM (1903–80) for an altar hanging in Coventry Cathedral, West Midlands. It cost £10,500, weighs ¾ ton *760 kg* and was delivered from Pinton Frères of Felletin, France, on 1 Mar 1962.

Longest embroidery

The famous Bayeux *Telle du Conquest, dite tapisserie de la reine Mathilde*, a hanging 19½ in *49,5 cm* wide by 231 ft *70,40 m* in length depicts events of the period 1064–6 in 72 scenes and was probably worked in Canterbury, Kent, in *c.* 1086. It was 'lost' for 2½ centuries from 1476 until 1724. The Overlord Embroidery of 34 panels each 8 × 3 ft *2,43 × 0,91 m*, commissioned by Lord Dulverton CBE, TD (b. 1915) from the Royal School of Needlework, London, was completed in 1979 after 100 man years of work and is 41 ft *12,49 m* longer than the Bayeaux and has the largest area of any embroidery with 816 ft² *75,8 m²*. An uncompleted 8 in *20,3 cm* deep 1200 ft *365,76 m* embroidery of scenes from C. S. Lewis's Narnia children's stories has been worked by Mrs Margaret S. Pollard of Truro, Cornwall to the order of Mr Michael Maine.

Most expensive

The highest price paid for a tapestry is £550,000 for a Swiss Medieval tapestry frieze in two parts dated 1468–1476 at Sotheby's, Geneva, on 10 Apr 1981 by the Basle Historische Museum.

Tartan *Earliest*

The earliest evidence of tartan is the so-called Falkirk tartan, found stuffed in a jar of coins in Bells Meadow, Falkirk, Scotland. It is of a dark and light brown pattern and dates from *c.* AD 245. The earliest reference to a specific named tartan has been to a Murray tartan in 1618 although Mackay tartan was probably worn earlier.

Tea Towels

The largest reported collection of unduplicated tea towels is 5000 by Mr Tony Judkin of Luton, Bedfordshire.

Thimble *Most expensive*

The record auction price for a thimble is £8,000 paid by the London dealer Winifred Williams at Christie's, London on 3 Dec 1979 for a Meissen dentil-shaped porcelain piece of *c.* 1740.

Time capsule

The world's largest time capsule is the Tropico Time Tunnel of 10,000 ft³ *283 m³* in a cave in Rosamond, California, sealed by the Kern Antelope Historical Society on 20 Nov 1966 and intended for opening in AD 2866.

Toy Construction

The tallest LEGO tower was one of 13,1 m *43 ft* with 100,000 'bricks' weighing 250 kg or ¼ ton put up at Central Milton Keynes Shopping Centre, Buckinghamshire on 9–25 Aug 1980. LEGO (from Danish *leg*, play; *godt*, well) was invented by a village carpenter Ole Christiansen of Billund, Denmark in 1930 and now exported to 106 countries.

Typewriters

The first patent for a typewriter was by Henry Mill in 1714 but the earliest known working machine was made by Pellegrine Turri (Italy) in 1808. The highest price paid for an antique machine is £3000 for an 1886 Daw and Tait machine auctioned at Sotheby's, London on 12 Dec 1980.

Vase *Largest*

The largest vase on record is one 8 ft *2,78 m*, in height, weighing 650 lb *294,8 kg*, thrown by Sebastiano Maglio at Haeger Potteries of Dundee, Illinois, USA (founded 1872) during August 1976.

Most Valuable

The Chinese ceramic authority Chingwah Lee of San Francisco was reported in Aug 1978 to have appraised a unique 39 in *99 cm*

The giant lego tower constructed between 9–25 August 1980 to a height of 13,1 m *43 ft* at Central Milton Keynes Shopping Centre, Bucks (see p. 168).

Kang Hsi 4-sided vase then in a bank vault in Phoenix, Arizona, at '$60 million' (*now £27.2 million*).

Wreath *Most expensive*
The most expensive wreath on record was that sent to the funeral of President Kennedy in Washington, DC on 25 Nov 1963 by the civic authority of Paris. It was handled by Interflora Inc and cost $1200 (*then £428*). The only rival was a floral tribute sent to the Mayor of Moscow in 1970 by Umberto Formichello, general manager of Interflora which is never slow to scent an opportunity.

Writing paper
The most expensive writing paper in the world is that sold by Cartier Inc on Fifth Avenue, New York City at $10,000 (*now £4545*) per 100 sheets with envelopes. It is of hand made paper from Tervakoski Osakeyhtiö, Finland, with deckle edges and a 'personalized' portrait watermark. Second thoughts and misspellings tend to be costly.

3. AGRICULTURE

Origins
It has been estimated that only 21 per cent of the world's land surface is cultivable and that only 7.6 per cent is actually under cultivation. Evidence adduced in 1971 from Non Nok Tha and Spirit Cave, Thailand tends to confirm plant cultivation and animal domestication was part of the Hoabinhian culture *c.* 11,000 BC. Reindeer may have been domesticated as early as *c.* 18,000 BC but definite evidence is still lacking.

Goat was domesticated at Asiab, Iran by *c.* 8050 BC and dog at Star Carr, North Yorkshire by *c.* 7700 BC: the earliest definite date for sheep is *c.* 7200 BC at Argissa-Magula, Thessaly, Greece and for pig and cattle *c.* 7000 BC at the same site. The earliest date for horse is *c.* 4350 BC from Dereivka, Ukraine, USSR.

FARMS
Earliest
The earliest dated British farming site is a neolithic one, enclosed within the Iron Age hill-fort at Hembury, Devon, excavated during 1934–5 and now dated to 4210–3990 BC. Pollen analysis from two sites Oakhanger, Hampshire, and Winfrith Heath, Dorset (Mesolithic *c.* 5000 BC) indicates that Mesolithic man may have had herds which were fed on ivy during the winter months.

Largest *World*
The largest farms in the world are collective farms (*sovkhozes*) in the USSR. These have been reduced in number from 235,500 in 1940 to only 18,000 in 1980 and have been increased in size so that units of over 60,000 acres *25 000 ha* are not uncommon. The pioneer farm of Laucidio Coelho near Campo Grande, Mato Grosso, Brazil in *c.* 1901 was 3358 miles² *8700 km²* 2.15 million acres with 250,000 head of cattle at the time of his death in 1975.

Great Britain
The largest farms in the British Isles are Scottish hill farms in the Grampians. The largest arable farm is that of Elveden, Suffolk, farmed by the Earl of Iveagh. Here 11,250 acres *4553 ha* are farmed on an estate of 22,926 acres *9278 ha*, the greater part of which was formerly derelict land. The 1980 production included 1,262,212 gal *5 737 890 litres* of milk, 4902 tons *4980 tonnes* of grain and 23,404 tons *23 780 tonnes* of sugar beet. The livestock includes 3074 cattle, 1017 ewes and 4551 pigs.

Cattle station
The world's largest cattle station is Alexandria Station, Northern Territory, Australia, selected in 1873 by Robert Collins, who rode 1600 miles *2575 km* to reach it. It has 99 working bores, a staff of 90 and originally extended over 7,207,608 acres *2 916 818 ha*—more than the area of England's four largest counties of North Yorkshire, Cumbria, Devon and Lincoln put together. The present area is 6252 miles² *16 192 km²* which is stocked with 60,000 shorthorn cattle. Until 1915 the Victoria River Downs Station, Northern Territory, was over three times larger, with an area of 22,400,000 acres (35,000 miles² *90 650 km²*).

Sheep station
The largest sheep station in the world is Commonwealth Hill, in the north-west of South Australia. It grazes between 70,000 and 90,000 sheep, *c.* 700 cattle and 54,000 uninvited kangaroos in an area of 4080 miles² *10 567 km²*, *i.e.* larger than the combined area of Norfolk and Suffolk.

The largest sheep move on record occurred when 27 horsemen moved a mob of 43,000 sheep 40 miles *64 km* from Barcaldine to Beaconsfield Station, Queensland, Australia, in 1886.

Rice Farming
The largest contiguous wild rice (*Zizania aquatica*) farm in the world is Clearwater Rice, Inc at Clearbrook, Minnesota, USA with 2000 acres *809 ha*. In 1972 it yielded 262,000 lb *118 87 tonnes*.

Turkey farm
The world's largest turkey farm is that of Bernard Matthews Ltd, centred at Gt Witchingham, Norfolk, with 1600 workers tending 6,400,000 turkeys.

Chicken ranch
The world's largest chicken ranch is the 345 acre *140 ha* 'Egg City' Moorpark, California established by Julius Goldman in 1961. Some 2,220,000 eggs are laid daily by 3.0 million hens.

Piggery
The world's largest piggery is the Sljeme pig unit in Yugoslavia which is able to process 300,000 pigs in a year. Even larger units may exist in Romania but details are at present lacking.

Cow shed
The longest cow shed in Britain is that of the Yorkshire Agricultural Society at Harrogate, North Yorkshire. It is 456 ft *139 m* in length with a capacity of 686 cows. The National Agricultural Centre, Kenilworth, Warwickshire, completed in 1967, has, however, capacity for 782 animals.

left: Part of the world's largest hopfield at Toppenish, Washington State, USA, which covers 1836 acres *743 ha*. (*F. J. Haas*) *right*: Britain's largest live litter of 30 piglets (see p. 172). (*Stephen Austin Newspapers Ltd*)

Foot-and-mouth disease

The worst outbreak of foot-and-mouth disease in Great Britain was that from Salop on 25 Oct 1967 to 25 June 1968 in which there were 2364 outbreaks and 429,632 animals slaughtered at a direct and consequential loss of £150,000,000. The outbreak of 1871, when farms were much smaller, affected 42,531 farms. The disease first appeared in Great Britain at Stratford, East London in August 1839.

Sheep shearing

The highest recorded speed for sheep shearing in a working day was that of G. Phillips who machine-sheared 694 lambs (average 77.1 per hour) in 9 hr at Tymawr Farm, Libanus, Powys on 25 June 1975. Peter Casserly of Christchurch, New Zealand, achieved a solo blade (i.e. hand-shearing) record of 353 lambs in 9 hours on 13 Feb 1976. In a shearing marathon, four men machine-shore 1649 sheep in 24 hr at Brecon, Powys, Wales on 13–14 July 1977.

Mr Lavor Taylor (b. 27 Feb 1896) of Ephraim, Utah claims to have sheared 512,000 sheep to mid 1980.

Great Britain

British records for 9 hr have been set at 555 by Roger Poyntz-Roberts (300) and John Savery (255) on 9 June 1971 (sheep caught *by* shearers), and 610 by the same pair (sheep caught *for* shearers) in July 1970.

Commonwealth Hill Sheep Station in South Australia, the largest in the world which grazes some 80,000 sheep, 700 cattle and an estimated 54,000 uninvited kangaroos.

Sheep *Survival*

On 2 Mar 1978, Peter Boa of Seiberscross, Strath Brora, Sutherland, Scotland dug out 9 sheep buried in snow for 33 days. Two ewes were alive.

Mushroom farm

The largest mushroom farm in the world is the Butler County Mushroom Farm, Inc, founded in 1937 in a disused limestone mine near West Winfield, Pennsylvania, USA. It employs over 1000 in a maze of underground galleries 110 miles *177 km* long producing over 45,000,000 lb *20 411 tonnes* of mushrooms per year.

Largest wheat field

The largest single fenced field sown with wheat was one of 35,000 acres *14 160 ha* sown in 1951 south west of Lethbridge Alberta, Canada.

Largest vineyard

The world's largest vineyard is that extending over the Mediterranean façade between the Rhône and the Pyrenees in the *départments* Hérault, Gard, Aude, and Pyrénées-Orientales in an area of 840 000 ha *2,075,685 acres* of which 52.3 per cent is *monoculture viticole*.

Largest hop field

The largest hop field in the world is one of 1836 acres *743 ha* near Toppenish, Washington State, USA. It is owned by John I. Haas, Inc, the world's largest hop growers, with hop farms in California, Idaho, Oregon and Washington State, with a total net area of 4112 acres *1664 ha*.

Community garden *Largest*

The largest recorded community garden project is that operated by the City Beautiful Council, and the Benjamin Wegerzyn Garden Center, Dayton, Ohio, USA. It comprises 1173 allotments each of 812¼ ft² *74,45 m²*.

CROP YIELDS

Wheat

Crop yields for highly tended small areas are of little significance. The British record is 92.08 cwt/acre *11 560 kg/ha* on a field of 26 acres *10,5 ha* by C. H. Warhurst & Sons Ltd, at Sutton under Brailes, Oxfordshire using Mardler wheat in 1980.

Barley

A yield of 83.2 cwt/acre *10 450 kg/ha* of Athene Winter Barley was achieved in 1980 by M. J. Leigh on behalf of R. M. Harris at Watcombe Manor, Watlington, Oxon. from a 30 acre *12,14 ha* field.

Corn

A yield of 352.64 US bushels (15½ per cent moisture) from an acre, using De Kalb XL-54, was achieved by Roy Lynn, Jr near Kalamazoo, Michigan on 30 Sept 1977.

Sugar beet

The highest recorded yield for sugar beet is 62.4 short tons (55.71 long tons) per acre *1139,8 tonnes/ha* by Andy Christensen and Jon Giannini in the Salinas Valley, California.

Potato picking

The greatest number of US barrels picked in a 9½ hr day is 235 by Walter Sirois (b. 1917) of Caribou, Maine, USA on 30 Sept 1950.

Ploughing

The world championship (instituted 1953) has been staged in 17 countries and won by ploughmen of ten nationalities of which the United Kingdom has been most successful with 7 championships. The only man to take the title three times has been Hugh Barr of Northern Ireland in 1954–5–6.

The fastest recorded time for ploughing an acre *0,404 ha* (minimum 32 right-hand turns and depth 9 in *22 cm*) is 12 min 9.5 sec by Martin Allum using a Ransomes 5 furrow 14 in *35,5 cm* plough towed by a Ford Model TW20 tractor at the Royal East Berkshire Agricultural Association's 126th Annual Ploughing Match on 29 Sept 1979 at Lower Mount Farm, Cookham, Berks.

The greatest recorded acreage ploughed in 24 hr is 123.4 acres *49,9 ha* by David Griffiths and Pat Neylan using a Lamborghini R-1056 DT tractor with a 6 furrow plough to a depth of 7 in *17,7 cm* in the Nakuru District, Kenya on 6–7 July 1978. Pat Bolger of Athy, Co. Kildare, Ireland ploughed for 181 hr 25 min on 1–8 Sept 1980.

Largest rick

A rick of some 66,000 bales was completed from summer 1977 to September 1978 by Geoffrey Woollard Ltd at Bottisham, Cambridge. It measured 400 × 60 × 18 ft *122 × 18 × 55 m* and weighed some 2050 tons *2100 tonnes*.

LIVESTOCK

Note: Some exceptionally high livestock auction sales are believed to result from collusion between buyer and seller to raise the ostensible price levels of the breed concerned. Others are marketing and publicity exercises with little relation to true market prices.

Highest Priced *Bull*

The highest price ever paid for a bull is $2,500,000 (*£1,087,000*) for the beefalo (a ⅜ bison, ⅜ charolais, ¼ Hereford) 'Joe's Pride' sold by D. C. Basolo of Burlingame, California to the Beefalo Cattle Co of Canada, of Calgary, Alberta, Canada on 9 Sept 1974.

The highest price ever paid for a bull in Britain is 60,000 guineas (*£63,000*), paid on 5 Feb 1963 at Perth, Scotland, by James R. Dick (1928–74) co-manager of Black Watch Farms, for 'Lindertis Evulse', an Aberdeen-Angus owned by Sir Torquil and Lady Munro of Lindertis, Kirriemuir, Tayside, Scotland. This bull failed a fertility test in August 1963 when 20 months old, thus becoming the world's most expensive piece of beef.

Cow

The highest price ever paid for a cow is $300,000 (*then £136,360*) for the Holstein-Friesian 'Pammies Citation Paula' by Dreamstreet Holsteins Inc., Walton, NY, USA at the Hilltop Hanover Farm sale on 21 Nov 1980. The British record is £14,910 for 'Fairthwaite Indiana', a pure-bred Chianina in-calf heifer sold to Mr Christopher Reeves of Taunton, Somerset by Harrison & Hetherington Ltd in Carlisle, Cumbria on 21 Sept 1974.

Sheep

The highest price ever paid for a sheep is $A46,000 (*£30,000*) for a Merino ram from John Collins & Sons, Mount Bryan, South Australia by Mrs P. L. Puckridge of White River, Port Lincoln, South Australia at the Royal Adelaide Show on 2 Sept 1976.

The British auction record is £21,000 paid by Mr W. Sheddon of Brighouse, Balmaclellan, Kirkcudbright, Dumfries and Galloway for A. W. Carswell & Son's Blackface ram on 4 Oct 1978.

The highest price ever paid for wool is $A46 per kg greasy (*£11.09 per lb*) for a bale of superfine Merino fleece from the Launceston, Tasmania sales in February 1973. It was sold by Mr C. Stephen of Mount Morrison estate to Fujii Keori Ltd of Osaka, Japan.

Pig

The highest price ever paid for a pig is $42,500 (*£21,250*) for a Duroc boar named 'Glacier', owned by Baize Durocs of Stamford, Texas, USA, by Wilbert & Myron Meinhart of Hudson, Iowa, on 24 Feb 1979. The UK record is 3300 guineas (*£3465*), paid by Malvern Farms for the Swedish Landrace gilt 'Bluegate Ally 33rd' owned by Davidson Trust in a draft sale at Reading, Berkshire on 2 Mar 1955.

Horse

The highest price for a draught horse is $47,500 (*£9,970*) paid for the 7-year-old Belgian stallion 'Farceur' by E. G. Good at Cedar Falls, Iowa on 16 Oct 1917.

A Welsh mountain pony stallion 'Coed Cock Bari' was sold to an Australian builder in Wales in September 1978 for 21,000 guineas (*then £22,050*).

Donkey

Perhaps the lowest ever price for livestock was at a sale at Kuruman, Cape Province, South Africa in 1934 where donkeys were sold for less than 2p each.

Heaviest *Cattle*

Of heavyweight cattle the heaviest on record was a Holstein-Durham cross named 'Mount Katahdin' exhibited by A. S. Rand of Maine, USA in 1906–10 and frequently weighed at an even 5000 lb *2267 kg*. He was 6 ft 2 in at the shoulder with a 13 ft *3,96 m* girth and died in a barn fire *c.* 1923. The British record is the 4480 lb *2032 kg* of 'The Bradwell Ox' owned by William Spurgin of Bradwell, Essex. He was 15 ft *4,57 m* from nose to tail and had a girth of 11 ft *3,35 m* when 6 years old in 1830. The largest breed of heavyweight cattle is the Chianini, brought to Italy from the Middle East in pre-Roman times. Mature bulls average 5 ft 8 in *1,73 m* at the forequarters and weigh 2865 lb *1300 kg*. In 1955 a bull named 'Donetto' tipped the scales at 3834 lb *1740 kg* at the Arezzo show—a world record for any bull of any breed.

The highest recorded birthweight for a calf is 225 lb *102 kg* from a British Friesian cow at Rockhouse Farm, Bishopston, Swansea, West Glamorgan, in 1961.

Pigs

The heaviest hog recorded was 'Big Bill' of 2552 lb *22¾ cwt 11 575 kg* measuring 9 ft *2,75 m* long with a belly on the ground, raised in Henderson County, Tennessee, USA and killed in 1933. He was mounted and displayed by the Wells family in Jackson, Tennessee until 1946. The British record is a hog of 12 cwt 66 lb *639,5 kg* bred by Joseph Lawton of Astbury, Cheshire. In 1774 it stood 4 ft 8½ in *1,43 m* in height and was 9 ft 8 in *2,94 m* long. The highest recorded weight for a piglet at weaning (8 weeks) is 81 lb *36,7 kg* for a boar, one of nine piglets farrowed on 6 July 1962 by the Landrace gilt 'Manorport Ballerina 53rd', *alias* 'Mary', and sired by a Large White named 'Johnny' at Kettle Lane Farm, West Ashton, Trowbridge, Wiltshire.

Sheep

The highest recorded birthweight for a lamb in the world is 38 lb *17,2 kg* at Clearwater, Sedgwick County, Kansas, USA in 1975, but neither this lamb nor the ewe survived.

Broiler growth

The record for growth for flocks of at least 2400 at 56 days is 2,767 kg *6.100 lb* by G. W. Gelden at Gemert, nr. Boekel, Netherlands on 15 July 1980 using Ross I broilers.

Prolificacy *Cattle*

On 25 Apr 1964 it was reported that a cow named 'Lyubik' had given birth to seven calves at Mogilev, USSR. Five live and one dead calf were recorded from a Friesian at Te Puke, North Island, New Zealand on 27 July 1980 but none survived. A case of five live calves at one birth was reported in 1928 by T. G. Yarwood of Manchester. The life-time prolificacy record is 30 in the case of a cross-bred cow owned by G. Page of Warren Farm, Wilmington, East Sussex, which died in November 1957, aged 32. A cross-Hereford calved in 1916 and owned by A. J. Thomas of West Hook Farm, Marloes, Dyfed, Wales, produced her 30th calf in May 1955 and died in May 1956, aged 40.

'Soender Jylland's Jens' a Danish black and white bull left 220,000 surviving progeny by artificial insemination when he was put down aged 11 in Copenhagen in September 1978. 'Bendalls Adema', a Friesan bull, died aged 14 at Clondalkin, County Dublin, Ireland on 8 Nov 1978 having sired an estimated 212,000 progeny by artificial insemination.

Pigs

The highest recorded number of piglets in one litter is 34, thrown on 25–26 June 1961 by a sow owned by Aksel Egedee of Denmark. In February 1955 a Wessex sow owned by Mrs E. C. Goodwin of Paul's Farm, Leigh, near Tonbridge, Kent, had a litter of 34, of which 30 were born dead. The highest reported number of live births in Britain is 30 by W. Ives of Dane End Fruit Farm, near Ware, Hertfordshire from a white Welsh sow in September 1979. A sow, 'Bessie' owned by Mr L. Witt of Bath, Avon farrowed litters of 19 on 12 Nov 1975, 19 (3 stillborn) on 5 Apr 1976 and 21 (3 stillborn) on 16 Sept 1976 making 59 in a 12 month period (53 reared).

Sheep

A case of eight lambs at a birth was reported by D. T. Jones of Priory Farm, Gwent, in June 1956 and by Ken Towse of Buckton near Bridlington in March 1981 but none lived. A case of a sheep living to 26 years was recorded in flock book records by H. Poole, Wexford, Ireland. Four cases of sextuplet lambs have been reported since 1977.

Egg-laying

The highest authenticated rate of egg-laying is by 'Princess Te Kawau', a Black Orpington, owned by Mrs D. M. Waddell, with 361 eggs in 364 days in an official test at Taranaki, New Zealand, ending on 31 Mar 1930. The UK record is 353 eggs in 365 days in a National Laying Test at Milford, Surrey in 1957 by a Rhode Island Red owned by W. Lawson of Welham Grange, Retford, Nottinghamshire.

The heaviest egg reported is one of 16 oz *454 g*, with double yolk and double shell, laid by a white Leghorn at Vineland, New Jersey, USA, on 25 Feb 1956. The largest recorded was one of 'nearly 12 oz' for a 5 yolked egg 12¼ in *31 cm* around the long axis and 9 in *22,8 cm* around the shorter axis laid by a Black Minorca at Mr Stafford's Damsteads Farm, Mellor, Lancashire in 1896.

The highest recorded annual average for a flock is 313 eggs in 52 weeks from a flock of 1000 Warren-Stadler SSL layers (from 21 weeks of age) by Eric Savage, White Lane Farm, Albury, Surrey, England in 1974–5.

Most yolks

The highest claim for the number of yolks in a chicken's egg is 9 reported by Mrs Diane Hainsworth of Hainsworth Poultry Farms, Mount Morris, New York, USA in July 1971 and also from a hen in Kirghizia, USSR in August 1977.

Goose egg

The white goose 'Speckle' owned by Donny Brandenberg, of Goshen, Ohio, USA, on 3 May 1977 laid a 24 oz *680 g* egg measuring 13½ × 9½ in *34 × 24 cm* in circumferences.

Milk yields *Cows*

The highest recorded world lifetime yield of milk is 363,979 lb (162.49 tons *165 096 kg*) by the US Holstein cow 'Breezewood Patsy Bar Pontiac' owned by Gelbke Bros. of Vienna, Ohio to late in 1980. The greatest yield of any British cow was that given by the British Friesian 'Guillyhill Janna 2nd', owned by S. H. West. This cow yielded 330,939 lb *150 111 kg* up to 1973. The greatest recorded yield for one lactation (365 days) is 55,661 lb *25 247 kg* by the Holstein 'Beecher Arlinda Ellen' owned by Mr and Mrs Harold L. Beecher of Rochester, Indiana, USA in 1975. The British and probably world record for milk yield in a day is 198¼ lb *89,92 kg* by R. A. Pierson's British Friesian 'Garsdon Minnie' in 1948.

Hand milking

Andy Faust at Collinsville, Oklahoma, USA in 1937 achieved 120 US gal *99.92 UK gal* in 12 hr.

Goats

The highest recorded milk yield for any goat is 7714 lb *3499 kg* in 365 days by 'Osory Snow-Goose' owned by Mr and Mrs G Jameson of Leppington, N.S.W. Australia in 1977. The part Nubian milk goat 'Lou' owned by Mrs Jonnie Stinson of Springtown, Texas was still lactating after 5 years on 15 Nov 1980.

Butter fat yield

The world record lifetime yield is 16,370 lb *7425 kg* by the US Holstein 'Breezewood Patsy Bar Pontiac' in 3979 days (see left also for yield record). Her lactation record for 365 days of 2230 lb *1011 kg* was reported on 8 Oct 1976. The British record butter fat yield in a lifetime is 12,166 lb *5518 kg* by the Ayrshire cow 'Craighead Welma' owned by W. Watson Steele from 273,072 lb at 4.45 per cent. The British record for 365 days is 761 kg *1677.7 lb* by 'Crookgate Aylwinia 7' a Fresian, owned by J. V. Machin of Hill Farm, Penley near Wrexham, Clwyd, set on 5 May 1973. The United Kingdom record for butter fat in one day is 9.30 lb *4,218 kg* (79 lb *35,8 kg* milk at 11.8 per cent) by Queens Letch Farms' Guernsey Cow 'Thisbe's Bronwen of Trewollack'.

Cheese

The most active cheese-eaters are the people of France, with an annual average in 1979 of 17,3 kg *38.1 lb* per person. The world's biggest producer is the United States with a factory production of 4,773,500,000 lbs (2,165,000 tons *2 200 000 tonnes*) in 1980. The UK cheese consumption in 1980 was 12.60 lb *5,71 kg* per head.

Oldest

The oldest and most primitive cheeses are the Arabian *kishk*, made of dried curd of goats' milk. There are today 450 named cheeses of 18 major varieties, but many are merely named after different towns and differ only in shape or the method of packing. France has 240 varieties.

Most expensive

The world's most expensive cheese is Le Leruns made from Ewes milk at 90 francs per kilo (*now £3.40 per lb*). Britain's most costly cheese is the illicitly made Dorset Vinny which has no fixed price but is unobtainable from bootleggers much under £3 per lb.

Largest

The largest cheese ever made was a cheddar of 34,591 lb *15 190 kg* made in 43 hr on 20–22 Jan 1964 by the Wisconsin Cheese Foundation for exhibition at the New York World's Fair, USA. It was transported in a specially designed refrigerated tractor trailer 'Cheese Mobile' 45 ft *13,71 m* long.

CHICKEN PLUCKING

Ernest Hausen (1877–1955) of Fort Atkinson, Wisconsin, USA, died undefeated after 33 years as a champion. On 19 Jan 1939 he was timed at 4.4 sec and reputedly twice did 3.5 sec a few years later.

The record time for plucking 12 chickens clean by a team of 4 women at the annual Chicken Plucking Championship at Marsaryktown, Florida, USA is 32.9 sec set on 9 Oct 1976 by Doreena Cary, Diane Grieb, Kathy Roads and Dorothy McCarthy.

TURKEY PLUCKING

Vincent Pilkington of Cootehill, County Cavan, Ireland killed and plucked 100 turkeys in 7 hr 32 min on 15 Dec 1978. His record for a single turkey is 1 min 30 sec on RTE Television in Dublin on 17 Nov 1980.

10. HUMAN ACHIEVEMENTS

Lunar conquest

Neil Alden Armstrong (b. Wapakoneta, Ohio, USA of Scoto-Irish and German ancestry, on 5 Aug 1930), command pilot of the Apollo XI mission, became the first man to set foot on the Moon on the Sea of Tranquility at 02.56 and 15 sec GMT on 21 July 1969. He was followed out of the Lunar Module *Eagle* by Col. Edwin Eugene Aldrin, Jr USAF (b. Glen Ridge, New Jersey, USA of Swedish, Dutch and British ancestry, on 20 Jan 1930), while the Command Module *Columbia* piloted by Lt Col Michael Collins, USAF (b. Rome, Italy, of Irish and pre-Revolutionary American ancestry, on 31 Oct 1930) orbited above.

Eagle landed at 20.17 and 42 sec. GMT on 20 July and lifted off at 17.54 GMT on 21 July, after a stay of 21 hr 36 min. The Apollo XI had blasted off from Cape Canaveral, Florida at 13.32 GMT on 16 July and was a culmination of the US space programme which, at its peak, employed 376,600 people and attained in the year 1966–7 a peak budget of $5,900,000,000 (*then £2460 million*).

There is evidence that Pavel Belgayev (USSR) was the cosmonaut selected by Russia for a manned lunar flight in *Zond 7* on 9 Dec 1968 but no launch took place.

Altitude *Man*

The greatest altitude attained by man was when the crew of the ill-fated Apollo XIII were at apocynthion (*i.e.* their furthest point) 158 miles *254 km* above the lunar surface and 248,655 miles *400 187 km* above the Earth's surface at 1.21 a.m. BST on 15 Apr 1970. The crew were Capt. James Arthur Lovell, Jr USN (b. Cleveland, Ohio 25 Mar 1928), Fred Wallace Haise Jr (b. Biloxi, Miss., 14 Nov 1933) and John L. Swigert Jr (b. Denver, Col., 30 Aug 1931).

Altitude *Woman*

The greatest altitude attained by a woman is 231 km *143.5 miles* by Jnr Lt (now Lt Col) Valentina Vladimirovna Tereshkova-Nikolayev (b. 6 Mar 1937) of the USSR, during her 48-orbit flight in *Vostok 6* on 16 June 1963. The record for an aircraft is 24 336 m *79,842 ft* by Natalia Prokhanova (USSR) (b. 1940) in an E-33 jet, on 22 May 1965.

Speed *Man*

The fastest speed at which humans have travelled is 24,791 mph *39 897 km/h* when the Command Module of Apollo X carrying Col (*now* Brig Gen) Thomas Patten Stafford, USAF (b. Weatherford, Okla. 17 Sept 1930), and Cdr Eugene Andrew Cernan (b. Chicago, 14 Mar 1934) and Cdr (*now* Capt) John Watts Young, USN (b. San Francisco, 24 Sept 1930), reached this maximum value at the 400,000 ft *121,9 km* altitude interface on its trans-Earth return flight on 26 May 1969.

Speed *Woman*

The highest speed ever attained by a woman is 28 115 km/h *17,470 mph* by Jnr Lt (now Lt Col) Valentina Vladimirovna Tereshkova-Nikolayev (b. 6 Mar 1937) of the USSR in *Vostok 6* on 16 June 1963. The highest speed ever achieved by a woman aircraft pilot is 2687,42 km/h *1669.89 mph* by Svetlana Savitskaya (USSR) reported on 2 June 1975.

Land speed *Man*

The highest speed ever achieved on land is 739.666 mph *1190,377 km/h* or Mach 1.0106 by Stan Barratt (US) in *The Budweiser Rocket*, a rocket engined 3 wheeled car at Edwards Air Force Base, California on 17 Dec 1979 (see also p. 137).

The official land speed record is 622.287 mph *1001,473 km/h* set by Gary Gabelich (b. San Pedro, Calif, 29 Aug 1940) on 23 Oct 1970 on the Bonneville Salt Flats, Utah, USA, in the rocket powered *The Blue Flame*, built by Reaction Dynamics Inc of Milwaukee, Wisconsin, USA.

24,790·8 mph Cdrs Eugene Andrew Cernan and John Watts Young, USN and Col Thomas P. Stafford, USAF *Apollo* X: **39 897,0 km/h Re-entry after lunar orbit** 26 May 1969

24,226 mph Col Frank Borman, USAF, Capt James Arthur Lovell, Jr, USN, Major William A. Anders, USAF *Apollo VIII*: **38 988 km/h Trans-lunar injection** 21 Dec 1968

17,560 mph Flt Maj Yuriy Alekseyevich Gagarin, *Vostok 1*: *c.***28 260 km/h Earth orbit** 12 Apr 1961

2905 mph Major Robert M. White, North American *X–15*: **4675,1 km/h Muroc Dry Lake, California** 7 Mar 1961

967 mph Capt Charles Elwood Yeager, USAF *Bell XS–1*: **1556 km/h Muroc Dry Lake, California** 26 Mar 1948

623·85 mph Flugkapitan Heinz Dittmar *Me. 163V–1*: **1004 km/h Peenemunde, Germany** 2 Oct 1941

415·2 mph Flt Lt (Later Wing Cdr) George Hedley Stainforth AFC *Supermarine S.6B*: **668,2 km/h Lee-on-Solent, England** 29 Sept 1931

210·64 mph Sadi Lecointe (France) Nieuport-Delage 29: **339 km/h Villesauvage, France** 25 Sept 1921

150 mph Frederick H. Marriott (fl. 1957) Stanley Steamer *Wogglebug*: *c.***257,5 km/h Ormond Beach, Florida, USA** 26 Jan 1907

130·61 mph Siemens and Halske electric engine: **210,2 km/h Marienfeld-Zossen, near Berlin** 27 Oct 1903

90 mph Midland Railway 4–2–2 7 ft 9 in single: **144,8 km/h Ampthill, Bedford, England** Mar 1897

87·8 mph Tommy Todd, downhill skier: **141,3 km/h La Porte, California, USA** Mar 1873

56·75 mph Grand Junction Railway 2–2–2: *Lucifer*: **95 km/h Madeley Banks, Staffs., England** 13 Nov 1830

50 mph Ice Yachts (earliest patent): **80 km/h Netherlands** AD 1600

45 mph Mountain Sledging: **70 km/h Island of Hawaii (now USA)** *ante* AD 1500

35 mph Horse-riding: **55 km/h Anatolia, Turkey** *c.*1400BC

25 mph Sledging: **40 km/h Heinola, Finland** *c.*6500BC

PROGRESSIVE SPEED RECORDS

Note: *A complete progressive table comprising entries from pre-historic times to date was published in the 23rd edition of 1977.*

The highest land speed attained in Britain is 251.19 mph *404,25 km/h* by Richard Nobel in his twin Rolls Royce jet-powered *Thrust 2* at Greenham Common, Berkshire on 25 Sept 1980.

Land speed *Woman*
The highest land speed recorded by a woman is 524.016 mph *843,323 km/h* by Mrs Kitty Hambleton *née* O'Neil (US) in the 48,000 hp rocket-powered 3-wheeled S.M.1 *Motivator* over the Alvard Desert, Oregon, USA on 6 Dec 1976. Her official two-way record was 512.710 mph *825,126 km/h* and she probably touched 600 mph *965 km/h* momentarily.

Water speed *Man*
The highest speed ever achieved on water is an estimated 300 knots (345 mph *556 km/h*) by Kenneth Peter Warby, MBE, (b. 9 May 1939) on the Blowering Dam Lake, NSW, Australia on 20 Nov 1977 in his unlimited hydroplane *Spirit of Australia*. The official world water speed record is 514,39 km/h *319.627 mph* set on 8 Oct 1978 by Warby on Blowering Dam Lake.

Woman
Sue Williams, 28, drove the unlimited hydroplane U-96 KYYX through a measured mile on Lake Washington, Seattle, USA at 163.043 mph *262,392 km/h* on 26 July 1978 for a women's world record.

The official feminine record is 109.40 mph *176,06 km/h* on Windermere, Cumbria on 8 Nov 1980 by Rosalind Nott.

Water speed *Propeller driven*
The world record for propeller-driven craft is 202.42 mph *325,76 km/h* set by Larry Hill in his supercharged hydroplane *Mr. Ed* off Long Beach, California. On a one-way run *Climax* recorded 205.19 mph *330,22 km/h*.

Most travelled *Man*
The man who had visited more countries than anyone was Jesse Hart Rosdail (1914–77) of Elmhurst, Illinois, USA, a teacher of children in the 5th grade. Of the 161 sovereign countries and 60 non-sovereign territories, listed by the *UN Population Report of 1981* making a total of 221, he had visited 219 excepting only North Korea and French Antarctic Territories. He estimated his mileage was 1,626,605 statute miles *2 617 766 km*.

Though he has not visited so many *currently* existing countries, Mehmet S. Ersöz (b. 1904 in Turkey) has travelled much more widely within some 210 countries and is the world's most travelled man. Mrs Ersöz's total was 163 by mid-1978.

Horseback
The most travelled man in the horseback era was probably the Methodist preacher Francis Asbury (b. Birmingham, England), who travelled 264,000 miles *424 850 km* in North America from 1771 to 1815 preaching 16,000 sermons.

Disabled person
The most countries visited by a disabled person is 120 sovereign and 63 non-sovereign countries by Professor Daniel J. Crowley of Davis, California, USA who has been confined to a wheelchair since March 1946.

Most isolated *Man*
The farthest any human has been removed from his nearest living fellow man is 2233.2 miles *3596,4 km* in the case of the Command Service Module pilot Alfred M. Worden on the US Apollo XV lunar mission of 30 July–1 Aug 1971.

Passport Records
The world's most expensive passports are those from the USSR which in 1974 at the official rate of exchange were priced at £225 payable in advance. If applications involved a whole family or travel to the West however the necessary accompanying visa was refused, 996 times in each 1000 applications.

Round the World
The fastest time for a round world trip on scheduled flights for a circumnavigation is 44 hr 6 min by David J Springbett, 41 of Taplow, Buckinghamshire, from Los Angeles eastabout *via*

London, Bahrain, Singapore, Bangkok, Manila, Tokyo and Honolulu on 8–10 Jan 1980 over a 23,068 mile *37 124 km* route.

The FAI allows any flight taking off and landing at the same point, which is as long as the Tropic of Cancer (viz 22,858.754 miles 36 787,599 km) as a circumnavigational flight.

North Pole conquest
The claims of neither of the two US Arctic explorers, Dr Frederick Albert Cook (1865–1940) nor Cdr (later Rear Ad.) Robert Edwin Peary (1856–1920), of the US Naval Civil Engineering branch in reaching the North Pole are subject to positive proof. Cook accompanied by the Eskimos, Ah-pellah and Etukishook, two sledges and 26 dogs, struck north from a point 60 miles *96,5 km* north of Svartevoeg, on Axel Heiberg I., Canada, 460 miles *740 km* from the Pole on 21 Mar 1908, allegedly reaching Lat. 89° 31′ N on 19 Apr and the Pole on 21 Apr. Peary, accompanied by his Negro assistant, Matthew Alexander Henson (1866–1955) and the four Eskimos, Ooqueah, Eginwah, Seegloo, and Ootah (1875–1955), struck north from his Camp Bartlett (Lat. 87° 44′ N.) at 5 a.m. on 2 Apr 1909. After travelling another 134 miles *215 km*, he allegedly established his final camp, Camp Jessup, in the proximity of the Pole at 10 a.m. on 6 Apr and marched a further 42 miles *67,5 km* quartering the sea-ice before turning south at 4 p.m. on 7 Apr. On excellent pack ice Wally Herbert's 1968–9 Expedition (see below) attained a best day's route mileage of 23 miles *37 km* in 15 hr. Cook claimed 26 miles *41,8 km* twice while Peary claimed a surely unsustainable average of 38 miles *61 km* for 8 consecutive days.

The earliest indisputable attainment of the North Pole over the sea-ice was at 3 p.m. (Central Standard Time) on 19 Apr 1968 by Ralph Plaisted (US) and three companions after a 42-day trek in four Skidoos (snow-mobiles). Their arrival was independently verified 18 hr later by a US Air Force weather aircraft. The sea bed is 13,410 ft *4087 m* below the North Pole.

Naomi Uemura (b. 1941) the Japanese explorer and mountaineer became the first person to reach the North Pole in a solo trek across the Arctic Ice Cap at 4.45 a.m., GMT on 1 May 1978. He had travelled 450 miles *725 km* setting out on 7 Mar from Cape Edward, Ellesmere Island in northern Canada. He averaged over 8 miles *13 km* per day with his sled 'Aurora' drawn by 17 huskies. He had hoped to average 17 km *10.5 miles* per day.

The first woman to set foot on the North Pole was Mrs Fran Phipps, wife of the Canadian bush pilot Weldy Phipps on 5 Apr 1971. Galina Aleksandrovna Lastovskaya (b. 1941) and Lilia Vladislavovna Minina (b. 1959) were crew members of the USSR atomic icebreaker Arktika which reached the Pole on 17 Aug 1977.

Seven polar explorers from the USSR, Dmitri Shparo 37, Yuri Khmelevsky, Vladimir Ledenev, Anatoly Melnikov, Vadim Davydov, Vladimir Rakhmanov and Vasily Shishkarev reached the North Pole across 900 miles *1448 km* of the ice cap from Henrietta Island on skis in 77 days from 15 Mar–31 May 1979.

South Pole conquest
The first ships to cross the Antarctic circle (Lat. 66° 30′ S.) were the 193 crew of the *Resolution* (462 tons/*tonnes*) (Capt James Cook RN (1728–79)) and *Adventure* (336 tons/*tonnes*) (Lt T. Furneaux) on 17 Jan 1773 in 39° E. The first person to sight the Antarctic *mainland*—on the best available evidence and against claims made for British and Russian explorers—was Nathaniel Brown Palmer (US) (1799–1877). On 17 Nov 1820 he sighted the Orleans Channel coast of the Palmer Peninsula from his 45 ton/*tonnes* sloop *Hero*.

The South Pole (alt. 9186 ft *2779 m* on ice and 336 ft *102 m* bed rock) was first reached at 11 a.m. on 16 Dec 1911 by a Norwegian party led by Capt. Roald Engebereth Gravning Amundsen (1872–1928), after a 53-day march with dog sledges from the Bay of Whales, to which he had penetrated in the *Fram*. Subsequent calculations showed that Olav Olavson Bjaaland (the last survivor, dying in June 1961, aged 88) and Helmer Hanssen probably passed within 400–600 m of the exact pole. The other two members were Sverre H. Hassell (d. 1928) and Oskar Wisting (d. 1936).

Women

The first woman to set foot on Antarctica was Mrs Karoline Mikkelsen on 20 Feb 1935. No woman stood on the South Pole until 11 Nov 1969. On that day Lois Jones, Eileen McSaveney, Jean Pearson, Terry Lee Tickhill (all US), Kay Lindsay (Australia) and Pam Young (NZ) arrived by air.

First on both Poles

David S Porter (b. 1938) of Hope, New Jersey USA visited the South Pole as a guest of the US Navy on 14 Dec 1970 (temperature −38°F −38,8°C). On 9 Apr 1979 he visited the North Pole where the temperature was −39°F −39,4°C.

Arctic crossing

The first crossing of the Arctic sea-ice was achieved by the British Trans-Arctic Expedition which left Point Barrow, Alaska on 21 Feb 1968 and arrived at the Seven Island Archipelago northeast of Spitzbergen 464 days later on 29 May 1969 after a haul of 2920 statute miles *4699 km* and a drift of 700 miles *1126 km* compared with the straight line distance of 1662 miles *2674 km*. The team was Wally Herbert (leader), 34, Major Ken Hedges, 34, RAMC, Allan Gill, 38, and Dr Roy Koerner, 36 (glaciologist), and 40 huskies. This was the longest sustained journey ever made on polar pack ice and the first indisputable attainment of the North Pole by sledge. Temperatures sank to −47°F −43,8° C during the trek.

Antarctic crossing

The first surface crossing of the Antarctic continent was completed at 1.47 p.m. on 2 Mar 1958, after a trek of 2158 miles *3473 km* lasting 99 days from 24 Nov 1957, from Shackleton Base to Scott Base *via* the Pole. The crossing party was led by Dr (now Sir) Vivian Ernest Fuchs (born 11 Feb 1908). The 2600 mile *4185 km* trans-Antarctic leg of the 1980–82 Trans Globe Expedition was achieved in 66 days on 11 Jan 1981 having passed through the South Pole on 23 Dec 1980. The 3 man party on snowmobiles was led by Sir Ranulph Fiennes (b. 1944).

Longest sledge journeys

The longest totally self-supporting Polar sledge journey ever made was one of 1080 miles *1738 km* from West to East across Greenland on 18 June to 5 Sept 1934 by Capt M. Lindsay (1905–1981) (later Sir Martin Lindsay of Dowhill, Bt, CBE, DSO; Lt Arthur S. T. Godfrey, RE, (later Lt Col, k. 1942), Andrew N. C. Croft (later Col, DSO) and 49 dogs. The first ice-cap crossing was that of Nansen who in 1888 travelled from South-east Greenland with man-hauled sledges to the West Coast.

Greatest ocean descent

The record ocean descent was achieved in the Challenger Deep of the Marianas Trench, 250 miles *400 km* south-west of Guam, in the Pacific Ocean, when the Swiss-built US Navy bathyscaphe *Trieste*, manned by Dr Jacques Piccard (b. 1914) (Switzerland) and Lt Donald Walsh, USN, reached the ocean bed 35,820 ft (6.78 miles *10 917 m*) down, at 1.10 p.m. on 23 Jan 1960 (see page 64). The pressure of the water was 16,883 lbf/in² *1183 kgf/cm²* and the temperature 37.4°F *3°C*. The descent required 4 hr 48 min and the ascent 3 hr 17 min.

Deep diving records

The record depth for the extremely dangerous activity of breath-held diving is 282 ft *85,9 m* by Jacques Mayol (France) off Elba, Italy, on 9 Nov 1973 for men and 147½ ft *45 m* by Giuliana Treleani (Italy) off Cuba in September 1967 for women. The pressure on Mayol's thorax was 136.5 lbf/in² *9,6 kg/cm²* and his pulse fell to 36. Enzo Maiorca (Italy) surfaced unconscious from a dive of 87 m *285 ft* off Sorrento, Italy on 27 Sept 1974. The record dive with Scuba (self-contained under-water breathing apparatus) is 437 ft *133 m* by John J. Gruener and R. Neal Watson (USA) off Freeport, Grand Bahama on 14 Oct 1968. The record dive utilizing gas mixtures (nitrogen, oxygen and helium) is a simulated dive of 2250 ft *685,8 m* in a dry chamber by Stephen Porter, Len Whitlock and Erik Kramer at the Duke University Medical Center in Durham, North Carolina on 3 Feb 1981 in a 43 day trial in a sphere of 8 ft *2,43 m*. Some divers have survived free swimming for short intervals at depths of 1400 ft *426 m*.

Deepest underwater escape

The deepest underwater rescue achieved was of the *Pisces III* in which Roger R. Chapman, 28 and Roger Mallinson, 35 were trapped for 76 hr when it sank to 1575 ft *480 m* 150 miles *240 km* south-east of Cork, Ireland on 29 Aug 1973. She was hauled to the surface by the cable ship *John Cabot* after work by Pisces V, Pisces II and the remote control recovery vessel US CURV on 1 Sept. The greatest depth of an actual escape without any equipment has been from 225 ft *68,58 m* by Richard A. Slater from the rammed submersible *Nekton Beta* off Catalina Island, California, USA on 28 Sept 1970.

Deepest salvage

The greatest depth at which salvage has been achieved is 16,500 ft *5029 m* by the bathyscaphe *Trieste II* (Lt Cdr Mel Bartels, USN) to attach cables to an 'electronic package' on the sea bed 400 miles *645 km* north of Hawaii on 20 May 1972. Project Jennifer by USS *Glomar Explorer* in June/July 1974 to recover a Golfclass USSR submarine, 750 miles *1200 km* NW of Hawaii, cost $550 million but was not successful.

Flexible dress divers

The deepest salvaging operation ever carried out was on the wreck of the SS *Niagara*, sunk by a mine in 1940, 438 ft *133,5 m*

MILESTONES IN ABSOLUTE HUMAN ALTITUDE RECORDS

Altitude Ft	m	Pilot	Vehicle	Place	Date	
80*	24	Jean François Pilâtre de Rozier (France)	Hot Air Balloon (tethered)	Fauxbourg, Paris	15 & 17 Oct	1783
c.330	c.100	de Rozier and the Marquis d'Arlandes (1742–1809) (France)	Hot Air Balloon (free flight)	LaMuette, Paris	21 Nov	1783
c.3,000	c.900	Dr Jacques-Alexander-Cesar Charles (1746–1823) and Ainé Robert (France)	Charliere Hydrogen Balloon	Tuileries, Paris	1 Dec	1783
c.9000	c.2750	J.-A.-C. Charles (France)	Hydrogen Balloon	Nesles, France	1 Dec	1783
c.13,000	c.4000	James Sadler (GB)	Hydrogen Balloon	Manchester	May	1785
25,400[1]	7740	James Glaisher (1809–1903) (UK)	Hydrogen Balloon	Wolverhampton	17 July	1862
31,500	9615	Prof. A. Berson (Germany)	Hydrogen Balloon Phoenix	Strasbourg, France	4 Dec	1894
36,565	11 145	Sadi Lecointe (France)	Nieuport Aircraft	Issy-les-Moulineaux, France	30 Oct	1923
51,961	15 837	Prof. Auguste Piccard and Paul Kipfer (Switzerland)	FNRS 1 Balloon	Augusburg, Germany	27 May	1931
72,395	22 066	Capts Orvill A. Anderson and Albert W. Stevens (US Army Air Corps)	US Explorer II Helium Balloon	Rapid City, South Dakota, USA	11 Nov	1935
79,600	24 262	William Barton Bridgeman (USA)	US Douglas D558—11 *Skyrocket*	California, USA	15 Aug	1951
126,200	38 465	Capt Iven C. Kincheloe, Jr (USAF)	US Bell X-2 Rocket 'plane	California, USA	7 Sept	1956
169,600	51 694	Joseph A. Walker (USA)	US X-15 Rocket 'plane	California, USA	30 Mar	1961

Statute miles	Km					
203.2	327	Flt-Major Yuriy A. Gagarin (USSR)	USSR. *Vostok I* Capsule	Orbital flight	12 Apr	1961
234,672	377 268,9	Col Frank Borman, USAF, Capt James Arthur Lovell, Jr, USN and Major William A. Anders, USAF	US *Apollo VIII* Command Module	Circum-lunar flight	25 Dec	1968
248,655	400 187	Capt James Arthur Lovell Jr, USN, Frederick Wallace Haise Jr and John L. Swigert Jr	US *Apollo XIII*	Abortive lunar landing mission	15 Apr	1970

* There is some evidence that Father Bartolomeu de Gusmao flew in his hot-air balloon in his 4th experiment post August 1709 in Portugal.
[1] Glaisher, with Henry Tracey Coxwell (1819–1900) claimed 37,000 ft *11 275 m* from Wolverhampton on 5 Sept 1862. Some writers accept 30,000 ft *9145 m*..
Note: A complete progressive table comprising entries from 1783 to date was published in the 23rd edition of 1977.

MARINE CIRCUMNAVIGATION RECORDS (Compiled by Sq Ldr D. H. Clarke, DFC, AFC)

A true circumnavigation entails passing through two antipodal points (which are at least 12,429 statute miles *20 000 km* apart).

CATEGORY	VESSEL	NAME	START PLACE AND DATE	FINISH DATE AND DURATION
Earliest*	*Vittoria* Expedition of Fernão de Magalhães, *c.* 1480–k. 1521	Juan Sebastion de Elcano or Del Cano (d. 1526) and 17 crew	Seville, Spain 20 Sept 1519	San Lucar, 6 Sept 1522 30,700 miles *49 400 km*
Earliest British	*Golden Hind* (ex *Pelican*) 100 tons/*tonnes*	Francis Drake (*c.* 1540–96) (Knighted 4 April 1581)	Plymouth, 13 Dec 1577	26 Sept. 1580
Earliest Woman	*Etoile*	Crypto-female valet of M. de Commerson, named Baré	St Malo, 1766	1769
Earliest fore-and-aft rigged vessel	*Union* 98 tons (Sloop)	John Boit Junior, 19–21, (US)	Newport, RI 1794 (via Cape Horn westabout)	Newport, RI 1796
Earliest Yacht	*Sunbeam* 170 ft *51,8 m* 3 Mast Topsail schooner	Lord and Lady Brassey (GB) passengers and crew	Cowes, Isle of Wight 1876	Cowes, Isle of Wight 1877
Earliest Solo	*Spray* 36¾ ft *11,20 m* gaff yawl	Capt Joshua Slocum, 51, (US) (a non-swimmer) (No 1 solo circum)	Newport, RI, *via* Magellan Straits, 24 Apr 1895	3 July 1898 46,000 miles *74 000 km*
Earliest Motor Boat	*Speejacks* 98 ft *29,87 m*	Albert Y. Gowen (US) wife and crew	New York City 1921	New York City 1922
Earliest Woman Solo	*Mazurek* 31 ft 2 in *9,5 m* Bermudan Sloop	Krystyna Chojnowska-Liskiewicz (Poland) (No 58 solo circum)	Las Palmas 28 Mar 1976 westabout *via* Panama	Tied knot 21 Mar 1978
Earliest Woman Solo (via Cape Horn)	*Express Crusader* 53 ft *16,15 m* Bermuda Sloop	Naomi James (NZ/GB) (later DBE) (No 59 solo circum)	Dartmouth 9 Sept 1977 (Cape Horn 19 Mar 1978)	Dartmouth 8 June 1978 (266 days 19 hr)
Smallest Boat	*Super Shrimp* 18 ft 4 in *5,58 m* Bermuda Sloop	Shane Acton (GB) Iris Derungs (Swiss)	Cambridge, England August 1972	Cambridge, England August 1980 (E–W *via* Panama Canal)
Earliest Submerged	*US Submarine Triton*	Capt Edward L. Beach USN plus 182 crew	New London, Connecticut 16 Feb 1960	10 May 1960 30,708 miles *49 422 km*
Earliest non-stop Solo (Port to Port)	*Suhaili* 32.4 ft *9,87 m* Bermudan Ketch	Robin Knox Johnston CBE (b. 1939) (No 25 solo circum)	Falmouth, 14 June 1968	22 Apr 1969 (312 days) Longest alone at sea
Fastest Solo (multihull)	*Manureva* (ex *Pen Duick IV*) 70 ft *21,33 m* Trimaran	Alain Colas (France) (No 40 solo circum)	Saint Malo *via* Sydney	29 Mar 1974 (167 days)
Fastest Solo time (monohull)	*Cor Caroli* 29 ft 9 in *9,06 m* Bermuda Sloop	George Georgier (Bulgaria) (No 57 solo circum)	Havana, Cuba 20 Dec 1976	Havana, Cuba, 20 Dec 1977. 201 days 21 hr 36 min
Fastest Solo Speed (monohull)	*Ocean Bound* 41 ft 8 in *12,69 m* Bermuda Cutter	David Cowper (GB) (No 63 solo circum)	Plymouth 19 Aug 1979 (W–E *via* Cape Horn)	224 days 12 hr 28 min (av speed 131.05 mpd)
Fastest time (yacht)	*Great Britain II* 77 ft 2 in *23,52 m* Ketch	1st Mike Gill (13 crew) 2nd R. Mullender (15 crew)	Thames 31 Aug 1975 *via* Sydney (Change crews)	67 days 5 hr 19 min 66 days 22 hr 31 min 196.9 mpd
Fastest speed (yacht)	*Great Britain II* (see above)	Rob James and crew	Plymouth 27 Aug 1977 via Cape Town Auckland, Rio de Janeiro	24 Mar 1978 134 days 12 hr 26,815 miles 199.4 mpd
Fastest (clipper)	*James Baines* 266 ft *81,07 m*	Capt C McDonald (GB) and crew	Liverpool to Melbourne (58 days) 1854	Melbourne to Liverpool (69 days) 1855
Fastest Solo Westabout (via Cape Horn)	*Mermaid III* 28 ft *8,80 m* sloop	Kenichi Horie (Japan) (b. 1939) (No 37 solo circum)	Osaka, Japan 1 Aug 1973	5 May 1974 (275 days 13 hr)
Fastest-ever (yacht) (Cape Horn)	*Awahnee II* 53 ft *16,15 m* Bermuda Cutter	Bob Griffith (US) (5 crew)	Bluff, NZ, 1970 (eastabout)	Bluff, NZ, 1971 (88 sailing days plus 23 days stopovers)
Fastest-ever (clipper)	*Red Jacket* 260 ft *79,24 m*	Capt S. Reid (GB) and crew	From/to Lat 26° 25′ W	62 days 22 hr 1854

* Eduard Roditi, author of *Magellan of the Pacific*, advances the view that Magellan's slave, Enrique, was the first circumnavigator. He had been purchased in Malacca but knew the Filipino dialect Vizayan, when he reached the Philippines from the east. He 'tied the knot' off Limasawa on 28 Mar 1521. The first to circumnavigate in both directions was Tobias Furneaux (GB) as second lieutenant aboard the *Dolphin* from/to Plymouth east to west *via* the Magellan Straits in 1766–68 and as captain of the *Adventure* from/to Plymouth west to east *via* Cape Horn in 1772–4.

down off Bream Head, Whangarei, the North Island, New Zealand. All but 6 per cent of the £2,250,000 of gold in her holds was recovered in 7 weeks. The record recovery was that from the White Star Liner *Laurentic*, which was mined in 132 ft *40,2 m* of water off Malin Head, Donegal, Ireland, in 1917, with £5,000,000 of gold ingots in her Second Class baggage room. By 1924, 3186 of the 3211 gold bricks had been recovered with immense difficulty.

Greatest penetration into the earth
Man's deepest penetration made into the ground is in the Western Deep Levels Mine at Carletonville, Transvaal, South Africa where a record depth of 3582 m *11,752 ft* (2.22 miles) has been attained. The rock temperature at this depth is 131° F *55° C*.

Shaft sinking record
The one month (31 days) world record is 1251 ft *381,3 m* for a standard shaft 26 ft *7,92 m* in diameter at Buffelsfontein Mine, Transvaal, South Africa, in March 1962. The British record of 410 ft *124,9 m* of 18 ft 1 in *5,51 m* diameter shaft was set in the Boulby Mine, Whitby, North Yorkshire on 18 Jan–17 Feb 1971 (30 days). The rock shaft at this potash mine at 3765 ft *1147,5 m* is the deepest in Great Britain.

Longest on a raft
The longest recorded survival alone on a raft is 133 days (4½ months) by Second Steward Poon Lim (born Hong Kong) of the UK Merchant Navy, whose ship, the SS *Ben Lomond*, was torpedoed in the Atlantic 565 miles *910 km* west of St Paul's Rocks in Lat. 00° 30′ N Long. 38° 45′ W at 11.45 a.m. on 23 Nov 1942. He was picked up by a Brazilian fishing boat off Salinópolis,

Brazil, on 5 Apr 1943 and was able to walk ashore. In July 1943, he was awarded the BEM and now lives in New York City.

Maurice and Maralyn Bailey survived 118⅓ days in an inflatable dinghy 4½ ft *1,37 m* in diameter in the north-east Pacific from 4 Mar to 30 June 1973.

Most marriages *World*
The greatest number of marriages accumulated in the monogamous world is 22 by the former minister of religion Glynn de Moss Wolfe (US) (b. 1908) who married for the 24th time since 1931 his 22nd wife and oldest Regina Santos, 25 of Brazil in October 1980. His total number of children is, he says, 40. He has long kept two wedding dresses (different sizes) in his closet for ready use. He has additionally suffered 19 mothers-in-law. The most often marrying millionaire was Thomas F. Manville (1894–1967) who contracted his 13th marriage to his 11th wife Christine Erdlen Popa (1940–71) aged 20, in New York City, USA, on 11 Jan 1960 when aged 65. His shortest marriage (to his seventh wife) effectively lasted only 7½ hr. His fortune of $20 million came from asbestos, neither of which he could take with him.

Mrs Beverly Nina Avery, then aged 48, a bar-maid from Los Angeles, California, USA, set a monogamous world record in October 1957 by obtaining her sixteenth divorce from her fourteenth husband, Gabriel Avery. She alleged outside the court that five of the 14 had broken her nose.

Had *Time Magazine* reported the wedding of Leonard Safley of Cedar City, Missouri in 1981 to Wynola Rockling it would or should have added—'he for the tenth, she for the ninth'.

Great Britain

The only monogamous citizen married eight times is Olive Joyce Wilson of Marston Green, Birmingham. She has consecutively been Mrs John Bickley; Mrs Don Trethowan; Mrs George Hundley; Mrs Raymond Ward; Mrs Harry Latrobe; Mrs Leslie Harris; Mrs Ray Richards and now Mrs John Grassick. All were divorced except Mr Hundley, who died.

Oldest bride and bridegroom

Dyura Avramovich reportedly aged 101, married Yula Zhivich, admitting to 95, in Belgrade, Yugoslavia in November 1963.

The British record was set by Sir Robert Mayer CH, KCVO (b. 1879) who married Jacqueline Noble, 51 in London on 10 Nov 1980 when aged 101 years.

Mrs Elsie Burtenshaw, 94 married Mr John Gatton, 85 at St. Werbergh's Church, Hoo, Kent on 5 June 1980.

Longest engagements

The longest engagement on record is one of 67 years between Octavio Guillen, 82 and Adriana Martinez, 82. They finally took the plunge in June 1969 in Mexico City, Mexico.

Longest marriage *World*

The longest recorded marriage is one of 86 years between Sir Temulji Bhicaji Nariman and Lady Nariman from 1853 to 1940 resulting from a cousin marriage when both were five. Sir Temulji (b. 3 Sept 1848) died, aged 91 years 11 months, in August 1940 at Bombay. The only reliable instance of an 83rd anniversary celebrated by a couple marrying at normal ages is that between the late Edd (105) and Margaret (99) Hollen, who celebrated their 83rd anniversary on 7 May 1972. They were married in Kentucky on 7 May 1889. Austin and Susie Roseberry of Center Point, Iowa, USA celebrated their 80th anniversary on 27 Mar 1981.

Great Britain

James Frederick Burgess (born 3 March 1861, died 27 Nov 1966) and his wife Sarah Ann, *née* Gregory (born 11 July 1865, died 22 June 1965) were married on 21 June 1883 at St James's, Bermondsey, London, and celebrated their 82nd anniversary.

The most recent example of a marriage with both partners being centenarians was that of John (1876–1981) and Harriet Orton (b. 1879) aged 105 and 102 of Great Gidding, Cambridgeshire, who celebrated their 80th anniversary on 9 July 1980.

Most married

Jack V. and Edna Moran of Seattle, Washington, USA have married each other 40 times since the original and only really necessary occasion on 27 July 1937 in Seaside, Oregon. Subsequent ceremonies have included those at Banff, Canada (1952), Cairo, Egypt (1966) and Westminster Abbey, London (1975).

Mass ceremony

The largest mass wedding ceremony was one of 1800 couples officiated over by Sun Myung Moon of the Holy Spirit Association for the Unification of World Christianity in Seoul, South Korea on 14 Feb 1975. The response to the question 'Will you swear to love your spouse for ever?' is 'Ye'. The Rev Moon was reported in January 1981 to be planning a mass ceremony in New York City for 10,000 couples.

Most Expensive Wedding

The most expensive private wedding is reputed to be that of Maria Niarchos, 20 to Alix Chevassus, 36 at her father Stavros's estate in Normandy, France on 16 June 1979. Though guests consumed an estimated 12,000 bottles of champagne and red wine, the supply of caviar outweighed the demand in four football field sized marquees. The cost was conservatively estimated at $500,000 (*then £250,000*).

Slowest Divorce

In March 1980 a divorce was reported in the Los Angeles Superior Court, California between Bernardine and Leopold Delpes in which both parties were aged 88. The British record age is 101 years by Harry Bidwell at Brighton, Sussex on 21 Nov 1980.

Dining out

The world champion for eating out is Fred E. Magel of Chicago, Illinois, USA who since 1928 has dined in 44,000 restaurants in 60 nations as a restaurant grader (to May 1981). He asserts the one serving the largest helpings is Zehnder's Hotel, Frankenmuth, Michigan, USA. Mr Magel's favourite dishes are South African rock lobster and mousse of fresh English strawberries.

Party giving

The most expensive private party ever thrown was that of Mr and Mrs Bradley Martin of Troy, NY, USA staged at the Waldorf Hotel, Manhattan in February 1897. The cost to the host and hostess was estimated to be $369,200 in the days when dollars were made of gold.

Estimates as high as $600 million (*then £325 million*) were made for the 49 nation Organization of African Unity summit conference staged in Libreville, Gabon in July 1977.

The 'International Year of the Child' children's party in Hyde Park, London was attended by Royal Family and 160,000 children on 30–31 May 1979.

The largest Christmas Party ever staged was that thrown by The Boeing Company in the 65,000 seat Kingdome, Seattle, Washington, USA, in two shows totalling 103,152 people on 15 Dec 1979, managed by general chairman John Mathiasen and produced by Greg Thompson with a cast of 2500. The floor was decorated with 1000 Christmas trees each with 100 lights; 150,000 snow white balloons and three ice ponds.

Toastmasters

The Guild of Professional Toastmasters (founded 1962) has only 12 members. Its founder and President, Ivor Spencer, listened to a speech in excess of 2 hr by the maudlin guest of honour of a retirement luncheon. The Guild also elects the most boring speaker of the year, but for professional reasons, will not publicize the winners' names until a decent interval has elapsed. Red coats were introduced by the pioneer professional, William Knight-Smith (d. 1932) *c.* 1900.

Lecture agency

The world's largest lecture agency is the American Program Bureau of Boston, Mass., USA, with 400 Personalities on 40 Topics and a turnover of some $5 million. The top rate *reported* in March 1981 was $40,000 (*£18,000*) reportedly commanded by Johnny Carson and Bob Hope.

Working week

A case of a working week of 142 hours was recorded in June 1980 by Dr Paul Ashton, 32 the anaesthetics registrar at Birkenhead General Hospital, Merseyside. This left an average each day of 3 hr 42 min 51 sec for sleep. Some non-consultant doctors are actually contracted to work 110 hours a week. Some contracts for University lecturers call for a 3 hr week or a 72 hr year spread over 24 weeks.

Working career

The longest working life has been that of 98 years by Mr Izumi (see Chapter 1 p16), who began work goading draft animals at a sugar mill at Isen, Tokunashima, Japan in 1872. He retired as a sugar cane farmer in 1970 aged 105.

The longest working life recorded in the United Kingdom was that of Susan O'Hagan (1802–1909) who was in domestic service with 3 generations of the Hall family of Lisburn, near Belfast, Northern Ireland for 97 years from the age of 10 to light duties at 107.

The longest recorded industrial career in one job in Britain was that of Miss Polly Gadsby who started work with Archibald Turner & Co of Leicester aged 9. In 1932, after 86 years service, she was still at her bench wrapping elastic, at the age of 95. Mr Theodore C. Taylor (1850–1952) served 86 years with J. T. & T. Taylor of Batley, West Yorkshire including 56 years as chairman. Currently the longest serving and the oldest chairman of any board of directors is Mrs Mary Henrietta Anne Moody (b. 7 Apr 1881) of Mark & Moody Ltd, printers and booksellers of Stourbridge, West Midlands.

Milkman, Longest serving

Britain's longest serving milkman was Mr John Baggs (b. August 1884) of Horndean, near Portsmouth, Hampshire, who had been on his round for over 80 years ('I don't like sitting about'). He was assisted by his boy John Baggs Junior, aged 64.

Most durable coal miner

David Davies (*né* David) (b. 19 Feb 1842 Pontrhyfen, Afan Valley, South Wales) worked underground as a collier for 73 years from 1849 to 1922 from the age of 7 to his retirement aged 80.

Longest pension

Miss Millicent Barclay, daughter of Col William Barclay was born posthumously on 10 July 1872 and became eligible for a Madras Military Fund pension to continue until her marriage.

TRANS-ATLANTIC AND PACIFIC MARINE RECORDS

(Compiled by Sq Ldr D. H. Clarke, DFC, AFC)

TRANS-ATLANTIC MARINE RECORDS

Earliest Canoe	'Finn-Man' (Eskimo)	Kayak 11 ft 10 in *3,6 m*	Greenland	Humber, England	Time not known	1613
Earliest Rowing (partial)	Six British deserters from garrison (fastest ever row)	Ship's boat c. 20 ft *6,1 m*	St Helena (10 June)	Belmonte, Brazil	28 days (83 mpd)	1799
Earliest Crossing (2 men)	C. R. Webb + 1 crew (US)	*Charter Oak* 43 ft *13,1 m*	New York	Liverpool	35 days	1857
Earliest Trimaran	John Mikes + 2 crew (US)	*Non Pareil*, 25 ft *7,62 m* (designed as a raft)	New York (4 June)	Southampton	51 days	1868
Earliest Solo Sailing (E–W)	Josiah Shackford (US)	15 ton gaff sloop	Bordeaux, France	Surinam (Dutch Guiana)	35 days	1786
Earliest Solo Sailing (W–E)	Alfred Johnson (US)	*Centennial* 20 ft *6,09 m*	Glos., Mass.	Wales	46 days	1876
Earliest Woman (with US husband)	Mrs Joanna Crapo (b. Scotland)	*New Bedford* 20 ft *6,09 m*	Chatham, Mass.	Newlyn, Cornwall	51 days	1877
Earliest Single-handed race	J. W. Lawlor (US) (winner)	*Sea Serpent* 15 ft *4,57 m*	Boston (21 June)	Coverack, Cornwall	45 days	1891
Earliest Rowing by 2 men	Georg Harboe and Frank Samuelsen (US)	*Fox* 18⅓ ft *5,58 m*	New York City (6 June)	Isles of Scilly (1 Aug)	55 days (56 mpd)	1897
Fastest Solo Sailing West-East	J. V. T. McDonald (GB)	*Inverarity* 38 ft *11,58 m*	Nova Scotia	Ireland	16 days (147 mpd)	1922
Earliest Canoe (with sail)	F. Romer (Germany)	*Deutscher Sport* 21½ ft *6,55 m*	Las Palmas	St Thomas	58 days (47 mpd)	1928
Earliest Woman Solo (East-West)	Mrs Ann Davison (GB)	*Felicity Ann* 23 ft *7,01 m*	Portsmouth Las Palmas	Dominica (20 Nov 1952)	65 days	1952/ 1953
Earliest Woman Solo (West-East)	Gladys Gradley (US)	Lugger 18 ft *5,5 m*	Nova Scotia	Hope Cove, Devon	60 days	1903
Fastest Woman Solo	Naomi James DBE	*Kriter Lady* 53 ft *16,15 m*	Plymouth	Newport, R.I.	25 days 19 hr 12 min	1980
Smallest (Across 2 oceans)	John Riding (GB)	*Sjo Ag* 12 ft *3,65 m*	Plymouth *via* Panama	New Zealand, 1973	Lost in Tasman Sea	1964/ 1974
Smallest West-East	Gerry Spiess (US)	*Yankee Girl* 10 ft *3,05 m*	Norfolk, Virginia (1 June)	Falmouth, Eng (24 July)	54 days	1979
Smallest (East-West) (Southern)	Hugo S. Vihlen (US)	*April Fool* 5 ft 11⅞ in *1,82 m*	Casablanca (29 Mar)	Ft Lauderdale, Florida (21 June)	85 days	1968
Fastest Crossing Sailing (multihull) (East–West)	Eric Tabarly (France) +2 crew	*Pen Duick IV* 67 ft *20,42 m*	Tenerife	Martinique	251.4 miles *404,5 km*/ day (10 days 12 hours)	1968
Fastest Crossing Sailing (monohull) (East-West)	Wilhelm Hirte & crew (Ger)	*Kriter II* 80 ft *24,38 m*	Canary Is.	Barbados	13 days 8 hr	1977
Fastest Crossing (multihull) (West–East)	Eric Tabarly (Fr) plus 3 crew	*Paul Ricard* 54 ft *16,4 m* (Tri)	Sandy Hook, NJ 22 July	Lizard, Cornwall 1 Aug	10 days 5 hr 14 min (av 12.3 kts)	1980
Fastest Crossing monohull (West-East)	Wilson Marshall (US) & crew	*Atlantic* 185 ft *56,38 m*	Sandy Hook, NJ	Lizard, Cornwall (3054 miles)	12 days 4 hr (fastest noon to noon 341 miles)	1905
Fastest Crossing Sail (West-East)	A. Eldridge (US) and crew	*Red Jacket* (Clipper) 260 ft *79,24 m*	Sandy Hook, NJ	Liverpool Bar	12 days 277.7 m.p.d.	1854
Fastest Solo East-West (Northern) (monohull)	Kazimierz Jaworski (Poland)	*Spaniel II* 56 ft *17,06 m*	Plymouth	Newport, R.I.	19 days 13 hr 25 min	1980
Fastest Solo East-West (Northern) (multihull)	Philip Weld (US)	*Moxie* 51 ft *15,54 m* (Tri)	Plymouth	Newport. R. I.	17 days 23 hr 12 min	1980
Fastest Solo East-West (Southern) (monohull)	Sir Francis Chichester KBE (GB)	*Gipsy Moth V* 57 ft *17,37 m*	Portuguese Guinea	Nicaragua	179.1 miles *288,2 km*/ day (22.4 days)	1970
Fastest Crossing Sail (East-West)	W. S. Johnson (US) and crew	*Andrew Jackson* (Clipper) 220 ft *67,05 m*	Liverpool	New York	15 days 202 m.p.d.	1860
Fastest Solo Rowing East-West	Sidney Genders, (51 years) (GB)	*Khaggavisana* 19¾ ft *6,02 m*	Penzance, Cornwall	Miami, Florida *via* Antigua	37.3 miles *60 km*/day 162 days 18 hr	1970
Fastest Solo Rowing West–East	Gérard d'Aboville (Fr)	*Captaine Cook* 5,60 m 18 ft 4 in	Chatham, Mass 10 July	Ushant, France 20 Sept	71 days 23 hr 72 km *44.8 mpd*	1980
Earliest Solo Rowing East-West	John Fairfax (GB)	*Britannia* 22 ft *6,70 m*	Las Palmas (20 Jan)	Ft Lauderdale, Florida (19 July)	180 days	1969
Earliest Solo Rowing West-East	Tom McClean (Ireland)	*Super Silver* 20 ft *6,90 m*	St John's, Newfoundland (17 May)	Black Sod Bay, Ireland (27 July)	70.7 days	1969
Youngest Solo Sailing	David Sandeman (17½ years)	*Sea Raider* 35 ft *10,67 m*	Jersey, C.I.	Newport, R.I.	43 days	1976
Oldest Solo Sailing	Jean Gau (72 years)	*Atom* 30 ft *9,14 m*	New York	France (wrecked N. Africa)	50 days	1975

TRANS-PACIFIC MARINE RECORDS

Fastest (Trans Pac)	Bill Lee (US)	*Merlin* 67 ft *20,42 m* sloop	Los Angeles, Cal	Honolulu, Hawaii	8 days 11 hr 1 min	1977
Fastest Yacht (Australia-Horn)	O.K. Pennendreft (Fr) plus 13 crew	*Kriter II* 80 ft *24,38 m*	Sydney	Cape Horn	21 days (275 mpd)	1975/6
Fastest Clipper (Australia-Horn)	Capt J. N. Forbes (GB) and crew	*Lightning* 244 ft *74,36 m*	Melbourne	Cape Horn	19 days 1 hr (315 mpd)	1854
Fastest Solo Monohull Australia-Horn	Chris Baranowski (Poland) (No 36 solo circum)	*Polonez* 45 ft 3 in *13,8 m*	Hobart	Cape Horn	45 days (135 mpd)	1973
Fastest Solo Multihull (Australia-Horn)	Alain Colas (Fr) (No 40 solo circum)	*Pen Duick IV* trimaran 70 ft *21,33 m*	Sydney	Cape Horn	37 days (160 mpd)	1973/4
Earliest Solo (Woman)	Sharon Sites Adams (US)	*Sea Sharp II* 31 ft *9,45 m*	Yokohama, Japan	San Diego, Cal	75 days (5911 miles)	1969
Earliest Rowing	John Fairfax (GB) Sylvia Cook (GB)	*Britannia II* 35 ft *10,66 m*	San Francisco, Cal. 26 Apr 1971	Hayman I., Australia 22 Apr 1972	362 days	1971/ 1972
Earliest Rowing Solo	Anders Svedlund (Sweden)	*Waka Moana* 24 ft *7,3 m*	Chile (2 June)	Samoa	118 days	1974

N.B.—The earliest single-handed Pacific crossings were achieved East-West by Bernard Gilboy (US) in 1882 in the 18 ft *5,48 m* double-ender *Pacific* to Australia and West-East by Fred Rebel (Latvia) in the 18 ft *5,48 m* *Elaine*, (from Australia) and Edward Miles (US) in the 36¾ ft *11,2 m* *Sturdy II* (from Japan) both in 1932, the latter via Hawaii.

Delmar Shelton, William Bell and Stephen Porter of the Duke University Medical Center, Durham, N. Carolina who set a simulated deep diving record of 2132 ft *649,8 m* on 14 Mar 1980. On 3 Feb 1981 Porter and two colleagues set a new record of 2250 ft *685,8 m* (see p. 176). (*M. Brenner*)

She died unmarried on 26 Oct 1969 having drawn the pension for every day of her life of 97 years 3 months.

Doctors *Oldest*
The oldest doctor currently known to be in practice is Dr Walter L Pannell, who graduated in Canada in 1903 and was seeing patients daily during 1980.

Doctors *Most in a family*
Eight sons of John Robertson of Benview, Dumbarton, Scotland graduated as medical doctors between 1892 and 1914. The family of David L. Bernie of Dayton, Ohio contains 27 members who are qualified MDs with 5 more in medical school.

MISCELLANEOUS ENDEAVOURS
Accordion playing
Norman English of Fanfare Music, Chorley, Lancs played an accordion for 82 hr 50 min on 6–9 Apr 1981.

Apple peeling
The longest single unbroken apple peel on record is one of 172 ft 4 in *52,51 m* peeled by Kathy Wafler, 17 of Wolcott, NY, USA in 11 hr 30 min at Long Ridge Mall, Rochester, NY on 16 Oct 1976. The apple weighed 20 oz *567 g*.

Apple picking
The greatest recorded performance is 365½ US bushels (354.1 Imperial bushels *128,80 hectolitres*) picked in 8 hr by George Adrian, 32 of Indianapolis, Indiana on 23 Sept 1980.

Bag-carrying
The greatest non-stop bag-carrying feat carrying 1 cwt *50,8 kg* of household coal in an open bag is 22.2 miles *35,72 km* by Brian Newton, 29 from Leicester to Rearsby and back in 6 hr 7 min on 12 Nov 1976.

The record for the 1012,5 m *1107.2 yd* course annual Gawthorpe, West Yorkshire race is 4 min 19 sec by Terry Lyons, 36 on 16 Apr 1979.

Bag-pipes
The longest duration pipe has been one of 100 hr by Neville Workman, Clive Higgins, Patrick Forth and Paul Harris, playing two at a time in shifts, of Churchill School Pipe Band, Salisbury, Rhodesia on 9–13 July 1976.

Balancing on one foot
The longest recorded duration for balancing on one foot is 33 hr by V S Kumar Anandan of Colombo, Sri Lanka on 15–17 May 1980. The disengaged foot may not be rested on the standing foot nor may any sticks be used for support or balance.

Ball punching
The world duration ball punching record is 146 hr 20 min by Pat McEnteggart of Shallon, Julianstown, Co. Meath, Ireland on 27 Feb–5 Mar 1981.

Balloon flights
The longest reported toy balloon flight is one of 9000 miles *14 500 km* from Atherton, California, USA, (released by Jane Dorst on 21 May 1972) and found on 10 June at Pietermaritzburg, South Africa. The longest recorded hydrogen-filled balloon flight from the geographical British Isles is one of 5880 miles *9460 km* from Jersey which was returned from Camps Bay, Cape Province, South Africa on 28 Apr 1974, 43 days after release by Gerard Wankling.

Balloon release
The largest ever balloon release has been one of 156,000 helium balloons from the Fuji Safari Park Japan, on 29 Mar 1981 on the occasion of the opening of the 8th *Guinness Museum of World Records*.

Band marathons
The longest recorded 'blow-in' is 100 hr 2 min by the Du Val Senior High School, Lanham, Maryland, USA on 13–17 May 1977.

Band One-man
Don Davis of Hollywood, California, USA, was the first one-man band able to play 4 melody and 2 percussion instruments simultaneously without electronics in 1974. For his rendition of the 4th movement of Beethoven's Fifth, he utilizes his unique 8-prong pendular perpendicular piano pounder and semicircular chromatic radially-operated centrifugally sliding left-handed glockenspiel. The greatest number of instruments played in a single tune is 75 in 2 min 11.2 sec by Rory Blackwell at the EMI Bingo and Social Club, Derry's Cross, Plymouth, Devon on 6 Sept 1977. The Professor of Music at the University of Connecticut, USA certified on 11 Aug 1978 that James Blain played 8 instruments (4 melodic and 4 percussion) simultaneously. Mik

Vallintine of New Romney, Kent, played his one-man band (which must include at least 3 instruments played simultaneously) for 42 hr 29 min on 16–18 June 1980 for charity at East Cliff Pavilion, Folkestone, Kent.

Barrel jumping

The official distance record is 28 ft 8 in *8,73 m* over 17 barrels by Kenneth Lebel at Liberty, New York, USA on 12 Feb 1965. Yvon Jolin (Canada) cleared 18 barrels (27 ft 8 in *8,43 m*) at the Quebec Provincial Championship of 1980.

The feminine record is 20 ft 4½ in *6,21 m* over 11 barrels by Janet Hainstock in Michigan on 15 Mar 1980.

Barrel rolling

The record for rolling a full 36 gallon metal beer barrel over a measured mile is 8 min 15 sec by a team of six from Tinwald Rugby Club, Ashburton, New Zealand on 3 Mar 1980.

Barrow pushing

The heaviest loaded barrow pushed for a minimum 20 ft is one loaded with 289 bricks weighing a gross 1.95 tons (*2347 lb 1064,5 kg*) by Bill Richardson of Pontefract, Yorks on 30 June 1979.

Barrow Racing

The fastest time reached for a 1 mile *1,609 km* wheelbarrow race is 5 min 1.59 sec by Bryan Zellweger ('charger') and Jack Zellweger ('rider') at the Ladner Centennial Sports Festival, Delta, BC, Canada on 1 July 1979

Bath tub racing

The record for the annual international 36 miles *57,9 km* Nanaimo to Vancouver, British Columbia bath tub race is 1 hr 29 min 40 sec by Gary Deathbridge (Australian) on 30 July 1978. Tubs are limited to 75 in *1,90 m* and 6 hp motors. The greatest distance for paddling a hand propelled bath tub in 24 hr is 55 miles 425 yd *88,90 km* by a team of 25 from Worcester Canoe Club on 28/29 Sept 1979.

Baton twirling

Three members of the Havant Hurricanes of Hayling Island, Hampshire twirled for 77 hr 45 min on 21–24 Apr 1981.

Beard of bees

A beard of bees estimated at not less than 21,000 swarmed on the chest and throat of Don Cooke, Ohio, USA on 20 June 1980. The British record is 20,000 on the bare chest and throat of Howard Davis of Bridgwater, Somerset in May 1952.

Bed making

The record time set under the rigorous rules of the Australian Bedmaking Championships is 28.2 sec by Wendy Wall, 34, of Hebersham, Sydney, NSW on 30 Nov 1978.

The British record with 1 blanket, 2 sheets, an undersheet, an uncased pillow, 1 counterpane and 'hospital' corners is 24.0 sec by Judith Strange and Catheryn Marsden of High Peak College, Buxton, Derbyshire on 11 Mar 1978.

Bed of nails

The duration record for non-stop lying on a bed of nails (sharp 6-inch *15,2 cm*; 2 in *5 cm* apart) is 102 hr 23½ min by the Rev Ken Owen at the YMCA, Port Talbot, W Glamorgan, Wales on 29 Sept–30 Oct 1980. The female record is 30 hr (non-stop) set by Geraldine Williams (Miranda, Queen of the *fakirs*) of Welwyn Garden City, Hertfordshire, on 18–19 Mar 1977. Much longer durations are claimed by uninvigilated *fakirs*—the most extreme case being *Silki* who claimed 111 days in São Paulo, Brazil ending on 24 Aug 1969.

Note: Now that weights in Bed of Nails contests have attained ¾ ton 762 kg the following category has been retired. No further claims for publication will be entertained or published.

The ultimate weight in an Iron Maiden, being sandwiched between two beds of nails, was 1642½ lb *745,02 kg* endured by Komar (Vernon E. Craig) at Old Chicago Towne, Chicago, Illinois, USA, on 6 Mar 1977.

Bed pushing

The longest recorded push of a normally sessile object is of 3233 miles 1150 yd *5204 km* in the case of a wheeled hospital bed by a team of 9 employees of Bruntsfield Bedding centre, Edinburgh on 21 June–26 July 1979.

Bed race

The record time for the annual Knaresborough Bed Race (established 1966) in North Yorkshire is 13 min 28 sec for the 2 mile 63 yd *3,27 km* course crossing the River Nidd by the ICI Fibres Flying Fiasco team on 9 June 1979.

Beer label collecting

The greatest collection of different British Beer labels is 22,000 by Keith Osborne, Hon Sec of The Labologists Society (founded by Guinness Exports Ltd in 1958). His oldest is a Bass label of 1869.

Beer mat flipping

Lack of standardisation of the size and weight of beer mats has bedevilled the chronicling of records in this international pursuit.

A figure of 102 was reported from Stephen Thornton, 22, of Romsey Hants on 16 Jan 1980.

Best man

The world's champion 'best man' is Mr Wally Gant, a bachelor fishmonger from Wakefield, West Yorkshire, who officiated for the 50th time since 1931 in December 1964.

Bicycle *Most mounting simultaneously*

In August 1977 Chinese circus acrobats demonstrated the ability of a troupe of 12 (sometimes 13) to mount and ride a single bicycle in Peking.

Big Wheel riding

The endurance record for riding a Big Wheel is 37 days by Rena Clark and Jeff Block at Frontier Village Amusement Park, San Jose, California, USA on 1 July–7 Aug 1978.

Howard Davis of Bridgwater, Somerset who allowed 20,000 bees to swarm on him as a 'living beard' in May 1952.

Billiard table jumping

Joe Darby (1861–1937) cleared a full-sized 12 ft *3,65 m* billiard table lengthwise, taking off from a 4 in *10 cm* high solid wooden block, at Wolverhampton, West Midlands on 5 Feb 1892.

Bomb defusing

The highest reported number of unexploded bombs defused by any individual is 8000 by Werner Stephan in West Berlin, Germany, in the 12 years from 1945 to 1957. He was killed by a small grenade on the Grunewald blasting site on 17 Aug 1957.

Bond signing

The greatest historical feat of bond signing was that performed by L. E. Chittenden (d. 1902), the Registrar of the United States Treasury. In 48 hr (20–22 Mar 1863) he signed 12,500 bonds worth $10,000,000 (*now £4.5 million*), which had to catch a steam packet to England. He suffered years of pain and the bonds were never used.

Boomerang throwing

The earliest mention of a word similar to *boomerang* is *wo-mur-rang* in Collins *Acct. N.S. Wales Vocab.* published in 1798. The earliest certain Australian account of a returning boomerang (term established, 1827) was in 1831 by Major (later Sir Thomas) Mitchell. Curved throwing sticks for wild fowl hunting were found in the tomb of Tutankhamun dating from the mid 14th century BC.

World championships and codified rules were not established until 1970. Jeff Lewry has won in 1970–71–72–73 and also the Australian title in 1974. The Boomerang Association of Australia's official record for distance reached from the thrower before the boomerang returns is 88,2 m *289 ft 4 in* diameter (orbital path 270 m *885 ft*) by Leo Meier (Switzerland) at Darlington Point, NSW on 6 Nov 1976. The longest out and return record on record is one of 370 ft *112,7 m* by Al Gerhards at Old Westbury, Long Island, NY on 20 Oct 1979.

Brick carrying

The greatest distance achieved for carrying a brick 8 lb 15 oz *4,053 kg* in a nominated ungloved hand in an uncradled downward pincher grip is 45 miles *72,4 km* by David and Kym Barger of Lamar, Missouri, USA on 21 May 1977.

The feminine record for a 9 lb 12 oz *4,422 kg* brick is 19.2 miles *30,89 km* by Cynthia Ann Smolko of Denville, New Jersey, USA on 14 May 1977. The British record for a 6 lb *2,72 kg* smooth-sided brick is 3 miles *4,82 km* by Karen Stevenson of Wallasey, Merseyside on 24 Jan 1981.

Bricklaying

Ralph Charnock of Benfleet, Essex set the National Bricklaying Championship record at Colindale, north-west London on 24 Oct 1979. He laid 698 bricks in 60 minutes, according to the strict rules of the Guild of Bricklayers.

Brick racing

The record times recorded at the Annual NFBTE Young Builders Dry-brick championship in Leicester are 100 metres: 1 min 7.0 sec + 11 penalty points giving a gross 1 min 18.0 sec by Ian Jones on 3 June 1979, and 1 mile (team): 21 min 25 sec + 118 penalties giving an overall time of 23 min 23 sec by William Davis & Company (Leicester) Ltd, on 15 June 1980.

Brick throwing

The greatest reported distance for throwing a standard 5 lb *2,268 kg* building brick is 44,54 m *146 ft 1 in* by Geoffrey Capes at Braybrook School, Orton Goldhay, Cambridgeshire on 19 July 1978.

Bubble gum blowing

The greatest reported diameter for a bubble gum bubble is 19¼ in *48,9 cm* by Susan Montgomery, 18 of Fresno, Calif, USA in April 1979. The British record also using 'Bubble Yum' is 16½ in *41,91 cm* by Nigel Fell, 13 from Derriaghy, N. Ireland in November 1979.

Burial alive

Voluntary burial alive (for which claims up to 217 days have been published) are inadmissible unless the depth of the coffin is a minimum 2 m *6 ft 6¾ in* below ground; the coffin has a maximum cubic capacity of 1,5 million cc or *54 ft³* and the aperture for communication and feeding has a maximum dimension of 10 cm or *4 inches*.

'Country' Bill White, 44, used an inadmissible 8 in square *20,3 × 20,3 cm* aperture in his 134 day 2 hr 5 min burial at New Bedford, Massachusetts on 29 Jan–12 June 1978 but the Sheriff of Bristol County certified that he remained underground throughout.

Camping Out

Two brothers Sven and Per and a sister Kari Heistad of Lebanon, New Hampshire, USA have never slept indoors since March 1974. The coldest they have experienced has been Christmas morning 1980 with a wind chill temperature of −67° F *−55° C*, which to them is a 'three-bag night'. Also remarkably the family have no television.

Canal Jumping

In the Channel 8 TV show *Challenge the Guinness '80* on 28 Mar 1980 Douwe Bult (Netherlands) leapt 13,33 m *43 ft 8¾ in* across water with a pole near Tokyo, Japan.

Can top collecting

The longest recorded one-man chain of can tops is one of 11.2 miles *18,02 km* collected since 4 July 1969 by Arthur J. Jordan Sr of Yorkstown, Virginia, USA to the estimated number of 710,000 as of 14 May 1979.

Card throwing

Kevin St Onge threw a standard playing card 185 ft 1 in *56,41 m* at the Henry Ford Community College Campus, Dearborn, Michigan, USA on 12 June 1979.

Carriage Driving

The only man to drive 48 horses in a single hitch is Dick Sparrow of Zearing, Iowa, USA in 1972–77. The lead horses were 135 ft *41 m* away.

Car wrecking

The greatest number of cars wrecked in a stunting career is 1514 to 1 July 1980 by Dick Sheppard of Gloucester, England.

Catapulting

The greatest recorded distance for a catapult shot is 1362 ft *415 m* by James F. Pfotenhauer using a patented 16½ ft *5,02 m* 'Monarch IV Supershot' and a 53 calibre lead shot on Ski Hill, Escanaba, Michigan, USA on 10 Sept 1977.

Champagne fountain

The tallest successfully filled column of champagne glasses is one 21 high filled from the top by Carl Groves and Keith Pepper at Frankston, Vic, Australia on 10 Mar 1981.

Clapping

The duration record for continuous clapping (sustaining an average of 140 claps per min audible at 100 yd *91 m*) is 42 hr 6 min by Pubudu Senanayaka of Ananda College, Colombo, Sri Lanka on 18–19 Jan 1980.

Club swinging

Bill Franks set a world record of 17,280 revolutions (4.8 per sec) in 60 min at Webb's Gymnasium, Newcastle, NSW, Australia on 2 Aug 1934. M. Dobrilla swung continuously for 144 hr at Cobar, NSW finishing on 15 Sept 1913.

Coal cutting

The most productive coal mine in Britain has been Bagworth Colliery, Leicestershire with 5.8 tonnes per man shift in the 41 weeks from April to 31 Dec 1980. The colliery dates from 1829. The individual record for filling is 218 tons in a week of 5 shifts by Jim Marley (b. 1914) at East Walbottle Colliery, Tyne and Wear, England in 1949. This included 47½ tons in 6 hr.

Coal shovelling

The record for filling a half-ton *508 kg* hopper with coal is 31.5 sec by Robert Taylor of Dobson, New Zealand on 7 Feb 1981.

Coin balancing

The greatest recorded feat of coin-balancing is the stacking of 170 Canadian coins on top of a Canadian Commemorative penny which was freestanding vertically on another coin by Bruce McConachy (b. 1963) of West Vancouver, BC, on 24 Aug 1979.

Coin snatching
The greatest number of 10p pieces clean caught from being flipped from the back of a forearm into the same palm is 62 by Andrew Gleed at the *Evening Star* offices, Ipswich on 22 Sept 1978. It is contended that claims beyond 100 coins (using US 25 cent pieces) are beyond the capacity of the human hand. Such claims remain under investigation.

Competition winnings
The largest individual competition prize win on record is $307,500 (*then £109,821*) by Herbert J. Idle, 55, of Chicago in an encyclopaedia contest run by Unicorn Press Inc on 20 Aug 1953. The highest value first prize offered in Britain has been a fully furnished Thatched Cottage worth 'over £30,000' by Country Life English Butter for an 'order of merit' contest with 3,628,880 permutations closing on 31 July 1980.

Complainer Most successful
Ralph Charell (b. 3 Dec 1929), author of *How I Turn Ordinary Complaints into Thousands of Dollars*, between January 1963 and June 1977 amassed a total of $80,710.46 (£42,480) ranging between $6.95 and $25,000 in refunds and compensations. A recent complaint was against this publication for failing to list his 51 consecutive profitable transactions in 'option trading'.

Cow chip tossing
The record distance for throwing a dried cow chip depends on whether or not the projectile may or may not be 'moulded into a spherical shape'. The greatest distance achieved under the 'non-sphericalization and 100% organic' rule (established in 1970) is 219 ft 6 in *66,9 m* by Mr Robert D. Fleming, of Taylorville, Illinois on 26 Aug 1978. These increasing distances are anxiously studied by party political campaign managers who are also in support of a rule which precludes the common practice of mixing cement kiln dust into the cow feed prior to contests.

Crawling
The longest continuous voluntary crawl (progression with one or other knee in unbroken contact with the ground) on record is 40,767 km *25.33 miles* by Michael Speed at Manly Oval, NSW, Australia on 28–30 Aug 1980.

Crochet
The longest recorded crocheted chain is one of 4 ply yarn measuring 25.70 miles *41,3 km* completed by Mrs Theresa Bloxsome of Mortlake in April 1978. Mrs Sybille Anthony bettered all knitting marathons in a 120 hr crochet marathon at Toombul Shopping-town, Queensland, Australia on 3–7 Oct 1977.

Cucumber slicing
Norman Johnson of Blackpool College of Art and Technology set a record of 24.2 sec for slicing a 12 in cucumber 1½ in diameter at 20 slices to the inch (total 240 slices) on BBC TV *Record Breakers* on 28 Sept 1973.

Custard pie throwing
The most times champion in the annual World Custard Pie Championships at Coxheath, Kent (instituted 1967) have been the 'The Birds' and the Coxheath Man each with 3 wins. The target (face) must be 8 ft 3⅞ in *2,53 m* from the thrower who must throw a pie no more than 10¾ in *27,3 cm* in diameter. Six points are scored for a square hit full in the face.

DANCING
Largest dance
The largest dance ever staged was that put on by the Houston Livestock Show at the Astro Hall, Houston, Texas, USA on 8 Feb 1969. The attendance was more than 16,500 with 4000 turned away.

Marathon dancing must be distinguished from dancing mania, which is a pathological condition. The worst outbreak of dancing mania was at Aachen, Germany, in July 1374, when hordes of men and women broke into a frenzied and compulsive choreomania in the streets which lasted for hours till injury or complete exhaustion ensued.

The most severe marathon dance staged as a public spectacle in the USA was one lasting 4152½ hr (24 weeks 5 days) completed by Tony Alteriri and Vera Mikus (now Mrs Oglesby of Springdale, Pennsylvania) at Motor Square Garden, Pittsburgh from 6 June to 30 Nov 1932. The rest allowance of 15 min per hour was progressively cut to 10, 7, 6, 5, and in the final weeks to 3 min per hour until this Marathon Dance 'Classic' was finally stopped by the authorities. The prize of $1000 was equivalent to 24 cents per hour.

Ballet
In the *entrechat* (a vertical spring from the fifth position with the legs extended criss-crossing at the lower calf), the starting and finishing position each count as one such that in an *entrechat douze* there are *five* crossings and uncrossings. This was performed by Wayne Sleep for the BBC *Record Breakers* programme on 7 Jan 1973. He was in the air for 0.71 sec.

Ballet *Most turns*
The greatest number of spins called for in classical ballet choreography is the 32 *fouettés rond de jambe en tournant* in 'Swan Lake' by Pyotr Ilyich Chaykovskiy (Tschaikovsky) (1840–93). Miss Rowena Jackson (later Chatfield), MBE (b. Invercargill, NZ, 1925) achieved 121 such turns at her class in Melbourne, Victoria, Australia, in 1940.

Ballet *Most curtain calls*
The greatest recorded number of curtain calls ever received by ballet dancers is 89 by Dame Margaret Evelyn Arias, DBE *née* Hookham (born Reigate, Surrey, 18 May 1919), *alias* Margot Fonteyn, and Rudolf Hametovich Nureyev (born on a train near Irkutsk, USSR, 17 Mar 1938) after a performance of 'Swan Lake' at the Vienna Staatsoper, Austria, in October 1964.

Ballet *Largest Cast*
The largest number of ballet dancers used in a production in Britain has been 2000 in the London Coster Ballet of 1962, directed by Lillian Rowley, at the Royal Albert Hall, London.

Ballroom *Marathon*
The individual continuous world record for ballroom dancing is 120 hr 17 min 10 sec by Janab Fareed Nazeer on 27 Feb–4 Mar 1981 at the Open Air Theatre, Jaffna, Sri Lanka. Three girls worked shifts as his partner.

Ballroom *Champions*
The world's most successful professional ballroom dancing champions have been Bill Irvine, MBE and Bobbie Irvine, MBE, who won 13 world titles between 1960 and 1972.

The most consecutive national titles won is 10 in the New Zealand Old Time Championship by Mr Maurice Fox and his wife Royce (*née* Miles) of Palmerston North in 1959–68.

The oldest competitive ballroom dancer is Albert J. Sylvester CBE, JP (b. 24 Nov 1889) of Corsham, Wiltshire. In 1977 he won the topmost amateur Alex Moore award for a 10 dance test with his partner Paula Smith in Bath on 26 Apr 1977. By 1981 he had won nearly 50 medals and trophies since he began dancing in 1964.

Belly dancing
The longest recorded belly dance was one of 100 hr by Sabra Starr at Teplitzki's Hotel, Atlantic City, New Jersey, USA on 4–8 July 1977.

Charleston
The Charleston duration record is 110 hr 58 min by Sabra Starr of Lansdowne, Pennsylvania, USA on 15–20 Jan 1979.

Conga
The longest recorded conga was one comprising a 'snake' of 8128 people in Sidmouth, Devon on 25 Aug 1978.

Disco
The longest recorded disco dancing marathon is one of 342 hr by George Thompson in Des Moines, Iowa, USA on 6–20 Mar 1980.

Flamenco
The fastest flamenco dancer ever measured is Solero de Jerez aged 17 who in Brisbane, Australia in September 1967 in an electrifying routine attained 16 heel taps per second or a rate of 1000 a minute.

Doris Rogers of Scarboro, Ontario, Canada who set the high kicking record on 16 Feb 1980 with 8491 in 4 hr 22 min.

High kicking

The world record for high kicks is 8491 in 4 hr 22 min by Doris Rogers, 26, at the Broom and Stone, Scarboro, Ontario, Canada on 16 Feb 1980.

Jiving

The duration record for non-stop jiving is 97 hr 42 min by Richard Rimmer (with a relay of partners) of Caterham, Surrey on 11–16 Nov 1979. Under the strict rules of the European Rock n' Roll Association the duration record is 22 hr by Mirco and Manuela Catalano at the Olympia Shopping Centre, Munich on 6–7 Feb 1981.

Limbo

The lowest height for a bar (flaming) under which a limbo dancer has passed is 6⅛ in *15,5 cm* off the floor by Marlene Raymond, 15 at the Port of Spain Pavilion, Toronto, Canada on 24 June 1973. Strictly no part of the body other than the sole or side of the foot should touch the ground though the brushing of a shoulder blade does not in practice usually result in disqualification.

Tap

The fastest *rate* ever measured for any tap dancer has been 1440 taps per min (24 per sec) by Roy Castle on the BBC TV *Record Breakers* programme on 14 Jan 1973.

The greatest ever assemblage of tap dancers in a single routine is 1801 organized by Beth Obermeyer in a single routine for the T. V. show 'Twin Cities Today' on 15 Oct 1979 in Minneapolis, USA.

Dance band

The most protracted session for a dance band is one of 321 hr (13 days 9 hr) by the Black Brothers of W. Germany at Bonn ending on 2 Feb 1968. Never less than a quartet were in action during the marathon.

Demolition work

Fifteen members of the International Budo Association (Japanese martial arts) led by Phil Milner (3rd Dan Karate), demolished a 6-roomed early Victorian house at Idle, Bradford, West Yorkshire by head, foot and empty hand in 6 hr on 4 June 1972. On completion they bowed to the rubble.

Domino toppling

The greatest number of dominoes (set up singlehanded) toppled is 169,713 by Michael Cairney, 23, at the Mid-Hudson Civic Center, Plaza, Poughkeepsie, New York on 9 June 1979 for the National Hemophilia Foundation. The dominoes stretching 4.3 miles *6,9 km* fell at 2¼ mph *3,6 km/h* having taken 13 days to set up.

The record for a team (maximum 4 people) is 255,389 falling in 53 min on 24 Aug 1980 at Hakone, Japan. The 2 team members, John Wickham and Erez Klein, spent 5 weeks setting up the dominoes.

Drumming

The world's duration drumming record is 720 hr by Clifford Marshall Van Buren of Ridgefield, Conn., USA on 26 Dec 1977 to 25 Jan 1978.

Ducks and drakes

The best accepted ducks and drakes (stone-skipping) record is 24 skips (10 plinkers and 14 pitty-pats) by Warren Klope, 20 of Troy, Michigan with a 4 in *10 cm* thin flat limestone at the annual Mackinac Island, Michigan, USA stone skipping tournament on 5 July 1975. This was equalled by John S. Kolar of Birmingham, Michigan and Glenn Loy Jr of Flint, Michigan on 4 July 1977.

Egg dropping

The greatest height from which fresh eggs have been dropped (to earth) and remained intact is 198 m *650 ft* by David S. Donoghue from a helicopter on 2 Oct 1979 over Tokyo Golf Course.

Egg Hunt

The greatest egg hunt on record involved 20,160 hard-boiled eggs hidden by The Georgia Civil Air Patrol in the meadow of Stone Mountain Park, Georgia, USA for a hunt on 26 Mar 1980 by 3000 children aged 3 to 9.

Egg and spoon racing

Chris Riggio of San Francisco, California, USA completed a 28.5 mile *45,86 km* fresh egg and dessert spoon marathon in 4 hr 34 min on 7 Oct 1979.

Egg shelling

Two kitchen hands, Harold Witcomb and Gerald Harding, shelled 1050 dozen eggs in a 7¼ hr shift at Bowyers, Trowbridge, Wiltshire on 23 Apr 1971. Both are blind.

Egg throwing

The longest recorded distance for throwing a fresh hen's egg without breaking is 350 ft *106,68 m* on their 58th exchange between William Cole and Jonathan Heller in Central Park, New York, USA on 17 Mar 1979.

The Thatched Country Cottage offered as first prize in a competition run by Country Life English Butter. Worth in excess of £30,000, it is the highest valued prize ever won in Britain (see p. 183).

Escapology
The most renowned of all escape artists has been Ehrich Weiss *alias* Harry Houdini (1874–1926), who pioneered underwater escapes from locked, roped and weighted containers while hand-cuffed and shackled with irons.

One of the major manufacturers of strait-jackets acknowledges that an escapologist 'skilled in the art of bone and muscle manipulation' could escape from a standard jacket in seconds. The extreme acknowledged claim is 1.68 sec by Bill Shirk on 19 June 1979 at the Marion County Sheriff's Dept Training Center, Indianapolis, Indiana, USA. Records claimed for the highest escapes effected by strait-jacketed escapologists suspended upside-down from helicopters have been discontinued since the altitudes now far exceed the heights for attaining terminal velocity.

Family tree
The largest family tree on record is the Borton tree of 6820 names compiled by Nellaray 'Borton' Holt of Union Gap, Washington, USA over 16 years. It measures 18 × 15 ft *5,48 × 4,57 m* and extends back to 1562. She also constructed a 340 ft *103,6 m* long pedigree chart covering 16 generations commissioned by Maxine Bremermans.

Fashion show *longest*
The longest fashion show ever recorded was one which lasted 48 hr on the Roseland catwalk, Sydney, Australia on 16–18 June 1977, compèred by Patrick Bollen. Lyn Snowdon, Kay Hammond and Virginia Connor all completed 41.4 miles *66,6 km* on the catwalk.

Faux pas
If measuring by financial consequence, the greatest *faux pas* on record was that of the young multi-millionaire, James Gordon Bennett, committed on 1 Jan 1877 at the family mansion of his demure fiancée one Caroline May, in Fifth Avenue, New York City. Bennett arrived in a two-horse cutter late and obviously in wine. By dint of intricate footwork, he gained the portals to enter the withdrawing room where he was the cynosure of all eyes. He mistook the fireplace for a plumbing fixture more usually reserved for another purpose. The May family broke the engagement and Bennett (1841–1918) was obliged to spend the rest of his foot-loose and fancy-free life based in Paris with the resultant non-collection of millions of tax dollars by the US Treasury.

Feminine beauty
Female pulchritude being qualitative rather than quantitative does not lend itself to records. It has been suggested that, if the face of Helen of Troy (*c.* 1200 BC) was capable of launching 1000 ships, a unit of beauty sufficient to launch one ship should be a millihelen. The pioneer beauty contest was staged at Atlantic City, New Jersey, USA in 1921 and was won by a thin blue-eyed blonde with a 30 in *76,2 cm* chest, Margaret Gorman. The Miss World contest began in London in July 1951. The maximum dimensions of any winner were those of Miss Egypt, Antigone Costanda, in 1954 whose junoesque characteristics were at 40–26–38 in *101–66–96 cm* and thus in advance of the classic Western idea of allure. The United Kingdom is the only country to have produced four winners. They were Rosemarie Frankland (1961); Ann Sidney (1964); Lesley Langley (1965) and Helen Morgan (1974), who resigned. The maximum number of contestants was 68 in November 1975. The shortest reign was that of 18 hours by Miss Germany (Gabriella Brum) in 1980.

The tallest girl to win the Miss United Kingdom title has been Madelene Stringer (now Mrs Chandler), the 6 ft *1,82 m* tall 1977 winner from Tyne and Wear.

The world's largest beauty pageant is the annual Miss Universe contest inaugurated in Long Beach California in 1952. The most successful country has been the USA with winners in 1954–56–60–67. The number of countries represented has reached 78 with Miss Venezuela reigning in 1979.

Fire pumping
The greatest gallonage stirrup-pumped by a team of 8 in an 80 hr charity pump is 7494 gal *340,6 hectolitres* by the Witney Brigade, Oxfordshire on 26–30 Aug 1977.

Fire pump pulling
The longest unaided tow of a fire appliance in excess of 10 cwt *508 kg* in 24 hr is 217.5 miles *350 km* by a team of 32 men from the Hamburg Fire Brigade in 23 hr 55 min on 22–23 June 1980.

Flute marathon
The longest recorded marathon by a flautist is 48 hr by Joe Silmon in HMS *Grampus* in Gosport, Hampshire on 19–20 Feb 1977.

Frisbee throwing
A Frisbee is a concave plastic throwing plate. Competitive Frisbee throwing began in 1957. The International Frisbee Association indoor records are Men: 363,5 ft *110,8 m* by Joseph Youngman; and Women: 229.6 ft *69,9 m* by Suzanne Fields, both at Cedar Falls, Iowa on 26 Apr 1981. The outdoor records are: Men: 500 ft *152,4 m* by Tetsuro Arita, 4 May 1980, Tokyo, Japan; and Women: 401.5 ft *122,3 m* by Liz Reeves, 14 June 1980, Surrey, England. The throw, run and catch record is 271.2 ft *82,6 m* by Tom Monroe on 24 Aug 1979 at Irvine, California. The group marathon record is 1001 hr by The Alhambra Frisbee disc club on 7 May–18 June 1978 at Alhambra, California.

Gladiatorial combat
Emperor Trajan of Rome (AD 98–117) staged a display involving 4941 pairs of gladiators over 117 days. Publius Ostorius, a freedman, survived 51 combats in Pompeii.

Gold panning
The fastest time recorded for 'panning' 8 planted gold nuggets in a 10 in *25,4 cm* diameter pan is 13.4 sec by Dick Huber of Ahwahnee, California in the 20th World Gold Panning Championship at Tropico Gold Mine, Rosamond, California, on 2 Mar 1980. The female record is 15.27 sec by Mrs Carolyn Box also of Ahwahnee, California in the 1978 18th Championship on 4–5 Mar 1978.

Golf ball balancing
Lang Martin balanced 7 golf balls vertically without adhesive at Charlotte, North Carolina, USA on 9 Feb 1980.

Grape catching
The longest recorded distance for catching a thrown grape in the mouth is 319 ft 8 in *97,43 m* by Arden Chapman of Pioneer, Louisiana, USA, on 18 July 1980. The thrower was Jerry 'Pete' Mercer.

Grave digging
It is recorded that Johann Heinrich Karl Thieme, sexton of Aldenburg, Germany, dug 23,311 graves during a 50-year career. In 1826 *his* understudy dug his grave.

Ground Breaking
The highest number of participants in a ground-breaking ceremony has been 5714 for the Owens-Illinois headquarters building at SeaGate, Toledo, Ohio, USA on 22 May 1979.

Guitar playing
The longest recorded solo guitar playing marathon is one of 230 hr by John D. Marshall of West Bridgford, Nottingham on 18–28 Feb 1981 at the Yorker Public House, Nottingham.

Gum boot throwing
The longest recorded distance (a Size 8 Challenger Dunlop Boot) for 'Wellie wanging' is 173 ft *52,73 m* by Tony Rodgers of Warminster, Wilts on 9 Sept 1978. Rosemary Payne established the feminine record at Cannon Hill Park, Birmingham on 21 June 1975 with 129 ft 11 in *39,60 m*.

Gun running
The record for the Royal Tournament Naval Field Gun competition (instituted 1907, with present rules since 1913) is 2 min 44.4 sec by the Fleet Air Arm at Earl's Court, Kensington & Chelsea, London on 17 July 1979. The barrel alone weighs 8 cwt *406 kg*. The wall is 5 ft *1,52 m* high and the chasm 28 ft *8,53 m* across. The Portsmouth crew returned 2 min 40.7 sec in a training practice run at Whale Island, Portsmouth, Hampshire in 1972.

Haggis Hurling
The longest recorded distance for throwing a haggis (min.

weight 1 lb 8 oz *680 g* is 158 ft 2 in *48,2 m* by Robin Durant in Edzell, Tayside, Scotland on 12 Aug 1978.

Hair-dressing
Gerry Stupple of Dover, Kent cut, set and styled hair continuously for 341 hr 58 min on 5–19 Mar 1979.

Hair splitting
The greatest reported achievement in hair splitting has been that of the former champion cyclist and craftsman Alfred West (b. London, 14 Apr 1901) who has succeeded in splitting a human hair 17 times into 18 parts on eight occasions. Examples of his work are exhibited in a number of Guinness Exhibit Halls and Museums.

Hammock Swinging
V. Paratore and B. Galvin maintained a hammock in constant swinging motion for 192 hours in San Francisco, California, USA in April 1979.

Handbell ringing
The longest recorded handbell ringing recital has been one of 50 hr by the Potomac English Handbell Ringers at Landover Shopping Mall, Maryland, USA, on 14–16 Feb 1981.

Handshaking
A world record for handshaking was set up by Theodore Roosevelt (1858–1919), President of the USA, when he shook hands with 8513 people at a New Year's Day, White House Presentation in Washington, DC, USA on 1 Jan 1907. Mayor Joseph Lazarow shook hands with 11,030 people on the Boardwalk, Atlantic City, New Jersey, USA in 11 hr 5 min on 3 July 1977. Outside public life the record has become meaningless because aspirants merely tend to arrange circular queues or wittingly or unwittingly shake the same hands repetitively.

Jean-Claude Droyer nearing completion of his 300 m *984 ft* climb up the Eiffel Tower on 21 July 1980 (see p. 187). (*David F. Hoy*)

The Potomac English Handbell Ringers during their 50 hour marathon which took place on 14–16 Feb 1981.

Hand writing
The longest recorded hand written letter writing marathon is one of 505 hr and 3998 letters with their envelopes by Raymond L. Cantwell of Littlemore, Oxford, England in raising money for the Radcliffe Infirmary on 25 Aug–16 Sept 1978.

High diving
The highest regularly performed dive is that of professional divers from La Quebrada ('the break in the rocks') at Acapulco, Mexico, a height of 118 ft *36 m*. The leader of the 27 divers in the exclusive Club de Clavadistas is Raul Garcia (b. 1928) with more than 35,000 dives. The base rocks, 21 ft *6,40 m* out from the take-off, necessitate a leap of 27 ft *8,22 m* out. The water is 12 ft *3,65 m* deep. On 30 Sept 1979 Dana Kunze (US) dived *48,77 m* *160 ft* from a crane jib in Tōkyō Wan, Japan, for Fuji TV.

On 8 May 1885, Sarah Ann Henley, aged 24, jumped from the Clifton Suspension Bridge, which crosses the Avon, England. Her 250 ft *76 m* fall was slightly cushioned by her voluminous dress and petticoat acting as a parachute. She landed, bruised and bedraggled, in the mud on the north bank and was carried to hospital by four policemen. On 11 Feb 1968 Jeffrey Kramer, 24, leapt off the George Washington Bridge 250 ft *76 m* above the Hudson River, New York City, NY and survived. Of the 696 (to 1 Jan 1980) identified people who have made 240 ft *73 m* suicide dives from the Golden Gate Bridge, San Francisco, California, USA since 1937, twelve survived of whom Todd Sherratt, 17, was the only one who managed to swim ashore unaided. On 10 July 1921 a stuntman named William H. Bailey leapt from a sea-plane into the Ohio River at Louisville, Kentucky. The alleged altitude was 310 ft *94,5 m*.

Samuel Scott (US) is reputed to have made a dive of 497 ft *151,48 m* at Pattison Fall (now Manitou Falls) in Wisconsin, USA, in 1840, but this would have entailed an entry speed of 86 mph *138 km/h*. The actual height was probably 165 ft *50,30 m*. Col Harry A. Froboess (Switzerland) jumped 110 m *360 ft* into the Bodensee from the airship *Graf Hindenburg* on 22 June 1936.

The greatest height reported for a dive into a flaming tank is one of 100 ft *20,4 m* into 7½ ft *2,28 m* by Bill McGuire, 48 at the Holiday Inn, Chicago City Center, Michigan, USA on 14 Aug 1975. Kitty O'Neil dived 180 ft *54,8 m* from a helicopter over Northridge, California on 9 Sept 1979 onto an air cushion measuring 30 × 60 ft *9,14 × 18,28 m* for a TV film stunt.

Highest shallow dive
Henri La Mothe (b. 1904) set a record by diving 28 ft *8,53 m* into 12⅜ in *31,43 cm* of water in a child's paddling pool in Northridge, California, on 7 Apr 1979. He struck the water chest first at a speed of more than 25 mph *40 km/h*.

High-wire act
The greatest height above street level of any high wire performance has been from a 140 ft *42,6 m* wire between the 1350 ft

411 m twin towers of the World Trade Center, New York City by Philippe Petit, 24 of Nemours, France on 7 Aug 1974. He was charged with criminal trespass after a 75 min display of at least 7 crossings. The police psychiatrist opined 'Anyone who does this 110 storeys up can't be entirely right'.

Hitch-hiking
The title of world champion hitch-hiker is claimed by Devon Smith who from 1947 to 1971 thumbed lifts totalling 291,000 miles *468 300 km*. In 1957 he covered all the then 48 US States in 33 days. It was not till his 6013th 'hitch' that he got a ride in a Rolls-Royce. The hitch-hiking record for the 874 miles *1406 km* from Land's End, Cornwall, to John o'Groats, Highland, Scotland, is 17 hr 50 min by Andrew Markham of Brigg, S Humbs. on 3–4 Sept 1979. The time before the first 'hitch' on the first day is excluded. The fastest time recorded for the round trip is 45 hr 34 min by Guy Hobbs of Bradford-on-Avon, Wiltshire on 14–16 June 1978.

Hod carrying
Jimmy Ford of Bury, Lancashire carried bricks totalling 314 lb *142,4 kg* up the minimum 12 foot *3,65 m* ladder on 24 Aug 1980 at Blackpool. Eric Stenman of Jakobstad, Finland carried 74 bricks of 4 kg *8.8 lb* each so totalling 296 kg *652½ lb* in a 4 kg *8.8 lb* hod 5 metres *16.4 ft* on the flat before ascending up a runged ramp to a height of 7 ft *2,13 m* on 25 July 1939.

Hoop rolling
In 1968 it was reported that Zolilio Diaz (Spain) had rolled a hoop 600 miles *965 km* from Mieres to Madrid and back in 18 days.

Hop scotch
The longest recorded hop scotch marathon is one of 72 hr by 5 couples, Philip Harris and Noel Scruton, Maureen Mulquiney and Vicki Binns, Helen Young and Halimah Young, Jenny Street and Dianne Wulff, Ian Gash and Ian Macrae at Mittagong Recreation Centre, NSW, Australia on 12–15 Mar 1981.

Hot water bottle bursting
Contests involving the bursting of hot water bottles by sheer lung power is regarded as medically most inadvisable and the category has been discontinued. Substituted for this activity will be the inflation of standardized meteorogical balloons to a diameter of 8 feet *2,43 m* against time. Noel Batten of Brisbane, Australia set an inaugural mark of 6 hr 6 min (gross) with a Totex 350 gram balloon on 13 Apr 1979.

House of cards
The greatest number of storeys achieved in building freestanding houses of playing cards is 61 in the case of a tower using 3650 cards to a height of 11 ft 7 in *3,53 m* built by James Warnock at Cantley, Quebec, Canada, on 8 Sept 1978.

Hula hooping
The highest claim for sustaining gyrating hoops between shoulders and hips is 63 by Peter Hernandez, at the "Olmec Olympics", Austin, Texas, USA on 1 Apr 1979. Three complete gyrations are mandatory. The longest recorded marathon for a single hoop is 54 hr by Kym Coberly of Denton, Texas, USA on 7–9 Oct 1978.

Human cannonball
The record distance for firing a human from a cannon is 175 ft *53,3 m* in the case of Emanuel Zacchini in the Ringling Bros and Barnum & Bailey Circus, Madison Square Gardens, New York City, USA, in 1940. His muzzle velocity has been estimated at 54 mph *86,9 km/h*. On his retirement the management were fortunate in finding that his daughter Florinda was of the same calibre. An experiment on Yorkshire TV on 17 Aug 1978 showed that when Miss Sue Evans, 17 was fired she was ⅜ in *9,5 mm* shorter on landing.

In the Halifax explosion of 6 Dec 1917 (p. 238) A. B. William Becker, AM (d. 1969) was blown some 1600 yd *1,46 km* but was found breathing in a tree.

Human Chain
An estimated 17,000 people linked hands in the 'Hands Around

The Wrekin', a 1335 ft *407 m* hill in Shropshire, England on 4 May 1981, when over £1300 was raised for the International Year of the Disabled, the British Red Cross and St John's Ambulance Brigade.

Human fly
The greatest climb achieved on the vertical face of a building occurred on 26 May 1977 when George Willig, 27, scaled the outside of the 1350 ft *411,48 m* high World Trade Centre, New York City in 3½ hr at a rate of 6.4 ft/min *1,95 m/min*. On descending by elevator he was led to a waiting police car and charged with criminal trespass and reckless endangerment. The name of the masked 'human fly', who has ridden at 380 km/h *240 mph* atop a DC-8 jetliner in April 1977 has not been disclosed. It is however believed unlikely that he is a member of the jet set. Lead climber Jean-Claude Droyer (b. 8 May 1946) of Paris and Pierre Puiseux (b. 2 Dec 1953) of Pau, France climbed up the outside of the Eiffel Tower to a height of 300 m *984 ft* with no dynamic mechanical assistance on 21 July 1980. Jean-Claude took 2 hr 18 min 15 sec to complete the climb.

Joke cracking
Bob Carroll cracked jokes unremittingly for 24 hr 5 min at the Castilian Lounge, Clifton Park, New York, USA on 19–20 Nov 1979. The duration record for a duo is 52 hr by Wayne Malton and Mike Hamilton at the Howard Johnson Motor Hotel, Toronto airport, Ontario, Canada on 13–16 Nov 1975.

Jumble Sale
Britain's largest Jumble Sale was 'Jumbly '79' sponsored by *Woman's Own* at Alexandra Palace, London on 5–7 May 1979 in aid of Save The Children Fund. The attendance was 60,000 and the gross takings in excess of £60,000. The Winnetka Congregational Church, Illinois, USA raised $91,890.17 (*then £41,770*) in a one-day rummage sale on 8 May 1980.

Karate Chop
Claims for breaking bricks and wooden slats etc. are unsatisfactory because of the lack of any agreed standards of friability and the spacing of fulcrums upon which comparisons can be made. Karatekas have been measured to exert a force of 3000 newtons *675 lb f* and can develop a downward chopping speed of 14,4 m/sec *32.2 mph*.

Kiss of life
Five members of the CPR team of the University of North Carolina, Greensboro, USA maintained a 'Kiss of Life' for 200 hr with 144,000 inflations on 16–25 Aug 1980. The 'patient' was a dummy.

Kissing
The most prolonged osculatory marathon in cinematic history is one of 185 sec by Regis Toomey and Jane Wyman in *You're In the Army Now* released in 1940. In the Valentine's Day 'Big Kiss Off' for charity Debbie Luray and Jim Schuyler kissed for 5 days 12 hr at the Ocean Mall, Singer Island, Florida, USA on 14–19 Feb 1980. James Whale, 27, of Metro Radio, Newcastle-upon-Tyne kissed 4049 girls in 8 hr in Tyneside on 22 Sept 1978—a rate of one per 7.11 sec.

Underwater
The most protracted kiss underwater was one of 2 min 18 sec by Toshiaki Shirai and Yukiko Nagata on Channel 8, Fuji TV in Tokyo, Japan on 2 Apr 1980.

Kite flying *Largest*
The largest kite ever flown was the Jalbert Parafoil measuring 52 × 70 ft *15,84 × 21,33 m* and 3640 ft² *338 m²*, which flew to an altitude of 300 ft *90 m* for 2 min 47 sec at Magnuson Park, Seattle, Washington, USA on 3 Oct 1980.

Kite flying *Greatest number*
The most kites flown on a single line is 4128 by Kazuhiko Asaba, 55 at Kamakura, Japan on 21 Sept 1978.

Kite flying *Altitude*
The single kite record is 22,500 ft (min)–28,000 ft (max) *6860–8535 m* by Prof. Phillip R. Kunz and Jay P. Kunz at Laramie, Wyoming, USA on 21 Nov 1967. Only rangefinder or radar verifications are permitted by the American Kitefliers Association.

187

Cheryl Tiegs who signed the largest ever modelling contract for $1,500,000 in December 1979 with Noxelle cosmetics.

Kite flying *Duration*
The longest recorded flight is one of 169 hr by the Sunrise Inn team, Fort Lauderdale, Florida managed by Will Yolen on 30 Apr–7 May 1977.

Knitting
The world's most prolific hand-knitter of all time has been Mrs Gwen Matthewman of Featherstone, West Yorkshire. She had attained a speed of 111 stitches per min in a test at Phildar's Wool Shop, Central Street, Leeds on 29 Sept 1980. Her technique has been filmed by the world's only Professor of Knitting—a Japanese.

Knot-tying
The fastest recorded time for tying the six Boy Scout Handbook Knots (square knot, sheet bend, sheep shank, clove hitch, round turn and two half hitches and bowline) on individual ropes is 8.1 sec by Clinton R. Bailey Sr, 52, of Pacific City, Oregon, on 13 Apr 1977.

Leap frogging
Fourteen members of the Phi Gamma Delta Club at the University of Washington, Seattle, USA, covered 602 miles *968,8 km* in 126 hr 46 min on 20–25 Mar 1981.

Life saving
In November 1974 the City of Galveston, Texas and the Noon Optimist Club unveiled a plaque to the deaf-mute lifeguard Leroy Colombo (1905–74) who saved 907 people from drowning in the waters around Galveston Island from 1917 to his death.

Lightning most times struck
The only living man in the world to be struck by lightning 7 times is ex-Park Ranger Roy C. Sullivan (US), the human lightning conductor of Virginia. His attraction for lightning began in 1942 (lost big toe nail), and was resumed in July 1969 (lost eyebrows), in July 1970 (left shoulder seared), on 16 Apr 1972 (hair set on fire), on 7 Aug 1973 (new hair refired and legs seared), on 5 June 1976 ankle injured, and sent to Waynesboro Hospital with chest and stomach burns on 25 June 1977 after being struck while fishing.

Lion-taming
The greatest number of lions mastered and fed in a cage by an unaided lion-tamer was 40, by 'Captain' Alfred Schneider in 1925. Clyde Raymond Beatty handled more than 40 'cats' (mixed lions and tigers) simultaneously. Beatty (b. Bainbridge, Ohio, 10 June 1903, d. Ventura, California, 19 July 1965) was the featured attraction at every show he appeared with for more than 40 years. He insisted upon being called a lion-trainer. More than 20 lion-tamers have died of injuries since 1900.

Log rolling
The record number of International Championships is 10 by Jubiel Wickheim (of Shawnigan Lake, British Columbia, Canada) between 1956 and 1969. At Albany, Oregon on 4 July 1956 Wickheim rolled on a 14 in. *35,5 cm* log against Chuck Harris of Kelso, Washington USA for 2 hr 40 min before losing.

Merry go round
The longest merry go round marathon on record is one of 312 hr 43 min by Gary Mandau, Chris Lyons and Dana Dover in Portland, Oregon, USA on 20 Aug–2 Sept 1976.

Message in a bottle
The longest recorded interval between drop and pick-up is 64 years between 7 Aug 1910 ('please write to Miss Gladys Potter') in Grand Lake and August 1974 from Lake Huron. Miss Potter was traced as Mrs Oliver Scheid, 76 of Columbus, Ohio. A bottle apparently bearing a message written on 19 Nov 1899 by Capt Charles Weieerishen of the SS *Crown Princess Cecilia* off Varberg, Sweden was reportedly picked up on the coast of Victoria, BC Canada on 9 Dec 1936.

Milk bottle balancing
The greatest distance walked by a person continuously balancing a full pint milk bottle on the head is 18 miles 880 yd *29,7 km* by Willie Hollingsworth of Freeport, New York, USA on 24 Mar 1979.

Model *Highest Paid*
The largest reported contract in the history of modelling is $1,500,000 (*now £652,000*) for 5 years' rights to the face, eyes and lips of Cheryl Tiegs (Mrs Stan Dragoti) of the California look paid by the cosmetic group Noxell in December 1979. *Fortune Magazine* says that her legs are still "up for grabs". Though God makes models he makes very few.

Morse
The highest recorded speed at which anyone has received morse code is 75.2 words per minute—over 17 symbols per second. This was achieved by Ted R. McElroy of the United States in a tournament at Asheville, North Carolina, USA on 2 July 1939. The highest speed recorded for hand key transmitting is 175 symbols a minute by Harry A. Turner of the US Army Signal Corps at Camp Crosder, Missouri on 9 Nov 1942.

Musical chairs
The largest game on record was one starting with 4378 participants and ending with Lisa Springer, on the last chair at Ohio State University, Ohio, USA on 27 Apr 1980.

Needle threading
The record number of times a strand of cotton can be threaded through a number 13 needle (eye ½ in, by 1⁄16 in, *12,7 mm × 1,6 mm*) in 2 hr is 3795 by Miss Brenda Robinson of the College of Further Education, Chippenham, Wiltshire on 20 Mar 1971.

Noodle making
Mark Pi of the China Gate Restaurant, Toledo, Ohio, USA made 1024 noodle strings (over 5 ft *1,52 m*) in 60 sec on WDHO-TV on 4 Mar 1981.

Omelette making
The greatest number of two-egg omelettes made in 30 min is 217 by Howard Helmer of New York City, USA, at Disneyland, Anaheim, California on 14 July 1978.

Onion peeling
The record for peeling 50 lb *22,67 kg* of onions is 3 min 18 sec by Alain St. John in Plainfield, Conn., USA, on 6 July 1980.

Organ

The longest recorded electric organ marathon is one of 411 hr by Vince Bull at the Comet Hotel, Scunthorpe, South Humberside on 2–19 June 1977. The longest church organ recital ever sustained has been 90 hr by Frank Hughes at Wesley College Chapel, Dublin, Ireland on 31 Oct–4 Nov 1975.

Paddle Boating

The longest recorded voyage in a paddle boat is 2226 miles *3582 km* in 103 days by the foot power of Mick Sigrist and Brad Rud down the Mississippi from the headwaters in Minnesota to the Gulf of Mexico on 4 Aug–11 Nov 1979.

Parachuting *Longest fall without*

The greatest altitude from which anyone has bailed out without a parachute and survived is 6700 m *21,980 ft*. This occurred in January 1942, when Lt (now Lt-Col) I. M. Chisov (USSR) fell from an Ilyushin 4 which had been severely damaged. He struck the ground a glancing blow on the edge of a snow-covered ravine and slid to the bottom. He suffered a fractured pelvis and severe spinal damage. It is estimated that the human body reaches 99 per cent of its low level terminal velocity after falling 1880 ft *573 m* which takes 13–14 sec. This is 117–125 mph *188–201 km/h* at normal atmospheric pressure in a random posture, but up to 185 mph *298 km/h* in a head down position.

Vesna Vulovic, 23, a Jugoslavenski Aerotransport hostess, survived when her DC–9 blew up at 33,330 ft *10 160 m* over the Czechoslovak village of Ceská Kamenice on 25 Jan 1972. She fell inside a section of tail unit. She was in hospital for 16 months after emerging from a 27 day coma and having many bones broken. She is now Mrs Breka.

The British record is 18,000 ft *5485 m* by Flt-Sgt Nicholas Stephen Alkemade, aged 21, who jumped from a blazing RAF *Lancaster* bomber over Germany on 23 Mar 1944. His headlong fall was broken by a fir tree near Oberkürchen and he landed without a broken bone in a snow bank 18 in *45 cm* deep.

Piano-playing

The longest piano-playing marathon has been one of 1172 hr 27 min (48 days 20 hr 27 min) playing 22 hr every day (with 5 min intervals each playing hour) from 6 Jan to 24 Feb 1978 by Roger Lavern at the Osborne Tavern, London.

David Parchment, making one of his 233 parachute drops over Shobdon Air Centre, near Leominster on 19 June 1979 (see p. 192). (*John Topham Picture Library*)

The Lightning Piano Tuner Steve Fairchild who raised and then lowered the pitch of a piano in 4 min 20 sec at the Dante Piano Factory, NY, USA.

The women's world record in the discontinued non-stop category was 133 hr (5 days 13 hr) by the 20 stone *127 kg* Mrs Marie Ashton aged 40, now of Bradford, in a theatre in Blyth, Northumberland, on 18–23 Aug 1958. Her last piece was 'Five minutes more'.

Piano smashing

The record time for demolishing an upright piano and passing the entire wreckage through a circle 9 in *22,8 cm* in diameter is 1 min 37 sec by six members of the Tinwald Rugby Football Club, Ashburton, New Zealand led by David Young on 6 Nov 1977. Messrs Anthony Fukes, Mike Newman and Terry Cuilington smashed a piano with bare hands and feet in 2 min 53 sec in Nottingham on 25 Aug 1979. (All wreckage was passed through the circle.)

Piano tuning

The record time for pitch raising (one semi-tone or 100 cents) and then returning a piano to a musically acceptable quality is 4 min 20 sec by Steve Fairchild at the Piano Technicians Guild contest at the Dante Piano Co factory, NY, USA on 5 Feb 1980.

Pillar box standing

The record number of people to pile on top of a pillar box (oval top of 6 ft^2 *0,55 m^2*) is 29, all students of the City of London College, Moorgate, in Finsbury Circus, City of London on 21 Oct 1971.

Pipe smoking

The duration record for keeping a pipe (3.3 g *0.1 oz* of tobacco) continuously alight with only an initial match under IAPSC (International Association of Pipe Smokers Clubs) rules is 126 min 39 sec by the four-time champion William Vargo of Swartz Creek, Michigan at the 27th World Championships in 1975. The only 5-time champion is Paul T. Spaniola (USA) (1951–66–70–73–77). Longer durations have been recorded in less rigorously invigilated contests in which 'tamping' and 'gardening' are not unknown.

Plate spinning

The greatest number of plates spun simultaneously is 55 by Shukuni Sasaki of Takamatsu, Japan on 2 Jan 1980. The British record is 54 set by Holley Gray set during BBC *Record Breakers* on 6 May 1980.

Pogo stick jumping

The greatest number of jumps achieved is 120,715 by Jeff Kane in 16 hr 12 min at Oaklawn, Illinois USA, on 9–10 June 1980.

above: Shukuni Sasaki of Takamatsu, Japan who spun 55 plates simultaneously on 2 Jan 1980 (see p. 189).

below: John Massis demonstrating the strength of his teeth when he pulled two water skiers along the River Seine in Paris on 19 July 1980 (see p. 193). (*David F. Hoy*)

bottom: Tom McRann, who cast a 'Skyro' 857 ft 8 in *261,42 m*, the greatest distance any object heavier than air has been thrown (see p. 193).

Pole-squatting

Modern records do not, in fact, compare with that of St Simeon the Younger, (*c.* 521–597 AD) called Stylites (Greek, *stylos* = pillar) a monk who spent his last 45 years up a stone pillar on The Hill of Wonders, near Antioch, Syria. This is probably the earliest example of record setting.

There being no international rules, the 'standards of living' atop poles vary widely. The record squat is 399 days by Frank Perkins from 1 June 1975–4 July 1976 in 8 × 8 ft *2,43 × 2,43 m* box atop a 50 ft *15,24 m* telegraph pole in San Jose, California, USA.

The British record is 32 days 14 hr by John Stokes, aged 32, of Moseley, West Midlands in a barrel on a 45 ft *13,70 m* pole in Birmingham, ending on 27 June 1966. This is claimed as a world record for a barrel.

Pop group

The duration record for a 4-man pop-playing group is 144 hr by 'Rocking Ricky and the Velvet Collars' at The Talardy Hotel, St Asaph, Clwyd, N. Wales on 12–18 Nov 1976.

Potato peeling

The greatest amount of potatoes peeled by 5 people to an institutional cookery standard with standard kitchen knives in 45 min is 417 lb *189,14 kg* by the International Stores team from Newark, on 3 Nov 1980.

Pram pushing

The greatest distance covered in pushing a pram in 24 hr is 345.25 miles *555,62 km* by Runner's Factory of Los Gatos, California, USA with an All-Star team of 57 California runners on 23–24 June 1979. A team of 10 students from Sir Joseph Banks and East Hills High Schools, Chipping Norton, NSW, Australia, with an adult 'Baby', covered 388,408 km *241,34 miles* in 24 hr on 16–17 Nov 1979.

'Psychiatrist' fastest

The world's fastest 'psychiatrist' was Dr Albert L. Weiner of Erlton, New Jersey, USA, who was trained solely in osteopathy but who dealt with up to 50 psychiatric patients a day in four treatment rooms. He relied heavily on narcoanalysis, muscle relaxants and electro-shock treatments. In December 1961 he was found guilty on 12 counts of manslaughter from using unsterilized needles.

Quoit throwing

The world's record for rope quoit throwing is an unbroken sequence of 4002 pegs by Bill Irby, Snr of Australia in 1968.

Ramp jumping

The longest distance ever achieved for motor cycle long jumping is *64,60 m* 212 ft by Alain Jean Prieur (b. 4 July 1939) of France at Montlhéry near Paris over 16 buses on 6 Feb 1977. The pioneer of this form of exhibition—Evel Knievel (b. Robert Craig Knievel, 17 Oct 1938 at Butte, Montana, USA) had suffered 433 bone fractures by his 1975 season. His abortive attempt to cross the Snake River Canyon, Idaho on 8 Sept 1974 in a rocket reputedly increased his life-time earnings by $6 million (*then £2½ million*). The longest jump achieved in Britain is 190 ft *57,9 m* by Eddie Kidd at Radlett Airfield, Hertfordshire on 4 Apr 1978.

Riding in armour

The longest recorded ride in full armour (8 stone *50,8 kg*) is one of 167 miles *268,7 km* from Edinburgh to Dumfries in 3 days (riding time 28 hr 30 min) by Dick Brown, 48, on 13–15 June 1979.

Riveting

The world's record for riveting is 11,209 in 9 hr by J. Moir at the Workman Clark Ltd shipyard, Belfast, Northern Ireland, in June 1918. His peak hour was his seventh with 1409, an average of nearly 23½ per min.

Rocking chair

The longest recorded duration of a 'Rockathon' is 432 hr by Mrs Maureen Weston of Petreburgh Athletics Club, Peterborough, Cambridge on 14 Apr–2 May 1977.

Rolling pin
The record distance for a woman to throw a 2 lb *907 g* rolling pin is 175 ft 5 in *53,4 m* by Lori La Deane Adams, 21 at Iowa State Fair on 21 Aug 1979.

Scooter riding
The greatest distance covered by a team of 25 in 24 hr is 336.11 miles *540,93 km* by Wimmera Young Farmers, Victoria, Australia on 22–23 Mar 1980.

Search *Longest*
Walter Edwin Percy Zillwood (b. Deptford, London SE8, Dec 1900) traced his missing sister Lena (now Mrs Elizabeth Eleanor Allen, b. Nov 1897) after 79 years through the agency of the Salvation Army on 3 May 1980.

See-saw
George Partridge and Tamara Marquez of Auburn High School, Washington, USA on a suspension see-saw completed 1101 hr 40 min (indoor) on 28 Mar–13 May 1977. Georgia Chaffin and Tammy Adams of Goodhope Jr. High School, Cullman Alabama, USA completed 730 hr 30 min (outdoor) on 25 June–25 July 1975.

Sermon
The longest sermon on record was delivered by the Rev Donald Thomas of Brooklyn, New York, USA on 18–22 Sept 1978 for 93 hr. From 31 May to 10 June 1969 the 14th Dalai Lama (b. 6 July 1934 as Tenzin Gyalto) the exiled ruler of Tibet, completed a sermon on Tantric Buddhism for 5–7 hr per day to total 60 hr in India.

Shaving
The fastest demon barber on record is Jerry Harley, who shaved 368 men in 60 min with a *cut-throat* razor at Command House, Chatham, Kent on 20 Aug 1979.

Sheaf tossing
The world's best performance for tossing a 3,63 kg *8 lb* sheaf for height is 19,77 m *64.86 ft* by Trond Ulleberg of Skolleborg, Norway on 11 Nov 1978. Such pitchfork contests date from 1914.

Shoeshine boys
In this category (limited to a team of 4 teenagers; duration of 8 hr; shoes 'on the hoof') the record is 6334 pairs by the Bedford North (Newnham) Scout Group on 16 July 1977.

Shorthand fastest
The highest recorded speeds ever attained under championship conditions are: 300 words per min (99.64 per cent accuracy) for 5 min and 350 wpm (99.72 per cent accuracy, that is, two insignificant errors) for 2 min by Nathan Behrin (USA) in tests in New York in December 1922. Behrin (b. 1887) used the Pitman system invented in 1837. Morris I. Kligman, official court reporter of the US Court House, New York has taken 50,000 words in 5 hr (a sustained rate of 166.6 wpm). Rates are much dependent upon the nature, complexity and syllabic density of the material. Mr G. W. Bunbury of Dublin, Ireland held the unique distinction of writing at 250 wpm for 10 min on 23 Jan 1894.

Mr Arnold Bradley achieved a speed of 309 words per minute without error using the Sloan-Duployan system with 1545 words in 5 minutes in a test in Walsall, West Midlands on 9 Nov 1920.

Shouting
The greatest number of wins in the national town criers' contest is 11 by Ben Johnson of Fowey, Cornwall, who won in 1939, 1949–55, 1966, 1969 and 1973. The first national feminine champion has been Mrs Henrietta Sargent, town-crier, of The Three Horse Shoes, Cricklade, Wiltshire in 1980. On being told she had beaten the other 31 contestants she said 'I'm speechless'. (See also Longest-ranged voice, Chapter I page 22.)

Showering
The most prolonged continuous shower bath on record is one of 336 hr by Arron Marshall of Rockingham Park, Western Australia on 29 July–12 Aug 1978. The feminine record is 120 hr 1 min by Penny Cresswell of Waikiki, Western Australia on 7–12 Sept 1977. Desquamation can be a positive danger.

Singing
The longest recorded solo singing marathon is one of 153 hr by Bob Anthony in Hayes, Middlesex on 2–8 Sept 1979. The marathon record for a choir has been 72 hr 2 min by the combined choir of Girl's High School and Prince Edward School, Salisbury, Zimbabwe on 7–10 Sept 1979. Acharya Prem Bhikuji started chanting the Akhand Ram Dhum in 1964 and devotees took this up in rotation completing their devotions 13 years later on 31 July 1977 at Jamnagar, India.

Skate boarding
'World' championships have been staged intermittently since 1966. Mike Kinney won a marathon contest at Reseda, California on 26 May 1979 with 217.3 miles *349,7 km* in 30 hr 35 min.

The highest speed recorded on a skate board is 71.79 mph *115,53 km/h* under USSA rules on a course at Mt Baldy, California in a prone position by Richard K. Brown, 33, on 17 June 1979. The stand-up record is 53.45 mph *86,01 km/h* by John Hutson, 23 at Signal Hill, Long Beach, California on 11 June 1978. The high jump record is 5 ft 3 in *1,60 m* by Trevor Baxter (b. 1 Oct 1962) of Burgess Hill, Sussex at the Skatepark, Southsea, Hants on 6 July 1980. At the 4th US Skateboard Association championship, at Signal Hill on 25 Sept 1977, Tony Alva, 19, jumped 17 barrels (17 ft *5,18 m*).

Skipping
The longest recorded non-stop skipping marathon was one of 9 hr 46 min by Katsumi Suzuki in Kumagaya Gymnasium, Saitama, Japan on 23 Mar 1980.

Other records made without a break:

Most quintuple turns	5 by Katsumi Suzuki, Saitama, Japan, 29 May 1975	
Most turns in 1 min	330 by Brian D. Christensen, Ridgewood Shopping Center, Tennessee, 1 Sept 1979	
Most turns in 10 sec	108 by Albert Rayner, Wakefield, W. Yorks, 28 June 1978	
Most doubles (with cross)	691 by Frank P Oliveri at Henrietta, NY, USA 6 Nov 1980	
Double turns	10 133 by Katsumi Suzuki, Saitama, Japan, 27 Sept 1979	
Treble turns	381 by Katsumi Suzuki, Saitama, Japan, 29 May 1975	
Quadruple turns	51 by Katsumi Suzuki, Saitama, Japan, 29 May 1975	
Duration	1264 miles *2034 km* by Tom Morris, Brisbane-Cairns, Queensland, 1963	
Most on single rope (32 turns)	88 (50 m rope) Todoroki Ground, Kanagawa, Japan 24 Oct 1980	
On a tightrope	55 (consecutive) by Bryan Andrew (*né* Dewhurst) BBC TV Centre, London 5 May 1980	

Slinging
The greatest distance recorded for a sling-shot is 1147 ft 4 in *349,70 m* using a 34 in *86 cm* long sling and a 7½ oz *212 g* stone by Melvyn Gaylor on Newport Golf Course, Shide, Isle of Wight on 25 Sept 1970.

Smoke ring blowing
The highest recorded number of smoke rings formed from the lips from a single pull of a cigarette (cheek-tapping is disallowed) is 355 by Jan van Deurs Formann of Copenhagen achieved in Switzerland in August 1979.

Snakes and Ladders
The longest recorded game of Snakes and Ladders has been one of 216 hr by two teams of six (playing independently) (four from each team always in play) from 13th Barking St. Patrick's Scout Group and Mayesbrook School, Dagenham, Essex on 19–28 July 1980.

Snow shoeing
The fastest officially recorded time for covering a mile *1609,34 m* is 6 min 23.8 sec by Richard Lemay (Frontenac Club, Quebec, Canada) at Manchester, New Hampshire, USA in 1973.

Parachuting Records

First from Tower	Louis-Sébastian Lenormand (1757–1839)	quasi-parachute	Montpellier France		1783
First from Balloon	André-Jacques Garnerin (1769–1823)	2230 ft *680 m*	Monceau Park, Paris	22 Oct	1797
Earliest Mid-air Rescue	Miss Louie May held by Miss Dolly Shepard on a single 'chute	from balloon at 11,000 ft *3350 m*	Longton, Staffordshire	9 June	1908
First from Aircraft (man)	Capt. Albert Berry	US Army	St. Louis, Missouri	1 Mar	1912
(woman)	Mrs Georgina 'Tiny' Broadwick (b. 1893)		Griffith Park, Los Angeles	21 June	1913
First Free Fall	Mrs Georgina 'Tiny' Broadwick	Pilot Glenn L. Martin	North Island, San Diego, California	13 Sept	1914
Lowest Escape	S/Ldr Terence Spencer, DFC, RAF	30–40 ft *9–12 m*	Wismar Bay, Baltic	19 April	1945
Longest Duration Fall	Lt Col Wm H. Rankin USMC	40 min due to thermals	North Carolina	26 July	1956
Highest Escape	Flt Lt J. de Salis and Fg Off P. Lowe, RAF	56,000 ft *17 068 m*	Monyash, Derby	9 April	1958
Longest Delayed Drop (man)	Capt Joseph W. Kittinger[1]	84,700 ft 16.04 miles *25 816 m* from balloon at 102,800 ft *31 333 m*	Tularosa, New Mexico	16 Aug	1960
(woman)	O. Kommissarova (USSR)	14 100 m *46,250 ft*	over USSR	21 Sept	1965
(civilian, over UK)	John Noakes (GB)	22,000 ft from 25,000 ft *7620 m*	Salisbury Plain, Wiltshire	15 May	1973
(civilian, world)	R. W. K. Beckett (GB) Harry Ferguson (GB)	30,000 ft *9144 m* from 32 000 ft *9753 m*	D. F. Malan Airport, Capetown	23 Nov	1969
Most Southerly	T/Sgt Richard J. Patton (d. 1973)	Operation Deep Freeze	South Pole	25 Nov	1956
Most Northerly	Raymond Zebulon Munro (Canada)	−39° F (−39,4° C)	In 89° 39′ N	31 Mar	1969
Cross Channel (Lateral fall)	Sgt. Bob Walters with 3 soldiers and 2 Royal Marines	22 miles *35,4 km* from 25,000 ft *7600 m*	Dover to Sangatte, France	31 Aug	1980
Career Total (man)	Yuri Baranov and Anatolyi Osipov (USSR)	10,000	over USSR	to Sept	1980
(woman)	Valentina Zakoretskaya (USSR)	8000	over USSR	1964–Sept	1980
Highest Landing	Ten USSR parachutists[2]	23,405 ft *7133 m*	Lenina Peak	May	1969
Heaviest Load	US Space Shuttle *Columbia* external rocket retrieval	80 ton capacity, triple array, each 120 ft *36,5 m* diameter	Atlantic off Cape Canaveral, Florida	12 Apr	1981
Highest from Bridge	Donald R. Boyles	1053 ft *320 m*	Royal Gorge, Colorado	7 Sept	1970
Highest Tower Jump	Herbert Leo Schmidtz (US)	KTUL-TV Mast 1984 ft *604 m*	Tulsa, Oklahoma	4 Oct	1970
Biggest Star (5 sec hold)	32 man Enquirer Team	Formation held 5 sec (FAI rules)	Tahlequah, Oklahoma	14 July	1975
Highest column	8 man Enquirer Team	170 ft *52 m*	over California, USA	Oct	1978
Most travelled	Kevin Seaman from a Cessna Skylane (pilot Charles E. Merritt)	12,186 miles *19 611 km*	Jumps in all 50 US States	26 July– 15 Oct	1972
Oldest Man	Bob Broadbere (GB) (1892–1977)	85 years (broke glasses)	Honiton, Devon, England	10 July	1977
Woman	Mrs. Ardath Evitt (US)	74 years 6 months	Mooresville, Indiana, USA	6 Aug	1978
24 Hr Total	David Parchment (GB)	233 (18 hr 7 min)	Shobdon Air Centre, nr Leominster, Hereford & Worcs.	19 June	1979

[1] *Maximum speed in rarefied air was 625.2 mph 1006 km/h. at 90,000 ft 27,430 m – marginally supersonic.*
[2] *Four were killed.*

Spinning

The duration record for spinning a clock balance wheel by hand is 5 min 26.8 sec by Philip Ashley, aged 16, of Leigh, Greater Manchester on 20 May 1968.

Spitting

The greatest distance achieved at the annual tobacco spitting classic (instituted 1955) at Raleigh, Mississippi is 31 ft 1 in *9,47 m* by Don Snyder, 28, on 26 July 1975. In the 3rd International Spittin', Belchin' and Cussin' Triathlon, Harold Fielden reached 34 ft 0¼ in *10,36 m* at Central City, Colorado USA on 13 July 1973. Distance is dependent on the quality of salivation, absence of cross wind, two finger pucker and the coordination of the back arch and neck snap. Sprays or wads smaller than a dime are not measured. Randy Ober of Bentonville, Arkansas, USA spat a tobacco wad 44 ft 6 in *13,56 m* at the Calico 3rd Annual Tobacco Chewing and Spitting Championships north of Barstow, California, USA on 30 Mar 1980. The record for projecting a melon seed under WCWSSCA rules is 59 ft 1½ in *18,02 m* by Brian Dunne at Savemore Centre, Yeppoon, Queensland, Australia on 11 Dec 1976. The highest reported distance for a cherry stone is 65 ft 2 in *19,86 m* by Rick Krause, at Eau Claire, Michigan, USA on 5 July 1980. Spitters who care about their image wear 12 in *30,4 cm* block-ended boots so practice spits can be measured without a tape.

Stair climbing

The 100 storey record for stair climbing was set by Dennis W. Martz in the Detroit Plaza Hotel, Detroit, Michigan, USA, on 26 June 1978 at 11 min 23.8 sec. Richard Black, 44, President of the Maremont Corporation ran a vertical mile on the stairs of Lake Point Tower, Chicago on 13 July 1978 in continuous action with 1 hr 25 min 6 sec ascent time and 44 min 39 sec descent time. *These records can only be attempted in buildings with a minimum of 70 storeys.*

The record for the 1760 steps in the world's tallest free-standing structure, Toronto's CN Tower, is 10 min 16 sec by Michael Round.

Pete Squires raced up the 1575 steps of the Empire State Building, New York City on 12 Feb 1981 in 10 min 59 sec.

In the line of duty Bill Stevenson has mounted 334 of the 364 steps of the tower in the Houses of Parliament, 3392 times in 12 years (1968–80)—equivalent to 21.13 ascents of Everest.

Standing

The longest period on record that anyone has continuously stood is for more than 17 years in the case of Swami Maujgiri Mahari when performing the *Tapasya* or penance from 1955 to November 1973 in Shahjahanpur, Uttar Pradesh, India. When sleeping he would lean against a plank. He died aged 85 in Sept 1980.

Stilt-walking

Hop stringers use stilts up to 15 ft *4.57 m*. In 1892 M. Garisoain of Bayonne stilt-walked 8 km *4.97 miles* into Biarritz in 42 min to average 11,42 km/h *7.10 mph*. In 1891 Sylvain Dornon stilt walked from Paris to Moscow *via* Vilno in 50 stages for the 1830 miles *2945 km*. Another source gives his time as 58 days. Even with a safety wire or Kirby wire very high stilts are extremely dangerous—25 steps are deemed to constitute 'mastery'. Eddy Wolf (also known as Steady Eddy) mastered stilts measuring 30 ft 3 in *9,22 m* from ground to ankle over a distance of 51 ft *15,54 m* in Loyal, Wisconsin, USA on 18 May 1978. Joe Long (b. Kenneth Caesar), who has suffered 5 fractures, mastered 56 lb *25,4 kg* 24 ft *7,31 m* stilts at the BBC TV Centre, London on 8 Dec 1978. John Russell of Ringling Bros and Barnum & Bailey Circus mastered 33 ft *10,05 m* aluminium stilts, with 34 steps at Madison Square Garden, New York, USA on 20 May 1981. The stilts weighed 35 lb *15,87 kg* each. The endurance record is 3008 miles *4840 km* from Los Angeles, California to Bowen, Kentucky from 20 Feb to 26 July 1980 by Joe Bowen. Masaharu Tatsushiro, 28, (Japan) ran 100 m *328 ft* on 1 ft *30,48 cm* high stilts in 14.15 sec in Tōkyō on 30 Mar 1980.

Stowaway

The most rugged stowaway was Socarras Ramirez who escaped from Cuba on 4 June 1969 by stowing away in an unpressurized wheel well in the starboard wing of a Douglas DC8 from Havana to Madrid in a 5600 mile *9010 km* Iberian Airlines flight. He survived 8 hr at 30,000 ft *9145 m* where temperatures were −8° F −22° C.

Stretcher bearing
The longest recorded carry of a stretcher case with a 10 st *63,5 kg* 'body' is 120 miles *193 km* in 41 hr 12 min by two four man teams from 1 Field Ambulance, Canadian Forces Base, Calgary, Alberta, Canada on 5–7 May 1979.

The record limited to Youth Organizations (under 20 years of age) and 8 hr carrying is 42.02 miles *67,62 km* by 8 members of the Henry Meoles School, Moreton, Wirral, Cheshire on 13 July 1980.

String ball largest
The largest balls of string on record are ones both of 11 ft *3,35 m* in diameter, weighing 5 tons/*tonnes* amassed by Francis A. Johnson of Darwin, Minnesota, USA, since 1950 and Frank Stoeber of Cawker City, Kansas since at least 1962.

Submergence
The most protracted underwater endurance record (excluding the use of diving bells) is 147 hr 15 min established by Robert Ingolia in tests in which the US Navy was the beneficiary of all data in 1961.

The continuous duration record (i.e. no rest breaks) for 'Scuba' (i.e. self-contained and without surface air hoses) is 68 hr by Mrs Ellen Curry of the Inner Space Dive School at the Oshawa Shopping Centre, Ontario, Canada on 20–23 Feb 1981. She predictably suffered severe desquamation.

Suggestion boxes
The most prolific example on record of the use of any suggestion box scheme is that of John Drayton (b. 18 Sept 1907) of Newport, Gwent who has plied British Rail and the companies from which it was formed with a total of 28,777 suggestions from 1924 to May 1980 of which one in seven were accepted.

Swinging
The record duration for continuous swinging is 185 hr by Mollie Jackson of Tarrytown, New York, USA on 25 Mar–1 Apr 1979.

Switchback riding
The endurance record for rides on a roller coaster is 368 hr by Jim King at the Miracle Strip Amusement Park, Panama City, Florida, USA, on 22 June–7 July 1980. He covered a distance of 10,425 miles *16 780 km*. The minimum required speed is 25 mph *40 km/h*.

Tailoring
The highest speed in which the making of a 2 piece suit has been made from sheep to finished article is 1 hr 52 min 18.5 sec to the order of Bud Macken of Mascot, NSW, Australia on 23 Dec 1931. The shearing took 35 sec, the carding and teasing 19 min and weaving 20 min.

Talking
The world record for non-stop talking is 150 hr by Raymond Cantwell at Trust House Forte's Travel Lodge, Oxford on 4–10 Dec 1977. A feminine non-stop talking record was set by Mrs Mary E. Davis, who on 2–7 Sept 1958 started at a radio station in Buffalo, New York and did not draw breath until 110 hr 30 min 5 sec later in Tulsa, Oklahoma, USA. The longest continuous political speech on record was one of 33 hr 5 min by Marvin Eakman of Minneapolis, Minnesota, USA on 6–7 Nov 1978. The longest recorded lecture was one of 59½ hr on 'Everything You Ever Wanted To Know About Sociology and People' by James Gray of Evergreen Valley College, San Jose, Calif, USA, on 11–14 Apr 1980.

Historically the longest recorded after-dinner speech with unsuspecting victims was one of 3 hr by the Rev. Henry Whitehead (d. March 1896) at the Rainbow Tavern, Fleet Street, London on 16 Jan 1874. Both Nicholas Parsons and Gyles Brandreth spoke for 11 hr from 8 p.m. to 7 a.m. on 13–14 Feb 1978 at the Hyde Park Hotel, London in aid of Action Research, to tie a longest after-dinner speech contest.

T-bone dive
The so-called T-bone dives or Dive Bomber crash by cars off ramps over and on to parked cars are often measured by the number of cars, but owing to their variable size and that their purpose is purely to cushion the shock, distance is more significant. The longest recorded distance in this highly dangerous activity is 196 ft 5 in *59,86 m* by Jean-Pierre Vignau in a Ford Capri 2600 at Montlhéry autodrome near Paris, France on 20 July 1980.

Teeth-pulling
The man with 'the strongest teeth in the world' is 'Hercules' John Massis (b. Wilfried Oscar Morbée, 4 June 1940) of Oostakker, Belgium, who raised a weight of 233 kg *513⅝ lb* 15 cm *6 in* from the ground with a teeth bit at Evrey, France on 19 Mar 1977. Massis prevented a helicopter from taking off using only a teeth-bit harness in Los Angeles on 7 Apr 1979 for a Guinness Spectacular TV Show. On 2 May 1981 Walter Arfeuille (Belgium) pulled 3 railway coaches and a goods wagon weighing 135,3 tonnes *133.1 tons* along a level track for 2,54 m *8 ft 3 in*.

Throwing
The greatest distance any inert object heavier than air has been thrown is 857 ft 8 in *261,42 m*, in the case of a plastic 'Skyro' by Tom McRann, 30, in Golden Gate Park, San Francisco, Calif, USA, on 9 June 1980.

Tightrope walking
The greatest 19th century tightrope walker was Jean François Gravelet, *alias* Charles Blondin (1824–97), of France, who made the earliest crossing of the Niagara Falls on a 3 in *76 mm* rope, 1100 ft *335 m* long, 160 ft *48,75 m* above the Falls on 30 June 1859. He also made a crossing with Harry Colcord, pick-a-back on 15 Sept 1860. Though other artists still find it difficult to believe, Colcord was his agent. The oldest wirewalker was 'Professor' William Ivy Baldwin (1866–1953), who crossed the South Boulder Canyon, Colorado, USA on a 320 ft *97,5 m* wire with a 125 ft *38,1 m* drop on his 82nd birthday on 31 July 1948.

Tightrope walking *Endurance*
The world tightrope endurance record is 185 days by Henri Rochetain (b. 1926) of France on a wire 394 ft *120 m* long, 82 ft *25 m* above a supermarket in Saint Etienne, France, on 28 Mar–29 Sept 1973. His ability to sleep on the wire has left doctors puzzled. He walked some 500 km *310 miles* on the wire to keep fit.

Tightrope walking *Highest and Steepest*
Steve McPeak (b. 21 April 1945) of Las Vegas, Nevada, USA ascended the 46,6 mm *1.83 in* diameter Zugspitzbahn cable for a vertical height of 705 m *2313 ft* in 3 stints aggregating 5 hr 4 min on 24/25/28 June 1981.

The maximum gradient over the stretch of 2282 m *7485 ft* was above 30 degrees. Earlier on 28 June 1981 he had walked on a thinner stayed cable 181 steps across a gorge at the top of the 2963 m *9721 ft* mountain with a sheer drop of 960 m *3150 ft* below him.

The first crossing of the River Thames was achieved by Charles Elleano (b. 1911) of Strasbourg, France on a 1050 ft *320 m* wire 60 ft *18,2 m* above the river in 25 min on 22 Sept 1951.

Tree-climbing
The fastest speed climb up a 100 ft *30,4 m* fir spar pole and return to the ground is one of 27.93 sec by Clarence Bartow of Grants Pass, Oregon, USA on 27 July 1980.

The fastest time up a 9 m *29.5 ft* coconut tree barefoot is 4.88 sec by Fuatai Solo, 17, in Sukuna Park, Fiji on 22 Aug 1980.

Tree-sitting
The duration record for sitting in a tree is 182 days 2 min by Glen T. Woodrich, 23, at Golf N'Stuff Amusement Park, Norwalk, Calif., USA from 1 Jan–2 July 1978.

Typewriting *Fastest*
The highest recorded speeds attained with a ten-word penalty per error on a manual machine are:

One Min: 170 words, Margaret Owen (US) (Underwood Standard), New York, 21 Oct 1918.
One Hour: 147 words (net rate per min) Albert Tangora (US) (Underwood Standard), 22 Oct 1923.

The official hour record on an electric machine is 9316 words (40 errors) on an IBM machine, giving a net rate of 149 words per min, by Margaret Hamma, now Mrs Dilmore (US), in Brooklyn, New York City, NY, USA on 20 June 1941. Mrs Barbara Blackburn of Everett, Washington can maintain 150 wpm for 50 min (37,500 key strokes) and attain speeds of 170 wpm using the Dvorak Simplified Keyboard (DSK) system.

In an official test in 1946 Stella Pajunas, now Mrs Garnard, attained a rate of 216 words in a minute on an IBM machine.

Typewriting *Longest*

The world duration record for typewriting on an electric machine is 214 hr by Violet Gibson Burns at Cremorne, Sydney, Australia on 18–27 Feb 1980. Mrs Marva Drew, 51, of Waterloo, Iowa, USA between 1968 and 30 Nov 1974 typed the numbers 1 to 1,000,000 in words on a manual typewriter on 2473 pages. Asked why, she replied 'But I love to type'.

The longest duration typing marathon on a manual machine is 120 hr 15 min by Mike Howell, a 23-year-old blind office worker from Greenfield, Oldham, Greater Manchester on 25–30 Nov 1969 on an Olympia manual typewriter in Liverpool. In aggregating 561,006 strokes he performed a weight movement of 2482 tons *2521 tonnes* plus a further 155 tons *157 tonnes* on moving the carriage for line spacing.

Tyre supporting

The greatest number of motor tyres supported in a free-standing 'lift' is 80 by Gary Windebank of Romsey, Hants on 27 Sept 1980 at Bayeux, Normandy, France. The total weight was 1182 lb *536,14 kg*. The tyres used were Michelin XZX 155 × 13.

Unsupported circle

The highest recorded number of people who have demonstrated the physical paradox of all being seated without a chair is an unsupported circle of 5810 staged by Channel 8, Fuji Telecasting of Tokyo, Japan in September 1980.

Hugo Dabbert during his world record marathon on the wall of death in Rüsselsheim, W Germany.

Clarence Bartow, world record holder of the speed tree climbing event, who returned a time of 27.93 sec on 27 July 1980 (see p. 193).

Waiters marathon

Beverly Hills restaurateur Roger Bourbon (b. Switzerland, 1934), the 'running waiter', ran a full marathon in full uniform in London on 29 Mar 1981 carrying a free standing open bottle on a tray in the same hand (gross weight 2 lb 11½ oz *1,24 kg*) in 3 hr 6 min 4 sec.

Walking on hands

The duration record for walking on hands is 1400 km *871 miles* by Johann Hurlinger, of Austria, who in 55 daily 10 hr stints, averaged 1.58 mph *2,54 km/h* from Vienna to Paris in 1900. Thomas P. Hunt of USAF Academy, Colorado Springs, completed a 50 m *54.68 yd* inverted sprint in 18.4 sec in Tokyo on 22 Sept 1979.

Wall of death

The greatest endurance feat on a wall of death was 6 hr 7 min 38 sec by Hugo Dabbert (b. Hildesheim, 24 Sept 1938) at Rüsselsheim, West Germany on 14 Aug 1980. He rode 6841 laps on the 10 m *32.8 ft* diameter wall on a Honda CM 400T averaging 35,2 km/h *21.8 mph* for the 214,8 km *133.4 miles*.

Whip cracking

The longest stock whip ever 'cracked' (*i.e.* the end made to travel above the speed of sound—760 mph *1223 km/h*) is one of 97 ft *29,66 m* wielded by Noel Harris on the steps of Parliament House, Melbourne, Australia on 7 Aug 1978. The dry weight of the red hide plaited whip was 12 kg *26.4 lb*.

Window cleaning

The fastest time in the Ettore Challenge Cup contest has been 24.0 sec plus ten ½ sec smear penalties to equal 29 sec by Nicholas Woolman of Braunstone, Frith, Leicester at the NEC, Birmingham on 29 Apr 1980 for 3 standard 1040 × 1153 mm *40.94 × 45.39 in* office windows with a 300 mm *11.8 in* long squeegee and 9 litres *15.83 pts* of water.

Wire Slide

The greatest distance recorded in a wire slide is from a height of 175 ft *53,3 m* over a distance of 300 ft *91,44 m* by Grant Page with Bob Woodham over his shoulder across the Australian landmark known as 'The Gap' for the filmed episode in 'The Stunt Men' in 1972.

Endurance and Endeavour

Wood-cutting

The earliest competitions date from Tasmania in 1874. The records set at the Lumberjack World Championships at Hayward, Wisconsin (founded 1960) are

Power Saw	11.36 sec	Ron Johnson (US)	1978
	11.36 sec	Dave Geer (US)	1978
One-Man Bucking	22.83 sec	Ron Hartill (NZ)	1976
Standing Block Chop	26.90 sec	Ron Wilson (Aust)	1973
Underhand Block Chop	20.30 sec	Jim Alexander (Aust)	1973
Two-Man Bucking	10.04 sec	Ron Hartill (Can) and	1977
		Merv Jensen (NZ)	

White pine logs 14 in *35,5 cm* diameter are used for chopping and 20 in *50,8 cm* for sawing.

Writing minuscule

In 1926 an account was published of Alfred McEwen's pantograph record in which the 56 word version of the Lord's Prayer was written by diamond point on glass in the space of 0.0016 × 0.0008 in *0,04 × 0,02 mm*. Frank C. Watts of Felmingham, Norfolk demonstrated for photographers on 24 Jan 1968, his ability, without mechanical or optical aid, to write the Lord's Prayer 34 times (9452 letters) within the size of a definitive UK postage stamp (viz.) 0.84 × 0.71 in *21,33 × 18,03 mm*.

Writing under handicap

The ultimate feat in 'funny writing' would appear to be the ability to write extemporaneously and decipherably backwards, upside down, laterally inverted (mirror-style) while blindfolded with both hands simultaneously. Three claims to this ability with both hands and feet simultaneously, by Mrs Carolyn Webb of Thirlmere, NSW, Australia, Mrs Judy Hall of Chesterfield, Virginia, USA, and Robert Gray of Toronto, Ontario, Canada are under investigation.

Yodelling

The most protracted yodel on record was that of Errol Bird for 10 hr 15 min in Lisburn, Northern Ireland on 6 Oct 1979.

Yo-yo

The yo-yo originates from a Filipino jungle fighting weapon recorded in the 16th century weighing 4 lb with a 20 ft *6 m* thong. The word means 'come-come'. Though illustrated in a book in 1891 as a bandalore the craze did not begin until it was started by Donald F. Duncan of Chicago, USA in 1926. The most difficult modern yo-yo trick is the 'Whirlwind' incorporating both inside and outside horizontal loop-the-loops. The individual continuous endurance record is 120 hr by John Winslow of Gloucester, Virginia, USA on 23–28 Nov 1977. Dr Allen Bussey in Waco, Texas on 23 Apr 1977 completed 20,302 loops in 3 hr (including 6886 in a single 60 min period). He used a Duncan Imperial with a 34½ in *87,6 cm* nylon string.

The largest yo-yo ever constructed was one by Dr Tom Kuhn weighing 256 lb *116,11 kg* test launched from a 150 ft *52,2 m* crane in San Francisco, California on 13 Oct 1979.

WEALTH AND POVERTY

The comparison and estimations of extreme personal wealth are beset with intractable difficulties. Quite apart from reticence and the element of approximation in the valuation of assets, as Jean Paul Getty (1892–1976) once said 'if you can count your millions you are not a billionaire'. The term millionaire was invented *c.* 1740 and billionaire in 1861. The earliest dollar billionaires were John Davison Rockfeller (1839–1937); Henry Ford (1863–1947) and Andrew William Mellon (1855–1937). In 1937, the last year in which all 3 were alive, a billion US dollars were worth £205 million but that amount of sterling would today have a purchasing power in excess of £2500 million.

Richest men *World*

The fortune of Daniel K. Ludwig (b. South Haven, Michigan, June 1897) was estimated as high as $3000 million in 1977. It is believed that his wood pulp investment in 4,000,000 acres *1 618 700 ha* of Amazonian jungle around Jari, Brazil in 1967 for $3 million had led to a drain of more than $1 billion by Apr 1981 by which time he was described by *Fortune Magazine* as an 'ex-billionaire'. The only other living US businessman to have experienced the problems of a ninth nought is (Henry) Ross

Half an hour after being reunited, Edwin Zillwood and his sister Lena Allen whom he traced after 79 years (see p. 191).

Ron Hartill, from Sooke, British Columbia, Canada who not only holds lumberjacking records but was also supreme World Champion of 1980.

Perot (b. Texarkana, Texas, 27 June 1930), who in December 1969 was briefly a billionaire on paper before the slump in Electronic Data Systems shares. The richest US millionaire is now believed to be Forrest E. Mars Sr (b. 1907) of Las Vegas, worth some $900 million.

Richest man *Great Britain*

The richest man in Great Britain is reputed to be John Moores, CBE the co-founder of Littlewoods football pools in 1923. In 1973 he was estimated to be worth about £400 million (hence £1200 million in 1981 £'s). His first job after leaving school at 14 was as a telephone operator. He was born in Eccles, Lancashire in 1896. He reassumed the chairmanship of Littlewoods on 17 Oct 1980.

Highest incomes

The greatest incomes derive from the collection of royalties per barrel by rulers of oil-rich sheikhdoms, who have not abrogated personal entitlement. Before his death in 1965, H. H. Sheikh Sir Abdullah as-Salim as-Sabah GCMG, CIE (b. 1895), the 11th Amir of Kuwait was accumulating royalties payable at a rate of £2.6 million per week or £135 million a year.

The highest gross income ever achieved in a single year by a private citizen is an estimated $105,000,000 (*then £21½ million*) in 1927 by the Neapolitan born Chicago gangster Alphonse ('Scarface Al') Capone (1899–1947). This was derived from illegal liquor trading and alky-cookers (illicit stills), gambling establishments, dog tracks, dance halls, 'protection' rackets and vice. On his business card Capone described himself as a 'Second Hand Furniture Dealer'. The highest gross earned income in a year by a UK subject is reputedly in excess of £25 million earned by Paul McCartney MBE in 1979/80.

CIRCUS RECORDS

Largest circus

The world's largest permanent circus is Circus Circus, Las Vegas, Nevada, USA opened on 18 Oct 1968 at a cost of $15,000,000 (*then £6,250,000*). It covers an area of 129,000 ft² *11 984 m²* capped by a tent-shaped flexiglass roof 90 ft *27,43 m* high. The largest travelling circus is the Circus Vargas in the USA which can accommodate 5000 people under its Big Top.

A table of historic circus records from 1859 to date was published in the 26th Edition at p. 233. New records set since 1975 are as follows

Flying Trapeze:	Downward circles or 'Muscle grinding'—306 by Denise La Grassa (US) Circus World Museum, Baraboo, Wisconsin, USA, 9 May 1977.
	Single heel hang on swinging bar, Angela Revelle (Angelique), Australia, 1977.
Triple Twisting Double Somersault:	Tom Edelston to catcher John Zimmerman, Circus World, Florida, 20 Jan 1981
Teeter Board:	Six man high perch pyramid, Emilia Ivanova (Bulgaria) of the Kehaiovi Troupe at Inglewood, California, USA, 21 July 1976.
Trampoline:	Septuple twisting back somersault to bed and quintuple twisting back somersault to shoulders by Marco Canestrelli to Belmonte Canestrelli at Madison Square, NY, USA on 5 Jan and 28 Mar 1979.
Flexible Pole:	Double full twisting somersault to a 2 in *5,08 cm* diameter pole by Roberto Tabak (aged 11) in Jarasota, Florida, USA in 1977.
Human Pyramid (or Tuckle):	Twelve (3 high) supported by a single understander. Weight 771 kg *1700 lb* or 121.4 stone by Tahar Davis of the Hassani Troupe at BBC TV Pebble Mill Studio, Birmingham, England, on 17 Dec 1979.

Juggling Records

7 clubs	Albert Petrovski (USSR), 1963
	Sorin Munteanu (Romania), 1975
	Jack Bremlov, currently
8 plates	Enrico Rastelli (Italy), 1896–1931
10 balls	Enrico Rastelli (Italy), 1896–1931
11 rings	Petrovski, 1963–66
	Eugene Belaur
	Sergei Ignatov (USSR)
Pirouettes with 3 cigar boxes	Kris Kremo (quadruple turn with 3 boxes in mid air)
Duration 5 clubs	16 min 20 sec, Igantov in USSR

Proved wills and death duties

Sir John Reeves Ellerman, 2nd Bt, (1909–73) left £53,238,370 on which all-time record death duties were payable. This is the largest will ever proved in the United Kingdom. The greatest will proved in Ireland was that of the 1st Earl of Iveagh (1847–1927), who left £13,486,146.

Millionairesses

The world's wealthiest woman was probably Princess Wilhelmina Helena Pauline Maria of Orange-Nassau (1880–1962), formerly Queen of the Netherlands from 1890 to her abdication, 4 Sept 1948, with a fortune which was estimated at over £200 million. The largest amount proved in the will of a woman in the United Kingdom has been the £4,075,550 (duty paid £3,233,454) of Miss Gladys Meryl Yule, daughter of Sir David Yule, Bt. (1858–1928), in August 1957. Mrs. Anna Dodge (later Mrs. Hugh Dillman) who was born in Dundee, Scotland, died on 3 June 1970 in the United States, aged 103, and left an estate of £40,000,000.

The cosmetician Madame Charles Joseph Walker *née* Sarah Breedlove (b. Louisiana Delta, USA 23 Dec 1867) is reputed to have become the first self-made millionairess. She was an uneducated Negro orphan scrub-woman whose fortune was founded on a hair straightener.

It was estimated by the United States Trust Co in 1980 that over half of the USA's 574,342 millionaires are in fact millionairesses. The highest density is in Idaho (264.6 per 10,000) and the lowest in Wyoming. New York (56,096) leads California (38,691).

Millionaire and millionairess *Youngest*

The youngest person ever to accumulate a million dollars was the child film actor Jackie Coogan (b. Los Angeles, 26 Oct 1914) co-star with Sir Charles Chaplin (1889–1977) in 'The Kid' made in 1920. Shirley Temple (b. Santa Monica, California 23 Apr 1928), formerly Mrs John Agar, Jr, now Mrs Charles Black, accumulated wealth exceeding $1,000,000 (*then £209,000*) before she was 10. Her child actress career spanned the years 1934–9.

Richest families

It has been tentatively estimated that the combined value of the assets nominally controlled by the Du Pont family of some 1600 members may be of the order of $150,000 million. The family arrived in the USA from France on 1 Jan 1800. Capital from Pierre Du Pont (1730–1817) enabled his son Eleuthère Irénée Du Pont to start his explosives company in the United States. Europeans with family assets reportedly in excess of a billion dollars include the Wallenbergs of Sweden.

Largest dowry

The largest recorded dowry was that of Elena Patiño, daughter of Don Simón Iturbi Patiño (1861–1947), the Bolivian tin millionaire, who in 1929 bestowed £8,000,000 from a fortune at one time estimated to be worth £125,000,000.

Greatest miser

If meanness is measurable as a ratio between expendable assets and expenditure then Henrietta (Hetty) Howland Green (*née* Robinson) (1835–1916), who kept a balance of over $31,400,000 (*then £6.2 million*) in one bank alone, was the all-time world champion. Her son had to have his leg amputated because of her delays in finding a *free* medical clinic. She herself lived off cold porridge because she was too thrifty to heat it. Her estate proved to be of $95 million (*then £19 million [and now worth £270 million]*).

Return of cash

The largest amount of *cash* ever found and returned to its owners was $500,000 (US) found by Lowell Elliott, 61 on his farm at Peru, Indiana, USA. It had been dropped in June 1972 by a parachuting hi-jacker.

Greatest bequests

The greatest bequests in a life-time of a millionaire were those of the late John Davison Rockefeller (1839–1937), who gave away sums totalling $750,000,000 (*now £350 million*). The greatest benefactions of a British millionaire were those of William Richard Morris, later the Viscount Nuffield, GBE, CH (1877–1963), which totalled more than £30,000,000 between 1926 and his death on 22 Aug 1963. The Scottish-born US citizen Andrew Carnegie (1835–1919) is estimated to have made benefactions totalling £70 million during the last 18 years of his life. These included 7689 church organs and 2811 libraries. He had started life in a bobbin factory at $1.20 per week.

The largest bequest made in the history of philanthropy was the $500,000,000 (*then £178,570,000*) gift, announced on 12 Dec 1955, to 4157 educational and other institutions by the Ford Foundation (established 1936) of New York City, NY, USA.

Salary Highest *World*

The highest reported remuneration of any US businessman in 1980 was an estimated $6 million in salary, bonus, stock awards and other benefits to William S. Paley, founder and chairman of CBS. The executive chairman of the Mobil Corporation, A. Rawleigh Warner, reportedly received $3,590,000.

Highest Fees

The highest paid investment consultant in the world is Dr Harry D. Schultz, who operates from Western Europe. His standard consultation fee for 60 minutes is $2000 on weekdays and $3000 at weekends. His quarterly retainer permitting companies to call him on a daily basis is $28,125. He writes and edits an information packed International Newsletter instituted in 1964 now sold at $25 or £11 per copy.

Salary Highest *Great Britain*

Britain's highest paid executives are the four directors of Queen Productions Ltd. whose accounts published in February 1981 showed drawings for between £660,000 and £697,000 by John Deacon, 29 (bass guitarist); Dr Brian May, 30 (lead guitarist); Freddie Mercury (lead singer) and Roger Taylor, 31 (drummer). The highest salary paid by any public company is £271,400 to Mr Dick Giordano (b. New York, 1931), chief executive of BOC International.

Golden handshake

The highest carat handshake approved in Britain was one of £180,000 for Nicholas Coral the resigning chairman of Coral Leisure when acquired by Bass in January 1981.

Lowest incomes

The poorest people in the world are the Tasaday tribe of cave-dwellers of central Mindanao, Philippines who were 'discovered' in 1971 without any domesticated animals, agriculture, pottery, wheels or clothes.

GLUTTONY RECORDS

Records for eating and drinking by trenchermen do not match those suffering from the rare disease of bulimia (morbid desire to eat) and polydipsia (pathological thirst). Some bulimia patients have to spend 15 hr a day eating, with an extreme consumption of 384 lb 2 oz *174,236 kg* of food in six days by Matthew Daking, aged 12, in 1743 (known as Mortimer's case). Fannie Meyer of Johannesburg, after a skull fracture, was stated in 1974 to be unsatisfied by less than 160 pints of water a day. By October 1978 he was down to 52 pints. Miss Helge Andersson (b. 1908) of Lindesberg, Sweden was reported in January 1971 to have been drinking 40 pints *22,73 litres* of water a day since 1922—a total of 87,600 gal *3982 hectolitres*.

The world's greatest trencherman has been Edward Abraham ('Bozo') Miller (b. 1909) of Oakland, California, USA. He consumes up to 25,000 calories per day or more than 11 times that recommended. He stands 5 ft 7½ in *1,71 m* tall but weighs from 20 to 21½ st *127–139 kg* with a 57 in *144 cm* waist. He had been undefeated in eating contests since 1931 (see below). The bargees on the Rhine are reputed to be the world's heaviest eaters with 5200 calories a day. However the New Zealand Sports Federation of Medicine reported in December 1972 that a long-distance road runner consumed 14,321 calories in 24 hr.

While no healthy person has been reported to have succumbed in any contest for eating non-toxic food or drinking non-alcoholic drinks, such attempts, from a medical point of view, must be regarded as *extremely* inadvisable, particularly among young people. Gluttony record attempts should aim at improving the *rate* of consumption rather than the *volume*. Guinness Superlatives will not list any records involving the consumption of more than 2 litres *3.52 Imperial pints* of beer nor any at all involving spirits. Nor will records for such potentially dangerous categories as live ants, chewing gum, marsh mallow or raw eggs with shells be published. The ultimate in stupidity—the eating of a bicycle—has however been recorded since it is unlikely to attract competition.

Specific records have been claimed as follows:

Baked Beans
2780 cold baked beans one by one with a cocktail stick in 30 min by Karen Stevenson, of Wallasey, Merseyside on 4 Apr 1981.

Bananas
17 (edible weight minimum 4½ oz *128 g* each) in 2 min by Dr Ronald L. Alkana at the University of California, Irvine on 7 Dec 1973.

Beer
Steven Petrosino drank one litre of beer in 1.3 sec on 22 June 1977 at 'The Gingerbreadman', Carlisle, Pennsylvania.
Peter G. Dowdeswell (b. London 29 July 1940) of Earls Barton, Northants holds the following records:

2 pints—2.3 sec Zetters Social Club, Wolverton, Bucks	11 June 1975
2 litres—6.0 sec Carriage Horse Hotel, Higham Ferrers, Northants	7 Feb 1975

Yards of Ale
2½ pints—5.0 sec RAF Upper Heyford, Oxfordshire	4 May 1975
3 pints—5.4 sec Corby Town S.C., Northamptonshire	23 Jan 1976

Upsidedown
2 pints—6.4 sec Top Rank Club, Northants	25 May 1975

Bicycle
15 days by Monsieur 'Mangetout' (M. Lotito) (stewed tyres and metal filings) at Evrey, France on 17 Mar–2 Apr 1977.

Champagne
1000 bottles per annum by Bobby Acland of the 'Black Raven', Bishopsgate, City of London.

Cheese
16 oz *453 g* of Cheddar in 1 min 13 sec by Peter Dowdeswell (see above) in Earls Barton, Northants on 14 July 1978.

Chicken
27 (2 lb *907 g* pullets) by 'Bozo' Miller (see above) at a sitting at Trader Vic's, San Francisco, California, USA in 1963.

Clams
424 (Littlenecks) in 8 min by Dave Barnes at Port Townsend Bay, Washington, USA on 3 May 1975.

Doughnuts
12¾ (51 oz *1,445 kg*) in 5 min 46 sec by James Wirth, and 13 (52 oz *1,474 kg*) in 6 min 1.5 sec by John Haight, both at the Sheraton Inn, Canandaigua, New York on 3 Mar 1981.

Eels
1 lb *453 g* of elvers in 13.7 sec by Peter Dowdeswell at Reeves Club, Bristol on 20 Oct 1978.

Eggs
(Hard Boiled) 14 in 58 sec by Peter Dowdeswell (see above) at the Stardust Social Club, Corby, Northants on 18 Feb 1977.
(Soft Boiled) 32 in 78 sec by Peter Dowdeswell in Northampton, on 8 Apr 1978.
(Raw) 13 in 2.2 sec by Peter Dowdeswell at BBC, Norwich on 26 Jan 1978.

Frankfurters
23 (2 oz *56,6 g*) in 3 min 10 sec by Lynda Kuerth, 21, at the Veterans Stadium, Philadelphia, on 12 July 1977.

Gherkins
1 lb *453 g* by Rex Barker of Elkhorn, Nebraska, USA on 30 Oct 1975.

Grapes
3 lb 1 oz of grapes in 34.6 sec by Jim Ellis of Montrose, Michigan, USA on 30 May 1976.

Haggis
26 oz *737 g* in 50 sec by Peter Dowdeswell at Reeves Club, Bristol on 21 Dec 1978.

Hamburgers
20¾ hamburgers (each weighing 3½ oz *100 g* totalling *2,07 kg* of meat) and buns in 30 min by Alan Peterson at Longview, Washington, USA on 8 Feb 1979.

Lynda Kuerth who consumed 23 frankfurters weighing a total of 2 lb 14 oz *1,3 kg* in 3 min 10 sec. *(Neil Benson)*

Ice Cream
3 lb 6 oz *1,530 kg* in 90 sec by Bennett D'Angelo at Dean Dairy, Waltham, Massachusetts, USA on 7 Aug 1977. The ice cream must be unmelted.

Kippers
25 (self-filleted) in 60 min by Bob Ibbotson at Scarborough, North Yorkshire on 10 Aug 1973.

Lemons
12 quarters (3 lemons) whole (including skin and pips) in 15.3 sec by Bobby Kempf of Roanoke, Virginia, USA on 2 May 1979.

Meat
One whole roast ox in 42 days by Johann Ketzler of Munich, Germany in 1880.

Meat Pies
22 (each weighing 5½ oz *156 g*) in 18 min 13 sec by Peter Dowdeswell of Earls Barton, Northants on 5 Oct 1978.

Milk
2 pt (1 Imperial quart or *113.5 centilitres*) in 3.2 sec by Peter Dowdeswell (see above) at Dudley Top Rank Club, West Midlands on 31 May 1975.

Oysters
7.08 lb *3,21 kg* (total number 250) in 3 min 56 sec by Thomas Greene of Tracy's Creek Marina, Deale, Maryland, USA, on 14 Feb 1980. The record for opening oysters is 100 in 3 min 1 sec by Douglas Brown, 31 at Christchurch, New Zealand on 29 Apr 1975.

Pancakes
(6 inch *15,2 cm* diameter buttered and with syrup) 62 in 6 min 58.5 sec by Peter Dowdeswell (see above) at The Drapery, Northampton on 9 Feb 1977.

Peanuts
100 (whole unshelled) singly in 46 sec by Jim Kornitzer, 21 at Brighton, Sussex on 1 Aug 1979.

Pickled Onions
91 pickled onions (total weight 30 oz *850 g*) in 1 min 8 sec by Pat Donahue in Victoria, British Columbia on 9 Mar 1978.

Potatoes
3 lb *1,36 kg* in 1 min 22 sec by Peter Dowdeswell in Earls Barton, Northants on 25 Aug 1978.

Potato Crisps
Thirty 2 oz *56,6 g* bags in 24 min 33.6 sec, without a drink, by Paul G. Tully of Brisbane University in May 1969. Charles Chip Inc of Mountville, Pennsylvania produced crisps 4 × 7 in *10 × 17,5 cm* from outsize potatoes in February 1977.

Prunes
144 in 53.5 sec by Peter Dowdeswell in Paris on 21 July 1980.

Ravioli
250 pieces (av. weight of each piece 8½ gr) in 66 min by John Keogh of Heaton, Bolton, Gtr Manchester on 16 Feb 1981.

Sandwiches
40 in 17 min 53.9 sec (jam 'butties' 6 × 3¾ × ½ in *15,2 × 9,5 × 1,2 cm*) by Peter Dowdeswell on 17 Oct 1977 at The Donut Shop, Reedley, California, USA.

Sausage Meat
96 sausages each 1 oz *28,3 g*, in 6 min by Steve Meltzer of Brooklyn, New York, USA on 14 Oct 1974. No 'Hot Dog' contest results have been remotely comparable.

Shrimps
3 lb *1,36 kg* in 4 min 8 sec by Peter Dowdeswell of Earls Barton, Northants on 25 May 1978.

Snails
144 in 11 min 30 sec by the late Marc Quinquandon, 27, in France July 1979. N.B. He died after consuming 72 in 3 min on 25 Nov 1979 some of which may have been toxic.

Spaghetti
100 yd *91,44 m* in 28.73 sec by Steve Weldon of Austin, Texas, USA, on 1 May 1977.

Tortilla
74 (total weight 4 lb 1½ oz *1,85 kg*) in 30 min by Tom Nall in the 2nd World Championship at Mariano's Mexican Restaurant, Dallas, Texas, USA on 16 Oct 1973.

Tree
11 ft *3,35 m* Birch (4.7 in 12 cm diameter trunk) in 89 hrs by Jay Gwaltney, 19 on WKQX's 'Outrageous Contest', Chicago, 11–15 Sept 1980.

Whelks
82 (unshelled) in 5 min 26 sec by John Fletcher at the Castle Inn, Dover, Kent on 27 July 1980.

2. HONOURS, DECORATIONS AND AWARDS

Oldest Order
The order which can trace its origins furthest back is the Military Hospitaller Order of St Lazarus of Jerusalem founded by St Basil the Great in the 4th Century AD. The prototype of the princely Orders of Chivalry is the Most Noble Order of the Garter founded by King Edward III in *c.* 1348. A date as early as AD 809 has been attributed to the Most Ancient Order of the Thistle but is of doubtful provenance.

Eponymous record
The largest object to which a human name is attached is the universe itself—in the case of the 'standard' cosmological model devised in 1922 by the Russian mathematician Aleksandr Aleksandrovitch Friedman (1888–1925) and known as Friedman's Universe. This model was undermined in January 1980 by the quadropole or isotrophy theory, which denies the Freidmanian model. The new model may be eventually named after F. Melchiori of the University of Florence.

Most titles
The most titled person in the world is the 18th Duchess of Alba (Alba de Tormes), Doña Maria del Rosario Cayetana Fitz-James Stuart y Silva. She is 8 times a duchess, 15 times a marchioness, 21 times a countess and is 19 times a Spanish grandee.

Versatility
The only person to win a Victoria Cross and an Olympic Gold Medal has been Lt Gen Sir Philip Neame VC, KBE, CB, DSO (1888–1978). He won the VC in 1914 and was an Olympic gold medallist for Britain for rifle shooting in 1924 though under the illusion at the time that he was shooting for the British Empire. The only George Cross holder who is also a Fellow of the Royal Society is Prof Peter Victor Danckwerts, GC, MBE, FRS (b. 1916) who diffused 16 parachute mines during the Battle of Britain as a Sub Lt RNVR.

Victoria Cross *Double awards*
The only three men ever to have been awarded a bar to the Victoria Cross (instituted 29 Jan 1856) are:

Surg-Capt (later Lt-Col) Arthur Martin-Leake, VC*, VD, RAMC (1874–1953) (1902 and bar 1915).

Capt Noel Godfrey Chavasse, VC*, MC, RAMC (1884–1917) (1916 and bar posthumously 14 Sep 1917).

Second Lieut (later Capt) Charles Hazlitt Upham, VC*, NZMF (b. 21 Sept 1908) (1941 and bar 1942).

The most VC's awarded in a war were the 634 in World War I (1914–18). The greatest number won in a single action was 11 at Rorke's Drift in the Zulu War on 22–23 Jan 1879.

Victoria Cross *Youngest*
The lowest established age for a VC is 15 years 100 days for Hospital Apprentice Andrew (wrongly gazetted as Arthur) Fitzgibbon (born at Peteragurh, northern India, 13 May 1845) of the Indian Medical Services for bravery at the Taku Forts in northern China on 21 Aug 1860. The youngest living VC is Lance-Corporal Rambahadur Limbu (b. Nepal, 1939) of the 10th Princess Mary's Own Gurkha Rifles. The award was for his courage while fighting in the Bau district of Sarawak, East Malaysia, on 21 Nov 1965.

Victoria Cross *Longest lived*
The longest lived of all the 1349 winners of the Victoria Cross was Captain (later General Sir) Lewis Stratford Tollemache Halliday, VC, KCB, of the Royal Marine Light Infantry. He was born on 14 May 1870, won his VC in China in 1900, and died on 9 Mar 1966, aged 95 years 299 days.

Most highly decorated
The only four living persons to have been twice decorated with any of the United Kingdom's topmost decorations are Capt C. H. Upham VC and bar; the Viscount De L'Isle VC, KG; HRH the Duke of Edinburgh KG, KT and HRH Prince Charles KG, KT. Britain's most highly decorated woman is the World War II British agent Mrs Odette Hallowes GC, MBE, Légion d'Honneur, who survived imprisonment and torture at the hands of the Gestapo in 1943–45.

Record Price
The highest ever paid for a VC group was £27,000 for the VC, DCM and MM group won by Pte Henry Tandy (1891–1977) of the West Riding Regt. at Sotheby's on 26 Nov 1980.

George Cross
The highest award ever given to a woman is the George Cross. The oldest female recipient was Miss Emma Josie Townsend (formerly EGM) aged 53 in 1932 and the youngest is Mrs Doreen Ashburnham-Ruffner (formerly AM) aged 11 in 1916.

Order of Merit
The Order of Merit (instituted on 23 June 1902) is limited to 24 members. Up to 30 June 1981 there have been 136 awards including only 3 women, plus 9 honorary awards to non-British citizens. The longest lived holder has been the Rt Hon. Bertrand Arthur William Russell, 3rd Earl Russell, who died on 2 Feb 1970 aged 97 years 260 days. The oldest recipient was Admiral of the Fleet the Hon. Sir Henry Keppel, GCB, OM, (1809–1904) who received the Order aged 93 years 56 days on 9 Aug 1902. The youngest recipient has been HRH the Duke of Edinburgh

KG, KT, OM, GBE, who was appointed on his 47th birthday on 10 June 1968.

Most mentions in despatches
The record number of 'mentions' is 24 by Field Marshal the Rt Hon Sir Frederick Sleigh Roberts Bt, the Earl Roberts, VC, KG, KP, GCB, OM, GCSI, GCIE, VD (1832–1914).

Most post-nominal letters
Lord Roberts was the only subject with 8 sets of *official* post-nominal letters. Currently the record number is seven by Marshal of the RAF the Rt Hon Lord Elworthy KG, GCB, CBE, DSO, MVO, DFC, AFC (b 23 Mar 1911) of New Zealand.

USSR
The USSR's highest award for valour is the Gold Star of a Hero of the Soviet Union. Over 10,000 were awarded in World War II. Among the 109 awards of a second star were those to Marshal Iosif Vissarionovich Dzhugashvili, *alias* Stalin (1879–1953) and Lt-General Nikita Sergeyevich Khrushchyov (1894–1971). The only war-time triple awards were to Marshal Georgiy Konstantinovich Zhukov, Hon GCB (1896–1974) (subsequently awarded a fourth Gold Star) and to the leading air aces Guards' Colonel (now Marshal of Aviation Aleksandr Ivanovich Pokryshkin) and Aviation Maj Gen Ivan Nikitovich Kozhedub. Zhukov also uniquely had the Order of Victory, twice, the Order of Lenin 6 times and the Order of the Red Banner, thrice.

Germany
The only man to be awarded the Knight's Cross of the Iron Cross with swords, diamonds and golden oak-leaves was Col Hans-Ulrich Rudel for services on the Eastern Front in 1941–5.

USA
The highest US decoration is the Congressional Medal of Honor. Five marines received both the Army and Navy Medals of Honor for the same acts in 1918 and 14 officers and men from 1863 to 1915 have received the medal on two occasions.

Top Scoring Air Aces (World Wars I and II)
The 'scores' of air aces in both wars are *still* hotly disputed. The highest figures officially attributed have been:

	World	United Kingdom
World War I	80 Rittmeister Manfred, Freiherr (Baron) von Richthofen (Germany)	73 Major Edward Mannock, VC, DSO**, MC*
World War II	352 Major Erich Hartmann (Germany)	38 Wg Cdr (Now AVM) James Edgar Johnson, CB, CBE, DSO**, DFC*[1]

[1] The greatest number of successes against flying bombs (V.1's) was by Sqn Ldr Joseph Berry, DFC** (b. Nottingham, 1920, killed 2 Oct 1944) who brought down 60 in 4 months. The most successful fighter pilot in the RAF was Sqn Ldr Marmaduke Thomas St John Pattle, DFC*, of South Africa, with a known total of at least 40.

Top jet ace
The greatest number of kills in jet to jet battles is 16 by Capt Joseph Christopher McConnell, Jr, USAF (b. Dover, New Hampshire, 30 Jan 1922) in the Korean war (1950–3). He was killed on 25 Aug 1954. It is possible that an Israeli ace may have surpassed this total in the period 1967–70 but the identity of pilots is subject to strict security.

Top woman ace
The record score for any woman fighter pilot is 12 by Jnr Lt Lydia Litvak (USSR) (b. 1921) on the Eastern Front between 1941 and 1943. She was killed in action on 1 Aug 1943.

Anti-tank successes
Col Hans-Ulrich Rudel, the German *Stuka* pilot, in 2530 combat missions destroyed 519 Soviet armoured vehicles and was uniquely awarded the golden oak-leaves to the Knight's Cross of the Iron Cross on 1 Jan 1945 (see Germany above).

Anti-submarine successes
The highest number of U-boat kills attributed to one ship in the 1939–45 war was 13 to HMS *Starling* (Capt Frederic J. Walker, CB, DSO***, RN). Captain Walker was in overall command at the sinking of a total of 25 U-boats between 1941 and the time of his death on 9 July 1944. The US Destroyer Escort *England* sank six Japanese submarines in the Pacific between 18 and 30 May 1944.

Most successful submarine captains
The most successful of all World War II submarine commanders was Leutnant Otto Kretschmer, captain of the U.23 and U.99 who up to March 1940 sank one destroyer and 44 Allied merchantmen totalling 266,629 gross registered tons.

In World War I Kapitän-Leutnant (later Vizeadmiral) Lothar von Arnauld de la Périère, in the U.35 and U.139, sank 195 allied ships totalling 458,856 gross tons. The most successful boats were U.35, which in World War I sank 54 ships of 90,350 grt in a single voyage and 224 ships of 539,711 grt all told, and U.48 which sank 51 ships of 310,007 grt in World War II. The largest target ever sunk by a submarine was the Japanese aircraft carrier *Shinano* (59,000 tons) by *USS Archerfish* (Cdr Joseph F. Enright, USN) on 29 Nov 1944.

NOBEL PRIZE
The Nobel Foundation of £3,200,000 was set up under the will of Alfred Bernhard Nobel (1833–96), the unmarried Swedish chemist and chemical engineer, who invented dynamite, in 1866. The Nobel Prizes are presented annually on 10 Dec, the anniversary of Nobel's death and the festival day of the Foundation. Since the first Prizes were awarded in 1901, the highest cash value of the award, in each of the six fields of Physics, Chemistry, Medicine and Physiology, Literature, Peace and Economics (inst. 1969) was Sw Kr 880 000 (£88,620) in 1980.

Most awards by countries (shared awards count as one)
United States citizens have won outright or shared in the greatest number of awards (including those made in 1980) with a total of 152 made up of 42 for Physics, 22 for Chemistry, 54 for Medicine-Physiology, 9 for Literature, 17 for Peace and 8 for Economics.

The United Kingdom has shared in 73 awards, comprising 20 for Physics, 22 for Chemistry, 14 for Medicine-Physiology, 9 for Peace, 5 for Literature and 3 for Economics.

By classes, the United States holds the record for Medicine-Physiology with 54, for Physics with 42, for Peace with 17 and Economics with 8; Germany, Britain and the US for Chemistry with 22 each. France has the record for Literature with 12.

Individuals
Individually the only person to have won two Prizes outright is Dr Linus Carl Pauling (b. 28 Feb 1901), Professor of Chemistry at the California Institute of Technology, Pasadena, California, USA since 1931. He was awarded the Chemistry Prize for 1954 and the Peace Prize for 1962. The only other persons to have won two prizes are Madame Marie Curie (1867–1934), who was born in Poland as Marja Sklodowska. She shared the 1903 Physics Prize with her husband Pierre Curie (1859–1906) and Antoine Henri Becquerel (1852–1908), and won the 1911 Chemistry Prize outright. Professor John Bardeen (b. 23 May 1908) shared the Physics Prize in 1956 and 1972. Professor Frederick Sanger, CBE, FRS (b. 13 Aug 1918) has twice shared the Chemistry Prize—in 1958 and 1980. The Peace Prize has been awarded three times to the International Committee of the Red Cross (founded 29 Oct 1863), of Geneva, Switzerland, namely in 1917, 1944 and in 1963, when it was shared with the International League of Red Cross Societies.

Oldest
The oldest prizeman has been Professor Francis Peyton Rous (1879–1970) of the United States. He shared the Medicine Prize in 1966, at the age of 87.

Youngest
The youngest laureate has been Professor Sir William Lawrence Bragg, CH, OBE, MC (1890–1971), of the UK, who at the age of 25, shared the 1915 Physics Prize with his father, Sir William Henry Bragg, OM, KBE (1862–1942), for work on X-rays and crystal structures. Bragg and also Theodore William Richards (1868–1928) of the USA, who won the 1914 Chemistry Prize, carried out their prize work when aged 23. The youngest Literature prizeman has been Joseph Rudyard Kipling (1865–1936) at

VC with the extra miniature replica denoting a second award or first bar won by only 3 officers.

DSO and 3 bars—won by 16 officers.

DSC and 3 bars—uniquely won by Col N. E. Morley, RNVR.

MC and 3 bars—won by 4 World War I officers.

DFC and 2 bars—won by 54 officers.

AFC and 2 bars—won by 12 officers.

DCM and 2 bars—won by 11 NCO's.

CGM (Naval) and bar—uniquely won by CPO A. R. Blore, MM.

George Medal and bar—won by 25 recipients.

King's Police Medal for Gallantry and 2 bars—uniquely won by Supt F. W. O'Gorman.

DSM and 3 bars—uniquely won by PO W. H. Kelly.

MM and 3 bars—uniquely won by Cpl E. A. Corey (Australia).

DFM and 2 bars—uniquely won by Group Capt D. E. Kingaby, DSO, DFC, AFC.

AFM and bar—won by 9 recipients.

SGM and bar—uniquely won by Chief Officer J. Whitely.

BEM (for Gallantry) and bar—3 military and 1 civil award.

The uniquely decorated holders of the VC: *left:* Capt Charles Upham (New Zealand) the only combatant to win the VC twice, and *right:* Lord De L'Isle the only VC who is also a Knight of the Garter (see p. 198).

the age of 41 in 1907. The youngest Peace prize-winner has been the Rev Dr Martin Luther King, Jr (1929–68) of the USA, in 1964 at the age of 35.

Most Valuable Annual Prize

The highest valued annual award is the Templeton Foundation Prize for Progress in Religion inaugurated in 1972 by Mr John M. Templeton (b. 1912). The award was increased to £100,000 for 1982.

Most statues

The world record for raising statues to oneself was set by Generalissimo Dr Rafael Leónidas Trujillo y Molina (1891–1961), former President of the Dominican Republic. In March 1960 a count showed that there were 'over 2000'. The country's highest mountain was named Pico Trujillo (now Pico Duarte). One province was called Trujillo and another Trujillo Valdez. The capital was named Ciudad Trujillo (Trujillo City) in 1936, but reverted to its old name of Santo Domingo de Guzmán on 23 Nov 1961. Trujillo was assassinated in a car ambush on 30 May 1961, and 30 May is now celebrated annually as a public holiday. The man to whom most statues have been raised is undoubtedly Vladimir Ilyich Ulyanov, *alias* Lenin (1870–1924), busts of whom have been mass-produced as also in the case of Mao Tse-tung (1893–1976) and Ho Chi Minh (1890–1969).

Air Vice Marshal 'Johnnie' Johnson, CB, CBE, DSO and two bars, DFC and bar, Britain's top scoring air ace. He was on operations from the Battle of Britain in 1940 in Spitfires to V.E. Day in 1945 destroying a total of 38 German aircraft (see p. 199). (*N. Broadhurst*)

PEERAGE

Most ancient
The oldest extant peerage is that of the premier Earl of Scotland, the Rt Hon Margaret of Mar, the Countess of Mar and 31st holder of this Earldom (b. 19 Sept 1940), who is the heir-at-law of Roderick or Rothri, 1st Earl (or Mormaer) of Mar, who witnessed a charter in 1114 or 1115 as 'Rothri *comes*'.

Oldest creation
The greatest age at which any person has been raised to the peerage is 93 years 337 days in the case of Sir William Francis Kyffin Taylor, GBE, KC (b. 9 July 1854), who was created Baron Maenan of Ellesmere, County Shropshire, on 10 June 1948, and died, aged 97, on 22 Sept 1951. The oldest elevation to a Life Peerage has been that of Emmanuel Shinwell CH (b. 18 Oct 1884) on 2 June 1970 when aged 85 years 227 days.

Longest lived peer
The longest lived peer ever recorded was the Rt Hon Frank Douglas-Pennant, the 5th Baron Penrhyn (b. 21 Nov 1865), who died on 3 Feb 1967, aged 101 years 74 days. The oldest peeress recorded was the Countess Desmond, who was alleged to be 140 when she died in 1604. This claim is patently exaggerated but it is accepted that she may have been 104. Currently the oldest holder of a peerage, and the oldest Parliamentarian, is the Rt Hon Robert William O'Neill, 1st Baron Rathcavan who was 98 on 18 June 1981. He contested the 1906 General Election.

Youngest peers
Twelve Dukes of Cornwall became (in accordance with the grant by the Crown in Parliament) peers at birth as the eldest son of a Sovereign; and the 9th Earl of Chichester posthumously inherited his father's (killed 54 days previously) earldom at his birth on 14 Apr 1944. The youngest age at which a person has had a peerage conferred on him is 7 days old in the case of the Earldom of Chester on HRH the Prince George (later George IV) on 19 Aug 1762.

Longest and shortest peerages
The peer who has sat longest in the House of Lords was Lt-Col Charles Henry FitzRoy, OBE, the 4th Baron Southampton (b. 11 May 1867), who succeeded to his father's title on 16 July 1872, took his seat on 23 Jan 1891, 18 months before Mr W. E. Gladstone's fourth administration began, and died, aged 91, on 7 Dec 1958, having held the title for 86 years 144 days.

The shortest enjoyment of a peerage was the 'split second' by which the law assumes that the Hon Wilfrid Carlyle Stamp (b. 28 Oct 1904), the 2nd Baron Stamp, survived his father, Sir Josiah Charles Stamp, GCB, GBE, the 1st Baron Stamp, when both were killed as a result of German bombing of London on 16 Apr 1941. Apart from this legal fiction, the shortest recorded peerage was one of 30 min in the case of Sir Charles Brandon, KB, the 3rd Duke of Suffolk, who died, aged 13 or 14, just after succeeding his brother, Henry, when both were suffering a fatal illness, at Buckden, Cambridgeshire, on 14 July 1551.

Highest numbering
The highest succession number borne by any peer is that of the present 35th Baron Kingsale (John de Courcy, b. 27 Jan 1941), who succeeded to the then 746-year-old Barony on 7 Nov 1969.

Most creations
The largest number of new hereditary peerages created in any year was the 54 in 1296. The record for all peerages (including 40 life peerages) is 55 in 1964. The greatest number of extinctions in a year was 16 in 1923 and the greatest number of deaths was 44 in 1935.

Most prolific
The most prolific peers of all time are believed to be the 1st Earl Ferrers (1650–1717) and the 3rd Earl of Winchilsea (*c.* 1620–89) each with 27 legitimate children. In addition, the former reputedly fathered 30 illegitimate children. Currently the peer with the largest family is the Rt Hon Bryan Walter Guinness, 2nd Baron Moyne (b. 27 Oct 1905) with 6 sons and 5 daughters.

The most prolific peeress is believed to be Elizabeth (*née* Barnard), who bore her husband, Lord Chandos of Sudeley (1642–1714), 22 children.

Baronets
The greatest age to which a baronet has lived is 101 years 188 days, in the case of Sir Fitzroy Donald Maclean, 10th Bt., KCB (1835–1936). He was the last survivor of the Crimean campaign of 1853–56. The only baronetess in her own right is Dame Maureen Dunbar of Hempriggs, who succeeded as 8th in line of a 1706 baronetcy in 1965.

Knights
The greatest number of knights dubbed in a single day was 432 by James I in the Royal Garden, Whitehall on 23 July 1603. On his coronation day two days later, he appointed 62 Knights of the Garter.

Youngest and oldest
The youngest age for the conferment of a knighthood is 29 days for HRH the Prince Albert Edward (b. 9 Nov 1841) (later Edward VII) by virtue of his *ex officio* membership of the Order of the Garter (KG) consequent upon his creation as Prince of Wales on 8 Dec 1841. The greatest age for the conferment of a knighthood is on a 100th birthday, in the case of the knight bachelor Sir Robert Meyer, additionally made a KCVO by the Queen at the Royal Festival Hall, London on 5 June 1979.

Most freedoms
Probably the greatest number of freedoms ever conferred on any man was 57 in the case of Andrew Carnegie (1835–1919), who was born in Dunfermline, Fife but emigrated to the United States in 1848. The most freedoms conferred upon any citizen of the United Kingdom is 42, in the case of Sir Winston Churchill (1874–1965).

Most honorary degrees
The greatest number of honorary degrees awarded to any individual is 89, given to Herbert Clark Hoover (1874–1964), former President of the United States (1929–33).

Greatest vote
The largest monetary vote made by Parliament to a subject was the £400,000 given to the 1st Duke of Wellington (1769–1852) on 12 Apr 1814. He received in all £864,000. The total received by the 1st, 2nd and 3rd Dukes to January 1900 was £1,052,000.

The Royal Society
The longest term as an FRS (Fellow of the Royal Society) has been 61 years in the case of Bertrand Russell, first Baron (1872–1970), who had been elected in 1908. The longest lived FRS has been Sir Rickard Christophers KT, CIE, OBE (1873–1978) aged 104 years 84 days. John Lubbock (1834–1913), later 1st Baron Avebury, was elected at the age of 23 in 1857.

Who's Who
The longest entry in *Who's Who* (founded 1848) was that of the Rt Hon Sir Winston Leonard Spencer Churchill, KG, OM, CH, TD (1874–1965), who appeared in 67 editions from 1899 (18 lines) and had 211 lines by the 1965 edition. Currently the longest entry is that of Barbara Cartland, the romantic novelist, with 114 lines. Apart from those who qualify for inclusion by hereditary title, the youngest entry has been Yehudi Menuhin, Hon. KBE (b. New York City, USA 22 Apr 1916), the concert violinist, who first appeared in the 1932 edition aged 15. The longest entry of the 66,000 entries in *Who's Who in America* is that of Dr Glen T. Seaborg (b. 12 Apr 1912) whose all-time record of 97 lines compares with the 16 line sketch on President Carter.

Most brothers
The most brothers having entries in *Who's Who* is five in the case of the Barrington-Wards: Frederick Temple (1880–1938), Sir Lancelot (1884–1953), Sir Michael (1887–1972), Robert McGowan (1891–1948) and John Grosvenor (1894–1946). Their father Canon Mark James Barrington-Ward (died 1924) of Duloe, Cornwall was himself in *Who's Who*.

Oxford and Cambridge Unions
Four brothers were Presidents of the Union in the case of the sons of the Rt Hon Isaac Foot. Sir Dingle Foot (Balliol, 1927–8); John (Lord Foot) (Balliol, 1930–1) and Rt Hon Michael (Wadham, 1933–4) at Oxford and Hugh (Lord Caradon) (St John's, 1929) at Cambridge. The last named's son Paul was President at Oxford (University College, 1960–1). The longest debate staged by the Oxford Union was one of 48 hr 6 min on the motion that 'This House will go on for ever' on 29–31 May 1981 chaired by their President, Alexandra Jones.

11. THE HUMAN WORLD

1. POLITICAL AND SOCIAL

Detailed information on all the sovereign and non-sovereign countries of the world is contained in *The Guinness Book of Answers* (3rd Edition) (Price £5.95).

The land area of the Earth is estimated at 57,506,000 miles^2 *148 940 000 km^2* (including inland waters), or 29.20 per cent of the world's surface area.

Largest political division

The British Commonwealth of Nations, a free association of 42 sovereign independent states together with their dependencies, and 4 associated states covers an area of 13,095,000 miles^2 *33 915 000 km^2* with a population which in 1980 surpassed 1,000,000,000.

COUNTRIES

Total

The total number of separately administered *de facto* territories in the world is 224, of which 167 were independent countries (as at 1 Aug 1981). Only 30 sovereign countries are entirely without a seaboard. The United Nations list 4 *de jure* territories— Palestine and Gaza Strip; East Timor and Western Sahara, but do not list Taiwan, Estonia, Latvia and Lithuania, Mayotte, the 4 Antarctic dependencies, Coral Island and Heard Island.

Largest

The country with the greatest area is the Union of Soviet Socialist Republics (the Soviet Union), comprising 15 Union (constituent) Republics with a total area of 22 402 200 km^2 *8,649,500 miles^2*, or 15.0 per cent of the world's total land area, and a total coastline (including islands) of 106 360 km *66,090 miles*. The country measures 8980 km *5580 miles* from east to west and 4490 km *2790 miles* from north to south and is 91.8 times the size of the United Kingdom. Its population on 1 Jan 1981 was 266.6 million.

The United Kingdom covers 94,221 miles^2 *244 030 km^2* (including 1197 miles^2 *3100 km^2* of inland water), or 0.16 per cent of the total land area of the world. Great Britain is the world's eighth largest island, with an area of 84,186 miles^2 *218 040 km^2* and a coastline 4928 miles *7930 km* long, of which Scotland accounts for 2573 miles *4141 km*, Wales 426 miles *685 km* and England 1929 miles *3104 km*.

Smallest

The smallest independent country in the world is the State of the Vatican City or Holy See (Stato della Città del Vaticano), which was made an enclave within the city of Rome, Italy on 11 Feb 1929. The enclave has an area of 44 hectares *108.7 acres*. The maritime sovereign country with the shortest coastline is Monaco with 3.49 miles *5,61 km* excluding piers and breakwaters.

The world's smallest republic is Nauru, less than 1 degree south of the equator in the Western Pacific, which became independent on 31 Jan 1968, has an area of 5263 acres *2129 ha* and a population of 8000 (latest estimate mid-1978). Tuvalu has an area of 6080 acres *2460 ha* but a population of 6000.

The smallest colony in the world is Gibraltar with an area of 2½ miles^2 *5,8 km^2*. Pitcairn Island, the only inhabited (62 people, 1978) island of a group of 4 (total area 18½ miles^2 *48 km^2*) has an area of 1½ miles^2 or 960 acres *388 ha*.

The official residence, since 1834, of the Grand Master of the Order of the Knights of Malta totalling 3 acres *1,2 ha* and comprising the Villa del Priorato di Malta on the lowest of Rome's seven hills, the 151 ft *46 m* Aventine, retains certain diplomatic privileges as does 68 Via Condotti. The order has accredited representatives to foreign governments and is hence sometimes cited as the smallest 'state' in the world.

Flattest and Most Elevated

The country with the lowest highest point is the Republic of the Maldives which attains 8 ft *2,4 m*. The country with the highest lowest point is Lesotho. The egress of the Senqu (Orange) riverbed is 4530 ft *1381 m* above sea level.

Most impenetrable boundary

The 'Iron Curtain' (858 miles *1380 km*) dividing the Federal Republican (West) and the Democratic Republican (East) parts of Germany, utilizes 2,230,000 land mines and 50,000 miles *80 500 km* of barbed wire, much of it of British manufacture, in addition to many watch-towers containing detection devices. The whole strip of 270 yd *246 m* wide occupies 133 miles^2 *344 km^2* of East German territory and cost an estimated $7000 million to build and maintain. It reduced the westward flow from more than 200,000 in 1961 to 5761 escapees in 1962 and to only 18 a month in 1980 including the 106th fatality.

Longest and Shortest frontier

The longest *continuous* frontier in the world is that between Canada and the United States, which (including the Great Lakes boundaries) extends for 3987 miles *6416 km* (excluding 1538 miles *2547 km* with Alaska). The frontier which is crossed most frequently is that between the United States and Mexico. It extends for 1933 miles *3110 km* and there are more than 120,000,000 crossings every year. The Sino-Soviet frontier, broken by the Sino-Mongolian border, extends for 4500 miles *7240 km* with no reported figure of crossings. The 'frontier' of the Holy See in Rome measures 2.53 miles *4,07 km*. The land frontier between Gibraltar and Spain at La Linea, closed since 1969, measures 1672 yd *1,53 km*. Zambia, Zimbabwe, Botswana and Namibia (South West Africa) meet at a point.

Most frontiers

The country with the most land frontiers is China, with 13—Mongolia, USSR, North Korea, Hong Kong, Macau, Vietnam, Laos, Burma, India, Bhutan, Nepal, Pakistan and Afghanistan. France, if all her *Départements d'outre-mer* are included, may, on extended territorial waters, have 20 frontiers.

POPULATIONS

World

Estimates of the world's population have hitherto largely hinged on the accuracy of the component figure for the population of the People's Republic of China, which published no census between 1953 (582.6 million) and mid-1979 (958.05 million). The daily increase in the world's population has been estimated at 215,850, or 149 per minute. It is estimated that 75,000,000,000 humans have been born and died in the last 600,000 years.

Most populous country

The largest population of any country is that of China, which in *pinyin* is written Zhogguo. The mid-1979 census was 958,050,000. The rate of natural increase in the People's Republic of China is now estimated to have been reduced from 2.3 in 1971 to less than 1.2 in 1978 so the 1000 million mark should not now be reached until mid 1983.

Least populous

The independent state with the smallest population is the Vatican City or the Holy See (see Smallest country, page 202), with 728 inhabitants at mid-1978 and a nil return for births.

Most densely populated

The most densely populated territory in the world is the Portuguese province of Macau (or Macao), on the southern coast of China. It has an estimated population of 272,000 (mid-1979) in an area of 6.2 miles^2 *16,05 km^2* giving a density of 43,860 per mile^2 *16 933 per km^2*.

The Principality of Monaco, on the south coast of France, has a population of 26,000 (30 June 1979) in an area of 369,9 acres *149,6 ha* giving a density of 37,230/mile^2 *15 073/km^2*. This is being relieved by marine infilling which will increase her area to 447 acres *180 ha*. Singapore has 2,363,000 (mid-1979 estimate) people in an inhabited area of 73 miles^2 *189 km^2*.

Of territories with an area of more than 1000 km^2, Hong Kong (405 miles^2 *1049 km^2*) contains 4,900,000 (estimated mid-1979), giving the territory a density of 12,097/mile^2 *4671/km^2*. Hong Kong is now the most populous of all colonies. The transcription of the name is from a local pronunciation of the Peking dialect version of Xiang gang (a port for incense). The 1976 by-census showed that the West Area of the urban district of Mong Kok on the Kowloon Peninsula had a density of 252,090/km^2 *652,910/mile^2*. In 1959, at the peak of the housing

WORLD POPULATION
— Progressive estimates

Date	Millions	Date	Millions
10 000 BC	c.5	1930	2070
AD 1	c.200	1940	2295
1000	c.275	1950	2533
1250	375	1960	3049
1500	420	1970	3704
1650	550–600	1975	4033
1700	615	1976	4107
1750	720	1977	4182
1800	900	1978	4258
1900	1625	1979	4336
1920	1862	1980	4410*
		2000	6200*†

* *Provisional Estimate for mid-year.*

† *Some demographers maintain that the figure will (or must) stabilize at 10–15,000 million but above 8000 million during the 21st century. The Tsui-Bogue estimate from the University of Chicago for AD 2000 is 5800 million, compared with the U.N. mid-estimate given.*

WORLD'S MOST POPULOUS CITIES
— Progressive List

Population	Name		Date
c. 150	Chemi Shanidar	Iraq	8910 BC
3,000	Jericho (Arihā)	Samaria	7800 BC
50,000	Uruk (Erech) (now Warka)	Iraq	3000 BC
250,000	Greater Ur	Iraq	2200 BC
350,000	Babylon (now al-Hillah)	Iraq	600 BC
500,000	Pataliputra (Paltna) Bihār	India	400–185 BC
600,000	Seleukia (near Baghdad)	Iraq	300 BC–165 AD
1,100,000	Rome	Italy	133 BC
1,500,000	Angkor	Cambodia	900 AD
1.0–1.5 million	Hang Chow	China	1279
707,000	Peking (Cambaluc), now Beijing	China	1578
1,117,290	Greater London	United Kingdom	1801
8,615,050	Greater London (peak)	United Kingdom	1939
11,700,000 (est.)	Tokyo	Japan	1980

Note: The UN projections for AD 2000 for Greater Mexico City and Tōkyō-Yokohama are 31,616,000 and 26,128,000.

crisis, it was reported that in one house designed for 12 people the number of occupants was 459, including 104 in one room and 4 living on the roof.

Of countries over 1000 miles^2 *2589 km^2* the most densely populated is Bangladesh with a population of 87,657,000 (1 Jan 1980, estimate) living in 55,126 miles^2 *142 775 km^2* at a density of 1589/mile^2 *612/km^2*. The Indonesian island of Java (with an area of 48,763 miles^2 *126 295 km^2*) had a population of 94,693,000 (1981 estimate), giving a density of 1941/mile^2 *750/km^2*.

The United Kingdom (94,221 miles^2 *244 030 km^2*) had an estimated census population of 55,671,000 at 5 Apr 1981, giving a density of 590.8 people/mile^2 *228,1/km^2*. The population density for the Greater London Borough of Kensington and Chelsea is 5312/km^2 *13,292/mile^2*.

Most sparsely populated

Antarctica became permanently occupied by relays of scientists from October 1956. The population varies seasonally and reaches 1500 at times.

The least populated territory, apart from Antarctica, is Kalaatdlit Nunaat (formerly Greenland), with a population of 52,000 (estimated mid-1979) in an area of 840,000 miles^2 *2 175 000 km^2* giving a density of one person to every 16.1 miles^2 *41,8 km^2*. Some 84.3 per cent of the island comprises an ice-cap.

The lowest population densities in the United Kingdom are in the Scottish Highlands and Islands with 13,1/km^2 *5.05/mile^2*. The most sparsely populated county in England is Cumbria with 69.4/km^2 *26.79/mile^2*.

Emigration

More people emigrate from Mexico than from any other country. An estimated 800,000 emigrated illegally into the USA in 1976 alone. A total of 210,300 emigrated from the UK in 1976. The largest number of emigrants in any one year was 360,000 in 1852, mainly from Ireland. The number of UK citizens leaving from mid 1979–mid 1980 was 139,400.

203

Immigration

The country which regularly receives the most legal immigrants is the United States, with more than 800,000 in 1980. It has been estimated that in the period 1820–1980, the USA has received more than 50 million *official* immigrants. One in 24 of the US population is however an *illegal* immigrant to which another 700,000 were added in 1980. The peak year for immigration into the United Kingdom was the 12 months from 1 July 1961 to 30 June 1962, when about 430,000 Commonwealth citizens arrived. The number of new Commonwealth and Pakistani immigrants in 1980 was 33,400 bringing the estimated total to 2.1 million or 3¾ per cent of the population.

Most patient 'Refusnik'

The USSR citizen who has waited longest for an exit visa is Beniamin Boyornolny (b. 7 Apr 1946) who first applied in 1966.

Tourism

In 1980 the United Kingdom received 12,393,000 visitors who spent an estimated £2965 million excluding fares to British carriers.

Birth rate *Highest and Lowest*

The highest estimated by the UN is 54.6 per 1000 for Kenya in 1980. The rate for the whole world was 29 per 1000 in 1978. A world wide survey published in July 1979 showed only Nepal (44.4) with a still rising birth rate.

Excluding Vatican City, where the rate is negligible, the lowest recorded rate is 9.5 for the Federal Republic of Germany (1979).

The 1980 rate in the United Kingdom was 13.4/1000 (13.3 in England and Wales, 13.3 in Scotland and 18.5 in Northern Ireland), while the 1978 rate for the Republic of Ireland was 21.1 registered births per 1000. The highest number of births in England and Wales (since registration in 1837) has been 957,782 in 1920 and the lowest this century 569,259 in 1977. After falling each year since 1964 (875,972) the figure started rising again at the end of 1977.

Death rate *Highest and Lowest*

The death rate for the whole world was 11 per 1000 in 1978. The highest of the latest available recorded death rates is 26.3 deaths per 1000 of the population in Yemen (1970–75).

The lowest of the latest available recorded rates is 1.9 deaths/1000 in Tonga in 1976.

The 1980 rate in the United Kingdom was 11.8/1000 (11.7 in England and Wales, 12.2 in Scotland and 10.8 in Northern Ireland). The highest SMI (Standard Mortality Index where the national average is 100) is in Salford, Greater Manchester with a figure of 133. The 1978 rate for the Republic of Ireland was 10.0 registered deaths per 1000.

Natural increase

The rate of natural increase for the whole world was 29−11 = 18 per 1000 in 1978. The highest of the latest available recorded rates is 40.4 (54.6 − 14.2) in Kenya in 1980.

The 1980 rate for the United Kingdom was 1.6 (1.6 in England and Wales, 1.1 in Scotland and 7.6 in Northern Ireland). The rate for the first time in the first quarter of 1975 became one of natural decrease. The figure for the Republic of Ireland was 10.5/1000 in 1977.

The lowest rate of natural increase in any major independent country is in W. Germany with a negative figure of −2.1 per 1000 (9.5 births and 11.6 deaths) for 1979.

Marriage ages

The country with the lowest average ages for marriage is India, with 20.0 years for males and 14.5 years for females. At the other extreme is Ireland, with 31.4 for males and 26.5 for females. In the People's Republic of China the *recommended* age for marriage for men has been 28 and for women 25. In England and Wales the peak ages for marriage are 22.8 years (male) and 19.6 years (female).

Divorces

The country with most divorces is the United States with a total of 1,170,000 in 1979—a rate of 50.49 per cent on the current annual total of marriages.

Sex ratio

There were estimated to be 1003.5 men in the world for every 1000 women (1975). The country with the largest recorded shortage of males is the USSR, with 1143 females to every 1000 males (1979 census). The country with the largest recorded woman shortage is Pakistan, with 885 to every 1000 males in 1972. The figures are, however, probably under-enumerated due to *purdah*. The ratio in the United Kingdom was 1054.7 females to every 1000 males at 30 June 1978, and is expected to be 1014.2/1,000 by AD 2000.

Infant mortality

Based on deaths before one year of age, the lowest of the latest available recorded rates is 7.3 deaths per 1000 live births in Sweden in 1979. The world rate in 1978 was 91.

The highest recorded infant mortality rate reported has been 195 to 300 for Burma in 1952 and 259 for Zaïre in 1950. In Ethiopia the infant mortality rate was unofficially estimated to be nearly 550/1000 live births in 1969. Many countries have ceased to make returns.

The United Kingdom figure for 1980 was 11.8/1000 live births (England and Wales 11.6, Scotland 11.9, Northern Ireland 13.1). The Republic of Ireland figure for 1977 was 15.7.

Life expectation

There is evidence that life expectation in Britain in the 5th century AD was 33 years for males and 27 years for females. In the decade 1890–1900 the expectation of life among the population of India was 23.7 years.

Based on the latest available data, the highest recorded expectation of life at age 12 months is 73.0 years for males and 79.2 years for females in Iceland (1975–6).

BRITISH AND IRISH LARGEST AND SMALLEST PRIMARY LOCAL GOVERNMENT AREAS
- By size and population

	By Area (in acres/hectares)						By Home/Population			
	Largest			**Smallest**			**Most Populous**		**Least Populous**	
England	North Yorkshire	2,055,109	*831 661*	Isles of Scilly	4,120	*1 667*	Greater London	6,849,100	Isles of Scilly	2,020
Wales	Dyfed	1,424,668	*576 534*	South Glamorgan	102,807	*41 604*	Mid Glamorgan	537,600[1]	Powys	107,600
Scotland[2]	Highland[3]	6,214,400	*2 514 880*	Orkney	217,600	*88 059*	Strathclyde[4]	2,504,909	Orkney	17,675
Northern Ireland	Tyrone	779,520	*315 460*	North Down	18,174	*7 354*	Belfast City	354,400	Moyle	13,400
Republic of Ireland	Cork	1,843,408	*745 990*	Louth	202,806	*82 071*	Dublin County	799,048	Longford	28,250

[1] *The most populous town in Wales—the City of Cardiff (pop. 278,900)—is in South Glamorgan.*
[2] *Scotland's 33 Counties were replaced on 16 May 1975 by nine regions and three Island Areas.*
[3] *The inclusion by Act of Parliament on 10 Feb 1972 of Rockall in the District of Harris in Western Isles put the extremities of that Authority at the record distance apart of 302 miles 486 km.*
[4] *Includes the most populous town in Scotland—the City of Glasgow (pop. 809,000).*

The lowest recorded expectation of life at birth is 27 years for both sexes in the Vallée du Niger area of Mali in 1957 (sample survey, 1957–8). The figure for males in Gabon was 25 years in 1960–1 but 45 for females.

The latest available figures for England and Wales (1975–7) are 69.9 years for males and 76.0 years for females; for Scotland (1976–8) 68.0 years for males and 74.37 years for females; for Northern Ireland (1975–7) 67.54 years for males and 73.84 years for females, and for the Republic of Ireland (1970–2) 68.77 years for males and 73.52 years for females. The British figure for 1901–10 was 48.53 years for males and 52.83 years for females.

Housing
For comparison, dwelling units are defined as a structurally separated room or rooms occupied by private households of one or more people and having separate access or a common passageway to the street.

The country with the greatest recorded number of private housing units is India, with 100,251,000 occupied in 1972.

Great Britain had a stock of 20,816,000 dwellings as at 1 Jan 1980. The record number of permanent houses built in a year has been 413,715 in 1968.

Physicians
The country with the most physicians is the USSR, with 831,300, or one to every 307 persons. China had an estimated 1.4 million para-medical personnel known as 'bare foot doctors' by 1981. In England and Wales there were 103,837 doctors qualified to work as specialists in general practice or in industry as at 30 Sept 1978.

The country with the lowest recorded proportion is Upper Volta, with 58 physicians (one for every 92,759 people) in 1970.

Dentists
The country with the most dentists is the United States, where 136,000 were registered members of the American Dental Association in 1979.

Psychiatrists
The country with the most psychiatrists is the United States. The registered membership of the American Psychiatric Association (inst. 1894) was 25,440 in 1979. The membership of the American Psychological Association (inst 1892) was 50,000 in 1979.

Hospital Largest *World*
The largest mental hospital in the world is the Pilgrim State Hospital, West Brentwood, Long Island, NY, USA, with 3618 beds. It formerly contained 14,200 beds.

The busiest maternity hospital in the world is the Mama Yemo Hospital, Kinshasa, Zaïre with 41,930 deliveries in 1976. The record 'birthquake' occurred on a day in May 1976 with 175 babies born. It has 599 beds.

Great Britain
The largest hospitals of any kind in Great Britain are Winwick Hospital near Warrington, with 1750 staffed beds, and Rainhill Hospital near Liverpool, which has 1550 staffed beds for mental patients.

The largest general hospital in Great Britain is the St James Hospital, Leeds, West Yorkshire, with 1398 staffed beds.

The largest maternity hospital in Great Britain is the Simpson Memorial Maternity Pavilion, Edinburgh with 219 staffed beds.

The largest children's hospital in Great Britain is Queen Mary's Hospital for Children, at Carshalton, Sutton, Greater London, with 522 staffed beds.

Longest stay in hospital
Miss Martha Nelson was admitted to the Columbus State Institute for the Feeble-Minded in Ohio, USA in 1875. She died in January 1975 aged 103 years 6 months in the Orient State Institution, Ohio after spending more than 99 years in institutions.

A set of stamps issued by the off-shore platform Sealand showing its owners 'Prince' Roy and 'Princess' Joan. They claim that their UDI outside territorial waters makes their abode the world's smallest sovereign territory.

Most Expensive
In mid-1980 the average daily cost of a day's stay in a California hospital was $411 (*£186*) or $2874 (*£1300*) per average stay.

CITIES
Oldest *World*
The oldest known walled town in the world is Arīhā (Jericho). The latest radio-carbon dating on specimens from the lowest levels reached by archaeologists indicate habitation there by perhaps 3000 people as early as 7800 BC. The village of Zawi Chemi Shanidar, discovered in 1957 in northern Iraq, has been dated to 8910 BC. The oldest capital city in the world is Dimashq (Damascus), the capital of Syria. It has been continuously inhabited since *c.* 2500 BC.

Great Britain
The oldest town in Great Britain is often cited as Colchester, the old British Camulodunum, headquarters of Belgic chiefs in the 1st century BC. However, the name of the tin trading post Salakee, St Mary's, Isles of Scilly, is derived from pre-Celtic roots and hence *ante* 550 BC. The oldest borough in Britain is reputed to be Barnstaple, Devon whose charter was granted by King Athelstan (927–939) in AD 930.

Most populous *World*
The most populous 'urban agglomeration' in the world is the 'Keihin Metropolitan Area' (Tōkyō-Yokohama Metropolitan Area) of 1081 miles² *2800 km²* containing an estimated 28,043,000 people in 1978. Of 'cities proper' both Tōkyō, Japan and Mexico City, Mexico have populations exceeding 8½ million while Greater Tōkyō, known as Tōkyō-to, and Greater Mexico City have populations exceeding 11½ million.

Great Britain
The largest conurbation in Britain is Greater London (established on 1 Apr 1965), with a population of 6,696,008 (1981 census). The residential population of the City of London (677.3 acres *274 ha* plus 61.7 acres *24,9 ha* foreshore) is 5893 compared with 128,000 in 1801. The peak figure for Greater London was 8,615,050 in 1939.

Largest in area
The world's largest town, in area, is Mount Isa, Queensland, Australia. The area administered by the City Council is 15,822 miles² *40 978 km²*. The largest conurbation in the United Kingdom is the county of Greater London with an area of 609.8 miles² *1579,5 km²*.

Smallest town and hamlet
The smallest place with a town council is Caerwys, Clwyd, Wales with a population of 801. The town has a charter dated 1284.

Highest *World*

The highest capital in the world, before the domination of Tibet by China, was Lhasa, at an elevation of 12,087 ft *3684 m* above sea-level. La Paz, the administrative and *de facto* capital of Bolivia, stands at an altitude of 11,916 ft *3631 m* above sea-level. The city was founded in 1548 by Capt Alonso de Mendoza on the site of an Indian village named Chuquiapu. It was originally called Ciudad de Nuestra Señora de La Paz (City of Our Lady of Peace), but in 1825 was renamed La Paz de Ayacucho, its present official name. Sucre, the legal capital of Bolivia, stands at 9301 ft *2834 m* above sea-level. The new town of Wenchuan, founded in 1955 on the Chinghai–Tibet road, north of the Tangla range, is the highest in the world at 5100 m *16,732 ft* above sea-level. The highest dwellings in the world are those at Bāsisi, India near the Tibet border at *c.* 19,700 ft *5988 m*.

Great Britain

The highest village in Britain is Flash, in northern Staffordshire, at 1518 ft *462 m* above sea-level. The highest in Scotland is Wanlockhead, in Dumfries and Galloway at 1380 ft *420 m* above sea-level.

Lowest

The settlement of Ein Bokek, which has a synagogue, on the shores of the Dead Sea is the lowest in the world at 1291 ft *393,5 m* below sea-level.

Northernmost

The world's most northerly town with a population of more than 10,000 is the Arctic port of Dikson, USSR in 73° 32′ N. The northernmost village is Ny Ålesund (78° 55′ N.), a coalmining settlement on King's Bay, Vest Spitsbergen, in the Norwegian territory of Svalbard, inhabited only during the winter season. The northernmost capital is Reykjavik, the capital of Iceland, in 64° 08′ N. Its population was estimated to be 83,887 (1978 est.). The northernmost permanent human occupation is the base at Alert (82° 31′ N.), on Dumb Bell Bay, on the north-east coast of Ellesmere Island, northern Canada.

Southernmost

The world's southernmost village is Puerto Williams (population about 350), on the north coast of Isla Navarino, in Tierra del Fuego, Chile, 680 miles *1090 km* north of Antarctica. Wellington, the North Island, New Zealand is the southernmost capital city on 41° 17′ S. The world's southernmost administrative centre is Port Stanley (51° 43′ S.), in the Falkland Islands, off South America.

Most remote from the sea

The largest town most remote from the sea is Wulumuch'i (Urumchi) formerly Tihwa, Sinkiang, capital of the Uighur Autonomous Region of China, at a distance of about 1400 miles *2250 km* from the nearest coastline. Its population was estimated to be 320,000 in 1974.

---

2. ROYALTY AND HEADS OF STATE

The *Guinness Book of Kings, Rulers and Statesmen* by Clive Carpenter (Guinness Superlatives, £7.95) contains much extra information.

Oldest ruling house

The Emperor of Japan, Hirohito (born 29 Apr 1901), is the 124th in line from the first Emperor, Jimmu Tenno or Zinmu, whose reign was traditionally from 660 to 581 BC, but more probably from *c.* 40 to *c.* 10 BC.

Her Majesty Queen Elizabeth II (b. 21 Apr 1926) represents dynasties historically traceable at least back until the 5th century AD; notably that of Elesa of whom Alfred The Great was a 13 greats grandson and the Queen is therefore a 49 greats granddaughter. If the historicity of some early Scoto-Irish and Pictish kings were acceptable, the lineage could be named to about 70 generations.

Reigns *Longest*

The longest recorded reign of any monarch is that of Pepi II, a Sixth Dynasty Pharaoh of ancient Egypt. His reign began in *c.* 2310 BC, when he was aged 6, and lasted *c.* 94 years. Musoma Kanijo, chief of the Nzega district of western Tanganyika (now part of Tanzania), reputedly reigned for more than 98 years from 1864, when aged 8, until his death on 2 Feb 1963. The 6th Japanese Emperor Koo-an traditionally reigned for 102 years (from 392 to 290 BC), but probably his actual reign was from about AD 110 to about AD 140. The reign of the 11th Emperor Suinin was traditionally from 29 BC to AD 71 (99 years), but probably from AD 259 to 291. The longest reign of any major European monarch was that of King Louis XIV of France, who ascended the throne on 14 May 1643, aged 4 years 231 days, and reigned for 72 years 110 days until his death on 1 Sept 1715, four days before his 77th birthday. Grand Duke Karl Friederich of Baden (1728–1811) ruled from 12 May 1738 for 73 years 29 days.

Currently the longest reigning monarch in the world is King Sobhuza II, KBE (b. 22 July 1899), the *Ngwenyama* (Paramount Chief) of Swaziland, who succeeded on 10 Dec 1899 at the age of 141 days and reigned under the regency of his grandmother Queen Labotsibeni until he assumed full powers on 6 Dec 1921. *Burke's Royal Families of the World* lists 28 wives and 85 children. Hirohito (see Oldest Ruling House) has been Emperor in Japan since 25 Dec 1926.

Roman Occupation

During the 369 year long Roman occupation of England, Wales and parts of Scotland there were 40 sole and 27 co-Emperors of Rome. Of these the longest reigning was Constantinus I (The Great) from 31 Mar 307 to 22 May 337–30 years 2 months.

Shortest

King Virabahu of the Kalinga Kshatriya dynasty of Ceylon (Sri Lanka) was assassinated a few hours after he was crowned at Polonnaruwa in 1196.

Highest post-nominal numbers

The highest post-nominal number ever used to designate a member of a Royal House was 75 briefly enjoyed by Count Heinrich LXXV Reuss (1800–1). All male members of this branch of this German family are called Heinrich and are successively numbered from I upwards *each* century.

The highest British regnal number is 8, used by Henry VIII (1509–1547) and by Edward VIII (1936) who died as HRH the Duke of Windsor, KG, KT, KP, GCB, GCSI, GCMG, GCIE, GCVO, GBE, ISO, MC, on 28 May 1972. Jacobites liked to style Henry Benedict, Cardinal York (b. 1725), the grandson of James II, as Henry IX in respect of his 'reign' from 1788 to 1807 when he died the last survivor in the male line of the House of Stuart.

Longest lived 'Royals'

The longest life among the Blood Royal of Europe has been that of the late HRH Princess Alicia of Bourbon who was born on 29 June 1876 and died on 20 Jan 1975 aged 98 years 206 days. The greatest age among European Royal Consorts is the 101 years 268 days of HSH Princess Leonilla Bariatinsky (b. Moscow, 9 July 1816), who married HSH Prince Louis of Sayn-Wittgenstein-Sayn and died in Ouchy, Switzerland on 1 Feb 1918. The longest-lived Queen on record has been the Queen Grandmother of Siam, Queen Sawang (b. 10 Sept 1862), 27th daughter of King Mongkut (Rama IV); she died on 17 Dec 1955 aged 93 years 3 months.

HRH Princess Alice Mary, VA, GCVO, GBE, Countess of Athlone (b. 25 Feb 1883) became the longest ever lived British 'royal' on 15 July 1977 and died aged 97 years 313 days on 3 Jan 1981. She fulfilled 20,000 engagements, including the funerals of five British monarchs.

Youngest King and Queen

Thirty-one of the world's 167 sovereign states have monarchical rule comprising 1 Emperor, 10 Kings, 3 Queens, 4 princely rulers and one elected monarch. Queen Elizabeth II is Head of State of 14 Commonwealth countries. That with the youngest King is Bhutan where King Jigme Singye Wangchuk was born 11 Nov 1955, succeeded on 24 July 1972 when aged 16 years and 8 months. That with youngest Queen is Denmark with Queen Margrethe II (b. 16 Apr 1940). Obi Keagboekuzi I of Agbor, Nigeria, the 18th obi since 1270, was born on 29 June 1977 and

BRITISH MONARCHY RECORDS

	Kings	Queens Regnant	Queens Consort
LONGEST REIGN OR TENURE	59 years 96 days[1] George III 1760–1820	63 years 216 days Victoria 1837–1901	57 years 70 days Charlotte 1761–1818 (Consort of George III)
SHORTEST REIGN OR TENURE	77 days[2] Edward V 1483	13 days[3] Jane, 6–19 July 1553	154 days Yoleta (1285–6) (second consort of Alexander III)
LONGEST LIVED	81 years 239 days[4] George III (b. 1738–d. 1820)	81 years 243 days Victoria (b. 1819–d. 1901)	85 years 303 days Mary of Teck (b. 1867–d. 1953) (Consort of George V)
MOST CHILDREN (LEGITIMATE)[5]	18 Edward I 1272–1307	9[6] Victoria (b. 1819–d. 1901)	15 Eleanor (c. 1244–90) and Charlotte (b. 1744–d. 1818)
OLDEST TO START REIGN OR CONSORTSHIP	64 years 10 months William IV 1830–7	37 years 5 months Mary I 1553–8	56 years 53 days Alexandra (b. 1844–d. 1925) (Consort of Edward VII)
YOUNGEST TO START REIGN OR CONSORTSHIP	269 days Henry VI in 1422	6 or 7 days Mary, Queen of Scots in 1542	6 years 11 months Isabella (second consort of Richard II in 1396)
MOST MARRIED	6 times Henry VIII 1509–47	3 times Mary, Queen of Scots 1542–67 (executed 1587)	4 times Catherine Parr (b. c. 1512–d. 1548) (sixth consort of Henry VIII)
MOST ALIVE SIMULTANEOUSLY	Between 30 Oct 1683 (birth of George Augustus of Hanover, later George II) and 6 Feb 1685 (death of Charles II) there were 7 monarchs living simultaneously (Charles II, James II, William and Mary, Anne, George I and II) and also Richard Cromwell (d. 1712) the 2nd Lord Protector and _de facto_ Head of State in 1658–59.		

Notes (Dates are dates of reigns or tenures unless otherwise indicated).

1 James Francis Edward, the Old Pretender, known to his supporters as James III, styled his reign from 16 Sept 1701 until his death 1 Jan 1766 (i.e. 64 years 109 days).
2 There is the probability that in pre-Conquest times Sweyn 'Forkbeard', the Danish King of England, reigned for only 40 days in 1013–14.
3 She accepted the allegiance of the Lords of the Council (9 July) and was proclaimed on 10 July so is often referred to as the '9 (or 10) day Queen'.
4 Richard Cromwell (b. 4 Oct 1626), the 2nd Lord Protector from 3 Sept 1658 until his abdication on 24 May 1659, lived under the alias John Clarke until 12 July 1712 aged 85 years 9 months and was thus the longest lived Head of State.
5 Henry I (1068–1135) in addition to one (possibly two) legitimate sons and a daughter had at least 20 bastard children (9 sons, 11 daughters), and possibly 22, by six mistresses.
6 Queen Anne (b. 1665–d. 1714) had 17 pregnancies, which produced only 5 live births.

succeeded his father, the 17th obi, on 31 Oct 1979 aged 2 years 4 months.

Heaviest monarch
The world's heaviest monarch is the 6 ft 3 in _1,90 m_ tall King Taufa'ahau of Tonga who in Sept 1976 was weighed on the only adequate scales in the country at the airport recording 33 st (462 lb) _209,5 kg_.

Most prolific
The most prolific monogamous 'royals' have been Prince Hartmann of Liechtenstein (1613–86) who had 24 children, of whom 21 were live born, by Countess Elisabeth zu Salm-Reifterscheidt (1623–88). HRH Duke Roberto I of Parma also had 24 children but by two wives.

Head of State _Oldest and Youngest_
The oldest head of state in the world is the President of Italy, Alessandro Pertini (b. 27 Sept 1896). The youngest non-royal head of state is Jean-Claude Duvalier, (b. 3 July 1951) President of Haiti since 21 Apr 1971 when he was 19 years and 10 months.

Earliest Elected Female
President Vigdis Finnbogadottir (b. 1930) of Iceland became the first democratically elected female head of state on 30 June 1980 and took office on 1 Aug 1980.

3. LEGISLATURES

PARLIAMENTS—WORLD
Earliest and Oldest
The earliest known legislative assembly was a bicameral one in Erech, Iraq c. 2800 BC. The oldest legislative body is the _Althing_ of Iceland founded in AD 930. This body, which originally comprised 39 local chieftains at Thingvellir, was abolished in 1800, but restored by Denmark to a consultative status in 1843 and a legislative status in 1874. The legislative assembly with the oldest continuous history is the Tynwald Court in the Isle of Man, which is believed to have originated more than 1000 years ago.

Largest
The largest legislative assembly in the world is the National People's Congress of the People's Republic of China. The fourth Congress, which was convened in 1979 had 3471 members.

Smallest quorum
The House of Lords has the smallest quorum, expressed as a percentage of eligible voters, of any legislative body in the world, namely less than one-third of 1 per cent. To transact business there must be three peers present, including the Lord Chancellor or his deputy. The House of Commons quorum of 40 MPs, including the Speaker or his deputy, is 20 times as exacting.

Highest paid legislators
The most highly paid of all the world's legislators are Members of the US Congress whose basic annual salary was raised on 12 Oct 1979 to $60,662.50 (now £27,570). In addition up to $1,021,167 (£464,000) per annum is allowed for office help, with a salary limit of $49,941 (_now £22,700_) for any one staff member (limited to 16 in number). Senators are allowed up to $143,000 (£65,000) per annum for an official office expense account from which official travel, telegram, long distance telephone, air mail, postage, stationery, subscriptions to newspapers, and office expenses in home state are paid. They also command very low rates for filming, speech and radio transcriptions and, in the case of women senators, beauty treatment. When abroad they have access to 'counterpart funds'. A retiring President electing to take also his congressional pension would enjoy a combined pension of $103,500 (£47,000) per annum.

Longest membership
The longest span as a legislator was 83 years by József Madarász (1814–1915). He first attended the Hungarian Parliament in 1832–6 as _oblegatus absentium_ (i.e. on behalf of an absent deputy). He was a full member in 1848–50 and from 1861 until his death on 31 Jan 1915.

Best attendance record
US Congressman William H. Natcher (Democrat) of Bowling Green, Kentucky on 6 Jan 1981 completed 27 years (1954–81) without missing a single vote (3901 quorum calls and 8242 votes) to 23 May 1981. State Representative Lucille H. McCollough

207

was elected to the Michigan House of Representatives on 1 Jan 1955 and had a perfect attendance record into June 1981.

UN Speech *Longest*
The longest speech made in the United Nations has been one of 4 hr 29 min by President Dr Fidel Castro Ruz (b. 13 Aug 1927) of Cuba on 26 Sept 1960.

Filibusters
The longest continuous speech in the history of the United States Senate was that of Senator Wayne Morse (1900–74) of Oregon on 24–25 Apr 1953, when he spoke on the Tidelands Oil Bill for 22 hr 26 min without resuming his seat. Interrupted only briefly by the swearing-in of a new senator, Senator Strom Thurmond (b. 1902) (South Carolina, Democrat) spoke against the Civil Rights Bill for 24 hr 19 min on 28–29 Aug 1957. The United States national record duration for a filibuster is 43 hr by Texas State senator Bill Meier against nondisclosure of industrial accidents in May 1977.

Treaty *Oldest*
The world's oldest treaty is the Anglo-Portuguese Treaty of Alliance signed in London over 600 years ago on 16 June 1373. The text was confirmed 'with my usual flourish' by John de Banketre, Clerk.

PARLIAMENTS—UNITED KINGDOM
Earliest
The earliest known use of the term 'parliament' in an official English royal document, in the meaning of a summons to the King's council, dates from 19 Dec 1241.

The Houses of Parliament of the United Kingdom in the Palace of Westminster, London, had 1801 members (House of Lords 1166, House of Commons 635) in June 1980.

Longest
The longest English Parliament was the 'Pensioners' Parliament of Charles II, which lasted from 8 May 1661 to 24 Jan 1679, a period of 17 years 8 months and 16 days. The longest United Kingdom Parliament was that of George V, Edward VIII and George VI, lasting from 26 Nov 1935 to 15 June 1945, a span of 9 years 6 months and 20 days.

Shortest
The parliament of Edward I, summoned to Westminster for 30 May 1306, lasted only 1 day. The parliament of Charles II at Oxford from 21–28 Mar 1681 lasted 7 days. The shortest United Kingdom Parliament was that of George III, lasting from 15 Dec 1806 to 29 Apr 1807, a period of only 4 months and 14 days.

Longest sittings
The longest sitting in the House of Commons was one of 41½ hr from 4 p.m. on 31 Jan 1881 to 9.30 a.m. on 2 Feb 1881, on the question of better Protection of Person and Property in Ireland. The longest sitting of the Lords has been 19 hr 16 min from 2.30 p.m. on 29 Feb to 9.46 a.m. on 1 Mar 1968 on the Commonwealth Immigrants Bill (Committee stage). The longest sitting of a Standing Committee occurred from 10.30 a.m. 11 May to 12.08 p.m. 13 May 1948 when Standing Committee D considered the Gas Bill through two nights for 49 hr 38 min.

Longest speech
The longest recorded continuous speech in the House of Commons was that of Henry Peter Brougham (1778–1868) on 7 Feb 1828, when he spoke for 6 hr on Law Reform. He ended at 10.40 p.m. and the report of this speech occupied 12 columns of the next day's edition of *The Times*. Brougham, created the 1st Lord Brougham and Vaux on 22 Nov 1830, then set the House of Lords record, also with 6 hours on 7 Oct 1831, when speaking on the second reading of the Reform Bill. The longest back bench speech under present, much stricter, Standing Orders has been one of 3 hr 16 min by Sir Bernard Braine (b. 1914) the Conservative member for Essex, South East concerning Canvey Island on 23–24 July 1974.

The longest speech in Stormont, Northern Ireland was one of 9½ hr by Tommy Henderson MP on the Appropriations Bill on 26–27 May 1936.

Greatest parliamentary petition
The greatest petition has been supposed to be the Great Chartist Petition of 1848 but of the 5,706,000 'signatures' only 1,975,496 were valid. The largest of all time was for the abolition of Entertainment Duty with 3,107,080 signatures presented on 5 June 1951.

Most time consuming legislation
The most profligate use of parliamentary time was on the Government of Ireland Bill of 1893–4, which required 82 days in the House of Commons of which 46 days was in Committee. The record for a standing committee is 58 sessions for the Aircraft and Shipbuilding Industries Bill which was re-presented to the House of Commons on 8 June 1976 after the 303–303 tied vote of 27 May 1976.

Divisions
The record number of divisions in the House of Commons is 64 on 23–24 Mar 1971 including 57 in succession between midnight and noon. The largest division was one of 350–310 on the vote of no confidence on 11 Aug 1892.

ELECTIONS—WORLD
Largest
The largest elections in the world are those for the 529 seat Indian *Lok Sabha* (House of the People). The in-coming Prime Minister Mrs Indira Gandhi was better known by her symbol (a cow) than by name among the 362 million voters.

Closest
The ultimate in close general elections occurred in Zanzibar (now part of Tanzania) on 18 Jan 1961, when the Afro-Shirazi Party won by a single seat, after the seat of Chake-Chake on Pemba Island had been gained by a single vote.

The narrowest recorded percentage win in an election would seem to be for the office of Southern District highway commissioner in Mississippi State, USA on 7 Aug 1979. Robert E. Joiner was declared the winner over W. H. Pyron with 133,587 votes to 133,582. The loser got more than 49.9999% of the votes.

Most one-sided
North Korea recorded a 100 per cent turn-out of electors and a 100 per cent vote for the Worker's Party of Korea in the general election of 8 Oct 1962. The previous record had been set in the Albanian election of 4 June 1962, when all but seven of the electorate of 889,875 went to the polls—a 99.9992 per cent turn-out. Of the 889,868 voters, 889,828 voted for the candidates of the Albanian Party of Labour, *i.e.* 99.9955 per cent of the total poll.

Most bent
In the Liberian presidential election of 1927 President Charles D. B. King (1875–1961) was returned with a majority over his opponent, Mr Thomas J. R. Faulkner of the People's Party, officially announced as 234,000. The total electorate at the time was less than a fifteenth of this at 15,000.

Highest personal majority
The highest ever personal majority by any politician has been 424,545 by Ram Bilas Paswan, 30, the Janata candidate for Hajipur in Bihar, India in March 1977. The electorate was 625,179.

Communist parties
The largest national Communist party outside the Soviet Union (15,000,000 members in 1975) and Communist states has been the Partito Comunista Italiano (Italian Communist Party), with a membership of 2,300,000 in 1946. The total was 1,700,000 in 1976. The membership in mainland China was estimated to be 28,000,000 in 1974.

The Communist Party of Great Britain, formed on 31 July 1920 in Cannon Street Station Hotel, London, attained its peak membership of 56,000 in December 1942, compared with 20,599 on 1 Jan 1980.

Longest term
Members of Taiwan's National Assembly elected in 1947 have been extended in office and include several hundred who celebrated their 32nd year in 1979.

Voting age Extremes
The eligibility for voting is 15 years of age in the Philippines and 25 years in Andorra.

Smallest vote
Mr Wideon Pyfrom (Free National Party) standing for the Rolleville constituency, in the Bahamas in the July 1977 elections secured a *nil* vote.

Most Coups
Statisticians contend Bolivia, since it became a sovereign country in 1825, has had 188 *coups*.

PRIME MINISTERS AND STATESMEN—WORLD
Oldest
The longest lived Prime Minister of any country is Christopher Hornsrud, Prime Minister of Norway from 28 Jan to 15 Feb 1928. He was born on 15 Nov 1859 and died on 13 Dec 1960, aged 101 years 28 days. The Hon. Richard Gavin Reid (b. Glasgow 17 Jan 1879), Premier of Alberta, Canada in 1934–35 died on 17 Oct 1980 aged 101 years 274 days.

El Hadji Muhammad el Mokri, Grand Vizier of Morocco, died on 16 Sept 1957, at a reputed age of 116 Muslim (*Hijri*) years, equivalent to 112.5 Gregorian years. The oldest age of appointment has been 81 years in the case of Morarji Ranchhodji Desai of India (b. 29 Feb 1896) in March 1977.

Longest term of office
Prof. Dr António de Oliveirar Salazar, GCMG (Hon.) (1889–1970) was the President of the Council of Ministers (*i.e.* Prime Minister) of Portugal from 5 July 1932 until 27 Sept 1968—36 years 84 days. He was superseded 11 days after going into coma. The longest serving democratically elected premier was Tage Erlander of Sweden for 22 years 357 days from 10 Oct 1946 to 1 Oct 1969.

Andrei Andreevich Gromyko (b. 6 July 1909) has been Minister of Foreign Affairs of the USSR since 15 Feb 1957 having been Deputy Foreign Minister since 1946.

EUROPEAN PARLIAMENTARY ELECTION RECORDS
In the first European Parliamentary elections of 7 June 1979 the highest majority in the 81 constituencies was 95,484 for M. Seligman (Con) in Sussex West. The lowest was 302 for W. Hopper (Con) in Greater Manchester West. The largest and smallest electorates were 575,991 in Wight and Hampshire East and 298,802 in Highlands and Islands. The latter had the highest turn out with 39.4 per cent. The lowest turn out was 20.4 per cent in London North East.

MAJORITIES—UNITED KINGDOM
Party
The largest party majorities were those of the Liberals, with 307 seats in 1832 and 356 seats in 1906. In 1931 the Coalition of Conservatives, Liberals and National Labour candidates had a majority of 491. The narrowest party majority was that of the Whigs in 1847, with a single seat.

The largest majority on a division was one of 463 (464 votes to 1), on a motion of 'no confidence' in the conduct of World War II, on 29 Jan 1942. Since the war the largest has been one of 461 (487 votes to 26) on 10 May 1967, during the debate on the government's application for Britain to join the European Economic Community (the 'Common Market').

Narrowest personal *All-time*
The closest result occurred in the General Election of 1886 at Ashton-under-Lyne, Greater Manchester when the Conservative and Liberal candidates both received 3,049 votes. The Returning Officer, Mr James Walker, gave his casting vote for John E. W. Addison (Con), who was duly returned while Alexander B. Rowley (Gladstone-Liberal) was declared unelected. On 13 Oct 1892 there was a by-election at Cirencester, Gloucestershire, which resulted in an election petition after which the number of votes cast for the Conservative and Liberal were found to have been equal. A new election was ordered.

Two examples of majorities of 1 have occurred. At Durham, in the 1895 General Election, Matthew Fowler (Lib) with 1111

Stephen James Dorrell, Tory MP for Loughborough, who was aged only 25 yr 39 days when elected for Parliament (see p. 211).

votes defeated the Hon. Arthur R. D. Elliott (Liberal-Unionist) (1110 votes) after a recount. At Exeter in the General Election of December 1910 a Liberal victory over the Conservatives by 4 votes was reversed on an election petition to a Conservative win by H. E. Duke KC (later the 1st Lord Merrivale) (Unionist) with 4777 votes to R. H. St Maur's (Lib) 4776 votes.

The smallest majority since 'universal' franchise was by two votes by Abraham John Flint (1903–71), the National Labour candidate at Ilkeston, Derbyshire, in the 1931 General Election. He received 17,587 votes, compared with 17,585 for G. H. Oliver, DCM (Lab).

Highest poll
The highest poll in any constituency since 'universal' franchise was 93.42 per cent in Fermanagh and South Tyrone, Northern Ireland, at the General Election of 25 Oct 1951, when there were 62,799 voters from an electorate of 67,219. The Anti-Partition candidate, Mr Cahir Healy (1877–1970), was elected with a majority of 2635 votes. The highest poll in any constituency in the May 1979 General Election was 86.97 per cent in Fermanagh and South Tyrone. The highest figure in Great Britain was 86.08 per cent in Cornwall North and the lowest in Chelsea with 57.30 per cent.

HOUSE OF LORDS
Oldest member
The oldest member ever was the Rt Hon the 5th Baron Penrhyn, who was born on 21 Nov 1865 and died on 3 Feb 1967, aged 101 years 74 days. The oldest now is the Rt Hon Hugh O'Neill, Bt, 1st Baron Rathcavan (b. 18 June 1883). The oldest peer to make a maiden speech was Lord Maenan (1854–1951) aged 94 years 123 days (see Oldest creation, Chapter 10).

Youngest member
The youngest present member of the House of Lords has been HRH the Prince Charles Philip Arthur George, KG, KT, GCB, the Prince of Wales (b. 14 Nov 1948). All Dukes of Cornwall, of whom Prince Charles is the 24th, are technically eligible to sit, regardless of age—in his case from his succession on 6 Feb 1952, aged 3. The 20th and 21st holders, later King George IV (b. 1762) and King Edward VII (b. 1841), were technically entitled to sit from birth. The youngest creation of a life peer or peeress under the Peerage Act 1958 has been that of Lady Masham (b. 14 Apr 1935) who was created Baroness Masham of Ilton at the age of 34 years 262 days.

The first woman to address the House was Mrs Elizabeth Robinson *née* Hastings (1695–1779) from Gibraltar to give testimony about slave trafficking.

POLITICAL OFFICE HOLDERS

Premiership *Longest term*

No United Kingdom Prime Minister has yet matched in duration the continuous term of office of Great Britain's first Prime Minister the Rt Hon Sir Robert Walpole, KG, later the 1st Earl of Orford (1676–1745), First Lord of the Treasury and Chancellor of the Exchequer for 20 years 326 days from 3 Apr 1721 to 12 Feb 1742. The office was not, however, formally recognized until 1905, since when the longest tenure has been that of Herbert Henry Asquith, later the 1st Earl of Oxford and Asquith (1852–1928), with 8 years 243 days from 8 Apr 1908 to 7 Dec 1916. This was 7 days longer than the three terms of Sir Winston Churchill, between 1940 and 1955.

Shortest term

The Rt Hon William Pulteney, the Earl of Bath (1684–1764) held office for 3 days, 10–12 Feb 1746, but was unable to form a ministry. The shortest term of any ministry was that of the 1st Duke of Wellington, KG, GCB, GCH. (1769–1852), whose third ministry survived only 22 days from 17 Nov to 9 Dec 1834.

Most times

The only Prime Minister to have accepted office five times was the Rt Hon Stanley Baldwin, later the 1st Earl Baldwin of Bewdley (1867–1947). His ministries were those of 22 May 1923 to 22 Jan 1924, 4 Nov 1924 to 5 June 1929, 7 June 1935 to 21 Jan 1936, from then until the abdication of 12 Dec 1936 and from then until 28 May 1937.

Longest lived

The longest lived Prime Minister of the United Kingdom has been the Rt Hon Sir Winston Leonard Spencer-Churchill, KG, OM, CH, TD, (b. 30 Nov 1874), who surpassed the age of the Rt Hon William Ewart Gladstone (1809–98) on 21 Apr 1963 and died on 24 Jan 1965, aged 90 years 55 days. Gladstone's last day in office on 3 Mar 1894 was when he was 84 years 64 days—having been elected on 18 Aug 1892.

Youngest

The youngest of Great Britain's 50 Prime Ministers has been the Rt Hon the Hon William Pitt (b. 28 May 1759), who accepted the King's invitation to be First Lord of the Treasury on 19 Dec 1783, aged 24 years 205 days. He had previously declined on 27 Feb 1783, when aged 23 years 275 days.

Chancellorship *Longest and shortest tenures*

The Rt Hon Sir Robert Walpole, KG, later the 1st Earl of Orford (1676–1745), served 22 years 5 months as Chancellor of the Exchequer, holding office continuously from 12 Oct 1715 to 12 Feb 1742, except for the period from 16 Apr 1717 to 2 Apr 1721. The briefest tenure of this office was 26 days in the case of the Baron (later the 1st Earl of) Mansfield (1705–93), from 11 Sept to 6 Oct

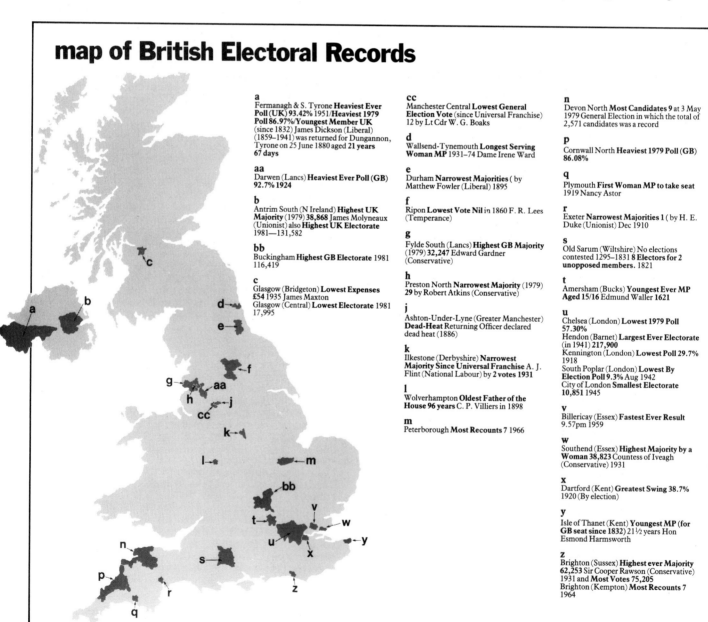

map of British Electoral Records

a
Fermanagh & S. Tyrone **Heaviest Ever Poll (UK) 93.42%** 1951/**Heaviest 1979 Poll 86.97%/Youngest Member UK** (since 1832) James Dickson (Liberal) (1859–1941) was returned for Dungannon, Tyrone on 25 June 1880 aged **21 years 67 days**

aa
Darwen (Lancs) **Heaviest Ever Poll (GB) 92.7% 1924**

b
Antrim South (N Ireland) **Highest UK Majority (1979) 38,868** James Molyneaux (Unionist) also **Highest UK Electorate** 1981—131,582

bb
Buckingham **Highest GB Electorate** 1981 116,419

c
Glasgow (Bridgeton) **Lowest Expenses £54** 1935 James Maxton
Glasgow (Central) **Lowest Electorate** 1981 17,995

cc
Manchester Central **Lowest General Election Vote** (since Universal Franchise) 12 by Lt Cdr W. G. Boaks

d
Wallsend-Tynemouth **Longest Serving Woman MP** 1931–74 Dame Irene Ward

e
Durham **Narrowest Majorities** (by Matthew Fowler (Liberal) 1895

f
Ripon **Lowest Vote Nil** in 1860 F. R. Lees (Temperance)

g
Fylde South (Lancs) **Highest GB Majority** (1979) **32,247** Edward Gardner (Conservative)

h
Preston North **Narrowest Majority** (1979) **29** by Robert Atkins (Conservative)

j
Ashton-Under-Lyne (Greater Manchester) **Dead-Heat** Returning Officer declared dead heat (1886)

k
Ilkestone (Derbyshire) **Narrowest Majority Since Universal Franchise** A. J. Flint (National Labour) by **2 votes 1931**

l
Wolverhampton **Oldest Father of the House 96 years** C. P. Villiers in 1898

m
Peterborough **Most Recounts 7** 1966

n
Devon North **Most Candidates 9** at 3 May 1979 General Election in which the total of 2,571 candidates was a record

p
Cornwall North **Heaviest 1979 Poll (GB) 86.08%**

q
Plymouth **First Woman MP to take seat** 1919 Nancy Astor

r
Exeter **Narrowest Majorities 1** (by H. E. Duke (Unionist) Dec 1910

s
Old Sarum (Wiltshire) No elections contested 1295–1831 **8 Electors for 2 unopposed members.** 1821

t
Amersham (Bucks) **Youngest Ever MP Aged 15/16** Edmund Waller **1621**

u
Chelsea (London) **Lowest 1979 Poll 57.30%**
Hendon (Barnet) **Largest Ever Electorate** (in 1941) **217,900**
Kennington (London) **Lowest Poll 29.7%** 1918
South Poplar (London) **Lowest By Election Poll 9.3%** Aug 1942
City of London **Smallest Electorate 10,851** 1945

v
Billericay (Essex) **Fastest Ever Result** 9.57pm 1959

w
Southend (Essex) **Highest Majority by a Woman 38,823** Countess of Iveagh (Conservative) 1931

x
Dartford (Kent) **Greatest Swing 38.7%** 1920 (By election)

y
Isle of Thanet (Kent) **Youngest MP (for GB seat since 1832)** 21½ years Hon Esmond Harmsworth

z
Brighton (Sussex) **Highest ever Majority 62,253** Sir Cooper Rawson (Conservative) 1931 and **Most Votes 75,205**
Brighton (Kempton) **Most Recounts 7** 1964

1767. The only man with four terms in this office was the Rt Hon William Ewart Gladstone (1809–98) in 1852–5, 1859–66, 1873–4 and 1880–2.

Foreign Secretaryship *Longest tenures*
The longest continuous term of office of any Foreign Secretary has been the 10 years 360 days of Sir Edward Grey KG, MP (later Viscount Grey of Fallodon) from 10 Dec 1905 to 5 Dec 1916. The Most Hon Robert Arthur Talbot Gascoyne-Cecil, Marquis of Salisbury, KG, GCVO, in two spells in 1887–92 and 1895–1900 aggregated 11 years 87 days in this office.

Colonial Secretaryship *Longest tenures*
The longest term of office has been 19 years 324 days by the Rt Hon Henry Bathurst, Earl Bathurst (1762–1834), who was Secretary of State for the Colonial and War Department from 11 June 1812 to 1 May 1827. The longest tenure this century has been the 5 years 78 days of the Rt Hon Alan Tindal Lennox-Boyd, Viscount Boyd of Merton, CH (b. 18 Nov 1904) from 28 July 1954 to 13 Oct 1959.

Speakership *Longest*
Arthur Onslow (1691–1768) was elected Mr Speaker on 23 Jan 1728, at the age of 36. He held the position for 33 years 43 days, until 18 Mar 1761 allowing for the 'lost' 11 days (3–13 Sept 1752).

MPs *Youngest*
Edmund Waller (1606–87) sat as the Member of Parliament for Amersham, Buckinghamshire, during the Parliament of 16 Jan 1621, which met before he was 15, though he himself said he did not sit till he was 16. He was undisputedly MP for Ilchester, Somerset from 12 Feb 1624 aged 17 years 11 months. In 1435 Henry Long (1420–90) was returned for an Old Sarum seat also at the age of 15. His precise date of birth is unknown. Minors were debarred in law in 1695 and in fact in 1832. Since that time the youngest Member of Parliament has been James Dickson (1859–1941) who was elected Liberal member for Dungannon in 1880. The youngest MP is Stephen James Dorrell (Con.) MP for Loughborough (b. 25 Mar 1952).

Oldest
The oldest of all members was Samuel Young (b. 14 Feb 1822), Nationalist MP for East Cavan (1892–1918), who died on 18 Apr 1918, aged 96 years 63 days. The oldest 'Father of the House' in Parliamentary history was the Rt Hon Charles Pelham Villiers (b. 3 Jan 1802), who was the member for Wolverhampton when he died on 16 Jan 1898, aged 96 years 13 days. He was a Member of Parliament for 63 years 6 days, having been returned at 17 elections. The oldest member and 'Father of the House' is John Parker CBE, MP (Lab) for Barking, Dagenham (b. 15 July 1906), having been first elected for Romford, Essex in 1935.

Longest span
The longest span of service of any MP is 63 years 10 months (1 Oct 1900 to 25 Sept 1964) by the Rt Hon Sir Winston Leonard Spencer-Churchill, KG, OM, CH, TD (1874–1965), with a break only from November 1922 to October 1924. The longest unbroken span was that of C. P. Villiers (see above). The longest span in the Palace of Westminster (both Houses of Parliament) has been 73 years by the 10th Earl of Wemyss and March GCVO, who, as Sir Francis Wemyss-Charteris-Douglas, served as MP for East Gloucestershire (1841–6) and Haddingtonshire (1847–83) and then took his seat in the House of Lords, dying on 30 June 1914, aged 95 years 330 days.

Women MPs *Earliest*
The first woman to be elected to the House of Commons was Mme. Constance Georgine Markievicz (*née* Gore Booth). She was elected as member (Sinn Fein) for St Patrick's Dublin, in December 1918. The first woman to take her seat was the Viscountess Astor, CH (1879–1964) (b. Nancy Witcher Langhorne at Danville, Virginia, USA; formerly Mrs Robert Gould Shaw), who was elected Unionist member for the Sutton Division of Plymouth, Devon, on 28 Nov 1919, and took her seat three days later. The first woman to take her seat from the island of Ireland was Lady Fisher *née* Patricia Smiles as unopposed Ulster Unionist for North Down in April 1953 as Mrs Patricia Ford.

Longest serving
The longest ever serving woman MP has been Baroness Irene

Mrs Elizabeth Robinson (1695–1779) from Gibraltar, the first woman to address the House of Lords, when she gave evidence on slave trafficking (see p. 209).

Mary Bewick Ward CH, DBE (d. 1980), who fought all 12 General Elections (1924–70) and who served as member for Wallsend (1931–45) and for Tynemouth (1950–74). She shared also the 20th century record for introducing 4 Private Members Bills which became Acts with Sir Robert Gower (1880–1953).

Heaviest and Tallest
The heaviest MP of all-time is believed to have been Cyril Smith MBE, Liberal member for Rochdale since October 1972, when in January 1976 his peak reported weight was 29 st 12 lb *189,60 kg*. Sir Louis Gluckstein GBE, TD, QC (1897–1979), who served for East Nottingham (1931–45), was an unrivalled 6 ft 7½ in *2,02 m*. Currently the tallest is the Hon. Archie Hamilton member for Epsom and Ewell at 6 ft 6 in *1,98 m*.

Mayoralties
The longest recorded mayoralty was that of Edmond Mathis (1852–1953) *maire* of Ehuns, Haute-Saône, France for 75 years (1878–1953). The longest established mayoralty in Britain is that of the City of London dating from 1192 with the 20 year term of Henry Fitz Ailwyn till 1212. The most elections, since these became annual in 1215, has been 8 by Gregory de Rokesley (1274/5 to 1280/1). Alderman G. T. Paine served as Mayor of Lydd, Kent for 29 consecutive years in 1931 to 1961.

Largest Agenda Item
All the weight of evidence indicates that the heaviest agenda item in the history of local government was a 950 page, 6 in *15,2 cm* thick, 6½ lb *2,95 kg* report produced for Lambeth Borough Council's Community Liaison Sub-Committee in May 1979 at a reproduction cost of £728.

Local Government Service Duration Records
Henry Winn (1816–1914) served as parish clerk for Fulletby near Horncastle, Lincolnshire for 76 years.

4. MILITARY AND DEFENCE

Guinness Superlatives Ltd. has published specialist volumes entitled *The Guinness History of Land Warfare* (£4.95) by Kenneth Macksey, *History of Sea Warfare* (£4.95) by Gervis Frere-Cook and Macksey, and *History of Air Warfare* (£6.50) by David Brown, Christopher Shores and Macksey.

WAR

Longest
The longest of history's countless wars was the 'Hundred Years War' between England and France, which lasted from 1338 to 1453 (115 years), although it may be said that the nine Crusades from the First (1096–1104) to the Ninth (1270–91), extending over 195 years comprised a single Holy War.

Shortest
The shortest war on record was that between the United Kingdom and Zanzibar (now part of Tanzania) from 9.02 to 9.40 a.m. on 27 Aug 1896. The UK battle fleet under Rear-Admiral (later Admiral Sir) Harry Holdsworth Rawson (1843–1910) delivered an ultimatum to the self-appointed Sultan Sa'īd Khalid to evacuate his palace and surrender. This was not forthcoming until after 38 minutes of bombardment. Admiral Rawson received the Brilliant Star of Zanzibar (first class) from the new Sultan Hamud ibn Muhammad. It was proposed at one time that elements of the local populace should be compelled to defray the cost of the ammunition used.

Bloodiest
By far the most costly war in terms of human life was World War II (1939–45), in which the total number of fatalities, including battle deaths and civilians of all countries, is estimated to have been 54,800,000 assuming 25 million USSR fatalities and 7,800,000 Chinese civilians killed. The country which suffered most was Poland with 6,028,000 or 22.2 per cent of her population of 27,007,000 killed. The total combatant death roll from World War I was 9,700,000 compared with the 15,600,000 of World War II.

In the case of the United Kingdom, however, the heaviest armed forces fatalities occurred in World War I (1914–18), with 765,399 killed out of 5,500,000 engaged (13.9 per cent), compared with 265,000 out of 5,896,000 engaged (4.49 per cent) in World War II.

In the Paraguayan war of 1864–70 against Brazil, Argentina and Uruguay, their population was reduced from 1,400,000 to 220,000 of whom only 30,000 were adult males.

Bloodiest civil
The bloodiest civil war in history was the T'ai-p'ing ('Great Peace') rebellion, in which peasant sympathizers of the Southern Ming dynasty fought the Manchu Government troops in China from 1851 to 1864. The rebellion was led by the deranged Hung Hsiu-ch'üan (executed) who imagined himself to be a younger brother of Jesus Christ. His force was named *T'ai-p'ing T'ien Kuo* (Heavenly Kingdom of Great Peace). According to the best estimates, the loss of life was between 20,000,000 and 30,000,000 including more than 100,000 killed by Government forces in the sack of Nanking on 19–21 July 1864.

Most costly
The material cost of World War II far transcended that of the rest of history's wars put together and has been estimated at $1.5 million million. The total cost to the Soviet Union was estimated in May 1959 at 2,500,000,000,000 roubles (*£100,000 million*) while a figure of $530,000 million has been estimated for the USA. In the case of the United Kingdom the cost of £34,423 million was over five times as great as that of World War I (£6700 million) and 158.6 times that of the Boer War of 1899–1902 (£217 million).

Last battle on British soil
The last pitched land battle in Britain was at Culloden Field, Drummossie Moor, near Inverness, Highland, on 16 Apr 1746. The last Clan battle in Scotland was between Clan Mackintosh and Clan MacDonald at Mulroy, Highland in 1689. The last battle on English soil was the Battle of Sedgemoor, Somerset, on 6 July 1685, when the forces of James II defeated the supporters of Charles II's illegitimate son, James Scott (formerly called Fitzroy or Crofts), the Duke of Monmouth (1649–85). During the Jacobite rising of 1745–6, there was a skirmish at Clifton Moor, Cumbria, on 18 Dec 1745, when the British forces under Prince William, the Duke of Cumberland (1721–65), brushed with the rebels of Prince Edward Stuart (1720–88) with about 12 killed on the King's side and 5 Highlanders. This was a tactical victory for the Scots under Lord George Murray.

Bloodiest battle *Modern*
The battle with the greatest recorded number of fatalities was the First Battle of the Somme, France from 1 July to 19 Nov 1916, with more than 1,030,000—614,105 British and French and *c.* 420,000 (*not* 650,000) German. The gunfire was heard on Hampstead Heath, London. The greatest battle of World War II and the greatest ever conflict of armour was the Battle of Kursk and Oryol which raged for 50 days on 5 July–23 Aug 1943 on the Eastern front, which involved 1,300,000 Red Army troops with 3600 tanks, 20,000 guns and 3130 aircraft in repelling a German Army Group which had 2700 tanks. The final investment of Berlin by the Red Army on 16 Apr–2 May 1945 involved 3,500,000 men; 52,000 guns and mortars; 7750 tanks and 11,000 aircraft on both sides.

Ancient
Modern historians give no credence to the casualty figures attached to ancient battles, such as the 250,000 reputedly killed at Plataea (Greeks v Persians) in 479 BC or the 200,000 allegedly killed in a single day.

British
The bloodiest battle fought on British soil was the Battle of Towton, in North Yorkshire, on 29 Mar 1461, when 36,000 Yorkists defeated 40,000 Lancastrians. The total loss has been estimated at between 28,000 and 38,000 killed. A figure of 80,000 British dead was attributed by Tacitus to the battle of AD 61 between Queen Boudicca (Boadicea) of the Iceni and the Roman Governor of Britain Suetonius Paulinus, for the reputed loss of only 400 Romans in an army of 10,000. The site of the battle is unknown but may have been near Borough Hill, Daventry, Northamptonshire, or more probably near Hampstead Heath, Greater London. Prior to this battle the Romans had lost up to 70,000 in Colchester and London.

Greatest naval battle
The greatest number of ships and aircraft ever involved in a sea-air action was 231 ships and 1996 aircraft in the Battle of Leyte Gulf, in the Philippines. It raged from 22 to 27 Oct 1944, with 166 Allied and 65 Japanese warships engaged, of which 26 Japanese and 6 US ships were sunk. In addition 1280 US and 716 Japanese aircraft were engaged. The greatest naval battle of modern times was the Battle of Jutland on 31 May 1916, in which 151 Royal Navy warships were involved against 101 German warships. The Royal Navy lost 14 ships and 6097 men and the German fleet 11 ships and 2545 men. The greatest of ancient naval battles was the Battle of Salamis, Greece on 23 Sept 480 BC. There were an estimated 800 vessels in the defeated Persian fleet and 310 in the victorious Greek fleet with a possible involvement of 190,000 men. The death roll at the Battle of Lepanto on 7 Oct 1571 has been estimated at 33,000.

Invasion Greatest *Seaborne*
The greatest invasion in military history was the Allied land, air and sea operation against the Normandy coasts of France on D-day, 6 June 1944. Thirty-eight convoys of 745 ships moved in on the first three days, supported by 4066 landing craft, carrying 185,000 men and 20,000 vehicles, and 347 minesweepers. The air assault comprised 18,000 paratroopers from 1087 aircraft. The 42 available divisions possessed an air support from 13,175 aircraft. Within a month 1,100,000 troops, 200,000 vehicles and 750,000 tons of stores were landed. The Allied invasion of Sicily on 10–12 July 1943 involved the landing of 181,000 men in 3 days.

Airborne
The largest airborne invasion was the Anglo-American assault of three divisions (34,000 men), with 2800 aircraft and 1,600 gliders, near Arnhem, in the Netherlands, on 17 Sept 1944.

Last on the soil of Great Britain

The last invasion of Great Britain occurred on 12 Feb 1797, when the Irish-American adventurer General Tate landed at Carreg Gwastad with 1400 French troops. They surrendered near Fishguard, Dyfed, to Lord Cawdor's force of the Castlemartin Yeomanry and some local inhabitants armed with pitchforks. The UK Crown Dependency of the Channel Islands were occupied by German armed forces from 30 June 1940 to 9 May 1945 when Vice Admiral Huffmeier signed the instrument of surrender.

Greatest evacuation

The greatest evacuation in military history was that carried out by 1200 Allied naval and civil craft from the beach-head at Dunkerque (Dunkirk), France, between 27 May and 4 June 1940. A total of 338,226 British and French troops were taken off.

Worst sieges

The worst siege in history was the 880-day siege of Leningrad, USSR by the German Army from 30 Aug 1941 until 27 Jan 1944. The best estimate is that between 1.3 and 1.5 million defenders and citizens died. The longest recorded siege was that of Azotus (now Ashdod), Israel which according to Herodotus was invested by Psamtik I of Egypt for 29 years in the period 664–610 BC.

DEFENCE

The estimated level of spending on armaments throughout the world in 1979 was $500,000 million *£225,000 million*. This represents £52 per person per annum, or more than 6 per cent of the world's total production of goods and services. It was estimated in 1980 that there were 22¾ million full-time armed force regulars or conscripts.

The budgeted expenditure on defence by the US government for the year ending 30 June 1981 was $142,700 million (*£64,800 million*) or 5.2 per cent of the country's Gross National Product. For the Financial Year 1982 this was raised to $185.8 billion (*£83,000 million*).

An extrapolation of the Chinese estimate into 1979 indicates that the defence burden on the USSR was in excess of 15 per cent of Gross National Product, *i.e.* then nearly treble that of the USA. The CIA estimate is 11 to 13 per cent.

The ISS estimates for 1980–81 list 2244 strategic warheads held by the USSR and 1811 by the US and NATO combined.

ARMED FORCES

Largest

Numerically the largest regular armed force in the world is that of the People's Republic of China with 4,450,000. Her paramilitary forces of armed and unarmed militias have been estimated also by the Institute of Strategic Studies at 12 million plus. Their mid-1980 estimates for the world's two principal military powers are USSR (3,568,000) and USA (2,050,000).

Navies *Largest*

The largest navy in the world in terms of manpower is the United States Navy, with a manpower of 528,000 and 189,000 Marines in mid-1980. The active strength in 1980 included 14 aircraft carriers, 41 strategic missile submarines, 74 attack nuclear submarines and 7 diesel attack submarines, 73 guided missile warships (25 cruisers, 80 destroyers and 13 frigates) and 65 amphibious warfare ships. The USSR navy has a larger submarine fleet of 338 boats with 115 in reserve. Eighty-eight carry offensive strategic nuclear weapons of which 72 are also nuclear-powered. It has 2 aircraft carriers, 38 cruisers and 75 destroyers.

The strength of the Royal Navy in mid-1980 included 4 nuclear submarines with strategic atomic missiles, 11 other nuclear and 16 diesel attack submarines and 2 anti-submarine commando carriers, a helicopter cruiser, 12 guided weapon destroyers, and 54 frigates in a fleet of 70 major surface combat vessels. The uniformed strength was 72,240 including Fleet Air Arm and Royal Marines in mid-1980. In 1914 the Royal Navy had 542 warships including 72 capital ships with 16 building.

Admiral *Longest serving*

Admiral of the Fleet Sir Provo Wallis GCB (1791–1892) first

Britain's longest ever serving officer—Admiral Sir Provo Wallis, who was 87 years 4 months on the Royal Navy's active list. (*John Frost*)

served on *HMS Cleopatra* in Oct 1804. Because of his command of *HMS Shannon* in 1813 during the French war he was kept on the active list in 1870 for life. He thus was 87 years 4 months on active service.

Armies *Oldest*

The oldest army in the world is the 83-strong Swiss Guard in the Vatican City, with a regular foundation dating back to 21 Jan 1506. Its origins, however, extend back before 1400.

Largest

Numerically, the world's largest army is that of the People's Republic of China, with a total strength of some 3,600,000 in mid-1980. The total size of the USSR's army in mid-1980 was estimated by The International Institute of Strategic Studies at 1,825,000 men, believed to be organised into 173 divisions. The strength of the British Army was 167,250 in mid-1980. The NATO agreement requires not less than 55,000 in West Germany. The basic strength maintained in Northern Ireland is 14,500 but this fluctuates.

Oldest soldiers

The oldest old soldier of all time was probably John B. Salling of the army of the Confederate States of America and the last accepted survivor of the US Civil War (1861–5). He died in Kingsport, Tennessee, USA on 16 Mar 1959, aged 113 years 1 day. The oldest Chelsea pensioner, based *only* on the evidence of his tombstone, was the 111-year-old William Hiseland (b. 6 Aug 1620, d. 7 Feb 1732). The longest serving British soldier has been Field Marshal Sir William Maynard Gomm GCB (1784–1875), who was an ensign in 1794 and the Constable of the Tower to his death aged 91. The United States longest serving officer was General of the Army, Omar Nelson Bradley (1893–1981) who served 69 years.

Youngest soldiers

Dr Kenneth Vernon Bailey MC (b. 14 Dec 1897) served as a 2nd Lieutenant in the 2/8th Btn Manchester Regt. for some 6 weeks before his 17th birthday. Probably the youngest enlistment in the 20th century was of William Frederick Price, (b. 1 June 1891), who was enlisted into the Army at Aldershot on 23 May 1903, aged 11 years 356 days.

Youngest conscripts
President Francisco Macias Nguema of Equatorial Guinea decreed in March 1976 compulsory military service for all boys between 7 and 14. Any parent refusing to hand over his or her son 'will be imprisoned or shot'.

Tallest soldiers
The tallest soldier of all time was Väinö Myllyrinne (1909–63) who was inducted into the Finnish Army when he was 7 ft 3 in *2,21 m* and later grew to 8 ft 1¼ in *2,47 m*. The British Army's tallest soldier was Benjamin Crow who was signed on at Lichfield in November 1947 when he was 7 ft 1 in *2,15 m* tall. Edward Evans (1924–58), who later grew to 7 ft 8½ in *235 cm* was in the Army when he was 6 ft 10 in *2,08 m*.

British regimental records
The oldest regular regiment in the British Army is the Royal Scots, raised in French service in 1633, though the Buffs (Royal East Kent Regiment) can trace back their origin to independent companies in Dutch pay as early as 1572. The Coldstream Guards, raised in 1650, were, however, placed on the establishment of the British Army before the Royal Scots and the Buffs. The oldest armed body in the United Kingdom is the Queen's Bodyguard of the Yeoman of the Guard formed in 1495. The Honourable Artillery Company, formed from the Fraternity of St. George, Southwark, received its charter from Henry VIII in 1537 but this lapsed until re-formed in 1610. The infantry regiment with most battle honours is The Queen's Lancashire Regiment with 188.

The most senior regiment of the Reserve Army is The Royal Monmouthshire Royal Engineers (Militia) formed on 21 Mar 1577 and never disbanded, with battle honours at Dunkirk, 1940 and Normandy, 1944.

Greatest mutiny
In the 1914–18 War 56 French divisions comprising some 650,000 men and their officers refused orders on the Nivelles sector.

Longest march
The longest march in military history was the famous Long March by the Chinese Communists in 1934–5. In 368 days, of which 268 days were of movement, from October to October, their force of 90,000 covered 6000 miles *9650 km* from Kiangsi to Yenan in Shensi *via* Yünnan. They crossed 18 mountain ranges and six major rivers and lost all but 22,000 of their force in continual rear-guard actions against Nationalist Kuo-min-tang (KMT) forces.

On the night of 12–13 Sept 1944 a team of nine from B Company 4th Infantry Battalion of the Irish Army made a night march of 42 miles *67,59 km* in full battle order carrying 40 lb *18,1 kg* in 11 hr 49 min.

Air Forces *Oldest*
The earliest autonomous air force is the Royal Air Force whose origin began with the Royal Flying Corps (created 13 May 1912); the Air Battalion of the Royal Engineers (1 Apr 1911) and the Corps of Royal Engineers Balloon Section (1878) which was first operational in Bechuanaland (now Botswana) in 1884. The Prussian Army used a balloon near Strasbourg, France as early as 24 Sept 1870.

Largest
The greatest Air Force of all time was the United States Army Air Force (now called the US Air Force), which had 79,908 aircraft in July 1944 and 2,411,294 personnel in March 1944. The US Air Force including strategic air forces had 555,100 personnel and 3700 combat aircraft in mid-1980. The USSR Air Force, including Air Defence Forces, with about 1,070,000 men in mid-1980, had 5850 combat aircraft. In addition, the USSR's Offensive Strategic Rocket Forces had about 385,000 operational personnel in mid-1980. The strength of the Royal Air Force was 89,714 with 713 combat aircraft in mid-1980.

214

BOMBS
Heaviest
The heaviest conventional bomb ever used operationally was the Royal Air Force's 'Grand Slam', weighing 22,000 lb *9975 kg* and measuring 25 ft 5 in *7,74 m* long, dropped on Bielefeld railway viaduct, Germany, on 14 Mar 1945. In 1949 the United States Air Force tested a bomb weighing 42,000 lb *19 050 kg* at Muroc Dry Lake, California, USA.

Atomic
The two atom bombs dropped on Japan by the United States in 1945 each had an explosive power equivalent to that of 20,000 short tons *20 kilotons* of trinitrotoluene ($C_7H_5O_6N_3$), called TNT. The one dropped on Hiroshima, known as 'Little Boy', was 10 ft *3,04 m* long and weighed 9000 lb *4080 kg*. The most powerful thermo-nuclear device so far tested is one with a power equivalent to 57,000,000 short tons of TNT, or 57 megatons, detonated by the USSR in the Novaya Zemlya area at 8.33 a.m. GMT on 30 Oct 1961. The shock wave was detected to have circled the world three times, taking 36 hr 27 min for the first circuit. Some estimates put the power of this device at between 62 and 90 megatons. On 9 Aug 1961, Nikita Khrushchyov, then the Chairman of the Council of Ministers of the USSR, declared that the Soviet Union was capable of constructing a 100-megaton bomb, and announced the possession of one in East Berlin, Germany, on 16 Jan 1963. The largest US H-Bomb tested was the 15 megaton 'Bravo' at Bikini Atoll on 1 Mar 1954.

Atom bomb theory began with Einstein's publication of the E = mc² formula in *Annalen der Physik* in Leipzig on 14 May 1907. It became a practicality with the mesothorium experiments of Otto Hahn, Fritz Strassman and Lise Meitner on 17 Dec 1938. Work started in the USSR on atomic bombs in June 1942 although their first chain reaction was not achieved until December 1945 by Dr Igor Vasilyevich Kurchatov. The patent for the fusion or H bomb was filed in the United States on 26 May 1946 by Dr Janos (John) von Neumann (1903–57), a Hungarian-born mathematician, and Dr Klaus Julius Emil Fuchs (born in Germany 29 Dec 1911), the physicist, who defected from Britain.

Largest nuclear weapons
The most powerful ICBM are the USSR's SS–18s, each with up to 10 one-megaton MIRVs (multiple independently-targetable re-entry vehicles), thus each of a power 50 times as great as the Hiroshima bomb. The US Minute-man III has 3 MIRVs each of 335 kiloton force.

No official estimate has been published of the potential power of the device known as Doomsday, but this far surpasses any tested weapon. If it were practicable to construct, it is mooted that a 50,000 megaton cobalt-salted device could wipe out the entire human race except people deep underground and who did not emerge for more than five years.

Largest 'conventional' explosion
The largest use of conventional explosive was for the blasting of 90 million ft³ *2.5 million³* of granite at a dam site at Medeo, Kazakhstan, USSR on 21 Oct 1966 with 5200 tonnes of high explosive.

Most bombed country
The most heavily bombed country in the world has been Laos. It has been estimated that between May 1964 and 26 Feb 1973 some 2½ million tons of bombs of all kinds were dropped along the North to South Ho Chi Minh Trail supply route to South Vietnam.

TANKS
Note—Guinness Superlatives Ltd. has published a specialist volume entitled *The Guinness Book of Tank Facts and Feats* (3rd edition) by Kenneth Macksey (£7.95). This work deals with all the aspects of the development and history of the tank and other armoured fighting vehicles in greater detail.

Earliest
The first tank was 'No 1 Lincoln' modified to become '*Little Willie*' built by William Foster & Co Ltd of Lincoln. It first ran on 6 Sept 1915. Tanks were first taken into action by the Heavy Section, Machine-Gun Corps, which later became the Royal Tank Corps, at the battle of Flers-Courcelette in France, on 15 Sept 1916. The Mark I Male tank, which was armed with a pair of 6-pounder guns and 4 machine-guns, weighed 28 tons *28,4 tonnes* and was driven by a motor developing 105 hp which gave it a maximum road speed of 3 to 4 mph *4,8–6,4 km/h*.

Heaviest

The heaviest tank ever constructed was the German Panzer Kampfwagen Maus II, which weighed 189 tons *192 tonnes*. By 1945 it had reached only the experimental stage and was not proceeded with.

The heaviest operational tank used by any army was the 74 ton *75,2 tonnes* 13-man French Char de Rupture 2C bis of 1922. It carried a 155 mm howitzer and had two 250 hp engines giving a maximum speed of 8 mph *12 km/h*. The DM3,6 million (£950,000) German Leopard 2 has the greatest fire-power with a 120 mm *4.72 in* gun. The world's fastest tank is the $1.8 million (£900,000) XM-1 due for US Army service. The prototype reached 45 mph *72,4 km/h*.

The heaviest British armoured vehicle ever built was the 78-ton *79 tonnes* prototype 'Tortoise'. With a crew of seven and a designed speed of 12 mph *19 km/h*, this tank had a width 2 in *5 cm* less than that of the one-time operational 65-ton *66 tonnes* 'Conqueror'. The most heavily armed is the 52-ton *52,8 tonnes* 'Chieftain', put into service in November 1966, with a 120 mm gun.

GUNS

Earliest

Although it cannot be accepted as proved, the best opinion is that the earliest guns were constructed in North Africa, possibly by Arabs, in *c*. 1250. The earliest representation of an English gun is contained in an illustrated manuscript dated 1326 at Oxford. The earliest anti-aircraft gun was an artillery piece on a high angle mounting used in the Franco-Prussian War of 1870 by the Prussians against French balloons.

Largest

The two most massive guns ever constructed were used by the Germans in the siege of Sevastopol on the Eastern Front. They were of a calibre of 800 mm *31.5 in* with barrels 28,87 m *94 ft 8½ in* long and named *Dore* and *Gustav*. Their remains were discovered, one near Metzenhof, Bavaria in Aug 1945 and the other in the Soviet zone. They were built by Krupp as railway guns carried on 24 cars two of which had 40 wheels each. The whole assembly of the gun was 42,9 m *141 ft* long and weighed 1323 tons *1344 tonnes* with a crew of 1500. The range for an 8¼ ton projectile was 29 miles *46,67 km*.

During the 1914–18 war the British Army used a gun of 18 in *457 mm* calibre. The barrel alone weighed 125 tons *127 tonnes*. In World War II the 'Bochebuster', a train-mounted howitzer with a calibre of 18 in *457 mm* firing a 2500 lb *1133 kg* shell to a maximum range of 22,800 yd *20 850 m*, was used from 1940 onwards as part of the Kent coast defences.

Greatest range

The greatest range ever attained by a gun was achieved by the HARP (High Altitude Research Project) gun consisting of two 16.5 in *419 mm* calibre barrels in tandem 36,4 m *119.4 ft* long weighing 150 tonnes/*tons* at Yuma, Arizona, USA. On 19 Nov 1966 an 84 kg *185 lb* projectile was fired to an altitude of 180 km *111.8 miles* or *590,550 ft*. The static V3 underground firing tubes built in 50 degree shafts near Mimoyecques, near Calais, France to bombard London were never operative due to RAF bombing.

The famous long range gun, which shelled Paris in World War I, was the *Kaiser Wilhelm geschütz* with a calibre of 220 mm (*8.66 in*), a designed range of 79.5 miles *127,9 km* and an achieved range of 76 miles *122 km* from the Forest of Cérpy in March 1918. The Big Berthas were mortars of 420 mm *16.53 in* calibre and with a range of less than 9 miles *14 500 m*.

Mortars

The largest mortars ever constructed were Mallets mortar (Woolwich Arsenal, London, 1857), and the 'Little David' of World War II, made in the USA. Each had a calibre of 36¼ in *920 mm*, but neither was ever used in action. The heaviest mortar used was the tracked German 600 mm *23.6 in* siege piece known as 'Karl' before Stalingrad, USSR.

Largest cannon

The highest calibre cannon ever constructed is the *Tsar Puchka* (King of Cannons), now housed in the Kremlin, Moscow, USSR. It was built in the 16th century with a bore of 920 mm

The British designed and built Shir 2 with its 120 mm *4.72 in* gun and special Chobham armour.

36.2 in and a barrel 10 ft 5 in *3,18 m* long. It weighs 2400 *pouds* (*sic*) or 40 tonnes. The Turks fired up to seven shots per day from a bombard 26 ft *7,92 m* long, with an internal calibre of 42 in *1066 mm* against the walls of Constantinople (now Istanbul) from 12 Apr to 29 May 1453. It was dragged by 60 oxen and 200 men and fired a stone cannon ball weighing 1200 lb *544 kg*.

Military engines

The largest military catapults, or onagers, were capable of throwing a missile weighing 60 lb *27 kg* a distance of 500 yd *457 m*.

Conscientious Objection

The only Conscientious Objector to be 6 times court martialled in World War II was Gilbert Lane of Wallington, Surrey. He served 31 months detention and 183 days imprisonment.

5. JUDICIAL

LEGISLATION AND LITIGATION

Statutes *Oldest*

The earliest known judicial code was that of King Ur-Hammu during the third dynasty of Ur, Iraq, in *c*. 2145 BC. The oldest English statute in the Statute Book is a section of the Statute of Marlborough of 1267, retitled in 1948 'The Distress Act, 1267'. Some statutes enacted by Henry II (d. 1189) and earlier kings are even more durable as they have been assimilated into the Common Law. An extreme example is Ine's Law concerning the administration of shires *c* 8 AD.

Longest in the United Kingdom

Measured in bulk the longest statute of the United Kingdom, is the Income Tax and Corporation Tax Act, 1970, which ran to 540 sections, 15 schedules and 670 pages. It is 1½ in *37 mm* thick and costs £2.80. However, its 540 sections are surpassed in number by the 748 of the Merchant Shipping Act, 1894. Of old statutes, 31 George III XIV, the Land Tax Act of 1791, written on parchment, consists of 780 skins forming a roll 1170 ft *360 m* long.

Shortest

The shortest statute is the Parliament (Qualification of Women) Act, 1918, which runs to 27 operative words—'A woman shall not be disqualified by sex or marriage from being elected to or sitting or voting as a Member of the Commons House of Parliament'. Section 2 contains a further 14 words giving the short title.

Most inexplicable

Certain passages in several Acts have always defied interpretation and the most inexplicable must be a matter of opinion.

215

A Judge of the Court of Session of Scotland once sent the Editor his candidate which reads, 'In the Nuts (unground), (other than ground nuts) Order, the expression nuts shall have reference to such nuts, other than ground nuts, as would but for this amending Order not qualify as nuts (unground) (other than ground nuts) by reason of their being nuts (unground).'

Earliest English patent

The earliest of all known English patents was that granted by Henry VI in 1449 to Flemish-born John of Utyman for making the coloured glass required for the windows of Eton College. The peak number of applications for patents filed in the United Kingdom in any one year was 63,614 in 1969. The shortest, concerning a harrow attachment, of 48 words was filed on 14 May 1956 while the longest, comprising 2318 pages of text and 495 pages of drawings, was filed on 31 Mar 1965 by IBM to cover a computer.

Most protracted litigation

The longest contested law suit ever recorded ended in Poona, India on 28 Apr 1966, when Balasaheb Patloji Thorat received a favourable judgement on a suit filed by his ancestor Maloji Thorat 761 years earlier in 1205. The points at issue were rights of presiding over public functions and precedences at religious festivals.

The dispute over the claim of the Prior and Convent (now the Dean and Chapter) of Durham Cathedral to administer the spiritualities of the diocese during a vacancy in the See grew fierce in 1283. It flared up again in 1672 and 1890; an attempt in November 1975 to settle the issue, then 692 years old, was unsuccessful. Neither side admit the legitimacy of writs of appointment issued by the other even though identical persons are named.

Fastest trial

The law's shortest delay occurred in *Duport Steel and Others v. Sirs and Others* heard in the High Court on 25 Jan 1980; the appeal was heard on 26 Jan and the appeal heard in the House of Lords on 1 Feb (am) with the decision given pm.

Longest British trial

The longest trial in the annals of British justice was the Tichborne personation case. The civil trial began on 11 May 1871, lasted 103 days and collapsed on 6 Mar 1872. The criminal trial went on for 188 days, resulting in a sentence on 28 Feb 1874 for two counts of perjury (two 7 year consecutive terms of imprisonment with hard labour) on the London-born Arthur Orton, *alias* Thomas Castro (1834–98), who claimed to be Roger Charles Tichborne (1829–54), the elder brother of Sir Alfred Joseph Doughty-Tichborne, 11th Bt (1839–66). The whole case thus spanned 1025 days. The jury were out for only 30 minutes.

The impeachment of Warren Hastings (1732–1818), which began in 1788, dragged on for seven years until 23 Apr 1795, but the trial lasted only 149 days. He was appointed a member of the Privy Council in 1814.

The £21 million claim against the UK government by the Ocean Islanders, Pacific before Mr Justice Megarry (Hon Sir Robert Megarry (b. 1910)) finished after 226 days on 3 Dec 1976 with 7,000,000 words of evidence and £7 million in compensation.

Murder

The longest murder trial in Britain was that at the Old Bailey, London of Reginald Dudley, 51, and Robert Maynard, 46 in the Torso Murder of Billy Moseley and Micky Cornwall which ran before Mr Justice Swanwick from 11 Nov 1976 to 17 June 1977 with 136 trial days. Both men were sentenced to life (minimum 15 years) imprisonment. The costs were estimated to exceed £500,000 and the evidence 3,500,000 words.

Divorce

The longest trial of a divorce case in Britain was *Gibbons v. Gibbons and Roman and Halperin*. On 19 Mar 1962, after 28 days, Mr Alfred George Boyd Gibbons was granted a decree *nisi* against his wife Dorothy for adultery with Mr John Halperin of New York City, NY, USA.

Shortest trials

The shortest recorded British murder hearings were *R. v. Murray* on 28 Feb 1957 and *R. v. Cawley* at Winchester assizes on 14 Dec 1959. The proceedings occupied only 30 sec on each occasion.

An ill-founded prosecution under the Air Navigation Order 1974 against a pilot at Edinburgh airport was timed at No. 1 Sheriff Court, Edinburgh on 1 Mar 1977 to have lasted 7 sec. Sheriff Skae uttered two words—'Not Guilty'.

Litigants in Person

Since the Union of Parliament in 1707 the only Scot to win an appeal in person before the House of Lords has been Mr Jock Malloch, an Aberdeen Schoolmaster in 1971. He was restored to his employment under the dormant but operative Teachers Act 1882 with costs.

Longest address

The longest address in a British court was in *Globe and Phoenix Gold Mining Co. Ltd. v. Amalgamated Properties of Rhodesia*. Mr William Henry Upjohn, KC (1853–1941) concluded his speech on 22 Sept 1916, having addressed the court for 45 days.

Highest bail *World*

The highest amount ever demanded as bail was $46,500,000 (*then £16,608,333*) against Antonio De Angelis in a civil damages suit by the Harbor Tank Storage Co. filed in the Superior Court, Jersey City, New Jersey, USA on 16 Jan 1964 in the Salad Oil Swindle. He was released on 4 June 1973. Abul Hassen Ebtehaj, later Chairman of the Iranian Bank in Teheran, was in 1967 granted bail in excess of $50 million.

Great Britain

The highest bail figure in a British court is £250,000 granted to the former Hong Kong policeman, chief superintendent Peter Godber, 52, at Bow Street Court, Greater London on 16 May 1974 when charged with bribery. This consisted of a maximum of four sureties aggregating £200,000 and £50,000 in his own recognisance.

Longest arbitration

The longest arbitration (under the 1950 Act) on record has been the Royce Arbitration. It lasted 239 days and concerned the Mitchell Construction Co. and the East Anglian Regional Hospital Board over the building of Peterborough Hospital.

The longest case before an Industrial Tribunal has been 44 days during more than 13 months (2 May 1977–29 June 1978) when the columnist C. Gordon Tether contested the fairness of his dismissal by *The Financial Times* in person.

Best attended trial

The greatest attendance at any trial was that of Major Jesús Sosa Blanco, aged 51, for an alleged 108 murders. At one point in the 12½ hr trial (5.30 p.m. to 6 a.m., 22–23 Jan 1959), 17,000 people were present in the Havana Sports Palace, Cuba.

Greatest damages *Personal injury World*

The greatest personal injury damages ever awarded were to Janelle Lynn Stearns, 12, against Park Avenue Hospital Inc and an anaesthetist Dr Howard K. Gifford in settlement for alleged medical malpractice resulting in severe brain damage following a tonsillectomy at Pomona, California in May 1973. If she lives to the average expectation of 63.9 additional years the payments will total $26,541,832. The largest single cash payment settlement for a single person has been $6,800,000 (*then £3.4 million*) to the lawyer John Coates, 42, of Austin, Texas, USA against Remington Arms Co. Inc *et al.* on 23 Oct 1978. The case concerned severe injury from a defectively made hunting rifle.

The highest damages ever actually paid have been $14,387,674, following upon the crash of a private aircraft at South Lake, Tahoe, California, USA on 21 Feb 1967, to the sole survivor Ray Rosendin, 45, by the Santa Clara Superior Court on 8 Mar 1972. Rosendin received *inter alia* $1,069,374 for the loss of both legs and disabling arm injuries; $1,213,129 for the loss of his wife and $10,500,000 punitive damages against Avco-Lyconing Corporation which allegedly violated Federal regulations when it rebuilt the aircraft engine owned by Rosendin Corporation.

Great Britain

The record damages in the High Court are £338,252 to Mr. Wijendra Watson, 32 for the bicyclist and Oxford post graduate student's 'devastating injuries' sustained in December 1976 in *Watson v. Murphy* on 7 Nov 1980.

Breach of contract

The greatest damages ever awarded for a breach of contract were

£610,392, awarded on 16 July 1930 to the Bank of Portugal against the printers Waterlow & Sons Ltd, of London, arising from their unauthorized printing of 580,000 five-hundred escudo notes in 1925. This award was upheld in the House of Lords on 28 Apr 1932. One of the perpetrators, Arthur Virgilio Alves Reis, served 16 years (1930–46) in gaol.

Breach of promise
The largest sum involved in a breach of promise suit in the United Kingdom was £50,000, accepted in 1913 by Miss Daisy Markham, *alias* Mrs Annie Moss (d. 20 Aug 1962, aged 76), in settlement against the 6th Marquess of Northampton DSO (1885–1978).

Defamation *World*
A sum of $16,800,000 (£6,720,000) was awarded to Dr John J. Wild, 58, at the Hennepin District Court, Minnesota, USA, on 30 Nov 1972 against The Minnesota Foundation and others for defamation, bad-faith termination of a contract, interference with professional business relationship and $10.8 million in punitive damages. These amounts are unappealed. The $39.6 million awarded in Columbus, Ohio on 1 Mar 1980 to Robert Guccione, publisher of *Penthouse*, for defamation against Lowry Flynt, publisher of *Hustler* was reduced by Judge Craig Wright to $4 million on 17 Apr 1980.

The greatest damages for defamation ever awarded in the United Kingdom have been £327,000 in the Courts in Edinburgh in favour of Capital Life Assurance Co against the *Scottish Daily Record* and the *Sunday Mail* for articles published in the latter in 1975.

The most expensive and longest defamation trial was *Orme v. Associated Newspapers Ltd.*, known as the Moonies case before Mr Justice Comyn from 6 Oct 1980 to 31 Mar 1981. The *Daily Mail*'s article of May 1978 was found not to be defamatory of the Unification Church. Costs exceeded £500,000.

Greatest compensation
William De Palma (b. 1938) of Whittier, California, agreed to a $750,000 (*then £34,000*) settlement for 16 months wrongful imprisonment in McNeil Island Federal Prison, on 12 Aug 1975 after a 15 year sentence for armed robbery in Buena Park on forged fingerprint evidence in 1968.

The greatest Crown compensation in Britain for wrongful imprisonment has been £17,500 paid to Laszio Virag, 35, who had been sentenced to 10 years imprisonment at Gloucester assizes in 1969 for theft and shooting and wounding a police officer. His acceptance of this sum was announced on 23 Dec 1974 after his having been released in April 1974 on grounds of mistaken identification.

Greatest Alimony
The highest alimony awarded by a court has been $2,261,000 (*then £983,000*) against George Storer Sr, 74, in favour of his third wife Dorothy, 73, in Miami, Florida on 29 Oct 1974. Mr Storer, a broadcasting executive, was also ordered to pay his ex-wife's attorney $200,000 (*then £86,950*) in fees.

Greatest Alimony Suit
Mrs Soraya Khashoggi (née Sandra Jarvis-Daley) filed the highest ever alimony claim of $2,500 million (*then £1136 million*) against her former husband Adnan Khashoggi in Los Angeles on 3 Aug 1979. Mr Marvin Mitchelson explaining the size of the settlement claim alluded to Mr Khashoggi's wealth which included 13 homes, 3 private Jumbo jets and a $24 million yacht *Khalidia*.

Greatest divorce settlement
The greatest amount ever reported in a divorce settlement is half of the estimated $100 million wealth of the publisher James Kent Cooke (b. Canada 1913) of Las Vegas, Nevada agreed by a Los Angeles court in March 1979 in favour of his wife Mrs Barbara Jean Cooke (b. 1917) after 42 years of marriage. The highest High Court divorce award was £700,000 on 13 Nov 1980 for 'Mrs P' after 23 years of marriage against her former husband from Jersey from whom she had been receiving £6000 per annum.

Patent case
The greatest settlement ever made in a patent infringement suit is $9,250,000 (*then £3,303,000*), paid in April 1952 by the Ford Motor Company to the Ferguson Tractor Co for a claim filed in January 1948.

Largest suit
The highest amount of damages ever sought is $675,000,000,000,000 (then equivalent to 10 times the US national wealth) in a suit by Mr I. Walton Bader brought in the US District Court, New York City on 14 Apr 1971 against General Motors and others for polluting all 50 states.

Highest costs
The highest costs in English legal history arose from the alleged infringement of a patent owned by General Tire and Rubber Co of America by the Firestone Tyre and Rubber Co. The case was heard by 17 judges over 5½ years ending on 16 Apr 1975 in a reduction of damages from £1,388,000 to £311,000 but costs were an estimated £500,000.

Longest lease
Part of the Cattle Market, Dublin, Ireland was leased by John Jameson to the city's corporation on a lease for 100,000 years expiring on 21 January AD 101,863.

Greatest lien
The greatest lien ever imposed by a court is 40,000 million lire (*then £27 million*) on 9 Apr 1974 upon Vittorio and Ida Riva in Milan for back taxes allegedly due on a chain of cotton mills around Turin, Italy, inherited by their brother Felice (who left for Beirut) in 1960.

Wills *Shortest*
The shortest valid will in the world is 'Vše zene', the Czech for 'All to wife', written and dated 19 Jan 1967 by Herr Karl Tausch of Langen, Hesse, Germany. The shortest will contested but subsequently admitted to probate in English law was the case of *Thorn v. Dickens* in 1906. It consisted of the three words 'All for Mother'.

Longest
The longest will on record was that of Mrs Frederica Cook (USA), in the early part of the century. It consisted of four bound volumes containing 95,940 words.

Judges *Most Durable*
The oldest recorded active judge was Judge Albert R. Alexander (1859–1966) of Plattsburg, Missouri, USA. He was the magistrate and probate judge of Clinton County until his retirement aged 105 years 8 months on 9 July 1965. Judge J. Frank Graff (b. 28 Dec 1888) was serving as a senior judge at Armstrong County Court House, Pennsylvania since 1 Jan 1923. Judge Vernon D. Hitchings of Norfolk, Virginia disposed of his millionth traffic case from January 1954 to 19 Jan 1977. Of these some 965,000 of his verdicts were unappealed or upheld on appeal. In more than 23 years of judgeship to his retirement in Dec 1968, Judge James Hardie Ferguson heard 13,000 cases in the Wilmington Juvenile and Domestic Relations Court, North Carolina, without a single appeal.

Great Britain
The greatest recorded age at which any British judge has sat on a bench was 93 years 9 months in the case of Sir William Francis Kyffin Taylor, GBE, KC (*later* Lord Maenan), who was born on 9 July 1854 and retired as presiding judge of the Liverpool Court of Passage in April 1948, having held that position since 1903. Sir Salathiel Lovell was, however, still sitting in 1713 in his 94th or 95th year. The greatest age at which a House of Lords judgement has been given is 92 in the case of the 1st Earl of Halsbury (b. 3 Sept 1823) in 1916.

The longest serving judge in Britain is the Rt Hon Lord Denning (b. 23 Jan 1899), who was appointed a High Court Judge in 1944, a Lord Justice of Appeal in 1948, a Law Lord in 1957 and Master of the Rolls in 1962.

Master of the Rolls
The longest tenure of the Mastership of the Rolls since the office was inaugurated in 1286 has been 24 years 7 months by David de Wollore from 2 July 1346 to 27 March 1371. The longest tenure

since the Supreme Court Judicature Act, 1881 has been that of Lord Denning (see above). William Morland held the office for 77 days while in 1629 Sir Humphrey May died 'soon after' his appointment on 10 April.

Judge Youngest

No collated records on the ages of judicial appointments exist. However Thomas J. Boynton (b. Amherst, Ohio on 31 Aug 1838) is known to have been appointed Federal Judge at Key West, Florida on 20 Jan 1864 aged 25 years 142 days. Judge Susan I. Broyles (b. Alamosa, Colorado, USA, 25 June 1949) was appointed County Judge of Conejos County, Colorado on 9 Jan 1973 aged 23 years 198 days.

The youngest certain age at which any English judge has been appointed is 31, in the case of Sir Francis Buller (b. 17 Mar 1746), who was appointed Second Judge of the County Palatine of Chester on 27 Nov 1777, and Puisne Judge of the King's Bench on 6 May 1778, aged 32 years 1 month. The lowest age of appointment this century has been 42 years 2 months of Lord Hodson in 1937.

Most Judges

Lord Balmerino was found guilty of treason by 137 of his peers on 28 July 1746. In R *v*. Canning at the Old Bailey in 1754 Elizabeth Canning was deported for wilful perjury by 19 judges voting 10 to 9. In *James, Young and Webster* v. *United Kingdom*, the British Rail 'Closed Shop' case before the European Court of Human Rights in Strasbourg on 3–4 Mar 1981, Sir Ian Percival QC and Mr David Calcutt QC faced 21 judges.

Youngest English QC

The earliest age at which a barrister has taken silk this century is 33 years 8 months in the case of Mr (later the Rt Hon Sir) Francis Raymond Evershed (1899–1966) in April 1933. He was later

Sir Lionel Luckhoo who has succeeded in obtaining 236 successive murder charge acquittals in Guyana.

Lord Evershed, Master of the Rolls. Buller (see above) wa nepotistically given silk aged 31, being a nephew of the the Lord Chancellor, Lord Bathurst.

Most successful

Sir Lionel Luckhoo KCMG CBE, senior partner of Luckhoo and Luckhoo of Georgetown, Guyana succeeded in getting his 236th successive murder charge acquittal by 1 May 1981.

Deadliest prosecutor

Joe Freeman Britt, District Attorney, Sixteenth Judicia District, North Carolina, USA obtained 23 death verdicts in 2 months to mid-1976 when he had 13 defendants simultaneously on death row.

CRIME
Mass Killings *China*

The greatest massacre ever imputed by the government of on sovereign nation against the government of another is that o 26,300,000 Chinese during the regime of Mao Tse-tung betwee 1949 and May 1965. This accusation was made by an agency o the USSR Government in a radio broadcast on 7 Apr 1969. Th broadcast broke down the figure into four periods:—2.8 million (1949–52); 3.5 million (1953–7); 6.7 million (1958–60); and 13. million (1961–May 1965). The highest reported death figures ir single monthly announcements on Peking radio were 1,176,00 in the provinces of Anhwei, Chekiang, Kiangsu, and Shantung and 1,150,000 in the Central South Provinces. Po I-po, Ministe of Finance, is alleged to have stated in the organ *For a lasting peace, for a people's democracy* 'in the past three years (1950–2 we have liquidated more than 2 million bandits'. Genera Jacques Guillermaz, a French diplomat estimated the total executions between February 1951 and May 1952 at between 1 million and 3 million. In April 1971 the Executive cabinet or *Yuan* of the implacably hostile government of The Republic of China in Taipei, Taiwan announced its official estimate of the mainland death roll in the period 1949–69 as 'at least 39,940,000'. This figure, however, excluded 'tens of thousands' killed in the Great Proletarian Cultural Revolution, which began in late 1966. The Walker Report published by the US Senate Committee of the Judiciary in July 1971 placed the parameters of the total death roll within China since 1949 between 32.25 and 61.7 million. An estimate of 63,784,000 was published by Jean-Pierre Dujardin in *Figaro* magazine of 19–25 Nov 1978.

USSR

The total death roll in the Great Purge, or *Yezhovshchina*, in the USSR, in 1936–8 has, not surprisingly, never been published. Evidence of its magnitude may be found in population statistics which show a deficiency of males from *before* the outbreak of the 1941–5 war. The reign of terror was administered by the *Narodny Kommissariat Vnutrennykh Del* (NKVD), or People's Commissariat of Internal Affairs, the Soviet security service headed by Nikolay Ivanovich Yezhov (1895–1939), described by Nikita Khrushchyov in 1956 as a 'degenerate'. S. V. Utechin, an expert on Soviet affairs, regarded estimates of 8,000,000 or 10,000,000 victims as 'probably not exaggerations'. On 17 Aug 1942 Stalin indicated to Churchill in Moscow that 10 million *kulaks* had been liquidated for resisting the collectivization of their farms.

Nazi Germany

Obersturmbannführer (Lt-Col) Karl Adolf Eichmann (b. Solingen, W. Germany 19 Mar 1906) of the SS was hanged in a small room inside Ramleh Prison, near Tel Aviv, Israel, at just before midnight (local time) on 31 May 1962, for his complicity in the deaths of an indeterminably massive number of Jews during World War II, under the instruction given in April 1941 by Adolf Hitler (1889–1945) for 'the Final Solution' (*Endlösung*).

At the SS (*Schutzstaffel*) extermination camp (*Vernichtungslager*) known as Auschwitz-Birkenau (Oświęcim-Brzezinka), near Oświęcim (Auschwitz), in southern Poland, where a minimum of 920,000 people (Soviet estimate is 4,000,000) were exterminated from 14 June 1940 to 18 Jan 1945, the greatest number killed in a day was 6000. The man who operated the release of the 'Zyklon B' cyanide pellets into the gas chambers there during this time was Sgt Major Moll (variously Mold). The Nazi

(*Nationalsozialistsche Deutsche Arbeiterpartei*) Commandant during the period 1940–3 was Rudolph Franz Ferdinand Höss who was tried in Warsaw from 11 Mar to 2 Apr 1947 and hanged, aged 47, at Oświeçim on 15 Apr 1947.

Forced labour

No official figures have been published of the death roll in Corrective Labour Camps in the USSR, first established in 1918. The total number of such camps was known to be more than 200 in 1946 but in 1956 many were converted to less severe Corrective Labour Colonies. An estimate published in the Netherlands puts the death roll between 1921 and 1960 at 19,000,000. The camps were administered by the *Cheka* until 1922, the OGPU (1922–34), the NKVD (1934–46), the MVD (1946–53) and the KGB since 1953. Solzhenitsyn's aggregate best estimate is that the number of inmates has been 66 million. The study by S. Grossu published 1975 stated there were then 2 million political prisoners in 96 camps. In China there are no published official statistics on the numbers undergoing *Lao Jiao* (Education through Labour) nor *Lao Dong Gai Zao* (Reform through manual labour). An estimate published by Bao Ruo-wang, who was released in 1964 due to his father having been a Corsican, was 16,000,000 which then approached 3 per cent of the population.

Genocide

In the genocide in Kampuchea, formerly Cambodia, according to the Khmer Rouge foreign minister Ieng Sarg, more than a third of the 8 million Khmers were killed between April 1975 and January 1979. Under the rule of Saloth Sar *alias* Pol Pot, a founder member of the CPK (Communist Party of Kampuchea, formed in September 1960) towns, money and property were abolished and economical execution by bayonet and club introduced for such offences as falling asleep during the day, asking too many questions, playing non-Communist music, being old and feeble, being the offspring of an 'undesirable' or being too well educated. Deaths at the Tuol Sleng interrogation centre reached 582 in a day.

Largest criminal organization

The largest syndicate of organized crime is the Mafia or La Cosa Nostra, which has infiltrated the executive, judiciary and legislature of the United States. It consists of some 3000 to 5000 individuals in 24 'families' federated under 'The Commission', with an annual turnover in vice, gambling, protection rackets, cigarettes, bootlegging, hijacking, narcotics, loan-sharking and prostitution estimated in the *Time* magazine survey of May 1977 at $48,000 million per annum of which $25.3 billion were profit—then 9½ times over than Exxon. The origin in the US dates from 1869 in New Orleans. The biggest Mafia (meaning *swank* from a Sicilian word for beauty or pride) killing was on 11–13 Sept 1931 when the topmost man Salvatore Maranzano, *Il Capo di Tutti Capi*, and 40 allies were liquidated.

Murder rate *Highest*

The country with the highest recorded murder rate is Mexico, with 46.3 registered homicides for each 100,000 of the population in 1970. It has been estimated that the total number of murders in Colombia during *La Violencia* (1945–62) was about 300,000, giving a rate over a 17-year period of more than 48 a day. A total of 592 deaths was attributed to one bandit leader, Teófilo ('Sparks') Rojas, aged 27, between 1948 and his death in an ambush near Armenia on 22 Jan 1963. Some sources attribute 3500 slayings to him.

The highest homicide rates recorded in New York City have been 58 in a week in July 1972 and 13 in a day in August 1972. In 1973 the total for Detroit, Michigan (pop. then 1.5 million) was 751.

Lowest

The country with the lowest officially recorded rate in the world is The Maldives with a nil rate among its naturals since its independence in July 1965. In the Indian state of Sikkim, in the Himalayas, murder is, however, practically unknown, while in the Hunza area of Kashmir, in the Karakoram, only one definite case by a Hunzarwal has been recorded since 1900.

Great Britain

In Great Britain the total number of homicides and deaths from injuries purposely inflicted by other persons in the year 1979–80

was 658. This figure compares with a murder total of 124 in 1937 and 125 in 1958.

Terrorist Outrages

The greatest death roll from a terrorist bomb was 76 killed and 200 injured at the central railway station, Bologna, Italy on 2 Aug 1980. Marco Affatigato was later held in France pending extradition.

Most prolific murderers *World*

It was established at the trial of Buhram, the Indian thug, that he had strangled at least 931 victims with his yellow and white cloth strip or *ruhmal* in the Oudh district between 1790 and 1840. It has been estimated that at least 2,000,000 Indians were strangled by Thugs (*burtotes*) during the reign of the Thugee (pronounced tugee) cult from 1550 until its final suppression by the British *raj* in 1853. The greatest number of victims ascribed to a murderess has been 610 in the case of Countess Erszebet Bathory (1560–1614) of Hungary. At her trial which began on 2 Jan 1611 a witness testified to seeing a list of her victims in her own handwriting totalling this number. All were alleged to be young girls from the neighbourhood of her castle at Csejthe where she died on 21 Aug 1614. She had been walled up in her room for the 3½ years after being found guilty.

20th century

The 20th century's most prolific one-at-a-time murderer has been Bruno Lüdke (Germany) (b. 1909), who confessed to 85 murders of women between 1928 and 29 Jan 1943. He was executed by injection without trial in a hospital in Vienna on 8 Apr 1944.

Pedro Alonso López (b. Columbia, 1949) known as the 'Columbian Monster', was reported captured by the villagers of Ambato, Ecuador in early March 1980. He admitted to more than 300 murders of pre-teen girls in Colombia, Peru and Ecuador since 1973. The remains of 53 victims of the 110 admitted to in Ecuador were rapidly detected after his confession.

John Wayne Gacy (b. 1943) was sentenced to death by electrocution on 13 Mar 1980 for murdering 33 males in Chicago. The first of the 33 bodies was found on 21 Dec 1978 under his house at Northwood Township, Illinois, USA.

Great Britain

Six men were each charged with 21 murders at Lancaster Crown Court on 9 June 1975 concerning the bombing of the two Birmingham public houses Mulberry Bush and Tavern in the Town on 21 Nov 1974. They were John Walker, Patrick Hill, Robert Hunter, Noel McIlkenny, William Power and Hugh Callaghan. The Home Office began, in February 1981, to investigate the attribution of 26 deaths between 1973 and 1979 to the confessed arsonist Bruce Lee. In January 1981 he was sent to a mental hospital by Leeds Crown Court.

Judith Minna Ward, 25, of Stockport, Cheshire was convicted on 11 separate murder charges on 4 Nov 1974 making 12 in all arising from the explosion in an army coach on the M.62 near Drighlington, West Yorkshire on 4 Feb 1974. Mary Ann Cotton (*née* Robson) (b. 1832, East Rainton, County Durham), hanged in Durham Jail on 24 Mar 1873 is believed to have poisoned 14, possibly 20, people.

'Smelling out'

The greatest 'smelling out' recorded in African history occurred before Shaka (1787–1828) and 30,000 Nguni subjects near the River Umhlatuzana, Zululand (now Natal, South Africa) in March 1824. After 9 hr, over 300 were 'smelt out' as guilty of smearing the Royal *Kraal* with blood, by 150 witch-finders led by the hideous female *isangoma* Nobela. The victims were declared innocent when Shaka admitted to having done the smearing himself to expose the falsity of the power of his diviners. Nobela poisoned herself with atropine ($C_{17}H_{23}NO_3$), but the other 149 witch-finders were thereupon skewered or clubbed to death.

Suicide

The estimated daily rate of suicides throughout the world surpassed 1000 in 1965. The country with the highest suicide rate is Hungary, with 42.6 per 100,000 of the population in 1977. The country with the lowest recorded rate is Jordan with a single case in 1970 and hence a rate of 0.04 per 100,000.

In England and Wales there were 4195 suicides in 1980, or an average of 11.49 per day. In the northern hemisphere April and May tend to be peak months.

Mass Suicide

The final total of the mass cyanide poisoning of the People's Temple cult near Port Kaituma, Guyana on 18 Nov 1978 was 913. The leader was the paranoid 'Rev.' Jim Jones of San Francisco, California who had deposited 'millions of dollars' overseas.

Robbery

The greatest robbery on record was that of the Reichsbank following Germany's collapse in April/May 1945. The largest haul consisted of negotiable securities valued at $400,000,000. In April 1979 three men were convicted and sentenced to terms of imprisonment at Brantford, Ontario on a number of conspiracy charges connected with some of these bonds.

Gold bullion, foreign exchange and jewels worth $20,000,000 (worth some $200 million (£91 million) today) were also stolen by members of the German and American armies. None of this loot was recovered and none of the perpetrators were ever brought to trial.

Art

The greatest recorded art robbery by market valuation was the removal of 19 paintings, valued at £8,000,000 taken from Russborough House, Blessington, County Wicklow, Ireland, the home of Sir Alfred and Lady Beit by 4 men and a woman on 26 Apr 1974. They included the £3 million Vermeer 'Lady Writing a Letter with her maid'. The paintings were recovered on 4 May near Glandore, County Cork. Dr Rose Bridgit Dugdale (b. 1941) was convicted. It is arguable that the value of the *Mona Lisa* at the time of its theft from The Louvre, Paris on 21 Aug 1911 was greater than this figure. It was recovered in Italy in 1913 when Vincenzo Perruggia was charged with its theft. On 1 Sept 1964 antiquities reputedly worth £10,000,000 were recovered from 3 warehouses near the Pyramids, Egypt.

Bank

During the extreme civil disorder prior to 22 Jan 1976 in Beirut, Lebanon, a guerilla force blasted the vaults of the British Bank of the Middle East in Bab Idriss and cleared out safe deposit boxes with contents valued by former Finance Minister, Lucien Dahadah, at $50 million and by another source as an 'absolute minimum' of $20 million.

Britain's greatest ever robbery was of an estimated £8,000,000 from the Bank of America, Mayfair, London on 24 Apr 1975. On 16 Nov 1976 five men were jailed for between 12 and 23 years. Leonard 'The Twirler' Wilde, 51, was the locksmith.

Train

The greatest recorded train robbery occurred between about 3.03 a.m. and 3.27 a.m. on 8 Aug 1963, when a General Post Office mail train from Glasgow, Scotland, was ambushed at Sears Crossing and robbed at Bridego Bridge near Mentmore, Buckinghamshire. The gang escaped with about 120 mailbags containing £2,631,784 worth of bank notes being taken to London for destruction. Only £343,448 was recovered.

Jewels

The greatest recorded theft of jewels was from the bedroom of the 'well-guarded' villa of Prince Abdel Aziz Bin Ahmed Al-Thani near Cannes, France on 24 July 1980 valued at $16,000,000 (*then £7¼ million*). The haul from Carrington & Co Ltd of Regent Street, London, on 21 Nov 1965 was estimated to be £500,000.

Greatest kidnapping ransom

Historically the greatest ransom paid was that for Atahualpa by the Incas to Francisco Pizarro in 1532–3 at Cajamarca, Peru which constituted a hall full of gold and silver worth in modern money some $170 million (*£95 million*).

The greatest ransom ever reported is 1500 million pesos (*£25,300,000*) for the release of the brothers Jorge Born, 40 and Juan Born, 39, of Bunge and Born, paid to the left wing urban guerilla group Montoneros in Buenos Aires, Argentina on 20 June 1975.

The youngest person kidnapped has been Carolyn Wharton born at 12.46 p.m. on 19 Mar 1955 in the Baptist Hospital, Texas, USA and kidnapped, by a woman disguised as a nurse, at 1.15 p.m. aged 29 min.

Greatest hijack ransom

The highest amount ever paid to aircraft hijackers has been $6 million (*then £3.42 million*) by the Japanese government in the case of a JAL DC-8 at Dacca Airport on 2 Oct 1977 with 38 hostages. Six convicted criminals were also exchanged. The Bangladesh government had refused to sanction any retaliatory action.

Largest narcotics haul

It was revealed on 29 Apr 1978 that 512.5 tons *529,7 tonnes* of marijuana was seized in raids on the Guajira peninsula, Colombia on 27–29 Apr 1978. The wholesale value was estimated at $200 million (*£105 million*).

The most valuable seizure was made on 20 Feb 1981 in Miami, Florida when 826 lb *374,6 kg* of processed cocaine was seized and two men arrested.

The Home Office disclosed on 23 Dec 1977 that 13 million LSD tablets with a street value approaching £100 million had been destroyed on the conclusion of 'Operation Julie'.

Greatest banknote forgery

The greatest forgery was the German Third Reich government's forging operation, code name 'Bernhard', engineered by SS Sturmbannfuhrer Alfred Naujocks of the Technical Dept of the German Secret Service Amt VI F in Berlin in 1940–1. It involved £150,000,000 worth of £5 notes.

Biggest bank fraud

The largest amount of money named in a defalcation case has been a gross £33,000,000 at the Lugano branch of Lloyd's Bank International Ltd in Switzerland on 2 Sept 1974. Mr Mark Colombo was arrested pending charges including falsification of foreign currency accounts and suppression of evidence.

Computer fraud

Between 1964 and 1973, 64,000 fake insurance policies were created on the computer of the Equity Funding Corporation involving $2000 million.

Stanley Mark Rifkin (b. 1946) was arrested in Carlsbad, California by the FBI on 6 Nov 1978 charged with defrauding a Los Angeles bank of $10.2 million (*then £4.85 million*) by manipulation of a computer system. He was sentenced to 8 years in June 1980.

Welfare swindle

The greatest welfare swindle yet worked was that of the gypsy Anthony Moreno on the French Social Security in Marseille. By forging birth certificates and school registration forms, he invented 197 fictitious families and 3000 children on which he claimed benefits from 1960 to mid-1968. Moreno, nicknamed 'El Chorro' (the fountain), was later reported free of extradition worries and living in luxury in his native Spain having absquatulated with an estimated £2,300,000.

Largest object ever stolen by a single man

On a moonless night at dead calm high water on 5 June 1966 armed with only a sharp axe, N William Kennedy slashed free the mooring lines at Wolfe's Cove, St Laurence Seaway, Quebec, Canada, of the 10,639 dwt S S *Orient Trader* owned by Steel Factors Ltd of Ontario. The vessel drifted to a waiting blacked out tug thus escaping a ban on any shipping movements during a violent wild-cat waterfront strike. She sailed for Spain.

CAPITAL PUNISHMENT

Capital punishment was first abolished *de facto* in 1798 in Liechtenstein. The death penalty for murder was formally abolished in Britain on 18 Dec 1969. Between the 5–4 Supreme Court decision against capital punishment in June 1972 and April 1975, 32 of the 50 States of the USA voted to restore it.

Capital punishment in the British Isles dates from AD 450, but was abolished by William I and re-imposed by Henry I, reaching a peak in the reign of Edward VI (1547–53), when an average of 560 persons were executed annually at Tyburn alone. Even into the 19th century, there were 223 capital crimes, though people were, in practice, hanged for just 25 of these. Between 1830 and 1955 the most murderers hanged in a year was 27 (24 men, 3 women) in 1903. The least was 5 in 1854, 1921 and 1930. In 1956 there were no hangings in England, Wales or Scotland, since when the highest number in any year to 1964 was 5.

Largest hanging

The most people hanged from one gallows was 38 Sioux Indians by William J. Duly outside Mankato, Minnesota, USA for the murder of unarmed citizens on 26 Dec 1862.

The Nazi Feldkommandant simultaneously hanged 50 Greek resistance men as a reprisal in Athens on 22 July 1944.

Last hangings

The last public execution in England took place outside Newgate Prison, London at 8 a.m. on 26 May 1868, when Michael Barrett was hanged for his part in the Fenian bomb outrage on 13 Dec 1867, when 12 were killed outside the Clerkenwell House of Detention, London. The earliest non-public execution was of the murderer Thomas Wells on 13 Aug 1868. The last public hanging in Scotland was that of the murderer Joe Bell in Perth in 1866. The last in the United States occurred at Owensboro, Kentucky in 1936. The last hangings in the United Kingdom were those of Peter Anthony Allen (b. 4 Apr 1943) at Walton Prison, Liverpool, and John Robson Walby (b. 1 Apr 1940), *alias* Gwynne Owen Evans, at Strangeways Gaol, Manchester both on 13 Aug 1964. They had been found guilty of the capital murder of John Alan West, on 7 Apr 1964. The 14th and last woman executed this century was Mrs Ruth Ellis (*née* Neilson), 28, for the murder of David Blakely, 25, shot outside the Magdala, Hampstead, on 10 Apr 1955. She was executed on 13 July at Holloway. The last hanging in the Republic of Ireland was in 1954.

Last from yard-arm

The last naval execution at the yard-arm was the hanging of Private John Dalliger, Royal Marines, aboard HMS *Leven* in the River Yangtze, China, on 13 July 1860. Dalliger had been found guilty of two attempted murders.

Youngest

Although the hanging of persons under 18 was expressly excluded only in the Children's and Young Person's Act, 1933 (Sec. 33), no person under that age was, in fact, executed more recently than 1887. The lowest satisfactorily recorded age was of a boy aged 8 'who had malice, cunning and revenge' in firing two barns and who was hanged at Abingdon, Oxfordshire in the 17th century. The youngest persons hanged since 1900 have been 18 years old, the most recent of whom was Francis Robert George ('Flossie') Forsyth on 10 Nov 1960.

Oldest

The oldest person hanged in the United Kingdom since 1900 was a man of 71 named Charles Frembd (*sic*) at Chelmsford Gaol on 4 Nov 1914, for the murder of his wife at Leytonstone, Waltham Forest, Greater London. In 1822 John Smith, said to be 80, of Greenwich, Greater London, was hanged for the murder of a woman.

Last public guillotining

The last person to be publicly guillotined in France was the murderer Eugen Weidmann before a large crowd at Versailles, near Paris, at 4.50 a.m. on 17 June 1939. In January 1978 Marcel Chevalier was nominated to succeed his uncle Andre Obrecht as executioner who had in turn succeeded his uncle Henri Desfourneaux. Dr Joseph Ignace Guillotin (1738–1812) died a natural death. He had advocated the use of the machine designed by Dr Antoine Louis in 1789 in the French constituent assembly. There were 6 guillotinings in the 1970's.

Death row

It was estimated that by mid-1980 some 600 prisoners in the United States were on 'Death Row'. Caryl Whittier Chessman, aged 38 and convicted of 17 felonies, was executed on 2 May 1960 in the gas chamber at the California State Prison, San Quentin, California, USA. In 11 years 10 months and one week on 'death row', Chessman had won eight stays. John Spenkelink, 30, was the first to be electrocuted since 1967 at Railford Jail, Florida on 25 May 1979. Samanichi Hirasawa celebrated his 88th birthday on death row in Sendai Prison, northern Japan on 18 Feb 1980.

Executioner

The longest period of office of a Public Executioner was that of William Calcraft (1800–79), who was in action from 1828 to 25 May 1874 and officiated at nearly every hanging outside and later inside Newgate Prison, London. On 2 Apr 1868 he hanged the murderess Mrs Frances Kidder, 25, outside Maidstone Jail, Kent—the last public execution of a woman.

From 1900 to abolition of hanging in 1964 the Pierrepoint family dominated the task of executing murderers and war criminals. Henry Albert (1876–1922) officiated from 1900–1911 with a record 20 executions in Britain in 1909 and the last double female execution (the baby farmers Mrs Amelia Sachs and Mrs Annie Walters) on 3 Feb 1903. The longest serving executioner has been his eldest brother Thomas Pierrepoint from 1903 to 1948. Albert Pierrepoint, son of Henry Albert, officiated at the hanging of 530 men and 20 women in his career in 9 countries including a record 27 war criminals in a day in Germany.

Lynching

The worst year in the 20th century for lynchings in the United States has been 1901, with 130 lynchings (105 Negroes, 25 Whites), while the first year with no reported cases was 1952. The last lynching recorded in Britain was that of Panglam Godolan, a suspected murderer, in London on 27 Oct 1958. The last case previous to this was of a kidnapping suspect in Glasgow in 1922.

Corporal punishment

The last use of corporal punishment in one of HM Prisons was on 26 June 1962 and it was abolished in the United Kingdom by the Criminal Justice Act, 1967. The treadmill which 14 prisons operated in 1878 was finally suspended on 1 Apr 1902. Men on the 36-man wheel at Northallerton, Yorkshire raised themselves 9639 ft *2937 m* in an 8-hr day, equivalent to reaching within 111 ft *33,8 m* of the summit of Everest in 3 days.

PRISON SENTENCES

Longest sentences *World*

The longest recorded prison sentence is one of 7109 years awarded to a pair of confidence tricksters by an Iranian court on 15 June 1969. The durations of sentences are proportional to the amount of the defalcations involved. A sentence of 384,912 years was *demanded* at the prosecution of Gabriel March Grandos, 22, at Palma de Mallorca, Spain on 11 Mar 1972 for failing to deliver 42,768 letters or 9 years per letter.

Juan Corona, a Mexican-American, was sentenced to 25 consecutive life terms, for murdering 25 farm workers in 1970–1 around Feather River, Yuba City, California, at Fairfield on 5 Feb 1973. His 20th century record was surpassed by Dean Corll (27) in 1974 and John Wayne Gacy (33 victims) in 1980.

United Kingdom

Robert Bates, 30, received 16 life sentences for his part in the Shankill butcher's murders of 1975–7 in Belfast from Lord Justice O'Donnell on 20 Feb 1979. It was recommended that he be held for the 'rest of his life'.

The longest single period served by a reprieved murderer in Great Britain this century was 40 years 11 months by John Watson Laurie, the Goat Fell or Arran murderer, who was reprieved on the grounds of insanity in November 1889 and who died in Perth Penitentiary on 4 Oct 1930.

The longest specific minimum period recommended by a judge under the Murder (Abolition of Death Penalty) Act 1965 has been 35 years in the case of Patrick Armstrong and Michael Hill on 22 Oct 1975 for pub bombings (7 killed, 99 injured) at Guildford and Woolwich in 1974.

The longest prison sentence ever passed under British law was one of three consecutive and two concurrent terms of 14 years, thus totalling 42 years, imposed on 3 May 1961 on George Blake *né* Behar (b. Rotterdam, 11 Nov 1922), for treachery. Blake, formerly UK vice-consul in Seoul, South Korea, had been converted to Communism during 34 months' internment there from 2 July 1950 to April 1953. It had been alleged that his betrayals may have cost the lives of up to 42 British agents. He was 'sprung' from Wormwood Scrubs Prison, Greater London, on 22 Oct 1966.

The longest single sentence passed on a woman under English law was 20 years for Mrs Lona Teresa Cohen *née* Petra (b. 1913) at the Old Bailey, City of London on 2 Mar 1961 for conspiring to commit a breach of the Official Secrets Act, 1911. The sentence of this KGB agent was remitted by the Foreign Secretary on no known lawful authority on 24 July 1969. Ward (see Most Prolific Murderers) was sentenced to 20 years for a single offence and an aggregate 30 years on 4 Nov 1974.

Longest time served
Paul Geidel, (b. 21 Apr 1894) was convicted of second degree murder on 5 Sept 1911 as a 17 year old porter in a New York Hotel. He was released from the Fishkill Correctional Facility, Beacon, New York aged 85 on 7 May 1980 having served 68 years 8 months and 2 days—the longest recorded term in US history. He first refused parole in 1974.

Longest in Broadmoor
The longest period for which any person has been detained in the Broadmoor hospital for the criminally insane, near Crowthorne, Berkshire, is 76 years in the case of William Giles. He was admitted as an insane arsonist at the age of 11 and died there on 10 Mar 1962, at the age of 87.

The longest escape from Broadmoor was one of 39 years by the Liverpool wife murderer James Kelly, who got away on 28 Jan 1888, using a pass key made from a corset spring. After an adventurous life in Paris, in New York and at sea he returned in April 1927, to ask for re-admission. After some difficulties this was arranged. He died in 1930.

Most appearances
There are no collated records on the greatest number of convictions on an individual but the highest recently reported is 1433 for the gentlemanly but alcoholic Edward Eugene Ebzery, who died in Brisbane Jail, Queensland, Australia on 23 Sept 1967.

Greatest mass arrest
The greatest mass arrest in the United Kingdom occurred on 17 Sept 1961, when 1314 demonstrators supporting the unilateral nuclear disarmament of the United Kingdom were arrested for wilfully disregarding the directions of the police and thereby obstructing highways leading to Parliament Square, London, by sitting down. As a consequence of the 1926 General Strike there were 3149 prosecutions: incitement (1760) and violence (1389).

FINES
Heaviest *World*
It was reported in January 1979 that Carlo Ponti, husband of Sophia Loren, was to be fined the equivalent of $26.4 million by the Italian courts in connection with claims for tax alleged to be due but unpaid.

UK
The heaviest fine ever imposed in the United Kingdom was one of £277,500 plus £3717 costs, by H. M. Customs and Excise on I. Hennig & Co. Ltd, the London diamond merchants, at Clerkenwell Magistrates' Court, London, on 14 Dec 1949. The amount was later reduced on appeal.

Rarest prosecution
There are a number of crimes in English law for which there have never been prosecutions. Among unique prosecutions are *Rex v. Crook* in 1662 for the praemunire of disputing the King's title and *Rex v. Gregory* for selling honours under the Honours (Prevention of Abuses) Act, 1924, on 18 Feb 1933. John Maundy Gregory (d. 3 Oct 1941 in France as 'Sir' 'Arthur Gregory) was an honours broker during 6 administrations from 1919 to 1932 and was sentenced to two months in Wormwood Scrubs, London.

PRISONS
Largest *World*
The largest prison in the world is Kharkov Prison, in the USSR which has at times accommodated 40,000 prisoners.

Great Britain
The largest prison in Great Britain is Wormwood Scrubs, West London, with 1208 cells. The highest prison walls in Great Britain are those of Lancaster Prison measuring 36–52 ft *11–15,85 m.*

The largest prison in Scotland is Barlinnie, Glasgow, with 75 single cells. Ireland's largest prison is Mountjoy Prison, Dublin with 808 cells.

Penal camps
The largest penal camp systems in the world were those near Karaganda and Kolyma, is the USSR, each with a population estimated in 1958 at between 1,200,000 and 1,500,000. The largest labour camp is now said to be the Dubrovlag Complex of 15 camps centred on Pot'ma, Mordovian SSR. The official NATO estimate for all Soviet camps was 'more than one million' in March 1960 compared with a peak of probably 12 million during the Stalinist era.

Devil's Island
The largest French penal settlement was that of St Laurent du Maroni, which comprised the notorious Îles du Diable, Royale and St Joseph (for incorrigibles) off the coast of French Guiana in South America. It remained in operation for 99 years from 1854 until the last group of repatriated prisoners, including Théodore Rouselle, who had served 50 years, was returned to Bordeaux on 22 Aug 1953. It has been estimated that barely 2000 *bagnards* (ex-convicts) of the 70,000 deportees ever returned. These, however, included the executioner Ladurelle (imprisoned 1921–37), who was murdered in Paris in 1938.

Highest population
The peak prison population, including Borstals and detention centres, for England and Wales was the figure for March 1980 with 44,223. In Scotland the prison population record was 5400 in 1972 and in Northern Ireland 2934 on 16 Nov 1975.

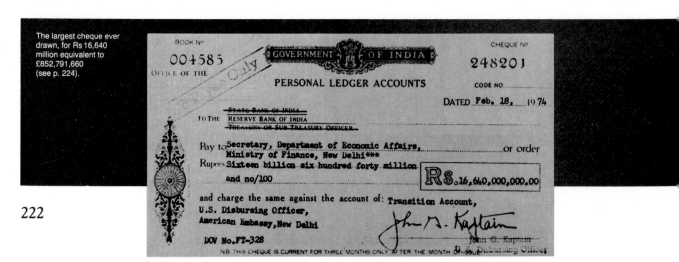

The largest cheque ever drawn, for Rs 16,640 million equivalent to £852,791,660 (see p. 224).

Most secure prison

After it became a maximum security Federal prison in 1934, no convict was known to have lived to tell of a successful escape from the prison of Alcatraz Island in San Francisco Bay, California, USA. A total of 23 men attempted it but 12 were recaptured, 5 shot dead, one drowned and 5 presumed drowned. On 16 Dec 1962, just before the prison was closed on 21 Mar 1963, one man reached the mainland alive, only to be recaptured on the spot. John Chase held the record with 26 years there.

Most expensive prison

Spandau Prison, Berlin, built 100 years ago for 600 prisoners is now used solely for the person widely and officially purported to be Nazi war criminal Rudolf Hess (b. 26 Apr 1894). The cost of maintenance of the staff of 105 has been estimated at $415,000 (*£245,000*) per annum.

Longest escape

The longest recorded escape by a recaptured prisoner was that of Leonard T. Fristoe, 77, who escaped from Nevada State Prison, USA, on 15 Dec 1923 and was turned in by his son on 15 Nov 1969 at Compton, California. He had had 46 years of freedom under the name Claude R. Willis. He had killed two sheriff's deputies in 1920. The longest period of freedom achieved by a British gaol breaker is more than 24 years by Irish-born John Patrick Hannan, who escaped from Verne Open Prison at Portland, Dorset, on 22 Dec 1955 and was still at large in June 1980. He had served only 1 month of a 21-month term for car-stealing and assaulting two policemen.

Greatest gaol break

In February 1979 a retired US Army Colonel Arthur 'Bull' Simons led a band of 14 to break into Gasre prison, Tehran, Iran to rescue two fellow Americans. Some 11,000 other prisoners took advantage of this and the Islamic revolution in what became history's largest ever gaol break.

In July 1971, Raoul Sendic and 105 other Tupamaro guerrillas escaped from a Uruguayan prison through a tunnel 91 m *298 ft* long.

The greatest gaol break in Britain was that from Brixton Prison, Lambeth, Greater London on 30 May 1973 when 20 men got out using a rubbish tipping lorry as a battering ram. Eighteen were captured immediately and one other 5 weeks later. Nine staff were injured.

6. ECONOMIC

MONETARY AND FINANCE

Largest budget *World*

The greatest annual expenditure budgeted by any country has been $615,800 million (*£279,900 million*) by the United States government for the fiscal year 1981. The highest budgeted revenue in the United States has been $600,000 million (*£272,700 million*) for the fiscal year 1981.

In the United States, the greatest surplus was $8,419,469,844 in 1947–8, and the greatest budgeted deficit was $61,800 million (*£30,900 million*) in 1978–9.

Largest budget *Great Britain*

The greatest budgeted current expenditure of Great Britain has been £91,500 million for the fiscal year 1981–82. The highest budgeted current receipts has been £82,500 million for the same fiscal year showing a General Government Borrowing Requirement of £9,000 million.

Foreign aid

The total net foreign aid given by the United States government between 1 July 1945 and 1 Jan 1980 was $177,681 million. The country which received most US aid in 1979 was Israel with $1539 million. US foreign aid began with $50,000 to Venezuela for earthquake relief in 1812.

Least taxed

The lowest income-taxed nations in the world include Bahrain, Kuwait and Qatar where the rate regardless of income is nil.

There is no income tax paid by residents on Lundy Island off North Devon, England. This 1062.4 acre *429,9 ha* island issued its own unofficial currency of Puffins and Half Puffins between the Wars, for which offence the owner was prosecuted. No tax is levied on the Sarkese (inhabitants of Sark) in the Channel Islands.

Highest taxation rates

The country with the most confiscatory taxation is Norway where in January 1974 the Labour Party and Socialist Alliance abolished the 80 per cent limit so that some 2000 citizens were listed in the *Lignings Boka* as paying more than 100 per cent of their taxable income. The shipping magnate Hilmer Reksten (1898–1980) was assessed at 491 per cent. In the United Kingdom the former top earned and unearned rates of 83 per cent and 98 per cent were reduced to 60 per cent and 75 per cent in the budget of 12 June 1979. The all-time record ruled in 1967–8, when a 'special charge' of up to 9s. (45p) in the £ additional to surtax brought the top rate to 27s. 3d. (or 136%) in the £ on investment income.

Tax demands highest

The highest recorded tax demand under litigation is one for $336 million (*then £164 million*) for 70 per cent of the estate of Howard Hughes. The highest income tax demand raised on an individual is one for £2,900,000 on Nicholas Hoogstratem, 34 of London reported on 19 Feb 1981. British Petroleum made a single payment of £854,400,000 in North Sea Taxes to the Inland Revenue on 27 Feb 1981.

Highest and lowest rates in Great Britain

Income tax was first introduced in Great Britain in 1799 for incomes above £60 per annum. It was discontinued in 1815, only to be re-introduced in 1842 at the rate of 7d. (2.91p) in the £. It was at its lowest at 2d. (0.83p) in the £ in 1875, gradually climbing to 1s. 3d. (6.24p) by 1913. From April 1941 until 1946 the record peak of 10s. (50p) in the £ was maintained to assist in the financing of World War II.

National Debt

The largest national debt of any country in the world is that of the United States, where the gross federal public debt of the Federal Government surpassed the 'half trillion' dollar mark in 1975 and reached $968,497 million (*£484,000 million*) by 1 June 1981. This amount in dollar bills would make a pile 52,550 miles *84 570 km* high, weighing 736,233 tons *748 042 tonnes*.

The National Debt in Great Britain was less than £1 million during the reign of James II in 1687. It was £112,780 million or £2,017 per person at 31 Mar 1981. This amount placed in a pile of brand new £1 notes would be 6872.2 miles *11060 km* in height.

Gross National Product

The country with the largest Gross National Product is the United States reaching $3 trillion ($3 \times 10^{12}$) in 1981. The GNP of the United Kingdom at factor cost was £222,962 million for 1980–81.

National wealth

The richest nation, measured by average per caput, is Kuwait with $US 17,270 in 1979. The USA which took the lead in 1910 was tenth behind also Switzerland, Sweden, Denmark, West Germany and Belgium. The United Kingdom stood 30th with $6340 (*£2760*) per head. It has been estimated that the value of all physical assets in the USA in 1976 was $6.2 trillion ($10^{12}$) or $28,800 (*£16,950*) per head. The figure for private wealth in the United Kingdom was £325,000 million (1976) or £5811 per head.

Poorest country

The lowest published annual income per caput of any country in the world is Bhutan but the World Bank has no data for Kampuchea, Laos or Somalia.

Gold reserves *World*

The country with the greatest monetary gold reserve is the United States, whose Treasury had 264.6 million fine oz of the world's 927.02 million fine oz on hand in January 1981. Valued at $500 per fine oz, these amounts translate to $132,300.0 million and $463,510 million respectively. The United States Bullion Depository at Fort Knox, 30 miles *48 km* south-west of Louisville, Kentucky, USA has been the principal Federal depository of US gold since Dec 1936. Gold is stored in 446,000 standard mint bars of 400 troy ounces *12,4414 kg* measuring 7 × 3⅝ × 1⅝ in, *17,7 × 9,2 × 4,1 cm*. As at 1 Jan 1981 Fort Knox housed 147,300,000 fine oz *3436 tonnes* or 55.66% of the United States total holding.

Gold and foreign currency reserves *Great Britain*
The lowest published figure for the sterling area's gold and convertible currency reserves was $298,000,000 (*then £74 million*) on 31 Dec 1940. The valuation on 1 Apr 1980 was a peak $28,008 million of which $1465 million was in gold.

Minimum Lending Rate
The highest ever figure for the British bank rate (since 13 Oct 1972, the Minimum Lending Rate) has been 17 per cent from 15 Nov 1979 to 3rd July 1980. The longest period without a change was the 12 years 13 days from 26 Oct 1939 to 7 Nov 1951, during which time the rate stayed at 2 per cent. This record low rate was first attained on 22 Apr 1852.

Balance of Payments
The most unfavourable current balance of payments figure for the United Kingdom has been a deficit of £3591 million in 1974. The 4th quarter of 1979 was the worst with £1401 million. The greatest surplus for a quarter has been £616 million for the 4th quarter of 1978. Monthly figures are regarded as too erratic to be significant.

Worst inflation *World*
The world's worst inflation occurred in Hungary in June 1946, when the 1931 gold pengö was valued at 130 trillion (1.3×10^{20}) paper pengös. Notes were issued for szazmillion billion (100 trillion or 10^{20}) pengös on 3 June and withdrawn on 11 July 1946. Notes for 1000 trillion or 10^{21} pengös were printed but not circulated. On 6 Nov 1923 the circulation of Reichsbank marks reached 400,338,326,350,700,000,000 and inflation 755,700 million fold on 1913 levels. Inflation in Israel in 1980 ran at 135 per cent and was thus ahead of Turkey and Argentina.

Worst inflation *Great Britain*
The United Kingdom's worst rate in a year has been for August 1974 to August 1975 when inflation ran at a rate of 26.9 per cent compared with 12.0 per cent for May 1980 to May 1981. The Tax and Price Index (allowing for tax reliefs) was 18.4 per cent. The peak TPI extrapolated figure was 31.9 per cent in August 1975. At a sustained 20 per cent inflation rate the £ would be worth 1p (1980 value) *before* the turn of the century.

The Kruger Kilo gold medallion of 22 carats which was issued in February 1981 and contains a kilogramme *35.27 oz* of pure gold.

PAPER MONEY
Earliest
Paper money is an invention of the Chinese first tried in AD 91 and prevalent by AD 970. The world's earliest bank notes (*banco sedlar*) were issued in Stockholm, Sweden, in July 1661. The oldest surviving banknote is one for 5 dalers dated 6 Dec 1662. The oldest surviving printed Bank of England note is one for £555 to bearer, dated 19 Dec 1699 (4½ × 7½ in, *11,4 × 19,6 cm*).

Largest and smallest
The largest paper money ever issued was the one kwan note of the Chinese Ming dynasty issue of 1368–99, which measured × 13 in *22,8 × 33,0 cm*. The smallest note ever issued by a ban was the 10 bani note of the Ministry of Finance of Romania issued in 1917. It measured (printed area) 27,5 × 38 mm *1.09 × 1.49 in*. Of German *notgeld* the smallest are the 1–3 pfg of Passau (1920–21) measuring 18 × 18,5 mm *0.70 × 0.72 in*.

Highest denominations *World*
The highest denomination notes in circulation are US Federal Reserve Bank notes for $10,000 (£5260). They bear the head of Salmon Portland Chase (1808–73). None has been printed since July 1944 and the US Treasury announced in 1969 that no further notes higher than $100 would be issued. Only some 400 $10,000 bills remain in circulation.

Great Britain
Two Bank of England notes for £1,000,000 still exist, dated before 1812, but these were used only for internal accounting. In November 1977 the existence of a Treasury £1 million note dated 30 Aug 1948 came to light and was sold by private treaty for $A18,500 (*then £11,300*) in Australia.

The highest issued denominations were £1000 notes, first printed in 1725, discontinued on 22 Apr 1943 and withdrawn on 30 Apr 1945. A total of 16 of these notes were still unretired up to Nov 1979 (last data to be published). Of these only 4 are known to be in the hands of collectors.

Lowest denomination *World*
The lowest denomination bank note issued is the 1 cent Hong Kong note which is worth 1/12th of one new penny.

Great Britain
The lowest denomination Bank of England notes ever printed were half-crown (now 12½p) black on pale blue notes in 1941 signed by K. O. Peppiatt. Very few examples have survived and they are now valued at from £750.

Highest circulation
The highest ever Bank of England note circulation in the United Kingdom was £10,647 million on 27 May 1981—equivalent to a pile of £1 notes 529.20 miles *851,67 km* high.

CHEQUES
Largest *World*
The greatest amount paid by a single cheque in the history of banking has been one for Rs. 16,640,000,000 equivalent to £852,791,660 handed over by Hon. Daniel P. Moynihan Ambassador of the USA to India in New Delhi on 18 Feb 1974. An internal US Treasury cheque for $4,176,969,623.57 was drawn on 30 June 1954.

Largest *Great Britain*
The largest cheque drawn in Britain was one for £590,700,000 drawn on 27 Feb 1981 by British Petroleum Oil Development Ltd, payable to the Inland Revenue and signed in a ballpoint pen by David Cobbold.

COINS
Oldest *World*
The earliest certainly dated coins are the electrum (alloy of gold and silver) staters of Lydia, in Asia Minor (now Turkey), which were coined in the reign of King Gyges (*c.* 690–650 BC). Primitive uninscribed 'spade' money of the Chou dynasty of China is now *believed* to date from *c.* 770 BC. A discovery at Tappe Nush-i-jan, Iran, of silver ingot currency in 1972 has been dated to as early as 760 BC. The earliest dated coin is the Danish coin

the Bishop of Roskilde dated MCCXXXIIII (1234) of which 6 are known. Laos is the only country today without coins. Kampuchea abolished money under the Pol Pot regime in 1975 but re-introduced it in March 1980 with the riel as the monetary unit.

Oldest *Great Britain*
The earliest coins to circulate in Britain were Gallo-Belgic gold imitations of the Macedonian staters of Philip II (359–336 BC). The Bellovaci type has been tentatively dated *c.* 130 BC. The earliest date attributed to coins minted *in* Britain is *c.* 95 BC for the Westerham type gold stater of which 51 examples have been found.

Heaviest
A Swedish 10 daler copper plate of 1644 attained a weight of 43 lb 7¼ oz *19,710 kg.* Of primitive exchange tokens, the most massive are the holed stone discs, or *Fé*, from the Yap Islands, in the western Pacific Ocean, with diameters of up to 12 ft *3,65 m* and weighing up to 185 lb *84 kg.* A medium-sized one was worth one Yapese wife or an 18 ft *5,18 m* canoe. The 22 carat gold Kruger Kilo medallion issued in Feb 1981 weighs 1090,9 grams *38.48 oz.*

Smallest
The smallest coins in the world have been the Nepalese ¼ dam or Jawa struck *c.* 1740 in silver in the reign of Jeya Prakash Malla. The Jawa of between 0.008 and 0.014 g measuring about 2 × 2 mm were sometimes cut into ½ and even ¼ Jawa of 0.002 g or 14,000 to the oz.

Highest denomination *World*
The 1654 Indian gold 200 Mohur (£500) coin of the Mughal Emperor Khurram Shihāb-ud-dīn Muhammad, Shāh Jahān (reigned 1628–57), had the greatest intrinsic worth ever struck. It weighed 2177 g *70 troy oz* and hence has an intrinsic worth of £2800. It had a diameter of 5⅜ in *136 mm.* The only known example disappeared in Patna, Bihar, India, in *c.* 1820, but a plastercast of this coin exists in the British Museum, London. Currently the highest denomination is the Bahamian $2500 1977 gold coin 72 mm *2.8 in* in diameter struck by the Royal Canadian Mint, Ottawa. Each of the 250 examples struck contain 1 lb troy *435,4 g* of 22 carat gold.

Highest denomination *Great Britain*
Gold 5-guinea pieces were minted from the reign of Charles II (1660–85) until 1753 in the reign of George II. A pattern 5-guinea piece of George III dated 1777 also exists.

Lowest denomination *Great Britain*
Quarter farthings (sixteen to the penny) were struck in copper at the Royal Mint, London, in the Imperial coinage for use in Sri Lanka (then Ceylon), in 1839 and 1851–3.

Rarest *World*
There are numerous coins of which but a single example is known. An example of a unique coin of threefold rarity (in alloy, denomination and reign) is one of the rare admixture of bronze with inlaid gold of Kaleb I of Axum (*c.* AD 500). Only 700 Axumite coins of any sort are known.

Rarest *Modern British*
Single examples of a Victoria farthing of 1889, a George VI half-crown of 1952 and an Elizabeth II penny of 1954 are known. The penny was sold privately in March 1978 for £23,000.

Most expensive *World*
The highest price paid at auction for a single coin is $725,000 (*then £329,500*) for the uncirculated Garrett specimen of the gold Brasher doubloon struck in New York by Ephraim Brasher in 1787 of which only 7 are known. The bid was by lawyer Martin Monas for an undisclosed American collector at St. Moritz Hotel, New York City on 29 Nov 1979.

Most expensive *Great Britain*
The highest asking price for a British coin is £55,000 for a James VI of Scotland £20 gold piece of 1576 by Spink & Son of London on 1 May 1981.

An unissued silver Crown (5 shillings) piece of Edward VIII owned by Richard Lobel & Co. in London, was sold privately in February 1979 for £50,000. One example of the Edward VIII £5 gold piece is known to be in private hands in Ohio, USA.

Legal tender coins *Oldest*
The oldest legal tender Imperial coins in circulation are the now rare silver shillings (now 5p) and sixpences (now 2½p) of the reign of George III, dated 1816. All gold coinage of or above the least current weight dated onward from 1838 is still legal tender. Scotland's separate coinage dated only between 1135 and 1709.

Legal tender coins *Heaviest and highest denomination*
The gold five-pound (£5) piece or quintuple sovereign is both the highest current denomination coin in the United Kingdom and also, at 616.37 grains *1.4066 oz 39,94 grams* the heaviest. The most recent specimens made available to the public were dated 1980, of which only 10,000 were minted. Their diameter is 36,02 mm *1.418 in.*

Legal tender coins *Lightest and smallest*
The silver Maundy (new) penny piece is the smallest of the British legal tender coins and, at 7.27 grains (*just under* 1/60 oz), the lightest. These coins were so used since 1670 and exist for each date since 1822. They are 0.453 in. *11,5 mm* in diameter.

Greatest collection
The highest price paid for a coin collection has been $7,300,000 (*then £3,550,000*) for a hoard of 407,000 US silver dollars from the La Vere Redfield estate in a courtroom auction in Reno, Nevada on 27 Jan 1976 by Steven C. Markoff of A-Mark Coin Co. Inc. of Beverly Hills, California.

Largest hoards
The largest hoard ever found was one of about 80,000 aurei in Brescello near Modena, Italy in 1814 believed to have been deposited *c.* 37 BC. The numerically largest hoard ever found was the Brussels hoard of 1908 containing *c.* 150,000 coins. A hoard of 56,500 Roman coins was found at Cunetio near Marlborough, Wiltshire on 15 Oct 1978.

The greatest discovery of treasure is the estimated $2000 million of gold coins and platinum ingots from the sunken Tsarist battleship *Admiral Nakhimov* 8524 tons/*tonnes* 200 ft *60 m* down off the Japanese island of Tsushima. She sank on 27 May 1905.

Largest mint
The largest mint in the world is the US Treasury's mint built in 1965–9 on Independence Mall, Philadelphia, covering 11½ acres *4,65 ha* with an annual capacity on a 3 shift 7-day week production of 8000 million coins. A single stamping machine can produce coins at a rate of 10,000 per hour.

Charity walks
The greatest recorded amount raised by a single charity walk is HK $1.9 million (*then £172,727*) in the Community Chest of Hong Kong Walk on 2 Dec 1979. The most participants on one course were 57,000 in the Kowloon Walk over 14 miles *22,5 km* on 6 Mar 1977. The record raised by a single walker is £71,210 for the Royal Institution of Chartered Surveyors Benevolent Fund, by the Institution's Secretary-General, Robert Steel CBE, in a 1001 mile *1611 km* walk from John O'Groats to Lands End on 10 May–16 June 1979.

Largest charity collection
The most valuable column of coins amassed for charity was a column of 206,147 coins worth £4122.94 collected in 10 months by the villagers of Houghton and Wyton, Huntingdon for The Gloucester Centre for the Mentally Handicapped, Peterborough, 'knocked over' by Lord Renton, QC, Brian Rix and Ann Severs at The Three Jolly Butchers on 12 Dec 1980. The longest line of coins is 6,68 km *4.15 miles* (390,210 coins) in length laid by pupils at Manor Farm School, Rushall, Walsall on 23 Feb 1981. The highest value line was one of 5p pieces valued at £3335.10 laid by the Parents and Friends Association of Oundle Middle School, nr. Peterborough on 29 Nov 1980.

The 1084 ft *330,41 m* cream slice made by Fritz Strübin–Keller and the Bäckermeisterkegel-club on 10 June 1979 in Leistel, Switzerland (see p. 229).

LABOUR

Trade union Oldest *Great Britain*

The oldest of the 108 trade unions affiliated to the Trades Union Congress (founded 1868) is the National Society of Brush-makers and General Workers (current membership 1505) founded in 1747.

Trade union Largest *World*

The world's largest union is Solidarnosc (Solidarity) in Poland which by October 1980 was reported to have 8,000,000 members. The union with the longest name is probably the International Association of Marble, Slate and Stone Polishers, Rubbers and Sawyers, Tile and Marble Setters' Helpers and Marble Mosaic and Terrazzo Workers Helpers of Washington DC, USA.

Trade union Largest *Great Britain*

The largest union in the United Kingdom is the Transport and General Workers' Union, with 2,086,281 members at 1 May 1981.

Trade union Smallest

The smallest TUC affiliated unions are the Wool Shear Workers' Trade Union of Sheffield and the Cloth Pressers Society both with a membership of 30. The unaffiliated London Handforged Spoon and Fork Makers' Society instituted in July 1874, has a last reported membership of 6.

Labour dispute *Earliest*

A labour dispute concerning monotony of diet and working conditions was recorded in 1153 BC in Thebes, Egypt. The earliest recorded strike was one by an orchestra leader from Greece named Aristos in Rome *c.* 309 BC. The cause was meal breaks.

Labour dispute *Largest*

The most serious single labour dispute in the United Kingdom was the General Strike of 4–12 May 1926, called by the Trades Union Congress in support of the Miners' Federation. During the nine days of the strike 1,580,000 people were involved and 14,500,000 working days were lost.

During the year 1926 a total of 2,750,000 people were involved in 323 different labour disputes and the working days lost during the year amounted to 162,300,000, the highest figure ever recorded. The figure for 1980 was 11,910,000 working days involving 789,400 workers.

Labour dispute *Longest*

The world's longest recorded strike ended on 4 Jan 1961, after

33 years. It concerned the employment of barbers' assistants i Copenhagen, Denmark. The longest recorded major strike wa that at the plumbing fixtures factory of the Kohler Co. in She boygan, Wisconsin, USA, between April 1954 and Octobe 1962. The strike is alleged to have cost the United Automobil Workers' Union about $12,000,000 (*then £4.8 million*) t sustain.

Longest dispatch to Coventry

The longest recorded instance of a worker being 'sent t Coventry' by his fellow workers is 4 years 11 months endured b Mr Tommy Seddon of Droylsden, Greater Manchester from Dec 1970 until 7 Nov 1975 at the Wellman Gas Engineering Co

Unemployment *Highest*

The highest recorded unemployment in Great Britain was on 2 Jan 1933, when the total of unemployed persons on the Employ ment Exchange registers was 2,903,065, representing 22.8 pe cent of the insured working population. The highest figure fo Wales was 244,579 (39.1 per cent) on 22 Aug 1932.

Unemployment *Lowest*

In Switzerland in December 1973 (pop. 6.6 million), the tot number of unemployed was reported to be 81. The lowes recorded peace-time level of unemployment in Britain was 0. per cent on 11 July 1955, when 184,929 persons were registered The peak figure for the total working population in the Unite Kingdom has been 26,503,000 in September 1977.

Association *Largest*

The largest single association in the world is the Blue Cros system, the US-based hospital insurance organization with membership of 83,504,952 on 1 Jan 1981. Benefits paid out i 1980 totalled $20,755,113,000 (*£9434 million*). The largest as sociation in the United Kingdom is the Automobile Associatio (formed 1905) with a membership which reached 5,305,200 on Jan 1981.

Oldest Club

Britain's oldest gentleman's club is White's, St James', Londor opened *c.* 1697 by Francis White (d. 1711), as a Chocolat House, and moved to its present site in 37 St. James's in 1755 This has been described as an 'oasis in a desert of democracy' Britain's oldest known dining club is the 'Corporation of S Pancras' of Chichester, West Sussex, known as The Wheelbar row Club. It was formed on 4 Aug 1689 and is still in being.

CONSUMPTION

Prohibition

The longest lasting imposition of prohibition has been 26 year in Iceland (1908–34). Other prohibitions have been Russia, late USSR (1914–24) and USA (1920–33). The Faroe Islands hav had a public (as opposed to private licensed) prohibition sinc 1918. By way of contrast the Northern Territory of Australia' annual intake has been estimated to be as high as 416 pints *23 litres* per person. A society for the prevention of alcoholism i Darwin had to disband in June 1966 for lack of support. It is per haps noteworthy that the only parliamentary candidate o record in Britain ever to receive a nil vote was Mr F. R. Lees who described himself as a Temperance Chartist.

Biggest round

The largest round of drinks ever recorded was one for 122 people stood by the *Sunday Sun* and shouted by Jack Amos i Newcastle upon Tyne, England, in October 1974 at the con clusion of the Jack o' Clubs road show.

Largest dish

The largest menu item in the world is roasted camel, prepare occasionally for Bedouin wedding feasts. Cooked eggs ar stuffed in fish, the fish stuffed in cooked chickens, the chicken stuffed into a roasted sheep carcass and the sheep stuffed into whole camel.

Most expensive food

The most expensively priced food (as opposed to spice) is Roya de luxe caviar retailed at £224.50 per 500 grams *17.6 oz* at Fort num and Mason, London W.1

Longest banana split

The longest banana split ever made was one of 7005 ft *2135,1 m*

World's greatest consumers

Of all the countries in the world, based on the latest available data, Belgium—Luxembourg has the largest available total of calories per person. The net supply averaged 3645 per day in 1974. The United Kingdom average was 3349 per day in 1974. The lowest *reported* supply figures are 1728 calories per day in Upper Volta in 1974. It has been estimated that Britons eat 7¼ times their own weight in food per annum or 70,000 tons/*tonnes* per day. The highest calorific value of any foodstuff is that of pure animal fat with 930 calories per 100 g *3.5 oz*. Pure alcohol provides 710 calories per 100 g.

Below: The World's greatest consumers per head, per day. Figures in square brackets refer to UK consumption.

PROTEIN Australia and New Zealand 106 g *3.79 oz* (1969) [*88 g 3.1 oz (1968–9)*]

CEREALS[1] Egypt—600 g *21.95 oz* (1966–7) [*7.14 oz 202 g (1977)*]

SUGARS Bulgaria—177 g *6.26 oz* (1977) [*4.1 oz 116 g (1977)*]

MEAT USA—308 g *10.89 oz* (1977) [*193 g 6.8 oz (1977)*]

SWEETS Britain—1.20 oz *4,01 g* (1979)

TEA[2] Ireland 0.36 oz *10,2 g* (1977) [*0.314 oz 8,9 g (1977)*]

COFFEE[3] Sweden—32,18 g *1.13 oz* (1979–80) [*7,08 g 0.25 oz (1979–80)*]

FRESH WATER USA—1544 gal *7021 l* (1974)

BEER W. Germany—39,7 cl *0.699 pints* (1980) [*0.584 pints 33,2 cl (1980)*]

WINE France—25,1 cl *0.44 pints* (1980) [*0.030 pints 1,7 cl (1978)*]

SPIRITS Poland—1,53 cl *0.026 pints* (1978) [*0.008 pints 0,47 cl (1978)*]

[1] Figures for 1977 from China suggest a possible consumption (including rice) of 890 g *31.3 oz.*
[2] The most expensive tea marketed in the UK is 'Oolong Leaf Bud', specially imported for Fortnum & Mason of Piccadilly, City of Westminster, London. In July 1980 it retailed for £17.00 per lb or *£3.74/100 g*. It is blended from very young Formosan leaves. Tea-bags were invented by Thomas Sullivan of New York in 1904.
[3] The most expensive coffee in the US is Jamaican Blue Mountain which retails for up to $16.80 per lb *$37 per kg*.

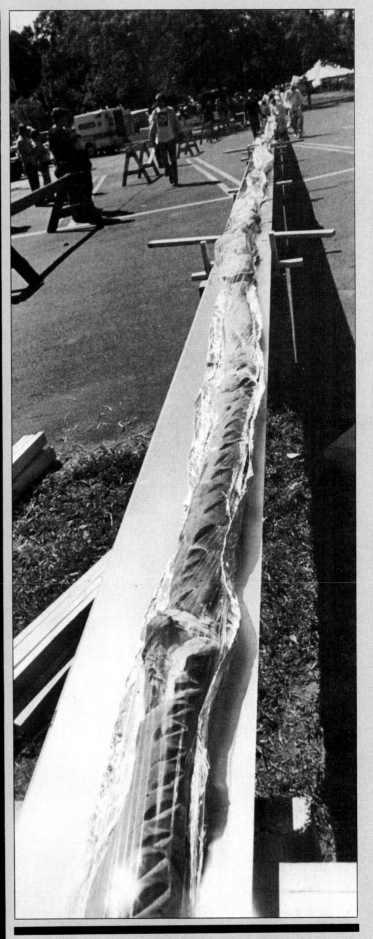

A loaf measuring just over ⅕th of a mile *322 m*, made by Franz Eichenauer and baked in one piece in an insulated aluminium pipe oven on 16 Sept 1979 at the Peekskill Riverfront Green in New York (see p. 228).

227

Economics

right: Over 4½ tons/*tonnes* of ice cream and toppings were used to concoct the world's largest sundae by students of the Mark Twain Summer Institute, Clayton, Missouri, USA (see p. 229).

below: The world's largest Yorkshire pudding, more than 60 ft² *5,5 m²*, baked for 7 hours on 4 June 1977 at Alwoodley, Leeds, W. Yorkshire (see p. 230).

(*1 mile 575 yd*) in length embracing 11,400 bananas, 1500 gal *6819 litres* of ice cream, 380 gal *1727 litres* of topping and 170 lb *77,1 kg* of nuts by the Alpha Phi Omega at Texas A & M University, Texas, USA, on 26 Apr 1980.

Largest barbecue
The most monumental barbecue has been one for 5,829 people at the West Pasco Sertoma Club of New Port Richey, Florida on 23 Mar 1980 serving 4036 lb *1830 kg* of meat. The 1979 annual Lancaster Sertoma in Pennsylvania, USA served 20,500 barbecued chickens.

Largest beefburger
The largest beefburger on record is one of 2859 lb *1293 kg* 27½ ft *8,38 m* in circumference exhibited by Tip Top Butchers and Noonan's Bakery Pty Ltd at the Perth Royal Show, Western Australia on 24 Sept 1975.

Largest cake
The largest cake ever assembled was the Baltimore City Bicentennial Cake on 4 July 1976 with ingredients weighing 69,860 lb or 31.18 tons *31,69 tonnes*. An estimated 10,000 dozen eggs, 21,600 lb *9797 kg* of sugar and a 415 lb *188 kg* pinch of salt were

used. The tallest recorded free-standing wedding cake was one of 48 tiers 32 ft 6 in *9,90 m* tall baked and constructed by Roy Butterworth and Frank Brennan for the incorporation of Bedford, Nova Scotia, Canada on 1 May 1980.

Largest Easter egg
The largest Easter egg ever made was one weighing 4737 lb *2148,6 kg*, measuring 12 ft *3,65 m* high, made outside The Royal Oak, Winterbourne, Bristol by Mark Harries and completed on 3 Apr 1980.

Largest haggis
The largest haggis (encased in 7 ox stomach linings) on record was one weighing 541½ lb *245,6 kg* for the CWS Hypermarket of Glasgow, Scotland by David A. Hall Ltd. of Broxburn Lothian, Scotland. The cooking time was 12 hr.

Longest loaf
The longest one-piece loaf ever baked was one of 1058 ft 10 in *322,7 m* created by Franz Eichenauer and baked at the Peekskill Riverfront Green, NY, USA, in an insulated aluminium pipe oven on 16 Sept 1979.

228

Largest apple pie
The largest apple pie ever baked was that in a 16 ft 8 in *5,08 m* diameter dish at the Orleans Country Fair, New York State, USA on 2–3 Aug 1977. Baking time of the 300 bushels of apples and 5950 lb *2,698 tonnes* of sugar was 4 hr 40 min. The total weight was 21,210 lb *9,62 tonnes*.

Largest cherry pie
The largest cherry pie ever made was one weighing a total of 6¼ tons *6350 kg* and containing 4950 lb *2245 kg* of cherries. It measured 14 ft 4 in *4,36 m* in diameter, 24 in *60,96 cm* in depth, and was baked in the grounds of the Medusa Cement Corporation, Charlevoix, Michigan on 15 May 1976, as part of the town's contribution to America's Bicentennial celebrations.

Largest meat pie
The largest meat pie ever baked weighed 5¾ tons, measuring 18 × 6 ft and 18 in deep *5,48 × 1,83 × 0,45 m*, the eighth in the series of Denby Dale, West Yorkshire pies, to mark four royal births, baked on 5 Sept 1964. The first was in 1788 to celebrate King George III's return to sanity, but the fourth (Queen Victoria's Jubilee, 1887) went a bit 'off' and had to be buried in quick-lime.

Largest mince pie
The largest mince pie recorded was one of 2260 lb *1025 kg* 20 × 5 ft *6,09 × 1,52 m*, baked at Ashby-de-la-Zouch, Leicestershire on 15 Oct 1932.

Largest omelette
The largest omelette in the world was one made of 12,440 eggs on a pan measuring 30 × 10 ft *9,1 × 3,04 m* cooked by students of Conestoga College, Kitchener, Ontario, Canada on 29 June 1979.

Longest pastry
The longest cream slice (*mille feuilles* invented in Florence in the 16th century) ever made was one 330,41 m *1084 ft* long by Fritz Strübin-Keller and the Bäckermeisterkegelclub in Liestel, Switzerland on 10 June 1979.

Largest pizza pie
The largest pizza ever baked was one measuring 80 ft 1 in *24,4 m* in diameter, hence 5037 ft² *468 m²* in area and 18,664 lb *8465 kg* in weight at the Oma Pizza Restaurant, Glen Falls, New York, USA owned by Lorenzo Amato on 8 Oct 1978. It was cut into 60,318 slices.

Potato mash
A single serving of 10,286 lb *4,66 tonnes* of potato mash was prepared at the Mantua Potato Festival, Ohio, USA in September 1980.

Largest iced lollipop
The world's largest iced lollipop was one of 5750 lb *2608 kg* constructed for the Westside Assembly of God Church, Davenport, Iowa, USA on 7 Sept 1975.

Blackpool rock
The mightiest piece of Blackpool lettered rock ever produced was a piece weighing more than 3 cwt *152 kg* delivered on 16 Apr 1975 to the Royal Variety Club of Great Britain in London by Ashton Candy Co. Ltd. of Blackpool.

Largest salami
The largest salami on record was one 18 ft 10 in *5,74 m* long with a circumference of 28 in *71 cm*, weighing 457 lb *207,2 kg* made by La Ron Meat Co., Cosby, Missouri, USA on 29 Jan 1978.

Longest sausage
The longest continuous sausage ever recorded was one of 2.37 miles *3,81 km*, made in the village of Trets, Aix-en-Provence, France for a local celebration on 21 May 1980.

Largest sundae
The largest ice cream sundae ever concocted is one of 9,616 lb *4361 kg* plus 90 lb *40,8 kg* of nuts, 250 lb *113,4 kg* of chocolate, 250 lb *113,4 kg* of strawberry topping and 65.6 lb *29,7 kg* of instant whip, constructed by students of the Mark Twain Summer Institute, Clayton, Mo., USA on 2 Sept 1979.

Preparing to bake the world's largest pizza, 80 ft 1 in *24,4 m* in diameter made by Lorenzo Amato of Glen Falls, NY, USA.

Largest Yorkshire pudding

The largest Yorkshire pudding on record is one measuring 16½ × 3¾ ft *5,02 × 1,14 m* baked for 7 hr at 'The Jester', Alwoodley, Leeds, West Yorkshire by Ian Ghiloni and Mark Harries on 4 June 1977.

Top selling sweet

The world's top selling sweets (candies) are Life Savers with 29,651,840,000 rolls between 1913 and 30 June 1980. A tunnel formed by the holes in the middle placed end to end would stretch to the moon and back 3 times. Paul Shirley, 21, of Sydney made one last for 4 hr 40 min on 15 Feb 1979.

Spice *Most expensive*

Prices for wild ginseng (root of *Panax quinquefolius*), from the Chan Pak Mountain area of China thought to have aphrodisiac qualities were reported in November 1977 to be as high as $23,000 (*then £10,454*) per ounce in Hong Kong. Total annual shipments from Jilin Province do not exceed 4 kg *140 oz* a year. The leading medical journal in the USA has likened its effects to 'corticosteroid poisoning'.

Spice *'Hottest'*

The hottest of all spices is claimed to be Siling labuyo from the Philippines.

Most Expensive fruit

On 5 Apr 1977 John Synnott of Ashford, Co. Wicklow, Ireland sold 1 lb *453 g* of strawberries (a punnet of 30 berries) to the restaurateur, Mr Leslie Cooke, at auction by Walter L. Cole Ltd. in the Dublin Fruit Market for £530 or £17.70 a berry.

Rarest condiment

The world's most prized condiment is Cà Cuong, a secretion recovered in minute amounts from beetles in northern Vietnam. Owing to war conditions, the price rose to $100 (*now £57*) per ounce *28 g* before supplies virtually ceased in 1975.

ENERGY CONSUMPTION

To express the various forms of available energy (coal, liquid fuels and water power, etc., but omitting vegetable fuels and peat), it is the practice to convert them all into terms of coal.

The highest consumption in the world is in the United States, with an average of 11 500 kg *226.0 cwt* per person. With only 5.3 per cent of the world's population the US consumes 28.6 per cent of the world's gasoline and 32.9 per cent of the world's electric power. The United Kingdom average was 6365 kg *125.2 cwt* per person in 1979. The lowest recorded average for 1974 was 13 kg *28.6 lb* per person in Rwanda.

MASS COMMUNICATIONS

Airline

The country with the busiest airlines system is the United States of America where 269,599,679,000 revenue passenger miles were flown on scheduled domestic and local services in 1979. This was equivalent to an annual trip of 1200.3 miles *1931,7 km* for every one of the inhabitants of the USA. It was estimated in 1978 that only 37% of adult Americans had not flown in their lives. The United Kingdom airlines flew 625,957,000 miles *1 007 380 100 km* and carried 35,172,279 passengers in 1980.

Merchant shipping

The world total of merchant shipping, excluding vessels of less than 100 tons gross, sailing vessels and barges, was 71,129 vessels of 413,021,426 tons gross on 1 July 1979. The largest merchant fleet in the world as at mid-1979 was that under the flag of Liberia with 2466 ships of 81,528,175 tons gross. The UK figure for mid-1979 was 3211 ships of 27,951,342 tons gross.

Largest and busiest ports

Physically, the largest port in the world is the Port of New York and New Jersey, USA. The port has a navigable waterfront of 755 miles *1215 km* (295 miles *474 km* in New Jersey) stretching over 92 miles² *238 km²*. A total of 261 general cargo berths and 130 other piers give a total berthing capacity of 391 ships at one time. The total warehousing floor space is 422.4 acres *170,9 ha*. The world's busiest port and largest artificial harbour is the

Rotterdam-Europoort in the Netherlands which cove 38 miles² *100 km²*. It handled 29,859 sea-going vessels carrying total of 286 million tonnes of sea-going cargo, and about 200,0 barges in 1980. It is able to handle 310 sea-going vessels sim taneously of up to 318,000 tonnes and 68 ft *20,72 m* draught.

Railways

The country with the greatest length of railway is the Unit States, with 213,835 miles *344 134 km* of track at 1 Jan 197 The farthest anyone can get from a railway on the mainla island of Great Britain is 110 miles *177 km* by road in the case Southend, Mull of Kintyre.

The number of journeys made on British Rail in 1980 w 760,192,000 (average 25.9 miles *41,6 km*) compared with t peak year of 1957, when 1101 million journeys (avera 20.51 miles *33 km*) were made.

Road *Oldest*

The oldest trackway yet discovered in the world is the Swe track, Shapwick, Somerset which has been dated to 4000 B The first sod on Britain's first motorway, the M6 Preston B Pass, was cut by bulldozer driver Fred Hackett on 12 June 19 on the section between junctions 29 and 32 opened in Decemb 1958.

Road *Mileages*

The country with the greatest length of road is the United Stat (all 50 States), with 3,885,452 miles *6 253 028 km* of grade roads at 1 Jan 1978. Regular driving licences are issuable at 1 without a driver education course only in Hawaii and Missis ippi. Thirteen US States issue restricted juvenile licences at 1

The United Kingdom has 224,612 miles *361 401 km* of ro including 1537 miles *2474 km* of motorway at 1 Apr 1979 a 18,625,000 vehicles in 1980.

The $3500 million Interstate 75, opened on 21 Dec 1977, no runs 1564 miles *2517 km* from Sault St Marie, Michigan Tampa, Florida without a traffic light. The longest uninterrupt ted dual carriageway is from Plymouth to Exeter (A38) a thence by the M5 and M6 for 515 miles *829 km* to Greenloanin north of Stirling, Scotland. The Interstate Highway I-80 f New York City to Salt Lake City, Utah is 2180 miles *3508 k* long.

Traffic volume *Highest*

The highest traffic volume of any point in the world is at the Ea Los Angeles interchange (Santa Ana, Pomona, Golden State a Santa Monica Freeways), California, USA with a 24-hr averag on weekdays of 547,600 vehicles in 1980—over 380 per minut The most heavily travelled stretch of road is between 43rd a 47th Street on the Dan Ryan Expressway, Chicago with a average daily volume of 254,700 vehicles.

The territory with the highest traffic density in the world Hong Kong. By 1 Jan 1977 there were 191,146 motor vehicles 678 miles *1091 km* of serviceable roads giving a density 6.24 yd *5,70 m* per vehicle. The comparative figure for Gre Britain in 1979 was 21.2 yd *19,40 m*.

The greatest traffic density at any one point in Great Britain is Hyde Park Corner, London. The average daytime 8 a.m 8 p.m. flow in 1970 (last census) was 164,338 vehicles eve 12 hr. The busiest Thames bridge in 1976 was Putney Bridg with a 24-hr average of 63,000 vehicles. The greatest reporte aggregation of London buses was 52, bumper to bumper, alor Oxford Street on 13 Feb 1976.

Traffic jams *Largest*

The longest traffic jam ever reported was that of 16 Feb 198 which stretched northwards from Lyon 176 km *109.3 mi* towards Paris. The longest traffic jam reported in Britain w one of 35 miles *56 km* out of 42.5 miles *75,6 km* road length b tween Torquay and Yarcombe, Devon, on 25 July 1964 a 35 miles *56 km* on the A30 between Egham, Surrey and Miche dever, Hampshire on 23 May 1970.

Road *Widest*

The widest street in the world is the Monumental Axis running for 1½ miles *2,4 km* from the Municipal Plaza to the Plaza of the Three Powers in Brasilia, the capital of Brazil. The six-lane Boulevard was opened in April 1960 and is 250 m *273.4 yd* wide. The San Francisco–Oakland Bay Bridge Toll Plaza has 23 lanes (17 west bound) serving the Bridge in Oakland, California.

The only instance of 17 carriageway lanes side by side in Britain occurs on the M61 at Linnyshaw Moss, Worsley, Greater Manchester.

Road *Narrowest*

The world's narrowest street is in Port Isaac, Cornwall at the junction of Temple Bar and Dolphin Street. It is popularly known as 'Squeeze-belly alley' and is 19⁵/₁₆ in *49 cm* wide at its narrowest point.

Road *Longest*

The longest motorable road in the world is the Pan-American Highway, which will stretch 17,018 miles *27 387 km* from North West Alaska to southernmost Chile. There remains a gap known as the Tapon del Darién, in Panama and the Atrato Swamp, Colombia. This was first traversed by the land rover La Cucaracha Carinosa (The Affectionate Cockroach) of the Trans-Darien Expedition 1959–60 crewed by former SAS man Richard E Bevir (UK) and engineer Terence John Whitfield (Australia). They left Chepo, Panama on 3 Feb 1960 and reached Quibdó, Colombia on 17 June averaging 220 yd *201 m* per hour of indescribable difficulty. The Range Rover VXC 868K of the British Trans-Americas Expedition was the first vehicle to cover the whole route leaving Alaska on 3 Dec 1971 and arriving in Tierra del Fuego on 9 June 1972.

Most complex interchange

The most complex interchange on the British road system is that at Gravelly Hill, north of Birmingham on the Midland Link Motorway section of the M6 opened on 24 May 1972. There are 18 routes on 6 levels together with a diverted canal and river, which consumed 26,000 tons/*tonnes* of steel, 250,000 tons/*tonnes* of concrete, 300,000 tons/*tonnes* of earth and cost £8,200,000.

Street *Longest World*

The longest designated street in the world is Yonge Street running north and west from Toronto, Canada. The first stretch completed on 16 Feb 1796 ran 34 miles 53 chains *55,783 km*. Its official length now extended to Rainy River at the Ontario–Minnesota border is 1178.3 miles *1896,2 km*

Longest *Great Britain*

The longest designated road in Great Britain is the A1 from London to Edinburgh of 404 miles *650 km*. The longest Roman roads were Watling Street, from Dubrae (Dover) 215 miles *346 km* through Londinium (London) to Viroconium (Wroxeter), and Fosse Way, which ran 218 miles *350 km* from Lindum (Lincoln) through Aquae Sulis (Bath) to Isca Dumnoniorum (Exeter). However, a 10 mile *16 km* section of Fosse Way between Ilchester and Seaton remains indistinct. The commonest street name in Greater London is High Street (119) followed by Station Road (100).

Shortest

The title of 'The Shortest Street in the World' has been claimed since 1907 by McKinley Street in Bellefontaine, Ohio, USA built of 'vitrified brick' and measuring 30 ft *9,14 m* in length. The shortest reported measurement of a street in Britain is 58 ft *17,67 m* of Tolbooth Street, Falkirk, Central, Scotland. The shortest length of restricted road is probably Kelbrook Road, Salterforth, Lancashire with 336½ ft *102,5 m* between 30 mph signs, seemingly too short to sustain a speeding conviction.

Steepest

The steepest streets in the world are Filbert Street, Russian Hill and 22nd Street, Dolores Heights, San Francisco with gradients of 31.5 per cent or 1 in 3.17. Lombard Street between Leavenworth and Hyde with 8 consecutive 90 degree turns of 20 ft *6,1 m* radius is described as the 'Crookedest street in the world'. Britain's steepest motorable road is the unclassified Chimney Bank which is signposted '1 in 3' at Rosedale Abbey, North Yorkshire. The County Surveyor states it is 'not quite' a 33 per cent gradient.

Longest hill

The longest steep hill on any road in the United Kingdom is on the road westwards from Lochcarron towards Applecross in Highland, Scotland. In 6 miles *9,6 km* this road rises from sea-level to 2054 ft *626 m* with an average gradient of 1 in 15.4, the steepest part being 1 in 4.

Of the five unclassified roads with 1 in 3 gradients the most severe is Hard Knott Pass between Boot and Ambleside, Cumbria.

Road *Highest World*

The highest trail in the world is an 8 mile *13 km* stretch of the Kang-ti-suu between Khaleb and Hsin-chi-fu, Tibet which in two places exceeds 20,000 ft *6080 m*. The highest carriageable road in the world is one 1180 km *733.2 miles* long between Tibet and south western Sinkiang, completed in October 1957, which takes in passes of an altitude up to 18,480 ft *5632 m* above sea-level. Europe's highest pass (excluding the Caucasian passes) is the Col de Restefond (9193 ft *2802 m*) completed in 1962 with 21 hairpins between Jausiers and Saint Etienne-de-Tinée, France. It is usually closed between early October and early June. The highest motor road in Europe is the Pico de Veleta in the Sierra Nevada, southern Spain. The shadeless climb of 36 km *22.4 miles* brings the motorist to 11,384 ft *3469 m* above sea-level and became, on completion of a road on its southern side in Summer 1974, arguably Europe's highest 'pass'.

Highest *Great Britain*

The highest road in the United Kingdom is the A6293 unclassified tarmac, private extension at Great Dun Fell, Cumbria, (2780 ft *847 m*) leading to a Ministry of Defence and Air Traffic Control installation. A permit is required to use it. The highest public classified road in England is the A689 at Killhope Cross (2056 ft *626 m*) on the Cumbria-Durham border near Nenthead. The highest classified road in Scotland is the A93 road over the Grampians through Cairnwell, a pass between Blairgowrie, Tayside, and Braemar, Grampian, which reaches a height of 2199 ft *670 m*. The highest classified road in Wales is the Rhondda-Afan Inter-Valley road (A4107), which reaches 1750 ft *533 m* 2½ miles *4 km* east of Abergwynfi, Mid Glamorgan. An estate track exists to the summit of Ben a'Bhuird (3860 ft *1176 m*) in Grampian, Scotland. The highest motorway in Great Britain is the trans-Pennine M62, which, at the Windy Hill interchange, reaches an altitude of 1220 ft *371 m*. Its Dean Head cutting is the deepest roadway cutting in Europe at 183 ft *55,7 m*.

Lowest

The lowest road in the world is that along the Israeli shores of the Dead Sea, 1290 ft *393 m* below sea-level. The lowest surface roads in Great Britain are just below sea-level in the Holme Fen area of Cambridgeshire. The world's lowest 'pass' is Rock Reef Pass, Everglades National Park, Florida which is 3 ft *91 cm* above sea-level.

Longest viaduct

The longest elevated road viaduct on the British road system is the 2.97 mile *4779 m* Gravelly Hill to Castle Bromwich section of the M6. It was completed in May 1972.

Biggest square

The Tian an men (Gate of Heavenly Peace) Square in Peking, described as the navel of China, extends over 98 acres *39,6 ha*. The Maiden e Shah in Isfahan, Iran extends over 20.1 acres *8,1 ha*. The oldest London Square is Lincoln's Inn Fields dating to the mid 17th century. The largest is the 6.99 acre *2,82 ha* Ladbroke Square (open to residents only) constructed in 1842–45 while Lincoln's Inn Fields measures 6.84 acres *2,76 ha*.

Traffic lights

Semaphore-type traffic *signals* had been set up in Parliament Square, London in 1868 with red and green gas lamps for night use. It was not an offence to disobey traffic signals until assent was given to the 1930 Road Traffic Bill. Traffic *lights* were introduced in Great Britain with a one-day trial in Wolverhampton on 11 Feb 1928. They were first permanently operated in Leeds,

POSTAGE STAMPS

EARLIEST	Put on sale at GPO 1 May 1840	1d Black of Great Britain, Queen Victoria, 68,158,080 printed. Available for pre-payment of postage on 6 May 1840.
HIGHEST PRICE (TENDER) (WORLD)	$1 million (£465,000)	5 cent Blue Alexandria USA cover, 1846 by George Normann *via* David Feldman, Geneva on 9 May 1981.
HIGHEST PRICE (AUCTION) (WORLD)	$850,000 (£380,000)	British Guiana 1c magenta provisional post-marked 'Ap.4 1856' by Irwin R. Weinberg syndicate to anonymous collector at Waldorf-Astoria, New York City on 5 Apr 1980.
HIGHEST PRICE (ERROR)	$500,000 (£227,500)	US 1918 24 cent airmail invert of Jenny biplane 'Princeton' block of 4, by Myron Kaller syndicate on 19 July 1979.
HIGHEST PRICE (AUCTION) (UK)	£50,000 £50,000	1d 'Perot' of Bermuda, 1854, at Stanley Gibbons, London on 4 Oct 1973. 1d orange-red of Mauritius, 1847, by M. René Berlingen at Stanley Gibbons, London on 25 Nov 1976.
HIGHEST PRICE (PHILATELIC ITEM) (UK)	£75,000	Pair of 2 cent 'Cotton Reels' of British Guiana (now Guyana) on envelope dated 26 Nov 1851 sold by F. T. Small, by Robson Lowe at Christie's, London on 21 Mar 1970.
LARGEST PHILATELIC PURCHASE	$11,000,000 (£4,545,000)	Marc Haas collection of 3000 US postal and pre-postal covers to 1869 by Stanley Gibbons International Ltd of London in August 1979.
LARGEST (SPECIAL PURPOSE) (STANDARD POSTAGE)	9¾ × 2¾ in *247,5 × 69,8 mm* 6.3 × 4.33 in *160 × 110 mm*	Express Delivery of China, 1913. Marshall Islands 75 cents issued 30 Oct 1979.
SMALLEST	0.31 × 0.37 in *8 × 9,5 mm*	10 cent and 1 peso Colombian State of Bolivar, 1863–6.
HIGHEST DENOMINATION (WORLD) (UK)	£100 £5	Red and black, George V, of Kenya, 1925–7. Orange, Victoria, issued 21 Mar 1882. Pink and Blue Elizabeth II definitive 2 Feb 1977.
LOWEST DENOMINATION	3,000 pengö of Hungary	Issued 1946 when 150 million million pengö = 1p.
RAREST (WORLD)	Unique examples include	British Guiana (now Guyana) 1 cent black on magenta of 1856 (see above); Swedish 3 skilling banco yellow colour error of 1855. Gold Coast provisional of 1885 and US postmaster stamps from Boscowen, New Haven and Lockport, NY.
RAREST (UK) (Issued for postal use)	11 or 12	6d dull purple Inland Revenue Edward VII, issued and withdrawn on 14 May 1904. Only unused specimen in private hands from W. H. Harrison-Cripps sold by Stanley Gibbons for £10,000 on 27 Oct 1972.

West Yorkshire on 16 Mar and in Edinburgh, Scotland on 19 Mar 1928. The first vehicle-actuated lights were installed at the Cornhill-Gracechurch Junction, City of London in 1932.

Parking meters
The earliest parking meters ever installed were those put in the business district of Oklahoma City, Oklahoma, USA, on 19 July 1935. They were the invention of Carl C. Magee (USA) and reached London in 1958.

Worst driver
It was reported that a 75-year-old *male* driver received 10 traffic tickets, drove on the wrong side of the road four times, committed four hit-and-run offences and caused six accidents, all within 20 minutes, in McKinney, Texas, USA, on 15 Oct 1966. The most heavily banned driver in Britain was John Hogg, 28, who, in the High Court, Edinburgh on 27 Nov. 1975, received 5¾ years in gaol and his 3rd, 4th and 5th life bans for drunken driving in a stolen car while disqualified. For his previous 40 offences he had received bans of 71½ years plus two life bans.

Milestone
Britain's oldest milestone *in situ* is a Roman stone dating from AD 150 on the Stanegate, at Chesterholme, near Bardon Mill, Northumberland.

Longest ford
The longest ford in any classified road in England is that at Bilbrook, Old Cleeve parish, Somerset which measures 90 yd *82 m* in width.

Inland waterways
The country with the greatest length of inland waterways is Finland. The total length of navigable lakes and rivers is about 50 000 km *31,000 miles*. In the United Kingdom the total length of navigable rivers and canals is 3940 miles *6340 km*.

Longest navigable river
The longest navigable natural waterway in the world is the River Amazon, which sea-going vessels can ascend as far as Iquitos, in Peru, 2236 miles *3598 km* from the Atlantic seaboard. On a National Geographic Society expedition ending on 10 Mar 1969,

Helen and Frank Schreider navigated downstream from San Francisco, Peru, a distance of 3845 miles *6187 km* to Bélem.

TELECOMMUNICATIONS
Telephones
There were 448,250,000 telephones in the world at 1 Jan 1979 as estimated by The American Telephone & Telegraph Co. The country with the greatest number was the United States, with 168,994,000 instruments, equivalent to 770 for every 1000 people or in 96 of every 100 households. This compares with the United Kingdom figure of 24,934,670 (third largest in the world to the USA and Japan), or 446 per 1000 people. The territory with fewest reported telephones is Pitcairn Island with 28 for a population of 70. The country with the lowest proportion is Upper Volta with less than 1 telephone per 100.

The greatest total of calls made in any country is in the United States, with 239,641 million (1090 calls per person) in 1978. The United Kingdom telephone service connected 19,352,400,000 calls, an average of 347 per person.

The city with most telephones is New York City, NY, USA with 5,847,731 (808 per 1000 people) at 1 Jan 1979. In 1979 Washington DC reached the level of 1588 telephones per 1000 people though in some small areas there are still higher densities such as Beverly Hills, Los Angeles County with an estimated level above 1600 per 1000.

Telephones *Busiest Phone*
The pay phone with the heaviest usage in the world is one in the Greyhound bus terminal, Chicago, which averages 270 calls a day. It is used each 5 min 20 sec round the clock all year.

Telephones *Longest telephone cable*
The world's longest submarine telephone cable is the Commonwealth Pacific Cable (COMPAC), which runs for more than 9000 miles *14 480 km* from Australia, *via* Auckland, New Zealand and the Hawaiian Islands to Port Alberni, Canada. It cost about £35,000,000 and was inaugurated on 2 Dec 1963.

Telephones *Bill Most Incorrect*
On 18 Aug 1975 the landlord of the Blue Bell Inn, Lichfield

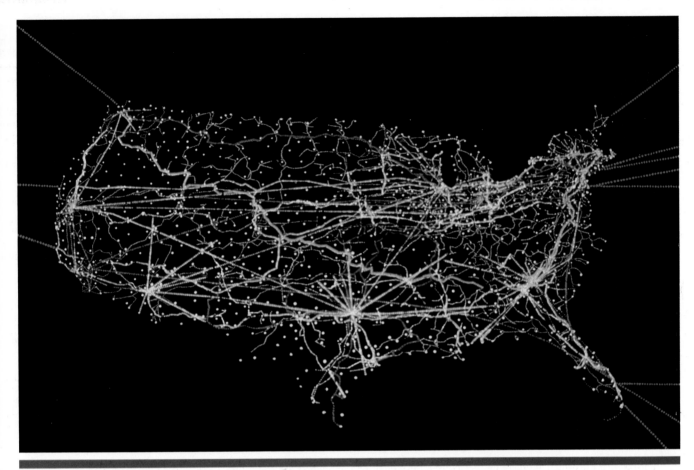

A graphic interpretation of the world's most extensive telecommunications network outlining the 48 coterminous United States. (*AT & T photo/Graphics Center*)

Staffordshire received a bill for £1,494,000,000. The Post Office admitted it contained 'an arithmetical error'.

Postal services

The country with the largest mail in the world is the United States, whose population posted over 106 billion letters and packages in 1980 when the US Postal Service employed 666,823 people. The United Kingdom total was 10,208 million letters and 180 million parcels in the year ending 31 Mar 1980.

The United States also takes first place in the average number of letters which each person posts during one year. The figure was 480 in 1980. The United Kingdom figure was 182 per head in 1979–80.

Postal address *Highest numbering*

The practice of numbering houses began in 1463 on the Pont Notre Dame, Paris, France. The highest numbered house in Britain is No 2679 Stratford Road, Hockley Heath, West Midlands, owned since 1964 by Mr and Mrs Howard Hughes. The highest numbered house in Scotland is No 2629 London Road, Mount Vernon, Glasgow, which is part of the local police station.

Pillar-boxes *Oldest*

The oldest site on which a pillar-box is still in service is one dating from 8 Feb 1853 in Union Street, St Peter Port, Guernsey, though the present box is not the original. The oldest original box (still in use) in Great Britain is another Victorian example at Barnes Cross, Holwell (postally in Bishop's Caundle), Dorset, also dating from probably later in 1853.

Post Offices

The Post Office's northernmost post office is at Haroldswick, Unst, Shetland Islands. The most southerly in the British Isles is at Samarès, Jersey. The oldest is at Sanquhar, Dumfries and Galloway which was first referred to in 1763. In England the Post Office at Shipton-Under-Wychwood, Oxfordshire dates back to April 1845.

The longest counter in Britain is one of 185 ft *56,38 m* with 33 positions opened in 1962 at Trafalgar Square, London. It is open 24 hr a day, 7 days a week. The biggest sorting office is that of 17½ acres *6,75 ha* in Birmingham with a capacity of 3,500,000 items per day.

Telegrams

The country where most telegrams are sent is the USSR, whose population sent 492,631,000 telegrams in 1978. The United Kingdom total was 7,833,000 including 4,461,000 sent overseas, in the year ending 31 Mar 1980.

7. EDUCATION

Illiteracy

Literacy is variously defined as 'ability to read simple subjects' and 'ability to read and write a simple letter'. The looseness of definition and the scarcity of data for many countries preclude anything more than approximations, but the extent of illiteracy among adults (15 years old and over) is estimated to have been 34.7 per cent in 1969. The continent with the greatest proportion of illiterates is Africa, where 81.5 per cent of adults are illiterate. The last published figure for Mali in 1960 showed 97.8 per cent of people over 15 were unable to read.

University Oldest *World*

Probably the oldest educational institution in the world is the University of Karueein, founded in AD 859 in Fez, Morocco. The University of Bologna was founded in 1088.

University Oldest *Great Britain*

The oldest university in the United Kingdom is the University of Oxford, which came into being in *c*. 1167. The oldest of the existing colleges is probably University College (1249), though its foundation is less well documented than that of Merton College in 1264. The earliest college at Cambridge University is Peterhouse, founded in 1284. The largest college at either

233

university is Trinity College, Cambridge. It was founded in 1546. The oldest university in Scotland is the University of St. Andrews, Fife. It was established in 1411.

University *Greatest enrolment*
The university with the greatest enrolment in the world is the State University of New York, USA, with 344,000 students enrolled in 1978. Its oldest college at Albany, New York was founded in 1844. Britain's largest university is the University of London with 40,539 internal students and 20,353 external students (in 1980–81) so totalling 60,892. The Open University, first called the University of the Air (Royal Charter 30 May 1969) at Walton Hall near Milton Keynes has 5520 part-time tutors and 75,000 students.

University *Largest*
Tenders for the $3.4 billion (*£1790 million*) University of Riyadh, Saudi Arabia closed in June 1978. The University will house 15,000 families and have its own mass transport system.

The largest existing university building in the world is the M. V. Lomonosov State University on the Lenin Hills, south of Moscow, USSR. It stands 240 m *787.4 ft* tall, has 32 storeys and contains 40,000 rooms. It was constructed in 1949–53.

University *Most northerly*
The world's most northerly university is Inupiat University of the Arctic Barrow, Alaska, USA in *Lat 71° 16′ N*. Eskimo subjects feature in the curricula.

Largest court or quadrangle
The largest College quadrangle at any Oxford or Cambridge college is the Great Court, Trinity College, Cambridge completed in 1605. Its dimensions average 325 ft × 273 ft *99,06 m × 83,2 m*.

Professor *Youngest*
The youngest at which anybody has been elected to a chair in a university is 19 years in the case of Colin MacLaurin (1698–1746), who was admitted to Marischal College, Aberdeen as Professor of Mathematics on 30 Sept 1717. In 1725 he was made Professor of Mathematics at Edinburgh University on the recommendation of Sir Isaac Newton. Dr Harvey Martin Friedman, PhD, (b. 23 Sept 1948) was appointed Assistant Professor of Logic at Stanford University, California, USA on 1 Sept 1967—3 weeks before his 19th birthday.

Professors *Most durable*
The longest period of which any professorship has been held is 63 years in the case of Thomas Martyn (1735–1825), Professor of Botany at Cambridge University from 1762 until his death. His father, John Martyn (1699–1768), had occupied the chair from 1733 to 1762. Dr Joel Hildebrand (b. 16 Nov 1881), Professor Emeritus of Physical Chemistry at the University of California, Berkeley, became first an Assistant Professor in 1913 and in 1981 published his 275th research paper.

Senior Wranglers
Since 1910 the Wranglers (first class honours students in the Cambridge University mathematical Tripos, part 2) have been placed in alphabetical order only. In 1890 Miss P. G. Fawcett of Newnham was placed 'above the Senior Wrangler'.

Youngest undergraduate and graduate
The most extreme recorded case of undergraduate juvenility was that of William Thomson (1824–1907), later Lord Kelvin, OM, GCVO, who entered Glasgow University aged 10 years 4 months in October 1834 and matriculated on 14 Nov 1834. Dr Merrill Kenneth Wolf (b. 28 Aug 1931) of Cleveland, Ohio took his B.A. in music from Yale University in September 1945 in the month of his 14th birthday.

School *Oldest in Britain*
The title of the oldest existing school in Britain is contested. It is claimed that King's School in Canterbury, Kent, was a foundation of Saint Augustine, some time between his arrival in Kent in AD 597 and his death in *c*. 604. Cor Tewdws (College of Theodosius) at Llantwit Major, South Glamorgan, reputedly burnt down in AD 446, was refounded, after an elapse of 62 years, by St Illtyd in 508 and flourished into the 13th century.

School Largest *World*
At the time of its highest enrolments the largest school in the world was the De Witt Clinton High School in the Bronx, New York City, NY, USA, with a peak of 12,000 in 1934. It was founded in 1897 and now has an enrolment of 4500.

Great Britain
The school with the most pupils in Great Britain was Exmouth Comprehensive, Devon with 2582 (1979-80). The highest enrolment in Scotland has been at Our Lady's Roman Catholic High School, Motherwell, Strathclyde with a peak of 2325 in August 1977. The total in Holy Child School, Belfast, Northern Ireland reached 2752 in 1973 before being split up. Britain's most cosmopolitan school is reputed to be Hallfield Infant's School, Queensway, London with 51 nationalities in 1979.

Correspondence School *Largest*
The Extension Course Institute of the US Department of the Air Forces at Gunter, Alabama founded on 1 May 1950 had, by 1 Jan 1980, over 8 million graduates. Enrolments have attained levels in excess of 430,000.

School Most Expensive *World*
L'Institut 'Le Rosey' at Rolle, Switzerland charges annual fees of at least 25,000 Sw Fr or £5820.

The most expensive US college in 1981 was Bennington College, Vermont at $10,560 (*£5280*) for tuition, room and board—$20 p.a. more than Harvard.

Great Britain
The most expensive school in Great Britain is Millfield (founded 1935) in Street, Somerset (headmaster C. R. M. Atkinson). The annual fee for boarding entries in 1981–2 is £5100. The most expensive girls' school in 1981 was Benenden, Kent (founded 1923) with annual fees of £3240.

Oldest old school tie
The practice of wearing distinctive neckties bearing the colours of registered designs of schools, universities, sports clubs, regiments, etc., appears to date from *c*. 1880. The practice originated in Oxford University, where boater bands were converted into use as 'ribbon ties'. The earliest definitive evidence stems from an order from Exeter College for college ties, dated 25 June 1880.

PTA Oldest
The Parent-Teacher Association with the earliest foundation date in Britain is St. Christopher School, Letchworth, Parents' Circle formed in 1919.

Most schools
The greatest documented number of schools attended by a pupil is 265 by Wilma Williams, now Mrs R. J. Horton, from 1933–43 when her parents were in show business in the USA.

Most 'O' and 'A' levels
Francis L. Thomason of Tottenham, London had by January 1977 accumulated 37 O, 8 A and 1 S levels making a total of 46. A. F. Prime, a prisoner in HM Prison Portsmouth, has a total of 10 A's and 36 O's to July 1980. Environmental difficulties make study far harder in prison than elsewhere.

Stephen Murrell of Crown Woods School, Eltham passed 8 A levels at one sitting in June 1978 achieving 7 at grade A. Robert Pidgeon (b. 7 Feb 1959) of St Peter's School, Bournemouth, secured 13 O level passes at grade A at one sitting in the summer of 1975. Subsequently he passed 3 A levels at grade A and 2 S levels with firsts. Andrew Maclaren of Chelmsford, Essex passed 14 O levels, 5 A levels all at grade A and 3 S levels at grade one—making 22 top grades.

Youngest headmaster
The youngest headmaster of a major public school was Henry Montagu Butler (b. 2 July 1833), appointed Headmaster of Harrow School on 16 Nov 1859, when aged 26 years 137 days. His first term in office began in January 1860.

Most durable teachers
David Rhys Davies (1835–1928) taught as a pupil teacher and

latterly as teacher and headmaster of Dame Anna Child's School, Whitton, Powys (1879–1928) for a total of 76 years 2 months. Col Ernest Achey Loftus CBE, TD, DL (b. 11 Jan 1884) served as a teacher over a span of 73 years from May 1901 in York, England until 18 Feb 1975 in Zambia retiring as the world's oldest civil servant aged 91 years 38 days. His father William was born in Hull in the reign of William IV in 1832.

Elsie Marguerite Touzel (b.1889) of Jersey began her teaching career aged 16 in 1905 and was still teaching at Les Alpes School, Faldonet in 1979.

ost durable don
Dr Martin Joseph Routh (b. Sept 1755) was President of Magdalen College, Oxford, from April 1791 for 63 years 8 months, until his death in his 100th year on 22 Dec 1854. He had previously been a fellow for 16 years and was thus a don for a span of 79 years.

8. RELIGIONS

ldest
The oldest major formal religion is Hinduism. Its Vedic precursor was brought to India by Aryans *c.* 1500 BC. The Rig Veda Hindu hymnal was codified *c.* 900 BC or earlier.

argest
Religious statistics are necessarily only approximate. The test of adherence to a religion varies widely in rigour, while many individuals, particularly in the East, belong to two or more religions.

Christianity is the world's prevailing religion, with some 1,070,000,000 adherents in 1979. The Vatican statistics office reported that in 1979 there were 739,126,000 Roman Catholics. The largest non-Christian religion is Islam (Muslim) with some 550,000,000 followers.

In the United Kingdom the Anglicans comprise members of the Established Church of England, the Dis-established Church in Wales, the Episcopal Church in Scotland and the Church of Ireland. In mid 1979 there were 26,800,000 (57.5 per cent of the home population) baptized in the Church of England, which has two provinces (Canterbury and York), 44 dioceses, 11,235 full-time diocesan clergymen (1980) and 13,762 parishes (1978).

In Scotland the most numerous group is the Church of Scotland (12 Synods, 46 Presbyteries), which had 987,196 members as at 1 Jan 1979.

argest clergies
The world's largest religious organization is the Roman Catholic Church, with 406,644 clergy (including 403,672 priests) and 938,881 nuns. The total number of cardinals, archbishops and bishops is 2947. There are about 420,000 churches.

ews
The total of world Jewry was estimated to be 14.3 million in 1979. The highest concentration is in the United States, with 5.8 million, of whom 2.0 million are in the New York area. The total in Israel is 3,076,000. The total of British Jewry is 410,000 of whom 280,000 are in Greater London, and 13,000 in Glasgow. The total in Tōkyō, Japan, is only 400.

PLACES OF WORSHIP
arliest *World*
The earliest known shrine dates from the proto-neolithic Natufian culture in Jericho, where a site on virgin soil has been dated to the ninth millennium BC. A simple rectilinear red-plastered room with a niche housing a stone pillar believed to be the shrine of a Pre-Pottery fertility cult dating from *c.* 6500 BC was also uncovered in Jericho (now Arīhā) in Jordan. The oldest surviving Christian church in the world is Qal'at es Salihiye in eastern Syria, dating from AD 232.

ldest *Great Britain*
The oldest ecclesiastical building in the United Kingdom is a 6th century cell built by St Brendan in AD 542 on Eileachan Naoimh (pronounced Noo), Garvelloch Islands, Strathclyde. The Church in Great Britain with the oldest origins is St Martin's Church in Canterbury, Kent. It was built in AD 560 on the foundations of a 1st century Roman church. The oldest church in Ireland is the Gallerus Oratory, built in *c.* 750 at Ballyferriter, near Kilmalkedar, County Kerry, Britain's oldest nunnery is St Peter and Paul Minster, on the Isle of Thanet, Kent. It was founded in *c.* 748 by the Abbess Eadburga of Bugga. The oldest wooden church in Great Britain is St Andrew's, Greensted, near Ongar, Essex dating to AD 845 though some of the timbers date to the original building of *c.* AD 650.

Temple Largest
The largest religious structure ever built is Angkor Wat (City Temple), enclosing 402 acres *162,6 ha* in Kampuchea, southeast Asia. It was built to the God Vishnu by the Khmer King Suryavarman II in the period 1113–50. Its curtain wall measures 1400 × 1400 yd *1280 × 1280 m* and its population, before it was abandoned in 1432, was 80,000. The largest Buddhist temple in the world is Borobudur, near Jogjakarta, Indonesia built in the 8th century. It is 103 ft *31,5 m* tall and 403 ft *123 m* square.

The largest Mormon temple is in Kensington, Maryland, USA dedicated in November 1974 with a floor area of 159,000 ft² *14 770 m²*.

Cathedral Largest *World*
The world's largest cathedral is the cathedral church of the Diocese of New York, St John the Divine, with a floor area of 121,000 ft² *11 240 m²* and a volume of 16,822,000 ft³ *476 350 m³*. The cornerstone was laid on 27 Dec 1892, and work on the Gothic building was stopped in 1941. Work re-started in earnest in July 1979. In New York it is referred to as 'Saint John the Unfinished'. The nave is the longest in the world, 601 ft *183,18 m* in length, with a vaulting 124 ft *37,79 m* in height.

The cathedral covering the largest area is that of Santa Mariá de la Sede in Sevilla (Seville), Spain. It was built in Spanish Gothic style between 1402 and 1519 and is 414 ft *126,18 m* long, 271 ft *82,60 m* wide and 100 ft *30,48 m* high to the vault of the nave.

Cathedral Largest *Great Britain*
The largest cathedral in the British Isles is the Anglican Cathedral Church of St James on the Mount, Liverpool. Built in modernized Gothic style, work was begun on 18 July 1904, and was completed in October 1978 after 74 years (*cf.* Exeter 95 years) using ½ million stone blocks and 12 million bricks at a cost of £65 million (1978 prices). The building encloses 100,000 ft² *9300 m²* and has an overall length of 671 ft *204,52 m*. The Vestey Tower is 331 ft *100,88 m* high.

Cathedral Smallest
The smallest cathedral in the world is the Cathedral Chapel of St Francis of the American Catholic Church built in 1933 at Laguna Beach, California with an area of 1008 ft² *93,6 m²* and seating for 42 people. The smallest cathedral in use in the United Kingdom (of old foundation) is St Asaph in Clwyd, Wales, it is 182 ft *55,47 m* long, 68 ft *20,72 m* wide and has a tower 100 ft *30,48 m* high. Oxford Cathedral in Christ Church (College) is 155 ft *47,24 m* long. The nave of the Cathedral of the Isles on the Isle of Cumbrae, Strathclyde measures only 40 × 20 ft *12,19 × 6,09 m*. The total floor area is 2,124 ft² *197,3 m²*.

Church Largest *World*
The largest church in the world is the basilica of St Peter, built between 1492 and 1612 in the Vatican City, Rome. The length of the church, measured from the apse, is 611 ft 4 in *186,33 m*. The area is 162,990 ft² *15 142 m²*. The inner diameter of the famous dome is 137 ft 9 in *41,98 m* and its centre is 119 m *390 ft 5 in* high. The external height is 457 ft 9 in *139,52 m*.

The elliptical Basilique of St Pie X at Lourdes, France, completed in 1957 at a cost of £2,000,000 has a capacity of 20,000 under its giant span arches and a length of 200 m *656 ft*.

The crypt of the underground Civil War Memorial Church in the Guadarrama Mountains, 45 km *28 miles* from Madrid, Spain, is 260 m *853 ft* in length. It took 21 years (1937–58) to build, at a reported cost of £140,000,000, and is surmounted by a cross 150 m *492 ft* tall.

Church Largest *Great Britain*
The largest Church in the United Kingdom is the Collegiate Church of St Peter at Westminster built AD 1050–1745. Its maximum dimensions are overall: length 530 ft *161,5 m*; breadth across transept 203 ft *61,87 m* and internal height 101 ft 8 in *30,98 m*. The largest parish church is the Parish Church of the Most Holy and Undivided Trinity at Kingston-upon-Hull covering 27,235 ft² *2530 m²* and with an external length and width of 288 ft × 124 ft *87,7 × 37,7 m*. It is also believed to be the country's oldest brick building serving its original purpose, dating from *c.* 1285. Both the former Cathedral of St Mungo, Glasgow and Beverley Minster, Humberside are now used as parish churches. The largest school chapel is that of the 150 ft *45,7 m* high Lancing College, West Sussex.

Church Smallest *World*
The world's smallest church is the Union Church at Wiscasset, Maine, USA, with a floor area of 31½ ft² *2,92 m²* (7 × 4½ ft *2,13 × 1,37 m*). St. Gobban's Church, Portbradden County Antrim, Northern Ireland measures 12 ft 1½ in by 6 ft 6 in *3,7 × 2,0 m*.

Church Smallest *Great Britain*
The smallest church in use in England is Bremilham Church, Cowage Farm, Foxley near Malmesbury, Wiltshire which measures 12 × 12 ft *3,65 × 3,65 m* and is used for service once a year. The smallest completed medieval English church in regular use is that at Culbone, Somerset, which measures 35 × 12 ft *10,66 × 3,65 m*. The smallest Welsh chapel is St Trillo's Chapel, Rhôs-on-Sea (Llandrillo-yn-Rhos), Clwyd, measuring only 12 × 6 ft *3,65 × 1,83 m*. The smallest chapel in Scotland is St Margaret's, Edinburgh, measuring 16½ × 10½ ft *5,02 × 3,20 m*, giving a floor area of 173¼ ft² *16,09 m²*.

Synagogue Largest *World*
The largest synagogue in the world is the Temple Emanu-El on Fifth Avenue at 65th Street, New York City, NY, USA. The temple, completed in September 1929, has a frontage of 150 ft *45,72 m* on Fifth Avenue and 253 ft *77,11 m* on 65th Street. The Sanctuary proper can accommodate 2500 people, and the adjoining Beth-El Chapel seats 350. When all the facilities are in use, more than 6000 people can be accommodated.

Synagogue Largest *Great Britain*
The largest synagogue in Great Britain is the Edgware Synagogue, Barnet, Greater London, completed in 1959, with a capacity of 1630 seats. That with highest registered membership is Ilford Synagogue with 2613 at 31 May 1980.

Mosque Largest
The largest mosque ever built was the now ruinous al-Malawiya mosque of al-Mutawakil in Samarra, Iraq built in AD 842–52 and measuring 9.21 acres *3,72 ha* with dimensions of 784 × 512 ft *238,9 × 156,0 m*. The world's largest mosque in use is the Umayyad Mosque in Damascus, Syria built on a 2000-year-old religious site measuring 157 × 97 m *515 × 318 ft* thus covering an area of 3.76 acres *1,52 ha*. The largest mosque will be the Merdeka Mosque in Djakarta, Indonesia, which was begun in 1962. The cupola will be 45 m *147.6 ft* in diameter and the capacity in excess of 50,000 people.

Minaret *Tallest*
The tallest minaret is one of 282 ft *86 m* at the Sultan Hassan Mosque (founded 1356 AD) in Cairo, Egypt. The world's tallest free-standing stone tower is the Qutb Minar, south of New Delhi, India, built in 1194 to a height of 238 ft *72,54 m*.

Pagoda *Tallest and Oldest*
The world's tallest pagoda is the Shwe Dagon Pagoda in Rangoon, Burma which was increased to its present height of 326 ft *99,36 m* and perimeter of 1420 ft *432,8 m* by Hsinbyu-shin, King of Ava (1763–76). The oldest pagoda in China is Sung-Yo Ssu in Honan built with 15 12-sided storeys, in AD 523.

Sacred Object *Most Valuable*
The sacred object with the highest intrinsic value is the 15th century gold Buddah in Wat Trimitr Temple in Bangkok,

Thailand. It is 10 ft *3,04 m* tall and weighs an estimated 5½ tons. At $500 per fine ounce its intrinsic worth has been calculated to be £28½ million.

Nave *Longest*
The longest nave in the United Kingdom is that of St Albans Cathedral, Hertfordshire, which is 285 ft *86,86 m* long. The central tower of Liverpool's Anglican Cathedral (internal overall length 619 ft *188,6 m*) interrupts the nave with an undertower space.

Spire Tallest *World*
The tallest cathedral spire in the world is that of the Protestant Cathedral of Ulm in Germany. The building is early Gothic and was begun in 1377. The tower, in the centre of the west façade, was not finally completed until 1890 and is 160,90 m *528 ft* high. The world's tallest church spire is that of the Chicago Temple of the First Methodist Church on Clark Street, Chicago, Illinois, USA. The building consists of a 22-storey skyscraper (erected in 1924) surmounted by a parsonage at 330 ft *100,5 m*, a 'Sky Chapel' at 400 ft *121,92 m* and a steeple cross at 568 ft *173,12 m* above street level.

Great Britain
The highest spire in Great Britain is that of the church of St Mary, called Salisbury Cathedral, Wiltshire. The Lady Chapel was built in the years 1220–5 and the main fabric of the cathedral was finished and consecrated in 1258. The spire was added later *ante* 1305, and reaches a height of 404 ft *123,13 m*. The central spire of Lincoln Cathedral completed in *c.* 1307 and which fell in 1548 was 525 ft *160,02 m* tall.

Stained glass *Oldest*
The oldest stained glass in the world represents the Prophets in a window of the cathedral of Augsburg, Bavaria, Germany, dating from *c.* 1050. The oldest datable stained glass in the United Kingdom is represented by 12th century fragments in the Tree of Jesse in the north aisle of the nave of York Minster, dated *c.* 1150, and medallions in Rivenhall Church, Essex which appear to date from the first half of that century. Dates late in the previous century have been attributed to glass in a window of the church at Compton, Surrey, and a complete window in St Mary the Virgin, Brabourne, Kent.

Stained glass *Largest*
The largest stained glass window is the complete mural of The Resurrection Mausoleum in Justice, Illinois, measuring 22,381 ft² *2079 m²* in 2448 panels completed in 1971. The largest single stained glass window in Great Britain is the East window in Gloucester Cathedral measuring 72 × 38 ft *21,94 × 11,58 m*, set up to commemorate the Battle of Crécy (1346), while the largest area of stained glass is 125 windows totalling 25,000 ft² *2 322 m²* in York Minster.

Brasses
The world's oldest monumental brass is that commemorating Bishop Yso von Wölpe in Andreaskirche, Verden, near Hanover, W. Germany, dating from 1231. An engraved coffin plate of St Ulrich (d. 973), laid in 1187, was found buried in the Church of SS Ulrich and Afra, Augsburg, W. Germany in 1979. The oldest brass in Great Britain is of Sir John D'Abernon (d. 1277) at Stoke D'Abernon, near Leatherhead, Surrey, dating from *c.* 1320.

CHURCH PERSONNEL
Saints
There are 1848 'registered' saints (including 60 St Johns) of whom 628 are Italians, 576 French and 271 from the British Isles. Of these 8 came from Cambridge and 7 from Oxford between 1535 and 1645 but none from the House of Commons. Britain's first Christian martyr was St Alban executed *c.* AD 209. The first US born saint is Mother Elizabeth Ann Bayley Seton (1774–1821) canonized 14 Sept 1975. The total includes 76 Popes.

Most and least rapidly canonized
The shortest interval that has elapsed between the death of a Saint and his canonization was in the case of St Anthony of Padua, Italy, who died on 13 June 1231 and was canonized 352 days later on 30 May 1232. The other extreme is represented by

St Bernard of Tiron for 20 years Prior of St Sabinus, who died in 1117 and was made a Saint in 1861—744 years later.

Pope *Reign Longest and Shortest*
The longest reign of any of the 264 Popes has been that of Pius IX (Giovanni Maria Mastai-Ferretti), who reigned for 31 years 236 days from 16 June 1846 until his death aged 85, on 7 Feb 1878. Pope Stephen II was elected on 24 Mar 752 and died two days later.

Pope *Oldest*
It is recorded that Pope St Agatho (reigned 678–81) was elected at the age of 103 and lived to 106, but recent scholars have expressed doubts. The oldest of recent Pontiffs has been Pope Leo XIII (Gioacchino Pecci), who was born on 2 Mar 1810, elected Pope at the third ballot on 20 Feb 1878 and died on 20 July 1903, aged 93 years 140 days.

Pope *Youngest*
The youngest of all Popes was Pope Benedict IX (d. 1056) (Theophylact), who had three terms as Pope; 1032–44; April to May 1045; and 8 Nov 1047 to 17 July 1048. It would appear that he was aged only 11 or 12 in 1032, though the Catalogue of the Popes admits only to his 'extreme youth'.

Last non-Italian, ex-Cardinalate and English Popes
The current Pope John-Paul II, elected on 16 Oct 1978, (born Karol Wojtyla, 18 May 1920 at Wadowice, nr. Cracow, Poland) is the first non-Italian pope since Cardinal Adrian Florenz Boeyens (Pope Adrian VI) of the Netherlands crowned on 31 Aug 1522. The last Pope elected from outside the College of Cardinals was Bartolomeo Prignano (1318–89), Archbishop of Bari, who was elected Pope Urban VI on 8 Apr 1378. The only Englishman to be elected Pope was Nicholas Breakspear (born at Abbots Langley, near Watford, Hertfordshire, in *c.* 1100), who, as Cardinal Bishop of Albano, was elected Pope Adrian IV on 4 Dec 1154, and died on 1 Sept 1159.

Last married Pope
The first 37 Popes had no specific obligation to celibacy. Pope Hormisdas (514–23) was the father of Pope Silverius (536–7). The last married Pope was Adrian II (867–72). Rodrigo Borgia (1431–1503) was the father of at least six children before being elected Pope Alexander VI in 1492.

Slowest papal election
After 31 months without declaring *Habemus Papam* ('We have a Pope'), the cardinals were subjected to a bread and water diet and the removal of the roof of their conclave by the Mayor of Viterbo before electing Tabaldo Visconti (*c.* 1210–76), the Archbishop of Liège, as Pope Gregory X on 1 Sept 1271. The papacy was, however, vacant for at least 3 years 214 days in AD 304–8. The shortest conclave was that of 21 Oct 1503 for the election of Pope Julius II on a first ballot.

Cardinal *Oldest*
By 2 Feb 1973 the Sacred College of Cardinals contained a record 145 declared members compared with 127 on 13 Apr 1981. The oldest is Carlos Carmelo de Vasconcellos Motta (b. 16 July 1890). The record length of service of any cardinal has been 60 years 10 days by the Cardinal Duke of York, a grandson of James VII of Scotland and II of England, from 3 July 1747 to 13 July 1807.

The oldest Cardinal of all time was reputedly Giorgio da Costa (b. Portugal, 1406), who died in Rome on 18 Sept 1508 aged 102.

Cardinal *Youngest*
The youngest Cardinal of all time was Luis Antonio de Bourbon (b. 25 July 1727) created on 19 Dec 1735 aged 8 years 147 days. His son Luis was also made a Cardinal but aged 23. The youngest Cardinal is Jaime L Sin, Archbishop of Manila (b. 31 Aug 1928).

Bishopric *Longest tenure*
The longest tenure of any Church of England bishopric is 57 years in the case of the Rt Rev. Thomas Wilson, who was consecrated Bishop of Sodor and Man on 16 Jan 1698 and died in office on 7 Mar 1755. Of English bishoprics the longest tenures, if one excludes the unsubstantiated case of Aethelwulf, reputedly Bishop of Hereford from 937 to 1012, are those of 47 years by Jocelin de Bohun (Salisbury) 1142–89 and Nathaniel Crew or Crewe (Durham) 1674–1721.

Bishop *Oldest*
The oldest serving bishop (excluding Suffragans and Assistants) in the Church of England at 1 May 1981 was the Right Reverend George Reindorp, Bishop of Salisbury, who was born on 19 Dec 1911.

The oldest Roman Catholic bishop in recent years has been Bishop Angelo Teutonico, formerly Bishop of Aversa (b. 28 Aug 1874), who died aged 103 years 276 days on 31 May 1978. He had celebrated Mass about 24,800 times. Bishop Herbert Welch of the United Methodist Church, who was elected a bishop for Japan and Korea in 1916, died on 4 Apr 1969 aged 106.

Bishop *Youngest*
The youngest bishop of all time was HRH The Duke of York and Albany, KG, GCB, GCH, the second son of George III, who was elected Bishop of Osnabrück, through his father's influence as Elector of Hanover, at the age of 196 days on 27 Feb 1764. He resigned after 39 years' enjoyment.

The youngest serving bishop (excluding Suffragans and Assistants) in the Church of England at 1 May 1981 was the Rt Rev David Young (b. 2 Sept 1931), Bishop of Ripon.

Longest incumbency
The longest Church of England incumbency on record is one of 75 years 357 days by the Rev. Bartholomew Edwards, Rector of St Nicholas, Ashill, Norfolk from 1813 to 1889. There appears to be some doubt as to whether the Rev. Richard Sherinton was installed at Folkestone from 1524 or 1529 to 1601. If the former is correct it would surpass the Norfolk record. The parish of Farrington, Hampshire had only two incumbents in a 122 year period *viz* Rev J. Benn (28 Mar 1797 to 1857) and Rev T. H. Massey (1857 to 5 Apr 1919).

Longest serving chorister
Leonard Thompson (b. 19 Feb 1883) sang with St. Mary's Church choir, Kidderminster, Shropshire for 88 years. Having become a chorister in 1876 at the age of 9, Thomas Rogers was appointed vicar's warden in 1966 at Montacute, Somerset.

Parishes *Largest and Smallest*
The smallest parish in the United Kingdom is The Scares which consists of rocky islets in Luce Bay with an area of 1.10 acres *0.44 ha* and included in Wigtown, Dumfries and Galloway. The largest parish is Kilmonivaig in Inverness, Highland with an area of 267,233.03 acres *108 145,46 ha*.

Oldest parish register
The oldest part of any parish register surviving in England is a sheet from that of Alfriston, East Sussex recording a marriage on 10 July 1504. Scotland's oldest surviving register is that for Anstruther-Wester, Fife, with burial entries from 1549.

Crowds *Largest*
The greatest recorded number of human beings assembled with a common purpose was an estimated 12,700,000 at the Hindu festival of Kumbh-Mela, which was held at the confluence of the Yamuna (formerly called the Jumna), the Ganges and the invisible 'Sarasvati' at Allahabad, Uttar Pradesh, India, on 19 Jan 1977. The holiest time during this holiest day since 1833 was during the planetary alignment between 9.28 and 9.40 a.m. during which only 200,000 achieved immersion to wash away the sins of a lifetime.

Largest funerals
The greatest attendance at any funeral is the estimated 4 million who thronged Cairo, Egypt, for the funeral of President Gamal Abdel Nasser (1918–70) on 1 Oct 1970. The longest funeral in Britain was probably that of Vice Admiral Viscount Nelson on 9 Jan 1806. Ticket-holders were seated in St Paul's Cathedral by 8.30 a.m. Many were unable to leave until after 9 p.m.

Biggest demonstrations
A figure of 2.7 million was published from China for the demonstration against the USSR in Shanghai on 3–4 Apr 1969 following the border clashes, and one of 10 million for the May Day celebrations of 1963 in Peking.

237

ACCIDENTS & DISASTERS

WORST IN THE WORLD

DATE	LOCATION	NUMBER KILLED	DISASTER
1347-51	Eurasia: The Black Death (bubonic, pneumonic and septicaemic plague)	75,000,000	**Pandemic**
April-Nov 1918	Worldwide: Influenza	21,640,000	**Famine**
1969-1971	Northern China	c. 20,000,000[1]	
1931 Aug	Hwang-ho River, China	3,640,000	**Flood**
12-13 Nov 1970	Ganges Delta Islands, Bangladesh	1,000,000	**Circular Storm**[2]
23 Jan 1556	Shensi Province, China (duration 2 hours)	830,000	**Earthquake**
16 Dec 1920	Kansu Province, China	180,000	**Landslide**
6 Aug 1945	Hiroshima, Japan	141,000	**Atomic Bomb**
13-15 Feb 1945	Dresden, Germany	c. 25,000	**Conventional bombing**[3]
31 May 1970	Yungay, Huascarán, Peru	c. 25,000[4]	**Alluvion Flood**
30 Jan 1945	Wilhelm Gustloff (25,484 tons) German liner torpedoed off Danzig by USSR submarine S-13	c. 7,700	**Marine (single ship)**
11 Aug 1979	Manchhu River Dam, Morvi, Gujarat, India	c. 5,000	**Dam Burst**
c. 8 June 1941	Chungking (Zhong qing) China air raid shelter	c. 4,000[5]	**Panic**
6 Dec 1917	Halifax, Nova Scotia, Canada	1,963[6]	**Explosion**
May 1845	The Theatre, Canton, China	1,670	**Fire**[7] **(single building)**
26 April 1942	Honkeiko Colliery, China (coal dust explosion)	1,572	**Mining**[8]
13-16 July 1942	New York City anti-conscription riots	c. 1,200	**Riot**
18 Nov 1978	People's Temple cult by cyanide, Jonestown, Guyana	913	**Mass Suicide**
19-20 Feb 1945	Japanese soldiers, Ramree I., Burma (disputed)	c. 900	**Crocodiles**
6 June 1981	Bagmati River, Bihar state, India	>800	**Railway**
16 May 1770	Dauphine's Wedding, Seine, Paris	>800	**Fireworks**
18 Mar 1925	South Central States, USA (3 hours)	689	**Tornado**
27 Mar 1977	KLM-Pan Am Boeing 747 ground crash, Tenerife	583	**Aircraft (Civil)**
April-May 1907	Champawat district, India, tigress shot by Col. Jim Corbett	436	**Man-eating Animal**
20 April 1888	Novosibirsk B & CW plant, USSR	c. 300	**Bacteriological & Chemical**
1888	Moradabad, Uttar Pradesh, India	246	**Hail**
27 Mar 1980	Alexander L. Kielland 'Flotel' (10,105 tons), North Sea	123	**Off-Shore Oil Plant**
18 Feb 1942	Le Surcouf rammed in Caribbean	130	**Submarine**
9 Aug 1973	Bus crashed into irrigation canal, Egypt	127	**Road (single vehicle)**[9]
10 May 1977	Israeli military 'Sea Stallion', West Bank	54	**Helicopter**
9 Mar 1976	Cavalese resort, Northern Italy	42	**Ski Lift (Cable car)**
Dec 1952	USSR Expedition on Mount Everest	40[10]	**Mountaineering**
27 Mar 1980	Vaal Reefs Gold mine lift fell 1.2 miles 1,93 km	23	**Elevator (Lift)**
23 Dec 1975	Hut in Chinamasa Kraal nr. Umtali, Rhodesia	21	**Lightning (single bolt)**
13-15 Aug 1979	28th Fastnet Race—25 boats sank, 19 abandoned in Force 11 gale	15	**Yacht Racing**
27 Jan 1967	Apollo oxygen fire, Cape Kennedy, Fla., USA	3	**Space Exploration**
29 June 1971	Soyuz II re-entry over USSR	3	
1957-58	Venting of plutonium waste, Kyshtym, USSR	high but unknown	**Atomic Accident**

WORST IN THE UNITED KINGDOM

DISASTER	NUMBER KILLED	LOCATION	DATE
Pandemic	800,000	The Black Death (bubonic, pneumonic and septicaemic plague)	1347-1350
Famine	225,000	Influenza	Sept-Nov 1918
	1,500,000[11]	Ireland (famine and typhus)	1846-1851
Flood	c. 2,000[12]	Severn Estuary	20 Jan 1606
Circular Storm	c. 8,000	'The Channel Storm'	26 Nov 1703
Earthquake	4	East Anglian Earthquake	22 April 1884
Landslide	144	Pantglas coal tip No 7, Aberfan, Mid Glamorgan	21 Oct 1966
Atomic Bomb			
Conventional bombing	1,436	London	10-11 May 1941
Alluvion Flood	8	Lewes, East Sussex (avalanche)	27 Dec 1836
Marine (single ship)	c. 800[13]	HMS Royal George, off Spithead	29 Aug 1782
Dam Burst	250	Bradfield Reservoir, Dale Dyke, near Sheffield, South Yorkshire (embankment burst)	12 Mar 1864
Panic	183	Victoria Hall, Sunderland, Tyne and Wear	16 June 1883
Explosion	134[14]	Chilwell, Notts. (explosives factory)	1 July 1918
Fire (single building)	188[15]	Theatre Royal, Exeter	5 Sept 1887
Mining	439	Universal Colliery, Senghenydd, Mid Glamorgan	14 Oct 1913
Riot	565 (min)	London anti-Catholic Gordon riots	2-13 June 1780
Railway	227[16]	Triple collision, Quintins Hill, Dumfries & Galloway	22 May 1915
Tornado	60	Widecombe, Devon (casualty figure)	21 Oct 1638
Aircraft (Civil)	118[17]	BEA Trident 1C, Staines, Surrey	18 June 1972
Off-Shore Oil Plant	24	Aboard North Sea pentagonal semi-submersible (see left)	27 Mar 1980
Submarine	99	HMS Thetis, during trials, Liverpool Bay	1 June 1939
Road (single vehicle)	33	Coach crash, River Dibb, nr Grassington, North Yorks	27 May 1975
Mountaineering	6	On Cairngorm, Scotland (4084ft)	21 Nov 1971
Yacht Racing	31	Worst year on record (annual av. 12)	1914
	15	(See left) Of 316 starters only 128 finished	13-15 Aug 1979

Footnotes

1. In 1770 the great Indian famine carried away a proportion of the population estimated as high as one third, hence a figure of tens of millions. The figure for Bengal alone was also probably about 10 million. The loss in the Northern China famine of Feb 1877-Sept 1878 was 9,500,000. It has been estimated that more than 5 million died in the post-World War I famine of 1920-1 in the USSR. The USSR government on 6 July 1923 informed Mr (later President) Herbert Hoover that the ARA (American Relief Administration) had saved 20 million lives from famine and famine diseases.

2. This figure published in 1972 for the Bangladeshi disaster was from Dr Afzal, Principal Scientific Officer of the Atomic Energy Authority Centre, Dacca. One report asserted that less than half of the population of the 4 islands of Bhola, Charjabbar, Hatia and Ramagati (1961 Census 1.4 million) survived. The most damaging hurricane recorded was the billion dollar Betsy (name now retired) in 1965 with an insurance pay-out of $715 million. Hurricane Frederic (Sept 1979) cost insurers $752 million in inflated dollars.

3. The number of civilians killed by the bombing of Germany has been put variously as 593,000 and 'over 635,000'. A figure of c. 140,000 deaths in the USAF fire raids on Tōkyō of 10 Mar 1945 has been attributed. Total Japanese fatalities were 600,000 (conventional) and 220,000 (nuclear).

4. A total of 10,000 Austrian and Italian troops is reported to have been lost in the Dolomite valley of Northern Italy on 13 Dec 1916 in more than 100 snow avalanches. The total is probably exaggerated though bodies were still being found in 1952. 4,000 killed, Santa Valley, below Huascarán, Peru, 10 Jan 1962.

5. It was estimated that some 5000 people were trampled to death in the stampede for free beer at the coronation celebration of Czar Nicholas II in Moscow in May 1896.

6. Some sources maintain that the final death roll was over 3000 on 6-7 Dec. Published estimates of the 11,000 killed at the BASF chemical plant explosion at Oppau, W. Germany on 21 Sept 1921 were exaggerated. The best estimate is 561 killed.

7. >200,000 killed in the sack of Moscow, freed by the Tartars in May 1571. Worst ever hotel fire 162 killed, Hotel Daeyungak, Seoul,

8. The worst gold mining disaster in South Africa was 152 killed due to flooding in the Witwatersrand Gold Mining Co. Gold Mine in 1909.

9. The worst ever years for road deaths in the USA and the UK have been respectively 1969 (56,400) and 1941 (9,169). The global aggregate death roll was put at 25 million by September 1975. The world's highest death rate is 29 per 100,000 in 1978 in Luxembourg and Portugal. The greatest pile-up on British roads was on the M6 near Lymm Interchange, near Thelwall, involving 200 vehicles on 13 Sept 1971 with 11 dead and 60 injured.

10. According to Polish sources, not confirmed by the USSR. Also 23 died on Mount Fuji, Japan, in blizzard and avalanche on 20 Mar 1972.

11. Based on the net rate of natural increase between 1841 and 1851, a supportable case for a loss of population of 3 million can be made out if rates of under-enumeration of 25 per cent (1841) and 10 per cent (1851) are accepted. Potato rot (Phytophthora infestans) was first reported on 13 Sept 1845.

12. Death rolls of 100,000 were reputed in England and Holland in the floods of 1099, 1421 and 1446.

13. c. 2800 were lost on HM Troopship Lancastria 16,243 tons off St. Nazaire on 17 June 1940. The Princess Alice collision in the Thames off the Bywell Castle off Woolwich on 6 Sept 1878 killed 786.

14. HM Armed Cruiser Natal blew up off Invergordon killing 428 on 30 Dec 1915.

15. In July 1212, 3000 were killed in the crush, burned or drowned when London Bridge caught fire at both ends. The death roll in the Great Fire of London of 1666 was only 8. History's first 'fire storm' occurred in the Quebec Yard, Surrey Docks, Southwark, London during the 300-pump fire in the Blitz on 7-8 Sept 1940. Dockland casualties were 306 killed.

16. The 213yd 194.7m long troop train was telescoped to 67 yd 61.2m. Signalmen Meakin and Tinsley were sentenced for manslaughter. Britain's worst underground train disaster was the Moorgate Tube disaster of 28 Feb 1975 when 43 were killed.

17. The worst crash by a UK operated aircraft was that of the Dan-Air Boeing 727 from Manchester which crashed into a mountain on

12.
SPORTS,
GAMES & PASTIMES

ALL SPORTS

See also The Guinness Book of Winners and Champions—£6.95 *by Chris Cook, Anne Marshall and Peter Matthews—published by Guinness Superlatives Ltd.*

Earliest
The origins of sport stem from the time when self-preservation ceased to be the all-consuming human preoccupation. Archery was a hunting skill in mesolithic times (by *c.* 8000 BC), but did not become an organised sport until *c.* AD 300, among the Genoese. The earliest dated evidence for sport is *c.* 2750–2600 BC for wrestling. Ball games by girls depicted on Middle Kingdom murals at Beni Hasan, Egypt have been dated to *c.* 2050 BC.

Fastest
The highest speed reached in a non-mechanical sport is in skydiving, in which a speed of 185 mph *298 km/h* is attained in a head-down free falling position, even in the lower atmosphere. In delayed drops speeds of 625 mph *1005 km/h* have been recorded at high rarefied altitudes. The highest projectile speed in any moving ball game is *c.* 188 mph *302 km/h* in pelota. This compares with 170 mph *273 km/h* (electronically-timed) for a golf ball driven off a tee.

Slowest
In wrestling, before the rules were modified towards 'brighter wrestling', contestants could be locked in holds for so long that a single bout once lasted for 11 hr 40 min. In the extreme case of the 2 hr 41 min pull in the regimental tug o' war in Jubbulpore, India, on 12 Aug 1889, the winning team moved a net distance of 12 ft *3,6 m* at an average speed of 0.00084 mph *0,00135 km/h*.

Longest
The most protracted sporting contest was an automobile duration test of 222,618 miles *358 268 km* by Appaurchaux and others in a Ford Taunus. This was contested over 142 days in 1963. The distance was equivalent to 8.93 times around the equator.

The most protracted non-mechanical sporting event is the *Tour de France* cycling race. In 1926 this was over 3569 miles *5743 km* lasting 29 days. The total effect on the French national economy due to the interest in this annual event, now reduced to 23 days, is immense.

Largest stadium
For details of the world's largest stadium see p. 118.

Largest pitch
The largest pitch of any ball game is that of polo, with 12.4 acres *5,0 ha*, or a maximum length of 300 yd *274 m* and a width, without side boards, of 200 yd *182 m*. Twice a year in the Parish of St Columb Major, Cornwall, a game called Hurling (not to be confused with the Irish game) is played on a 'pitch' which consists of the entire Parish, approximately 25 square miles *64,7 km²*.

Largest trophy
The world's largest trophy for a particular sport is the Bangalore Limited Handicap Polo Tournament Trophy. This massive cup is 6 ft *1,83 m* tall and was presented in 1936 by the Raja of Kolanka.

Youngest and oldest world record breakers
The youngest age at which any person has broken a non-mechanical world record is 12 years 298 days in the case of Gertrude Caroline Ederle (USA) (b. 23 Oct 1906) who broke the women's 880 yd freestyle world record with 13 min 19.0 sec at Indianapolis, USA, on 17 Aug 1919. Irish-born John J. Flanagan (1868–1938), triple Olympic hammer-throw champion for the US, 1900–8, set his last world record of 184 ft 4 in *56,18 m* at New Haven, Conn., USA, on 24 July 1909 aged 41 years 196 days.

Youngest and oldest champions
The youngest successful competitor in a world title event was a French boy, whose name is not recorded, who coxed the Netherlands' Olympic pair at Paris on 26 Aug 1900. He was not more than ten and may have been as young as seven. The youngest individual Olympic winner was Marjorie Gestring (USA) (b. 18 Nov 1922), who took the springboard diving title at the age of 13

years 268 days at the Olympic Games in Berlin on 12 Aug 1936. Oscar Gomer Swahn (Sweden) (1847–1927) was aged 65 years 258 days when he won a gold medal in the 1912 Olympic Running Deer team shooting competition.

Youngest and oldest internationals

The youngest age at which any person has won international honours is eight years in the case of Joy Foster, the Jamaican singles and mixed doubles table tennis champion in 1958. The youngest British international has been diver Beverley Williams (b. 5 Jan 1957), who was 10 years 268 days old when she competed against the USA at Crystal Palace, London, on 30 Sept 1967. It would appear that the greatest age at which anyone has actively competed for his country was 72 years 280 days in the case of Oscar Swahn (see above) who won a silver medal for shooting in the Olympic Games at Antwerp on 26 July 1920. He qualified for the 1924 Games but was unable to participate due to illness. Britain's oldest international was Hilda Lorna Johnstone (b. 4 Sept 1902) who was 70 years 5 days when she was placed twelfth in the Dressage competition at the 1972 Games.

Most versatile

All-round ability is measured by level of attainment in highly varied pursuits. By these parameters Charlotte 'Lottie' Dod (1871–1960) stands supreme. She won the Wimbledon Singles title five times between 1887 and 1893, the British Ladies Golf Championship in 1904, an Olympic silver medal for archery in 1908, and represented England at hockey in 1899. She also excelled at skating and tobogganing. Charles Burgess Fry (GB) (1872–1956) was probably the most versatile male sportsman at the highest level. On 4 Mar 1893 he equalled the world long jump record of 23 ft 6½ in *7,17 m*. He represented England *v* Ireland at soccer (1901) and played first-class Rugby for the Barbarians. His greatest achievements were at cricket, where he headed the English batting averages in six seasons and captained England in 1912. He was an excellent angler and tennis player.

Most prolific record breaker

Between 24 Jan 1970 and 1 Nov 1977 Vasili Alexeyev (USSR) (b. 7 Jan 1942) broke 80 official world records in weightlifting.

Longest reign

The longest reign as a world champion is 33 years (1829–62) by Jacques Edmond Barre (France) (1802–73) at real tennis. The longest reign as a British champion is 41 years by the archer Alice Blanche Legh (1855–1948) who first won the Championship in 1881 and for the 23rd and final time in 1922 aged 67.

Shortest reign

Olga Rukavishnikova (USSR) (b. 13 Mar 1955) held the pentathlon world record for only 0.4 sec at Moscow on 24 July 1980. That is the difference between her second place time of 2 min 04.8 sec in the final 800 m event of the Olympic five-event competition, and that of the third-placed Nadezda Tkachenko (USSR), whose overall points came to more than Rukavishnikova's total—5083 points to 4937 points.

Heaviest sportsmen

The heaviest sportsman of all-time was the professional wrestler William J. Cobb of Macon, Georgia, USA, who in 1962 was billed as the 802 lb (57 st 4 lb *363 kg*) 'Happy Humphrey'. The heaviest player of a ball-game was the 487 lb *221 kg* Bob Pointer, the US Football tackle formerly on the 1967 Santa Barbara High School Team, California, USA. The current heaviest in British sport are professional wrestlers 'The Masked Bulk' (Terry Thomas) and 'Giant Haystacks' (Luke McMasters), both fluctuating up to 550 lb *247 kg* (39 stone).

Greatest earnings

The greatest fortune amassed by an individual in sport is an estimated $68 million by the boxer Muhammad Ali Haj (USA) to Oct 1980. The highest paid woman athlete in the world is tennis player Martina Navratilova (b. Prague, Czechoslovakia, 18 Oct 1956) who is reported to have had total earnings in excess of $800,000 in 1980.

Most expensive

The most expensive of all sports is the racing of large yachts—'J'

Twice Wimbledon Singles champion, Martina Navratilova earned more than any other sportswoman in 1980. (*Don Morley, All-Sport*)

type boats, last built in 1937, and International 12-metre boats. The owning and racing of these is beyond the means of individual millionaires and is confined to multi-millionaires or syndicates.

Largest crowd

The greatest number of live spectators for any sporting spectacle is the estimated 2,500,000 who lined the route of the New York Marathon on 21 Oct 1979. The race was won by Bill Rodgers (USA) for the fourth consecutive time. However, spread over 23 days, it is estimated that more than 10,000,000 see the annual *Tour de France* along the route (see also above).

The largest crowd travelling to any single sporting venue is 'more than 400,000' for the annual *Grand Prix d'Endurance* motor race on the Sarthe circuit near Le Mans, France. The record stadium crowd was one of 199,854 for the Brazil *v.* Uruguay soccer match in the Maracaña Municipal Stadium, Rio de Janeiro, Brazil, on 16 July 1950.

Most participants

The *Round the Bays*, 6.5 mile *10,5 km* run in Auckland, New Zealand attracted an estimated 70,000 runners on 28 Mar 1981. In May 1971, the 'Ramblin' Raft Race' on the Chattahoochee River, at Atlanta, Georgia, USA, attracted 37,683 competitors on 8304 rafts. The most runners in a marathon were the 14,012 in the New York marathon on 26 Oct 1980, of whom 12,512 finished.

Most officials

Lawn tennis is the sport with the highest ratio of officials to participants. For a singles match there should be 13—ten line, one net-cord and one foot-fault judge, in addition to the umpire.

Largest following

The sport with most regular participants in Britain is angling with 3¾ million in 1980. About 22 million spectators watched Association Football matches in Britain in 1980–1. The largest television audience for a single sporting event, excluding Olympic events, was an estimated 400 million who saw the final of the 1978 Soccer World Cup (see also p. 112).

Most sportsmen

According to a report in 1978, 55 million people are active in sports in the USSR. The country has 3282 stadiums, 1435 swimming pools and over 66,000 indoor gymnasia. It is estimated that some 29 per cent of the population of E. Germany participate in sport regularly.

Worst disasters

The worst sports disaster in recent history was when an estimated 604 were killed after some stands at the Hong Kong Jockey Club racecourse collapsed and caught fire on 26 Feb 1918. During the reign of Antoninus Pius (AD 138–161) the upper wooden tiers in the Circus Maximus, Rome, collapsed during a gladiatorial combat killing some 1112 spectators. Britain's worst sports disaster was when 66 were killed and 145 injured at the Rangers *v.* Celtic football match at Exit 13 of Ibrox Park stadium, Glasgow on 2 Jan 1971.

AEROBATICS

Earliest

The first aerobatic 'manoeuvre' is generally considered the sustained inverted flight in a Bleriot of Célestin-Adolphe Pégoud (1889–1915), at Buc, France on 21 Sept 1913, but Lieut. Peter Nikolayevich Nesterov (1887–1914), of the Imperial Russian Air Service, performed a loop in a Nieuport Type IV monoplane at Kiev, USSR on 27 Aug 1913.

World Championships

Held biennially since 1960 (excepting 1974), scoring is based on the system devised by Col José Aresti of Spain. The competitions consist of two compulsory and two free programmes. The Team competition has been won on four occasions by the USSR. No individual has won more than one title, the most successful competitor being Igor Egorov (USSR) who won in 1970, was second in 1976, fifth in 1972 and eleventh in 1968. The most successful in the women's competition has been Lidia Leonova (USSR) with first place in 1976, second in 1978, third in 1972 and fifth in 1970. The only medal achieved by Britain has been a bronze in the team event at Kiev, USSR in 1976. The highest individual placing by a Briton is fourth by Neil Williams (1935–77) in 1976.

Inverted flight

The duration record for inverted flight is 4 hr 9 min 5 sec by John 'Hal' McClain in a Swick Taylorcraft on 23 Aug 1980 over Houston International Raceways, Texas, USA.

Loops

On 21 June 1980, R. Steven Powell performed 2315⅝ inside loops in a Bellanca Decathlon over Almont, Michigan, USA. John McClain achieved 180 outside loops in a Bellanca Super Decathlon on 2 Sept 1978 over Houston, Texas, USA.

ANGLING

For further information on fishing see The Guinness Guides to Fresh and Salt Water Angling *by Brian Harris and to* Game Fishing *by Dr William Currie, published by Guinness Superlatives at £6.95, £8.95 and £9.95 respectively.*

Catch *Largest Single*

The largest officially ratified fish ever caught on a rod is a man-eating great white shark (*Carcharodon carcharias*) weighing 2664 lb *1208 kg* and measuring 16 ft 10 in *5,13 m* long, caught on a 130 lb *58 kg* test line by Alf Dean at Denial Bay, near Ceduna, South Australia, on 21 Apr 1959. A white pointer shark

Paul Kerry has beaten the British Surfcasting record for the second year running. (*Tony Duffy, All-Sport*)

weighing 3388 lb *1537 kg* was caught by Clive Green off Albany, Western Australia, on 26 Apr 1976 but will remain unratified as whale meat was used as bait. The biggest ever rod-caught fish by a British angler is a 1260 lb *571,5 kg* black marlin caught by Edward A. Crutch off Cairns, Queensland, Australia on 19 Oct 1973.

In June 1978 a great white shark measuring 29 ft 6 in *9,00 m* in length and weighing over 10,000 lb *4536 kg* was harpooned and landed by fishermen in the harbour of San Miguel, Azores.

The largest marine animal ever killed by *hand* harpoon was a blue whale 97 ft *29,56 m* in length, killed by Archer Davidson in Twofold Bay, New South Wales, Australia, in 1910. Its tail flukes measured 20 ft *6,09 m* across and its jaw bone 23 ft 4 in *7,11 m*.

The largest fish ever caught in a British river was a 388 lb *175,99 kg* sturgeon landed by Alec Allen (1895–1972), helped by David Price, from the River Towy, between Llandilo and Carmarthen, S Wales, on 25 July 1933. It was 9 ft 2 in *2,79 m* in length.

Catch *Smallest*

The smallest fish to win a competition is a smelt, weighing 1/16 oz *1 dram*, caught by Peter Christian at Buckenham Ferry, Norfolk, England on 9 Jan 1977, in defeating 107 other competitors. For the smallest full-grown fish see p. 43.

Spear fishing

The largest fish ever taken underwater was an 804 lb *364 kg* giant black grouper or jewfish by Don Pinder of the Miami Triton Club, Florida, USA, in 1955. The British spear-fishing record is 89 lb *40,36 kg* for an angler fish by James Brown (Weymouth Association Divers) in 1969.

Championship records *World*

The *Confederation Internationale de la Pêche Sportive* championships were inaugurated as European championships in 1953. They were recognised as World Championships in 1957. France won eleven times between 1956 and 1979 and Robert Tesse (France) took the individual title uniquely three times, in 1959–60, 1965. The record weight (team) is 76 lb 8 oz 8 dr *34 kg 715* in 3 hr by West Germany on the Neckar at Mannheim, West Germany on 21 Sept 1980. The individual record is 37 lb 7 oz 3 dr *16 kg 990* by Wolf-Rüdiger Kremkus (West Germany) at Mannheim on 20 Sept 1980. The most fish caught is 652 by Jacques Isenbaert (Belgium) at Dunajvaros, Yugoslavia on 27 Aug 1967.

Championship records *British*

The National Angling Championship (instituted 1906) has been won seven times by Leeds (1909–10, 1914, 1928, 1948–9, 1952). Only James H. R. Bazley (Leeds) has ever won the individual title twice (1909, 1927). The record catch is 76 lb 9 oz *34 kg 720* by David Burr (Rugby) in the Huntspill, Somerset in 1965. The largest single fish caught in the Championships is a carp of 14 lb 2 oz *6 kg 406* by John C. Essex on 13 Sept 1975 on the River Nene, Peterborough. The team record is 136 lb 15¼ oz *62 kg 120* by Sheffield Amalgamated, also in the Huntspill in 1955.

Match fishing

In a sweepstake on the Sillees River, a tributary of the Erne, Co. Fermanagh, Ulster, on 14 May 1981, Peter Burrell weighed in 258 lb 9½ oz *117,29 kg* of fish in the five hour open event.

Casting records

The longest freshwater cast ratified under ICF (International Casting Federation) rules is 175,01 m *574 ft 2 in* by Walter Kummerow (W. Germany), for the Bait Distance Double-Handed 30 g event held at Lenzerheide, Switzerland in the 1968 Championships. The British National record is 148,78 m *488 ft 1 in* by Andy Dickison on the same occasion. The longest Fly Distance Double-Handed cast is 78,38 m *257 ft 2 in* by Sverne Scheen (Norway), also at Lenzerheide in September 1968. Peter Anderson set a British National professional record of 70,50 m *231 ft 3 in* on water at Scarborough on 11 Sept 1977, and Hugh Newton cast 80,47 m *264 ft* on land at Stockholm, Sweden on 20 Sept 1978. The UK Surfcasting Federation record (150 gr *5¼ oz* weight) is 723 ft 7 in *220,54 m* by Paul Kerry at Norwich, Norfolk on 7 Sept 1980.

Longest fight

The longest recorded individual fight with a fish is 32 hr 5 min by Donal Heatley (b. 1938) (New Zealand) with a black marlin (estimated length 20 ft *6,09 m* and weight 1500 lb *680 kg*) off Mayor Island off Tauranga, North Island on 21–22 Jan 1968. It towed the 12 ton/*tonnes* launch 50 miles *80 km* before breaking the line.

WORLD RECORDS

New all-tackle records ratified since January 1980 by the International Game Fish Association. For the complete list see the 27th edition of the *Guinness Book of Records*.

Species	Weight lb oz	kg/g	Name of Angler	Location	Date
FRESHWATER FISH					
Bass, peacock	21 00	9,52	David Orndorf	Orinoco River, Columbia	6 Feb 1981
Bowfin	21 08	9,75	Robert L. Harmon	Forest Lake, Florence, SC, USA	29 Jan 1980
Buffalo, bigmouth	70 05	31,89	Delbert Sisk	Bussey Brake Bastrop, Los Angeles, Cal, USA	21 Apr 1980
Gar, Florida	4 00	1,82	W. R. Haynes	Hillsborough, Florida, USA	13 Apr 1980
Huchen	70 12	32,09	Martin F. Pesterl	Carinthia, Austria	1 Jan 1980
Pike, Northern	62 08	28,35	Jürg Nötzli	Reuss-Weiher, Rickenbach, Switzerland	15 June 1979
Redhorse, silver	5 14	2,67	Ernest Harley, Jr	Shelbyville, Indiana, USA	20 Oct 1980
SEA FISH					
Bonito, Atlantic	16 12	7,60	Rolf Fedderies	Puerto Rio, Gran Canaria, Canary Is	6 Dec 1980
Cubera snapper	60 12	27,55	Dr Richard A. Klein	Miami Beach, Florida, USA	27 Feb 1980
Kawakawa	26 00	11,80	Wally Elfring	Merimbula, NSW, Australia	26 Jan 1980
Marlin, White	181 14	82,49	Evando Luiz Coser	Vitoria, Brazil	8 Dec 1979
Shark, hammerhead	717 00	325,23	Richard Edward Morse	Jacksonville Beach, Florida, USA	27 July 1980
Spearfish	90 13	41,20	Joseph Larkin	Madeira Is	2 June 1980
Tuna, dogtooth	194 00	88,00	Kim Chul I	Kwan-Tall Es, Che Ju-Do, Korea	27 Sept 1980

BRITISH RECORDS

The complete list ratified by the British Record [rod caught] Fish Committee of the National Anglers Council as at January 1981

Species	Weight lb oz dr	kg/g	Name of Angler	Location	Date
FRESHWATER FISH					
Barbel	13 12 00	6,237	J. Day	Royalty Fishery, Hants.	1962
Bleak	03 15	0,111	D. Pollard	Staythorpe Pond, nr Newark, Notts.	1971
Bream (Common, Bronze)	13 08 00	6,123	A. R. Heslop	Private water, Staffs.	1977
Bullhead (Millers's Thumb)	10	0,017	E. Harrison	Leeds and Liverpool Canal, Leach Bridge	1978
Carp	44 00 00	19,957	R. Walker	Redmire Pool	1952
Carp, Crucian	5 10 08	2,565	G. Halls	nr King's Lynn, Norfolk	1976
Catfish (Wels)	43 08 00	19,730	R. J. Bray	Wilstone Reservoir, Tring, Herts	1970
Char	1 12 04	0,801	C. Imperiale	Loch Insh, Inverness-shire	1974
Chub	7 06 00	3,345	W. L. Warren	Royalty Fishery, Hants	1957
Dace	1 04 04	0,574	J. L. Gasson	Little Ouse, Thetford, Norfolk	1960
Eel	11 02 00	5,046	S. Terry	Kingfisher Lake, nr Ringwood, Hants	1978
Grayling	2 09 04	1,169	D. Hauxwell	River Teviot, Jedburgh, Borders	1980
Gudgeon	4 04	0,120	M. J. Brown	Fish Pond, Ebbw Vale, Gwent	1977
Gwyniad (Whitefish)	1 04 00	0,567	J. R. Williams	Llyn Tegid, Gwynedd	1965
Loch Lomond Powan	1 07 00	0,652	J. M. Ryder	Loch Lomond, Scotland	1972
Minnow	11	0,020	I. S. Collinge	River Calder, Padiham, Lancs	1979
Orfe, Golden	4 03 00	1,899	B. T. Mills	River Test, Hants	1976
Perch	4 12 00	2,154	S. F. Baker	Oulton Broad, Suffolk	1962
Pike[1]	40 00 00	18,143	P. D. Hancock	Horsey Mere, Norfolk	1967
Pikeperch (Walleye)	11 12 00	5,329	F. Adams	The Delph, Welney, Norfolk	1934
Pikeperch (Zander)	17 04 00	7,824	D. Litton	Great Ouse Relief Channel	1977
Pumpkinseed	2 10	0,074	A. Baverstock	GLC Highgate Pond, London	1977
Roach	4 01 00	1,842	R. G. Jones	Gravel Pit, Notts	1975
Rudd	4 08 00	2,041	Rev E. C. Alston	Thetford, Norfolk	1933
Ruffe	5 00	0,141	P. Barrowcliffe	River Bure, St Benets Abbey, Norfolk	1977
Salmon[2]	64 00 00	29,029	Miss G. W. Ballantyne	River Tay, Scotland	1922
Schelly (Skelly)	1 10 00	0,737	W. Wainwright	Ullswater, Cumbria	1976
Tench	10 01 02	4,567	L. W. Brown	Peterborough Brick Pit, Cambs	1975
Trout, American Brook	5 06 00	2,438	A. Pearson	Avington Fishery, Hants	1979
Trout, Brown[3]	19 09 04	8,880	J. A. F. Jackson	Loch Quoich, Inverness-shire	1978
Trout, Rainbow	19 08 00	8,844	A. Pearson	Avington Fishery, Hants	1977

[1] *A pike of allegedly 52 lb 23 kg was recovered when Whittlesea Mere, Cambridgeshire was drained in 1851. A pike of reputedly 72 lb 32 kg 650 was landed from Loch Ken, Dumfries and Galloway, by John Murray in 1777.*

[2] *The 8th Earl of Home is recorded as having caught a 69¾ lb 31 kg 638 specimen in the River Tweed in 1730. J. Wallace claimed a 67-pounder 30 kg at Barjarg, Dumfries and Galloway in 1812.*

[3] *In 1866 W. C. Muir caught a 39½ lb 17 kg 916 specimen in Loch Awe, Strathclyde and in 1816 a 36 lb 16 kg specimen was reported from the R. Colne, near Watford, Hertfordshire.*

BRITISH RECORDS
(continued)

SEA FISH

Fish	Weight	grams	Angler	Location	Year
Angler Fish	82 12 00	37,533	K. Ponsford	off Mevagissey, Cornwall	1977
Bass	18 06 00	8,334	R. G. Slater	off Eddystone Reef	1975
Black-fish	3 10 08	1,658	James Semple	off Heads of Ayr, Strathclyde	1972
Bluemouth	3 02 08	1,431	Anne Lyngholm	Stornoway, Western Isles	1976
Bogue	1 15 04	0,885	S. G. Torode	Pembroke, Guernsey, CI	1978
Bream, Black	6 14 04	3,125	J. A. Garlick	off Devon Coast	1977
Bream, Gilthead	6 15 00	3,146	H. Solomons	Salcombe Estuary, Devon	1977
Bream, Ray's	7 15 12	3,621	G. Walker	Crimdon Beach, Hartlepool, Cleveland	1967
Bream, Red	9 08 12	4,330	B. H. Reynolds	off Mevagissey, Cornwall	1974
Brill	16 00 00	7,257	A.H. Fisher	Isle of Man	1950
Bull Huss	21 03 00	9,610	J. Holmes	Looe, Cornwall	1955
Catfish	15 12 00	7,144	E. Fisher	off Filey, Yorks	1973
Coalfish	33 07 00	15,166	L. M. Saunders	Start Point, off Dartmouth, Devon	1980
Cod	53 00 00	24,039	G. Martin	Start Point, Devon	1972
Comber	1 13 00	0,822	B. Phillips	off Mounts Bay, Cornwall	1977
Common Skate	226 08 00	102,733	R. S. Macpherson	Duny Voe, Shetland	1970
Conger	109 06 00	49,609	R. W. Potter	SE of Eddystone Light	1976
Dab	2 12 04	1,254	R. Islip	Gairloch, Wester Ross, Scotland	1975
Dogfish, Black-mouthed	2 13 08	1,288	J. H. Anderson	NW Poll Point, Loch Fyne, Scotland	1977
Dogfish, Lesser Spotted	4 08 00	2,040	J. Beattie	off Ayr Pier, Strathclyde	1969
Flounder	5 11 08	2,593	A. G. L. Cobbledick	Fowey, Cornwall	1956
Forkbeard, Greater	4 11 04	2,133	Miss M. Woodgate	Falmouth Bay, Cornwall	1969
Garfish	2 15 09	1,347	M. Wills	The Lizard, Coverack, Cornwall	1979
Greater Weaver	2 04 00	1,020	P. Ainslie	Brighton, E Sussex	1927
Gurnard, Grey	2 07 00	1,105	D. Swinbanks	Caliach Point, Mull, Scotland	1976
Gurnard, Red	5 00 00	2,268	B. D. Critchley	off Rhyl, Clwyd	1973
Gurnard, Streaked	1 06 08	0,637	H. Livingstone Smith	Loch Goil, Firth of Clyde	1971
Gurnard, Yellow or Tubfish	12 03 00	5,528	G. J. Reynolds	Langland Bay, W Glamorgan	1976
Haddock	13 11 04	6,215	G. Bones	off Falmouth, Cornwall	1978
Haddock, Norway	1 13 08	0,836	T. Barrett	off Southend-on-Sea, Essex	1975
Hake	25 05 08	11,494	H. W. Steele	Belfast Lough, N Ireland	1962
Halibut	234 00 00	106,136	C. Booth	Dunnett Head, off Scrabster, Highland	1979
Herring	1 01 00	0,481	Brett Barden	off Bexhill-on-Sea, E Sussex	1973
John Dory (St Peter's Fish)	11 14 00	5,386	J. Johnson	off Newhaven, E Sussex	1977
Ling	57 02 08	25,924	H. Solomons	off Mevagissey, Cornwall	1975
Lumpsucker	14 03 00	6,435	W. J. Burgess	off Felixstowe, Suffolk	1970
Mackerel	5 06 08	2,452	S. Beasley	north of Eddystone Light	1969
Megrim	3 12 08	1,715	Paul Christie	Loch Gairloch, Scotland	1973
Monkfish	66 00 00	29,936	C. G. Chalk	Shoreham, W Sussex	1965
Mullet, Golden Gray	2 10 00	1,190	R. J. Hopkins	Burry Port, Nr Llanelli, Dyfed	1976
Mullet, Red	3 10 00	1,644	J. E. Martel	Guernsey, CI	1967
Mullet, Thick-lipped	14 02 12	6,427	R. S. Gifford	The Leys, Aberthaw, Glamorgan	1979
Mullet, Thin-lipped	5 11 00	2,579	D. E. Knowles	River Rother, Sussex	1975
Opah	128 00 00	58,057	A. R. Blewett	Mounts Bay, Cornwall	1973
Pelamid	8 13 04	4,004	J. Parnell	Torbay, Devon	1969
Perch, Dusky	28 00 00	12,700	D. Cope	off Durlston Head, Dorset	1973
Plaice	10 03 08	4,635	H. Gardiner	Longa Sound, Scotland	1974
Pollack	25 00 12	11,360	R. J. Vines	Lyme Bay, Devon	1980
Pouting	5 08 00	2,494	R. S. Armstrong	off Berry Head, Devon	1969
Ray, Blonde	37 12 00	17,122	H. T. Pout	off Start Point, Devon	1973
Ray, Bottle-nosed	76 00 00	34,471	R. Bulpitt	off The Needles, Isle of Wight	1970
Ray, Cuckoo	5 11 00	2,579	V. Morrison	off Causeway Coast, N Ireland	1975
Ray, Eagle	52 08 00	23,812	R. J. Smith	off Nab Tower, Isle of Wight	1972
Ray, Electric	96 01 00	43,571	N. J. Cowley	off Dadman Point, Cornwall	1975
Ray, Small-eyed	16 04 00	7,370	H. T. Pout	Salcombe, Devon	1973
Ray, Spotted	7 12 00	3,515	P. R. Dower	Plymouth, Devon	1977
Ray, Sting	61 08 00	27,894	V. W. Roberts	Cardigan Bay, Gwynedd	1979
Ray, Thornback	38 00 00	17,236	J. Patterson	Rustington, W Sussex	1935
Ray, Undulate	19 06 13	8,811	L. R. Le Page	Herm, CI	1970
Rockling, 3-bearded	3 02 00	1,417	N. Docksey	off Portland Breakwater, Dorset	1976
Rockling, Shore	1 01 04	0,488	A. Bayes	Gristhorpe, N Yorks	1976
Salmon, Coho	1 08 01	0,681	R. J. McCracken	St Sampsons, Guernsey, CI	1977
Sea Scorpion, Short-spined	2 03 00	0,992	R. Stephenson	Gt Cumbrae I, Strathclyde	1973
Scad (Horse Mackerel)	3 05 03	1,507	M. A. Atkins	Torbay, Devon	1978
Shad, Allis	4 12 07	2,166	P. B Gerrard	off Chesil Beach, Dorset	1977
Shad, Twaite	3 02 00	1,417	T. Hayward	Deal, Kent	1949
			S. Jenkins	Torbay, Devon	1954
Shark, Blue	218 00 00	98,878	N. Sutcliffe	Looe, Cornwall	1959
Shark, Mako	500 00 00	226,786	Mrs J. M. Yallop	off Eddystone Light	1971
Shark, Porbeagle	465 00 00	210,910	J . Potier	off Padstow, Cornwall	1976
Shark, Six-gilled	9 08 00	4,309	F. E. Beeton	off Plymouth, Devon	1976
Shark, Thresher	295 00 00	133,804	H.J. Aris	Dunose Head, Isle of Wight	1978
Smoothound, Starry	23 02 00	10,488	D. Carpenter	Bradwell-on-Sea, Essex	1972
Smoothound	28 00 00	12,700	A. T. Chilvers	Heacham, Norfolk	1969
Sole	4 14 09	2,225	P. Smart	Guernsey, CI	1980
Sole, Lemon	2 07 11	1,126	W. N. Callister	Douglas, Isle of Man	1980
Spanish Mackerel	1 00 06	0,464	P. Jones	off Guernsey, CI	1972
Spurdog	21 03 07	9,622	P. R. Barrett	off Porthleven, Cornwall	1977
Sunfish	108 00 00	48,986	T. F. Sisson	off Saundersfoot, Dyfed	1976
Tadpole-fish	1 03 12	0,559	D. A. Higgins	Browns Bay, Whitley Bay, Tyne & Wear	1977
Tope	74 11 00	33,876	A. B. Harries	Caldy I, Dyfed	1964
Torsk	12 01 00	5,471	D. Pottinger	Shetland	1968
Trigger Fish	4 09 05	2,077	E. Montacute	Weymouth Bay, Dorset	1975
Tunny	851 00 00	385,989	L. Mitchell-Henry	Whitby, N Yorks	1933
Turbot	33 12 00	15,308	R. Simcox	Salcombe, Devon	1980
Whiting	6 04 00	2,834	S. Dearman	West Bay, Bridport, Devon	1977
Whiting, Blue (Poutassou)	1 12 00	0,793	J. H. Anderson	Loch Fyne, Strathclyde	1977
Witch	1 02 13	0,533	T. J. Barathy	Colwyn Bay, Clwyd	1967
Wrasse, Ballan	8 06 06	3,808	R. W. Le Page	Bordeaux Beach, Guernsey, CI	1976
Wrasse, Cuckoo	2 00 08	0,921	A. M. Foley	off Plymouth, Devon	1973
Wreckfish	7 10 00	3,458	Cdr E. St John Holt	Looe, Cornwall	1974

ARCHERY

Earliest references

Though the earliest evidence of the existence of bows is seen in the Mesolithic cave paintings in Spain, archery as an organized sport appears to have developed in the 3rd century AD. The oldest archery body in the British Isles is the Royal Company of Archers, the Sovereign's bodyguard for Scotland, dating from 1676, though the Society of Kilwinning Archers, in Scotland, have contested the Papingo Shoot since 1488. The world governing body is the *Fédération Internationale de Tir à l'Arc* (FITA), founded in 1931.

World records

The world records for a single FITA Round are: men 1341 points (possible 1440) by Darrell Pace (USA) at Kumamoto, Japan, on 3–4 Nov 1979 and women 1321 points (possible 1440) by Natalia Butuzova (USSR) in Poland in Aug 1979.

Highest Championship scores

There are no world records for Double FITA Rounds but the highest scores achieved in either a world or Olympic championship were: men, 2571 points (possible 2880) by Darrell Pace (USA) at the 1976 Olympic Games in Montreal, Canada, on 29–30 July 1976; and women, 2515 points by Luann Ryon (USA) at Canberra, Australia, 11–12 Feb 1977.

British records

York Round—possible 1296 pts: Single Round, 1142, Peter Waterton at Oxford on 29 June 1977. Double Round, 2238, Peter Waterton at Oxford on 29 June 1977.

Hereford (Women)—possible 1296 pts: Single Round, 1182, Eileen Tomkinson at Manchester on 9 Aug 1980. Double Round, 2331, Sue Willcox at Oxford on 27–28 June 1979.

FITA Round (Men): Single Round, 1258, Mark Blenkarne at Strasbourg, France, 24 June 1979. Double Round, 2466, Dennis Savory at Welshpool, Powys, on 23–24 May 1980.

FITA Round (Women's): Single Round, 1271, Rachel Fenwick at Southampton, Hants., 3 June 1979. Double Round, 2520, Rachel Fenwick at Brussels, Belgium, 12–13 Aug 1978.

Most titles *World*

The greatest number of world titles (instituted 1931) ever won by a man is four by Hans Deutgen (b. 28 Feb 1917) (Sweden) in 1947–50. The greatest number won by a woman is seven by Janina Spychajowa-Kurkowska (b. 8 Feb 1901) (Poland) in 1931–4, 1936, 1939 and 1947. Oscar Kessels (Belgium) (1904–68) participated in 21 world championships.

Most titles *Olympic*

Hubert van Innis (1866–1961) (Belgium) won six gold and three silver medals in archery events at the 1900 and 1920 Olympic Games.

Most titles *British*

The greatest number of British Championships is 12 by Horace Alfred Ford (1822–80) in 1849–59 and 1867, and 23 by Alice Blanche Legh (1855–1948) in 1881, 1886–92, 1895, 1898–1900, 1902–9, 1913 and 1921–2. Miss Legh was inhibited from winning from 1882 to 1885—because her mother Piers Legh was Champion—and also for four further years 1915 to 1918 because there were no Championships held owing to the First World War.

Flight shooting

Sultan Selim III (1761–1808) shot 1400 Turkish *Pikes* or *gez* near Istanbul, Turkey in 1798. The equivalent is arguably between 953 and 972 yd *871–888 m*. The longest recorded distance ever shot is 1 mile 268 yd *1854,40 m* in the unlimited footbow class by the professional Harry Drake (b. 7 May 1915) of Lakeside, California, USA at Ivanpah Dry Lake, California on 24 Oct 1971. The female footbow record is 1113 yd 2 ft 6 in *1018,48 m* by Arlyne Rhode (b. 4 May 1936) at Wendover, Utah, USA on 10 Sept 1978. Don Brown (b. 13 Nov 1945) (USA) set the flight record for the handbow with 1227 yd 11 in *1122,25 m* on 5 Oct 1980 and April Moon (USA) set a women's record of 923 yd 1 ft 6 in *844,45 m* on 4 Oct 1980, both at Ivanpah Dry Lake. Drake holds the crossbow flight record with 1359 yd 2 ft 5 in *1243,4 m* at Ivanpah Dry Lake on 14 Oct 1967.

The British record (Men) is 789 yd 1 ft 9 in *721,99 m* by Alan Webster at Burton Constable, nr Hull, Humberside on 6 July 1980 and (Women) 456 yd *417,47 m* by Julie Ingleby at Burton Constable, on 15 Sept 1979.

Greatest draw

Gary Sentman, of Roseburg, Oregon, USA drew a longbow weighing a record 176 lb *79,83 kg* to the maximum draw on the arrow of 28¼ in *72 cm* at Forksville, Penn., on 20 Sept 1975.

24 Hours

The highest recorded score over 24 hours by a pair of archers is 51,633 during 48 Portsmouth Rounds by Jimmy Watt and Gordon Danby at the Epsom Showgrounds, Auckland NZ, on 18–19 Nov 1977.

BADMINTON

Origins

A similar game was played in China in the 2nd millennium BC. The modern game may have evolved *c* 1870 at Badminton Hall in Avon, the seat of the Dukes of Beaufort or from a game played in India. The first modern rules were codified in Poona in 1876. The oldest club is the Newcastle Badminton Club formed as the Armstrong College Club on 24 Jan 1900.

Thomas Cup

The International Championship or Thomas Cup (instituted 1948) has been won seven times by Indonesia in 1958, 1961, 1964, 1970, 1973, 1976 and 1979.

Uber Cup

The Ladies International Championship or Uber Cup (instituted 1956) has been won five times by Japan (1966, 1969, 1972, 1978 and 1981).

Inter County Championship

The most successful county has been Surrey with 19 wins between 1955 and 1975. The championships were instituted on 30 Oct 1930.

MOST INTERNATIONAL APPEARANCES		
	Times	Men
England	100	Anthony Derek Jordan, MBE, 1951–70
Scotland	67	Robert S. McCoig, MBE, 1956–76
Ireland	52	Clifford McIlwaine, 1972–81
Wales	51	David Colmer, 1964–80
	Times	Women
England	69	Gillian M. Gilks MBE (*née* Perrin), 1966–80
Ireland	57	Yvonne Kelly, 1955–76
Wales	52	Sue Brimble, 1969–80
Scotland	50	Christine Stewart (*née* Evans), 1970–78

Most titles

The men's singles in the All-England Championships (instituted 1899) have been won a record eight times by Rudy Hartono Kurniawan (Indonesia) (b. 18 Aug 1948) in 1968–74 and 1976. The greatest number of championships won (incl. doubles) is 21 by G. A. Thomas (later Sir George Alan Thomas, Bt.) (1881–1972) between 1903 and 1928. The women's title has been won ten times by Judy Hashman (*née* Devlin) (USA) (b. 22 Oct 1935) in 1954, 1957–8, 1960–4, 1966–7. She also equalled the greatest number of championships won of 17 by Muriel Lucas (later Mrs King Adams) from 1899 to 1910.

Shortest game

In the 1969 Uber Cup in Jakarta, Indonesia, Noriko Takagi (later Mrs Nakayama) (Japan) beat Poppy Tumengkol (Indonesia) in 9 min.

Longest hit

Frank Rugani drove a shuttlecock 79 ft 8½ in *24,29 m* in indoor tests at San José, California, USA, on 29 Feb 1964.

Marathon

The longest singles match is 73 hr 20 min by Richard P. Cuthbert at Queen Elizabeth's Grammar School, Horncastle, Lincolnshire on 23–26 Apr 1979. (*This category will now be confined to two players only.*) Two teams of four from the Royal Air Force Badminton Association played doubles for 74 hr 1 min at Rheindahlen, Germany on 25–28 June 1981.

BASEBALL

Earliest game

The Rev Thomas Wilson, of Maidstone, Kent, England, wrote disapprovingly, in 1700, of baseball being played on Sundays. It is also referred to in *Northanger Abbey* by Jane Austen, *c.* 1798. The earliest baseball game under the Cartwright (Alexander Joy Cartwright Jr 1820–92) rules was at Hoboken, New Jersey, USA, on 19 June 1846, with the New York Nine beating the Knickerbockers 23–1 in four innings.

Highest batting average

The highest average in a career is 0.367 by Tyrus Raymond Cobb (1886–1961), the 'Georgia Peach' from Augusta who played with Detroit (1905–26) and Philadelphia (1927–8). During his career Ty Cobb made a record 2244 runs from a record 4191 hits made in 3033 major league games. Lin Wen-Nsiung (Taiwan) was reported to have an average of 0.727.

Home runs *Most*

Henry Louis 'Hank' Aaron (Atlanta Braves) (b. 5 Feb 1934) holds the major league career home run record of 755 from 1954 to 1976. When he retired in Nov 1980, Japan's Sadaharu Oh (b. 20 May 1940) (Yomuiri Giants) had hit his 868th home run in a 21-yr career. George Herman 'Babe' Ruth's (1895–1948) record for home runs in one year is 60 in 154 games between 15 Apr and 30 Sept 1927. Roger Eugene Maris (b. 10 Sept 1934) (New York Yankees) hit 61 homers in a 162-game schedule in 1961. Joshua Gibson (1911–47) of Homestead Grays and Pittsburgh Crawfords, Negro League clubs, achieved a career total of 800 homers and 84 in one season, and in 1972 was elected to the Hall of Fame.

Longest home run

The longest home run ever measured was one of 618 ft *188,4 m* by Roy Edward 'Dizzy' Carlyle (1900–56) in a minor league game at Emeryville Ball Park, California, USA, on 4 July 1929. In 1919 Babe Ruth hit a 587 ft *178,9 m* homer in a Boston Red Sox *v.* New York Giants match at Tampa, Florida, USA.

Longest throw

The longest throw (ball weighs 5–5¼ oz *141–148 g*) is 445 ft 10 in *135,88 m* by Glen Edward Gorbous (b. Canada 8 July 1930) on 1 Aug 1957. The longest throw by a woman is 296 ft *90,2 m* by Mildred Ella 'Babe' Didrikson (later Mrs George Zaharias) (US) (1914–56) at Jersey City, New Jersey, USA on 25 July 1931.

Fastest base runner

The fastest time for circling bases is 13.3 sec by Ernest Evar Swanson (1902–73) at Columbus, Ohio, in 1932, at an average speed of 18.45 mph *29,70 km/h*.

Pitching

The only 'perfect game' (no hits, no runs, no walks) pitched in a World Series was by Don Larsen (New York Yankees) (b. 7 Aug 1929) with 97 pitches (71 in the strike zone) against Brooklyn Dodgers on 8 Oct 1956.

Fastest pitcher

The fastest pitcher in the world is Lynn Nolan Ryan (California Angels, Houston Astros) (b. 31 Jan 1947) who, on 20 Aug 1974 at Anaheim Stadium, California, USA, was measured to pitch at 100.9 mph *162,3 km/h*.

Youngest player

The youngest major league player of all time was the Cincinnati

pitcher, Joseph Henry Nuxhall (b. 30 July 1928) who started his career in June 1944, aged 15 years 10 months 11 days.

Record attendances and receipts

The World Series record attendance is 420,784 (six games with total receipts of $2,626,973.44) when the Los Angeles (ex-Brooklyn) Dodgers beat the Chicago White Sox 4–2 on 1–8 Oct

BATTING RECORDS			
Batting av., season	.438	Hugh Duffy (NL)	1894
,, ,,	.422	Napoleon Lajoie (AL)	1901
RBIs, career	2297	Henry 'Hank' Aaron	1954–76
,, season	190	Lewis Rober 'Hack' Wilson	1930
,, game	12	James LeRoy Bottomley	16 Sept 1924
,, innings	7	Edward Cartwright	23 Sept 1890
Base hits, season	257	George Harold Sisler	1920
Hits, consecutive	12	Michael Franklin 'Pinky' Higgins	19–21 June 1938
,, ,,	12	Walter 'Moose' Dropo	14–15 July 1952
Consecutive games batted safely	56	Joseph Paul DiMaggio	15 May–16 July 1941
Stolen bases, career	938	Louis Clark Brock	1961–79
,, season	118	Louis Clark Brock	1974
Consecutive games played	2130	Henry Louis 'Lou' Gehrig	1 June 1925– 30 April 1939
PITCHING RECORDS			
Games won, career	511	Denton True 'Cy' Young	1890–1911
,, ,, season	60	Charles Gardner Radbourne	1884
Consecutive games won	24	Carl Owen Hubbell	1936–37
Shutouts, career	113	Walter Perry Johnson	1907–27
,, season	16	George W. Bradley	1876
	16	Grover Cleveland Alexander	1916
Strikeouts, career	3508	Walter Perry Johnson	1907–27
,, season	383	Lynn Nolan Ryan	1973
No-hit games, career	4	Sanford 'Sandy' Koufax	1955–66
	4	Lynn Nolan Ryan	1966–77
Earned run av., season	0.90	Ferdinand Schupp (140 inn)	1916
,, ,,	1.01	Hubert 'Dutch' Leonard (222 inn)	1914
,, ,,	1.12	Robert Gibson (305 inn)	1968
Complete games, career	751	Denton True 'Cy' Young	1890–1911

Hank Aaron's record breaking 715th home run, which brought him another world record of 900,000 letters from fans and others (see p. 98).

1959. The single game record is 92,706 for the fifth game (receipts $552,774.77) at the Memorial Coliseum, Los Angeles, California, on 6 Oct 1959. The highest seating capacity in a baseball stadium is 76,977 in the Cleveland Municipal Stadium, Ohio, USA. The all-time season record for attendances for both leagues has been 29,193,417 in 1971.

An estimated 114,000 spectators watched a game between Australia and an American Services team in a 'demonstration' event during the Olympic Games at Melbourne, 1 Dec 1956.

BASKETBALL

Origins
The game of 'Pok-ta-Pok' was played in the 10th century BC, by the Olmecs in Mexico, and closely resembled basketball in its concept. 'Ollamalitzli' was a variation of this game played by the Aztecs in Mexico as late as the 16th century. If the solid rubber ball was put through a fixed stone ring the player was entitled to the clothing of all the spectators. Modern basketball (which may have been based on the German game of *Korbball*) was devised by the Canadian-born Dr James A. Naismith (1861–1939) at the Training School of the International YMCA College at Springfield, Massachusetts, USA, in mid-December 1891. The first game played under modified rules was on 20 Jan 1892. The International Amateur Basketball Federation (FIBA) was founded in 1932, and the English Basket Ball Association was founded in 1936.

Most titles *Olympic*
The USA won all seven Olympic titles from the time the sport was introduced to the Games in 1936 until 1968, without losing a single match. In 1972 in Munich their run of 63 consecutive victories in matches in the Olympic Games was broken when they lost 50–51 to the USSR in the disputed Final match. They won their eighth title in 1976.

Most titles *World*
Brazil, USSR and Yugoslavia have won the World Men's Championship (instituted 1950) twice. Brazil won in 1959 and 1963, the USSR in 1967 and 1974 and Yugoslavia in 1970 and 1978. In 1975 the USSR won the Women's Championship (instituted 1953) for the fifth consecutive time since 1959.

Most titles *European*
The most European Champions Cup (instituted 1957) wins is seven by Real Madrid, Spain. The women's title has been won 17 times by Daugawa, Riga, USSR. The most wins in the European Nations Championships for men is 12 by the USSR, and in the women's event 15 also by the USSR.

Most titles *British*
England has won seven British Championship titles, out of the 14 competitions since the championship was introduced in 1960.

Most titles *American Professional*
The most National Basketball Association titles (instituted 1947), played for between the leading professional teams in the United States, have been won by the Boston Celtics with 14 victories between 1957 and 1981.

Most titles *English*
The most English National championship wins (instituted 1936) have been by London Central YMCA, with eight wins in 1957–8, 1960, 1962–4, 1967 and 1969. On 6 Apr 1974 Sutton and Crystal Palace beat Embassy All Stars in a record score for the final of 120–100. The English National League title has been won five times by Crystal Palace 1974, 1976–8 and 1980.

Most titles *English Women's Cup*
Most English Women's cups (instituted 1965) have been won by Tigers (Hertfordshire) with seven wins, 1972–3, 1976–80.

Highest score *International*
The highest score recorded in an international match is 167 by S. Korea against Thailand (50) in Hong Kong on 13 Sept 1980, in the Asian Women's Championships. The highest in a British Championship is 125 by England when beating Wales (54) on 1 Sept 1978. England beat Gibraltar 130–45 on 31 Aug 1978.

Highest score *match*
The highest aggregate score in an NBA match is 316 between the Philadelphia Warriors (169 points) and the New York Knickerbockers (147 points) at Hershey, Pennsylvania on 2 Mar 1962, and between the Cincinnati Royals (165 points) and the San Diego Rockets (151 points) on 12 Mar 1970. In an ABA match between the San Diego Conquistadors (176 points) and the New York Nets (166 points) on 14 Feb 1975, the score totalled 342 points after four periods of overtime.

Highest score *United Kingdom*
The highest score recorded in a match is 250 by the Nottingham YMCA Falcons v. Mansfield Pirates at Nottingham, on 18 June 1974. It was a handicap competition and Mansfield received 120 points towards their total of 145. The highest score in a senior National League match is 165 by Crystal Palace v. Bedford (40) on 3 Dec 1977. The highest in the National Cup is 146 by Doncaster v Cleveland (109) on 11 Feb 1976.

Highest score *Individual*
Mats Wermelin, 13, (Sweden) scored all 272 points in a 272–0 win in a regional boys' tournament in Stockholm, Sweden on 5 Feb 1974. The highest single game score in an NBA game is 100 points by Wilton Norman Chamberlain (b. 21 Aug 1936) for Philadelphia v. New York on 2 Mar 1962. The most in a college game is 113 points by Clarence 'Bevo' Francis, for Rio Grande College, Ohio v. Hillsdale at Jackson, Ohio on 2 Feb 1954. The record score by a woman is 70 points by Annette Kennedy of SUNY-Purchase in a 116-21 defeat of Pratt, New York, USA on 23 Jan 1981.

The highest individual score in an English National League (Div. One) or Cup match is 68 points by Bobby Cooper of London Central YMCA v. Exeter on 2 Mar 1979.

Most points
Wilt Chamberlain scored a career total of 31,419 points in NBA matches between 1960 and 1973. The record for the most points scored in a college career is (women): 4061, Pearl Moore of Francis Marion College, Florence, S. Carolina, 1975–9, (men): 4045 by Travis Grant for Kentucky State in 1969–72. In the English National League, Ian Day has scored 2314 points in 136 games, 1973–81.

Tallest players
The tallest player of all time is reputed to be Suleiman Ali Nashnush (b. 1943) who played for the Libyan team in 1962 when measuring 2,45 m *8 ft*. The tallest woman player is Iuliana Semenova (USSR) (b. 9 Mar 1952) at a reported 7 ft 2 in *2,18 m* and weighing 281 lb *127,4 kg*. The tallest British player has been the 7 ft 6¼ in *229 cm* tall Christopher Greener (see p. 11) of London Latvians whose International debut for England was v. France on 17 Dec 1969.

Most accurate
The greatest goal shooting demonstration has been by Ted St Martin of Jacksonville, Florida, who, on 25 June 1977, scored 2036 consecutive free throws. In a 24-hr period, 31 May–1 June 1975 Fred L. Newman of San José, California, USA scored 12,874 baskets out of 13,116 throws (98.15 per cent accuracy). Newman also holds the record for consecutive blindfold free throws with 88 straight at the San José YMCA on 5 Feb 1978.

Longest recorded goal
The longest recorded field goal in a match is a measured 89 ft 3 in *27,20 m* by Les Henson for Virginia Tech v Florida State on 21 Jan 1980. A British record of 75 ft 9½ in *23,10 m* is claimed by David Tarbatt (b. 23 Jan 1949) of Altofts Aces v Harrogate Demons at Featherstone, West Yorkshire on 27 Jan 1980.

Most travelled team
The Harlem Globetrotters (USA) have travelled over 6,000,000 miles *9 600 000 km*, visited 94 countries on six continents, and have been watched by an estimated 80,000,000 since their foundation on 7 Jan 1927 at Hinckley, Illinois. They have won over 12,000 games (losing less than 350), but many were not truly competitive.

Largest ever gate
The Harlem Globetrotters (USA) played an exhibition in front

of 75,000 in the Olympic Stadium, West Berlin, Germany, in 1951. The largest indoor basketball attendance was at the Astrodome, Houston, Texas, USA, where 52,693 watched the match between University of Houston and University of California at Los Angeles (UCLA), on 20 Jan 1968.

Marathon
The longest game is 90 hr 2 min by PE3 at Jordanhill College of Education, Glasgow on 23–27 Mar 1981.

BILLIARDS AND SNOOKER

BILLIARDS
Earliest mention
The earliest recorded mention of billiards was in France in 1429, while Louis XI, King of France 1461–83, is reported to have had a billiard table. The first recorded public billiards room in England was the Piazza, Covent Garden, London, in the early part of the 19th century. Rubber cushions were introduced in 1835 and slate beds in 1836.

Most titles *Professional*
The greatest number of world championship titles (instituted 1870) won by one player is eight by John Roberts, Jnr (1847–1919) (England) in 1870 (twice), 1871, 1875 (twice), 1877 and 1885 (twice). The greatest number of United Kingdom titles (instituted 1934) won by any player is seven (1934–39 and 1947) by Joe Davis, OBE (1901–78) (England), who also won four world titles (1928–30 and 1932). William F. Hoppe (USA) (1887–1959) won 51 'world' titles in the United States variant of the game between 1906 and 1952.

Most titles *Amateur*
The record for world amateur titles is four by Robert James Percival Marshall (Australia) (b. 10 Apr 1910) in 1936, 1938, 1951 and 1962. The greatest number of English Amateur Championships (instituted 1888) ever won is 12 by Norman Dagley (b. 27 June 1930) in 1965–66, 1970–75, 1978–81. The record number of women's titles is eight by Vera Selby (b. 13 Mar 1930) 1970–8.

Highest breaks
Tom Reece (1873–1953) made an unfinished break of 499,135, including 249,152 cradle cannons (two points each), in 85 hr 49 min against Joe Chapman at Burroughes' Hall, Soho Square, London, between 3 June and 6 July 1907. This was not recognized because press and public were not continuously present. The highest certified break made by the anchor cannon is 42,746 by William Cook (England) from 29 May to 7 June 1907. The official world record under the then baulk-line rule is 1784 by Joe

Davis, OBE in the United Kingdom Championship on 29 May 1936. Walter Albert Lindrum OBE (Australia) (1898–1960) made an official break of 4137 in 2 hr 55 min against Joe Davis at Thurston's on 19–20 Jan. 1932, before the baulk-line rule was in force. Davis has an unofficial personal best of 2502 (mostly pendulum cannons) in a match against Tom Newman (1894–1943) (England) in Manchester in 1930. The highest break recorded in amateur competition is 1149 by Michael Ferreira (India) at Calcutta, India on 15 Dec 1978, but a rule amendment which now permits only three consecutive pot reds from its spot instead of five has reduced the size of breaks. The record under current rules is 506 by Norman Dagley at Nottingham on 23 Feb 1980.

Fastest century
Walter Lindrum, OBE of Australia made an unofficial 100 break in 27.5 sec in Australia on 10 Oct 1952. His official record is 100 in 46.0 sec set in Sydney in 1941.

3 CUSHION
This pocketless variation dates back to 1878. The world governing body, the *Union Mondiale de Billiard* (UMB) was formed in 1928. The most successful exponent spanning the pre and post international era from 1906 to 1952 was Willie Hoppe who won 51 billiards championships in all forms. Most UMB titles have been won by Raymond Ceulemans (Belgium) (b. 1937) with 16 (1963–6, 1968–73, 1975–80), with a peak average of 1.679 in 1978.

SNOOKER
Further information is available in the Guinness Book of Snooker *by Clive Everton (£7.50) published by Guinness Superlatives Ltd.*

Origins
Research shows that snooker was originated by Colonel Sir Neville Francis Fitzgerald Chamberlain, KCB, KCVO (1856–1944) as a hybrid of 'black pool', 'pyramids' and billiards, in the Ootacamund Club, Nilgiris, Madras, India in the summer of 1875. It did not reach England until 1885, where the modern scoring system was adopted in 1891. Championships were not instituted until 1916. The World Professional Championship was instituted in 1927.

Most titles *World*
The world professional title (inst 1927) was won a record 15 times by Joe Davis OBE (1901–78), 1927–40 and 1946. The most wins in the amateur championships (inst 1963) have been two by Gary Owen (England) in 1963 and 1966, and Ray Edmonds (England) 1972 and 1974.

World Championships *Youngest*
The youngest player to win a world title is Jimmy White (GB) (b. 2 May 1962) who was 18 yr 191 days when he won the World

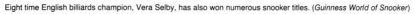

Eight time English billiards champion, Vera Selby, has also won numerous snooker titles. (*Guinness World of Snooker*)

top: Peter Kantor and Colin McCormack acknowledge congratulations for beating the snooker marathon record after nearly six days play. *(Lancashire Evening Post)*

centre: Swiss engineer, Poldi Berchtold, smashed all the records as well as winning four of the major competitions on the Cresta Run in 1975. *(St Moritz Tobogganing Club)*

bottom: In addition to their Olympic successes, Manfred Nehmer and Bernhard Germeshausen have won four world title medals between them. *(Tony Duffy, All-Sport)*

Amateur Snooker championship at Launceston, Tasmania, Australia on 9 Nov 1980.

Highest breaks

It is possible in a combination of highly unlikely circumstances to score 155. Alex Higgins (b. 18 Mar 1949) (N. Ireland) became the first player ever to make a '16 red' clearance with a break of 146 at Leicester YMCA, Leicester, England in 1976. The official world record break (commonly referred to as a maximum) is 147 set by Joe Davis, OBE (1901–78) against Willie Smith at Leicester Square Hall, London on 22 Jan 1955, and by Rex Williams (b. 30 July 1933) (GB) against Manuel Francisco at Cape Town, South Africa, on 22 Dec 1965. Over 150 other 'perfect' frames have been achieved under less rigorous conditions. The only maximum compiled in a major tournament was by John Spencer at Slough, Berks, on 13 Jan 1978. The first man to compile a 147 break was E. J. 'Murt' O'Donoghue (b. New Zealand, 1901) in Griffiths, NSW, Australia, on 26 Sept 1934.

The official world amateur record break is 140 set by Joe Johnson (b. 29 July 1952) (England) in the TUC Club, Middlesbrough, Cleveland in 1978. David Taylor (b. 9 July 1943) made three consecutive frame clearances of 130, 140, and 139 (total 409) at Minehead, Somerset, on 1 June 1978.

Marathon

The snooker endurance record is 140 hr 25 min by Peter Kantor and Colin McCormack at Preston Polytechnic, Lancashire on 20–26 Feb 1981.

POOL

Pool or championship pocket billiards with numbered balls began to become standardised *c.* 1890. The greatest exponents were Ralph Greenleaf (USA) (1899–1950) who won the 'world' professional title 19 times (1919–37) and William Mosconi (USA) (b. 27 June 1913) who dominated the game from 1941 to 1957.

The longest consecutive run in an American straight pool match is 625 balls by Michael Eufemia at Logan's Billiard Academy, Brooklyn, NY, on 2 Feb 1960. The greatest number of balls pocketed in 24 hr is 11,700 (a rate of one per 7.38 sec) by Gary Mounsey (b. 1947) at Hamilton, NZ, on 30 June–1 July 1979.

Marathon

The longest game is 203 hr by Peter McDermott and Stephen Rhodes at Keighley, W. Yorkshire on 13–21 Sept 1980.

BAR BILLIARDS
Highest scoring rate

The record scoring rate in a league game has been 24,340 in 17 min by John Stevens at the Ampthill Hotel, Freemantle, Southampton, Hampshire on 25 Jan. 1979.

24 hours

The highest bar billiards score in 24 hr by a team of five is 1,383,870 at The Magpie, Goring-on-Thames, Berkshire on 30–31 May 1981.

BOBSLEIGH AND TOBOGGANING

BOBSLEDDING
Origins

The oldest known sledge is dated *c.* 6500 BC and came from Heinola, Finland. The first known bobsleigh race took place at Davos, Switzerland in 1889. The International Federation of Bobsleigh and Tobogganing was formed in 1923, followed by the International Bobsleigh Federation in 1957.

Most titles *Olympic*

The Olympic four-man bob title (inst. 1924) has been won four times by Switzerland (1924, 1936, 1956 and 1972). The USA (1932, 1936), Switzerland (1936, 1980), Italy (1956, 1968) and W. Germany (1952, 1972) have won the Olympic boblet (inst. 1932) event twice. The most gold medals won by an individual is three by Meinhard Nehmer (GDR) and Bernhard Germeshausen (GDR) in the 1976 two-man, 1976 and 1980 four-man events. The most medals won is six (two gold, two silver, two bronze) by Eugenio Monti (Italy) (b. 23 Jan 1928) from 1956 to 1968. The only British victory has been the two-man bob in 1964 by Hon.

Robin Thomas Valerian Dixon (b. 21 Apr 1935) and Anthony James Dillon Nash (b. 18 Mar 1936).

Most titles *World*
The world four-man bob title has been won 12 times by Switzerland (1924, 1936, 1939, 1947, 1954–7, 1971–3 and 1975). Italy won the two-man title 14 times (1954, 1956–63, 1966, 1968–9, 1971 and 1975). Eugenio Monti has been a member of eleven world championship crews, eight two-man and three four-man.

TOBOGGANING
Cresta Run
The word toboggan comes from the Micmac American Indian word *tobaakan*. The St Moritz Tobogganing Club, Switzerland, founded in 1887 is the oldest toboggan club in the world. It is unique in being the home of the Cresta Run, which dates from 1884, and for the introduction of the one-man racing toboggan skeleton. The course is 3977 ft *1212,25 m* long with a drop of 514 ft *157 m* and the record is 53.24 sec (av. 50.92 mph *81,96 km/h*) by Poldi Berchtold of Switzerland on 9 Feb 1975. The record from the Junction (2913 ft *888 m*) is 42.96 sec, by Berchtold on 22 Feb 1975. Speeds of 90 mph *145 km/h* are occasionally attained.

The greatest number of wins in the Grand National (inst. 1885) is eight by the 1948 Olympic champion Nino Bibbia (Italy) (b. 9 Sept 1924) in 1960–4, 1966, 1968 and 1973. The greatest number of wins in the Curzon Cup (inst. 1910) is eight by Bibbia in 1950, 1957–8, 1960, 1962–4, and 1969, who hence won the double in 1960 and 1962–4. The most descents made in a season is 7915 during 70 days in 1980.

Lugeing
In lugeing the rider adopts a sitting, as opposed to a prone, position. Official international competition began at Klosters, Switzerland, in 1881. The first European championships were at Reichenberg, E. Germany, in 1914 and the first world championships at Oslo, Norway, in 1953. The International Luge Federation was formed in 1957. Lugeing became an Olympic sport in 1964. Speeds of more than 80 mph *128 km/h* have been recorded at Krynica, Poland.

Most titles *World and Olympic*
The most successful rider in the world championships is Thomas Köhler (E. Germany) (b. 25 June 1940), who won the single-seater title in 1962, 1964 (Olympic), 1966 and 1967 and shared the two seater title in 1967 and 1968 (Olympic). In the women's championship Margit Schumann (E. Germany) (b. 14 Sept 1952) has won five times, in 1973–5, 1976 (Olympic) and 1977.

BOWLING (TENPIN)

Origins
The ancient German game of nine-pins (*Heidenwerfen*—knock down pagans) was exported to the United States in the early 17th century. In about 1845 the Connecticut and New Haven State Legislatures prohibited the game so a tenth pin was added to evade the ban; but there is some evidence of ten pins being used in Suffolk about 300 years ago. The first body to standardise rules was the American Bowling Congress (ABC), established in New York on 9 Sept 1895.

In the United States there were 8699 bowling establishments with 154,077 bowling lanes and 65,000,000 bowlers in 1979. The world's largest bowling centre (now closed) was the Tōkyō World Lanes Centre, Japan with 252 lanes. Currently the largest centre is the Willow Grove Park Lanes, Philadelphia, USA which has 116 lanes. The largest in Europe is the Nottingham Bowl at Nottingham, England, where the game was introduced in 1960, with 48 lanes on two floors (24 on each floor).

World championships
The world (Fédération Internationale des Quilleurs) championships were instituted in 1954. The highest pinfall in the individual men's event is 5963 (in 28 games) by Ed Luther (US) at Milwaukee, Wisconsin, on 28 Aug 1971. In the women's championships (instituted 1963) the record is 4720 pins (in 24 games) by Bong Coo (Philippines) at Manila, Philippines in Dec 1979.

British tenpin record holder Daniel Smith who bowled a three-game series of 785. (*British Tenpin Bowling Association*)

Highest scores *World*
The highest individual score for three sanctioned games (possible 900) is 886 by Albert 'Allie' Brandt of Lockport, New York, USA, on 25 Oct 1939. The record by a woman is 831 by Anne Splain in Boardman, Ohio, USA, on 7 Dec 1979. The record for consecutive strikes in sanctioned match play is 33 by John Pezzin (b. 1930) at Toledo, Ohio, USA on 4 Mar 1976. The highest number of sanctioned 300 games is 27 (till 1980) by Elvin Mesger of Sullivan, Missouri, USA. The maximum 900 for a three-game series has been recorded four times in unsanctioned games—by Leo Bentley at Lorain, Ohio, USA, on 26 Mar 1931; by Joe Sargent at Rochester, New York State, USA, in 1934, by Jim Margie in Philadelphia, Pennsylvania, USA, on 4 Feb 1937 and by Bob Brown at Roseville Bowl, California, USA on 12 Apr 1980. Such series must have consisted of 36 consecutive strikes (*i.e.* all pins down with one ball).

The highest average for a season attained in sanctioned competition is 239 by Jim Lewis, of Schenectady, NY, USA, for 88 games in 1975–6.

Highest scores *Great Britain*
The United Kingdom record for a three-game series is 785 by Daniel John Smith (b. 15 June 1955) at the Charrington Bowl, Tolworth, Surrey on 18 Dec 1980. The record score for a single game is 300, first achieved by Albert Kirkham (b. 1931) of Burslem, Staffordshire, on 5 Dec 1965, which has since been equalled on several occasions. The best by a woman is 299 by Carole Cuthbert at the Airport Bowl, Hayes, Middx on 16 Mar 1972, and Patricia Dew also at the Airport Bowl on 5 July 1978. The three-game series record for a woman player is 724 by Joyce Presland at the Humber Bowl, Ilkeston, Derby on 8 Oct 1974.

Marathon
John Francis Damiani bowled for 155 hr 4 min on 15–21 Aug 1980 at the Lancaster Lanes, New York, USA.

SKITTLES
24 Hours
Eight players from Torquay United Social Club Blues knocked down 77,904 West Country skittles on 6–7 June 1980 at the Belgrave Hotel, Torquay, Devon. The highest hood skittle score in 24 hr is 107,487 pins by 12 players from the Plume of Feathers, Daventry, Northamptonshire, on 19–20 Mar 1976. The highest table skittle score in 24 hr is 90,446 skittles by 12 players at the Finney Gardens Hotel, Hanley, Staffs on 27–28 Dec 1980.

Marathon
The duration record for knocking down skittles (9-pins) is 146 hr by the Exiles at the Horseshoe Inn, Combe Down, Bath, Avon on 24-30 Aug 1979.

BOWLS

OUTDOOR
Origins
Bowls can be traced back to at least the 13th century in England. The Southampton Town Bowling was formed in 1299. A green dating back to 1294 is claimed by the Chesterfield Bowling Club. After falling into disrepute, the game was rescued by the bowlers of Scotland who, headed by William W. Mitchell (1803–84), framed the modern rules in 1848–9.

Most titles *World*
The only man to win two singles titles is David John Bryant CBE

(b. 27 Oct 1931) (England) in 1966 and 1980. Australia has won the doubles event on two occasions, 1966 and 1980. At Johannesburg, South Africa, in February 1976, the South African team achieved an unprecedented clean sweep of all four titles and the team competition (Leonard Trophy).

Most titles *International Championship*

In the annual International Championships (instituted 1903) Scotland have won 34 times to England's 19. The most consecutive wins are 11 by Scotland from 1965 to 1975.

Most titles *English*

The record number of English Bowls Association (founded 8 June 1903) championships is 15 won or shared by David Bryant, CBE, including six singles, three pairs (1965, 1969, 1974), and two triples (1966, 1977), who uniquely was involved in all four titles with four rinks or fours championships (1957, 1968, 1969 and 1971). He has also won six British Isles titles (four singles, one pairs, one fours) in the period 1957–74.

Highest score

The highest score achieved in an international bowls match is the 63–1 victory by Swaziland *v* Japan during the World Championships at Melbourne, Australia on 16 Jan 1980.

Most eights

Freda Ehlers and Linda Bertram uniquely scored three consecutive eights in the Southern Transvaal pairs event at Johannesburg, South Africa on 30 Jan 1978.

International appearances

The greatest number of international appearances outdoors by any bowler is 78 reached by Syd Thompson (b. 29 Aug 1912) for Ireland 1947–73. He also has had 45 indoor caps. The youngest bowler to represent England was David J. Cutler (b. 1 Aug 1954) on 16 July 1975, who was the youngest ever EBA champion. Norman Thomas Amos (b. 20 Sept 1958) represented Scotland aged 20 years 299 days in Wales on 16 July 1979.

Marathon

The longest game is 81 hr 35 min by two fours teams of the River Park Bowling Club, Johannesburg, South Africa on 17–20 Apr 1981.

INDOOR

The English Indoor Bowling Association became an autonomous body in 1971. Prior to that it was part of the English Bowling Association.

Most titles

The four-corner international championship was first held in 1936. England have won most titles with 18 wins. The National Singles title (inst. 1960) has been won most often by David Bryant, CBE with eight wins (1960, 1966, 1971–3, 1975, 1978–9). David Bryant has won the World Indoor Championship (inst 1979) on all three occasions it has been held, 1979–81.

Highest score

The highest score in a British International match is 52 by Scotland *v.* Wales (3) at Teeside in March 1972.

Marathon

Two fours teams from the Tauranga District Indoor Bowling Association, NZ, played for 73 hr 30 min on 13–16 Apr 1979.

BOXING

below left: Larry Holmes, World heavyweight champion, who finally caused Mohammad Ali to quit boxing after earning an estimated $68 million. (*Steve Powell, All-Sport*)

below: When Sugar Ray Leonard won the Olympic light-welterweight title in 1976 he could hardly have dreamed he would receive a record $8.5 million despite losing a fight. (*Tony Duffy, All-Sport*)

Earliest references

Boxing with gloves was depicted on a fresco from the Isle of Thera, Greece which has been dated 1520 BC. The earliest prizering code of rules was formulated in England on 16 Aug 1743 by the champion pugilist Jack Broughton (1704–89), who reigned from 1734 to 1750. Boxing, which had, in 1867, come under the Queensberry Rules formulated for John Sholto Douglas, 9th Marquess of Queensberry (1844–1900) was not established as a legal sport in Britain until after the ruling, R. v. Roberts and Others, of Mr Justice Grantham, following the death of Billy Smith (Murray Livingstone) as the result of a fight on 24 Apr 1901.

Longest fights

The longest recorded fight with gloves was between Andy Bowen of New Orleans (k. 1894) and Jack Burke in New Orleans, Louisiana, USA, on 6–7 Apr 1893. The fight lasted 110 rounds and 7 hr 19 min (9.15 p.m.–4.34 a.m), and was declared no contest (later changed to a draw) when both men were unable to continue. The longest bare knuckle fight was 6 hr 15 min between James Kelly and Jack Smith at Fiery Creek, Dalesford, Victoria, Australia on 3 Dec 1855. The longest bare knuckle fight in Britain was 6 hr 3 min (185 rounds) between Bill Hayes and Mike Madden at Edenbridge, Kent, on 17 July 1849. The greatest number of rounds was 276 in 4 hr 30 min when Jack Jones beat Patsy Tunney in Cheshire in 1825.

Shortest fights

There is a distinction between the quickest knock-out and the shortest fight. A knock-out in 10½ sec (including a 10 sec count) occurred on 26 Sept 1946, when Al Couture struck Ralph Walton while the latter was adjusting a gum shield in his corner at Lewiston, Maine, USA. If the time was accurately taken it is clear that Couture must have been more than half-way across the ring from his own corner at the opening bell. The shortest fight on record appears to be one in a Golden Gloves tournament at Minneapolis, Minnesota, USA, on 4 Nov 1947 when Mike Collins floored Pat Brownson with the first punch and the contest was stopped, without a count, 4 sec after the bell.

The fastest officially timed knock-out in British boxing is 11 sec (including a doubtless fast 10 sec count) when Jack Cain beat Harry Deamer, both of Notting Hill, London at the National Sporting Club on 20 Feb 1922.

The shortest world heavyweight title fight occurred when Tommy Burns (b. Noah Brusso) (1881–1955) of Canada knocked out Jem Roche in 1 min 28 sec in Dublin, Ireland, on 17 Mar 1908. The duration of the fight between Cassius Clay (b. Louisville, Kentucky, USA, 17 Jan 1942 who later took the name Muhammad Ali Haj) and Charles 'Sonny' Liston (1932–70) at Lewiston, Maine, USA, on 25 May 1965 was 1 min 52 sec (including the count) as timed from the video tape recordings, despite a ringside announcement giving a time of 1 min. The shortest world title fight was when Al McCoy knocked out George Chip in 45 sec for the middleweight crown in New York on 7 Apr 1914. The shortest ever British title fight was one of 40 sec (including the count), when Dave Charnley knocked out David 'Darkie' Hughes in a lightweight championship defence in Nottingham on 20 Nov 1961.

Most British titles

The most defences of a British heavyweight title is 14 by 'Bombardier' Billy Wells (1889–1967) from 1911 to 1919. The only British boxer to win three Lonsdale Belts outright has been Henry William Cooper, OBE (b. Camberwell, London, 3 May 1934), heavyweight champion (1959–69, 1970–1). He retired after losing to Joe Bugner (b. Hungary, 13 Mar 1950), having held the British heavyweight title from 12 Jan 1959 to 28 May 1969 and from 24 Mar 1970 to 16 Mar 1971.

Tallest

The tallest boxer to fight professionally was Gogea Mitu (b. 1914) of Romania in 1935. He was 7 ft 4 in *223 cm* and weighed 23 st 5 lb (327 lb) *148 kg*. John Rankin, who won a fight in New Orleans, Louisiana, USA, in November 1967, was reputedly also 7 ft 4 in *223 cm*.

Longest career

The heavyweight Jem Mace (GB), known as 'the gypsy' (1831–1910), had a career lasting 35 years from 1855 to 1890, but there were several years in which he had only one fight. Bobby Dobbs (USA) (1858–1930) is reported to have had a 39 year career from 1875 to 1914. Walter Edgerton, the 'Kentucky Rosebud', knocked out John Henry Johnson aged 45 in four rounds at the Broadway AC, New York City, USA, on 4 Feb 1916, when aged 63.

Most fights

The greatest recorded number of fights in a career is 1024 by Bobby Dobbs (USA) (see above). Abraham Hollandersky, *alias* Abe the Newsboy (USA) is reputed to have had up to 1309 fights from 1905 to 1918, but many of them were exhibition bouts.

Most fights without loss

Hal Bagwell (b. 18 Dec 1918), a lightweight, of Gloucester, was reputedly undefeated in 183 consecutive fights, of which only five were draws, between 15 Aug 1938 and 29 Nov 1948. His record of fights in the war-time period (1939–46), is however very sketchy. He never contested a British title. Of boxers with complete records Packey McFarland (USA) (1888–1936) had 97 fights in 1905–15 without a defeat.

Most knock-outs

The greatest number of finishes classed by the rules prevailing as 'knock-outs' in a career (1936–63) is 141 by Archie Moore (b. Archibald Lee Wright, Benoit, Mississippi, USA, 13 Dec 1913 or 1916). The record for consecutive KO's is 44, set by Lamar Clark of Utah at Las Vegas, Nevada, USA, on 11 Jan 1960. He knocked out six in one night (five in the first round) at Bingham, Utah, on 1 Dec 1958.

Largest purse

The greatest purse received is a reported $8,500,000 by Sugar Ray Leonard (USA) when he lost the welterweight title to Roberto Duran (Panama) in the Olympic Stadium, Montreal, Canada on 20 June 1980.

Highest bare knuckle stake

The largest stake ever fought for in this era was £4500 in the 27-round fight when Jack Cooper beat Wolf Bendoff at Port Elizabeth, South Africa on 26 July 1889.

Highest earnings in career

The largest fortune ever made in a fighting career is an estimated $68 million (including exhibitions) amassed by Muhammad Ali from October 1960 to October 1980 in 60 fights comprising 539 rounds.

Attendances *Highest*

The greatest paid attendance at any boxing fight has been 120,757 (with a ringside price of $27.50) for the Tunney v. Dempsey world heavyweight title fight at the Sesquicentennial Stadium, Philadelphia, Pennsylvania, USA, on 23 Sept 1926. The indoor record is 63,350 at the Ali v. Leon Spinks fight in the Superdome, New Orleans, Louisiana, on 15 Sept 1978. The British attendance record is 82,000 at the Len Harvey v. Jock McAvoy fight at White City, London, on 10 July 1939.

The highest non-paying attendance is 135,132 at the Tony Zale v. Billy Pryor fight at Juneau Park, Milwaukee, Wisconsin, USA, on 18 Aug 1941.

Attendances *Lowest*

The smallest attendance at a world heavyweight title fight was 2434 at the Clay v. Liston fight at Lewiston, Maine, USA, on 25 May 1965.

WORLD HEAVYWEIGHT CHAMPIONS

Earliest title fight

The first world heavyweight title fight, with gloves and 3 min rounds, was that between John Lawrence Sullivan (1858–1918) and 'Gentleman' James John Corbett (1866–1933) in New Orleans, Louisiana, USA, on 7 Sept 1892. Corbett won in 21 rounds.

Longest and shortest reigns

The longest reign of any world heavyweight champion is 11 years 8 months and 7 days by Joe Louis (b. Joseph Louis Barrow, 1914–81), from 22 June 1937, when he knocked out

James Joseph Braddock in the eighth round at Chicago, Illinois, USA, until announcing his retirement on 1 Mar 1949. During his reign Louis made a record 25 defences of his title. The shortest reign was by Leon Spinks (USA) (b. 11 July 1953) for 212 days from 15 Feb to 15 Sept 1978. Ken Norton (USA) (b. 6 Aug 1945) was recognised by the WBC as champion for 83 days from 18 Mar–9 June 1978.

Most recaptures
Muhammad Ali Haj is the only man to regain the heavyweight championship twice. Ali first won the title on 25 Feb 1964 defeating Sonny Liston. He defeated George Foreman on 30 Oct 1974 having been stripped of the title by the world boxing authorities on 28 Apr 1967. He then won the WBA title from Leon Spinks on 15 Sept 1978 having previously lost to him on 15 Feb 1978.

Undefeated
Rocky Marciano (b. Rocco Francis Marchegiano) (1923–69) is the only world heavyweight champion to have been undefeated during his entire professional career (1947–56).

Oldest and Youngest
The oldest man to win the heavyweight crown was Jersey Joe Walcott (b. Arnold Raymond Cream, 31 Jan 1914 at Merchantville, New Jersey, USA) who knocked out Ezzard Mack Charles (1921–75) on 18 July 1951 in Pittsburgh, Pennsylvania, when aged 37 years 168 days. Walcott was the oldest holder at 38 years 7 months 23 days, losing his title to Rocky Marciano (1923–69) on 23 Sept 1952. The youngest age at which the world title has been won is 21 years 331 days by Floyd Patterson (b. Waco, North Carolina, 4 Jan 1935). After the retirement of Marciano, Patterson won the vacant title by beating Archie Moore in five rounds in Chicago, Illinois, USA, on 30 Nov 1956.

Heaviest and lightest
The heaviest world champion was Primo Carnera of Italy, the 'Ambling Alp', who won the title from Jack Sharkey in six rounds in New York City, NY, USA, on 29 June 1933. He scaled 267 lb *121 kg* for this fight but his peak weight was 270 lb *122 kg*. He had an expanded chest measurement of 53 in *134 cm*, the longest reach at 85½ in *217 cm* (finger tip to finger tip) and also the largest fists with a 14¾ in *37 cm* circumference. The lightest champion was Robert James 'Bob' Fitzsimmons (1863–1917), from Helston, Cornwall, who at a weight of 167 lb *75 kg*, won the title by knocking out James Corbett in 14 rounds at Carson City, Nevada, USA, on 17 Mar 1897.

The greatest differential in a world title fight was 86 lb *39 kg* between Carnera (270 lb *122 kg*) and Tommy Loughran (184 lb *83 kg*) of the USA, when the former won on points at Miami, Florida, USA, on 1 Mar 1934.

Tallest and shortest
The tallest world champion according to measurements by the Physical Education Director of the Hemingway Gymnasium, Harvard University, was Carnera at 6 ft 5.4 in *196,59 cm* although he was widely reported and believed to be up to 6 ft 8½ in *204 cm*. Jess Willard (1881–1968) who won the title in 1915, often stated to be 6 ft 6¼ in *199 cm* was in fact 6 ft 5¼ in *196,21 cm*. (Willard was the longest lived of heavyweight champions at 86 years 351 days). The shortest was Tommy Burns, world champion from 23 Feb 1906 to 26 Dec 1908, who stood 5 ft 7 in *170 cm* and weighed 179 lb *81 kg*.

WORLD CHAMPIONS (any weight)
Longest and shortest reign
Joe Louis's heavyweight duration record of 11 years 252 days stands for all divisions. The shortest reign has been 33 days by Tony Canzeroni (USA) (1908–59) who was Junior Welterweight champion from 21 May to 23 June 1933.

Youngest and oldest
The youngest age at which any world championship has been won is 17 years 180 days by Wilfred Benitez (b. 8 Sept 1958) of Puerto Rico, who won the WBA light welterweight title in San Juan, PR, on 6 Mar 1976. The oldest world champion was Archie Moore who was recognised as a light heavyweight champion up to 10 Feb 1962 when his title was removed. He was then

believed to be between 45 and 48. Bob Fitzsimmons had the longest career of any official world titleholder with over 32 years from 1882 to 1914. He won his last world title aged 40 years 183 days in San Francisco, California on 25 Nov 1903. He was an amateur from 1880 to 1882.

Longest fight
The longest world title fight (under Queensberry Rules) was that between the lightweights Joe Gans (1874–1910), of the USA, and Oscar Matthew 'Battling' Nelson (1882–1954), the 'Durable Dane', at Goldfield, Nevada, USA, on 3 Sept 1906. It was terminated in the 42nd round when Gans was declared the winner on a foul.

Most recaptures
The only boxer to win a world title five times at one weight is 'Sugar' Ray Robinson (b. Walker Smith, Jr, in Detroit, 3 May 1920) of the USA, who beat Carmen Basilio (USA) in the Chicago Stadium on 25 Mar 1958, to regain the world middleweight title for the fourth time. The other title wins were over Jake LaMotta (USA) in Chicago on 14 Feb 1951, Randolph Turpin (United Kingdom) in New York on 12 Sept 1951, Carl 'Bobo' Olson (USA) in Chicago on 9 Dec 1955, and Gene Fullmer (USA) in Chicago on 1 May 1957. The record number of title bouts in a career is 33 or 34, at bantam and featherweight, by George Dixon (1870–1909), *alias* 'Little Chocolate', of Canada, between 1890 and 1901.

Greatest weight span
The only man to hold world titles at three weights *simultaneously* was Henry 'Homicide Hank' Armstrong (b. 12 Dec 1912), now the Rev Henry Jackson, of the USA, at featherweight, lightweight and welterweight from August to December 1938.

Greatest 'tonnage'
The greatest 'tonnage' recorded in any fight is 700 lb *317 kg* when Claude 'Humphrey' McBride (Oklahoma) 340 lb *154 kg* knocked out Jimmy Black (Houston), who weighed 360 lb *163 kg* in the third round at Oklahoma City on 1 June 1971. The greatest 'tonnage' in a world title fight was 488¾ lb *221½ kg*, when Carnera, then 259¼ lb *117½ kg* fought Paolino Uzcudun 229½ lb *104 kg* of Spain in Rome on 22 Oct 1933.

Smallest champion
The smallest man to win any world title has been Pascual Perez (1926–77) who won the flyweight title in Tōkyō on 26 Nov 1954 at 107 lb *48½ kg* and 4 ft 11½ in *1,51 m*. Jimmy Wilde (1892–1969) who held the flyweight title from 1916 to 1923 was reputed never to have fought above 108 lb *49 kg*.

Most knock-downs in Title fights
Vic Toweel (South Africa) knocked down Danny O'Sullivan of London 14 times in ten rounds in their world bantamweight fight at Johannesburg on 2 Dec 1950, before the latter retired.

AMATEUR
Most Olympic titles
Only two boxers have won three Olympic gold medals: southpaw László Papp (b. 25 Mar 1926) (Hungary), middleweight 1948, light-middleweight 1952 and 1956; Teofilio Stevenson (b 23 Mar 1952) (Cuba), heavyweight 1972, 1976 and 1980. The only man to win two titles in one celebration was Oliver L. Kirk (USA), who took both the bantam and featherweight titles in St Louis, Missouri, USA, in 1904, when the US won all the titles. In 1908 Great Britain won all the titles. Henry William 'Harry' Mallin (1892–1969) (GB) was in 1924 the first boxer ever to defend successfully an Olympic title in retaining the middleweight title.

Oldest gold medallist
Richard K. Gunn (1870–1961) (GB) won the Olympic featherweight gold medal on 27 Oct 1908 in London aged 38.

Most titles
The greatest number of ABA titles won by any boxer is six by Joseph Steers at middleweight and heavyweight between 1890 and 1893. Alex 'Bud' Watson (b. 27 May 1914) of Leith, Scotland won the Scottish heavyweight title in 1938, 1942–3, and the light-heavyweight championship 1937–9, 1943–5 and

MOST ABA TITLES WON IN EACH CLASS

Class	Instituted	Wins	Name	Years
Light-Flyweight (7 st 8 lb. *48 kg* or under)	1971	3	Michael Abrams	1971–3
Flyweight (8 st *51 kg* or under)	1920	5	Thomas Pardoe	1929–33
Bantamweight (8 st 7 lb *54 kg* or under)	1884	4	William W. Allen	1911–12, 1914, 1919
Featherweight (9 st *57 kg* or under)	1884	5	George R. Baker	1912–14, 1919, 1921
Lightweight (9 st 7 lb *60 kg* or under)	1881	4	Matthew Wells	1904–7
		4	Frederick Grace	1909, 1913, 1919–20
Light-Welterweight (10 st *63,5 kg* or under)	1951	2	David Stone	1956–7
		2	Robert Kane	1958–9
		2	L/Cpl. Brian Brazier	1961–2
		2	Richard McTaggart	1963, 1965
Welterweight (10 st 8 lb *67 kg* or under)	1920	3	Nicky Gargano	1954–6
		3	Terry Waller	1970, 1973–4
Light-Middleweight (11 st 2 lb *71 kg* or under)	1951	2	Bruce Wells	1953–4
		2	Bernard Foster	1952, 1955
		2	Stuart Pearson	1958–9
		2	Thomas Imrie	1966, 1969
		2	Robert Maxwell	1973–4
Middleweight (11 st 11 lb *75 kg* or under)	1881	5	Reuben C. Warnes	1899, 1901, 1903, 1907, 1910
		5	Harry W. Mallin	1919–23
		5	Frederick Mallin	1928–32
Light-Heavyweight (12 st 10 lb *81 kg* or under)	1920	4	Harry J. Mitchell	1922–5
Heavyweight (over 12 st 10 lb *81 kg*)	1881	5	Frederick Parks	1899, 1901–2, 1905-6

1947, making ten in all. He also won the ABA light-heavyweight title in 1945 and 1947.

Longest span

The greatest span of ABA title-winning performances is that of the heavyweight Hugh 'Pat' Floyd (b. 23 Aug 1910), who won in 1929 and gained his fourth title 17 years later in 1946.

Alex Watson with some of the trophies won in his highly successful amateur boxing career.

BULLFIGHTING

Earliest

In the latter half of the second millennium BC bull leaping was practised in Crete. Bullfighting in Spain was first reported by the Romans in Baetica (Andalusia) in the third century BC.

The first renowned professional *espada* was Francisco Romero of Ronda, in Andalusia, Spain, who introduced the *estoque* and the red muleta *c.* 1700. Spain now has some 190 active matadors. Since 1700, 42 major matadors have died in the ring.

Most successful matadors

The most successful matador measured by bulls killed was Lagartijo (1841–1900), born Rafael Molina, whose lifetime total was 4867. The longest career as a full matador was by Bienvenida (1922–75), born Antonio Mejías, from 1942 to 1974. Spanish law requires compulsory retirement at 55 years of age.

Most kills in a day

In 1884 Romano set a record by killing 18 bulls in a day in Seville and in 1949 El Litri (Miguel Báes) set a Spanish record with 114 *novilladas* in a season.

Highest paid

The highest paid bullfighter in history was El Cordobés (b. Manuel Benítez Pérez, probably on 4 May 1936, Palma del Rio, Spain), who became a sterling millionaire in 1965, when he fought 111 *corridas* up to 4 Oct of that year. In 1970 he received an estimated £750,000 for 121 fights. Paco Camino (b. 19 Dec 1941) has received up to 2,000,000 pesetas £16,000 for a *corrida*. He retired in 1977.

Largest stadiums

The world's largest bullfighting ring, the Plaza, Mexico City, with a capacity of 48,000, was closed in March 1976. The largest of Spain's 312 bullrings is Las Ventas, Madrid with a capacity of 24,000.

CANOEING

Origins

The acknowledged pioneer of canoeing as a modern sport was John Macgregor, a British barrister, in 1865. The Canoe Club was formed on 26 July 1866.

Most titles *Olympic*

Gert Fredriksson (b. 21 Nov 1919) of Sweden has won most Olympic gold medals with six in 1948, 1952, 1956 and 1960. The most by a woman is three by Ludmila Pinayeva (*née* Khvedosyuk) (b. 14 Jan 1936) (USSR), in 1964, 1968, and 1972.

Most titles *World*

Yuri Lobanov (USSR) (b. 29 Sept 1952) has won a record 11 titles from 1972 to 1979, Ludmila Pinayeva (see above) added

DOWNSTREAM CANOEING

River	Miles	Km	Name and Country	Route	Date	Duration
Rhine	714	*1149*	Sgt Charles Kavanagh (GB)	Chur, Switzerland to Willemstad, Neth.	13 Feb–2 Apr 1961	17½ days
	714	*1149*	Four RAF canoeists (GB)	Chur to Willemstad	28 Apr–7 May 1981	8 days 16 hr
Murray-Darling	1980	*3186*	Six students of St Albert's College, UNE. (Australia)	Gunnedah, NSW to Lake Alexandrina, SA	Dec 1975	—
Mississippi	2320	*3733*	Royal Air Force team of three two-man canoes (GB)	Lake Itasca, Minnesota to Gulf of Mexico	23 Aug–4 Oct 1978	42 days 5 hr
Zaire (Congo)	2600	*4185*	John and Julie Batchelor (GB)	Moasampanga to Banana	8 May–12 Sept 1974	128 days
Amazon	3400	*5470*	Stephen Zsolnay Bezuk (US) (Kayak)	Atalaya to Ponta do Céu	21 June–4 Nov 1970	136 days
Mississippi-Missouri	3810	*6132*	Nicholas Francis (GB)	Three Forks, Montana to New Orleans, La.	13 July–25 Nov 1977	135 days
Nile	4000	*6500*	John Goddard (US), Jean Laporte and André Davy (France)	Kagera to the Delta	Nov 1953–July 1954	9 months

six other world titles to her three Olympic golds, from 1966 to 1973 for a female record.

British world title winners have been the late Paul Farrant, the canoe slalom in 1959, Alan Emus, the canoe sailing in 1961, 1965 and 1969, and Albert Kerr, the Whitewater kayak slalom in 1977. Kerr, Alan Edge and Richard Fox won the slalom team title in 1979.

Most titles *British*
The most British Open titles (instituted 1936) ever won is 32 by John Laurence Oliver (Lincoln Canoe Club) (b. 12 Jan 1943) from 1966 to 1976 including 12 individual events. David Mitchell (Chester S&CC) won eight British slalom titles in 1963–8, 1970–1.

Highest speed
The Olympic 1000 m best performance of 3 min 02.70 sec set in a heat by the USSR K4 at Moscow on 31 July 1980, represents an average speed of 12.24 mph *19,70 km/h*. They achieved 13.14 mph *21,15 km/h* over the first quarter of the course.

Longest journey
The longest journey ever made by canoe is one of 7516 miles *12 096 km* around the eastern USA by paddle and portage, from Lake Itasca, Minnesota via New Orleans, Miami, New York and Lake Ontario, by Randy Bauer (b. 15 Aug 1949) and Jerry Mimbach (b. 22 May 1952) of Coon Rapids, Minn. from 8 Sept 1974 to 30 Aug 1976.

The longest journey without portages or aid of any kind is one of 6102 miles *9820 km* by Richard H. Grant and Ernest 'Moose' Lassy circumnavigating the eastern USA via Chicago, New Orleans, Miami, New York and the Great Lakes from 22 Sept 1930 to 15 Aug 1931.

Cross-Channel
The singles record across the English Channel is 3 hr 33 min 47 sec by Andrew William Dougall Samuel (b. 12 July 1937) of Glasgow, from Shakespeare Bay, Dover, to Wissant, France, on 5 Sept 1976. The doubles record is 2 hr 54 min 54 sec by Andrew Samuel and Sgt John David Anderson (RAF) (b. 18 Mar 1957) in a K2 *Accord*, from Shakespeare Bay, Dover to Cap Gris Nez, France on 22 Aug 1980.

The record for a double crossing is 12 hr 47 min in K1 canoes by nine members of the Canoe Camping Club, GB, on 7 May 1976.

North Sea
On 4–5 June 1976 Derek Hutchinson, Tom Caskey and Dave Hellawell paddled solo kayaks from Felixstowe, Suffolk to Ostend Belgium, over 100 miles *160 km* across open sea, in 31 hr.

Longest open sea voyage
Beatrice and John Dowd, Ken Beard and Steve Benson (Richard Gillett replaced him mid-journey) paddled 2170 miles *3491 km* (of a total 2192 miles *3527 km*) from Venezuela to Miami, Florida, USA, via the West Indies, 11 Aug 1977–29 Apr 1978 in two Klepper Aerius 20 kayaks.

Devizes-Westminster
The Senior Class record for the annual Challenge Cup race (instituted officially 1949) over 125 miles *201 km* with 76 locks is 15 hr 34 min 12 sec by Brian R. Greenham and Timothy J. Cornish (Reading/Leighton Park/Richmond) to win the 1979 race. The Junior Class record is 15 hr 34 min 43 sec by Anthony R. Ayres and Jeremy Q. West (Royal CC) to win the 1979 race from 60 crews.

Loch Ness
The fastest time for a K.1 from Fort Augustus to Lochend (22. miles *36,5 km*) is 3 hr 33 min 4 sec by Andrew Samuel (Trossachs Canoe and Boat Club) on 19 Oct 1975.

Highest altitude
In September 1976 Dr Michael Leslie Jones (1951–78) and Michael Hopkinson of the British Everest Canoe Expedition canoed down the River Dudh Kosi, Nepal from an altitude of 17,500 ft *5334 m*.

Longest race
The longest regularly held canoe race in the USA is the Texas Water Safari (inst. 1963), 419 miles *674 km* from San Marcos to Seadrift on the San Marcos and Guadalupe rivers. Butch Hodges and Robert Chatham set a record of 37 hr 18 min on 5–6 June 1976.

Eskimo rolls
The record for Eskimo rolls is 1000 in 53 min 5.7 sec by Terry Russell (b. 1956) at Swanley, Kent on 20 Apr 1980. A 'hand rolling' record of 100 rolls in 3 min 23 sec was set in the Crystal Palace Pool, London on 25 Feb 1980 by John Bouteloup (21).

CAVING
Duration (trogging)
The endurance record for staying in a cave is 463 days by Milutin Veljkovic (b. 1935) (Yugoslavia) in the Samar Cavern, Svrljig Mountains, northern Yugoslavia from 24 June 1969 to 30 Sep 1970. The British record is 130 days by David Lafferty, (b 1939) of Hampstead, who stayed in Boulder Chamber, Gough's Cave, Cheddar Gorge, Somerset, from 27 Mar to 4 Aug 1966. He was alone until 1 Aug when he thought it was 7 July.

COURSING
Origins
The sport of dogs chasing hares was probably of Egyptian origin in c. 3000 BC and brought to England by the Normans in 1067. The first club was the Swaffham Coursing Club formed in 1776. The classic event is the annual Waterloo Cup, instituted at Altcar, Merseyside in 1836. A government bill to declare the sport illegal was 'lost' owing to the dissolution of Parliament on 29 May 1970. The number of clubs in Britain had dwindled from 169 in 1873 to 25 in 1973.

Most successful dog
The most successful Waterloo Cup dog recorded was Colonel North's *Fullerton*, sired by *Greentich*, who tied for first in 1889 and then won outright in 1890–2. He died on 4 June 1899.

The only man in Olympic boxing history to win the same title three times, Teofilio Stevensoh of Cuba (*Don Morley, All-Sport*)

above: Channel record-breakers, Drew Samuel and John Anderson.

right: Descending the Ruiz shaft in the Gouffre Berger, France. (*Martin Farr, All-Sport*)

CAVING—PROGRESSIVE WORLD DEPTH RECORDS

Compiled by Dr A. C. Waltham, Trent Polytechnic, Nottingham.

ft	m	Cave	Country	Cavers	Date
453	138	Macocha	Czechoslovakia	J. Nagel *et al.*	1748
741	226	Grotta di Padriciano	Italy	A. Lindner *et al.*	1839
1076	328	Grotta di Trebiciano	Italy	A. Lindner *et al.*	1841
1509	460	Geldloch	Austria	—	1923
1574	480	Antro di Corchia	Italy	E. Fiorentino Club	1934
1978	603	Trou du Glaz	France	P. Chevalier *et al.*	1947
2418	737	Reseau de la Pierre St Martin	France	G. Lepineux *et al.*	July 1953
2962	903	Gouffre Berger	France	F. Petzl *et al.*	Sept 1954
3123	952	Gouffre Berger	France	L. Potié *et al.*	Aug 1955
3681	1122	Gouffre Berger	France	F. Petzl *et al.*	July 1956
3715	1133	Gouffre Berger	France	K. Pearce	Aug 1963
3842	1171	Reseau de la Pierre St Martin	France	A.R.S.I.P.	Aug 1966
4335	1321	Reseau de la Pierre St Martin	France	A.R.S.I.P.	Aug 1975
4457	1358	Gouffre Jean Bernard	France	Groupe Vulcain	July 1979
4600	1402	Gouffre Jean Bernard	France	P. Penez	Mar 1980
4773	1455	Gouffre Jean Bernard	France	P. Penez & F. Vergier	Feb 1981

N.B. The Gouffre Jean Bernard and the Reseau de la Pierre St Martin have both been explored via multiple entrances. The Jean Bernard has never been entirely descended, and the Pierre St Martin was only completely descended in one visit in 1978; consequently after August 1963 the 'sporting' records for the greatest descent into a cave should read:

3743	1141	Gouffre Berger	France	Spéléo Club de Seine	July 1968
4335	1321	Reseau de la Pierre St Martin	France	P. Courbon *et al.*	Sept 1978
4457	1358	Gouffre Jean Bernard	France	A. Ciezewski *et al.*	Feb 1980

Longest course
The longest authenticated course is one of 4 min 24.5 sec by *Hypeddars Reah*, owned and trained by Mr and Mrs M Campbell, Ayr, Ayrshire, with his litter brother *Hypeddars Angus*, owned and trained by Mr and Mrs Giles nr Kings Lynn, Norfolk, at Crowland, Lincs on 13 Oct 1979.

BEAGLING

The oldest beagle hunt is the Royal Rock Beagle Hunt, Wirral, Merseyside, whose first outing was on 28 Mar 1845. The Newcastle and District Beagles claim their origin from the municipally-supported Newcastle Harriers existing in 1787. The Royal Agricultural College beagle pack killed 79½ brace of hares in the 1968–9 season.

CRICKET

Origins
The earliest evidence of the game of cricket is from a drawing depicting two men playing with a bat and ball dated *c*. 1250. The game was played in Guildford, Surrey, at least as early as 1550. The earliest major match of which the full score survives was one in which a team representing England (40 and 70) was beaten by Kent (53 and 58 for 9) by one wicket at the Artillery Ground in Finsbury, London, on 18 June 1744. Cricket was played in Australia as early as 1803. The first international match was played between Canada and USA in 1844. Fifteen years later those countries were host to the first English touring team. The first touring team to visit England was an Australian Aborigine XI in 1868.

FIRST-CLASS CRICKET (1815 to 1981)
A substantial reduction in the English first-class cricket programme since 1968 has rendered many of the record aggregates for a season unassailable.

BATTING RECORDS—TEAMS
Highest innings *World*
The highest recorded innings by any team was one of 1107 runs by Victoria against New South Wales in an Australian Sheffield Shield match at Melbourne on 27–28 Dec 1926.

Highest innings *England*
The highest innings made in England is 903 runs for 7 wickets declared, by England in the Fifth Test against Australia at Kennington Oval, London, on 20, 22 and 23 Aug 1938. The highest innings in a county championship match is 887 by Yorkshire *v*. Warwickshire at Edgbaston, Birmingham on 7–8 May 1896.

Lowest innings
The lowest recorded innings is 12 made by Oxford University *v*. the Marylebone Cricket Club (MCC) at Oxford on 24 May 1877, and 12 by Northamptonshire *v*. Gloucestershire at Gloucester on 11 June 1907. On the occasion of the Oxford match, however, the University batted a man short. The lowest score in a Test innings is 26 by New Zealand *v*. England in the second innings of the Second Test at Auckland on 28 Mar 1955.

The lowest aggregate for two innings is 34 (16 in first and 18 in second) by Border *v*. Natal in the South African Currie Cup at East London on 19 and 21 Dec 1959.

Greatest victory
The greatest recorded margin of victory is an innings and 851 runs, when Pakistan Railways (910 for 6 wickets declared) beat Dera Ismail Khan (32 and 27) at Lahore on 2–4 Dec 1964. The largest margin in England is one of an innings and 579 runs by England over Australia in the Fifth Test at The Oval on 20–24 Aug 1938 when Australia scored 201 and 123 with two men short in both innings. The most one-sided county match was when Surrey (698) defeated Sussex (114 and 99) by an innings and 485 runs at The Oval on 9–11 Aug 1888.

Most runs in a day *World*
The greatest number of runs scored in a day is 721 all out (ten wickets) in 5 hr 48 min by the Australians *v*. Essex at Southchurch Park, Southend-on-Sea on 15 May 1948.

Most runs in a day *Test match*
The Test record for runs in a day is 588 at Old Trafford, Manchester, on 27 July 1936 when England added 398 and India were 190 for 0 in their second innings by the close.

Fastest 200 or more
The fastest recorded exhibition of hitting occurred in a Kent *v*. Gloucestershire match at Dover on 20 Aug 1937, when Kent scored 219 runs for two wickets in 71 min, at the rate of 156 runs for each 100 balls bowled.

BATTING RECORDS—INDIVIDUALS
Highest innings
The highest individual innings recorded is 499 in 10 hr 40 min by Hanif Mohammad (b. 21 Dec 1934) for Karachi *v*. Bahawalpur at Karachi, Pakistan, on 8, 9 and 11 Jan 1959. The highest score in England is 424 in 7 hr 50 min by Archibald Campbell MacLaren (1871–1944) for Lancashire *v*. Somerset at Taunton on 15–16 July 1895. The record for a Test match is 365 not out in 10 hr 8 min by Sir Garfield St Aubrun Sobers (b. 28 July 1936) playing for West Indies in the Third Test against Pakistan at Sabina Park, Kingston, Jamaica, on 27 Feb–1 Mar 1958. The England Test record is 364 by Sir Leonard Hutton (b. 23 June 1916) *v*. Australia in the Fifth Test at The Oval on 20, 22 and 23 Aug 1938.

1000 in May
The most recent example of scoring 1000 runs *in May* was by Charles Hallows (Lancashire) (1895–1972), who made precisely 1000 between 5 and 31 May 1928. Dr William Gilbert Grace (1848–1915) 9–30 May 1895, and Walter Reginald Hammond (1903–65) 7–31 May 1927, surpassed this feat with 1016 and 1042 runs. The greatest number of runs made *before the end of May* was by Thomas Walter Hayward (1871–1939) with 1074 from 16 Apr to 31 May in 1900.

Longest innings
The longest innings on record is one of 16 hr 10 min for 337 runs by Hanif Mohammad (Pakistan) *v*. West Indies in the First Test at Bridgetown, Barbados, on 20–23 Jan 1958. The English record is 13 hr 17 min by Len Hutton in his record Test score of 364.

Most runs *Season*
The greatest number of runs ever scored in a season is 3816 in 50 innings (8 not out) by Denis Charles Scott Compton CBE (b. 23 May 1918) of Middlesex and England in 1947. His batting average was 90.85.

Most runs *Career*
The greatest aggregate of runs in a career is 61,237 in 1315 innings (106 not out) between 1905 and 1934 by Sir John 'Jack' Berry Hobbs (1882–1963) of Surrey and England. His career average was 50.65.

Most runs *Test matches*
The greatest number of runs scored in Test matches is 8032 in 160 innings (21 not out) by Sir Garfield Sobers of West Indies between 1954 and 1974. His average was 57.78.

Most runs *Off an over*
The only batsman to score 36 runs off a six-ball over was Sir Garfield Sobers (Nottinghamshire) off Malcolm Andrew Nash (Glamorgan) at Swansea on 31 Aug 1968. The ball (recovered from the last hit from the road by a small boy) resides in Nottingham's Museum.

Most runs *Off a ball*
The most runs scored off a single hit is ten by Albert Neilson Hornby (1847–1925) off James Street (1839–1906) for Lancashire *v*. Surrey at The Oval on 14 July 1873, and ten by Samuel Hill Wood (later Sir Samuel Hill Hill-Wood) (1872–1949) off Cuthbert James Burnup (1875–1960) in the Derbyshire *v*. MCC match at Lord's, London, on 26 May 1900.

Most sixes *In an innings*
The highest number of sixes hit in an innings is 15 by John Richard Reid, OBE (b. 3 June 1928), in an innings of 296, lasting 3 hr 40 min, for Wellington *v*. Northern Districts in the Plunket

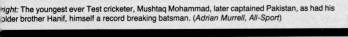

above: Record breaker in the field, Greg Chappell, here captaining Australia in the Centenary Test at Lord's, scored a remarkable 108 on his debut in Test cricket. (*Adrian Murrell, All-Sport*)

right: The youngest ever Test cricketer, Mushtaq Mohammad, later captained Pakistan, as had his older brother Hanif, himself a record breaking batsman. (*Adrian Murrell, All-Sport*)

Shield Tournament at Wellington, New Zealand, on 14–15 Jan 1963. The Test record is ten by Walter Hammond in an innings of 336 not out for England v. New Zealand at Auckland on 31 Mar and 1 Apr 1933.

Most sixes *In a match*

The highest number of sixes in a match is 17 (ten in the first and seven in the second innings) by William James Stewart (b. 31 Aug 1934) for Warwickshire v. Lancashire at Blackpool on 29–31 July 1959. His two innings were of 155 and 125.

Most boundaries in an innings

The highest number of boundaries was 68 (all in fours) by Percival Albert Perrin (1876–1945) in an innings of 343 not out for Essex v. Derbyshire at Chesterfield on 18–19 July 1904.

Highest score by a No. 11

The highest score by a No. 11 batsman is 163 by Thomas Peter Bromly Smith (1908–67) for Essex v. Derbyshire at Chesterfield in August 1947.

Most hundreds *Season*

The record for the greatest number of hundreds in a season is held by Denis Compton with 18 in 1947.

Most hundreds *Career*

The most hundreds in a career is 197 by Sir Jack Hobbs between 1905 and 1934.

Most hundreds *Test matches*

The greatest number of hundreds scored in Test matches is 29 by Sir Donald George Bradman (Australia) (b. 27 Aug 1908) between 1928 and 1948. The England record is 22 by Walter Hammond of Gloucestershire, between 1927 and 1947, and 22 by Michael Colin Cowdrey, CBE (b. 24 Dec 1932) (Kent) between 1954 and 1975.

Double hundreds

The only batsman to score double hundreds in both innings is Arthur Edward Fagg (1915–77), who made 244 and 202 not out for Kent v. Essex at Colchester on 13–15 July 1938. Sir Donald Bradman scored a career record 37 double hundreds 1927–49.

'Carrying bat'

Cecil John Burditt Wood (1875–1960), of Leicestershire, is the only batsman to carry his bat through both completed innings of a match, and score a hundred in both innings, (107 not out, 117 not out) on 12–14 June 1911 v. Yorkshire at Bradford.

Father and Son

The only case of a father and son both scoring hundreds in the same innings is that of George Gunn (1879–1958) (183) and George Vernon Gunn (1905–57) (100 no) for Nottinghamshire v. Warwickshire at Edgbaston on 23–24 July 1931.

Highest averages

The highest seasonal batting average in England is 115.66 for 26 innings (2429 runs including 13 hundreds) by Sir Donald Bradman (Australia) in England in 1938. The English record is 102.53 by Geoffrey Boycott OBE (b. 21 Oct 1940) of Yorkshire and England for 20 innings (1538 runs) including 6 hundreds in 1979. The world record for a complete career is 95.14 for 338 innings (28,067 runs) by Bradman between 1927 and 1949. The record for Test matches is 99.94 in 80 innings (6996 runs) by Bradman between 1928 and 1948. The English career record is 56.69 for 799 innings by Geoffrey Boycott with 38,442 runs between 1962 and the start of the 1981 season.

Fastest scoring

The fastest 50 was completed off 13 balls in 8 min (1.22 to 1.30 p.m.) and in 11 scoring strokes by Clive Clay Inman (b. 29 Jan 1936) in an innings of 57 not out for Leicestershire v. Nottinghamshire at Trent Bridge, Nottingham on 20 Aug 1965. Full tosses were bowled to expedite a declaration.

The fastest hundred was completed in 35 min by Percy George Herbert Fender (b. 22 Aug 1892), when scoring 113 not out for Surrey v. Northamptonshire at Northampton on 26 Aug 1920. The most prolific scorer of hundreds in an hour or less was Gilbert Laird Jessop (1874–1955), with 11 between 1897 and 1913. The fastest Test hundred was one of 70 min by Jack Morrison Gregory (1895–1973) of New South Wales, for Australia v. South Africa in the Second Test at Johannesburg on 12 Nov 1921. Edwin Boaler Alletson (1884–1963) scored 189 runs in 90 min for Nottinghamshire v. Sussex at Hove on 20 May 1911.

A double hundred in 120 min was achieved by Gilbert Jessop (286) for Gloucestershire v. Sussex at Hove on 1 June 1903 and equalled by Clive Hubert Lloyd (West Indies) (b. 31 Aug 1944) v. Glamorgan at Swansea, on 9 Aug 1976.

The fastest treble hundred was completed in 181 min by Denis Compton, who scored 300 for the MCC v. North-Eastern Transvaal at Benoni on 3–4 Dec 1948.

Slowest scoring

The longest time a batsman has ever taken to score his first run is 1 hr 35 min by Thomas Godfrey Evans (b. 18 Aug 1920) of Kent, who scored 10 not out for England v. Australia in the Fourth Test at Adelaide on 5–6 Feb 1947. The longest innings without scoring is 87 minutes by Vincent Richard Hogg for Zimbabwe-Rhodesia 'B' v. Natal 'B' at Pietermaritzburg in the South African Castle Bowl competition on 20 Jan 1980.

The slowest hundred on record is by Mudassar Nazar (b. 6 Apr 1956) of Pakistan in the First Test v. England at Lahore on 14–15 Dec 1977. He required 9 hr 51 min for 114, reaching the 100 in 9 hr 17 min. The slowest double hundred recorded is one of 10 hr 22 min by The Nawab Mansur Ali of Pataudi (now Mansur Ali Khan) (b. 5 Jan 1941), during an innings of 200 for South Zone v. West Zone in the Duleep Trophy Final at Bombay on 29–31 October 1967.

Highest partnership

The record partnership for any wicket is the fourth wicket stand of 577 by Gul Mahomed (b. 15 Oct 1921), who scored 319, and Vijay Samuel Hazare (b. 11 Mar 1915) 288 in the Baroda v. Holkar match at Baroda, India, on 8–10 Mar 1947.

The highest stand in English cricket is the first-wicket partnership of 555 by Percy Holmes (1886–1971) (224 not out) and Herbert Sutcliffe (1894–1978) (313) for Yorkshire v. Essex at Leyton on 15–16 June 1932.

Longest hit

The longest measured drive is one of 175 yd *160 m* by Walter (later the Rev.) Fellows (1834–1901) of Christ Church, Oxford University, in a practice on their ground off Charles Rogers in 1856. J. E. C. Moore made a measured hit of 170 yd 1 ft 5 in *155,59 m* at Griffith, New South Wales, Australia, in February 1930.

BOWLING

Most wickets *Season*

The largest number of wickets ever taken in a season is 304 by Alfred Percy 'Tich' Freeman (1888–1965) of Kent, in 1928. Freeman bowled 1976.1 overs, of which 423 were maidens, for an average of 18.05 runs per wicket.

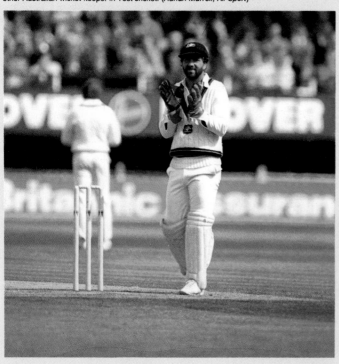

right: Wasim Bari's credentials include eight catches v. England in 1971, as well as his Test innings record of seven dismissals. (*Adrian Murrell, All-Sport*)

below: As well as setting records for dismissals, Rodney Marsh has also scored more runs than any other Australian wicket-keeper in Test cricket. (*Adrian Murrell, All-Sport*)

Most wickets *Career*
The greatest wicket-taker in history was Wilfred Rhodes (1877–1973) of Yorkshire and England, who took 4187 wickets for 69,939 runs (average 16.70 runs per wicket) between 1898 and 1930. He also holds the record for most first-class appearances with 1107. The highest percentage of wickets gained unassisted is 73.50 per cent (1479 from 2012) by Schofield Haigh (1871–1921), who played for Yorkshire from 1895 to 1913.

Most wickets *Tests*
The greatest number of wickets taken in Test matches is 309 for 8989 runs (average 29.09) by Lancelot Richard Gibbs (b. 29 Sept 1934) in 79 Tests for West Indies between 1958 and 1976. The lowest bowling average in a Test career (minimum 15 wickets) is 112 wickets for 1205 runs (10.75 runs per wicket) by George Alfred Lohmann (1865–1901) in 18 Tests for England between 1886 and 1896.

Most wickets *In an innings*
The taking of all ten wickets by a single bowler has been recorded many times but only one bowler has achieved this feat on three occasions—Alfred Freeman of Kent, against Lancashire at Maidstone on 24 July 1929, against Essex at Southend on 13–14 Aug 1930 and against Lancashire at Old Trafford on 27 May 1931. The fewest runs scored off a bowler taking all ten wickets is ten, when Hedley Verity (1905–43) of Yorkshire dismissed (eight caught, one lbw, one stumped) Nottinghamshire at Leeds on 12 July 1932. The only bowler to have 'clean bowled' a whole side out was John Wisden (1826–84) of Sussex, playing for the North *v.* the South at Lord's in 1850.

Most wickets *Match*
James Charles Laker (b. 9 Feb 1922) of Surrey took 19 wickets for 90 runs (9–37 and 10–53) for England *v.* Australia in the Fourth Test at Old Trafford, on 26–31 July 1956. No other bowler has taken more than 17 wickets in a first class match.

Most wickets *In a day*
The greatest number of wickets taken in a day's play is 17 by Colin Blythe (1879–1917) for 48 runs, for Kent against Northamptonshire at Northampton on 1 June 1907; by Hedley Verity for 91 runs, for Yorkshire *v.* Essex at Leyton on 14 July 1933; and by Thomas William John Goddard (1900–66) for 106 runs, for Gloucestershire *v.* Kent at Bristol on 3 July 1939.

Most consecutive wickets
No bowler in first-class cricket has yet achieved five wickets with five consecutive balls. The nearest approach was that of Charles Warrington Leonard Parker (1882–1959) (Gloucestershire) in his own benefit match against Yorkshire at Bristol on 10 Aug 1922, when he struck the stumps with five successive balls but the second was called as a no-ball. The only man to have taken four wickets with consecutive balls more than once is Robert James Crisp (b. 28 May 1911) for Western Province *v.* Griqualand West at Johannesburg on 23–24 Dec 1931 and against Natal at Durban on 3 Mar 1934.

Most 'hat tricks'
The greatest number of 'hat tricks' is seven by Douglas Vivian Parson Wright (b. 21 Aug 1914) of Kent, on 3 and 29 July 1937, 18 May 1938, 13 Jan and 1 July 1939, 11 Aug 1947 and 1 Aug 1949. In his own benefit match at Lord's on 22 May 1907, Albert Edwin Trott (1873–1914) of Middlesex took four Somerset wickets with four consecutive balls and then later in the same innings achieved a 'hat trick'.

Most expensive bowling
The greatest number of runs hit off one bowler in one innings is 362, scored off Arthur Alfred Mailey (1886–1967) in the New South Wales *v.* Victoria match at Melbourne on 24–28 Dec 1926. The greatest number of runs ever conceded by a bowler in one match is 428 by Cottari Subhann Nayudu (b. 18 April 1914) in the Holkar *v.* Bombay match at Bombay on 4–9 Mar 1945, when he also made the record number of 917 deliveries.

Most consecutive maidens
Hugh Tayfield (b. 30 Jan 1929) bowled 16 consecutive eight-ball maiden overs (137 balls without conceding a run) for South Africa *v.* England in the Third Test at Durban on 25–26 Jan 1957. The greatest number of consecutive six-ball maiden overs bowled is 21 (131 balls) by Rameshchandra Gangaram 'Bapu' Nadkarni (b. 4 Apr 1932) for India *v.* England in the First Test at Madras on 12 Jan 1964. The English record is 17 overs (105 balls) by Horace Leslie Hazell (b. 30 Sept 1909) for Somerset *v.* Gloucestershire at Taunton on 4 June 1949, and 17 (104 balls) by Graham Anthony 'Tony' Richard Lock (b. 5 July 1929) of Surrey, playing for the MCC *v.* the Governor-General's XI at Karachi, Pakistan, on 31 Dec 1955. Alfred Shaw (1842–1907) of Nottinghamshire bowled 23 consecutive four-ball maiden overs (92 balls) for the North *v.* the South at Trent Bridge on 17 July 1876.

Most balls
The greatest number of balls sent down by any bowler in one season is 12,234 (651 maidens: 298 wickets) by Alfred Freeman in 1933. The most balls bowled in an innings is 588 (98 overs) by Sonny Ramadhin (b. 1 May 1930) of Trinidad, playing for West Indies in the First Test *v.* England at Edgbaston on 30 May and 1, 3 and 4 June 1957.

Best average
The lowest recorded bowling average for a season is one of 8.54 runs per wicket (186 wickets for 1589 runs) by Alfred Shaw of Nottinghamshire in 1880.

Fastest
The highest electronically measured speed for a ball bowled by any bowler is 99.7 mph *160,45 km/h* by Jeffrey Robert Thomson (b. 16 Aug 1950) (Australia) during the Second Test *v.* the West Indies in December 1975. Albert Cotter (1883–1917) of New South Wales, Australia, is reputed to have broken a stump on more than 20 occasions.

ALL-ROUNDERS
The 'double'
The 'double' of 1000 runs and 100 wickets in the same season was performed a record number of 16 times by Wilfred Rhodes between 1903 and 1926. The greatest number of consecutive seasons in which a player has performed the 'double' is 11 (1903–13) by George Herbert Hirst (1871–1954), of Yorkshire and England. Hirst is also the only player to score 2000 runs (2385) and take 200 wickets (208) in the same season (1906).

Test Cricket
The only players to achieve 2000 runs and 200 wickets in their Test careers are Richard 'Richie' Benaud, OBE (b. 6 Oct 1930), of Australia, with 2201 runs and 248 wickets in 63 matches between 1952 and 1964, and Sir Garfield Sobers, of West Indies, with 8032 runs and 235 wickets in 93 matches between 1954 and 1974. The only player to score a hundred and take eight wickets in a single innings in the same Test is Ian Terrence Botham (b. 24 Nov 1955) with 108 and eight for 34 for England v Pakistan in the Second Test at Lord's on 15–19 June 1978. He is also alone in scoring a hundred (114) and taking ten wickets (6–58 and 7–48) in the same Test, for England *v.* India in the Golden Jubilee Test at Bombay on 15–19 February 1980. He also completed the double of 1000 runs and 100 wickets in the fewest Test matches (21) on 30 Aug 1979.

FIELDING
Most catches *Innings and Match*
The greatest number of catches in an innings is seven, by Michael James Stewart (b. 16 Sept 1932) for Surrey *v.* Northamptonshire at Northampton on 7 June 1957, and by Anthony Stephen Brown (b. 24 June 1936) for Gloucestershire *v.* Nottinghamshire at Trent Bridge on 26 July 1966.

The most catches in a Test match is seven by Gregory Stephen Chappell MBE (b. 7 Aug 1948) for Australia *v.* England at Perth on 13–17 Dec 1974, and by Yajurvindra Singh (b. 1 Aug 1952) for India *v.* England at Bangalore on 28 Jan–2 Feb 1977.

Walter Hammond held a record total of ten catches (four in the first innings, six in the second) for Gloucestershire *v.* Surrey at Cheltenham on 16–17 Aug 1928. The record for a wicket-keeper is 11 (see wicket-keeping).

Most catches *Season and career*
The greatest number of catches in a season is 78 by Walter Hammond in 1928, and 77 by Michael Stewart in 1957. The most

259

catches in a career is 1018 by Frank Edward Woolley (1887–1978) of Kent between 1906 and 1938. The Test record is 120 by Colin Cowdrey in 114 matches between 1954 and 1975.

Longest throw

A cricket ball (5½ oz *155 g*) was reputedly thrown 140 yd 2 ft *128,6 m* by Robert Percival, a left-hander, on Durham Sands Racecourse on Easter Monday, 18 Apr 1881.

WICKET-KEEPING

Most dismissals *Season*

The record number of dismissals for any wicket-keeper in a season is 127 (79 caught, 48 stumped) by Leslie Ethelbert George Ames, CBE (b. 3 Dec 1905) of Kent in 1929. The record for the number stumped is 64 by Ames in 1932. The record for catches is 96 by James Graham Binks (b. 5 Oct 1935) of Yorkshire in 1960.

Most dismissals *Career*

The highest total of dismissals in a wicket-keeping career is 1526 (a record 1268 catches plus 258 stumpings) by John Thomas Murray, MBE (b. 1 Apr 1935) of Middlesex between 1952 and 1975. The most stumpings in a career is 415 by Leslie Ames between 1926 and 1951. The Test record is 271 dismissals (260 catches, 11 stumpings) in 72 Tests by Rodney William Marsh (b. 4 Nov 1947) for Australia between November 1970 and 2 Aug 1981.

Most dismissals *Innings*

The most dismissals by a wicket-keeper in an innings is eight (all caught) by Arthur Theodore Wallace 'Wally' Grout (1927–68) for Queensland against Western Australia at Brisbane on 15 Feb 1960. The most stumpings in an innings is six by Henry 'Hugo' Yarnold (1917–74) for Worcestershire *v.* Scotland at Broughty Ferry, Tayside, on 2 July 1951. The Test record is seven (all caught) by Wasim Bari (b. 23 Mar 1948) for Pakistan in the Third Test *v.* New Zealand at Auckland on 23 Feb 1978, and by Robert William Taylor MBE (b. 17 July 1941) for England *v.* India in the Golden Jubilee Test at Bombay on 15 Feb 1980.

Most dismissals *Match*

The greatest number of dismissals by a wicket-keeper in a match is 12 by Edward Pooley (1838–1907), eight caught, four

stumped, for Surrey *v.* Sussex at The Oval on 6–7 July 1868 nine caught, three stumped by Donald Tallon (b. 17 Feb 1916 of Australia for Queensland *v.* New South Wales at Sydney o 2–4 Jan 1939; and also nine caught, three stumped by Hedle Brian Taber (b. 29 Apr 1940) for New South Wales *v.* Sout Australia at Adelaide 17–19 Dec 1968. The record for catches i 11, seven in the first innings and four in the second, by Arnol Long (b. 18 Dec 1940), for Surrey *v.* Sussex at Hove on 18 an 21 July 1964, and also by Rodney Marsh for Western Australi *v.* Victoria at Perth on 15–17 Nov 1975. The most stumpings in match is nine by Frederick Henry Huish (1869–1957) for Ken *v.* Surrey at The Oval on 21–23 Aug 1911. The Test record fo dismissals is ten, all caught, by Robert Taylor MBE for Englan *v.* India at Bombay, 15–19 Feb 1980.

TEST RECORDS

Most Test appearances

The record number of Test appearances is 114 by Colin Cow drey, for England between November 1954 and February 1975 The highest number of Test captaincies is 46 by Clive Lloyd wh captained West Indies from 1974 to April 1981 and played in total of 82 Tests. The most innings batted in Test matches is 18 in 114 Tests by Colin Cowdrey. Sir Garfield Sobers (Wes Indies) holds the record for consecutive Tests, with 85 from April 1955 to April 1972.

Longest match

The lengthiest recorded cricket match was the 'timeless' Tes between England and South Africa at Durban on 3–14 Ma 1939. It was abandoned after ten days (eighth day rained off because the boat taking the England team home was due t leave. The lengthiest in England have been the six-day Fift England *v.* Australia Test on 16–22 Aug 1930, when rain pre vented play on the fifth day, the six-day Fifth England *v.* Austra lia Test on 10–16 Aug 1972, and the six-day Fourth England *v* Australia Test on 28 Aug–3 Sep 1975.

Largest crowds

The greatest recorded attendance at a cricket match is 350,53 (receipts £30,124) for the Third Test between Australia an England at Melbourne on 1–7 Jan 1937. For the whole series th figure was a record 933,513 (receipts £87,963). The greates recorded attendance at a cricket match on one day was 90,800 o

Record-breaking wicket-keeper Bob Taylor (see also Stop Press) exhibiting his acrobatic skill against Australia in the 5th Test at Adelaide in January 1979. (*Adrian Murrell, All-Sport*)

NAT WEST BANK TROPHY (formerly GILLETTE CUP), JOHN PLAYER LEAGUE AND BENSON & HEDGES CUP RECORDS

	Gillette Cup (instituted 1963) now Nat West Bank Trophy – 60 overs matches	John Player League (instituted 1969) – 40 overs matches	Benson and Hedges Cup (instituted 1972) – 55 overs matches
Highest Individual Innings	177—C. G. Greenidge, Hampshire v. Glamorgan, Southampton, 1975	163*—C. G. Greenidge, Hampshire v. Warwickshire, Edgbaston, 1979	173*—C. G. Greenidge, Hampshire v. Minor Counties (South), Amersham, 1973
Best Individual Bowling	7-15—A. L. Dixon, Kent v. Surrey, Oval, 1967	8-26—K. D. Boyce, Essex v. Lancashire, Old Trafford, 1971. NB A. Ward, Derbyshire v. Sussex, Derby, 1970, 4 wickets in 4 balls	7-12—W. W. Daniel, Middlesex v. Minor Counties (East), Ipswich, 1978
Highest Innings Total	371 for 4 (off 60 overs), Hampshire v. Glamorgan, Southampton, 1975	307 for 4 (off 38 overs), Worcestershire v. Derbyshire, Worcester, 1975	350 for 3 (off 55 overs), Essex v. Combined Universities, Chelmsford, 1979
Lowest Innings Total	41 (off 20 overs), Cambridgeshire v. Buckinghamshire, Cambridge, 1972 41 (off 19.4 overs), Middlesex v. Essex, Westcliff, 1972 41 (off 36.1 overs), Shropshire v. Essex, Wellington, 1974	23 (off 19.4 overs), Middlesex v. Yorkshire, Headingley, 1974	61 (off 26 overs), Sussex v. Middlesex, Hove, 1978
Highest Partnership	234* for 4th wicket—D. Lloyd and C. H. Lloyd, Lancashire v. Gloucestershire, Old Trafford, 1978	218 for 1st wicket—A. R. Butcher and G. P. Howarth, Surrey v. Gloucestershire, Oval, 1976	285* for 2nd wicket—C. G. Greenidge and D. R. Turner, Hampshire v. Minor Counties (South), Amersham, 1973

*Not Out

the second day of the Fifth Test between Australia and West Indies at Melbourne on 11 Feb 1961, when the receipts were £A13,132 *£10,484 sterling*. The English record is 159,000 for the Fourth Test between England and Australia at Headingley, Leeds, on 22–27 July 1948, and the record for one day probably a capacity of 46,000 for a match between Lancashire and Yorkshire at Old Trafford on 2 Aug 1926. The English record for a Test series is 549,650 (receipts £200,428) for the series against Australia in 1953.

Greatest receipts
The world record for receipts from a match is £292,595 at the Second Test between England and West Indies at Lords 19–24 June 1980. The Test series record is £993,295 for the five England v. West Indies Tests of June–August 1980.

WORLD CUP
The Prudential World Cup held in 1975 and 1979, was won both times by West Indies. The highest team score was 334 for 4 by England v. India at Lords on 7 June 1975, and the lowest 45 by Canada v. England at Old Trafford on 14 June 1979. The highest individual score was 171 not out by Glenn Maitland Turner (b. 26 May 1947) for New Zealand v. East Africa at Edgbaston on 7 June 1975. The best bowling was six wickets for 14 runs by Gary John Gilmour (b. 26 June 1951) for Australia v. England at Headingley on 18 June 1975.

ENGLISH COUNTY CHAMPIONSHIP
The greatest number of victories since 1890, when the championship was officially constituted, has been secured by Yorkshire with 29 outright wins, and one shared with Nottinghamshire and Middlesex in 1949. The most 'wooden spoons' have been won by Northamptonshire, with ten since 1923. They did not win a single match between May 1935 and May 1939. The record number of consecutive title wins is seven by Surrey from 1952 to 1958. The greatest number of consecutive appearances for one county in county championship matches is 423 by Kenneth George Suttle (b. 25 Aug 1928) of Sussex between 1954 and 1969. James Binks of Yorkshire played in every county championship match for his side between his debut in 1955 and his retirement in 1969—412 matches. The seven sons of the Rev Henry Foster, of Malvern, uniquely all played county cricket for Worcestershire between 1899 and 1934.

Oldest and youngest
The oldest man to play in a Test match was Wilfred Rhodes, aged 52 yr 165 days, when he played for England v. West Indies at Kingston, Jamaica on 12 April 1930. The youngest was Mushtaq Mohammad (b. 22 Nov 1943), aged 15 yr 124 days, when he played for Pakistan v. West Indies at Lahore on 26 March 1959. England's youngest player was Dennis Brian Close (b. 24 Feb 1931) aged 18 yr 149 days v. New Zealand at Old Trafford on 23 July 1949.

The oldest player in first-class cricket was Col Cottari Kanakaiya Nayudu (1895–1967) (India), aged 68 yr 4 days, when he played

for the Maharashtra Governor's XI v. Chief Minister's XI at Nagpur, India on 4 Nov 1963. The youngest is reputed to be Qasim Feroze (Pakistan) (b. 21 Jan 1958) who played for Bahawalpur v. Karachi Whites on 19 Jan 1971 aged 12 yr 363 days. The oldest Englishman was George Robert Canning, the 4th Lord Harris (1851–1932) who played for Kent v All India at Catford on 4 July 1911 aged 60 yr 151 days. The youngest English first-class player was George Frederick Grace (1850–80) when he played for Gentlemen of England v. Oxford University at Oxford on 21 May 1866, aged 15 yr 159 days. The youngest player to represent his county was William Wade Fitzherbert Pullen (1866–1937), for Gloucestershire v. Middlesex at Lord's on 5 June 1882 when aged 15 yr 346 days.

WOMEN'S CRICKET
Earliest
The first recorded women's match took place at Gosden Common, Surrey, England on 26 July 1745. *Circa* 1807 Christina Willes is said to have introduced the roundarm bowling style. The first Test match was Australia v. England at Brisbane on 28 Dec 1934. The International Women's Cricket Council was formed in 1958.

Batting *Individual*
The highest individual innings recorded is 224 not out by Mabel Bryant for Visitors v. Residents at Eastbourne, East Sussex, in August 1901. The highest innings in a Test match is 189 by Elizabeth Alexandra 'Betty' Snowball for England v. New Zealand at Christchurch, NZ on 16 Feb 1935. The highest Test innings in England is 179 by Rachael Flint, MBE (née Heyhoe) for England v. Australia at The Oval, London on 27–28 July 1976. Rachael Flint also has scored the most runs in Test cricket with 1789 in 22 matches from December 1960 to July 1979.

Batting *Team*
The highest innings score by any team is 567 by Tarana v. Rockley, at Rockley, NSW Australia in 1896. The highest Test innings is 503 for five wickets declared by England v. New Zealand at Christchurch, NZ on 16 Feb 1935. The most in a Test in England is 379 by Australia v. England at The Oval, London on 26–27 July 1976. The highest innings total by any team in England is 406 by the South v. Australia at Hove, East Sussex on 17–19 July 1937.

The lowest innings in a Test is 35 by England v. Australia at Melbourne, Australia on 22–24 Feb 1958. The lowest in a Test in England is 63 by New Zealand at Worcester on 3, 5–6 July 1954.

Bowling
The greatest number of wickets taken in Test matches is 77 by Mary Duggan (England) in 16 Tests from 1949 to 1963.

On 26 June 1931 Rubina Winifred Humphries (b. 19 Aug 1915), for Dalton Ladies v. Woodfield SC, took all ten wickets for no runs. (She also scored all her team's runs.) This bowling feat was equalled by Rosemary White for Wallington LCC v. Beaconsfield LCC in July 1962.

MINOR CRICKET RECORDS
(where excelling those in First Class Cricket)

Highest individual innings
In a Junior House match between Clarke's House (now Poole's) and North Town, at Clifton College, Bristol, 22–23, 26–28 June 1899, Arthur Edward James Collins (b. India, 1885—k. Flanders, November 1914) scored an unprecedented 628 not out in 6 hr 50 min, over five afternoons' batting, carrying his bat through the innings of 836. The scorer, E. W. Pegler, gave the score as '628—plus or minus 20, shall we say'.

Fastest individual scoring
Stanley Keppel 'Shunter' Coen (South Africa) (1902–67) scored 50 runs (11 fours and one six) in 7 min for Gezira v. the RAF in 1942. The fastest hundred by a prominent player in a minor match was by Vivian Frank Shergold Crawford (1879–1922) in 19 min at Cane Hill, Surrey on 16 Sept 1899. Greg Beacroft (b. 20 Jan 1958) scored 268 (including 29 sixes and 11 fours) in 92 min for Yass Wallaroos v. Williamsdale at Canberra, ACT, Australia on 21 Jan 1979.

Successive sixes
Cedric Ivan James Smith hit nine successive sixes for a Middlesex XI v. Harrow and District at Rayner's Lane, Harrow, Greater London in 1935. This feat was repeated by Arthur Dudley Nourse (b. 12 Nov 1910) in a South African XI v. Military Police match at Cairo, Egypt in 1942–3. Nourse's feat included six sixes in one over.

Fastest and Slowest scoring rates
In the match Royal Naval College, Dartmouth v. Seale Hayne Agricultural College in 1923, Kenneth Anderson Sellar (now Cdr 'Monkey' Sellar, DSO, DSC, RN) (b. 11 Aug 1906) and Leslie Kenneth Allen Block (later Judge Block, DSC) (1906–80) were set to score 174 runs in 105 min but achieved this total in 33 min, so averaging 5.27 runs per min. Playing for Gentlemen of Leicestershire CC v. Free Foresters, at Oakham, Rutland, on 19 Aug 1963, Ian H. S. Balfour batted for 100 min without adding to his score of five runs. He went on to make 39.

Consecutive not out hundreds
Gerald Vivian William Lukehurst (b. 5 Oct 1917) of Kent, hit six consecutive not out hundreds for Gore Court and F. Day's XI between 3 July and 20 July 1955.

Most runs off a ball
A scoring stroke of 11 (all run, with no overthrows) was achieved by Lt (later Lt-Col) Philip Mitford (1879–1946), QO Cameron Highlanders, in a Governor's Cup match in Malta on 28 May 1903.

Greatest stand
T. Patten and N. Rippon made a third wicket stand of 641 for Buffalo v. Whorouly at Gapsted, Victoria, Australia, on 19 Mar 1914.

Twenty-year-old wicket-keeper Welihinda Bennett, who responded to some brief coaching by Sir Learie Constantine by dismissing all ten opposition batsmen in one innings.

Bowling
Stephen Fleming bowling for Marlborough College 'A' XI, New Zealand v. Bohally Intermediate at Blenheim, New Zealand in December 1967 took nine wickets in nine consecutive balls. In February 1931 in a schools match in South Africa Paul Hugo also took nine wickets with nine consecutive balls for Smithfield School v. Aliwal North. In the Inter-Divisional Ships Shield at Purfleet, Essex, on 17 May 1924, Joseph William Brockley (b. 9 Apr 1907) took all ten wickets, clean bowled, for two runs in 11 balls—including a triple hat trick.

In 1881 Frederick Robert Spofforth (1853–1926) in Australia clean bowled all ten wickets in *both* innings. J. Bryant for Erskine v. Deaf Mutes in Melbourne on 15 and 22 Oct 1887, and Albert Rimmer for Linwood School v. Cathedral GS at Canterbury, New Zealand in December 1925 repeated the feat. In 1910, H. Hopkinson, of Mildmay CC London, took 99 wickets for 147 runs.

Maurice Hanes bowled 107 consecutive balls (17 overs and five balls) for Bedworth II v. A P Leamington II at Bedworth, Warwickshire on 16 June 1979, without conceding a run.

Wicket-keeping
In Ceylon, playing for Mahinda College v. Galle CC, at the Galle Esplanade, Welihinda Badalge Bennett (b. 25 Jan 1933) caught four and stumped six batsmen in one innings, on 1 March 1953.

Fielding
In a Wellington, New Zealand secondary schools 11-a-side match on 16 Mar 1974, Stephen Lane, 13, held 14 catches in the field (seven in each innings) for St Patrick's College, Silverstream v. St Bernard's College, Lower Hutt.

Marathon
A match under MCC rules was played by 22 members of St Peter's School, Bournemouth, Dorset for 137 hr, on 25 June–1 July 1980.

CROQUET

Earliest references
Croquet was probably derived from the French game *Jeu de Mail* first mentioned in the 12th century. In its present-day form, it originated as a country-house lawn game in Ireland in the 1830s when it was called 'crokey' and was introduced to Hampshire 20 years later. The first club was formed in the Steyne Gardens, Worthing, West Sussex in 1865.

Most championships
The greatest number of victories in the Open Croquet Championships (instituted at Evesham, Hereford & Worcester, 1867) is ten by John William Solomon (b. 1932) (1953, 1956, 1959, 1961, 1963–8). He has also won the Men's Championship on ten occasions (1951, 1953, 1958–60, 1962, 1964–5, 1971 and 1972), the Open Doubles (with Edmond Patrick Charles Cotter) on ten occasions (1954–5, 1958–9, 1961–5 and 1969) and the Mixed Doubles once (with Freda Oddie) in 1954, making a total of 31 titles. Solomon has also won the President's Silver Cup (inst. 1934) on nine occasions (1955, 1957–9, 1962–4, 1968 and 1971). He has also been Champion of Champions on all four occasions that this competition has been run (1967–70).

Dorothy Dyne Steel (1884–1965), fifteen times winner of the Women's Championship (1919–39), won the Open Croquet Championship four times (1925, 1933, 1935–36). She had also five Doubles and seven Mixed Doubles titles making a total of 31 titles.

International trophy
The MacRobertson International Shield (instituted 1925) has been played for ten times. It has been won most often by Great Britain with six wins (in 1925, 1937, 1956, 1963, 1969 and 1974). The players to make five international appearances are J. C. Windsor (Australia) in 1925, 1928, 1930, 1935 and 1937 and John Solomon (GB) in 1951, 1956, 1963, 1969 and 1974.

Lowest handicap
Historically the lowest playing handicap has been that of

Humphrey Osmond Hicks (Devon) (b. 1904) with minus 5½. In 1974 the limit was however fixed at minus 5. The player holding the lowest handicap is G. Nigel Aspinall with minus 5.

Marathon
The longest croquet match on record is one of 106 hr by Craig Calvert, Andrew Cooksey, Stephen Foden and Peter Wood at Rossall School, Fleetwood, Lancashire on 1–5 July 1981.

CROSS-COUNTRY RUNNING

International championships
The earliest recorded international cross-country race took place over 14,5 km *9 miles 18 yd* from Ville d'Avray, outside Paris, on 20 Mar 1898, between England and France (England won by 21 points to 69). The inaugural International Cross-Country Championships took place at the Hamilton Park Racecourse, Scotland, on 28 Mar 1903. The greatest margin of victory is 56 sec or 390 yd *356 m* by John 'Jack' Thomas Holden (England) (b. 13 Mar 1907) at Ayr Racecourse, Scotland, on 24 Mar 1934. The narrowest win was that of Jean-Claude Fayolle (France) (b. 10 Nov 1937) at Ostend, Belgium, on 20 Mar 1965, when the timekeepers were unable to separate his time from that of Melvyn Richard Batty (England), who was placed second. Since 1973 the race has been run under the auspices of the International Amateur Athletic Federation.

The greatest team wins have been those of England, with a minimum of 21 points (the first six runners to finish) on two occasions, at Gosforth Park, Newcastle, Tyne and Wear, on 22 Mar 1924, and at the Hippodrome de Stockel, Brussels, Belgium, on 20 Mar 1932.

Most international appearances
The runners of participating countries with the largest number of international championship appearances are:

Belgium	20	Marcel Van de Wattyne, 1946–65
Wales	14	Danny Phillips, 1922, 1924, 1926–37
Spain	14	Mariano Haro, 1962–5, 1967–9, 1971–7
Scotland	14	Jim N. C. Alder, 1962, 1964–76
France	14	Noel Tijou, 1963–75, 1977
England	12	Jack T. Holden, 1929–39, 1946

Two women have competed in 14 of the 15 races held: Margaret Coomber (*née* MacSherry) (b. 13 June 1950) (Scotland), 1967–80; and Jean Lochhead (b. 24 Dec 1946) (Wales), 1967–79, 1981.

Most wins
The greatest number of victories in the International Cross-Country Race is four by Jack Holden (England) in 1933–5 and 1939, by Alain Mimoun-o-Kacha (France) (b. 1 Jan 1921) in 1949, 1952, 1954 and 1956 and Gaston Roelants (Belgium) (b. 5 Feb 1937) in 1962, 1967, 1969 and 1972. England have won 45 times to 1980. Doris Brown-Heritage (USA) (b. 17 Sept 1942) has won the women's race five times, 1967–71.

English championship
The English Cross-Country Championship was inaugurated at Roehampton, Wandsworth, London, in 1877. The most individual titles won is four by Percy H. Stenning (1854–92) (Thames Hare and Hounds) in 1877–80 and Alfred E. Shrubb (1878–1964) (South London Harriers) in 1901–4. The most successful club in the team race has been Birchfield Harriers from Birmingham with 27 wins and one tie between 1880 and 1953. The largest field was the 1710 starters in 1980 at Leicester, of whom all but 83 finished.

Largest field
The largest recorded field in any cross-country race was 9093 starters (8834 finished) in the 30 km *18.6 miles* Lidingöloppet, near Stockholm, Sweden, on 5 Oct 1980.

CURLING

Origins
Although a 15th century bronze figure in the Florence Museum appears to be holding a curling stone, the earliest illustration of the sport was in one of the Flemish painter Pieter Bruegel's winter scenes *c.* 1560. The game was probably introduced into Scotland by Flemings in the 15th century. The earliest documented club is Muthill, Tayside, Scotland, formed in 1739. The game was introduced into Canada in 1759. Organized administration began in 1838 with the formation in Edinburgh of the Grand (later Royal) Caledonian Curling Club, the international legislative body until the foundation of the International Curling Federation in 1966. The first indoor ice rink to introduce curling was in Montreal, Canada in 1807, and the first in Britain was at Southport, Merseyside in 1878.

The USA won the first Gordon International Medal series of matches, between Canada and the USA, at Montreal in 1884. The first Strathcona Cup match between Canada and Scotland was won by Canada in 1903. Although demonstrated at the Winter Olympics of 1924, 1932 and 1964, curling has never been included in the official Olympic programme.

Most titles
The record for World championships (inst. 1959) for the Air Canada Silver Broom is 13 wins by Canada, in 1959–64, 1966, 1968–72, 1980. The most Strathcona Cup wins is seven by Canada (1903, 1909, 1912, 1923, 1938, 1957, 1965) against Scotland. A Ladies World Championships was instituted in 1979 and the title has been won by Switzerland, Canada and Sweden.

'Perfect' games
Stu Beagle, of Calgary, Alberta, Canada, played a perfect game (48 points) against Nova Scotia in the Canadian championships (Brier) at Fort William (now Thunder Bay), Ontario, on 8 Mar 1960. Bernice Fekete, of Edmonton, Alberta, Canada, skipped her rink to two consecutive eight-enders on the same sheet of ice at the Derrick Club, Edmonton, on 10 Jan and 6 Feb 1973. Andrew McQuistin, of Stranraer, skipped a Scotland rink to a 1–0 victory over Switzerland, scoring in the tenth end after nine consecutive blank ends, in the Uniroyal World Junior Championships at Kitchener-Waterloo, Ontario, Canada on 16 Mar 1980.

Largest bonspiel
The largest bonspiel in the world is the Manitoba Bonspiel held in Winnipeg, Canada. There were 736 teams, or rinks, of four players in the January 1981 tournament.

Largest rink
The world's largest curling rink is the Big Four Curling Rink, Calgary, Alberta, Canada opened in 1959 at a cost of $Can. 2,250,000 *£867,050*. Each of the two floors has 24 sheets of ice, the total accommodating 96 teams and 384 players.

Marathons
The longest recorded curling match is one of 64 hr 28 min by eight members of the Pine Point Curling Club, NWT, Canada on 13–15 Jan 1979.

The record for two curlers is 36 hr 30 min by Glen James and Gary Grant at the Uxbridge Curling Club, Ontario, Canada on 11–12 Apr 1981. The weight handled was 104.639 tons.

CYCLING

See also The Guinness Guide to Bicycling *published by Guinness Superlatives at £8.50*

Earliest race
The earliest recorded bicycle race was a velocipede race over 2 km *1.24 miles* at the Parc de St Cloud, Paris, on 31 May 1868, won by Dr James Moore (GB) (1847–1935) (later Chevalier de la Legion d'Honneur).

Highest speed
The highest speed ever achieved on a bicycle is 140.5 mph *226,1 km/h* by Dr Allan V. Abbott, 29, of San Bernadino, California, USA, behind a wind-shield mounted on a 1955 Chevrolet over ¾ mile *1,2 km* at Bonneville Salt Flats, Utah, USA on 25 Aug 1973. His speed over a mile *1,6 km* was 138.674 mph *223,174 km/h*. It should be noted that considerable help is provided by the slipstreaming effect of the lead vehicle. The first Mile a Minute was achieved by Charles Minthorne Murphy (b. 1872) behind a pacing locomotive on the Long Island Railroad

Nineteen-year-old Tony Michetschläger raised nearly £5000 for the Guide Dogs for the Blind Association with his cycle trip around the coast of Great Britain.

on 30 June 1899 in 57⅘ sec for an average of 62.28 mph *100,23 km/h*. Fred Markham recorded an official unpaced 8.80 sec for 200 m (50.84 mph *81,81 km/h*) on a streamlined bicycle at Ontario, California, USA, on 6 May 1979.

The greatest distance ever covered in one hour is 122,771 km *76 miles 504 yd* by Leon Vanderstuyft (Belgium) (1890–1964) on the Montlhery Motor Circuit, France, on 30 Sept 1928, achieved from a standing start paced by a motorcycle. The 24 hr record behind pace is 860 miles 367 yd *1384,367 km* by Hubert Ferdinand Opperman (later Hon Sir) (b. 29 May 1904) in Melbourne, Australia on 23 May 1932.

Most titles *Olympic*

Cycling has been on the Olympic programme since the revival of the Games in 1896. The most gold medals won is three by Paul Masson (France) in 1896, Francisco Verri (Italy) (1885–1945) in 1906 and Robert Charpentier (France) (1916–66) in 1936. In the 'unofficial' 1904 cycling programme, Marcus Hurley (USA) (1884–1950) won four events.

Most titles *British*

Beryl Burton, OBE (b. 12 May 1937), 21 times British all-round time trial champion (1959–80), has won 12 BCF road race titles, 14 track pursuit titles and 65 RTTC titles. Mrs Burton's career overshadows all male achievements. Albert White (1889–1965) gained 12 individual National track championships from the ¼ mile to 25 miles in 1920–5 and also shared in three tandem titles.

Tour de France

The greatest number of wins in the Tour de France (inaugurated 1903) is five by Jacques Anquetil (b. 8 Jan 1934) of France, 1957, 1961–4 and by Eddy Merckx (b. Belgium, 17 June 1945), 1969–72 and 1974. The closest race ever was that of 1968 when after 4665 km *2898.7 miles* over the 25 days (27 June–21 July) Jan Janssen (Netherlands) (b. 19 May 1940) beat Herman van Springel (Belgium) in Paris by 38 sec. The fastest average speed was 37,84 km/h *23.51 mph* by Bernard Hinault (France) (b. 1955) in 1981. The longest race was 5745 km *3569 miles* in 1926, and most participants were in 1928 when 162 started—only 41 finished.

Tour of Britain (Milk Race)

Three riders have won the Tour of Britain twice each—Bill Bradley (1959–60), Les West (1965, 1967) and Fedor den

Hertog (Netherlands) (1969, 1971). The closest race ever was in 1976 when after 1035 miles *1665,67 km* over 14 days (30 May–1 June) Bill Nickson (GB) (b. 30 Jan 1953) beat Joe Waugh (GB) by 5 sec. Den Hertog recorded the fastest average speed of 25.20 mph *40,55 km/h* in the 1971 race (1096 miles *1763,84 km*). The longest Milk Race was in 1969 (1515 miles *2438,16 km* although the longest ever Tour of Britain was in 1953 (163 miles *2624,84 km* starting and finishing in London) under *Daily Express* sponsorship.

Six-day races

The greatest number of wins in 6-day races is by Patrick Sercu (b. 27 June 1944), of Belgium, who by February 1981 had taken his total number of victories to 79.

Longest one-day race

The longest single-day 'massed start' road race is the 551-620 km *342–385 miles* Bordeaux–Paris, France, event. Paced over all or part of the route, the highest average speed was in 1979 with 47,06 km/h *29.24 mph* by Andre Chalmal (France).

The longest unpaced single day race is the Bristol–Bradford England, 245 mile *394 km* event. The now-defunct London–Holyhead race was over a distance of 265 miles *426 km*.

Land's End to John o' Groats

The 'end to end' record for the 861 miles *1414 km* is 1 day 23 hr 23 min 2 sec (average speed 18.17 mph *29,24 km/h*) by Paul Carbutt (b. 4 July 1950) on 11–13 July 1979. The feminine record is 2 days 11 hr 7 min by Eileen Sheridan (b. 18 Oct 1923) on 9–11 June 1954. She completed 1000 miles *1609 km* in 3 days 1 hr.

Endurance

Tommy Edward Godwin (1912–75) (GB) in the 365 days of 1939 covered 75,065 miles *120 805 km* or an average of 205.65 miles *330,96 km* per day. He then completed 100,000 miles *160 934 km* in 500 days to 14 May 1940.

The greatest mileage amassed in a cycle tour was more than 402,000 miles *643 700 km* by the itinerant lecturer Walter Stolle (b. Sudetenland, 1926) from 24 Jan 1959 to 12 Dec 1976. He visited 159 countries starting from Romford, Essex, England. Among his many misadventures were over 1000 punctures. From 1922 to 25 Dec 1973 Tommy Chambers (b. 1903) of Glasgow, had ridden a verified total of 799,405 miles *1 286 517 km*. On Xmas Day he was badly injured and has not ridden since.

Ray Reece (b. 13 July 1930), of Alverstoke, Hants, circumnavigated the world (13,325 road miles *21 444 km*) between 14 June and 5 Nov (143 days) in 1971. Visiting every continent, John W. Hathaway (b. England, 13 Jan 1925) of Vancouver, Canada covered 50,600 miles *81 300 km* from 10 Nov 1974 to 6 Oct 1976. John Joseph Marino (b. 26 Nov 1948) rode from Santa Monica to New York City, 2861 miles *4604 km* in a record 12 days 3 hr 41 min on 14–28 June 1980. Tony Michetschläger, of London, cycled 8339 miles *134,20 km* around the coast of Great Britain in 165 days (5 July–16 Dec 1979). Veronica and Colin Scargill, of Bedford, travelled 18,020 miles *29 000 km* around the world, on a tandem, 25 Feb 1974–27 Aug 1975.

Vivekananda Selva Kumar Anandan (Sri Lanka) cycled for 187 hr 28 min non-stop around Vihara Maha Devi Park, Colombo, on 2–10 May 1979. The distance covered was 1476.8 miles and he was moving 99.6% of the time.

Cyclo-cross

The greatest number of world championships (inst. 1950) have been won by Eric de Vlaeminck (Belgium) (b. 23 Aug 1945) with the amateur and Open in 1966 and six professional titles in 1968–73. British titles (inst. 1955) have been won most often by John Atkins (b. 7 Apr 1942) with five amateur (1961–2, 1966–8), seven professional (1969–75) and one Open title in 1977.

Pennine Way

John North (b. 18 Aug 1943) of Rawtenstall, Lancashire, cycled or carried his machine along the 271 mile *436 km* Pennine Way from Edale, Derbyshire to Kirk Yetholm, Borders in 2 days 8 hr 45 min on 9–11 June 1978.

tationary cycling

David Steed, of Tucson, Arizona, USA, stayed stationary without support for 9 hr 15 min on 25 Nov 1977.

Roller cycling

The four-man 12 hr record is 717.9 miles *1155,5 km* by a Northampton team at the Guildhall, Northampton, on 28 Jan 1978. The 24 hr solo record is 792.7 miles *1275,7 km* by Bruce W. Hall at San Diego University, Calif., USA on 22–23 Jan 1977.

Most World titles

The greatest number of world titles for a particular event won since the institution of the amateur championships in 1893 and the professional championships in 1895 are:

Amateur Sprint	7	Daniel Morelon (France)	1966–7, 1969–71, 1973, 1975
Amateur 100 km Paced	7	Leon Meredith (UK)	1904–5, 1907–9, 1911, 1913
Amateur Road Race	2	Giuseppe Martano (Italy)	1930, 1932
	2	Gustave Schur (East Germany)	1958–9
Professional Sprint	7	Jef Scherens (Belgium)	1932–7, 1947
	7	Antonio Maspes (Italy)	1955–6, 1959–62, 1964
Amateur Pursuit	3	Guido Messina (Italy)	1947–8, 1953
	3	Tiemen Groen (Netherlands)	1964–6
Professional Pursuit	4	Hugh Porter, MBE (UK)	1968, 1970, 1972–3
Professional 100 km Paced	6	Guillermo Timoner (Spain)	1955, 1959–60, 1962, 1964–5
Professional Road Race	3	Alfredo Binda (Italy)	1927, 1930, 1932
	3	Henri 'Rik' Van Steenbergen (Belgium)	1949, 1956–7
	3	Eddy Merckx (Belgium)	1967, 1971, 1974
Women's titles	7	Beryl Burton, OBE (UK)	1959–60, 1962–3, 1966 (pursuits) 1960, 1967 (Road)
	7	Yvonne Reynders (Belgium)	1961, 1964–5 (pursuits) 1959, 1961, 1963, 1966 (Road)

WORLD RECORDS *(In events contested by professional and amateur riders only the better mark is given)*

OPEN AIR TRACKS

MEN

Distance	min sec	Name and Country	Place	Date
Professional unpaced standing start:				
10 km	11:53.2	Eddy Merckx (Belgium)	Mexico City	25 Oct 1972
20 km	24:06.8	Eddy Merckx (Belgium)	Mexico City	25 Oct 1972
100 km	2 hr 14:02.5	Ole Ritter (Denmark)	Mexico City	18 Nov 1971
1 hour	30 miles 1258 yd *49,431 km*	Eddy Merckx (Belgium)	Mexico City	25 Oct 1972
Professional motor-paced:				
100 km	1 hr 03:40.0	Walter Lohmann (W. Germany)	Wuppertal, W. Germany	24 Oct 1955
1 hour	58 miles 737 yd *94,016 km*	Walter Lohmann (W. Germany)	Wuppertal, W. Germany	24 Oct 1955
Amateur unpaced standing start:				
1 km	1:02.547	Marc Malchow (GDR)	Mexico City	3 Nov 1980
5 km	5:50.68	Hans-Hendrick Oersted (Denmark)	Mexico City	31 Oct 1979
Amateur unpaced flying start:				
200 metres	10.58	Gordon Singleton (Canada)	Mexico City	9 Oct 1980
500 metres	27.31	Gordon Singleton (Canada)	Mexico City	9 Oct 1980
1 km	59.682	Alan Cuff (NZ)	Mexico City	7 July 1980

WOMEN

	min sec	Name and Country	Place	Date
Unpaced standing start:				
1 km	1:15.1	Irena Kirichenko (USSR)	Yerevan, USSR	8 Oct 1966
5 km	6:44.75	Keetie Van Oostenhage (Netherlands)	Munich, W. Germany	16 Sept 1978
10 km	13:34.39	Keetie Van Oostenhage (Netherlands)	Munich, W. Germany	16 Sept 1978
20 km	27:26.66	Keetie Van Oostenhage (Netherlands)	Munich, W. Germany	16 Sept 1978
100 km	2 hr 41:32.6	Maria Cressari (Italy)	Milan, Italy	17 Oct 1974
1 hour	26 miles 1355 yd *43,082 km*	Keetie Van Oostenhage (Netherlands)	Munich, W. Germany	16 Sept 1978
Unpaced flying start:				
200 metres	11.753	Natalia Kruchelnitskaya (USSR)	Tbilisi, USSR	14 Sept 1980
500 metres	31.7	Galina Tzareva (USSR)	Tbilisi, USSR	6 Oct 1978
1 km	1:12.9	Lyubov Brovina (USSR)	Irkutsk, USSR	17 July 1955

INDOOR TRACKS

MEN

	min sec	Name and Country	Place	Date
Professional unpaced standing start:				
1 hour	29 miles 192 yd *46 847 km*	Siegfried Adler (W. Germany)	Zürich, Switzerland	2 Aug 1968
5 km	5:59.099	Hans-Henrik Oersted (Denmark)	Copenhagen, Denmark	28 Oct 1980
Professional unpaced flying start:				
500 metres	28.6	Oscar Plattner (Switzerland)	Zürich, Switzerland	17 Aug 1956
1000 metres	1:01.23	Patrick Sercu (Belgium)	Antwerp, Belgium	3 Feb 1967
Professional motor-paced:				
100 km	1 hr 23:59.8	Guillermo Timoner (Spain)	San Sebastian, Spain	12 Sept 1965
1 hour	46 miles 669 yd *74,642 km*	Guy Solente (France)	Paris, France	13 Feb 1955
Amateur unpaced standing start:				
1 km	1:02.955	Lothar Thoms (E. Germany)	Moscow, USSR	22 July 1980
10 km	12:06.29	Hans-Henrik Oersted (Denmark)	Copenhagen, Denmark	28 Nov 1978
20 km	25:14.6	Ole Ritter (Denmark)	Zürich, Switzerland	30 Oct 1966
Amateur unpaced flying start:				
200 metres	10.72	Daniel Morelon (France)	Zürich, Switzerland	4 Nov 1967
500 metres	28.163	Heinz Isler (Switzerland)	Zürich, Switzerland	9 July 1979

WORLD RECORDS *continued*

WOMEN

	min sec	Name and Country	Place	Date
Unpaced standing start:				
1 km	1:07.031	Rosella Galbiati (Italy)	Milan, Italy	14 Nov 198■
Unpaced flying start:				
200 metres	11.914	Galina Tzareva (USSR)	Moscow, USSR	11 June 198■
500 metres	32.302	Galina Tzareva (USSR)	Moscow, USSR	24 Apr 198■
1 km	1:09.077	Galina Tzareva (USSR)	Moscow, USSR	10 June 1980

BRITISH RECORDS

OPEN AIR TRACKS

MEN

Distance	min sec	Name	Place	Date
Professional unpaced-standing start:				
5 km	6:20.9	Ian Hallam, MBE	Leicester, Leicestershire	30 July 197■
Amateur unpaced flying start:				
500 m	31.2	Shaun Wallace	Leicester, Leicestershire	23 Aug 198C
Amateur unpaced standing start:				
1 km	1:08.86	Trevor Gadd	Leicester, Leicestershire	24 July 197■
10 km	13:01.08	Dave Lloyd	Leicester, Leicestershire	14 July 198■
20 km	26:01.05	Dave Lloyd	Leicester, Leicestershire	14 July 198■
1 hour	28 miles 513 yd *45,531 km*	Dave Lloyd	Leicester, Leicestershire	28 July 198■
Amateur motor-paced standing start:				
50 km	42:58.0	Rik Notley	Leicester, Leicestershire	31 July 197■
1 hour	43 miles 1426 yd *70 506 km*	Rik Notley	Leicester, Leicestershire	31 July 197■

WOMEN

Distance	min sec	Name	Place	Date
Unpaced standing start:				
1 km	1:21.2	Amanda Jones	Leicester, Leicestershire	30 June 198■
3 km	3:59.10	Amanda Jones	Leicester, Leicestershire	1 Aug 198■
5 km	6:52.4	Amanda Jones	Leicester, Leicestershire	30 June 198■
10 km	28:31.3	Amanda Jones	Leicester, Leicestershire	30 June 198■
20 km	28:31.3	Amanda Jones	Leicester, Leicestershire	30 June 198■
1 hour	25 miles 1190 yd *41,322 km*	Amanda Jones	Leicester, Leicestershire	30 June 198■

ROAD CYCLING RECORDS
(British) as recognised by the Road Time Trials Council (out-and-home records)

MEN

Distance	hr min sec	Name	Course area	Date
10 miles	19 41	Martin Pyne	Eaton Socon, Cambridgeshire	18 July 198■
25 miles	49 24	Alf Engers	Kelvedon, Essex	5 Aug 1978
30 miles	1 00 11	Martin Pyne	Kelvedon, Essex	30 May 1981
50 miles	1 43 46	John Watson	Boroughbridge, North Yorkshire	23 Aug 197C
100 miles	3 38 39	Ian Cammish	Doncaster-Newark	2 Aug 198■
12 hours	286.85 miles *461,64 km*	Peter Wells	Shefford, Bedfordshire	9 Sept 1979
24 hours[1]	507.00 miles *815,93 km*	Roy Cromack	Cheshire	26–27 July 196■

[1] On 10 Sept 1974 Teuvo Louhivuori (Finland) cycled from Tampere to Kolari, 830,1 km 515.8 miles *in 24 hours—an unofficial world best performance.*

WOMEN

Distance	hr min sec	Name	Course area	Date
10 miles	21 25	Beryl Burton, OBE	Blyth, Nottinghamshire	29 Apr 1973
25 miles	53 21	Beryl Burton, OBE	Catterick, North Yorkshire	17 June 197■
30 miles	1 8 48	Ann Illingworth	Kelvedon, Essex	30 May 198■
50 miles	1 51 30	Beryl Burton, OBE	Boroughbridge, North Yorkshire	25 July 197■
100 miles	3 55 05	Beryl Burton, OBE	Essex	4 Aug 196■
12 hours	277.25 miles *446,19 km*	Beryl Burton, OBE	Wetherby, West Yorkshire	17 Sept 1967
24 hours	427.86 miles *688,57 km*	Christine Minto (*née* Moody)	Cheshire	26–27 July 196■

ROAD RECORDS ASSOCIATION'S STRAIGHT-OUT DISTANCE RECORDS

Distance	hr min sec	Name	Date
25 miles	46 23	Alan Richards	1 Sept 1977
50 miles	1 35 45	David Lloyd	26 Oct 1974
100 miles	3 28 40	Ray Booty	28 Sept 1956
1000 miles	2 days 10 40 0	Reg Randell	19–21 Aug 1960

PLACE TO PLACE RECORDS
(British) as recognised by the Road Records Association

	hr min sec	Name	Date
London to Edinburgh (380 miles *610 km*)	18 49 42	Cliff Smith	2 Nov 1965
London to Bath and back (212 miles *341 km*)	9 03 07	John Woodburn	13 June 1981
London to York (197 miles *317 km*)	7 41 13	Bob Addy	6 Aug 1972
London to Brighton and back (107 miles *172 km*)	4 15 8	Phil Griffiths	20 July 1977
Land's End to London (287 miles *461 km*)	12 34 0	Robert Maitland	17 Sept 1954

Captain Mark Phillips, here winning his third Badminton title on *Lincoln*, was a member of Britain's gold medal Olympic team at Munich in 1972. *(John Starr, All-Sport)*

EQUESTRIAN SPORTS

See also The Guinness Guide to Equestrianism *by Dorian Williams, published by Guinness Superlatives Ltd. (price £8.95).*

Origins

Evidence of horse-riding dates from a Persian engraving dated *c.* 3,000 BC. Pignatelli's academy of horsemanship at Naples dates from the 16th century. The earliest jumping competition was at the Agricultural Hall, Islington, London, in 1869. Equestrian events have been included in the Olympic Games since 1912.

Most Olympic medals

The greatest number of Olympic gold medals is five by Hans-Günter Winkler (b. 24 July 1926) (W. Germany) who won four team gold medals as captain in 1956, 1960, 1964 and 1972 and won the individual Grand Prix in 1956. The most team wins in the Prix des Nations is five by Germany in 1936, 1956, 1960, 1964 and 1972. The lowest score obtained by a winner is no faults by Frantisek Ventura (1895–1969) (Czechoslovakia) on *Eliot*, 1928 and Alwin Schockemöhle (b. 29 May 1937) (W. Germany) on *Warwick Rex*, 1976. Pierre Jonqueres d'Oriola (b. 1 Feb 1920) (France) is the only two time winner of the individual gold medal in 1952 and 1964. Richard John Hannay Meade, OBE (b. 4 Dec 1938) (Great Britain) is the only British rider to win three gold medals—as an individual in 1972 and team titles in 1968 and 1972, all in the 3-day event.

Most titles *World*

The men's world championships (inst. 1953) have been won twice by Hans-Günter Winkler (W. Germany) (1954–5) and Raimondo d'Inzeo (Italy) (1956 and 1960). The women's title (inst. 1965) has been won twice by Jane 'Janou' Tissot (*née* Lefebvre) (France) (b. Saigon, 14 May 1945) on *Rocket* (1970 and 1974).

Most titles *BSJA*

The most BSJA championships won is five by Alan Oliver (b. 8 Sept 1932) (1951, 1954, 1959, 1969–70). The only horses to have won twice are *Maguire* (Lt-Col Nathaniel Kindersley) (1900–80) in 1945 and 1947, *Sheila* (Seamus Hayes) in 1949–50, *Red Admiral* (Oliver) in 1951 and 1954 and *Stroller* (Marion Mould) in 1968 and 1971. The record for the Ladies' Championship is eight by Patricia Smythe (b. 22 Nov 1928), now Mrs Samuel Koechlin, OBE (1952–3, 1955, 1957–9, 1961–2). She won on *Flanagan*, owned by Robert Hanson, CBE, in 1955, 1958 and 1962—the only three-time winner.

George V Gold Cup and Queen Elizabeth II Cup

David Broome (b. 1 Mar 1940) has won this award (first held 1911) a record five times, 1960 on *Sunsalve*, 1966 on *Mister Softee*, 1972 on *Sportsman*, 1977 on *Philco* and 1981 on *Mr Ross*. The Queen Elizabeth Cup (first held 1949), for women, has been won three times by Marion Mould (*née* Coakes) (GB) (1965, 1971 on *Stroller* and 1976 on *Elizabeth Ann*. The only horse to win both these trophies is *Sunsalve* in 1957 (with Elisabeth Anderson) and 1960.

President's Trophy

Instituted in 1965, the Trophy has been won most times by Great Britain with nine in 1965, 1967, 1970, 1972–4, 1977–9.

Three-day event

The Badminton Three-Day Event (inst. 1949) has been won four times by Lucinda Prior-Palmer, MBE (b. 7 Nov 1953) in 1973 (on *Be Fair*), 1976 (*Wide Awake*), 1977 (*George*), and 1979 (*Killaire*) and by Capt. Mark Anthony Peter Phillips, CVO (b. 22 Sept 1948) in 1971 and 1972 (*Great Ovation*), 1974 (*Columbus*) and 1981 (*Lincoln*).

Jumping records

The official *Fédération Equestre Internationale* high jump record is 8 ft 1¼ in *2,47 m* by *Huasó*, ridden by Capt Alberto Larraguibel Morales (Chile) at Vina del Mar, Santiago, Chile, on 5 Feb 1949, and 27 ft 2¾ in *8,30 m* for long jump over water by *Amado Mio* ridden by Lt-Col Lopez del Hierro (Spain), at Barcelona, Spain on 12 Nov 1951. *Heatherbloom*, ridden by Dick Donnelly was reputed to have covered 37 ft *11,28 m* in clearing an 8 ft 3 in *2,51 m puissance* jump at Richmond, Virginia, USA in 1903. H. Plant on *Solid Gold* cleared 36 ft 3 in *11,05 m* over water at the Wagga Show, New South Wales, Australia on 28 Aug 1936. The official Australian record is 32 ft 10 in *10,00 m* by *Monarch* in Brisbane in 1951. *Jerry M.* allegedly cleared 40 ft *12,19 m* over the water at Aintree, Liverpool in 1912.

At Cairns, Queensland, *Golden Meade* ridden by Jack Martin cleared an unofficially measured 8 ft 6 in *2,59 m* on 25 July 1946. *Ben Bolt* was credited with clearing 9 ft 6 in *2,89 m* at the 1938 Royal Horse Show, Sydney, Australia. The Australian record is 8 ft 4 in *2,54 m* by *Flyaway* (Colin Russell) in 1939 and *Golden Meade* (A. L. Payne) in 1946. The world's unofficial best for a woman is 7 ft 8 in *2,34 m* by Katrina Towns (now Musgrove) (Australia) on *Big John* at Cairns, Queensland, Australia in 1978. The greatest recorded height reached bareback is 6 ft 7 in *2,00 m* by *Silver Wood* at Heidelberg, Victoria, Australia, on 10 Dec 1938.

The highest British performance is 7 ft 7⁵⁄₁₆ in *2,32 m* by the 16.2 hands *167 cm* grey gelding *Lastic* ridden by Nick Skelton

(b. 30 Dec 1957) at Olympia, London, on 16 Dec 1978. On 25 June 1937, at Olympia, the Lady Wright (*née* Margery Avis Bullows) set the best recorded height for a British equestrienne on her liver chestnut *Jimmy Brown* at 7 ft 4 in *2,23 m*.

Driving
The biennial World Driving Championships have been held five times since 1972. Great Britain won the team gold medal in 1972, 1974 and 1980 and the team bronze in 1978. The best individual performances by Britons have been silver medals won by Col Sir John Miller in 1972, and George Bowman in 1980.

Longest ride
Aimé Felix Tschiffely (b. Switzerland) rode 10,000 miles *16 093 km* from Buenos Aires, Argentina to Washington DC, USA in 504 days starting on 23 Apr 1925, with two horses, *Mancha* and *Gato*.

Horsemanship marathon
Michael Grealy of Australia rode at all paces (including jumping) for 62 hr at Blackwater, Queensland on 8–10 May 1981.

FENCING

Origins
'Fencing' (fighting with single sticks) was practised as a sport, or as a part of a religious ceremony, in Egypt as early as *c*. 1360 BC. The first governing body for fencing in Britain was the Corporation of Masters of Defence founded by Henry VIII before 1540 and fencing has been practised as sport, notably in prize fights, since that time. The foil was the practice weapon for the short court sword from the 17th century. The épée was established in the mid-19th century and the light sabre was introduced by the Italians in the late 19th century.

Most titles *World*
The greatest number of individual world titles won is four by Christian d'Oriola (see details in table), but note that he also won two individual Olympic titles. Of the three women foilists with three world titles, Helène Mayer (Germany) (1929, 1931, 1937), Ellen Muller-Preis (Austria) (1947, 1949, 1950) and Ilona Schacherer-Elek (Hungary), (1934–5, 1951), only Elek won two individual Olympic titles (1936 and 1948).

Most titles *Olympic*
The most individual Olympic gold medals won is three by Ramón Fonst (Cuba) (1883–1959) in 1900 and 1904 (two) and by Nedo Nadi (Italy) (1894–1952) in 1912 and 1920 (two). Nadi also won three team gold medals in 1920 making a then unprecedented total of five gold medals at one celebration. Edoardo Mangiarotti (Italy) (b. 7 Apr 1919) with six gold, five silver and two bronze, holds the record of 13 Olympic medals. He won them for foil and épée from 1936 to 1960. The most gold medals by a woman is four (one individual, three team) by Elena Novikova-Belova (USSR) (b. 28 July 1947) from 1968 to 1976,

and the record for all medals is seven (two gold, three silver, two bronze) by Ildikó Sagi-Retjö (formerly Ujlaki-Retjö) (Hungary) (b. 11 May 1937) from 1960 to 1976.

British Olympic records
The only British fencer to win a gold medal is Gillian Mary Sheen (b. 21 Aug 1928) in the 1956 foil. A record three Olympic medals has been won by Edgar Seligman (1867–1958) with silver medals in the épée team event in 1906, 1908 and 1912. Henry William Furse Hoskyns, MBE (b. 19 Mar 1931) has competed most often for Great Britain with six Olympic appearances, 1956–76.

FIVES

ETON FIVES
A handball game against the buttress of Eton College Chapel was first recorded in 1825. New courts were built at Eton in 1840, the rules were codified in 1877, rewritten laws were introduced in 1931 and the laws were last drawn up in 1950. There are courts in several countries besides England, with more than a dozen in northern Nigeria.

Most titles
Only one pair has won the Amateur Championship (Kinnaird Cup) eight times—Anthony Hughes and Arthur James Gordon Campbell (1958, 1965–8, 1971, 1973 and 1975). Hughes was also in the winning pair in 1963 making nine titles in all. The Clubs championship (the Barber Cup) has been won six times by Old Cholmeleians out of ten final appearances.

RUGBY FIVES
As now known, this game dates from *c*. 1850 with the first inter-public school matches recorded in the early 1870s. The Oxford *v*. Cambridge contest was inaugurated in 1925 and the Rugby Fives Association was founded in the home of Dr Edgar Cyriax (1874–1954), in Welbeck Street, London, on 29 Oct 1927. The dimensions of the Standard Rugby Fives court were approved by the Association in 1931.

Most titles
The greatest number of Amateur Singles Championships (instituted 1932) ever won is eight by Wayne Enstone in 1973–8 and 1980–1. The record for the Amateur Doubles Championship (instituted 1925) is seven shared by John Frederick Pretlove (1952, 1954, 1956–9, 1961) and David E. Gardner (1960, 1965–6, 1970–2, 1974).

FOOTBALL (ASSOCIATION)

A specialist volume The Guinness Book of Soccer Facts and Feats *(4th ed.) by Jack Rollin has been published by Guinness Superlatives Ltd. (price £6.95).*

Origins
A game with some similarities termed *Tsu-chu* was played in China in the 4th and 3rd centuries BC. One of the earliest

---

MOST OLYMPIC AND WORLD FENCING TITLES

Event	Olympic Gold Medals		World Championships (not held in Olympic years)	
Men's Foil, Individual	2	Christian d'Oriola (France) (b. 3 Oct 1928) 1952, 56	4	Christian d'Oriola (France) (b. 3 Oct 1928) 1947, 49, 53–4
	2	Nedo Nadi (Italy) (1894–1952) 1912, 20		
Men's Foil, Team	6	France 1924, 32, 48, 52, 68, 80	12	Italy 1929–31, 33–5, 37–8, 49–50, 54–5
Men's Épée, Individual	2	Ramón Fonst (Cuba) (1883–1959) 1900, 04	3	Georges Buchard (France) (b. 21 Dec 1893) 1927, 31, 33
			3	Aleksey Nikanchikov (USSR) (1940–72) 1966–7, 70
Men's Épée, Team	6	Italy 1920, 28, 36, 52, 56, 60	10	Italy 1931, 33, 37, 49–50, 53–5, 57–8
Men's Sabre, Individual	2	Dr Jenő Fuchs (Hungary) (b. 29 Oct 1882) 1908, 12	3	Aladár Gerevich (Hungary) (b. 16 Mar 1910) 1935, 51, 55
	2	Rudolf Kárpáti (Hungary) (b. 17 July 1920) 1956, 60	3	Jerzy Pawlowski (Poland) (b. 25 Oct 1932) 1957, 65–6
	2	Jean Georgiadis (Greece) (b. 1874) 1896, 1906	3	Yakov Rylsky (USSR) (b. 25 Oct 1928) 1958, 61, 63
	2	Viktor Krovopouskov (USSR) 1976, 80		
Men's Sabre, Team	9	Hungary 1908, 12, 28, 32, 36, 48, 52, 56, 60	15	Hungary 1930–1, 33–5, 37, 51, 53–5, 57–8, 66, 73, 78
Women's Foil, Individual	2	Ilona Schacherer-Elek (Hungary) (b. 1907) 1936, 48	3	Helène Mayer (Germany) (1910–53) 1929, 31, 37
			3	Ilona Schacherer-Elek (Hungary) (b. 17 May 1907) 1934–5, 51
			3	Ellen Muller-Preis (Austria) (b. 6 May 1912) 1947, 49, 50 (shared)
Women's Foil, Team	4	USSR 1960, 68, 72, 76	13	USSR 1956, 58, 61, 63, 65–6, 70–1, 74–5, 77–9

MOST AMATEUR FENCING ASSOCIATION TITLES

Foil	(Instituted 1898)	7	John Emrys Lloyd OBE (b. 8 Sept 1905)		1928, 1930–3, 1937–8
Épée	(Instituted 1904)	6	Edward O. 'Teddy' Bourne (b. 30 Sept 1948)		1966, 1972, 1974, 1976–8
Sabre	(Instituted 1898)	6	Dr Roger F. Tredgold (1912–75)		1937, 1939, 1947–9, 1955
Foil (Ladies)	(Instituted 1907)	10	Gillian M. Sheen (now Mrs R. G. Donaldson)		1949, 1951–8, 1960

references to the game in England is a Royal Proclamation by Edward II in 1314 banning the game in the City of London. The earliest clear representation of the game is an Edinburgh print dated 1672–3. The game was standardised with the formation of the Football Association in England on 26 Oct 1863. The oldest club is Sheffield FC, formed on 24 Oct 1857. Eleven per side became standard in 1870.

PROFESSIONAL

Longest match

The duration record for first class fixtures was set in the Copa Libertadores in Santos, Brazil, on 2–3 Aug 1962, when Santos drew 3–3 with Penarol FC of Montevideo, Uruguay. The game lasted 3½ hr (with interruptions), from 9.30 p.m. to 1 a.m.

The longest British match on record was one of 3 hr 23 min between Stockport County and Doncaster Rovers in the second leg of the Third Division (North) Cup at Edgeley Park, Stockport, Greater Manchester on 30 Mar 1946.

Longest unbeaten streak

Nottingham Forest were undefeated in 42 consecutive Division I matches from 20 Nov 1977 to 9 Dec 1978. In Scottish Football Glasgow Celtic were undefeated in 62 matches (49 won, 13 drawn), 13 Nov 1915–21 April 1917.

Most postponements

The Scottish Cup tie between Inverness Thistle and Falkirk during the winter of 1978–9 was postponed a record 29 times due to weather conditions. Finally Falkirk won the game 4–0.

GOAL SCORING

Teams

The highest score recorded in a first-class match is 36. This occurred in the Scottish Cup match between Arbroath and Bon Accord on 5 Sept 1885, when Arbroath won 36–0 on their home ground. But for the lack of nets and the consequent waste of retrieval time the score must have been even higher.

The highest margin recorded in an international match is 17. This occurred in the England v. Australia match at Sydney on 30 June 1951, when England won 17–0. This match is not listed by England as a *full* international. The highest in the British Isles was when England beat Ireland 13–0 at Belfast on 18 Feb 1882.

The highest score in an FA Cup match is 26, when Preston North End beat Hyde 26–0 at Deepdale, Lancashire on 15 Oct 1887. This is also the highest score between English clubs in any major competition. The biggest victory in a final tie is six when Bury beat Derby County 6–0 at Crystal Palace on 18 Apr 1903, in which year Bury did not concede a single goal in the five Cup matches.

The highest score by one side in a Football League (Division I) match is 12 goals when West Bromwich Albion beat Darwen 12–0 at West Bromwich, West Midlands on 4 Apr 1892; when Nottingham Forest beat Leicester Fosse by the same score at Nottingham on 21 Apr 1909; and when Aston Villa beat Accrington 12–2 at Perry Barr, West Midlands on 12 Mar 1892.

The highest aggregate in League Football was 17 goals when Tranmere Rovers beat Oldham Athletic 13–4 in a Third Division (North) match at Prenton Park, Merseyside, on Boxing Day, 1935. The record margin in a League match has been 13 in the Newcastle United 13, Newport County 0 (Division II) match on 5 Oct 1946 and in the Stockport County 13, Halifax 0 (Division III (North)) match on 6 Jan 1934.

The highest number of goals by any British team in a professional league in a season is 142 in 34 matches by Raith Rovers (Scottish Division II) in the 1937–8 season. The English League record is 134 in 46 matches by Peterborough United (Division IV) in 1960–1.

Individual

The most scored by one player in a first-class match is 16 by Stephan Stanis (né Stanikowski, b. Poland, 15 July 1913) for Racing Club de Lens v. Aubry-Asturies, in Lens, France, in a wartime French Cup game on 13 Dec 1942. The record for any British first-class match is 13 by John Petrie in the Arbroath v. Bon Accord Scottish Cup match in 1885 (see above). The record

in League Football is ten by Joe Payne (1914–77) for Luton Town v. Bristol Rovers in a Division III (South) match at Luton on 13 Apr 1936. The English Division I record is seven goals by Ted Drake (b. 16 Aug 1912) for Arsenal v. Aston Villa at Birmingham on 14 Dec 1935, and James David Ross ('The Little Demon') for Preston North End v. Stoke at Preston on 6 Oct 1888. The Scottish Division I record is eight goals by James Edward McGrory (b. 26 Apr 1904) for Celtic v. Dunfermline Athletic at Celtic Park, Glasgow, on 14 Jan 1928.

The record number of goals scored by one player in an international match is ten by Gottfried Fuchs (1889–1972) for Germany who beat Russia 16–0 in the 1912 Olympic tournament (consolation event) in Sweden.

The record for individual goal-scoring in a British home international is six by Joe Bambrick (b. 3 Nov 1905) for Ireland v. Wales at Belfast on 1 Feb 1930.

Career

Artur Friedenreich (1892–1969) (Brazil) scored an undocumented 1329 goals in a 43 year first class football career. The most goals scored in a specified period is 1216 by Edson Arantes do Nascimento (b. Baurú, Brazil, 23 Oct 1940), known as Pelé, the Brazilian inside left, from 7 Sept 1956 to 2 Oct 1974 in 1254 games. His best year was 1959 with 126 and the *milesimo* (1000th) came in a penalty for his club Santos in the Maracaña Stadium, Rio de Janeiro on 19 Nov 1969 when playing his 909th first-class match. He later played for New York Cosmos and on his retirement on 1 Oct 1977 his total had reached 1281, in 1363 games. Franz 'Bimbo' Binder (b. 1 Dec 1911) scored 1006 goals in 756 games in Austria and Germany between 1930 and 1950.

The best season League records are 60 goals in 39 League games by William Ralph 'Dixie' Dean (1907–80) for Everton (Division I) in 1927–8 and 66 goals in 38 games by James Smith (1902–76) for Ayr United (Scottish Division II) in the same season. With three more in Cup ties and 19 in representative matches Dean's total was 82.

The international career record for England is 49 goals by Robert 'Bobby' Charlton, OBE (b. Ashington, Northumberland, 11 Oct 1937). His first was v. Scotland on 19 Apr 1958 and his last on 20 May 1970 v. Colombia.

The greatest number of goals scored in British first-class football is 550 (410 in Scottish League matches) by James McGrory of Glasgow Celtic (1922–38). The most scored in League matches is 434, for West Bromwich Albion, Fulham, Leicester City and Shrewsbury Town, by George Arthur Rowley (b. Wolverhampton, 21 Apr 1926) between 1946 and April 1965. Rowley also scored 32 goals in the F.A. Cup and one for England 'B'.

Fastest goals

The fastest goals on record were scored in 6 sec by Albert Mundy (Aldershot) in a Division IV match v. Hartlepools United at Victoria Ground, Hartlepool, Cleveland on 25 Oct 1958, by Barrie Jones (Notts Co) in a Division III match v. Torquay United on 31 Mar 1962, by Keith Smith (Crystal Palace) in a Division II match v. Derby County at the Baseball Ground, Derby on 12 Dec 1964 and by Tommy Langley (Queen's Park Rangers) in a Division II match v. Bolton Wanderers on 11 Oct 1980.

The fastest confirmed hat-trick is in 2½ minutes by Ephraim 'Jock' Dodds for Blackpool v Tranmere Rovers on 28 Feb 1943, and by Jimmy Scarth for Gillingham v Leyton Orient in Div III (Southern) on 1 Nov 1952. A hat-trick in 1 min 50 sec is claimed for Maglioni of Independiente v. Gimnasia y Escrima de la Plata in Argentina on 18 Mar 1973. John McIntyre (Blackburn Rovers) scored four goals in 5 min v. Everton at Ewood Park, Blackburn, Lancashire on 16 Sept 1922. William 'G.' 'Ginger' Richardson (West Bromwich Albion) scored four goals in 5 min against West Ham United at Upton Park on 7 Nov 1931. Frank Keetley scored six goals in 21 min in the 2nd half of the Lincoln City v. Halifax Town league match on 16 Jan 1932. The international record is three goals in 3½ min by Willie Hall (Tottenham Hotspur) for England against Ireland on 16 Nov 1938 at Old Trafford, Greater Manchester.

The fastest goal in World Cup competition was one in 30 sec by Olle Nyberg for Sweden *v.* Hungary in Paris, 16 June 1938.

Fastest own goal

Torquay United's Pat Kruse equalled the fastest goal on record when he headed the ball into his own net only 6 sec after kick-off *v.* Cambridge United on 3 Jan 1977.

FA CHALLENGE CUP
Most wins

The greatest number of FA Cup wins is seven by Aston Villa in 1887, 1895, 1897, 1905, 1913, 1920 and 1957 (nine final appearances). Newcastle United have been in the final 11 times and Tottenham Hotspur have won six times in six appearances. The highest aggregate scores have been 6–1 in 1890, 6–0 in 1903 and 4–3 in 1953.

The greatest number of Scottish FA Cup wins is 25 by Celtic in 1892, 1899, 1900, 1904, 1907–8, 1911–12, 1914, 1923, 1925, 1927, 1931, 1933, 1937, 1951, 1954, 1965, 1967, 1969, 1971, 1972, 1974, 1975 and 1977.

Youngest player

The youngest player in a FA Cup Final was Paul Allen (b. 28 Aug 1962) of West Ham United, who played against Arsenal on 10 May 1980 aged 17 years 256 days. Note however, that Derek Johnstone (Rangers) (b. 4 Nov 1953) was 16 years 11 months old when he played in the Scottish League Cup Final against Celtic on 24 Oct 1970. The youngest goal scorer in the FA Cup Final was John Sissons (b. 30 Sept 1945) who scored for West Ham United *v.* Preston North End on 2 May 1964. The youngest player ever in the FA Cup competition was Scott Endersby (b. 20 Feb 1962) who was only 15 years 288 days old when he played in goal for Kettering *v.* Tilbury on 26 Nov 1977.

Most medals

Three players have won five FA Cup Winner's Medals: James Forrest (Blackburn Rovers) (1884–6, 1890–1); the Hon Sir Arthur Fitzgerald Kinnaird, KT (Wanderers) (1873, 1877–8) and Old Etonians (1879, 1882) and Charles H. R. Wollaston (Wanderers) (1872–3, 1876–8).

Longest tie

The most protracted FA Cup tie in the competition proper was that between Stoke City and Bury in the third round with Stoke winning 3–2 in the fifth meeting after 9 hr 22 min of play in January 1955. The matches were at Bury (1–1) on 8 Jan; Stoke on Trent on 12 Jan (abandoned after 22 min of extra time with the score 1–1); Goodison Park (3–3) on 17 Jan; Anfield (2–2) on 19 Jan; and finally at Old Trafford on 24 Jan. In the 1972 final qualifying round Alvechurch beat Oxford City after five previous drawn games.

FOOTBALL LEAGUE CUP
Most Wins

The most Football League Cup wins is three by Aston Villa in 1961, 1975 and 1977.

MOST LEAGUE CHAMPIONSHIPS
World

The world record number of successive national League championship wins is nine by Celtic (Scotland) 1966–74, CSKA, Sofia (Bulgaria) 1954–62 and MTK Budapest (Hungary) 1917–25. The Sofia club hold a European postwar record of 21 league titles.

English

The greatest number of League Championships (Division I) is 12 by Liverpool in 1901, 1906, 1922, 1923, 1947, 1964, 1966, 1973, 1976–7 and 1979–80. The record number of points in Division I is 68 by Liverpool in 1978–9. The most in Division II is 70 by Tottenham Hotspur in 1919–20. Doncaster Rovers scored 72 points from 42 games in Division III (North) in 1946–7. Lincoln City achieved 74 points from 46 games in Division IV in 1975–6. The lowest in the League has been eight by Doncaster Rovers (Division II) in 1904–5.

'Double'

The only FA Cup and League Championship 'doubles' are those of Preston North End in 1889, Aston Villa in 1897, Tottenham

Hotspur in 1961 and Arsenal in 1971. Preston won the League without losing a match and the Cup without having a goal scored against them throughout the whole competition. Glasgow Rangers have won the Scottish League Championship 35 times between 1899 and 1976 and were joint champions on another occasion. Their 76 points in the Scottish Division I in 1920–1 represents a record in any division.

Closest win

In 1923–4 Huddersfield won the Division I championship over Cardiff by 0.02 of a goal with a goal average of 1.81.

TOURNAMENT RECORDS

World Cup

The *Fédération Internationale de Football Association* (FIFA) was founded in Paris on 21 May 1904 and instituted the World Cup Competition on 13 July 1930, in Montevideo, Uruguay.

The only country to win three times has been Brazil in 1958, 1962 and 1970. Brazil was also second in 1950 and third in 1938 and 1978, and is the only one of the 45 participating countries to have played in all eleven competitions. Antonio Carbajal (b. 1923) played for Mexico in goal in the five competitions from 1950 to 1966. The record goal scorer has been Just Fontaine (b. Marrakesh, Morocco, 18 Aug 1933) (France) with 13 goals in six games in the final stages of the 1958 competition in Sweden. The most goals scored in a final is three by Geoffrey Charles Hurst, MBE (b. Ashton-under-Lyne, Greater Manchester, 8 Dec 1941) (West Ham United) for England *v.* W. Germany on 30 July 1966. Gerd Müller (W. Germany) (b. 3 Nov 1945) holds the aggregate record for goals scored in the World Cup Finals with 14 in 1970 and 1974.

World Club Championship

This club tournament was started in 1960 between the winners of the European Cup and the Copa Libertadores, the South American equivalent. Three clubs have won it twice: Penarol, Uruguay in 1961, 1966; Santos, Brazil in 1962, 1963; and Inter-Milan in 1964, 1965.

European Championship *(formerly Nations Cup)*

The European equivalent of the World Cup started in 1958 and is staged every four years. Each tournament takes two years to run with the semi-finals and final in the same country. W. Germany have won twice in 1972 and 1980.

European Champion Clubs Cup

The European Cup for the League champions of the respective nations was approved by FIFA on 8 May 1955 and was run by the European governing body UEFA (Union of European Football Associations) which came into being in the previous year. Real Madrid won the first final, and have won a record six times, including five times consecutively, 1956–60, 1966.

Glasgow Celtic became the first British club to win the Cup beating Inter-Milan 2–1 in Lisbon, Portugal, on 25 May 1967. They also became the only British club to win the European Cup and the two senior domestic tournaments (League and Cup) in the same season. On 10 May 1978 Liverpool won the Cup for the second successive year, beating FC Bruges 1–0 at Wembley. Nottingham Forest also won successively in 1979 and 1980.

European Cup Winners Cup

A tournament for the national Cup winners started in 1960–1 with ten entries. Fiorentina beat Glasgow Rangers 4–1 on aggregate in a two-leg final in May 1961. Tottenham Hotspur were the first British club to win the trophy, beating Atletico Madrid 5–1 in Rotterdam in 1963.

UEFA Cup

Originally known as the International Inter-City Industrial Fairs Cup, this club tournament began in 1955. The first competition lasted three years, the second two years. In 1960–1 it became an annual tournament and since 1971–2 has been replaced by the UEFA Cup. The first British club to win the trophy were Leeds United in 1968. The most wins is three by Barcelona in 1958, 1960 and 1966.

above: The empty terraces at Upton Park for the West Ham *v.* Castilla match in 1980 were in sharp contrast to the record crowd which cheered the English club to its third FA Cup victory earlier that year. *(Duncan Raban, All-Sport) right:* Totalling 1534 appearances for their respective clubs, John Trollope (Swindon) receiving the Mecca Loyalty Award from former record holder, Jimmy Dickinson (Portsmouth) at the County Ground in January 1981. *(Mecca Leisure)*

PLAYERS

Most international appearances

The greatest number of appearances for a national team is 145 by Hector Chumpitaz (b. 12 Apr 1943) (Peru) from 1963 to 1981. This includes all matches played by the national team. The record for full internationals against other national teams is 115 by Bjorn Nordqvist (Sweden) (b. 6 Oct 1942) from 1963 to 1979.

Most appearances *Home Countries*

Robert Frederick 'Bobby' Moore, OBE (b. Barking, Greater London, 12 Apr 1941) of West Ham United and Fulham set up a new record of full international appearances by a British footballer by playing in his 108th game for England *v.* Italy on 14 Nov 1973 at Wembley. His first appearance was *v.* Peru on 20 May 1962 and he retired from professional football on 14 May 1977 on his 1000th appearance in all matches.

Ivor Allchurch, MBE (b. 29 Dec 1929) of Swansea, Newcastle, Cardiff City and Worcester City played 68 times for Wales, including 37 times against the home countries, between 15 Nov 1950 and February 1968.

Kenny Dalglish (b. Glasgow, 4 Mar 1951), of Celtic and Liverpool, has a record total of 78 appearances for Scotland between November 1971 and June 1981.

The greatest number of appearances for N. Ireland is 87 by Patrick Jennings (b. Newry, 12 June 1945) (Watford, Tottenham Hotspur, Arsenal) April 1964 to June 1981.

Oldest and youngest caps

The oldest cap has been William Henry 'Billy' Meredith (1874–1958) (Manchester City and United) who played outside right for Wales *v.* England at Highbury, London, on 15 Mar 1920 when aged 45 years 229 days. He played internationally for a record span of 26 years (1895–1920).

The youngest cap in the four home countries internationals has been Norman Kernaghan (Belfast Celtic) who played for Ireland *v.* Wales in 1936 aged 17 years 80 days. It is possible, however, that W. K. Gibson (Cliftonville) who played for Ireland *v.* Wales on 24 Feb 1894 at 17 was slightly younger. England's youngest home international was Duncan Edwards (b. Dudley, West Midlands, 1 Oct 1936, d. 21 Feb 1958, 15 days after the Munich air crash) the Manchester United left half, against Scotland at Wembley on 2 Apr 1955, aged 18 years 183 days. The youngest Welsh cap was John Charles (b. Swansea, 27 Dec 1931) the Leeds United centre half, against Ireland at Wrexham on 8 Mar 1950, aged 18 years 71 days. Scotland's youngest international has been Denis Law of Huddersfield Town, who played against Wales on 18 Oct 1958, aged 18 years 236 days. David Black of Hurlford, Strathclyde, may have been 17 when he played for Scotland *v.* Ireland in 1889.

 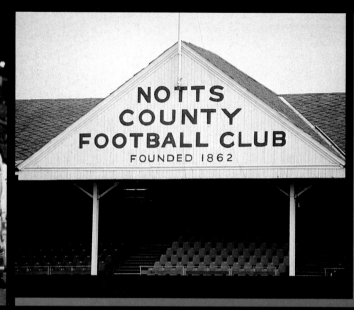

left: Nottingham Forest with the European Champion Clubs Cup in 1980 which they had just successfully retained against SV Hamburg (*Provincial Sports Photography*); and right: their local rivals, Notts County, who are proud that they are the oldest existing club in the Football League. (*Peter Robinson/Mick Alexander*)

Most durable player

The most durable player in League history has been Terence Lionel Paine, MBE (b. 23 Mar 1939) who made 824 league appearances from 1957 to 1977 playing for Southampton FC and Hereford Utd FC. Norman John Trollope, MBE (b. 14 June 1943) made 770 League appearances for one club, Swindon Town, between 1960 and 1980.

Transfer fees *British*

The record fee received by a British club was £1,469,500 (incl VAT and other levies) by Aston Villa from Wolverhampton Wanderers for Andy Gray (b. 30 Nov 1955), on 12 Sept 1979.

Heaviest goalkeeper

The biggest goalkeeper in representative football was the England international Willie J. 'Fatty' Foulke (1874–1916), who stood 6 ft 3 in *1,90 m* and weighed 22 st 3 lb *141 kg*. His last games were for Bradford City, by which time he was 26 st *165 kg*. He once stopped a game by snapping the cross bar.

Most successful national coaches

The teams of Helmut Schoen (b. Dresden 15 Sept 1915) of W. Germany won the 1972 European championship and the 1974 World Cup, as well as finishing second in the 1966 World Cup and 1976 European championships, and third in the 1970 World Cup. George Raynor's (b. Hoyland, West Yorkshire, 1907) Swedish teams won the 1948 Olympic competition and were second in the 1958 World Cup and third in both the 1950 World Cup and in the 1952 Olympic competition.

ATTENDANCES
Greatest crowds

The greatest recorded crowd at any football match was 205,000 (199,854 paid) for the Brazil *v.* Uruguay World Cup match in the Maracaña Municipal Stadium, Rio de Janeiro, Brazil on 16 July 1950. The record attendance for a European Cup match is 136,505 at the semi-final between Glasgow Celtic and Leeds United at Hampden Park, Glasgow on 15 Apr 1970.

The British record paid attendance is 149,547 at the Scotland *v.* England international at Hampden Park, Glasgow, on 17 Apr 1937. It is, however, probable that this total was exceeded (estimated 160,000) on the occasion of the FA Cup Final between Bolton Wanderers and West Ham United at Wembley Stadium on 28 Apr 1923, when the crowd broke in on the pitch and the start was delayed 40 min until the pitch was cleared. The counted admissions were 126,047.

The Scottish Cup record attendance is 146,433 when Celtic played Aberdeen at Hampden Park on 24 Apr 1937. The record attendance for a League match in Britain is 118,567 for Rangers *v.* Celtic at Ibrox Park, Glasgow on 2 Jan 1939.

For details of the largest football stadiums, see p. 118.

Smallest crowd

The smallest crowd at a full home international was 4946 for the Northern Ireland *v.* Wales match of 19 May 1973 at Goodison Park, Everton, Merseyside. The smallest paying attendance at a Football League fixture was for the Stockport County *v.* Leicester City match at Old Trafford, Greater Manchester, on 7 May 1921. Stockport's own ground was under suspension and the 'crowd' numbered 13 but an estimated 2000 gained free admission. When West Ham beat Castilla, of Spain (5–1) in the European Cup Winners Cup at Upton Park, Greater London, on 1 Oct 1980, there were no paying spectators due to disciplinary action by the European Football Union.

Greatest receipts

The record gross FA Cup receipts at Wembley, London, is £729,000 (excluding radio and television fees) for the final on 10 May 1980. The 'gate' at the first FA Cup Final at Kennington Oval, London on 16 Mar 1872 was £100.

The greatest receipts at any World Cup final were £204,805, from an attendance of 96,924 for England *v.* W. Germany at Wembley, on 30 July 1966.

The record for a British international match is £550,000 for the England *v.* Argentina match at Wembley on 13 May 1980 (attendance 92,000). The receipts for the Manchester United *v.* Benfica match at Wembley on 29 May 1968 were £118,000 (attendance 100,000).

Most peripatetic fans

In a period of 264 days (10 Aug 1968–30 Apr 1969) Michael Jones and Bob Wilson of Shrewsbury, viewed league matches at all 93 English Football League grounds (inc. Berwick Rangers).

AMATEUR AND MINOR LEAGUES
Most Olympic wins

The only country to have won the Olympic football title three times is Hungary in 1952, 1964 and 1968. The United Kingdom won the unofficial tournament in 1900 and the official tournaments of 1908 and 1912. The highest Olympic score is Denmark 17 *v.* France 'A' 1 in 1908.

Most FA Amateur Cup wins

The greatest number of FA Amateur Cup (1893–1974) wins is

The current representatives of the best behaved club in football, Coleridge FC, with their chairman Frank Wilson (centre left), the man who has kept the players on the straight and narrow, and president.

ten by Bishop Auckland who won in 1896, 1900, 1914, 1921–2, 1935, 1939, 1955–7.

Most caps

The record number of England amateur caps is held by Rod Haider (b. 23 Jan 1943), the Hendon captain and half-back, who made his 65th amateur international appearance for England *v.* Scotland on 5 Apr 1974.

Largest crowd

The highest attendance at an amateur match has been 120,000 in Senayan Stadium, Jakarta, Indonesia, on 26 Feb 1976 for the Pre-Olympic Group II final, North Korea *v.* Indonesia.

Highest scores *Teams*

The highest aggregate score in a home Amateur International is 11 goals in the England *v.* Scotland match (8–3) at Dulwich on 11 Mar 1939. The foreign record was when England beat France 15–0 in Paris on 1 Nov 1906.

The highest score in an FA Amateur Cup Final was eight when Northern Nomads beat Stockton 7–1 at Sunderland, Tyne and Wear in 1926, and when Dulwich Hamlet beat Marine (Liverpool) by the same score at Upton Park in 1932.

In 1975, in a Scottish ladies league match, Edinburgh Dynamos FC beat Lochend Thistle 42–0.

In an under-14 league match between Midas FC and Courage Colts, in Kent, on 11 Apr 1976, the full time score after 70 min play was 59–1. Top scorer for Midas was Kevin Graham with 17 goals. Courage had scored the first goal.

Needing to improve their goal 'difference' to gain promotion in 1979, Ilinden FC of Yugoslavia, with the collusion of the opposition, Mladost, and the referee, won their final game of the season by 134–1. Their rivals in the promotion race won their match, under similar circumstances by 88–0.

Highest scores *Individual*

The highest individual score in amateur internationals is six: by William Charles Jordan (1885–1949) for England *v.* France (12–0) at Park Royal, London on 23 Mar 1908; by Vivian John Woodward (1879–1954) for England *v.* Holland (9–1) at Stamford Bridge, London, on 11 Dec 1909; and by Harold A. Walden (1889–1949) for Great Britain *v.* Hungary, in Stockholm, Sweden, on 1 July 1912. Kim Barker, 11, of South Hobart, Tasmania, Australia scored 21 goals in his team's 25–0 win over Hutchins in the under-12 competition on 11 May 1974.

Highest scores *International Schoolboys*

The most prolific schoolboy international scorer has been Richard Smith Bell (b. 9 Oct 1921) of Crook, Co Durham, who in the 1935–6 season scored 12 goals for England in three internationals: three *v.* Scotland, three *v.* Wales and six *v.* Ireland.

Highest scores *Season*

The greatest number of goals in a season reported for an individual player in junior professional league football is 96 by Tom Duffy (b. 7 Jan 1937), who played centre forward for Ardeer Thistle FC, Strathclyde in the 1960–1 season. The highest season figure reported in any class of competitive football for an individual is 294 goals in 67 matches by centre forward Michael Jones for Afan Lido FC, St Joseph's School and Port Talbot Boys XI in 1972–3. His total (65 headers, 120 right foot and 109 left foot) included an 11, a ten and six triple hat-tricks. David King (b. 11 Sept 1968) scored 143 goals in 28 league and cup matches for Coed Eva Junior FC, Gwent, Wales in 1978–79.

Fastest goals

Wind-aided goals in 3 sec after kick-off have been scored by a number of players. Tony Bacon, of Schalmont HS scored three goals *v.* Icabod Crane HS in 63 sec at Schenectady, New York, USA on 8 Oct 1975.

Fastest own goal

The fastest own goal on record was one in 5 sec 'scored' by Peter

Johnson of Chesham United in a match against Wycombe Wanderers on 21 Feb 1976.

Longest match

A match between Simon Fraser Univ. Clansmen and Quincy College Hawks lasted 4 hr 25 min (221 min 43 sec playing time) at Pasadena, Cal, USA in November 1976.

Longest ties

The aggregate duration of ties in amateur soccer have not been collated but it is recorded that in the London FA Intermediate Cup first qualifying round Highfield FC Reserves had to meet Mansfield House FC on 19 and 26 Sept and 3, 10 and 14 Oct 1970 to get a decision after 9 hr 50 min play with scores of 0–0, 1–1, 1–1, 3–3, and 0–2.

In the Hertfordshire Intermediate Cup, London Colney beat Leavesden Hospital after 12 hr 41 min play and seven ties from 6 Nov to 17 Dec 1971.

Largest tournament

The Metropolitan Police 5-a-side Youth Competition in 1981 attracted an entry of 7008 teams, a record for an FA sanctioned competition.

Most and Least successful teams

The Home Farm FC, Dublin, Ireland, between 12 Oct 1968 and 10 Oct 1970 won 79 consecutive matches. Winlaton West End FC, Tyne and Wear, completed a run of 95 league games without defeat between 1976 and 1980. In six successive years the Larkswood County Junior School team of 1959–60 was unbeaten, winning 118 games and drawing three. Stockport United FC, of the Stockport Football League, lost 39 consecutive League and Cup matches from September 1976 to 18 Feb 1978.

In 5-a-side football, Hebburn Argyle Juniors won 115 successive games from 17 Oct 1977 to 5 Jan 1980. Steven Foster played in every game.

Most disciplined

Coleridge FC of the Cambridgeshire FA completed 27 years without a single member having been cautioned, sent off or otherwise disciplined since its formation in 1954.

Most indisciplined

In the local Cup match between Tongham Youth Club, Surrey and Hawley, Hampshire, on 3 Nov 1969 the referee booked all 22 players including one who went to hospital, and one of the linesmen. The match, won by Tongham 2–0, was described by a player as 'A good, hard game'.

The two Royal Marine five-a-side soccer teams, scoreline to the fore, after their record breaking efforts. (*Jim Ratcliffe*)

In a Gancia Cup match at Waltham Abbey, Essex on 23 Dec 1973, the referee, Michael J. Woodhams, sent off the entire Juventus-Cross team and some club officials. Glencraig United, Faifley, nr Clydebank, had all 11 team members and two substitutes for their match against Goldenhill Boy's Club on 2 Feb 1975 booked in the dressing room before a ball was kicked. The referee, Mr Tarbet of Bearsden, took exception to the chant which greeted his arrival. It was not his first meeting with Glencraig. The teams drew 2–2.

Ball control

Mikael Palmqvist (20) juggled a regulation soccer ball for 10 hr non-stop at Träffens Sporthall, Gävle, Sweden on 8 May 1980. He did 80,357 repetitions with feet, legs and head without the ball ever touching the ground.

Mikael Palmqvist headed a regulation football non-stop for 2 hr 33 min (22,900 repetitions) at the Kristianstad, Sweden on 25 Mar 1981.

Marathon *11-a-side*

The longest recorded 11-a-side football match is 65 hr 1 min by Callinafercy Soccer Club, Co Kerry, Ireland on 1–3 Aug 1980.

Marathon *5-a-side*

The longest 5-a-side games have been: outdoors; 73 hr by two teams of five from Three Medical Troop, Commando Logistic Regiment, Royal Marines at Arbroath, Scotland, on 24–26 Oct 1980, and indoors; 100 hr 5 min by The Friends of Powys at Yale Sixth Form College, Wrexham, Clwyd on 4–8 Apr 1980.

FOOTBALL (GAELIC)

Earliest references

The game developed from inter-parish 'free for all' with no time-limit, no defined playing area nor specific rules. The earliest reported match was Meath v. Louth, at Slane in 1712. Standardisation came with the formation of the Gaelic Athletic Association in Thurles, Ireland, on 1 Nov 1884.

Most titles

The greatest number of All Ireland Championships ever won by one team is 26 by Ciarraidhe (Kerry) between 1903 and 1980. The greatest number of successive wins is four by Wexford (1915–18) and four by Kerry (1929–32). Leinster has won most Inter-provincial championships (Railway Cup) with 18 between 1928 and 1974. Sean O'Neill (Down) holds the record of eight medals with Ulster (1960–71).

Highest scores

The highest team score in an All-Ireland final was when Dublin, 27 (5 goals, 12 points) beat Armagh, 15 (3 goals, 6 points) on 25 Sept 1977. The highest combined score was 45 points when Cork (26) beat Galway (19) in 1973. A goal equals three points. The highest individual score in an All-Ireland final has been 2 goals, 6 points by Jimmy Keaveney (Dublin) in the match against Armagh in 1977, and by Michael Sheehy (Kerry) v. Dublin in 1979.

Lowest scores

In four All-Ireland finals the combined totals have been 7 points; 1893 Wexford (1 goal, till 1894 worth 5 points, 1 point) v. Cork (1 point); 1895 Tipperary (4 points) v. Meath (3 points); 1904 Kerry (5 points) v. Dublin (2 points); 1924 Kerry (4 points) v. Dublin (3 points).

Most appearances

The most appearances in All-Ireland finals is ten by Dan O'Keeffe (Kerry) of which seven (a record) were on the winning side.

Largest crowd

The record crowd is 90,556 for the Down v. Offaly final at Croke Park, Dublin, in 1961.

FOOTBALL (RUGBY LEAGUE)

Origins

The Rugby League was formed originally on 29 Aug 1895 at

Huddersfield, Lancs as 'The Northern Rugby Football Union' by the secession of 22 clubs in Lancashire and Yorkshire from the parent Rugby Union. Though payment for loss of working time was a major cause of the breakaway the 'Northern Union' did not itself embrace full professionalism until 1898. A reduction in the number of players per team from 15 to 13 took place in 1906 and the present title of 'Rugby League' was adopted in 1922.

Most titles
There have been eight World Cup Competitions. Australia were winners in 1957, 1968, 1970, 1975 and 1977. Great Britain/England won in 1954, 1960 and 1972.

Under the one-league Championship system (1907–62 and 1965–71) the club with the most wins was Wigan with nine (1909, 1922, 1926, 1934, 1946, 1947, 1950, 1952 and 1960).

In the Rugby League Challenge Cup (inaugurated 1896–7) the club with the most wins is Leeds with ten in 1910, 1923, 1932, 1936, 1941–2 (wartime), 1957, 1968, 1977–8. Oldham is the only club to appear in four consecutive Cup Finals (1924–7).

Only three clubs have won all four major Rugby League trophies (Challenge Cup, League Championship, County Cup and County League) in one season: Hunslet in 1907–8, Huddersfield in 1914–15 and Swinton in 1927–8.

In addition to the three 'All Four Cup clubs', on only five other occasions has a club taken the Cup and League honours in one season: Broughton Rangers (1902); Halifax (1903); Huddersfield (1913); Warrington (1954); and St Helens (1966). Warrington (1974) and St Helens (1976) have won the Cup and the newly constituted Club championship.

HIGHEST TEAM SCORES
World Cup
The record aggregate score in a World Cup match is 72 points when Great Britain beat New Zealand at Hameau Stadium, Pau, France by 53 points to 19 on 4 Nov 1972.

Senior match
The highest aggregate score in Cup or League football in a game where a senior club has been concerned, was 121 points, when Huddersfield beat Swinton Park Rangers by 119 points (19 goals, 27 tries) to 2 points (one goal) in the first round of the Northern Union Cup on 28 Feb 1914.

Cup Final
The record aggregate in a Challenge Cup Final is 47 points when Featherstone Rovers beat Bradford Northern 33–14 at Wembley, London, on 12 May 1973.

The greatest winning margin was 34 points when Huddersfield beat St Helens 37–3 at Oldham on 1 May 1915.

Touring teams
The record score for a British team touring the Commonwealth is 101 points by England v. South Australia (nil) at Adelaide in May 1914.

The record for a Commonwealth touring team in Britain is 92 points (10 goals, 24 tries) by Australia against Bramley's 7 points (2 goals, 1 try) at the Barley Mow Ground, Bramley, near Leeds, on 9 Nov 1921.

Most points *Season*
Leeds scored a record 1220 points in the 1972–73 season, in all competitive matches.

HIGHEST INDIVIDUAL SCORES
Most points *Cup*
George Henry 'Tich' West (1882–1927) of Hull Kingston Rovers scored 53 points (10 goals and 11 tries) in a First Round Challenge Cup-tie v. Brookland Rovers on 4 Mar 1905.

Most points *League*
Jimmy Lomas (Salford) scored a record 39 points (5 tries, 12 goals) against Liverpool City (78–0) on 2 Feb 1907.

Most points *Season*
The official record number of points in a season was scored by Benjamin Lewis Jones (Leeds) (b. 11 Apr 1931) with 496 (194 goals, 36 tries) in season 1956–7. He also scored 9 points in a friendly game). However, including 14 points in friendly games, David Watkins (Salford) (b. 5 Mar 1942) scored 507 points in season 1972–3.

Most points *Career*
Neil Fox (Bradford Northern) scored 6220 points (2575 goals, 358 tries, 4 drop goals) in a senior Rugby League career from 10 Apr 1956 to the end of the 1979–80 season.

Most tries *Season*
Albert Aaron Rosenfeld (1885–1970) (Huddersfield), an Australian-born wing-threequarter, scored 80 tries in 42 matches in the 1913–14 season.

Most tries *Career*
Brian Bevan (b. Australia, 24 Apr 1924) a wing-threequarter, scored 796 tries in the 18 seasons (16 with Warrington, two with Blackpool Borough) from 1946 to 1964. He scored 740 for Warrington, 17 for Blackpool and 39 in representative matches.

Most goals *Season*
The record number of goals in a season is 221 by David Watkins (Salford) in the 1972–3 season. His total was made up in League, Cup, other competitions, and a Salford v. New Zealand match.

Most international appearances
Test Matches between Great Britain (formerly England) and Australia are regarded as the highest distinction for a RL player in either hemisphere and Jim Sullivan (1903–77) (Wigan) holds the Test record for a British player with 15 appearances between 1924 and 1933, though Mick Sullivan (no kin) (b. 12 Jan 1934) of Huddersfield, Wigan, St Helens and York, played in 16 GB v. Australia games in 1954–64, of which 13 were Tests and three World Cup matches.

In all Tests, including those against New Zealand and France, Mick Sullivan made the record number of 46 appearances and scored 43 tries.

Most Cup Finals
Two players have appeared in seven Cup Finals: Alan Edwards (Salford, Dewsbury, and Bradford Northern) between 1938 and 1949, and Eric Batten (Leeds, Bradford Northern and Featherstone Rovers) between 1941 and 1952.

Alex Murphy (b. 22 Apr 1939) (St Helens, Leigh and Warrington) between 1961 and 1974, and Brian Lockwood (b. 8 Oct 1946) (Castleford, Hull Kingston Rovers and Widnes) between 1969 and 1981, have both been in four Challenge Cup-winning sides.

Youngest player
The youngest player in a Cup Final was Reg Lloyd (Keighley) (b. 1 Sept 1919) who was 17 years 249 days when he played at Wembley on 8 May 1937.

Most durable player
David Watkins (Salford) played and scored in every club game during seasons 1972–3 and 1973–4—a total of 92 games contributing 41 tries and 403 goals—a total of 929 points. Together with seasons 1970–1 and 1971–2 he played 140 consecutive games.

Gilbert Austin (Hull Kingston Rovers) played in 190 consecutive games (plus five friendlies) for his club between 1918 and 1924.

Most and least successful teams
Hull FC won all 26 League Division II matches in the 1978–9 season. Doncaster hold the unenviable record of losing 40 consecutive League games from 16 Nov 1975 to 21 Apr 1977.

Record transfer fees
The highest RL transfer fee is £72,500 paid to Wigan for full-back, George Fairbain (b. 1955) by Hull Kingston Rovers on 7 June 1981.

HIGHEST SCORE   The highest aggregate scores in international Rugby League football are:

Match	Points	Score
Great Britain v. Australia (*Test Matches*)	62	Australia won 50–12 (Swinton, 9 Nov 1963)
Great Britain v. New Zealand (*Test Matches*)	72	Great Britain won 52–20 (Wellington, 30 July 1910)
Great Britain v. France (*Test Matches*)	65	Great Britain won 50–15 (Leeds, 14 Mar 1959)
England v. Wales	73	England won 60–13 (St. Helens, 28 May 1978)
England v. France	55	France won 42–13 (Marseille, 25 Nov 1951)
England v. Other Nationalities	61	England won 34–27 (Workington, 30 Mar 1933)
Wales v. France	50	France won 29–21 (Bordeaux, 23, Nov 1947)
Wales v. Other Nationalities	48	Other Nationalities won 27–21 (Swansea, 31 Mar 1951)
Australia v. Great Britain	76	Australia won 63–13 (Paris, 31 Dec 1933)
Australia v. Wales	70	Australia won 51–19 (Wembley, 30 Dec 1933)
Australia v. France (*Test Matches*)	62	Australia won 56–6 (Brisbane, 2 July 1960)
Australia v. New Zealand (*Test Matches*)	74	New Zealand won 49–25 (Brisbane, 28 June 1952)
New Zealand v. France (*Test Matches*)	53	France won 31–22 (Lyon, 15 Jan 1956)

Greatest crowds

The greatest attendance at any Rugby League match is 102,569 for the Warrington v. Halifax Cup Final replay at Odsal Stadium, Bradford, on 5 May 1954.

Greatest receipts

The highest receipts for a match in the world have been £591,117 for the Hull Kingston Rovers v. Widnes Final at Wembley on 2 May 1981.

FOOTBALL (RUGBY UNION)

For a more comprehensive survey of world rugby see The Guinness Book of Rugby Facts and Feats *by Terry Godwin, published by Guinness Superlatives Ltd, at £7.95.*

Records are determined in terms of present day scoring values, i.e. a try at 4 points; a dropped goal, penalty or goal from a mark at 3 points; and a conversion at 2 points. The actual score, in accordance with which ever of the eight earlier systems was in force at the time, is also given, in brackets.

Origins

Though there are records of a game with many similarities to Rugby dating back to the Roman occupation, the game is traditionally said to have originated from a breach of the rules of the football played in November 1823 at Rugby School by William Webb Ellis (later the Rev) (c. 1807–72). This handling code of football evolved gradually and was known to have been played at Cambridge University by 1839. The Rugby Football Union was founded on 26 Jan 1871.

Most Olympic Gold Medals

Rugby Football was included four times in the Olympic Games: 1900, 1908, 1920 and 1924. Four United States players, in the 1920 winning team, won second gold medals in 1924: Charles W. Doe, John T. O'Neil, John C. Patrick and Rudolph J. Scholz. Daniel Brendan Carroll, who was in the winning Australian team in 1908, won a second gold medal in the 1920 US team.

HIGHEST TEAM SCORES
Internationals

The highest score in any full International was when France beat Spain by 92 points (including 19 tries) to nil on 4 Mar 1979.

The International Championship record is 75 points when Wales beat France at Swansea in 1910 by 59 points (8 goals, 1 penalty goal, 2 tries) to 16 (1 goal, 2 penalty goals and 1 try) (49–14).

The highest aggregate score for any International match between the Four Home Unions is 69 when England beat Wales by 69 points (7 goals, 1 drop goal and 6 tries) to 0 at Blackheath, London in 1881. (Note: there was no point scoring in 1881).

The highest score by any Overseas side in an International in the British Isles is 53 points (7 goals, 1 drop goal and 2 tries) to 0 when South Africa beat Scotland at Murrayfield, Edinburgh, on 24 Nov 1951 (44–0).

Tour match

The record score for any international tour match is 125–0 (17 goals, 5 tries and 1 penalty goal) (103–0) when New Zealand beat Northern New South Wales at Quirindi, Australia, on 30 May 1962.

Match

In Denmark, Comet beat Lindo by 194–0 on 17 Nov 1973. The highest British score is 174–0 by 7th Signal Regiment v. 4 Armoured Workshop, REME, on 5 Nov 1980 at Herford, W. Germany.

Scores of over 200 points have been recorded in school matches, for example Radford School beat Hills Court 214 points (31 goals and 7 tries) to 0 (200–0) on 20 Nov 1886.

Season

The highest number of points accumulated in a season by a rugby club is 1454 points by Pontypridd RFC, Mid Glamorgan, in 1975–6. In 1970–1 Solihull RUFC's 1st XV scored a record 247 tries.

HIGHEST INDIVIDUAL SCORES
Internationals

The highest individual points score in any match between members of the International Board is 24 by William Fergus 'Fergie' McCormick (b. 1940)—1 drop goal, 3 conversions and 5 penalty goals for New Zealand against Wales at Auckland on 14 June 1969.

Ian Scott Smith (Scotland) (1903–72) scored a record six consecutive international tries in 1925; comprised of the last three v. France and two weeks later, the first three v. Wales.

The most points scored in an international career is 232 by Andrew Robertson Irvine (Heriots), (b. 16 Sept 1951), for Scotland and the British Lions, 1973–81.

Season

The first class rugby scoring record for a season is 581 points by Samuel Arthur Doble (1944–77) of Moseley, in 52 matches in 1971–2. He also scored 47 points for England in South Africa out of season.

Career

William Henry 'Dusty' Hare (b. 29 Nov 1952) of Leicester, scored 3711 points in first class games from 1971–81, comprising 1800 for Nottingham, 1548 for Leicester, 94 for England and 269 in other representative matches.

Match

Jannie van der Westhuizen (S Africa) scored 80 points (14 tries, 9 conversions, 1 dropped goal, 1 penalty goal) for Carnarvon (88) v. Williston (12) at North West Cape, on 11 March 1972.

In a junior house match in February 1967 at William Ellis School, Edgware, Greater London, between Cumberland and Nunn, Thanos Morphitis, 12, contributed 90 points (13 tries and 19 conversions) (77) to Cumberland's winning score.

All-rounder

Canadian international, Barrie Burnham, scored all possible ways—try, conversion, penalty goal, drop goal, goal from mark—for Meralomas v. Georgians (20–11) at Vancouver, BC, on 26 Feb 1966.

Most international appearances

The following totals are limited to matches between the seven member countries of the 'International Rugby Football Board' and France. Including 12 appearances for the British Lions, Mike Gibson (b. 3 Dec 1942) has played in 81 international matches. Willie John McBride, MBE (b. Co. Antrim, 6 June, 1940) made a record 17 appearances for the British Lions.

Widnes after their sixth Challenge Cup win in 1981, a game which took receipts of nearly £600,000. (*Tony Duffy, All-Sport*)

Ireland	69	Cameron Michael Henderson Gibson	1964–79
New Zealand	55	Colin Earl Meads	1957–71
Wales	55	John Peter Rhys 'JPR' Williams	1969–81
France	50	Benoit Dauga	1964–72
	50	Roland Bertranne	1971–81
Scotland	50	Alexander 'Sandy' B. Carmichael MBE	1967–78
England	43	Anthony Neary	1971–80
Australia	39	Peter G. Johnson	1958–72
	39	Gregory Victor Davis	1963–72
South Africa	38	Frederick Christoffel Hendrick Du Preez	1960–71
	38	Jan Hendrik Ellis	1965–76

Youngest International

Edinburgh Academy pupils Ninian Jamieson Finlay (1858–1936) and Charles Reid (1864–1909) were both 17 years 36 days old when they played for Scotland *v.* England in 1875 and 1881 respectively. However, as Finlay had one less leap year in his lifetime up to his first cap, the outright record must be credited to him. Daniel Brendan Carroll (b. 17 Feb 1892) was aged only 16 yr 149 days when he played for Australia in the 1908 Olympic Games Rugby tournament—not considered to be a 'full' international.

County Championships

The County Championships (instituted in 1889) have been won most often by Gloucestershire with 13 titles (1910, 1913, 1920–2, 1930–2, 1937, 1972, 1974, 1975 and 1976). The most individual appearances is 104 by Richard Trickey (Sale) (b. 6 Mar 1945) for Lancashire between 1964 and 1978.

Seven-a-sides *Origins*

Seven-a-side rugby dates from 28 Apr 1883 when Melrose RFC Borders in order to alleviate the poverty of a club in such a small town staged a Seven-a-side tournament. The idea was that of Ned Haig, the town's butcher. The popularity of this variation

of the game culminated in a world record 20 countries competing in an international Seven-a-side tournament in Hong Kong on 28–29 Mar 1981.

Middlesex Seven-a-sides

The Middlesex Seven-a-sides were inaugurated in 1926. The most successful sides have been Harlequins with eight wins (1926–9, 1933, 1935, 1967, 1978) and Richmond (incl once by their second Seven) (1951, 1953, 1955, 1974–5, 1977, 1979–80).

The only players to be in five winning 'sevens' have been Norman Macleod Hall (1925–73) (St Mary's Hospital 1944, 1946 and Richmond 1951, 1953, 1955), and James Alexander Pirie Shackleton and Iain Hugh Page Laughland both of London Scottish (1960–3, 1965).

Greatest crowd

The record paying attendance is 104,000 for Scotland *v.* Wales at Murrayfield, Edinburgh, on 1 Mar 1975. Scotland won 12 points to 10.

Highest posts

The world's highest Rugby Union goal posts are 110 ft ½ in *33,54 m* high at the Roan Antelope Rugby Union Club, Luanshya, Zambia. The posts at Brixham RFC, Devonshire, are 57 ft *17,37 m* high with an additional 1 ft *0,30 m* spike on top.

Longest kicks

The longest recorded successful drop-goal is 90 yd *82 m* by Gerald Hamilton 'Gerry' Brand (b. 8 Oct 1906) for South Africa *v.* England at Twickenham, Greater London, on 2 Jan 1932. This was taken 7 yd *6 m* inside the England 'half' 55 yd *50 m* from the posts and dropped over the dead ball line.

The place kick record is reputed to be 100 yd *91 m* at Richmond Athletic Ground, Greater London, by Douglas Francis Theodore Morkel (b. 1886) in an unsuccessful penalty for South

Dusty Hare who helped his club, Leicester, to its third John Player Cup win with his record breaking achievements. (*Steve Powell, All-Sport*)

Andy Irvine kicking against France in January 1981, and taking sole possession of the career international points scoring record. (*Sporting Pictures*)

ALL TIME SCORING RECORDS—AGGREGATE and MARGIN OF VICTORY in the ten annual matches in the 'International Championship'
Note headnote on page 276 on Scoring systems

		Aggregate Record Present Day pts Value		Record Margin Present Day pts Value
England v. Scotland	Scotland (28) beat England (19) in 1931	57	England (19) beat Scotland (0) in 1924	21
			England (24) beat Scotland (5) in 1947	21
England v. Ireland	England (36) beat Ireland (14) in 1938	61	Ireland (22) beat England (0) in 1947	27
England v. Wales	England beat Wales by 7 goals, 1 drop goal and 6 tries to nil in 1881	69*	England beat Wales by 7 goals, 1 drop goal and 6 tries to nil in 1881	69
England v. France	England (49) beat France (15) in 1907	64	England (37) beat France (0) in 1911	44
Scotland v. Ireland	Scotland (29) beat Ireland (14) in 1913	51	Scotland beat Ireland by 6 goals and 2 tries to nil in 1877	44
Scotland v. Wales	Scotland (20) beat Wales (0) in 1887	56	Scotland (20) beat Wales (0) in 1887	56
Scotland v. France	Scotland (31) beat France (3) in 1912	41	Scotland (31) beat France (3) in 1912	33
Ireland v. Wales	Wales (24) beat Ireland (21) in 1979	45	Wales (29) beat Ireland (0) in 1907	34
Ireland v. France	France (27) beat Ireland (6) in 1964	40	Ireland (24) beat France (0) in 1913	30
Wales v. France	Wales (49) beat France (14) in 1910	75	Wales (47) beat France (5) in 1909	52

* Point scoring was not introduced until 1886.

Africa *v.* Surrey on 19 Dec 1906. This was not measured until 1932.

In the match Bridlington School 1st XV *v.* an Army XV at Bridlington, Humberside on 29 Jan 1944, Ernie Cooper (b. 21 May 1926), captaining the school, landed a penalty from a measured 81 yd *74 m* from the post with a kick which carried over the dead ball line.

Fastest try
The fastest try in an international game was when H. L. 'Bart' Price scored for England *v.* Wales at Twickenham on 20 Jan 1923 less than 10 sec after kick off.

Most tries
Dan Jones, of Neath, scored a record 73 tries in a season in 1928–29. In his last game on 4 May 1979 Andy Hill (b. 17 Jan 1945) scored his 312th try for Llanelli, a British Club Rugby record, since his debut on 3 Nov 1967.

Longest try
The longest 'try' ever executed is by 15 members of Sedgley Park RUFC Manchester, who scored on 5 May 1979 from a 'move' which carried the ball 736 miles 637 yd *1185,06 km*. There were no forward passes or knock-ons, and the ball was touched down between the posts in the prescribed manner (Law 12).

FOX HUNTING

For further reading see The Guinness Guide to Field Sports *by Wilson Stevens published by Guinness Superlatives at £10.50.*

Earliest references
Hunting the fox in Britain became popular from the second half of the 18th century though it is mentioned very much earlier. Prior to that time hunting was confined principally to the deer and the hare. It is estimated that foxhunters account for some 10,000 of the 50,000 foxes killed each year.

Pack *Oldest*
The Old Charlton Hunt (later the Goodwood) in West Sussex, now extinct, the Duke of Monmouth and Lord Grey of Werke at Charlton, Sussex, and the Duke of Buckingham in north Yorkshire, owned packs which were entered to fox only during the reign (1660–85) of Charles II.

Pack *Largest*
The pack with the greatest number of hounds has been the Duke of Beaufort's hounds maintained at Badminton, Avon, since 1786. At times hunting six days a week, this pack once had 120 couples at hounds.

Longest span
Jean Bethel 'Betty' McKeever (neé Dawes) (b. 26 Feb 1901) has been Master of the Blean Beagles in Kent since 1909. The 10th Duke of Beaufort has been Master of Foxhounds since 1924.

Longest hunt
The longest recorded hunt was one led by Squire Sandys which ran from Holmbank, northern Lancashire to Ulpha, Cumbria, a total of nearly 80 miles *128 km* in reputedly only 6 hr, in January or February 1743. The longest hunt in Ireland was probably a run of 24 miles *38 km* made by the Scarteen Hunt, County Limerick, from Pallas to Knockoura in 1914. The longest duration hunt was one of 10 hr 5 min by the Charlton Hunt of West Sussex, which ran from East Dean Wood at 7.45 a.m. to a kill over 57¼ miles *92 km* away at 5.50 p.m. on 26 Jan 1738.

Largest fox
The largest fox ever killed by a hunt in England was a 23¾ lb. *10 kg 770* dog on Cross Fell, Cumbria, by an Ullswater Hunt in 1936.

GAMBLING

World's biggest win
The world's biggest gambling win is $3,003,532 in the Brazilian football pools Loteria Esportiva by Tadeu Resende of Volta Redonda, (23), on the results of 13 games in February 1981. By winning a state lottery in January 1976, Eric C. Leek, of North Arlington, New Jersey, USA, won $1776 a week for life. Aged 26, he will receive a total of $4.6 million should he live a further 50 years.

World's biggest loss
An unnamed Italian industrialist was reported to have lost £800,000 in 5 hr at roulette in Monte Carlo, Monaco on 6 Mar 1974. A Saudi Arabian prince was reported to have lost more than $1 million in a single session at the Metro Club, Las Vegas, USA in December 1974.

Largest casino
The largest casino in the world is the Resorts International Casino, Atlantic City, NJ, USA, with an annual win in 1979 of $232,945,748. The Casino comprises 60,000 ft² *5574 m²*, containing 127 gaming tables and 1640 slot machines. Attendances total over 35,000 daily at peak weekends.

BACKGAMMON
Forerunners of the game have been traced back to a dice and a board game found in excavations at Ur, dated to 3000 BC. Later the Romans played a game remarkably similar to the modern one. The name 'Backgammon' is variously ascribed to Welsh "little battle", or Saxon "back game". Modern variations include the American Acey Deucey.

At present there are no world championships held, but a points rating system may soon be introduced internationally, thereby enabling players to be ranked.

Marathon
Dick Newcomb and Greg Peterson of Rockford, Illinois, played backgammon for 151 hr 11 min on 30 June–6 July 1978.

BINGO
Origins
Bingo is a lottery game which, as keno, was developed in the 1880s from lotto, whose origin is thought to be the 17th century

Brewery worker David Preston and his wife Jean, holding the record breaking cheque for his Football Pools win. His future plans included a trip to Las Vegas. (*John Topham Picture Library*)

Italian game *tumbule*. It has long been known in the British Army (called Housey-Housey) and the Royal Navy (called Tombola). The winner was the first to complete a random selection of numbers from 1 to 90. The USA version called Bingo differs in that the selection is from 1 to 75. There are six million players in the United Kingdom.

Largest house
The largest 'house' in Bingo sessions was staged at the Empire Pool, Wembley, London, on 25 Apr 1965 when 10,000 attended.

Earliest and latest Full House
A 'Full House' call occurred on the 15th number by Norman A. Wilson at Guide Post Workingmen's Club, Bedlington, Northumberland on 22 June 1978. 'House' was not called until the 85th number at the Devoran Hotel, Sidmouth, Devon on 3 May 1981. There were eleven winners.

Marathon
A session of 240 hr 30 min was held at the Top Rank Club, Kingston-upon-Thames, Surrey, on 4–14 May 1979 with Philip Carter and Timothy Mann calling.

ELECTIONS
The highest ever individual bet was £50,000 on Labour to win the 1964 Election by Sir Maxwell Joseph. He made £37,272 on the odds offered. A bet of £5000 at 200–1 was placed by Frank Egerton in April 1975 that his political Centre Party would win the next General Election. It didn't.

FOOTBALL POOLS
The winning dividend paid out by Littlewoods Pools in their first week in February 1923 was £2 12s 0d (£2.60). In 1979–80

British Football Pools firms had a total record turnover of £338,818,865 of which Littlewoods contributed over two-thirds.

Biggest win

The greatest sum won from the British Pools is £953,874.10 by David Preston, 47, of Burton-on-Trent, Staffs, on 23 Feb 1980. This total comprised £804,573.35 from Littlewoods Pools and £149,300.75 from Vernons Pools. In order to earn such a sum post-tax in 1980/81, a single person would have to be paid a salary of £2,369,810.25.

The odds for selecting 8 draws (if there are only 8 draws) from 55 matches for an all-correct line are 217,566,350 to 1 against. (In practice, the approximate odds of winning a dividend of any size on Littlewoods Pools are 80 to 1.)

HORSE RACÍNG
Highest ever odds

The highest recorded odds ever secured were 1,099,299 to 1 by a backer from Otley, West Yorkshire on a seven horse accumulator on 10 May 1975. On a stake of £1.76 in penny bets, he won a total of £12,578.14. The world record odds on a 'double' are 31,793 to 1 paid by the New Zealand Totalisator Agency Board on a five shilling tote ticket on *Red Emperor* and *Maida Dillon* at Addington, Christchurch, in 1951.

Biggest tote win

The best recorded tote win was one of £341 2s 6d to 2s (*£341.12½ to 10p*) representing odds of 3,410¼ to 1, by Catharine Unsworth of Blundellsands, Liverpool at Haydock Park on a race won by *Coole* on 30 Nov 1929. The highest odds in Irish tote history were £184 7s 6d on a 2s 6d (*£184.37½ on a 12½p*) stake, *viz.* 1474 to 1 on *Hillhead VI* at Baldoyle on 31 Jan 1970.

Largest bookmaker

The world's largest bookmaker is Ladbroke's of London with a turnover from gambling in 1980 of £514 million. The largest chain of betting shops is that of Ladbrokes with 1144 shops in the United Kingdom in 1981.

Topmost tipster

The only recorded instance of a racing correspondent forecasting ten out of ten winners on a race card was at Delaware Park, Wilmington, Delaware, USA on 28 July 1974 by Charles Lamb of the *Baltimore News American*.

Greatest pay-out

The greatest published 'pay-out' on a single bet is £69,375 by Ladbroke's to the late Bernard Sunley on the Derby victory of *Santa Claus* in 1964. The greatest on a day's racing is £100,000 to Peter Joliffe on 19 Aug 1978. On 12 Dec 1976 Mr Lim Chooi

Seng won Malaysian $1,112,400 *£258,700* on *Freedom Fighter* in the sixth race at Penang.

ROULETTE

The longest run on an ungaffed (*i.e.* true) wheel reliably recorded is six successive coups (in No. 10) at El San Juan Hotel, Puerto Rico on 9 July 1959. The odds with a double zero were 1 in 38^6 or 3,010,936,383 to 1.

Longest marathon

The longest 'marathon' on record is one of 31 days from 10 Apr to 11 May 1970 at The Casino de Macao, to test the validity or invalidity of certain contentions in 20,000 spins.

SLOT MACHINES

The world's biggest slot machine (or one-armed bandit) is Super Bertha (555 ft^3 *15,71 m^3*) installed by Si Redd at the Four Queens Casino, Las Vegas, Nevada, USA in September 1973. Once in every 25,000 million plays it may yield $1 million for a $10 feed. The total gambling 'take' in 1979 in Nevada casinos was estimated at $2,100,000,000. The biggest beating handed to a 'one-armed bandit' was $355,000 by Lawrence 'Chuck' Balentine (USA) aged 61, at the Flamingo Hilton, Las Vegas on 18 Apr 1981.

GLIDING

Emanuel Swedenborg (1688–1772) of Sweden made sketches of gliders *c.* 1714.

The earliest man-carrying glider was designed by Sir George Cayley (1773–1857) and carried his coachman (possibly John Appleby) about 500 yd *457 m* across a valley in Brompton Dale, North Yorkshire in the summer of 1853. Gliders now attain speeds of 200 mph *322 km/h* and the Jastrzab aerobatic sailplane is designed to withstand vertical dives at up to 280 mph *450 km/h*.

Highest standard

A gold C with three diamonds (for goal flight, distance and height) is the highest standard in gliding. This has been gained by 114 British pilots up to June 1981.

Most titles *World*

The most World individual championships (inst. 1948) won is three by Helmut Reichmann (b. 1942) (W. Germany) in 1970, 1974, 1978 and Douglas George Lee, MBE (GB) (b. 7 Nov 1945) in 1976, 1978 and 1981.

Most titles *British*

The British national championship (inst. 1939) has been won five times by John Delafield (b. 31 Jan 1938) in 1968, 1972, 1976, 1978 and 1981. The first woman to win this title was Anne Burns (b. 23 Nov. 1915) of Farnham, Surrey on 30 May 1966.

SELECTED WORLD RECORDS (Single-seaters)

Distance	907.7 miles *1460,8 km*	Hans-Werner Grosse (W. Germany) in an ASW-12 on 25 Apr 1972 from Lübeck to Biarritz
Declared Goal Flight	779.4 miles *1254,26 km*	Bruce Drake, David Speight, S. H. 'Dick' Georgeson (all NZ) all in Nimbus 2s, Te Anau to Te Araroa, 14 Jan 1978
Absolute Altitude	46,266 ft *14 102 m*	Paul F. Bikle, Jr (USA) in a Schweizer SGS 1–23E over Mojave, California (released at 3963 ft *1207 m*) on 25 Feb 1961 (also record altitude gain—42,303 ft *12 894 m*)
Goal and Return	1015.7 miles *1634,7 km*	Karl H. Striedieck (USA) in an ASW 17 from Lock Haven, Penn. to Tennessee, on 9 May 1977
Speed over Triangular Course		
100 km	102.74 mph *165,35 km/h*	Ross Briegleb (USA) in a Kestrel 17 over the USA on 18 July 1974
300 km	98,59 mph *158,67 km/h**	Hans-Werner Grosse (W. Germany) in an ASW-17 over Australia on 24 Dec 1980.
500 km	94.00 mph *151,28 km/h*	George Eckle (W. Germany) in an ASW-17 over South Africa on 10 Dec 1980.
750 km	87.69 mph *141,13 km/h*	Georg Eckle (W. Germany) in a Nimbus 2 over South Africa, 7 Jan 1978
1000 km	90.29 mph *145,32 km/h*	Hans-Werner Grosse (W. Germany) in an ASW-17 over Australia on 3 Jan 1979
1250 km	82.79 mph *133,24 km/h**	Hans-Werner Grosse (W. Germany) in an ASW-17 over Australia on 9 Dec 1980

* awaiting homologation

BRITISH NATIONAL RECORDS[1] (Single-seaters)

	589.9 miles *949,47 km*	Karla Karel in a LS-3 over Australia on 23 Jan 1980
	360 miles *579,36 km*	H. C. N. Goodhart in a Skylark 3, Lasham, Hants, to Portmoak, Scotland on 10 May 1955
	37,729 ft *11 500 m*	H. C. N. Goodhart in a Schweizer 1-23 over California, USA on 12 May 1955
	497.7 miles *801,3 km*	Christopher Garton in a Kestrel 19: Lasham to Durham on 22 July 1976
	88.99 mph *143,3 km/h*	E. Paul Hodge in a Standard Cirrus over Rhodesia on 30 Oct 1976
	91.2 mph *146,8 km/h*	Edward Pearson in a Nimbus 2 over S. W. Africa on 30 Nov 1976
	88.6 mph *142,6 km/h*	Michael R. Carlton in an ASW-17 over South Africa on 24 Dec 1980
	68.2 mph *109,8 km/h*	Michael R. Carlton in a Kestrel 19 over South Africa on 5 Jan 1975

[1] *British National Records may be set up by British pilots in any part of the world.*

Glider pilots extraordinary (from left to right)—Karl Striedieck, the only pilot to have covered over 1000 miles; Ross Briegleb, 100 km triangle record holder; Paul Bikle, who experienced −65° C temperatures in his altitude record (*George Uveges/SSA*); and Jeff Scott, who set a hang glider height gain record.

HANG GLIDING

Origins
In the eleventh century the monk, Elmer, is reported to have flown from the 60 ft *18,3 m* tower of Malmesbury Abbey, Wiltshire. The earliest modern pioneer was Otto Lilienthal (1848–96) (Germany) with numerous flights between 1893 and 1896. In the 1950s Professor Francis Rogallo of the National Space Agency, USA, developed a 'wing' from his space capsule re-entry researches.

Championships
The World Team Championships, held at Chattanooga, Tenn, USA in 1978 and 1979 have been won by Great Britain.

Greatest distance
The official FAI record is 110.65 miles *178,07 km* by George Worthington (b. 1920) (USA) in a Moyes Maxi II, from Cerro Gordo, Cal, to Boundary Peak, Nevada, on 25 July 1980. The British record is 82.58 miles *132,9 km* by John Stirk in a Solar Wings Typhoon from Hawes, N. Yorkshire to Hawick, Borders, on 10 Apr 1981.

Greatest ascent and descent
The official FAI height gain record is 12,139 ft *3700 m* by Jeff Scott (USA) in a Wills Harrier over California on 9 Aug 1980.

The greatest altitude from which a hang-glider has descended is 31,600 ft *9631 m* by Bob McCaffrey, 18 (USA) in an experimental design from a balloon over the Mojave Desert, California, USA on 21 Nov 1976.

GOLF

The Guinness Book of Golf Facts and Feats *by Donald Steel, published by Guinness Superlatives, at £7.95 contains more information on this sport.*

Origins
Although a stained glass window in Gloucester Cathedral, dating from 1350 portrays a golfer-like figure, the earliest mention of golf occurs in a prohibiting law passed by the Scottish Parliament in March 1457 under which 'goff be utterly cryit doune and not usit'. The Romans had a cognate game called *paganica* which may have been carried to Britain before AD 400. The Chinese Nationalist Golf Association claim the game is of Chinese origin ('*Ch'ui Wan*—the ball hitting game') in the 3rd or 2nd century BC. Gutta percha balls succeeded feather balls in 1848 and by 1902 were in turn succeeded by rubber-cored balls, invented in 1899 by Coburn Haskell (USA). Steel shafts were authorised in the USA in 1925 and in Britain in 1929.

Club *Oldest*
The oldest club of which there is written evidence is the Gentlemen Golfers (now the Honourable Company of Edinburgh Golfers) formed in March 1744—ten years prior to the institution of the Royal and Ancient Club of St Andrews, Fife. However the Royal Burgess Golfing Society of Edinburgh claim to have been founded in 1735.

Club *Largest*
The club with the highest membership in the British Isles is the Royal and Ancient Golf Club of St Andrews, Fife, Scotland with 1800 members. The largest in England is 1600 at the Moor Park GC, Rickmansworth, Herts., and the largest in Ireland is Royal Portrush, Co. Antrim with 1215 members.

Course *Highest*
The highest golf course in the world is the Tuctu Golf Club in Morococha, Peru, which is 4369 m *14,335 ft* above sea-level at its lowest point. Golf has, however, been played in Tibet at an altitude of over 4875 m *16,000 ft.*

The highest golf course in Great Britain is one of nine holes at Leadhills, Strathclyde, 1500 ft *457 m* above sea-level.

Course *Lowest*
The lowest golf course in the world was that of the now defunct Sodom and Gomorrah Golfing Society at Kallia (Qulya) on the northern shores of the Dead Sea, 380 m *1250 ft* below sea-level. Currently the lowest is the Rotterdam Golf Club's 9-hole course at 8 m *26 ft* below sea-level.

Longest hole
The longest hole in the world is the 7th hole (par 7) of the Sano Course, Satsuki GC, Japan, which measures 831 m *909 yd.* In August 1927 the sixth hole at Prescott Country Club in Arkansas, USA, measured 838 yd *766 m.* The longest hole on a championship course in Great Britain is the sixth at Troon, Strathclyde, which stretches 577 yd *528 m.*

Largest green
Probably the largest green in the world is the fifth green at International GC Bolton, Massachusetts, USA with an area greater than 28,000 ft² *2600 m².*

Biggest bunker
The world's biggest bunker (called a trap in the USA) is Hell's Half Acre on the 585 yd *535 m* seventh hole of the Pine Valley course, Clementon, New Jersey, USA, built in 1912 and generally regarded as the world's most trying course.

Longest course
The world's longest course is at Dub's Dread GC, Piper, Kansas, USA and is a 78-par 8101 yd *7407 m.* Floyd Satterlee Rood used the United States as a course, when he played from the Pacific surf to the Atlantic surf from 14 Sept 1963 to 3 Oct 1964 in 114,737 strokes. He lost 3511 balls on the 3397.7 mile *5468 km* trail.

Longest drives
In long-driving contests 330 yd *300 m* is rarely surpassed at sea-level. In officially regulated long driving contests over level ground the greatest distance recorded is 392 yd *358 m* by William Thomas 'Tommie' Campbell (b. 24 July 1927) (Foxrock Golf Club) made at Dun Laoghaire, Co. Dublin, in July 1964. On an airport runway Valentin Barrios (Spain) drove a Slazenger

B51 ball 568½ yd *520 m* at Palma, Majorca on 7 Mar 1977. The greatest recorded drive on an ordinary course is one of 515 yd *471 m* by Michael Hoke Austin (b. 17 Feb 1910) of Los Angeles, California, USA, in the US National Seniors Open Championship at Las Vegas, Nevada, on 25 Sept 1974. Austin, 6 ft 2 in *1,88 m* tall and weighing 210 lb *92,250 kg* drove the ball to within a yard of the green on the par-4 450 yd *412 m* fifth hole of the Winterwood Course and it rolled 65 yd *59 m* past the flagstick. He was aided by an estimated 35 mph *56 km/h* tailwind.

A drive of 2640 yd (1½ miles) *2414 m* across ice was achieved by an Australian meteorologist named Nils Lied at Mawson Base, Antarctica, in 1962. Arthur Lynskey claimed a drive of 200 yd *182 m* horizontal and 2 miles *3200 m* vertical off Pikes Peak, Colorado (14,110 ft *4300 m*) on 28 June 1968. On the Moon the energy expended on a mundane 300 yd *274 m* drive would achieve, craters permitting, a distance of 1 mile *1,6 km*.

Longest hitter
The golfer regarded as the longest consistent hitter the game has ever known is the 6 ft 5 in *195 cm* tall, 17 st 2 lb *108 kg 86* George Bayer (USA) (b. 17 Sept 1925), the 1957 Canadian Open Champion. His longest measured drive was one of 420 yd *384 m* at the fourth in the Las Vegas Invitational, Nevada, in 1953. It was measured as a precaution against litigation since the ball struck a spectator. Bayer also drove a ball pin high on a 426 yd *389 m* hole at Tucson, Arizona in 1955. Radar measurements show that an 87 mph *140 km/h* impact velocity for a golf ball falls to 46 mph *74 km/h* in 3 sec.

Longest putt
The longest recorded holed putt in a major tournament was one of 86 ft *26 m* on the vast 13th green at the Augusta National, Georgia by Cary Middlecoff (b. January 1921) (USA) in the 1955 Masters' Tournament. Robert Tyre 'Bobby' Jones Jr (1902–71) was reputed to have holed a putt in excess of 100 ft *30 m* at the fifth green in the first round of the 1927 Open at St. Andrews.

SCORES
Lowest 9 holes and 18 holes *Men*
The lowest recorded score on any 18-hole course with a par score of 70 or more is 55 (15 under bogey) first achieved by Alfred Edward Smith (b. 1903) the Woolacombe professional, on his home course on 1 Jan 1936. The course measured 4248 yd *3884 m*. The detail was 4, 2, 3, 4, 2, 4, 3, 4, 3 = 29 out, and 2, 3, 3, 3, 3, 2, 5, 4, 1 = 26 in. At least three players are recorded to have played a long course (over 6000 yd *5846 m*) in a score of 58. The lowest recorded score on a long course in Britain is 58 by Harry Weetman (1920–72) the British Ryder Cup golfer, for the 6171 yd *5642 m* Croham Hurst Course, Croydon, Surrey, on 30 Jan 1956.

Nine holes in 25 (4, 3, 3, 2, 3, 3, 1, 4, 2) was recorded by A. J. 'Bill' Burke in a round in 57 (32 + 25) on the 6389 yd *5842 m* par 71 Normandie course St Louis, Missouri, USA on 20 May 1970. The tournament record is 27 by Mike Souchak (USA) (b. May 1927) for the second nine (par-35) first round of the 1955 Texas Open, Andy North (USA) (b. 9 Mar 1950) second nine (par-34), first round, 1975 BC Open at En-Joie GC, Endicott, NY and Jose Maria Canizares (Spain) (b. 18 Feb 1947), first nine, third round, in the 1978 Swiss Open on the 6811 yd *7228 m* Crans-Sur course.

The United States PGA tournament record for 18 holes is 59 (30 + 29) by Al Geiberger (b. 1 Sept 1937) in the second round of the Danny Thomas Classic, on the 72-par 7249 yd *6628 m* Colonial CC course Memphis, Tennessee on 10 June 1977. Three golfers have recorded 59 over 18 holes in non-PGA tournaments; Samuel Jackson Snead (b. 27 May 1912) in the third round of the Sam Snead Festival at White Sulphur Springs, West Virginia, USA on 16 May 1959; Gary Player (South Africa) (b. 1 Nov 1935) in the second round of the Brazilian Open in Rio de Janeiro on 29 Nov 1974, and David Jagger (GB) (b. 9 June 1949) in a Pro-Am tournament prior to the 1973 Nigerian Open at Ikoyi Golf Club, Lagos.

Lowest 9 holes and 18 holes *Women*
The lowest recorded score on an 18-hole course (over 6000 yd *5486 m*) for a woman is 62 (30 + 32) by Mary 'Mickey' Kathryn Wright (b. 14 Feb 1935) (USA) on the Hogan Park Course

(par-71, 6286 yd *5747 m*) at Midland, Texas, USA, in November 1964. Wanda Morgan (b. 22 Mar 1910) recorded a score of 60 (31 + 29) on the Westgate and Birchington Golf Club course Kent, over 18 holes (5002 yd *4573 m*) on 11 July 1929.

Lowest 9 holes and 18 holes *Great Britain*
The British tournament 9-hole record is 28 by John Panton (b. Oct 1916) in the Swallow-Penfold Tournament at Harrogate North Yorkshire, in 1952; by Bernard John Hunt, MBE (b. 2 Feb 1930) of Hartsbourne in the Spalding Tournament at Worthing West Sussex, in August 1953; by Peter Mills (b. 7 June 1931) in the Bowmaker Tournament at Sunningdale, Berkshire in 1958 by Lionel Platts (b. 10 Oct 1934, Yorkshire) of Wanstead in the Ulster Open at Shandon Park, Belfast, on 11 Sept 1965; and by Richard W. Seamer in the Kent Cob at Knole Park, Sevenoaks Kent on 3 Sept 1977. This last is the best by an Amateur player The lowest score recorded in a first class professional tournament on a course of more than 6000 yd *5486 m* in Great Britain was set at 61 (29 + 32), by Thomas Bruce Haliburton (1915–75 of Wentworth GC in the Spalding Tournament at Worthing West Sussex, in June 1952. Peter J. Butler (b. 25 Mar 1932) equalled this record with 61 (32 + 29) in the Bowmaker Tournament on the Old Course at Sunningdale, Berkshire, on 4 July 1967.

Lowest 36 holes
The record for 36 holes is 122 (59 + 63) by Snead in the 1959 Sam Snead Festival on 16–17 May 1959. Horton Smith (1908–1963), twice US Masters Champion, scored 121 (63 + 58) on a short course on 21 Dec 1928 (see below). The lowest score by a British golfer has been 124 (61 + 63) by Alexander Walter Barr 'Sandy' Lyle (b. 9 Feb 1958) in the Nigerian Open at the 6024 yd *5508 m* (par-71) Ikoyi Golf Club, Lagos in 1978.

Lowest 72 holes
The lowest recorded score on a first-class course is 255 (29 under par) by Leonard Peter Tupling (b. 6 Apr 1950) (GB) in the Nigerian Open at Ikoyi Golf Club, Lagos in February 1981 made up of 63, 66, 62 and 64 (average 63.75 per round).

Horton Smith scored 245 (63, 58, 61 and 63) for 72 holes on the 4700 yd *4297 m* course (par 64) at Catalina Country Club, California, USA, to win the Catalina Open on 21–23 Dec 1928.

The lowest 72 holes in a national championship is 262 (67, 66 66, 63) by Percy Alliss (GB) (1897–1975) in the 1932 Italian Open at San Remo, and by Lu Liang Huan (Taiwan) (b. 10 Dec 1935) in the 1971 French Open at Biarritz. Kelvin D. G. Nagle (b. 21 Dec 1920) of Australia shot 261 in the Hong Kong Open in 1961. The lowest for four rounds in a British first class tournament is 262 (66, 63, 66 and 67) by Bernard Hunt in the Piccadilly Stroke Play tournament on par-68, 6184 yd *5655 m* Wentworth East Course, Virginia Water, Surrey on 4–5 Oct 1966.

Eclectic record
The lowest recorded eclectic (from the Greek *eklektikos* = choosing) score, i.e. the sum of a player's all-time personal low scores for each hole, for a course of more than 6000 yd *5486 m* is 33 by the club professional Jack McKinnon on the par-72 6538 yd *5978 m* Capilano Golf and Country Club course, Vancouver, British Columbia, Canada. This was compiled over the period 1937–64 and reads 2–2–2–1–2–2–2–2–1 (16 out) and 2–1–2–2–1–2–2–2–3 (17 in) = 33. The British record is 34 by John Harrowar 'Jock' Morrison (b. 3 Oct 1929) at West Kilbride GC Strathclyde, (par-70, 6348 yd *5804 m*) from 1951 to 1978. This is made up of fourteen 2s, three aces and one 3.

Highest score
The highest score for a single hole in the British Open is 21 by a player in the inaugural meeting at Prestwick in 1860. Double figures have been recorded on the card of the winner only once when Willie Fernie (1851–1924) scored a ten at Musselburgh Lothian, in 1883. Ray Ainsley of Ojai, California, took 19 strokes for the par-4 16th hole during the second round of the US Open at Cherry Hills Country Club, Denver, Colorado, on 10 June 1938. Most of the strokes were used in trying to extricate the ball from a brook. Hans Merell of Mogadore, Ohio, took 19 strokes on the par-3 16th (222 yd *203 m*) during the third round of the Bing Crosby National Tournament at Cypress Point Club Del Monte, California, USA, on 17 Jan 1959. It is recorded tha

When Gary Wright 'played' a round of golf in twenty-eight minutes he beat former world mile record holder, Herb Elliott, in the process.

Fourteen years after winning the British Boys title in 1967, Peter Tupling recorded a remarkable 255 for four rounds of golf. (*Steve Powell, All-Sport*)

Chevalier von Cittern went round 18 holes in 316, averaging 17.55 per hole, at Biarritz, France in 1888. Steven Ward took 222 strokes for the 6212 yd *5680 m* Pecos Course, Reeves County, Texas, USA, on 18 June 1976—but he was only aged 3 years 286 days.

Most shots for one hole

A woman player in the qualifying round of the Shawnee Invitational for Ladies at Shawnee-on-Delaware, Pennsylvania, USA, in *c.* 1912, took 166 strokes for the short 130 yd *118 m* 16th hole. Her tee shot went into the Binniekill River and the ball floated. She put out in a boat with her exemplary, but statistically minded husband at the oars. She eventually beached the ball 1½ miles *2,4 km* downstream but was not yet out of the wood. She had to play through one on the home run. In a competition at Peacehaven, Sussex, England in 1890, A. J. Lewis had 156 puts on one green without holing out.

Rounds fastest *Individual*

With such variations in lengths of courses, speed records, even for rounds under par, are of little comparative value. Rick Baker completed 18 holes (6142 yd *5616 m*) in 26 min 20.55 sec at the Metropolitan Golf Club, Melbourne, Australia, on 14 Feb 1981, during the Victorian Open, but this test permitted the striking of the ball whilst still moving. The record for a still ball is 28.09 min by Gary Wright at Tewantin-Noosa Golf Club, Queensland, Australia (18 holes, 6039 yd *5522 m*) on 9 Dec 1980.

Rounds fastest *Team*

Eighty-three players completed the 18-hole 6421 yd *5871 m* Prince George Golf and Country Club course, British Columbia, Canada in 12 min 14.5 sec in 1973, using only one ball.

MOST TITLES

The most titles won in the world's major championships are as follows:

The Open	Harry Vardon (1870–1937)	6	1896, 1898–9, 1903, 11, 14
The Amateur	John Ball (1861–1940)	8	1888, 90, 92, 94, 99, 1907, 10, 12
US Open	Willie Anderson (1880–1910)	4	1901, 03–5
	Robert Tyre Jones, Jr. (1902–71)	4	1923, 26, 29–30
	William Ben Hogan (b. 13 Aug 1912)	4	1948, 50–1, 53
	Jack William Nicklaus (b. 21 Jan 1940)	4	1962, 67, 72, 80
US Amateur	Robert Tyre Jones, Jr. (1902–71)	5	1924–25, 27–8, 30
PGA Championship (USA)	Walter Charles Hagen (1892–1969)	5	1921, 24–7
	Jack William Nicklaus (b. 21 Jan 1940)	5	1963, 71, 73, 75, 80
Masters' Championship (USA)	Jack William Nicklaus (b. 21 Jan 1940)	5	1963, 65–6, 72, 75
US Women's Open	Elizabeth 'Betsy' Earle-Rawls (b. 4 May 1928)	4	1951, 53, 57, 60
	'Mickey' Wright (b. 14 Feb 1935)	4	1958–59, 61, 64
US Women's Amateur	Glenna C. Vare (*née* Collett) (b. 20 June 1903)	6	1922, 25, 28–30, 35
British Women's	Charlotte Cecilia Pitcairn Leitch (1891–1977)	4	1914, 20–1, 26
	Joyce Wethered (b. 17 Nov 1901) (now Lady Heathcoat-Amory)	4	1922, 24–5, 29

Note: Nicklaus is the only golfer to have won five different major titles (The Open, US Open, Masters, PGA and US Amateur titles) twice and a record 19 all told (1959–80). His remarkable record in The US Open is four firsts, seven seconds and two thirds. In 1930 Bobby Jones achieved a unique 'Grand Slam' of the US and British Open and Amateur titles.

Beth Daniel won the US Amateur title twice before turning professional and setting an earnings record in 1980. (*Tony Duffy, All-Sport*)

Isao Aoki kissing the ball which he aced to win a £50,000 flat, was only two strokes behind when the legendary Jack Nicklaus won the 1980 US Open with a record low score. (*Steve Powell, All-Sport*)

Rounds slowest

The slowest stroke play tournament round was one of 6 hr 45 min taken by South Africa in the first round of the 1972 World Cup at the Royal Melbourne GC, Australia. This was a four-ball medal round, everything holed out.

Most rounds

The greatest number of rounds played on foot in 24 hr is 22 rounds and five holes (401 holes) by Ian Colston, 35, at Bendigo GC Victoria (par-73, 6061 yd *5542 m*) on 27–28 Nov 1971. The most holes played on foot in a week (168 hr) is 1128 by Steve Hylton at the Mason Rudolph Golf Club (6060 yd *5541 m*), Clarkesville, Tennessee, USA, from 25–31 Aug 1980.

Most peripatetic golfer

George S. Salter, of Carmel, California, USA has played in 110 different 'countries' around the world from 1964 to 1977.

Throwing the golf ball

The lowest recorded score for throwing a golf ball round 18 holes (over 6000 yd or 5500 m) is 82 by Joe Flynn (USA), 21, at the 6228 yd *5694 m* Port Royal Course, Bermuda, on 27 Mar 1975.

CHAMPIONSHIP RECORDS
The Open

The Open Championship was inaugurated in 1860 at Prestwick, Strathclyde, Scotland. The lowest score for 9 holes is 29 by Tom Haliburton (Wentworth) and Peter W. Thomson, CBE (Australia) (b. 23 Aug 1929) in the first round at Lytham St Anne's, Lancashire on 10 July 1963, by Tony Jacklin, OBE (b. 7 July 1944) in the first round at St Andrews, Fife, on 8 July 1970 and by Bill Longmuir (b. 10 June 1953) in the first round on the Royal Lytham and St Anne's course on 18 July 1979.

The lowest round in The Open is 63 by Mark Hayes (b. 12 July 1949) (USA) at Turnberry, Strathclyde, on 7 July 1977, and Isao Aoki (b. 31 Aug 1942) (Japan) at Muirfield, East Lothian on 19 July 1980. Thomas Henry Cotton, MBE (b. Holmes Chapel, Cheshire, 26 Jan 1907) at Royal St George's, Sandwich, Kent completed the first 36 holes in 132 (67 + 65) on 27 June 1934. The lowest 72-hole aggregate is 268 (68, 70, 65, 65) by Tom Watson (b. 4 Sept 1949) (USA) at Turnberry, ending on 9 July 1977.

US Open

The United States Open Championship was inaugurated in 1894. The lowest 72-hole aggregate is 272 (63, 71, 70, 68) by Jack Nicklaus (b. 21 Jan 1940) on the Lower Course (7015 yd *6414 m*) at Baltusrol Country Club, Springfield, New Jersey, on 12–15 June 1980. The lowest score for 18 holes is 63 by Johnny Miller (b. 29 Apr 1947) on the 6921 yd *6328 m* par-71 Oakmont Country Club course, Pennsylvania on 17 June 1973, Jack Nicklaus (see above) and Tom Weiskopf (USA) (b. 9 Nov 1942), both on 12 June 1980.

US Masters'

The lowest score in the US Masters' (instituted on the par-72 6980 yd *6382 m* Augusta National Golf Course, Georgia, in 1934) has been 271 by Jack Nicklaus in 1965 and Raymond Floyd (b. 4 Sept 1942) in 1976. The lowest rounds have been 64 by Lloyd Mangrum (1914–74) (first round, 1940), Jack Nicklaus (third round, 1965), Maurice Bainbridge (GB) (b. 21 Feb 1945) (fourth round, 1974), Hale Irwin (b. 3 June 1945) (fourth round, 1975), Gary Player (S. Africa) (fourth round, 1978) and Miller Barber (b. 31 Mar 1931) (second round, 1979).

Amateur

The lowest score for nine holes in the Amateur Championship (inaugurated in 1885) is 29 by Richard Davol Chapman (1911–78) of the USA at Royal St George's, Sandwich, Kent (par-70 6633 yd *6065 m*), on 27 May 1948.

Michael Francis Bonallack, OBE (b. 31 Dec 1934) shot a 61 (32 + 29) on the par-71 6905 yd *6313 m* course at Ganton, North Yorkshire, on 27 July 1968 in the first 18 of the 36 holes in the final round of the English Amateur championship.

World Cup (formerly Canada Cup)

The World Cup (instituted as the Canada Cup in 1953) has been won most often by the USA with 15 victories between 1955 and

1979. The only men to have been on six winning teams have been Arnold Palmer (b. 10 Sept 1929) (1960, 1962–4, 1966–7) and Jack Nicklaus (1963–4, 1966–7, 1971 and 1973). Only Nicklaus has taken the individual title three times (1963–4, 1971). The lowest aggregate score for 144 holes is 545 by Australia, Bruce Devlin (b. 10 Oct 1937) and David Graham (b. 23 May 1946), at San Isidro, Buenos Aires, Argentina on 12–15 Nov 1970. The lowest individual score has been 269 by Roberto de Vicenzo (b. Buenos Aires, Argentina, 14 Apr 1923) also in 1970.

Ryder Trophy
The biennial Ryder Cup professional match between USA and the British Isles or Great Britain (Europe in 1979) was instituted in 1927. The USA have won 19½ to 3½ to date. William Earl 'Billy' Casper (b. San Diego, California, USA, 24 June 1931) has the record of winning most matches in the Trophy with 20 in 1961–75. Christy O'Connor Sr (b. 21 Dec 1924) (GB) played in ten matches up to 1973.

Walker Cup
The USA v. GB series instituted in 1921 (for the Walker Cup since 1922 and now biennially) has been won by the USA 26½–2½ to date. Joseph Boynton Carr (GB&I) (b. February 1922) played in ten contests (1947–67).

Youngest and oldest champions
The youngest winner of The Open was Tom Morris, Jr. (1851–75) at Prestwick, Strathclyde in 1868 aged 17 years 249 days. The youngest winners of The Amateur title were John Charles Beharrell (b. 2 May 1938) at Troon, Strathclyde, on 2 June 1956, and Robert 'Bobby' Cole (b. 11 May 1958) (South Africa) at Carnoustie, Tayside, on 11 June 1966, both aged 18 years 1 month. The oldest Open Champion was 'Old Tom' Morris (1821–1908), aged 46 years 99 days when he won at Prestwick in 1867. In recent times the 1967 champion, Roberto de Vicenzo was aged 44 years 93 days. The oldest winner of The Amateur was the Hon Michael Scott (1879–1959) at Hoylake, Merseyside in 1933, when 54. The oldest United States Amateur Champion was Jack Westland (b. 14 Dec 1904) at Seattle, Washington, on 23 Aug 1952, aged 47 yr 253 days.

Longest span
Jacqueline Ann Mercer (née Smith) (b. 5 Apr 1929) won her first South African title at Humewood GC, Port Elizabeth in 1948, and her fourth title at Port Elizabeth GC on 4 May 1979, 31 years later.

Most club championships
Bernard Charles Cusack (b. 24 Jan 1920) has won a record total of 32 Club championships, including 31 consecutively, at the Narembeen GC, Western Australia, between 1943 and 1980. The women's record is 31 by Molly St John Pratt (b. 19 Oct 1912) at the Stanthorpe GC, Queensland, Australia from 1931 to 1979. The British record for amateur club championships is 27 wins between 1925 and 1969 by Eileen Nairn (née Ashton) (b. 3 June 1905) at the Worsley GC, Manchester. The record for consecutive wins is 22 (1959–80) by Patricia Mary Shepherd (b. 7 Jan 1940) at Turriff GC, Aberdeenshire, Scotland.

Record tie
The longest delayed result in any National Open Championship occurred in the 1931 US Open at Toledo, Ohio. George von Elm (1901–61) and Billy Burke (1902–72) tied at 292, then tied the first replay at 149. Burke won the second replay by a single stroke after 72 extra holes.

Largest tournament
The Dunhill Trophy Open Amateur Championship in Great Britain attracted a record 124,509 competitors in 1981.

Richest prizes
The greatest first place prize money was $100,000 (total purse $500,000) in the World Open played at Pinehurst, North Carolina, USA, over 144 holes on 8–17 Nov 1973 won by Miller Barber, of Texas, USA. The World Series of Golf also carries a prize of $100,000. The highest British prize was £25,000 in the John Player Golf Classic at Hollinwell, Nottinghamshire, on 3–6 Sept 1970 won by Christy O'Connor Sr. Probably the greatest

prize for one shot was the £50,000 home won by Isao Aoki (Japan) by aceing the 155 yd *142 m* second hole in the World Match Play Championship at Wentworth on 12 Oct 1979.

Highest earnings *US PGA and LPGA circuits*
The all time professional money-winner is Jack Nicklaus who, up to 31 Dec 1980, has won $3,581,213. The record for a year is $530,808 by Tom Watson in 1980. The record for a woman is $231,000 by Beth Daniel (b. 14 Oct 1956) in 1980. The record career earnings for a woman is $906,854 by Kathy Whitworth (USA) (b. 27 Sept 1939) up to 31 Dec 1980. The most won in a year by a British golfer is £66,060 by 'Sandy' Lyle in 1980.

Most tournament wins
The record for winning tournaments in a single season is 18 (plus one unofficial), including a record 11 consecutively, by John Byron Nelson (b. 4 Feb 1912) (USA), from 8 Mar–4 Aug 1945. Sam Snead has won 84 official US PGA Tour events to December 1979, and has been credited with a total 134 tournament victories since 1934. Mickey Wright has won 82 professional tournaments from 1955 to December 1979, including a record 13 in 1963.

Biggest winning margin
The greatest margin of victory in a major tournament is 17 strokes by Randall Colin Vines (b. 22 June 1945) of Australia, in the Tasmanian Open with 274 in 1968, and by Bernhard Langer (b. 27 Aug 1957) (W. Germany) in the 1979 World Under-25 tournament at Nimes, France on 30 Sept 1979, also with 274 (73, 67, 67, 67).

HOLES IN ONE
Longest
The longest straight hole ever holed in one shot is the tenth (447 yd *408 m*) at Miracle Hills Golf Club, Omaha, Nebraska, USA by Robert Mitera (b. 1944) on 7 Oct 1965. Mitera stands 5 ft 6 in *1,68 m* tall and weighs 165 lb *74,842 kg* (11 st 11 lb). He is a two handicap player who can normally drive 245 yd *224 m*. A 50 mph *80 km/h* gust carried his shot over a 290 yd *265 m* drop-off. The longest 'dog-leg' hole achieved in one is the 480 yd *439 m* fifth at Hope Country Club, Arkansas by L. Bruce on 15 Nov 1962. The feminine record is 393 yd *359 m* by Marie Robie on the first hole of the Furnace Brook Golf Club, Wollaston, Mass., USA, on 4 Sept 1949. The longest hole in one performed in the British Isles is the seventh (par-4, 393 yd *359 m*) at West Lancashire GC by Peter Richard Parkinson (b. 26 Aug 1947) on 6 June 1972.

In 1980 *Golf Digest* magazine recorded 31,559 'aces' reported in the US, which averages over 80 per day.

Most
The greatest number of holes-in-one in a career is 47 by Norman L. Manley (b. 1923) up to 1980. The British record is 31 by Charles T. Chevalier (1902–73) of Heaton Moor Golf Club, Stockport, Greater Manchester between 20 June 1918 and 1970. Douglas Porteous, 28, holed-in-one four times over 39 consecutive holes (3rd and 6th on 26 Sept; 5th on 28 Sept at Ruchill Golf Club, Glasgow; 6th at the Clydebank and District Golf Course on 30 Sept 1974). Robert John Taylor (b. 25 Mar 1944) (Leicestershire) holed the par-3 188 yd *172 m* 16th at Hunstanton, Norfolk on three successive days—31 May, 1 and 2 June 1974—in the Eastern Inter-Counties foursomes. Joseph Felix Vituello (USA) (b. 4 Jan 1916), holed the 130 yd *119 m* 16th at the Hubbard Golf Course, Ohio, in one for the tenth time on 26 June 1979.

Consecutive
There are at least 15 cases of 'aces' being achieved in two consecutive holes, of which the greatest was Norman L. Manley's unique 'double albatross' on the par-4 330 yd *301 m* seventh and par-4 290 yd *265 m* eighth holes on the Del Valle Country Club Course, Saugus, California, on 2 Sept 1964. The only woman to record consecutive 'aces' is Sue Prell, on the 13th and 14th holes at Chatswood Golf Club, Sydney, Australia on 29 May 1977.

There is no recorded instance of a golfer performing three consecutive holes in one. The closest to achieving it was by the late Dr Joseph Boydstone on the 3rd, 4th and 9th at Bakersfield GC,

California, USA, on 10 Oct 1962 (the year he recorded a record 11 aces), and by the Rev Harold Snider (b. 4 July 1900) who aced the 8th, 13th and 14th holes of the par-3 Ironwood course, Arizona, USA on 9 June 1976.

Youngest and oldest

The youngest golfer recorded to have shot a hole-in-one was Coby Orr (5 years) of Littleton, Colorado on the 103 yd *94 m* fifth at the Riverside Golf Course, San Antonio, Texas in 1975. The oldest golfers to have performed the feat are (men): 93-year-olds George Henry Miller, on the 116 yd *106 m* 11th at Anaheim GC, California on 4 Dec 1970; Charles Youngman, at the Tam O'Shanter Club, Toronto in 1971; and William H. Diddel, on the 142 yd *130 m* 8th at the Royal Poinciana GC, Naples, Florida on 1 Jan 1978. The oldest woman to perform the feat is Maude Bridget Hutton (b. 7 Apr 1892) when she holed the 102 yd *93 m* 14th at Kings Inn Golf and Country Club, Sun City Center, Florida on 7 Aug 1978.

Shooting your age

The lowest under his age score recorded on the PGA Circuit is 66, at age 67, by Sam Snead (USA) in the Ed McMahon Quad Cities Open, Oakwood CC, Coal Valley, Illinois on 23 June 1979. In a less important tournament he had scored 64, at Onion Creek GC (6585 yd *6021 m*, par 70), Austin, Texas, in April 1978 when one month short of his 66th birthday.

The oldest player to score his age is C. Arthur Thompson (1869–1975) of Victoria, British Columbia, Canada, who scored 103 on the Uplands course of 6215 yd *5682 m* aged 103 in 1973. The youngest player to score his age is Robert Leroy Klingaman (b. 22 Oct 1914) who shot a 58 when aged 58 on the 5654 yd *5170 m* course at the Caledonia GC, Fayetteville, Penn., USA, on 31 Aug 1973. Bob Hamilton shot 59, aged 59, on the 6233 yd *5699 m* blue course, Hamilton GC, Evansville, Indiana, USA, on 3 June 1975.

GREYHOUND RACING

Earliest meeting

In September 1876 a greyhound meeting was staged at Hendon, North London with a railed hare operated by a windlass. Modern greyhound racing originated with the perfecting of the mechanical hare by Owen Patrick Smith at Emeryville, California, USA, in 1919. The earliest greyhound race behind a mechanical hare in the British Isles was at Belle Vue, Manchester, opened on 24 July 1926.

Derby

The only two greyhounds to have won the English Greyhound Derby twice (instituted 1927, now over 500 m *546 yd*) are *Mick the Miller* (whelped in Ireland, June 1926 and died 1939) on 25 July 1929, when owned by Albert H. Williams, and on 28 June 1930 (owned by Mrs Arundel H. Kempton), and *Patricia's Hope* on 24 June 1972 (when owned by Gordon and Basil Marks and Brian Stanley) and 23 June 1973 (when owned by G. & B. Marks and J. O'Connor). The highest prize was £35,000 to *Indian Joe* for the Derby on 28 June 1980. The only greyhounds to win the English, Scottish and Welsh Derby 'triple' are *Trev's Perfection*, owned by Fred Trevillion, in 1947, *Mile Bush Pride*, owned by Noel W. Purvis, in 1959, and *Patricia's Hope* in 1972. The only greyhound to win the American Derby, at Taunton, Mass., twice was *Real Huntsman* in 1950–51.

Grand National

The only greyhound to have won the Grand National (inst. 1927 over 525 yd *480 m*, now 500 m, and five flights) three times is *Sherry's Prince*, a 75 lb *32 kg* dog (whelped in April 1967, died July 1978) owned by Mrs Joyce Mathews of Sanderstead, Surrey, in 1970, 1971 and 1972 when he won by 6¼ lengths.

Fastest greyhound

The highest speed at which any greyhound has been timed is 41.72 mph *67,14 km/h* (410 yd *374 m* in 20.1 sec) by *The Shoe* on the then straightaway track at Richmond, NSW, Australia on 25 Apr 1968. It is estimated that he covered the last 100 yd *91,44 m* in 4.5 sec or at 45.45 mph *73,14 km/h*. The highest speed recorded for a greyhound in Great Britain is 39.13 mph *62,97 km/h* by *Beef Cutlet*, when covering a straight course of 500 yd *457 m* in 26.13 sec at Blackpool, Lancashire, on 13 May 1933.

Fastest 500 m timings

The fastest *photo*-timing is 28.96 sec (38.62 mph *62,15 km/h*) at Brighton and Hove Stadium, Sussex by *Monday's Bran* on 4 Aug 1979. The fastest *photo*-timing over hurdles is 29.71 sec (37.64 mph *60,58 km/h*) also at Brighton by *Wotchit Buster* on 22 Aug 1978.

Winning streak

The world record is 31 consecutive victories by an American greyhound *Joe Dump* from 18 Nov 1978 to 1 June 1979. *Westpark Mustard*, owned by Mr and Mrs Cyril Scotland, set a British record of 20 consecutive wins between 7 Jan and 28 Oct 1974.

GYMNASTICS

Earliest references

A primitive form of gymnastics was practised in ancient Greece and Rome during the period of the ancient Olympic Games (776 BC to AD 393) but Johann Friedrich Simon was the first teacher of modern gymnastics at Basedow's School, Dessau, Germany in 1776.

Most titles *World*

The greatest number of individual titles won by a man in the World Championships is ten by Boris Shakhlin (b. 27 Jan 1932) (USSR) between 1954 and 1964. He also won three team titles. The female record is ten individual wins and five team titles by Larissa Semyonovna Latynina (b. 27 Dec 1934, retired 1966) of the USSR, between 1956 and 1964. Japan has won the men's team title a record five times (1962, 1966, 1970, 1974, 1978) and the USSR the women's team title on six occasions (1954, 1958, 1962, 1970, 1974, 1978).

The most overall titles in Modern Rhythmic Gymnastics is three by Maria Guigova (Bulgaria) in 1969, 1971 and 1973 (shared). Galina Shugurova (USSR) (b. 1955) won eight apparatus titles from 1969–77.

Most titles *Olympic*

Japan (1960, 1964, 1968, 1972 and 1976) have won the men's team title most often. The USSR have won the women's title eight times (1952–80). The only men to win six individual gold medals are Boris Shakhlin (USSR), with one in 1956, four (two shared) in 1960 and one in 1964, and Nikolai Andrianov (USSR) (b. 14 Oct 1952), with one in 1972, four in 1976 and one in 1980.

Vera Caslavska-Odlozil (b. 3 May 1942) (Czechoslovakia) has won most individual gold medals with seven, three in 1964 and four (one shared) in 1968. Larissa Latynina won six individual gold medals and was in three winning teams in 1956–64 making nine gold medals. She also won five silver and four bronze medals making 18 in all—an Olympic record for either sex in any sport. The most medals for a male gymnast is 15 by Nikolai Andrianov (USSR), 7 gold, 5 silver and 3 bronze in 1972–80. Alexander Ditiatin (USSR) (b. 7 Aug 1957) is the only man to win a medal in all eight categories in the same Games, with 3 gold, 4 silver and 1 bronze at Moscow in 1980.

Highest score *Olympics*

Nadia Comaneci (b. Romania, 12 Nov 1961) achieved seven perfect scores of 10.00 at the Montreal Olympics in July 1976. Six other girls have received perfect scores in the 1979 and 1980 Games.

Youngest International

Anita Jokiel (Poland) was aged only 11 years 2 days when she competed at Brighton, East Sussex, on 6 Dec 1977.

Most titles *British*

The British Gymnastic Championship was won ten times by Arthur John Whitford (b. 2 July 1908) in 1928–36 and 1939. He was also in four winning teams. Wray 'Nik' Stuart, MBE (b. 20 July 1927) equalled the record of nine successive wins, 1956–64. The women's record is eight by Mary Patricia Hirst (b. 18 Nov 1918) (1947, 1949–50 and 1952–6).

Most titles *World Cup*

In the first World Cup Competition, in London in 1975, Ludmilla Tourischeva (now Mrs Valeriy Borzov) (b. 7 Oct 1952) (USSR) won all five gold medals available.

Rope climbing
The United States Amateur Athletic Union records are tantamount to world records: 20 ft *6,09 m* (hands alone) 2.8 sec, Don Perry (USA) at Champaign, Illinois, USA, on 3 Apr 1954; 25 ft *7,62 m* (hands alone) 4.7 sec, Garvin S. Smith at Los Angeles, California, USA, on 19 Apr 1947.

Chinning the bar
The greatest number of continuous chin-ups (from a dead hang position) is 135 by Joe Hernandez (b. 1961) at Dysart Junior H. S., Cashion, Arizona, USA on 22 May 1980. William Aaron Vaught (b. 1959) performed 20 one-arm (his right) chin-ups at Finch's Gymnasium, Houston, Texas, USA, on 3 Jan 1976. Francis Lewis (b. 1896) of Beatrice, Nebraska, USA in May 1914 achieved seven consecutive chins using only the middle finger of his left hand. His bodyweight was 158 lb *71 kg 667* (11 st 4 lb).

Parallel bar dips
Thomas Gildert (b. 1944) performed a record 533 consecutive parallel bar dips on 1 July 1980 at the Coloroll Leisure Centre, Nelson, Lancashire. Jack La Lanne (b. 1914) is reported to have done 1000, in Oakland, Calif., USA in 1945.

Press-ups (Push-ups)
Tommy Gildert did 9105 consecutive press-ups at the Burnley Boys' Club, Lancashire, on 1 July 1979. Harry Lee Welch Jr, 32, performed 392 one-armed push-ups at WTIK Broadcasting Station, Durham, N Carolina, USA on 17 Apr 1980. Noel Barry Mason, did 267 finger tip press-ups on 10 June 1979 at Burton-on-Trent, Staffs. Carl A White did 90 consecutive hand-stand push-ups at Baltimore, Maryland, USA, on 7 Dec 1979.

Sit-ups *Straight-legged*
The greatest recorded number of sit-ups without feet pinned down or knees bent is 26,000 by Angel Bustamonte (b. 28 Feb 1959) at Sacramento, Calif., USA on 17 Dec 1977.

Jumping Jacks
The greatest recorded number of side-straddle hops is 27,000 by Ashrita Furman (b. 16 Sept 1954) at the Jack LaLanne Health Spa, New York, USA on 14 Aug 1979.

Vertical jumps
The greatest height in a vertical jump (Sargent Jump) *i.e.* the differential between the height of the finger-tip reach static and in jumping is 42 in *1,06 m* by David 'Dr. D' Thompson (USA) of North Carolina State and the Denver Nuggets, 1.94 m *6 ft 4½ in* tall, in 1972. Reported higher jumps by athletes Franklin Jacobs (USA) and Greg Joy (Canada) were probably with an initial run. Olympic Pentathlon champion Mary Peters MBE (GB) (b. 6 July 1939) is reported to have done 30 in *76,2 cm* in California in 1972.

Luckily Ashrita Furman didn't encounter too many patches like this when he did his ten miles of somersaults in New York's Central Park.

Multi Olympic medallist Nikolai Andrianov won the 1978 World Rings and Combined Exercises titles. *(All-Sport)*

Somersaults
Ashrita Furman performed 6,773 forward rolls over 10 miles *16,09 km* in Central Park, New York, USA on 19 Nov 1980. Lance Corporal Wayne Wright of the Royal Engineers, made a successful dive and tucked somersault over 37 men at Old Park Barracks, Dover, Kent on 30 July 1980. Shigeru Iwasaki (b. 1960) backwards somersaulted over 50 m *54.68 yd* in 10.8 sec at Tokyo, Japan on 30 Mar 1980.

Largest gymnasium
The world's largest gymnasium is Yale University's nine-storey, Payne Whitney Gymnasium at New Haven, Connecticut, USA, completed in 1932 and valued at $18,000,000 *£10,285,000.*

Largest crowd
The largest recorded crowd was approximately 18,000 people who packed the Forum, Montreal, Canada, for the final of the women's individual apparatus competitions at the XXI Olympic Games on 22 July 1976. Comparable audiences are reported for the Shanghai Stadium, People's Republic of China.

HANDBALL

Origins
Handball, similar to association football, with hands substituted for feet, was first played *c.* 1895. It was introduced into the Olympic Games at Berlin in 1936 as an 11-a-side outdoor game with Germany winning, but when re-introduced in 1972 it was an indoor game with seven-a-side, the standard size of team since 1952.

By 1980 there were 75 countries affiliated to the International Handball Federation (founded 1946), and an estimated ten million participants. The earliest international match was when Sweden beat Denmark on 8 Mar 1935.

Olympic titles
The most victories in Olympic competition have been those by the USSR in winning the men's and women's titles at Montreal, Canada in 1976, and the women's title at Moscow in 1980.

World titles
The most victories won in World championship (inst. 1938) competition are by Romania with four men's and three women's titles from 1956 to 1974.

287

HANDBALL (COURT)

Origins

Handball played against walls or in a court is a game of ancient Celtic origin. In the early 19th century only a front wall was used but gradually side and back walls were added. The earliest international contest was in New York City, USA, in 1887 between the champions of the USA and Ireland. The court is now a standardised 60 ft *18 m* by 30 ft *9 m* in Ireland, Ghana and Australia, and 40 ft *12 m* by 20 ft *6 m* in Canada, Mexico and the USA. The game is played with both a hard and soft ball in Ireland and soft ball only in Australia, Canada, Ghana, Mexico and the USA.

Championships

World championships were inaugurated in New York in October 1964 with competitors from Australia, Canada, Ireland, Mexico and the USA. The most wins have been two by the USA in 1964 and 1967 (shared with Canada).

Most titles

The US Championship 4-wall singles has been won six times by Jimmy Jacobs (b. 1931) in 1955–7, 1960, 1964–5. He also shared in six doubles titles, 1962–3, 1965, 1967–8, 1975.

HARNESS RACING

Origins

Trotting races were held in Valkenburg, Netherlands in 1554. In England the trotting gait (the simultaneous use of the diagon-

ally opposite legs) was known in the 16th century. The sulky first appeared in harness racing in 1829. Pacers thrust out their fore and hind legs simultaneously on one side.

Most successful driver

The most successful sulky driver in North American harness racing history has been Herve Filion (b. 1 Feb 1940) of Quebec, Canada who reached a record 7553 wins and $32.3 million in purse money by the end of the 1980 season. He won his eleventh North American championship in 1980. The most wins in a year is 637 by Herve Filion in 1974. The greatest earnings in a year is $3,732,306 by John Campbell in 1980.

Highest price

The highest price paid for a trotter is $3,200,000 for *Green Speed* by the Pine Hollow Stud of New York from Beverley Lloyds, Florida in 1977. The highest price ever paid for a pacer is $5,000,000 for *Niatross* by Lou Guida in September 1979 putting the total value of the horse at $10 million.

Greatest winnings

The greatest amount won by a trotting horse is $1,960,945 by *Bellino II* (France) up to retirement in 1977. The record for a pacing horse is $2,019,213 by *Niatross* (USA) to end of 1980 season. The greatest amount won by a harness horse in a single season is $1,414,313 by *Niatross* (USA) during 1979.

The largest ever purse was $2,011,000 for the Woodrow Wilson Two-year-old race at Meadowlands, New Jersey on 6 Aug 1980 of which a record $1,005,000 went to the winner *Land Grant* driven by Del Insko.

Harness Horse of the Year in 1977, *Green Speed* was sold for $3.2 million after having won nearly a million dollars in racing. (*US Trotting Association*)

HOCKEY

MEN

Origins

A representation of two players with curved snagging sticks apparently in an orthodox 'bully' position was found in Tomb No. 17 at Beni Hasan, Egypt and has been dated to *c.* 2050 BC. There is a British reference to the game in Lincolnshire in 1277. The English Hockey Association was founded at Cannon Street Hotel, City of London on 16 Apr 1875. The Federation Internationale de Hockey was formed on 7 Jan 1924.

The first organised club was the Blackheath Rugby and Hockey Club founded in 1861. The oldest club with a continuous history is Teddington HC formed in the autumn of 1871. They played Richmond on 24 Oct 1874 and used the first recorded circle *versus* Surbiton at Bushey Park on 9 Dec 1876. The first international match was the Wales *v*. Ireland match at Rhyl on 26 Jan 1895. Ireland won 3–0.

Most Olympic medals

The Indians were Olympic Champions from the re-inception of Olympic hockey in 1928 until 1960, when Pakistan beat them 1–0 at Rome. They had their eighth win in 1980. Of the six Indians who have won three Olympic team gold medals two have also won a silver medal—Leslie Walter Claudius (b. 25 Mar 1927) in 1948, 1952, 1956 and 1960 (silver) and Udham Singh (b. 4 Aug 1928) in 1952, 1956, 1964 and 1960 (silver).

Highest international score

The highest score in international hockey was when India defeated the United States 24–1 at Los Angeles, California, USA in the 1932 Olympic Games. The greatest number of goals in

HARNESS RACING RECORDS AGAINST TIME

TROTTING

World (mile track)	1:54.8	*Nevele Pride* (driver, Stanley Dancer) (US) at Indianapolis, Indiana	31 Aug 1969
	1;54.8	*Lindy's Crown* (driver, Howard Beissinger) (US) at Du Quoin, Illinois	30 Aug 1980
World race record (mile)	1:54.8	*Lindy's Crown* (driver, Howard Beissinger) (US) at Du Quoin, Illinois	30 Aug 1980
British record (mile)	2:06.8	*Ted Trot* (driver, John Blisset) at Chasewater, West Midlands	21 June 1975

PACING

World (mile track)	1:49.2	*Niatross* (driver, Clint Galbraith) (US) at Lexington, Kentucky	1 Oct 1980
World race record (mile)	1:52.2	*Niatross* (driver, Clint Galbraith) (US) at Inglewood, California	15 Nov 1980
British record (mile)	2:04.3	*Bomber* (driver, Thomas Brown) at Chasewater, West Midlands	7 July 1978

home international match was when England defeated France 16–0 at Beckenham on 25 Mar 1922. The World Cup has been won twice by Pakistan in 1971 and 1978.

Most international appearances

Avtar Singh Sohal (b. 22 Mar 1938) represented Kenya 167 times between 1957 and 1972. The most by a home countries player is 139 by H. David Judge (b. 19 Jan 1936) with 124 for Ireland and 15 for Great Britain from 1957 to 1978.

Ireland	124	H. David Judge	1957–78
Wales	100	D. Austin Savage (b. 15 Dec 1940)	1962–81
Scotland	78	Christopher Sutherland (b. 6 Dec 1949)	1969–81
England	73	Bernard J. Cotton (b. 30 June 1948)	1970–78
Great Britain	56	John W. Neill (England) (b. 15 May 1934)	1959–68

Greatest scoring feats

The greatest number of goals scored in international hockey is 150 by Paul Litjens (Netherlands) (b. 9 Nov 1947) in 112 games to April 1979. M. C. Marckx (Bowdon 2nd XI) scored 19 goals against Brooklands 2nd XI (score 23–0) on 31 Dec 1910. He was selected for England in March 1912 but declined due to business priorities. Between 1923 and 1958, Fred H. Wagner scored 1832 goals for Beeston HC, Nottingham Casuals and the Nottinghamshire county side.

The fastest goal in an international was in 7 sec by John French for England v. W. Germany at Nottingham, on 25 Apr 1971.

Greatest goalkeeping

Richard James Allen (b. 4 June 1902) (India) did not concede a goal during the 1928 Olympic Tournament and only a total of three in the following two Olympics of 1932 and 1936. In these three games India scored a total of 102 goals.

Longest game

The longest international game on record was one of 145 min (into the sixth period of extra time), when Netherlands beat Spain 1–0 in the Olympic tournament at Mexico City on 25 Oct 1968. The longest recorded club match occurred in the Hong Kong Hockey Association Holland Cup semi-final between HKFC 'C' and Prisons Sports Dept HC on 11 Mar 1979 which ended at 2–2 at full time. After 20 min of extra time, it took 115 min of 'sudden death' play before the Football Club scored.

WOMEN

Origins

The earliest women's club was East Molesey in Surrey, England formed in *c.* 1887. The Wimbledon Ladies Hockey Club, founded one year later, is still in existence. The first national association was the Irish Ladies' Hockey Union founded in 1894. The All England Women's Hockey Association held its first formal meeting in Westminster Town Hall, London, on 23 Nov 1895. The first international match was an England v. Ireland game in Dublin in 1896. Ireland won 2–0. The first IFWHA Championship Tournament of 21 nations was at Edinburgh, Scotland in 1975, when England won the Silver Quaich.

Most international appearances

Wales	138	Ann Ellis, MBE (b. 21 Sept 1940)	1963–80
England	111	Valerie Robinson	1963–81
Scotland	63	Margaret Brown (b. 7 June 1946)	1967–79
Ireland	55	Marie Bartlett (b. 7 Aug 1945)	1969–81

Highest scores

The highest score in a women's international match was when England beat France 23–0 at Merton, Greater London, on 3 Feb 1923. In club hockey, Ross Ladies beat Wyeside, at Ross-on-Wye, Herefordshire, 40–0 on 24 Jan 1929, when Edna Mary Blakelock (b. 22 Oct 1904) scored a record 21 goals.

Highest attendance

The highest attendance at a women's hockey match was 65,165 for the match between England and the USA at the Empire Stadium, Wembley, London, on 11 Mar 1978.

Marathon

Two teams of eleven from Epsom Girls Grammar School, Auckland, NZ played for 35 hr 3 min 50 sec on 21–22 Apr 1980.

HORSE RACING

Origins

Horsemanship was an important part of the Hittite culture of Anatolia, Turkey dating from 1400 BC. The 33rd ancient Olympic Games of 648 BC in Greece featured horse racing. The earliest horse race recorded in England was one held in about AD 210 at Netherby, North Yorkshire, among Arabians brought to Britain by Lucius Septimius Severus (AD 146–211), Emperor of Rome.

Racecourse *Largest*

The world's largest racecourse is the Newmarket course (founded 1636). It now comprises the Rowley Mile Course and the July Course, whose grandstands are about a mile apart, although a portion of the course is common to both. The Beacon Course of 4 miles 397 yd *6,80 km* long, is no longer in use. The course, mainly unfenced, is situated in the middle of Newmarket Heath, *c* 2500 acres, the largest turfed training area in the world. The world's largest grandstand was opened in 1968 at Belmont Park, Long Island, NY, USA at a cost of $30,700,000 *£12.8 million*. It is 110 ft *33 m* tall, 440 yd *402 m* long, contains 908 mutuel windows and seats 30,000.

Largest prizes

The richest race ever held is the All-American Futurity, a race for quarter-horses over 440 yd *402 m* (400 yd *366 m* before 1973) at Ruidoso Downs, New Mexico, USA. The prizes in 1978 and 1979 totalled $1,280,000 *£218,750*. The richest first prize for any horse race was the $600,000 announced for the winner of the Arlington Million, Chicago, USA, on 30 Aug 1981.

The richest prize on the British Turf was £166,820 in the 201st Derby, won by *Henbit*, ridden by William 'Willie' Hunter

Willie Shoemaker, who rode his 8000th winner *War Allied* at Hollywood Park, California on 27 May 1981. (*All-Sport*)

Carson (b. 16 Nov 1942), owned by Mme Arpad Plesch and trained by Major William Richard 'Dick' Hern, on 4 June 1980.

Longest race

The longest recorded horse race was one of 1200 miles *1925 km* in Portugal, won by a horse *Emir* bred from Egyptian-bred Blunt Arab stock. The holder of the world record for long distance racing and speed is *Champion Crabbet*, who covered 300 miles *482 km* in 52 hr 33 min carrying 17½ st *111,130 kg*, in 1920.

Most runners

The most horses in a race is 66 in the Grand National of 22 Mar 1929. The record for the flat is 58 in the Lincolnshire Handicap on 13 Mar 1948. The most runners at a meeting were 214 (flat) in seven races at Newmarket on 15 June 1915 and 229 (National Hunt) in eight races at Worcester on 13 Jan 1965.

Dead heats

There is no recorded case in turf history of a quintuple dead heat. The nearest approach was in the Astley Stakes, at Lewes, Sussex, on 6 Aug 1880 when *Mazurka, Wandering Nun* and *Scobell* triple dead-heated for first place a head in front of *Cumberland* and *Thora*, who dead-heated for fourth place. Each of the five jockeys thought he had won. The only three known examples of a quadruple dead heat were between *Honest Harry, Miss Decoy, Young Daffodil* and *Peteria* at Bogside, on 7 June 1808, between *Defaulter, The Squire of Malton, Reindeer* and *Pulcherrima* in the Omnibus Stakes at The Hoo, Hertfordshire, on 26 Apr 1851, and between *Overreach, Lady Golightly, Gamester* and *The Unexpected* at Newmarket on 22 Oct 1855. Since the introduction of the photo-finish, the highest number of horses deadheating has been three, on several occasions.

Horse *Greatest record*

The horse with the best recorded win-loss record was *Kincsem*, a Hungarian mare foaled in 1874, who was unbeaten in 54 races (1876–9), including the Goodwood Cup of 1878. *Camarero* owned by Don José Coll Vidal of Puerto Rico, foaled in 1951, had a winning streak of 56 races from 19 Apr 1953 to 17 Aug 1955. He died 'from a colic' on 26 Aug 1956, the day after his 73rd win in 77 starts.

Bob Champion and *Aldaniti* clearing the highest jump—The Chair, 5 ft 2 in *1,57 m*—on the way to winning the 1981 Grand National. *(John Starr, All-Sport)*

Triple Crown Winners

The English 'Triple Crown' (2000 Guineas, Derby, St Leger) has been won 15 times, most recently by *Nijinsky* in 1970. The American 'Triple Crown' (Kentucky Derby, Preakness Stakes, Belmont Stakes) has been achieved 11 times, most recently by *Affirmed* in 1978.

Horse *Highest price*

The most expensive horse ever is the 1969 All-American Futurity winner *Easy Jet* (foaled 1967). It was reported in October 1980 that he had been syndicated for $30 million, in 50 shares of $600,000 each. The highest price for a yearling is $3.5 million for a colt by *Northern Dancer—South Ocean*, on 20 July 1981 at Keeneland, Kentucky, USA, by Robert Sangster and partners.

Horse *Greatest winnings*

The greatest amount ever won by a horse is $2,781,608 by *Spectacular Bid* from 1978 to his retirement on 4 Oct 1980. The leading money-winning mare is *Dahlia* (foaled 1970) who, from 1973 to 1976, earned $1,535,443. The most won in a year is $1,279,334 by *Spectacular Bid* in 1979.

Jockey *Wins on one card*

The most winners ridden on one card is eight by Hubert S Jones, 17, from 13 rides at Caliente, Cal., USA on 11 June 1944 and by Oscar Barattuci, at Rosario City, Argentina, on 15 Dec 1957. The longest winning streak is 12 by Sir Gordon Richards (b. Oakengates, Salop, 5 May 1904) (one race at Nottingham on 3 Oct, six out of six at Chepstow on 4 Oct and the first five races next day at Chepstow) in 1933.

Jockey *Youngest and oldest*

The youngest jockey was Frank Wootton (1893–1940) (English champion jockey 1909–12), who rode his first winner in South Africa aged 9 years 10 months. The oldest jockey was Levi Burlingame (USA), who rode his last race at Stafford, Kansas, in 1932 aged 80.

Jockey *Lightest*

The lightest recorded jockey was Kitchener (d. 1872), who won the Chester Cup on *Red Deer* in 1844 at 3 st 7 lb *22,226 kg*. He was said to have weighed only 2 st 7 lb *15,875 kg* in 1840.

Jockey *Most successful*

The most successful jockey of all time has been William Lee 'Willie' Shoemaker (USA) (b. weighing 2½ lb *1,133 kg*, nr Fabens, Texas 19 Aug 1931) now weighing 94 lb *43 kg* and standing 4 ft 11 in *1,50 m*. From March 1949 to 27 May 1981 he has ridden 8000 winners from 34,623 mounts earning over $8 million.

The greatest amount ever won by any jockey in a year is $8,183,535 by Laffit Pincay Jr (b. Panama 29 Dec 1946) in 1979. The most winners ridden in a year is 546, from a record 2199 mounts, by Chris McCarron (USA) (b. 1955) in 1974.

Trainers

The greatest number of wins by a trainer in one year is 494 by Jack Van Berg (USA) in 1976. The greatest amount won in a year is $3,563,147 by Lazaro S. Barrera (USA) in 1979.

Owners

The most winners in a year by an owner is 494 by Dan R. Lasater (USA) in 1974 when he also won a record $3,022,960 in prize money.

BRITISH TURF RECORDS
Most successful *Horses*

As the 1000 Guineas and the Oaks are restricted to fillies, only they can possibly win all five classics. *Sceptre* (foaled 1899) came closest in 1902 when she won the 2000 Guineas, 1000 Guineas, Oaks and St Leger. In 1868 *Formosa* won the same four but dead-heated in the 2000 Guineas. The most races won in a season is 23 by three-year-old *Fisherman* in 1856. *Catherina* (foaled 1830) won a career record 79 out of 176 races, 1832–41. The record for this century is by *Le Garcon d'Or* (foaled 1958) with 34 wins out of 181 flat races 1960–73. The only horse to win the same race in seven successive years was *Dr Syntax* (foaled 1811) in the Preston Gold Cup (1815–21). The most successful sire was *Stockwell* (foaled 1849) whose progeny won 1153 races (1858–

MAJOR RACE RECORDS

Race	Record Time	Jockey	Trainer	Owner	Largest Field
FLAT					
Derby (1780) 1½ miles *2414 m* Epsom	2 min 33.8 sec *Mahmoud* 1936	8—Lester Piggott OBE 1954, 57, 60, 68, 70, 72, 76, 77	7—John Porter 1868, 82, 83, 86, 90, 91, 99 7—Robert Robson 1793, 1802, 09, 10, 15, 17, 23 7—Fred Darling 1922, 25, 26, 31, 38, 40, 41	5—3rd Earl of Egremont 1782, 1804, 05, 07, 26 5—H. H. Aga Khan III 1930, 35, 36, 48, 52	34 (1862)
1000 Guineas (1814) 1 mile *1609 m* Newmarket	1 min 37 sec *Camarée* 1950	7—George Fordham 1859, 61, 65, 68, 69, 81, 83	8—Robert Robson 1819, 20, 21, 22, 23, 25, 26, 27	8—4th Duke of Grafton 1819, 20, 21, 22, 23, 25, 26, 27	29 (1926)
2000 Guineas (1809) 1 mile *1609 m* Newmarket	1 min 35.8 sec *My Babu* 1948	9—Jem Robinson 1825, 28, 31, 33, 34, 35, 36, 47, 48	5—Fred Darling 1925, 31, 38, 42, 47	5—4th Duke of Grafton 1820, 21, 22, 26, 27 5—Lord Jersey 1831, 34, 35, 36, 37	28 (1930)
Oaks (1779) 1½ miles *2414 m* Epsom	2 min 34.33 sec *Bireme* 1980	9—Frank Buckle 1797, 98, 99, 1802, 03, 05, 17, 18, 23	8—Alec Taylor 1910, 17, 18, 19, 21, 22, 25, 26	6—4th Duke of Grafton 1813, 15, 22, 23, 28, 31	26 (1848)
St Leger (1776) 1 m 6 f 127 yd *2932 m* Doncaster	3 min 01.6 sec *Coronach* 1926 *Windsor Lad* 1934	9—Bill Scott 1821, 25, 28, 29, 38, 39, 40, 41, 46	16—John Scott 1827, 28, 29, 32, 34, 38, 39, 40, 41, 45, 51, 53, 56, 57, 59, 62	7—9th Duke of Hamilton 1786, 87, 88, 92, 1808, 09, 14	30 (1825)
King George VI and Queen Elizabeth Stakes (1951) 1½ miles *2414 m* Ascot	2 min 26.98 sec *Grundy* 1975	6—Lester Piggott 1965, 66, 69, 70, 74, 77	3—Noel Murless 1966, 67, 68 3—Vincent O'Brien 1958, 70, 77 3—Dick Hern 1972, 79, 80	2—Nelson Bunker Hunt 1973, 74	19 (1951)
Prix de l'Arc de Triomphe (1920) 2400 metres *1 mile 864 yd* Longchamp	2 min 28 sec *Detroit* 1980	4—Jacques Doyasbère 1942, 44, 50, 51 4—Frédéric Head 1966, 72, 76, 79	4—Charles H. Semblat 1942, 44, 46, 49	6—Marcel Boussac 1936, 37, 42, 44, 46, 49	30 (1967)
VRC Melbourne Cup (1861) 3200 metres *1 mile 1739 yd* Flemington, Victoria	3 min 19.1 sec *Rain Lover* 1968	4—Bobby Lewis 1902, 15, 19, 27 4—Harry White 1974, 75, 78, 79	7—Bart Cummings 1965, 66, 67, 74, 75, 77, 79	4—Etienne de Mestre 1861, 62, 67, 78	39 (1890)
Washington, D.C. International (1952) 1½ miles *2414 m* Laurel Park	2 min 23.8 sec *Kelso* 1964	3—Manuel Ycaza 1959, 60, 67 3—Lester Piggott 1968, 69, 80	4—Maurice Zilber 1973, 75, 76, 80	3—Paul Mellon 1967, 70, 71 3—Nelson Bunker Hunt 1973, 75, 76	13 (1955, 1962)
Kentucky Derby (1875) 1¼ miles *2012 m* Churchill Downs	1 min 59.4 sec *Secretariat* 1973	5—Eddie Arcaro 1938, 41, 45, 48, 52 5—Bill Hartack 1957, 60, 62, 64, 69	6—Ben A. Jones 1938, 41, 44, 48, 49, 52	8—Calumet Farm 1941, 44, 48, 49, 52, 57, 58, 68	23 (1974)
NATIONAL HUNT					
Grand National (1839) 4½ miles *7242 m* Liverpool	9 min 01.9 sec *Red Rum* 1973	5—George Stevens, 1856, 63, 64, 69, 70	4—Fred Rimell, 1956, 61, 70, 76 4—Hon Aubrey Hastings, 1906, 15, 17 (at Gatwick), 24	3—Capt Henry Machell, 1873, 74, 76 3—Sir Charles Assheton-Smith, 1893, 1912, 13 3—Noel Le Mare, 1973, 74, 77	66 (1929)
Cheltenham Gold Cup (1924) 3¼ miles *5230 m*[2] Cheltenham	—[1]	4—Pat Taaffe, 1964, 65, 66, 68	5—Tom Dreaper, 1946, 64, 65, 66, 68	7—Dorothy Paget, 1932, 33, 34, 35, 36, 40, 52	16 (1945)
Champion Hurdle (1927) 2 miles *3218 m*[2] Cheltenham	—[1]	4—Tim Molony, 1951, 52, 53, 54	5—Peter Easterby, 1967, 76, 77, 80, 81	4—Dorothy Paget 1932, 33, 40, 46	24 (1964)

[1] It would be unrealistic to include time records for these two races because they have been run over a variety of distances and, although always held at Cheltenham, several different courses have been used.

[2] 1980 distances

76) and in 1866 set a record of 132 races won. The greatest amount ever won by an English-trained horse is £450,428 by *Troy* (foaled 1976) in 1978–9 and by a filly, £281,379 by *Mrs Penny* (foaled 1977) to June 1981.

Most successful *Owners*
H H Aga Khan III (1877–1957) was leading owner a record 13 times between 1924 and 1952. The record for a season was set by Robert Sangster, who won £348,023 in first-prize money in 1977. The most wins in a season is 115 by David Robinson in 1973. The most English classics won is 20 by the 4th Duke of Grafton, KG (1760–1844), from 1813 to 1831.

Most successful *Trainers*
The record first-prize money earned in a season is £831,964 by Dick Hern in 1980. The most classics won by a trainer is 41 by John Scott (1794–1871) including 16 St Leger winners between 1827 and 1862. Alec Taylor of Manton, Wiltshire headed the trainers' list for a record 12 seasons between 1907 and 1925. In 1867 John Day won 146 races.

Most successful *Jockeys*
Sir Gordon Richards won 4870 races from 21,834 mounts from his first mount at Lingfield on 16 Oct 1920 to his last at Sandown on 10 July 1954. His first win was on 31 Mar 1921. In 1953, at his 28th and final attempt, he won the Derby, six days after his knighthood. In 1947 he won a record 269 races. He was champion jockey a record 26 times between 1925 and 1953. The most classic races won by a jockey is 27 by Francis 'Frank' Buckle (1766–1832), between 1792 and 1827.

Horses *Oldest winners*
The oldest horse to win a flat race was *Marksman*, aged 18 when he won at Ashford, Kent in 1826. Also aged 18, *Sonny Somers* became the oldest horse this century to win over jumps at Lingfield Park, Surrey on 28 Feb 1980.

291

SPEED RECORDS

Distance	Time min sec	mph	km/h	Name	Age	Weight carried lb	kg	Course	Date
¼ mile	20.8	43.26	69,62	Big Racket (Mexico)	4	114	51,7	Mexico City, Mexico	5 Feb 1945
½ mile	44.4	40.54	65,24	Sonido (Venezuela)	2	111	50,3	‡Caracas, Venezuela	28 June 1970
⅝ mile	53.6†	41.98	67,56	Indigenous (GB)	4	131	59,4	‡*Epsom Surrey	2 June 1960
	53.89††	41.75	67,19	Raffingora (GB)	5	140	63,5	‡*Epsom, Surrey	5 June 1970
	55.4	40.61	65,36	Zip Pocket (USA)	3	122	55,3	Turf Paradise, Phoenix, Arizona, USA	22 Apr 1967
¾ mile	1:06.2	40.78	65,62	Gelding by Blink—Broken Tendril (GB)	2	123	55,7	*Brighton, East Sussex	6 Aug 1929
	1:07.2	40.18	64,66	Grey Papa (USA)	6	112	59,8	Longacres, Seattle, Washington, USA	4 Sept 1972
1 mile	1:31.8	39.21	63,10	Soueida (GB)	4	126	57,1	*Brighton, East Sussex	19 Sept 1963
	1:31.8	39.21	63,10	Loose Cover (GB)	3	110	49,8	*Brighton, East Sussex	9 June 1966
	1:32.2	39.04	62,82	Dr Fager (USA)	4	134	60,7	Arlington, Illinois, USA	24 Aug 1968
1¼ miles	1:57.4	38.33	61,68	Double Discount (USA)	4	116	52,6	Santa Anita, Arcadia, California, USA	9 Oct 1977
1½ miles	2:23.0	37.76	60,76	Fiddle Isle (USA)	5	124	56,2	Santa Anita, Arcadia, California, USA	21 Mar 1970
				John Henry (USA)	5	126	57,1	Santa Anita, Arcadia, California, USA	16 Mar 1980
2 miles**	3:15.0	36.93	59,43	Polazel (GB)	3	142	64,4	Salisbury, Wiltshire	8 July 1924
2½ miles	4:14.6	35.35	56,90	Miss Grillo (USA)	6	118	53,5	Pimlico, Baltimore, Maryland, USA	12 Nov 1948
3 miles	5:15.0	34.29	55,18	Farragut (Mexico)	5	113	51,2	Aguascalientes, Mexico	9 Mar 1941

*Epsom and Brighton courses include a sharp descent of ¼ mile.
** A more reliable modern record is 3 min 16.75 sec by Il Tempo (NZ) (7 yr, 130 lb) at Trentham, Wellington, New Zealand on 17 Jan 1970.
† Hand timed.   †† Electrically timed.   ‡ Straight courses.

THE DERBY

For more details see Derby 200 *by Michael Seth-Smith and Roger Mortimer, published by Guinness Superlatives Ltd. (price £5.95).*

The greatest of England's five classics is the Derby Stakes, inaugurated on 4 May 1780, and named after the 12th Earl of Derby (1752–1834). The distance was increased in 1784 from a mile to 1½ miles *2414 m*. The race has been run at Epsom Downs, Surrey, except for the two war periods, when it was run at Newmarket, and is for three-year-olds only. Since 1884 the weights have been: colts 9 st *57 kg 152*, fillies 8 st 9 lb *54 kg 884*. Geldings were eligible until 1904.

Largest and Smallest winning margins
Shergar won the Derby by a record ten lengths in 1981. There have been two dead-heats: in 1828 when *Cadland* beat *The Colonel* in the run-off, and in 1884 between *St Gatien* and *Harvester* (stakes divided).

Longest and shortest odds
Three winners have been returned at odds of 100–1: *Jeddah* (1898), *Signorinetta* (1908) and *Aboyeur* (1913). The shortest priced winner was *Ladas* (1894) at 2–9 and the hottest losing favourite was *Surefoot*, fourth at 40–95 in 1890.

NATIONAL HUNT

For more details see The Guinness Guide to Steeplechasing *by Gerry Cranham, Richard Pitman and John Oaksey, published by Guinness Superlatives Ltd. (price £11.95).*

Jockeys *Most successful*
The only National Hunt jockey to reach 1000 wins is Stan Mellor, MBE (b. Manchester, 10 Apr 1937). This he achieved on *Ouzo* at Nottingham on 18 Dec 1971 and he retired on 18 June 1972 after 1049 wins (incl. 14 abroad) in 20 years. He also won three flat races.

The record number of wins in a season is 149 by John 'Jonjo' O'Neill (b. 13 Apr 1952) in 1977–8. The record number of successive wins is ten by John Alnam Gilbert (b. 26 July 1920), 8–30 Sept 1959. The record number of National Hunt championships is seven by Gerald Wilson (1903–68) from 1933 to 1938 and 1941. Capt Kenyon Goode owned, trained and rode three successive winners under National Hunt rules at Torquay, Devon on 7 Apr 1931.

Trainers *Most successful*
The most first-prize money earned in a season is £235,867 by Peter Easterby in 1980–1. The record number of wins in a season is 114 by Arthur Stephenson in 1969–70. Fred Winter, CBE, won a record seven trainers' championships between 1971 and 1978.

Horse *Greatest winnings*
The greatest amount earned by a British-trained jumper is £154,149 by dual champion hurdler *Sea Pigeon* (foaled 1970) to the end of 1980–1.

GRAND NATIONAL

The first Grand National Steeplechase may be regarded as the Grand Liverpool Steeplechase of 26 Feb 1839 though the race was not given its present name until 1847. It became a handicap in 1843. Until 1930 five-year-olds were eligible, but since then it has been for six-year-olds and above. Except for the two war periods (1916–18 and 1941–5) the race has been run at Aintree, near Liverpool, over a course of 30 jumps.

Most wins
The only horse to win three times is *Red Rum* (foaled 1965) in 1973–4, and 1977. He also came second in 1975 and 1976 from five runs. *Manifesto* ran eight times (1895–1904) and won twice, came third three times and fourth once.

Highest prize
The highest prize and the richest ever under National Hunt rules was £51,324 won by *Aldaniti* ridden by Bob Champion on 4 Apr 1981.

Highest Weight
The highest weight ever carried to victory is 12 st 7 lb (175 lb) *385.8 kg* by *Cloister* (1893), *Manifesto* (1899), *Jerry M* (1912) and *Poethlyn* (1919).

HURLING

Earliest reference
A game of very ancient origin, hurling was included in the Tailteann Games (inst 1829 BC). It only became standardised with the formation of the Gaelic Athletic Association in Thurles, Ireland, on 1 Nov 1884. The Irish Hurling Union was formed on 24 Jan 1879.

Most titles *All-Ireland*
The greatest number of All-Ireland Championships won by one team is 24 by Cork between 1890 and 1978. The greatest number of successive wins is the four by Cork (1941–4).

Most titles *Inter-provincials*
Munster holds the greatest number of inter-provincial (Railway Cup) championships with 34 (1928–77).

Most appearances
The most appearances in All-Ireland finals is ten shared by Christy Ring (Cork and Munster) and John Doyle (Tipperary). They also share the record of All-Ireland medals won with eight each. Ring's appearances on the winning side were in 1941–4,

Tipperary on their way to beating Wexford in the 1965 All-Ireland Hurling Final, with John Doyle (third from the left) gaining his eighth winners' medal. (*Hopkins Photo Agency*)

1946 and 1952–4, while Doyle's were in 1949–51, 1958, 1961–2 and 1964–5. Ring also played in a record 22 inter-provincial finals (1942–63) and was on the winning side 18 times.

Highest scores

The highest score in an All-Ireland final (60 min) was in 1896 when Tipperary (8 goals, 14 points) beat Dublin (no goals, 4 points). The record aggregate score was when Cork (6 goals, 21 points) defeated Wexford (5 goals, 10 points) in the 80 min final of 1970. A goal equals three points.

The highest recorded individual score was by Nick Rackard (Wexford), who scored 7 goals and 7 points against Antrim in the 1954 All Ireland semi-final.

Lowest score

The lowest score in an All-Ireland final was when Tipperary (1 goal, 1 point) beat Galway (nil) in the first championship at Birr in 1887.

Longest stroke

The greatest distance for a 'lift and stroke' is one of 129 yd *117 m* credited to Tom Murphy of Three Castles, Kilkenny, in a 'long puck' contest in 1906. The record for the annual *An Poc Fada* (Long Puck) contest (instituted 1961) in the ravines of the Cooley Hills, north of Dundalk, County Louth, is 65 pucks (drives) plus 87 yd *79 m* over the course of 3 miles 320 yd *5120 km* by Fionnbar O'Neill (Cork) in 1966. This represents an average of 84.8 yd *77,5 m* per drive.

Largest crowd

The largest crowd was 84,856 for the final between Cork and Wexford at Croke Park, Dublin, in 1954.

ICE HOCKEY

Origins

There is pictorial evidence that a hockey-like game (*Kalv*) was played on ice in the early 16th century in The Netherlands. The game was probably first played with a puck in North America in 1855 at Kingston, Ontario, Canada, but Halifax also lays claim to priority. The International Ice Hockey Federation was founded in 1908. The National Hockey League of North America was inaugurated 1917. The World Hockey Association was formed in 1971 and disbanded in 1979.

Olympic Games and World Championships

Canada has won the Olympic Championship six times (1920, 1924, 1928, 1932, 1948 and 1952) and the world title 19 times, the last being at Geneva in 1961. The longest Olympic career is that of Richard Torriani (b. 1 Oct 1911) (Switzerland) from 1928 to 1948. The most gold medals won by any player is three achieved by Vitaliy Davidov, Anatoliy Firssov, Viktor Kuzkin and Aleksandr Ragulin of the USSR teams that won the Olympic titles in 1964, 1968 and 1972. World amateur championships began at Antwerp, Belgium in 1920, and were first opened to professionals in 1976.

Stanley Cup

The Stanley Cup, presented by the Governor-General, Lord Stanley (original cost $48.67), became emblematic of National Hockey League supremacy 33 years after the first contest at Montreal in 1893. It has been won most often by the Montreal Canadiens with 22 wins in 1916, 1924, 1930–1, 1944, 1946, 1953, 1956–60, 1965–6, 1968–9, 1971, 1973, 1976–9.

British Competitions

The defunct English (later British) League championship (inst. 1934) was won most often by the Wembley Lions with four victories in 1936–7, 1952 and 1957. Murrayfield Racers have won the Northern League (inst. 1966) six times, 1970–2, 1976, 1979 and 1980. Streatham Redskins have won the Southern League (inst. 1970) four times, 1975–8. The Icy Smith Cup (first held 1966), emblematic of British club supremacy, has been won by Murrayfield Racers nine times, 1966, 1969–72, 1975 and 1979–81.

Most goals *Team*

The greatest number of goals recorded in a world championship match has been 47–0 when Canada beat Denmark in Stockholm, Sweden on 12 Feb 1949. The National Hockey League record is 21 goals when Montreal Canadiens beat Toronto St Patrick's, at Montreal, 14–7 on 10 Jan 1920.

Most goals *Individual*

The most goals scored in a season in the NHL is 76 by Phil Esposito (b. 20 Feb 1942) (Boston Bruins) on a record 550 shots in the 1970–1 season. The most NHL goals in one season *including* playoffs is 85 by Mike Bossy (b. 22 Jan 1957) (New York Islanders) in 1980–1. The most points in a season is 164, a record

above: The Knights of Columbus team from Kamloops, British Columbia, who averaged a goal every 20 seconds against their Prince George rivals.

below: Natalia Petruseva has added two world records to the Olympic gold medal she won at Lake Placid in 1980. (*Tony Duffy, All-Sport*)

average of better than two points per game, by Wayne Gretzky (b. 26 Jan 1961) (Edmonton Oilers), on 55 goals and a record 109 assists in 1980–1. Including the playoffs, his record assist and point totals are 123 and 185 respectively. The North American career record for goals is 1071 (801 in the NHL) by Gordie Howe (b. 31 Mar 1928) (Detroit Red Wings, Houston Aeros, New England Whalers and Hartford Whalers) from 16 Oct 1946 in 32 seasons ending in 1979–80. He took 2204 games to achieve the 1000th goal, but Robert Marvin 'Bobby' Hull, OC (b. 3 Jan 1939) (Chicago Black Hawks and Winnipeg Jets) scored his 1000th in 1600 games on 12 Mar 1978.

Most goals *British*

The highest score and aggregate in a League match has been 34–0 when Streatham beat Deeside Dragons on 1 Nov 1975. The most individual goals scored in a senior League game is 13 by John Hudson for Durham Wasps *v.* Paisley Mohawks on 20 Feb 1977.

Fastest scoring *World*

In major leagues the fastest goal was after 4 sec in the second period by Joseph Antoine Claude Provost (b. 17 Sept 1933) (Montreal Canadiens) *v.* Boston Bruins at Montreal on 9 Nov 1957. Canadian William George 'Bill' Wilson (b. 8 May 1919) (Tulsa Oilers) scored three goals in 20 sec *v.* Fort Worth Rangers at Tulsa, Oklahoma, USA on 22 Nov 1945. Toronto scored eight goals in 4 min 52 sec *v.* New York Americans on 19 Mar 1938.

In minor leagues, Kim D. Miles scored in 3 sec for Univ of Guelph *v.* Univ of W Ontario on 11 Feb 1975. Three goals in 13 sec was achieved by Gregory Kueneman for Hanover *v.* Kincardine at Hanover, Ontario, Canada on 13 Feb 1978. The Kamloops Knights of Columbus scored seven goals in 2 min 22 sec *v.* Prince George Vikings on 25 Jan 1980.

Fastest scoring *Great Britain*

Kenny Westman (Nottingham Panthers) scored a hat trick in 30 sec *v.* Brighton Tigers on 3 Mar 1955.

Most points one game

The North American major league record for most points scored in one game is ten (3 goals, 7 assists) by Jim Harrison (b. 9 Jul 1947) (for Alberta, later Edmonton Oilers) in a WHA match at Edmonton on 30 Jan 1973, and by Darryl Sittler (b. 18 Sep 1950) (6 goals, 4 assists) for Toronto Maple Leafs in a NHL match at Toronto on 7 Feb 1976. In Britain, Richard Bacon scored 15 (10 goals, 5 assists) for Streatham *v.* Deeside on 1 Nov 1975.

Most successful goaltending

The most matches played by a goaltender without conceding a goal is 103 by Terrance 'Terry' Gordon Sawchuck (b. 28 Dec 1929) of Detroit Red Wings, Boston Bruins, Toronto Maple Leafs, Los Angeles Kings and New York Rangers, between 1950 and 1967. Gerry Cheevers (b. 2 Dec 1940), Boston Bruins, went a record 33 games without defeat in 1971–2.

Fastest player

The highest speed measured for any player is 29.7 mph *47,7 km/h* for Bobby Hull. The highest puck speed is also attributed to Hull, whose left-handed slap shot has been timed at 118.3 mph *190,3 km/h.*

Longest match

The longest match was 2 hr 56 min 30 sec (playing time) when Detroit Red Wings beat Montreal Maroons 1–0 in the sixth period of overtime at the Forum, Montreal, at 2.25 a.m. on 25 Mar 1936. Norm Smith, the Red Wings goaltender, turned aside 92 shots for the NHL's longest single shutout.

ICE SKATING

Origins

The earliest reference to ice skating is in early Scandinavian literature referring to the 2nd century though its origins are believed, on archaeological evidence, to be ten centuries earlier still. The earliest English account of 1180 refers to skates made of bone. The earliest known illustration is a Dutch woodcut of 1498. The earliest skating club was the Edinburgh Skating Club formed in 1742. The first recorded race was from Wisbech to Whittlesea, East Anglia, in 1763. The earliest artificial ice rink in the world was opened at the Baker Street Bazaar, Portman Square, London, on 7 Dec 1842. The National Skating Association of Great Britain was founded in 1879. The International Skating Union was founded at Scheveningen, Netherlands in 1892.

FIGURE SKATING

Most titles *Olympic*

The most Olympic gold medals won by a figure skater is three by Gillis Gråafstrom (1893–1938) of Sweden in 1920, 1924, and 1928 (also silver medal in 1932); by Sonja Henie (1912–69) of Norway in 1928, 1932 and 1936; and by Irina Rodnina (b. USSR 12 Sept 1949) in the Pairs event in 1972, 1976, and 1980.

Most titles *World*

The greatest number of individual world figure skating titles (instituted 1896) is ten by Ulrich Salchow (1877–1949) of Sweden, in 1901–5 and 1907–11. The women's record (instituted 1906) is also ten individual titles by Sonja Henie between 1927 and 1936. Irina Rodnina has won ten pairs titles (inst. 1908), four with Aleksiy Ulanov (b. 4 Nov 1947) 1969–72, and six with her husband Aleksandr Zaitsev (b. 16 June 1952) 1973–8. Most ice dance titles (inst. 1950) won is six by Aleksandr Gorshkov (b. 8 Dec 1946) and Ludmila Pakhomova (b. 31 Dec 1946) (USSR) 1970–4 and 1976.

Most titles *British*

The most individual British titles is 11 by Jack Page (1900–47) (Manchester SC) in 1922–31 and 1933, and six by Cecilia Colledge (b. 28 Nov 1920) (Park Lane FSC, London) in 1935–7 (two), 1938 and 1946. Page also won nine pairs titles, 1923–31.

Triple Crown

The only British skater to win the 'Grand Slam' of World, Olympic and European titles in the same year is John Anthony Curry, OBE (b. 9 Sept 1949) in 1976.

Karl Schäfer (Austria) (1909–76) and Sonja Henie achieved double 'Grand Slams', both in the years 1932 and 1936.

Highest marks

The highest number of maximum six marks awarded for one performance in an international championship was 12 to Alek-

After three Olympic victories and ten world titles, Sonja Henie became one of the highest paid film stars in Hollywood. The city of Oslo has a museum in her honour. (*Sonje Henie og Niels Onstads Stiftelser*)

sandr Zaitsev and Irina Rodnina (USSR) in the European pairs in Cologne, W. Germany on 7 Feb 1978. The most by a soloist was seven to Donald Jackson (b. 2 Apr 1940) (Canada) in the world men's championship at Prague, Czechoslovakia, in 1962.

Most difficult jump

The first ever triple Axel jump in competition was by Vern Taylor (b. 1 Mar 1958) (Canada) in the World Championships at Ottawa on 10 Mar 1978. The quadruple twist lift has been performed by only one pair, Sergei Shakrai (b. 28 June 1958) and Marina Tcherkasova (b. 17 Nov 1964), of USSR, in an international championship, at Helsinki, on 26 Jan 1977. They also were the first skaters to accomplish simultaneous triple jumps at that level, at Strasbourg, France on 1 Feb 1978.

SPEED SKATING WORLD OUTDOOR RECORDS	Distance	min sec	Name and Country	Place	Date
MEN	500 metres	36.91	Evgeni Kulikov (USSR)	Medeo, USSR	28 Mar 1981
	1000 metres	1:13.39	Gaetan Boucher (Canada)	Davos, Switzerland	31 Jan 1981
	1500 metres	1:54.79	Eric Heiden (USA)	Davos, Switzerland	19 Jan 1980
	3000 metres	4:04.06	Dmitrij Ogloblin (USSR)	Medeo, USSR	28 Mar 1979
	5000 metres	6:56.90	Kay Arne Stenshjemmet (Norway)	Medeo, USSR	29 Mar 1980
	10,000 metres	14:26.71	Dmitrij Ogloblin (USSR)	Medeo, USSR	29 Mar 1980
WOMEN	500 metres	40.18	Christa Rothenburger (E. Germany)	Medeo, USSR	28 Mar 1981
	1000 metres	1:20.81	Natalia Petruseva (USSR)	Medeo, USSR	28 Mar 1981
	1500 metres	2:05.39	Natalia Petruseva (USSR)	Medeo, USSR	27 Mar 1981
	3000 metres	4:21.70	Gaby Schönbrunn (E. Germany)	Medeo, USSR	28 Mar 1981

BRITISH OUTDOOR RECORDS	Distance	min sec	Name	Place	Date
MEN	500 metres	39.41	Archie Marshall	Davos, Switzerland	20 Jan 1980
	1000 metres	1:19.23	Archie Marshall	Davos, Switzerland	20 Jan 1980
	1500 metres	2:05.99	Steve Pearce	Madonna di Campiglio, Italy	16 Jan 1977
	3000 metres	4:27.53	Geoff Sandys	Madonna di Campiglio, Italy	10 Jan 1978
	5000 metres	7:35.42	Geoff Sandys	Inzell, W. Germany	6 Jan 1977
	10,000 metres	15:45.45	Geoff Sandys	Innsbruck, Austria	9 Jan 1980
WOMEN	500 metres	46.53	Kim Ferran	Inzell, W. Germany	5 Jan 1980
	1000 metres	1:31.85	Kim Ferran	Madonna di Campiglio, Italy	10 Jan 1979
	1500 metres	2:21.86	Amanda Horsepool	Inzell, W. Germany	27 Dec 1980
	3000 metres	4:54.74	Kim Ferran	Inzell, W. Germany	6 Jan 1979

Largest rink
The world's largest indoor ice rink is in the Moscow Olympic indoor arena which has an ice area of 8064 m² *86,800 ft²*. The largest artificial outdoor rink is the quintuple complex of the Fujikyu Highland Promenade Rink, Japan (opened 1967) with an area of 26 500 m² *285,244 ft²*.

Marathon
The longest recorded skating marathon is one of 109 hr 5 min by Austin McKinley, of Christchurch, New Zealand on 21–25 June 1977.

SPEED SKATING
Most titles *Olympic*
The most Olympic gold medals won in speed skating is six by Lidia Skoblikova (b. 8 Mar 1939) of Chelyabinsk, USSR, in 1960 (two) and 1964 (four). The male record is by Clas Thunberg (1893–1973) (Finland) with five gold (including one tied), and also one silver and one tied bronze in 1924 and 1928. Eric Heiden (USA) (b. 14 June 1958) also won five gold medals, all at Lake Placid, NY, USA, in 1980.

Most titles *World*
The greatest number of world overall titles (instituted 1893) won by any skater is five by Oscar Mathisen (Norway) (1888–1954) in 1908–9 and 1912–14, and Clas Thunberg in 1923, 1925, 1928–9 and 1931. The most titles won by a woman is four by Inga Voronina (*née* Artomonova) (1936–66) of Moscow, USSR, in 1957, 1958, 1962 and 1964 and Atje Keulen-Deelstra (b. 31 Dec 1938) (Netherlands) 1970, 1972–4.

The record score achieved in the world overall title is 162,973 points by Eric Heiden (USA) at Oslo, Norway, 10–11 Feb 1979.

Longest race
The longest race regularly held is the 'Elfstedentocht' ('Tour of the Eleven Towns') in the Netherlands. It covers 200 km *124 miles 483 yd* and the fastest time is 7 hr 35 min by Jeen van den Berg (b. 8 Jan 1928) on 3 Feb 1954.

ICE AND SAND YACHTING

Origins
The sport originated in the Low Countries from the year 1600 (earliest patent granted) and along the Baltic coast. The earliest authentic record is Dutch, dating from 1768. Land or sand yachts of Dutch construction were first reported on beaches (now in Belgium) in 1595. The earliest International championship was staged in 1914.

Christian Nau and *Mobil*, in which he set a world speed record of 107 km/h *66.48 mph* on the sands of Le Touquet. (*Mobil Oil Co Ltd*)

Highest speeds *Ice*
The largest known ice yacht was *Icicle*, built for Commodore John E. Roosevelt for racing on the Hudson River, New York, in 1869. It was 68 ft 11 in *21 m* long and carried 1070 ft² *99 m²* of canvas. The highest speed officially recorded is 143 mph *230 km/h* by John D. Buckstaff in a Class A stern-steerer on Lake Winnebago, Wisconsin, USA, in 1938. Such a speed is possible in a wind of 72 mph *115 km/h*.

Highest speeds *Sand*
The official world record for a sand yacht is 107 km/h *66.48 mph* set by Christian Yves Nau (France) in *Mobil* at Le Touquet, France on 22 Mar 1981. A speed of 88.4 mph *142,26 km/h* was attained by Nord Embroden of USA in *Midnight at the Oasis* at Superior Dry Lake, California, USA on 15 Apr 1976.

INDOOR PASTIMES

CHESS
Origins
The game originated in ancient India under the name Chaturanga (literally 'four-corps' – an army game). The name chess is derived from the Persian word *shah* (a king or ruler). The earliest reference is from the Middle Persian Karnamak (c. AD 590–628), though in December 1972, two ivory chessmen were found in the Uzbek Soviet Republic dateable to AD 200. It reached Britain in c. 1255. The *Fédération Internationale des Echecs* was established in 1924. There were an estimated 7,000,000 competitive players in the USSR in 1973.

Most World titles
World champions have been generally recognised since 1886. The longest undisputed tenure was 27 years by Dr Emanuel Lasker (1868–1941) of Germany, from 1894 to 1921. The women's world championship was held by Vera Menchik-Stevenson (1906–44) (USSR, later GB) from 1927 till her death, and was successfully defended a record seven times. Nona Gaprindashvili (USSR) (b. 3 May 1941) held the title from 1962 to 1978 and defended successfully four times. Robert J. 'Bobby' Fischer (b. Chicago, Illinois, USA, 9 Mar 1943) is reckoned on the officially adopted Elo System to be the greatest Grand Master of all-time with a 2785 rating. The USSR has won the men's team title a record 13 times and the women's title eight times.

Youngest and Oldest
The youngest World champion was Mikhail Nekhemevich Tal (USSR) (b. 9 Nov 1936) when he took the title on 7 May 1960 aged 23 yr 180 days. The oldest was Wilhelm Steinitz (1836–1900) who was 58 yr old when he lost his title to Lasker in 1894.

Most British titles
Most British titles have been won by Dr Jonathan Penrose, OBE (b. 7 Oct 1933) of East Finchley, London with ten titles in 1958–63, 1966–9. Rowena Mary Bruce (*née* Dew) (b. 15 May 1919) of Plymouth, Devon won 11 titles between 1937 and 1969. The first British player to attain official International Grand Master status was Anthony Miles (b. 23 Apr 1955), on 24 Feb 1976.

Winning streak
Bobby Fischer won 20 games in succession in Grand Master chess from 2 Dec 1970 to 30 Sept 1971. From 1966 to December 1977 Anatoli Evgenyevich Karpov (USSR) (b. 23 May 1951) lost only 4.3 per cent of his 597 games.

Most opponents
Vlastimil Hort (b. 12 Jan 1944) (Czechoslovakia), in Seltjarnes, Iceland on 23–24 Apr 1977, played 550 opponents including a record 201 simultaneously. He only lost ten games. The record for most consecutive games played is held by Branimir Brebrich (Canada) who played 575 games (533 wins, 27 draws, 15 losses) in Edmonton, Alberta on 27–28 Jan 1978, during 28 hr of play. Georges Koltanowski (Belgium, now of USA) (b. 17 Sept 1903) tackled 56 opponents 'blindfold', won 50, and drew six in 9¾ hr at the Fairmont Hotel, San Francisco, California, USA, on 13 Dec 1960.

Slowest and longest games
The slowest reported move (before modern rules) was one of

11 hr between Paul Charles Morphy, (1837–84) the US Champion, and the German chess master Louis Paulsen (1833–91). Grandmaster Friedrich Sämisch (1896–1975) (Germany) ran out of the allotted time (2½ hr for 45 moves) after only 12 moves, in Prague, Czechoslovakia, in 1938.

The Master game with most moves on record was when Yedael Stepak (Israel) (b. 21 Aug 1940) beat Yaakov Mashian (Iran, later Israel) (b. 17 Dec 1943) in 193 moves in Tel Aviv, Israel on 23 Mar–16 Apr 1980. The total playing time was a record 24½ hr.

Marathon

The longest recorded session is one of 168 hr by Stan Zygmunt and Ilya Schwartzman at the 45th Avenue Shopping Centre, Munster, Indiana, USA on 28 Dec 1979–4 Jan 1980.

CONTRACT BRIDGE

Origins

Bridge (a corruption of Biritch) is thought to be either of Levantine origin, similar games having been played there in the early 1870s, or to have come from the East—probably India.

Auction Bridge (highest bidder names trump) was invented *c.* 1902. The contract principle, present in several games (notably the French game *Plafond, c.* 1917) was introduced to Bridge by Harold S. Vanderbilt (USA) on 1 Nov 1925 during a Caribbean voyage aboard the *SS Finland*. It became a world-wide craze after the USA *v.* Great Britain challenge match between Romanian-born Ely Culbertson (1891–1955) and Lt-Col Walter Thomas More Buller (1887–1938) at Almack's Club, London, in September 1930. The USA won the 200 hand match by 4845 points.

Most World titles

The World Championship (Bermuda Bowl) has been won most often by Italy's Blue Team (*Squadra Azzurra*), 1957–9, 1961–3, 1965–7, 1969, 1973–5, whose team also won the Olympiad in 1964, 1968 and 1972. Giorgio Belladonna (b. 1923) was in all these winning teams.

HIGHEST POSSIBLE SCORES: BRIDGE

Opponents bid 7 of any suit or 7 No Trumps doubled and redoubled and vulnerable

	Opponents make no trick	
Above Line	1st undertrick	400
	12 subsequent undertricks at 600 each	7200
	All Honours	150
		7750

Bid 1 No Trump, doubled and redoubled, vulnerable

Below Line	1st trick (40 × 4)	160
Above Line	6 over tricks (400 × 6)	2400
	2nd game of 2-Game Rubber	*350
	All Honours	150
	Bonus for making redoubled contract	50
	(Highest Possible Positive Score)	3110

* In practice, the full bonus of 700 points is awarded after the completion of the second winning game rather than 350 after each game.

Most master points

In the latest ranking list based on Master Points awarded by the World Bridge Federation, the leading male player in the world was Giorgio Belladonna a member of Italy's Blue Team with 1767 points, followed by five more Italians. The leading Briton is Boris Schapiro (b. 22 Aug 1909) in 17th place with 353 points. The world's leading woman player is Dorothy Hayden Truscott (USA) with 318 points, followed by Rika 'Rixi' Markus, MBE (Austria, later GB) with 269 points.

Most brilliant play

Richard Cummings (Australia) was awarded the Bols Brilliancy Prize by the International Bridge Press Association, for the most outstanding play at the World Bridge Olympiad in 1980.

Perfect deals

The mathematical odds against dealing 13 cards of one suit are 158,753,389,899 to 1, while the odds against receiving a 'perfect hand' consisting of all 13 spades are 635,013,559,596 to 1. The odds against each of the four players receiving a complete suit (a 'perfect deal') are 2,235,197,406,895,366,368,301,559,999 to 1.

Marathon

The longest recorded session is one of 180 hr by four students at Edinburgh University, Scotland on 21–28 Apr 1972.

CRIBBAGE

Origins

The invention of the game (once called Cribbidge) is credited to the English dramatist Sir John Suckling (1609–42). It is estimated that some ten million people play in the United States alone.

Rare hands

F. Art Skinner, of Alberta, Canada is reported to have had three maximum 29 point hands. Paul Nault of Athol, Mass, USA had two such hands within eight games in a tournament on 19 Mar 1977. At Blackpool, Lancashire, Derek Hearne dealt two hands of six clubs with the turn-up the remaining club on 8 Feb 1976. Bill Rogers of Burnaby, BC, Canada scored 29 in the crib in 1975.

Marathon

Nick Whitechurch and John Dudley played for 109 hr at the Chequers Inn, Bath, Avon on 12–17 Apr 1981.

DARTS

Further information can be obtained from the Guinness Book of Darts *by Derek Brown, published by Guinness Superlatives Ltd at £7.50*

Origins

The origins of darts date from the use by archers of heavily weighted ten-inch throwing arrows for self-defence in close quarters fighting. The 'dartes' were used in Ireland in the 16th century and darts was played on the *Mayflower* by the Plymouth pilgrims in 1620. The modern game dates from at least 1896 when Brian Gamlin of Bury, Lancashire, is credited with inventing the present numbering system on the board. The first recorded score of 180 was by John Reader at the Highbury Tavern in Sussex in 1902. Today there are an estimated 6,000,000 dart players in the British Isles.

Most titles

Re-instituted in 1947, the annual *News of the World* individual Championships consist of the best of three legs 501 up, 'straight' start and finish on a double with an 8 ft *2,4 m* throwing distance. The only men to win twice are Tommy Gibbons (Ivanhoe Working Men's Club) of Conisbrough, South Yorkshire, in 1952 and 1958; Tom Reddington (b. 1922) of New Inn, Stonebroom, Derbyshire in 1955 and of George Hotel, Alfreton, Derbyshire 1960, Tom M. Barrett (1909–81) (Odco Sports Club, London) in 1964 and 1965; and Stefan Lord (b. 1954) of the Stockholm Super Darts Club, Sweden in 1978 and 1980.

The National Darts Association of Great Britain Individual title was won by Tom O'Regan of the Northern Star, New Southgate, Greater London in 1970–2.

Eric Bristow (b. 1957) has won the World Masters Championships (inst 1974) twice, in 1977 and 1979. He has also won the World Professional Championship (inst 1978) twice, in 1980 and 1981.

Barbara Higgs, of the Brunswick Arms, Reading has won the Landladies Trophy of the Courage Darts League (Reading) 19 times, 1958–80.

Longest unbeaten run

Mike Bowell (b. 31 May 1947) of Paulton Darts League, Avon, won 152 successive competition games from 9 Feb 1971 to 29 Nov 1974.

Fastest match

The fastest time taken for a match of three games of 301 is 1 min 58 sec by Ricky Fusco (GB) at the Perivale Residents Association Club, Middlesex, on 30 Dec 1976.

Fastest 'round the board'

The record time for going round the board clockwise in 'doubles' at arm's length is 9.2 sec by Dennis Gower at the Millers

High scoring Scrabble® champion, Philip Nelkon, an accountant from North London, with the cup he won for the second time in 1981. (*Daily Telegraph*)

Arms, Hastings, East Sussex on 12 Oct 1975 and 14.5 sec in numerical order by Jim Pike (1903–60) at the Craven Club, Newmarket in March 1944. The record for this feat at the 9 ft 2,7 m throwing distance, retrieving own darts, is 2 min 13 sec by Bill Duddy (b. 1932) at The Plough, Harringey, London on 29 Oct 1972.

Least darts

Scores of 201 in four darts, 301 in six darts, 401 in seven darts and 501 in nine darts, have been achieved on various occasions. The lowest number of darts thrown for a score of 1001 is 19 by Cliff Inglis (b. 1935) (160, 180, 140, 180, 121, 180, 40) at the Bromfield Men's Club, Devon on 11 Nov 1975. A score of 2001 in 52 darts was achieved by Alan Evans (b. 1949) at Ferndale, Glamorgan on 3 Sept 1976. 3001 in 79 darts was thrown by Charlie Ellix (b. 1941) at The Victoria Hotel, Tottenham, London on 29 April 1977.

Ten hour scores

The record number of trebles scored in 10 hr is 2190 by Corporal David Leslie Bentley (b. 25 July 1947) at RAF Stanmore Park, Middlesex on 1 Mar 1980. On 19 Mar 1978 Nick Korn scored a record 2814 doubles (out of 9285 darts) in 10 hr at Newquay, Cornwall. The greatest score amassed in 10 hr is 487,588 by Bruce Campbell and Peter Dawson at the Waikiki Hotel, Safety Bay, Western Australia, on 14 Oct 1978.

24 hr scores

Eight players from the Royal Hotel, Newsome, Huddersfield scored 1,358,731 in 24 hr on one board on 26–27 May 1981.

Million and one up

Eight players from The Sir John Barleycorn, Bitterne, Hampshire scored 1,000,001 with 39,566 darts in one session from 4–6 Apr 1980.

Marathon

John Yates, Stuart Neie, Quentin Smith and Nigel Lucas played doubles for 116 hr at Chigwell School, Essex on 8–13 Jan 1981.

DOMINOES
Origins

The National Museum in Baghdad, Iraq contains artifacts from Ur called 'dominoes' dated *c.* 2450 BC. Though unknown in Europe in *c.* 1750, the game reached England *via* France *c.* 1795. The Eskimo game requires 148 pieces while that in Europe utilises only 28.

Marathon

The longest session is 123 hr 4 min by Alan Mannering and David Harrison of Stoke on Trent, Staffs, on 8–13 Feb 1978.

DRAUGHTS
Origins

Draughts, known as checkers in North America, has origins earlier than chess. It was played in Egypt in the second millennium BC. The earliest book on the game was by Antonio Torquemada of Valencia, Spain in 1547. There have been three US *v.* Great Britain international matches (crossboard) 1905, 1927 and 1973 two won by the United States and one by Great Britain.

The British Championship (biennial) was inaugurated in 1926 The only man to win five titles has been Jim Marshall (Fife) in 1948, 1950, 1952, 1954 and 1966. Melvin Pomeroy (US), was internationally undefeated from 1914 until his death in 1933.

Most opponents

Newell W. Banks (b. Detroit, USA, 10 Oct 1887) played 140 games simultaneously, winning 133 and drawing seven, in Chicago, Illinois in 1933. His playing time was 145 min, so averaging about one move per sec. In 1947 he played blindfold for 4 hr per day for 45 consecutive days, winning 1331 games, drawing 54 and losing only two, while playing six games at a time. Patrick Moore, OBE (b. 4 Mar 1923) played 149 games simultaneously, at Twickenham, Greater London on 30 May 1981, winning 118 losing 27 and drawing four.

Longest and shortest games

In competition the prescribed rate of play is not less than 30 moves per hour with the average game lasting about 90 min. In 1958 a match between Dr Marion Tinsley (US) and Derek Oldbury (GB) lasted 7½ hr. The shortest possible game is one of 20 moves composed by Alan M. Beckerson (b. 21 Feb 1938) (GB) on 2 Nov 1977.

MONOPOLY ®
Origins

The patentee of Monopoly ® the world's most popular proprietary board game of which Parker Brothers has sold in excess of 80,000,000 copies, was Charles Darrow (1889–1967). He invented the patented version of the game in 1933, while an unemployed heating engineer, using the street names of Atlantic City New Jersey where he spent his vacations.

Marathon

The longest game by four players ratified by Parker Brothers is 408 hr by Peter Callon, Paul Taplin, John Cresswell and Lesley De Wahl of Shanklin, Isle of Wight on 5–22 Feb 1981.

SCRABBLE ® Crossword Game
Origins

The crossword game was invented by Alfred M. Butts in 1931 and was developed, refined and trademarked as Scrabble ® Crossword Game by James Brunot in 1948. He sold the North American rights to Selchow & Richter Company, New York the European rights to J. W. Spears & Sons, London, and the Australian rights to Murfett Pty Ltd, Melbourne.

Highest scores

The highest competitive league game score is 774 by Allan Simmons (GB) on 1 July 1981. His opponent scored 285. The highest competitive single turn score recorded is 380.

Most titles

British National Championships were instituted in 1971. Olive Behan, 1972 and 1975, and Philip Nelkon, 1978 and 1981, have both won twice. The highest score in the Championship has been 1551 (three games total) by Philip Nelkon in 1981.

Marathon

The longest Scrabble ® Crossword Game is 120 hr by Norman Hazeldean, Alan Giles, Tom Barton and Keith Ollett at Uckfield, East Sussex, on 4–9 Aug 1975, and Mark Morris, Jean Pierre Burdinat, Robert Emmanuel and Gary Dolton in Sydney Australia on 27 Aug–1 Sept 1975.

TABLE FOOTBALL

Sean and Roger Connolly played for 42 hr 38 min at Warrenpoint, Co. Down, N. Ireland on 24–26 Apr 1981.

TIDDLYWINKS

Origins

This game was only espoused by adults in 1955 when Cambridge University issued a challenge to Oxford.

National Championships

Alan Dean (Southampton) (b. 22 July 1949) has won the singles title a record five times, 1971–3, 1976, 1978. He has also won the pairs title three times. Jonathan Mapley (b. 1947) has won the pairs title a record four times, 1972, 1975, 1977, and 1980.

Guinness Trophy

England has remained unbeaten against Scotland, Ireland and Wales since the Trophy's inception on 7 May 1960. The closest result has been their 59½–52½ win over Wales at Warwick on 7 Apr 1968.

Silver Wink Trophy

The *Silver Wink*, presented by HRH The Duke of Edinburgh, for the British University championship has been won a record six times by Cambridge University to 1979.

Speed records

The record for potting 24 winks from 18 in *45 cm* is 21.8 sec by Stephen Williams (Altrincham Grammar School) in May 1966. Allen R. Astles (University of Wales) potted 10,000 winks in 3 hr 51 min 46 sec at Aberystwyth, Cardiganshire in February 1966.

Four pot relay

The greatest number of winks potted in 3 min by a relay of four is 29 by Paul Light, Paul Hoffman, Andrew James and Geoff Thorpe at 'The Castle', Cambridge on 6 Dec 1974.

Marathon

The longest game on record is 300 hr by six players from the Southampton University Tiddlywinks Club, Hampshire, on 20 Feb–5 March 1981.

WHIST

Origins

Whist, first referred to in 1529 (as *trump*), was the world's premier card game until 1930. The rules were standardised in 1742.

Highest score

The highest score claimed for 24 hands is 209 by Mrs E. Heslop in the Shaldon Over 60 Club, Teignmouth, Devon on 5 Jan 1973 and by Mrs A. Lulham at Hurstmonceux, East Sussex, on 21 Jan 1978.

JUDO

Origins

Judo is a modern combat sport which developed out of an amalgam of several old (pre-Christian era) Japanese fighting arts, the most popular of which was ju-jitsu (jiu-jitsu), which is thought to be of pre-Christian Chinese origin. Judo has greatly developed since 1882, when it was first devised by Dr Jigoro Kano (1860–1938).

Most titles *World and Olympic*

World championships were inaugurated in Tōkyō on 5 May 1956. Two men have won four world titles, Wilhelm Ruska (b. 29 Aug 1940) (Netherlands), 1967, 1971 Heavyweight and the 1972 Olympic Heavyweight and Open titles, and Shozo Fujii (Japan) (b. 12 May 1950), the Middleweight title 1971, 1973, 1975, and 1979. In the European championships (instituted in 1951) only Great Britain (1957–9) and the USSR (1972–4) have won three consecutive team titles.

Most titles *British*

The greatest number of titles (inst. 1966) won is nine by David Colin Starbrook, MBE (b. 9 Aug 1945) (5th dan) who won the Middleweight title 1969–70, the Light-heavyweight 1971–5 and the Open division 1970–1. The women's championships were instituted in 1971. Christine Child (b. 1946) (5th dan) has won a record six times: the Heavyweight in 1971–5 and the Open division in 1973.

Highest grades

The efficiency grades in Judo are divided into pupil (*kyu*) and master (*dan*) grades. The highest awarded is the extremely rare red belt *Judan* (10th dan), given only to seven men so far. The highest awarded to a woman is 6th dan, achieved by three Japanese women. The Judo protocol provides for an 11th dan (*Juichidan*) who also would wear a red belt, a 12th dan (*Junidan*) who would wear a white belt twice as wide as an ordinary belt and the highest of all, *Shihan*, but these have never been bestowed. The highest British native Judo grades are 8th dan by Charles Stuart Palmer, OBE (b. 1930).

Marathon

The longest recorded continuous Judo marathon, by two of six Judoka in 5 min stints, is 216 hr by the Wanganui Judo Club, New Zealand on 29 Aug–7 Sept 1980.

KARATE

Origins

Based on techniques devised from the sixth century Chinese art of Shaolin boxing (Kempo), Karate was developed by an unarmed populace in Okinawa as a weapon against armed Japanese oppressors *c.* 1500. Transmitted to Japan in the 1920s by Funakoshi Gichin, this method of combat was refined into Karate and organised into a sport with competitive rules. The five major styles of Karate in Japan are: *Shotokan*, *Wado-ryu*, *Goju-ryu*, *Shito-ryu* and *Kyokushinkai*, each of which place different emphasis on speed and power, etc. Other styles include *Sankukai*, *Shotokai* and *Shukokai*. The military form of *Tae kwon-do* with nine dans is a Korean equivalent of Karate. *Wu shu* is a comprehensive term embracing all Chinese martial arts. *Kung fu* is one aspect of these arts popularised by the cinema. (See also p. 187).

The Governing Body for the sport in Britain is the Martial Arts Commission upon which all the martial arts are represented.

Great Britain became the first country ever to defeat the Japanese in competition when they beat them in the 1972 World championships in Paris. They repeated the feat in the final of the 1975 World championships at Long Beach, California, USA and during the 1977 World championships in Tōkyō.

Most titles

The only winner of three All-Japanese titles has been Takeshi Oishi who won in 1969–71. David 'Ticky' Donovan (6th dan) has won the British title on three consecutive occasions 1973–5.

Top exponents

The leading exponents among karatekas are a number of 10th dans in Japan. The leading exponents in the United Kingdom are Tatsuo Suzuki (8th dan, *Wado-ryu*) (b. 27 Apr 1928) chief instructor to the European Karatedo Wadokai; Keinosuke Enoeda (8th dan, *Shotokan*), resident instructor to the Karate Union of Great Britain and Steve Arneil (7th dan, *Kyokushinkai*) British national born in South Africa.

LACROSSE

Origins

The game is of American Indian origin, derived from the intertribal game *baggataway*, and was played before 1492 by Iroquois Indians in lower Ontario, Canada and upper New York State, USA. The French named it after their game of *Chouler à la crosse*, known in 1381. It was introduced into Great Britain in 1867. The English Lacrosse Union was formed in 1892. It was included in the Olympic Games of 1908 and featured as an exhibition sport in the 1928 and 1948 Games.

Most titles *World*

The United States won the first two World Championships in 1967 and 1974. Canada won the third in 1978 beating the USA 17–16 after extra time—this was the first drawn international match.

Most titles *English*

The English Club Championship (Iroquois Cup), instituted in

1890, has been won most often by Stockport with 15 wins between 1897 and 1934. The record score in a final was in 1979 when Cheadle beat Buckhurst Hill, 28–6.

Highest scores

The highest score in any international match was the United States' 28–4 win over Canada at Stockport, Greater Manchester on 3 July 1978. England's highest score was their 19–11 win over Canada at Melbourne in 1974. The highest score in the annual North of England v. South of England match was when the North won 29–9 in 1980.

Most international appearances *Men*

The record number of international representations is 26 for England by James Michael 'Mike' Roberts (Urmston) (b. 22 Feb 1946), to 1978. He is the only person to play in all three World Championships.

Most international appearances *Women*

The record for women is 52 for Scotland by Caro MacIntosh (b. 18 Feb 1932), 1952–69.

Fastest scoring

Rod Burns scored only 4 sec into the game for South Manchester and Wythenshawe v. Sheffield Univ. on 6 Dec 1975.

LAWN TENNIS

Origins

The modern game is generally agreed to have evolved as an outdoor form of the indoor game of Tennis (see separate entry). 'Field Tennis' is mentioned in an English magazine—*Sporting Magazine*—of 29 Sept 1793. The earliest club for such a game, variously called Pelota or Lawn Rackets, was the Leamington Club founded in 1872 by Major Harry Gem. The earliest attempt to commercialise the game was by Major Walter Clopton Wingfield, MVO (1833–1912) who patented a form called 'sphairistike' on 23 Feb 1874. It soon became called Lawn Tennis. Amateur players were permitted to play with and against professionals in 'Open' tournaments in 1968.

Greatest domination

The grand slam is to hold at the same time all four of the world's major championship singles: Wimbledon, the United States, Australian and French championships. The first man to have won all four was Frederick John Perry (GB) (b. 18 May 1909) with the French title in 1935. The first man to hold all four championships simultaneously was John Donald Budge (USA) (b. 13 June 1915) with the French title in 1938. The first man to achieve the grand slam twice was Rodney George Laver, MBE (Australia) (b. 9 Aug 1938) having won in 1962 as an amateur and again in 1969 when the titles were 'open' to professionals.

Only two women have achieved the grand slam: Maureen Catherine Connolly (USA) (1934–69), later Mrs Norman E. Brinker, in 1953; and Margaret Jean Court, MBE (*née* Smith) (Australia) (b. 16 July 1942) in 1970.

Most Olympic medals

Lawn Tennis was part of the Olympic programme at the first eight celebrations of the Games (including the 1906 Games). The winner of most medals was Max Decugis (1882–1978) (France) with six (a record four gold, one silver and one bronze) in the 1900, 1906 and 1920 tournaments. The most won by a woman is five by Kitty McKane (later Mrs L. A. Godfree) (b. 7 May 1897) (GB), with one gold, two silver and two bronze in 1920 and 1924.

Davis Cup

The most wins in the Davis Cup (instituted 1900) have been

left: John McEnroe's million dollar earnings in 1980 didn't include a Wimbledon championship. He corrected that in 1981 with both the singles and the doubles titles. (*Tony Duffy, All-Sport*)

below: The youngest ever player to be seeded at Wimbledon, Andrea Jaeger (USA) who achieved that distinction in 1980, aged 15 yr 19 days. (*Tony Duffy, All-Sport*) (inclusive of 1980) by the USA with 26. The British Isles/Great Britain have won nine times, in 1903–6, 1912, 1933–6.

Nicola Pietrangeli (b. 11 Sept 1933) (Italy) played 164 rubbers, 1954 to 1972, winning 120. He played 110 singles (winning 78) and 54 doubles (winning 42). He took part in 66 ties.

Wightman Cup
The most wins in the Wightman Cup (inst 1923) have been 44 by the United States. Virginia Wade (GB) (b. 10 July 1945) played in a record 17 ties between 1965 and 1981.

Fastest service
The fastest service timed with modern equipment is 137 mph *220 km/h* by Scott Carnahan (USA) at Los Angeles, California, USA, in Sept 1976. The fastest *ever* measured was one of 163.6 mph *263 km/h* by William Tatem Tilden (1893–1953) (USA) in 1931. Some players consider the service of Robert Falkenburg (USA) (b. 29 Jan 1926), the 1948 Wimbledon champion, as the fastest ever produced.

Longest game
The longest known singles game was one of 37 deuces (80 points) between Anthony Fawcett (Rhodesia) and Keith Glass (GB) in the first round of the Surrey championships at Surbiton, Surrey, on 26 May 1975. It lasted 31 min.

Greatest crowd
The greatest crowd at a tennis match was 30,472 at the Astrodome, Houston, Texas, on 20 Sept 1973, when Billie-Jean King (*née* Moffitt) (b. 22 Nov 1943) (USA) beat Robert Larimore Riggs (b. 25 Feb 1918) (USA). The record for an orthodox match is 25,578 at Sydney, NSW, Australia on 27 Dec 1954 in the Davis Cup Challenge Round (first day) Australia *v.* USA.

Highest earnings
John Patrick McEnroe Jr (USA) (b. 16 Feb 1959) won a record $1,026,383 in 1980. The record for a woman player is $747,548 in 1979 by Martina Navratilova (b. Prague, 18 Oct 1956). Earnings from special restricted events and team tennis salaries are not included.

The one match record is $500,000 *£217,400* won by James Scott Connors (USA) (b. 2 Sept 1952) when he beat John Newcombe (Australia) (b. 23 May 1944) in a challenge match at Caesars Palace, Las Vegas, USA on 26 Apr 1975.

The highest total prize money is $680,000 for the Dubai Golden Tournament in November 1980.

Longest span
The championship career of C. Alphonso Smith (b. 18 Mar 1909) of Charlottesville, Virginia, USA, extended from winning the United States National Boys' title at Chicago, on 14 Aug 1924, to winning the National 70-and-over Hard Court Doubles title at Santa Barbara, California, in Aug 1979. Smith has won 31 US National Titles in all.

Marathons
The longest recorded lawn tennis singles match is one of 105 hr by Ricky Tolston and Jeff Sutton at Bill Faye Park, Kinston, NC, USA, on 7–11 May 1979. The duration record for doubles is 84 hr 7 min by Daryl Murray, Richard Munao, Stephen Duerden and Stephen Foord at the Racquet Centre, Silverwater, NSW, Australia on 7–10 Jan 1980.

WIMBLEDON RECORDS
For more details see 100 Years of Wimbledon *by Lance Tingay, published by Guinness Superlatives Ltd. (price £8.50)*

Most wins *Women*
Six time singles champion Billie-Jean King has won ten women's doubles and four mixed doubles during the period 1961 to 1979, to total a record 20 titles. Elizabeth Montague Ryan (USA) (1892–1979) won a record 19 doubles titles from 1914 to 1934.

Most wins *Men*
The greatest number of wins by a man at Wimbledon has been 13 by Hugh Laurence Doherty (GB) (1875–1919) who won five

singles titles (1902–6) and a record eight men's doubles (1897–1901, 1903–5) partnered by his brother Reginald Frank (1872–1910).

Most wins *Singles*
The greatest number of singles wins was eight by Helen N. Moody (*née* Wills) (USA) (b. 6 Oct 1905), who won in 1927–30, 1932–3, 1935 and 1938. The most men's singles wins since the Challenge Round was abolished in 1922 is five consecutively, by Bjorn Rune Borg (Sweden) (b. 6 June 1956) in 1976–80. William Charles Renshaw (GB) (1861–1904) won seven singles in 1881–6 and 1889.

Most wins *Mixed doubles*
The male record is four wins shared by Elias Victor Seixas (USA) (b. 30 Aug 1923) in 1953–6, Kenneth N. Fletcher (Australia) (b. 15 June 1940) in 1963, 1965–6, 1968 and Owen Keir Davidson (Australia) (b. 4 Oct 1943) in 1967, 1971, 1973–4. The female record is seven by Elizabeth Ryan (USA) from 1919 to 1932.

Most appearances
Arthur William Charles 'Wentworth' Gore (1868–1928) (GB) made a record 36 appearances at Wimbledon between 1888 and 1927, and was in 1909 at 41 years 6 months the oldest ever singles winner. In 1964, Jean Borotra (b. 13 Aug 1898) of France, made his 35th appearance since 1922. In 1977 he appeared in the Veterans' Doubles aged 78.

Youngest champions
The youngest champion was Charlotte 'Lottie' Dod (1871–1960), who was 15 years 9 months when she won in 1887 (see also p. 240). Richard Dennis Ralston (b. 27 July 1942) of Bakersfield, California, USA, was 25 days short of his 18th birthday when he won the men's doubles with Rafael H. Osuna (1938–69) of Mexico in 1960. The youngest male singles champion was Wilfred Baddeley (1872–1929) who won the Wimbledon title in 1891 aged 19 years 175 days. The youngest ever player at Wimbledon is reputedly Mita Klima (Austria) who was 13 years old in the 1907 singles competition. The youngest of modern times is Kathy Rinaldi (b. 24 Mar 1967) (USA), who was only 14 years 91 days at the start of the 1981 tournament.

Greatest crowd
The record crowd for one day is 38,291 on 27 June 1979. The record for the whole championship is 358,250 in 1981.

MARBLES

Origins
Marbles may have been a children's game in Ancient Egypt, and was introduced into Britain by the Romans in the 1st Century AD. It became a competitive sport under the British Marbles Board of Control at the Greyhound Hotel, Tinsley Green, Crawley, West Sussex in 1926. The governing body now is the British Isles Marbles Association.

The game is also played on the Continent (especially Belgium) and in Australia, Brazil (as *Gude*), Canada, China, India, Iran, New Zealand, Syria, the United States and the West Indies.

Most championships
The British Championship (established 1926) has been won most often by the Toucan Terribles with 20 consecutive titles (1956–75). Three founder members, Len Smith, Jack and Charlie Dempsey, have played in every title win. They were finally beaten in 1976 by the Pernod Rams, captained by Len Smith's son, Paul. Len Smith (b. 13 Oct 1917) has won the individual title 15 times (1957–64, 1966, 1968–73) but lost in 1974 to his son Alan.

Speed record
The record for clearing the ring (between 5¾ and 6¼ ft *1,75–1,90 m* in diameter) of 49 marbles is 2 min 57 sec by the Toucan Terribles at Worthing, West Sussex in 1971.

MODERN PENTATHLON

Points scores in riding, fencing, cross country and hence overall scores have no comparative value between one competition and another. In shooting and swimming (300 m) the scores are of record significance and the best achievements are shown.

The Modern Pentathlon (Riding, Fencing, Shooting, Swimming and Running) was inaugurated into the Olympic Games at Stockholm in 1912. The Modern Pentathlon Association of Great Britain was formed in 1922.

Most titles *World*
The record number of world titles won is six by András Balczó (b. 16 Aug 1938) (Hungary) in 1963, 1965–7 and 1969. In Olympic years this title also rates as the world title, thus giving Balczó his sixth in 1972. The best British placing is the bronze medal by Sgt. (now Capt) Jeremy Robert 'Jim' Fox, MBE (b. 19 Sept 1941) at Mexico in 1975.

Most titles *Olympic*
The greatest number of Olympic gold medals won is three by András Balczó, a member of the winning team in 1960 and 1968 and the 1972 individual champion. Lars Hall (b. 30 Apr 1927) (Sweden) has uniquely won two individual Championships (1952 and 1956). Balczó has won a record number of five medals (three gold and two silver). The best British performance is the team gold medal at Montreal, Canada 18–22 July 1976 by Jim Fox, Adrian Philip Parker and Daniel Nightingale. The best individual placing is fourth by Jim Fox at Munich in 1972.

Probably the greatest margin of victory was by William Oscar Guernsey Grut (b. 17 Sept 1914) (Sweden) in the 1948 Games in London, when he won three events and was placed fifth and eighth in the other two events.

Most titles *British*
The pentathlete with most British titles is Jim Fox, with ten (1963, 1965–8, 1970–4).

HIGHEST SCORES (In major competition)				
	Performance	Points		
WORLD				
Shooting	200/200	—[1]	Charles Leonard (USA) Berlin, Germany	3 Aug 1936
	200/200	1132	Danieli Massala (Italy) Jönkoping, Sweden	21 Aug 1978
	200/200	1132	George Horvath (Sweden) Moscow, USSR	22 July 1980
Swimming	3 min 10.856 sec	1348	Ivar Sisniega (Mexico) Moscow, USSR	23 July 1980
BRITISH				
Shooting		1066	Robert Lawson Phelps MBE Leipzig, E. Germany	21 Sept 1965
Swimming		1240	Adrian Philip Parker, Montreal, Canada	21 July 1976
[1] *points not given in 1936 Olympic Games*				

MOTORCYCLE RACING

See also The Guinness Book of Motorcycling Facts and Feats by L. J. K. Setright, published by Guinness Superlatives Ltd (price £6.95) and The Guinness Guide to Motorcycling by Peter Carrick, published by Guinness Superlatives at £10.95.

Earliest race
The first motorcycle race was held over a mile *1,6 km* on an oval track at Sheen House, Richmond, Surrey, on 29 Nov 1897, won by Charles Jarrott (1877–1944) on a Fournier. The oldest motorcycle races in the world are the Auto-Cycle Union Tourist Trophy (TT) series, first held on the 15.81 mile *25,44 km* 'Peel' ('St John's') course in the Isle of Man on 28 May 1907, and still run in the island on the 37.73 mile *60,72 km* long 'Mountain' circuit.

Fastest circuits *World*
The highest average lap speed attained on any closed circuit is 160.288 mph *257,958 km/h* by Yvon du Hamel (Canada) (b. 1941) on a modified 903 cc four-cylinder Kawasaki Z1 at the 31 degree banked 2.5 mile *4,02 km* Daytona International Speedway, Florida, USA, in March 1973. His lap time was 56.149 sec.

The fastest road circuit is the Francorchamps circuit near Spa,

Belgium. It is 8.74 miles *14,120 km* in length and was lapped in 3 min 50.3 sec (average speed 137.150 mph *220,721 km/h*) by Barry Stephen Frank Sheene, MBE (b. Holborn, London, 11 Sept 1950) on a 495 cc four-cylinder Suzuki during the Belgian Grand Prix on 3 July 1977.

Fastest circuits *United Kingdom*
The fastest circuit in the United Kingdom is the Portstewart-Coleraine-Portrush circuit in Londonderry, N. Ireland. The lap record (10.1 mile *16,26 km* lap) is 4 min 53.2 sec (average speed 124.060 mph *199,655 km/h*) by John Glyn Williams (1946–78) on a 747 cc four-cylinder Yamaha on lap five of the 750 cc event of the North West 200, on 21 May 1977.

The lap record for the outer circuit (2.767 miles *4,453 km*) at the Brooklands Motor Course, near Weybridge, Surrey (open between 1907 and 1939) was 80.0 sec (average speed 124.51 mph *200,37 km/h*) by Noel Baddow 'Bill' Pope (later Major) (1909–71) of the United Kingdom on a Brough Superior powered by a supercharged 996 cc V-twin '8-80' JAP engine developing 110 bhp, on 4 July 1939.

Fastest races *World*
The fastest track race in the world was held at Grenzlandring, near Wegberg, W. Germany in 1939. It was won by Georg 'Schorsh' Meier (b. Germany, 9 Nov 1910) at an average speed of 134 mph *215 km/h* on a supercharged 495 cc flat-twin BMW.

The fastest road race is the 500 cc Belgian Grand Prix held on the Francorchamps circuit (see above). The record time for this ten lap (87.74 mile *141,20 km*) race is 38 min 58.5 sec (average speed 135.068 mph *217,370 km/h*) by Barry Sheene, on a 495 cc four-cylinder Suzuki, on 3 July 1977.

Fastest races *United Kingdom*
The fastest race in the United Kingdom is the 750 cc event of the North-West 200 held on the Londonderry circuit (see above). The record time for this five lap (50.52 mile *81,30 km*) race is 24 min 53.8 sec (average speed 121.751 mph *195,939 km/h*) by John Williams on a 747 cc four-cylinder Yamaha, on 21 May 1977.

Most successful riders *Tourist Trophy*
The record number of victories in the Isle of Man TT races is 14 by Stanley Michael Bailey Hailwood, MBE, GM (1940–81) between 1961 and 1979. The first man to win three consecutive TT titles in two events was James A. Redman, MBE (Rhodesia) (b. Hampstead, London, 8 Nov 1931). He won the 250 cc and 350 cc events in 1963–5. Mike Hailwood is the only man to win three events in one year, in 1961 and 1967.

Most successful riders *World championships*
The most world championship titles (instituted by the *Fédération Internationale Motocycliste* in 1949) won are 15 by Giacomo Agostini (b. Lovere, Italy, 16 June 1942), the 350 cc in 1968–74, and 500 cc in 1966–72, 1975. He is the only man to win two world championships in five consecutive years (350 and 500 cc titles in 1968–72).

Agostini won 122 races in the world championship series between 24 Apr 1965 and 29 Aug 1976, including a record 19 in 1970, also achieved by Mike Hailwood in 1966. Klaus Enders (Germany) (b. 1937) won six world side-car titles, 1967, 1969–70, 1972–4.

Most successful riders *Trials*
Samuel Hamilton Miller (b. Belfast, N. Ireland, 11 Nov 1935) won eleven A-CU Solo Trials Drivers' Stars in 1959–69.

Most successful riders *Moto-cross and Scrambles*
Joël Robert (b. Chatelet, Belgium, 11 Nov 1943) has won six 250 cc moto-cross world championships (1964, 1968–72). Between 25 Apr 1964 and 18 June 1972 he won a record fifty 250 cc Grands Prix. He became the youngest moto-cross world champion on 12 July 1964 when he won the 250 cc championship aged 20 years 8 months.

Jeffrey Vincent Smith, MBE (b. Colne, Lancashire, 14 Oct 1934) won nine A-CU 500 cc Scrambles' Stars in 1955–6, 1960–5 and 1967.

Most successful machines

Italian MV-Agusta machines won 37 world championships between 1952 and 1973, and 276 world championship races between 1952 and 1976. Japanese Honda machines won 29 world championship races and five world championships in 1966. In the seven years they contested the championship (1961–7) their annual average was 20 race wins.

Youngest and oldest world champions

Alberto 'Johnny' Cecotto (b. Caracas, Venezuela, 25 Jan 1956) is the youngest to win a world championship. He was 19 years 211 days when he won the 350 cc title on 24 Aug 1975. The oldest was Hermann-Peter Müller (1909–76) of W. Germany, who won the 250 cc title in 1955 aged 46.

Highest speeds

Official world speed records must be set with two runs over a measured distance made in opposite directions within a time limit. This limit is 1 hr for FIM records and 2 hr for AMA records.

Donald A. Vesco (b. Loma Linda, Calif, USA, 8 Apr 1939) riding his 21 ft long 1500 cc *Silver Bird* streamliner, powered by two Yamaha TZ750 four-cylinder engines developing 180 bhp, on Bonneville Salt Flats, Utah, USA on 28 Sept 1975 set AMA and FIM absolute records. His average time was 11.8495 sec (303.810 mph *488,935 km/h*) for the AMA record and 11.884 sec (302.928 mph *487,516 km/h*) for the FIM record. (For details of the individual runs see the 23rd Edition). On the same day he covered a flying quarter mile in 2.925 sec (307.692 mph *495,183 km/h*), the highest speed ever achieved on a motor-cycle.

The highest speed achieved over two runs in the UK is 189.873 mph *305,571 km/h* by Frederick James Cooper (b. London, 9 Mar 1925) on his 1267 cc supercharged twin-engined Triumph *Cyclotron* at RAF Fairford, Gloucester, on 23 Sept 1972. Average time for the flying 440 yd *402 m* runs was 4.74 sec.

The world record for 1 km *1,093.6 yd* from a standing start is 16.68 sec by Henk Vink (b. 24 July 1939) (Netherlands) on his supercharged 984 cc four-cylinder Kawasaki, at Elvington Airfield, North Yorkshire on 24 July 1977. The faster run was made in 16.09 sec.

The world record for 440 yd *402 m* from a standing start is 8.805 sec by Henk Vink on his supercharged 1132 cc four-cylinder Kawasaki at Elvington Airfield, North Yorkshire on 23 July 1977. The faster run was made in 8.55 sec.

The fastest time for a single run over 440 yd *402 m* from a standing start is 7.62 sec by Russ Collins of Gardena, California, USA riding a nitro-burning 2000 cc 8-cylinder Honda, *Sorcerer*, in the National Hot Rod Association's World Finals at Ontario Motor Speedway, Ontario, California, on 7 Oct 1978. The highest terminal velocity recorded at the end of a 440 yd *402 m* run from a standing start is 199.55 mph *321,14 km/h* by Russ Collins at the above meeting on 7 Oct 1978.

Longest race

The longest race is the Liège 24 hr. The greatest distance ever covered is 2761.9 miles *4444,8 km* (average speed 115.08 mph *185,20 km/h*) by Jean-Claude Chemarin and Christian Leon, both of France, on a 941 cc four-cylinder Honda on the Francorchamps circuit on 14–15 Aug 1976.

Longest circuit

The 37.73 mile *60,72 km* 'Mountain' circuit, over which the principal TT races have been run since 1911 (with minor amendments in 1920), has 264 curves and corners and is the longest used for any motorcycle race.

MOTOR RACING

Additional information can be obtained from The Guinness Guide to Grand Prix Motor Racing *by Eric Dymock published by Guinness Superlatives Ltd at £11.95.*

Earliest races

There are various conflicting claims, but the first automobile race was the 201 mile *323 km* Green Bay to Madison, Wisconsin,

USA run in 1878 won by an Oshkosh steamer. In 1887 Count Jules Felix Philippe Albert de Dion de Malfiance (1856–1946) won the *La Velocipede* 19.3 miles *31 km* race in Paris in a De Dion steam quadricycle in which he is reputed to have exceeded 37 mph *59 km/h.* The first 'real' race was from Paris to Bordeaux and back (732 miles *1178 km*) on 11–13 June 1895. The first to finish was Emile Levassor (1844–97) of France, in a Panhard-Levassor two-seater, with a 1.2 litre Daimler engine developing 3½ hp. His time was 48 hr 47 min (average speed 15.01 mph *24,15 km/h*). The first closed circuit race was held over five laps of a mile *1,6 km* dirt track at Narragansett Park, Cranston, Rhode Island, USA, on 7 Sept 1896, won by A. H. Whiting, driving a Riker electric.

The oldest race in the world, still regularly run, is the RAC Tourist Trophy, first staged on 14 Sept 1905, in the Isle of Man. The oldest continental race is the French Grand Prix first held on 26–27 June 1906. The Coppa Florio, in Sicily, has been irregularly held since 1900.

Fastest circuits *World*

The highest average lap speed attained on any closed circuit is 250.958 mph *403,878 km/h* in a trial by Dr Hans Liebold (b. 12 Oct 1926) (Germany) who lapped the 7.85 mile *12,64 km* high-speed track at Nardo, Italy in 1 min 52.67 sec in a Mercedes-Benz C111-IV experimental coupé on 5 May 1979. It was powered by a V8 engine with two KKK turbochargers with an output of 500 hp at 6,200 rpm.

The highest average race lap speed for a closed circuit is 214.158 mph *344,654 km/h* by Mario Gabriele Andretti (USA) (b. Trieste, Italy, 28 Feb 1940) driving a 2.6 litre turbocharged Viceroy Parnelli-Offenhauser on the 2 mile *3,2 km*, 22 degree banked oval at Texas World Speedway, College Station, Texas, USA on 6 Oct 1973.

The fastest road circuit was the Francorchamps circuit near Spa, Belgium, then 8.761 miles *14,100 km* in length which was lapped in 3 min 13.4 sec (average speed 163.086 mph *262,461 km/h*) on lap seven of the Francorchamps 1000 km sports car race on 6 May 1973, by Henri Pescarolo (b. Paris, France, 25 Sept 1942) driving a 2993 cc V12 Matra-Simca MS670 Group 5 sports car. The race lap average speed record at Berlin's AVUS track was 171.75 mph *276,38 km/h* by Bernd Rosemeyer (Germany) (1909–38) in a 6-litre V16 Auto Union in 1937.

The fastest World championship GP circuit in current use is the 2.932 miles *4,719 km* circuit at Silverstone, Northamptonshire, England opened in 1948. The race lap record is 1 min 14.40 sec (average speed 141.87 mph *228,31 km/h*) by Gianclaudio 'Clay' Regazzoni (Switzerland) (b. 5 Sept 1939) driving a Saudia-Williams FW07 on 14 July 1979. The practice lap record is 1 min 11.00 sec (148.66 mph *239,24 km/h*) by Rene Arnoux (France) (b. 4 July 1948) in a Renault Elf Turbo RE30 on 17 July 1981. A test run of 1 min 10.8 sec (average speed 149.08 mph *239,92 km/h*) was recorded by Nelson Piquet Soutomaior (Brazil) in a Brabham–Cosworth BT48 on 17 June 1980.

The Motor Industry Research Association (MIRA) High Speed Circuit (2.82 mile *4,53 km* lap with 33-degree banking on the bends) at Lindley, Warwickshire, was lapped in 1 min 2.8 sec (average speed 161.655 mph *260,158 km/h*) by David Wishart Hobbs (b. Leamington, Warwickshire, 9 June 1939) driving a 4994 cc V12 Jaguar XJ13 Group 6 prototype sports car in April 1967.

Fastest races *World*

The fastest race was the NASCAR Grand National 125 mile *201 km* (a qualifying event for the Daytona 500) on the 2.50 mile *4,02 km*, 31-degree banked tri-oval at Daytona International Speedway, Florida, USA. The record time for this race is 40 min 55 sec (average speed 183.295 mph *294,985 km/h*) by William Caleb 'Cale' Yarborough (b. 27 Mar 1939) of Timmonsville, S Carolina, USA, driving a 1969 Mercury V8, on 19 Feb 1970.

The fastest road race was the Francorchamps 1000 km sports car race held on the Francorchamps circuit. The record time for this 71-lap (622.055 mile *1001,100 km*) race was 4 hr 1 min 9.7 sec (average speed 154.765 mph *249,070 km/h*) by Pedro Rodriguez

left: Belgian driver Jacky Ickx celebrating his fifth Le Mans win in 1981 with British co-driver Derek Bell, who had his second victory and, *above:* the Porsche 936 in which Ickx and Bell averaged over 125 mph *200 km/h* to finish 14 laps ahead of their nearest rival. (*Sporting Pictures (UK) Ltd*)

(1940–71) of Mexico, and Keith Jack 'Jackie' Oliver (b. Chadwell Heath, London, 14 Aug 1942) driving a 4998 cc flat-12 Porsche 917K Group 5 sports car, on 9 May 1971.

Fastest races *United Kingdom*

The fastest currently held race in the United Kingdom is the British Grand Prix race. The record time is 1 hr 26 min 11.17 sec (average speed 138.80 mph *223,37 km/h*) by Clay Regazzoni (Switzerland) driving a Saudia-Williams FW07 over 68 laps (199.37 miles *320,85 km*) at Silverstone on 14 July 1979.

Fastest pit stop

Robert William 'Bobby' Unser (b. Colorado Springs, Colorado, USA, 20 Feb 1934) took 4 sec to take on fuel on lap 10 of the Indianapolis 500 on 30 May 1976.

Toughest circuit *World*

The Targa Florio (first run 9 May 1906) was widely acknowledged to be the most arduous race. Held on the Piccolo Madonie Circuit in Sicily, it covered eleven laps (492.126 miles *792,000 km*) and involved the negotiation of 9350 corners, over severe mountain gradients, and narrow rough roads. The record time was 6 hr 27 min 48.0 sec (average speed 76.141 mph *122,537 km/h*) by Arturo Francesco Merzario (b. Civenna, Italy, 11 Mar 1943) and Sandro Munari (b. Venice, Italy, 1940) driving a 2998.5 cc flat-12 Ferrari 312P Group 5 sports car in the 56th race on 21 May 1972. The lap record was 33 min 36.0 sec (average speed 79.890 mph *128,570 km/h*) by Leo Juhani Kinnunen (b. Tampere, Finland, 5 Aug 1943) on lap 11 of the 54th race on 3 May 1970 driving a 2997 cc flat-8 Porsche 908/3 Spyder Group 6 prototype sports car.

Toughest circuit *Grand Prix*

The most gruelling and slowest Grand Prix circuit is that for the Monaco Grand Prix (first run on 14 Apr 1929), round the streets and the harbour of Monte Carlo. It is 2.058 miles *3,312 km* in length and has eleven pronounced corners and several sharp changes of gradient. The race is run over 76 laps (156.4 miles *251,7 km*) and involves on average about 1600 gear changes. The record time for the race is 1 hr 55 min 22.48 sec (average speed 81.338 mph *130,901 km/h*) by Jody Scheckter (b. S. Africa, 29 Jan 1950) driving a Ferrari 312T4 on 27 May 1979. The race lap record is 1 min 28.65 sec (average speed 83.67 mph *134,649 km/h*) by Andreas-Nikolaus 'Niki' Lauda (b. Austria, 22 Feb 1949) driving a Brabham-Alfa Romeo BT46 on 7 May 1978. The

practice lap record is 1 min 26.45 sec (average speed 85.69 mph *137,92 km/h*) by Jody Scheckter in a Ferrari 312T4 on 26 May 1979.

Le Mans

The greatest distance ever covered in the 24 hour *Grand Prix d'Endurance* (first held on 26–27 May 1923) on the old Sarthe circuit at Le Mans, France is 3315.208 miles *5335,313 km* by Dr Helmut Marko (b. Graz, Austria, 27 Apr 1943) and Jonkheer Gijs van Lennep (b. Bloemendaal, Netherlands, 16 Mar 1942) driving a 4907 cc flat-12 Porsche 917K Group 5 sports car, on 12–13 June 1971. The record for the current circuit is 3134.52 miles *5044,52 km* by Didier Pironi (b. 26 Mar 1952) and Jean-Pierre Jaussaud (b. 3 June 1937) (France) (av. speed 130.60 mph *210.18 km/h*) in an Alpine Renault on 10–11 June 1978. The race lap record (8.475 mile *13,64 km* lap) is 3 min 34.2 sec (average speed 142.44 mph *229,244 km/h*) by Jean Pierre Jabouille (b. France, 1 Oct 1942) driving an Alpine Renault on 11 June 1978. The practice lap record is 3 min 27.6 sec (av. speed 146.97 mph *236,53 km/h*) by Jacques-Bernard 'Jacky' Ickx (b. Belgium, 1 Jan 1945) in a turbocharged 2.1 litre Porsche 936/78 on 7 June 1978.

Le Mans *Most wins*

The race has been won by Ferrari cars nine times, in 1949, 1954, 1958 and 1960–5. The most wins by one man is five by Jacky Ickx, 1969, 1975–7 and 1981.

Le Mans *British wins*

The race has been won 13 times by British cars: Bentley in 1924 and 1927–30, Lagonda in 1935, Jaguar in 1951, 1953 and 1955–7, Aston Martin in 1959 and a Gulf-Ford in 1975.

Indianapolis 500

The Indianapolis 500 mile *804 km* race (200 laps) was inaugurated in the USA on 30 May 1911. The most successful driver has been Anthony Joseph 'A.J.' Foyt, Jr (b. Houston, Texas, USA, 16 Jan 1935) who won in 1961, 1964, 1967 and 1977. The record time is 3 hr 4 min 5.54 sec (average speed 162.962 mph *262,261 km/h*) by Mark Donohue, Jr driving a 2595 cc 900 bhp turbocharged Sunoco McLaren M16B-Offenhauser on 27 May 1972. The race lap record is 46.71 sec (average speed 192.678 mph *310,085 km/h*) by Danny Ongais (b. Hawaii, 21 May 1942), driving a 2.6 litre turbocharged Parnelli-Cosworth DFX on lap 42 of the race held on 29 May 1977. The 4-lap qualifying record is 2 min 58.08 sec (average speed 202.156 mph *325,338 km/h*) by Tom Sneva (b. USA, 1 June 1948) driving a Penske-Cosworth DFX turbocharged PC6 on 20 May 1978.

The record prize fund was $1,502,425 for the 64th race on 25 May 1980. The individual prize record is $318,819 by Johnny Rutherford on 25 May 1980.

Drivers *Most successful*
Based on the World Drivers' Championship, inaugurated in 1950, the most successful driver is Juan-Manuel Fangio (b. Balcarce, Argentina, 24 June 1911) who won five times in 1951, 1954–7. He retired in 1958, after having won 24 Grand Prix races (two shared). The most successful driver in terms of race wins is Richard Lee Petty (b. Randleman, N. Carolina, USA, 2 July 1937) with 186 NASCAR Grand National wins between 1960 and April 1979. His best season was 1967 with 27 wins.

The most Grand Prix victories is 27 by John Young 'Jackie' Stewart, OBE (b. Milton, Dunbartonshire, 11 June 1939) between 12 Sept 1965 and 5 Aug 1973. James 'Jim' Clark, OBE (1936–68) of Scotland holds the record for Grand Prix victories in one year with seven in 1963. He won a record 61 Formula One and Formula Libre races between 1959 and 1968. The most Grand Prix starts is 176 (out of a possible 184) between 18 May 1958 and 26 Jan 1975 by the British driver Norman Graham Hill, OBE (1929–75). Between 20 Nov 1960 and 5 Oct 1969 he took part in 90 consecutive Grands Prix.

Oldest and youngest *World champions*
The youngest world champion was Emerson Fittipaldi (b. São Paulo, Brazil, 12 Dec 1946) who won his first world championship on 10 Sept 1972 aged 25 years 273 days. The oldest world champion was Juan-Manuel Fangio who won his last world championship on 18 Aug 1957 aged 46 years 55 days.

Oldest and youngest *GP winners and drivers*
The youngest Grand Prix winner was Bruce Leslie McLaren (1937–70) of New Zealand, who won the United States Grand Prix at Sebring, Florida, USA, on 12 Dec 1959 aged 22 years 104 days. The oldest Grand Prix winner was Tazio Giorgio Nuvolari (1892–1953) of Italy, who won the Albi Grand Prix at Albi, France on 14 July 1946 aged 53 years 240 days. The oldest Grand Prix driver was Louis Alexandre Chiron, O. St-C., L.d'H., C.d'I., (Monaco) (1899–1979), who finished 6th in the Monaco Grand Prix on 22 May 1955 aged 55 years 292 days. The youngest Grand Prix driver was Michael Christopher Thackwell (b. New Zealand, 30 Mar 1961) who took part in the Canadian GP on 28 Sept 1980, aged 19 yr 182 days).

Hill climbing *Pikes Peak race*
The Pikes Peak Auto Hill Climb, Colorado, USA (instituted 1916) has been won 13 times by Bobby Unser between 1956 and 1974 (ten championship, two stock and one sports car title). On 30 June 1968, in the 46th race, he set a record time of 11 min 54.9 sec in his 5506 cc Chevrolet championship car for the 12.42 mile *19,98 km* course rising from 9402 ft to 14,110 ft *2865–4300 m* through 157 curves.

Hill climbing *Most successful drivers*
The British National Hill Climb Championship (inaugurated in 1947) has been won six times by Anthony Ernest Marsh (b. Stourbridge, West Midlands, 20 July 1931) 1955–7, 1965–7. Raymond Mays, CBE (1899–1980) won the Shelsley Walsh hill climb, near Worcester, 19 times between 1923 and 1950.

Rallies *Earliest*
The earliest long rally was promoted by the Parisian daily *Le Matin* in 1907 from Peking, China to Paris over about 7500 miles *12 000 km* on 10 June. The winner, Prince Scipione Borghese (1871–1927), of Italy, arrived in Paris on 10 Aug 1907 in his 40 hp Itala accompanied by his chauffeur, Ettore, and Luigi Barzini.

Rallies *Longest*
The longest ever rally was the *Singapore Airlines* London-Sydney Rally over 19,329 miles *31 107 km* from Covent Garden, London on 14 Aug 1977 to Sydney Opera House, won on 28 Sept 1977 by Andrew Cowan, Colin Malkin and Michael Broad

in a Mercedes 280E. The longest held annually is the East African Safari (first run 1953 through Kenya, Tanzania and Uganda) which is up to 3874 miles *6234 km* long, as in the 17th Safari held between 8 and 12 Apr 1971. It has been won a record four times by Shekhar Mehta (b. Uganda) in 1973, 1979-81.

Rallies *Monte Carlo*
The Monte Carlo Rally (first run 1911) has been won a record four times by Sandro Munari (Italy) in 1972, 1975, 1976 and 1977. The smallest car to win was an 851 cc Saab driven by Erik Carlsson (b. Sweden 5 Mar 1929) and Gunnar Häggbom of Sweden on 25 Jan 1962, and by Carlsson and Gunnar Palm on 24 Jan 1963.

Rallies *Britain*
The RAC Rally (first held 1932) has been recognised by the FIA since 1957. Most wins have been three each by Erik Carlsson driving a Saab in 1960–2 and Timo Makinen (Finland) (b. 18 Mar 1938) in a Ford Escort, 1973–5.

Dragging *Piston engined*
The lowest elapsed time recorded by a piston-engined dragster is 5.637 sec (terminal velocity 250.69 mph *403,45 km/h*) by Donald Glenn 'Big Daddy' Garlits (b. 1932) of Seffner, Florida, USA driving his rear-engined AA/F dragster, powered by a 7948 cc supercharged Dodge V8 engine, during the National Hot Rod Association's Super-nationals at Ontario Motor Speedway, Ontario, California, USA, on 11 Oct 1975. The highest terminal velocity recorded is 255.58 mph *411,31 km/h* by Shirley Muldowney (b. 1940) (USA) at Pomona, Cal., in January 1979.

The world record for two runs in opposite directions over 440 yd *402 m* from a standing start is 6.70 sec by Dennis Victor Priddle (b. 1945) of Yeovil, Somerset, driving his 6424 cc supercharged Chrysler dragster developing 1700 bhp using nitromethane and methanol, at Elvington Airfield, North Yorkshire on 7 Oct 1972. The faster run was made in 6.65 sec.

Dragging *Rocket or jet-engined*
The highest terminal velocity recorded by any dragster is 392.54 mph *631,732 km/h* by Kitty O'Neil (USA) at El Mirage Dry Lake, California, USA on 7 July 1977. The lowest elapsed time was 3.72 sec also by Kitty O'Neil on the same occasion.

Terminal velocity is the speed attained at the end of a 440 yd 402 m run made from a standing start and elapsed time is the time taken for the run.

Highest speeds
For details of the land speed record see pp 137 and 173.

The world speed record for compression ignition engined cars is 190.344 mph *306,328 km/h* (average of two runs in opposite directions over a measured mile *1,6 km*) by Robert Havemann of Eureka, California, USA driving his *Corsair* streamliner, powered by a turbocharged 6981 cc 6-cylinder GMC 6-71 diesel engine developing 746 bhp, at Bonneville Salt Flats, Utah, USA, in August 1971. The faster run was made at 210 mph *337 km/h*.

The most successful land speed record breaker was Major Sir Malcolm Campbell (1885–1948) of the United Kingdom. He broke the official record nine times between 25 Sept 1924, with 146.157 mph *235,216 km/h* in a Sunbeam, and 3 Sept 1935, when he achieved 301.129 mph *480,620 km/h* in the Rolls-Royce engined *Bluebird*.

Duration records
The greatest distance ever covered in one year is 400 000 km *248,548.5 miles* by François Lecot (1879–1949), an innkeeper from Rochetaillée, near Lyon, France, in a 1900 cc 66 bhp Citroën 11 sedan, mainly between Paris and Monte Carlo, from 22 July 1935 to 26 July 1936. He drove on 363 of the 370 days allowed.

The world's duration record is 185,353 miles 1741 yd *298 298 km* in 133 days 17 hr 37 min 38.64 sec (average speed 58.07 mph *93,45 km/h*) by Marchand, Presalé and six others in a Citroën on the Montlhéry track near Paris, France, during March-July 1933.

MOUNTAINEERING

See also Mountains and Mountaineering Facts and Feats *by Edward Pyatt published by Guinness Superlatives Ltd at £8.95*

Origins

Although bronze-age artifacts have been found on the summit of the Riffelhorn, Switzerland (9605 ft *2927 m*), mountaineering, as a sport, has a continuous history dating back only to 1854. Isolated instances of climbing for its own sake exist back to the 13th century. The Atacamenans built sacrificial platforms near the summit of Llullaillaco (22,058 ft *6723 m*) in late pre-Columbian times *c.* 1490. The earliest recorded rock climb in the British Isles was of Stac na Biorrach, St Kilda (236 ft *71,9 m*) by Sir Robert Moray in 1698.

Mount Everest

Mount Everest (29,028 ft *8848 m*) was first climbed at 11.30 a.m. on 29 May 1953, when the summit was reached by Edmund Percival Hillary (b. 20 July 1919), created KBE, of New Zealand, and the Sherpa, Tenzing Norgay (b., as Namgyal Wangdi, in Nepal in 1914, formerly called Tenzing Khumjung Bhutia), who was awarded the GM. The successful expedition was led by Col (later Hon Brigadier) Henry Cecil John Hunt, CBE, DSO (b. 22 June 1910), who was created a Knight Bachelor in 1953, a life Baron on 11 June 1966 and KG on 23 Apr 1979.

Since the first ascent, another 105 climbers have succeeded to end 1980 including five who have done it twice. Franz Oppurg (Austria) was the first to make the final ascent solo on 15 May 1978 while Reinhold Messner (Italy) was the first to succeed solo without oxygen on 20 Aug 1980. The first Britons to reach the summit were Douglas Scott (b. 29 May 1941) and Dougal Haston (1940–77) on 24 Sept 1975. Four women have reached the summit, the first being Junko Tabei (b. 1939) (Japan) on 16 May 1975. The oldest person was Dr Gerhard Schmatz (W. Germany) (b. 5 June 1929) aged 50 years 88 days on 1 Oct 1979.

Greatest walls

The highest final stage in any wall climb is that on the south face of Annapurna I (26,545 ft *8091 m*). It was climbed by the British expedition led by Christian John Storey Bonington, CBE (b. 6 Aug 1934) when from 2 Apr to 27 May 1970, using 18,000 ft *5500 m* of rope, Donald Whillans (b. 1934) and Dougal Haston scaled to the summit. The longest wall climb is on the Rupal-Flank from the base camp at 3560 m *11,680 ft* to the South Point 8042 m *26,384 ft* of Nanga Parbat—a vertical ascent of 4482 m *14,704 ft*. This was scaled by the Austro-Germano-Italian Expedition led by Dr Karl Maria Herrligkoffer in April 1970.

Europe's greatest wall is the 6,600 ft *2000 m* north face of the Eigerwand (Ogre wall) first climbed by Heinrich Harrer and Fritz Kasparek of Austria and Anderl Heckmair and Wiggerl Vörg of Germany on 21–24 July 1938. The north-east face of the Eiger had been climbed on 20 Aug 1932 by Hans Lauper, Alfred Zurcher, Alexander Graven and Josef Knubel. The greatest alpine solo climb was that of Walter Bonatti (b. Bergamo, Italy, 22 June 1930) of the South West Pillar of the Dru, Montenvers now called the Bonatti Pillar, with five bivouacs in 126 hr 7 min on 17–22 Aug 1955.

There are climbs in the Yosemite Valley, California with a severity rating of 5.12, regarded as the most demanding free climbs in the world.

Highest bivouac

Douglas Scott and Dougal Haston bivouaced in a snow hole at 28,700 ft *8747 m* on the South Summit of Everest on the night of 24 Sept 1975.

MOUNTAIN RACING
Mount Cameroun

Ndumbe Evambe Amos descended from the summit 13,353 ft *4070 m* to Buea at 3000 ft *914 m* in 78 min 4 sec on 26 Feb 1978 achieving a vertical rate of 132 ft *40,4 m* per min. In winning for the third successive year, Father Walter Stifter (Italy) ran to the summit and back in a record 4 hr 18 min 16 sec in 1978.

Ben Nevis

The record time for the race from Fort William Town Park to the Cairn on the summit of Ben Nevis (4418 ft *1346,6 m*) and return is 1 hr 26 min 55 sec by David Cannon (b. 7 Aug 1950) (Gateshead H) on 4 Sept 1976. The feminine record is 1 hr 53 min 23 sec by Ros Coates (Lochaber AC) (b. 17 Jan 1950) on 2 Sept 1978. The full course by the bridle path is about 14 miles *22 km* but distance is saved by crossing the open hillside. The mountain was first climbed *c.* 1720 and the earliest run, by William Swan in 2 hr 41 min, was in 1895.

Peak racing

In the 1972 Skiddaw Fell Race (3053 ft to 250 ft *930 to 107 m*) a vertical descent rate of 128 ft *39 m* per min was achieved by George Jeffrey Norman (b. 6 Feb 1945) (Altrincham AC).

Joss Naylor MBE (b. 10 Feb 1936) won the Ennerdale mountain race (23 miles *37 km*) nine times, 1968–1977. The fastest time is 3 hr 21 min 4 sec by Billy Bland (Keswick AC) in 1980.

The Yorkshire three peak record is 2 hr 29 min 53 sec by Jeff Norman on 28 Apr 1974.

Bill Teasdale, MBE (b. 12 Oct 1924), won the Guides Race at the Grasmere Sports, Cumbria, for the eleventh time in 1966. It involves running to a turning point on Butter Crag (966 ft *294 m* above sea level) and back, a distance of about 1½ miles *2,4 km*. The record time for this race is 12 min 21.6 sec by Frederick Leslie Reeves (b. 25 Feb 1945) on 24 Aug 1978.

Holder of the Scottish Munros record, Chris Dodd (left), with companion Howard Artiss, who had to retire from the attempt due to injury.

PROGRESSIVE MOUNTAINEERING ALTITUDE RECORDS (See also pp. 68–69)

ft	m	Mountain	Climbers	Date	
17,887	5452	Popocatépetl, Mexico	Francisco Montano		1521
18,400	5608	Mana Pass, Zaskar Range	A. de Andrade, M. Morques	July	1624
18,893	5758	On Chimborazo, Ecuador	Dr Alexander Von Humboldt, Aimé Bonpland, Carlos Montufar	23 June	1802
19,411	5916	On Leo Pargyal Range, Himalaya	Gerrard and Lloyd		1818
22,260	6784	On E. Abi Gamin, Garhwal Himalaya	A. & R. Schlagintweit	Aug	1855
22,606	6890	Pioneer Peak on Baltoro Kangri	William M. Conway, Matthias Zurbriggen	23 Aug	1892
22,834	6960	Aconcagua, Andes	Matthias Zurbriggen	14 Jan	1897
23,394	7130	On Pyramis Peak, Karakoram	William H. Workman, J. Petigax Snr & Jnr, C. Savoie	12 Aug	1903
23,787	7250	On Gula Mandhata, Tibet	Thomas G. Longstaff, Alexis & Henri Brocherel	23 July	1905
c.23,900	c.7285	On Kabru, Sikkim-Nepal	Carl W. Rubenson and Monrad Aas	20 Oct	1907
24,607	7500	On Chogolisa, Karakoram	Duke of the Abruzzi, J. Petigax, H. & E. Brocherel	18 July	1909
c.24,900	c.7590	Camp V, Everest, Tibet-Nepal	G. L. Mallory, E. F. Norton, T. H. Somervell, H. T. Morshead	20 May	1922
26,986	8225	On Everest (North Face), Tibet	George L. Mallory, Edward F. Norton, T. Howard Somervell	21 May	1922
c.27,300	c.8320	On Everest (North Face), Tibet	George I. Finch, J. Granville Bruce	27 May	1922
28,126	8570	On Everest (North Face), Tibet	Edward Felix Norton	4 June	1924
28,126	8570	On Everest (North Face), Tibet	P. Wynn Harris, Lawrence R. Wager	30 May	1933
28,126	8570	On Everest (North Face), Tibet	Francis Sydney Smythe	1 June	1933
28,215	8599	South Shoulder on Everest, Nepal	Raymond Lambert, Tenzing Norgay	28 May	1952
28,721	8754	South Shoulder on Everest, Nepal	Thomas D. Bourdillon, Robert C. Evans	26 May	1953
29,028*	8848*	Everest, Nepal-Tibet	Edmund P. Hillary, Tenzing Norgay	29 May	1953

* *First attained without oxygen, by Reinhold Messner (Italy) and Peter Habeler (Austria), 8 May 1978.*

PROGRESSIVE LIST OF HIGHEST SUMMITS CLIMBED

The progressive list of highest summits climbed after Aconcagua in 1897 is as follows:

ft	m		Climbers	Date
23,360	7120	Trisul, Garhwal Himalaya	Thomas G. Longstaff, Alexis & Henri Brocherel, Karbir	12 June 1907
23,385*	7127	Pauhunri, Sikkim Himalaya	A. M. Kellas, Sonam and another porter	16 June 1911
23,383	7127	Pik Lenin, Trans-Alai Pamir	E. Allwein, K. Wien, E. Schneider	25 Sept 1928
23,442	7145	Nepal Peak, Sikkim-Nepal	E. Schneider	24 May 1930
24,344	7417	Jongsong Peak, Nepal-Sikkim-Tibet	E. Schneider, H. Hoerlin	3 June 1930
25,447	7756	Kamet, Garhwal Himalaya	Francis S. Smythe, R. L. Holdsworth, Eric E. Shipton, Lewa	21 June 1931
25,645	7816	Nanda Devi, Garhwal Himalaya	N. E. Odell, Harold W. Tilman	29 Aug 1936
26,492	8047	Annapurna I, Nepal	Maurice Herzog, Louis Lachenal	3 June 1950
29,028	8848	Mount Everest, Nepal-Tibet	Edmund P. Hillary, Tenzing Norgay	29 May 1953

* *Survey of India height now listed as 23,180 ft 7065 m.*

Peak running

The Lakeland 24-hr record is 72 peaks achieved by Joss Naylor, on 22–23 June 1975. He covered 105 miles *168 km* with 37,000 ft *11 227 m* of ascents and descents in 23 hr 11 min.

The record for traversing the 85 mile *136.79 km* cross-country route of the nine 4000 ft *1219,2 m* Scottish Munros is 23 hr 14 min by Christopher John Dodd (Dark Peak Fell Runners) (b. 5 Dec 1950) on 19-20 July 1980.

The 'Three Thousander' record over the 14 Welsh peaks of over 3000 ft *914 m* is 4 hr 46 min 22 sec with pacemakers, by Joss Naylor on 17 June 1973 despite misty conditions.

The Ten Peaks run is from Burnthwaite Farm, Wasdale Head, Cumbria to the top of Skiddaw *via* England's nine other highest mountains and tops. The record time is 6 hr 56 min by Joss Naylor, wholly on foot, in May 1975.

Ernest Roger Baumeister (Dark Peak Fell Runners Club) (b. 17 Dec 1941) of Sheffield, S. Yorkshire, twice ran the 42 Lakeland Peaks, known as a Bob Graham Round, in 46 hr 34½ min on 30 June–1 July 1979, covering a total distance of 144 miles *231 km* and 54,000 ft *16 459 m* of ascent and descent.

Three peaks record

The Three Peaks route from sea level at Fort William, Inverness-shire, to sea level at Caernarvon, *via* the summits of Ben Nevis, Scafell Pike and Snowdon, was covered by Metropolitan Police Constable Arthur Eddleston BEM (b. 6 Dec 1939) (Cambridge H) who walked it in 5 days 23 hr 37 min on 11–17 May 1980. Five members of the Vauxhall Motors Recreation Club, Luton, Beds., ran the distance in relay in 54 hr 57 min 47 sec, on 21–23 May 1977.

The fastest individual total time for climbing the three mountains is 4 hr 16 min by Joss Naylor on 8–9 July 1971.

Pennine Way

The record for traversing the 271 mile *436 km* long Pennine Way is 3 days 42 min by Brian Harney (Rotherham H) (b. 11 May 1945) on 9–12 Aug 1979.

NETBALL

Origins

The game was invented in the USA in 1891 and introduced into England in 1895 by Dr Toles. The All England Women's Netball Association was formed in 1926. The oldest club in continuous existence is the Polytechnic Netball Club of London founded in 1907.

Most titles *World*

World championships were inaugurated in August 1963. Australia has won on four occasions, 1963, 1971, 1975 and 1979.

Most titles *National*

The National Championships (inst. 1966) have been won most often by Sudbury Netball Club with five titles (1968–70, 1971 (shared) and 1973).

England's Judy Heath practising the shot which brought her record goal scoring figures in the 1971 World Netball Tournament. (*Sunday Times*)

307

Most titles *County*

Surrey have won the County Championships (inst 1932) a record 18 times 1949–64, 1966, 1969 (shared) and 1981.

Most international appearances

The record number of internationals is 65 by Anne Miles (b. 9 Apr 1942) of England 1965–75.

Highest scores

The World Tournament record score was in Auckland, New Zealand in 1975 when England beat Papua New Guinea 114 goals to 16. The record number of goals in the World Tournament is 402 by Judith Heath (England) (b. 1942) in 1971. The highest international score recorded was when New Zealand beat Singapore 117–9 in Oct 1974.

Marathon

Two teams of seven girls from the Dharruk Panthers Netball Club played for 24 hr 1 min at Whalan Reserve, Mount Druitt, NSW, Australia on 29–30 Sept 1979.

OLYMPIC GAMES

See also The Guinness Book of Olympic Records published by Penguin (April 1980) (price £1.95)

Note: These records include the un-numbered Games held at Athens in 1906.

Origins

The earliest celebration of the ancient Olympic Games of which there is a certain record is that of July 776 BC, when Coroibos, a cook from Elis, won the foot race, though their origin dates from *c.* 1370 BC. The ancient Games were terminated by an order issued in Milan in AD 393 by Theodosius I, 'the Great' (*c.* 346–95), Emperor of Rome. At the instigation of Pierre de Fredi, Baron de Coubertin (1863–1937), the Olympic Games of the modern era were inaugurated in Athens on 6 Apr 1896.

Modern celebrations

Modern celebrations have been voted for by the International Olympic Committee as follows. Dates indicate the span of Olympic competitions (excluding elimination contests). The first date is not necessarily that of the opening ceremony.

I	1896	Athens, Greece	6–15 April
II	1900	Paris, France	20 May–28 Oct
III	1904	St Louis, USA	1 July–23 Nov
*	1906	Athens, Greece	22 Apr–2 May
IV	1908	London, England	27 Apr–31 Oct
V	1912	Stockholm, Sweden	5 May–22 July
VI	1916	Berlin, Germany	not celebrated owing to war
VII	1920	Antwerp, Belgium	20 Apr–12 Sept
VIII	1924	Paris, France	4 May–27 July
IX	1928	Amsterdam, Holland	17 May–12 Aug
X	1932	Los Angeles, USA	30 July–14 Aug
XI	1936	Berlin, Germany	1–16 Aug
XII	1940	Tōkyō, then Helsinki, Finland	not celebrated owing to war
XIII	1944	London, England	not celebrated owing to war
XIV	1948	London, England	29 July–14 Aug
XV	1952	Helsinki, Finland	19 July–3 Aug
XVI	1956	Melbourne, Australia[1]	22 Nov–8 Dec
XVII	1960	Rome, Italy	25 Aug–11 Sept
XVIII	1964	Tōkyō, Japan	10–24 Oct
XIX	1968	Mexico City, Mexico	12–27 Oct
XX	1972	Munich, W. Germany	26 Aug–10 Sept
XXI	1976	Montreal, Canada	17 July–1 Aug.
XXII	1980	Moscow, USSR	19 July–3 Aug
XXIII	1984	Los Angeles, USA	28 July–12 Aug

* *This celebration (to mark the tenth anniversary of the modern Games) was officially intercalated but is not numbered.*
[1] *The equestrian events were held in Stockholm, Sweden, 10–17 June 1956.*

Separate Winter Olympics (there had been ice skating events in 1908 and 1920 and ice hockey in 1920) were inaugurated in 1924 and have been voted for as follows:

I	1924	Chamonix, France	25 Jan–4 Feb
II	1928	St Moritz, Switzerland	11–19 Feb
III	1932	Lake Placid, New York, USA	4–15 Feb
IV	1936	Garmisch-Partenkirchen, Germany	6–16 Feb
V	1948	St. Mortiz, Switzerland	30 Jan–8 Feb
VI	1952	Oslo, Norway	14–25 Feb
VII	1956	Cortina d'Ampezzo, Italy	26 Jan–5 Feb
VIII	1960	Squaw Valley, California, USA	18–28 Feb
IX	1964	Innsbruck, Austria	29 Jan–9 Feb
X	1968	Grenoble, France	6–18 Feb
XI	1972	Sapporo, Japan	3–13 Feb
XII	1976	Innsbruck, Austria	4–15 Feb
XIII	1980	Lake Placid, New York, USA	13–24 Feb
XIV	1984	Sarajevo, Yugoslavia	8–19 Feb

The first Winter Games in 1924 attracted 294 competitors from 16 nations.

Most medals *Individual gold*

In the ancient Olympic Games victors were given a chaplet of wild olive leaves. Leonidas of Rhodos won 12 running titles 164–152 BC. The most individual gold medals won by a male competitor in the modern Games is ten by Raymond Clarence Ewry (USA) (1874–1937) (see Track and Field Athletics). The female record is seven by Vera Caslavska-Odlozil (Czechoslovakia) (see Gymnastics). The most gold medals won by a British competitor is four by Paul Radmilovic (1886–1968) in water polo, 1908, 1912 and 1920 and the 4 × 200 m freestyle relay in 1908, and swimmer Henry Taylor (1885–1951) in 1906 and 1908. The Australian swimmer Iain Murray Rose, who won four gold medals, was born in Birmingham, England on 6 Jan 1939. The only Olympian to win four consecutive individual titles in the same event has been Alfred A. Oerter (b. 19 Sept 1936, Astoria, NY) of the USA, who won the discus title in 1956–68.

Swimmer Mark Andrew Spitz (USA) (b. 10 Feb 1950) won a record seven golds at one celebration, at Munich in 1972, including three in relays. The most won in individual events at one celebration is five by speed skater Eric Heiden (USA) (b. 14 June 1948) at Lake Placid, USA, in 1980.

The only man to win a gold medal in both the Summer and Winter Games is Edward F Eagan (USA) (1898–1967) who won the 1920 Light-Heavyweight boxing title and was a member of the winning four-man bob in 1932.

Most medals *National*

The total figures for medals for all Olympic events (including those now discontinued) for the Summer (1896–1980) and Winter Games (1924–80):

	Gold	Silver	Bronze	Total
1. USA[1]	660[2]	511	444	1615
2. USSR (formerly Russia)	402	330	296	1028
3. GB (including Ireland to 1920)[1]	169	205	186	560

[1] *Excludes medals won in Official Art competitions in 1912–48.*
[2] *The AAU (US) reinstated James Francis Thorpe (1888–1953) the disqualified highest scorer in the 1912 decathlon and pentathlon events on 12 Oct 1973 but no issue of medals has yet been authorised by the IOC.*

(A unique table of all medals won by nations is contained in The Guinness Book of Answers, 1982 edition).

Youngest and oldest gold medallists

The youngest ever winner was a French boy (whose name is not recorded) who coxed the Netherlands pair in 1900. He was 7–10 years old and he substituted for Dr Hermanus Brockmann, who coxed in the heats but proved too heavy. The youngest-ever female champion is Marjorie Gestring (USA) (b. 18 Nov 1922, now Mrs Bowman), aged 13 years 267 days, in the 1936 women's springboard event. Oscar Swahn (see p. 240) was in the winning Running Deer shooting team in 1912 aged 65 years 258 days.

Youngest and oldest *Great Britain*

The youngest competitor to represent Britain in the Olympic Games was Magdalena Cecilia Colledge (b. 28 Nov 1920) aged 11 years 24 days when she skated in the 1932 Games. The oldest was Hilda Lorna Johnstone (b. 4 Sept 1902) aged 70 years 5 days in the Equestrian Dressage in the 1972 Games.

Longest span

The longest span of an Olympic competitor is 40 years by Dr Ivan Osiier (Denmark) (1888–1965) in fencing, 1908–32 and 1948, and Magnus Konow (Norway) (1887–1972) in yachting, 1908–20, and 1936–48. The longest feminine span is 24 years (1932–56) by the Austrian fencer Ellen Müller-Preis (b. 6 May 1912). Raimondo d'Inzeo (b. 8 Feb 1925) competed for Italy in equestrian events at a record eight celebrations from 1948 to 1976, gaining one gold, two silver and three bronze medals.

Janice Lee York Romary (b. 6 Aug 1928) the US fencer, competed in all six Games from 1948 to 1968, and Lia Manoliu (Romania) (b. 25 Apr 1932) competed from 1952 to 1972 winning the discus in 1968.

The longest span of any British competitor is 28 years by Enoch Jenkins (b. 6 Nov 1892) who appeared in the 1924 and the 1952 Games in the clay pigeon shooting event, and the longest feminine span by Dorothy J. B. Tyler (*née* Odam) (b. 14 Mar 1920) who high-jumped from 1936 to 1956. The record number of appearances for Great Britain is six by fencer Bill Hoskyns from 1956 to 1976. Durward Randolph Knowles (b. 2 Nov 1917) competed in yachting for Britain in 1948 and in the following six Games for the Bahamas.

Most and least countries and participants
The greatest number of competitors in any summer Olympic Games has been 7147 at Munich in 1972. A record 122 countries competed at Munich in 1972. The fewest was 311 competitors from 13 countries in 1896. In 1904 only 12 countries participated. France entered the largest ever team of 880 men and four women in the 1900 Games at Paris.

Ever present
Four countries have never failed to be represented at the 20 celebrations of the Summer Games: Australia, Greece, Great Britain and Switzerland. Of these only Great Britain has been present at all Winter celebrations as well.

Largest crowd
The largest crowd at any Olympic site was 150,000 at the 1952 ski-jumping at the Holmenkollen, outside Oslo, Norway. Estimates of the number of spectators of the marathon race through Tōkyō, Japan on 21 Oct 1964 were 500,000 to 1,500,000.

ORIENTEERING

Origins
Orienteering as now known was invented by Major Ernst Killander in Sweden in 1918. It was based on military exercises of the 1890s. The term was first used for an event at Oslo, Norway on 7 Oct 1900. World championships were instituted in 1966. Annual British championships were instituted in 1967 following the formation of the British Orienteering Federation.

Most titles *World*
Sweden has won the men's relay six times between 1966 and 1979 and the women's relay four times, 1966, 1970, 1974–6. Ulla Lindkvist (Sweden) gained the women's individual titles in 1966 and 1968. The men's title has been won twice by Age Hadler (Norway) in 1966 and 1972 and Egil Johansen (Norway) 1976 and 1978.

Most titles *British*
The men's relay has been won twice by Oxford University, 1975, 1979, and the women's relay three times by Derwent Valley Orienteers, 1975, 1979 and 1980. Geoffrey Peck (b. Blackpool, 27 Sept 1949) (Interlopers) has won the men's individual title a record five times, 1971, 1973, 1976–7 and 1979. Carol McNeill (b. 20 Feb 1944) of the same club has won the women's title six times, 1967, 1969, 1972–76.

PARACHUTING

Origins
Parachuting became a regulated sport with the institution of world championships in 1951. A team title was introduced in 1954 and women's events were included in 1956.

Most titles *World*
The USSR won the men's team titles in 1954, 1958, 1960, 1966, 1972, 1976, and 1980, and the women's team title in 1956, 1958, 1966, 1968, 1972, and 1976. Nikolai Ushamyev (USSR) has won the individual title twice, 1974 and 1980.

Most titles *British*
John Meacock (Peterborough) (b. 30 Aug 1938) has won the British title four times in 1969, 1971–2 and 1975.

The Soviet ice hockey team congratulating the United States team at Lake Placid after they had won America's 660th Olympic gold medal. (*Steve Powell, All-Sport*)

Greatest accuracy
Jacqueline Smith (GB) (b. 29 Mar 1951) scored ten consecutive dead centre strikes (10 cm *4 in* disc) in the World Championships at Zagreb, Yugoslavia, 1 Sept 1978. At Yuma, Arizona, USA, in March 1978, Dwight Reynolds scored a record 105 daytime dead centres, and Bill Wenger and Phil Munden tied with 43 nighttime DCs, competing as members of the US Army team, the Golden Knights. With electronic measuring the official FAI record is 50 DCs by Alexander Aasmiae (USSR) at Ferghana, USSR, Oct 1979.

Most jumps
The greatest number of consecutive jumps completed in 24 hr is 233 by David Parchment at Shobdon Airfield, Hereford, on 19 June 1979.

A record 10,000 jumps have been made by Anatoli Ossipov (USSR) to end-1979. The women's record is 8000 by Valentina Zakoretskaya (USSR) since 1964.

Phil Munden, record breaking member of the crack US Army Parachute team, the Golden Knights. (*United States Army*)

Paragliding
Six men of a British Joint Services team paraglided across the English Channel from an aeroplane 25,000 ft *7620 m* over Dover, Kent to Sangatte, France on 31 Aug 1980.

PELOTA VASCA *(Jaï Alaï)*

Origins
The game, which originated in Italy as *longue paume* and was introduced into France in the 13th century, is said to be the fastest of all ball games. The glove or *gant* was introduced *c.* 1840 and the *chistera* was invented by Jean 'Gantchiki' Dithurbide of Ste Pée, France. The *grand chistera* was invented by Melchior Curuchague of Buenos Aires, Argentina in 1888.

The world's largest *frontón* (enclosed stadium) is the World Jaï-Alaï at Miami, Florida, USA, which had a record attendance of 15,052 on 27 Dec 1975.

Various games are played in a *frontón*, the most popular being *main nue, remonte, rebot, pala, grand chistera* and *cesta punta.* Internationally the sport is governed by the Federación Internacional de Pelota Vasca in Madrid, Spain.

Highest speed
An electronically measured ball velocity of 188 mph *302 km/h* was recorded by José Ramon Areitio at the Newport Jai Alai, Rhode Island, USA on 3 Aug 1979.

Longest domination
The longest domination as the world's No. 1 player was enjoyed by Chiquito de Cambo (*né* Joseph Apesteguy) (France), (1881–1955) from the beginning of the century until succeeded in 1938 by Jean Urruty (France) (b. 19 Oct 1913).

PIGEON RACING

Earliest references
Pigeon racing developed from the use of homing pigeons for carrying messages—a quality utilised in the ancient Olympic Games (776 BC–AD 393). The sport originated in Belgium and the earliest long-distance race was from London to Antwerp in 1819, involving 32 pigeons. The earliest recorded occasion on which 500 miles *804 km* was flown in a day was by *Motor* (owned by G. P. Pointer of Alexander Palace Racing Pigeon Club) which was released from Thurso, Scotland on 30 June 1896 and covered 501 miles *806 km* at an average speed of 1454 yd *1329 m* per min (49½ mph *79,6 km/h*).

Longest flights
The greatest recorded homing flight by a pigeon was made by one owned by the 1st Duke of Wellington (1769–1852). Released from a sailing ship off the Ichabo Islands, West Africa, on 8 April, it dropped dead a mile from its loft at Nine Elms, Wandsworth, London on 1 June 1845, 55 days later, having flown an airline route of 5400 miles *8700 km*, but an actual distance of possibly 7000 miles *11 250 km* to avoid the Sahara Desert. The official British duration record (into Great Britain) is 1173 miles *1887 km* in 15 days by C.S.O. (owned by Rosie and Bruce of Wick) in the 1976 Palamos Race. In the 1975 Palamos Race, *The Conqueror*, owned by Alan Raeside, homed to Irvine, Strathclyde, 1010 miles *1625 km*, in 43 hr 56 min.

Greatest mileage
A red chequer cock *Concord* owned by Gerry Holten, of Taupiri, NZ has flown a record competitive 15,033 miles *24.193 km.*

Highest speeds
In level flight in windless conditions it is very doubtful if any pigeon can exceed 60 mph *96 km/h*. The highest race speed recorded is one of 3229 yd *2952 m* per min (110.07 mph *177,14 km/h*) in the East Anglian Federation race from East Croydon on 8 May 1965 when the 1428 birds were backed by a powerful south south-west wind. The winner was owned by A. Vidgeon & Son, Wickford, Essex.

The highest race speed recorded over a distance of more than 1000 km *621.37 miles* is 2432.70 yd *2224,5 m* per min

(82.93 mph *133,46 km/h*) by a hen pigeon in the Central Cumberland Combine race over 683 miles 147 yd *1099,316 km* from Murray Bridge, South Australia to North Ryde, Sydney on 2 Oct 1971.

24 hr records
The world's longest reputed distance in 24 hr is 803 miles *1292 km* (velocity 1525 yd *1394 m* per min) by E. S. Petersen's winner of the 1941 San Antonio R.C. event in Texas, USA.

The best 24-hr performance into the United Kingdom is 724 miles 219 yd *1165,3 km* by E. Cardno's *Mormond Lad*, on 2 July 1977, from Nantes, France to Fraserburgh, Grampian. Average speed was 1648 yd *1507 m* per min (56.18 mph *90,41 km/h*).

Lowest speed
A pigeon *Blue Clip*, belonging to Harold Hart released in Rennes, France arrived home in its loft in Leigh, Greater Manchester, on 29 Sept 1974, 7 years and 2 months later. It had covered the distance of 370 miles *595 km* at an average speed of 0.00589 mph *0,00948 km/h* which is slower than the world's fastest snail (see page 48).

Most first prizes
Owned by R. Green, of Walsall Wood, West Midlands, *Champion Breakaway* won 56 first prizes from 1972 to May 1979.

Highest priced bird
The highest recorded price paid for a pigeon is approximately £25,000 by a Japanese fancier for *De Wittslager* to Georges Desender (Belgium) in October 1978.

POLO

Earliest games
Polo is usually regarded as being of Persian origin having been played as *Pulu c.* 525 BC. Other claims have come from Tibet and the Tang Dynasty of China AD 250. The earliest polo club of modern times was the Kachar Club (founded in 1859) in Assam, India. The game was introduced into England from India in 1869 by the 10th Hussars at Aldershot, Hampshire and the earliest match was one between the 9th Lancers and the 10th Hussars on Hounslow Heath, Greater London, in July 1871. The earliest international match between England and the USA was in 1886.

The game is played on the largest pitch of any ball game in the world. A ground measures 300 yd *274 m* long by 160 yd *146 m* wide with side boards, or 200 yd *182 m* wide without boards.

Most Olympic medals
Polo has been part of the Olympic programme on five occasions: 1900, 1908, 1920, 1924, and 1936. Of the 21 gold medallists, a 1920 winner, the Rt Hon. Sir John Wodehouse, Br., CBE, MC, the 3rd Earl of Kimberley (b. 1883–k. 1941) uniquely also won a silver medal (1908).

Most international appearances
The most times any player has represented England is four in the case of (later Sir) Frederick Maitland Freake (1876–1950) in 1900, 1902, 1909 and 1913. Thomas Hitchcock, Jr. (1900–44) played five times for the USA *v.* England (1921, 1924, 1927, 1930, 1939) and twice *v.* Argentina (1928 and 1936).

Highest handicap
The highest handicap based on eight 7½-min 'chukkas' is ten goals introduced in the USA in 1891 and in the United Kingdom and in Argentina in 1910. The latest of the 39 players ever to receive ten-goal handicaps are Alberto Heguy and Alfredo Harriott of Argentina, and in England, Eduardo Moore (Argentina). The last (of six) ten-goal handicap players from Great Britain was Gerald Balding in 1939. A match of two 40-goal teams was staged for the first time ever, at Palermo, Buenos Aires, Argentina, in 1975.

The highest handicap of the United Kingdom's current 500 players is nine by Julian Hipwood (b. 23 June 1946). Claire Tomlinson of Gloucestershire has a handicap of four, the highest ever attained by a British woman.

Julian Hipwood (left), competing here in the 1973 International Trial match at Cowdray Park, Sussex, is Britain's highest handicap player. His brother Howard is also a top ranked player. (*Desmond O'Neill*)

Highest score
The highest aggregate number of goals scored in an international match is 30, when Argentina beat the USA 21–9 at Meadow Brook, Long Island, New York, USA, in September 1936.

Largest trophy
For details see p. 239.

Largest crowd
World record crowds of more than 50,000 have watched floodlit matches at the Sydney Agricultural Show, Australia. A crowd of 40,000 watched a game played at Jaipur, India, in 1976 using elephants instead of ponies. The length of the polo sticks used has not been ascertained.

POWERBOAT RACING

See also The Guinness Book of Motorboating Facts and Feats *by Kevin Desmond, published by Guinness Superlatives Ltd (price £7.95).*

Origins
The earliest application of the petrol engine to a boat was by Jean Joseph Etienne Lenoir (1822–1900) on the River Seine, Paris, France, in 1865. The sport was given impetus by the presentation of an international championship cup by Sir Alfred Harmsworth in 1903, which was also the year of the first off-shore race from Calais to Dover.

Harmsworth Trophy
Of the 25 Anglo-American contests from 1903 to 1961, the United States won the most with 16. The greatest number of wins is eight, by Commodore Garfield A. Wood (1881–1971) 1920–1, 1926, 1928–30, 1932–3. The only boat to win three times is *Miss Supertest III*, owned by James G. Thompson (Canada), driven by the late Bob Hayward (Canada), in 1959–61. This boat also achieved the record speed of 119.27 mph *191,94 km/h* at Picton, Ontario, Canada in 1961.

Gold Cup
The Gold Cup (instituted 1903) has been won eight times by Bill Muncey (b. 1929) (USA), 1956–7, 1961–2, 1972, 1977–9. The record speed is 128.338 mph *206,539 km/h* for a 2½ mile *4 km* lap by the unlimited hydroplane *Atlas Van Lines*, driven by Bill Muncey in a qualifying round on the Columbia River, Washington, USA, in July 1977, and again in July 1978.

Cowes–Torquay–Cowes race
The record average for this International Off-shore Race (instituted 1961) is 79.64 mph *128,16 km/h* by *Satisfaction* driven by Bill Elswick (USA) over the 245 mile *394,2 km* course in 3 hr

4 min 35 sec on 23 Aug 1980. The only three time winner has been Thomas Edward Brodie 'Tommy' Sopwith (b. 15 Nov 1932) (GB) in 1961, 1968 and 1970.

Highest speeds
The fastest off-shore record, as recognised by the Union Internationale Motonautique, is 97.20 mph *156,43 km/h* in the IIID class by Robert Cook on Lake Windermere, Cumbria, on 15 Oct 1979. The R6 inboard engine record of 128.375 mph *206,599 km/h* was set by the hydroplane *Vladivar I*, driven by Tony Fahey (GB) on Lake Windermere, on 23 May 1977. The Class ON record is 136.38 mph *219,48 km/h* by James F. Merten (USA) 1973. (For the world water speed record see p. 175).

Longest races
The longest race has been the Port Richborough London to Monte Carlo Marathon Off-Shore International event. The race extended over 2947 miles *4742 km* in 14 stages on 10–25 June 1972. It was won by *H.T.S.* (GB) driven by Mike Bellamy, Eddie Chater and Jim Brooks in 71 hr 35 min 56 sec (average 41.15 mph *66,24 km/h*). The *Daily Telegraph and BP* Round Britain race, 26 July–7 Aug 1969, 1403 miles *2257 km* (from Portsmouth in ten stages west and *via* the Caledonian Canal) was won by *Avenger Too* (Timo Makinen, Alan Pascoe Watson and Brian Hendicott) in 39 hr 9 min 37.7 sec. Of 42 starters, 24 finished.

Longest jump
The longest jump achieved by a powerboat has been 120 ft *36,57 m* by Peter Horak (USA) (b. 7 May 1943) in a Glastron Carlson CVX 20 Jet Deluxe with a 460 Ford V8 engine (take-off speed 55 mph *88 km/h*) for a documentary TV film 'The Man who fell from the Sky', at Salton Sea, California, USA on 26 Apr 1980.

Dragsters
The first drag boat to attain 200 mph *321 km/h* was Sam Kurtovich's *Crisis* which attained 200.44 mph *322,57 km/h* in California in October 1969 at the end of a one-way run. *Climax* has since been reported to have attained 205.19 mph *330,22 km/h*.

RACKETS

Origins
There is record of the sale of a racket court at Southernhay, Exeter, Devon dated 12 Jan 1798. The game which is of 17th century origin was played by debtors in the Fleet Prison, London in the middle of the 18th century, and an inmate, Robert Mackay, claimed the first 'world' title in 1820. The first closed court champion was Francis Erwood at Woolwich in 1860. A new court was constructed at the Sea Court Club, Hayling Island, Hampshire in 1979.

Longest reign
Of the 20 world champions since 1820 the longest reign is by

The 120 foot jump by Peter Horak in the film 'The Man who fell from the Sky'. (*Greg Meny*)

Relaxing prior to competing, six-time World all-round Rodeo champion Tom Ferguson from Oklahoma. (*Association of Professional Rodeo Cowboys*)

The standard required time to stay on in bareback, saddle bronc and bull riding events is 8 sec. In the now discontinued ride-to-a-finish events, rodeo riders have been recorded to have survived 90 + min, until the mount had not a buck left in it.

The highest score in bull riding was made by Don Gay on *Oscar* at The Cow Place, San Francisco, California, in 1977, when he was awarded 97 points.

Champion bull
The top bucking bull was probably *Honky Tonk*, an 11-year-old Brahma, who unseated 187 riders in an undefeated eight-year career to his retirement in September 1978.

Champion bronc
Traditionally a bronc called *Midnight* owned by Jim McNab of Alberta, Canada was never ridden in 12 appearances at the Calgary Stampede.

ROLLER SKATING

Origins
The first roller skate was devised by Joseph Merlin of Huy, Belgium, in 1760 and first worn by him in public in London. James L. Plimpton of New York produced the present four-wheeled type and patented it in January 1863. The first indoor rinks were opened in London, in the Strand and at Floral Hall, Covent Garden, in 1857. The great boom periods were 1870–5, 1908–12 and 1948–54, each originating in the United States.

Most titles *Speed*
Most world speed titles have been won by Alberta Vianello (Italy) with 16 between 1953 and 1965. Leslie E. Woodley of Birmingham won 12 British national individual titles between 1957 and 1964, a feat equalled by Michael McGeogh, 1966–79, and John Fry, 1967–79. Chloe Ronaldson (b. 30 Nov 1939) has won 37 ladies' titles from 1958 to 1979.

Most titles *Figure*
The records for figure titles are five by Karl Heinz Losch in 1958–9, 1961–2 and 1966, and four by Astrid Bader, both of W. Germany, in 1965–8. Most world pair titles have been taken by Dieter Fingerle (W. Germany) with four in 1959, 1965–7.

Speed skating
The fastest speed put up in an official world record is 25.78 mph *41,48 km/h* when Giuseppe Cantarella (Italy) (b. 13 Aug 1944) recorded 34.9 sec for 440 yd *402 m* on a road at Catania, Sicily on 28 Sept 1963. The world mile record on a rink is 2 min 25.1 sec by Gianni Ferretti (Italy) (b. 11 May 1948) at Inzell, W. Germany on 28 Sept 1968. The greatest distance skated in 1 hr on a rink by a woman is 35,399 km *21.995 miles* by Marisa Anna Danesi (Italy) (b. 25 Nov 1935) at Inzell, W. Germany on 28 Sept 1968. The men's record on a track is 37,230 km *23,133 miles* by Alberto Civolani (Italy) (b. 16 Mar 1933) at Inzell, W. Germany on 28 Sept 1968, who went on to skate 50 miles *80,46 km* in 2 hr 20 min 33.1 sec.

Roller hockey
Roller hockey (previously known as Rink Hockey in Europe) was first introduced in this country as Rink Polo, at the old Lava rink, Denmark Hill, London in the late 1870s. The Amateur Rink Hockey Association was formed in 1908, and in 1913 became the National Rink Hockey (now Roller Hockey) Association. Britain won the inaugural World Championship in 1936 since when Portugal has won most titles with 11 between 1947 and 1974. The European Championship (inst. 1926) was won by Portugal a record 15 times between 1947 and 1977.

Largest rink
The greatest indoor rink ever to operate was located in the Grand Hall, Olympia, London. Opened 1890 and closed in 1912 it had an actual skating area of 68,000 ft² *6 300 m²*. The current largest is the Fireside Roll-Arena, Illinois, USA which has a total skating surface of 29,859 ft² *2774 m²*.

Endurance
Theodore James Coombs (b. 1954) of Hermosa Beach, Califor-

Geoffrey Willoughby Thomas Atkins (b. 20 Jan 1927) who held the title after beating the professional James Dear in 1954 and retired, after defending it four times, in April 1972.

Most Amateur titles
Since the Amateur singles championship was instituted in 1888 the most titles won by an individual is nine by Edgar Maximilian Baerlein (1879–1971) between 1903 and 1923. Since the institution of the Amateur doubles championship in 1890 the most shares in titles has been eleven by David Sumner Milford (b. 7 June 1905), between 1938 and 1959 and John Ross Thompson (b. 10 May 1918) between 1948 and 1966. Milford has also seven Amateur singles titles (1930–51), an Open title (1936) and held the World title from 1937 to 1946. Thompson has additionally won an Open singles title and five Amateur singles titles.

RODEO

Origins
Rodeo which developed from 18th century *fiestas* came into being in the early days of the North American cattle industry. The earliest reference to the sport is at Santa Fe, New Mexico, USA, on 10 June 1847. Steer wrestling came in with Bill Pickett (1870–1932) of Texas, in 1900.

The largest rodeo in the world is the Calgary Exhibition and Stampede at Calgary, Alberta, Canada. The record attendance has been 1,069,830 on 8–17 July 1977. The record for one day is 148,486 on 7 July 1979. The oldest continuously held rodeo is that at Payson, Arizona, first held in August 1887.

Most world titles
The record number of all-round titles in the Association of Professional Rodeo Cowboys world championships is six by Larry Mahan (USA) (b. 21 Nov 1943) in 1966–70 and 1973 and, consecutively, 1974–9 by Tom Ferguson (b. 20 Dec 1950). Jim Shoulders (b. 1928) of Henryetta, Oklahoma, USA has won a record 16 world championships between 1949 and 1959. The record figure for prize money with bonuses in a single season is $131,233 by Tom Ferguson from Miami, Oklahoma, USA in 1978.

Youngest champion
The youngest winner of a world title is Metha Brorsen, of Oklahoma, USA, who was only 11 years when she won the International Rodeo Association Cowgirls barrel racing event in 1975.

Time records
Records for timed events, such as calf-roping and steer-wrestling, are meaningless, because of the widely varying conditions due to the size of arenas and amount of start given the stock. The fastest time recorded for roping a calf is 5.7 sec by Bill Reeder at Assiniboia, Saskatchewan, Canada in 1978, and the fastest time for overcoming a steer is 2.4 sec by James Bynum of Waxahachie, Texas, at Marietta, Oklahoma, USA, in 1955.

nia, skated 5193 miles *8357 km* from Los Angeles to New York and back to Yates Center, Kansas from 30 May to 14 Sept 1979.

Marathon

The longest recorded continuous roller skating marathon was one of 331 hr 20 min by Lou Sergi at the Majestic Rink, Sydney, Australia on 22 June–6 July 1980.

ROWING

Oldest race

The Sphinx stela of Amenhotep II (1450–1425 BC) records that he *stroked* a boat for some three miles. The earliest established sculling race is the Doggett's Coat and Badge, which was first rowed on 1 Aug 1716 from London Bridge to Chelsea and is still contested annually. Although rowing regattas were held in Venice in 1300 the first English regatta probably took place on the Thames by the Ranelagh Gardens, near Putney in 1775. Boating began at Eton in 1793, 72 years before the 'song'. The Leander Club was formed *c.* 1818.

Most Olympic medals

Five oarsmen have won three gold medals: John B. Kelly (USA) (1889–1960), father of HSH Princess Grace of Monaco, in the sculls (1920) and double sculls (1920 and 1924); his cousin Paul Vincent Costello (USA) (b. 27 Dec 1899) in the double sculls (1920, 1924 and 1928); Jack Beresford, Jr, CBE (GB) (1899–1977) in the sculls (1924), coxless fours (1932) and double sculls (1936), Vyacheslav Ivanov (USSR) (b. 30 July 1938) in the sculls (1956, 1960 and 1964) and Siegfried Brietzke (E. Germany) (b. 12 June 1952) in the coxless pairs (1972) and coxless fours (1976, 1980).

Boat Race

The earliest University Boat Race, which Oxford won, was from Hambledon Lock to Henley Bridge on 10 June 1829. Outrigged eights were first used in 1846. In the 127 races to 1981, Cambridge won 68 times, Oxford 58 times and there was a dead heat on 24 Mar 1877.

The race record time for the course of 4 miles 374 yd *6779 km* (Putney to Mortlake) is 16 min 58 sec by Oxford on 20 Mar 1976. This represents an average speed of 14.89 mph *23,97 km/h*. The smallest winning margin has been by a canvas by Oxford in 1952 and 1980. The greatest margin (apart from sinking) was Cambridge's win by 20 lengths in 1900.

The record to the Mile Post is 3 min 31 sec (Oxford 1978) an average speed of 17.06 mph *27,45 km/h*; Hammersmith Bridge 6 min 24 sec (Oxford 1978); Chiswick Steps 10 min 18 sec (Oxford 1976); and Barnes Bridge 14 min 09 sec (Oxford 1976).

The heaviest man ever to row in a University boat has been Stephen G. H. Plunkett (Queen's) the No. 5 in the 1976 Oxford boat at 16 st 5 lb *104 kg*. The 1976 Oxford crew averaged a record 14 st 0⅝ lb *89 kg*. The lightest oarsman was the 1882 Oxford Stroke, Alfred Herbert Higgins, at 9 st 6½ lb *60 kg*. The lightest coxes, Francis Henry Archer (Cambridge) (1843–89) in 1862 and Hart Parker Vincent Massey (Oxford) (b. Canada, 30 Mar 1918) in 1939, were both 5 st 2 lb *32,6 kg*.

Head of the River

A processional race for eights instituted in 1926, the Head has an entry limit of 420 crews (3780 competitors). The record for the course Mortlake–Putney (the reverse of the Boat Race) is 17 min 17.40 sec by the ARA National Squad in 1980.

Henley Royal Regatta

The annual regatta at Henley-on-Thames, Oxfordshire, was inaugurated on 26 Mar 1839. Since then the course, except in 1923, has been about 1 mile 550 yd *2212 m* varying slightly according to the length of boat. In 1967 the shorter craft were 'drawn up' so all bows start level.

The most wins in the Diamond Challenge Sculls (inst. 1844) is six consecutively by Stuart A. Mackenzie (b. 5 Apr 1937) (Australia and GB) 1957–62. The record time is 7 min 40 sec by Sean Drea (Neptune RC, Ireland) on 5 July 1975. The Grand Challenge Cup (inst. 1839) for eights, has been won 27 times by Leander C crews between 1840 and 1953. The record time for the event is 6 min 13 sec by Harvard Univ, USA, and a combined Leander/Thames Tradesmen crew, both on 5 July 1975.

Sculling

The record number of wins in the Wingfield Sculls (Putney to Mortlake) (instituted 1830) is seven by Jack Beresford, Jr. from 1920 to 1926. The fastest time has been 21 min 11 sec by Leslie Frank Southwood (b. 18 Jan 1906) on 12 Aug 1933. The most world professional sculling titles (instituted 1831) won is seven by William Beach (Australia) between 1884 and 1887.

Highest speed

The highest recorded speed on non-tidal water for 2000 m *2187 yd* is by an East German eight in 5 min 32.17 sec (13.46 mph *21.67 km/h*) at Montreal, Canada on 18 July 1976. A team from Penn AC, USA, was timed in 5 min 18.8 sec (14.03 mph *22,58 km/h*) in the FISA Championships on the River Meuse, Liege, Belgium, on 17 Aug 1930.

Cross Channel

The Rev Sidney Swann (1862–1942) sculled across the Channel in a record 3 hr 50 min on 12 Sept 1911. *For trans-Atlantic rowing records see p. 179.*

River Thames

A crew of five from 'F' Division of the London Fire Brigade rowed the navigable length of the Thames, 209 miles *336 km*, from Lechlade Bridge, Gloucestershire to Southend Pier, Essex in 53 hr 2 min on 2–4 July 1981. The fastest time from Folly Bridge, Oxford to Westminster Bridge, London (112 miles *180 km*) is 14 hr 35 min 46 sec by an eight from Guy's Hospital on 28 Apr 1974.

Loch Ness

Loch Ness, (22.7 miles *36,5 km*), was rowed by George G. Parsonage, 31, of Whitehill Secondary School, Glasgow in 2 hr 43 min 34.1 sec on 17 May 1975. A coxed junior eight (average age 15 yr 7 months) from Sir Thomas Rich's School, Gloucester, took 2 hr 35 min 38.2 sec on 25 Aug 1975.

Longest race

The longest annual rowing race is the Ringvaart Regatta 100 km

MEN—Fastest times over 2 000 m course (still water)				
	min sec	Country	Place	Date
Single Sculls	6:49.68	Nikolai Dovgan, USSR	Amsterdam, Netherlands	26 Aug 1978
Double Sculls	6:12.48	Norway	Montreal, Canada	23 July 1976
Coxed Pairs	6:56.94	E. Germany	Copenhagen, Denmark	—Aug 1971
Coxless Pairs	6:33.02	E. Germany	Montreal, Canada	23 July 1976
Coxed Fours	6:09.17	E. Germany	Amsterdam, Netherlands	30 June 1979
Coxless Fours	5:53.65	E. Germany	Montreal, Canada	23 July 1976
Quadruple Sculls	5:47.38	W. Germany	Lucerne, Switzerland	4 June 1980
Eights	5:32.17	E. Germany	Montreal, Canada	18 July 1976

WOMEN—Fastest times over 1 000 m course (still water)				
Single Sculls	3:34.31	Christine Scheiblich, E. Germany	Amsterdam, Netherlands	21 Aug 1977
Double Sculls	3:16.27	USSR	Moscow, USSR	26 July 1980
Coxless Pairs	3:26.32	E. Germany	Amsterdam, Netherlands	21 Aug 1977
Coxed Fours	3:14.03	E. Germany	Lucerne, Switzerland	15 June 1980
Quadruple Sculls	3:08.49	E. Germany	Montreal, Canada	19 July 1976
Eights	2:57.38	E. Germany	Lucerne, Switzerland	15 June 1980

62 miles for eights, at Delft, Netherlands. The record time is 7 hr 2 min 41 sec by the Rijnland team on 29 May 1980. The annual Tour du Lac Leman, Geneva, Switzerland for coxed four gigs is over 150–160 km *93–99 miles*.

Punting

The earliest reference to punting as a sport was in 1793. Amateur and professional championships were instituted in the 1870s. Victorians argued about the two styles of pole planting and running *versus* pricking. Abel Beasley, the foremost exponent of the latter, won the Professional Championship 14 times (1877–90). In winning the 1896 Amateur title B. Rixon achieved a record average speed of 7.6 mph *12,2 km/h*. The longest recorded punt is one of 721 miles *1160 km*, Oxford–Leeds–Oxford by John Pearse, aided mainly by John Charles and three other alternative crew members from Jesus College, Oxford, on 19 June–10 Aug 1965. A trip of 694 miles *1116 km* was made by Michael Wigney and Christopher Smith, of Magdalen College, Oxford on 28 June–3 Aug 1980.

SHINTY

Origins

Shinty (from the Gaelic *sinteag*, a leap) was recorded in the West and Central Highlands in 1769 when it was known as *lomain* (driving forward). Games were contested between whole clans or parishes without limit as to numbers or time until darkness stopped play among the walking wounded. The field of play was undelineated except by the occasional pail of *uisge-beatha* 'breath of life' (i.e. whisky). In an inter-clan match a combatant who had failed to disable at least one opponent within a reasonable time had his curved stick (*caman*) confiscated as a punishment by the Chieftain so that he could only kick the ball (*cnaige*) or his opponents.

This ungovernable game was first given rules in 1879 and the Camanachd Association was set up by Charles Julian Brewster Macpherson of Balavil near Kingussie, Highland on 10 Oct 1893.

Most titles

Newtonmore, Highland has won the Camanachd Association Challenge Cup (instituted 1896) a record 21 times (1896–1975). In 1923 the Furnace Club, Argyll won the Cup without conceding a goal throughout the competition.

Highest scores

The highest Cup Final score was in 1909 when Newtonmore beat Furnace 11–3 at Glasgow, Dr Johnnie Cattanach scoring eight hails or goals. In 1938 John Macmillan Mactaggart scored ten hails for Mid-Argyll in a Camanachd Cup match.

SHOOTING

Earliest club

The Lucerne Shooting Guild (Switzerland) was formed *c.* 1466 and the first recorded shooting match was at Zurich in 1472.

Most Olympic medals

The record number of medals won is 11 by Carl Townsend Osburn (USA) (1884–1966) in 1912, 1920 and 1924, consisting of five gold, four silver and two bronze. Six other marksmen have won five gold medals. The only marksman to win three individual gold medals has been Gudbrand Gudbrandšonn Skatteboe (Norway) (1875–1965) in 1906.

Bisley

The National Rifle Association was instituted in 1859. The Queen's (King's) Prize has been shot since 1860 and has only once been won by a woman—Marjorie Elaine Foster, MBE (1894–1974) (score 280) on 19 July 1930. Arthur George Fulton, MBE (1887–1972) won a record three times (1912, 1926, 1931). Both his father and his son also won the Prize.

The highest score (possible 300) for the final of the Queen's Prize, which is an aggregate of the last two stages of the competition, is 294 by Alain Marion (Canada) on 26 July 1980. The record for the Silver Medal is 150 (possible 150) by Martin John Brister (City Rifle Club) (b. 1951) and the Lord Swansea on 24 July 1971. This was equalled by John Henry Carmichael (WRA Bromsgrove RC) on 28 July 1979 and Robert Stafford on 26 July 1980, with the size of the bullseyes reduced.

Small Bore

The National Small-Bore Rifle Association, of Britain, was formed in 1901. The British team record (1966 target) is 1988 × 2000 by Lancashire in 1968–9 and London in 1980–1. The British individual record is by John Palin (b. 16 July 1934) who shot 600 × 600 prone with a .22 rifle in Switzerland in 1972, Barry Dagger (b. 19 May 1937) at Bisley, in June 1976 and Alistair Allan at Bisley in 1977. The record score for a round in the

INDIVIDUAL WORLD RECORDS
(as ratified by the International Shooting Union (UIT)).

Event			Possible—Score	Name	Country	Date
Free Rifle	300 m	3 × 40 shots	1200—1160	Lones W. Wigger (USA)	Seoul, S. Korea	Oct 1978
		60 shots prone	600— 592	Gennadi Lushikov (USSR)	Oulu, Finland	17 June 1981
			592	Alexander Mastrianin (USSR)	Oulu, Finland	17 June 1981
Standard Rifle	300 m	3 × 20 shots	600— 577	David Kimes (USA)	Seoul, S. Korea	Oct 1978
Small-bore Rifle	50 m	3 × 40 shots	1200—1173	Viktor Vlasov (USSR)	Moscow, USSR	23 July 1980
		60 shots prone	600— 599	Eight men		
Free Pistol	50 m	60 shots	600— 581	Alexander Melentev (USSR)	Moscow, USSR	20 July 1980
Rapid Fire Pistol	25 m	60 shots	600— 598	Giovanni Liverzani (Italy)	Phoenix, USA	1970
			598	Ion Corneliu (Romania)	Bucharest, Romania	1977
Centre Fire Pistol	25 m	60 shots	600— 597	Thomas D. Smith (USA)	São Paulo, Brazil	1963
Standard Pistol	25 m	60 shots	600— 583	Ragnar Skanaker (Sweden)	Seoul, S. Korea	Oct 1978
Running Target	50 m	60 shots 'normal runs'	600— 589	Igov Sokolov (USSR)	Moscow, USSR	24 July 1980
			589	Thomas Pfeffer (E. Germany)	Moscow, USSR	24 July 1980
Trap	—	200 birds	200— 199	Angelo Scalzone (Italy)	Munich, W. Germany	29 Aug 1972
			199	Michel Carrega (France)	Thun, Switzerland	23 Sept 1974
Skeet	—	200 birds	200— 199	J. Clemmons (USA)	Mexico City	1977
Air Rifle	10 m	60 shots	600— 584	Harald Stanvaag (Norway)	Athens, Greece	Feb 1981
Air Pistol	10 m	60 shots	600— 582	Valdas Tourla (USSR)	Athens, Greece	Feb 1981
			582	Ivan Mandov (Bulgaria)	Athens, Greece	Feb 1981

LARGEST BRITISH BAGS
See also The Guinness Guide to Field Sports *by Wilson Stevens published by Guinness Superlatives Ltd at £10.50*

Hare	1,215	11 guns	Holkham, Norfolk	19 Dec 1877
Rabbit	6,943	5 guns	Blenheim, Oxfordshire	17 Oct 1898
Geese (Brent)	704[1]	32 punt-guns	Colonel Russell i/c, River Blackwater, Essex	*c.* 1860
Grouse	1,070	1 gun	Thomas, 6th Baron Walsingham in Yorkshire	30 Aug 1888
Grouse	2,929	8 guns	Littledale and Abbeystead, Lancashire	12 Aug 1915
Partridge (Wild)	2,015[2]	6 guns	Rothwell, Lincolnshire	3 Oct 1952
Pheasant	3,937	7 guns[3]	Hall Barn, Beaconsfield, Buckinghamshire	18 Dec 1913
Pigeon	561	1 gun	K. Ransford, Salop-Powys	22 July 1970
Snipe	1,108	2 guns	Tiree, Inner Hebrides	25 Oct–3 Nov 1906
Woodcock	228	6 guns	Ashford, County Galway, Ireland	28 Jan 1910
Woodpigeon	550	1 gun	Major A. J. Coates, near Winchester, Hampshire	10 Jan 1962

[1] *Plus about 250 later picked up.*
[2] *Plus 104 later picked up.*
[3] *Including H.M. King George V.*

British Schools' Small Bore Rifle Association (B.S.S.R.A.) contest is a team possible of 500 × 500 by Gresham's School, Holt, Norfolk in Lent Term, 1972. Simon John Carter (b. 7 May 1954) scored 500 × 500 in the five rounds in this .22 contest. Richard Hansen shot 5000 bullseyes in 24 hr at Fresno, Cal, USA on 13 June 1929.

Clay pigeon

Most world titles have been won by Susan Nattrass (Canada) (b. 5 Nov 1950) with five in 1974–5, 1977–9. The most by a man is four by Michael Carrega (France) (b. 26 Sept 1934) in 1970–1, 1974 and 1979. The record number of clay birds shot in an hour is 1904 by Tom Kreckman, 36, at Cresco, Penn, USA, on a Skeet range, 28 Sept 1975. Graham Douglas Geater (b. 21 July 1947) shot 2264 targets in an hour on a Trapshooting range at the NILO Gun Club, Papamoa, New Zealand on 17 Jan 1981.

Bench rest shooting

The smallest group on record at 1000 yd *914 m* is 5.093 in *12.936 cm* by Rick Taylor with a 300 Weatherby at Williamsport, Penn., USA on 24 Aug 1980.

Highest score in 24 hr

The Central Lancashire Rifle Club team of John Jepson, Graham Sharples, Derek Byron and Joseph Graham, scored 85,752 points (averaging 94.03 per card) on 26–27 Nov 1976.

Rapid firing

Using a Soper single-loading rifle, Private John Warrick, 1st Berkshire Volunteers, loaded and fired 60 rounds in one minute at Basingstoke, Hants, in April 1870.

Trick shooting

The greatest revolver firing feat was that of Ed McGivern (USA), who twice fired from 15 ft *4,5 m* five shots which could be covered by a silver half-dollar piece (diameter 1.205 in *3,060 cm*) in 0.45 sec at the Lead Club Range, South Dakota, USA, on 20 Aug 1932. On 13 Sept 1932 at Lewiston, Montana, McGivern fired ten shots in 1.2 sec from two guns at the same time double action (no draw) all ten shots hitting two 2¼ × 3½ in *5,7 × 8,9 cm* playing cards at 15 ft *4,57 m*.

The most renowned trick shot of all-time was Phoebe Anne Oakley Mozee (Annie Oakley) (1860–1926). She demonstrated the ability to shoot 100 × 100 in trap shooting for 35 years aged between 27 and 62. At 30 paces she could split a playing card end-on, hit a dime in mid-air or shoot a cigarette from the lips of her husband—one Frank Butler.

Record heads

The world's finest head is the 23-pointer stag in the Maritzburg collection, E. Germany. The outside span is 75½ in *191 cm*, the length 47½ in *120 cm* and the weight 41½ lb *18 kg 824*. The greatest number of points is probably 33 (plus 29) on the stag shot in 1696 by Frederick III (1657–1713), the Elector of Brandenburg, later King Frederick I of Prussia.

Biggest bag

The largest animal ever shot by any big game hunter was a bull African elephant (*Loxodonta africana africana*) shot by E. M. Nielsen, of Columbus, Nebraska, USA, 25 miles *40 km* north-northeast of Mucusso, Angola, on 7 Nov 1974. The animal, brought down by a Westley Richards 0.425 stood 13 ft 8 in *4,16 m* at the shoulders (see also p. 28). In November 1965 Simon Fletcher, 28, a Kenyan farmer, claimed to have killed two elephants with one 0.458 bullet.

The greatest recorded lifetime bag is 556,000 birds, including 241,000 pheasants, by the 2nd Marquess of Ripon (1852–1923). He himself dropped dead on a grouse moor after shooting his 52nd bird on the morning of 22 Sept 1923.

Largest shoulder guns

The largest bore shoulder guns made were 2-bore. Less than a dozen of these were made by two English wildfowl gunmakers *c.* 1885. Normally the largest guns made are double-barrelled 4-bore weighing up to 26 lb *11 kg* which can be handled only by men of exceptional physique. Larger smooth-bore guns have been made, but these are for use as punt-guns.

above: Michael Wigney and Chris Smith back at Oxford after their 694 mile, 20 mile a day, punting achievement.

below: New Zealander, Graham Geater, averaged a hit every 1½ seconds in his trap-shooting record.

SKIING

Origins

The most ancient ski in existence was found well preserved in a peat bog at Höting, Sweden, dating from *c.* 2500 BC. A rock carving of a skier at Bessovysledki, USSR, dates from 6000 BC. The earliest recorded military use of skiing was in Norway in 1199. Skiing did not develop into a sport until 1843 at Tromsø, Norway. The Trysil Shooting and Skiing Club, founded in

315

left: The nearest man gets to unaided flying. Armin Kogler who holds the official world's ski jumping record of 180 m. (*Don Morley, All-Sport*)

below: One of the few men in Olympic history to win four consecutive medals in the same event, Biathlon expert, Alexander Tikhonov, here in the shooting element. (*Steve Powell, All-Sport*)

Norway in 1861, claims it is the world's oldest. Skiing was not introduced into the Alps until 1883, though there is some evidence of earlier use in the Carniola district. The earliest formal downhill race was staged at Montana, Switzerland in 1911. The first Slalom event was run at Mürren, Switzerland, on 21 Jan 1922. The International Ski Federation (FIS) was founded on 2 Feb 1924. The Winter Olympics were inaugurated on 25 Jan 1924. The Ski Club of Great Britain was founded on 6 May 1903. The National Ski Federation of Great Britain was formed in 1964.

Most titles *World Championships*

The world Alpine championships were inaugurated at Mürren, Switzerland, in 1931. The greatest number of titles won is 12 by Christel Cranz (b. 1 July 1914) of Germany, with four Slalom (1934, 1937–9), three Downhill (1935, 1937, 1939) and five Combined (1934–5, 1937–9). She also won the gold medal for the Combined in the 1936 Olympics. The most won by a man is seven by Anton 'Toni' Sailer (b. 17 Nov 1935) (Austria) who won all four in 1956 (Giant Slalom, Slalom, Downhill and the non-Olympic Alpine Combination) and the Downhill, Giant Slalom and Combined in 1958.

In the Nordic events Sixten Jernberg (b. 6 Feb 1929) (Sweden) won eight titles, including relays, in 1956–64. Johan Grøttumsbraaten (1899–1942) of Norway won six individual titles in 1926–32. The most by a woman is nine by Galina Koulakova (b. 29 Apr 1942) (USSR) in 1968–78. The record for a jumper is five by Birger Ruud (b. 23 Aug 1911) of Norway, in 1931–2 and 1935–7.

Most titles *World Cup*

The Alpine World Cup, (inst. 1967), has been won four times by Gustavo Thoeni (Italy) (b. 28 Feb 1951) in 1971–3 and 1975. The women's cup has been won six times by the 1,67 m *5 ft 6 in* 68 kg *150 lb* Annemarie Moser *née* Proell (b. 27 Mar 1953) of Austria in 1971–5 and 1979. From Dec 1972 to Jan 1974 she completed a record sequence of 11 consecutive downhill wins and in ten seasons, 1970–9, has won a total of 62 individual events. The most by a man is also 62 (from 127 races) by Ingemar Stenmark (Sweden) (b. 18 Mar 1956) in 1974–81, including a record 14 in one season in 1979. The Nordic World Cup (inst. 1979) was first won by Oddvar Braa (Norway) with the women's title won by Galina Koulakova (USSR).

Most titles *British*

The most British skiing overall titles won is four by Stuart Fitzsimmons (b. 28 Dec 1956) in 1973, 1975–6 and 1979.

The most ladies' titles won is four by Isobel M. Roe (1938–9, 1948–9) and Gina Hathorn (b. 6 July 1949) (1966, 1968–70), and Valentina Iliffe (b. 17 Feb 1956) (1975–6, 1979–80).

Ski-jumping

The longest ski-jump ever recorded is one of 181 m *593 ft 10 in* by Bogdan Norcic (Yugoslavia) (b. 19 Sept 1953) who fell on landing at Planica, Yugoslavia in February 1977. The official record is 180 m *590 ft 6 in* by Armin Kogler (b. 4 Sept 1959) (Austria) at Oberstdorf, W. Germany, on 26 Feb 1981. The female record is 98 m *321 ft 6 in* jumped by Anita Wold (b. 21 Sept 1956) (Norway) at Okura, Sapporo, Japan on 14 Jan 1975. The longest jump achieved in the Olympics is 117 m *384 ft* by Juoko Tormanen (Finland) (b. 10 Apr 1954) at Lake Placid, USA, on 23 Feb 1980. The greatest jump ever recorded on a 90 m hill is 128,5 m *421 ft 6 in* by Steve Collins (b. 1936) at Thunder Bay, Canada on 15 Dec 1980.

The British record is 61 m *200 ft 1 in* by Guy John Nixon (b. 9 Jan 1909) at Davos on 24 Feb 1931. The record at Hampstead, London, on artificial snow is 28 m *91 ft 10 in* by Reidar Anderson (b. 20 Apr 1911) of Norway on 24 Mar 1950.

The most wins in the British Ski-jumping championship (discontinued 1936) was three, by Colin Wyatt (1931, 1934 and 1936).

Highest speed
The highest speed claimed for any skier is 124.412 mph *200,222 km/h* by Steve McKinney (b. 18 Aug 1953) (USA) at Portillo, Chile on 1 Oct 1978. The fastest by a woman is 105.217 mph *169,332 km/h* by Catherine Breyton (b. 31 May 1965) (France) at Silverton, Colorado, USA in April 1981. The highest average speed in the Olympic downhill race was in 1976 on the Patscherkofel course, Innsbruck, Austria by Franz Klammer (b. 3 Dec 1953) of Austria with 102,828 km/h *63.894 mph* on 5 Feb 1976.

Closest Verdict
The narrowest winning margin in a championship ski race was one hundredth of a second by Thomas Wassberg (Sweden) (b. 23 Mar 1956) over Juha Mieto (Finland) in the Olympic 15 km Cross-country race at Lake Placid, USA on 17 Feb 1980. His winning time was 41 min 57.63 sec.

Highest altitude
Yuichiro Miura (Japan) (b. 1933) skied 2,5 km *1.6 miles* down Mt Everest on 6 May 1970 starting from 8100 m *26,574 ft*.

Greatest descent
The greatest reported aggregate elevation descended in 12 hr is 416,000 ft *126 796 m* by Sarah Ludwig, Scott Ludwig and Timothy B. Gaffney at Mount Brighton, Brighton, Michigan, USA on 16 Feb 1974.

Steepest descent
The steepest descents in alpine skiing history have been by Sylvain Saudan. At the start of his descent from Mont Blanc on the north-east side down the Couloir Gervasutti from 4248 m *13,937 ft* on 17 Oct 1967 he skied to gradients in excess of 60°.

Longest run
The longest all-downhill ski run in the world is the Weissfluhjoch-Kublis Parsenn course, near Davos, Switzerland, which measures 12,23 km *7.6 miles*. The run from the Aiguille du Midi top of the Chamonix lift (vertical lift 2492 m *8176 ft*) across the Vallée Blanche is 20,9 km *13 miles*.

The longest downhill race is the *Inferno* in Switzerland, 14 km *8.7 miles* from the top of the Schilthorn to Lauterbrunnen. In 1981 there was a record entry of 1401, with Heinz Fringer (Swit) winning in a record 15 min 44.57 sec.

Largest race
The world's greatest Nordic ski race is the 'Vasa Lopp', which commemorates an event of 1521 when Gustav Vasa (1496–1560), later King Gustavus Eriksson, skied 85,8 km *53.3 miles* from Mora to Sälen, Sweden. The re-enactment of this journey in reverse direction is now an annual event, with a record 11,596 starters on 5 Mar 1978. The fastest time is 4 hr 5 min 58 sec by Ola Hassis (Sweden) on 4 Mar 1979.

24 hours
In 24 hr Ahti Nevala (Finland) covered 280,90 km *174,5 miles* at Rovaniemi, Finland on 30 Mar 1977.

Longest lift
The longest chair lift in the world is the Alpine Way to Kosciusko Chàlet lift above Thredbo, near the Snowy Mountains, New South Wales, Australia. It takes from 45 to 75 min to ascend the 3.5 miles *5,6 km*, according to the weather. The highest is at Chacaltaya, Bolivia, rising to 5029 m *16,500 ft*. The longest gondola ski lift, at Killington, Vermont, USA, is 3.4 miles *5,48 km* long.

Backflip
The greatest number of skiers to perform a back layout flip while holding hands is 21 at Mont St Saveur, Quebec, Canada, on 12 Mar 1977.

Marathons
The longest non-stop nordic skiing marathon was one lasting 48 hr by Onni Savi, aged 35, of Padasjoki on 19–21 Apr 1966.

Pat Purcell and John McGlynn (USA) completed 81 hr 12 min of alpine skiing at Holiday Mountain, Monticello, NY, USA on 1–4 Feb 1979.

Ski-Parachuting
The greatest recorded vertical descent in parachute ski-jumping is 3300 ft *1006 m* by Rick Sylvester (b. 3 Apr 1942) (US) who on 28 July 1976 skied off the 6600 ft *2011 m* summit of Mt Asgard in Auyuittuq National Park, Baffin Island, Canada, landing on the Turner Glacier, the jump for a sequence in the James Bond film 'The Spy Who Loved Me'.

Ski-Bob *Origins*
The ski-bob was invented by J. C. Stevenson of Hartford, Connecticut, USA in 1891, and patented (No. 47334) on 19 Apr 1892 as a 'bicycle with ski-runners'. The Fédération Internationale de Skibob was founded on 14 Jan 1961 in Innsbruck, Austria and the first world championships were held at Bad Hofgastein, Austria in 1967. The Ski-Bob Association of Great Britain was registered on 23 Aug 1967. The highest speed attained is 166 km/h *103.4 mph* by Erich Brenter (b. 1940) (Austria) at Cervinia, Italy, in 1964.

Ski-Bob *World Championships*
The only ski-bobbers to retain a world championship are Alois

MOST OLYMPIC TITLES

Men Alpine	3	Anton 'Toni' Sailer (Austria) (b. 17 Nov 1935)	Downhill, slalom, giant slalom, 1956
	3	Jean-Claude Killy (France) (b. 30 Aug 1943)	Downhill, slalom, giant slalom, 1968
Men Nordic	4[1]	Sixten Jernberg (Sweden) (b. 6 Feb 1929)	50 km, 1956; 30 km, 1960; 50 km and 4 × 10 km, 1964
	4[2]	Alexander Tikhonov (USSR) (b. 2 Jan 1947)	Biathlon relay, 1968, 1972, 1976, 1980
Women Alpine	2	Andrea Mead-Lawrence (USA) (b. 19 Apr 1932)	Slalom, giant slalom, 1952
	2	Marielle Goitschel (France) (b. 28 Sept 1945)	Giant slalom, 1964; slalom, 1968
	2	Marie-Therese Nadig (Switz) (b. 8 Mar 1954)	Downhill, giant slalom, 1972
	2[3]	Rosi Mittermaier (now Neureuther) (W. Germany) (b. 5 Aug 1950)	Downhill, slalom, 1976
	2[4]	Hanni Wenzel (Liechtenstein) (b. 14 Dec 1956)	Giant slalom, slalom 1980
Women Nordic	4[5]	Galina Koulakova (USSR) (b. 29 Apr 1942)	5 km, 10 km and 3 × 5 km relay, 1972; 4 × 5 km relay, 1976.

[1] Jernberg also won three silver and two bronze medals for a record nine Olympic medals.
[2] Tikhonov also won a silver in the 1968 20 km Biathlon.
[3] Also won silver medal in Giant Slalom in 1976.
[4] Wenzel won a silver in the 1980 Downhill and a bronze in the 1976 Slalom.
[5] Koulakova also won two silver and two bronze medals in 1968, 1976 and 1980.

Fischbauer (Austria), (b. 6 Oct 1951), 1973 and 1975, Robert Mühlberger (W. Germany), 1979 and 1981, Gerhilde Schiffkorn (Austria), (b. 22 Mar 1950) the women's title, 1967 and 1969, and Gertrude Geberth (Austria), (b. 18 Oct 1951), 1971 and 1973.

Snowmobile
A record speed of 135.93 mph *218,75 km/h* was set by Donald J. Pitzen (USA) at Union Lake, Michigan, USA, on 27 Feb 1977.

SOFTBALL

Origins
Softball, the indoor derivative of baseball, was invented by George Hancock at the Farragut Boat Club of Chicago, Illinois in 1887. Rules were first codified in Minneapolis, Minnesota in 1895 as Kitten Ball. International rules were set in 1933 when the name Softball was officially adopted and the ISF was formed in 1952 as governing body for both fast pitch and slow pitch.

Most titles
The USA has won the men's world championship (inst. 1966) four times, 1966, 1968, 1976 (shared), and 1980. The USA has twice won the women's title (inst. 1965) in 1974 and 1978.

Marathon
The longest fast pitch marathon is 56 hr 4 min by two BIC Softball teams at Coolidge Park, Fitchburg, Massachusetts, USA on 3–5 July 1981. The longest for slow pitch is 90 hr 5 min 7 sec by two teams of ten players at Ballou Park Field, Danville, Virginia, USA on 4–8 Sept 1980.

WORLD CHAMPIONSHIP RECORDS

MEN

Most runs	12	Generoso Lopez (Venezuela)	1966
Most home runs	4	Robert 'Bob' Burrows (Canada)	1976
Most hits	17	Basil McLean (New Zealand)	1976
RBIs	14	Chuck Teuscher (USA)	1966
,,	14	Robert 'Bob' Burrows (Canada)	1976
Highest average	.556	Seiichi Tanaka (Japan)	1980
Most wins	6	Owen Walford (New Zealand)	1976
	6	Owen Walford (New Zealand)	1980
Most innings pitched	59	Ty Stofflet (USA)	1976
Most strikeouts	98	Ty Stofflet (USA)	1976
Most perfect games	1	Joe Lynch (USA); Chuck Richard (USA);	1976
		Dave Ruthowsky (Canada)	1968

WOMEN

Most runs	13	Kathy Elliott (USA)	1974
Most hits	17	Miyoko Naruse (Japan)	1974
RBIs	11	Miyoko Naruse (Japan); Keiko Usui (Japan);	
		Kathy Elliott (USA)	1974
Highest average	.550	Tamara Bryce (Panama)	1978
Most wins	6	Lorraine Wooley (Australia)	1965
,, ,,	6	Nancy Welborn (USA)	1970
Most innings pitched	50	Nancy Welborn (USA)	1970
Most strikeouts	76	Joan Joyce (USA)	1974
Most perfect games	2	Joan Joyce (USA)	1974

SPEEDWAY

Origins
Motorcycle racing on large dirt track surfaces has been traced back to 1902 in the United States. The first organized 'short track' races were at the West Maitland (New South Wales, Australia) Agricultural Show in November 1923. The sport evolved in Great Britain with small diameter track racing at Droylsden, Greater Manchester on 25 June 1927 and a cinder track event at High Beech, Essex, on 19 Feb 1928. The National League was instituted in 1932. The best record is that of the Wembley Lions who won in 1932, 1946–7, 1949–53, making a record total of eight victories. Since the National Trophy knock-out competition was instituted in 1931, Belle Vue (Manchester) have been most successful with nine victories in 1933–7, 1946–7, 1949 and 1958. In 1965 the National League was replaced by the British League which Belle Vue have won three times in succession (1970–2).

Most world titles
The world speedway championship was inaugurated at Wembley, London in September 1936. The most wins have been six

by Ivan Gerald Mauger, MBE (b. Christchurch, NZ, 4 Oct 1939) in 1968–70, 1972, 1977 and 1979. Barry Briggs, MBE (b. Christchurch, NZ, 30 Dec 1934) made a record 17 consecutive appearances in the finals (1954–70) and won the world title in 1957–8, 1964 and 1966. He also scored a record 201 points in world championship competition. New Zealanders have won the title on 12 occasions.

Most points
In League racing the highest score recorded was when Bristol defeated Glasgow (White City) in National League Division 2 by 70–14 in 1949. In the current National League, Crayford beat Workington by 65–12 on 15 July 1980. The highest number of League points scored by an individual in a season was 480 by Pete Lansdale for Plymouth in National League Division 3 in 1949.

SQUASH RACKETS

Earliest champion
Although rackets (US spelling racquets) with a soft ball was played in 1817 at Harrow School, Harrow, Greater London, there was no recognised champion of any country until John A Miskey of Philadelphia won the American Amateur Singles Championship in 1907.

Most World Amateur titles
Australians have won the individual title (inst. 1967) five times and the team title four times. Geoffrey B. Hunt (b. 11 Mar 1947) (Australia) won the individual title three times (1967, 1969 and 1971).

World Open title
The world Open championship (inst. 1976) has been won four times by Geoffrey Hunt (Australia) in 1976, 1977, 1979 and 1980.

Most titles *Open Championship*
The most wins in the Open Championship (amateurs or professionals), held annually in Britain, is eight by Geoffrey Hunt in 1969, 1974, 1976–81. Hashim Khan (Pakistan) (b. 1915) won seven times and has also won the Vintage title four times in 1978–81.

The most wins in the Women's Squash Rackets Championship is 16 by Heather Pamela McKay, MBE (*née* Blundell) (b. Australia, 31 July 1941) from 1961 to 1976. She also won the World Open title in 1976 and 1979. In her career from 1959 to 1980 she only lost two games.

Most titles *Amateur Championship*
The most wins in the Amateur Championship is six by Abdel Fattah Amr Bey (b. Egypt, 14 Feb 1910) later appointed Ambassador in London, who won in 1931–3 and 1935–7. Norman Francis Borrett (b. 1 Oct 1917) of England won in 1946–50.

Most titles *Professional Championship*
The most wins in the Professional Championship of Britain is ten by John Henry 'Jack' Giles, MBE from 1954 to 1963. He relinquished the title in 1964 undefeated.

Longest and shortest championship matches
The longest recorded championship match was one of 2 hr 35 min in the British Amateur Championships at Wembley on 12 Dec 1976 when Murray Lilley (NZ) beat Barry O'Connor (Kent) 9–3, 10–8, 2–9, 7–9, 10–8. The second game lasted 58 min and there were 98 lets in the match. Deanna Murray beat Christine Rees in only 9½ min in a Ladies Welsh title match at Rhos-on-Sea, Clwyd, on 21 Oct 1979.

Most international appearances

Men

Scotland	75	Christopher Wilson	1970–81
Wales	68	Robert Anthony Dolman	1960–80
England	60	Philip Norman Ayton	1968–79
N. Ireland	53	Robert Weir	1969–77

Women

Scotland	65	Dorothy Sharp (*née* McNeill)	1964–81
Wales	48	Pat Connies-Laing	1954–76
		Rachel Campin (*née* Byrne)	1947–69

Longest span of internationals

Sheila Macintosh (*née* Speight) (b. 8 Sept 1930), the 1960 British Champion, played for England *v.* Wales in April 1949 and in December 1971—a span of 22 years 8 months. Among men Lawrence John Verney (b. 19 July 1924) was only marginally less, representing Wales on 3 Feb 1950 and on 17 Feb 1972.

Marathons

The longest squash marathon has been 120 hr 51 min by Peter Fairlie (b. 18 Dec 1957) at the Bridge of Allan Sports Club, Stirling, Scotland on 30 June–5 July 1979. George Deponselle and William de Bruin played for 106 hr 43 min at Sutterheim Country Club, Cape Province, South Africa on 1–5 Oct 1978. (*This category will now be confined to two players only.*)

SURFING

Origins

The traditional Polynesian sport of surfing in a canoe (*ehorooe*) was first recorded by Captain James Cook, RN, FRS (1728–79) on his first voyage at Tahiti in December 1771. Surfing on a board (*Amo Amo iluna ka lau oka nalu*) was first described 'most perilous and extraordinary ... altogether astonishing and is scarcely to be credited' by Lt (later Capt) James King, RN, FRS in March 1779 at Kealakekua Bay, Hawaii Island. A surfer was first depicted by this voyage's official artist John Webber. The sport was revived at Waikiki by 1900. Hollow boards were introduced in 1929 and the light plastic foam type in 1956.

Most titles

World Championships were inaugurated in May 1964 at Sydney, Australia. The only surfer to win two titles has been Joyce Hoffman (US) in 1965 and 1966.

Highest waves ridden

Makaha Beach, Hawaii provides the reputedly highest consistently high waves often reaching the rideable limit of 30–35 ft *9–10 m*. The highest wave ever ridden was the *tsunami* of 'perhaps 50 ft *15,24 m*', which struck Minole, Hawaii on 3 Apr 1868, and was ridden to save his life by a Hawaiian named Holua.

Longest ride *Sea wave*

About four to six times each year rideable surfing waves break in Matanchen Bay near San Blas, Nayarit, Mexico which makes rides of *c.* 5700 ft *1700 m* possible.

Longest ride *River bore*

The longest recorded rides on a river bore have been set on the Severn bore, England. The official British Surfing Association record is 2.6 miles *4,1 km* by Stuart Matthews and Peter James on 15 Apr 1980. In 1968 a ride of 4–6 miles *6–9 km* was claimed by Rodney Sumpter of Sussex. In September 1971 Mick Evans of Towyn Surfing Club, Gwynedd succeeded in making a run from Rea to Maisemore Weir a distance of 4 miles *6,4 km* in a canoe.

SWIMMING

Earliest references

In Japan, swimming in schools was ordered by Imperial edict of Emperor Go-Yozei (1586–1611) in 1603 but competition was known from 36 BC. Sea water bathing was fashionable at Scarborough, North Yorkshire as early as 1660. In Great Britain competitive swimming originated in London *c.* 1837, at which time there were five or more pools, the earliest of which had been opened at St George's Pier Head, Liverpool in 1828.

Largest pools

The largest swimming pool in the world is the sea-water Orthlieb Pool in Casablanca, Morocco. It is 480 m *1547 ft* long and 75 m *246 ft* wide, and has an area of 3.6 ha *8.9 acres*. The largest land-locked swimming pool with heated water was the Fleishhacker Pool on Sloat Boulevard, near Great Highway, San Francisco, California, USA. It measured 1000 × 150 ft *304,8 × 45,7 m* and up to 14 ft *4,26 m* deep and contained 7,500,000 US gal *28 390 hectolitres* of heated water. It was opened on 2 May 1925 but has now been abandoned to a few ducks. The world's largest competition pool is that at Osaka, Japan, which accommodates 13,614 spectators. The largest in use in the United

Record breaking softball pitcher, America's Nancy Welborn, of the Orange Lionettes. (*American Softball Association*)

Kingdom is the Royal Commonwealth Pool, Edinburgh, completed in 1970 with 2000 permanent seats, but the unused pool at Earls Court, London (opened 1937) is 195 ft *59,50 m* by 95 ft *29 m* and has seating for some 12,000 spectators.

Fastest swimmer

The fastest 50 m in a 50 m pool is 22.71 sec by Joe Bottom (b. 18 Apr 1955) (USA), averaging 4.92 mph *7,92 km/h*, at Honolulu, Hawaii on 15 Aug 1980. The fastest by a woman is 25.79 sec by Jill Sterkel (b. 1961) (USA), averaging 4.34 mph *6,98 km/h* at Austin, Texas, USA on 3 Apr 1981.

Most world records

Men, 32, Arne Borg (Sweden) (b. 18 Aug 1901), 1921–9. Women, 42, Ragnhild Hveger (Denmark) (b. 10 Dec 1920), 1936–42. Under modern conditions (only metric distances in 50 m pools) the most is 26 by Mark Andrew Spitz (USA) (b. 10 Feb 1950), 1967–72, and 23 by Kornelia Ender (now Matthes) (b. Plauen, E. Germany, 25 Oct 1958), 1973–6.

Most world titles

In the world championships (inst 1973) the most medals won is

Fifteen year old Tracy Caulkins (USA) with her record medal haul in the 1978 World Swimming Championships. (*Tony Duffy, All-Sport*)

ten by Kornelia Ender (E. Germany) with eight gold and two silver in 1973 and 1975. The most by a man is seven by James Montgomery (USA) (b. 24 Jan 1955), six gold and a bronze in 1973 and 1975. The most medals in a single championships is six by Tracy Caulkins (USA) (b. 11 Jan 1963) in 1978 with five golds and a silver.

OLYMPIC RECORDS
Most gold medals *Men*
The greatest number of Olympic gold medals won is nine by Mark Spitz (USA).

100 m and 200 m freestyle	1972
100 m and 200 m butterfly	1972
4 × 100 m freestyle	1968 and 1972
4 × 200 m freestyle	1968 and 1972
4 × 100 m medley	1972

All but one of these performances (the 4 × 200 m freestyle of 1968) were also new world records.

Most gold medals *Women*
The record number of gold medals won by a woman is four shared by Patricia McCormick (*née* Keller) (USA) (b. 12 May 1930) with the high and springboard diving double in 1952 and 1956 (also the female record for individual golds), Dawn Fraser, OBE (b. Sydney, Australia, 4 Sept 1937) with the 100 m freestyle (1956, 1960 and 1964) and the 4 × 100 m freestyle (1956) and Kornelia Ender (E. Germany) with the 100 and 200 m freestyle, 100 m butterfly and 4 × 100 m medley in 1976. Dawn Fraser is the only swimmer to win the same event on three successive occasions.

Most gold medals *British*
The record number of gold medals won by a British swimmer (excluding Water Polo, *q.v.*) is four by Henry Taylor (1885–1951) in the mile freestyle (1906), 400 m freestyle (1908), 1500 m freestyle (1908) and 4 × 200 m freestyle (1908). None of the seven British women who have won a gold medal won a second title.

Most medals *Men*
The most medals won is 11 by Mark Spitz who in addition to his nine golds (see above), won a silver (100 m butterfly) and a bronze (100 m freestyle) both in 1968.

Most medals *Women*
The most medals won by a woman is eight by Dawn Fraser, who in addition to her four golds (see above) won four silvers (400 m freestyle 1956, 4 × 100 m freestyle 1960 and 1964, 4 × 100 m medley 1960), Kornelia Ender (see above) who in addition to her four golds won four silvers (200 m individual medley 1972, 4 × 100 m medley 1972, 4 × 100 m freestyle 1972 and 1976) and Shirley Babashoff (USA) (b. 3 Jan 1957), who won two golds (4 × 100 m freestyle 1972 and 1976) and six silvers (100 m freestyle 1972, 200 m freestyle 1972 and 1976, 400 m and 800 m freestyle 1976, 4 × 100 m medley 1976).

Most medals *British*
The British record is eight by Henry Taylor who in addition to his four golds (see above) won a silver (400 m freestyle 1906) and three bronzes (4 × 200 m freestyle 1906, 1912, 1920). The most medals by a British woman is four by M. Joyce Cooper (later Mrs John Badcock) (b. 18 Apr 1909) with one silver (4 × 100 m freestyle 1928) and three bronze (100 m freestyle 1928, 100 m backstroke 1928, 4 × 100 m freestyle 1932).

Most individual gold medals
The record number of individual gold medals won is four by Charles M. Daniels (USA) (1884–1973) (100 m freestyle 1906 and 1908, 220 yd freestyle 1904, 440 yd freestyle 1904); Roland Matthes (E. Germany) (b. 17 Nov 1950) with 100 m and 200 m backstroke 1968 and 1972; Mark Spitz and Pat McCormick (see above). The most individual golds by a British swimmer is three by Henry Taylor (see above).

Closest verdict
The closest recorded win in the Olympic Games was in the Munich 400 m individual medley final of 30 Aug 1972 when Gunnar Larsson (Sweden) (b. 12 May 1951) got the verdict over Tim McKee (USA) (b. 14 Mar 1953) by 2/1000th of a second in 4 min 31.981 sec to 4 min 31.983 sec—a margin of 3 mm or the

length grown by a finger nail in three weeks. This led to a change in international rules with timings and places decided only to hundredths.

DIVING
Most Olympic medals *World*
The most medals won by a diver are five (three gold, two silver) by Klaus Dibiasi (b. Austria, 6 Oct 1947) (Italy) in four Games from 1964 to 1976. He is also the only diver to win the same event (highboard) at three successive Games (1968, 1972 and 1976). Pat McCormick (see above) won four gold medals.

Most Olympic medals *British*
The highest placing by a Briton has been the silver medal by Beatrice Eileen Armstrong (later Purdy) (1894–1981) in the 1920 highboard event. The best placings by male divers are the bronze medals by Harold Clarke (b. 1888) (plain high diving 1924) and Brian Phelps (b. 21 Apr 1944) (highboard, 1960).

Most world titles
Phil Boggs (USA) (b. 29 Dec 1949) has won three gold medals in 1973, 1975 and 1978 but Klaus Dibiasi (Italy) won four medals (two gold, two silver) in 1973 and 1975. Irina Kalinina (USSR) (b. 8 Feb 1959) has won five medals (three gold, one silver, one bronze) in 1973, 1975 and 1978.

Perfect dive
In the 1972 US Olympic Trials, in Chicago, Illinois, Michael Finneran (b. 21 Sept 1948) was awarded a score of 10 by all seven judges for a backward 1½ somersault, 2½ twist, from the 10 m board, an achievement without precedent. (See also p. 186).

CHANNEL SWIMMING
Earliest
The first to swim the English Channel from shore to shore (without a life jacket) was the Merchant Navy captain Matthew Webb (1848–83) who swam breaststroke from Dover, England to Calais Sands, France, in 21 hr 45 min from 12.56 p.m. to 10.41 a.m., 24–25 Aug 1875. He swam an estimated 38 miles *61 km* to make the 21-mile *33 km* crossing. Paul Boyton (USA) had swum from Cap Gris-Nez to the South Foreland in his patent life-saving suit in 23 hr 30 min on 28–29 May 1875. There is good evidence that Jean-Marie Saletti, a French soldier, escaped from a British prison hulk off Dover by swimming to Boulogne in July or August 1815. The first crossing from France to England was made by Enrico Tiraboschi, a wealthy Italian living in Argentina, in 16 hr 33 min on 12 Aug 1923, to win the *Daily Sketch* prize of £1000. At the end of 1980, 220 persons on 349 occasions have succeeded.

The first woman to succeed was Gertrude Caroline Ederle (b. 2 Oct 1906) (USA) who swam from Cap Gris-Nez, France to Deal, England on 6 Aug 1926, in the then overall record time of 14 h. 39 min. The first woman to swim from England to France was Florence Chadwick (b. 1918) of California, USA, in 16 h 19 min on 11 Sept 1951. The first Englishwoman to succeed was Mercedes Gleitze (later Carey) (1900–81) who swam from France to England in 15 hr 15 min on 7 Oct 1927.

Fastest and Slowest
The official Channel Swimming Association (founded 1927) record is 7 hr 40 min by Penny Dean (b. 21 Mar 1955) of California, USA, from Shakespeare Beach, Dover to Cap Gris-Nez, France, on 29 July 1978.

The slowest crossing was the third ever made, when Henry Sullivan (USA) swam from England to France in 26 hr 50 min on 5–6 Aug 1923. It is estimated that he swam 56 miles *90 km*.

Earliest and latest
The earliest date in the year on which the Channel has been swum is 6 June by Dorothy Perkins (England) (b. 1942) in 1961 and the latest is 28 Oct by Michael Peter Read (GB) (b. 9 July 1941) in 1979.

Youngest and Oldest
The youngest conqueror is Marcus Hooper (b. 14 June 1967) of Eltham, Kent who swam from Dover to Sangatte, France in 14 hr 37 min on 5–6 Aug 1979, when he was aged 12 yr 53 days

Swimming

The oldest has been James Edward 'Doc' Counsilman (USA) (b. 28 Dec 1920), former US Olympic coach, who was aged 58 years 260 days when he swam from England to France in 13 hr 7 min on 14 Sept 1979. The youngest woman was Abla Adel Khairi (b. Egypt, 26 Sept 1960), aged 13 yr 326 days when she swam from England to France in 12 hr 30 min on 17 Aug 1974, and the oldest was Stella Ada Rosina Taylor (b. Bristol, Avon, 20 Dec 1929) aged 45 yr 350 days when she did the swim in 18 hr 15 min on 26 Aug 1975.

Double crossing

Antonio Abertondo (b. Buenos Aires, Argentina, 1919), swam from England to France in 18 hr 50 min (8.35 a.m. on 20 Sept to 3.25 a.m. on 21 Sept 1961) and after about 4 min rest returned to England in 24 hr 16 min, landing at St Margaret's Bay at 3.45 a.m. on 22 Sept 1961, to complete the first 'double crossing' in 43 hr 10 min. Kevin Murphy (b. Bushey Heath, Herts, 1949) completed the first double crossing by a Briton in 35 hr 10 min on 6 Aug 1970. The first swimmer to achieve a crossing both ways was Edward Harry Temme (1904–78) on 5 Aug 1927 and 19 Aug 1934.

The fastest double crossing was one of 19 hr 12 min by Cynthia 'Cindy' Nicholas (b. 20 Aug 1957) of Scarborough, Ont., Canada, on 4–5 Aug 1979. The fastest by a relay team is 16 hr 5½ min (including a 2 min rest) by six Saudi Arabian men on 11 Aug 1977.

Most conquests

The greatest number of Channel conquests is 22 by Michael Read, (GB) to 10 Aug 1981, including a record six in one year. Cindy Nicholas made her first crossing on 29 July 1975 and her tenth on 1 Sept 1979.

Underwater

The first underwater cross-Channel swim was achieved by Fred Baldasare (b. 1924) (USA), who completed a 42 mile *67,5 km* distance from France to England with Scuba equipment in 18 hr 1 min on 10–11 July 1962.

LONG DISTANCE SWIMMING

Longest ocean swim

The longest ocean swim claimed is one of 128.8 miles *207,3 km* by Walter Poenisch Snr (USA) (b. 1914) who started from Havana, Cuba, and arrived at Little Duck Key, Florida, USA (in a shark cage and wearing flippers) 34 hr 15 min later on 11–13 July 1978.

In 1966 Mihir Sen of Calcutta, India uniquely swam the Palk Strait from Sri Lanka to India (in 25 hr 36 min on 5–6 Apr); the Straits of Gibraltar (in 8 hr 1 min on 24 Aug); the length of the Dardanelles (in 13 hr 55 min on 12 Sept), the Bosphorus (in 4 hr on 21 Sept) and the length of the Panama Canal (in 34 hr 15 min on 29–31 Oct). He swam the English Channel in 14 hr 45 min on 27 Sept 1958.

Irish Channel

The swimming of the 23 mile *37 km* wide North Channel from Donaghadee, Northern Ireland to Portpatrick, Scotland was first accomplished by Tom Blower of Nottingham in 15 hr 26 min in 1947. A record time of 11 hr 21 min was set by Kevin Murphy on 11 Sept 1970. The first Irish-born swimmer to achieve the crossing was Ted Keenan on 11 Aug 1973 in 52–56°F *11–13°C* water in 18 hr 27 min.

Bristol Channel

The first person to achieve a crossing of the Bristol Channel was Kathleen Thomas (now Mrs F. Day) (b. Apr 1906) who swam from Penarth, South Glamorgan to Weston-super-Mare, Avon in 7 hr 20 min on 5 Sept 1927. The record for the longer swim from Glenthorne Cove, Devon to Porthcawl, Mid-Glamorgan is 10 hr 46 min by Jane Luscombe (b. 13 Jan 1961) of Jersey, CI, on 19 Aug 1976.

Lake swims

The fastest time for swimming the 22.7 mile *36,5 km* long Loch Ness, is 10 hr 30 min by Kevin Murphy on 14 July 1976. The first successful swim was by Brenda Sherratt (b. 1948) of West Bollington, Cheshire on 26–27 July 1966. The fastest time for

(*top*) World record holder and Olympic 100 metres champion, Barbara Krause, is now Mrs Wanja. (*Tony Duffy, All-Sport*)
(*bottom*) Victory salute from Duncan Goodhew, Olympic 100 metres Breaststroke champion, the event at which he holds the British record. (*Provincial Sports Photography*)

the Lake Windermere International Championship, 16.5 miles *26,5 km*, is 6 hr 10 min 33 sec by Mary Beth Colpo (USA) (b. 1961) on 5 Aug 1978.

Longest swims

The greatest recorded distance ever swum is 1826 miles *2938 km* down the Mississippi, USA between Ford Dam near Minneapolis and Carrollton Ave, New Orleans, Louisiana, by Fred P. Newton, (b. 1903) of Clinton, Oklahoma from 6 July to 29 Dec 1930. He was 742 hr in the water.

The greatest distance covered in a continuous swim is 292 miles *469,9 km* by Joe Maciag (b. 26 Mar 1956) from Billings to Glendive, Montana in the Yellowstone River in 64 hr 50 min on 1–4 July 1976.

The longest swim using the highly exhausting butterfly stroke exclusively was an officially measured 10 miles *16,09 km* by twins James and Jonathan di Donato (USA) (b. 24 Oct 1953) off Fort Lauderdale, Florida, USA on 27 Aug 1980.

Longest duration

The longest duration swim ever achieved was one of 168 con-

The first swimmer to break 15 minutes for 1500 metres, Vladimir Salnikov added the Olympic titles to the World 400 metres and 1500 metres championships he already held. (*Tony Duffy, All-Sport*)

Irina Kalinina exhibiting the form which has won her Russian, European, World and Olympic titles in Springboard diving. (*Tony Duffy, All-Sport*)

tinuous hours, ending on 24 Feb 1941, by the legless Charles Zibbelman, *alias* Zimmy (b. 1894) of the USA, in a pool in Honolulu, Hawaii, USA. The longest duration swim by a woman was 87 hr 27 min in a salt-water pool by Myrtle Huddleston (USA) at Raven Hall, Coney Island, NY, USA, in 1931. Margaret 'Peggy' Byrne (USA) (b. 17 Dec 1949), a Minnesota State Representative, swam for 60 hr 15 min in a freshwater pool at Saint Paul, Minn, on 18–20 Dec 1978.

24 hours
Bertrand Malègue (France) (21) swam 87,529 km *54.38 miles* in a pool at Saint Etienne, France, on 31 May–1 June 1980.

Relays
The longest recorded mileage in a 24 hr swim relay is 89 miles 1455.3 yd *144,562 km* by a team of five from Loughborough University, Leicestershire on 13–14 May 1980. The fastest time recorded for 100 miles *160 km* by a team of 20 swimmers is 22 hr 8 min 15 sec at Menzieshill High School, Dundee, Scotland on 23–24 Feb 1980. Four swimmers from the Darien YMCA, Connecticut, USA covered 300 miles *483 km* in relay in 122 hr 59 min 40 sec on 25–30 Nov 1980.

Underwater relay
Peter Saville, John Mason, Robert Mortimer and Duncan Moulder, of Stratford upon Avon Sub Aqua Club, swam a relay of 279,099 miles *499 166 km* underwater in 168 hr at the Holiday Inn, Birmingham on 30 June–7 July 1979.

Sponsored swimming
The greatest amount of money collected in a charity swim was £36,563.92 by the Lions Club of Jersey, CI on 20–22 Feb 1981 at the Fort Regent Pool, St Helier.

Treading water marathon
The duration record for treading water (vertical posture without touching the lane markers in an 8 ft *2,43 m* square) is 72 hr 13 sec by Kenton D. Smith (20) at California State University, Chico, California, USA on 28 Aug–31 Aug 1980.

WORLD RECORDS
recognised by the *Fédération Internationale de Natation Amateur* as at 16 Aug 1981

MEN

Event	Time Min. sec.	Name and Country	Place	Date
FREESTYLE				
100 metres	49.36	Ambrose 'Rowdy' Gaines (USA)	Austin, Texas, USA	3 Apr 19
200 metres	1:49.16	Ambrose 'Rowdy' Gaines (USA)	Austin, Texas, USA	11 Apr 19
400 metres	3:50.49	Peter Szmidt (Canada)	Toronto, Canada	16 July 19
800 metres	7:56.49	Vladimir Salnikov (USSR)	Minsk, USSR	24 Mar 19
1500 metres	14:58.27	Vladimir Salnikov (USSR)	Moscow, USSR	22 July 19
4 × 100 metres relay	3:19.74	United States: (Jack Babashoff, Ambrose Gaines, James Montgomery, David McCagg)	West Berlin	22 Aug 19
4 × 200 metres relay	7:20.82	United States: (Bruce Furniss, William Forrester, Bobby Hackett, Ambrose Gaines)	West Berlin	24 Aug 19
BREASTSTROKE				
100 metres	1:02.86	Gerald Moerken (W. Germany)	Jonkoping, Sweden	17 Aug 19
200 metres	2:15.11	David Andrew Wilkie, MBE (GB)	Montreal, Canada	24 July 19

BUTTERFLY

100 metres	53.81	William Paulus (USA)	Austin, Texas, USA	3 Apr	1981
200 metres	1:58.21	Craig Beardsley (USA)	Irvine, California, USA	30 July	1980

BACKSTROKE

100 metres	55.49	John Naber (USA)	Montreal, Canada	19 July	1976
200 metres	1:59.19	John Naber (USA)	Montreal, Canada	24 July	1976

MEDLEY

200 metres	2:02.78	Alex Baumann (Canada)	Heidelberg, W. Germany	29 July	1981
400 metres	4:20.05	Jesse Vassallo (USA)	West Berlin	22 Aug	1978
4 × 100 metres relay	3:42.22	United States: (John Naber, John Hencken, Matthew Vogel, James Montgomery)	Montreal, Canada	22 July	1976

WOMEN

FREESTYLE

100 metres	54.79	Barbara Krause (E. Germany)	Moscow, USSR	21 July	1980
200 metres	1:58.23	Cynthia Woodhead (USA)	Tokyo, Japan	3 Sept	1979
400 metres	4:06.28	Tracey Wickham, MBE (Australia)	West Berlin	24 Aug	1978
800 metres	8:24.62	Tracey Wickham, MBE (Australia)	Edmonton, Canada	6 Aug	1978
1500 metres	16:04.49	Kim Linehan (USA)	Fort Lauderdale, Florida, USA	19 Aug	1979
4 × 100 metres relay	3:42.71	E. Germany: (Barbara Krause, Caren Metschuck, Ines Diers, Sarina Hulsenbeck)	Moscow, USSR	27 July	1980

BREASTSTROKE

100 metres	1:09.39	Ute Geweniger (E. Germany)	East Berlin	2 July	1981
200 metres	2:28.36	Lina Kachushite (USSR)	Potsdam, E. Germany	6 Apr	1979

BUTTERFLY

100 metres	57.93	Mary Meagher (USA)	Milwaukee, Wisconsin, USA	16 Aug	1981
200 metres	2:05.96	Mary Meagher (USA)	Milwaukee, Wisconsin, USA	13 Aug	1981

BACKSTROKE

100 metres	1:00.86	Rica Reinisch (E. Germany)	Moscow, USSR	23 July	1980
200 metres	2:11.77	Rica Reinisch (E. Germany)	Moscow, USSR	27 July	1980

MEDLEY

200 metres	2:11.73	Ute Geweniger (E. Germany)	East Berlin	4 July	1981
400 metres	4:36.29	Petra Schneider (E. Germany)	Moscow, USSR	26 July	1980
4 × 100 metres relay	4:06.67	E. Germany: (Rica Reinisch, Ute Geweniger, Andrea Pollack, Caren Metschuck)	Moscow, USSR	20 July	1980

World records can only be set in 50 m pools. FINA has not recognised records for Imperial distances since 30 Apr 1969.

BRITISH NATIONAL (long course) RECORDS
as ratified by the Amateur Swimming Federation of Great Britain as at 16 Aug 1981

MEN

Event	Time Min. sec.	Name	Place	Date	
FREESTYLE					
100 metres	51.88	Martin Smith	Moscow, USSR	26 July	1980
200 metres	1:52.47	Gordon Downie	Montreal, Canada	19 July	1976
400 metres	3:56.46	Andrew Astbury	Fort Lauderdale, Florida, USA	17 Aug	1979
800 metres	8:13.83	Simon Gray	Blackpool, Lancashire	23 May	1980
1500 metres	15:31.42	Simon Gray	West Berlin	24 Aug	1978
4 × 100 metres relay	3:28.76	National team: (Martin Smith, Mark Taylor, Ricky Burrell, David Dunne)	West Berlin	22 Aug	1978
4 × 200 metres relay	7:30.81	United Kingdom Team: (Douglas Campbell, Philip Hubble, Martin Smith, Andrew Astbury)	Moscow, USSR	23 July	1980
BREASTSTROKE					
100 metres	1:03.31	Duncan Goodhew	Edinburgh, Scotland	24 Apr	1980
200 metres	2:15.11	David Andrew Wilkie, MBE	Montreal, Canada	24 July	1976
BUTTERFLY					
100 metres	55.42	Gary Abraham	Moscow, USSR	23 July	1980
200 metres	2:00.75	Philip Hubble	Moscow, USSR	20 July	1980
BACKSTROKE					
100 metres	57.72	Gary Abraham	Moscow, USSR	24 July	1980
200 metres	2:04.23	Douglas Campbell	Moscow, USSR	26 July	1980
INDIVIDUAL MEDLEY					
200 metres	2:06.25	David Andrew Wilkie, MBE	Long Beach, California, USA	4 Apr	1976
400 metres	4:27.70	Simon Gray	Edmonton, Canada	5 Aug	1978
4 × 100 metres relay	3:47.71	United Kingdom Team: (Gary Abraham, Duncan Goodhew, David Lowe, Martin Smith)	Moscow, USSR	24 July	1980
WOMEN					
FREESTYLE					
100 metres	57.01	June Croft	Cardiff, Wales	4 May	1981
200 metres	2:02.95	June Croft	Blackpool, Lancashire	11 July	1981
400 metres	4:16.27	Jackie Willmott	Blackpool, Lancashire	20 Apr	1980
800 metres	8:38.56	Jackie Willmott	Leeds, Yorkshire	7 Aug	1981
1500 metres	16:46.48	Jackie Willmott	Edinburgh, Scotland	25 Apr	1980
4 × 100 metres relay	3:51.71	United Kingdom Team: (Sharron Davies, Kaye Lovatt, Jackie Willmott, June Croft)	Moscow, USSR	27 July	1980

BREASTSTROKE					
100 metres	1:11.48	Margaret Mary Kelly, MBE	Moscow, USSR	26 July	1980
200 metres	2:34.43	Susan Brownsdon	Kiev, USSR	3 July	1981
BUTTERFLY					
100 metres	1:01.93	Ann Osgerby	Moscow, USSR	23 July	1980
200 metres	2:14.83	Ann Osgerby	Moscow, USSR	21 July	1980
BACKSTROKE					
100 metres	1:04.60	Helen Jameson	Moscow, USSR	20 July	1980
200 metres	2:17.84	Helen Jameson	Moscow, USSR	27 July	1980
INDIVIDUAL MEDLEY					
200 metres	2:17.31	Sharron Davies	Blackpool, Lancashire	20 Apr	1980
400 metres	4:46.83	Sharron Davies	Moscow, USSR	26 July	1980
4 × 100 metres relay	4:12.24	United Kingdom Team: (Helen Jameson, Margaret Kelly Ann Osgerby, June Croft)	Moscow, USSR	20 July	1980

TABLE TENNIS

MOST WINS IN WORLD CHAMPIONSHIPS (Instituted 1926–7)

Event	Name and Nationality	Times	Years
Men's Singles (St Bride's Vase)	G. Viktor Barna (Hungary) (1911–72)	5	1930, 1932–5
Women's Singles (G. Geist Prize)	Angelica Rozeanu (Romania) (b. 15 Oct 1921)	6	1950–5
Men's Doubles	G. Viktor Barna (Hungary)	8	1929–35, 1939
Women's Doubles	Maria Mednyanszky (Hungary) (1901–79)	7	1928, 1930–5
Mixed Doubles (Men)	Ferenc Sido (Hungary) (b. 1923)	4	1949–50, 1952–3
(Women)	Maria Mednyanszky (Hungary)	6	1927–8, 1930–1, 1933–4

G. Viktor Barna gained a personal total of 15 world titles, while 18 have been won by Maria Mednyanszky.
Note: With the staging of championships biennially the breaking of the above records would now be virtually impossible

MOST TEAM TITLES

Event	Team	Times	Years
Men's Team (Swaything Cup)	Hungary	12	1927–31, 1933–5, 1938, 1949, 1952, 1979
Women's Team (Marcel Corbillon Cup)	Japan	8	1952, 1954, 1957, 1959, 1961, 1963, 1967, 1971

MOST WINS IN ENGLISH OPEN CHAMPIONSHIPS (Instituted 1921)

Event	Name and Nationality	Times	Years
Men's Singles	Richard Bergmann (Austria, then GB) (1920–70)	6	1939–40, 1948, 1950, 1952, 1954
Women's Singles	Maria Alexandru (Romania) (b. 1941)	6	1963–4, 1970–2, 1974
Men's Doubles	G. Viktor Barna (Hungary, then GB)	7	1931, 1933–5, 1938–9, 1949
Women's Doubles	Diane Rowe (GB) (now Scholer) (b. 14 Apr 1933)	12	1950–6, 1960, 1962–5
Mixed Doubles (Men)	G. Viktor Barna (Hungary, then GB)	8	1933–6, 1938, 1940, 1951, 1953
(Women)	Diane Rowe (GB) (now Scholer)	4	1952, 1954, 1956, 1960

Seven times English Singles champion, Jill Hammersley won the European title in 1976. *(Don Morley, All-Sport)*

Origins

The earliest evidence relating to a game resembling table tennis has been found in the catalogues of London sports goods manufacturers in the 1880s. The old Ping Pong Association was formed in 1902 but the game proved only a temporary craze until resuscitated in 1921. The English Table Tennis Association was formed on 24 Apr 1927.

Most English titles

The highest total of English men's titles (instituted 1921) is 20 by G. Viktor Barna (1911–72) (b. Hungary, Gyözö Braun). The women's record is 17 by Diane Rowe (b. 14 Apr 1933), now Mrs Eberhard Scholer. Her twin Rosalind (now Mrs Cornett) has won nine (two in singles).

The most titles won in the English Closed Championships is seven by Jill Patricia Hammersley, MBE (b. 6 Dec 1951) in 1973–6, 1978–9, 1981.

Youngest international

The youngest ever international was Joy Foster, aged 8, when she represented Jamaica in the West Indies Championships at Port of Spain, Trinidad in Aug 1958.

Longest match

In the Swaythling Cup final match between Austria and Romania in Prague, Czechoslovakia, in 1936, the play lasted for 11 h beginning on Sunday 15 March and completed on the following Wednesday.

Longest rally

In a Swaythling Cup match in Prague on 14 Mar 1936 between Alex Ehrlich (Poland) and Farcas Paneth (Romania) the opening rally lasted 1 hr 58 min. On 30 July 1978 Robert Siegel and Donald Peters staged an 8 hr 33 min rally at Stamford, Conn, USA.

Counter hitting

The record number of hits in 60 sec is 162 by English Internationals Nicky Jarvis (b. 7 Mar 1954) and Desmond Douglas (b. 20 July 1955) at the Eccentric Club, London on 1 Dec 1976. This was equalled by Douglas and Paul Day (b. 20 Oct 1958) at Butlins, Blackpool, Lancs, on 21 Mar 1977. The most by women is 148 by Linda Howard and Melodi Ludi at Blackpool, Lancs, on 11 Oct 1977. With a bat in each hand, Gary D. Fisher of Olympia, Wash., USA, completed 5000 consecutive volleys over the net in 44 min 28 sec on 25 June 1979.

Highest speed

No conclusive measurements have been published but in a lecture M. Sklorz (W. Germany) stated that a smashed ball had been measured at speeds up to 170 km/h *105,6 mph.*

Marathons

The longest marathon singles match is 132 hr 31 min by Danny Price and Randy Nunes at Cherry Hill, NJ, USA, on 20–26 Aug 1978.

The longest doubles marathon is 101 hr 1 min 11 sec by Lance, Phil and Mark Warren and Bill Weir at Sacramento, Calif., USA on 9–13 Apr 1979.

TENNIS *(Real or Royal)*

Origins

The game originated as *jeu de paume* in French monasteries *c.* 1050. A tennis court is mentioned in the sale of the Hôtel de Nesle, Paris in 1308. The oldest court in the world is one built in Paris in 1496.

The oldest of the 18 surviving active Tennis Courts in the British Isles is the Royal Tennis Court at Hampton Court Palace, which was built in 1529–30 and rebuilt in 1660. There are estimated to be 3000 players and 30 active courts throughout the world. The court at Jesmond Dene, Newcastle upon Tyne was reactivated for play in 1981.

Most titles *World*

The first recorded World Tennis Champion was Clerge (France) *c.* 1740. Jacques Edmond Barre (France) (1802–73) held the title for a record 33 yr from 1829 to 1862. Pierre Etchebaster (1893–1980) a Basque, holds the record for the greatest number of successful defences of the title with eight between 1928 and 1952.

Most titles *British*

The Amateur Championship of the British Isles (instituted 1888) has been won 15 times by Howard Rea Angus MBE (b. 25 June 1944) consecutively 1966–80. Angus, a left-hander, is also the first British amateur to win a World title, in 1975.

TRACK AND FIELD ATHLETICS

See also The Official Centenary History of the A.A.A. *by Peter Lovesey, published by Guinness Superlatives Ltd (price £8.95).*

Origins

Track and field athletics date from the ancient Olympic Games. The earliest accurately known Olympiad dates from July 776 BC, at which celebration Coroibos won the foot race. The oldest surviving measurements are a long jump of 7,05 m *23 ft 1½ in* by Chionis of Sparta in *c.* 656 BC and a discus throw of 100 cubits (about 46.30 m *152 ft*) by Protesilaus.

Earliest landmarks

The first time 10 sec ('even time') was bettered for 100 yd under championship conditions was when John Owen, then aged 30, recorded 9⅘ sec in the AAU Championship at Analostan Island, Washington, DC, USA, on 11 Oct 1890. The first recorded instance of 6 ft *1,83 m* being cleared in the high jump was when Marshall Jones Brooks (1855–1944) jumped 6 ft 0⅛ in *1,832 m* at Marston, near Oxford, on 17 Mar 1876. The breaking of the 'four-minute barrier' in the 1 mile *1609,34 m* was first achieved by Dr (now Sir) Roger Gilbert Bannister, CBE (b. Harrow, London, 23 Mar 1929), when he recorded 3 min 59.4 sec on the Iffley Road track, Oxford, at 6.10 p.m. on 6 May 1954. Since then it has been broken by another 349 runners to end-June 1981, including 66 Britons.

Fastest runner

Robert Lee Hayes (b. 20 Dec 1942) of Jacksonville, Florida, USA, may have reached a speed of over 27 mph *43,5 km/h* during his then world record run of 9.1 sec in a 100 yd event at St Louis, Missouri, on 21 June 1963. Marlies Göhr (*née* Oelsner) (b. E. Germany, 21 Mar 1958) reached a speed of over 24 mph *38,6 km/h* in her world record 100 m in 10.88 sec at Dresden, E. Germany on 1 July 1977.

Highest jumper

There are several reported instances of high jumpers exceeding the official world record height of 7 ft 8¾ in *2,36 m.* The earliest of these came from unsubstantiated reports of Tutsi tribesmen in Central Africa (see page 12) clearing up to 8 ft 2½ in *2,50 m,* definitely however, from inclined take-offs. The greatest height cleared above an athlete's own head is 23¼ in *59 cm* by Franklin Jacobs (US) (b. 31 Dec 1957), who cleared 7 ft 7¼ in *2,32 m* at New York, USA, on 28 Jan 1978. He is only 5 ft 8 in *1,73 m* tall. The greatest height cleared by a woman above her own head is 27 cm *10½ in* by Marina Sisoyeva (b. 10 July 1959) (USSR) who stands 1,66 m *5 ft 5½ in* and jumped 1,93 m *6 ft 4 in* at Moscow, USSR, on 5 July 1980.

Most Olympic titles *Men*

The most Olympic gold medals won is ten (an absolute Olympic record) by Ray C. Ewry (USA) (1874–1937) in the Standing High, Long and Triple Jumps in 1900, 1904, 1906 and 1908.

Most Olympic titles *Women*

The most gold medals won by a woman is four shared by Francina 'Fanny' E. Blankers-Koen (Netherlands) (b. 26 Apr 1918) with 100 m, 200 m, 80 m hurdles and 4 × 100 m relay, 1948, Betty Cuthbert (Australia) (b. 20 Apr 1938) with 100 m, 200 m, 4 × 100 m relay, 1956 and 400 m, 1964, and Barbel Wöckel (*née* Eckert) (b. 21 Mar 1955) (E. Ger) with 200 m and 4 × 100 m relay in 1976 and 1980.

Most wins at one Games

The most gold medals at one celebration is five by Paavo Johannes Nurmi (Finland) (1897–1973) in 1924, and the most individual is four by Alvin C. Kraenzlein (USA) (1876–1928) in 1900, with 60 m, 110 m hurdles, 200 m hurdles and long jump.

Most Olympic titles *British*

The most gold medals won by a British athlete (excluding Tug of War and Walking, *q.v.*) is two by: Charles Bennett (1871–1949) (1500 m and 5000 m team, 1900); Alfred Tysoe (1874–1901) (800 m and 5000 m team, 1900); John Rimmer (1879–1962) (4000 m steeplechase; and 5000 m team, 1900); Albert G. Hill (1889–1969) (800 m and 1500 m, 1920) and Douglas Gordon Arthur Lowe (1902–81) (800 m 1924 and 1928).

Most Olympic medals *Men*

The most medals won is 12 (nine gold and three silver) by Paavo Nurmi (Finland) in the Games of 1920, 1924 and 1928.

Most Olympic medals *Women*

The most medals won by a woman athlete is seven by Shirley de la Hunty (*née* Strickland), MBE (Australia) (b. 18 July 1925) with three gold, one silver and three bronze in the 1948, 1952 and 1956 Games. A recently discovered photo-finish indicates that she finished third, not fourth, in the 1948 200 metres event, thus unofficially increasing her medal haul to eight. Irena Szewinska (*née* Kirszenstein) (Poland) (b. 24 May 1946) won three gold, two silver and two bronze in 1964, 1968, 1972 and 1976, and is the only woman athlete to win a medal in four successive games.

Most Olympic medals *British*

The most medals won by a British athlete is four by Guy M. Butler (1899–1981) with a gold medal for the 4 × 400 m relay and a silver in the 400 m in 1920 and a bronze medal for each of these events in 1924. Two British women athletes have won three medals: Dorothy Hyman, MBE (b. 9 May 1941) with a silver (100 m, 1960) and a bronze (200 m, 1960 and 4 × 100 m relay, 1964) and Mary Denise Rand, MBE (now Toomey, *née* Bignal), (b. 10 Feb 1940) with a gold (long jump), a silver (pentathlon) and a bronze (4 × 100 m relay) all in 1964.

Olympic champions *Oldest and youngest*

The oldest athlete to win an Olympic title was Irish-born Patrick

J. 'Babe' McDonald (USA) (1878–1954) who was aged 42 years 26 days when he won the 56 lb *25,4 kg* weight throw at Antwerp, Belgium on 21 Aug 1920. The oldest female champion was Lia Manoliu (Romania) (b. 25 Apr 1932) aged 36 years 176 days when she won the discus at Mexico City on 18 Oct 1968. The youngest gold medallist was Barbara Jones (USA) (b. 26 Mar 1937) who was a member of the winning 4 × 100 m relay team, aged 15 years 123 days, at Helsinki, Finland on 27 July 1952. The youngest male champion was Robert Bruce Mathias (USA) (b. 17 Nov 1930) aged 17 years 263 days when he won the decathlon at London on 5–6 Aug 1948.

World record breakers *Oldest and youngest*

For the greatest age at which anyone has broken a world record in a standard Olympic event see p. 239. The female record is 35 years 255 days in the case of Dana Zátopkova, *née* Ingrova (b. 19 Sept 1922) of Czechoslovakia, who broke the women's javelin record with 182 ft 10 in *55,73 m* at Prague, Czechoslovakia, on 1 June 1958. The youngest individual record breaker is Ulrike Meyfarth (b. 4 May 1956) of W. Germany who equalled the women's high jump mark with 1.92 m *6 ft 3½ in* in winning the gold medal on 4 Sept 1972 at the Munich Olympics aged 16 years 123 days. Barbara Jones (see Olympic champions above), aged 15 years 123 days, was in a team event.

Most records in a day

Jesse Owens (1913–80) (USA) set six world records in 45 min at Ann Arbor, Michigan on 25 May 1935 with a 9.4 sec 100 yd at 3.15 p.m., a 26 ft 8¼ in *8,13 m* long jump at 3.25 p.m., a 20.3 sec 220 yd (and 200 m) at 3.45 p.m. and a 22.6 sec 220 yd low hurdles (and 200 m) at 4.00 p.m.

Most national titles

The greatest number of national AAA titles (excluding those in tug of war events) won by one athlete is 14 individual and one relay title by Emmanuel McDonald Bailey (b. Williamsville, Trinidad 8 Dec 1920), between 1946 and 1952. The most won in a single event is 13 by Denis Horgan (Ireland) (1871–1922) in the shot putt between 1893 and 1912.

The greatest number of consecutive title wins is seven by Denis Horgan (1871–1922) (Ireland) (shot putt, 1893–99), Albert Arthur Cooper (1910–74) (2 miles walk, 1932–8), Donald Osborne Finlay, DFC, AFC (1909–70) (120 yd hurdles, 1932–8),

Three-legged record holders for over seventy years, Harry Hillman (left) and Lawson Robertson both won medals in the 1904 Olympic Games.

Harry Whittle (b. 2 May 1922) (440 yd hurdles, 1947–53) and Maurice Herriott (b. 8 Oct 1939) (3000 m steeplechase 1961–7). The record for consecutive WAAA titles is nine by Judy Undine Farr (Trowbridge & District AC) (b. 24 Jan 1942) who won the 1½ mile *2414 m*/2500 m *1 mile 974 yd* walk from 1962 to 1970.

Most international appearances

The greatest number of full Great Britain outdoor internationals won by a British male athlete is 61 by Andrew Howard Payne (b. South Africa, 17 Apr 1931) from July 1960 to Sept 1974. Geoffrey Lewis Capes (b. 23 Aug 1949) has made 67 full international appearances, including indoor matches, between 6 July 1969 and 12 Sept 1980. The feminine record is 65 full internationals including indoor matches, by Brenda Rose Bedford (*née* Sawyer) (b. 4 Sept 1937, London) from September 1961 to June 1978.

Oldest and youngest internationals

Of full Great Britain (outdoor) internationals the oldest have been Hector Harold Whitlock (b. 16 Dec 1903) at the 1952 Olympic Games, aged 48 years 218 days, and Rosemary Payne (*née* Charters) (b. 19 May 1933) in the Great Britain v. Finland match on 26 Sept 1974, aged 41 yr 130 days. The youngest have been Ross Hepburn (b. 14 Oct 1961) v. the USSR on 26 Aug 1977, aged 15 years 316 days, and Janis Walsh (b. 28 Mar 1960) v. Belgium (indoor) at 60 m and 4 × 200 m relay on 15 Feb 1975, 41 days short of her 15th birthday.

Longest career

Duncan McLean (1884–1980) of Scotland set a world age—92—record of 100 m in 21.7 sec in August 1977, over 73 years after his best ever sprint of 100 yd in 9.9 sec in South Africa in February 1904. At Athens, Greece, on 10 Oct 1976, Dimitrion Yordanidis, aged 98, completed a marathon race in 7 hr 33 min.

Ambidextrous shot putt

The best recorded distance is 121 ft 6¾ in by Allan Feuerbach (b. 14 Jan 1948) (USA) (left 51 ft 5 in *15,67 m*, right 70 ft 1¾ in *21.38 m*) at Malmo, Sweden on 24 Aug 1974.

Highland Games

The weight and height of cabers (Gaelic *cabar*) vary considerably. Extreme values are 25 ft *7,62 m* and 280 lb *127 kg*. The Braemar caber (19 ft 3 in *5,86 m* and 120 lb *54,4 kg*) in Grampian, Scotland, was untossed from 1891 until 1951 when it was tossed by George Clark. The best authentic mark recorded for throwing the 56 lb weight for height, using one hand only is 17 ft *5,18 m* over a bar by Bishop Dolegiewicz (Canada) (b. 8 Jul 1953) at Great Gorge, New Jersey, USA on 19 Aug 1980. The best throw recorded for the Scots hammer is 151 ft 2 in *46,08 m* by William Anderson, MBE, (b. 6 Oct 1938) at Lochearnhead, 2 July 1969.

Standing jumps

The best high jump is 6 ft 2¾ in *1,90 m* by Rune Almen (b. 2 Oct 1952) (Sweden) at Karlstad, Sweden on 3 May 1980. Joe Darby (1861–1937), the famous Victorian professional jumper (see also p. 182), long jumped a measured 12 ft 1½ in *3,69 m* *without* weights at Dudley Castle, on 28 May 1890. Johan Christian Evandt (Norway) achieved 3,65 m *11 ft 11¾ in* as an amateur in Reykjavik, Iceland on 11 Mar 1962.

The best high jump by a woman is 1,50 m *4 ft 11 in* by Grete Bjørdalsbakke (b. 23 June 1960) (Norway) at Orsta, Norway on 12 Dec 1979. The best long jump is 2,92 m *9 ft 7 in* by Anneli Mannes (Norway) at Flisa, Norway on 7 Mar 1981.

Highest one-legged jump

One-legged Arnie Boldt, (b. 1958) of Saskatchewan, Canada cleared 2.04 m *6 ft 8¼ in* in Rome, Italy on 3 Apr 1981.

Fastest three-legged race

The fastest recorded time for a 100 yd three-legged race is 11.0 sec by Olympic medallists Harry Livingstone Hillman (1881–1945) and Lawson Robertson (1883–1951) at Brooklyn, New York City, NY USA, on 24 Apr 1909.

Backwards running

The fastest time recorded for running the 100 yd backwards is

13.1 sec by Paul Wilson (NZ) at Tokyo, Japan on 22 Sept 1979. He clocked 14.4 sec for 100 m. Ernest C. Conner jr (b. 1944) ran the New York Marathon backwards in 5 hr 18 min on 26 Oct 1980.

Fastest blind sprinting
Graham Henry Salmon (b. 5 Sept 1952) of Loughton, Essex, England ran 100 m *109 yd* in 11.4 sec at Grangemouth, Scotland on 2 Sept 1978.

Pancake race record
The annual Shrove Tuesday Housewives' Pancake Race at Olney, Buckinghamshire, was first mentioned in 1445. The record for the winding 415 yd *380 m* course (three tosses mandatory) is 61.0 sec, set by Sally Ann Faulkner, (b. 1958) on 26 Feb 1974. The record for the counterpart race (inst. 1949) at Liberal, Kansas, USA is 58.5 sec by Sheila Turner (b. 9 July 1953) on 11 Feb 1975.

Longest runs
Ernst Mensen (Norway) (1799–1841), a former seaman in the British Navy is reputed to have run from Istanbul, Turkey, to Calcutta, in West Bengal, India, and back in 59 days in 1836, averaging an improbable 100 miles *161 km* per day. Max Telford (NZ) (b. Hawick, Scotland, 2 Feb 1935) ran 5110 miles *8224 km* from Anchorage, Alaska to Halifax, Nova Scotia, in 106 days 18 hr 45 min from 25 July to 9 Nov 1977. The fastest time reported for the cross-America run is 46 days 8 hr 36 min by Frank Giannino Jr (USA) (b. 1952) for the 3100 miles *4989 km* from San Francisco to New York on 1 Sept–17 Oct 1980. Terry Fox (1958–81), a Canadian with an artificial leg, ran 3339 miles *5374 km* from St John's, Newfoundland to Thunder Bay, Ontario, in 143 days, from 12 Apr–2 Sept 1980, raising nearly $10m for cancer research.

Longest non-stop run
The greatest non-stop run recorded is 352.9 miles *568 km* in 121 hr 54 min by Bertil Järläker (Sweden) (b. 1936) at Norrköping, Sweden, 26–31 May 1980. He was moving for 95.04 per cent of the time.

Longest running race
The longest race ever staged was the 1929 Trans-continental Race (3665 miles *5898 km*) from New York City, NY, to Los Angeles, California, USA. The Finnish-born Johnny Salo (1893–1931) was the winner in 79 days, from 31 Mar to 18 June. His elapsed time of 525 hr 57 min 20 sec (averaging 6.97 mph *11,21 km/h*) left him only 2 min 47 sec ahead of Englishman Pietro 'Peter' Gavuzzi (1905–81).

Six-day races
The greatest distance covered by a man in six days (*i.e.* the 144 permissible hours between Sundays in Victorian times) was 623¾ miles *1003,828 km* by George Littlewood (England), who required only 141 hr 57 min 30 sec for this feat on 3–8 Dec 1888 at the old Madison Square Gardens, New York City, USA.

London to Brighton race
Ian Thompson (b. 16 Oct 1949) (Luton United H) won the 54.3 miles *87,4 km* race (inst 1951) in 5 hr 15 min 15 sec on 28 Sept 1980, averaging 10.33 mph *16,62 km/h*.

Greatest mileage
Jay F Helgerson (b. 3 Feb 1955) of Foster City, California, ran a certified marathon (26 miles 385 yd) or longer, each week for 52 weeks from 28 Jan 1979 to 19 Jan 1980, totalling 1418 racing miles *2282 km*.

The greatest life-time mileage recorded by any runner is 195,855 miles *315 198 km* by Earle Linwood Dilks (b. 24 Sept 1894) of New Castle, Pennsylvania, USA, up to end-1977.

Oldest race
The oldest continuously held foot race is the 'Red Hose Race' held at Carnwath, Strathclyde, Scotland since 1508. The prize is a pair of hand-knitted knee length red hose. Michael Glen, of Bathgate, won a record 14 times, 1951–66.

24 hour record
The greatest distance run on a standard track in 24 hr is 169

miles 705 yd *272,624 km* by Jean-Gilles Boussiquet (France) (b. 1944) at Lausanne, Switzerland on 2–3 May 1981. The best by a woman is 123 miles 675 yd *198,566 km* by Sue Ellen Trapp (USA) (b. 3 Mar 1946) at Miami, Florida, 29 Feb–1 Mar 1980.

Fastest 100 miles
On 15 Oct 1977 Donald A. Ritchie (b. 6 July 1944) (Birchfield H) ran 100 miles *160,9 km* in a record 11 hr 30 min 51 sec at Crystal Palace, London. The best by a woman is 15 hr 44 min 27 sec by Marcy Schwamm (USA) at Greenwich, Conn, USA on 1–2 Nov 1980.

Mass relay records
The record for 100 miles *160,9 km* by 100 runners belonging to one club is 7 hr 53 min 52.1 sec by Baltimore Road Runners Club, Towson, Maryland, USA, on 17 May 1981. The feminine record is held by a team from San Francisco Dolphins Southend Running Club, USA with 10 hr 47 min 9.3 sec on 3 Apr 1977. The best club time for a 100 × 400 metres relay is 1 hr 29 min 11.8 sec (average 53.5 sec) by the Physical Training Institute, Leuven, Belgium on 19 Apr 1978.

Thirteen runners from the Melbourne Fire Brigade, Australia ran 6290 km *3908 miles* in relay from Darwin, NT, to Melbourne, Victoria, in 18 days 20 hr 25 min from 25 May–13 June 1979.

The longest relay ever run, and that with the most participants, was by 1607 students and teachers who covered 6014.65 miles *9679,645 km* at Trondheim, Norway, 21 Oct–23 Nov 1977

(top) The late Terry Fox greatly moved the Canadian public with his 3339 mile charity run. *(Canada-Wide)*
(bottom) Grete Waitz winning her third consecutive New York Marathon and setting her third world record for this distance. *(John Topham Picture Library)*

WORLD RECORDS - MEN

A list of World's Records for the 32 scheduled men's events (excluding the walking records—see under WALKING) passed by the International Amateur Athletic Federation as at 19 Aug 1981. Fully automatic electric timing is mandatory for the six events up to the 400 metre distance. * Denotes awaiting ratification.

RUNNING	Min sec	Name and Country	Place	Date
100 metres	9.95	James Ray Hines (USA)	Mexico City, Mexico	14 Oct 1968
200 metres	19.72	Pietro Mennea (Italy)	Mexico City, Mexico	12 Sept 1979
400 metres	43.86	Lee Edward Evans (USA)	Mexico City, Mexico	18 Oct 1968
800 metres	1:41.72*	Sebastian Newbold Coe (GB & NI)	Florence, Italy	10 June 1981
1000 metres	2:12.18*	Sebastian Newbold Coe (GB & NI)	Oslo, Norway	11 July 1981
1500 metres	3:31.36	Steven Michael James Ovett (GB & NI)	Coblenz W. Germany	27 Aug 1980
1 mile	3:48.53	Sebastian Newbold Coe (GB & NI)	Zurich, Switzerland	19 Aug 1981
2000 metres	4:51.4	John George Walker, OBE (NZ)	Oslo, Norway	30 June 1976
3000 metres	7:32.1	Henry Rono (Kenya)	Oslo, Norway	27 June 1978
5000 metres	13:08.4	Henry Rono (Kenya)	Berkeley, California, USA	8 Apr 1978
10,000 metres	27:22.4	Henry Rono (Kenya)	Vienna, Austria	11 June 1978
20,000 metres	57:24.2	Josephus Hermens (Netherlands)	Papendal, Netherlands	1 May 1976
25,000 metres	1 hr 13:55.8	Toshihiko Seko (Japan)	Christchurch, New Zealand	22 Mar 1981
30,000 metres	1 hr 29:18.8*	Toshihiko Seko (Japan)	Christchurch, New Zealand	22 Mar 1981
1 hour	20 944 m *13 miles 24 yd 2 ft*	Josephus Hermens (Netherlands)	Papendal, Netherlands	1 May 1976

(*left*) World mile record holder and Olympic 800 metres champion Steve Ovett, wearing number 11, won 45 consecutive 1500 m/mile races from 1977 to 1980. (*Tony Duffy, All-Sport*)

(*above*) Hungary's Ferenc Paragi, who broke the World javelin record previously held by his countryman, Miklos Nemeth. (*John Topham Picture Library*)

(*right*) Olympic relay bronze medallist Joslyn Hoyte-Smith, whose British best at 400 metres is also the Commonwealth record. (*Bob Martin, All-Sport*)

HURDLING	Min sec	Name and Country	Place	Date
110 metres (3′ 6″ *106 cm*)	12.93	Renaldo Nehemiah (USA)	Zurich, Switzerland	19 Aug 1981
400 metres (3′ 0″ *91,4 cm*)	47.13	Edwin Corley Moses (USA)	Milan, Italy	3 July 1980
3000 metres steeplechase	8:05.37	Henry Rono (Kenya)	Seattle, Washington, USA	13 May 1978

MARATHON

There is no official marathon record because of the varying severity of courses. The best time recorded over 26 miles 385 yd *42,195 km* (standardised in 1924) is 2 hr 08 min 33.6 sec (av. 12.28 mph *19,77 km*) by Derek Clayton (b. 17 Nov 1942, Barrow-in-Furness, England) of Australia, at Antwerp, Belgium, on 30 May 1969. The best time by a British international is 2 hr 09 min 12 sec by Ian Thompson (b. 16 Oct 1949) at Christchurch, New Zealand, 31 Jan 1974. The fastest time by a female is 2 hr 25 min 42 sec (av 10.79 mph *17,37 km/h*) by Grete Waitz (Norway) (b. 1 Oct 1953) at New York, USA on 26 Oct 1980. The fastest by a British woman is 2 hr 29 min 57 sec by Joyce Esther Smith (*née* Byatt) (b. 26 Oct 1937) at London on 29 Mar 1981.

RELAYS

4 × 100 metres (two turns)	38.03	United States National Team: (William Collins, Steven Earl Riddick, Clifford Wiley, Steven Williams)	Dusseldorf, W. Germany	3 Sept 1977
4 × 200 metres	1:20.26†	University of Southern California, USA: (Joel Andrews, James Sanford, William Mullins, Clancy Edwards)	Tempe, Arizona, USA	27 May 1978
4 × 400 metres	2:56.16	United States National Team: (Vincent Edward Matthews, Ronald J. Freeman, George Lawrence James, Lee Edward Evans)	Mexico City, Mexico	20 Oct 1968

RELAYS (continued)	Min Sec	Name and Country	Place	Date
4 × 800 metres	7:08.1	USSR Team: (Vladimir Podoliakov, Nikolai Kirov, Vladimir Malosemlin, Anatoli Reschetniak)	Podolsk, USSR	13 Aug 1978
4 × 1,500 metres	14:38.8	W. German Team: (Thomas Wessinghage, Harald Hudak, Michael Lederer, Karl Fleschen)	Cologne, W. Germany	17 Aug 1977

† *The time of 1:20.23 achieved by the Tobias Striders (Guy Abrahams, Mike Simmons, Donald O'Riley Quarrie, James Gilkes) at Tempe, Aríz., USA on 27 May 1978 was not ratified as the team was composed of varied nationalities.*

FIELD EVENTS	ft	in	m	Name and Country	Place	Date
High Jump	7	8¾	2,36	Gerd Wessig (E. Germany)	Moscow, USSR	1 Aug 1980
Pole Vault	19	0¾	5,81*	Vladimir Poliakov (USSR)	Tbilisi, USSR	26 June 1981
Long Jump	29	2½	8,90	Robert Beamon (USA)	Mexico City, Mexico	18 Oct 1968
Triple Jump	58	8½	17,89	João Carlos de Oliveira (Brazil)	Mexico City, Mexico	15 Oct 1975
Shot Putt	72	8	22,15‡	Udo Beyer (E. Germany)	Gothenburg, Sweden	6 July 1978
Discus Throw	233	5	71,16†	Wolfgang Schmidt (E. Germany)	East Berlin	9 Aug 1978
Hammer Throw	268	4	81,80	Yuri Sedykh (USSR)	Moscow, USSR	31 July 1980
Javelin Throw	317	4	96,72	Ferenc Paragi (Hungary)	Tata, Hungary	23 Apr 1980

‡ *Note: One professional performance is superior to the IAAF mark, but the same highly rigorous rules as to measuring and weighing were not necessarily applied.*

| | 75 | 0 | 22,86 | Brian Ray Oldfield (USA) | El Paso, Texas, USA | 10 May 1975 |

† *Ben Plucknett (USA) threw 237 ft 4 in 72,34 m at Oslo, Norway on 7 July 1981 but was subsequently disqualified from competition.*

DECATHLON

8649 points	Guido Kratschmer (W. Germany) (1st day: 100 m 10.58 sec, Long Jump 7,80 m *25' 7¼"*, Shot Putt 15,47 m *50' 9¼"*, High Jump 2,00 m *6' 6¾"*, 400 m 48.04 sec)	Bernhausen, W. Germany (2nd day: 110 m hurdles 13.92 sec, Discus 45,25 m *149' 4"*, Pole Vault 4,60 m *15' 1"*, Javelin 66,50 m *218' 2"*, 1500 m 4:24.15 sec)	14–15 June 1980

WORLD RECORDS - WOMEN

A list of World's Records for the 22 scheduled women's events passed by the International Amateur Athletic Federation as at 19 Aug 1981. The same stipulation about automatically timed events applies in the six events up to 400 metres as in the men's list. * Denotes awaiting ratification.

RUNNING	Min sec	Name and Country	Place	Date
100 metres	10.88	Marlies Oelsner (now Göhr) (E. Germany)	Dresden, E. Germany	1 July 1977
200 metres	21.71	Marita Koch (E. Germany)	Karl Marx Stadt, E. Germany	10 June 1979
400 metres	48.60	Marita Koch (E. Germany)	Turin, Italy	4 Aug 1979
800 metres	1:53.43	Nadezda Olizarenko [née Mushta] (USSR)	Moscow, USSR	27 July 1980
1500 metres	3:52.47	Tatyana Kazankina (USSR)	Zurich, Switzerland	13 Aug 1980
1 mile	4:21.68†	Mary Decker (USA)	Auckland, New Zealand	26 Jan 1980
3000 metres	8:27.12	Ludmila Bragina (USSR)	College Park, Maryland, USA	7 Aug 1976
5000 metres	15:28.43	Ingrid Christensen (Norway)	Oslo, Norway	11 July 1981
10000 metres	31:45.35	Loa Olofsson (Denmark)	Copenhagen, Denmark	6 Apr 1981

† *Mary Decker ran 4:17.55 indoors at Houston, USA on 16 Feb 1980.*

HURDLING	Min sec	Name and Country	Place	Date
100 metres (2' 9" 84 cm)	12.36	Grazyna Rabsztyn (Poland)	Warsaw, Poland	13 June 1980
400 metres (2' 6" 76 cm)	54.28	Karin Rossley (E. Germany)	Jena, E. Germany	18 May 1980

RELAYS	Min sec	Name and Country	Place	Date
4 × 100 metres	41.60	E. German Team: (Romy Müller [née Schneider], Barbel Wöckel [née Eckert], Ingrid Auerswald, Marlies Göhr [née Oelsner])	Moscow, USSR	1 Aug 1980
4 × 200 metres	1:28.15	E. German Team: (Marlies Göhr [née Oelsner], Romy Muller [née Schneider], Barbel Wöckel [née Eckert], Marita Koch)	Jena, E. Germany	9 Aug 1980
4 × 400 metres	3:19.23	E. German National Team: (Doris Maletzki, Brigitte Röhde, Ellen Streidt [née Stropahl], Christina Brehmer [now Lathan])	Montreal, Canada	31 July 1976
4 × 800 metres	7:52.3	USSR National Team: (Tatyana Providokhina, Valentina Gerasimova, Svetlana Styrkina, Tatyana Kazankina)	Podolsk, USSR	16 Aug 1976

FIELD EVENTS	ft	in	m	Name and Country	Place	Date
High Jump	6	7	2,01	Sara Simeoni (Italy)	Brescia, Italy	4 Aug 1978
Long Jump	23	3¼	7,09	Vilma Bardauskiene (USSR)	Prague, Czechoslovakia	29 Aug 1978
Shot Putt	73	8	22,45†	Ilona Slupianek [née Schoknecht] (E. Germany)	Potsdam, E. Germany	11 May 1980
Discus Throw	235	7	71,80	Maria Petkova [née Vergova] (Bulgaria)	Sofia, Bulgaria	13 July 1980
Javelin Throw	235	10	71,88	Antoaneta Todorova (Bulgaria)	Zagreb, Yugoslavia	15 Aug 1981

† *Helena Fibingerova (Czechoslovakia) set an indoor record of 22,50 m 73 ft 10 in at Jablonec, Cz. on 19 Feb 1977.*

PENTATHLON (with 800 m)

5083 points (1971 Scoring Tables)	Nadezda Tkachenko (USSR) (100 m hurdles 13.29 sec; Shot Putt 16,84 m *55' 3"*; High Jump 1,84 m *6' 0½"*; Long Jump 6,73 m *22' 1"*; 800 m 2:05:20 sec)	Moscow, USSR	24 July 1980

HEPTATHLON

6716 points	Ramona Neubert (E. Germany) (100 m hurdles 13.70 sec: Shot Putt 15,41 m *50' 6¾"*; High Jump 1,86 m *6' 1¼"*; 200 m 23.58 sec; Long Jump 6,82 m *22' 4½"*; Javelin 40,62 m *133' 3"*; 800 m 2 min 06.72 sec)	Kiev, USSR	27–28 June 1981

UNITED KINGDOM (NATIONAL) RECORDS - MEN (as at 19 Aug 1981)

* Denotes awaiting ratification.

RUNNING	min sec	Name	Place	Date
100 metres	10.11	Allan Wipper Wells	Moscow, USSR	24 July 1980
200 metres (turn)	20.21	Allan Wipper Wells	Moscow, USSR	28 July 1980
400 metres	44.93	David Andrew Jenkins	Eugene, Oregon, USA	21 June 1975
800 metres	1:41.72*	Sebastian Newbold Coe	Florence, Italy	10 June 1981
1000 metres	2:12.18*	Sebastian Newbold Coe	Oslo, Norway	11 July 1981
1500 metres	3:31.36	Steven Michael James Ovett	Coblenz, W. Germany	27 Aug 1980
1 mile	3:48.53	Sebastian Newbold Coe	Zurich, Switzerland	19 Aug 1981
2000 metres	4:57.82	Steven Michael James Ovett	London (Crystal Palace)	3 June 1978
3000 metres	7:35.2	Brendan Foster, MBE	Gateshead, Tyne and Wear	3 Aug 1974
5000 metres	13:14.6	Brendan Foster, MBE	Christchurch, New Zealand	29 Jan 1974
10,000 metres	27:30.5†	Brendan Foster, MBE	London (Crystal Palace)	23 June 1978
20,000 metres	58:39.0	Ronald Hill	Leicester	9 Nov 1968
25,000 metres	1 hr 15:22.6	Ronald Hill	Bolton, Lancashire	21 July 1965
30,000 metres	1 hr 31:30.4	James Noel Carroll Alder	London (Crystal Palace)	5 Sept 1970
1 hour	12 miles 1268 yd *20 472 m*	Ronald Hill	Leicester	9 Nov 1968

† *Film evidence indicates that time should be 27:30.3*

HURDLING		Name	Place	Date
110 metres	13.69	Berwyn Price	Moscow, USSR	18 Aug 1973
400 metres	48.12	David Peter Hemery, MBE	Mexico City, Mexico	15 Oct 1968
3000 metres Steeplechase	8:18.95	Dennis Malcolm Coates	Montreal, Canada	25 July 1976

RELAYS		Name	Place	Date
4 × 100 metres	38.62	United Kingdom Team: (Michael Anthony McFarlane, Allan Wipper Wells, Robert Cameron Sharp, Andrew Emlyn McMaster)	Moscow, USSR	1 Aug 1980
4 × 200 metres	1:24.1	Great Britain: (Brian William Green, Roger Wilfred Walters, Ralph Banthorpe, Martin Edward Reynolds)	Paris, France	2 Oct 1971
4 × 400 metres	3:00.46	United Kingdom National Team: (Martin Edward Reynolds, Alan Peter Pascoe, MBE, David Peter Hemery, MBE, David Andrew Jenkins)	Munich, West Germany	10 Sept 1972
4 × 800 metres	7:17.4†	United Kingdom National Team: (Martin Bilham, David Cropper, Michael John Maclean, Peter Miles Browne)	London (Crystal Palace)	5 Sept 1970
4 × 1500 metres	14:56.8	United Kingdom Team: (Alan David Mottershead, Geoffrey Michael Cooper, Stephen John Emson, Roy Wood)	Bourges, France	24 June 1979

† *A time of 7:14.6 by a UK team (Graeme Grant, G. Michael Varah, Christopher Carter, John Peter Boulter) at Crystal Palace, London on 22 June 1966 was not ratified on a technicality.*

FIELD EVENTS	ft	in	m	Name	Place	Date
High Jump	7	4¼	2,24	Mark Naylor	Plymouth, Devon	28 June 1980
Pole Vault	18	6½	5,65*	Keith Stock	Oslo, Norway	7 July 1981
Long Jump	27	0	8,23	Lynn Davies, MBE	Bern, Switzerland	30 June 1968
Triple Jump	56	3¾	17,16†	Keith Leroy Connor	Melbourne, Australia	17 Jan 1980
Shot Putt	71	1½	21,68	Geoffrey Lewis Capes	Cwmbran, Gwent	18 May 1980
Discus Throw	211	0	64,32	William Raymond Tancred	Woodford, Essex	10 Aug 1974
Hammer Throw	246	0	74,98	Christopher Francis Black	Edinburgh, Scotland	21 Aug 1976
Javelin Throw	280	7	85,52	David Charles Ottley	Isleworth, Middlesex	28 May 1980

† *Connor jumped 56 ft 9½ in 17,31 m indoors at Detroit, Michigan, USA on 13 March 1981.*

DECATHLON (1962 Scoring Table)

8622 points	Francis Morgan 'Daley' Thompson	Götzis, W. Germany	17–18 May 1980

(1st day: 100 m 10.55 sec　　　　　　　　　　(2nd day: 110 m Hurdles 14.37 sec,
Long Jump 7,72 m *25' 4"*　　　　　　　　　　Discus 42,98 m *141' 0"*
Shot Putt 14,46 m *47' 5"*　　　　　　　　　　Pole Vault 4,90 m *16' 0¾"*
High Jump 2,11 m *6' 11"*　　　　　　　　　　Javelin 65,38 m *214' 6"*,
400 m 48.04 sec)　　　　　　　　　　　　　　1500 m 4:25.49 sec)

UNITED KINGDOM (NATIONAL) RECORDS - WOMEN (as at 19 Aug 1981)

* Denotes awaiting ratification.

RUNNING	Min sec	Name	Place	Date
100 metres	11.16	Andrea Joan Caron Lynch, MBE	London (Crystal Palace)	11 June 1975
200 metres	22.31	Kathryn Jane Smallwood	London (Crystal Palace)	8 Aug 1980
400 metres	50.88	Joslyn Hoyte-Smith	Oslo, Norway	1 July 1980
800 metres	1:59.05	Christina Tracy Boxer	Turin, Italy	4 Sept 1979
1500 metres	4:01.53	Christine Mary Benning [*née* Tranter]	Zurich, Switzerland	15 Aug 1979
1 mile	4:30.20	Christina Tracy Boxer	Gateshead, Tyne and Wear	8 July 1979
3000 metres	8:48.74	Paula Fudge [*née* Yeoman]	Prague, Czechoslovakia	29 Aug 1978
5000 metres	15:49.6	Kathryn Binns	Stretford, Greater Manchester	5 Apr 1980
10000 metres	32:57.17	Kathryn Binns	Sittard, Netherlands	14 Aug 1980

RELAYS		Name	Place	Date
4 × 100 metres	42.43	United Kingdom Team: (Heather Regina Hunte, Kathryn Jane Smallwood, Beverley Lanita Goddard, Sonia May Lannaman)	Moscow, USSR	1 Aug 1980
4 × 200 metres	1:31.57	United Kingdom National Team: (Donna-Marie Louise Hartley [*née* Murray], Verona Marolin Elder [*née* Bernard], Sharon Colyear, Sonia May Lannaman)	London (Crystal Palace)	20 Aug 1977
4 × 400 metres	3:26.6	United Kingdom National Team: (Jannette Veronica Roscoe [*née* Champion], Gladys Taylor [now McCormack], Verona Marolin Elder [*née* Bernard], Donna-Marie Louise Murray [now Hartley])	Nice, France	17 Aug 1975

RELAYS (continued)	Min sec	Name	Place	Date
4× 800 metres	8:23.8	Great Britain: (Joan Florence Allison, Sheila Janet Carey [*née* Taylor], Patricia Barbara Lowe [now Cropper], Rosemary Olivia Stirling [now Wright])	Paris, France	2 Oct 1971

HURDLING		Name	Place	Date
100 metres	13.06	Shirley Strong	Stuttgart, W. Germany	11 July 1980
400 metres	56.06	Christine Anne Warden [*née* Howell]	London (Crystal Palace)	28 July 1979

FIELD EVENTS	ft	in	m	Name	Place	Date
High Jump	6	4¼	1,94	Louise Ann Miller	Naples, Italy	25 May 1980
Long Jump	22	2¼	6,76	Mary Denise Rand, MBE [now Toomey, *née* Bignal]	Tokyo, Japan	14 Oct 1964
Shot Putt	58	6½	17,84*	Venissa Head	Cwmbran	6 June 1981
Discus Throw	221	5	67,48*	Margaret Elizabeth Ritchie	Walnut, California, USA	26 April 1981
Javelin Throw	228	8	69,70	Theresa Ione Sanderson	Stuttgart, W. Germany	5 June 1980

PENTATHLON (with 800 m)		Name	Place	Date
4408 points (1971 Tables)		Susan Jane Longden [*née* Wright]	Cwmbran, Gwent	24 May 1980

HEPTATHLON		Name	Place	Date
6110 points		Theresa Ione Saunderson	Brussels, Belgium	11–12 July 1981

TRAMPOLINING

Origins
Trampolines were used in show business at least as early as 'The Walloons' of the period 1910–12. The sport of trampolining (from the Spanish word *trampolin*, a springboard) dates from 1936, when the prototype 'T' model trampoline was developed by George Nissen (USA).

Most titles
Four men have won a world title (instituted 1964) twice; Dave Jacobs (USA) in 1967–8, Wayne Miller (b. 1946) (USA), in 1966 and 1970, Richard Tison (France) in 1974 and 1976 (shared), and Evgeni Janes (USSR), 1976 (shared) and 1978. Judy Wills (b. 1948) (USA) won the first five women's titles (1964–8). Two European titles (1969 and 1971) have been won by Paul Luxon (b. 1952) (GB), the 1972 world champion. A record seven United Kingdom titles have been won by Wendy Wright (1969–70, 1972–5, 1977). The most by a man have been five by Stewart Matthews (1976–80).

Marathons
The longest trampoline bouncing marathon is one of 1248 hours (52 days) set by a team of six in Phoenix, Arizona, USA on 24 June to 15 Aug 1974. The solo record is 240 hr by Darlene Blume, at Matraville RSL Youth Club, NSW, Australia, on 8–18 May 1980.

TUG OF WAR

Origins
Though ancient China and Egypt have been suggested as the originators of the sport, it is known that neolithic flint miners in Norfolk, England practised 'rope-pulling'. The first rules were those framed by the New York AC in 1879. In 1958 the Tug-of-War Association was formed to administer Britain's 600 clubs.

Most Olympic medals
An Olympic event from 1908 to 1920, three men won two gold medals (1908 and 1920) (all also won a silver medal in 1912)— John James Shepherd (1884–1954), Frederick H. Humphreys (1878–1954) and Edwin A. Mills (1878–1946) (all GB).

Most titles
The Wood Treatment team (formerly the Bosley Farmers) of Cheshire, have represented England since 1964, winning two World and ten European Championships at 720 kg *1587 lb*. They also won 20 consecutive AAA Catchweight Championships 1959–78. Hilary Brown (b. 13 Apr 1934) was in every team. Trevor Brian Thomas (b. 1943), of British Aircraft Corporation Club is the only holder of three winners medals in the European Open club championships.

Longest pulls
The longest recorded pull (prior to the introduction of AAA rules) is one of 2 hr 41 min between 'H' Company and 'E' Company of the 2nd Battalion of the Sherwood Foresters (Derbyshire Regiment) at Jubbulpore, India, on 12 Aug 1889. 'H' Company won. The longest recorded pull under AAA Rules (in which lying on the ground or entrenching the feet is not permitted) is one of 11 min 23 sec for the first pull between the Isle of Oxney and St Claret's at Chertsey, Surrey on 26 May 1979. The record time for 'The Pull' (inst. 1898), across the Black River, between freshman and sophomore teams at Hope College, Holland, Mich, USA, is 3 hr 51 min on 23 Sept 1977, but the method of bracing the feet precludes the replacing of the preceding records.

VOLLEYBALL

Origins
The game was invented as *Minnonette* in 1895 by William G. Morgan at the YMCA gymnasium at Holyoke, Massachusetts, USA. The International Volleyball Association was formed in Paris in April 1947. The Amateur (now English) Volleyball Association of Great Britain was formed in May 1955.

Most world titles
World Championships were instituted in 1949. The USSR has won five men's titles (1949, 1952, 1960, 1962 and 1978). The USSR won the women's championship in 1952, 1956, 1960 and 1970.

Most Olympic medals
The sport was introduced to the Olympic Games for both men and women in 1964. The only player to win four medals is Inna Ryskal (USSR) (b. 15 June 1944), who won silver medals in 1964 and 1976 and golds in 1968 and 1972. The record for men is held by Yuriy Poyarkov (USSR) (b. 10 Feb 1937) who won gold medals in 1964 and 1968 and a bronze in 1972.

Highest attendance
The record crowd is 60,000 for the 1952 world title matches in Moscow, USSR.

Marathon
The record by two teams of six is 75 hr 30 min by twelve players from Kinston, North Carolina, USA, on 31 Jan–3 Feb 1980.

WALKING

Most Olympic medals
Walking races have been included in the Olympic events since 1906 but walking matches have been known since 1589. The only walker to win three gold medals has been Ugo Frigerio (Italy) (1901–68) with the 3000 m and 10,000 m in 1920 and 1924. He also holds the record of most medals with four (having additionally won the bronze medal in the 50,000 m in 1932) which total is shared with Vladimir Golubnichiy (USSR) (b. 2

Frenchman Jean-Gilles Boussiquet twice improved on the 24 hour track running record within 203 days. (Sculptural—Club de Niort)

1958 to 1976, plus four Canadian championships. The greatest number of UK National titles won by a British walker is 27 by Vincent Paul Nihill, MBE (b. 5 Sept 1939) from 1963 to 1975.

Longest race

The Strasbourg-Paris event (inst. 1926 in the reverse direction) over 504–554 km *313–344 miles* is the world's longest annual race walk. The fastest performance is by Robert Pietquin (Belgium) (b. 1938) who walked 507 km *315 miles* in the 1980 race in 60 hr 1 min 10 sec (deducting 4 hr compulsory stops). This represents an average speed of 8.45 km/h *5.25 mph*. Gilbert Roger (France) (b. 1914) won six times (1949, 1953–4, 1956–8). The only Briton to have completed the course is Colin Young (b. 20 Jan 1935) (Essex Beagles) in 1971 averaging 7.46 km/h *4.63 mph*, covering 520 km *323.1 miles* in 73 hr 38 min.

Dumitru Dan (1890–1978) of Romania was the only man of 200 entrants to succeed in a contest in walking 100,000 km *62,137 miles* organised by the Touring Club de France on 1 Apr 1910. He covered 96,000 km *59,651 miles* up to 24 Mar 1916 so averaging 43,85 km *27.24 miles* a day.

Longest walks

The first person reported to have 'walked round the world' is George Matthew Schilling (USA) from 3 Aug 1897 to 1904, but the first verified achievement was by David Kunst (b. 1939) (USA) from 10 June 1970 to 5 Oct 1974. Tomas Carlos Pereira (b. Argentine, 16 Nov 1942) spent ten years, 6 Apr 1968–8 Apr 1978, walking 29,825 miles *48,000 km* around all five continents. Sean Eugene Maguire (b. USA 15 Sept 1956) walked 7327 miles *11791 km* from the Yukon River, north of Livengood, Alaska, to Key West, Florida, USA, in 307 days, 6 June 1978–9 April 1979. The Trans-Canada (Halifax to Vancouver) record walk of 3764 miles *6057 km* is 96 days by Clyde McRae, 23, from 1 May to 4 Aug 1973. John Lees, (b. 23 Feb 1945) of Brighton, East Sussex, England between 11 Apr and 3 June 1972, walked 2876 miles *4628 km* across the USA from City Hall, Los Angeles to City Hall, New York City in 53 days 12 hr 15 min (average 53.746 miles *86,495 km* a day). The longest continuous walk in Britain is one of 6824 miles *10 982 km*, around the British coast by John N. Merrill, (b. 19 Aug 1943) from 3 Jan to 8 Nov 1978.

'End to end'

Ann Sayer (b. 16 Oct 1936) walked the 840 miles *1352 km* from Land's End to John o' Groats in 13 days 17 hr 42 min on 20 Sept-3 Oct 1980. The Irish 'End to End' record over the 376 miles *605 km* from Mizen Head, Cork to Malin Head, Donegal is 7 days 16 hr 34 min, set by Roy Dickson on 2–9 June 1979.

June 1936), who won gold medals for the 20,000 m in 1960 and 1968, the silver in 1972 and the bronze in 1964.

The best British performance has been two gold medals by George Edward Larner (1875–1949) for the 3500 m and the 10 miles in 1908, but Ernest J. Webb (1872–1937) won three medals being twice 'walker up' to Larner and finishing second in the 10,000 m in 1912.

Most titles

Four time Olympian, Ronald Owen Laird (b. 31 May 1938) of the New York AC, USA, won a total of 65 National titles from

Sean Maguire, with *Sweden*, at the beach in Key West, Florida, having walked an average of 25 miles a day for 307 days.

OFFICIAL WORLD RECORDS (Track Walking)

(As recognised by the International Amateur Athletic Federation)

Distance	Time hr min sec	Name and Country	Place	Date	
MEN					
20,000 metres	1 20 06.8	Daniel Bautista (Mexico) (b. 4 Aug 1952)	Montreal, Canada	17 Oct	1979
30,000 metres	2 08 00.0	Jose Marin (Spain) (b. 21 Jan 1950)	Barcelona, Spain	8 Apr	1979
50,000 metres	3 41 39.0	Raul Gonzalez (Mexico) (b. 29 Feb 1952)	Fana, Norway	25 May	1979
2 hours	28 165 m *17 miles 881 yd*	Jose Marin (Spain)	Barcelona, Spain	25 May	1979
WOMEN					
3000 metres	13 20.7	Sue Cook (Australia)	Doncaster, Australia	8 Mar	1980
5000 metres	22 40.6	Ludmilla Khrusheva (USSR)	Kishinev, USSR	17 May	1981
10,000 metres	48 11.0	Marion Fawkes (GB) (b. 3 Dec 1948)	Harnosand, Sweden	8 July	1979

UNITED KINGDOM RECORDS

	Time hr min sec	Name and Country	Place	Date	
MEN					
20,000 metres	1 26 22	Steven John Barry (b. 25 Oct 1950)	Brighton, Sussex	29 June	1981
30,000 metres	2 22 55	Dennis Jackson (b. 29 June 1945)	Brighton, Sussex	29 June	1981
50,000 metres	4 11 22	Robert William Dobson (b. 4 Nov 1942)	Paris, France	10 Aug	1974
2 hours	26 037 m *16 miles 314 yd*	Ronald Edward Wallwork (b. 26 May 1941)	Stretford, Lancashire	31 July	1971
WOMEN					
3000 metres	13 25.2	Carol Tyson (b. 15 Dec 1957)	Hofgangens, Sweden	6 July	1979
5000 metres	23 11.2	Carol Tyson	Ostersund, Sweden	30 June	1979

London to Brighton

The record time for the 53 miles *85 km* walk is 7 hr 35 min 12 sec by Donald James Thompson, MBE (b. 20 Jan 1933) on 14 Sept 1957. The record time to Brighton and back is 18 hr 5 min 51 sec by William Frederick Baker (1889–1980) on 18–19 June 1926. Richard Esmond Green (b. 22 Apr 1924) has completed the course a record 45 times from 1950 to 1980.

Longest non-stop walk

Edward George 'Fred' Jago (b. 22 Mar 1935) walked 349.98 miles *563,23 km* in 152 hr 40 min at Plymouth, Devon on 13–19 Sept 1980. He was not permitted any stops for rest and was moving 98.33 per cent of the time.

1 Hour

The greatest distance covered on the track in one hour is 15121 m *9 miles 696 yd* by Daniel Bautista (Mexico) at Monterey, Mexico on 27 Mar 1980.

24 hours

The best official performance for distance walked in 24 hr is 133 miles 21 yd *214,06 km* by Huw Nielson (GB) at Walton-on-Thames, Surrey, on 14–15 Oct 1960. The best by a woman is 190,7 km *118.5 miles* by Ann Sayer (GB) at Torcy, France on 4–5 May 1980.

Walking backwards

The greatest ever exponent of reverse pedestrianism has been Plennie L. Wingo (b. 24 Jan 1895) then of Abilene, Texas, who completed his 8000 mile *12,875 km* trans-continental walk from Santa Monica, California to Istanbul, Turkey, from 15 Apr 1931 to 24 Oct 1932. The longest distance recorded for walking backwards in 24 hr is 80.5 miles *129,55 km* by Veikko Matias (b. 23 Apr 1941) of Kangasala, Finland, at Kankaapää Airfield, Niinisalo, Finland on 7–8 Oct 1978.

WATER POLO

Origins

Water Polo was developed in England as 'Water Soccer' in 1869 and first included in the Olympic Games in Paris in 1900.

Most Olympic titles

Hungary has won the Olympic tournament most often with six wins in 1932, 1936, 1952, 1956, 1964 and 1976. Great Britain won in 1900, 1908, 1912 and 1920.

Members of the Manly-Warringah Water Polo Club during their successful record attempt.

Five players share the record of three gold medals: Britons, George Wilkinson (1879–1946) in 1900, 1908, 1912; Paulo 'Paul' Radmilovic (1886–1968), and Charles Sidney Smith (1879–1951) in 1908, 1912, 1920; and Hungarians Deszo Gyarmati (b. 23 Oct 1927) and György Kárpáti (b. 23 June 1935) in 1952, 1956, 1964. Gyarmati's wife (Eva Szekely) and daughter (Andrea) won gold and silver medals respectively in swimming. Paul Radmilovic also won a gold medal for the 4 × 200 m freestyle relay in 1908.

ASA championships

The greatest number of Amateur Swimming Association titles is eleven, by Plaistow United SC from 1928 to 1954 and London Polytechnic from 1956 to 1978. The National League (formed 1963) has been won a record nine times by London Polytechnic.

Most goals

The greatest number of goals scored by an individual in a home international is eleven by Terry Charles Miller (b. 2 Mar 1932) (Plaistow United), when England defeated Wales 13–3 at Newport, Gwent, in 1951.

Most international appearances

The greatest number of international appearances is 412 by Alexei Barkalov (USSR) (b. 18 Feb 1946) from 1965–80. The British record is 126 by Martyn Thomas, of Cheltenham, 1964–78.

Marathon

Two teams of seven from Manly-Warringah Amateur Water Polo Club played for 24 hr 10 min at the Aquatic Centre, French's Forest, NSW, Australia on 3–4 Oct 1980.

WATER SKIING

A specialist volume entitled The Guinness Guide to Water Skiing *by David Nations, OBE and Kevin Desmond has been published by Guinness Superlatives Ltd. (price £8.50).*

Origins

The origins of water skiing lie in walking on planks and aquaplaning. A 19th century treatise on sorcerers refers to Eliseo of Tarentum who, in the 14th century, 'walks and dances' on the water. The first report of aquaplaning was on America's Pacific coast in the early 1900s. At Scarborough, Yorkshire, on 15 July 1914, a single plank-gliding contest was won by H. Storry.

The present day sport of water skiing was pioneered by Ralph W. Samuelson (1904–77) on Lake Pepin, Minnesota, USA, on two curved pine boards in the summer of 1922, though claims have been made for the birth of the sport on Lake Annecy (Haute Savoie), France at about the same time. The first world organisation, the Union Internationale de Ski Nautique, was formed in Geneva on 27 July 1946. The British Water Ski Federation was founded in London in 1954.

Most titles

World Overall championships (instituted 1949) have been won twice by Alfredo Mendoza (USA) in 1953 and 1955, Mike Suyderhoud (USA) in 1967 and 1969 and George Athans (Canada) in 1971 and 1973, and three times by Willa McGuire (*née* Worthington) of the USA in 1949–50 and 1955 and Elizabeth 'Liz' Allan-Shetter (USA) in 1965, 1969 and 1975. Liz Allan-Shetter has won a record eight individual championship events. The USA has won the team championship on 12 successive occasions since 1957. The most British Overall titles (instituted 1953) ever won by a man is six by Michael Hazelwood, MBE (b. Lincolnshire 14 Apr 1958) in 1974, 1976–9, 1981; the most by a woman is eight by Karen Jane Morse (b. 1956) in 1971–6, 1978, 1981.

Jumping

The first recorded jump on water skis was made by Ralph Samuelson off a greased ramp, on Lake Pepin in 1925. The longest jump ever recorded is one of 59,84 m *196 ft 4 in* by Michael Hazelwood MBE (GB) at Kirtons Farm, Reading, Berks. on 2 Aug 1981. The women's record is 41,20 m *135 ft 2 in* by Sue Lipplegoes (*née* Wright) (Australia) at Kirtons Farm on 2 Aug 1981.

Slalom and Tricks

The world record for slalom is 3 buoys on a 10,75 m *35 ft 3 in* line at 58 km/h *36 mph* by Bob LaPoint (USA) at McCormick Lake, Seffner, Florida on 21 Sept 1980. The record for women is 4 buoys on a 12 m *39 ft* line at 55 km/h *34 mph* by Cindy Hutcherson Todd (USA) at Calloway Gardens, Georgia on 3 Sept 1978. The tricks record is 8660 points by Cory Pickos (b. USA, 1964) at Groveland, Florida on 5 July 1980. The women's record is 6660 points by Natalia Rumyantzeva (USSR) at Thorpe Water Park on 27 June 1981 (awaiting ratification). The British records for tricks are: (men) 7730 points by Mike Hazelwood at Groveland, Florida on 5 July 1980; (women) 4270 points by Philippa Roberts at Thorpe on 29 June 1980.

Highest speed

The unofficial water skiing speed record is 206,25 km/h *128.16 mph* by Craig Wendt (USA) (b. 1953) at the Long Beach Marine Stadium, California, USA on 19 Aug 1979. Donna Patterson Brice (b. 1953), set a feminine record of 178,81 km/h *111.11 mph* at Long Beach, California on 21 Aug 1977. The fastest recorded speed by a British skier over a measured kilometre is 131,217 km/h *81.535 mph* (average) on Lake Windermere, Cumbria on 18 Oct 1973 by Billy Rixon. The fastest by a British woman is 111,80 km/h *69.47 mph* by Elizabeth Hobbs on Windermere, 19 Oct 1979.

Longest run

The greatest distance travelled is 1190 miles *1916 km* by Helge Johansen (22) and Trond Georg Larsen (23) of Narvik, Norway, in the harbour, on 14–16 Aug 1980.

Barefoot

The first person to water ski barefoot is reported to be Dick Pope Jr at Lake Eloise, Florida, on 6 Mar 1947. The barefoot duration record is 2 hr 42 min 39 sec by Billy Nichols (USA) (b. 1964) on Lake Weir, Florida, on 19 Nov 1978. The backward barefoot record is 39 min by Paul McManus (Aust). The British duration record is 67 min 5 sec by John Doherty on 1 Oct 1974. The official barefoot speed record (two runs) is 177,06 km/h *110.02 mph* by Lee Kirk (USA) at Firebird Lake, Phoenix, Ariz, on 11 June 1977. His fastest run was 182,93 km/h *113.67 mph*. The fastest by a woman is 109,72 km/h *68.18 mph* by Lorraine Nelson (USA) at Long Beach, California on 24 Aug 1980. Richard Mainwaring (GB) reached 114,86 km/h *71.37 mph* at Holme Pierrepoint, Nottinghamshire on 2 Dec 1978.

The best officially recorded barefoot jump is 17.20 m *56 ft 5 in* by Peter Lindenberg (S. Africa) in Natal, on 27 Apr 1980.

WEIGHTLIFTING

Origins

Amateur weightlifting is of comparatively modern origin and the first 'world' championship was staged at the Café Monico, Piccadilly, London, on 28 Mar 1891. Prior to that time, weightlifting consisted of professional exhibitions in which some of the advertised poundages were open to doubt. The first to raise 400 lb *181 kg* was Karl Swoboda (1882–1933) (Austria), in Vienna, with 401¼ lb *182 kg* in 1910, using the Continental clean and jerk style.

Most Olympic Medals

The winner of most Olympic medals is Norbert Schemansky (USA) (b. 30 May 1924) with four: Gold, middle-heavyweight

School teacher, Sultan Rakhmanov, from the Central Asian area of the Soviet Union, is Olympic champion and a world record holder in the super-heavyweight class. (*Don Morley, All-Sport*)

WORLD WEIGHTLIFTING RECORDS (as at 16 Aug 1981)

Bodyweight Class	Lift	Lifted kg	lb	Name and Country	Place	Date	
Flyweight	Snatch	113	249¾	Han Gien Shi (N. Korea)	Moscow, USSR	20 July	1980
(*52 kg* 114½ lb)	Jerk	142,5	314	Alexander Senyshin (USSR)	Moscow, USSR	14 May	1980
	Total	247,5	545½	Alexander Voronin (USSR)	Stuttgart, W. Germany	17 Sept	1977
Bantamweight	Snatch	126,5	278¾	Wu Shu-Teh (China)	Nagoya, Japan	16 Aug	1981
(*56 kg* 123¼ lb)	Jerk	157,5	347	Yuri Sarkisian (USSR)	Moscow, USSR	21 July	1980
	Total	277,5	611¾	Andreas Letz (E. Germany)	Meissen, E. Germany	10 Apr	1981
Featherweight	Snatch	134,5	296½	Daniel Nunez (Cuba)	Camaguey, Cuba	17 May	1981
(*60 kg* 132¼ lb)	Jerk	168	370¼	Yuri Sarkissian (USSR)	Lignano Sabbiadore, Italy	16 June	1981
	Total	297,5	655¾	Viktor Mazin (USSR)	Moscow, USSR	5 July	1980
Welterweight	Snatch	150,5	331¾	Joachim Kunz (E. Germany)	Karl Marx Stadt, E. Germany	27 June	1981
(*67,5 kg* 148¾ lb)	Jerk	196	432	Joachim Kunz (E. Germany)	Karl Marx Stadt, E. Germany	27 June	1981
	Total	345	760½	Joachim Kunz (E. Germany)	Karl Marx Stadt, E. Germany	27 June	1981
Middleweight	Snatch	161	354¾	Nedelcho Kolev (Bulgaria)	Varna, Bulgaria	1 Feb	1980
(*75 kg* 165¼ lb)	Jerk	205,5	453	Asen Zlatev (Bulgaria)	Moscow, USSR	24 July	1980
	Total	360	793½	Asen Zlatev (Bulgaria)	Moscow, USSR	24 July	1980
Light-heavyweight	Snatch	177,5	391¼	Yurik Vardanyan (USSR)	Moscow, USSR	26 July	1980
(*82,5 kg* 181¾ lb)	Jerk	222,5	490½	Yurik Vardanyan (USSR)	Moscow, USSR	26 July	1980
	Total	400	881¾	Yurik Vardanyan (USSR)	Moscow, USSR	26 July	1980
Middle-heavyweight	Snatch	183,5	404½	Yuri Zakharevitch (USSR)	Lignano Sabbiadore, Italy	20 June	1981
(*90 kg* 198¼ lb)	Jerk	224	493¾	Yurik Vardanyan (USSR)	Novosibirsk, USSR	15 May	1981
	Total	405	892¾	Yuri Zakharevitch (USSR)	Lignano Sabbiadore, Italy	20 June	1981
(*100 kg* 220½ lb)	Snatch	187,5	413¼	Ota Zaremba (Czechoslavakia)	Sturovo, Czechoslavakia	28 June	1981
	Jerk	232	511¼	Viktor Sotz (USSR)	Novosibirsk, USSR	16 May	1981
	Total	415	914¾	Ota Zaremba (Czechoslavakia)	Sturovo, Czechoslavakia	28 June	1981
Heavyweight	Snatch	190,5	419¾	Vyacheslav Klokov (USSR)	Moscow, USSR	5 July	1980
(*110 kg* 242½ lb)	Jerk	240	529	Leonid Taranenko (USSR)	Moscow, USSR	29 July	1980
	Total	422,5	931¼	Leonid Taranenko (USSR)	Moscow, USSR	29 July	1980
Super-heavyweight	Snatch	201	443	Sultan Rakhmanov (USSR)	Novosibirsk, USSR	16 May	1981
(Over 110 kg *242½ lb*)	Jerk	257,5	567½	Vladimir Marchuk (USSR)	Lvov, USSR	22 Mar	1981
	Total	445	981	Vasili Alexeyev (USSR)	Podolsk, USSR	1 Sept	1977

WORLD POWERLIFTING RECORDS (as recognised by the International Powerlifting Federation), as at 17 Feb 1981

	Lift	kg	lb	Name and Country	Place	Date	
52 kg	Squat	232,5	512½	Hideaki Inaba (Japan)	Arlington, Texas, USA	7 Nov	1980
	Bench Press	142,5	314	Chuck Dunbar (USA)	Arlington, Texas, USA	7 Nov	1980
	Dead Lift	232,5	512½	Haruji Watanabe (Japan)	Tokyo, Japan	21 Sept	1980
	Total	567,5	1251	Hideaki Inaba (Japan)	Arlington, Texas, USA	7 Nov	1980
56 kg	Squat	232.5	512½	Precious McKenzie (NZ)	Arlington, Texas, USA	7 Nov	1980
	Bench Press	145	319½	Lamar Gant (USA)	Auburn, Alabama, USA	19 Apr	1980
	Dead Lift	287,5	633½	Lamar Gant (USA)	Auburn, Alabama, USA	19 Apr	1980
	Total	620	1366½	Lamar Gant (USA)	Auburn, Alabama, USA	19 Apr	1980
60 kg	Squat	295	650½	Joe Bradley (USA)	Arlington, Texas, USA	7 Nov	1980
	Bench Press	180	397	Joe Bradley (USA)	Phoenix, Arizona, USA	12 Jan	1980
	Dead Lift	285	628½	Lamar Gant (USA)	Arlington, Texas, USA	7 Nov	1980
	Total	705	1554	Lamar Gant (USA)	Arlington, Texas, USA	7 Nov	1980
67,5 kg	Squat	285	628½	Rick Crain (USA)	Arlington, Texas, USA	7 Nov	1980
	Bench Press	187,5	413	Armington Rafael (USA)	Tollhouse, Cal., USA	16 Feb	1980
	Dead Lift	300	661½	Rick Crain (USA)	Arlington, Texas, USA	7 Nov	1980
	Total	730	1609	Mike Bridges (USA)	Turku, Finland	3 Nov	1979
75 kg	Squat	327,5	722	Mike Bridges (USA)	Auburn, Alabama, USA	19 Apr	1980
	Bench Press	217,5	479½	James Rouse (USA)	Arlington, Texas, USA	8 Nov	1980
	Dead Lift	315	694	Rick Gaugler (USA)	Ft. Worth, Texas, USA	10 Feb	1980
	Total	835	1840½	Mike Bridges (USA)	Auburn, Alabama, USA	19 Apr	1980
82,5 kg	Squat	377,5	832	Mike Bridges (USA)	Arlington, Texas, USA	8 Nov	1980
	Bench Press	232,5	512½	Mike McDonald (USA)	Brookings, S. D., USA	17 Feb	1979
	Dead Lift	357,5	788	Veli Kumpuniemi (Finland)	Zurich, Switzerland	17 May	1980
	Total	940	2072½	Mike Bridges (USA)	Arlington, Texas, USA	8 Nov	1980
90 kg	Squat	375	826½	Fred Hatfield (USA)	Arlington, Texas, USA	8 Nov	1980
	Bench Press	250	551	Mike MacDonald (USA)	Honolulu, Hawaii, USA	5 May	1979
	Dead Lift	370	815½	Vince Anello (USA)	Turku, Finland	4 Nov	1978
	Total	937,5	2066½	Mike Bridges (USA)	Huber Heights, Ohio, USA	4 Oct	1980
100 kg	Squat	367,5	810	Chip McCain (USA)	Arlington, Texas, USA	9 Nov	1980
	Bench Press	261,5	576½	Mike MacDonald (USA)	Santa Monica, Cal., USA	21 Aug	1977
	Dead Lift	365	804½	Vince Anello (USA)	Culver City, Cal., USA	19 June	1977
	Total	935	2061	Larry Pacifico (USA)	Perth, Australia	4 Nov	1977
110 kg	Squat	382,5	843	Marvin Phillips (USA)	Honolulu, Hawaii, USA	17 Mar	1980
	Bench Press	264,5	583	Mike MacDonald (USA)	Whittier, Cal., USA	15 Nov	1980
	Dead Lift	395	870½	John Kuc (USA)	Arlington, Texas, USA	9 Nov	1980
	Total	1000	2204½	John Kuc (USA)	Arlington, Texas, USA	9 Nov	1980
125 kg	Squat	400,5	882½	Ernie Hackett (USA)	Bay St. Louis, Miss., USA	19 Aug	1979
	Bench Press	268	590½	Tom Hardman (USA)	Jasper, Alabama, USA	15 Dec	1979
	Dead Lift	373,5	823	Terry McCormick (USA)	Arizona, USA	12 June	1980
	Total	977,5	2155	Larry Kidney (USA)	Madison, Wisc., USA	13 July	1980
Over 125 kg	Squat	440	970	Dave Waddington (USA)	Kent, Ohio, USA	17 May	1980
	Bench Press	287,5	633½	Bill Kazmier (USA)	Auburn, Alabama, USA	19 Apr	1980
	Dead Lift	400	881½	Don Reinhoudt (USA)	Chattanooga, Tenn., USA	3 May	1975
	Total	1097,5	2420	Don Reinhoudt (USA)	Chattanooga, Tenn., USA	3 May	1975

1952; Silver, heavyweight 1948; Bronze, heavyweight 1960 and 1964.

Most titles *World*

The most world title wins is eight by John Davis (USA) (b. 12 Jan 1921) in 1938, 1946–52; by Tommy Kono (USA) (b. 27 June 1930) in 1952–9; and by Vladimir Alexeyev (USSR) (b. 7 Jan 1942) 1970–7.

Most successful British lifter

The only British lifter to win an Olympic title has been Launceston Elliot (1874–1930), the open one-handed lift champion in 1896 at Athens.

Louis George Martin, MBE (b. Jamaica, 11 Nov 1936) won four World and European mid-heavyweight titles in 1959, 1962–3, 1965. He won an Olympic silver medal in 1964 and a bronze in 1960 and also three Commonwealth gold medals in 1962, 1966, 1970. His total of British titles was 12.

Greatest lift

The greatest weight ever raised by a human being is 6270 lb *2844 kg* (2.80 tons *2,84 tonnes*) in a back lift (weight raised off trestles) by the 26 st *165 kg* Paul Anderson (USA) (b. 17 Oct 1932), the 1956 Olympic heavyweight champion, at Toccoa, Georgia, USA, on 12 June 1957. The greatest lift by a woman is 3564 lb *1616 kg* with a hip and harness lift by Josephine Blatt (*née* Schauer) (1869–1923) at the Bijou Theatre, Hoboken, New Jersey, USA, on 15 Apr 1895.

Greatest overhead lifts

The greatest overhead lifts made from the ground are the clean and jerks achieved by super-heavyweights which now exceed 5 cwt (560 lb) *254 kg*. The greatest overhead lift ever made by a woman is 286 lb *129 kg* in a continental jerk by Katie Sandwina (*née* Brummbach, later Mrs Max Heymann) (1884–1952) of Germany, in *c.* 1911. She stood 5 ft 11 in *1,80 m* tall, weighed 210 lb 95 kg (15 st) and is reputed to have unofficially lifted 312½ lb *141,747 kg* and to have shouldered a cannon, which allegedly weighed 1200 lb *544 kg*.

Greatest power lifts

Paul Anderson, as a professional, has bench-pressed 627 lb *284 kg* and has achieved 1200 lb *544 kg* in a squat so aggregating, with an 820 lb *371 kg* dead lift, a career total of 2647 lb *1200 kg*. Precious McKenzie (b. 6 June 1936) was the first to total 11 times his bodyweight (55 kg *121 lb*) with 607,5 kg *1339 lb* at Honolulu, Hawaii on 5 May 1979. Lamar Gant (USA) deadlifted five times his bodyweight (56 kg *123¼ lb*) with 280 kg *617 lb* at Dayton, Ohio on 2 Nov 1979. Mike Bridges (USA) is the first to hold the total records in three classes simultaneously on 8 Nov 1980. The newly instituted two-man deadlift record was raised to 1448 lb *656.8 kg* by Clay and Doug Patterson in Arlington, Texas, USA, on 15 Dec 1979.

Hermann Görner (1891–1956) (Germany) performed a one-handed dead lift of 734½ lb *333,1 kg* in Dresden on 20 July 1920. Peter B. Cortese (USA) achieved a one-armed dead lift of 370 lb *167 kg* i.e. 22 lb *9,9 kg* over triple his bodyweight at York, Pennsylvania on 4 Sept 1954. Görner also raised 24 men weighing 4123 lb *1870 kg* on a plank on the soles of his feet in London on 12 Oct 1927 and carried on his back a 1444 lb *654 kg* piano for 52½ ft *16 m* at Leipzig on 3 June 1921.

The greatest power lift by a woman is a squat of 545½ lb *247 kg* by Jan Suffolk Todd (b. 22 May 1952) (USA) (weighing 88,5 kg *195 lb*) at Columbus, Georgia, USA in Jan 1981. The official record for the three-lift total is 1267 lb *574,5 kg* by Bev Francis (Australia) at Honolulu, Hawaii on 12 May 1981.

A deadlifting record of 2,650,837 lb *1,202,400 kg* in 24 hr was set by a team of ten at the Wealden Weightlifting Centre, Cowbeech, E. Sussex on 3–4 Apr 1981.

Cue Levering

Traffic warden Jim Mills (b. 24 May 1923) levered twenty 16 oz *453 g* billiard cues simultaneously by their tips through 90 degrees to the horizontal, at Alfreton Carnival, Alfreton Park, Derbyshire, on 1 Aug 1981. Following this he levered a 22 oz *623 g* cue 720 times consecutively at Alfreton Park, by the same method.

Strandpulling

The International Steel Strandpullers' Association was founded by Gavin Pearson (Scotland) in 1940. The greatest ratified poundage to date is a super-heavyweight right arm push of 815 lb *369,5 kg* by Malcolm Bartlett (b. 9 June 1955), of Oldham, Lancashire. He has also won a record 14 British Open titles. The record for the Back Press Anyhow is 645 lb *292,5 kg* by Barry Anderson, of Leeds, in 1975.

Harry Sawyer (Ashford Common) set a world 12 st dislocation record of 353 lb *160 kg* in 1972 aged 52 and David Hoar (Ossett, West Yorkshire) set a world 11 st right arm push record of 601 lb *272,5 kg* aged 17.

WRESTLING

Origins

The earliest depictions of wrestling holds and falls on wall plaques and a statue indicate that organised wrestling dates from *c.* 2750–2600 BC. It was the most popular sport in the ancient Olympic Games and victors were recorded from 708 BC. The Greco-Roman style is of French origin and arose about 1860. The International Amateur Wrestling Federation (FILA) was founded in 1912.

Most titles *Olympic*

Three wrestlers have won three Olympic titles: Carl Westergren (1895–1958) (Sweden) in 1920, 1924, 1932; Ivar Johansson (1903–79) (Sweden) in 1932 (two), 1936; and Aleksandr Medved (b. 16 Sept 1937) (USSR) in 1964, 1968, 1972.

The only wrestler with more medals is Imre Polyák (Hungary) (b. 16 Apr 1932) who won the silver medal for the Greco-Roman featherweight class in 1952, 1956, 1960 and the gold in 1964.

Most titles *World*

The greatest number of world championships won by a wrestler is ten by the freestyler Aleksandr Medved (USSR) (b. 16 Sept 1937) with the light-heavyweight titles in 1962–4 (Olympic) and 1966, the heavyweight 1967–8 (Olympic), and the super-heavyweight in 1969–72 (Olympic). The only wrestler to win the same title in six successive years has been Abdollah Movahed (Iran) (b. 10 Mar 1940) in the lightweight division in 1965–70. The record for successive Greco-Roman titles is five by Roman Rurua (USSR) (b. 25 Nov 1942) with the featherweight 1966–8 (Olympic), 1969 and 1970.

Most titles *British*

The most British titles won is ten by heavyweight Kenneth Alan Richmond (b. 10 July 1926) between 1949 and 1960.

Longest span

The longest span for BAWA titles is 24 years by George Mackenzie (1890–1957) who won his first in 1909 and his last in 1933. Mackenzie represented Great Britain in five successive Olympiads from 1908 to 1928.

Most wins

In international competition, Osamu Watanabe (b. 21 Oct 1940), of Japan, the 1964 Olympic freestyle featherweight champion, was unbeaten and unscored-upon in 187 consecutive matches. Wade Schalles (USA) has won 668 bouts from 1964 to 1980.

Longest bout

The longest recorded bout was one of 11 hr 40 min between Martin Klein (1885–1947) (Estonia representing Russia) and Alfred Asikáinen (1888–1942) (Finland) for the Greco-Roman middleweight 'A' event silver medal in the 1912 Olympic Games in Stockholm, Sweden. It was won by Klein.

Heaviest heavyweight

The heaviest wrestler in Olympic history is Chris Taylor (1950–79), bronze medallist in the super-heavyweight class in 1972, who stood 6 ft 5 in *1,96 m* and weighed over 420 lb *190 kg*. The record for a British heavyweight champion is held by Archibald 'Archie' Dudgeon (1914–73) (Scotland), who won the 1936–7 BAWA heavyweight titles at 6 ft 2 in *1,88 m*, 308 lb *139 kg*.

The giant Sumo wrestler Jesse Kuhaulau takes on two US Marines in a charity match in the Kuramae arena, Tokyo. (*John Topham Picture Library*)

Cumberland and Westmorland wrestling
The British amateur championships were established in 1904. The only six time champions have been J. Baddeley (middleweight in 1905–6, 1908–10, 1912) and Ernest Aubrey Bacon (b. 1893) (lightweight in 1919, 1921–3, 1928–9).

Professional wrestling
Professional wrestling dates from 1874 in the USA. Georges Karl Julius Hackenschmidt (USSR) (1877–1968), Estonian-born, was undefeated at Greco-Roman contests from 1900 to his retirement in 1911. (See also p. 109).

Sumo wrestling
The sport's origins in Japan certainly date from *c.* 23 BC. The heaviest ever *sumotori* is Hawaiian-born 6 ft 3¼ in *1,91 m* Jesse Kuhaulua (b. 16 June 1944)—now a Japanese citizen named Daigoro Watanabe—*alias* Takamiyama, who in 1980 attained 443 lb *201 kg*. Weight is amassed by over alimentation with a high protein stew called *chankonabe*. The tallest was probably Ozora, an early 19th century performer, who stood 7 ft 3 in *2,20 m* tall. The most successful wrestlers have been Sadaji Akiyoshi (b. 1912) *alias* Futabayama, winner of 69 consecutive bouts in the 1930s, Koki Naya (b. 1940) *alias* Taiho ('Great Bird'), who won the Emperor's Cup 32 times up to his retirement in 1971 and the *ozeki* Torokichi *alias* Raiden who in 21 years (1789–1810) won 254 bouts and lost only ten for the highest ever winning percentage of .962. The youngest of the 56 men to attain the rank of *Yokozuna* (Grand Champion) was Toshimitsu Ogata (b. 16 May 1953) *alias* Kitanoumi, in July

1974 aged 21 years and two months. He set a record in 1978 winning 82 of the 90 bouts that top *rikishi* fight annually. Takamiyama was the first non-Japanese to win an official tournament in July 1972 and has had a record of 1230 consecutive top division bouts to end-July 1981.

YACHTING
The Guinness Book of Yachting Facts and Feats (£4.95) *and* The Guinness Guide to Sailing *(£11.95), both by Peter Johnson, published by Guinness Superlatives Ltd provide more data on the sport.*

Origins
Yachting in England dates from the £100 stake race between Charles II and his brother James, Duke of York, on the Thames on 1 Sept. 1661 over 23 miles from Greenwich to Gravesend. The oldest club in the world is the Royal Cork Yacht Club (formerly the Cork Harbour Water Club), established in Ireland in 1720. The oldest active club in Britain is the Starcross Yacht Club at Powderham Point, Devon. Its first regatta was held in 1772. The word yacht is from the Dutch to hunt or chase.

Olympic titles *World*
The first sportsman ever to win individual gold medals in four successive Olympic Games was Paul B. Elvström (b. 24 Feb 1928) (Denmark) in the Firefly class in 1948 and the Finn class in 1952, 1956 and 1960. He has also won eight other world titles in a total of six classes. The lowest number of penalty points by the winner of any class in an Olympic regatta is three points (five wins, one disqualified and one second in seven starts) by *Superdocius* of the Flying Dutchman class (Lt. Rodney Stuart Pattisson, MBE RN (b. 5 Aug 1943) and Iain Somerled Macdonald-Smith, MBE (b. 3 July 1945)) at Acapulco Bay, Mexico in October 1968.

Olympic titles *British*
The only British yacht to win two titles was *Scotia* in the Open class and Half-One Ton class at the 1900 Regatta with Lorne Campbell Currie (1871–1926), helmsman and crewed by John H. Gretton (1867–1947) and Linton Hope (1863–1920). The only British yachtsman to win in two Olympic regattas is Rodney Pattisson in 1968 (see above) and again with *Superdoso* crewed by Christopher Davies (b. 29 June 1946) at Kiel, W. Germany in 1972. He gained a silver medal in 1976 with Julian Brooke Houghton (b. 16 Dec 1946).

Admiral's Cup
The ocean racing series with the most participating nations (three boats allowed to each nation) is the Admiral's Cup held by the Royal Ocean Racing Club. A record 19 nations competed in 1975, 1977 and 1979. To 1979, Britain had won the most times with seven wins.

America's Cup
The America's Cup was originally won as an outright prize by the schooner *America* on 22 Aug 1851 at Cowes and was later offered by the New York Yacht Club as a challenge trophy. On 8 Aug 1870 J. Ashbury's *Cambria* (GB) failed to capture the trophy from the *Magic*, owned by F. Osgood (USA). Since then the Cup has been challenged by Great Britain in 16 contests, in 2 contests by Canada, and by Australia six times, but the United States have never been defeated winning 77 races and only losing eight. The closest race ever was the fourth race of the 1962 series, when the 12 metre sloop *Weatherly* beat her Australian challenger *Gretel* by about three and a half lengths, a margin of only 26 sec, on 22 Sept 1962. The fastest time ever recorded by a 12 metre boat for the triangular course of 24.3 sea miles is 2 hr 46 min 58 sec by *Gretel* in 1962.

London to Sydney
The *Great Britain II*, a 77 ft 2 in *23,5 m* ketch manned by a British joint services crew, sailed from the Thames estuary to Sydney, Australia in 67 days 5 hr 19 min 49 sec from 31 Aug–7 Nov 1975, beating the previous record of the clipper *Patriarch* in 1870 by nearly two days. The return journey to Dover took only 66 days 22 hr 31 min 35 sec. The total round-the-world passage of up to 30,000 miles *42,280 km* was accomplished in a record time of 134 days 3 hr 51 min 24 sec. For other record passages see pp. 177 and 179.

Covering an area of 126 acres *51 hectares* the Brighton Marina is the largest yacht facility in Europe. *(Taylor Woodrow Construction Ltd)*

Longest race

The longest regular sailing race is the quadrennial Whitbread Round the World race (inst. Aug 1973) organized by the Royal Naval Sailing Association. The distance is 26,180 nautical miles from Portsmouth, and return with stops and re-starts at Cape Town, Auckland and Mar del Plata.

24 Hour Dinghy Race

The greatest distance covered in the West Lancashire Y.C. 24 hr race is 158.8 statute miles by an Enterprise from the Tynemouth Sailing Club on 13–14 Sept 1980. The Betio Boating Community sailed an Osprey, *Tamaroa*, 171.5 statute miles at Tarawa, Gilbert Islands, on 24–25 Sept 1977.

Highest speeds

The official world sailing speed record is 36.04 knots (41.50 mph *66,78 km/h*) by the 73½ ft *22,40 m* proa *Crossbow II* over a 500 m *547 yd* course in Portland Harbour, Dorset, on 17 Nov 1980. The vessel (sail area 1400 ft² *130,06 m²*) was designed by Rod McAlpine-Downie and owned and steered by Timothy Colman. In an unsuccessful attempt on the record in October 1978, *Crossbow II* is reported to have momentarily attained a speed of 45 knots (51 mph *83 km/h*).

The fastest 24 hr single-handed run by a sailing yacht was recorded by Nick Keig (b. 13 June 1936), of the Isle of Man, who covered 340 nautical miles in a 37½ ft *11,43 m* trimaran *Three Legs of Mann I* during the Falmouth to Punta, Azores race on 9–10 June 1975, averaging 14.16 knots (16.30 mph *26,23 km/h*). The fastest bursts of speed reached were about 25 knots (28.78 mph *46,32 km/h*).

The record speed for boardsailing, often termed windsurfing, is 24.63 knots (28.36 mph *45.64 km/h*) by Jaap van der Rest (Netherlands) at Maalaea Bay, Maui, Hawaii on 18 July 1980.

Most successful yacht

The most successful racing yacht in history was the Royal Yacht *Britannia* (1893–1935), owned by King Edward VII, when Prince of Wales and subsequently by King George V, which won 231 races in 625 starts.

Marinas, *Largest*

The largest marina in the world is that of Marina Del Rey, Los Angeles, California, USA, which has 7500 berths. The largest in Britain is the Brighton Marina, East Sussex, with 2313 berths.

Most competitors

The most competitors ever to start in a single race was 1261 sailing boats in the Round Zealand (Denmark) race in June 1976, over a course of 375 km *233 miles*. The greatest number to start in a race in Britain was 1055 keeled yachts and multihulls on 27 June 1981 from Cowes in the Annual Round-the-Island race.

Highest

The greatest altitude at which sailing has taken place is 16,109 ft *4910 m* on Laguna Huallatani, Bolivia, in Mirror Dinghy 55448, variously by Peter Williams, Gordon Siddeley, Keith Robinson and Brian Barrett, on 19 Nov 1977.

STOP PRESS

CHAPTER 1

Heaviest man UK (p 13). In June 1981 an unconfirmed weight of 40 st *254 kg* was reported for the 6 ft 11 in *210,8 cm* professional wrestler Luke McMasters ('Giant Haystacks').

Oldest Ever Human (p 17). Mr Izumi was still living on 15 Aug 1981 aged 116 years 47 days or 2.09 per cent longer than the next longest proven life. This seemingly very high margin compares however with Robert Wadlow (see pp 9–10). who was 3.2 per cent taller than the next tallest medically measured human of all-time.

Motionlessness (p 24). Melody A Schick remained motionless for 8 hr 33 min at the National Association of Broadcasters convention in Las Vegas, Nevada, USA on 15 Apr 1981.

CHAPTER 2

Animal Most Valuable (p 28). In October 1980 the racehorse *Easy Jet* was syndicated for $30 million (*£14.2 million*).

Rarest Pinniped (p 30). In 1976 a Caribbean monk seal was sighted between Punta Gorda, Belize and Livingston, Guatemala.

Smallest Deer (p 33). 2nd line. For Columbia read Colombia.

Dog Highest Jump (p 35). On 17 July 1981 'Young Sabre', a German Shepherd dog handled by Cpl David Smith scaled an 11 ft 8 in *3,55 m* wall at RAF Newton, Nottinghamshire.

Dog Strength and Endurance (p 35). The record time for the Anchorage to Nome Sled race is 12 days 7 hr 45 min by a dog owned by Rick Swenson in the 1981 race.

Mouse Oldest (p 37). 'Dixie' owned by A Newton of Sheffield, S. Yorks died on 25 Apr 1981 aged 6½ years.

Oldest Gerbil (p 37). 'Sahara' owned by Aaron Milstone of Lathrap Village, Michigan, USA born April 1973 was reportedly living on 6 May 1981 having passed her 8th birthday.

Champion Bird Spotter (p 39). In May 1981 Stuart Stokes of Perth, Australia was reported to have logged a total of 6125 species. Stuart Keith's total rose to 5530.

Reptiles Fastest (p 40). 6th line. For below read see p 41.

Chelonians longest lived (p 41). 1st line. For see p 26 read see p 27.

Smallest Marine Fishes (p 43). The smallest British marine fish is Guillet's goby (*Lebutus guilleti*) which does not exceed 24 mm *0.94 in.*

Most Valuable Goldfish (p 44). 1st line. For Benchana read Benihana.

Crustaceans – Vertical Distribution (p 45). In Nov 1980 the American research vessel *Thomas Washington* recovered a number of *live* amphipods from a depth of 10,500 m *34,450 ft* in the Challenger Deep, Marianas Trench, W. Pacific.

Butterflies and Moths – Rarest (p 46). Britain's rarest butterfly is now the Chequered Skipper (*Carterocephalus palaemon*) which is now confined to one site near Fort William, Inverness-shire, Scotland.

Extinct Animals – Largest flying bird (p 50). *Argentavis magnificens*, as it has been named, had a calculated wingspan of 23-24 ft *7,0-7,6 m* and weighed an estimated 264 lb *120 kg.*

Longest Daisy Chain (p 52). The longest daisy chain made by a team of 16 (for 'Books for Your Children') was one of 4529½ ft *1380,5 m* at the Museum of Childhood, Sudbury, Derbyshire on 6 June 1981.

Largest Orange (p 55). The largest orange ever recorded has been one of 2.50 kg *5 lb 8 oz* reported from Nelspruit, South Africa on 19 June 1981.

Tree greatest girth (p 55). 3rd line for Wimbourne read Wimborne.

Tallest Tree in England (p 56). A Douglas Fir (*Pseudotsuga taxifolia*) at Cedig Bridge near Oswestry, Shropshire was measured to be 188 ft 9 in *57,53 m* on 1 Mar 1981.

CHAPTER 3

Greatest Temperature ranges (p 59). 1st line. For great read greatest.

Coldest Place (p 61). 4th line. For Antartica read Antarctica.

Deepest Cave (p 68). In February 1981 the Reseau de Foillis in France was penetrated to 1455 m *4773 ft.*

Mountains Highest World (p 68). 13th line. For Tibeten read Tibetan.

Sea Cliffs Highest (p 70). 12th line for Coombe read Combe.

Greatest Avalanches (p 70). 8th line. For Chapter 10 read Chapter 11.

Largest Desert (p 70). For Sahara Desert read the Sahara.

CHAPTER 4

Meteorites Largest (p 72). 2nd Paragraph. For stoney read stony.

Surface features (p 75). 2nd line. After 'region' read 'of Mars'.

Largest and Smallest Satellites (p 75). Voyager I's measurements established that the diameter of Titan is 3194 miles *5140 km.* The largest satellite is thus Ganymede (Jupiter 3) with a diameter of 3275 miles *5270 km.*

Duration Record on Moon (p 78). 2nd line for acitivity read activity.

First extra-terrestrial vehicle (p 78). 3rd line. For .54 miles read 6.54 miles.

Highest Velocity (p 78). 9th line. For 2845 miles, read 2845 *million* miles.

CHAPTER 5

Most Expensive Perfume (p 80). 3rd line for flagrent read fragrant.

Most Expensive Wine (p 81). 4th line for San Fransisco read San Francisco.

Numerology – Cubism (p 85). A pioneer of Rubik's cube speed contest (with standardized dislocation and inspection time) was won in Munich, West Germany on 13 Mar 1981 in a 38.0 sec tie between Ronald Brinkman and Jury Fröschl. Ernö Rubik (Hungary) patented the device in 1975 with 43,252,003,274,489,856,856,000 possible combinations.

Extremes – Highest Velocity (p 85). The highest velocity at which any solid object has been projected is 150 km/sec or *335 500 mph* in the case of a plastic disc at the Naval Research Laboratory, Washington DC, reported in August 1980.

CHAPTER 6

Most and least consonants and vowels (p 93). 5th line for 'those' read 'that'.

Longest words – French (p 93). Anthropoclimatologiquement is not considered by *savants* to be an acceptable word.

Longest Palindrome (p 94). Edward Benbow has extended his palindromic composition to 33,333 words.

Longest surname (p 95). For Pensylvania read Pennsylvania.

Autographs and Signatures (p 98). The earliest known surviving signature is that of the French King Clotaire I (Le Vieux) of Soissons (558–561) born *c* 497. Hamilton Galleries sold a letter signed by President Reagan praising Frank Sinatra on 22 Jan 1981 for $12,500.

Diaries (p 98). Mrs P Joyce Evans of Swansea, Glamorgan, South Wales, (b. 6 May 1890) completed the first 75 years of her diary in 1981.

High Printings (p 100). The aggregate print of The Highway Code (instituted 1931) reached 90,000,000 by mid-1981.

Longest Editorship (p 101). M S Krishna Rao (b. *c* 1894) celebrated his 64th year as editor of *Satyavadi* of Mysore, India which was established in 1917.

Music Single Performer – Largest audience (p 103). Elton John (GB) entertained an estimated 400,000 in Central Park, New York City, USA in the summer of 1980.

Greatest Span (p 104). For 1953 read 1943.

Long Runs Broadway (p 108). *Grease* continued for 3388 performances.

Most Ardent Theatregoers (p 109). 7th line. For 27 read 28.

Cinema Box Office (p 110). Superman II grossed $5.6 million (*£2.8 million*) in the single day of 20 June 1981 in 1395 North American cinemas.

Cinemas – Largest Screen (p 111). A screen 103 ft *31,3 m* wide by 77 ft *23,4 m* tall built by Harkness Screens Ltd is to be installed at the Parques Interama S.A., Buenos Aires, Argentina.

TV Audience Largest (p 112). The estimated world audience of the wedding of TRH the Prince and Princess of Wales in London on 29 July 1981 was 700 million of which a record 39 million was in the United Kingdom.

Most Successful Appeals (p 113). The total raised in the Jerry Lewis Telethon was $31,103,787 (*£14,138,000*).

CHAPTER 7

Pleasure Piers Earliest (p 118–19). A predecessor to the 1808 Yarmouth jetty was one built in 1560 but neither was a pleasure pier. Both were washed away.

Night Clubs (p 120). The seating capacity of Gilley's Club is now reported to be 6,000 under one roof covering 4 acres *1,6 ha.*

Largest Bridge (p 121). The overall cost of the Humber Bridge on completion was revised to £91 million.

Demolitions (p 126). A 275 m *902 ft* tall smokestack at Matla Power Station, Kriel, South Africa was demolished on 19 July 1981 by The Santon (Steeplejack) Co. Ltd, of Manchester, England.

Largest Barn (p 126). The Cholsey barn has now been demolished. The barn at Frindsbury, Kent is the largest barn extant which is still wholly roofed. Its length is 219 ft *66,7 m.*

Bonfire Largest (pp 126 & 132). For Arrowthwhaite and Arrowhaite read Arrowthwhaite.

Oil Platform Largest (p 132). The world's most massive oil platform is the Statfjord B Condeep platform built at Stavanger, Norway and operated by Mobil Exploration Norway Inc. Tow-out to its permanent field began on 1 Aug 1981 and it was the heaviest object ever moved – 816,000 tonnes/tons ballasted weight. She was towed by 8 tugs with a combined power of 115,000 hp. The height of the concrete structure is 204 m *670 ft* and the overall height 271 m *890 ft.*

America's roller coaster competitive war now involves speeds nearing 70 mph *112 km/h.* The peak speed on this example completed in May 1981 is attained in a trough 20 ft *6,09 m* below ground level.

CHAPTER 8

Longest Bus Route (p 140). 'Across Australia Coach Lines' inaugurated a regular scheduled service between Perth and Brisbane on 9 Apr 1980. The route is 5455 km *3389 miles* taking 75 hr 55 min.

Road Load Heaviest & Longest GB (p 141). The heaviest and longest road load moved in the United Kingdom has been a 476 tonnes *468.4 tons* 194 ft *59,13 m* long Vacuum Distillation Column from Fawley Power Station to the Esso Refinery at Fawley by Mammoet-Econofreight on 24 July 1981. The gross weight of the load plus bogies (excluding tractors) was 696 tonnes *685 tons.*

Snowmobile (p 141). Richard and Raymond Moore and Loren Matthews drove their snowmobile 5876 miles *9456 km* from Fairbanks, Alaska to Fenton, Michigan in 39 days from 3 Feb–13 Mar 1980.

Largest Bicycle (p 142) The Pedaalstompers rode *c* 60 m *195 ft* in practice on 20 Apr 1979.

London Underground Record (p 144). Robert Robinson and Finn Gleeson of 20th Enfield Scout Troop toured all the stations on 23 June 1981 in 17 hr 57 min.

Largest Wing Span (p 146). 8th line. For hanger read hangar.

Lightest Aeroplane (p 146). *Solar Challenger* piloted by Stephen Ptacek, 28, made the first crossing of the English Channel on 7 July 1981. The 180 mile *290 km* journey from Clergy-Pontaise near Paris to Manston, Kent took 5½ hr. The aircraft has a wingspan of 47 ft *14,3 m.*

Computer Most Powerful (p 155). The CRAY – 1/S system, introduced in 1981, has an additional 8 million words of buffer memory and a storage capacity of 19 gigabytes or 1.55136×10^{11} bits with a system cost of up to $17 million for the maximum configuration.

Greatest Roll (p 137). The sloop Josephine II, 10m *32 ft 9½ in* double rolled on 15 Apr 1978.

CHAPTER 9

Oldest Companies British (p 156). The Shore Porters' Society of Aberdeen, a haulier, shipping and warehouse partnership, is known to have been established before 4 June 1498.

Greatest Loss (p 156). On 7 July 1981 British Steel Chairman Ian MacGregor announced a loss of £668 million in 1980–81 or £1270 per minute or £5520 *per caput* for the remaining 121,000 workers.

Largest Merger (p 157). The largest ever merger agreement signed has been that between Du Pont and Co. and Conoco Inc. at 1 am in Stamford, Connecticut on 6 July 1981 involving $7300 million in cash and stock for the latter.

Land highest rent (p 160). 3rd line for £120 read £1200.

Capital Issue Largest (p 161). American Telephone and Telegraph Co's 1981 capital issue realized a record $1034 million.

Art Nouveau (p 162). 1st line. For noveau read nouveau.

Largest Chair (p 163). The world's largest chair is the 33 ft 1 in *10,08 m* tall, 19 ft 7 in *5,96 m* wide chair constructed by Anniston Steel & Plumbing Co. Inc for Miller Office Furniture in Anniston, Alabama, USA and completed in May 1981.

Cattle Station (p 169). The world's largest cattle station is Strangeray Springs, South Australia extending over 11,594 miles² 7,420,160 acres *3 002 790 ha* – more than the area of England's four largest counties of North Yorkshire, Cumbria, Devon and Lincolnshire with Nottinghamshire 'thrown in'. Until 1915 the Victoria River Downs Station, Northern Territory had an area of 22,400,000 acres (35,000 miles² *90 650 km²*), the same as England's 20 largest counties put together.

Milk Yields Cows (p 172). 'Breezewood Patsy Bar Pontiac' (born 11 June 1964) reached 403,439 lb (180.10 tons *182 990 kg*) on 22 June 1981.

CHAPTER 10

Most Travelled Person (p 175). Fred Specovius (West Germany) has visited every sovereign country except Angola, São Tomé and North Korea and every non-sovereign territory except 13, making a total of 205 countries.

Longest period alone at sea (p 177). Les Powles (*né* Thomas) (GB) sailed round the world from Lymington Hants. westabout on 9 July 1980 returning on 3 June 1981 thus 329 days non-stop at sea.

Longest Marriage (p 178). The last person to be married in the 19th century Mrs Harriet Orton, 103, died on 28 Apr 1981 after a marriage lasting 80 years 293 days. The new claimants to the British record are Sam Loveridge (b. Taunton, 1881) and Annie Pocock (b. Bridgwater, 1884) married at Taunton, Somerset on 1 June 1904.

Working Career (p 178). Edward William Beard (b. 18 Apr 1878), a builder of Swindon, Wiltshire was still working in August 1981 in the firm he founded in 1896.

Trans Atlantic Records (p 179). Fastest Crossing (multihull) (West–East) – Marc Pajôt (Fr) plus 3 crew – *Elf Aquitaine* 18,6 m *61 ft* catamaran – New York to Brest – 9 days 10 hr 6 min – 4–14 July 1981.

Bag Carrying (p 180). Alan M Jones (b. 17 Mar 1947) carried an open 120 lb *54,4 kg* bag for 23 miles *37,01 km* in 5 hr 53 min at the Family Fitness Center, Bellevue, Washington, USA on 6 May 1981.

Baton Twirling (p 181). Four members of the Brownhills Majorettes, Walsall, W. Midlands twirled for 78 hr 2 min on 20–23 July 1981.

Boomerang Throwing (p 182). The Boomerang Association of Australia's Championship record for distance reached from the thrower before the boomerang returns is 107 m *351 ft* by Bob Burwell in the 1981 Championship.

Canal Jumping (p 182). In the 1979 Fierljeppen Championship at Winsam, Friesland, Catharinus Hoekstra reached 17,39 m *57 ft.* A distance of 18,40 m *60 ft 4 in* has been attributed to Aarth de Wit.

Car Wrecking (p 182). Dick Sheppard's total had increased to 1577 by 1 Aug 1981.

Champagne Fountain (p 182). Joseph Achenback, Steven Arnold, Donald Milonowski and Timothy Tweddale of F.E.A.S.T. equalled the world record with 21 on 26 Apr 1981 at the Hilton Hotel, Grand Rapids, Michigan, USA.

Club Swinging (p 182). 17,512 in one hour on 27 July 1981 by Albert Rayner at Wakefield, W. Yorkshire.

Cow Chip Tossing (p 183). David L Roenigk, 18, threw 232 ft 1 in *70,73 m* at the Butler Fair, Pennsylvania on 24 July 1980.

Cucumber Slicing (p 183). Mr Johnson improved his time to 19.1 sec at RAF Scampton, Lincolnshire on 30 May 1981.

Largest Dance (p 183). A total of 18,520 dancers (2315 squares) took part in the 30th National Square Dance Convention in the Memorial Stadium, Seattle, Washington. The caller was Marv K.

Marathon Dance (p 183). Mike Ritof and the Edith Boudreaux logged 5148 hr 28½ min to win $2000 at Chicago's Merry Garden Ballroom, Belmont and Sheffield, Illinois USA from 29 Aug 1930 to 1 Apr 1931. Rest periods were progressively cut from 20 to 10 to 5 to nil minutes per hour with 10 inch steps and a maximum of 15 seconds for closure of eyes.

Disco Dancing (p 183). The longest recorded disco dancing marathon is one of 347 hr by Babs Spear and Bridget Powe at Tempo, Queen Street, Barnstaple, Devon on 5–19 Apr 1981.

High Kicking (p 184). V S Kumar Anandan achieved 9100 high kicks at Galle Face, Colombo, Sri Lanka on 31 Dec 1980 – 1 Jan 1981. He took 6 hr 51 min non-stop.

Haggis Hurling (p 185). Alan Pettigrew reached 163 ft 9½ in *49,92 m* at the Ardrossan Highland Games on 14 June 1981.

Feminine Beauty (p 185). Miss USA won the Miss Universe contest in 1980.

Highest Shallow Dive (p 186). Henri la Mothe struck the water at a speed of 28.4 mph *45,7 km/h.*

Human Fly (p 187). Jaromir Wagner (b. Czechoslovakia 1941) became the first man to fly the Atlantic standing on the wing of an aircraft. He took off from Aberdeen, Scotland on 28 Sept 1980. Daniel Goodwin, 25 became the first to climb Sears Tower (1454 ft *443 m*) on 25 May 1981. It took from 3 am to 10.25 am.

Jumble Sale (p 187). The Winnetka Congregational Church raised $114,479.52 (*then £57,240*) at their 49th sale on 14 May 1981.

Kiss of Life (p 187). Five members of the St John Ambulance Clifton Combined Division, York, N. Yorkshire maintained a Kiss of Life for 240 hr with 224,029 inflations on 26 July–5 Aug 1981.

Onion Peeling (p 188). Alfonso Salvo of York, Pennsylvania, USA peeled 50 lb *22,67 kg* of onions (52 onions) in 5 min 23 sec on 28 Oct 1980.

Organ (p 189). Robert A Hawkins of New Longton, Preston, Lancs played a church organ for 92 hr on 15–19 June 1981.

Plate Spinning (p 189). Shukuni Sasaki spun 72 plates simultaneously on 16 July 1981 at Nio Town Taiyo Exhibition, Kagawa, Japan.

Potato Peeling (p 190). J Mills, M McDonald, P Jennings, E Gardiner and V McNulty peeled 266,5 kg *587 lb 8 oz* of potatoes in 45 min at Bourke Street Mall, Melbourne, Vic, Australia on 17 Mar 1981.

Singing (p 191). Pat Power sang for 171 hr 15 min at the Blue Anchor Lounge, Bellurgan, Co. Louth, Ireland on 24 July–1 Aug 1981.

Skateboarding (p 191). Trevor Baxter jumped 5 ft 4 in *1,625 m* on 26 July 1981 at Farnborough, Hants.

Skipping Non Stop (p 191). Frank P Oliveri achieved 12 hr 8 min (est. 120,744 turns) at Great Lakes Training Center, North Chicago, Illinois, USA on 13 June 1981.

Spitting (p 192). At the National Tobacco Spitting Contest, Raleigh, Miss on 25 July 1981 Jeff Barker achieved a distance of 33 ft 7½ in *10,24 m*. In 1980 he reached 45 ft *13,71 m* at Fulton, Miss, USA.

Stretcher Carrying (p 193). The longest recorded carry of a stretcher with a 10 st *63,5 kg* 'body' is 127 miles *204,3 km* by two four man teams from the Sri Chinmoy marathon team of Jamaica, New York, USA on 17–19 Apr 1981 in 45 hr 45 min.

Suggestion Boxes (p 193). Mr Drayton raised his total to 29,153 by 1 January 1981 of which more than 4,000 were adopted.

Oldest Clown (p 196). The longest career of anyone in show business is 82 years by the world's oldest clown Charlie Revel (b. Andrea Lasserre in Spain, 24 Apr 1896). He first appeared as a child performer in 1899 and performed at the Tivoli, Stockholm in July 1981.

Circus – Trampoline (p 196). Richard Tison (France) performed a triple twisting triple back somersault for television near Berchtesgarden, West Germany on 30 June 1981.

Golden Handshake (p 197). Malcolm Anson, 57, received £300,000 on 9 July 1981 from Imperial Group of which he had been the Chairman.

Most valuable Prize (p 200). Templeton Prize 1981 (US $200,000) won by Dame Cicely Saunders DBE FRCP (b. 22 June 1918).

Who's Who (p 201). Miss Cartland's entry now comprises 133 lines in the 1981 edition.

CHAPTER 11

Countries Total Number (p 202). After Belize (23 Sept 1981), Antigua became the 168th sovereign country on 1 Nov 1981.

Communist Parties (p 208). The membership of the Communist Party of the Soviet Union was stated to be more than 17 million in Feb 1981.

Most Coups (p 209). Bolivia had a 189th coup (by General Luis Garcia Mesa) on 17 July 1980.

Most Candidates (p 210). The record of 11 candidates in the Lambeth Central by-election in 1978 was equalled at the Warrington by-election of 16 July 1981.

Highest Costs (p 217). The trial judge in R *v* Sinclair and others (the handless corpse murder) ordered the international drug trafficker Alexander James Sinclair, 36 of N.Z. (sentenced to a minimum term of 20 years for the murder of Marty Johnstone found in a quarry at Chorley, Lancashire) to pay £1 million towards the Crown's costs.

Largest Charity Collection (p 225). The most valuable column of coins amassed for charity was a column of 10p pieces worth £5119.70 created between 15–22 July 1981 at Denham for the Licensed Victuallers' National Homes.

Largest Barbecue (p 228). West Pasco Sertoma Club of New Port Richey, Florida held a barbecue for 10,335 people on 28–29 Mar 1981 where 8274 lb *3753 kg* of meat was served.

Largest Beefburger (p 228). A beefburger of 3020 lb *1369 kg* was served in 13,083 portions in City Part, Towner, 'Cattle Capitol of North Dakota', USA on 19 June 1981.

Longest Sausage (p 229) A 4607,76 m *2.86 miles* long sausage weighing 1979,5 kg *1.94 tons* was completed by Auckland Farmers' Freezing Cooperative Ltd, New Zealand on 26 June 1981. Over $4000 was raised for Telethon.

Strawberry Bowl (p 229). The largest bowl of strawberries with a net weight of 349½ lb *158,5 kg* was served with 10 gallons *45 litres* of cream to 1500

people at the Greathouse Cheshire Home, Kington Langley, Wiltshire on 11 July 1981.

Largest Sundae (p 229). The largest ice cream sundae ever concocted is one of 10,808 lb *4902,40 kg* plus 180 lb *81,64 kg* of strawberries, 100 lb *45,35 kg* of nuts and 16 gal *72,73 litres* of whipped topping constructed by the Friendly Ice Cream Co and students from the High School at Troy, Ohio, USA on 8 June 1980.

Street – Longest Great Britain and Commonest name (p 231). The commonest street name in Greater London is High Street (122) followed by Station Road (100).

Oldest Pillar Box in Ireland (p 233). The hexagonal roof pillar box in Kent Railway Station, Glanmere, Cork dates from 1857.

Most 'O' and 'A' Levels (p 234). Arthur Prime's total rose to 47 (10 A and 37 O levels) in January 1981.

Most Durable Teacher (p 235). Miss Touzel retired on 30 Sept 1980 after 75 years.

Slowest Saint (pp 236–7). Pope St Leo III died on 12 June 816. His name was added to the Roman Martyrology in 1673 – 857 years later.

Accidents and Disasters (p 238). Tornado U.K. Meteorologists are increasingly of the view that the Tay Bridge collapsed under the impact of two tornadic vortices, on 28 Dec 1879. Death roll 75. *Footnote 13*: For 6 Sept 1878 read 3 Sept 1878.

CHAPTER 12

Aerobatics (p 241). The RAF aerobatic display team Red Arrows (formed 1915), based at Kemble, Gloucestershire uniquely perform a nine aircraft 'Wine Glass' manoeuvre in their 700 mph *1126,5 km/h* British Aerospace Hawk jets in which they are at times separated by less than 10 ft *3,04 m*.

Angling – World Records (p 242). Freshwater Fish: Burbot 18 lb 4 oz *8,27 kg* Thomas Courtemanche Pickford, Michigan, USA 31 Jan 1980; Sea Fish: Jack, horse-eye 22 lb *9,97 kg* Donald C Ball Miami Beach, Florida, USA 26 Aug 1980; Weakfish 17 lb 14 oz *8,10 kg* William H Herold Rye, New York, USA 31 May 1980.

Angling – British Records (pp 242–3) as at July 1981 – Freshwater Fish: Grayling 2 lb 13 oz *1,275 kg* P B Goldsmith River Test, Romsey, Hants 1981; Ruffe 5 oz 4 dms *0,148 kg* R J Jenkins West View Farm, Cumbria 1980; Sea Fish: Catfish 24 lb 3 oz *10,971 kg* N Trevelyan Whitby, Yorkshire 1980; Ray, Spotted 8 lb 5 oz *3,770 kg* P G Bowen Mewslade Bay, S. Wales 1980; Smoothhound, Starry 28 lb *12,700 kg* R Grady Maplin Sands, Essex 1980; Sole 5 lb 7 oz *2,467 kg* L Dixon Alderney, Channel Is 1980; Whiting 6 lb 12 oz *3,061 kg* N R Croft Falmouth, Cornwall 1981; Wreckfish 10 lb 10 oz *4,819 kg* B McNamara S of Eddystone 1980.

Cricket – Most Runs, Test Matches (p 256). Geoff Boycott scored 7628 runs in 103 Test Matches (182 innings, av. 47.30) to 13 Aug 1981, to better the English record.

Cricket – Wicket-keeping, Most dismissals, career (p 260). The record for most catches is 1273 by Bob Taylor to 2 Aug 1981.

Cycling – World Records, indoor track: amateur unpaced flying start (p 265). 200 m 10.369 Sergei Kopylov (USSR) Moscow, USSR 2 Aug 1981.

Cycling – British Records (p 266). Men's amateur unpaced standing start 1 km 1 min 08.45 sec Terry Tinsley Leicester, Leicestershire 3 Aug 1981; women's unpaced standing start 1 km 1 min 16.893 sec Brenda Atkinson Leicester, Leicestershire 4 Aug 1981.

Football (Minor League) – Highest scores, season (p 273). Paul Anthony Moulden (b. 6 Sept 1967) scored 157 goals in 30 league and cup matches for the Bolton Boys Federation in 1980–81.

Football (Minor League) – Ball control (p 273). Uno Lindstrom juggled a regulation soccer ball for 10 hr 6 min 38 sec (103,000 repetitions) at Sorbyn's Athletic Club, Sweden on 30 Nov 1980.

Gambling – Slot Machines (p 280). Jeff Randolph (31), (US) won $992,012.15 on 17 July 1981. Caesars Tahoe Casino, South Lake Tahoe, Nevada, USA, decided to round this figure to 'an even million'.

Golf – Most Club Championships (p 285). Bernard Cusack won his 32nd consecutive club championship on 26 July 1981, making 33 in all.

Mountaineering – Three peaks (p 307). Peter and David Ford, David Robinson, Kevin Duggan and John O'Callaghan, of Luton and Dunstable, ran the distance in relay in 54 hr 39 min 14 sec on 7–9 Aug 1981.

Skiing – Ski jumping (pp 316–7). The longest dry ski jump is 92 m *301 ft 10 in* by Hubert Schwarz (W. Germany) at Berchtesgarten, W. Germany on 30 June 1981.

Swimming – Fastest (p 319). Robin Leamy (USA) (b. 1 April 1961) swam 50 m in 22.54 sec averaging 4.96 mph *7,98 km/h* at Milwaukee, Wisconsin, USA on 15 Aug 1981.

Swimming – Channel, Fastest (p 320). 7 hr 22 min by six swimmers in relay from England to France on 9 Aug 1981.

Swimming – Channel, Triple Crossing (p 321). The first triple crossing was by Jon Erikson (USA) (b. 6 Sept 1954) in 38 hr 27 min on 11–12 Aug 1981.

SUBJECT INDEX

An asterisk indicates a further reference in the Stop Press

ABBREVIATION, *longest 94*
A-BOMB, *see* **Atomic Bomb**
ACCELERATOR, *most powerful 86*
ACCENTS, *word with most 94*
ACCIDENTS AND DISASTERS, *worst world*, U.K. 238, sports 241*
ACCORDION, *marathon 180*
ACE, *air 199*
ACID, *strongest 80*
ACROBATIC RECORDS, *196*
ACRONYM, *longest 94*
ACTOR, *highest earnings 110, 113, most durable, most roles 109*
ACTRESS, *most durable 109*
ADDRESS, *longest legal 216, highest numbered postal 233*
ADMIRAL, *longest serving 213*
ADVERTISER, *most durable 101, biggest 157*
ADVERTISING, *highest rate, expenditure 102, highest T.V. rates 113, largest agents 157, sign: greatest ever, largest, highest world: Great Britain 126*
ADVOCATE, *most successful 218*
AERIALIST, *feats 196*
AEROBATICS*, *241*
AEROFLORA, *57*
AEROPLANE, *see* **Aircraft**
AGE, *see* **Longevity**
AGENDA ITEM, *largest 211*
AGRICULTURE, *169–72*
AIR ACE, *top scoring, world, U.K., top jet, top woman 199*
AIRCRAFT, *Mach scale, earliest flights world, Great Britain, cross-Channel, jet-engined world, Great Britain, supersonic flight, trans-Atlantic first 145, first non-stop 145–6, solo most, first trans-Pacific, circumnavigation first, fastest, smallest aircraft, largest wing span*, heaviest, lightest*, smallest, fastest bombers, airliner largest world, G.B. 146, fastest 146–7, most capacious, largest propeller; longest, shortest scheduled flight, speed records, official, air-launched, jet, biplane 147, piston-engined 147–8, propeller-driven, fastest trans-Atlantic, greatest altitude, flight duration record, helicopter fastest, largest, smallest, highest 148, autogyros: earliest 148–9, speed, altitude, distance records, flying-boat, fastest, airship: earliest, largest, greatest passenger load, distance, duration, 149 hovercraft: earliest, largest, fastest warship. longest and highest flight 150, model aircraft, speed, duration records, altitude, first cross-Channel flight smallest, paper aircraft duration record, take-offs and landings, human-powered 151*
AIRCRAFT CARRIER, *largest world 135*
AIRCRAFT DISASTER, *worst world, U.K. 238*
AIRCRAFT MANUFACTURER, *largest 157*
AIR FORCE, *earliest, greatest 214*
AIRLINE, *largest commercial, most passengers, greatest mileage of routes, oldest 157, country with busiest system 230*
AIRLINER, *largest world, G.B. 146, fastest 146–7, most capacious 147*
AIRPORT, *largest world, G.B., busiest, highest, lowest, farthest, nearest to city centre, longest runway in world, G.B. 148*
AIRSHIP, *earliest, largest rigid, non-rigid, greatest passenger load, distance duration records 149*
AIR SPEED RECORDS, *world 147–8*
AIR SUPPORTED BUILDING *largest 116*
ALBATROSS, *largest wing span 38, longest incubation 39*
ALCOHOL, *most in blood 22, strongest, weakest 81, most expensive drink, beer, wine, liqueurs, spirits 81*
ALCOHOLIC, *greatest, youngest 22*
ALE, *yard of 197*
ALIMONY, *highest awards, suit 217*
ALKALI, *strongest 80*
ALPHABET, *oldest 92, longest, shortest 92–3*
ALPHORN, *longest 103*
ALTITUDE RECORDS, *mammal (dog) 35, bird 39, rocket 77, aircraft 148, balloon 149–50, man, woman 173, progressive records 176, kite 187, parachute 192, canoe 254, gliding 280, hang gliding, golf course 281, mountaineering 306–7, skiing 317, yachting 339*
ALUMINIUM, *largest producer, largest smelter 157*
AMBER, *largest piece 84*
AMBERGRIS, *heaviest 27*
AMBULANCE, *largest 140–1*
AMPHIBIANS, *largest world, British, smallest world, British, longest lived, highest, lowest, most poisonous 42, longest frog jump 43, earliest 46, most southerly, largest extinct 50*
AMPHIBIOUS VEHICLE, *first circumnavigation 141*
AMPHITHEATRE, *earliest, largest 108*
AMPUTATION, *fastest 25*
AMUSEMENT RESORT, *largest 118*
ANAESTHESIA, *earliest 25*
ANAGRAM, *longest 94*
ANCHORAGE, *deepest 137*
ANCIENT MONUMENT, *youngest 129*
ANGLING, *largest and smallest catch 241, championships 241–2, casting, longest fight 242, world records* 242, British records* 242–3*
ANIMAL, *kingdom 26–50, largest, heaviest, tallest, longest 26, rarest 26–7, commonest, fastest, longest lived, heaviest brain, largest eye, largest egg, longest gestation, fastest, slowest growth, greatest size difference between sexes, highest g force, blood temperatures, most prodigious eater, most valuable furs, heaviest ambergris 27, most valuable animals*, largest mammal, world, Britain, deepest dive, largest land, tallest, smallest, rarest 28, fastest land world 28–9, Britain, slowest, longest lived, highest living, longest, shortest gestation 29, longest extinct, heaviest, largest predator, most brainless 49, smallest organism, highest 57, earliest husbandry, order of domestication 169, man-eating 238*
ANNUAL GENERAL MEETING, *largest 156*
ANTARCTIC CONTINENT, *most northerly iceberg 65, first ship, first sighting, landing, conquest South Pole 175, first woman, first crossing, longest sledge journey 176*
ANTELOPE, *fastest 28–9, largest, smallest, rarest, oldest 32*
ANTHEM, *National, oldest, longest, shortest, longest rendition 105*
ANTIQUE, *largest sold 162*
ANTLERS, *largest span 33, 50, 315*
APE, *earliest 46*
APPEAL, *most successful T.V. 113*
APPENDICECTOMY, *earliest 25*
APPLAUSE, *greatest 182*
APPLE PEELING, *record 180*
APPLE PICKING, *record 180*
APPLE PIE, *largest 229*
AQUAMARINE, *largest 84*
AQUARIUM, *largest, record attendances 58*
AQUEDUCT, *longest ancient, modern, U.K. 123*
ARACHNIDS, *44–5*
ARBITRATION, *longest 216*
ARCH, *longest natural bridge, highest 70*
ARCH BRIDGE, *longest steel 122*
ARCHERY, *244*
ARCHIPELAGO, *greatest 67*
ARCTIC CONTINENT, *most southerly iceberg 65, first crossing 176*
ARIA, *longest 104*
ARMED FORCES, *largest 213*
ARMOUR, *most expensive, heaviest 162, longest ride in 190*
ARMY, *largest, oldest, oldest old soldier 213, youngest soldiers 213–14, youngest conscript, tallest soldier, oldest British regiment, most senior, greatest mutiny, longest march 214*
ARREST, *greatest mass 222*
ART, *painting 88–91, sculpture 91*
ART AUCTIONEERING, *largest, oldest firm 157*
ARTESIAN WELL, *deepest Britain, highest record flow 132*
ART GALLERY, *largest 90*
ARTIFICIAL MOUND, *largest prehistoric 129*
ARTIFICIAL SATELLITES, *first escape velocities, earliest successful manned, first woman in space, first in flight fatality, first 'walk' in space, longest manned space flight, oldest, youngest astronauts, longest stay on moon, first extra-terrestrial vehicle, closest to sun, largest space object, most expensive project 78*
ARTIFICIAL SEAWAY, *longest 124*
ARTILLERY, *see* **Gun, cannon,**
ART NOUVEAU*, *highest auction price 162*
ARTS FESTIVAL, *largest, 109*
ASCENDANTS, *most 18*
ASPIDISTRA, *largest 51*
ASSETS, *business, greatest 156, biggest write-off 157*
ASSOCIATION, *largest world, U.K. 226*
ASSOCIATION FOOTBALL, *highest scores* 269, 273, fastest goals 269, 273, most and least successful teams 269, 274, challenge cups 270, most caps 271, largest and smallest crowds 272–3, most disciplined and indisciplined 274*
ASTEROIDS, *largest, only visible, closest, most distant 75*
ASTRONAUT, *earliest, first woman, first fatality, walk, longest flight, oldest, youngest, number of, duration on moon* 78, maximum speed 173*
ASYLUM, *see* **Mental Hospital**
ATHLETICS, *235–332*
ATLANTIC CROSSING, *first, fastest* world 136, first amphibious vehicle, 141, first air 145, non-stop 145–6, solo, most 146, fastest 148, smallest boat, first rowing, record solo Britain—U.S.A., fastest solo sail, marine records 179*
ATLAS, *most expensive 97*
ATOLL, *largest, largest land area 67*
ATOMIC BOMB, *most deadly, largest arsenal 214, most casualties 238*
ATOMIC PILE, *earliest 151*
ATOMIC POWER STATION, *largest 151, worst disaster 238*
ATOMIC REACTOR, *largest 151*
ATOM SMASHER, *see* **Accelerator**
AUCTION, *greatest art 157, land 160, wine 81*
AUDIENCE, *greatest*, pop festival, concert 103, television, 112*
AURORA, (Borealis and Australis), *most frequent, highest, lowest, lowest latitudes, noctilucent clouds 73*
AUTHOR, *see* **Writer**
AUTOGRAPH, *earliest royal*, most expensive, most valuable 98*
AUTOGYROS, *earliest 148–9, speed, altitude, distance records 149*
AUTOMOBILE, *see* **Car**
AVALANCHE, *greatest* 70*
AVES, *see* **Birds**
AVIATION, *oldest, youngest passengers 150, see also* **Flight**
AWARDS, *Versatility Showbusiness 110, largest annual 200, see also* **Medals**
AXEMANSHIP, *records 195*

BABIES, *most by one mother in world, Britain 16–17, multiple births 18–19, heaviest world, U.K., most proximate 19, most bouncing 19–20, lightest, test tube 20*
BACKGAMMON, *279*
BACTERIA, *largest, smallest free living, highest, longest lived, toughest 57, biggest disaster 238*
BADMINTON, *244–5*
BAG-CARRYING*, *180*
BAGPIPES, *longest duration record 180*
BAIL, *highest world, G.B. 216*
BAKED BEANS, *eating record 197*
BALANCE, *finest 86*
BALANCE OF PAYMENTS, *highest, lowest 224*
BALANCING ON ONE FOOT, *180*
BALLET DANCING, *records 183*
BALLOON, *earliest, distance record 149, highest unmanned 149–50, manned, largest 150, human powered flight 151*
BALLOON FLIGHTS (toy), *180*
BALLOONING, *earliest distance record 149, highest unmanned 149–50, manned, largest, hot-air distance, altitude, endurance records 150*
BALLOON RACING, *largest release 180*
BALL PUNCHING, *duration record 180*
BALLROOM, *largest 118*
BALLROOM DANCING, *marathon record, most successful champions 183*
BAMBOO, *tallest, fastest growing 57*
BANANA, *eating record 197*
BANANA SPLIT, *longest 226, 228*
BAND, *largest marching, most successful brass 103, longest playing 180, greatest one-man 180–1, longest dance band session 184*
BANK, *largest 157, largest building 157–8, largest vault 158, biggest fraud, 220*
BANK NOTE, *greatest forgery 220, earliest, oldest surviving, largest, smallest, highest denomination, lowest denomination, highest circulation 224*
BANK RATE, *lowest, highest 224*
BANK ROBBERY, *greatest 220*
BANKRUPTCY, *greatest 157*
BANK VAULT, *largest 158*
BANQUET, *largest world outdoor, indoor, most expensive 158*
BAR, *longest world, U.K., Ireland 120*
BARBECUE, *largest* 228*
BARBER'S, *largest 158*
BAR BILLIARDS, *248*
BARBITURATE, *quickest poison 80*
BAREFOOT WATER SKIING, *335*
BARGE, *largest, 135*
BARLEY, *record yield 170*
BARN, *largest*, longest tithe G.B. 126*
BAROMETRIC PRESSURE, *highest, lowest 61*
BARONET, *oldest 201*
BARRACKS, *oldest 118*
BARREL-JUMPING, *greatest number 181*
BARREL ROLLING, *181*
BARROW, *largest, largest long 129*
BARROW-PUSHING, *heaviest load 181*
BARROW RACING, *fastest 181*
BASEBALL, *245–6*
BASIN, *largest river 71*
BASKETBALL, *246–7*
BATH TUB RACING, *fastest, greatest distance 181*
BATON TWIRLING*, *181*
BATS, *smallest mammal 28, largest, smallest 30, rarest 30–31, fastest, longest lived, highest detectable pitch 31*
BATTERY, *longest lasting 152*
BATTLE, *Britain, last pitched land, clan, worst, worst in Britain, greatest naval 212*
BATTLE HONOURS, *most 214*
BATTLESHIP, *largest world, Britain, largest guns, thickest armour 135*
BAY, *largest world, Great Britain 64*
BEACH, *pleasure, largest 118*
BEAGLING, *256*
BEAR, *largest 29*
BEARD, *longest 21, of bees 181*
BEAUTY, *feminine* 185*
BED, *largest, heaviest 162*
BED MAKING, *fastest 181*
BED OF NAILS, *duration record on 181*
BED PUSHING, *record push 181*
BED RACE, *181*
BEE, *hive record, 47, longest beard 181*
BEECH, *tallest hedge 51–2*
BEEFBURGER, *largest* 228*
BEER, *strongest world, Great Britain, weakest 81, largest exporter 158, consumption 227, drinking records 197*
BEER CANS, *largest collection, most expensive 162*
BEER LABEL COLLECTING, *largest collection 181*
BEER MAT FLIPPING, *181*
BEER MATS, *largest collection 163*
BEETLES, *largest, heaviest 45–6, longest, smallest 46, longest lived 47*
BELL, *oldest, heaviest, world, Great Britain, largest, heaviest carillon 105*
BELL-RINGING, *most changes rung 106*
BELLY DANCING, *marathon 183*
BENCH, *longest 165*
BEQUEST, *greatest 196–7*
BEST MAN, *most often 181*
BEST SELLER, *world non-fiction, fiction 100, gramophone records 107–8*
BETTING, *280*
BIBLE, *earliest printed 26, most valuable, oldest, earliest printed English, longest and shortest books, longest, shortest psalm, verse, total letters, words, longest name 97, print figures 99–100*
BICYCLE, *earliest, longest tandem, smallest, largest*, fastest, tallest unicycle, Penny-farthing record 142, most on one 181, eating record 197, fastest 263–4*
BICYCLE FACTORY, *largest 158*
BIG BEN, *longest stoppage 154*
BIG WHEEL, *largest 119, riding endurance record 181*
BILLIARDS, *247*
BILLIARD TABLE, *jumping 182*
BILLIONAIRES, *195–6*
BINGO, *279*
BIPLANE, *fastest 147*
BIRD, *36, 38–40, fastest 27, largest 36, 38, heaviest, largest wing span, smallest, most abundant, rarest 38, fastest flying 38–9, fastest and slowest wing-beats, longest lived, largest eggs, smallest eggs, shortest and longest incubation, longest flights, highest flying, most airborne, fastest swimmer, most acute vision, highest g force, longest feathers, most feathers, earliest and latest cuckoo 39, largest nests 39–40, domesticated birds, heaviest chicken, flying record, heaviest, most expensive turkey, longest lived, most talkative 40, extinct, earliest 46, largest* 50, most expensive stuffed 167*
BIRD SPOTTER, *champion* 39*
BIRTH DATES, *coincident 20, most proximate 19*
BIRTHDAY CARD, *most parsimonious 98*
BIRTH RATE, *highest, lowest, natural increase 204*
BIRTHS, *16–20, multiple 18–19, most proximate 19, most southerly, test tube 20*
BISHOP, *oldest Church of England, Roman Catholic, youngest 237*
BISHOPRIC, *longest tenure 237*
BITTEREST SUBSTANCE, *80*
BLACK HOLE, *76*
BLACK-OUT, *biggest 152*
BLACKPOOL ROCK, *largest 229*
BLADES, *penknife with greatest number 166*
BLANKET, *largest 163*
BLAST FURNACE, *largest 152*
BLINDNESS, Colour, *highest and lowest rate 21*
BLOOD, *richest, most alcohol in 22*
BLOOD ANTIBODY, *highest count 22*
BLOOD DONOR, *lifetime record 22*
BLOOD GROUP, *commonest, rarest 22*
BLOOD TEMPERATURE, *highest, lowest mammalian, 27*
BLOOM, *largest world, Great Britain, largest inflorescence, largest blossoming plant 52*
BOARDSAILING, *339*
BOAT, *see* **Ship**
BOAT RACE, *313*
BOBSLEIGH, *248–9*
BOILER, *largest 152*
BOMB, *heaviest conventional, most powerful atom, largest nuclear weapons 214, defusing record 182, most bombed country 214*
BOMBER, *heaviest, fastest 146*
BOMBING, *worst in world 238*
BOND SIGNING, *greatest feat 182*
BONE, *oldest fragment 14–15, longest, smallest human 20*
BONFIRE, *largest* 126*
BOOK, *oldest mechanically printed, largest, smallest printed 96, most valuable 97, best-sellers; world, non-fiction, fiction, slowest seller, shortest review 100, most overdue 100*
BOOK SHOP, *largest 158*
BOOKMAKER, *largest 280*
BOOMERANG, *greatest throws* 182*
BORES, River, *greatest world, Great Britain 71, surfing 319*
BORING, *deepest world 131*
BOTTLE, *largest, smallest (spirit) 81, largest collections 82, message in 188*
BOUNDARY, *see* **Frontiers**
BOWLING (Ten Pin), *249*
BOWLS, *249–50*
BOXING, *250–3*
BOX-OFFICE, *biggest film* 110*
BRAIN, *(human), largest, smallest (animal), heaviest 27, least 49*
BRAIN OF BRITAIN, *youngest, oldest 111*

INDEX

An asterisk indicates a further reference in the Stop Pres

BRASS, oldest monumental 236
BRASS INSTRUMENT, largest 102–3
BREACH OF CONTRACT, highest damages 216–17
BREACH OF PROMISE, highest damages 217
BREAKWATER, longest world, U.K. 126
BREEDER, fastest, youngest 29
BREWERY, oldest, largest world, Europe, G.B., greatest exports 158
BRICK-CARRYING, record for man, woman 182
BRICKLAYING, fastest, 182
BRICK RACING, 182
BRICK-THROWING, greatest distance 182
BRICKWORKS, largest 158–9
BRIDGE, longest natural 70, oldest world, British 121, longest suspension world* 121–2, U.K., longest cantilever, longest steel arch, longest floating 122, longest covered 122–3, railway longest, railway, widest, longest bridging, highest 123
BRIDGE (Contract), 297
BRIDGE-TUNNEL, longest 125
BROADCAST (Radio), first advertised, trans-Atlantic, longest 111
(Television) first 112
BROADCASTER, fastest 22, most durable, 111
BROADCASTING, see **Radio**
BROADMOOR, longest detention, longest escape 222
BROADSHEET, highest price 97
BROILER, record growth 171
BROTHERS, most in 'Who's Who' 201
BRUSH, finest 90
BUBBLE CHAMBER, largest world 86
BUBBLE GUM, blowing 182
BUDGERIGAR, oldest 37, 40
BUDGET, largest world, G.B., greatest surplus, deficit 223
BUILDING, (see also **Structure**), largest theatre 108, largest cinema 110, earliest world, Great Britain, Ireland, largest commercial, scientific 114, administrative 114–15, office world, G.B., tallest, most storeys, highest, northernmost, southernmost 115, wooden, air-supported 116, for living 116–18, entertainment 118–21, tallest (progressive records) 122, largest demolished by explosive* 126, largest university, oldest 233–4
BUILDING CONTRACTOR, largest 159
BUILDING SOCIETY, largest, 159
BULB, most powerful, most durable light 87
BULL, heaviest world, G.B., highest priced 171
BULLFIGHTING, 253
BURIAL ALIVE, record 182
BUS, earliest, longest, longest route* 140
BUSH-CRICKET, largest 47
BUSINESS, oldest, greatest assets, sales 156, profits, losses 156–7
BUTTER FAT, record lifetime, one lactation, day yields 172
BUTTERFLY, heaviest world, Britain 45, largest 45–6, smallest, rarest*, most acute sense of smell, 46

CABARET, highest fee 109
CABER TOSS, see **Highland Games,** 326
CABLE, Telephone, longest submarine 232
CACTUS, largest 51
CAKE, largest 228
CALF, highest birthweight 171, most at one birth 171–2, roping 312
CALORIES, most and least calorific fruit 54, highest, lowest consumption, largest available total 227
CAMBRIDGE, union presidents, 201
CAMERA, earliest, largest, smallest, fastest cine, most expensive 83
CAMP, concentration 218–19, largest penal 222
CAMPANOLOGY, 106
CAMPING OUT, longest 182
CANAL, earliest world, British, longest world, longest 123, busiest big ship, inland waterways U.K., irrigation, largest cut 124, longest tunnel world, British 125–6
CANAL JUMPING, longest*, 182
CANCER, most durable patient, 25
CANDLE, biggest, 163
CANNON, largest 215
CANNONBALL, Human, record distance 187
CANOE, longest dug-out 136
CANOEING, 253–4
CANTILEVER BRIDGE, longest world, Great Britain 122
CAN TOP, biggest collection 182
CANYON, deepest, deepest submarine 70
CAPE HORN, fastest solo rounding 177
CAPITAL CITY, oldest, most populous, largest 205, highest, northernmost, southernmost 206
CAPITAL PUNISHMENT, see **Execution**
CAPSULE, TIME, largest 168
CAR, largest ferry 135, most cars, earliest model, passenger carrying, first internal combustion, earliest petrol driven, earliest British, earliest, most expensive 137, registration, diesel-engined 137, fastest, rocket-engined, fastest jet driven, wheel driven, piston engine, racing car 137, fastest production car, largest, longest, largest engines, petrol consumption, most durable car, most expensive special, most expensive production, used, cheapest 138, longest in production 138–9, longest skid marks, longest tow, rubber powered 141, largest manufacturers, largest single plant, salesmanship record 160, wrecking* 182, greatest T-bone dive 193, see also **Driver**
CARAVAN, longest journey, largest, fastest 140
CARD HOUSES, largest number of storeys, tallest tower 187
CARDINAL, oldest, youngest 237
CARD PLAYING, 297, 299
CARD THROWING, longest 182
CAR FERRY, largest 135
CARGO VESSEL, largest 135
CARILLON, largest, heaviest 105
CAR MANUFACTURER, largest world, G.B., largest single plant 160
CARNIVORE, largest land 29–30, sea, smallest, largest, smallest feline 30, largest fish 43
CAR PARKING METERS, earliest 232
CARPET, earliest, largest, most expensive, most finely woven 163
CARRIAGE DRIVING, 268, 182
CARRIER, typhoid, most notorious 23
CARTOON, largest 91, longest lived strip 101
CARTOONIST, most syndicated, 101
CAR WRECKING, record 182
CASH, most found and returned 196
CASINO, biggest world 279
CASTLE, earliest world, British, Irish, largest world, U.K. and Ireland 116, thickest walls 116–17
CAT, heaviest U.K., smallest, oldest, largest litter, most prolific, richest and most valuable, best climber, population, mousing 36
CATALYST CRACKER, largest 152
CATAPULTING, record distance 182
CATHEDRAL, tallest (progressive records) 122, largest, smallest 235, longest nave, tallest spire 236
CATTLE, longest horns 33, heaviest, highest birthweight 171, record prices 171, prolificacy record 171–2
CATTLE STATION, largest* 169
CAVE, most extensive system, deepest by countries* 68
CAVERN, largest 68
CAVING, 254–5
CELLO, most valuable 103
CEMETERY, largest world, U.K. 126
CENTENARIAN, oldest 16
CENTIPEDE, longest, shortest, most legs, fastest 47
CENTRIFUGE, fastest 86
CERAMICS, auction record 163
CEREAL, biggest consumers 227
CHAIN, human longest 187
CHAIN STORE, largest department, grocery 159
CHAIR, largest*, most expensive 163
CHAMPAGNE, largest bottles, cork flight 81, tallest fountain* 182, drinking record 197
CHAMPIONS, (Sports), youngest and oldest world, Olympics 239–40, longest reign 240
CHANCELLORSHIP, longest–shortest tenure, most appointments 210–11
CHANDELIER, largest 163
CHANNEL CROSSING, see **Cross Channel**
CHAPEL, smallest U.K. 236
CHARITY COLLECTION, largest* 225
CHARITY WALK, most raised 225
CHARLESTON, duration record 183
CHEESE, heaviest eaters, biggest producer, oldest, varieties, most expensive, largest 172, eating record 197
CHELONIANS, largest, longest lived*, slowest moving 41, largest prehistoric 50
CHEMICAL COMPOUNDS, 80
CHEMICAL NAME, longest 94
CHEMIST SHOP, largest chain 159
CHEQUE, largest 224
CHERRY PIE, largest 229
CHESS, 296–7
CHEST MEASUREMENT, largest 20
CHESTNUT, greatest girth 55
CHICKEN, heaviest, flying 40, largest ranch 169, fastest growing 171, plucking record 172, eating record 197
CHILDREN, greatest number of siblings 16–17
CHILDREN'S HOSPITAL, largest U.K. 205
CHIMNEYS, tallest world, Great Britain 115
CHINNING THE BAR, 287
CHOCOLATE, largest factory 159
CHORISTER, longest serving 237
CHORUS LINE, longest 109
CHRISTIAN NAME, longest, most 95, commonest 95–6
CHRISTMAS, "white", most recent 60, most cards 98, largest cracker 163
CHRISTMAS TREE, tallest 56
CHURCH, tallest (progressive records) 122, oldest 235, largest 235–6, smallest, tallest spire 236, most bombed 214
CIGAR, largest, most expensive, most voracious smoker 163
CIGARETTE, consumption 163, highest tar/nicotine content, most popular, longest and shortest, largest collection, earliest and largest collection of cards, most expensive lighter, earliest, rarest packets (cartons) 164
CINEMA, earliest 109–10, most, least expensive film, film rights, longest film, highest box office gross*, largest loss, highest earning actor, stuntman, largest studios, most Oscars, oldest, largest, most seats, most 110, highest attendance by population 110–11, biggest screen* 111
CIRCLE, unsupported 194
CIRCULAR STORM, worst in world, U.K. 238
CIRCULATION, highest periodical 100–101, newspaper 101
CIRCUMNAVIGATION, first orbital 78, car, lorry 139, amphibious 141, air fastest, smallest aircraft 146, fastest commercial flight 175, sea; earliest, first solo, motorboat, woman, non-stop, fastest solo, longest voyage, submarine 177
CIRCUS, largest, acrobatic records* 196
CITY, longest name 94, oldest world, G.B., most populous, largest, smallest 205, highest world, G.B., lowest northernmost, southernmost, capitals, farthest from sea 206
CIVIC BUILDINGS, oldest G.B. 115
CIVIL WAR, bloodiest 212
CLAMS, eating record 197
CLAPPING, longest continuous 182
CLERGIES, largest 235
CLIFFS, highest* 70
CLIMB, vertical building 187
CLOCK, oldest, largest world, public, G.B., longest stoppage Big Ben 154, most accurate 154–5, most expensive 155
CLOTH, finest 165
CLOUDS, highest, lowest, greatest vertical range 63, noctilucent 73
CLOVER, most-leafed 55
CLOWN, oldest*
CLUB, oldest U.K. 226
CLUB SWINGING, duration record* 182
COACHING, 137
COAL CARRYING, record time 244–5
COAL CUTTING, record 182
COAL MINE largest open cast 132
COAL MINER, most durable 179
COAL SHOVELLING, record 182
COFFEE, greatest drinkers 227, most expensive 227
COIN, oldest 224–5, heaviest, smallest, highest, lowest denomination, rarest, most expensive, legal tender, oldest, heaviest, highest current denomination, lightest, smallest, greatest collection, hoard, largest mint, largest charity collection* 225, balancing 182–3, snatching 183
COLDEST PLACE, world*, U.K., annual mean 61
COLLEGE, oldest, largest university 233–4
COLLIERY TIP, largest U.K. 132
COLLISION, biggest marine 136
COLONIAL SECRETARYSHIP, longest tenures 211
COLONY, most populous 203
COLOUR BLINDNESS, highest, lowest rate 21
COLOUR SENSITIVITY, 21
COLUMN, tallest monumental, tallest, tallest stone 126
COMA, longest 23
COMET, earliest, speed, closest, largest, shortest, longest period 75
COMIC STRIP, (newspaper), most durable 101
COMMENTATOR, most durable, fashion shows 109
COMMERCE, 156–62
COMMON, largest U.K. 58
COMMUNICATIONS, 230–33
COMMUNIST PARTY, largest* 208
COMPANY, oldest, greatest assets world, G.B.* 156, greatest profit, loss* world, G.B. 156–7, greatest sales, work force, largest takeover, merger, biggest write off, number of companies registered, most directorships 157, largest manufacturing 160, largest investment house 162
COMPENSATION, (legal) greatest 217
COMPETITIONS, champion winner, largest single prize 183
COMPLAINER, most successful 183
COMPOSER, most prolific 103, most rapid 103–4
COMPOSITION, longest piano, longest silence 104
COMPUTER, human 21, oldest, most powerful*, fastest, world, largest G.B. 155, largest company 159, fraud 220
CONCENTRATION CAMP, worst 218–19
CONCERT, greatest attendance classical, pop festival 103
CONDIMENT, rarest 230
CONGA, longest 183
CONKER, most conquering 55
CONSCIENTIOUS OBJECTOR, most determined 215
CONSCRIPT, youngest 214
CONSONANTS, language with most*, least 93
CONSTELLATIONS, largest smallest 76
CONSULTATION FEE, highest 197
CONSUMPTION, food and drink 226–30
CONTINENT, largest, smallest 66, area 202
CONTRACT, biggest T.V. 112–13
CONTRACT, Breach of, highest damages 216–17
CONTRACT BRIDGE, 297
CONURBATION, largest 205
CONVEYOR BELT, longest 152
CONVICTIONS, most 222
COOLING TOWERS, largest world and U.K. 115
COPPER MINE, largest underground, opencast 132
CORK, champagne distance record 81
CORN, record yield 171
CORPORAL PUNISHMENT, last 221
CORPORATION, greatest sales, profit and loss 156–7
CORRESPONDENCE, shortest 98
COSMONAUT, see **Astronaut**
COSTS, highest legal* 217
COUNTRY, total number of*, largest, smallest 202, most impenetrable boundary 203, flattest and most elevated 202, most frontiers, longest, shortest frontiers, population, largest, smallest, densest, sparsest 203, poorest 223
COUPS, most* 209
COURSING, 254–6
COURT, most appearances in 222
COVENTRY, longest dispatch to 226
COW, record price 171, prolificacy record 171–2, record milk yield*, hand milking, butterfat yields 172,
COW CHIP, tossing record* 183
COW SHED, largest 169
CRAB, largest, smallest U.K., most abyssal 45
CRANE, most powerful, most powerful gantry, tallest mobile, greatest weight lifted 152
CRATER, largest volcano 64, meteoric 73, largest and deepest lunar 73–4
CRAWL, longest 183
CREATURE, largest flying (extinct) 49, most southerly 50
CREDIT CARD, largest collection 164
CREMATION, first legal 126
CREMATORIUM, oldest U.K., first legal cremation, largest world 126
CRESTA-RUN, records 249
CRIBBAGE, 297
CRICKET, batting* 256–8, bowling 258–9, fielding 259–60, wicket keeping* 260, women's 261, minor 262
CRIME AND PUNISHMENT, 218–23
CRIMINAL ORGANISATION, largest 219
CRISPS, potato, eating record 198
CROCHET, longest chain 183
CROCODILE, largest and heaviest 40, largest extinct 49–50, disaster 238
CROP YIELD, record wheat, barley 170, corn, sugar beet, potato, 171
CROQUET, 262
CROSS-CHANNEL, fastest ferry, 137, earliest flight 145, canoeing 253, rowing 313, swimming* 320–1
CROSS-COUNTRY RUNNING, 263
CROSSING THE LINE ceremony, largest 137
CROSSWORD, first, longest, largest, fastest, slowest, most durable compilers 102
CROWD, largest 257, sports 240, 245, 246, 251, 260, 272, 273, 274, 276, 277, 287, 289, 293, 301, 309, 311, 332
CRUSTACEANS, largest world, British, smallest, oldest, deepest* 45, earliest 46
CRYPT, church, largest 235–6
CRYSTAL, largest 84
CUCKOO, earliest, latest 39
CUCUMBER, slicing* 183
CURLING, 263
CURRENT, greatest, strongest 65, most powerful electric 86
CURTAIN, largest 164–5
CUSTARD PIE, throwing record 183
CUT, finest 86, largest canal 124
CUTLER, oldest firm 166
CYCLING*, 142, 263–6
CYCLO-CROSS, 264

DAISY CHAIN, longest* 52
DAM, earliest, most massive, largest concrete, highest, longest river, sea, strongest world, most massive, highest and longest U.K. 124
DAMAGES, personal injury, world, G.B. 216, highest breach of contract 216–17, breach of promise, defamation, wrongful imprisonment, alimony, divorce, greatest patent infringement, largest suit, highest costs 217
DAM DISASTER, worst world, U.K. 238
DANCE, largest* 183
DANCE BAND, longest playing 184
DANCING, marathon*, ballet; most turns, most curtain calls, largest cast; ballroom, belly dancing, dancing, modern, marathon, Charleston, Conga, disco*, flamenco 183, high kicking*, jiving, limbo, fastest tap 184
DANCING MANIA, worst outbreak 183
DARTS, 297–8
DEATH, leading cause of 23
DEATH DUTIES, highest 196
DEATH RATE, highest, lowest, infant mortality 204
DEATH ROW, longest stay 221
DEBT, largest National 223
DECAPLETS, 19
DECATHLON, world record 330, U.K. 331
DECORATIONS, see Medals 198–200
DEEP SEA DIVING, record depth 176
DEER, largest wild 28, fastest, largest herd 29, largest 32–3, largest antler span, smallest*, rarest, oldest 33, record heads 315
DEFAMATION, highest damages 217
DEFENCE, world expenditure 213
DEGREES, most honorary 201
DELTA, largest 71
DEMOLITION WORK, by hand 184
DEMONSTRATION, largest 237

INDEX

An asterisk indicates a further reference in the Stop Press

DENTISTS, most dedicated 21, most 205
DEPARTMENT STORE, largest world, U.K., most profitable 159
DEPRESSIONS, deepest world, G.B. 67, largest 67–8
DESCENDANTS, most 17–18
DESCENT, greatest ocean 176, caving 255
DESERT, largest* 70
DESPATCHES, most mentions 199
DESTROYER, fastest 135
DEVICE, most accurate 87
DIAMOND, hardest, largest, rarest coloured, price, highest auction price 84
DIARY, longest* 98
DICTIONARY, largest 96
DINING OUT, 178
DINOSAUR, longest world, Britain, heaviest, largest predator, most brainless, largest eggs 49
DIRECTORSHIPS, most 157
DISASTERS AND ACCIDENTS, worst world, U.K. 238, sports 241
DISCO, dancing marathon* 183
DISEASE, commonest, contagious and non-contagious 22–3, rarest, most and least infectious, Parkinson's 23
DISH, largest 226
DISTILLERY, largest 159
DIVE, deepest animal 28, highest* 186
DIVING (Deep Sea), record depth 176 **(Sport)** 320
DIVORCE, highest rate 204, longest case 216, highest damages, settlements 217, slowest, 178
DOCK, largest dry 128, largest gate 126, 128
DOCTORS, highest percentage 205, oldest, most in family 180
DOG, largest, tallest, smallest 34, oldest 34–5, strongest*, rarest, guide, largest litter, most prolific, most valuable, record altitude, highest and longest jump*, ratting record, tracking feat record 35, top show dog 35–6, top trainer, police records, greatest funeral 36
DOLLS, most expensive, largest 165
DOME, largest world U.K. 128
DOMESTICATED ANIMALS, 33–6
DOMESTICATED BIRDS, longest lived, heaviest, most expensive, most talkative 40
DOMESTICATION, animal 33–6, time sequence 169
DOMINOES, 184, 298
DON, most durable, 235
DONKEY, lowest price 171
DOOR, largest world, G.B., oldest G.B. 128
DOUBLE-BASS, largest 103
DOUGHNUTS, eating record 197
DOW JONES AVERAGE, peak 161
DOWRY, biggest 196
DRAGLINE, largest world, G.B. 152–3
DRAGONFLY, largest, smallest 47, largest extinct 50
DRAUGHTS, 298
DRAWING, highest price 90
DREAM, longest 23
DREDGER, largest 136
DRESS, most expensive 165
DRIEST PLACE, world, U.K., Ireland, annual mean 61
DRILLING, deepest world, deepest ocean 131
DRINK, most alcoholic, oldest vintage wine, strongest beer world, G.B., weakest beer, greatest wine auction, most expensive, wine, spirits, liqueurs 81, top-selling brand (spirits) 159, (soft) 161, biggest round 226
DRINKER, hardest 22
DRINKING, records 197–8
DRIVER (car) oldest, youngest 139, worst 232, (racing car) 303
DRIVING, fastest round the world, G.B., fastest mountain driving, farthest in reverse, longest on two wheels, 139, longest tow 141, equestrian 268, motor racing 303–5
DRIVING TEST, most failures 139–40
DROUGHT, longest 61
DRUG, most powerful, most prescribed 81, haul 220
DRUM, largest 103
DRUMMING, duration record 184
DRY DOCK, largest 128
DUCKS AND DRAKES, 184
DUMPER TRUCK, largest 140
DUNES, highest sand 70
DWARF, shortest, lightest, oldest 11–12
DWELLING UNITS, largest number 205
EARNINGS, see **Income**
EARTH, largest diameter, greatest circumference, area, axial rotation, weight, density, volume, most abundant element 59, sea area 64, depth, weight and volume 64, land surface, age 65–6, land area 202, deepest penetration 177 (see also **Structure and Dimensions** 64–71)
EARTH MOVER, largest 140
EARTHQUAKE, greatest, worst world, G.B., Ireland 63, highest seismic (tidal) wave or tsunami 65, worst world, U.K. 238
EARTHWORK, most massive, most extensive single site G.B. 128
EARTHWORM, longest in world, G.B. 48
EASTER EGG, largest 228
EATING, most prodigious animal 27, records 197–8
EATING OUT, world champion 178
ECHO, longest 87
ECLIPSES, earliest, most recent in G.B., longest 74, most and least frequent 74–5
ECONOMICS, 223–5
EDITORSHIP, longest* 101
EDUCATION, 233–5
EELS, eating record 197, largest caught 242
EGG, largest animal 27, largest, smallest bird 39, most (fish) 44, largest extinct 49, laying records, largest hen's, most yolks, goose 172, dropping, hunting, shelling, longest distance thrown 184, eating records 197
EGG AND SPOON RACE, marathon 184
ELECTION, largest, closest, most one-sided, most bent, highest personal majority 208, U.K. highest majority, party, personal, narrowest, highest poll 209, British records* 210, betting 279
ELECTORATES, British records 210, European Parliament 209
ELECTRIC CURRENT, most powerful 86
ELECTRIC GENERATOR, largest 152
ELECTRIC LIGHT BULB, oldest 87
ELECTRIC RAILWAY, first, fastest train, regular run, world, G.B., longest line 143, underground 144
ELECTRIC SHOCK, highest voltage 25
ELECTRODES, Glass, sharpest objects 86
ELECTRONIC BRAIN, see **Computer**
ELECTRON MICROSCOPE, most powerful 86
ELEMENTS, 79–81, number, lightest, heaviest sub-nuclear particles, newest 79, commonest, rarest, lightest, densest, heaviest, newest, purest, hardest, most expensive, most, least stable, most, least isotopes, most ductile, highest tensile strength, lowest, highest melting, boiling points, lowest, highest expansion, most poisonous, most, least stable 80
ELEPHANT, largest 28, longest lived 29, longest, heaviest tusks 33, largest shot 316
ELEVATOR, worst disaster 238, **Grain,** largest, largest collection 116, **lock,** highest 124
EMBASSY, largest 115
EMBROIDERY, longest 168
EMERALD, largest 84
EMIGRATION, most, U.K. most 203
EMPEROR, longest dynasty 206
EMPLOYMENT, highest 226
ENCORE, longest operatic 105
ENCYCLOPAEDIA, earliest 96, largest, most comprehensive 97
ENDURANCE/ENDEAVOUR 173–98
ENERGY, world average, highest, lowest consumption 230
ENGAGEMENT, longest 178
ENGINE, Car, largest 138
ENGINE, Jet, see **Jet Engine**
ENGINE, Military, largest 215
ENGINE, Railway, first, fastest electric, steam, most powerful 143
ENGINE, Ship, earliest steam 133
ENGINE, Steam, oldest 151
ENGINEERING, 152–5
ENGLISH CHANNEL, (first crossing) aircraft 145, canoeing 254, rowing 313, swimming 320–1
EPONYMOUS RECORD, largest object, object named after human 198
EQUESTRIAN SPORTS, 267–8
EQUITY, largest, smallest 161
ERUPTION, greatest volcanic 63
ESCALATOR, first, longest, Britain, world 153
ESCAPE, longest prison asylum 222, longest prison, greatest gaol break 223
ESCAPE-VELOCITY, terrestrial, solar 78
ESCAPOLOGY, greatest artist 185
ESKIMO ROLLS, 254
E.S.P., best performance 25
ESTUARY, longest 71
ETON FIVES, 268
EUROPEAN PARLIAMENT, election records, 209
EVACUATION, greatest military 213
EXAMINATIONS, most 'O' and 'A' levels passed* 234
EXCAVATOR, largest 153
EXECUTION, greatest number in Communist China, U.S.S.R., 218, Nazi Germany 218–19, most 219, largest hanging, last public hanging, last from yard-arm, last public guillotining, youngest, oldest, longest stay in Death Row 221
EXECUTIONER, longest in office 221
EXECUTIVE, highest paid 197
EXHIBITION, largest centre G.B. 115, largest international 119
EXPECTATION OF LIFE, highest and lowest at birth 204–5
EXPLOSION, greatest volcanic 63–4, largest 'conventional' 214, worst world, U.K. 238
EXPOSITION, largest international 119
EXTINCT ANIMALS, longest world, G.B., heaviest, largest predator, most brainless, largest dinosaur eggs, flying creature, marine reptile 49, crocodile 49–50, chelonians, tortoise, longest snake, largest amphibian, fish, insect, most southerly, largest bird*, largest mammal, mammoth, longest, heaviest tusks, longest horns 50, earliest of their types 46
EXTRA-SENSORY PERCEPTION, see **E.S.P.**
EYE, smallest visible object, colour sensitivity, colour blindness 21, largest animal 27

FABRIC, earliest, most expensive, finest cloth, 165
FACTORY, largest whale ship 135, earliest motor-cycle 141, largest bicycle 158, largest chocolate 159
FAIR, earliest, largest, record attendance, big wheel 119, fastest switchback, longest slide 120
FALL, greatest altitude without parachute 189
FAMILY, richest 196
FAMILY TREE, largest 185
FAMINE, worst world, U.K. 238
FANGS, largest (snake) 42
FARM, earliest site, largest world, G.B., largest arable, largest cattle, sheep station, largest rice, turkey, chicken, pig, 169, mushroom 170
FASHION SHOW, most prolific producer and durable commentator 109, longest 185
FAST, longest 24
FATTEST, man 12–13, woman 13
FAUX PAS, greatest 185
FEATHERS, longest, most 39
FELINE, largest, smallest 36
FELL RUNNING, 306–7
FENCE, longest 128
FENCING, 268
FERMENTATION VESSEL, largest 130
FERN, largest, smallest 55
FERRIS WHEEL, largest 119, endurance record 181
FERRY, largest car 135, fastest cross channel 137
FIDDLER, most durable 103
FIELD, oil 131, largest wheat, hop 170
FIELD GUN, competition 185
FIGURE SKATING, 296
FILIBUSTER, longest 208
FILLING STATION, largest 116
FILM, earliest 109–10, most expensive, most expensive rights, longest, highest box office gross, largest studios, most Oscar Awards 110
FINE, heaviest 222
FINGER NAILS, longest 21
FINGERS, greatest number, most sensitivity of 21
FIRE, human endurance 24, greatest gas 129, worst disaster 238
FIREBALL, brightest 73
FIRE-EATER, most voracious 24
FIRE ENGINE, most powerful 140
FIRE PUMP, greatest gallonage, pulling 185
FIREWORK, largest 165, worst disaster 238
FIRST NIGHTS, most 109
FISH, largest sea, largest carnivorous, world, G.B., largest freshwater, smallest* sea, freshwater 43, fastest 43–4, longest lived, shortest lived, most abundant, deepest, most, least eggs, most valuable* 44, most venomous, most electric, first salmon in R. Thames 44, earliest 46, largest extinct 50
FISH AND CHIPS, largest shop 161
FISHERIES, highest recorded catch, highest national haul 159
FISHING*, 241–3
FISHING NET, largest 159
FIVES, 268
FJORD, longest 64
FLAG, oldest, largest 165
FLAGSTAFF, tallest world, U.K. 128
FLAME, hottest 86, Olympic 307
FLAMENCO, fastest dancer 183
FLARE, greatest 132
FLATS, largest, tallest block world, G.B. 117
FLEA, largest, longest and highest jumps, varieties 47
FLIGHT, fastest 27, 38–9, longest, highest (bird) 39, space 78, aircraft, earliest world, G.B., cross-channel, jet-engined, world, G.B., supersonic, trans-Atlantic 145, first non-stop 145–6, solo, most flights, first trans-Pacific, circumnavigational 146, fastest 146–7, longest, shortest scheduled 147, duration record 148, greatest distance human-powered 151, kite 187–8, gliding 280–1
FLOAT, largest 165
FLOATING BRIDGE, longest 122
FLOOD, worst world, U.K., alluvion 238
FLOWER, rarest 50–51, northernmost, southernmost, highest, earliest 51, record dimensions 53, largest bloom world, G.B., largest blossoming plant, smallest, rarest, fastest growth, slowest flowering plant, largest, tallest, orchid 52, smallest, highest priced orchid, largest rhododendron, largest rose 54, tallest hollyhock, lupin, sunflower 53
FLUTE, marathon 185
FLYING-BOAT, first North Atlantic air crossing 145, largest aircraft wing span 146, fastest, highest 149
FLYING CREATURE, largest extinct 49
FLYING TRAPEZE, 196
FOG, longest 61
FOOD, survival without 24, most expensive 226
FOOD CONSUMPTION, highest, lowest calorie consumers, protein, tea, cereals, coffee, sugars, fresh water, meat, beer, sweets, wine, spirits, world & U.K. consumption, most expensive tea, coffee 227, gluttony records 197–8
FOOT-AND-MOUTH DISEASE, worst outbreak 170
FOOTBALL, Association 268–74, Five-a-side 274, Gaelic 274, Rugby League 274–6, Rugby Union 276–8, Seven-a-Side 277
FOOTBALL POOLS, 279–80
FOOTBALL STADIUM, largest 118
FOOTWAY, longest moving 153
FORCED LABOUR, 219
FORD, longest in England 232
FOREIGN AID, total given by U.S. 223
FOREIGN SECRETARYSHIP, longest tenures 211
FOREST, largest world, G.B. 56
FORGERY, greatest 220
FORGING, largest 153
FORT, largest 116
FOSSIL, oldest human 14, oldest animal 49
FOUNTAIN, tallest world, G.B. 128, tallest champagne* 182
FOXHUNTING, 278–9
FRANKFURTERS, eating record 197
FRAUD, biggest bank, largest computer 220
FREEDOMS, most conferred 201
FREEZE, longest 60
FREIGHT TRAIN, longest, heaviest 143
FREQUENCY, highest 87
FRESHWATER LAKE, largest world, U.K. 69, G.B. 69–70, Ireland 70
FRICTION, lowest 86
FRISBEE THROWING, 185
FROG, smallest, most poisonous, largest 42, longest jump 43, see also **Tree Frog**
FROGMAN, longest submergence 193, farthest underwater 176
FRONTIERS, most impenetrable, longest continuous, shortest, country with most 203
FROST FAIR, first recorded 60
FROSTS, earliest U.K. 59
FRUIT, most and least nutritive 54, record dimensions and weight U.K. 53, most expensive 230
FUEL ECONOMY, world car record 138
FUNERAL, largest attendance 237
FUNGUS, largest, most poisonous 57
FUNICULAR, longest, largest car 154
FURNACE (blast), largest 152, solar 151
FURNITURE, most expensive, oldest British, largest item 165
FURS, most valuable 27

GAELIC FOOTBALL, 274
GALAXIES, most distant 76, number of, Milky Way, remotest objects 76, progressive records 77
GALLERY, largest art 90
GALLEY, largest, 136
GAMBLING*, 279–80
GAOL, see **Prison**
GARAGE, largest, largest underground, largest private 116 see also **Filling Station**
GARBAGE DUMP, biggest 128
GARDEN, largest community 170
GAS, most powerful nerve gas 80, lightest, heaviest, lowest melting point, commonest 80
GAS FLARE, greatest 132
GAS HOLDER, largest world, G.B. 128
GAS PIPELINE, longest 153
GASTROPODS, largest, fastest 48
GAS WELL, deepest well 131
GAS WORKS, largest 152
GAUGE, widest and narrowest railway track 143, highest standard 143–4
GEMS, most precious, largest, rarest, hardest, densest, diamond, highest auction price, emeralds, sapphires, rubies, pearl, opal, crystal, topaz, amber, turquoise, jade, marble, gold, silver nuggets, 84
GENERATING PLANT, see **Power Station**
GENERATOR, largest 152
GENOCIDE, greatest, 219
GEORGE CROSS, oldest, youngest woman 198
GERBIL, largest litter 36, oldest* 37
GESTATION PERIOD, longest animal 27, mammalian longest and shortest 29
GEYSER, tallest 64
G FORCE, highest sustained, momentary 24–5, highest animal 27, highest bird 39
GHERKINS, eating record 197
GHOSTS, most durable 25
GIANT, tallest 9–11
GIANTESS, tallest 11
GIRAFFE, tallest 26
GLACIER, longest 70
GLADIATOR, greatest combat 185
GLASS, largest sheet 130–31, most priceless example 165
GLASSHOUSE, largest U.K. 116
GLIDING, 280
GLOBE, largest revolving 128
GLUTTONY, records 197–8
GOATS, record milk yield 172
GOLD, largest nugget 84, greatest reserves, accumulation 223–4
GOLDEN DISC, earliest, most awarded 107
GOLDEN HANDSHAKE, biggest* 197
GOLDFISH, oldest 37, 44, most expensive* 44
GOLD MEDALS (Olympic), most 308
GOLD MINE, largest world, G.B., richest 132
GOLD PANNING, 185
GOLD PLATE, highest auction price 165
GOLD RESERVES, greatest 223–4
GOLF, clubs, courses, longest drives 281, scores 282, championship records*, tournaments 284–5, holes in one 285–6, age shooting 286
GOLF BALL BALANCING, 185
GOOSE, oldest 40, biggest egg 172
GORGE, largest, deepest 70
GORILLA, largest 31, strength 32
GRADIENT, steepest, shallowest

railway 144
GRADUATE, *youngest 234*
GRAIN ELEVATOR, *largest, largest collection 116*
GRAMOPHONE, *106–8, invention, greatest number 106*
GRAMOPHONE RECORDS, *smallest 106, oldest, largest library, earliest jazz records, most successful solo artists, platinum disc award, most successful group, golden disc award, most recorded song, most recordings, biggest seller 107, best-sellers' charts 107–8, top-selling L.P., fastest-selling L.P.s, advance sales 108, longest running radio programme 111*
GRANDPARENTS, *most greats 18*
GRAPES, *catching distance record 185, eating record 197*
GRASS, *commonest, fastest growing, longest, shortest 55, pollen count 57*
GRASSHOPPER, *largest 47*
GRAVE DIGGING, *record 185*
GREAT GRANDPARENTS, *multiple 18*
GREENHOUSE, *largest 116*
GREYHOUND RACING, *286*
GROCERY STORE, *largest chain 159*
GROSS NATIONAL PRODUCT, *largest 223*
GROUND BREAKING, *185*
GROUND FIGURES, *91*
GROWTH, *fastest, slowest animal 27, fastest, slowest tree 55, fastest flower 52, fastest grass 55*
GUILLOTINING, *last public 221*
GUINEA PIG, *biggest litter 36, oldest 37*
GUITAR, *largest, most expensive 103, longest solo marathon 185*
GULF, *largest 64*
GUM BOOT, *throwing 185*
GUN, *largest Naval 135, most expensive 165; earliest, largest, greatest range 215, largest shoulder 315*
GUN RUN, *competition record 185*
GUSHER, *oil, most prolific 131*
GYMNASIUM, *largest 287*
GYMNASTICS, *chinning, dips, press-ups, sit-ups, jumping jacks, somersaults 286–7*

HABITATION, *greatest altitude, northernmost, southernmost 115*
HAGGIS, *largest 228, throwing* 185–6, eating record 197*
HAIL DISASTER, *238*
HAILSTONES, *heaviest 61*
HAIR, *longest 21*
HAIRDRESSING, *largest barbers 158, duration record 186*
HAIR SPLITTING, *186*
HALF-LIFE (Isotopes), *most and least 80*
HALITE, *highest 69*
HAMBURGER, *eating record 197*
HAMMOCK, *longest swinging 186*
HAMSTER, *largest litter 36, oldest 37*
HANDBALL, *287–8*
HANDBELL RINGING, *longest recital 186*
HANDBUCKING, *see* **Sawing**
HANDCLAPPING, *182*
HANDSHAKING, *world records 186*
HANDWRITING, *marathon 186*
HANGAR, *largest world, G.B. 115–16*
HANG GLIDING, *281*
HANGING, *see* **Execution**
HARBOUR, *biggest artificial 230*
HARDEST SUBSTANCE, *80*
HARE, *largest 36, coursing 256*
HARNESS RACING, *288*
HAT, *most expensive 165*
H-BOMB, *see* **Bomb**
HEAD OF STATE, *oldest, youngest, female 207*
HEADMASTER, *youngest 234*
HEARING RANGE, *limits 22*
HEART, *heaviest whale 28*
HEART STOPPAGE, *longest 23*
HEART TRANSPLANT, *first, longest surviving 25*
HEAT, *human endurance of 24*
HEDGE, *tallest 51–2*
HELICOPTER, *fastest, largest, smallest, highest 148, worst disaster 238*
HENGES, *largest 128*
HERB, *largest, fastest growth, slowest flowering 52*
HERD (Animals), *largest 29*
HICCOUGHING, *longest attack 24*
HIGH DIVING, *highest, highest shallow 186*
HIGH KICKING*, *184*
HIGHLAND GAMES, *326*
HIGHWAY, *most lanes 231*
HIGH WIRE, *highest act 186–7*
HIJACK RANSOM, *greatest 220*
HILL, *lowest 69, steepest 231*
HILL FIGURE, *largest, oldest, ground 91*
HILL-FORT, *largest Celtic 128*
HITCH-HIKING, *records 187*
HIVE, *greatest amount of honey 47*
HOARD, *largest coin 225*
HOCKEY, *288–9, Ice 293–4, Roller 312*
HOD CARRYING, *record 187*
HOLE, *smallest 87, deepest in world, U.K. 131*
HOLES IN ONE, *see* **Golf**
HOLIDAY CAMP, *largest U.K. 118*
HOLLYHOCK, *tallest 53*
HOLY BIBLE, *see* **Bible**
HOMINID, *earliest 14*
HOMOPHONES, *most 94*
HONEY, *highest yield from single hive 47*
HONORARY DEGREES, *most 201*
HONOURS, DECORATIONS, AND AWARDS, *198–200*
HOOP ROLLING, *world record 187*
HOP FIELD, *largest 170*
HOP SCOTCH, *marathon 187*
HORNS, *longest 33, extinct 50, longest musical, longest blow, 103*
HORSE, *most valuable* 28, largest, heaviest draught 33, tallest 33–4, smallest, oldest, strongest draught 34, highest price 171, 288, draught 171, showjumping 267–8, racing 289–92*
HORSEBACK, *most travelled man 175, longest ride 268*
HORSEPOWER (Car), *highest 138*
HORSE RACING, *289–92, racecourses 289, Derby, Grand National 291, 292, speed records 292, betting 280*
HOSPITAL, *largest world, G.B., mental, maternity, children's, longest stay, most expensive 205*
HOTEL, *largest in world, G.B., largest room, tallest, most expensive 117*
HOTELIER, *largest company 159*
HOTTEST PLACE, *world, U.K., Ireland, annual mean 61*
HOT WATER BOTTLE BURSTING, *187*
HOUSE, *earliest 114, largest world 117–18, G.B. 118, smallest, most expensive, oldest 118*
HOUSE OF CARDS, *largest number of storeys, tallest tower 187*
HOUSE OF COMMONS, *see* **Parliament**
HOUSE OF LORDS, *see* **Parliament**
HOUSING, *see* **Dwelling Units**
HOUSING ESTATE, *largest U.K. 117*
HOVERCRAFT, *inventor, earliest patent, first flight, public service, largest, fastest warship, longest flight, altitude 150*
HULA-HOOPING, *187*
HUMAN BEING, *(see also* **Man***), 9–25*
HUMAN CANNON BALL, *record distance 187*
HUMAN CHAIN, *187*
HUMAN FLY, *greatest climb* 187*
HUMAN MEMORY, *most retentive 21*
HUMIDITY, *and discomfort 62*
HUNGER STRIKE, *longest 24*
HURLING, *292–3*
HYDRO-ELECTRIC PLANT *largest world, G.B. 151*
HYDRO-ELECTRIC STATION, *largest world, G.B. 151*
HYDRO-ELECTRIC TUNNEL, *longest world, G.B. 125*
HYDROFOIL, *largest 135–6*
HYDROPLANE, *fastest 175*
HYMN, *earliest, longest, shortest, most prolific writer 105*

ICE, *thickest 62*
ICEBERG, *largest, most southerly Arctic, most northerly Antarctic 65*
ICEBREAKER, *most powerful, largest 136*
ICE CREAM, *eating record 198*
ICE HOCKEY, *293–4*
ICE RINK, *largest 296*
ICE SHOWS, *most costly 109*
ICE SKATING, *295–6, powered 138*
ICE SLED, *rocket powered 138*
ICE YACHTING, *296*
ICED LOLLIPOP, *largest 229*
ICON, *most expensive, 165*
ILLITERACY, *extent of 233*
ILLNESS, *commonest 22–3, rarest 23*
IMMIGRATION, *most in U.S. 204*
IMPEACHMENT, *longest 216*
IMPRISONMENT, *longest world, G.B. 222*
INCOME, *actor 110, 113, richest country, lowest 223, highest individual, highest in one year, world, U.K. 195–6, lowest 197, sport 240*
INCOME TAX, *lowest rate 223, see also* **Taxation**
INCUBATION, *longest, shortest 39*
INCUMBENCY, *longest 237*
INDEX, *longest 97*
INDOOR PASTIMES, *296–9*
INDUSTRIAL DISPUTE, *earliest, largest, most serious, longest 226*
INDUSTRIAL STRUCTURES, *tallest chimneys world, G.B., largest cooling tower 115*
INDUSTRY, *oldest 156*
INFANT MORTALITY, *lowest, highest 204*
INFLATION, *worst 224*
INFLORESCENCE, *largest 52*
INJECTIONS, *most 25*
INJURY, *personal, highest damages, world, G.B. 216*
INLAND SEAS, *largest 69*
INLAND WATERWAYS, *longest G.B. 124, country with greatest, greatest navigable length 232*
INSECT, *heaviest world, G.B. 45, largest 45–6, longest, smallest, smallest eggs 46, commonest, fastest flying, longest lived, loudest, southernmost, largest swarm, fastest, slowest wing beat, largest grasshopper, dragonfly, largest flea, longest flea jump 47, earliest 46, largest extinct 50*
INSECTIVORES, *largest, smallest, longest lived 32*
INSTRUMENTS (musical), *oldest, largest, loudest 102, highest and lowest notes, easiest and most difficult 103, greatest number played in single tune 180–81*
INSTRUMENTS (surgical), *largest, smallest 25*
INSURANCE COMPANY, *largest in world G.B., largest life policy, highest payout, marine insurance, 159*
INTELLIGENCE QUOTIENT, *highest 21*
INTERNATIONAL (Sport), *youngest and oldest 240*
INVASION, *greatest seaborne, airborne 212, most recent British 213*
INVESTMENT COMPANY, *largest 162*
I.Q., *highest 21*
IRON LUNG, *longest in 24*
IRON MINE, *largest 132*
IRRIGATION CANAL, *longest 124*
ISLAND, *largest world, G.B., largest freshwater, largest inland, remotest, remotest inhabited, remotest G.B., northernmost, southernmost, greatest archipelago, newest island, largest atoll 67, circumnatation 320*
ISOLATION, *longest period, farthest 25, 175*
ISOTOPES (Elements), *most and least, gaseous, heaviest, rarest, metallic, lightest, heaviest, rarest, longest and longest half-lives 80*

JACKING SYSTEM, *greatest lift 153*
JADE, *largest piece 84, highest price 165–6*
JAI-ALAI, *310*
JAIL, *see* **Prison**
JAZZ RECORD, *earliest 107*
JELLYFISH, *largest 48–9, smallest, most venomous 49*
JET ACE, *most kills 199*
JET AIRCRAFT, *first world, G.B. 145, fastest airliner 146–7, fastest 147–8, fastest flying boat 149*
JET ENGINE, *fastest car 137, earliest, first flight 145, fastest 147*
JETTY, *longest 128*
JEWELS, *highest price 166, record theft 220*
JEWS, *world total 235*
JIG-SAW, *largest 166*
JIVING, *duration record 184*
JOCKEY, *lightest, youngest, oldest, most successful 290–92*
JOKE CRACKING, *longest 187*
JOURNEY, *longest train 144*
JUDGE, *oldest world, 217, youngest, most 218*
JUDICIAL CODE, *earliest 215*
JUDO, *299*
JUGGLING, *record 196, football 274*
JUMBLE SALE, *largest* 187*
JUMP, *highest and longest kangaroo 33, dog 35, frog 43, flea 47, horse 267–8, high 325–32, long 326–32*
JUMPING, *billiard table, canal* 182, pogo stick 189*
JUNCTION, *railway, busiest 144*
JUNK, *largest 136*

KANGAROO, *largest, highest and longest jump 33*
KARATE, *299, demolition work 184, chop 187*
KIDNAPPING, *highest ransom 220*
KIDNEY, *earliest transplant, 25*
KIDNEY STONE, *largest 23–4*
KILLINGS, *greatest mass 218–19*
KING, *longest reign, shortest reign, longest lived 206, youngest 206–7, most children, heaviest 207*
KIPPERS, *eating record 198*
KISS, *most prolonged screen, underwater, marathon 187*
KISS OF LIFE, *longest* 187*
KITCHEN, *largest 128–9*
KITE-FLYING, *largest, greatest number, record altitude 187, duration 188*
KNIGHT, *youngest, oldest, most dubbed 201*
KNITTING, *most prolific hand-knitter, fastest 188*
KNOT-TYING, *fastest 188*

LABELS, *oldest matchbox 166*
LABOUR CAMPS, *total number 219*
LABOUR DISPUTES, *see* **Strike**
LACROSSE, *299–300*
LAGOON, *largest 70*
LAKE, *largest, largest freshwater world, U.K. 69, G.B. 69–70, Ireland, largest lagoon, deepest world, G.B., highest world, U.K. 70, lake in a lake, underground 69*
LAMB, *highest birthweight 171, prolificacy record 172*
LAMP, *most powerful 87*
LAND, *remotest spot from 65, Earth's land surface 65–6, remotest from the sea world, G.B. 66, northernmost, southernmost 67, largest owner, longest tenure, highest values, greatest auction, highest*, lowest rent 160, area 202*
LAND DIVING, *186*
LAND'S END TO JOHN O'GROATS, *hitch-hiking 187, cycling 264, walking 333*
LANDSLIDE, *worst world, UK, 238*
LAND SPEED RECORDS, *137–8, 173–5, 305*
LAND YACHTING, *296*
LANGUAGE, *earliest, oldest, English words, commonest, rarest, most complex, most and least irregular verbs, rarest and commonest sounds, vocabulary, greatest linguist, oldest alphabet 92, longest, shortest alphabet 92–3, most and least consonants and vowels, largest letter, longest words world, English, longest palindromes, longest chemical name, longest anagram, abbreviation, acronym, commonest words and letters, most meanings, most homophones, most accents, shortest holo-alphabetic sentence, longest sentence 93*
LARYNGECTOMY, *25*
LASER, *highest note, highest frequency 86, first illumination of moon, brightest light 86–7*
LATHE, *largest 153*
LAVA FLOW, *longest 63*
LAW, *215–23*
LAW CASE, *longest 216*
LAWN BOWLS, *249–50*
LAWN MOWER, *largest, racing 141*
LAWN TENNIS, *300–1*
LEAD, *largest mine 132*
LEAF, *most on tree 56, largest world, G.B., clover, 55*
LEAP-FROGGING, *188*
LEASE, *longest 217*
LECTURING, *largest agency, top rate 178*
LEGAL COSTS, *highest English 217*
LEGISLATION, *most time consuming 208*
LEGISLATORS, *highest paid, longest span 207, best attendance 207–8*
LEGISLATURE, *see* **Parliament**
LEGS, *creatures with most 47*
LEMONS, *53, eating record 198*
LENGTH, *shortest unit 85*
LENS, *earliest use, largest astronomical 82*
LEPIDOPTERA, *largest 45–6, smallest world, G.B., rarest, most acute sense of smell 46*
LETTERS, *most (alphabet) 32, largest 93, most frequently used in English 94, longest 97, most to an Editor, most personal mail, most durable pen pals, shortest, highest price 98, most sent 233*
LETTERS, *most post-nominal 199*
LEVEES, *largest 125*
LIBRARY, *largest world, G.B., oldest Scotland, most overdue book 100, largest gramophone 107*
LICENCES, *television, U.S., U.K. 112*
LIEN, *largest 217*
LIFE, *most basic, earliest 57*
LIFE EXPECTATION, *highest and lowest at birth 204–5*
LIFE POLICY, *largest 159*
LIFE SAVINGS, *most 188*
LIFT, *greatest mechanical 153, fastest passenger world, longest G.B. 153*
LIGHT, *brightest artificial 87, greatest visible range 129*
LIGHT BULB, *most durable 87*
LIGHTHOUSE, *most powerful world, brightest, remotest G.B., tallest world, 129, earliest 130*
LIGHTNING, *greatest length, speed, temperature 62, most times struck 188, worst disaster, 238*
LIGHT-YEAR, *72*
LIMBO DANCING, *lowest bar 184*
LINEAR UNIT, *shortest 85*
LINER, *passenger largest, fastest, longest 134–5*
LINGUIST, *greatest 92*
LION, *heaviest African 30*
LION TAMING, *most lions mastered 188*
LIQUEUR, *most expensive 81*
LIQUOR, *most alcoholic, largest, smallest bottle 81, largest collection 82*
LITERACY, *233*
LITERATURE, *smallest 92*
LITIGATION, *most protracted in person 216*
LITTER, *largest 29, puppies, kittens, rabbits, guinea pigs, hamsters, mice, gerbils 36*
LIVESTOCK RECORDS, *171–2*
LIVING STANDARD, *highest income per head 223*
LIZARD, *largest 40–41, oldest 41, largest extinct 49*
LOAD, *heaviest draught 34, heaviest and largest* (overland) 141, heaviest (railway) 143, greatest air 147, heaviest pushed in a barrow 181, parachute 192*
LOAF, *longest 228*
LOBSTER, *largest 45*
LOCAL GOVERNMENT AREA, *largest, smallest 204, service duration record 211*
LOCH, *longest sea 64, largest inland G.B., longest 69, deepest, highest 70*
LOCK, *largest, deepest, highest lock elevator, longest flight 124*
LOCOMOTIVE, *see* **Engine, Railway**
LOCUSTS, *largest swarm 47*
LOG ROLLING, *longest contest 188*
LOLLIPOP, *largest iced 229*
LONGEVITY, *human* 15–16, pet 37*
LOUDEST POP GROUP, *108*
LUGEING, *249*
LUNAR CONQUEST, *173*
LUPIN, *tallest 53*
LYNCHING, *worst, last in G.B. 221*

MACHINERY, *oldest 153*
MACH NUMBER, *highest attained with air 87, scale for aircraft speeds 145*
MAGAZINE, *largest circulation 100–101 highest advertising rates 102*
MAGNET, *strongest and heaviest 86*
MAGNETIC FIELD, *strongest, weakest 86*
MAGNITUDE, *Stellar 72*
MAIL, *greatest robbery 220*
MAJORITY, *Electoral see* **Elections,** *Parliamentary see* **Parliament**
MAMMALS, *28–36, largest marine, largest and heaviest, tallest, smallest, rarest 28, fastest 28–9, slowest, longest lived, highest living, largest herd, gestation periods, largest litter, youngest breeder 29, earliest 46, largest prehistoric 50, (see also* **Animal, Carnivore***)*

MAMMOTH, *largest, longest, heaviest tusks 50*
MAN, *tallest 9–11, shortest 11–12, most variable stature 12, heaviest world 12–13, heaviest G.B.*, Ireland 13, thinnest, lightest 13, greatest slimming feat 14, greatest weight gain 14, earliest 14–15, oldest* 15–16, largest chest 20, most fingers, longest fingernails, longest hair, beard, moustache 21, richest natural resources, most alcoholic, highest, lowest temperature 22, first space flight 78, greatest altitude 173, most travelled, most isolated 175, most married 178, richest in world, Britain 195–6, highest salary in world, G.B., highest income 196, most statues 200*
MANUFACTURING COMPANY, *largest 160*
MANUSCRIPT, *highest price at auction 97, most rejected 99*
MAP, *oldest 97*
MARATHON, *fastest 329 (see also* **separate activities)**
MARBLE, *largest slab 84*
MARBLES, *301*
MARCH (Military) *longest, fastest 214,* **(Musical)** *103*
MARINE DISASTER, *worst world, U.K.* 238*
MARQUEE, *largest world, G.B. 129*
MARRIAGE, *lowest, highest average ages 204, most 177–8, oldest bride and groom, longest*, most married, largest mass ceremony, most expensive 178*
MARSUPIALS, *largest, smallest, rarest, longest lived, highest, longest jumps 33*
MASER, *first illumination of moon 86–7*
MASSACRES, *greatest 218–19*
MASS ARREST, *greatest 222*
MASS KILLINGS, *greatest 218–19*
MASTER OF THE ROLLS, *longest 217–18*
MASTS, *radio and T.V., tallest world, G.B. 121, 122*
MATCHBOX LABELS, *oldest 166*
MATERNITY HOSPITAL, *largest world, G.B. 205*
MATTER, *rarest form 80*
MAYORALTY, *longest 211*
MAYPOLE, *tallest 129*
MAZE, *largest 129,*
MEASURE OF LENGTH, *shortest 85*
MEASURE OF TIME, *longest, shortest 85*
MEASURE OF WEIGHT, *earliest 85*
MEAT, *biggest consumers 227, eating record 198*
MEAT PIES, *largest 229, eating record 198*
MEDALS, *highest price 166, 198, V.C.—most bars, youngest, longest lived, most decorated, George Cross 198, most mentions in despatches, highest decorations U.S.S.R., Germany, U.S.A. 199, Olympic 308*
MEDICAL CENTRE, *largest 205*
MELON, *heaviest 54*
MELTING POINT, *lowest and highest for gases, metals 80*
MEMBER OF PARLIAMENT, *longest speech 208, largest, narrowest personal majority, highest poll 209, youngest, oldest, longest span of service, earliest and longest serving women M.P.s, heaviest, tallest M.P. 211*
MEMORIAL, *tallest (progressive records) 122, 123, tallest 130*
MEMORY (human), *most retentive 21*
MENTAL ARITHMETIC, *greatest feat 21*
MENTAL HOSPITAL, *largest 205, longest sentence in Broadmoor, longest escape 222*
MERCHANT SHIPPING, *world total, largest fleet 230*
MERGER, *largest* 157*
MERRY GO ROUND, *marathon 188*
MESSAGE, *in bottle, 188*
METAL, *lightest, densest, lowest, and highest melting and boiling points, highest and lowest expansion, highest ductility, highest tensile strength, rarest, commonest, most non-magnetic, newest, purest 80*
METAZOANS, *earliest, 46*
METEOR, *greatest shower 72*
METEORITE, *oldest, largest* world 72, U.K., Ireland 72–3, largest craters 73*
METEOROIDS, *72*
MICROBE, Bacteria: *largest, smallest free living, highest, longest lived, toughest 57,* **Viruses:** *largest, smallest 58*
MICROSCOPE, *most powerful 86*
MIDGET, *shortest 11–12, lightest 13*
MILESTONE, *oldest 232*
MILITARY ENGINE, *largest 215*
MILITARY SERVICE, *212–15*
MILK, *drinking record 198*
MILK BOTTLE BALANCING, *greatest distance 188*
MILKING, *record by hand 172*
MILKMAN, *longest serving 179*
MILK YIELD, *cows*, lifetime, one lactation, day; goats 172*
MILLIONAIRESSES, *world, U.K., youngest 196*
MILLIPEDE, *longest, shortest, most legs 47*
MINARET, *tallest 236*
MINCE PIE, *largest 229*
MINE, *earliest, deepest world, G.B., largest copper, lead, gold world, G.B., Ireland, richest gold, largest iron, platinum, uranium, tungsten, spoil heap, largest open cast, winding cage speed 150, greatest depth, shaft sinking record 177*
MINERALS, *see* **Gems**
MINERAL WATER, *largest firm 160*
MINIMUM LENDING RATE, *lowest, highest 224*
MINING, *disaster world, U.K. 238, winding cage speed 150, greatest depth shaft sinking record 177*
MINT, *largest 225*
MIRAGE, *largest 62*
MIRROR-WRITING, *195*
MISER, *greatest 196*
MISPRINTS, *most newspaper, 101*
MISS WORLD, *contest 185*
MISSING PERSONS, see Search
MOATS, *world's largest 117*
MOBILE, *most massive 91*
MODEL, *highest paid 188*
MODEL AIRCRAFT, *altitude, speed, duration records, first cross channel helicopter, smallest, paper aircraft duration record 151*
MODEL RAILWAYS, *duration record, longest train 144–5*
MODERN PENTATHLON, *301–2*
MOLLUSC *largest, largest squid, most ancient, longest lived, shells: largest, smallest, most valuable, snail: largest, smallest, speed 48, earliest 46*
MONARCH, *longest descent, longest reign, shortest reign, longest lived 206, youngest 206–7, heaviest, most prolific 207*
MONARCHY, *British records, 207*
MONETARY VOTE, *largest Paliamentary 201*
MONEY, *224–5*
MONKEY, *largest, smallest, oldest 32*
MONOPOLY, *298*
MONORAIL, *highest speed 145*
MONUMENT, *largest prehistoric, youngest ancient, tallest, largest 129*
MOON, *distance extremes, diameter, speed, first direct hit, first photographs hidden side, first soft landing, blue moon 73, largest and deepest craters 73–4, highest mountains, temperature extremes, oldest samples, eclipses; earliest, longest 74, most, least frequent 74–5, duration record on* 78, first man on 173*
MORSE, *highest speed 188*
MORTALITY, *highest 23, infant, lowest, highest 204*
MORTAR, *largest 215*
MOSAIC, *largest 91*
MOSQUE, *largest 236*
MOSS, *smallest, longest 52*
MOTH, *largest world 45–6, G.B., smallest, rarest, most acute sense of smell 46*
MOTHER, *most prolific in world, G.B. 16–17, oldest in world, G.B., Ireland 17*
MOTIONLESSNESS, *longest* 24*
MOTOR CAR, *see* **Car**
MOTOR CARAVAN, *longest journey 140*
MOTOR RACING, *303–5*
MOTOR RALLY, *earliest, longest 305*
MOTORCYCLE, *earliest, earliest factory, fastest road machine, track machines, duration record, most on one machine 141, most expensive 141–2, round Britain 142, most successful 303, fastest 303, 303*
MOTORCYCLE RACING, *302–3*
MOTOR VEHICLE, *see* **Car**
MOTORWAY, *most complex, interchange, highest 231*
MOUND, *largest artificial 129*
MOUNTAIN, *highest submarine 64, tallest by continent 66, highest world*, farthest from Earth's centre, highest insular, steepest slope, highest U.K. and Ireland, highest unclimbed, largest 68, greatest ranges 68–9, longest lines of sight, greatest plateau, sheerest wall, lowest, highest halite 69, lunar 74, climbing* 306–7, racing 306*
MOUNTAIN DRIVING, *fastest 139*
MOUNTAINEERING, *worst disaster world, U.K. 238 also 306–7*
MOUSE, *smallest 32, largest litter 36, oldest*, 37*
MOUSTACHE, *longest 21*
MULTIPLE BIRTHS, *18–19*
MULTIPLE GREAT grandparents, *18*
MUMMY, *oldest 16*
MURAL, *earliest 90, largest 90–91*
MURDER, *trial, longest, shortest, best attended 216, highest, lowest rate, most prolific murderer, world, G.B. 219*
MURDERESS, *most prolific 219*
MUSCLE, *largest, smallest 20, fastest movements 24*
MUSEUMS, *oldest, largest 91*
MUSHROOM, *largest farm 170*
MUSIC, *102–6, longest silence 104*
MUSICAL CHAIRS, *largest game 188*
MUSICAL FILM, *best-selling record 107, highest price rights, most Oscars 110*
MUSICAL INSTRUMENTS, *oldest, earliest, largest, loudest 102, highest and lowest notes, easiest, most difficult 103*
MUSICAL NOTATION, *oldest 102*
MUSICAL NOTE, *generated by "laser" beam 86, highest and lowest orchestral 103*
MUSICAL SHOW, *longest runs 108–9, shortest run 109,*
MUSICIANS, *highest paid 104*
MUTINY, *greatest 214*

NAILS (finger), *longest 21*
NAME, *longest chemical 94, place; earliest 94, longest* 94–5, shortest, most spellings, personal; earliest, longest, shortest 95, commonest 95–6, most versions, most contrived 96, longest Biblical 97*
NARCOTICS, *greatest haul 220*
NATION, *largest 202, richest 223, poorest 223*
NATIONAL ANTHEM, *oldest, longest, shortest, longest rendition 105*
NATIONAL DEBT, *largest 223*
NATIONAL INCOMES, *highest 223*
NATIONAL PRODUCT, *largest 223*
NATIONAL WEALTH, *total 223*
NATURAL BRIDGE, *longest, highest 70*
NATURAL INCREASE (population), *highest, lowest rates 204*
NATURISTS, *first and largest camps 129*
NAVAL BATTLE, *greatest 212*
NAVE, *longest, world, U.K. 236*
NAVY, *largest 213, greatest battle 212*
NECK, *longest 20*
NEEDLE THREADING, *record strands 188*
NERVE, *fastest impulses 24*
NERVE GAS, *most powerful 80*
NEST, *largest 39–40*
NETBALL, *307–8*
NEWSPAPER, *oldest, world, G.B., largest and smallest, most expensive British, most in world, longest editorship, most durable feature, most syndicated cartoonist, earliest, most durable comic strip, most misprints, highest circulation world, G.B., most read 101, highest advertising rates 102*
NEWT, *largest, smallest Britain, world 42*
NEW TOWN, *largest 117*
NIGHT CLUB, *highest fee 109, oldest, largest*, lowest 120*
NOBEL PRIZE, *highest cash value, most awards by country, individual, oldest prize-man 199, youngest 199–200*
NOISE, *loudest 86*
NONUPLETS, *19*
NOODLE MAKING, *most 188*
NORTH POLE, *conquest 175*
NOTE, *highest and lowest attained by human voice 21–2, highest generated by laser beam 86, highest and lowest orchestral 103*
NOUNS, *most cases 92*
NOVEL, *longest 96, highest sales 99*
NOVELIST, *most prolific, fastest, top-selling, youngest 99*
NUCLEAR ARSENAL, *largest 214*
NUCLEAR EXPLOSION, *greatest 214*
NUDIST CAMP, *first, largest 129*
NUGGET, *largest gold, silver 84*
NUMBER, *fastest calculating 21, highest named, longest Roman, lowest and highest prime; lowest and highest perfect, most innumerate people, most decimal places 85*
NUMBER PLATE (Car), *earliest, most expensive 137*
NUMEROLOGY, *expression of large numbers 85*
NUT (Engineering), *largest 153*
NYLON, *sheerest 166*

OAK, *largest U.K. 55, tallest 56*
OARS, *earliest 133*
OBELISK, *oldest, largest 129*
OBJECT, *smallest visible to human eye 21, farthest visible, remotest (universe) 76, sharpest 86*
OBSERVATORY, *highest, oldest 83*
OCEAN, *(see also* **Sea***), largest (area, depth, weight, volume), deepest, world, British 64, remotest spot from land, most southerly, longest voyage, temperature 65, crossings 136–7, greatest descent 176*
OCEANARIUM, *earliest, largest 58*
OCTOPUS, *largest 48*
ODDS (Gambling), *280, 292*
OFFICE BUILDING, *largest ground area, largest, tallest world, G.B. 115*
OIL COMPANY, *largest 160*
OIL FIELD, *largest world, greatest gusher 131*
OIL GUSHER, *most prolific 131*
OIL PIPELINE, *longest world, longest submarine, most expensive 153*
OIL PLANT, *off shore disaster, worst world, U.K. 238*
OIL PLATFORM, *largest* 131*
OIL REFINERY, *largest 160*
OIL SPILL, *greatest 131–2*
OIL TANK, *largest 153*
OLD SCHOOL TIE, *oldest 234*
OLD SOLDIERS, *oldest 213*
OLYMPIC GAMES, *308–9*
OMELETTE, *largest 229, greatest number 188*
ONAGER, *largest 215*
ONIONS, *peeling record* 188, pickled, eating record 198*
OPAL, *largest 84*
OPERA, *longest, shortest, longest aria, youngest, oldest singers 104, longest encore 105*
OPERA HOUSE, *largest, most tiers 104*
OPERATION, *longest, most major, oldest subject, heart, kidney transplants, earliest appendicectomy, anaesthesia, most durable cancer patient, laryngectomy, fastest amputation, instruments 25*
ORANGE, *heaviest world* 53*
ORCHESTRA, *highest and lowest notes, largest, largest attendance 103*
ORCHID, *largest, tallest 52, smallest, highest priced 54, smallest seed 55*
ORDER OF MERIT, *longest lived holder, oldest recipient 198, youngest recipient 198–9*
ORDERS AND MEDALS, *198–200*
ORGAN, *largest world, G.B., largest church, loudest stop 102, marathon* 189, highest and lowest notes 103*
ORGANISM, *smallest, largest, earliest 57*
ORGANIST, *most durable 102*
ORIENTEERING, *309*
OSCARS, *most 110*
OSTRICH, *largest 36, 38, largest egg 39*
OWL, *rarest 38*
OX, *heaviest, England 171, eating record 198*
OXFORD, *union presidents, debate 201*
OYSTERS, *eating record 198*

PACIFIC CROSSING, *fastest 136–7, earliest flight 146, marine records 179*
PACING, *288*
PADDLE BOAT, *longest voyage 189*
PAGODA, *tallest, oldest 236*
PAINTER, *most prolific, most repetitious portraitist, oldest, youngest R.A., 90*
PAINTING, *earliest, largest world, G.B. 88, most valuable 88–9, highest price auction, highest price miniature, modern 89, living artist 89–90, oldest and youngest R.A., youngest exhibitor 90, earliest 90–91, largest mural painting 90–91, progressive price records 90*
PALACE, *largest world, G.B., largest ever 117*
PALINDROME, *longest* 93–4*
PANCAKE, *eating record 198, race 327*
PANDEMIC, *worst world, U.K. 238*
PANIC, *worst world, U.K. 238*
PAPER, *most expensive writing 169*
PAPER MILL, *largest 160*
PAPER MONEY, *earliest, largest, smallest notes, highest denominations, highest value, lowest denomination, highest circulation 224*
PAPERWEIGHT, *highest auction price 166*
PARACHUTING, *longest fall without parachute 189, parachuting records 192, sport 309, ski 317*
PARALLEL BAR DIPS, *287*
PARISH, *longest incumbency, largest, smallest 237*
PARISH REGISTER, *oldest 237*
PARK, *largest world, Britain 58*
PARKING LOT, *largest 116*
PARKING METERS, *earliest 232*
PARKINSON'S DISEASE, *most protracted case 23*
PARLIAMENT, *world, earliest, oldest largest, smallest quorum, highest paid legislators, longest membership 207, best attendance 207–8, longest UN speech, filibusters, oldest treaty; U.K., earliest, longest, shortest, longest sittings, longest speech, greatest petition, most time-consuming legislation, most divisions, largest elections, closest, most one-sided, most bent, highest personal majority, communist parties, longest term 208, voting age extremes, smallest vote, most coups; Prime Ministers, world, longest lived, longest term, European records, party majorities, largest personal, narrowest, highest poll; Lords, oldest member, youngest member 209; Premiership, longest, shortest term, most times, longest lived, youngest 210; Chancellorship, longest and shortest tenures 210–11, most appointments; Foreign Secretaryship, longest tenures; Colonial Secretaryship, longest tenures; Speakership; longest; M.P.s youngest, oldest, longest span, earliest women, longest serving, heaviest, tallest, M.P. 211*
PARROT, *longest lived 39, most talkative 40*
PARTICIPANTS, *most (sport) 240*
PARTICLE, *number, lightest and heaviest sub-nuclear, newest 79, shortest lived nuclear 80*
PARTICLE ACCELERATOR, *most powerful 86*
PARTY GIVING, *most expensive, largest 178*
PASS, *highest 231*
PASSENGER, *oldest, youngest air 150*
PASSENGER LIFT, *fastest world, longest U.K. 153*
PASSENGER LINER, *largest 134–5, longest 135*
PASSPORT, *most expensive, 175*
PASTRY, *longest, 229*
PATENT, *earliest radio 111, television 112, earliest H Bomb 214, earliest English, most applications, shortest, longest 216, greatest infringement damages 217*
PEANUTS, *eating record 198*
PEARL, *largest 84*
PEDIGREE, *longest 95*
PEELING, *records, onion 188, potato 190*
PEER, *most ancient peerage, oldest creation, longest lived, youngest, longest and shortest, highest succession number, most creations, most prolific 201*
PEERAGE, *most ancient, oldest creation, longest, shortest, highest numbering, most creations, most prolific 201*
PEERESS, *most prolific 201*
PELOTA VASCA, *310*
PENAL CAMPS, *largest 222*
PENAL SETTLEMENT, *largest French 222*
PENCIL, *longest 166*
PENINSULA, *largest 66*
PENKNIFE, *most blades 166*

PENNINE WAY, cycling 264, running 307
PENNY, largest pile* 225
PENNY FARTHING, records 142
PENPALS, most durable 98
PENS, most expensive 166
PENSION, longest 179–80
PENTATHLON, 330, 332
PENTHOUSE, most expensive 118
PERFECT DEALS (Bridge), 297
PERFECT NUMBERS, lowest, highest 85
PERFORMER, highest paid T.V. 113
PERFUME, most expensive* 80
PERIODICAL, oldest world, G.B. 100, largest circulation, world 100–101, G.B., annual 101, highest advertising rates 102
PERMANENT WAY, longest, line, longest continuous stretch, longest straight line, widest, narrowest gauge 143, highest 143–4, lowest, steepest gradients world, G.B., shallowest G.B. 144
PERSONAL INJURY, highest damages world, G.B. 216
PERSONAL NAMES, earliest, longest pedigree, longest single Christian name, surname; world, U.K., most Christian names, shortest, commonest, surname 95, commonest Christian name 95–6, most versions of, most contrived 96
PETITION, greatest parliamentary 208
PETROL, largest station 116, consumption 138, most sold from single pump 141
PETUNIA, tallest 53
PHARMACEUTICALS, biggest sales 160
PHILODENDRON, largest 51
PHONE, see **Telephone**
PHONOGRAPH, see **Gramophone**
PHOTOGRAPHIC STORE, largest 160
PHOTOGRAPHY, earliest world, U.K., earliest aerial 83
PHYSICAL EXTREMES, 85–7
PHYSICIANS, most, highest, lowest proportion 205
PI, number of places memorized 21, most accurate, inaccurate version 85
PIANIST, highest paid, greatest span* 104
PIANO, earliest, grandest, most expensive 102, highest notes 103
PIANO COMPOSITION, longest 104
PIANO PLAYING, world, U.K., woman's record 189
PIANO SMASHING, record 189
PIANO TUNING, record 189
PICKLED ONIONS, eating record 198
PIE, largest apple, cherry, meat, mince, pizza 229
PIER, longest pleasure 118–19, longest world, G.B. 129–30
PIG, highest price, heaviest 171, prolificacy record 172
PIGEON RACING, 310
PIGGERY, largest 169
PILLAR BOX, oldest* 233
PILLAR BOX STANDING, record number of people 189
PILLAR OF PENNIES, 225
PILL-TAKER, greatest 25
PILOT, most flying hours, most take offs and landings 151, oldest and youngest 150–51, human powered flight 151, ace 199
PINEAPPLE, largest 55
PINNIPEDS, largest world, G.B., smallest, most abundant, rarest*, fastest, deepest dive, longest lived 30
PIPE, most expensive 166
PIPELINE, longest oil, submarine, natural gas, most expensive 153
PIPE SMOKING, duration record 189
PISTOLS, most expensive 166
PISTOL SHOOTING, 314
PIT, deepest 132
PITCH, (sound), highest detectable 22, highest 86, **(sport)** largest 239
PIZZA PIE, largest 229
PLACE-NAMES, earliest, longest world 94, G.B. 94–5, shortest world, G.B., most spellings 95
PLAGUE, most infectious disease 23
PLANET, largest, shortest 'day', smallest, highest orbital speed, hottest, coldest, nearest, surface features*, brightest and faintest, densest and least dense, conjunctions, most dramatic, next conjunction 75
PLANETARIUM, first, largest, earliest world, G.B. 83
PLANT KINGDOM, 50–58, oldest 50, rarest 50–51, northernmost, southernmost, highest, roots depth, length, worst weeds, most spreading 51, largest blossoming world, G.B. smallest flowering, slowest flowering 52, largest leaves world G.B. 55
PLASTICS, most refractory, strongest 80
PLATEAU, greatest 69
PLATE SPINNING, record* 189
PLATFORM, Railway, longest 144
PLATINUM, largest refinery 132
PLATINUM DISC, unique award 107
PLAY, longest 108–9, shortest runs, longest, Shakespeare 109
PLAYING CARDS, rarest and most expensive 166
PLAY READING, fastest, Shakespeare 109
PLEASURE BEACH, biggest 118
PLEASURE PIER*, longest 118–19
PLOUGHING, championship, greatest acreage ploughed, fastest 171
PLUCKING, chicken, turkey record 172
POEM, longest, most successful 99
POET LAUREATE, youngest, oldest 99
POGO-STICK JUMPING, 189
POISON, most potent 80, (also most poisonous snake 42, most active frog venom 42, most venomous fish 44, most poisonous spider 45)
POLAR CONQUESTS, first North, South 175–6
POLAR LIGHT, see **Aurora**
POLDER, largest 125
POLE SQUATTING, records 190
POLICY (Life assurance), largest, highest pay-out 159
POLITICAL DIVISION, largest 202
POLITICAL SPEECH, longest on record 193, 208
POLL, highest (general election) 209
POLLEN COUNT, highest 57
POLO, 310–11
POOL, 248
POP-CORN PLANT, largest 160
POPE, longest, shortest reign, oldest, youngest, last non-Italian, last ex-Cardinalate, English, last married,, quickest and slowest election 237
POP FESTIVAL, greatest attendance 103
POP GROUP, most successful 107, loudest 108, non-stop playing 190
POPULATION, world, progressive mid-year estimates, largest, smallest, densest, U.K., sparsest, cities, 203
PORCELAIN, highest price English, European 166
PORT, largest, busiest 230
PORTRAIT, most expensive miniature 89
PORTRAITIST, most prolific 90
POST OFFICE, northernmost U.K., and southernmost, oldest, longest counter 233
POSTAGE STAMPS, see **Stamps**
POSTAL SERVICE, largest and highest average letter mail, highest numbered address, oldest pillar-boxes, northernmost and southernmost, oldest post office, most telegrams 233
POSTCARDS, 166
POSTER, largest 88
POTATO, record display 55, picking record 171, peeling record* 190, eating record 198
POTATO CRISPS, eating record 198
POTATO MASH, largest serving 229
POT LID, highest price 166
POTTERY, highest price English 166
POWDER, finest 81
POWERBOAT RACING, 311
POWER FAILURE, greatest 152
POWERLIFTING, 336–7
POWER PRODUCERS, 151–2
POWER STATION, largest world, non-hydro-electric, largest G.B., atomic, solar 151, tidal 151–2
PRAM PUSHING, record distance 190
PREDATOR, largest 49
PREGNANCY, longest 18–19, shortest 19
PREHISTORIC ANIMALS, see **Extinct Animals**
PREHISTORIC MONUMENT, largest 129
PREMIER, see **Prime Minister**
PREMIUM (Insurance), largest 159
PRESS, largest 153
PRESS UPS, see **Gymnastics**
PRESSURE, highest, lowest Barometric 61, laboratory 85–6
PRIMATE, largest, heaviest 31, smallest 31–2, rarest, longest lived, strongest 32, earliest 14, 46
PRIME MINISTER, oldest, longest term of office 209, U.K., records; longest terms of office, shortest, most times, oldest, youngest 210
PRIME NUMBER, lowest, highest 85
PRINTER, largest 100, fastest 153–4
PRINTING, earliest, earliest books, largest, smallest 96, most valuable books 97, highest print order* 99–100
PRISON, longest sentences, world 221, G.B. 221–2, longest time served, longest detention, and escapes from Broadmoor, largest world, G.B., highest population 222, most secure, most expensive, longest escape, greatest break 223
PRISONER, oldest, most convictions 222
PRIZE, largest T.V. 113, competition 183, annual* 200
PROCARYOTA, 57
PROFESSOR, youngest, most durable 234
PROFIT AND LOSS, greatest 156–7
PROHIBITION, longest lasting 226
PROMISE, Breach of, highest damages 217
PROPELLER, largest aircraft 147
PROPER MOTION, 72
PROPERTY, most valuable 160
PROSECUTION, rarest 222
PROSECUTOR, deadliest 218
PROTEIN, most and least proteinous fruit 54, highest consumption 227
PROTISTA, largest, smallest, fastest moving, fastest reproduction 57
PROTOPHYTE, smallest 57
PROTOZOAN, largest, smallest, fastest moving, fastest reproduction 57
PRUNES, eating record 198
PSALM, longest, shortest 97
PSYCHIATRIST, most 205, fastest 190
PSYCHIC FORCES, 25
PUBLICATION, largest 96
PUBLIC HOUSE, oldest, U.K., largest world, G.B., smallest, longest bars world, U.K., Ireland, 120, longest tenure, longest name, shortest name, commonest name, highest, most visits 121
PUBLIC RELATIONS, largest firm 160
PUBLISHERS, fastest, most prolific 100
PUBLISHING, largest enterprise 160
PULSARS, first, fastest 76
PULSE RATES, highest, lowest 23
PUMP-TURBINE, largest 152
PUNTING, 314
PURGE, greatest 218–19
PYGMIES, smallest 12
PYRAMID, tallest (progressive records) 122, oldest, largest 130

Q.C. see **Queen's Counsel**
QUADRUPLETS, heaviest, most sets 19
QUARRY, deepest, largest world, England 132
QUASAR, 76
QUAY, longest 129–30
QUEEN, longest lived 206, youngest 206–7
QUEEN'S COUNSEL, youngest 218
QUIETEST PLACE, 86
QUINDECAPLETS, 18
QUINTUPLETS, heaviest 19
QUIZ, largest T.V. prize 113
QUOIT THROWING, record 190
QUORUM, smallest parliamentary 207

RABBITS, largest breed, heaviest specimen, most prolific, largest litter 36, oldest 37
RACE (Ethnology), poorest 197
RACKETS, 311–12
RADAR INSTALLATION, largest 154
RADIO, origins, earliest patent, earliest broadcast world, G.B., earliest trans-Atlantic, longest broadcast, most durable programmes, earliest Antipodal reception 111, most stations 111–12, highest listenership, highest response 112, tallest masts 121
RADIO-MICROPHONES, earliest 111
RADIO TELESCOPE, first fully steerable, largest 82–3
RAFT, longest survival alone 177, race 240
RAILWAY, longest, highest bridge 123, tunnel, subway tunnel 125, earliest, fastest, longest non-stop, most powerful engine, longest freight train, greatest load; longest run, straight, widest, narrowest gauge 143, highest 143–4, lowest, steepest (world, G.B.) shallowest gradients, busiest rail system, calling all stations, most countries, railroad handcar pumping, longest journey, stations, largest world, G.B., busiest, highest; largest waiting rooms, longest platform, underground most extensive, greatest depth, longest, quickest journey*, busiest subway, model railway duration record 144, longest model train 144–5, monorail highest speed 145, country with greatest length, furthest place from in G.B., number of journeys on British Rail 230, disasters 238
RAILWAY DISASTERS, worst world, U.K. 238
RAILWAY ENGINE, see **Engine, Railway**
RAINBOW, longest lasting 62
RAINFALL, most intense 62, greatest, least 61
RAINY DAYS, most in year 61
RALLY (motor), earliest, longest 305
RAMP JUMPING, longest 190
RANSOM, highest 220
RAT, oldest 37
RATTING, record by dog 35
RAVIOLI, eating record 198
REACTOR, largest single atomic 151
REAL ESTATE, most valuable 160
REAL TENNIS, 325
RECORD, Gramophone, see **Gramophone Record**
RECORD, longest held 190
RECORD BREAKERS (sport), youngest and oldest 239
RECORDING ARTIST, most successful, earliest golden disc, most golden discs, most recordings, best-selling 107, charts 107–8, fastest sellers, greatest advance sales 108
RECORD PLAYERS, most 106
REDWOOD, tallest 55
REED, tallest 55
REEF, longest 67
REFINERY (Oil), largest 160
REFLECTING TELESCOPE, largest and most powerful 82
REFLEXES, fastest 24
REFRACTING TELESCOPE, largest 82
REGIMENT, British: oldest, most senior 214
REGISTRATION PLATE, earliest, most expensive 137
REIGN, number lived through 16, longest, shortest, highest post-nominal numbers; longest lived 'Royals' 206
RELIGION, oldest, largest Christian, largest non-Christian, largest clergies, total world Jewry, earliest, oldest buildings, largest temple, largest, smallest cathedral 235, largest, smallest church 235–6, synagogue, mosque 236
RENT, highest*, lowest 160
REPTILE, largest, heaviest, smallest, fastest* 40; lizards; largest 40–41, oldest; chelonians; largest, longest lived, slowest, snakes; longest, shortest 41, heaviest 41–2, longest, shortest venomous, oldest, fastest moving, most poisonous, longest fangs 42, largest extinct, most brainless, largest extinct egg, winged, marine 49, earliest 46
REPUBLIC, smallest 202
RESERVOIR, largest world, G.B., deepest Europe 125
RESTAURANT, highest world, G.B. 120
RESTAURATEURS, largest 160–61
RETAILER, largest 161
RETIREMENT, longest pension 179–80
RHINOCEROS, longest anterior horn 33
RHODODENDRON, largest 54
RIBBON WORMS, longest 48
RICE, biggest farm 169
RICHEST, man 195–96, family 196
RICK, largest 171
RIDING IN ARMOUR, 190
RINK, largest ice 296, roller 312
RIOT, worst disaster 238
RIVER, longest world, Ireland, G.B., shortest world, largest basin, longest tributary, sub-tributary, longest estuary, largest delta, greatest flow, longest submarine, subterranean, greatest bores 71, longest dam 124, longest navigable 232
RIVETING, world record 190
ROAD, longest tunnel 125, oldest, youngest driver, driving tests, most failures 139, oldest, greatest length, vehicle density, busiest, worst jams 230, widest, narrowest, longest straight road, longest world, longest G.B., most complex interchange, longest street world, G.B., shortest street, longest hill, steepest street, highest world, G.B., lowest, longest viaduct, biggest square 231, first traffic lights 231–2, parking meters, worst driver, oldest milestone, longest ford 232
ROAD DISASTER, worst world, U.K. 238
ROAD TUNNEL, longest world, G.B. (sub-aqueous) largest diameter 125
ROAD VEHICLE, (see also individual road vehicles), most driving test failures 139–40, heaviest and largest load, longest skid marks 141, greatest density per mile, worst traffic jams 230
ROBBERY, greatest art, bank, mail-train, jewels 220
ROCK, oldest world, G.B., largest 66
ROCK CRYSTAL, largest 84
ROCK PINNACLE, highest 67
ROCKET, altitude records, earliest, longest ranges 77, most powerful world 77–8, highest pay load, velocity*, ion 78
ROCKING CHAIR, duration record 190
RODENTS, largest, smallest, rarest, longest living, fastest breeder 32
RODEO, 312
ROLL*, greatest 137
ROLLER COASTER, fastest* 119
ROLLER CYCLING, 265
ROLLER HOCKEY, 312
ROLLER SKATING, 312–3
ROLLING PIN, women's greatest throw 191
ROOF, largest 118
ROOTS, deepest 51
ROOTS (Mathematical), extraction 21
ROPE, longest wire 154, largest and longest 166, climbing 287
ROPEWAY, highest, longest, longest single span, largest cable cars 154
ROSE TREE, largest 54
ROTARY SPEED, highest man-made 86
ROTATING-WING AIRCRAFT, earliest 148–9, speed, distance and altitude record 149
ROULETTE, 280
ROUND, biggest 226
ROUNDING THE HORN, fastest, solo 177
ROWING, Atlantic crossing 177, sport 313–4
ROYAL SOCIETY, longest term 201
ROYAL TENNIS, 325
ROYALTY, oldest ruling house 206, longest, shortest reign, longest lived 206, youngest 206–7, most children 207
RUBIK'S CUBE*
RUBY, value, largest 84
RUGBY FIVES, 268
RUGBY LEAGUE, 274–6
RUGBY UNION, 276–8
RULER, most durable 206, richest 196
RULING HOUSE, oldest 206
RUMINANT, smallest 33
RUNNING, see **Track & Field Athletics**
RUNWAY, longest world, U.K. 148

SACRED OBJECT, most valuable 236
SAIL, largest 136
SAILING, Ice and sand 296, yachting 338–9
SAILING SHIP, earliest vessel 133, largest, largest junks, longest day's run, highest recorded speed, largest sails 136, (see also **Yachting**)
SAINT, total 236, most and least rapidly canonized* 236–7
ST. SWITHIN'S DAY, falsest 62
SALAMANDER, largest, longest lived 42, smallest, 43, human 24
SALAMI, biggest 229
SALARY, highest world, G.B. 197
SALES, Corporation, greatest 157
SALESMANSHIP, automobile record 160
SALMON, first caught in Thames (since 1883) 44, largest 242
SALVAGING, deepest operation, record recovery 176
SAND DUNES, highest 70

SANDWICHES, eating record 198
SAND YACHTING, 296
SAPPHIRE, largest 84
SATELLITE ARTIFICIAL, first escape velocities, records, earliest successful manned, first woman in space, first admitted fatality, first walk in space, longest manned space flight, oldest, youngest astronaut, duration record on Moon, first extra-terrestrial vehicle, closest approach to the Sun, largest space object, most expensive project 78
SATELLITE, NATURAL, most, least largest and smallest* 75
SAUSAGE, longest* 229, eating record 198
SAWING, world record 195
SCAFFOLDING, greatest 130
SCALE OF TIME, 14
SCALES, most accurate 86
SCENIC RAILWAY, see **Switchback**
SCHOOL, oldest G.B., largest world, G.B. correspondence, most expensive world, G.B. oldest old school tie, oldest PTA, most attended, most 'O' and 'A' level exams, youngest headmaster 234, most durable teacher 234–5, don 235
SCOOTER RIDING, greatest distance covered 191
SCRABBLE, 298
SCRAMBLING (Motorcycling), 302
SCRIPTWRITER, most prolific T.V. 113
SCROLLS, earliest 96
SCULLING, 313
SCULPTURE, earliest world, G.B., most expensive, largest, ground figures, hill figures 91
SEA (see also **Ocean**), largest 64, remotest spot from land, temperature, highest wave 65, longest alone at sea*
SEA CLIFFS, highest* 70
SEA DAM, longest 124
SEAL, see **Pinnipeds**
SEA-LION, see **Pinnipeds**
SEA-LOCH, longest world, G.B. 64
SEAMOUNT, highest 64
SEARCH, longest 191
SEARCHLIGHT, most powerful 87
SEAWAY, longest artificial 124
SEAWEED, longest 52
SEED, largest, smallest, most viable 55
SEE-SAW, duration record 191
SEGMENTED WORMS, longest, shortest 48
SEISMIC SEA WAVE, highest, fastest 65
SENIOR WRANGLER, order of 234
SENSITIVITY, of touch, colour 21
SENTENCE, shortest holoalphabetic, longest (classical literature) 94, longest Bible 97, longest prison, world, U.K. longest time served 221–2
SERMON, longest 191
SETTLEMENT, highest legal 217, largest French penal 222
SEVEN WONDERS OF THE world, 130
SEWAGE WORKS, largest world, G.B. 116
SEX RATIO, largest woman surplus, shortage 204
SHAFT, deepest, world, deepest U.K. 131–2, sinking record 177
SHAKESPEARE, fastest reading 109
SHARES, see **Stock Exchanges**
SHARK, largest 43, 241–3
SHARPEST OBJECTS, 86
SHAVING, fastest barber 191
SHEAF TOSSING, best performance 191
SHEARING (Sheep), fastest, biggest total 170
SHEEP, largest station, move 169, shearing record, survival 170, highest birthweight 171, prolificacy record 172, highest price auction 171
SHEET MUSIC, top-selling 105
SHELL, largest, smallest, rarest, 48
SHINTY, 314
SHIP, earliest, earliest power, oldest steam 133, earliest turbine 134, largest active liner 134–5, largest ever, largest battleships, guns, thickest armour, fastest destroyer, largest aircraft carrier, largest, fastest, deepest submarine, largest tanker, cargo vessel, largest whale factory, barge, most powerful tug, largest car ferry 135, largest hydrofoil 135–6, most powerful ice-breaker, most expensive yacht, largest dredger, heaviest, longest wooden ship, biggest human-powered, longest canoe, largest sailing, largest junks, longest day's run, highest speed, largest sails, largest wreck, largest collision, earliest, fastest Atlantic crossing 136, fastest Pacific crossing 136–7, fastest cross-channel, farthest south, deepest anchorage, greatest roll*, largest crossing the line ceremony 137, largest object stolen 220
SHIP-BUILDING, annual launching, leading firm, largest shipyard 161
SHIP CANAL, longest 123, busiest 124
SHIPPING, largest merchant fleet 161, 230
SHIPPING LINE, largest 161
SHOCK, highest voltage electric 25
SHOE, most expensive, largest 166
SHOE-SHINING, 191
SHOOTING, 314–5
SHOP, largest book 158, largest department store world, G.B., most profitable department store 159, largest shopping centre 161, largest store, supermarket, toy shop 162
SHOPPING CENTRE, largest 161
SHORTHAND, speed records 191
SHOUTING, 191
SHOW (Theatre), longest run 108–9, shortest run, one-man, most costly 109
SHOWERING, most prolonged bath 191
SHOW JUMPING, 267–8
SHREW, smallest 28, 31
SHRIMPS, eating record 198
SHRINE, oldest 235
SIAMESE TWINS, original 18
SIEGE, longest 213
SIGN (Advertising), greatest ever, largest, highest world, G.B. 126
SIGNALLING, Morse, record receiving 188
SIGNATURE, see **Autograph**
SILENCE, longest musical 104
SILK, see **Queen's Counsel**
SILVER, largest nugget 84, most expensive piece 166
SINGER, greatest earnings, finest middle register, worst singer, youngest and oldest opera 104
SINGING, longest marathon* 191
SIT UPS, 287
SKATEBOARDING*, 191
SKATING (Ice), 295–6
SKATING (Roller), 312–3
SKI-BOB, 317
SKI LIFT, worst disaster 238, longest, highest 317
SKID MARKS, longest 141
SKIING, Alpine, Nordic 316
SKIING, Water, 335
SKIJUMPING*, 316
SKIPPING, records* 191
SKITTLES, 249
SKULL, oldest 14
SKY-JACK RANSOM, greatest 220
SKYSCRAPERS, tallest 115
SLAG HEAP, largest 132
SLEDGE JOURNEY, longest, longest Antarctic 176
SLEEPLESSNESS, longest period 24
SLIDE, longest 120
SLIDE RULE, longest 85
SLIMMING, greatest feat 14
SLINGING, greatest distance 191
SLOGAN, most successful 99
SLOPE, steepest mountain 68
SLOT MACHINE, largest* 280
SMELL, most acute sense of 46, most unpleasant 80
'SMELLING OUT', greatest 219
SMELTER, largest aluminium 157
SMOKE RING BLOWING, most rings 191
SMOKESTACK, tallest world, U.K. 115
SMOKING, heaviest, 163
SNAIL, largest, fastest 48, eating record 198
SNAKE, longest, shortest 41, heaviest 41–2, longest, shortest, venomous, oldest, fastest, most poisonous world, Britain, longest fangs 42, longest extinct 50
SNAKES AND LADDERS, most protracted game 191
SNEEZING, longest fit, highest speed 24
SNOOKER, 247–8
SNORING, loudest 24
SNOW AVALANCHE, greatest 70
SNOWFALL, greatest 61
SNOWMOBILE, longest journey* 141, fastest speed 318
SNOW SHOEING, 191
SNUFF, most expensive 167
SNUFF BOX, record price 167
SOCCER, 268–74
SOCIAL INSECT, earliest 46
SOFA, largest 167
SOFTBALL, 318
SOFT DRINK, top selling 161
SOLAR FURNACE, largest world 151
SOLAR POWER PLANT, largest world 151
SOLAR TELESCOPE, largest 83
SOLDIER, oldest old 213, youngest 213–14, youngest conscript, tallest 214
SOLITARY CONFINEMENT, longest period 25
SOMERSAULTS, see **Gymnastics**
SONG, oldest, most frequently sung, top-selling, most successful writers, Eurovision contest 105, most recorded 107
SONGWRITER, most successful 105
SOUND, lowest, highest pitch 22, rarest and commonest (speech) 92
SOUNDING, deepest 64
SOUTH POLE, first crossing, sighting, landing, conquest 175, women, first both poles 176
SPA, largest, highest 117
SPACE FLIGHT, records, earliest successful manned, first woman, first admitted fatality, first space 'walk', longest manned, duration record on Moon, first extra-terrestrial vehicle, closest approach to Sun, largest object, most expensive project 78, worst disaster 238
SPAGHETTI, eating record 198
SPAN, Bridge, longest world, G.B. 121, **Parliamentary** longest service 208
SPEAKER, most boring of the year 178, **House of Commons,** longest in office 211
SPEECH, fastest 22, earliest 92, longest filibuster, longest parliamentary UN 208, longest political 193
SPEED RECORDS, car 137, 305, motorcycle 141, 303, railway progressive speed records 143, monorail 145, bomber 146, airliner 146–7, aircraft 147, fastest man, woman, space 173, land 173, 175, fastest water 175, 309, other records 174, fastest sport 239, cycling 263, 265–6, greyhound 286, racehorse 292, pigeon 310, rowing 313, skiing 317, swimming 319, running 325, water skiing 335, sailing 293, 339
SPEED SKATING, Ice 295–6, Roller 312
SPEEDWAY, 318
SPICE, most expensive, hottest 230
SPIDERS, largest world, Britain, heaviest 44, smallest 44–5, rarest, fastest, longest lived, largest web, most poisonous 45, earliest 46
SPINNING (balance wheel), duration record 192
SPIRE, tallest cathedral, church 122, 236
SPIRIT, highest strength, most expensive 81, largest collection 82, top-sellling brands 159, consumption 227
SPITTING, greatest distance* 192
SPOIL DUMP, largest 132
SPONGE, largest, smallest, deepest 49
SPOONS, record price 167
SPORT, 239–339 (see also individual sports)
SPORTS DISASTER, worst in world, U.K. 241
SPORTSMAN, youngest, oldest record breaker 239, internationals, most versatile, youngest, oldest champion, longest reign, heaviest, greatest earnings 240
SPUTNIK, see **Satellite**
SQUARE, biggest 231
SQUASH RACKETS 318–9
SQUATTING, Pole, records 190
SQUID, heaviest, longest 48
STADIUM, largest, largest football, covered, roofed, indoor 118
STAG, heaviest 28, hunting 314
STAGE, largest 108
STAINED GLASS (window), oldest, largest 236
STAIRS, longest, world, G.B. 130, climbing record 192
STALACTITE, longest 68
STALAGMITE, tallest 68
STAMPS, Postage, earliest adhesive, largest, smallest, highest and lowest denominations, highest price world, G.B., most valuable, unique and rarest British 232
STANDARDS OF LIVING, 223
STANDING, endurance record 192
STAR, magnitude 72, largest, most massive 75–6, smallest, brightest, farthest, nearest, most and least luminous, brightest supernova, constellations, stellar planets, longest name, Black Holes 76, progressive records 77
STARFISHES, largest, smallest, deepest 44
STATE, see **Country**
STATELY HOME, most visited 118
STATION, RAILWAY, largest world, G.B., busiest, highest 144
STATUE, tallest, longest 130, most 200
STATURE, most variable 12
STATUTE, oldest, longest U.K., shortest 215, most inexplicable 215–16
STEAM ENGINE, oldest 151
STEAMER, oldest 133
STEAM LOCOMOTIVE, fastest, most powerful 143
STEEL, largest company 161
STEEL ARCH BRIDGE, longest, world, G.B. 122
STEEL COMPANY, largest, largest works 161
STEER, heaviest 171
STELLAR MAGNITUDE, 72
STELLAR PLANETS, 76
STILTS, highest mastered 192
STOCK EXCHANGE, oldest, most markings, greatest overall daily movements, highest share index figure, highest par values, U.S. records, largest, smallest equity 161, greatest personal loss 161–2, largest new issue, largest investment house 162
STONE, tallest load-bearing columns 126
STONE, human largest 23–4
STORE, see **Shop**
STORM, Circular, worst world, U.K. 238
STOWAWAY, most rugged 192
STRAITS, longest, broadest, narrowest 65
STRATOSPHERE, lowest temperature 60, earliest penetration 173
STRAWBERRY BOWL, largest*
STREET, widest, narrowest, longest, shortest, steepest world, commonest name* 231
STRETCHER-BEARING, longest carry* 193
STRIKE, longest hunger 24, earliest, largest, most serious, biggest annual total, longest 226
STRING BALL, largest 193
STRINGED INSTRUMENTS, largest 103
STRUCTURE, (see also **Buildings**), earliest known human world, G.B., Ireland 114, tallest world, G.B., tallest towers, world, G.B. 121, tallest progressive records 122, 123, T.V. and Radio masts 121, largest concrete 124, oldest religious 235
STUFFED BIRD, most expensive 167
STUNTMAN, highest paid 110
SUB-ATOMIC PARTICLES, number and pattern 79
SUBMARINE, largest, fastest, deepest 135, first circumnavigation 177, most anti-submarine kills, most successful captain 199
SUBMARINE DISASTER, worst world, U.K. 238
SUBMERGENCE, record, human greatest descent, deep sea diving 176, longest by frogman 193
SUB-NUCLEAR PARTICLES, lightest and heaviest 79
SUBSTANCES, smelliest, most expensive, most poisonous, strongest, hardest, sweetest, bitterest 80, most absorbent 81
SUB-TRIBUTARY, longest 71
SUBWAY, longest tunnel 125, busiest 144
SUGAR, consumption world, G.B., 227
SUGAR BEET, record yield 171
SUGAR MILL, highest output 162
SUGGESTION BOX, most prolific user* 193
SUICIDE, highest, lowest rate 219–20, mass 220, 238
SUIT, fastest made 193, longest lawsuit 216, largest lawsuit, 217
SUMMER, earliest hot 59, best and worst British 62
SUMO WRESTLING, 338
SUN, distance extremes, temperature, core pressure, luminosity, density, diameter, mass, sun spot largest, most frequent, eclipses; earliest, most recent total, next G.B., longest 74, most and least frequent 74–5, closest approach by spacecraft 78
SUNDAE, largest* 229
SUNFLOWER, tallest 53
SUNSHINE, maximum, minimum 61
SUN-SPOT, largest, most frequent 74
SUPERMARKET, largest U.K. 162
SUPER-NOVA, brightest 76
SUPERSONIC FLIGHT, Mach scale, first 145, bomber 146, airliner 146–7, speed records, jet 147
SURFING, 319
SURGICAL INSTRUMENTS, largest, smallest 25
SURNAME, longest*, shortest, commonest 95, most contrived, most versions 96
SURTAX, highest 223
SUSPENSION BRIDGE, longest, world 121–2, highest 123
SWALLOWING, compulsive swallowing, sword swallowing 24
SWAMP, largest 71
SWARM, largest (insects) 47
SWEETEST SUBSTANCE, 80
SWEETS, biggest consumers 227, top-selling 230
SWIMMING, (bird) fastest 39, fastest* 319, most medals, diving 320, channel and long distance swimming* 320–22, world records 322–3, British records 323–4
SWIMMING POOL, largest 319
SWINDLE, greatest welfare 220
SWINGING, 193
SWITCHBACK, fastest* 120, longest ride 193
SWORD, highest price 167
SWORD SWALLOWING, longest 24
SYMPHONY, longest 104
SYNAGOGUE, largest world, G.B. 236

TABLE, longest, 168
TABLE CLOTH, largest 168
TABLE SKITTLES, 249
TABLE TENNIS, 324–5
TAILORING, fastest made suit 193
TAKE-OVER, largest 157
TALKING, fastest 22, longest non-stop 193
TANDEM BICYCLE, longest 142, endurance 264
TANK (military), earliest 214, heaviest 215, most anti-tank kills 199
TANK (oil), largest 153
TANK (water), largest 58
TANKER, largest world 135, largest wreck 136
TAP DANCING, fastest rate 184
TAPESTRY, earliest, largest, longest, most expensive 168
TARTAN, earliest 168
TATTOOS, most 25
TAXATION, least taxed country, highest world, highest, lowest rates in G.B. 223
TAXI, largest fleet 138
T-BONE DIVE, greatest 193
TEA, most expensive, consumption U.K. 227
TEACHING, longest career* 234–5
TEA TOWEL, largest collection 168
TEETER BOARD, feats 196
TEETH, earliest, most 21
TEETH-PULLING, greatest weight pulled 193
TEKTITE, largest 73
TELEGRAM, most sent 233
TELEPHERIQUE, highest, longest, longest single span, longest G.B. 154
TELEPHONE, world total, country with greatest number, smallest number, country with most, least per head, most calls, city, state, area with most, busiest, longest submarine cable 232, most incorrect bill 232–3
TELESCOPE, earliest, largest reflecting world, G.B., refracting world, G.B. 82, largest radio 82–3, solar 83
TELEVISION, earliest, first public service, first trans-Atlantic transmission, longest telecast, video tape, most durable show and B.B.C. programme, most sets, least TV, greatest audience*, largest production 112, largest contracts, world 112–13, G.B., highest paid performer, largest prize, world, most successful appeal*, biggest sale, most prolific scriptwriter, highest advertising rates, most takes, most for commercial, highest paid commercial, smallest set 113, tallest mast, (progressive records)

An asterisk indicates a further reference in the Stop Pre

transmitting tower G.B. 121
TEMPERATURE, *progressive extremes highest, lowest* 60, 61, most equable 59, greatest ranges* 59–60, longest freeze, lowest atmospheric 60, thickest ice, humidity and discomfort 62, highest shade, lowest screen 61, lunar, sun 74, man made, highest, lowest 85*
TEMPERATURE, *animal, highest, lowest 27*
TEMPERATURE, *human, highest, lowest 22, highest endured 24*
TEMPERATURE, *sea 65*
TEMPLE, *largest 235, tallest Chinese 236*
TENNIS (Lawn), *300–1,* **(Real or Royal)**, *325*
TEN PIN BOWLING, *249*
TENSILE STRENGTH, *highest 79*
TENT, *largest world, G.B. 129*
TERRORISM, *greatest toll 219*
TEXT, *oldest written, printed, largest book, publication, dictionary, smallest, longest novel 96, most valuable book, broadsheet, manuscript, atlas 97*
TEXTBOOKS, *most successful writer 99*
THEATRE, *earliest, oldest world, G.B., largest world, G.B., smallest G.B., largest amphitheatre, stage 108, longest runs* 108–9, shortest runs, most durable actor, leading actress, most roles, longest play, longest by Shakespeare, longest chorus line, most ardent theatre-goer* 109*
THEFT, *largest object stolen, 220*
THIMBLE, *most expensive 168*
THREE-LEGGED RACE, *326*
THROWING, *longest 193, basketball 246, cricket ball 260, golf ball 284*
THUNDER-DAYS, *most 61*
TIDAL POWER STATION, *world's first 151–2*
'TIDAL WAVE', *highest, fastest 65*
TIDDLYWINKS, *299*
TIDE, *greatest world, G.B., Ireland 65*
TIE, *oldest old school 234*
TIERS, *most in opera-house 104*
TIGER, *largest 30, man-eating 238*
TIGHTROPE WALKING, *greatest walker, endurance record, highest and steepest 193, high wire act 186–7*
TIME, *scale of 14, longest, shortest measure 85, most accurate measure 155*
TIME CAPSULE, *largest 168*
TIME MEASURER, *most accurate world, G.B. 155*
TITHE BARN, *longest Britain 126*
TITLE, *highest selling book 99, most titled person 198*
TOAD, *largest world, British, smallest world 43*
TOASTMASTERS, *founder, most boring speaker 178*
TOBACCO, *largest company 162, heaviest smokers 163, most expensive snuff 167*
TOBOGGANING, *249*
TOMATO, *largest 53*
TOMB, *largest 130*
TONGUE, *heaviest and longest 28*
TOPAZ, *largest 84*
TORNADO, *highest speed 61, strongest U.K.* 63, worst world, U.K. 238*
TORTILLA, *eating record 198*
TORTOISE, *longest lived 27, 41, slowest, largest 41, largest extinct 50*
TOSSING THE CABER, *see* **Highland Games** *326*
TOTE WIN, *biggest 278*
TOTEM POLE, *tallest 130*
TOUCH, *sensitivity 21*
TOURISTS, *most, highest spending 204*
TOW, *car longest 141*
TOWER, *tallest world, U.K. 121*
TOWN, *largest, smallest (earliest walled), oldest, world, Great Britain 205, highest, northernmost, southernmost, most remote from sea 206*
TOWN CRIER, *most title wins 191*
TOXIN, *most deadly 80*
TOY CONSTRUCTION, *tallest 168*
TOY MANUFACTURER, *largest 162*
TOY SHOP, *biggest world, G.B. 162*
TRACK AND FIELD ATHLETICS, *325–32*
TRACKING, *greatest feat 35*
TRACTOR, *largest 140*
TRADE UNION, *oldest, largest world, G.B., smallest 226*
TRAFFIC, *highest density, worst jams*

230, lights—first in U.K. 231–2
TRAIN, *see* **Railway**
TRAM, *longest journey, oldest 145*
TRAMPOLINING, *(circus)* 196, (sport) 332*
TRANS-ATLANTIC CROSSING, *see* **Atlantic Crossing**
TRANSFER FEES, *Association Football 272, Rugby League 275*
TRANSFORMER, *largest 154*
TRANSMISSION LINE, *longest, highest world, G.B., highest voltages 154*
TRANSMISSIONS, *earliest radio broadcasts world, G.B., earliest trans-Atlantic wireless 111, television; earliest, earliest trans-Atlantic, earliest satellite 112*
TRANSMITTERS, *greatest number radio 111–12, earliest television 112*
TRANSPORTER, *largest road 140*
TRAVEL (person), *most on land*, woman, disabled person, on horseback, passport records, in space 175*
TREADING WATER, *322*
TREASURE TROVE, *largest 225*
TREATY, *oldest 208*
TREE, *largest, most massive living thing, greatest girth world, Britain*, greatest oaks Britain, fastest growing, slowest growing, tallest world 55, tallest all-time, by species, G.B., Ireland, Christmas tree, oldest world, G.B., earliest, most leaves, remotest, most expensive 56, largest rose 54, eating record 198*
TREE-CLIMBING, *fastest 193*
TREE-FROG, *largest, smallest 43*
TREE SITTING, *longest 193*
TRENCHERMAN, *greatest 197*
TRIAL, *longest; longest shortest; murder, shortest, longest divorce trial, best attended 216*
TRIBES, *tallest, shortest 12*
TRIBUTARY, *longest 71*
TRIPLETS, *oldest 16, heaviest, most 19, fastest birth 18*
TROGGING, *254*
TROPHY, *largest 239*
TROTTING AND PACING, *288*
TSUNAMI, *highest, fastest 65*
TUBA, *largest 102–3*
TUBE, *see* **Underground**
TUBING, *smallest 154*
TUG, *first power-driven vessel 133, most powerful 135*
TUG OF WAR, *332*
TUNGSTEN MINE, *largest 132*
TUNNEL, *largest, most powerful wind world, G.B. 87, longest water supply world, G.B., longest passenger railway world, mainline, G.B., sub-aqueous, subway, longest road, world, G.B., largest diameter road, longest hydro-electric, irrigation, world, G.B., longest bridge-tunnel 125, longest canal world 125–6, G.B., tunnelling record 126*
TURBINE, *first ship 134, largest, reversible pump 152*
TURKEY, *largest, most expensive 40, largest farm, 169, plucking record 172*
TURQUOISE, *largest 84*
TURTLE, *fastest 40, largest, heaviest 41, largest extinct 50*
TUSKS, *longest, heaviest 33, (extinct animals) 50*
TWINS, *tallest 11, oldest, world, G.B. 16, lightest 18, heaviest, 13, 19, Siamese, rarest 18, most sets 19*
TYPEWRITER, *earliest, most expensive 168*
TYPEWRITING, *fastest 193–4, longest 194*
TYPHOID CARRIER, *most notorious 23*
TYPING, *see* **Typewriting**
TYRE LIFTING, *record 194*
TYRES, *largest 141*

U-BOAT, *See* **Submarine**
UNCONSCIOUSNESS, *longest 23*
UNDERGRADUATE, *youngest 234*
UNDERGROUND CHAMBER, *largest 68*
UNDERGROUND RAILWAY, *most extensive, oldest, passenger records*, greatest depth, busiest subway, tour record 144*
UNDERWATER, *longest stay 24, 322, deepest escape 176, swimming 322*
UNEMPLOYMENT, *highest, lowest, U.K. 226*
UNICYCLE, *tallest, distance records, place to place 142*

UNION, *see* **Trade Union**
UNITED NATIONS (UN), *longest speech 208*
UNIT OF LENGTH, *earliest, shortest 85*
UNIVERSE, *72, 76, farthest visible object, quasars, 'pulsars' 76, remotest object 76–7, age of 77*
UNIVERSITY, *oldest 233, oldest colleges G.B. 233–4, greatest enrolment, largest, building, most northerly, largest quad, youngest, most durable professor, senior wranglers, youngest undergraduate, graduate 234, union presidents 201, boat race 313*
UNSUPPORTED CIRCLE, *biggest 194*
URANIUM, *largest mine, 132*

VACUUM, *highest 86*
VALVE, *largest 154*
VASE, *most expensive 163, 165, 168–9, largest 168*
VAT, *largest 130*
VAULT, *Bank, largest 158*
V.C., *see* **Victoria Cross**
VEGETABLES, *record dimensions and weights U.K. 53, potato display 55*
VEHICLE, *extra-terrestrial* 78, most massive 140, rubber-powered 141, Road, see* **Road Vehicle**
VEIN, *largest human 22*
VELOCIPEDE, *see* **Bicycle**
VENOM, *most active snake, frog 42, fish 44, spider 45, jellyfish 49*
VERBS, *most forms, most and least irregular 92*
VERSE, *longest, shortest Bible 97*
VERTEBRATE, *earliest 46*
VIADUCT, *longest, longest in world 122, G.B. 231, rail, longest in world 122*
VICTORIA CROSS, *most expensive 166, most bars, youngest person awarded, longest lived 198*
VIDEO TAPE, *first recording 112*
VILLAGE, *shortest name 95, oldest, smallest 205, highest, northernmost, southernmost 206*
VINE, *largest 52*
VINEYARD, *most northerly, southerly 52, largest 170*
VINTAGE, *oldest 81*
VINTNERS, *oldest 162*
VIOLIN, *most valuable 103*
VIOLINIST, *underwater, most durable 103, highest paid 104*
VIRUS, *largest, smallest 58*
VISCOSITY, *lowest 86*
VISION, *most acute (bird) 39*
VOCABULARY, *richest 92*
VOICE, *highest, lowest 21–2, greatest range 22*
VOLCANO, *total number, greatest eruption, longest lava flow 63, greatest explosion 63–4, highest extinct, highest dormant, highest active, northernmost, southernmost, largest crater 64*
VOLLEYBALL, *332*
VOTE, *fewest received by Parliamentary candidate 209, largest parliamentary monetary 201*
VOTING AGE, *extremes 209*
VOWELS, *language with most*, least 93*
VOYAGE, *longest possible 65, longest by sailing boat 177*

WAIST, *smallest 20*
WAITER, *marathon 194*
WAITING ROOM, *railway, largest 144*
WALKING, *in space 78, on stilts 192, tightrope 193, on hands 194, track records, backwards, endurance, non-stop 332–4, round the world 333*
WALL, *sheerest mountain 69, thickest 116–17, longest world, G.B. 130, mountaineering 306*
WALL OF DEATH, *endurance feat 194*
WALRUS, *see* **Pinnipeds**
WAR, *longest, shortest, bloodiest, bloodiest civil war, most costly, last battle in Britain, bloodiest battle modern, ancient, British, greatest naval battle, greatest invasions seaborne, airborne 212, last invasion of Great Britain, greatest evacuation, worst sieges, largest armed forces 213*
WARSHIP, *largest, fastest 135*
WASP, *smallest, smallest eggs 46*
WATCH, *oldest, smallest, thinnest, most expensive 155*

WATER, Fresh, *survival without 24, biggest consumers 227*
WATERFALL, *highest world, U.K. 70, Ireland, greatest, widest 71*
WATERFLUME, *first 130*
WATERMILL, *oldest 152*
WATER POLO, *334–5*
WATER SKI-ING, *335*
WATER SPEED RECORDS, *174–5, 311*
WATERSPOUT, *highest 62–3*
WATER TREADING, *322*
WATERWAY, *(inland), longest world 123, G.B. 124, artificial seaway, irrigation canal, country with greatest navigable length, longest navigable river 123*
WATER WELL, *deepest world, Britain, greatest flow 132*
WATER WHEEL, *largest world, G.B. 130*
WAVE, *highest, highest and fastest seismic 65*
WEALTH, *national 223, individual 195–6*
WEATHER, *records 59–63*
WEB, *largest 45*
WEDDING CEREMONY, *largest mass, most expensive 178*
WEED, *worst 51*
WEIGHT, *heaviest men* 12–13, women, twins 13, lightest 13, slimming 14, gaining, greatest differential 14, greatest lifted 153, 336–7, heaviest sportsman 240*
WEIGHTLIFTING, *335–7*
WEIGHT-MEASURE, *earliest 85*
WELFARE, *greatest swindle 220*
WELL, *deepest oil world, British 131, deepest water world, G.B., greatest flow 132*
WETTEST PLACE, *world, U.K., Ireland annual mean 61*
WHALE, *largest, heaviest 26, 28, fastest growth 27, greatest recorded depth 28*
WHALE FACTORY SHIP, *largest 135*
WHEAT, *largest field, record yield 170*
WHELKS, *eating record 198*
WHIP, *longest cracked 194*
WHISKY, *smallest bottle 81, largest collection 82*
WHIST, *299*
WHISTLE, *greatest range 22*
'WHITE' CHRISTMAS, *60*
WHITE HORSE, *oldest in Britain 91*
WHO'S WHO, *longest entry*, youngest entrant, most brothers 201*
WILL, *shortest, longest 217, greatest in U.K., Ireland 196*
WINDIEST PLACE, *61*
WINDMILL, *largest, earliest recorded, oldest still complete, largest in Holland, England 152*
WINDOW, *largest 130–31, stained glass, oldest, largest 236, cleaning record 194*
WIND-SPEED, *highest surface 61*
WINDSURFING, *339*
WIND-TUNNEL, *largest, most powerful 87*
WINE, *oldest vintage, most expensive*, largest bottles, greatest auction 81, highest consumption 227*
WINE CELLAR, *largest 131*
WING BEAT, *fastest, slowest (bird) 39, fastest, slowest (insect) 47*
WING SPAN, *longest (bird) 38, (aeroplane)* 146*
WINTER, *earliest severe, worst in Britain 60, sports 248–9, 263, 293–6, 315–8*
WIRE, *high and low 186–7, 196, 193*
WIRELESS, *see* **Radio**
WIRE-ROPE, *longest, strongest 154*
WIRE SLIDE, *longest 194*
WOMEN, *tallest 11, shortest 11–12, heaviest 13, oldest 16, reproductivity 16–20, smallest waists, longest necks 20, lowest temperature 22, longest coma 23, first cosmonaut 78, greatest altitude, fastest 173, highest climb 306, longest delayed, oldest parachute drop, longest fall without parachute 192, piano playing record 189, richest 196, most titles 198, leading air ace 199, greatest surplus, shortage 204, earliest, longest serving M.P.s 211, oldest, youngest George Cross 198*
WOMEN'S CRICKET, *261*
WOMEN'S HOCKEY, *289*
WONDERS OF THE WORLD, *seven 130*
WOOD, *heaviest 56–7, lightest 57*

WOOD-CUTTING, *world record, sawing 195*
WOODEN BUILDINGS, *largest, oldest 116*
WOODEN SHIP, *heaviest, longest 136*
WOOL, *highest price 171*
WORD, *oldest English 92, longest, longest in various languages*, longest English 93, longest palindrome 93–4, longest chemical name, anagrams, commonest, most meanings, most homophones, most accents 94*
WORK FORCE, *biggest 157*
WORKING CAREER, *longest* 178*
WORKING WEEK, *longest, shortest 178*
WORLD RECORD BREAKER, (Sport), *youngest and oldest 239*
WORM, *longest, shortest earthworm 48, longest ribbon 26, 48*
WORSHIP, *oldest places of 235*
WRANGLER, *Senior order of 234*
WREATH, *largest 52, costliest 169*
WRECK, *largest 136, oldest ship 133*
WRECKER, *most powerful 140*
WRESTLING, *109, 337–8*
WRIST WATCH, *earliest, most expensive 155*
WRITE-OFF, *biggest 157*
WRITER, *most prolific 98, most novels 98–9, most textbooks, highest paid, top-selling, highest selling title, most publishers' rejections, oldest authoress, youngest author, longest gestation, youngest, oldest Poet Laureate 99*
WRITING, *handicapped, minuscule 195*
WRITING PAPER, *most expensive 169*

YACHT, *most expensive 136, most successful 339, racing disaster 238*
YACHTING, *Atlantic crossing 179, sport 338–9*
YARD-ARM, *last execution 221*
YAWNING, *most persistent 24*
YEW, *tallest tree, oldest G.B. 56*
YODELLING, *endurance record 195*
YOLKS, *most 172*
YORKSHIRE PUDDING, *largest 230*
YO-YO, *records 195*

ZIQQURAT, *largest 131*
ZOO, *largest game reserve, oldest, oldest privately owned, most comprehensive in U.K., greatest attendances 58*

Indexing by

Anna Pavord